CORPORATE

FINANCIAL

ACCOUNTING

CHARLES L. McDONALD, PhD, CPA

Associate Professor and Director,
Center for Accounting Research and Professional Education
University of Florida

ROBERT G. MAY, PhD

KMPG Peat Marwick Centennial Professor of Accounting
Associate Dean, College of Business Administration
and Graduate School of Business
The University of Texas at Austin

SOUTH-WESTERN College Publishing

An International Thomson Publishing Company

DEDICATION
To our families
Charles L. McDonald and Robert G. May

AO88AA
Copyright © 1995
by South-Western Publishing Co.
Cincinnati, Ohio

I Ⓣ P
International Thomson Publishing
South-Western College Publishing is an ITP Company.
The ITP trademark is used under license

Sponsoring Editor: David L. Shaut
Developmental Editor: Minta Berry
Production Editor: Mark Sears
Production House: Berry Publication Services
Cover Design: Paul Neff
Internal Design: Lesiak/Crampton Design
Photographer, Chapter Openers: Kessler Photography
Photo Editor: Jennifer Mayhall
Marketing Manager: Michael O'Brien

Credits:

123	Robert Morris Associates cautions that the Studies be regarded only as a general guidelines and not as an absolute industry norm. This is due to limited samples within categories, the categorization of companies by their primary Standard Industrial Classification (SIC) number only, and different methods of operations by companies within the same industry. For these reasons, Robert Morris Associates recommends that the figures be used only as general guidelines in addition to other methods of financial analysis.
210–217	ClickArt®Images Copyright © 1984–1994® T/Maker Company. All Rights Reserved.
759–785	Copyright J.C. Penney Company, Inc.–1994.

ISBN: 0-538-83074-3
1 2 3 4 5 6 7 VH 0 9 8 7 6 5 4
Printed in the United States of America

Library of Congress Cataloging-in-Publication Data
McDonald, Charles L.
     Corporate financial accounting / Charles L. McDonald, Robert G. May.
          p.   cm.
     Includes bibliographical references and index.
     ISBN 0-538-83074-3
     1. Corporations—Accounting.   I. May, Robert G.
     II. Title.
     HF5686.C7M3917   1994
     657'.95—dc20   94-37340
                                                                              CIP

PREFACE

According to the Accounting Education Change Commission (AECC):

> The primary objective of the first course in accounting is for students to learn about accounting as an information development and communication function that supports economic decision-making. The knowledge and skills provided by the first course in accounting should facilitate subsequent learning even if the student takes no additional academic work in accounting or directly related disciplines. For example, the course should help students perform financial analysis; derive information for personal or organization decisions; and understand business, governmental, and other organizational entities.[1]

Corporate Financial Accounting directly addresses the AECC's recommendations in the following ways:

1. A decision-making focus is evident in every chapter.
2. Financial analysis is integrated with the presentation of accounting concepts and practices.
3. Accounting is discussed in a way that provides insight into how businesses and other organizations function.

This text is suitable for a one-semester or a two-quarter course covering principles of financial accounting. Material is presented in sufficient depth so that students who aspire to major in accounting will have more than adequate preparation for their intermediate accounting courses. However, the text is aimed primarily at the majority of students who will major in other disciplines. The text stresses basic concepts and presents analytical tools in contexts that students will find appealing. Students will appreciate the clear prose, helpful graphics, and emphasis on decision making.

Decision-Making Focus

Each chapter opens with a brief, believable story about a decision maker facing a realistic business decision or dilemma. In the body of the chapter, we introduce accounting information related to the decision maker's problem. By the end of the chapter, we close the loop, describing and illustrating financial ratios and other analyses that specifically address the decision maker's concerns. The scenarios provide a context that aids understanding of the material, and they emphasize the role of accounting information in economic decision making.

Financial Analysis

Throughout the text, we illustrate the tools of financial analysis along with the development of related accounting information. For example, in Chapter 3, which deals with accrual concepts, students are introduced to the profit margin as a measure of profitability. Students compare the profit margin of the business in Chapter 3's opening scenario to the profit margin of other service businesses. This

---

[1]Accounting Education Change Commission, *The First Course in Accounting*, Position Statement No. Two, (June 1992).

comparison helps students understand the usefulness of accounting information. Another example of our approach is in Chapter 4, where students learn about sales revenue and cost of goods sold for merchandising entities. To emphasize how these important components affect profitability, students are introduced to the cost of goods sold and gross profit ratios.

Insights into Organizations

For many students, financial accounting is their first business course. Since accounting procedures track business activity, a great opportunity is lost if the financial text and course do not enhance students' understanding of underlying business processes as they learn financial accounting. In the context of our chapter scenarios, we find it natural to implicitly cover important aspects of various business activities as we introduce financial accounting. For example, Chapters 1 through 3 present a continuing scenario of a start-up business, how its financial statements are developed, and how accounting information is used in assessing its relative profitability and liquidity as it goes through its early growth stage. In Chapter 4, we emphasize how merchandising businesses earn profits in contrast to service businesses—by buying and selling goods. We follow the income statement of a merchandising business and introduce the transactions making up net sales and cost of goods sold (and gross profit). Each type of transaction is introduced in the context of running a merchandising business and the importance of managing gross profit is brought home at the end of the chapter where we close the loop on the motivating scenario.

In Chapter 6, we cover accounts and notes receivable. In a progression motivated by the opening scenario, we examine why a business grants credit and how bank card sales and notes receivable represent alternative ways of managing customer credit. The chapter winds up with an analysis of the contribution of credit sales to a business—an analysis, incidentally, that is echoed by a note to J.C. Penney's 1993 financial statements that is the focus of a critical thinking case in the end-of-chapter material.

Similarly in Chapter 9, we cover current liabilities and how they are used to provide short-term funds in a business. The scenario sets up the common business need to manage inventory purchases and collection lags for a peak selling season. In the process of covering accounting for a variety of current liabilities, we cover the features and tradeoffs of different strategies for managing the short-term financing problem.

Far from being distractions, these business activities and the decision contexts that apply are covered subtly and unobtrusively. This is an accounting text, but it enriches and motivates the student's first learning experience in the accounting discipline by presenting accounting in an organizational context that demonstrates a need for accounting information. Throughout the text, we have scattered feature boxes that provide insight into the functioning of businesses and other organizations. They include ethical dilemmas, insights into real-world accounting applications, historical perspectives, and global insights. We use these features judiciously; they season the text without distracting from its main lines of thought.

Analyzing, Thinking, and Communicating

Throughout this text, we emphasize decision making and thinking about problems in a rich business context. The thinking-in-context emphasis is reinforced in the end-of-chapter materials. At the end of each chapter are a set of Critical

Thinking and Communicating cases. They range from thought-provoking ethical situations, to scenarios that promote critical thinking about the limitations of accounting and the motives of managers who choose accounting methods, to cases requiring the analysis and interpretation of financial statements. In most cases, a substantial writing exercise is required or implied. The following icons are used to identify the cases:

Decision
Case

Ethical
Dilemmas

Financial Analysis
Case

Communication
Case

Supplementary Material for the Instructor

Solutions Manual The comprehensive manual contains solutions to questions, exercises, and problems. Suggested solutions and key points of discussion are provided for all cases. All exercises and problems are correlated to the appropriate learning objectives and time estimates are provided for all problems. The manual is also available in electronic media.

Solution Transparencies The solutions to exercises and problems are available on transparency for ease of classroom presentation.

Test Bank A printed test bank includes true/false, multiple choice, and problem materials for all chapters. All items are correlated to the appropriate learning objectives. The level of difficulty for the items is also identified.

MicroExam 4.0 Computerized Test Bank The test bank is available in a MicroExam version. All items that appear in the print test bank are available electronically. Among the features of the electronic version are the ability to customize the test, the ability to prepare multiple versions of the same questions, and the ability to add or edit questions and problems.

Videos *Financial Accounting* explores activities of the firm through interviews with people who use accounting data.

Supplementary Material for the Student

Working Papers Appropriate forms for students to use in solving end-of-chapter problems are available.

Study Guide A study guide is available for stduents to gain additional insights into their study of corporate financial accounting.

Practice Sets and Cases The following practice sets and cases provide additional exposure to the accounting systems of various business entities: *Ice Inc.: An Interactive, Corporate Financial Accounting Practice Case; Cool Company: An Interactive Sole Proprietorship Financial Accounting Practice Case; Mountain Bikes, Inc.*, a merchandising business using perpetual inventory; an *Annual Report Project;* and *Cases in Financial Accounting.*

Solutions Software This general ledger software, prepared by Warren W. Allen and Dale H. Klooster of Educational Technical Systems, may be used to solve selected end-of-chapter problems. The software may be used with DOS or Windows systems.

Acknowledgements

Throughout the text, relevant professional statements of the Financial Accounting Standards Board and other authoritative publications are discussed, quoted, or footnoted. We are indebted to the American Institute of Certified Public Accountants, the Financial Accounting Standards Board, and the American Accounting Association for material from their publications.

During the development of this text, many individuals contributed significant insights and provided guidance to us as we wrote and refined the text. We especially thank Jill Cunningham and Susan Crosson for their time and effort in assisting with the content development and review of the end of chapter material. We are also grateful for the assistance of Steven Rice in the preparation of the tax appendix.

We sincerely appreciate the efforts of all who have contributed to the final product. The following faculty served as reviewers and class testers during the project:

James Abbott	Broome Community College
Michael Adkins	Lexington Community College
Rainer Albright	The University of Alabama
Herman Andress	Santa Fe Community College
Sue Atkinson	Tarleton State University
Debra Barbeau	Southern Illinois University at Carbondale
Donald J. Barnett	California State University–Dominguez Hills
Homer L. Bates	University of North Florida
Susan Shannon Bates	Boise State University
Anne Connell Baucom	University of North Carolina–Charlotte
Kathleen Bindon	University of Alabama
Dorothy Binger	Tallahassee Community College
Sallie Branscom	Virginia Western Community College
Ronald P. Brooker	Phoenix College
Howard Bryan	Santa Rosa Junior College
James I. Bryant	Catonsville Community College
Carol Buchl	Northern Michigan University
Leon Button	Scottsdale Community College
David Bydalek	Mesa Community College
Eric Carlson	Kean College of New Jersey
Charles F. Chanter	Grand Rapids Junior College
Michael C. Chester	Norfolk State University
C. David Coffee	Western Carolina University
Kenneth L. Coffey	Johnson County Community College
A. Carter Cogle	Southside Virginia Community College
Judith Considine	Rutgers University
Grace M. Conway	Adelphi University
Judith M. Cook	Grossmont College
Tomas Cooper	Parkland College
Fredonna Cox	Eastern Kentucky University
Alan E. Davis	Philadelphia Community College
Paul L. Donohue	Delaware County Community College
Joseph G. Doser	Truckee Meadows Community College
Lola A. Dudley	Eastern Illinois University
Dean Edmiston	Emporia State University
Randy Edwards	Appalachian State University
John A. Elfrink	Southeast Missouri State University
David Fetyko	Kent State University
Carl J. Fisher	Foothill College
R. Leigh Frackelton, Jr.	Mary Washington College
Joseph Gallo	Cuyahoga Community College–Metro Campus
Helen Gernon	University of Oregon
Shirley Glass	Macomb Community College–South
Robert F. Godfrey	Marshall University
Maxwell P. Godwin	Southwest Texas State University

Harold Goedde	North Carolina A & T University
William D. Goodman	Bluefield State College
Donald J. Griffin	Cayuga Community College
Joyce Griffin	Kansas City Kansas Community College
Donald D. Gusarson	Cabrillo College
William T. Hall, Sr.	Fayetteville Technical Community College
Linda Herrington	Community College of Allegheny County
George Holdren	University of Nebraska
Cynthia L. Holloway	Tarrant County Junior College–Northeast
Patty Holmes	Des Moines Area Community College
Anita V. Hope	Tarrant County Junior College–Northeast
George Ihorn	El Paso Community College
Randy Johnston	Penn State University
Brent Joyce	Virginia Highlands Community College
Bruce Koch	University of North Texas
Edward Krohn	Miami-Dade Community College
Michael Layne	Nassau Community College
Marcella Y. Lecky	The University of Southwestern Louisiana
Albert Y. Lew	Wright State University
Norbert Lindskog	Harold Washington College
Johanna D. Lyle	Kansas State University
Thomas Lynch	Hocking Technical College
Rene Manes	The Florida State University
Ken Mark	Kansas City Kansas Community College
Thomas J. McCoy	Middlesex County College
William McFarland	Illinois Central College
Maria Trini U. Melcher	California State University–Fullerton
Phillip Mills	Miami-Dade Community College–South Campus
Thomas P. Moncada	Eastern Illinois University
Paula Morris	Kennesaw State College
C. Lynn Murray	Florida Community College–South Campus
M. Salah Negm	Prince George's Community College
Cletus O'Drobinak	South Suburban College
Leslie Oakes	Rutgers University
Frances Aileen Ormiston	Mesa Community College
John Overton	University of New Hampshire
John Palipchak	Penn State–Beaver Campus
Lynn M. Paluska	Nassau Community College
Joseph S. Patterson	DeKalb Community College–South Campus
Deborah Dianne Payne	Roosevelt University
A. George Petrie	University of Texas–Pan American
Rose Marie Pilcher	Richland College
Sharyll A.B. Plato	Central State University–Oklahoma
Norma C. Powell	Bryant College
Barbara Powers	Wytheville Community College
Robert D. Reid	Germanna Community College
Reg Rezac	Texas Women's University
Carla Lemley Rich	Pensacola Junior College
Juan Rivera	University of Notre Dame
Lawrence A. Roman	Cuyahoga Community College–Eastern
David L. Rozelle	Western Michigan University
Leo Ruggle	Mankato State University
Pearl B. Sandelman	De Anza College
Wallace James Satchell	St. Philip's Community College
John Schryver	Bentley College
Robbie Sheffy	Tarrant County Junior College
Michael T. Stein	Rutgers University
John R. Stewart	University of Northern Colorado
Linda Sugarman	University of Akron
Thomas Sullivan	Quincy College
Lisa Tahlier	North Carolina Wesleyan College
Greg Thom	Parkland College
Ingrid R. Torsay	DeKalb Community College–Central Campus
Charles L. Vawter	Glendale Community College
Vicki S. Vorell	Cuyahoga Community College–Western
DuWayne M. Wacker	University of North Dakota

Lori A. Wahila   Broome Community College
Al Walczak   Linn-Benton Community College
Thomas C. Waller   University of Houston–Clear Lake
Sharon Walters   Morehead State University
Peter R. Wilson   New York University
Frank Zattich   Lincoln Land Community College
Karl M. Zehms   University of Wisconsin–Green Bay

ABOUT THE AUTHORS

Charles L. McDonald is Associate Professor and Director of the Center for Accounting Research and Professional Education of the Fisher School of Accounting at the University of Florida. He received a Ph.D. in accounting from Michigan State University. Articles by Professor McDonald have appeared in *The Accounting Review, Accounting Horizons, Corporate Accounting,* and the *Journal of Business Research*. Professor McDonald is a CPA and a member of the American Accounting Association, American Institute of Certified Public Accountants, and the Florida Institute of Certified Public Accountants. He has served on numerous committees of those organizations including the Financial Accounting Standards Committee of the AAA and is currently a member of the Accounting Standards Executive Committee of the AICPA.

Robert G. May is the KPMG Peat Marwick Centennial Professor of Accounting at The University of Texas at Austin and Associate Dean for Academic Affairs. He has also held appointments at the University of Washington and at Stanford University. He received his Ph.D. from Michigan State University.

Professor May has published articles in scholarly journals and was co-winner of the 1976 AICPA Notable Contribution to the Accounting Literature Award. He has served as Associate Editor of *The Accounting Review*. He has coauthored three textbooks: *A New Introduction to Financial Accounting, A Brief Introduction to Managerial and Social Uses of Accounting,* and *Evaluating Business Ventures*. He is the co-developer of SCAD, a Simulated Case for Audit Decisions, under a grant from Price Waterhouse Foundation and developer of Variables Sampling Education Support Software (VSESS) under a grant from Coopers & Lybrand Foundation.

Professor May has taught a variety of graduate and undergraduate courses in accounting. He received teaching awards at the University of Washington and at the University of Texas. He was co-recipient of the American Accounting Association Innovation in Accounting Education Award in 1991 and 1993. Professor May has had public accounting experience and is active in the American Accounting Association.

CONTENTS IN BRIEF

CONTENTS

CORPORATE

FINANCIAL

ACCOUNTING

Introduction

Have you ever looked around your home town or city and wondered what makes everything work? When you shop for groceries, why is food on the shelves? Why do the streets (eventually) get repaired? Why do you have power available in your house, apartment, or dorm room? Why is a seat available for you in your accounting class? Why can you buy most things that you need when you need them—without waiting unreasonably long in lines? What holds all these essential goods and services together and makes them work in a coordinated manner? It takes thousands, tens of thousands, millions, or even hundreds of millions of individual economic decisions to make a town or city work. And, to be effective—in order for towns, cities, states, and whole economies to work well—these decisions must be based on sound information about their economic consequences.

Accounting supplies the informational basis for economic decisions. It provides quantitative—usually financial—information about past events and activities that are relevant to current decisions. Whether or not you become an accountant, you will find your knowledge of accounting to be of value in your personal as well as your professional life. Accountants hold many of the most rewarding and best paying jobs, and many top managers of our largest businesses are accountants.

In this Introduction, we describe what accounting information is about and specific ways it is used, by whom it is used, and what kinds of accounting professionals produce it. We also raise the important issue of business ethics and truth in accounting.

1. Define accounting and describe the process of accounting.
2. Identify the users and uses of accounting information.
3. Describe what accountants do in the private sector, in government, and in public accounting practice.
4. Identify the important relationships among ethics, business, and accounting.

Define accounting and
describe the process of
accounting.

ACCOUNTING INFORMATION PROCESSING

Accounting systematically and selectively captures financial data, records these data, summarizes them, and prepares statements that communicate to decision makers relevant information about economic entities, transactions, and events.

The Focus of Accounting Information—Economic Entities

Fundamentally, accounting focuses on economic entities. **Economic entities** carry on economic activities such as buying or selling products or providing or consuming services. Every person, every business, every government organization, every charitable organization, and every educational institution is an economic entity. By systematically processing data, accounting produces information about the transactions economic entities undertake and about the events that happen to them. A **transaction**, a voluntary exchange between economic entities, typically occurs when one entity sells a product or service that the other entity buys.

The transactions of an economic entity make up a large part of its history and constitute most of the raw material in the accounting process. However, the histories of entities are incomplete unless we also take into account the events that affect them involuntarily. These events can be natural such as fires, floods, and storms; political, such as condemnation of land for a freeway right-of-way; or social, such as a boycott of products produced by a company that has been polluting the environment.

The Accounting Process

As Illustration I-1 shows, business documents capture transaction data. For example, the sales slip, a common business document, captures the essential facts about an individual sale. Accountants generally do not record the actual transaction data on documents. Instead, they design procedures and documents so that other employees can gather transaction data accurately. It is much more efficient for employees directly involved in transactions (such as sales clerks) to gather data about transactions. Generally, *everyone who participates in transactions also participates in the accounting process.*

Second, the accounting process selects essential data from the business documents and records these data in chronological records. A cash register tape, a familiar accounting record, contains a listing of all the daily transactions in the order they occurred. In many cases today, employees enter transaction data directly into electronic computer files at the time of the transaction.

Third, accountants (or computers) total the data about individual transactions of each type and then carry these totals forward to record them to various

ILLUSTRATION I-1 The Accounting Process

Data gathering	Recording	Summarizing	Communicating
Facts about individual transactions and events are written on business documents.	Facts are recorded selectively in business records or computer files.	Recorded transaction data are totaled, and totals are tabulated into summary records.	Reports are prepared, relating summary data to decisions to be made.

summary records. If computers summarize accounting data, accountants direct the programming of the computers to ensure that the correct accounting result is obtained.

Finally, accountants prepare reports from the summary records for decision makers' use. To be useful to decision makers, accounting reports must convey information relevant to decisions. Thus, an important dimension of accounting—one that we emphasize in this text—is how accounting information can be used to facilitate decision making. *Accountants have a responsibility to construct reports that contain relevant information and to communicate that information to the decision maker.*

Accounting and Computer-Based Information Systems

Until after World War II, bookkeepers, accountants, or other employees performed all accounting functions manually or used bookkeeping machines. Now, computers assist in varying degrees in accounting for all but the smallest organizations—from handling the mechanics of recording accounting data to integrating accounting functions fully with the entity's operations. The more extensively computers are used, the more profoundly they affect the way accounting objectives are accomplished. For example, computers make some types of accounting reports economical or possible for the first time. However, computers have not changed the objectives of the accounting process or the principles and standards governing the preparation of accounting reports.

Accounting information is generally quantitative and predominantly financial in nature. The system many organizations use to accomplish the accounting process also provides managers with a wider range of information than just accounting information. For example, airlines use computers to manage their passenger reservations—clearly one of the most important management functions in an airline. Ultimately, however, when the passengers board a plane and the plane takes off, the data in the passengers' reservation records can be transferred directly to the sales (accounting) record for the day, thus supporting the accounting process as well. In developing such sophisticated systems, organizations should include accountants as part of the team. This way, the systems can fulfill both their accounting and other business objectives.

Accountants and Bookkeepers

Many people often confuse bookkeeping with accounting. **Bookkeeping** includes the mechanical and clerical aspects of the entire accounting process. Bookkeepers work under the supervision of accountants and record accounting data, summarize these data, and prepare routine financial reports. Illustration I-2 contrasts the responsibilities of accountants and bookkeepers.

ILLUSTRATION I-2 Responsibilities of Accountants and Bookkeepers

Accountants	Bookkeepers
• Determine data to be gathered and design business documents and controls to facilitate accurate data gathering.	• Gather data as needed, according to established procedures.
• Design accounting records and advise management about whether data should be recorded manually or by computer.	• Record data and apply control procedures over computer input preparation.
• Establish controls over recorded data to ensure accurate summarization and error detection either by manual procedures or by computer.	• Summarize recorded data and perform control procedures to detect and correct errors.
• Design relevant accounting reports that conform to established standards and design manual or computer procedures for preparing them.	• Prepare draft reports or review computer drafts as needed.
• Perform high-level control procedures to ensure the integrity of the accounting process and the computer-based information system.	• Assist with control procedures as directed.

LO 2
Identify the users and uses of accounting information.

USERS AND USES OF ACCOUNTING INFORMATION

Economic entities are accounting's focus, because they are the subjects of many economic decisions. Accounting supplies valuable information, by recognizing who wants what kinds of information and about what entities.

Information About Individuals

Individuals need information to manage their own financial affairs and frequently ask themselves the following questions:

- How much cash do I have on hand?
- How much cash could I raise if I sold everything I have?
- Will I be able to borrow additional funds to buy a house (or car) and still meet all of my other obligations?

Individuals are not the only ones interested in their financial affairs. In particular, when an individual wants to borrow money to buy a car or a house or take a vacation, a lender of some type enters the picture. The lender wants the answers to such questions as:

- How much income does this individual earn?
- How has the individual performed in paying back previous loans?
- How much of the individual's income is available after personal expenses to pay back a new loan?

- Does the individual own valuable property to pledge as collateral for a loan?

If the individual is an elected public official, then voters feel a need for and have a right to answers to questions such as:

- Does the individual have income from sources other than his or her salary in public office? What sources?
- Do conflicts of interest exist between the other sources of the individual's income and his or her duty to the public?

Information About Businesses

Businesses are private organizations operated to earn profits for their owners. Financial affairs can be much more complex for businesses than they are for most individuals. Hence, the users of information about businesses are numerous, and the questions they ask are more varied. Illustration I-3 summarizes three major classes of users of accounting information managers, owners, and lenders—and gives examples of the questions they ask.

ILLUSTRATION I-3 Users of Accounting Information About Businesses

Managers:
- Will sufficient cash be available to pay bills and retire debts as needed?
- Did expenditures exceed budgets or plans? In which areas?
- Should the business buy or rent new facilities and equipment?
- Should selling prices be increased or decreased?
- Are goods selling as quickly as expected?
- What product lines offer the best prospects for future profitability?

Owners and prospective owners:
- Is the business as profitable as it can be?
- Have sales grown or diminished?
- Is the business performing better or worse than its competition? Why?
- What is the risk that the business will fail financially (not be able to pay its debts)?
- Is it worthwhile making or continuing an investment in this business?

Lenders:
- Is the business profitable?
- Has the business paid its bills and retired its past debts on time?
- Does the business appear to be generating sufficient cash to handle additional debt in the future?
- What is the risk that the business will fail financially?

Besides managers, owners, and lenders, many others use accounting information about businesses. Employees and suppliers naturally want to know whether businesses can generate sufficient cash flows to pay them on time. Customers want to know whether businesses will survive and be steady sources of needed goods and services. The Internal Revenue Service wants to know if businesses (and individuals) have recognized all income, deducted only allowable deductions, and paid the actual amount of taxes owed. Regulators such as public utility commissions want to know if businesses are profiting excessively by charging unfairly high rates to consumers.

Information About Other Entities

Users of accounting information ask many of the same questions about other organizations such as charities and governmental units as they ask about businesses. However, since these entities differ from businesses in certain fundamental ways, some questions applicable to businesses do not apply to them.

For example, **charities** are private organizations that are operated not for profit but for humanitarian purposes. Therefore, questions of profitability do not apply. However, managers, creditors, suppliers, donors, and beneficiaries all want to know whether charities will continue to pay their bills on time and survive. They also want to know what percentages of total donations flow through from donors to beneficiaries and what percentages charities use for operations.

Governments are public organizations formed to supply essential public services to the citizenry and to the state (nation). Generally, financial failure is not an issue with government units—that is, they do not go out of business when they cannot pay their bills. Nevertheless, managers of government units take their ability to pay bills and repay debts very seriously—as do the constituents of the unit, its employees, and suppliers—because vital services and the ability to borrow for capital improvements are affected. Managers and citizens alike want to know whether a government unit spends too much or too little on current services and whether it makes sufficient capital investments to maintain or expand services as needed in the future.

LO 3

Describe what accountants do in the private sector, in government, and in public accounting practice.

PROVIDING ACCOUNTING INFORMATION— ACCOUNTING CAREERS

Accountants pursue two very broad career paths. The vast majority of accountants (close to 85 percent of the approximately one million accountants in the United States) are employed in private or government accounting occupations within economic organizations.[1] **Private accounting** consists of all accounting activities required to meet the information needs of managers of private-sector organizations and of outside users such as prospective owners and lenders. **Government accounting** consists of the same activities as private accounting but is performed in cities, counties, and state and federal agencies. The outside users of information about government organizations are lenders and taxpayers. Other accountants engage in **public accounting**, which consists of providing professional accounting services to individuals, businesses, government units, and other entities for fees—much like the practices of medicine and law.

Accountants and Accounting Within Organizations

Accountants perform the full variety of functions described in Illustration I-2 in all types of economic organizations. Accounting is a "staff function"; that is, it is not a direct part of providing products or services. However, it is a vital and indispensable staff function and usually enjoys a status within the organizational hierarchy that reflects its importance.

Large businesses, charities, education institutions, and government units recognize the persons responsible for the accounting function as high-ranking

---

[1]Economic organizations consist of all economic entities other than individuals.

members of management. These people generally have the status of vice president and the title of *controller*. In a business, a charity, or an education institution, the controller typically reports to the chief financial officer or CFO (an executive vice president) or to the chief executive officer or CEO (the president). Illustration I-4 shows the relationships among the executive vice president and CFO of J.C. Penney Company, Inc. and the various vice presidents, including the vice president and controller. In a government unit such as a city, the controller reports to an equally high-ranking officer such as the treasurer, city manager, or mayor.

ILLUSTRATION I-4 J.C. Penney Company, Inc., CFO Organization (March 1, 1990)

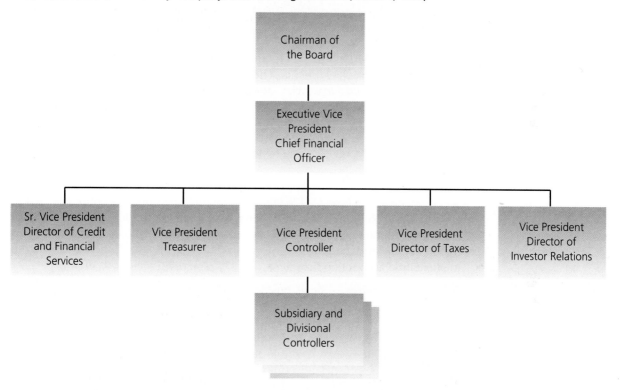

Accounting Specializations Within Organizations

Accountants tend to work in one of four areas within organizations. Financial accountants and managerial accountants prepare information directed at two major classes of users, outsiders and managers, respectively. In addition, accountants work as internal auditors and tax specialists.

Financial Accounting. This text presents the basics of financial accounting. **Financial accounting** consists of the processes and principles used to prepare financial statements. **Financial statements** are standardized reports organizations prepare for use by outsiders such as owners and prospective owners of a business, bankers who have loaned or are considering lending money to a business, and customers and suppliers of a business.

Managerial Accounting. Managers also find financial statements to be quite relevant in their work; however, they need more detailed information to guide their day-to-day decisions. **Managerial accounting** is the process by which information is prepared for use by managers in making decisions about the current and future activities of economic entities. Managerial accounting must accommodate a wide variety of managerial decision making; and, therefore, the reports produced are less standardized than they are in financial accounting. They may be one-of-a-kind reports, tailored to a specific use. Managerial accounting is presented in other accounting texts.

Internal Auditing.   Accountants also conduct internal audits within their organizations. An **internal audit** is an investigation intended to determine whether:

1. Employees and departments conform to management (or government) policies.
2. Functions in the organization are performed at reasonable cost.
3. A department or division is fully meeting its goals and objectives.

Internal Tax Management.   Larger corporations employ accountants and attorneys in internal tax departments. They plan transactions and structure entities to maximize *profits after taxes* (i.e., they minimize the effect of taxes on profits). While these departments may not be part of the accounting function (for example, they may be part of the treasury function), they employ many accountants who specialize in taxation.

Public Accounting

We estimate that close to 170,000 accountants are public accountants in the United States. Public accountants perform accounting, auditing, tax, and management advisory services for their clients. They practice alone, as sole practitioners, or in firms ranging from two practitioners to several thousand in large multinational accounting firms.

Accounting Services.   Small businesses do not always have the resources to hire skilled accountants internally. Until they grow large enough to justify expenditures on accounting salaries, small businesses often hire public accountants to prepare their financial statements and other reports. As businesses become larger, they may be able to hire accountants, but they might not be able to afford sophisticated computer-based accounting information systems. Once again, small businesses may turn to public accountants who operate centralized computer service bureaus to handle their clients' computing needs.

Auditing Services.   **Financial auditing** is an *independent* investigative activity through which public accountants lend credibility to the financial statements or other representations of economic entities. Independent auditing services are the most distinguishing feature of public accounting. Because it provides a basis for economic decisions, accounting information is valuable. However, *if information is not trusted, it will neither influence decisions to its full potential nor achieve its full value.*

Managers who prepare financial statements for outsiders realize that it is in their interests to improve the credibility of their organizations' financial statements. They demand the services of independent auditors who test the content of financial statements for conformity with underlying facts and with standards such as Generally Accepted Accounting Principles (defined later in this text). Auditors make an independent report to accompany the financial statements, which contains their opinion about the fairness of presentation of the information contained in the statements. Because fairness in financial reporting is in the public interest, the federal government and many states have passed statutes that require publicly-owned corporations to have independent audits of their financial statements. Banks also require audits of their medium- and large-loan customers.

Tax Services.   Public accountants offer tax services that consist of assisting clients in filing tax returns, helping them comply with tax laws and regulations, and advising them about ways to maximize their profits after taxes. State and federal tax laws are voluminous and complex and affect both business and individual profitability. Therefore, many businesses and individuals find it beneficial to consult with tax experts. Increasingly, businesses are operating globally and need expert advice on how to balance the tax provisions of several different countries.

Management Advisory Services.   Public accountants also provide management advisory services (MAS) to help their clients with many other aspects of running their businesses. As part of every audit, they make suggestions about ways to improve their clients' information systems and their business practices. If clients do not have the expertise to design new information systems or to implement other suggestions themselves, they may hire the MAS division of the public accounting firm that suggested the improvements. Public accountants also perform MAS services for non-audit clients.

Accounting Designations (Certifications)

The public and the managers of organizations rely on the integrity and expertise of accountants. Professional designations or certifications distinguish accountants who meet high standards of qualification and professional conduct.

The CPA Certificate and License to Practice Public Accounting.   Because the independent audit function protects a dimension of the public interest, public accounting is the only aspect of accounting practice that requires a license. Each state licenses individuals to practice public accounting as certified public accountants (CPAs).

According to the Department of Labor, there were about 400,000 CPAs in the United States in 1990. Approximately 40 percent of these CPAs practice public accounting, and the other 60 percent are employed in private accounting, government accounting, or other occupations.[2] Although states differ somewhat in their requirements, a candidate for the CPA certificate and license to practice must generally satisfy an education requirement (minimum of a bachelor's degree, with some minimum number of accounting credits), pass the Uniform CPA Examination (administered by the American Institute of Certified Public Accountants), and obtain work experience under a CPA's supervision.[3]

State Boards of Accountancy issue the licenses to practice and the CPA Certificates in most states, and they also enforce codes of conduct and stipulate continuing education requirements for retention of the licenses and certificates. You may wish to contact your State Board of Accountancy to find out the specific requirements and procedures for becoming a CPA in your state.

---

[2]*Occupational Outlook Handbook*, 1992–1993 Edition (U.S. Government Printing Office: U.S. Department of Labor, May, 1992), p. 15.

[3]Increasingly states are requiring more education. For example, as of January 1994, over 30 states were phasing in minimum requirements of 150 semester hours of college credit as well as a bachelor's degree.

Other Professional Accounting Certifications.   Accountants who practice in industry and government have recognized the benefits of setting high professional standards for all accounting practices rather than just for public accounting. They have formed institutes to administer rigorous standardized examinations and to award certificates to individuals who meet their standards. Two such institutes are the Institute of Management Accountants (IMA) and the Institute of Internal Auditors (IIA). They administer examinations to accountants aspiring to be certified management accountants (CMAs) and certified internal auditors (CIAs), respectively.[4]   According to the Department of Labor, in 1990, there were 17,000 CIAs and 10,000 CMAs in the United States.[5]

Professional Accounting Organizations

Most professional accounting organizations have several things in common. They all wish to protect and enhance the reputation of the accounting profession and the productivity of their members. To this end, they set standards of conduct for their members, set technical standards for accounting and auditing practice, represent their members in public forums such as legislative hearings, conduct or support research to improve the discipline of accounting, develop technology for practice, publish books and monographs on professional topics, and publish journals (magazines) to keep their members abreast of current developments. The names, members, and journals of the most influential professional accounting organizations are listed in Illustration I-5.

ILLUSTRATION I-5 Accounting Organizations

Organization Name	Primary Membership	Journal
American Institute of Certified Public Accountants (AICPA)	CPAs	Journal of Accountancy
Institute of Management Accountants (IMA)	Managerial accountants	Management Accounting
Financial Executives Institute (FEI)	Chief financial officers	The Financial Executive
American Accounting Association (AAA)	College and university teachers of accounting	The Accounting Review
The Association of Government Accountants (AGA)	Accountants in all branches of government	The Government Accountants Journal

Opportunities in Accounting

New entrants to the accounting field find both immediate employment and career-long opportunities very favorable. The Bureau of Labor Statistics expects faster than average growth in accounting and auditing jobs through the year

---

[4]Further information may be obtained by writing the following addresses: American Institute of Certified Public Accountants, 1211 Avenue of the Americas, New York, NY 10036; Institute of Internal Auditors, 249 Maitland Avenue, Altamonte Springs, FL 32701-4201; and Institute of Management Accountants, 10 Paragon Drive, Montvale, NJ 07645-1759.

[5]*Op. cit.*

2005 and estimates that approximately 304,000 new accounting and auditing jobs will be created between 1992 and 2005.[6]

The 1991 College Placement Council Survey reported an average *starting* salary of $26,600 for a graduate with a bachelor's degree in accounting and no prior accounting work experience—approximately 40 percent higher than the average personal income in the United States.[7] Of course, actual starting salaries of accountants vary, depending on the region of employment (and its cost of living), the prestige of the school granting the degree, the type of employer, and the performance of the individual earning the degree. Persons with advanced degrees and previous accounting experience generally receive significant premiums. The salaries of top accounting executives and partners in international public accounting firms average as much as ten times the starting salaries. This provides a significant range for upward economic mobility in accounting practice.

LO 4
Identify the important relationships among ethics, business, and accounting.

ETHICS IN BUSINESS AND TRUTH IN ACCOUNTING

Many people believe the phrase "business ethics" is a contradiction in terms. Perhaps this cynicism is understandable. In a free-enterprise, market economy, businesses compete vigorously for sales and profits with other businesses; and we know they sometimes bend the rules. In all types of organizations, managers and employees compete with each other for jobs, advancement, bonuses, etc. Hence, we hear expressions such as: "It's a dog-eat-dog world out there." Yet, we are wrong to assume that business and ethics do not mix.

To the contrary, most successful businesspeople know that integrity and ethical behavior are essential ingredients. Why? Because business is actually built on trust. Owners and lenders entrust their money to managers. Employees entrust their safety and future employment to managers. Managers, in turn, entrust employees with valuable resources for which the managers are themselves responsible. Such essential trust relationships cannot work effectively without a high level of confidence that the individuals involved have integrity. As most astute businesspeople know, in the long run, loss of other people's confidence means loss of business, loss of profit, loss of opportunity, etc.

Accountability and Business Ethics

Accountants are acutely aware of the relationship between successful business and integrity. Accounting is the heart of **accountability**, the process by which individuals and groups demonstrate to others that they have properly or effectively discharged their responsibilities. Financial statements, for example, show owners and lenders what management has done with the business's resources. Internal accounting reports show managers where employees are performing well or poorly and may reveal such crucial information as whether stocks of goods are shrinking due to theft or poor handling.

Thus, managers or employees who engage in fraud or other misconduct may attempt to compromise the organization's accountability system by falsify-

---

[6]*Occupational Outlook Quarterly* (U.S. Government Printing Office: U.S. Department of Labor, Fall 1993), p. 15.

[7]*Occupational Outlook Handbook*, 1990–1991 Edition, *ibid.*

ing accounting data or reports.[8] Unethical managers and employees pressure accountants to aid them in the latter. Accountants may also discover managers' or employees' unethical behavior and must decide when and how to "blow the whistle." Thus, accountants—as much or more than other members of society— need to have well-developed senses of ethics and abilities to cope with ethical dilemmas.

Individual and Group Ethics

Webster's defines ethics as "dealing with values relating to human conduct, with respect to the rightness and wrongness of actions."[9] Most of us know what is right and wrong. However, we can be influenced by feelings such as greed, jealousy, ambition, and pride. We know that moral and ethical standards require us to control or overcome our baser feelings. It takes discipline and self-denial to succeed. However, group pressure often works against our best efforts.

For example, during their college careers, most students witness at least one case of scholastic dishonesty such as cheating on examinations. However, these students report only a very few cases. Why? Because they believe their peer group will think less of the person who blows the whistle than of the person who commits the act of dishonesty. As we grow more mature, we should become less sensitive to peer pressure. However, it is also present in the business environment, and you must consider how you will handle it.

Black and White Versus Gray

The "gray zone" is another problem people face in ethical decisions. It is easy to know what one should do if one alternative is clearly right and the other one is clearly wrong. Unfortunately, many situations confront us in which both (all) alternatives have some aspects of right and some of wrong.

Consider an example. Your good friend, through a series of financial misfortunes, has fallen behind on her car payments. Unless she makes a payment immediately, the car will be repossessed. She has tried to borrow money from many sources, including friends, but no one has the money to spare. You are responsible for the office petty cash fund, and she asks you to advance her the money from the fund. Only a few days remain until payday when she says she will repay the money. Your co-workers agree that this is a good solution to her problem. Most people know in their minds that to make a loan from petty cash is wrong. However, in their hearts, they feel it is wrong for their friend to lose something as important as a car because she is late with a payment by just a few days. What would you do?

When you consider gray-zone dilemmas similar to the one above, review alternative ways to look at the situation. That way, you can ultimately do what you know is right and feel right about it. For example, in the case of your friend's car payment, no individual in the office can make a sufficient loan, but what about taking up a collection of smaller loans? Also, consider seeking advice from more experienced individuals who might know more ways to solve the problem. In this case, perhaps a supervisor knows whether your friend can receive an advance against her next paycheck.

---

[8]Clearly, not all unethical behavior within organizations involves accountability and the accounting system. For example, sexual harassment may occur with no compromise of accounting data or reports.

[9]*Webster's College Dictionary* (New York: Random House, Inc.), 1991.

Ethics in This Text

Because ethics in business and accounting are important, and because ethical situations in real life are not black and white and involve peer pressure, we have placed windows entitled "Insights Into Ethics" in many of the chapters of the text. Each contains an ethical decision situation that relates to the contents of the chapter and is printed on a purple background. No right answers are expected or given—reflecting the nature of many ethical choices.

SUMMARY

Define accounting and describe the process of accounting.   Accounting is a process of systematically and selectively capturing, recording, and summarizing data and preparing statements that communicate relevant information about economic entities, transactions, and events to decision makers. Accounting focuses on economic entities such as individuals, businesses, and government units and records data about the transactions they enter into. Accountants have a responsibility to construct reports that contain relevant information and to communicate that relevance to decision makers.

Identify the users and uses of accounting information.   The users of accounting information include managers, employees, and suppliers of all kinds of organizations and various outside decision makers such as owners and creditors of a business, citizens of a town or city, and donors and beneficiaries of charities. Accounting information about an entity is used to answer questions about its financial condition, its best future alternatives, whether it will be able to pay its bills and debts, and its performance—profitability in the case of a business.

Describe what accountants do in the private sector, in government, and in public accounting practice.   Accountants work within organizations to design and operate accounting systems to produce relevant information for managers and outsiders. They also perform internal audits and contribute to tax management. Accountants who practice public accounting perform accounting, auditing, and tax and management advisory services for fees.

Identify the important relationships among ethics, business, and accounting. Successful business is built on many relationships of trust and is impeded when individuals cannot rely on the integrity of others, either within their own organizations or outside. Accounting's central role in accountability puts accountants under pressure to falsify accounting information. Accountants often discover wrongdoing and must decide when and how to blow the whistle on wrongdoers.

KEY TERMS

accountability, *13*

accounting, *4*

bookkeeping, *5*

businesses, *7*

charities, *8*

economic entities, *4*

financial accounting, *9*

financial auditing, *10*

financial statements, *9*

government accounting, *8*

governments, *8*

internal audit, *10*

managerial accounting, *9*

private accounting, *8*

public accounting, *8*

transaction, *4*

QUESTIONS

QI-1   What is the difference between the accountant's role in data gathering and recording?

QI-2   What is the purpose of each of the four steps in the accounting process?

QI-3   What are the differences between the roles of accountants and bookkeepers?

QI-4   What functions do accountants perform within an organization?

QI-5   What type of accounting information might individuals need about their own finances?

QI-6   Name the three major classes of users of accounting information about businesses.

QI-7   What type of accounting information do managers need about their business?

QI-8   What type of accounting information do owners and prospective owners need about a business?

QI-9   What type of accounting information do lenders need about a business?

QI-10   What are the differences between financial and managerial accounting?

QI-11   What services do public accountants typically perform?

QI-12   What major certifications are available to accountants?

QI-13   What are five professional accounting organizations?

QI-14   Why are business ethics important?

QI-15   What is accountability?

CRITICAL THINKING AND COMMUNICATING

CI-1   You are the controller of Wings Corporation, a large manufacturer of military aircraft. As a result of an internal audit, you discover that a large monetary contribution was made to the spouse of a cousin of the President of Barunda. The cousin is the representative of Wings Corporation in Barunda. Your audit revealed that the purpose of the contribution was to secure the sale of a large number of aircraft to Barunda. Such a payment, though minor in amount to Wings, is illegal in both Barunda and the United States. What actions should you take regarding the payment of the cash?

CI-2   After visiting, observing, and interviewing the manager of a local business explain:

a. The business documents primarily used.
b. Whether the business uses a manual or computerized accounting system.
c. The reports prepared by the business and how often they are produced.
d. What information needs are being met by each of the reports and who are its users (managers, owners, lenders, or others).

CI-3   Contact and arrange to interview someone who is an accountant or who graduated with an accounting degree. Ask for a copy of this person's resume and use it to help you structure the questions you would like to ask in your interview regarding his or her career development. Share the resume and your write-up of the interview with your class in a brief oral presentation.

CHAPTER 1

Introduction to Corporate Financial Accounting

At a recent University Alumni Association event, Judy Martinez, Sharon Simpson, and Paul Shell complained to each other about their jobs in large cities and how much they disliked commuting to and from work. Besides the commuting, they found affordable parking nearly impossible to locate. Having been classmates at the University and having remained close friends since graduation, they reminisced about the "good old days" as college students and when problems such as commuting were nonexistent. They all agreed that it would be wonderful to relocate to and live in the University city.

For several weeks after the alumni event, Judy kept recalling their conversation about returning to the University community. She decided to do some research on business opportunities there. By talking to people familiar with the community, she discovered that few photocopying facilities were available for students and the University community. She asked herself, "Why don't Sharon, Paul, and I form a photocopying business in the University city?"

Excited with her idea, Judy called Sharon and Paul and discussed the idea of a photocopying business. They all agreed that the idea sounded promising, and they decided to go ahead with the business. Each invested $2,000 in the business to get it started. They formed a corporation called PhotoCopy, Inc., and the business came into existence.

After only one month, the business proved so successful that Judy, Sharon, and Paul considered opportunities for improving it. However, they faced a difficult decision. They could just continue operating the business as is indefinitely. They could borrow money to add additional capacity to the current location. Or, they could possibly borrow money to purchase another location for a photocopying business on the opposite side of campus.

What kind of information will they need to make such a decision? Accounting information—specifically, information about the amounts they can expect to receive and to pay under each of the alternatives. If they have to borrow money from a bank to pay for expansion or for an additional location, they will need accounting information to convince the bank that making the loan is a sound investment. Financial accounting provides information that is relevant to the owners of PhotoCopy, Inc., and potential lenders in such situations. So, let us look at its basic elements.

LEARNING OBJECTIVES

1. Define or describe the basic elements of financial accounting.
2. Apply the financial accounting equation and the double-entry technique to processing business transactions.
3. Describe the four basic financial statements.
4. Analyze the profitability of a business from an owner's perspective.
5. Recognize the limitations of accounting information for decision making.

LO 1

Define or describe the basic elements of financial accounting.

THE FOUNDATION OF FINANCIAL ACCOUNTING

Records similar to those of modern accounting were used in Northern Italy as early as the Middle Ages—at least a century before Columbus discovered America.[1] Begun as a means of keeping track of what a merchant owed and what was owed to a merchant, accounting has evolved over several centuries into a more sophisticated way of capturing and transforming data. Its objectives are to report on the financial position and performance of any business and to support the varied management decisions of that business. However, since the business world is ever-changing and increases in complexity each year, authorities, who the government designates directly or indirectly, continuously adapt accounting to the changing environment.

Generally Accepted Accounting Principles

Financial statements that a U.S. business publishes and distributes to outsiders must conform to professional standards called **Generally Accepted Accounting Principles** (GAAP). Before the mid-1930s, GAAP consisted of relatively few foundation elements, including broad assumptions, concepts, and definitions, that had evolved over several centuries. Much judgment was required to apply GAAP to individual businesses and circumstances. In fact, managers of U.S. firms made most judgments regarding what constituted GAAP and how to conform financial statements with them.[2]

The Stock Market Crash of 1929 and the ensuing Great Depression, however, uncovered many abuses of managements' discretion.[3] Although the Crash

[1]A. C. Littleton, *Essays on Accountancy* (Urbana: University of Illinois Press, 1961), p. 22. Littleton notes the existence of the 500-year-old account books of the Florentine merchant, Francesco di Marco, 1358–1412.

[2]Companies whose securities were listed on the New York Stock Exchange had to conform to some financial reporting requirements imposed by the Exchange in its listing agreement.

[3]A colorful description of some of the pre-Depression abuses of financial reporting in the United States is given in William Z. Ripley, *Main Street and Wall Street* (Lawrence, Kansas: Scholars Book Co., 1972), pp. 162–64. This book was published originally in 1927.

and Depression were not caused by accounting abuses, such abuses apparently were considered contributing factors. In the mid-1930s, the U. S. government passed the Securities Act of 1933 and the Securities Exchange Act of 1934. Both acts gave the newly formed Securities and Exchange Commission (SEC) the authority to set accounting standards for financial statements filed with the SEC, that is, for financial statements of virtually all large, publicly-owned U.S. corporations.

Interestingly, the SEC has exercised its authority only indirectly. In 1938, the SEC turned to the accounting profession, represented by the American Institute of Certified Public Accountants (AICPA). The AICPA's Committee on Accounting Procedure (CAP) and later its Accounting Principles Board (APB) set standards for financial statements until 1973. In 1973, the Financial Accounting Standards Board (FASB), a new body and independent of the AICPA, was formed to bring representatives of businesses and users of financial statements, as well as CPAs, directly into the standard-setting process. The CAP issued 51 Accounting Research Bulletins, the APB issued 31 Opinions, and the FASB had issued over 100 Statements of Financial Accounting Standards by the early 1990s.[4] As a consequence, Generally Accepted Accounting Principles now include the original foundation elements, those that evolved over centuries, plus an ever-expanding set of authoritative pronouncements on the ways to apply them to specific situations.

Key Financial Accounting Concepts

In spite of all the complexities in the business world – and the related complexities in setting accounting standards – a small and cohesive set of concepts, simple equations, definitions, measurement principles, and assumptions form the foundation of GAAP. These foundation elements guide accountants in recording the activities of businesses and in preparing their financial statements. To understand financial accounting, you must begin with the most fundamental of elements.

Three key concepts of financial accounting are: the accounting entity, the accounting period, and monetary measurement. These concepts give the accounting process its focus.

The Accounting Entity Concept. The **accounting entity concept** states that the accounting process focuses on specific, separate economic entities. The *focus of financial accounting is on specific business entities, separate from other entities*, including their owners. For example, if Dr. Jessica Brown purchased a new car for her personal use, she would account for the expenditure as a personal expenditure, not as an expenditure of her medical practice.

In the United States, business entities are organized into three basic forms: proprietorships, partnerships, and corporations.

A **proprietorship** is a business owned by an individual. Proprietorships have no legal status apart from their owners; their relationships to other parties (customers, suppliers, employees, etc.) are all interpreted legally as relationships between the owner, as an individual, and the other parties. For example, if the government found a proprietorship had not paid all of its payroll taxes on time, it would bring legal action against the owner, not the business itself. However, for accounting purposes, the proprietor is a separate entity from the

---

[4]CAP and APB standards are still considered authoritative, unless superceded by FASB Statements.

business. For example, the proprietor should keep personal funds separate from business funds. This way, the proprietor would know how much cash is available for business expenses and how much is available for personal spending.

Partnerships are businesses conducted by two or more entities acting as co-owners. Like proprietorships, partnerships are not separate, legal entities. The relationships between partnerships and others are interpreted legally as relationships between the partners, individually and collectively, with the other entities. For example, if a customer is injured by a product purchased from a partnership, he or she would sue the partners "jointly and severally" to recover

INTERNATIONAL PERSPECTIVES

The world is about to close the books on the 20th century amid a rapid-fire series of historic changes. Europe's markets are uniting. Eastern Bloc countries are embracing capitalist values. The Japanese are aggressively investing abroad. Medium and small companies are scrambling for new international opportunities. And in the midst of all this, issuers, investors, and analysts around the world are grappling with some surprisingly fundamental accounting questions.

For example: If the price/earnings ratio of a Japanese company is dramatically higher than that of an otherwise comparable U.S. company, is it because the cost of funds in Japan is lower? Is it because real prices charged to Japanese customers are higher than those charged to non-Japanese customers in overseas markets, presumably resulting in higher profit margins? Or is it due to an accounting distortion? If so, to what degree? And which of the two markets – U.S., Japan, or both – is distorted?

Granted, the volume of international financial transactions has exploded in recent years and may grow much larger if the United States Securities and Exchange Commission (SEC) eases restrictions on the sale of foreign debts and equity in the U.S. to sophisticated buyers. But what effect has accounting diversity had on the global capital markets so far? And if the purpose of accounting is to portray economic reality, are the economics driving the accounting or vice versa?

Because accountants of the world are not united by a single language like Esperanto or measurement standard like the metric system, cross-border financial participants must translate a bewildering array of financial information with great dispatch and hope nothing important gets lost in the translation. As one executive of a major credit rating agency put it, "Ten years ago, our primary readership was a U.S. audience. Today, it is very much an international market because of the recent explosion in Euro-bond and Euro-commercial paper offerings by companies in the U.S., Europe and Asia. And these international issuers are no longer brand names such as ICI or Siemens. It's a lot of companies that investors don't know, and frankly we're a little worried about this."

Can there be a single standard of comparison? Definite answers are still elusive. The SEC, the U.S.-based Financial Accounting Standards Board (FASB) and many organizations outside the U.S., most significantly the International Accounting Standards Committee, have publicly stated that harmonization of international accounting standards is a priority. But others are more skeptical. As one issuer [of financial statements] stated, "An international set of accounting standards would be a good idea, but we won't see it in our lifetime."

Meanwhile, the world must cope with accounting diversity.

Source: "Valuing Global Securities: Is Accounting Diversity a Mountain or a Molehill?" Arthur Andersen & Co., S.C., and Salomon Brothers, Inc., 1990.

damages for the injury. Nevertheless, for accounting purposes, partnerships are treated as entities that are separate and distinct from the partners.

Corporations are business entities that are legally separate from their owners. Corporations are nonpersons; they do not exist naturally. A person may not simply begin a business and call it a corporation; a corporation must be chartered under a state's corporation statutes. Corporations can have any number of owners (including one) and still be corporations. Since corporations are separate legal entities, no inconsistency exists between their legal status and their treatment as separate business entities in accounting. In this textbook, we emphasize the corporation form of business.

The Accounting Period Concept. The **accounting period concept** states that financial statements or other reports should be prepared at regular intervals such as every month, quarter, or year. Virtually all businesses prepare annual financial statements. Many also prepare statements at more frequent intervals because users of financial statements, particularly managers, need information more frequently to make decisions.

The Monetary Measurement Concept. An almost infinite variety of information could appear in accounting reports—from the business's physical characteristics and appearance to its personnel to the specific ways it provides services or products to customers. Accounting cuts through the infinite set of possibilities and focuses on the business's financial essentials. A business is a pool of financial resources provided by its owners and creditors (lenders). Accounting focuses on the flow of resources through a business and only measures and reports on those business events, resources, and obligations that can be expressed in money terms. This idea is known as the **monetary measurement concept** that underlies GAAP.

Accounting Equations and Definitions[5]

Fundamental equations bind the elements of financial accounting together into a logical whole. The definitions of the elements tell us what aspects of a business are actually recognized and measured by the financial accounting process.

The Accounting Equation. The **accounting equation** states that assets equal liabilities plus stockholders' equity and governs the relationship between these three elements. It is expressed as follows:

Assets = Liabilities + Stockholders' Equity

Assets. **Assets** are future economic benefits a business owns or controls. In a word, an asset is a resource of the business. Assets include anything that can be used for the business's benefit or any right to receive benefits. Examples of assets are cash, land, buildings, and equipment. **Accounts receivable** are payments due from customers for products or services previously provided on a credit basis. An account receivable is an asset because it represents a right to receive a future payment.

Liabilities. **Liabilities** are the business's debts and other obligations to transfer cash, other assets, or services to other entities at some time in the future. Debts to lenders are liabilities because they require payment of specific,

---

[5]To avoid unnecessary abstraction, definitions in this section are not direct quotes from *Statement on Financial Accounting Concepts No. 6*, "Elements of Financial Statements of Business Enterprises," (Stamford, Connecticut: FASB, 1985), but are based on the FASB definitions.

future amounts to repay and erase the debts. **Accounts payable**, amounts owed to suppliers for goods purchased on credit (charged), are also liabilities.

Stockholders' equity. The **stockholders' equity** of a corporation is the residual interest owners have in the business's assets after deducting its liabilities. Both creditors and owners supply the funds to buy assets. According to the accounting equation, the total assets of a business are matched by the combined claims of the owners and creditors. However, the claims of creditors come before the claims of owners. For example, if a business is liquidated (say, in bankruptcy proceedings), the creditors' claims must be paid in full before the owners can receive any of the business's assets. Therefore, stockholders' equity is a *residual* amount. It equals the net assets of the business, or the difference between the assets and the liabilities.

Stockholders' Equity = Net Assets = Assets − Liabilities

Stockholders' equity changes when the owners make investments in or receive dividends from the business. When owners contribute cash or other assets to the business, we call the contributions **investments**. Owners of a corporation make investments in the business by purchasing shares of stock. For this reason, the owners of a corporation are called **stockholders**. Investments increase stockholders' equity because they increase assets without increasing liabilities. When the business gives cash or other assets to the owners, we call the assets given **distributions**. Distributions of proprietorships and partnerships are also called **withdrawals**, while distributions by corporations are called **dividends**. Dividends decrease stockholders' equity because they decrease assets without decreasing liabilities. In addition, stockholders' equity is increased by revenues and decreased by expenses as defined below.

Stockholders' equity has two components. **Capital stock** is the amount of the investments in the business that stockholders make. **Retained earnings** is the cumulative amount of net income (defined below) less dividends paid to the stockholders since the corporation began operations.

The assets, liabilities, and stockholders' equity of a corporation make up its **financial position**. The financial position of a business is communicated in the **balance sheet** (formally known as a **statement of financial position**). The balance sheet takes its name from the accounting equation, which guarantees that assets will be balanced exactly by liabilities and stockholders' equity. We present a balance sheet later in the chapter as one of the outputs of the financial accounting process.

The Income Equation.   **Net income** is defined by a very important equation in accounting:

Revenues − Expenses = Net Income

Revenues. **Revenues** are the increases in net assets (stockholders' equity) that result directly from providing products or services to customers during a specific period. In most cases, the assets received for providing products or services to customers are cash or the rights to receive cash in the future (accounts receivable). Thus, for example, when you buy clothing from a department store, the amount of the sale is revenue to the store, regardless of whether you pay cash or charge your purchase.

Expenses. **Expenses** are decreases in net assets (stockholders' equity) caused by the revenue-producing activities during a specific period. Examples of expenses are employees' wages, supplies, utilities, and rent. Many expenses represent decreases in cash. However, not all expenses are direct decreases in cash. For example, wages earned by employees during a period but not yet paid as of the end of the period are an obligation to pay. The increase in the liability, called salaries and wages payable, is an expense of the period in which the wages are earned.

The revenues, expenses, and net income of a business are communicated in the **income statement**. The income statement follows the income equation —expenses are subtracted from revenues to derive net income. We present an income statement later in the chapter.

Measurement Principles

Several measurement principles have evolved over many years of financial accounting practice. The most pervasive is the cost principle, which guides us in deciding the values to assign to assets, liabilities, revenues, and expenses. We introduce additional measurement principles in later chapters.

According to the **cost principle**, the amounts of assets recorded in the accounting records should be the amounts paid (or promised to be paid) for them when acquired. Also, the amounts of liabilities recorded should be the amounts of assets received when the liabilities are incurred. Suppose, for example, that a convenience store such as 7-Eleven purchases a piece of land for a new store site at a cost of $100,000. For accounting purposes, the value of the land is $100,000, which is also the "fair value" of the land at the date it is acquired. That is, the business presumably paid no more or less than necessary to acquire it. The land may increase in fair value over time, and while its later fair value will be a matter of opinion, its cost remains unchanged and is more objective. Because various users of financial statements such as owners and creditors have different interests in a business, objectivity is an important criterion for accounting information. Thus, the cost principle is often favored over alternatives such as "fair value."

TRANSACTION ANALYSIS USING THE ACCOUNTING EQUATION

LO 2

Apply the financial accounting equation and the double-entry technique to processing business transactions.

The financial accounting process consists of capturing transaction data, recording transactions, summarizing their effects on financial position, and, ultimately, transforming their effects into financial statements. **Transactions** consist of purchases, sales, and other exchanges that change the business's financial position. When a business purchases a piece of equipment, its financial position changes —equipment increases and cash decreases. When a business borrows money, its financial position changes—cash increases and a liability increases.

Maintaining the Equality Condition

Since transactions change the business's financial position, they are subject to the accounting equation, which defines the relationship between the elements of financial position. Therefore, *transactions are recorded according to the equation, and the equation holds both before and after each transaction is recorded.*

Before a business comes into being, its financial position consists of all zeros:

$$\textbf{Assets = Liabilities + Stockholders' Equity}$$
$$0 = \quad 0 \quad + \quad 0$$

Since the accounting equation is satisfied by the all-zero beginning position, we know that the business's future financial positions will satisfy the equality condition *if, and only if*, all of the changes recognized from this point meet the equality condition. Thus, the rule for recording transactions is: *Each change in an element of the accounting equation must be matched by at least one change that has an equal, but opposite, effect*. Hence, the rule is often called the **double-entry rule**, and financial accounting is often referred to as double-entry accounting.

Suppose, for example, that a house painter buys a paint sprayer for $1,250 on credit. To record the transaction, the asset, equipment, is increased by $1,250; and the liability, accounts payable, is increased by $1,250. The change in assets equals the change in liabilities with no change in stockholders' equity—so, the equation is satisfied.

$$\textbf{Assets = Liabilities + Stockholders' Equity}$$
$$+\$1,250 = \quad +\$1,250 \quad + \quad 0$$

Processing Transactions

Now, let us address PhotoCopy, Inc. They need to prepare financial statements for the month of January 19X1, both for their own information and possibly to convince a bank to loan them money for expansion of the business. The business had no assets, no liabilities, and no stockholders' equity just before Judy, Sharon, and Paul make their initial investment.

$$\textbf{Assets = Liabilities + Stockholders' Equity}$$
$$\text{1/1/X1} \qquad 0 = \quad 0 \quad + \quad 0$$

We now apply the double-entry rule to the transactions and events that took place during January 19X1.

Transaction 1—Owners' Investments.   On January 2, 19X1, the three owners (Judy, Sharon, and Paul) invested $2,000 each of their own money in the new business, PhotoCopy, Inc. They opened a separate checking account for the business at the bank and deposited their personal checks in the company's account. These investments immediately give life to the business by endowing it with an asset, cash. The corresponding change is an increase in stockholders' equity.

Transaction	Cash	=	Stockholders' Equity	
1/1/X1	0	=	0	
(1)	6,000	=	6,000	Investment
New Bal.	6,000	=	6,000	

The equality condition is satisfied by this change in the business's financial position. The new financial position consists of $6,000 cash and $6,000 stockholders' equity.

Transaction 2—Rental of Building Space and Copying Equipment.   On January 2, 19X1, PhotoCopy completed the rental of building space and copying equipment from Asset Management Co. The rental agreement is for 12 months from the beginning of January, and PhotoCopy paid the rent for January in the amount of $1,000. This transaction decreased an asset, cash, due to the business's revenue-producing activities—in other words, an expense. Therefore, it is recognized with a decrease to cash and an equal decrease to stockholders' equity.

Transaction	Cash	=	Stockholders' Equity	
Prev. Bal.	6,000	=	6,000	
(2)	(1,000)	=	(1,000)	Rent Expense
New Bal.	5,000	=	5,000	

Notice the result of processing every change so that it satisfies the double-entry rule. The equality condition is met by the new financial position each time. After Transaction 2, the asset cash is $5,000 and stockholders' equity is $5,000.

Transaction 3—Purchase of Copying Supplies for Cash. PhotoCopy purchased $800 of copying supplies, paper and toner, for cash. These supplies are an expense because they are used in the business's revenue-producing activities during January. This transaction decreased cash and decreased stockholders' equity by $800.

Transaction	Cash	=	Stockholders' Equity	
Prev. Bal.	5,000	=	5,000	
(3)	(800)	=	(800)	Copying Supplies Expense
New Bal.	4,200	=	4,200	

Transaction 4—Revenues Received in Cash. During January, PhotoCopy earned $4,000 in cash revenues from customers for copying services. These transactions increase cash and increase stockholders' equity by the amount of revenues earned.

Transaction	Cash	=	Stockholders' Equity	
Prev. Bal.	4,200	=	4,200	
(4)	4,000	=	4,000	Revenues
New Bal.	8,200	=	8,200	

Transaction 5—Salaries Expense. The three owners of PhotoCopy manage the business and perform copying services for customers. They agreed to pay themselves salaries of $1,000 each per month for the services they provide. On January 20, they wrote themselves checks from the PhotoCopy's checking account for January salaries. When owners of a corporation are paid for services performed for the business, these payments are not classified as dividends. This is a decrease in the asset, cash, due to an expense of the business. Therefore, it is recognized with a decrease to cash and an equal decrease to stockholders' equity for salaries expense.

Transaction	Cash	=	Stockholders' Equity	
Prev. Bal.	8,200	=	8,200	
(5)	(3,000)	=	(3,000)	Salaries Expense
New Bal.	5,200	=	5,200	

Transaction 6—Uncollected Revenues. On January 25, PhotoCopy received and produced an order for 2,000 student orientation handouts from the College of Liberal Arts and Sciences at the University. The price agreed to for the handouts is $1,000. The College agreed to pay by February 15. We record the revenues for January, because they were earned in January and the right to receive payment in February is an asset as of January 31. To record the revenues earned, we increase a new asset, accounts receivable, and increase stockholders' equity by $1,000.

Transaction	Cash	+	Accounts Receivable	=	Stockholders' Equity	
Prev. Bal.	5,200	+		=	5,200	
(6)			1,000	=	1,000	Revenue
New Bal.	5,200	+	1,000	=	6,200	

Transaction 7—Advertising Expense. During January, PhotoCopy ran the following ad daily in the campus newspaper:

> **NOW OPEN**—PhotoCopy, Inc., 1503 University Avenue. Open 8:00 a.m. to 10:00 p.m. daily. We provide all copying services, both black and white and color. Binding available. Convenient to dorms, apartment complexes, and all of main campus.

The bill for $100 is due February 15. This transaction results in a decrease in stockholders' equity for advertising expense and an increase in the liability, accounts payable.

Transaction	Cash	+	Accounts Receivable	=	Accounts Payable	+	Stockholders' Equity	
Prev. Bal.	5,200		1,000	=			6,200	
(7)		+			100		(100)	Advertising Expense
New Bal.	5,200	+	1,000	=	100	+	6,100	

Transaction 8—Purchase of Office Equipment. On January 31, PhotoCopy purchased a computer system for $1,200 cash. PhotoCopy purchased the computer system to use in keeping the company's records. The computer system is an asset of the company. We record the transaction by increasing a new asset, office equipment, and decreasing the asset cash.

Transaction	Cash	+	Accounts Receivable	+	Office Equipment	=	Accounts Payable	+	Stockholders' Equity	
Prev. Bal.	5,200	+	1,000	+		=	100	+	6,100	
(8)	(1,200)	+		+	1,200	=		+		Off. Equip. Purch.
New Bal.	4,000	+	1,000	+	1,200	=	100	+	6,100	

Illustration 1-1 summarizes all of the transactions of PhotoCopy, Inc., for January 19X1. It starts with a hypothetical financial position that satisfies the equality condition with all zeros as of January 1, 19X1. Each transaction of January is processed to satisfy the equality condition (double entry).

ILLUSTRATION 1-1 Accounting History of PhotoCopy, Inc.—January 19X1

Transaction	Cash	+	Accounts Receivable	+	Office Equipment	=	Accounts Payable	+	Stockholders' Equity
			ASSETS			=	LIABILITIES	+	STOCKHOLDERS' EQUITY
1/1/X1	0	+	0	+	0	=	0	+	0
(1)	6,000	+		+		=		+	6,000
(2)	(1,000)	+		+		=		+	(1,000)
(3)	(800)	+		+		=		+	(800)
(4)	4,000	+		+		=		+	4,000
(5)	(3,000)	+		+		=		+	(3,000)
(6)		+	1,000	+		=		+	1,000
(7)		+		+		=	100	+	(100)
(8)	(1,200)	+		+	1,200	=		+	
1/31/X1	4,000	+	1,000	+	1,200	=	100	+	6,100
			6,200			=		6,200	

After the last transaction of January, we draw a line. Down each column of PhotoCopy's accounting equation, we sum the beginning balance and the effects, if any, of Transactions 1 through 8. The results shown below the line are the balances in the equation elements as of January 31, 19X1. Below the balances, note that the sum of the assets ($6,200) does indeed equal the sum of the liability ($100) and stockholders' equity ($6,100).

LO 3

Describe the four basic financial statements.

BASIC FINANCIAL STATEMENTS

The four basic financial statements—income statement, retained earnings statement, statement of cash flows, and balance sheet—can be prepared directly from the transaction analysis summary in Illustration 1-1.

Income Statement

The income statement displays the business's revenues, expenses, and net income for a specific time period. Transactions 2–7 represent revenues and expenses of PhotoCopy, Inc. for January 19X1. They are increases and decreases, respectively, in the Stockholders' Equity column of Illustration 1-1. To prepare the income statement of PhotoCopy, Inc. for January 19X1, we format the revenues and expenses from the Stockholders' Equity column of Illustration 1-1 into the statement shown in Illustration 1-2. The income statement lists revenues first, followed by expenses, which are summed and subtracted from revenues to derive net income.

ILLUSTRATION 1-2 Income Statement

PhotoCopy, Inc. Income Statement For the Month Ended January 31, 19X1		
Revenues		$5,000
Expenses:		
Advertising expense	$ 100	
Copying supplies expense	800	
Rent expense	1,000	
Wages and salaries expense	3,000	
Total expenses		4,900
Net income		$ 100

We label every financial statement with a heading that gives three items of information: the name of the business, the type of statement, and either the date for which it was prepared or the period it covers. Notice that the heading on the income statement in Illustration 1-2 indicates that it covers the month of January 19X1. This label is appropriate because an income statement reports about events that happened *during a period*.

The Retained Earnings Statement

Illustration 1-3 shows the retained earnings statement. The **retained earnings statement** reflects the effects on the business of net income and dividends *for a period of time*. Earlier we said that revenues increase stockholders' equity and dividends and expenses decrease stockholders' equity. These changes affect stockholders' equity through the retained earnings component of stockholders' equity as distinct from the capital stock component. The retained earnings statement reflects these changes. It can be prepared from the detail of the Stockholders' Equity column of Illustration 1-1, except that it is customary to offset revenues and expenses and show net income as a single change in retained earnings. Thus, we add net income of $100 to the beginning balance of zero. For January, PhotoCopy did not distribute dividends to the stockholders. If PhotoCopy had distributed dividends to the stockholders, we would next subtract them to arrive at the net change in retained earnings for the period.

ILLUSTRATION 1-3 Retained Earnings Statement

PhotoCopy, Inc. Retained Earnings Statement For the Month Ended January 31, 19X1	
Retained earnings, January 1, 19X1	$ 0
Add: Net income for January 19X1	100
Retained earnings, January 31, 19X1	$100

Statement of Cash Flows

A **statement of cash flows** explains the change in the business's cash balance for the period by presenting the increases and decreases in cash due to the company's operating, investing, and financing activities. The definitions of these activities, the techniques for preparing the statement, and the perceived useful-ness of the statement are subjects of a later chapter. However, the statement for PhotoCopy, Inc. for January 19X1 appears in Illustration 1-4. While you may not know how to format such a statement at this time, you can trace all figures in it to the Cash column of Illustration 1-1.

ILLUSTRATION 1-4 Statement of Cash Flows

PhotoCopy, Inc. Statement of Cash Flows For the Month Ended January 31, 19X1		
Operating activities:		
Cash collections for copying services	$4,000	
Expenditure for rent	(1,000)	
Expenditure for copying supplies	(800)	
Expenditures for salaries	(3,000)	
Cash provided by operations		$ (800)
Investing activities:		
Purchase of office equipment		(1,200)
Financing activities:		
Owners' investments		6,000
Net increase in cash		$4,000

Balance Sheet

The balance sheet presents a business's financial position *as of a specific date*. A balance sheet is like a snapshot, presenting a picture of the business's financial position at an instant in time. In this case, the point in time is January 31, 19X1. Illustration 1-5 contains PhotoCopy, Inc.'s balance sheet as of January 31, 19X1.

To prepare the balance sheet in Illustration 1-5, we format the January 31, 19X1, balances at the bottom of the transaction analysis worksheet in Illustration 1-1. The cash balance of $4,000 from Illustration 1-1 is the cash figure in Illustration 1-5; and the accounts receivable balance from Illustration 1-1 is the accounts receivable balance in Illustration 1-5. Likewise, the office equipment, accounts payable, and stockholders' equity figures in Illustration 1-5 are all from the bottom line of Illustration 1-1.

ILLUSTRATION 1-5 Balance Sheet

PhotoCopy, Inc. Balance Sheet January 31, 19X1	
Assets	
Cash	$4,000
Accounts receivable	1,000
Office equipment	1,200
Total assets	$6,200
Liabilities and Stockholders' Equity	
Accounts payable	$ 100
Stockholders' equity	6,100
Total liabilities and stockholders' equity	$6,200

LO 4

Analyze the profitability of a business from an owner's perspective.

INTERPRETATION OF FINANCIAL STATEMENTS

What can be learned from the financial statements that represent PhotoCopy, Inc. for January? First, the business's cash position improved from a zero balance at the beginning of January to a balance of $4,000 at the end of January. Second, the balance sheet shows that the business's total assets equal $6,200 at the end of January and its stockholders' equity equals $6,100. Third, seemingly the business was profitable. It earned $100 in net income in one month with an original investment of $6,000. But just how profitable is this?

Profitability from the Owners' Perspective—Rate of Return

To judge profitability, we like to use a relative measure—one that can be compared to alternative uses of the owners' money. One of the important relative measures of profitability is **rate of return** (ROR) **on stockholders' equity**:

$$\text{Rate of Return on Stockholders' Equity} = \frac{\text{Net Income}}{\text{Average Stockholders' Equity}}$$

By this measure, PhotoCopy's rate of return for January was:

$$\frac{\$100}{(\$6,000 + \$6,100) \div 2} = \frac{\$100}{\$6,050} = 1.65\%$$

The annual equivalent rate of return is 1.65% x 12 (months) = 19.8%, which is very impressive indeed when compared with the likely interest rate on the savings accounts from which the owners of PhotoCopy withdrew their investment funds.

However, it is important to recognize the nature and limitations of the accounting information used in the calculation. PhotoCopy's income for the month of January is unique to this first month of business. For example, January required no maintenance of the copying equipment, whereas future months will surely see some expenditures for maintenance.

INSIGHTS INTO ETHICS

John Washington started a successful business delivering fast foods for several small restaurants in his college town. Now, about to graduate and move on in his life, John has put his business up for sale. John is negotiating to sell it to James Caldwell, a retired postal worker who has some money he wants to invest. John knows Mr. Caldwell has a limited knowledge of accounting. John also knows that he provided a substantial amount of the actual delivery driving in his business for which he received no salary. Thus, the wages and salaries expense on his income statements do not reflect his services as owner. Mr. Caldwell, however, will not be driving deliveries himself and is relying on John's financial statements to estimate future profits and establish a price he is willing to pay.

What will happen to Mr. Caldwell's estimates of future profitability if he learns of John's role in making deliveries?

What should John do?

Limitations of Accounting Information as a *Basis* for Decisions

The lesson is that financial accounting information does not provide answers to decision problems by itself. It merely tracks the history of a business. To make decisions, a user of financial statements must learn to analyze historical accounting information, understand it in the context of the business, and then use it as a basis for projections into the future. It is the projections of past results into the future (with appropriate modifications for expected changes) that are the foundation for actual choices between decision alternatives.

For example, PhotoCopy may find that, not only will the maintenance costs of the business be substantial in the future, but that it will also incur additional costs such as wages of employees hired to handle increasing numbers of customers. Thus, the business may face higher wages expenses as well as significant maintenance expenses in the future. Such projected differences from the brief past history of the business should influence:

1. The owners' projections about the business in the future.
2. Whether they choose to expand their business.
3. Whether they choose to start a second location across campus.

When they compare the rates of return that they *project* for the business for these alternatives to the rate on, say, a savings account, they should consider the risk of their expanded business relative to the safety of a savings account.

SUMMARY

Define or describe the basic elements of financial accounting.   Financial accounting is built on concepts of the accounting entity, the accounting period, and monetary measurement; on definitions of assets, liabilities, stockholders' equity, revenues, and expenses; on the cost principle; and on two central equations:

$$\text{Assets} = \text{Liabilities} + \text{Stockholders' Equity}$$
$$\text{Revenues} - \text{Expenses} = \text{Net Income}$$

Apply the financial accounting equation and the double-entry technique to processing business transactions.   Transactions are processed from the business's inception according to the double-entry rule that says for each change in one element of the accounting equation one or more changes must be made in other elements that equal it in total and have the opposite effect.

Describe the four basic business financial statements.   The four basic financial statements of businesses are the income statement, the retained earnings statement, the statement of cash flows, and the balance sheet (statement of financial position).

Analyze the profitability of a business from an owner's perspective.   Owners wish to know whether a business is relatively as profitable as other alternatives that they may have for investing funds. The rate of return on stockholders' equity (net income ÷ average stockholders' equity) for a period is a relevant measure of profitability for owners.

Recognize the limitations of accounting information for decision making.   Accounting information tracks the history of a business. As such, it does not provide answers to business decision problems directly. Rather, accounting information provides a basis for the projections of future consequences of decisions necessary to decide about which courses of action to take.

REVIEW PROBLEM

John Crown, the owner of Crown's Dental Clinic, Inc. started his practice after graduating from dental school on July 1, 19X1. At that time, the practice had no assets, liabilities, or stockholders' equity. The transactions for the month of July are given below:

July 1   John Crown invested $28,000 of his own money in Crown's Dental Clinic by purchasing capital stock in the corporation.

      3   John paid $800 for July's office rent.

      5   John rented used dental equipment and paid $400 for July.

    31   John billed his patients $5,200 during July. $4,000 of fees were received in cash at the time services were performed, and the remaining $1,200 was still owed by patients as of July 31.

    31   John was billed $1,100 for utilities.

    31   John paid wages of $1,400 to himself, the receptionist, and the hygienist.

    31   John purchased $1,200 of used dental equipment, signing a note payable for the amount.

    31   Crown's Dental Clinic, Inc., paid John a $1,000 cash dividend.

REQUIRED:

a. Determine the effect of each transaction on the accounting equation for Crown's Dental Clinic, Inc., and total each part of the equation for July.

b. Prepare an income statement for the month of July.

c. Prepare a retained earnings statement for the month of July.

d. Prepare a balance sheet as of July 31.

SOLUTION:

Planning and Organizing Your Work

1. Analyze each transaction.
2. Enter the effect of each transaction in the appropriate columns of the accounting equation following the double-entry rule.
3. Total each column.
4. Verify that the equation is in balance.
5. Select the items to include on the income statement.
6. Prepare the income statement.
7. Select the items to include on the retained earnings statement.
8. Prepare the retained earnings statement.
9. Select the items to include on the balance sheet.
10. Prepare the balance sheet.

(a) *Determine the effect of each transaction.*

Transaction	Cash	+ Accounts Receivable	+ Equipment	= Accounts Payable	+ Notes Payable	+ Stockholders' Equity	
1.	28,000					28,000	Investment
2.	(800)					(800)	Rent exp.
3.	(400)					(400)	Rent exp.
4.	4,000	1,200				5,200	Revenue
5.				1,100		(1,100)	Utilities exp.
6.	(1,400)					(1,400)	Wages and salaries exp.
7.			1,200		1,200		Notes payable
8.	(1,000)					(1,000)	Dividend
7/31 Total	28,400 +	1,200 +	1,200	= 1,100 +	1,200 +	28,500	

(b) *Prepare an income statement.*

Crown's Dental Clinic, Inc. Income Statement For the Month Ended July 31, 19X1		
Fee revenue		$5,200
Expenses:		
Rent expense, office	$ 800	
Rent expense, equipment	400	
Utilities expense	1,100	
Wages and salaries expense	1,400	
Total expenses		3,700
Net income		$1,500

(c) *Prepare a retained earnings statement.*

Crown's Dental Clinic, Inc. Retained Earnings Statement For the Month Ended July 31, 19X1	
Beginning balance	$ 0
Add: Net income	1,500
Less: Dividends	(1,000)
Ending balance	$ 500

(d) *Prepare a balance sheet.*

Crown's Dental Clinic, Inc. Balance Sheet July 31, 19X1	
Assets	
Cash	$28,400
Accounts receivable	1,200
Equipment	1,200
Total assets	$30,800
Liabilities and Stockholders' Equity	
Accounts payable	$ 1,100
Notes payable	1,200
Capital stock	28,000
Retained earnings	500
Total liabilities and stockholders' equity	$30,800

KEY TERMS

accounting entity concept, *21*

accounting equation, *23*

accounting period concept, *23*

accounts payable, *24*

accounts receivable, *23*

assets, *23*

balance sheet, *24*

capital stock, *24*

corporations, *23*

SELF-QUIZ

LO 1 1. Which accounting concept requires accountants to separate the owners from their business entities?
- a. Individual concept
- b. Accounting period concept
- c. Monetary concept
- d. Accounting entity concept

LO 1 2. Which accounting relationship is incorrect?
- a. Assets = Liabilities + Stockholders' Equity
- b. Net Income – Expenses = Revenues
- c. Net Assets = Assets – Liabilities
- d. Stockholders' Equity = Assets – Liabilities

LO 1 3. Which type of business entities are legally separate from their owners?
- a. Corporations
- b. Proprietorships
- c. Partnerships
- d. Both b and c

LO 3 4. Which of the following is *not* one of the basic financial statements of a business?
- a. Income statement
- b. Statement of cash flows
- c. Liability statement
- d. Retained earnings statement

LO 2 5. What items in the accounting equation (assets, liabilities, or stockholders' equity) are increased or decreased as a result of an owner investing $15,000 cash in the business?

LO 2 6. What items in the accounting equation are increased or decreased as a result of paying wages of $1,500?

LO 2 7. What items in the accounting equation are increased or decreased as a result of receiving $9,000 cash for services performed?

LO 2 8. What items in the accounting equation are increased or decreased as a result of a corporation paying its stockholders $3,900 of dividends?

LO 4 9. How is the rate of return on stockholders' equity calculated?
- a. Dividing cash from operating activities by total assets
- b. Dividing net income by 2 and adding stockholders' equity
- c. Dividing net income by average stockholders' equity
- d. Dividing net income by average assets

LO 5 10. True or False? A decision maker can rely solely on accounting information to make a decision.

LO 1 11. Match the definitions with these terms that appear on an income statement:
- ___ Revenues
- ___ Net income
- ___ Expenses
- a. Decreases in net assets caused by generating revenues
- b. Increases in net assets from providing goods or services to customers
- c. Revenues minus expenses

LO 3 12. Match these definitions with the different financial statements:
- ___ Balance sheet
- ___ Retained earnings statement
- ___ Statement of cash flows
- ___ Income statement
- a. Presents revenues and expenses
- b. Presents cumulative amount of net income less dividends
- c. Presents assets, liabilities, and stockholders' equity
- d. Presents operating, investing, and financing cash flows

LO 1 13. Match the definitions with the different types of business entities.
- ___ Partnership
- ___ Proprietorship
- ___ Corporation
- a. A business legally separate from its owners
- b. A business not legally separate from its several owners
- c. A business not legally separate from the single owner

LO 1 14. The balance sheet is also known as the _____ of _____ _____ .

LO 1 15. The _____ _____ prevents an accountant from recording an asset's value greater than the price paid when it was acquired.

LO 3 16. The _____ _____ is the only basic statement prepared as of a specific time instead of for a period of time.

LO 1 17. Distributions of proprietorships are called _____, whereas distributions of corporations are called _____.

LO 2 18. The _____ rule states that at least two elements of the accounting equation must be increased or decreased for each transaction.

SOLUTIONS TO SELF-QUIZ

1. d   2. b   3. a   4. c   5. assets increase; stockholders' equity increases   6. assets decrease; stockholders' equity decreases   7. assets increase; stockholders' equity increases   8. assets decrease; stockholders' equity decreases   9. c   10. false   11. revenues = b; net income = c; expenses = a   12. balance sheet = c; retained earnings statement = b; statement of cash flows = d;   income statement = a   13. partnership = b; proprietorship = c; corporation = a   14. statement of financial position   15. cost principle   16. balance sheet   17. withdrawals, dividends   18. double-entry

QUESTIONS

Q1-1 What government body has the right to make accounting rules, even though it has only indirectly exercised this authority?

Q1-2 What do CAP, FASB, and APB have in common?

Q1-3 What are the important differences among a proprietorship, a partnership, and a corporation?

Q1-4 What are the four basic financial statements of businesses?

Q1-5 Why is the accounting period concept necessary?

Q1-6 What are the definitions of the three elements of the accounting equation?

Q1-7 What is the difference between a withdrawal and a dividend?

Q1-8 What is the general rule for recording accounting transactions?

Q1-9 What specific information can you learn about a company from each of its four financial statements?

Q1-10 What feature distinguishes a balance sheet from the other three basic financial statements?

Q1-11 Name a measure that can help stockholders judge profitability.

Q1-12 How should a decision maker effectively use financial accounting information?

EXERCISES

LO 1   **E1-1   Accounting Relationships**   Determine stockholders' equity if total assets are $86,000 and total liabilities are $31,000.

LO 1   **E1-2   Accounting Relationships**   Determine the ending balance of retained earnings if you know the following information:

Dividends to owners	$9,100
Beginning retained earnings	9,800
Net income	5,100

LO 1   **E1-3   Accounting Relationships**   Determine revenues if you know the following information:

Total assets (ending)	$13,500
Expenses	3,100
Capital stock	4,000
Total liabilities (ending)	3,600
Beginning stockholders' equity	6,000
Dividends to owners	1,100

LO 2

E1-4 **Processing Business Transactions** Ann Fernandez started operating U Rent-All, Inc. on January 1, 19X1. During the month of January, U Rent-All entered into a number of transactions. On a separate sheet of paper, show the effect that each transaction had on assets, liabilities, and stockholders' equity by using a + for increase; a − for decrease; and an N for no effect. Use the format below for your answer. The first transaction is completed for you.

Transaction	Assets	Liabilities	Stockholders' Equity
(0)	+	+	N

(0) Borrowed money from the bank.

a. Ann Fernandez invested her own money in U Rent-All, Inc. by purchasing capital stock.

b. Paid wages.

c. Collected cash from renting equipment.

d. Corporation paid dividends to Ann.

e. Paid the utility bill for January.

f. Paid the rent for January.

LO 3

E1-5 **Financial Statement Items** On a separate sheet of paper, place the correct letters next to the following items to show that they belong on the (*B*) balance sheet, (*I*) income statement, or (*RE*) retained earnings statement. It is possible that an item may belong on more than one statement.

Cash	Utilities expense
Fee revenue	Capital stock
Net income	Notes payable
Stockholders' equity	Dividends
	Wages and salaries expense

LO 3

E1-6 **Income Statement Preparation** Using the following data, prepare an income statement for the Clyde Corporation for the year ended December 31, 19X4.

Rent expense	$17,500	Utilities expense	$3,700
Fee revenue	48,900	Advertising expense	7,700
Wages and salaries expense	23,800	Insurance expense	2,000
Interest revenue	9,600		

LO 3

E1-7 **Balance Sheet Preparation** Using the following data, prepare a balance sheet for the Rolf Corporation for the year ended December 31, 19X7. Calculate any unknown amounts needed to complete the balance sheet.

Bank loan payable	$35,000	Cash	$16,600
Land	18,000	Accounts receivable	13,900

LO 3

E1-8 **Retained Earnings Statement Preparation** Using the following data, prepare a retained earnings statement for the Yolanda Corporation for the year ended December 31, 19X3.

Retained earnings, 1/1/X3	$14,000	Revenues	27,500
Dividends	3,800	Expenses	15,500

LO 4

E1-9 **Compute Rate of Return on Stockholders' Equity** Using the following data, compute the rate of return on stockholders' equity for Silverheels Corporation for the year ended December 31, 19X9.

Stockholders' equity, 1/1/X9	$ 8,000
Assets, 12/31/X9	65,000
Liabilities, 12/31/X9	41,000
Net income, 19X9	4,000

PROBLEM SET A

LO 2

P1-1A **Understanding Business Transactions** Transactions for Home Decorators, Inc. for the month ended October 31, 19X5 (the first month of operations), are shown below in equation form.

	Cash	+	Land	=	Bank Loan	+	Stockholders' Equity
Beg. Bal.	0		0		0		0
1.	191,000						191,000
2.	134,000				134,000		
3.	(107,300)		107,300				
4.	6,200						6,200
5.	(1,100)						(1,100)
6.	(2,500)				(2,500)		
7.	(2,300)						(2,300)

REQUIRED:

Describe the probable nature of each transaction that occurred during the month of October. For example, Transaction 1 could be described as the owner investing $191,000 cash in Home Decorators, Inc. by purchasing capital stock. Each transaction is different. Assume that Transaction 4 was with customers, Transaction 5 was with employees, and Transaction 7 was with the stockholders.

LO 2,3

P1-2A **Process Business Transactions** Janet Jones, the owner of Rent-a-Disk, Inc., started her business on May 1, 19X4. At that time, the business had no assets, liabilities, or stockholders' equity. The transactions for the month of May are given below:

May 1   Janet Jones invested $9,600 of her own money to establish her new business, Rent-a-Disk, Inc., by purchasing capital stock of the corporation.

      2   Janet borrowed $5,000 from the bank.

    31   Janet collected $1,900 for rentals in May.

    31   Janet rented a store. She paid $500 for May's rent.

    31   Janet paid her assistant $600 in wages.

    31   Janet rented CDs to the Phi Kappa Psi fraternity but will not be paid until next month. The total rental amount is $85.

    31   Janet received a utility bill for $160 for the month of May. The bill will be paid in June.

    31   Rent-A-Disk, Inc., paid Janet cash dividends of $700.

REQUIRED:

a. Determine the effect of each transaction on the accounting equation for Rent-a-Disk, Inc., and summarize their total effects on each part of the equation for May. The elements of the accounting equation for the store are cash, accounts receivable, accounts payable, bank loan payable, and stockholders' equity.

b. Prepare an income statement for the month of May.

c. Prepare a retained earnings statement for the month of May.

d. Prepare a balance sheet as of May 31.

LO 3

P1-3A **Financial Statement Preparation** The following data are presented for Clifton's Auto Repair Shop, Inc., for 19X1:

Capital stock	$10,000	Rent expense	$10,800
Bank loan payable, 12/31/X1	35,000	Wages or salaries expense	25,600
Land, 12/31/X1	38,000	Utilities expense	3,500
Cash, 12/31/X1	26,600	Advertising expense	4,200
Accounts receivable, 12/31/X1	24,500	Insurance expense	7,100
Repairs revenue	87,400	Dividends	6,800

REQUIRED:

Prepare an income statement, retained earnings statement, and balance sheet for Clifton's Auto Repair Shop, Inc., for 19X1. Calculate any unknown amounts needed to complete the financial statements.

LO 1,4   **P1-4A   Accounting Relationships and Return on Stockholders' Equity**   The following information is from Hal's Printing Services, Inc., for 19X1 and 19X2:

	19X1	19X2
Total assets (ending)	$ 90,000	$?
Total liabilities (ending)	25,000	41,000
Stockholders' equity (beginning)	31,000	?
Revenues	110,000	130,000
Expenses	?	85,000
Dividends	7,000	?
Stockholders' equity (ending)	?	79,000

REQUIRED:

a. Determine the unknown information for 19X1 and 19X2.
b. Calculate the rate of return on stockholders' equity for 19X1 and 19X2.

PROBLEM SET B

LO 2   **P1-1B   Understanding Business Transactions**   Transactions for The Appliance Service Center, Inc., for the month ended March 31, 19X8 (the first month of operations), are shown below in equation form:

	Cash	+	Equipment	=	Bank Loan	+	Stockholders' Equity
Beg. Bal.	0		0		0		0
1.	118,500						118,500
2.	(86,900)		86,900				
3.	45,000				45,000		
4.	7,900						7,900
5.	(4,000)				(4,000)		
6.	(2,100)						(2,100)
7.	(3,300)						(3,300)

REQUIRED:

Describe the nature of each transaction during the month of March. For example, Transaction 1 could be described as stockholders investing $118,500 cash in The Appliance Service Center, Inc. Each transaction is different. Assume that Transaction 4 was with customers, Transaction 6 was with employees, and Transaction 7 was with the stockholders.

LO 2,3   **P1-2B   Process Business Transactions**   Nancy Doubrava, the owner of Nancy's Landscape Design Shop, Inc., started her business after graduating with a degree in botany on August 1, 19X7. At that time, the business had no assets, liabilities, or stockholders' equity. The transactions for the month of August are given below:

Aug. 1 Nancy Doubrava invested $11,200 of her own money to establish Nancy's Landscape Design Shop, Inc., by purchasing capital stock in the corporation.

  2 Nancy borrowed $7,000 from the bank.

  31 Nancy collected $3,800 for designs prepared for clients in August.

  31 Nancy billed customers $1,800 for additional designs prepared in August that will be collected in September.

Aug. 31 Nancy paid her two assistants $550 each in wages.
   31 Nancy received a utility bill for $240 for the month of August. Nancy will pay the bill in early September.
   31 Nancy paid August's rent for the shop of $600.
   31 Nancy's Landscape Design Shop, Inc., paid Nancy $1,100 in cash dividends.

REQUIRED:

a. Determine the effect of each transaction on the accounting equation for Nancy's Landscape Design Shop, Inc., and total each part of the equation for August. The elements of the accounting equation for the design shop are cash, accounts receivable, accounts payable, bank loan payable, and stockholders' equity.
b. Prepare an income statement for the month of August.
c. Prepare a retained earnings statement for the month of August.
d. Prepare a balance sheet as of August 31.

LO 3 **P1-3B** **Financial Statement Preparation** The following data are presented for Dara's Rental Storage, Inc., for 19X1:

Capital stock	$ 5,000	Rent revenue	$23,700
Building, 12/31/X1	19,000	Dividends	3,400
Accounts receivable, 12/31/X1	12,250	Utilities expense	2,250
Rent expense	3,700	Advertising expense	1,600
Wages and salaries expense	2,800	Cash, 12/31/X1	13,300
Bank loan payable, 12/31/X1	17,500	Insurance expense	3,550

REQUIRED:

Prepare an income statement, retained earnings statement, and balance sheet for Dara's Rental Storage, Inc. for 19X1. Calculate any unknown amounts needed to complete the financial statements.

LO 1,4 **P1-4B** **Accounting Relationships and Return on Stockholders' Equity** The following information is from Milano's Computer Training School, Inc., for 19X8 and 19X9:

	19X8	*19X9*
Total assets (ending)	$270,000	$360,000
Total liabilities (ending)	105,000	?
Stockholders' equity (beginning)	163,000	?
Revenues	?	290,000
Expenses	147,000	225,000
Dividends	51,000	?
Stockholders' equity (ending)	?	137,000
Net income	?	?

REQUIRED:

a. Determine the unknown information for 19X8 and 19X9.
b. Calculate the rate of return on stockholders' equity for 19X8 and 19X9.

CRITICAL THINKING AND COMMUNICATING

C1-1 John Chang is thinking about investing half of his savings account to purchase an existing motorcycle maintenance business. Before investing, John requested a copy of the company's annual report. John would also like to study additional information about the company before making a decision to invest.

REQUIRED:

a. Determine the information that he should examine from the annual report.
b. What other information should John examine before making his decision?

C1-2   Carol Higgins was upset after she examined her business's balance sheet. She feels that the total assets shown in the balance sheet are significantly under fair value.

REQUIRED:

Write a memo to Carol explaining why historical cost may lead to underevaluation of assets. Include in the memo a discussion of the advantages and disadvantages of the historical cost principle versus fair value.

C1-3   The chapter discusses three key concepts of financial accounting.

REQUIRED:

a. Identify the three financial accounting concepts and discuss their effects on current financial reporting practice.
b. Discuss how the financial accounting concepts relate to yourself or to a business with which you are familiar.

C1-4   An important component of the financial accounting process is the double-entry rule.

REQUIRED:

a. Explain how you might use the double-entry technique when you run errands or go shopping.
b. Identify three personal transactions and discuss how they impact your financial position.

C1-5   The financial statements of J.C. Penney Company are reprinted in Appendix A at the end of this text. For this case you will need to locate the income statements and the balance sheets.

REQUIRED:

a. Calculate the rate of return on stockholders' equity for 1993 and 1992.
b. Comment on the change in the ratios that you calculated in a. above.
c. Determine the cause of the change in the ratios. Hint: Calculate the percentage changes in the numerator and the denominator of the ratios.

CHAPTER 2

Recording Transactions and Accounting Income

The owners of PhotoCopy, Inc., decide that before they expand the business's physical facilities, they could generate new business by acquiring a delivery van. The van could be used for both deliveries and pickups of copying business. The owners visit several car and truck dealers to look at and to price vans. It quickly becomes obvious that PhotoCopy does not have enough cash to purchase a van and that financing will be necessary. The owners decide to take the financial statements for January, which you saw in the previous chapter, to the local banks to apply for a loan.

The owners realize that the size of their business and the number of transactions that it enters into will expand as a result of adding the new volume of copying business. They recall how tedious it was during the first month of operations to record just the few transactions directly into the accounting equation. They wonder if there is a more efficient means of recording the transactions. Can you imagine just how many transactions a business such as General Electric enters into each day? They believe that there has to be a better system.

This chapter begins a more thorough examination of the financial accounting process to which you were introduced previously. The financial accounting process tracks business events and transactions by recording their effects on the business's financial position. The end product of this process is the financial statements of the business. In this chapter, you are introduced to accounts. Accounts are records used to store and summarize information about business transactions. Through the use of double-entry accounting, information about transactions that offset the business's financial position is recorded in the accounts. By using accounts and being shown how some common transactions are recorded in them, you are introduced to the mechanics of double entry. Then, we will examine in more detail the concept of accounting net income.

1. Describe accounts and recognize commonly used accounts.
2. Explain the rules of debit and credit and how they relate to the accounting equation.
3. Apply the rules of debit and credit to business transactions.
4. Identify the procedures in the accounting cycle.
5. Apply the procedures to record in the accounting records the effects of business transactions.
6. Explain the relationship between the general journal and the general ledger.
7. Prepare a trial balance.
8. Analyze the various types of errors a trial balance identifies and apply procedures to correct the errors.
9. Define accounting net income and distinguish among the cash basis, accrual basis, and income tax basis of accounting.

LO 1

Describe accounts and recognize commonly used accounts.

ACCOUNTS

Using the accounting equation directly, you previously examined the effects of business transactions on assets, liabilities, and stockholders' equity. While this procedure may be acceptable for a small number of transactions, most businesses need a more efficient and convenient means of storing and summarizing the effects of a variety of transactions. Many large businesses have thousands of transactions daily; obviously, for them the use of individual accounting equations is impractical.

In actual practice, the device businesses use for storing and summarizing information about the effects of transactions is the account. Using accounts is PhotoCopy, Inc.'s solution to the inefficiency of recording transactions directly in the accounting equation. An **account**, a subclassification of the accounting equation, is used for storing and summarizing information about transactions that affect a particular element of the business's financial position. Hence, there are asset accounts, liability accounts, and stockholders' equity accounts. Accounts are a part of the business's formal accounting records and are located in a general ledger, which we discuss later in this chapter.

T-Accounts

In its simplest form, an account resembles the letter T and is referred to as a **T-account**. The basic format of the T-account is illustrated below:

Account Title	
Left side	Right side

The T-account consists of three components:

1. the account title
2. the left side
3. the right side

The account title names an asset, a liability, or an item of stockholders' equity. We record increases in accounts on one side and decreases on the other side. We use the cash account to record the increases and decreases in cash.

For example, recall the transactions of PhotoCopy, Inc. If those transactions that affected cash are recorded in a T-account, they appear as follows:

Cash			
Investment by owners	6,000	Payment of rent	1,000
Revenues collected	4,000	Purchase of supplies	800
		Payment of salaries	3,000
		Purchase of equipment	1,200

Account Balance

When we place increases in an account on one side and decreases on the other side, it is easy to sum the increases and the decreases. Then we determine the **account balance** at the end of a period as follows:

> **Balance at the beginning of the period**
> **Add: Increases during the period**
> **Less: Decreases during the period**
> _____
> **Equals: Balance at the end of the period**

The balance in the cash account of PhotoCopy, Inc., is $4,000, and the account is shown below:

		Cash				
Jan.	1	Beginning balance	0	Jan.	2	Payment of rent	1,000
	2	Investment by owners	6,000		2	Purchase of supplies	800
	31	Revenues collected	4,000		20	Payment of salaries	3,000
					31	Purchase of equipment	1,200
		Beginning Bal. + Increases	10,000			Decreases	6,000
	31	Ending balance	4,000				

Notice that the T-account for cash now has the dates of the beginning balance, the cash transactions, and the ending balance. Also, the account balance of $4,000 is calculated in the T-account. Recall that the amount of cash shown in the January 31, 19X1, balance sheet for PhotoCopy, Inc. is $4,000.

Commonly Used Accounts

The types of accounts a business uses depend on the nature of its operations. For example, a service business such as PhotoCopy, Inc. will have accounts for the assets it uses to provide copying services to its customers. A manufacturing business will have accounts for the assets it uses in its manufacturing operations —factory buildings and equipment. A retail clothing store will have asset accounts different than either those of service or manufacturing businesses. For example, a retail clothing store's assets might include display cases, mannequins, and cash registers. Similarly, liability accounts will vary, depending on the form of the business's borrowing; and owners' equity accounts will vary, depending on how the business is organized—proprietorship, partnership, or corporation. While accounts do vary from business to business, those discussed in the following section are common to most businesses.

Asset Accounts.   Conceivably, a business could have just one account called Assets, one account called Liabilities, and one account called Stockholders'

Equity. However, the result of accounting for the business with only three accounts would not be very informative. For example, neither management nor outside users of financial statements would be able to tell how much of its total assets the business holds in cash and how much it holds in accounts receivable, equipment, buildings, etc. There is no rule that says exactly how many different accounts a business should have. However, it should use as many different asset, liability, and stockholders' equity accounts as needed to distinguish between the elements of its financial position. These accounts will have different implications for management purposes and for evaluation by outside users of the financial statements. Therefore, a business should have a separate account for each distinctly different category of assets that it uses.

Cash. We use a cash account to record increases and decreases in the business's cash. The term *cash* includes money or any medium of exchange that a bank will accept at face value for deposit. Common components of cash include coins, currency, checks, and money orders. A cash account includes both cash deposited in a bank and cash on the premises of the business in a cash register or safe.

Accounts receivable. Many businesses sell goods or provide services to customers for an implied promise to pay in the future. These types of transactions commonly are called *sales on credit* or *sales on account*. The amounts due from customers for sales on credit are called *accounts receivable*, which we record in the accounts receivable account. Sales on credit increase accounts receivable, and collections of amounts due from customers decrease accounts receivable.

Notes receivable. We use a notes receivable account to record formal written promises of other entities to pay amounts of money at specific future dates.

Prepaid expenses. A business often pays for goods and services before using or receiving them. These payments create assets called *prepaid expenses*. Common types of prepaid expenses include insurance and rent. A business may have a separate account for each type of prepaid expense.

Equipment. Each type of equipment that a business uses in its operations should be recorded in a separate equipment account. The types of equipment used in operations and the types of equipment accounts depend on the nature of the business's operations. A service business has equipment accounts for the equipment needed to provide its services to customers. A manufacturing business uses equipment such as drill presses and lathes and records increases and decreases in this type of equipment in a manufacturing equipment account. Items such as typewriters, photocopying machines, and microcomputers are recorded in an office equipment account. A retail store would record display cases, cash registers, and similar items in a store equipment account. A business that uses trucks and automobiles in its operations would have a transportation equipment account.

Land. A business often owns land that it uses in operations. For example, a business may own the land on which a factory, retail store, or office building is located. We use a separate land account to record each type of land the business owns.

Land improvements. A business sometimes adds improvements to the land it owns. We record the cost of the improvements in a land improvements account. Examples of land improvements include driveways, sidewalks, fences, and lighting.

Buildings. A business also commonly owns buildings that it uses in operations. Types of buildings a business uses include manufacturing plants, office buildings, warehouses, retail stores, and garages. Although a building is physically inseparable from the land on which it is located, we record land in a separate account from the building. The reason for recording land and buildings in separate accounts is that buildings are subject to wear and deterioration and are used up over time, while land is not used up. The using up of a building is called *depreciation* and is discussed in a subsequent chapter. A business should have a separate building account for each type of building it owns and uses in its operations.

To illustrate the variety of assets that a business may have, *The Walt Disney Company's* 1992 annual report listed the following assets in its balance sheet:

> Cash and cash equivalents
> Investments
> Receivables
> Merchandise inventories
> Film and television costs
> Theme parks, resorts, and other property

You may not understand all of the asset titles at this point or how they are combined in the balance sheet; but as you continue your study of accounting, the titles will become familiar. For example, the theme parks, resorts, and other property includes attractions, buildings, projects in progress, and land, all of which were recorded in Disney's actual accounting records. These assets were shown at a total amount of $10.8 billion.

Liability Accounts.   Managers and outside users of financial statements such as bankers are aware that different obligations may have entirely different implications for a business. For example, as a business pays accounts payable, it usually replaces them by new accounts payable through continuous purchases of supplies and services needed for operations. However, a business must pay off a bank loan without assuming any other liability to take its place automatically. Thus, the business must have sufficient cash, that is not required for other purposes, to pay off a bank loan. Once again, there is no clear rule as to how many different liability accounts a business should have. However, because different liabilities have different financial implications, a business should have a separate liability account for each distinctly different type of obligation.

Accounts payable.   Accounts payable are amounts owed to others as a result of an implied promise to pay in the future. Accounts payable generally are the result of purchases of goods and services on credit (on account). When a business purchases goods or services on account, it increases Accounts Payable. When a business pays cash to the vendor, it decreases Accounts Payable by the amount of the payment.

Notes payable.   We record increases and decreases in the amounts owed to others in the form of written promises to pay in Notes Payable.

Other payables.   The types of other liabilities that a business has depend on the nature of its operations. Examples of other liability accounts include Wages and Salaries Payable, Interest Payable, Rent Payable, and Mortgage Payable.

Stockholders' Equity Accounts.   Stockholders' equity accounts represent the owners' residual interest in the business's net assets (assets – liabilities). This residual interest may be seen in the following version of the accounting equation:

$$\text{Stockholders' Equity} = \text{Assets} - \text{Liabilities}$$

The right side of the equation represents the business's net assets, and the left side represents the owners' interest. To keep the equation in balance, transactions that increase the business's net assets must increase stockholders' equity and, conversely, transactions that decrease the business's net assets must decrease stockholders' equity. We use a separate stockholders' equity account to record the effects of each type of transaction that affects stockholders' equity.

Capital stock. We use a capital stock account to record the investment of the owners in the business. When Judy Martinez, Sharon Simpson, and Paul Shell invested $6,000 in PhotoCopy, Inc., they established a capital stock account to record the investment. The capital stock account represents the owners' claims to the business's net assets as a result of their investments in the business.

Retained earnings. Retained earnings is the increase in stockholders' equity as a result of the business's profitable operations. Retained earnings is increased by net income (revenues – expenses) and decreased by dividends. Retained earnings represent the stockholders' claims to the business's net assets as a result of profitable operations.

Revenues. Revenue accounts are stockholders' equity accounts used to accumulate the business's revenues for a particular period. For purposes of determining net income (or loss) and preparing income statements, separate accounts for each of the various sources of revenue are maintained. The types of revenue accounts a business uses depend on the nature of its operations. Examples of revenue accounts are Sales, Parking Revenue, Repairs Revenue, Rent Revenue, and Interest Revenue. Generally, the titles of revenue accounts are descriptive of the types of revenue recorded in each account.

The realization principle tells us how much revenue to recognize for a given period. To **recognize** means to record in an account. According to the **realization principle**, we should recognize revenues in a period only if:

1. They are *earned* during the period.
2. They either are collected in cash, or they will be collected from customers in the future.

Generally, we consider revenues as earned if the business has provided products or services to customers.

Expenses. Expense accounts are stockholders' equity accounts used to accumulate the business's expenses for a particular period. We use a separate expense account for each type of expense a business incurs. Different types of businesses will have different expense accounts. Examples of expense accounts are Wages and Salaries Expense, Rent Expense, Interest Expense, and Utilities Expense.

The matching principle governs when to recognize expenses. According to the **matching principle**, we should recognize as expenses the costs incurred to produce products and services, which the business sells to its customers, in the same period we recognize the revenues from those products and services.

Dividends. Dividends are distributions of assets—usually cash—to the stockholders of the business. Dividends are reductions in the stockholders' equity of the business that reflect reductions in *net* assets due to the payments of assets to the owners. Therefore, *dividends are not expenses of the business.*

LO 2
Explain the rules of debit and credit and how they relate to the accounting equation.

DEBIT AND CREDIT

Debit and credit rules determine on which side of an account we record the increases and decreases. In practice, accountants refer to the left side of a

T-account as the **debit** side; the right side, as the **credit** side. Debit is abbreviated as *Dr.* and credit is abbreviated as *Cr.* When we record an amount in the left side of an account, we have **debited** the account; and the amount itself is called a debit. Conversely, when we record an amount in the right side of an account, we have **credited** the account; and the amount itself is called a credit. If the sum of the debits exceeds the sum of the credits in an account, the account has a **debit balance**. On the other hand, in an account with a **credit balance**, the sum of the credits exceeds the sum of the debits. Examples of debit-balance and credit-balance accounts follow:

Debit-Balance Account			Credit-Balance Account	
1,250	250		800	1,900
100				1,000
1,100				2,100

Remember: The terms *debit* and *credit* simply refer to the left side and the right side of a T-account. These terms do not mean increases or decreases. Whether a debit or a credit increases or decreases an account depends on the account involved. Illustration 2-1 summarizes the rules for how debits and credits affect the accounts. As shown in Illustration 2-1, assets normally have debit balances. Conversely, liabilities and stockholders' equity normally have credit balances.

ILLUSTRATION 2-1 Debits and Credits and Changes in Accounts

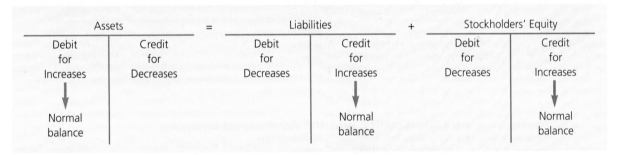

The rules in Illustration 2-1 are generally straightforward. However, experience tells us that you must initially memorize them at this point in your accounting education.

Debits, Credits, and Stockholders' Equity Accounts

Because some stockholders' equity accounts accumulate distinctly different types of changes in stockholders' equity, the debit and credit rules for them need further explanation. Illustration 2-1 indicates that stockholders' equity is increased by credits and decreased by debits. This translates into the following detailed rules for the different types of stockholders' equity accounts:

1. The owners' initial investments and any subsequent investments increase stockholders' equity, and we record them as credits to Capital Stock.
2. Dividends decrease net assets and stockholders' equity and we record them as debits to Dividends.

3. Revenues increase net assets and stockholders' equity, and we record them as credits to the appropriate revenue accounts.
4. Expenses decrease net assets and stockholders' equity, and we record them as debits to the appropriate expense accounts.

The T-account representation in Illustration 2-2 of the elements of stockholders' equity summarizes which accounts are increased by debits (left side) and which accounts are increased by credits (right side). Illustration 2-3 summarizes how the various accounts are affected by debits and credits.

ILLUSTRATION 2-2 Application of Debits and Credits to Stockholders' Equity Accounts

ILLUSTRATION 2-3 Summary of Rules of Debit and Credit

	Assets	Liabilities	Capital Stock	Dividends	Revenues	Expenses
Increases	Debit	Credit	Credit	Debit	Credit	Debit
Decreases	Credit	Debit	Debit	Credit	Debit	Credit
Normal balance	Debit	Credit	Credit	Debit	Credit	Debit

Debits, Credits, and the Accounting Equation

The rules for how debits and credits affect the accounts, summarized in Illustration 2-3, are a direct result of applying the accounting equation to transaction analysis. Consider again the accounting equation and the reasoning behind the double-entry rule introduced previously. The accounting equation must hold at all times:

Assets = Liabilities + Stockholders' Equity

Recall that as we record each transaction, we maintain the accounting equation. If we increase assets by debits (entries to the left side of the account), then it follows that we must increase liabilities and stockholders' equity by credits (entries to the right side of the account) since they are on the opposite side of the equation. Similarly, if we decrease assets by credits, then we must decrease liabilities and stockholders' equity by debits. When we apply these rules in recording transactions and events, the result is that *the debits must equal the credits* each time we process a transaction or event. Thus, the accounting equation will always hold.

In the example of PhotoCopy, Inc., when the owners invested $6,000 in the business, we increased the asset, cash, by $6,000. We also increased the stock-

PACIOLI—THE FATHER OF THE BALANCE SHEET

Centuries have elapsed since Fra Pacioli, an Italian Renaissance man, first outlined some of the fundamental principles of accounting. Pacioli, an Italian mathematician who is considered the "Father of the Balance Sheet," lived from about 1445 to 1520 and was a close friend of Renaissance master Leonardo da Vinci. Pacioli is best known for publishing *Summa de Arithmetica, Geometria, Proportione et Proportionalita*, which included a special supplement on double-entry record keeping for merchants. This supplement — a slender tract entitled *De Compatis et Scripturis* — proved to be the most useful and lasting part of the book since it detailed for the first time the system of accounting that had been in wide use in the commercial center of Venice for years.

What sort of man was the monk Luca Pacioli, and how did he acquire such knowledge and background about business? Pacioli was born in Borgo San Sepolcro, a small town in central Italy, and was early apprenticed to a wealthy merchant family. When he was 20, he went to Venice to tutor the sons of a rich merchant named Rompiasi. Later he studied at the great universities of his time. In the 1470s he joined the Franciscans and began to teach both mathematics and theology.

Pacioli was a skilled observer and noticed that Italian merchants kept track of their business affairs by making two entries, a debit and a credit. Each transaction was viewed separately, but the concept of "balance" was then unknown. Also, no attempt was made to find out if a business was operating profitably over a specific period such as a year. Pacioli added an important refinement by recording and classifying transactions and setting forth the necessary elements of a balance sheet.

The system described by Pacioli in his tract was not originated by him but had been employed in Venice as far back as the thirteenth century. But Pacioli was the first to bring many diverse elements together into a coordinated system, which proved to be the foundation of the modern double-entry bookkeeping system.

Source: *Journal of Accountancy* (May 1987), pp. 195–197. Reprinted with permission from the *Journal of Accountancy*, copyright © 1987 by American Institute of Certified Public Accountants, Inc.

holders' equity account, Capital Stock, by $6,000. Because we increase assets by debits and we increase stockholders' equity by credits, we record this transaction in the accounts by debiting Cash for $6,000 and crediting Capital Stock for $6,000. We maintained the equality of debits and credits in recording this transaction.

LO 3
Apply the rules of debit and credit to business transactions.

ANALYZING TRANSACTIONS USING THE RULES OF DEBIT AND CREDIT

Earlier you saw how we use the financial accounting process to track events and transactions by recording their effects on the business's financial position. Analyzing and recording effects of transactions is an essential part of the process by which financial statements are derived. Recording the effects of transactions requires us to analyze each transaction. First, we decide which accounts the transaction affects. Then, we decide by what amounts. Finally, we record these effects in the accounts by applying the rules of debit and credit.

Recording Transactions in T-Accounts

We continue the example of PhotoCopy, Inc. to illustrate analyzing and recording transactions. We record the transactions in T-accounts, and the entries to the accounts are numbered parenthetically with the same number as the related transaction. Illustration 2-4 shows the beginning balances for February 19X1, recorded in the accounts. The beginning balances are from the financial statements presented in Chapter 1.

ILLUSTRATION 2-4 T-Accounts at the Beginning of February

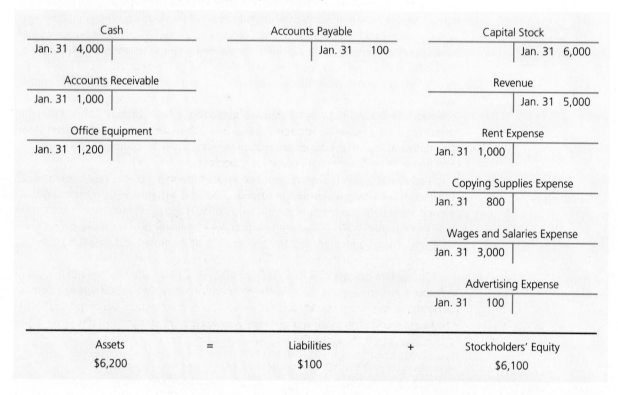

Cash		Accounts Payable		Capital Stock	
Jan. 31 4,000			Jan. 31 100		Jan. 31 6,000

Accounts Receivable				Revenue	
Jan. 31 1,000					Jan. 31 5,000

Office Equipment				Rent Expense	
Jan. 31 1,200				Jan. 31 1,000	

				Copying Supplies Expense	
				Jan. 31 800	

				Wages and Salaries Expense	
				Jan. 31 3,000	

				Advertising Expense	
				Jan. 31 100	

Assets	=	Liabilities	+	Stockholders' Equity
$6,200		$100		$6,100

Transaction 1—Bank Loan. PhotoCopy chose to purchase a delivery van from Town Motors for $13,000. Since PhotoCopy does not have sufficient cash for the purchase, the owners decided to borrow money for the van from the bank. Based on the January financial statements that PhotoCopy presented, North National Bank agreed to lend the company $10,000 to use in purchasing the van. The interest rate on the loan is 7.2% per year and interest is payable on the first of each month beginning March 1, 19X1. The borrowing transaction increased cash and increased the liability, notes payable, $10,000 each. We record the transaction as a debit to Cash for $10,000 and a credit to Notes Payable for $10,000.

Cash		Notes Payable	
Jan. 31 4,000			(1) 10,000
(1) 10,000			

Transaction 2—Purchase of Asset. On February 3, PhotoCopy completed the purchase of the van by paying Town Motors $13,000. PhotoCopy classifies the van as delivery equipment. We record the transaction by debiting Delivery Equipment for $13,000 and crediting Cash for $13,000.

Delivery Equipment		Cash	
(2) 13,000		Jan. 31 4,000	(2) 13,000
		(1) 10,000	

Transaction 3—Prepaid Expense. The owners of PhotoCopy decided that with the purchase of the delivery van they should acquire some insurance. On February 3, they paid $900 for a 12-month policy. This transaction creates an asset called prepaid insurance. The prepaid insurance will become an expense as the period of time covered by the policy expires. We record the transaction as a debit to Prepaid Insurance and as a credit to Cash for $900 each.

Prepaid Insurance		Cash	
(3) 900		Jan. 31 4,000	(2) 13,000
		(1) 10,000	(3) 900

Transaction 4—Account Receivable Collection. On February 4, PhotoCopy collects the $1,000 account receivable from the College of Liberal Arts and Sciences. The account receivable was shown as an asset on the January 31, 19X1, balance sheet. The collection increases cash and decreases accounts receivable. We record the transaction as a debit to Cash for $1,000 and as a credit to Accounts Receivable for $1,000.

Cash		Accounts Receivable	
Jan. 31 4,000	(2) 13,000	Jan. 31 1,000	(4) 1,000
(1) 10,000	(3) 900		
(4) 1,000			

Transaction 5—Rent Expense. On February 4, PhotoCopy paid rent of $1,000 for the month of February. Expenses are increased by debits. We record the payment by debiting Rent Expense and crediting Cash for $1,000.

Rent Expense		Cash	
Jan. 31 1,000		Jan. 31 4,000	(2) 13,000
(5) 1,000		(1) 10,000	(3) 900
		(4) 1,000	(5) 1,000

Transaction 6—Payment of Account Payable. On February 8, PhotoCopy pays the campus newspaper for the amount owed for advertising in January. The payment decreases cash and decreases the liability, accounts payable. We record the transaction by debiting Accounts Payable and crediting Cash for $100 each.

Accounts Payable		Cash	
(6) 100	Jan. 31 100	Jan. 31 4,000	(2) 13,000
		(1) 10,000	(3) 900
		(4) 1,000	(5) 1,000
			(6) 100

Transaction 7—Purchase of Copying Supplies. On February 8, PhotoCopy purchased copying supplies on credit for $2,400. This amount of supplies should last more than one month; however, by purchasing a larger amount, PhotoCopy received a quantity discount. The transaction creates an asset, copy-

ing supplies, that will become an expense as the supplies are used in providing copying services to customers. We record the transaction as a debit to Copying Supplies and as a credit to Accounts Payable for $2,400 each.

Copying Supplies			Accounts Payable		
Jan. 31	800		(6)	100	Jan. 31	100
(7)	2,400				(7)	2,400

Transaction 8—Unearned Revenue. The Student Government Association of the University arranged with PhotoCopy to allow its members to have copies made as needed. PhotoCopy agreed to the arrangement only because the Association agreed to pay in advance. On February 15, PhotoCopy received the $600 advance payment from the Association. The amount received, however, is not revenue to be recognized at the time it is received because it has not been earned. Rather, the amount received creates a liability called unearned revenue. The liability will be satisfied—and revenue will be earned—when PhotoCopy makes the agreed-to copies for the members of the Association. We record the transaction as a debit to Cash and as a credit to Unearned Revenue for $600 each.

Cash				Unearned Revenue	
Jan. 31	4,000	(2)	13,000	(8)	600
(1)	10,000	(3)	900		
(4)	1,000	(5)	1,000		
(8)	600	(6)	100		

Transaction 9—Wages Expense. During February, PhotoCopy had to hire an employee to make deliveries and pickups and to help make copies for customers. PhotoCopy agreed to pay the employee at the rate of $200 per week and that the wages would be paid at the end of each two weeks. On February 21, the company paid the employee $400 for the first two weeks that the employee worked. This transaction decreases the asset cash and increases the expense, wages and salaries expense. We record the transaction as a debit to Wages and Salaries Expense and as a credit to Cash for $400 each.

Wages and Salaries Expense			Cash		
Jan. 31	3,000		Jan. 31	4,000	(2)	13,000
(9)	400		(1)	10,000	(3)	900
			(4)	1,000	(5)	1,000
			(8)	600	(6)	100
					(9)	400

Transaction 10—Revenues Received in Cash. During February, PhotoCopy, Inc., earned $6,200 in cash revenues from customers. These transactions increased cash and increased revenues. We record these transactions by debiting Cash and crediting Revenue by $6,200 each.

Cash				Revenue	
Jan. 31	4,000	(2)	13,000	Jan. 31	5,000
(1)	10,000	(3)	900	(10)	6,200
(4)	1,000	(5)	1,000		
(8)	600	(6)	100		
(10)	6,200	(9)	400		

Transaction 11—Salaries Paid to the Owners. On February 28, the owners were paid their monthly salaries totaling $3,000. The transaction decreases the asset cash and increases the expense, wages and salaries expense. We record the transaction as a debit to Wages and Salaries Expense and as a credit to Cash for $3,000 each.

Wages and Salaries Expense			Cash			
Jan. 31	3,000		Jan. 31	4,000	(2)	13,000
(9)	400		(1)	10,000	(3)	900
(11)	3,000		(4)	1,000	(5)	1,000
			(8)	600	(6)	100
			(10)	6,200	(9)	400
					(11)	3,000

February Account Balances

At the end of February, the owners of PhotoCopy, Inc. determined the account balances. Illustration 2-5 shows the balances in the accounts at the end of February. Notice that we have maintained the equality of the accounting equation during the process of recording the transactions for February. Assets of $20,900 equal the sum of liabilities and stockholders' equity of $20,900 ($13,000 + $7,900).

ILLUSTRATION 2-5 Account Balances at End of February

Cash				Accounts Payable				Capital Stock		
Jan. 31	4,000	(2)	13,000	(6)	100	Jan. 31	100		Jan. 31	6,000
(1)	10,000	(3)	900			(6)	2,400		Bal.	6,000
(4)	1,000	(5)	1,000			Bal.	2,400		**Revenue**	
(8)	600	(6)	100	**Unearned Revenue**					Jan. 31	5,000
(10)	6,200	(9)	400			(8)	600		(10)	6,200
		(11)	3,000			Bal.	600		Bal.	11,200
Bal.	3,400			**Notes Payable**					**Rent Expense**	
Accounts Receivable						(1)	10,000	Jan. 31	1,000	
Jan. 31	1,000	(4)	1,000			Bal.	10,000	(5)	1,000	
Bal.	0							Bal.	2,000	
Copying Supplies								**Copying Supplies Expense**		
(7)	2,400							Jan. 31	800	
Bal.	2,400							Bal.	800	
Prepaid Insurance								**Wages and Salaries Expense**		
(3)	900							Jan. 31	3,000	
Bal.	900							(9)	400	
Office Equipment								(11)	3,000	
Jan. 31	1,200							Bal.	6,400	
Bal.	1,200							**Advertising Expense**		
Delivery Equipment								Jan. 31	100	
(2)	13,000							Bal.	100	
Bal.	13,000									

Assets	=	Liabilities	+	Stockholders' Equity
$20,900		$13,000		$7,900

LO 4

Identify the procedures in the accounting cycle.

THE ACCOUNTING CYCLE

The **accounting cycle** is the sequence of procedures accountants follow to complete the financial accounting process. Illustration 2-6 presents the accounting cycle as a loop, or a continuous process. When one accounting cycle ends—with preparing the annual financial statements and closing appropriate accounts—another accounting cycle begins anew with analyzing and recording transactions.

ILLUSTRATION 2-6 The Accounting Cycle

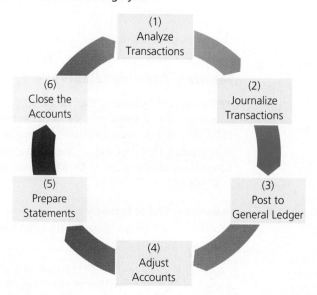

The following procedures are represented in Illustration 2-6.

1. Analyze the transactions.
2. Record the transactions in the general journal.
3. Post the general journal entries to the general ledger accounts.
4. Adjust the general ledger accounts.
5. Prepare the financial statements.
6. Close the revenue, expense, and dividends ledger accounts.

So far in this chapter, we analyzed the transactions for PhotoCopy, Inc. Next, we prepare general journal entries for those transactions. The posting of general journal entries to the general ledger accounts is also illustrated in this chapter. Then, in the next chapter, we present the procedures for adjusting the accounts and preparing financial statements. Adjusting accounts is necessary to bring them into conformity with GAAP so that we may prepare appropriate financial statements. In that chapter, we also illustrate the final procedure in the accounting cycle—closing the revenue and expense accounts.

LO 5

Apply the procedures to record in the accounting records the effects of business transactions.

RECORDING TRANSACTIONS

The first step in recording transactions is preparing general journal entries. We then post those entries to the general ledger.

The General Journal

A **general journal** is a chronological listing of transactions. We describe each transaction that affects the business's financial position in an *entry* in the general journal. The entry for Transaction 1 of February for PhotoCopy, Inc. is shown in Illustration 2-7.

ILLUSTRATION 2-7 General Journal Entry

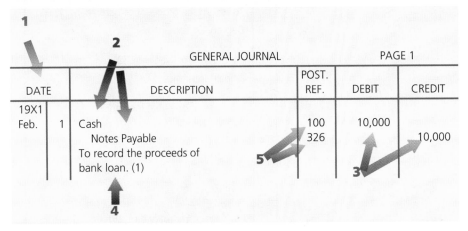

Each general journal entry provides the following information about the transaction or event:

1. The date of the transaction or event.
2. The names of the accounts debited and credited.
3. The amounts debited and credited to each account.
4. An explanation of the transaction.
5. A reference to the posting of the transaction (to be explained later).

The general journal provides a place to record information about transactions and events that affect the business. As we illustrated earlier, we can record transactions as debits and credits directly in the T-accounts. When we use this method, however, it is difficult to observe all the effects of a transaction. Since each transaction affects at least two accounts (by the double-entry rule), at most, we record only half of the information about a transaction in any one account.

As transactions take place, we first record them in the general journal. Therefore, it is sometimes called the *book of original entry*. We record each transaction as a separate **journal entry** in the general journal, and the process of recording a transaction is **journalizing**.

Illustration 2-8 shows the general journal entries for the February transactions of PhotoCopy, Inc. The numbers in parentheses correspond to the transaction numbers listed on pages 54–57.

We can summarize the procedures for recording transactions in the general journal as follows:

a. Record the year at the top of the Date column; record the month in the first column and the day in the second column. You do not need to repeat the year and month for subsequent entries, unless a new year or new month begins or when you begin a new page in the general journal.

ILLUSTRATION 2-8 General Journal

				POST.		
		GENERAL JOURNAL			PAGE 1	
DATE		DESCRIPTION		POST. REF.	DEBIT	CREDIT
19X1 Feb.	1	Cash			10,000	
		Notes Payable				10,000
		To record the proceeds of bank loan. (1)				
	3	Delivery Equipment			13,000	
		Cash				13,000
		Purchase of delivery van. (2)				
	3	Prepaid Insurance			900	
		Cash				900
		Purchase of one-year insurance policy. (3)				
	4	Cash			1,000	
		Accounts Receivable				1,000
		Collection of account receivable. (4)				
	4	Rent Expense			1,000	
		Cash				1,000
		Payment of February rent. (5)				
	8	Accounts Payable			100	
		Cash				100
		Payment of amount owed for ad in campus newspaper. (6)				
	8	Copying Supplies			2,400	
		Accounts Payable				2,400
		Purchase of copying supplies. (7)				
	15	Cash			600	
		Unearned Revenue				600
		Receipt of advance payment for copying services. (8)				
	21	Wages and Salaries Expense			400	
		Cash				400
		Payment of employee wages. (9)				
	28	Revenue			6,200	
		Cash				6,200
		Cash receipts for copying services for February. (10)				
	28	Wages and Salaries Expense			3,000	
		Cash				3,000
		Payment of monthly salaries to owners. (11)				

b. In the Description column, record the names of all accounts debited and credited and a brief description of the transaction. Record the names of the accounts debited first, aligned with the left margin, followed by the names of the accounts credited, indented a few spaces. For some transactions, more than one account will be debited and/or more than one account credited.

c. In the Debit column, record the amount debited on the same line as the related account name; and in the Credit column, record the amount credited on the same line as the related account name. Do not use dollar signs in the general journal.

d. After each entry, it is common practice to provide a brief explanation and then to skip a line. The explanation reflects the analysis of the transaction or other event.

The General Ledger

Regardless of the number of accounts, they are organized in a **general ledger**, which is the collection of all a business's accounts. For some businesses, the general ledger is a large book with a separate page for each account. However, many businesses maintain their general ledgers in a data storage medium such as a computer disk or tape. We recorded the previous examples of transactions in this chapter in T-accounts. While T-accounts are useful for textbook and classroom presentations, they are not used in practice. Rather, accountants use a ledger account form similar to the one presented in Illustration 2-9.

ILLUSTRATION 2-9 Ledger Account

GENERAL LEDGER ACCOUNT					
NAME:			ACCOUNT NO.:		
DATE	DESCRIPTION	POST. REF.	DEBIT	CREDIT	BALANCE

The general ledger account presents the account name, account number, date of the transaction, amount debited or credited, and the account balance. The Post. Ref. column provides a reference to the source of entry in the ledger account. The process of recording transactions in the general ledger accounts is **posting**.

Account Numbers

To locate accounts quickly within the general ledger, businesses have systems of numbering accounts. A three-digit numbering system numbers the accounts as follows:

Asset accounts, 100–299
Liability accounts, 300–499
Stockholders' equity accounts, 500–599
Revenue accounts, 600–699
Expense accounts, 700–799

In the three-digit numbering system, all asset account numbers begin with the digit 1 or 2; all liability account numbers, with the digit 3 or 4; and so forth. The second and third digits are used to identify the account further. In the general ledger, accounts are kept in numerical order. Organizing the accounts numerically is more efficient than ordering them alphabetically by account title. Also, using numbers to identify accounts increases the efficiency of data entry for those businesses that use computerized accounting systems. Only the numbers need be used to identify the accounts; the computer keeps a master list with the corresponding account titles in storage.

The numbering system illustrated above is common for a service business. Larger and more complex businesses need an expanded numbering system.

A business maintains a list of account names and their corresponding account numbers with a **chart of accounts**. A chart of accounts for PhotoCopy, Inc. is shown in Illustration 2-10. When you analyze transactions and work with the accounting records, a chart of accounts is useful for determining the accounts affected. For example, consider Transaction 3 of PhotoCopy, Inc. The purchase of an insurance policy for cash indicates that the asset account, Prepaid Insurance, should be debited and the asset account, Cash, should be credited. The chart of accounts shows that Prepaid Insurance can be found in the general ledger as account number 150; Cash, as account number 100. The chart of accounts is usually accompanied by a description of the types of transactions that are recorded in each account. For recording unusual transactions and new employees' reference, this description is particularly useful and significantly improves the efficiency of posting to the general ledger. Note that a list of the accounts used in this text is printed on the inside front cover of your text. You may use the list as a reference when completing the exercises and problems.

ILLUSTRATION 2-10 Chart of Accounts

PhotoCopy, Inc. Chart of Accounts			
Assets		*Owner's Equity*	
Cash	100	Capital Stock	519
Accounts Receivable	110	Retained Earnings	550
Copying Supplies	133	Dividends	598
Prepaid Insurance	150	Income Summary	599
Delivery Equipment	238	*Revenues*	
Accumulated Depreciation—		Revenue	600
Delivery Equipment	239		
Office Equipment	242	*Expenses*	
Accumulated Depreciation—		Advertising Expense	700
Office Equipment	243	Copying Supplies Expense	703
Liabilities		Depreciation Expense—	
Accounts Payable	302	Delivery Equipment	710
Income Taxes Payable	314	Depreciation Expense—	
Interest Payable	318	Office Equipment	716
Notes Payable	326	Insurance Expense	728
Unearned Revenue	342	Rent Expense	762
Wages and Salaries Payable	346	Utilities Expense	780
		Wages and Salaries Expense	784

Review the chart of accounts shown in Illustration 2-10. In subsequent chapters, you will learn more about these accounts. You do not need to understand them all at this point.

LO 6

Explain the relationship between the general journal and the general ledger.

Relationship Between the General Journal and General Ledger

Both the general journal and the general ledger are important components of the accounting records, and we record the effects of transactions in both of them.

Listing transactions chronologically, we record all debit and credit effects of each transaction in the general journal. Then, we post the information about the effects of the entry to the appropriate individual general ledger accounts.

Illustration 2-11 demonstrates the journalizing *and posting* of Transaction 1 from the set of transactions analyzed earlier in the chapter. The procedures for journalizing and posting transactions can be summarized as follows:

ILLUSTRATION 2-11 Posting the General Ledger

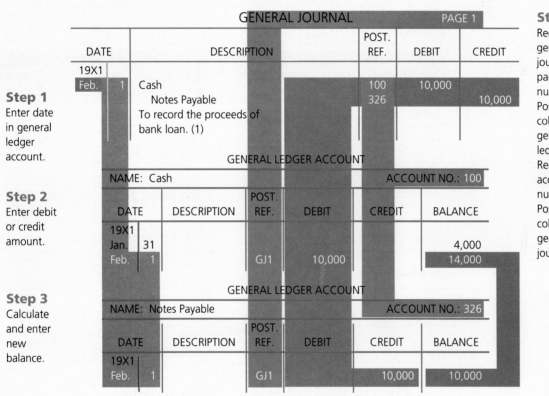

a. Record transactions in the general journal as described on pages 59–61.
b. Periodically, such as at the end of a day or the end of a week, post the journal entries to the ledger accounts. In the ledger, locate the account to be debited. In the Date column, enter the date of the transaction. Next, enter the amount of the debit in the Debit column and adjust the balance to reflect the debit. In the Post. Ref. column, enter the page in the general journal on which the journal entry is located. The page number is preceded by the letters *GJ* to indicate that the source of the posting is the *General Journal*. Do not use dollar signs in either the journal or the ledger. The last step in posting is to record in the general journal's Post. Ref. column the number of the account to which you posted the debit entry. This last step provides a cross-reference between the journal and the ledger. Should your posting process be interrupted, you can then determine which journal entries you have already posted.
c. For the credits, repeat the procedures you followed for the debits.

Prepare a trial balance.

THE TRIAL BALANCE

The double-entry requirement of equal debits and credits provides a useful means for finding errors. If the total amounts of those accounts with debit balances and the total amount of those accounts with credit balances do not equal, then we have made a recording error.

We test the equality of debits and credits periodically by preparing a trial balance such as the one shown in Illustration 2-12. A **trial balance** lists in columns and then totals all the debit balances and all the credit balances in the general ledger accounts. In preparing a trial balance, use the following four procedures:

ILLUSTRATION 2-12 Trial Balance

PhotoCopy, Inc. Trial Balance February 28, 19X1		
	Debits	*Credits*
Cash	$ 3,400	
Copying Supplies	2,400	
Prepaid Insurance	900	
Delivery Equipment	13,000	
Office Equipment	1,200	
Accounts Payable		$ 2,400
Notes Payable		10,000
Unearned Revenue		600
Capital Stock		6,000
Revenue		11,200
Advertising Expense	100	
Copying Supplies Expense	800	
Rent Expense	2,000	
Wages and Salaries Expense	6,400	
Totals	$30,200	$30,200

1. Determine the balance of each account in the ledger.
2. List the ledger account titles in the column at the left side of the trial balance. For debit-balance accounts, enter the balances in the Debits column on the same line as the related account titles. For credit-balance accounts, enter the balances in the Credits column on the same line as the related account titles.
3. Sum the Debits column and the Credits column.
4. Compare the sums of the two columns.

Illustration 2-12 shows a trial balance for PhotoCopy, Inc. You can trace each balance back to one of the T-accounts in Illustration 2-5. For example, the balance of Prepaid Insurance in the trial balance is $900 debit, which is the same balance as for the Prepaid Insurance T-account in Illustration 2-5.

LO 8

Analyze the various types of errors a trial balance identifies and apply procedures to correct the errors.

ERROR ANALYZING

In the trial balance in Illustration 2-12, the debits of $30,200 equal the credits of $30,200. The equality provides a check that the debits equal the credits in the general ledger. However, you must take care in interpreting the trial balance. The fact that debits equal credits does *not* ensure that all transactions are recorded, that the analysis of transactions is correct, or that the transactions are recorded in the correct accounts. *If the total debits do not equal total credits, however, we know that one or more of the following errors may have occurred:*

1. Debits and credits of unequal amounts were journalized and/or posted for a transaction.
2. A debit was recorded in an account as a credit, or vice versa.
3. An account balance was determined incorrectly.
4. An error occurred in recording account balances in the trial balance.
5. The Debits and/or Credits columns of the trial balance were summed incorrectly.

You may discover the source of the error by checking the correctness of journalizing, posting, and trial balance preparation procedures. You will find it more efficient to check those procedures in the reverse order that you originally performed them.

A common error is recording a debit-balance amount as a credit in the trial balance, or vice versa. If this type of error occurs, the amount by which the trial balance is "out of balance" is divisible by 2. A second common error is a transposition error. A **transposition error** occurs when two digits are reversed during the process of recording the number. For example, the debit amount of $1,319 is recorded in the trial balance as a debit of $1,391. If you make a transposition error, the amount by which the trial balance is out of balance is evenly divisible by 9. In our example, ($1,391 − $1,319) = $72 ÷ 9 = $8. A third common error is a slide. A **slide** is an error that results from adding or dropping one or more zeros from a number. For example, recording $100 as $1,000 or recording $8,000 as $800. For a slide, the differences between the correct number and the incorrect number is evenly divisible by 9: ($1,000 − $100 = $900 ÷ 9 = $100); or ($8,000 − $800 = $7,200 ÷ 9 = $800).

Correcting Entries

When we discover an error, we must correct it. We do not correct errors in the general journal or general ledger by simply erasing the error because such action may raise questions concerning the integrity of the recording process. The procedures for correcting errors in the general journal and general ledger depend on the nature of the error and at what point in the recording and posting process the error occurs.

Two types of errors may occur in the general journal and general ledger:

1. We recorded an incorrect amount in the general journal, and/or we posted an incorrect amount to a general ledger account.
2. We recorded a transaction as a debit or credit to an incorrect account in the general journal, and/or we posted the transaction to the incorrect account in the general ledger.

To correct the first type of error, the appropriate procedure is to draw a line through the incorrect amount, and then to enter the correct amount directly above the incorrect amount. For the second type of error, you must make a correcting journal entry. For example, assume an enterprise collects an account receivable and makes the following journal entry:

Feb. 12	Cash	75	
	Repairs Revenue		75
	To record the collection of an account receivable.		

The journal entry obviously is in error because the collection of an account receivable requires a credit to Accounts Receivable. If we do not correct the error, both Accounts Receivable and Repairs Revenue will be overstated by $75. The correcting general journal entry for the error is:

Feb. 19	Repairs Revenue	75	
	Accounts Receivable		75
	To correct an error of Feb.12 in which the collection of an account receivable was erroneously recorded as Repairs Revenue.		

Posting the correcting journal entry in the general ledger reduces both Repairs Revenue and Accounts Receivable to their correct balances. The full explanation in the correcting entry provides a complete record of what occurred for anyone who questions the journal entry.

ACCOUNTING NET INCOME

LO 9

Define accounting net income and distinguish among the cash basis, accrual basis, and income tax basis of income.

A business enterprise's primary objective is to earn a profit for the owners. Profit, however, means different things to different people—to investors and creditors, economists and accountants. An investor, for example, might consider profit as the increase in the market price of shares of stock that the investor owns. An accountant, on the other hand, considers profit to be the increase in a business enterprise's net assets from operations during a period. Accountants use the concept of net income (rather than profit) to report on the results of a business's operations. **Net income** is the excess of revenues over expenses for a period and may be expressed by the equation:

Net Income = Revenues – Expenses

If expenses exceed revenues for a period, the business has incurred a **net loss**. For 1992, General Motors Corporation reported the largest net loss, $23 billion, in the history of American business. As you saw previously, we report the business's net income (or net loss) in the income statement.

The income statement provides a measure of the business's performance during a period. Net income is important to both the owner and to other users of the financial statements such as creditors. When a business reports net income in its income statement, it means that operations have resulted in an increase in the business's net assets. This information is important to the owners because it signifies the degree of success the business has experienced during the period. The information about net income is important to creditors because it provides one basis for them to assess the business's financial health.

Revenues

Revenues are defined as the increases in net assets that result directly from providing products or services to customers during a specific period. In other words, revenues are increases in *net assets* due to the business's operations. For example, PhotoCopy, Inc. earns revenues by providing copying services to customers. IBM earns revenues by selling computers and related products to customers, while McDonald's earns revenues by providing fast-food to customers. Revenues increase assets by increasing cash (through cash sales) or accounts and notes receivable (through credit sales).

However, not all increases in cash or other assets are revenues. For example, borrowing from the bank increases cash, but this cash is not revenue because the transaction does not involve providing products or services to customers. Also, collection of accounts receivable is not revenue because the transaction does not increase net assets. Consider the following example. Cooper's Computer Repair Shop repairs several computers and bills the customers $1,200. Illustration 2-13 shows the effects of this transaction.

The $1,200 is considered revenue because Cooper's has increased its net assets (accounts receivable) by providing repair services to customers. However, when Cooper's collects $300 of the amount owed, the transaction does not result in revenue because net assets have not changed. Notice that in Illustration 2-13 the collection of the account receivable has no effect on stockholders' equity. The $300 increase in Cash is offset by the $300 decrease in Accounts Receivable so that there is no change in net assets.

ILLUSTRATION 2-13 Revenue Transactions and Net Assets

	Assets		Stockholders' Equity
	Cash	Accounts Receivable	Repairs Revenue
Revenue - $1,200 sales on credit		1,200	1,200
Collection of $300 of accounts receivable	300	300	

Expenses

Expenses are defined as decreases in assets and increases in liabilities the business's revenue-producing activities cause during a specific period. In other words, expenses are decreases in *net assets* due to the business's operations. We may view expenses as the sacrifices the business makes to earn the revenues of the period. Examples of expenses include wages and salaries, rent, depreciation, and utilities. When PhotoCopy, Inc. pays the employee wages of $400, we record the expense as follows:

Feb. 21	Wages and Salaries Expense	400	
	Cash		400
	Payment of employee wages.		

The payment is an expense because assets (cash) are decreased by revenue-producing activities—providing copying services for customers.

Transactions other than expenses can decrease assets or increase liabilities. For example, when PhotoCopy, Inc. borrowed from the bank to purchase the delivery van, we record the following entry:

Feb. 1	Notes Payable	10,000	
	Cash		10,000
	To record the proceeds of bank loan.		

This transaction increases liabilities (notes payable). However, because borrowing money does not involve the business's revenue-producing activities, it is not an expense.

ACCOUNTING BASES

In practice, more than one concept exists for measuring the business's performance during a period. Below we discuss three concepts—the cash basis, the accrual basis, and the income tax basis.

Cash Basis

Some small businesses prepare financial statements on the cash basis of accounting. Under the **cash basis of accounting**, revenues are recorded only in the period that cash payments are received from customers; and expenses are recorded only in the period that cash payments are made. This method measures the business's performance by the difference between cash receipts and cash disbursements. The primary advantage of the cash basis of accounting is its simplicity.

Accrual Basis

GAAP require the accrual basis of accounting for the preparation of income statements and balance sheets. The **accrual basis of accounting** means that revenues are recorded in the period that they are earned, and expenses are recorded in the period that they are incurred. The period that revenues are earned may be different from the period of the related cash receipts. For example, PhotoCopy, Inc. provided copying service to a customer on credit in one period but did not receive the cash payment until the following period. Under accrual accounting, we record revenue in the period that the business provides the service because that is when the business earns the revenue. Advocates of

HISTORICAL PERSPECTIVES

QUEEN ELIZABETH I

BLAME THIS LADY

She's Queen Elizabeth I, who in 1600 chartered the East India Company, one of the world's first "joint stock" companies. The joint stock company had owners who were merely investors and did not participate in the management of the trading ventures of the company. Initially, the company made distributions of all income (if any) to the investors at the end of a trading venture. But in 1661 the company's governor announced that future distributions would be paid periodically out of net income.

All of a sudden, measuring net income was a job for the accountants, who had to start making judgment calls. Assets and net income had to be apportioned among many voyages in different stages of completion. Many subjective judgments were required before calculating each period's net income—the life expectancy of ships, how much capital to retain to keep ships in tip-top shape, when to write off bad debts, etc.

In short, trading companies like East India Company introduced accrual accounting, periodic net income, and most of the accounting problems we face today.

Source: *Forbes* (November 12, 1990), pp. 8, 112. Reprinted by permission of FORBES magazine © Forbes Inc., 1990.

accrual accounting believe that recording the revenues in the period they are *earned*, rather than in the period that the *cash payments are received*, better measures enterprise performance. The basis for this viewpoint is that providing the product or service to customers is generally the critical event in the earning process. Accountants view the collection of the cash payment as only an incidental (but necessary) part of the earning process.

Under accrual accounting and the matching principle, we record expenses in the period that they are incurred, which may be a period different from the one in which the business makes the cash payment for the expense. For example, assume that an employee works for a business in one period but is not paid until the following period. Under accrual accounting, we record wages and salaries expense in the period the employee works for the business, rather than in the following period when the business pays the employee. An employee's salary increases liabilities because the business is obligated to pay the salary. Accrual accounting advocates believe that recording expenses in the period they are incurred—rather than in the period paid—is a superior measure of the sacrifices the business makes in earning the revenues of the period. The important event in the business's earning process is incurring wages and salaries expense for the service the employee provides during the period, not for the payment of the obligation to the employee. Illustration 2-14 summarizes the recording of revenues and expenses under the cash basis and the accrual basis of accounting.

ILLUSTRATION 2-14 Cash Basis and Accrual Basis

	Cash Basis	Accrual Basis
Revenue recorded	In period cash is received	In period earned (when product or service is provided)
Expense recorded	In period cash is paid	In period expense is incurred

Many businesses keep their records, on a day-to-day basis, using a method similar to the cash basis of accounting. That is, most transactions recorded involve either cash receipts or cash payments. At the end of an accounting period, these businesses must adjust their records to the accrual basis of accounting to prepare financial statements. For example, assume that on January 2, a painter contracts with an apartment complex to paint the interiors of the 20 units that make up the complex. The agreed-upon price for the job is $4,000, to be paid upon completion of all 20 units. In addition, the complex agrees to provide the paint. On the same day, the painter purchases for cash a spray-painting machine at a cost of $900. The painter expects to use the painting machine for 5 years. At the end of January, the painter has completed 15 of the units.

On the cash basis of accounting, the painter has no revenues for January because cash receipts are zero. On the other hand, expenses on a cash basis are $900—the cash payment for the spray-painting machine. In this case, the cash basis of accounting does not accurately reflect the painter's performance for the month. During January, he earned 75 percent of the contract price (15 ÷ 20 units), and he used only 1/60 [1 month ÷ (5 years x 12 months)] of the machine's service potential. To adjust to the accrual basis of accounting for January, the painter should record revenues of $3,000 (75% x $4,000). Expenses should be recorded at only $15 ($900 ÷ 60 months), and the machine should be shown as an asset at the cost of its remaining service potential of $885 ($900 – $15).

In the next chapter, we provide a full description of the adjustment process that accomplishes accrual basis accounting for such events. Note that even though income statements and balance sheets are prepared on the accrual basis, cash flow information is also important; and the statement of cash flows is a required financial statement. Statements of cash flows are discussed in a subsequent chapter.

Income Tax Basis

Because corporations are separate legal entities, they must pay federal income taxes just as individuals do. Federal income taxes were permanently imposed on corporations in the United States in 1913. In addition, most states impose an income tax on corporations that operate within their borders. The rules for the federal taxation of corporations are derived from the **Internal Revenue Code**, and the two primary factors in determining the amount of income taxes due are taxable income and the applicable tax rates.

Taxable Income. Under the Internal Revenue Code, corporate income taxes are assessed based on **taxable income**. Taxable income is calculated as follows:

Gross Income − Deductions = Taxable Income

For most corporations, taxable income is similar to net income on the accrual basis. Gross income approximates revenues and deductions approximate expenses. Taxable income is probably described best as net income on the accrual basis with certain specified differences. For example, interest earned on investments in certain state and municipal bonds is included in net income, but this interest is not subject to federal income taxes. The tax rules for merchandise inventories and for plant assets, in particular, are important considerations for management in making certain decisions. Those considerations are included in the discussions of those topics in later chapters and in Appendix A to the text.

Tax Rates. To determine the amount of income taxes due, a **tax rate** is applied to taxable income. Currently, the tax rate for corporations with taxable income of $15 million or more is 35%, as specified by the Internal Revenue Code. For example, Star Imports, Inc. has taxable income of $20 million and would pay federal income taxes of $7 million ($20,000,000 x 35%). Corporations with income of less than $15 million pay income taxes at a lower rate that varies according to the amount of taxable income.

SUMMARY

Describe accounts and recognize commonly used accounts.   Businesses store and summarize information about the effects of transactions in accounts. They use separate accounts for each category of assets, liabilities, and stockholders' equity that are relevant for management purposes or for analysis by outside users of the financial statements.

Explain the rules of debit and credit and how they relate to the accounting equation.   The rules of debit and credit dictate how we increase and decrease accounts for the effects of transactions and other events that affect the business's financial position. We increase asset accounts with debits, and we decrease them with credits. We increase liability and stockholders' equity accounts with credits, and we decrease them with debits. Observing the rule that debits must always equal credits as we record transactions in the business's accounts is equivalent to preserving the accounting equation.

Apply the rules of debit and credit to business transactions. Recording the effects of transactions requires us to analyze each transaction. First, we decide which accounts are affected. Then, we decide by what dollar amounts. Finally, we record these effects in the accounts, applying the rules of debit and credit.

Identify the procedures in the accounting cycle. Analyzing, journalizing, and posting transactions and events constitute three of the six stages in the accounting cycle—the process that maintains the accounting records according to GAAP and leads to periodic preparation of financial statements. Later, you are introduced to the next two procedures in the accounting cycle. To prepare financial statements that conform to GAAP, it is necessary to make adjustments to certain accounts at the end of an accounting period. These adjustments are explained, and the preparation of financial statements from the adjusted accounts is illustrated in a subsequent chapter. In that chapter, the last phase of the process, closing temporary accounts, is also described.

Apply the procedures to record in the accounting records the effects of business transactions. These procedures consist of (1) analyzing the transactions, (2) journalizing an entry in the general journal, and (3) posting the entries in the general journal to the general ledger.

Explain the relationship between the general journal and the general ledger. Businesses store their accounts in General Ledgers. As transactions and events that affect financial position occur, businesses analyze them and record their effects by entries in the general journal. The information in general journal entries consists of the date, accounts affected by the event or transaction, the amounts to be debited and credited to the accounts, and a brief description. The debit and credit amounts are then posted to the individual accounts in the general ledger.

Prepare a trial balance. The accuracy of the journalizing and posting process can be periodically checked by preparing a trial balance. The trial balance is a listing of all general ledger accounts, with debit balances in one column and credit balances in another. If the sums of the two columns are equal, the double-entry rule has been applied accurately. Otherwise, the accountant is alerted that there has been a recording or posting error.

Analyze the various types of errors a trial balance identifies and apply procedures to correct the errors. Errors may occur in the process of journalizing and posting transactions, in determining account balances, or in the preparation of the trial balance. When we discover an error, we should correct it, which often involves making a correcting entry.

Define accounting net income and distinguish among the cash basis, accrual basis, and income tax basis of income. Net income is the excess of revenues over expenses for a period. Net income provides a measure of the business's performance for a period. When a business reports net income in its income statement, it means that the business's operations have increased its net assets.

Businesses that use the cash basis of accounting recognize revenues when they receive cash and recognize expenses when they make cash payments. Businesses that use the accrual basis of accounting recognize revenues when they are earned and recognize expenses in the period they are incurred. GAAP require the use of the accrual basis of accounting for the preparation of financial statements. The income tax basis of accounting is similar to the accrual basis with differences specified in the Internal Revenue Code. The amount of income taxes a corporation owes is determined by multiplying taxable income by the specified income tax rate.

REVIEW PROBLEM: RECORDING BUSINESS TRANSACTIONS AND PREPARING THE TRIAL BALANCE

Computerworld, Inc., a computer repair shop, began business on January 2, 19X6, by issuing $30,000 of capital stock. You have been asked to prepare all the necessary accounting records.

Computerworld uses the following chart of accounts:

ASSETS
100 Cash
110 Accounts Receivable
139 Repair Parts
150 Prepaid Insurance
158 Utility Deposits

LIABILITIES
302 Accounts Payable

STOCKHOLDERS' EQUITY
519 Capital Stock
550 Retained Earnings
598 Dividends

REVENUE
608 Repairs Revenue

EXPENSES
744 Repair Parts Expense
762 Rent Expense
775 Telephone Expense
780 Utilities Expense
784 Wages and Salaries Expense

The following information is available for the month of January:

Jan. 2 Capital stock of Computerworld is sold for $30,000, cash.
      3 Two employees were hired by the Board of Directors to manage Computerworld. It is agreed that the employees will be paid $600 and $800, respectively, semimonthly.
      4 One of the new employees finds an appropriate storefront for Computerworld and signs a 1-year lease for it. He also pays the first month's rent in the amount of $1,000.
      4 The other employee arranges for telephone and utility service for Computerworld's store. A $150 deposit is required. This deposit may be refunded to Computerworld after it pays its bills on time for 2 years.
      4 Computerworld purchased an insurance policy for six months beginning January 2, 19X6, to protect itself against losses from fire and theft. The policy costs $1,200.
      5 Parts that will be used to repair computers are purchased for $400 on account from Modern Computer Parts.
      10 Computerworld opens its doors for business. Repairs are performed on 6 computers, and a total of $500 in revenue is earned and received in cash. To perform these repairs, Computerworld used repair parts that cost $60.
      12 Additional customers bring their computers in for repair. Computerworld performs the repairs and receives cash in the amount of $1,200 and will bill the remainder for $3,000.

Jan. 15 The two employees are paid their semimonthly salaries by check.

16 Parts are ordered from Micro Tek, a supplier of computer parts.

21 Computerworld receives checks totalling $800 from the customers billed on January 12.

22 The parts from Micro Tek are received with a bill for $400.

23 Additional repair services are performed, and $320 is received in cash.

24 A Computerworld check for $200 is written to Modern Computer Parts as a partial payment for the parts previously purchased.

26 Additional checks totaling $740 are received from customers on account.

28 A telephone bill in the amount of $46 is received from Eastern Bell, and a check is issued immediately.

30 The two employees are paid their semimonthly salaries by check.

31 A utility bill from City Electric is received in the amount of $187 for January's electricity, gas, and water.

REQUIRED:

a. Prepare a general journal entry for each transaction as appropriate.

b. Open a general ledger account for each account shown in the chart of accounts.

c. Post each transaction to the proper accounts in the general ledger.

d. Prepare a trial balance as of January 31, 19X6.

e. Calculate the totals for the trial balance that would have occurred if the balance of Parts Expense was incorrectly copied into the trial balance as $600.

f. Calculate the difference between the trial balance totals (the Debits column and the Credits column) as a result of the error in e.

g. Explain how the difference calculated in f indicates that a slide error was made.

SOLUTION:

Planning and Organizing Your Work

1. Analyze each transaction to determine which accounts, if any, are increased or decreased and by what amount.

2. Determine whether the effect would be a debit or credit to each of the accounts involved.

3. Prepare general journal entries based on the analysis in 1 and 2.

4. Open a general ledger account for each account in the chart of accounts.

5. Post each transaction in the general journal to the appropriate general ledger accounts.

6. Prepare a trial balance.

7. Analyze the effect of the error in the trial balance.

(a) *Prepare a general journal entry for each transaction as appropriate.*

GENERAL JOURNAL   PAGE 1

DATE		DESCRIPTION	POST. REF.	DEBIT	CREDIT
19X6					
Jan.	2	Cash	100	30,000	
		Capital Stock	519		30,000
		To record stock issuance.			
	4	Rent Expense	762	1,000	
		Cash	100		1,000
		To record payment of January rent.			

GENERAL JOURNAL   PAGE 2

DATE		DESCRIPTION	POST. REF.	DEBIT	CREDIT
19X6 Jan.	4	Utility Deposits	158	150	
		Cash	100		150
		To record payment of refundable utility deposit.			
	4	Prepaid Insurance	150	1,200	
		Cash	100		1,200
		To record the purchase of a 6-month insurance policy.			
	5	Repair Parts	139	400	
		Accounts Payable	302		400
		To record the purchase of repair parts from Modern Computer Parts.			
	10	Cash	100	500	
		Repairs Revenue	608		500
		To record repair revenues.			
	10	Parts Expense	744	60	
		Repair Parts	139		60
		To record repair parts used.			
	12	Cash	100	1,200	
		Accounts Receivable	110	3,000	
		Repairs Revenue	608		4,200
		To record repair revenues.			
	15	Wages and Salaries Expense	784	1,400	
		Cash	100		1,400
		To record wages and salaries expense for January 1–15.			
	21	Cash	100	800	
		Accounts Receivable	110		800
		To record receipts from January 12 billing.			
	22	Repair Parts	139	400	
		Accounts Payable	302		400
		To record receipt of parts from Micro Tek.			
	23	Cash	100	320	
		Repairs Revenue	608		320
		To record the receipt of repair revenue.			
	24	Accounts Payable	302	200	
		Cash	100		200
		To record partial payment to Modern Computer for January 5 purchase.			
	26	Cash	100	740	
		Accounts Receivable	110		740
		To record receipt from January 12 billing.			
	28	Telephone Expense	275	46	
		Cash	100		46
		To record the receipt and payment of January's telephone bill.			

GENERAL JOURNAL　　　　　　　PAGE 3

DATE		DESCRIPTION	POST. REF.	DEBIT	CREDIT
19X6					
Jan.	30	Wages and Salaries Expense	284	1,400	
		Cash	100		1,400
		To record wages and salaries expense for January 16–30.			
	31	Utilities Expense	780	187	
		Accounts Payable	302		187
		To record January's utility bill.			

Note: The events of January 3 and 16 are not recordable transactions.

(b), (c) *Open general ledger accounts and post each transaction to the proper accounts.*

GENERAL LEDGER

NAME:　Cash　　　　　　　　　　　　　　　　ACCOUNT NO.:　100

DATE		DESCRIPTION	POST. REF.	DEBIT	CREDIT	BALANCE
19X6						
Jan.	2		GJ1	30,000		30,000
	4		GJ1		1,000	29,000
	4		GJ2		150	28,850
	4		GJ2		1,200	27,650
	10		GJ2	500		28,150
	12		GJ2	1,200		29,350
	15		GJ2		1,400	27,950
	21		GJ2	800		28,750
	23		GJ2	320		29,070
	24		GJ2		200	28,870
	26		GJ2	740		29,610
	28		GJ2		46	29,564
	30		GJ3		1,400	28,164

NAME:　Accounts Receivable　　　　　　　　　ACCOUNT NO.:　110

DATE		DESCRIPTION	POST. REF.	DEBIT	CREDIT	BALANCE
19X6						
Jan.	12		GJ2	3,000		3,000
	21		GJ2		800	2,200
	26		GJ2		740	1,460

NAME:　Repair Parts　　　　　　　　　　　　ACCOUNT NO.:　139

DATE		DESCRIPTION	POST. REF.	DEBIT	CREDIT	BALANCE
19X6						
Jan.	5		GJ2	400		400
	10		GJ2		60	340
	22		GJ2	400		740

NAME: Prepaid Insurance   ACCOUNT NO.: 150

DATE		DESCRIPTION	POST. REF.	DEBIT	CREDIT	BALANCE
19X6 Jan.	4		GJ2	1,200		1,200

NAME: Utility Deposits   ACCOUNT NO.: 158

DATE		DESCRIPTION	POST. REF.	DEBIT	CREDIT	BALANCE
19X6 Jan.	4		GJ2	150		150

NAME: Accounts Payable   ACCOUNT NO.: 302

DATE		DESCRIPTION	POST. REF.	DEBIT	CREDIT	BALANCE
19X6 Jan.	5		GJ2		400	400
	22		GJ2		400	800
	24		GJ2	200		600
	31		GJ3		187	787

NAME: Capital Stock   ACCOUNT NO.: 519

DATE		DESCRIPTION	POST. REF.	DEBIT	CREDIT	BALANCE
19X6 Jan.	2		GJ1		30,000	30,000

NAME: Repairs Revenue   ACCOUNT NO.: 608

DATE		DESCRIPTION	POST. REF.	DEBIT	CREDIT	BALANCE
19X6 Jan.	10		GJ2		500	500
	12		GJ2		4,200	4,700
	23		GJ2		320	5,020

NAME: Parts Expense   ACCOUNT NO.: 744

DATE		DESCRIPTION	POST. REF.	DEBIT	CREDIT	BALANCE
19X6 Jan.	10		GJ2	60		60

NAME: Rent Expense   ACCOUNT NO.: 762

DATE		DESCRIPTION	POST. REF.	DEBIT	CREDIT	BALANCE
19X6 Jan.	4		GJ1	1,000		1,000

NAME: Telephone Expense   ACCOUNT NO.: 775

DATE		DESCRIPTION	POST. REF.	DEBIT	CREDIT	BALANCE
19X6 Jan.	28		GJ2	46		46

NAME: Utilities Expense ACCOUNT NO.: 780

DATE	DESCRIPTION	POST. REF.	DEBIT	CREDIT	BALANCE
19X6 Jan. 31		GJ3	187		187

NAME: Wages and Salaries Expense ACCOUNT NO.: 784

DATE	DESCRIPTION	POST. REF.	DEBIT	CREDIT	BALANCE
19X6 Jan. 15		GJ2	1,400		1,400
30		GJ3	1,400		2,800

(d) *Prepare a trial balance for January 31, 19X6.*

Computerworld, Inc.
Trial Balance
January 31, 19X6

		Debits	Credits
100	Cash	$28,164	
110	Accounts Receivable	1,460	
139	Repair Parts	740	
150	Prepaid Insurance	1,200	
158	Utility Deposits	150	
302	Accounts Payable		$ 787
519	Capital Stock		30,000
608	Repairs Revenue		5,020
744	Parts Expense	60	
762	Rent Expense	1,000	
775	Telephone Expense	46	
780	Utilities Expense	187	
784	Wages and Salaries Expense	2,800	
		$35,807	$35,807

(e) *Calculate the totals for the trial balance that would have occurred if the balance of Parts Expense was incorrectly copied into the trial balance as $600.*

Total debits would be $35,807 − $60 + $600 = $36,347.
Total credits would be unchanged at $36,347.

(f) *Calculate the difference between trial balance totals (the Debits column and the Credits column) as a result of the error in e.*

Total debits exceed total credits by $540. ($36,347 − $35,807)

(g) *Explain how the difference calculated in f indicates that a slide error was made.*
The difference between the Debits and Credits columns, $540, is evenly divisible by 9 ($540 ÷ 9 = $60) and the incorrect amount recorded was $600.

KEY TERMS

account, *46*	debit balance, *51*	posting, *61*
account balance, *47*	debited, *51*	realization principle, *50*
accounting cycle, *58*	dividends, *50*	recognize, *50*
accrual basis of accounting, *68*	general journal, *59*	slide error, *65*
capital stock, *50*	general ledger, *61*	T-account, *46*
cash basis of accounting, *68*	Internal Revenue Code, *70*	taxable income, *70*
chart of accounts, *62*	journal entry, *59*	tax rate, *70*
credit, *51*	journalizing, *59*	transposition error, *65*
credit balance, *51*	matching principle, *50*	trial balance, *64*
credited, *51*	net income, *66*	
debit, *51*	net loss, *66*	

SELF QUIZ

LO 1,2   1. Indicate which of the following statements about accounts are true (*T*) and which are false (*F*).
   a. Accounts are used to summarize accounting information.
   b. Accounts are always increased by debits.
   c. Accounts are used to store accounting information.
   d. All accounts appear in the balance sheet.

LO 1   2. Indicate whether the following accounts belong in a balance sheet (*B*) or in an income statement (*I*).
   a. Cash
   b. Utilities Expense
   c. Notes Payable
   d. Retained Earnings
   e. Land
   f. Service Revenue
   g. Prepaid Insurance
   h. Capital Stock

LO 1,2   3. Indicate the normal balances for the following types of accounts. Use *Dr.* for debit or *Cr.* for credit.
   a. Assets
   b. Liabilities
   c. Capital Stock
   d. Retained Earnings
   e. Revenues
   f. Expenses
   g. Dividends

LO 1,2   4. Identify each of the following accounts as to whether it is an asset (*A*), liability (*L*), revenue (*R*), or expense (*E*):
   a. Interest Revenue
   b. Prepaid Insurance
   c. Wages and Salaries Expense
   d. Buildings
   e. Wages and Salaries Payable
   f. Rent Receivable

LO 1,2   5. Indicate whether each of the following accounts would normally have a debit balance (*Dr.*) or a credit balance (*Cr.*).
   a. Cash
   b. Prepaid Rent
   c. Notes Payable
   d. Fee Revenue
   e. Advertising Expense
   f. Capital Stock
   g. Dividends
   h. Retained Earnings

LO 2   6. Complete the following statement: Debits will increase _____ accounts, decrease _____ accounts, and decrease _____ accounts.

LO 2   7. Complete the following statement: Credits will increase _____ accounts, increase _____ accounts, and decrease _____ accounts.

LO 2,3,6,9 8. Match the following accounting terms with the definitions shown below.
   a. Account
   b. General journal
   c. Compound journal entry
   d. Asset
   e. Dividends
   f. Credit
   g. Debit balance
   h. Journalizing
   i. Accrual accounting
   j. Cash basis accounting
   (1) Amount by which the total debits in an account exceed the total credits in that same account
   (2) Book of original entry that provides a complete description of a business transaction in one place
   (3) Method of accounting where revenues are recorded when earned

and expenses are recorded as incurred

(4) Right side of an account

(5) Process of recording business transactions in a general journal

(6) Something with future benefits

(7) Journal entry that affects three or more accounts or, in other words, contains more than one debit and/or more than one credit

(8) Subclassification of the accounting equation that is used for storing and summarizing transaction data that affect a particular account—i.e., Cash or Rent Expense

(9) Method of accounting that allows for the recording of revenues when received and expenses when paid

(10) Distributions of assets, usually cash, to the stockholders of a corporation

LO 3 9. An example of a transaction that increases one asset, decreases another asset, and has no effect on the liabilities or stockholders' equity is

a. Purchase of equipment on credit

b. Payment of an account payable

c. Recording of revenue

d. Contribution of cash by the owner

e. Purchase of supplies for cash

LO 3 10. An example of a transaction that increases an asset, increases a liability, and has no effect on stockholders' equity is

a. Purchase of equipment on credit

b. Payment of an account payable

c. Recording of revenue

d. Declaration of cash dividend

e. Purchase of supplies for cash

LO 3 11. An example of a transaction that decreases an asset, decreases a liability, and has no effect on stockholders' equity is

a. Purchase of equipment on credit

b. Payment of an account payable

c. Recording of revenue

d. Contribution of cash by the owner

e. Purchase of supplies for cash

LO 4 12. Indicate the proper order of the six steps in the accounting cycle listed below by placing the numbers 1 through 6 in the spaces provided.

___ a. Prepare financial statements.

___ b. Analyze business transactions.

___ c. Post to the general ledger.

___ d. Adjust the accounts.

___ e. Close the accounts.

___ f. Journalize transactions.

LO 4,6,7,9 13. Match the following accounting terms with the definitions that follow:

a. Matching principle

b. Realization principle

c. General ledger

d. T-account

e. Trial balance

f. Posting

(1) Abbreviation of a general ledger account that is used to simplify problem solutions and to explain how an account is used

(2) Process of transferring transactions data from the book of original entry to the general ledger

(3) Requires that the costs incurred to generate revenues should be recognized in the same accounting period in which the related revenue is recognized

(4) Group of accounts consisting of all of the accounts listed in the chart of accounts.

(5) Requires that revenues should only be recognized during an accounting period if (a) they are earned during the period and (b) cash is collected or expected be collected

(6) Statement that lists in one column the debit balances of general ledger accounts and lists in another column the credit balances

LO 5 14. The Womack Company purchased land for $25,000, paying cash of $10,000 and giving a note payable for the remaining $15,000. Which of the following journal entries would be correct?

a. Notes Payable   15,000
   Cash   10,000
       Land   25,000
   Purchased land.

b. Land   25,000
       Cash   10,000
       Notes Payable   15,000
   Purchased land.

c. Land   10,000
       Cash   10,000
   Purchased land,
   still owe $15,000.

d. Land   25,000
   Cash   10,000
       Notes Payable   15,000
   Purchased land.

LO 6 15. Indicate whether the following statements are true (*T*) or false (*F*).

a. Transaction data are entered directly into the general ledger.

b. Transaction data are entered directly into the general journal.

c. Transaction data are entered into the general ledger from the general journal.

LO 8 16. An example of a transposition error is

a. A check for $4,512.00 recorded as $451.20

b. A check for $4,512.00 recorded as $4,215.00

c. A check for $4,512.00 recorded as $5,512.00

d. None of the above are transposition errors

LO 8 17. Which of the following recording or posting errors would require a correcting journal entry?

a. Posting a $300 Cash debit as a debit to Rent Expense

b. Posting a $500 Cash debit as a $50 debit to Cash

c. Recording a journal entry for the payment of a $500 Account Payable as a debit to Accounts Receivable and a credit to Cash

d. Posting a $72 debit to Cash as a $27 debit to Cash in the general ledger

LO 8 18. In preparing a trial balance, the $10,000 Accounts Payable balance is listed in the debit column. Therefore,

a. The trial balance will be in balance because the $10,000 is included in the trial balance.

b. The trial balance will be out of balance, with the Debits column $10,000 greater than the Credits column.

c. The trial balance will be out of balance with the Debits column $20,000 greater than the Credits column.

d. The trial balance will be out of balance by one-half the amount of the error, $5,000.

LO 8 19. A cash dividend of $5,000 is declared and distributed to the stockholders. The payment of the dividend is recorded by a debit to Cash of $5,000 and a credit to Accounts Payable of $5,000. Therefore,

a. The trial balance will be out of balance by $5,000.

b. The trial balance will be out of balance by $10,000.

c. The trial balance will be in balance, but incorrect.

d. The trial balance will be out of balance by $2,500.

LO 9 20. Total revenue of $3,000 was earned during the month; and cash payments totaling $2,200 were received, $1,400 of which related to revenues earned this month. How much revenue should you report under GAAP?

a. $5,200

b. $3,000

c. $2,200

d. $1,400

LO 9 21. Ace Corp. had gross income for the year of $400,000 and deductions from income totaling $366,000. Ace's income is currently taxed at 28%. What will Ace's income taxes be for the year?

a. $12,000

b. $11,200

c. $ 9,520

d. $ 8,640

SOLUTIONS TO SELF-QUIZ

1. a. T   b. F   c. T   d. F   2. a. B   b. I   c. B   d. B   e. B   f. I   g. B   h. B   3. a. Dr.   b. Cr.   c. Cr.   d. Cr.   e. Cr.   f. Dr.
g. Dr.   4. a. R   b. A   c. E   d. A   e. L   f. A   5. a. Dr.   b. Dr.   c. Cr.   d. Cr.   e. Dr.   f. Cr.   g. Dr.   h. Cr.
6. asset, liability, stockholders' equity   7. liability, stockholders' equity, asset   8. a. 8   b. 2   c. 7   d. 6   e. 10   f. 4   g. 1
h. 5   i. 3   j. 9   9. e   10. a   11. b   12. a. 5   b. 1   c. 3   d. 4   e. 6   f. 2   13. a. 3   b. 5   c. 4   d. 1   e. 6   f. 2
14. b   15. a. F   b. T   c. T   16. b   17. a and c   18. c   19. c   20. b   21. c

QUESTIONS

Q2-1   What is the purpose of an account?

Q2-2   What is a ledger?

Q2-3   List five asset accounts and three liability accounts that businesses commonly use.

Q2-4 What is a debit?

Q2-5 Does a debit always increase an account? Explain.

Q2-6 How does a debit affect a liability account?

Q2-7 What is a credit?

Q2-8 What effect would a credit have on an asset account?

Q2-9 Comment on the following statement: "The whole premise of accounting is unnecessarily complex. Why not be consistent with debits and credits. If I designed the system, debits would always increase accounts and credits would always decrease accounts. This would make accounting much simpler."

Q2-10 Accounting transactions are first entered in the general journal and then posted to the general ledger accounts. Some view this as recording the transaction twice. Could time be saved by eliminating the general journal and making entries directly in the general ledger? Discuss.

Q2-11 When you have analyzed a business transaction in preparation for making a journal entry, is it true that one account will always increase and another account will always decrease?

Q2-12 Explain how the balance of a general ledger account is determined.

Q2-13 If all debits and credits recorded in the general journal are posted to the general ledger, is it reasonable to assume that the total of the debit balances in the general ledger will be equal to the total of the credit balances in the general ledger? Discuss.

Q2-14 What is a trial balance and what does it prove?

Q2-15 A credit to Accounts Receivable is inadvertently posted to Cash. What effect will this error have on your trial balance totals?

Q2-16 The trial balance that you prepare does not balance. Where might you look to find your error?

Q2-17 At the end of the accounting period, the trial balance is in balance. Does this ensure that the accounting records are correct? Explain.

Q2-18 A trial balance is taken at the end of the accounting period and is out of balance. The Debits column exceeds the Credits column by $810. Suggest possible errors that might have caused this difference.

Q2-19 Give an example of an error in the accounting records that will not cause the trial balance to be out of balance.

Q2-20 Comment on the following statement: "Taking a trial balance is a waste of time. It doesn't prove that the accounting records are correct; so, why bother?"

Q2-21 How does accrual accounting differ from the cash basis of accounting? Which method follows GAAP?

Q2-22 Does taxable income most closely approximate net income calculated under the cash or accrual basis of accounting?

EXERCISES

LO 1,2

E2-1 **Recognizing Common Accounts and Their Normal Balances**   The following accounts were selected from the chart of accounts of the Top Shop, Inc. Identify each account as an element of assets (*A*), liabilities (*L*), or stockholders' equity (*SE*) and indicate whether its normal balance is a debit (*Dr.*) or credit (*Cr.*).

a. Dividends
b. Accounts Receivable
c. Equipment
d. Notes Payable
e. Prepaid Insurance
f. Wages and Salaries Payable
g. Accounts Payable
h. Sales
i. Rent Expense
j. Capital Stock

LO 1,2

E2-2 **The Rules of Debit and Credit** Indicate whether you would debit (*Dr.*) or credit (*Cr.*) each of the following accounts to increase their balances. (First identify the account as an asset, liability, or stockholders' equity account.)

a. Fee Revenue

b. Notes Receivable

c. Utilities Expense

d. Notes Payable

e. Buildings

f. Cash

g. Accounts Payable

h. Capital Stock

i. Office Supplies

j. Dividends

LO 3,5

E2-3 **The Effect of Business Transactions on Accounts** Apex Apple Farm, Inc. borrowed $25,000 from the N.B.C. Bank at the beginning of the harvesting season to cover labor costs during the picking and packing process. What effect would this transaction have on the company's

a. Assets

b. Liabilities

c. Revenues

d. Expenses

e. Stockholders' equity

LO 3,5

E2-4 **Compound Journal Entry** A company purchases equipment costing $10,000 by paying $3,000 down and signing a note payable for the balance ($7,000).

REQUIRED:

a. Prepare the necessary journal entry.

b. Explain how you are reasonably sure that you have included all of the elements of the transaction in your entry.

LO 3,5

E2-5 **Applying the Rules of Debit and Credit** Each of the following unrelated business transactions occurred:

(1) The Too-Sweet Corporation paid salaries for the week in the amount of $575.

(2) Camping World, Inc. issued 100 shares of stock in its company for $1,000.

(3) Cat Corporation borrowed $15,000 from the bank to add a new building to its facilities.

(4) Camping World, Inc., paid $7,000 in insurance premiums for the first 6 months of the year on January 2.

(5) Cat collected $2,500 of amounts due from customers' open accounts.

(6) Too-Sweet purchased a new candy oven for $6,000, paying $2,000 in cash and signing a note payable for the $4,000 balance.

REQUIRED:

a. Determine the accounts involved

b. Determine if the account is increased or decreased

c. Determine if the account is debited or credited

Use the following format to complete your analysis:

0. The Flaming Arrow Campground received camping fees from patrons totaling $1,500 for the weekend.

(1)	(2)	(3)
0. Accounts Involved	Increase/Decrease	Debit/Credit
Cash	Increase	Debit
Fee Revenue	Increase	Credit

LO 5,6

E2-6 **The Relationship Between the General Journal and the General Ledger** The following T-accounts summarize the effect of 5 business transactions on the general ledger accounts of Mountain City Spas, Inc.:

Cash					Fee Revenue			
(1)	2,500	(4)	1,000				(1)	2,500
(3)	1,750	(5)	250				(2)	3,000

Accounts Receivable					Notes Payable			
(2)	3,000	(3)	1,750				(4)	2,000

Equipment			Rent Expense		
(4)	3,000		(5)	250	

REQUIRED:

a. Review the information contained in the accounts and write descriptions of the 5 transactions that were involved.

b. Prepare general journal entries to match your descriptions of the transactions.

LO 3,5,6

E2-7 **Journalizing and Posting Transactions** The following business events of the Cullowhee Collection Corporation occurred in March:

Mar. 1 $500 of common stock was issued to start the business.

3 Tim Trainor was hired by the Board of Directors to run the company.

5 $100 was paid to rent desk space in the office of the Paradise Travel Agency for the month of March.

16 $125 refundable deposit was paid for a three-line telephone from Mountain Phone Company and a one month's local service fee of $35. Tim wrote one check for these services.

19 A bill was collected for the Climber Tree Company, and $500 was received from the company for this service.

29 An old account for the accounting firm of Drew, Grimes, and Brown was collected. Cullowhee billed Drew, Grimes, and Brown $400 for this service.

30 Payment was received from Drew, Grimes, and Brown.

REQUIRED:

a. Prepare the journal entry for each transaction.

b. Post the journal entries to the general ledger.

LO 7

E2-8 **Preparing a Trial Balance** The following list of accounts and related balances is taken from the records of the Optical Shop Corporation on June 30, 19X3:

Accounts Payable	$ 12,650
Accounts Receivable	34,630
Advertising Expense	4,800
Buildings	50,000
Cash	7,800
Capital Stock	80,000
Dividends	16,000
Office Supplies	9,700
Laboratory Expense	45,000
Mortgage Payable	50,000
Retained Earnings	15,000
Office Equipment	58,000
Professional Fees Expense	17,500
Wages and Salaries Expense	18,000
Fee Revenue	120,000
Prepaid Insurance	12,000
Utilities Expense	4,220

REQUIRED:

Prepare a trial balance in proper form.

LO 7,8   **E2-9**   **Identifying and Correcting Trial Balance Errors**   A temporary bookkeeper, who worked while Save-All Corporation's accountant was on vacation, prepared the trial balance shown below.

REQUIRED:

Identify the three errors in this trial balance and prepare a corrected trial balance.

Save-All Corporation Trial Balance August 31, 19X4		
	Debits	*Credits*
Cash	$ 5,000	
Accounts Receivable	7,200	
Equipment	12,500	
Truck	9,500	
Prepaid Insurance		$ 400
Notes Payable		4,000
Capital Stock		21,300
Retained Earnings		1,000
Dividends		1,500
Lawn Service Revenue		17,000
Maintenance Expense	700	
Wages and Salaries Expense	6,500	
	$41,400	$41,400

LO 3,5,8   **E2-10**   **Correcting Errors**   The following unrelated journal entries have been recorded:

(1) On June 4, Jim Green paid $400 on an account payable.

Accounts Receivable	400	
Cash		400

(2) On June 23, Janet Dyer collected $750 from a customer in full payment of a note.

Cash	750	
Accounts Receivable		750

(3) On July 15, Kerri Middlehopf purchased a computer and printer for $4,000 cash.

Office Equipment	4,000	
Cash		4,000

(4) On August 15, Ajax Scaffold Rental Corporation paid $350 to a welder who did routine minor repairs to a number of its rental items.

Rental Equipment	350	
Cash		350

REQUIRED:

a. Review each transaction narrative and the related entry to determine if an error has been made.

b. Prepare correcting entries for transactions that have been improperly recorded.

c. Indicate the effect the error would have on: total assets, total liabilities, and stockholders' equity.

Date any required entries the last day of the month in which the error occurred.

LO 9   **E2-11   Cash and Accrual Bases of Accounting**   Amos Corporation had the following transactions during the month of June:

(1) Collected $500 of accounts receivable from customers.

(2) Had cash sales totaling $1,200.

(3) Had credit sales of $300.

(4) Paid bills totaling $600, $400 of which related to June's expenses and $200 of which related to May's expenses.

REQUIRED:

a. Calculate Amos's net income for the month of June using accrual accounting.

b. Calculate Amos's net income for the month of June using the cash basis of accounting?

c. Which of the above methods follows the realization and matching principles?

LO 9   **E2-12   Taxable Income**   The Holmes Company had gross income for the year of $1,600,000 and deductions of $1,200,000. The Holmes Company is subject to a 22% tax rate.

REQUIRED:

a. What was Holmes' taxable income for the year?

b. How much will Holmes have to pay in income taxes this year?

PROBLEM SET A

LO 1,2,3   **P2-1A   Account Recognition and Applying Rules of Debit and Credit**   Joanne Williams runs the Mountain Go-Cart Track Co. Mountain completed the following transactions during the month of June 19X5:

June   7 Mountain received an invoice from State Oil Company for gasoline delivered today, $2,500. The payment is due June 23, 19X5.

11 Additional stock was issued in the amount of $1,000.

14 Mountain borrowed $15,000 from 2nd National Bank of Asheville to finance a second track. A 1-year, 8%, note payable was signed, and the cash was deposited to the company's account.

15 Mountain paid $4,000 wages and salaries to Joanne and its other 6 employees for the first half of the month.

16 Track fees received in cash for the first half of June, $2,800.

18 A small, used Spacestar van was purchased to transport riders from area hotels to the track. The purchase price was $11,500. Mountain paid $3,000 in cash and financed the balance through 2nd National Bank of Asheville at 6%.

21 Purchased a 3-acre tract of land next to the current property as a site for the second track, at a cost of $10,000.

23 Issued a check to State Oil Company for the invoice received on June 7.

30 Bills were mailed to local hotels for providing go-cart rides for hotel patrons, $26,840.

30 Mountain paid $4,000 wages and salaries for the second half of June.

30 Paid $2,000 for monthly repairs and maintenance on the go-carts.

30 Track fees received in cash for the second half of June, $2,500.

REQUIRED:

Use the following format to analyze each transaction. The first transaction is completed as an example.

Date	Account Used	Increase/Decrease	Debit/Credit
June 7	Supplies	Increase	Debit
	Accounts Payable	Increase	Credit

LO 1,3,5

P2-2A **Analyzing and Journalizing Transactions** Jackson Meter Corporation specializes in repairing and adjusting gasoline and other dispensing pumps for service stations and other vendors in the area. The following selected business events are from the company's activities during December 19X6:

Dec. 3 Adjusted 14 gasoline pumps, 2 diesel pumps, and a kerosene dispenser for Super-Five Truck Stop, Inc. A bill was mailed to Super-Five Truck Stop, Inc., for the work in the amount of $850.

7 Repair parts costing $540 were purchased from Wend Pump Products Company on credit.

10 Purchased a new cellular phone for a repair truck at a cost of $850 installed. It was paid for at this time.

15 Paid the December 7, Wend Pump Products Company invoice, in the amount of $540.

20 Dividends of $1,500 were declared and paid to Jackson's stockholders.

21 Two gasoline pumps for Red's Super Serve were repaired. Red paid Jackson $110 in cash for the repairs.

23 Distributed annual bonus checks to the employees totaling $800.

27 Called to T. M.'s Self-Serve Gas Company by the fire department to repair a leaking propane dispensing unit. A bill was mailed to T. M.'s Self-Serve Gas Company for $350.

30 December salary checks were issued for $3,200.

REQUIRED:

a. Analyze each event to determine if a business transaction has occurred.

b. If the event is a business transaction and can be recorded in the accounting records, use the following format to analyze the transactions.

Date	Recordable Transaction	Account Used	Increase/ Decrease	Debit/ Credit
Dec. 3	Yes	Accounts Receivable	Increase	Debit
		Fee Revenue	Increase	Credit

c. Prepare general journal entries for the business transactions.

d. Is this information useful in its present form? How could its usefulness be enhanced?

LO 1,2,3,5

P2-3A **Journalizing and Posting Transactions** The following business transactions are from the August 19X7 activities of Johnson's Used Sporting Goods Company. The company accepts used sporting goods, such as roller blades, skis, and tennis rackets from clients to be sold at prices the clients set. The shop is liable to the client for the amount collected from the sale of the goods less a commission, which represents a fee for selling the items in the store. The store owns no merchandise of its own and does not accept responsibility for goods that are stolen.

Aug. 1 1,000 shares of stock of Johnson were sold for $10 per share. The stock sold quickly since many of the potential investors thought this was a great business idea and that it should be successful if properly managed.

Aug. 2 A business checking account was opened in Johnson's name by Sam Cortez who had been hired to manage the store. $2,500 was deposited in this account, and the balance was put into a certificate of deposit .

3 Sam gave a $200 check to Tarpon Springs Realty Management for one month's rent on a small store.

4 An advertisement for the store was placed in the *Clearwater Sun* to run during the month and paid $100.

9 Several groups of used items were received from clients to sell. The clients set the prices. The agreement provides for Johnson's to receive a commission equal to 25% of the sales price when the item is sold.

10 Two flea market buffs went through all of the goods received yesterday and purchased items totaling $460. The commission was recorded as revenue, and the amount owed to the client was recorded as accounts payable.

14 Several additional groups of used items were received to be sold. Johnson's sales during the day totaled $988.

20 Sam hired his brother-in-law, Fred, to run the store in the afternoon for $35. The wages are to be paid later. Sales totaling $748 were made during the afternoon while Fred was tending the store.

31 Six used display gondolas were purchased for $900.

REQUIRED:

a. Prepare general journal entries for the transactions.

b. Open T-accounts as needed and post from the general journal to the T-accounts. Determine the account balances at the end of the month.

c. Discuss how the T-accounts improve the information in terms of usefulness.

LO 3,4,5,6,7   **P2-4A**   **Recording Business Transactions, Explaining the Purpose of the Procedures, Preparing a Trial Balance**   A group of downtown businesspeople decided it would be nice if they had a place to work out near their offices. They believed there was a lot of interest for such a place and that it would be highly utilized at lunch and immediately after work. Since many of these businesspeople were attorneys, they decided the best route to take would be to form a small corporation and hire someone with experience in the field of fitness training to manage their facility.

The Uptown Fitness Center, Inc. uses the following accounts:

100 Cash
158 Utilities Deposits
230 Equipment
302 Accounts Payable
326 Notes Payable
519 Capital Stock
598 Dividends
604 Fee Revenue
700 Advertising Expense
734 Maintenance Expense
762 Rent Expense

The following business activities occurred during November 19X8:

Nov. 1 500 shares of Uptown Fitness Center, Inc., common stock were issued for $40 each.

2 Dave Morik, an ex-Marine with a lot of fitness training experience, was hired to manage the fitness center.

3 The $20,000 proceeds from the sale of the stock was deposited in Uptown's business checking account at the Valley Bank.

Nov.   4 A line of credit for up to $80,000 was arranged at the Valley Bank. Notes would be signed for any funds borrowed, and an interest rate of 12% was agreed upon.

4 Two complete fitness machines were purchased for Uptown Fitness Center, Inc. at a cost of $26,000, from International Sports Equipment, Inc. The payment is due November 15.

5 Twelve large gym mats were purchased from Warner Company. An Uptown check was written for $2,400 for the mats.

8 A 5,000-square foot building was rented at an annual cost of $12 per square foot, per year. Dave paid the first month's rent in advance.

9 $100 was deposited with the local utility company (refundable) to guarantee payment since Uptown was a new customer. The utilities were connected.

11 Tidy-Up, a local cleaning company was paid $250 to do general cleanup that needed to be done before the equipment could be installed.

15 Paid the November 4, International Sports Equipment, Inc. invoice, $26,000 by writing a check for $10,000 and borrowing the balance from Uptown's line of credit.

21 Warner delivered the mats.

22 Dave installed the equipment and the mats.

22 A radio spot was placed on KMOC to run 4 times per day through the end of November, at a cost of $300. It was paid for today.

23 A liability insurance policy was taken out with County Insurance. The $ 400 annual premium was paid. The policy covered the period from December 1, 19X8 through November 30, 19X9.

24 Five persons inquired about Uptown's program, and three of them signed up for classes, paying $40 each for the first week.

REQUIRED:

a. Journalize the transactions of Uptown Fitness Center, Inc. for the month of November.
b. Explain the advantage of first recording the transaction data in a general journal.
c. Set up T-accounts and post the information from the general journal. Determine the balances of the accounts.
d. Prepare a trial balance.
e. Explain how the general ledger makes accounting information easier to use.

LO 5,6,7   **P2-5A**   **The Effect of Business Transactions in the Accounting Records, Posting to the Ledger, and Preparing a Trial Balance**   Chocolate Mountains Trail Rides, Inc. was started by a group of outdoor enthusiasts as a weekend adventure program during the winter months.

You will use the following accounts for Chocolate Mountains Trail Rides:

100 Cash
134 Maintenance Supplies
230 Equipment
245 Livestock
519 Capital Stock
604 Fee Revenue
700 Advertising Expense
728 Insurance Expense
762 Rent Expense
784 Wages and Salaries Expense

The following business events occurred during the first month of activity, October 19X9:

Oct.   2 Six investors decided they would start the corporation by issuing 1,000 shares of common stock for $30 each. The stock was sold, and the proceeds were deposited in a business checking account in the name of Chocolate Mountains Trail Rides, Inc.

Oct. 3 The three largest stockholders agreed to serve as the Chocolate Mountains' Board of Directors, and they hired Ed Martin to manage the new business.

4 A base camp facility was rented at D. R. Dudley's ranch, which was located at the base of the Chocolate Mountains. $1,000 was paid for the 6-month season from Chocolate Mountains' checking account.

8 Ed began the process of acquiring the necessary assets on behalf of the corporation. He purchased 20 horses from a dude ranch that had closed for $4,000 and had them delivered to the base camp. Ed wrote a check on Chocolate Mountains' account to pay for the horses.

9 Ed went to an auction where he acquired a single lot of tack that included 25 saddles, 40 headstalls with bits, 6 pack saddles, and an array of repair leather, straps, etc., for $1,400. The auctioneer required cash, which Ed took out of Chocolate Mountains' account.

11 An advertisement was placed in the *Times* announcing trail rides. The ad cost $120 for 2 weeks.

14 Ed purchased cooking utensils and 25 sleeping bags and arranged for food staples to be delivered to the base camp on Saturday. The camping gear cost $2,600, and the food cost $460. The food is considered to be a part of the company's supplies.

19 A trip liability policy was purchased for the two planned trips for a premium of $150 per trip. Sara Brown, formerly with the dude ranch, was also hired to be the angler and trail guide.

23 Fourteen people had signed in for the ride and paid the $200 fee.

26 Ed sent Sara to buy 6 more horses advertised for $250 each. She returned with 5 sound horses, having given the seller a company check for $1,000 for the 5 horses.

29 Sara purchased food for tomorrow's trip for $410.

30 Sixteen riders registered for the trip, each paying the $200 fee.

31 Sara was paid her biweekly wages of $300.

REQUIRED:

a. Prepare general journal entries for the business transactions above.

b. Post the general journal entries to T-accounts and determine the balances of the accounts.

c. Prepare a trial balance as of October 31, 19X9.

LO 3,5,6,7   **P2-6A**   **Journalizing and Posting Business Transactions and Preparing a Trial Balance**
Great Plains Charter Service has been operating for 12 months out of Council Bluffs Airpark. They have been flying a leased Cherokee-Six all year. The trial balance for December 31, 19X9 is as follows.

Great Plains Charter Service **Trial Balance** **December 31, 19X9**		
	Debits	*Credits*
Cash	$15,500	
Accounts Receivable	12,800	
Office Supplies	200	
Accounts Payable		$ 700
Capital Stock		20,000
Retained Earnings		7,800
	$28,500	$28,500

The following events occurred in January 19X0:

Jan.   4 Great Plains' President, Harold Whealon, found an ad for a Piper Lance Turbo II, which was for sale by Roberta Randall in Omaha. He flew over with a friend to see the plane and negotiated a purchase price of $48,000. He immediately called 1st National of Council Bluffs and arranged for a loan on behalf of the corporation, pledging the plane as collateral. The bank insisted that Great Plains should put $6,000 of its own cash into the plane and agreed to finance the balance.

        5 A $42,000, five-year, 15 percent note was issued to Great Plains and Harold returned to Omaha with a $42,000 bank check and a $6,000 company check payable to Roberta Randall. Harold closed the deal and flew the plane home to Council Bluffs.

        5 Harold called Avemco and had the plane covered with insurance. He mailed the first quarter's premium check for $800 that same day.

        6 Harold paid Ted Eure, an aviation mechanic, $600 to service and inspect the plane to certify it for charter service.

        8 Harold and Ted took off for a shakedown cruise to Illinois, stopping to top off the tanks to check the fuel burn rate. The refueling cost $48 cash. After the return trip, they were both satisfied to place the aircraft in service.

       11 Harold called the leasing company to cancel the lease on the leased plane. The lessor advised Harold of the penalty clause in the contract, and they agreed to a $1,200 final lease payment in settlement. Harold mailed the check.

       16 Harold got a call at 11:00 p.m. for an air-ambulance run to pick up a patient in Iowa City for transport to the Memphis Burn Center.

       17 Harold returned from Memphis, via Iowa City, arriving back in Council Bluffs at 7:00 a.m. He mailed out a bill to Aero-Ambulance Booking Service for $960 for the plane and pilot.

       22 Harold picked up electronic parts at Lambert Field, in St. Louis, for delivery to Mulke Corp. of Janesville, Wisconsin. He billed the Mulke Corp. $600.

       24 Harold flew a group of 5 sightseers out to view the Black Hills from the air, stopping for fuel on the way back. The fuel cost, $96, was paid by check. The group paid $720 for the 6 hours of flying time.

       31 Harold received his fuel bill from Airpark for aviation fuel and oil totaling $620 for the month. He delivered a company check to their office.

REQUIRED:

a. Read the event information for an understanding of the company's activities and then develop a chart of accounts. Create a numbering system for the chart of accounts and assign an account number to each account. Enter the account titles, account numbers, and the beginning balances dated January 1, 19X0, in the general ledger accounts.

b. Prepare entries in a general journal to record each of the business transactions that you identify in the above listed events.

c. Post the journal entries to the ledger accounts.

d. Prepare a trial balance dated January 31, 19X0.

▌PROBLEM SET B

LO 1,2,3   **P2-1B**   **Account Recognition and Applying Rules of Debit and Credit**   Each of the following events in the activity of the Center City Realty Company occurred during March 19X1:

Mar.   1 Paid March rent of $500.

        3 Three homes were listed for sale. The contract provides for Center City to receive a commission equal to 6% of the sales price, provided the home is sold in 6 months.

Mar. 9 Paid $250 for ads for the 3 homes. The ads will appear in the *Center City News* during March.

11 Purchased office supplies for $300.

15 Salaries of $1,200 were paid for the first half of the month.

18 Sold 1 of the listed homes for $150,000.

25 Dividends of $2,500 were declared and distributed to the stockholders.

29 Collected half of the commission from the March 18 sale.

31 Salaries of $1,200 were paid for the second half of the month.

31 Paid $175 for March utilities to the landlord.

REQUIRED:

Use the following format to analyze each transaction. The first transaction is completed as an example.

Date	Account Used	Increase/Decrease	Debit/Credit
Mar. 1	Rent Expense	Increase	Debit
	Cash	Decrease	Credit

LO 1,3,5

P2-2B   **Analyzing and Journalizing Transactions**   The Hayes Printing Company has been in business in Hayesville for 6 years. The following events occurred during the month of February 19X2:

Feb. 1 Ink and assorted papers was purchased on credit from Printers' Supply for $980.

2 Vargo Corporation placed an order with Hayes for 10,000 sheets of imprinted billing paper. The cost estimate given to Vargo was $850.

5 The Vargo Corporation order was delivered, along with a bill for $850.

8 An order from RealeX Realty Co. was received for 5,000 color brochures to be used in selling property in a new recreational development. The estimate given to RealeX for the job was $6,250.

11 A check for $980 was mailed to Printers' Supply in payment of the February 1 shipment.

12 The mockups were taken to RealeX for approval. They approved the brochures for production. $2,500 was collected as an advance payment at this time.

15 The mail included a check from Vargo Corporation for the balance due from the February 2 order.

18 The RealeX job was completed.

22 The brochures was delivered to RealeX, and the balance of the $6,250 estimate was collected.

25 An order for 10,000 business cards was taken. It was to consist of 1,000 cards for each of Vargo Corporation's 10 salespeople. The cost to Vargo was estimated to be $550.

26 Vargo's sales manager delivered the check for $550 and picked up the business cards.

26 Dividends were declared and paid to Hayes' stockholders in the amount of $2,000.

REQUIRED:

a. Analyze each event to determine if a business transaction has occurred.

b. If the event is a business transaction, determine what accounts would be involved and whether they would increase or decrease.

c. Prepare general journal entries for the business transactions, complete with appropriate explanations.

d. What could be done with this information to make it more useful?

LO 3,5

P2-3B   **Journalizing and Posting Transactions**   The Finley Corporation was organized and started in January 19X4. Finley plans to operate a parking lot.

Finley uses the following general ledger accounts:

100 Cash
110 Accounts Receivable
136 Office Supplies
152 Prepaid Rent
242 Office Equipment
302 Accounts Payable
326 Notes Payable
519 Capital Stock
598 Dividends
604 Fee Revenue
780 Utilities Expense

The following business events occurred during the month.

Jan.   4 Common stock was issued for $8,000, and the Board of Directors was elected by the stockholders.
       5 Jeanne Jackson was hired as president of Finley. She rented a small office for $500 per month and paid the first 6 months' rent in advance.
       7 Jeanne purchased a parking lot for Finley. The total cost of the lot was $10,000. Finley paid $1,000 in cash and signed a note on behalf of Finley for the balance.
      10 Supplies needed to operate the lot were purchased on account at a cost of $300. Payment is due on February 10.
      12 Reserved parking spaces were sold for $3,000. Checks were received from customers for that amount.
      14 A check for $100 was issued in partial payment for the supplies purchased on January 10.
      17 Additional spaces were reserved. Bills for $3,000 were sent to the customers.
      27 The lighting bill of $150 was received, and a check was immediately issued and mailed.
      31 Checks for $1,000 are received for the sales made on account on January 17.
      31 Since the business was successful in its first month, dividends of $500 were paid to the stockholders.

REQUIRED:

a. Prepare general journal entries for the transactions.
b. Open T-accounts and post from the general journal to the T-accounts.
c. Discuss how the T-accounts improve the usefulness of the information.

LO 3,4,5,6,7   **P2-4B**   **Recording Business Transactions, Explaining the Purpose of the Procedures, Preparing a Trial Balance**   The DeSoot Chimney Service Corporation began in September 19X5.

You will use the following accounts for the DeSoot Chimney Service Corporation:

100 Cash
230 Equipment
519 Capital Stock
600 Revenue
700 Advertising Expense
733 Licenses Expense
784 Wages and Salaries Expense

The following events occurred during the month:

Sept. 1 Stock of DeSoot was issued for $3,000. The proceeds from the sale of the stock were deposited at Maine State Bank in the name of DeSoot Chimney Sweep Corporation.
       1 A city business license was purchased at the Rockland City Hall for $50.

Sept. 1 An ad was placed in the *Rockland Gazette* to run each day in September. The cost was $100, which was paid by check.

      1 Charlene Smider, DeSoot's president, purchased chimney cleaning equipment from Booklins Hardware at a cost of $1,450, and paid for it with one of DeSoot's checks.

      2 A used van was purchased for $450, and $150 was spent to paint DeSoot's logo on it.

      6 DeSoot got 5 calls to clean chimneys. Charlene cleaned 3 today and scheduled the other 2 for the 7th. She collected a total of $180 for the 3 chimneys.

      7 The other 2 chimneys were cleaned, and $145 was collected.

      8 Because Charlene felt that she needed to spend more time in the office and less time cleaning chimneys, she hired a part-time employee to work on an as-needed basis at $7.50 per hour.

    13 Twenty-five calls were received during the day to schedule chimney cleaning services between the 16th and the 30th.

    17 Nine chimneys were cleaned, and $640 in cash and checks was received.

    24 Fourteen chimneys were cleaned during the week of September 18–24. Cash totaling $940 was collected for these services and was deposited into DeSoot's account.

    30 Five additional chimneys were cleaned; 2 that had been previously scheduled and 3 new ones. The total fees collected amounted to $350.

    30 The part-time employee was paid for the 60 hours that he worked.

REQUIRED:

a. Journalize the transactions of DeSoot Chimney Service Corporation for the month of September.

b. Explain the advantage of first recording the transaction data in a general journal.

c. Set up T-accounts and post the information from the general journal. Determine the balances of the accounts.

d. Prepare a trial balance.

e. Explain how the general ledger makes accounting information more useful.

LO 5,6,7   **P2-5B**   **The Effect of Business Transactions in the Accounting Records, Posting to the Ledger, and Preparing a Trial Balance**   The Highway 107 Flea Market, Inc. was started by issuing $13,000 of common stock. The stock sold quickly since there were market studies indicating that a flea market would do well in the area. A very large barn was purchased on Highway 107. The market will be open only on weekends. The 90 small stalls will rent for $15 per day. The 10 large stalls will be rented to commercial vendors at $250 per month, payable on the first of the month. All collections are considered revenue when received as no refunds are made.

    Highway 107 Flea Market, Inc., uses the following accounts:

100 Cash
150 Prepaid Insurance
158 Utilities Deposits
220 Buildings
230 Equipment
408 Notes Payable—Noncurrent
519 Capital Stock
598 Dividends
610 Rent Revenue
700 Advertising Expense
734 Maintenance Expense
738 Miscellaneous Expense
780 Utilities Expense

The following events occurred during the month of July 19X6.

July 1 The stock of Highway 107 was sold, and the proceeds were used to open a company bank account at First Mountain Bank.

2 The barn was purchased by writing a check for $5,000 from the company checking account and giving a 5-year note for $25,000.

2 Karen's Cleaning Service was hired to clean up the barn and was paid $150. This is maintenance expense.

2 Craft Carpenters were hired to repair loose boards. A check was drawn for $260. This cost was treated as maintenance expense.

3 The building inspector and the fire marshall examined the building for safety considerations. They approved the barn for use as a flea market after recommending that 12 fire extinguishers be purchased and installed. The inspection fee of $350 was paid by check. Treat it as a miscellaneous expense.

3 Liability insurance was purchased for the balance of the year at a premium of $900.

5 Mountain Area Fire and Safety installed the fire extinguishers at a cost of $300. This was paid to the installers. The extinguishers are classified as equipment.

6 Coop Telephone Service installed a phone booth. The required deposit of $250 and the first months' service charge of $50 were paid.

8 A half-page ad was placed to run in the *Sunday Chronicle*, offering to rent the stalls. The $250 cost for the ad was paid.

12 Eight commercial vendors came by during the day to look over the facilities. Six rented large stalls for $150 for the rest of the month.

13 During the day, 75 different individuals signed up for booths for Saturday; 50 of these also signed up for Sunday. All monies were collected and deposited in the checking account.

14 A variety of balloons, small toys, and soft drinks were purchased to give away at Highway 107's grand opening. The cost was $350.

15 An additional 20 of the Saturday renters signed up for booths for Sunday, July 16. The cash was collected and deposited at the bank.

17 Karen's Cleaning Service was hired to clean up on July 17, 24, and 31, after the weekend activities. Karen was paid a total of $350 for these services. This should be treated as a maintenance expense.

21 On Friday, 3 more commercial vendors signed up for large stalls at $100 each for the balance of the month and paid in full. All 90 small stalls were rented for Saturday, and 80 were rented for Sunday. All of the cash was collected and deposited.

28 On Friday, all 90 small stalls were rented for both Saturday and Sunday. The cash was collected and deposited.

31 Because the Flea Market had such a successful first month, dividends totaling $1,500 were declared and distributed to the stockholders.

REQUIRED:

a. Prepare general journal entries to record the above business transactions.

b. Set up T-accounts for each account in the chart of accounts, post the general journal entries, and determine the balances of the accounts.

c. Prepare a trial balance dated July 31, 19X6.

LO 3,5,6,7 **P2-6B** **Journalizing and Posting Business Transactions and Preparing a Trial Balance**
Smelter's Seamless Guttering Co. of Deep Woods, OK, has been hanging gutters and installing aluminum soffit since 19X1. The January 1, 19X7, balances are listed on the following page.

The following events occurred during the month of January 19X7.

Jan. 4 Guttering and soffit supplies were purchased from White Metals & Supply on account. The invoice for the supplies totaled $6,500 and was due to be paid in 10 days.

Smelter's Seamless Guttering Co. Trial Balance December 31, 19X6		
	Debits	*Credits*
Cash	$16,000	
Accounts Receivable	6,000	
Equipment	40,000	
Notes Payable		$ 2,500
Capital Stock		20,000
Retained Earnings		39,500
	$62,000	$62,000

Jan.   4 Smelter's signed a contract with Wallart Construction Co. for the installation of gutters and soffits on a large townhouse development. The job is expected to generate revenues of approximately $45,000. Smelter's crew began the installation.

   8 Smelter's billed the Wallart Construction Co. $8,000 for work done on the townhouses during the week.

   13 Received a check from Wallart Construction for the amount billed on January 8.

   14 Issued a check to White Metals & Supply for the supplies purchased on January 4.

   15 Billed Wallart Construction $12,000 for the second week's work.

   25 Received an electric and water bill from the City of Deep Woods for $175, which was promptly paid.

   29 Sent a bill to Wallart Construction for two weeks' work in the amount of $19,000.

   29 Paid $12,500 wages for the month.

   29 Paid dividends to Smelter's stockholders in the amount of $1,800.

REQUIRED:

a. Read the event information for an understanding of the company's activities and then develop a chart of accounts. Create a numbering system for the chart of accounts and assign a number to each account. Enter the account titles, account numbers, and the beginning balances dated January 1, 19X7, in the general ledger accounts.

b. Prepare entries in a general journal to record each of the business transactions that are identified in the above events.

c. Post the journal entries to the ledger accounts.

d. Prepare a trial balance.

CRITICAL THINKING AND COMMUNICATING

C2-1   You are considering investing in the stock of a local business that sells locally manufactured crockery dinnerware for a commission. You have looked through its last two years' annual reports. Although there has been a sufficient level of income, you still believe that the company's overall financial health is not good. You have asked to look at its detailed accounting records, and you have been presented with the following trial balance for the year just ended. The financial statements are not yet complete.

The Crockery Shop Trial Balance December 31, 19X9		
	Debits	Credits
Cash	$17,350	
Accounts Receivable	23,000	
Supplies	900	
Prepaid Rent	2,500	
Accounts Payable		$11,450
Notes Payable		1,500
Capital Stock		5,000
Retained Earnings		1,000
Sales Commissions Revenue		50,000
Miscellaneous Expense	1,500	
Rent Expense	17,000	
Sales Supplies Expense	4,500	
Utilities Expense	2,200	
	$68,950	$68,950

REQUIRED:

a. What does the trial balance tell you about the possible income you might earn should you decide to purchase the business?

b. What kind of a financial statement would provide you with information concerning profitability?

c. What can you tell about the value of the assets listed, and would this information be important in determining the amount of your offer?

d. What kind of financial statement might provide you with information concerning the value of the assets?

C2-2 You have been hired by Quick Clean, a local carpet cleaning business, to maintain its accounting records. Quick Clean had previously used another accountant but was unhappy with the firm because it always seemed unable to answer questions. Sandra Potts, president of Quick Clean, has brought you last month's trial balance that the previous accountant prepared. Last month's financial statements have not been prepared, and this will be your first task. First, you want to verify the quality of the previous accountant's work.

Quick Clean Trial Balance September 30, 19X8		
	Debits	Credits
Cash		$ 1,000
Accounts Receivable	$ 2,000	
Cleaning Supplies	500	
Prepaid Insurance	400	
Equipment	90,000	
Notes Payable		80,000
Accounts Payable		1,900
Capital Stock		14,000
Dividends	1,000	
Revenue		6,000
Expenses	8,000	
	$102,900	$102,900

REQUIRED:

Examine the trial balance and make a list of items you should discuss with Sandra. Include items that she needs to clarify for you.

C2-3 Refer to the financial statements of J.C. Penney reprinted in Appendix B.

REQUIRED:

a. Using the information from the income statement and balance sheet provided, prepare the trial balance that J.C. Penney's accountants would have prepared for 1993 to assist them in preparing these financial statements.

b. What was J.C. Penney's income tax expense for each year presented? What was the income tax expense as a percent of net income each year?

CHAPTER 3

Accrual Adjustments, Preparing Financial Statements, and Completing the Accounting Cycle

The owners of PhotoCopy, Inc. consider investing in additional facilities to increase the volume of their copying business. An important consideration is the profitability of the current business. You saw that in January the company appeared quite profitable. In February, PhotoCopy added a delivery van. This addition increased revenues, but it also increased expenses. The owners of PhotoCopy are anxious to prepare financial statements at the end of February to assess the profitability of their business for the two-month period.

This chapter discusses the procedures that are necessary to prepare financial statements at the end of an accounting period. The end-of-period procedures are necessary because many revenue and expense transactions extend beyond one accounting period. As a result, we must *adjust* the accounts so that they are correct for the preparation of the financial statements for the period. Accounting apportions the effects of multiperiod transactions among accounting periods based on the fundamental elements of financial accounting, most of which were introduced previously. Also, we discuss in this chapter the additional end-of-period procedures that are necessary to complete the accounting cycle. These procedures involve the closing of revenue and expense accounts to begin the accounting cycle for the next accounting period.

1. Explain the concepts, assumptions, and principles underlying the accrual basis of accounting.
2. Prepare adjusting entries at the end of an accounting period.
3. Prepare financial statements using an adjusted trial balance.
4. Explain the closing process and prepare closing entries.
5. Prepare a post-closing trial balance.
6. Describe the various steps in the accounting cycle.
7. Calculate and interpret a business's profit margin.
8. Prepare adjusting entries when certain cash transactions are recorded initially as revenues and expenses (Appendix 3-A).
9. Complete the accountant's worksheet and prepare financial statements using the worksheet (Appendix 3-B).

ACCRUAL CONCEPTS, ASSUMPTIONS, AND PRINCIPLES

LO 1

Explain the concepts, assumptions, and principles underlying the accrual basis of accounting.

In previous chapters, we introduced the fundamental elements that compose the foundations of financial accounting. Several of those elements are essential to understanding the role of the accrual basis of accounting and the adjustment of accounts for preparation of financial statements. We review these key elements in this chapter to provide the basis for the discussion of the adjustment process. The elements that we review are: accounting period concept, realization principle, and matching principle. In addition to reviewing these elements, we introduce a new element—the going-concern assumption.

Accounting Period Concept

The previous discussion of accounting net income referred to the business's net income for a period. The period of time for which we determine net income is called the **accounting period**. The accounting period commonly is a year, but we may measure and report income for periods as short as a month. The development of a year as the accounting period may be traced to the requirement for businesses to file income tax returns with federal and state governments on an annual basis. Also, federal and state regulatory agencies require many businesses to file financial statements on an annual basis. In any event, the annual accounting period for businesses is an established practice. When we determine net income for a period of less than a year, the process is usually less formal than that for an annual determination and involves more estimates and assumptions. We present financial information such as net income for a period shorter than a year in reports called **interim financial reports**.

Various Business Fiscal Periods. A **fiscal year** is the specific twelve-month accounting period a business adopts. Many businesses adopt the calendar year, January 1 to December 31, as their fiscal year. Other businesses, however, use fiscal years different from the calendar year such as July 1 to June 30 or October 1 to September 30. The reason a business often cites for adopting a different fiscal year is to match the end of the fiscal year with a slack season.

The preparation of annual financial statements and annual tax returns requires many procedures and significant effort by the employees. For example, in this chapter, we describe how a business must undertake additional account-

INSIGHTS INTO ACCOUNTING

The American Institute of CPAs (AICPA) conducts an annual survey of financial reporting practices of 600 large U.S. businesses. For the years 1988 – 91, the businesses had fiscal years ending in months of the year as follows:

	1991	1990	1989	1988
January	21	22	22	20
February	14	15	15	13
March	12	14	16	15
April	7	7	8	7
May	16	16	15	16
June	62	62	57	54
July	16	16	16	14
August	18	17	16	15
September	31	33	37	38
October	21	21	20	22
November	18	17	17	15
December	364	360	361	371
Total	600	600	600	600

Source: *Accounting Trends and Techniques* (AICPA, 1992), p. 30. Reprinted with permission of the American Institute of Certified Public Accountants, Inc.

ing procedures to adjust its accounts to prepare formal financial statements. Other procedures also may be required—namely a physical check for the assets that the accounting records indicate the business owns. Therefore, if the end of the fiscal year comes during the business's slack season, the required additional efforts to prepare its annual financial statements can be accommodated more conveniently.

Income Determination and Multiperiod Transactions.   Determining net income for the accounting period, whether it is the annual period or an interim period, is one of the most difficult problems accountants face. Many transactions extend beyond one accounting period. That is, the transaction begins in one accounting period and concludes in a subsequent accounting period. Some transactions may conclude in the next accounting period; other transactions may span several accounting periods.

   To determine net income for a period, the accountant must apportion to the appropriate periods the effects of transactions that extend beyond one period. For example, PhotoCopy, Inc. purchased a delivery van costing $13,000 in February 19X1, that will benefit the business for several years—the estimated time period that the business can use the van. Since PhotoCopy will use the van to earn revenues over several years, we allocate the cost of the van to the years that the business benefits from the expenditure.

   We accomplish the required apportionment of the cost of the van by the adjustment process that we illustrate later in this chapter. After the adjustment process, the accounts should reflect the revenues earned and the expenses incurred during the period. To accomplish this objective, however, the adjustment process requires the accountant to make certain critical assumptions.

Going-Concern Assumption

An important assumption accountants make is whether the business is a going-concern. The **going-concern assumption** states that, in the absence of evidence to the contrary, we assume that the enterprise will continue to operate as a viable business. The going-concern assumption is the basis of the adjustment process. To apportion the effects of multiperiod transactions to current and future periods, the accountant assumes that the enterprise is a going-concern, even though thousands of businesses fail each year. Of course, the going-concern assumption is not appropriate if evidence is available that the enterprise is about to go out of business.

Accounting for the van PhotoCopy, Inc. purchased provides an excellent example of the application of the going-concern assumption. At the date of purchase, we record the van as an asset. As PhotoCopy uses the van, a portion of the asset expires and becomes an expense. If we estimate that the van can be used for 6 years, we apportion the cost of the van through the adjustment process to the 6-year period as an expense called *depreciation expense*. For example, we might recognize one-sixth of the total cost as an expense in each of the 6 years. But, the process of spreading the cost of the van over 6 years is appropriate only if the accountant can reasonably assume that the business will continue and, thereby, utilize the van to earn revenues in all 6 years.

Realization Principle and Revenue Apportionment

Some revenue transactions extend beyond one accounting period. Earlier we discussed that according to the realization principle, we recognize revenue in the period it is earned. Accountants apportion the effects of multiperiod revenue transactions to current and future periods by recognizing revenues in the period they are earned from delivering goods or providing services.

Matching Principle and Expense Apportionment

Some expense transactions, like some revenue transactions, extend beyond one accounting period. Accountants apportion the effects of multiperiod expense transactions to current and future periods by recognizing expenses in the period they are incurred. An expense is incurred in the period that the business uses up its assets or incurs liabilities from delivering goods or providing services in connection with its normal operations.

According to the matching principle, we should recognize expenses in the same period as the related revenues. Some expenses such as sales commissions are related directly to the revenues of a period. We recognize expenses that are related directly to revenues in the same period we recognize the revenues. Other expenses are only indirectly related to revenues, and their recognition involves much approximation. We allocate these expenses such as rent and insurance *to the periods* in which the business benefits from occupancy and insurance coverage.

ADJUSTING ENTRIES

LO 2
Prepare adjusting entries at the end of an accounting period.

The adjustment process requires the accountant to make adjusting entries at the end of an accounting period. **Adjusting entries** are those necessary to adjust the accounts to their proper balances to conform with GAAP for purposes of preparing appropriate financial statements. The adjustment process involves apportioning multiperiod revenues and expenses to the periods in which they are earned and incurred. The need for adjusting entries does not mean that the account balances are in error. All general journal entries to date may be correct, and all transactions may have been posted correctly to the general ledger accounts. We need adjusting entries because some revenues may have been earned but not yet recorded, and some expenses may have been incurred but not yet recorded. Also, some cash receipts may initially be recorded as revenues, but they are not yet earned; and some cash payments may initially be recorded as expenses, but the expenditures may not be expenses of the current period.

The adjusting entries needed at the end of an accounting period are for the following items:

Expiration of Prepaid Expenses
Recognition of Depreciation Expense
Accrual of Unpaid Expenses
Recognition of Revenues Previously Unearned
Accrual of Revenues Earned

Using PhotoCopy, Inc. from previous chapters, we discuss and illustrate adjusting entries for these items. Illustration 3-1 reproduces the trial balance at the end of February 19X1. The account balances reflect the transactions analyzed and recorded previously, but they do not reflect the adjusting entries. A trial balance prepared before posting the adjusting entries is an **unadjusted trial balance**.

ILLUSTRATION 3-1 Unadjusted Trial Balance

PhotoCopy, Inc. Trial Balance February 28, 19X1		
	Debits	*Credits*
Cash	$ 3,400	
Copying Supplies	2,400	
Prepaid Insurance	900	
Delivery Equipment	13,000	
Office Equipment	1,200	
Accounts Payable		$ 2,400
Unearned Revenue		600
Notes Payable–Noncurrent		10,000
Capital Stock		6,000
Revenue		11,200
Advertising Expense	100	
Copying Supplies Expense	800	
Rent Expense	2,000	
Wages and Salaries Expense	6,400	
Totals	$30,200	$30,200

Expiration of Prepaid Expenses

Prepaid expenses are those that have been paid but not yet incurred. Examples of prepaid expenses include insurance and rent. When prepaid expenses are for periods beyond one accounting period, we need adjusting entries to apportion the expenses to the periods they are incurred.

Prepaid Insurance.   Insurance policies cover a future period of time and usually require that the amount of the premium be paid in advance. The payment of the premium creates an asset—insurance coverage for the period of the policy—and we record the asset in Prepaid Insurance. As time passes, a portion of the asset expires and becomes insurance expense. At the end of an accounting period, we make an adjusting entry to record the expiration of the prepaid insurance. On February 3, 19X1, PhotoCopy paid for an insurance policy that provides coverage from the beginning of February 19X1 to the end of January 19X2. The transaction created an asset that we record in Prepaid Insurance in the amount of $900. On February 28, 19X1, we need an adjusting entry to recognize the expiration of one month's prepaid insurance. The amount of the expired insurance is $75 ($900 x 1/12). The adjusting entry is:

Feb. 28	Insurance Expense	75	
	Prepaid Insurance		75
	To record the expiration of prepaid insurance.		

Posting the adjusting entry to the general ledger affects the accounts as follows:

Prepaid Insurance				Insurance Expense		
Feb. 3	900	Feb. 28	75	Feb. 28	75	
Bal.	825					

The entry reduces (credits) the asset account, Prepaid Insurance, by the amount of the insurance expense ($75)—which we debit to Insurance Expense.

Copying Supplies.   On February 8, PhotoCopy purchased copying supplies costing $2,400. PhotoCopy recorded the copying supplies as an asset at their cost of $2,400. On February 28, the owners of PhotoCopy counted the remaining copying supplies and determined that supplies originally costing $1,500 were still on hand. This means that PhotoCopy had used $900 ($2,400 – $1,500) of the supplies during the month of February. Using the copying supplies is an expense since an asset was used up in the process of generating revenues. To recognize the expense, PhotoCopy records an adjusting entry at the end of February that debits Copying Supplies Expense for the $900 cost of the supplies used during the month and reduces the asset account, Copying Supplies, by the $900.

Feb. 28	Copying Supplies Expense	900	
	Copying Supplies		900
	To record the cost of copying supplies used during February.		

As shown in the T-accounts below, this entry leaves a balance in Copying Supplies of $1,500, which is the cost of the supplies that remain on hand at the end of February. The balance in Copying Supplies Expense is the total cost of copying supplies used during January and February.

Copying Supplies				Copying Supplies Expense		
Feb. 8	2,400	Feb. 28	900	Jan. 31	800	
Bal.	1,500			Feb. 28	900	
				Bal.	1,700	

Depreciation

We recognize an expense, called **depreciation expense**, for expiration of portions of the total lifetime usefulness of certain assets such as equipment and buildings. As time passes, a portion of the usefulness of such an asset expires, due to physical wear and such other forces as eventual obsolescence. Generally, it is not possible to observe the diminishing usefulness of assets on a day-to-day basis. However, management knows that a significant amount will expire during the estimated time that the business will use the assets. The matching principle requires that we apportion the cost of the assets to the accounting periods during the assets' useful lives. Apportioning the cost of an asset involves much estimation. Management must estimate both the useful life of the asset and the pattern of the expiration of the asset's usefulness during its useful life.

At the end of an accounting period, we make an adjusting entry to record the portion of the asset's cost that has expired during the period. The entry is a debit to Depreciation Expense. However, the credit is not made directly to the asset account, as you might have expected. Instead, a credit is made to an account called Accumulated Depreciation. **Accumulated Depreciation** represents the cumulative depreciation of the asset since it was acquired. Accumulated depreciation is a **valuation** (or **contra-asset**) **account** that reduces the asset to its correct balance for presentation in the balance sheet. The balance sheet presentation of these accounts is shown in Illustration 3-2.

ILLUSTRATION 3-2 Undepreciated Cost of an Asset

Asset Account	Original Cost of the Asset
Less: Accumulated Depreciation	Cumulative Depreciation
Carrying Amount	Undepreciated Cost of Asset

We credit Accumulated Depreciation for the amount of current depreciation expense so that the asset's original purchase cost will be preserved in the asset account. The balance in the asset account retains the cost of the *total* service potential purchased when the asset was new. The balance of Accumulated Depreciation represents the cost of the estimated service potential *used up* as of the current balance sheet date. The *net* amount, the difference between the asset account balance and Accumulated Depreciation balance, represents the cost of the asset's estimated *remaining* service potential. You should note that the net amount is *not* the current price of similar service potential. Rather, it is the *original cost* of the asset's unused service potential. The net amount is the asset's undepreciated cost and is called the **carrying amount**, **carrying value**, or the **net book value**. We record each category of assets that last multiple periods in separate accounts, and we maintain separate accumulated depreciation accounts for them. This separate identity is maintained because each asset conceivably depreciates over a different number of periods according to a different pattern. We discuss the varying patterns of depreciation in a subsequent chapter.

Office Equipment. PhotoCopy purchased a computer on January 31 at a cost of $1,200. Assume PhotoCopy estimates that the computer can be used for 4 years. The **useful life of an asset** is the period of time the business estimates it can use the asset in its operations. The expense of using the computer for 1 year is one-fourth of $1,200, or $300. The expense of using the computer for 1 month is one-twelfth of $300, or $25.

Depreciation Expense—Office Equipment. PhotoCopy, Inc. classifies the computer as office equipment. Note that there is no depreciation expense for January because PhotoCopy purchased the computer on the last day of the month and any usage of the asset would have been insignificant. The depreciation expense for office equipment for February as calculated above is $25. At the end of February, PhotoCopy should record depreciation expense by making the following adjusting entry:

Feb. 28	Depreciation Expense—Office Equipment	25	
	Accumulated Depreciation—Office Equipment		25
	To record February depreciation.		

After we post the adjusting entry to the general ledger, the accounts will appear as follows:

Office Equipment
Jan. 31	1,200	

Accumulated Depreciation— Office Equipment		Depreciation Expense— Office Equipment	
	Feb. 28 25	Feb. 28 25	

We include Depreciation Expense—Office Equipment in the income statement that we prepare at the end of February. Office Equipment and the contra-asset account, Accumulated Depreciation—Office Equipment, are shown in the February 28 balance sheet as follows:

Office equipment	$1,200	
Less: Accumulated depreciation	25	$1,175

The balance sheet presentation informs the reader that the cost of the service potential of the computer when purchased is $1,200. This amount gives the users of the financial statements some idea of the computer's total service capacity. The cost of the service potential used up is $25, and the cost of the remaining service potential is $1,175. The latter figure gives the users of the financial statements some idea of the computer's remaining capacity to provide service to the business. In subsequent months, the periodic depreciation continues to accumulate in Accumulated Depreciation—Office Equipment at the rate of $25 per month. Therefore, the carrying amount of the asset declines each month by $25.

Delivery Equipment. On February 3, PhotoCopy purchased a van to use in the business at a cost of $13,000. PhotoCopy's owners estimate that the van can be used in the business for 6 years. At the end of the van's estimated useful life, the owners estimate it will be worth $4,000 as a trade-in on a new van. We call an asset's estimated value at the end of its estimated useful life the **estimated residual value**. In this case, the cost of the van to apportion to the years that the business benefits from its services is $9,000 ($13,000 − $4,000). We call the asset's original cost less its estimated residual value the **depreciable cost**. For the van, annual depreciation is $1,500 ($9,000 ÷ 6) and monthly depreciation is $125 ($1,500 ÷ 12). The adjusting entry for February depreciation for the van is:

Feb. 28	Depreciation Expense—Delivery Equipment	125	
	Accumulated Depreciation—Delivery Equipment		125
	To record depreciation for February.		

The presentation of Delivery Equipment and Accumulated Depreciation—Delivery Equipment would be similar to the presentation of the computer. The accounts appear as follow after posting to the general ledger:

Delivery Equipment

| Feb. 3 13,000 | |

Accumulated Depreciation—
Delivery Equipment

| | Feb. 28 125 |

Depreciation Expense—
Delivery Equipment

| Feb. 28 125 | |

Accrued Expenses

As previously discussed, the transactions processing methods in most accounting systems are designed to record expenses at the time they are paid. At the end of an accounting period, some expenses may have been incurred but not recorded because they have not been paid. Incurred but unpaid expenses are called **accrued expenses**. Common examples of accrued expenses include wages and salaries, interest, and utilities.

Wages and Salaries Expense. On February 21, PhotoCopy paid its employee $400 for her services through February 21. Assume that for the period February 22 through February 28 the employee earned an additional $200. Since these wages are unpaid, they are unrecorded. To prepare financial statements at the end of February, however, we must record the employee's wages that have been incurred since she was last paid. We record the earned but unpaid wages with the following adjusting entry:

Feb. 28	Wages and Salaries Expense	200	
	Wages and Salaries Payable		200
	To record earned but unpaid wages.		

After we post the adjusting entry to the general ledger, the accounts appear as follows:

Wages and Salaries Expense

Jan. 31	3,000	
Feb. 21	400	
Feb. 28	3,000	
Feb. 28	200	
Bal.	6,600	

Wages and Salaries Payable

| | Feb. 28 200 |

The effect of the adjusting entry is to increase Wages and Salaries Expense to $6,600, which is the amount of wages and salaries expense PhotoCopy actually incurred during January and February. Also, we record Wages and Salaries Payable of $200. PhotoCopy is obligated to pay this amount as of the end of February because the employee has worked during February after the date she was last paid.

Interest expense. On February 1, PhotoCopy borrowed $10,000 from the bank to purchase the van. Recall that the interest rate on the loan is 7.2% per year. As of the end of February, PhotoCopy has incurred one month's interest. Even though the interest is not due to be paid until March 1, PhotoCopy incurs the interest expense in February. The amount of interest expense for February is $60 ($10,000 x 7.2% x 1/12). We record the interest expense for February with the following adjusting entry:

Feb. 28	Interest Expense	60	
	Interest Payable		60
	To record interest expense for February.		

After posting the entry to the general ledger, the accounts appear as follows:

Interest Expense		Interest Payable	
Feb. 28 60			Feb. 28 60

The adjusting entry records the interest expense for February and the liability (interest payable) to pay the interest to the bank.

Unearned Revenue

When a business receives a cash payment for goods or services before it delivers the goods or performs the services, we record **unearned revenue**. For example, if you subscribe to a magazine at a cost of $36 per year for 12 monthly issues, you pay the subscription price in advance. The magazine company records your payment as unearned revenue. The revenue is unearned until the magazines are delivered to you. Each month, the company earns one-twelfth of the subscription price when it delivers an issue of the magazine to you. Therefore, each month the company decreases unearned revenue and increases revenues by $3 (1/12 of $36).

PhotoCopy entered into an agreement with the Student Government Association to provide copying services to its members. The Association paid $600 in advance for the copying. We record the receipt of the payment on February 15 as a debit to Cash and a credit to Unearned Revenue. Remember: Unearned Revenue is a liability account because PhotoCopy is obligated to provide the copying services or else refund the advance payment to the customer. As of the end of February, however, PhotoCopy has earned a portion of the revenue because the members of the Association have made copies that used $400 of the advance payment. Therefore, PhotoCopy recognizes the revenue with the following adjusting entry:

Feb. 28	Unearned Revenue	400	
	Revenue		400
	To record revenue earned.		

The $400 is classified properly as revenue because net assets have increased (due to a decrease in liabilities) from the business's revenue-producing activities. After we post the adjusting entry to the general ledger, the accounts appear as follows:

Unearned Revenue			Revenue	
Feb. 28 400	Feb. 15 600		Jan. 31 5,000	
	Bal. 200		Feb. 28 6,200	
			Feb. 28 400	
			Bal. 11,600	

The adjusting entry decreases Unearned Revenue to reflect the partial satisfaction of the obligation to provide copying services and increases Revenue by the amount that has been earned under the agreement.

Accrued Revenue

A business sometimes earns revenue before receiving payment from the customer. Under the accrual basis of accounting, we record the revenue because it is earned. At the end of the accounting period, we record an adjusting entry for **accrued revenue**—revenue that the business has earned but not yet received. Also, as part of the adjusting entry, we record an account receivable representing the business's right to receive payment from the customer for the services performed. Examples of accrued revenues include interest earned, rent earned, and many types of revenues for services.

On February 23, the Chairperson of the Microbiology Department at the University entered into an agreement for PhotoCopy to make numerous copies of research grant applications for faculty and graduate students. It is expected that the copies will be needed over the next two weeks. The Chairperson agreed to make payment for the copies by March 15. As of February 28, PhotoCopy has made copies in the amount of $300. To record the revenue, we make the following adjusting entry:

Feb. 28	Accounts Receivable	300	
	Revenue		300
	To record revenue earned.		

After the adjusting entry is posted to the general ledger, the accounts appear as follows:

Accounts Receivable					Revenue	
Jan. 31	1,000	Feb. 5	1,000		Jan. 31	5,000
Feb. 28	300				Feb. 28	6,200
Bal.	300				Feb. 28	400
					Feb. 28	300
					Bal.	11,900

The adjusting entry increases Accounts Receivable and Revenue by the $300 that PhotoCopy has earned in February under the agreement with the Microbiology Department.

Accrued Income Tax Expense

After all the other adjusting entries have been prepared, the final adjusting entry is for income tax expense. This adjusting entry is actually an accrued expense of the type discusssed earlier. However, the amount of the entry cannot be determined until the amount of income is known, which depends on the other adjusting entries. PhotoCopy's owners determine that the amount of income taxes for the first two months of operation are $200. This amount is an expense that we debit to Income Tax Expense and credit to the liability account, Income Taxes Payable, for the same amount.

Feb. 28	Income Tax Expense	200	
	Income Taxes Payable		200
	To record income taxes for Jan. and Feb.		

After we post the adjusting entry to the general ledger, the accounts appear as follows:

Income Tax Expense	Income Taxes Payable
Feb. 28 200	Feb. 28 200

Summary of Adjustments

One way to think of adjusting entries is: Without them, the business's accounts would be misstated. We present a summary of the adjustment process reflecting this view in Illustration 3-3.

ILLUSTRATION 3-3 Summary of Adjustments

Type	Accounts	Account Balances Without Adjustment	Adjusting Entry
1. Expiration of prepaid expenses	Expenses and Assets	Expenses understated Assets overstated	Dr. Expenses Cr. Assets
2. Depreciation expense	Expenses and Assets	Expenses understated Assets overstated	Dr. Expenses Cr. Accumulated Depreciation
3. Accrued expenses	Expenses and Liabilities	Expenses understated Liabilities understated	Dr. Expenses Cr. Liabilities
4. Previously unearned revenue	Liabilities and Revenues	Liabilities overstated Revenues understated	Dr. Liabilities Cr. Revenues
5. Accrued revenue	Assets and Revenues	Assets understated Revenues understated	Dr. Assets Cr. Revenues

Journalizing and Posting Adjusting Entries

To complete the adjustment process, we must record the adjusting entries in the general journal and post them to the general ledger accounts. The adjusting entries as they would appear in the general journal for PhotoCopy, Inc. are shown in Illustration 3-4. The stockholders' equity, revenue, and expense general ledger accounts of PhotoCopy are shown in Illustration 3-5. These accounts show the balances after we have posted the adjusting entries.

ILLUSTRATION 3-4 Adjusting Entries

	GENERAL JOURNAL		PAGE 4	

DATE		DESCRIPTION	POST. REF.	DEBIT	CREDIT
19X1 Feb.	28	Insurance Expense		75	
		Prepaid Expense			75
		To record the expiration of prepaid insurance.			
	28	Copying Supplies Expense		900	
		Copying Supplies			900
		To record the cost of copying supplies used during February.			*(Continues)*

ILLUSTRATION 3-4 (Concluded) Adjusting Entries

GENERAL JOURNAL   PAGE 4

DATE		DESCRIPTION	POST. REF.	DEBIT	CREDIT
19X1 Feb.	28	Depreciation Expense–Office Equipment		25	
		Accumulated Depreciation–Office Equipment			25
		To record depreciation for February.			
	28	Depreciation Expense–Delivery Equipment		125	
		Accumulated Depreciation–Delivery Equipment			125
		To record depreciation for February.			
	28	Wages and Salaries Expense		200	
		Wages and Salaries Payable			200
		To record earned but unpaid wages.			
	28	Interest Expense		60	
		Interest Payable			60
		To record interest expense for February.			
	28	Unearned Revenue		400	
		Revenue			400
		To record revenue earned.			
	28	Accounts Receivable		300	
		Revenue			300
		To record revenue earned.			
	28	Income Tax Expense		200	
		Income Taxes Payable			200
		To record income taxes for January and February.			

ILLUSTRATION 3-5 General Ledger Accounts After Adjustments

GENERAL LEDGER

NAME: Capital Stock   ACCOUNT NO.: 519

DATE		DESCRIPTION	POST. REF.	DEBIT	CREDIT	BALANCE
19X1 Jan.	2		GJ1		6,000	6,000

NAME: Revenue   ACCOUNT NO.: 600

DATE		DESCRIPTION	POST. REF.	DEBIT	CREDIT	BALANCE
Jan.	31		GJ1		5,000	5,000
Feb.	28		GJ2		6,200	11,200
	28	Adjusting	GJ4		400	11,600
	28	Adjusting	GJ4		300	11,900

(Continues)

ILLUSTRATION 3-5 (Concluded) General Ledger Accounts After Adjustments

NAME: Advertising Expense   ACCOUNT NO.: 700

DATE		DESCRIPTION	POST. REF.	DEBIT	CREDIT	BALANCE
Jan.	31		GJ1	100		100

NAME: Copying Supplies Expense   ACCOUNT NO.: 703

DATE		DESCRIPTION	POST. REF.	DEBIT	CREDIT	BALANCE
Jan.	4		GJ1	800		800
Feb.	28	Adjusting	GJ4	900		1,700

NAME: Depreciation Expense–Delivery Equipment   ACCOUNT NO.: 710

DATE		DESCRIPTION	POST. REF.	DEBIT	CREDIT	BALANCE
Feb.	28	Adjusting	GJ4	125		125

NAME: Depreciation Expense–Office Equipment   ACCOUNT NO.: 716

DATE		DESCRIPTION	POST. REF.	DEBIT	CREDIT	BALANCE
Feb.	28	Adjusting	GJ4	25		25

NAME: Income Tax Expense   ACCOUNT NO.: 726

DATE		DESCRIPTION	POST. REF.	DEBIT	CREDIT	BALANCE
Feb.	28	Adjusting	GJ4	200		200

NAME: Insurance Expense   ACCOUNT NO.: 728

DATE		DESCRIPTION	POST. REF.	DEBIT	CREDIT	BALANCE
Feb.	28	Adjusting	GJ4	75		75

NAME: Interest Expense   ACCOUNT NO.: 730

DATE		DESCRIPTION	POST. REF.	DEBIT	CREDIT	BALANCE
Feb.	28	Adjusting	GJ4	60		60

NAME: Rent Expense   ACCOUNT NO.: 762

DATE		DESCRIPTION	POST. REF.	DEBIT	CREDIT	BALANCE
Jan.	2		GJ1	1,000		1,000
Feb.	4		GJ1	1,000		2,000

NAME: Wages and Salaries Expense   ACCOUNT NO.: 784

DATE		DESCRIPTION	POST. REF.	DEBIT	CREDIT	BALANCE
Jan.	31		GJ1	3,000		3,000
Feb.	21		GJ2	400		3,400
	28		GJ3	3,000		6,400
	28	Adjusting	GJ4	200		6,600

THE ADJUSTED TRIAL BALANCE

A trial balance prepared after posting the adjusting entries is an **adjusted trial balance**. Illustration 3-6 shows the adjusted trial balance for PhotoCopy, Inc. If we have correctly posted the adjusting entries, the debits and credits will be equal in the trial balance. Illustration 3-6 shows they are equal.

ILLUSTRATION 3-6 Adjusted Trial Balance

PhotoCopy, Inc. Trial Balance February 28, 19X1		
	Debits	*Credits*
Cash	$ 3,400	
Accounts Receivable	300	
Copying Supplies	1,500	
Prepaid Insurance	825	
Delivery Equipment	13,000	
Accumulated Depreciation—Delivery Equipment		$ 125
Office Equipment	1,200	
Accumulated Depreciation—Office Equipment		25
Accounts Payable		2,400
Income Taxes Payable		200
Interest Payable		60
Unearned Revenue		200
Wages and Salaries Payable		200
Notes Payable—Noncurrent		10,000
Capital Stock		6,000
Revenue		11,900
Advertising Expense	100	
Copying Supplies Expense	1,700	
Depreciation Expense—Delivery Equipment	125	
Depreciation Expense—Office Equipment	25	
Income Tax Expense	200	
Insurance Expense	75	
Interest Expense	60	
Rent Expense	2,000	
Wages and Salaries Expense	6,600	
Totals	$31,110	$31,110

LO 3
Prepare financial statements using an adjusted trial balance.

PREPARING FINANCIAL STATEMENTS FROM THE ADJUSTED TRIAL BALANCE

The account balances in the adjusted trial balance conform with GAAP and, therefore, are appropriate for the preparation of financial statements. We can prepare the income statement as shown in Illustration 3-7, by extracting the revenue and expense accounts from the adjusted trial balance. We prepare the retained earnings statement as shown in Illustration 3-8 using the net income figure from the income statement. Finally, we prepare the balance sheet, as shown in Illustration 3-9, by extracting the balance sheet accounts from the

ILLUSTRATION 3-7 Preparation of the Income Statement

PhotoCopy, Inc.
Trial Balance
February 28, 19X1

	Debits	Credits
Cash	$ 3,400	
Accounts Receivable	300	
Copying Supplies	1,500	
Prepaid Insurance	825	
Delivery Equipment	13,000	
Accumulated Depreciation—Delivery Equipment		$ 125
Office Equipment	1,200	
Accumulated Depreciation—Office Equipment		25
Accounts Payable		2,400
Income Taxes Payable		200
Interest Payable		60
Unearned Revenue		200
Wages and Salaries Payable		200
Notes Payable—Noncurrent		10,000
Capital Stock		6,000
Revenue		11,900
Advertising Expense	100	
Copying Supplies Expense	1,700	
Depreciation Expense—Delivery Equipment	125	
Depreciation Expense—Office Equipment	25	
Income Tax Expense	200	
Insurance Expense	75	
Interest Expense	60	
Rent Expense	2,000	
Wages and Salaries Expense	6,600	
Totals	$31,110	$31,110

PhotoCopy, Inc.
Income Statement
For the Two Months Ended February 28, 19X1

Revenue		$11,900
Expenses:		
Advertising expense	$ 100	
Copying supplies expense	1,700	
Depreciation expense—delivery equipment	125	
Depreciation expense—office equipment	25	
Income tax expense	200	
Insurance expense	75	
Interest expense	60	
Rent expense	2,000	
Wages and salaries expense	6,600	
Total expenses		10,885
Net income		$ 1,015

ILLUSTRATION 3-8 Preparation of the Retained Earnings Statement

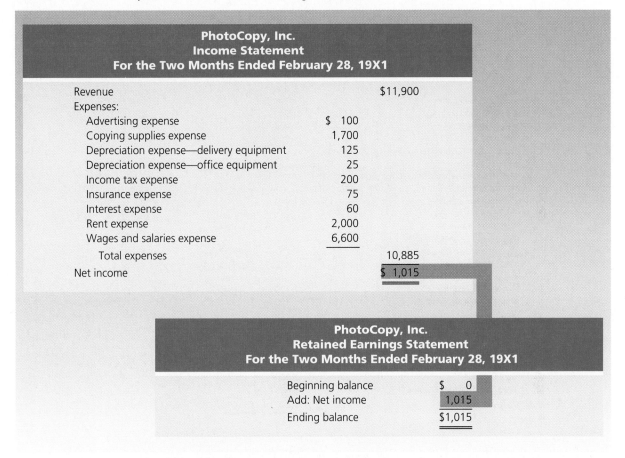

adjusted trial balance and the ending balance for retained earnings from the retained earnings statement.

LO 4

Explain the closing process and prepare closing entries.

CLOSING THE TEMPORARY ACCOUNTS

After we have journalized and posted the adjusting entries and have prepared the financial statements, the final step in the accounting cycle is to close the revenue and expense accounts. This section discusses the need for closing entries, describes the closing process, and shows the closing entries for PhotoCopy, Inc.

The Need for Closing Entries

Revenues and expenses could be recorded directly as increases and decreases in stockholders' equity. In practice, however, the detailed amounts and types of the business's individual revenues and expenses must be conveniently available to the accountant to facilitate calculating and presenting net income. To satisfy this requirement, we use a separate account for each type of revenue and expense.

ILLUSTRATION 3-9 Preparation of the Balance Sheet

PhotoCopy, Inc.
Trial Balance
February 28, 19X1

	Debits	Credits
Cash	$ 3,400	
Accounts Receivable	300	
Copying Supplies	1,500	
Prepaid Insurance	825	
Delivery Equipment	13,000	
Accumulated Depreciation—Delivery Equipment		$ 125
Office Equipment	1,200	
Accumulated Depreciation—Office Equipment		25
Accounts Payable		2,400
Income Taxes Payable		200
Interest Payable		60
Unearned Revenue		200
Wages and Salaries Payable		200
Notes Payable—Noncurrent		10,000
Capital Stock		6,000
Revenue		11,900
Advertising Expense	100	
Copying Supplies Expense	1,700	
Depreciation Expense—Delivery Equipment	125	
Depreciation Expense—Office Equipment	25	
Income Tax Expense	200	
Insurance Expense	75	
Interest Expense	60	
Rent Expense	2,000	
Wages and Salaries Expense	6,600	
Totals	$31,110	$31,110

PhotoCopy, Inc.
Balance Sheet
February 28, 19X1

Assets

Cash			$ 3,400
Accounts receivable			300
Copying supplies			1,500
Prepaid insurance			825
Delivery equipment		13,000	
Accumulated depreciation		(125)	12,875
Office equipment		1,200	
Accumulated depreciation		(25)	1,175
Total assets			$20,075

Liabilities and Stockholders' Equity

Liabilities:		
Accounts payable		$ 2,400
Income taxes payable		200
Interest payable		60
Unearned revenue		200
Wages and salaries payable		200
Notes payable—noncurrent		10,000
Total liabilities		$13,060
Stockholders' equity:		
Capital stock		6,000
Retained earnings		1,015
Total stockholders' equity		7,015
Total liabilities and stockholders' equity		$20,075

The revenue and expense accounts are **temporary accounts**. During an accounting period, we record revenues and expenses in the appropriate accounts, which always begin the period with zero balances. The net income measured in the revenue and expense accounts is for that period only. At the end of the period, we transfer the temporary account balances to stockholders' equity to state correctly the business's financial position as of the end of the period. Retained Earnings is the stockholders' equity account to which revenues and expenses are transferred. Therefore, at both the beginning and the end of an accounting period, temporary accounts have zero balances. We simply use temporary accounts in the interim to accumulate information in convenient form for the preparation of the financial statements. We call the process of transferring temporary account balances to stockholders' equity **closing temporary accounts**, or simply **closing the accounts**.

The Closing Process

The closing process for a corporation involves transferring net income and dividends to the retained earnings account. The revenue and expense accounts contain the information about net income. We could close (transfer) the revenue and expense accounts directly to Retained Earnings, but this would result in too much detailed information in Retained Earnings. For this reason, we close the revenue and expense accounts first to an account called **Income Summary**. After we close the revenue and expense account balances to Income Summary, the balance of Income Summary is equal to the net income or net loss for the period.

The closing process for a corporation is shown in Illustration 3-10. The process consists of four entries that we journalize in the general journal and post to the general ledger. The four entries are:

1. Close the revenue accounts by debiting each revenue account with the amount of its credit balance and crediting Income Summary with an amount equal to the sum of the debits. After posting this entry, the revenue accounts have zero balances.
2. Close the expense accounts by crediting each expense account with the amount of its debit balance and debiting Income Summary with an amount equal to the sum of the credits. After posting this entry, the expense accounts have zero balances. After the first two entries, the balance of Income Summary is equal to the net income (credit balance) or net loss (debit balance) for the period.
3. Close Income Summary to Retained Earnings. For net income (assumed in Illustration 3-10), the entry is a debit to Income Summary in an amount equal to its credit balance and a credit to Retained Earnings for the same amount. For a net loss, the entry is a credit to Income Summary and a debit to Retained Earnings in the amount of the debit balance in Income Summary. After this closing entry, Income Summary has a zero balance and the net income (loss) has been added to (subtracted from) Retained Earnings.
4. Close Dividends to Retained Earnings. This closing entry is illustrated here even though PhotoCopy has not declared dividends. The entry is a credit to Dividends and a debit to Retained Earnings in an amount equal to the debit balance in Dividends. After this entry, Dividends has a zero balance.

ILLUSTRATION 3-10 Closing Process

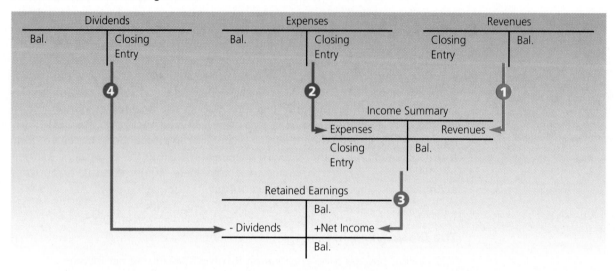

Closing Entries for PhotoCopy, Inc.

You may find the information necessary to prepare closing entries in the general ledger or in the adjusted trial balance. We base the closing entries for PhotoCopy, Inc. on the information in the adjusted trial balance in Illustration 3-6.

Closing the Revenue Account. PhotoCopy only has one revenue account and the closing entry is:

Feb. 28	Revenue	11,900	
	Income Summary		11,900
	To close revenue account to Income Summary.		

The effect of the closing entry for revenue is shown below:

Income Summary			Revenue		
	11,900 ◄**❶**	11,900	Bal.	11,900

Closing the Expense Accounts. The closing entry for PhotoCopy's expense accounts is:

Feb. 28	Income Summary	10,885	
	Advertising Expense		100
	Copying Supplies Expense		1,700
	Depreciation Expense–Delivery Equipment		125
	Depreciation Expense–Office Equipment		25
	Income Tax Expense		200
	Insurance Expense		75
	Interest Expense		60
	Rent Expense		2,000
	Wages and Salaries Expense		6,600
	To close expense accounts to Income Summary.		

The effects of the closing entry for expenses may be illustrated as follows:

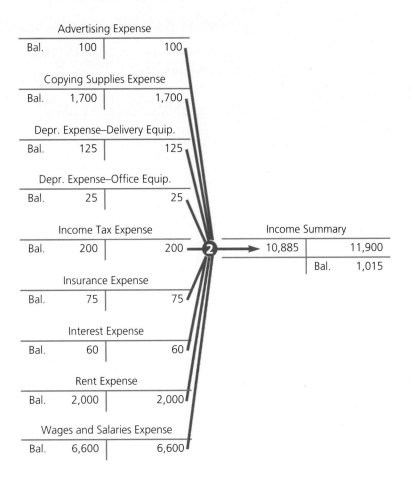

Closing the Income Summary Account. After the first two closing entries above, the balance of $1,015 in Income Summary is equal to the net income for the period. The closing entry for Income Summary is:

Feb. 28	Income Summary	1,015	
	Retained Earnings		1,015
	To close Income Summary.		

The effect of closing Income Summary may be illustrated as follows:

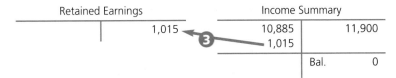

The General Ledger Accounts After Closing

Illustration 3-11 presents the retained earnings, revenue, and expense general ledger accounts for PhotoCopy, Inc., after we post the closing entries.

Notice that the temporary accounts—the revenue and expense accounts—have zero balances after we post the closing entries. The permanent accounts—the asset, liability, and stockholders' accounts—have non-zero balances.

ILLUSTRATION 3-11 General Ledger Accounts After Closing

GENERAL LEDGER

NAME: Retained Earnings   ACCOUNT NO.: 550

DATE		DESCRIPTION	POST. REF.	DEBIT	CREDIT	BALANCE
19X1 Feb.	28	Closing	GJ4		1,015	1,015

NAME: Revenue   ACCOUNT NO.: 600

DATE		DESCRIPTION	POST. REF.	DEBIT	CREDIT	BALANCE
Jan.	31		GJ1		5,000	5,000
Feb.	28		GJ2		6,200	11,200
	28	Adjusting	GJ4		400	11,600
	28	Adjusting	GJ4		300	11,900
	28	Closing		11,900		0

NAME: Advertising Expense   ACCOUNT NO.: 700

DATE		DESCRIPTION	POST. REF.	DEBIT	CREDIT	BALANCE
Jan.	31		GJ1	100		100
Feb.	28	Closing	GJ4		100	0

NAME: Copying Supplies Expense   ACCOUNT NO.: 703

DATE		DESCRIPTION	POST. REF.	DEBIT	CREDIT	BALANCE
Jan.	4		GJ1	800		800
Feb.	28	Adjusting	GJ4	900		1,700
	28	Closing	GJ4		1,700	0

NAME: Depreciation Expense–Delivery Equipment   ACCOUNT NO.: 710

DATE		DESCRIPTION	POST. REF.	DEBIT	CREDIT	BALANCE
Feb.	28	Adjusting	GJ4	125		125
	28	Closing	GJ4		125	0

NAME: Depreciation Expense–Office Equipment   ACCOUNT NO.: 716

DATE		DESCRIPTION	POST. REF.	DEBIT	CREDIT	BALANCE
Feb.	28	Adjusting	GJ4	25		25
	28	Closing	GJ4		25	0

NAME: Income Tax Expense   ACCOUNT NO.: 726

DATE		DESCRIPTION	POST. REF.	DEBIT	CREDIT	BALANCE
Feb.	28	Adjusting	GJ4	200		200
	28	Closing	GJ4		200	0

(Continues)

ILLUSTRATION 3-11 (Concluded) General Ledger Accounts After Closing

NAME: Insurance Expense　　　　　　　　　ACCOUNT NO.: 728

DATE		DESCRIPTION	POST. REF.	DEBIT	CREDIT	BALANCE
19X1						
Feb.	28	Adjusting	GJ4	75		75
	28	Closing	GJ4		75	0

NAME: Interest Expense　　　　　　　　　　ACCOUNT NO.: 730

DATE		DESCRIPTION	POST. REF.	DEBIT	CREDIT	BALANCE
Feb.	28	Adjusting	GJ4	60		60
	28	Closing	GJ4		60	0

NAME: Rent Expense　　　　　　　　　　　ACCOUNT NO.: 762

DATE		DESCRIPTION	POST. REF.	DEBIT	CREDIT	BALANCE
Jan.	2		GJ1	1,000		1,000
	4		GJ1	1,000		2,000
	28	Closing	GJ4		2,000	0

NAME: Wages and Salaries Expense　　　　　ACCOUNT NO.: 784

DATE		DESCRIPTION	POST. REF.	DEBIT	CREDIT	BALANCE
Jan.	31		GJ1	3,000		3,000
Feb.	21		GJ2	400		3,400
	28		GJ3	3,000		6,400
	28	Adjusting	GJ4	200		6,600
	28	Closing	GJ4		6,600	0

A Note About Preparing Financial Statements

As demonstrated in this chapter, accountants may prepare financial statements for relatively simple businesses such as PhotoCopy, Inc. directly from the adjusted trial balance. The preparation of financial statements from the adjusted trial balance requires knowledge of

1. Which accounts are listed in each financial statement.
2. The format of the financial statements.

For more complex businesses, accountants use a worksheet, which we demonstrate in Appendix 3-B at the end of this chapter.

LO 5

Prepare a post-closing trial balance.

The Post-Closing Trial Balance

A **post-closing trial balance** is a trial balance prepared after we have posted the closing entries to the general ledger. A post-closing trial balance for PhotoCopy, Inc. is presented in Illustration 3-12. Since revenue and expense accounts have zero balances after closing, the post-closing trial balance lists

ILLUSTRATION 3-12 Post-Closing Trial Balance

PhotoCopy, Inc. Post-Closing Trial Balance February 28, 19X1		
	Debits	*Credits*
Cash	$ 3,400	
Accounts Receivable	300	
Copying Supplies	1,500	
Prepaid Insurance	825	
Delivery Equipment	13,000	
Accumulated Depreciation—Delivery Equipment		$ 125
Office Equipment	1,200	
Accumulated Depreciation—Office Equipment		25
Accounts Payable		2,400
Income Taxes Payable		200
Interest Payable		60
Unearned Revenue		200
Wages and Salaries Payable		200
Notes Payable—Noncurrent		10,000
Capital Stock		6,000
Retained Earnings		1,015
Totals	$20,225	$20,225

only the balance sheet accounts—asset, liability, and stockholders' equity. The purpose of the post-closing trial balance is to serve as a check that no errors occurred in preparing and posting the closing entries.

THE ACCOUNTING CYCLE

LO 6

Describe the timing of the various steps in the accounting cycle.

You have seen the six steps in the accounting cycle. These steps are summarized in Illustration 3-13. Not all of the steps are performed at equal time intervals. On a daily basis, we perform the first three steps. That is, we analyze transactions, enter them in the general journal, and post them to the general ledger. We adjust the accounts whenever the business prepares financial statements. Most businesses prepare statements for interim periods such as monthly or quarterly; and we adjust the accounts to prepare the financial statements for those time intervals. We close the temporary accounts annually, so that the accumulation of revenue and expense information is for the annual accounting period. In this chapter, we closed the temporary accounts at the end of the second month of operations for discussion purposes only.

PROFITABILITY OF PHOTOCOPY, INC.

LO 7

Calculate and interpret a business's profit margin.

Now that the owners of PhotoCopy, Inc. have prepared financial statements, just how profitable was the business during January and February? The income statement for the two months shows net income of $1,015. But how does this amount compare to the profitability of other service businesses? One measure

ILLUSTRATION 3-13 The Accounting Cycle

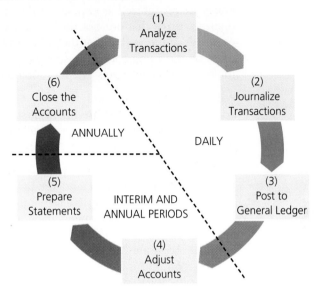

of profitability is the profit margin. **Profit margin** is the amount of net income as a percent of revenues, or:

Profit Margin = Net Income ÷ Revenues

The profit margin is an indication of the business's ability to generate revenues that are profitable. For the two-month period, PhotoCopy's profit margin is 8.5% ($1,015 ÷ $11,900). How does an 8.5% profit margin compare to those of other service businesses? The following data represent the average profit margins of certain service industries for 1992.

Industry	Profit Margin
Advertising agencies	1.9%
Car washes	3.5%
Auto repair	3.7%
Legal services	12.8%
Accounting services	15.4%

Reprinted with permission, copyright Robert Morris Associates 1992.

Compared to other service businesses, PhotoCopy, Inc. appears to be reasonably profitable. However, one must be careful in interpreting these data. For example, is January—February a typical period? Will the same level of business continue throughout the year? Also, other investors may open copying centers in the area and take away some of PhotoCopy's business.

SUMMARY

Explain the concepts, assumptions, and principles underlying the accrual basis of accounting. The accrual basis of accounting relies on the principles of revenue realization and expense recognition. Costs that are associated directly with revenues are recognized as expenses in the period that the related revenues are recognized. Costs that are not directly associated with revenues are recognized as expenses in the period that the business benefits from the costs. The accountant relies on the going-concern assumption as well as on assumptions about the useful lives of specific assets in apportioning the effects of multiperiod transactions.

Prepare adjusting entries at the end of the accounting period. Accountants use adjusting entries to prepare financial statements. Adjusting entries apportion the effects of multiperiod transactions to the proper periods. Adjusting entries are entered in the general journal and posted to the general ledger.

Prepare financial statements using an adjusted trial balance. An adjusted trial balance reflects the debit and credit effects of the adjusting entries; and the resulting adjusted account balances are appropriate for preparing the financial statements. Financial statements may be prepared directly from the adjusted trial balance. The income statement is prepared by using the adjusted revenue and expense accounts. The retained earnings statement is prepared by using the net income from the income statement. The balance sheet uses adjusted asset, liability, and capital stock accounts from the adjusted trial balance and retained earnings from the retained earnings statement.

Explain the closing process and prepare closing entries. The final step in the accounting cycle is to close the temporary accounts to Retained Earnings. The temporary accounts are the income statement accounts—revenue and expense accounts—and the dividends account. The temporary accounts begin each annual accounting period with zero balances and are used to accumulate information about net income and dividends for the year. At the end of the year, the temporary accounts are returned to zero balances by transferring (closing) their balances to Retained Earnings. After closing, the temporary accounts are ready to accumulate the applicable information for the next year.

Prepare a post-closing trial balance. An optional procedure after closing is to check the equality of the permanent (balance sheet) accounts by preparing a post-closing trial balance.

Describe the timing of the various steps in the accounting cycle. We perform the steps in the accounting cycle at varying time intervals. We daily analyze transactions, enter them in the general journal, and post them to the general ledger. We adjust the accounts whenever the business prepares financial statements. We close the accounts annually so that the accumulation of net income information is for the annual accounting period.

Calculate and interpret a business's profit margin. A business's profit margin is the ratio of net income to revenues. The profit margin is an indication of the business's ability to generate revenues that are profitable.

LO 8

Prepare adjusting entries when certain cash transactions are recorded initially as revenues and expenses.

APPENDIX 3-A: UNEARNED REVENUE AND PREPAID EXPENSES INITIALLY RECORDED AS REVENUES AND EXPENSES

The discussion of payments for services received before rendering them showed that a business initially records such payments as liabilities—Unearned

Revenue. Similarly, when a business makes payments for expenses before incurring them, it initially records the payments as assets—Prepaid Expenses. When revenues are earned and expenses are incurred, a business records adjusting entries to recognize them. However, some businesses find it more convenient to reverse the order of recording because most revenues are earned and most expenses are incurred by the end of the accounting period. Therefore, they first record all such cash transactions as revenues or expenses. Then, they make adjustments at the end of the period to recognize the remaining liability and asset amounts as of that time.

UNEARNED REVENUE

Consider the case of Southeastern Computing Services, Inc.. Assume that on January 24, 19X1, Southeastern received $2,400 in advance for one month's computing services. Under the method used in the chapter, Southeastern would initially record the payment in a liability account as follows:

Jan. 24	Cash	2,400	
	Unearned Revenue		2,400
	Receipt of advance payment for computing agreement.		

On January 31, we record the following adjusting entry to recognize that one-fourth of the services have been performed:

Jan. 31	Unearned Revenue	600	
	Revenue		600
	To record computing revenue earned.		

Assume instead that Southeastern initially records the receipt as revenue with the following entry:

Jan. 24	Cash	2,400	
	Revenue		2,400
	To record receipt of cash for computing services.		

At the end of the January accounting period, the following relationships indicate the need for adjustment:

1. Revenues are overstated by $1,800 ($2,400 – $600).
2. Liabilities are understated by $1,800.

Therefore, on January 31, we record the following adjusting entry:

Jan. 31	Revenue	1,800	
	Unearned Revenue		1,800
	To adjust Revenue for unearned revenue.		

The ultimate effects of the two alternative treatments are identical, as illustrated with T-accounts below. These T-accounts reflect the effects of only the one transaction.

Initial recording as a liability:

Revenue			Unearned Revenue		
	Jan. 31 600 ⟵—	Jan. 31 600	Jan. 24 2,400		
				Bal. 1,800	

Initial recording as a revenue:

Revenue				Unearned Revenue	
Jan. 31 1,800	Jan. 24 2,400				Jan. 31 1,800
	Bal. 600				

Notice that in both cases, after adjustment, the balance of Revenue is $600 and the balance of Unearned Revenue is $1,800.

PREPAID EXPENSES

On January 2, 19X1, Southeastern paid $12,000 in advance for rent for 19X1. Under the method used in the chapter, Southeastern would record the following entry:

Jan. 2	Prepaid Rent	12,000	
	Cash		12,000
	Payment in advance for 19X1 rent.		

On January 31, $1,000 ($12,000 ÷ 12) of the prepaid rent has expired; and we record the following entry to recognize the partial expiration of the asset prepaid rent:

Jan. 31	Rent Expense	1,000	
	Prepaid Rent		1,000
	To record rent for January.		

Assume instead that Southeastern initially records the prepaid rent as an expense with the following entry:

Jan. 2	Rent Expense	12,000	
	Cash		12,000
	To record rent expense.		

At the end of the January accounting period, the following relationships indicate the need for adjustment:

1. Expenses are overstated by $11,000 ($12,000 − $1,000).
2. Assets are understated by $11,000.

Therefore, on January 31, the following adjusting entry is required:

Jan. 31	Prepaid Rent	11,000	
	Rent Expense		11,000
	To record unexpired rent.		

The ultimate effects of the two alternative treatments are identical, illustrated with T-accounts. Notice that in both cases, after adjustment, the balance of Prepaid Rent is $11,000 and the balance of Rent Expense is $1,000.

Initial recording as an asset:

Prepaid Rent			Rent Expense	
Jan. 2 12,000	Jan. 31 1,000	→	Jan. 31 1,000	
Bal. 11,000				

Initial recording as an expense:

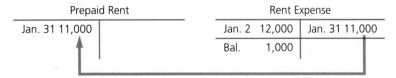

Prepaid Rent			Rent Expense		
Jan. 31 11,000			Jan. 2 12,000	Jan. 31 11,000	
			Bal. 1,000		

LO 9

Complete the accountant's worksheet and prepare financial statements using the worksheet.

APPENDIX 3-B: THE ACCOUNTANT'S WORKSHEET

A worksheet, as shown in Illustration 3-14, is a tool accountants use at the end of an accounting period to prepare financial statements; it is *not* a formal part of the accounting records. The worksheet begins with the unadjusted trial balance, then adjusting entries, and then extensions of the amounts to an adjusted trial balance. Finally, the worksheet includes Income Statement and Balance Sheet columns. Using these columns, accountants can prepare these two financial statements. Using the worksheet to prepare financial statements is not only more convenient than preparing them from an adjusted trial balance, but it also minimizes the chances of errors in the end-of-period procedures. In fact, accountants generally prepare adjusting entries on the worksheet *and then journalize and post the entries* to the general journal and general ledger after completing the worksheet.

Procedures for Preparing the Worksheet

The worksheet format presented in Illustration 3-14 has 11 columns. The first column, starting from the left, is for listing account titles. The next five pairs of columns are for entering monetary amounts. Each pair of columns has a left column Dr. (debits) and a right column Cr. (credits). The sequence of procedures below for preparing the worksheet are as follows:

1. Prepare the unadjusted trial balance in Illustration 3-15 by entering all general ledger account titles in the first column. Then, enter the unadjusted account balances in the first pair of monetary columns, Trial Balance. The trial balance is the same as the one you saw previously for PhotoCopy, Inc., except that accounts with zero balances are also listed here. After entering all account balances, check the equality of debits and credits to make sure the account balances have equal debits and credits and that the balances are entered correctly in the worksheet.

2. Next, prepare adjusting entries as shown in Illustration 3-15 by entering the adjustments (same as you saw previously) in the second pair of monetary columns, Adjustments. In the column with each part of an adjusting entry is a letter reference enclosed in parentheses. These references allow you to match the debit and credit parts of each adjusting entry so that the entire entry can be assessed. After entering all adjusting entries, check the equality of debits and credits in the Adjustments columns. By checking for equality, you can quickly discover and easily correct adjusting entries with unequal debits and credits.

3. Prepare the Adjusted Trial Balance as shown in Illustration 3-15 by summing each account across the Trial Balance and Adjustments columns. This process involves taking the trial balance amount of each account,

ILLUSTRATION 3-14 Format of a Worksheet for the Financial Statements

(WORKSHEET HEADING)

ACCOUNTS	TRIAL BALANCE		ADJUSTMENTS		ADJUSTED TRIAL BALANCE		INCOME STATEMENT		BALANCE SHEET	
	Dr.	Cr.	Dr.	Cr.	Dr.	Cr.	Dr.	Cr.	Dr.	Cr.
(Account titles)	(Account balances)		(Amounts of adjustments)		(Account balances for the adjusted trial balance)		(Income statement accounts from the adjusted trial balance)		(Balance sheet accounts from the adjusted trial balance)	

ILLUSTRATION 3-15 Worksheet for PhotoCopy, Inc.

PhotoCopy, Inc.
Worksheet for Financial Statements
February 28, 19X1

ACCOUNTS	TRIAL BALANCE Dr.	TRIAL BALANCE Cr.	ADJUSTMENTS Dr.	ADJUSTMENTS Cr.	ADJUSTED TRIAL BALANCE Dr.	ADJUSTED TRIAL BALANCE Cr.	INCOME STATEMENT Dr.	INCOME STATEMENT Cr.	BALANCE SHEET Dr.	BALANCE SHEET Cr.
Cash	3,400				3,400				3,400	
Accounts Receivable			(h) 300		300				300	
Copying Supplies	2,400			(b) 900	1,500				1,500	
Prepaid Insurance	900			(a) 75	825				825	
Delivery Equipment	13,000				13,000				13,000	
Acc. Depr.–Delivery Equip.				(c) 125		125				125
Office Equipment	1,200				1,200				1,200	
Acc. Depr.–Office Equip.				(d) 25		25				25
Accounts Payable		2,400				2,400				2,400
Income Taxes Payable				(i) 200		200				200
Interest Payable				(f) 60		60				60
Unearned Revenue		600	(g) 400			200				200
Wages and Salaries Payable				(e) 200		200				200
Notes Payable–Noncurrent		10,000				10,000				10,000
Capital Stock		6,000				6,000				6,000
Retained Earnings										0
Revenue		11,200		(g) 400 (h) 300		11,900		11,900		
Advertising Expense	100				100		100			
Copying Supplies Expense	800		(b) 900		1,700		1,700			
Depr. Exp.–Delivery Equip.			(c) 125		125		125			
Depr. Exp.–Office Equip.			(d) 25		25		25			
Income Tax Expense			(i) 200		200		200			
Insurance Expense			(a) 75		75		75			
Interest Expense			(f) 60		60		60			
Rent Expense	2,000				2,000		2,000			
Wages and Salaries Expense	6,400		(e) 200		6,600		6,600			
	30,200	30,200	2,285	2,285	31,110	31,110	10,885	11,900	20,225	19,210
Net Income (Retained Earn.)							1,015			1,015
							11,900	11,900	20,225	20,225

adding and subtracting the adjustments to that account, and then entering the adjusted balance in the appropriate column of the Adjusted Trial Balance. For accounts with zero balances in the Trial Balance columns, the amount entered in the Adjusted Trial Balance columns is composed solely of the amounts entered in the account in the Adjustments columns. After entering all adjusted account balances, check the equality of debits and credits in the Adjusted Trial Balance columns.

4. Complete the Income Statement columns as shown in Illustration 3-15 by transferring adjusted revenue and expense account balances to the Income Statement pair of columns. The revenue accounts have credit balances, so enter them in the Cr. column. Similarly, expense accounts have debit balances, so enter them in the Dr. column.

Compute net income by summing the Dr. and Cr. columns and finding the difference in the balances. The amount by which the balance of the Cr. (revenues) column exceeds the balance of the Dr. (expenses) column is the amount of net income. If the business incurred a net loss, the balance of the Dr. (expenses) column would exceed the balance of the Cr. (revenues) column.

When the Dr. and Cr. columns of the Income Statement in Illustration 3-15 are summed, the credits exceed the debits by $1,015 ($11,900 − $10,885). The $1,015 is net income. Enter the title "Net income" in the Accounts column at the left, and enter $1,015 in the Dr. column of the Income Statement *and* in the Cr. column of the Balance Sheet. Entering the amount of net income in the Dr. column of the Income Statement balances the sums of the Dr. and Cr. columns. Net income represents an increase in stockholders' equity due to the business's operations, and it has not yet been added to Retained Earnings. Also, this balances the sums of the Dr. and Cr. Balance Sheet columns.

5. Complete the Balance Sheet columns as shown in Illustration 3-15 by transferring the adjusted asset, liability, and stockholders' equity account balances to the Balance Sheet columns. Assets have debit balances, so enter them in the Dr. column. Liability accounts have credit balances, so enter them in the Cr. column. Take special care to enter accumulated depreciation account balances in the Balance Sheet Cr. column, even though accumulated depreciation is related to assets.

Capital Stock has a credit balance, so enter it in the Cr. column of the Balance Sheet. However, Retained Earnings from the adjusted trial balance is not the correct account balance for the balance sheet. (For PhotoCopy, Inc., the balance in Retained Earnings in the adjusted trial balance is in effect zero since this is the first period of operations.) It does not reflect the income for the period. This amount has been accumulated in the revenue and expense accounts, and ultimately you must transfer this amount to Retained Earnings. The transfer takes place through the closing entries (described earlier), after you complete the worksheet. In the worksheet, we accomplish the same effect on Retained Earnings by including the amount of net income in the Cr. column by the procedures described in 4 above.

Next, sum the balance sheet pair of columns. If you have made no errors in completing the worksheet, the sum of the Dr. column should equal the sum of the Cr. column. Notice the equality of debits and credits for each pair of the financial statement columns in Illustration 3-15.

Preparing Financial Statements Using a Worksheet

The completed worksheet in Illustration 3-15 contains all the information necessary to prepare the formal financial statements for PhotoCopy, Inc. We prepare the income statement from the information in the Income Statement columns, and we prepare the retained earnings statement and balance sheet from the information in the Balance Sheet columns. While all the information necessary for the financial statements is in the worksheet, the financial statement columns are *not* in financial statement format *per se*. That is, the columns do not show the proper headings. Therefore, we prepare the financial statements by extracting the information from the completed worksheet and then arranging the information in the proper format for the financial statements.

REVIEW PROBLEM: ADJUSTING ENTRIES, TRIAL BALANCE, FINANCIAL STATEMENTS, CLOSING ENTRIES, AND PROFIT MARGINS

Jack Ford organized Wildwater Expeditions, Inc. several years ago to provide raft trips down the Big South Fork of the Cumberland River. Wildwater has an annual accounting period based on the calendar year. Jack Ford provides the unadjusted trial balance and additional information shown below.

Wildwater Expeditions, Inc. Trial Balance December 31, 19X3		
	Debits	*Credits*
Cash	$ 6,500	
Accounts Receivable	4,500	
Prepaid Insurance	2,400	
Office Supplies	500	
Equipment	50,000	
Accumulated Depreciation–Equipment		$ 20,000
Accounts Payable		3,000
Unearned Fees		80,000
Capital Stock		10,000
Retained Earnings		4,400
Dividends	25,000	
Fee Revenue		32,000
Miscellaneous Expense	4,000	
Rent Expense	15,000	
Utilities Expense	1,500	
Wages and Salaries Expense	40,000	
	$149,400	$149,400

Additional Information:

1. The balance in Prepaid Insurance is the result of a comprehensive river liability policy that was purchased on April 1, 19X3. The policy cost $2,400 and covers the period of April 1, 19X3, through March 31, 19X4.
2. The equipment, purchased on January 1, 19X1, consists of 25 River Supply Scout Rafts at a cost of $2,000 each. These rafts have an estimated useful life of 5 years and are estimated to be worthless at the end of the 5-year period.

3. Wildwater records walk-in trip ticket sales (which result from customers purchasing trip tickets on the days of the trip) by crediting Fee Revenue. Most of its business, however, consists of trips booked and paid for in advance. Advance bookings are recorded with a credit to Unearned Fees. Unearned Fees is adjusted at the end of the accounting year based on the amount of advance booking customers that have completed the raft trip. On December 31, $65,000 of the $80,000 advance booking revenue is earned.

4. Wildwater rents paddles, helmets, and wetsuits from Whitewater Sales and Service. The bill for December rentals is $1,500 and is due January 31, 19X4.

5. Office supplies on hand on December 31 total $200.

REQUIRED:

a. Prepare and post the necessary adjusting entries.
b. Prepare an adjusted trial balance.
c. Prepare an income statement, a retained earnings statement, and a balance sheet for Wildwater as of December 31, 19X3.
d. Prepare and post closing entries.
e. Prepare a post-closing trial balance.
f. Calculate the profit margin for the 19X3 operations and comment on what it tells us about Wildwater's operations.

SOLUTION:

Planning and Organizing Your Work

1. Analyze the information in the problem to determine which accounts require adjustment.
2. Journalize the adjusting entries.
3. Post the adjusting entries to the T-accounts in the general ledger.
4. Prepare an adjusted trial balance. Make sure the debits equal the credits.
5. Prepare the financial statements.
6. Journalize the closing entries.
7. Post the closing entries to the T-accounts in the general ledger.
8. Prepare a post-closing trial balance. Make sure the debits equal the credits.
9. Use the appropriate figures to determine the profit margin from 19X3 operations.

(a) *Prepare and post adjusting entries.*

Dec. 31	Insurance Expense	1,800	
	Prepaid Insurance		1,800
	To record expired insurance.		
	($2,400 x 9/12 = $1,800)		
31	Depreciation Expense—Equipment	10,000	
	Accumulated Depreciation–Equipment		10,000
	To record 19X3 depreciation.		
	((25 x $2,000)/5 = $10,000)		
31	Unearned Fees	65,000	
	Fee Revenue		65,000
	To record advance booking revenues		
	that have been earned.		
31	Rent Expense	1,500	
	Accounts Payable		1,500
	To accrue rental expense.		
31	Office Supplies Expense	300	
	Office Supplies		300
	To record office supplies used.		

Note: A worksheet, presented in Appendix 3-B at the end of Chapter 3, will simplify the preparation of an adjusted trial balance. Without the worksheet, two approaches are possible: (1) Use T-accounts and place the balance from the trial balance in the accounts and then post the adjusting entries to the accounts and prepare an adjusted trial balance from the resulting account balances. (2) Use an "eyeball" approach, increasing and decreasing the account balances in the trial balance as required by the adjustments and adding account balances as required. The T-account approach is illustrated.

TB = Trial balance; Bal. = Balance; ( ) = Adjustment; keyed to "Additional Information"

Cash				Accounts Receivable		
TB	6,500			TB	4,500	
Bal.	6,500			Bal.	4,500	

Prepaid Insurance				Office Supplies		
TB	2,400	(1)	1,800	TB	500	(5)	300
Bal.	600			Bal.	200	

Equipment			Accumulated Depreciation— Equipment		
TB	50,000				
Bal.	50,000		TB	20,000
			(2)	10,000
			Bal.	30,000

Accounts Payable			Unearned Fees		
		TB	3,000	(3)	65,000	TB	80,000
		(4)	1,500			Bal.	15,000
		Bal.	4,500			

Capital Stock			Retained Earnings		
		TB	10,000			TB	4,400
		Bal.	10,000			Bal.	4,400

Dividends			Fee Revenue		
TB	25,000					TB	32,000
Bal.	25,000					(3)	65,000
						Bal.	97,000

Depreciation Expense–Equipment			Insurance Expense		
(2)	10,000			(1)	1,800	
Bal.	10,000			Bal.	1,800	

Miscellaneous Expense			Rent Expense		
TB	4,000			TB	15,000	
Bal.	4,000			(4)	1,500	
				Bal.	16,500	

Office Supplies Expense			Wages and Salaries Expense		
(5)	300			TB	40,000	
Bal.	300			Bal.	40,000	

Utilities Expense		
TB	1,500	
Bal.	1,500	

(b) *Prepare an adjusted trial balance.*

Wildwater Expeditions, Inc.
Trial Balance
December 31, 19X3

	Debits	Credits
Cash	$ 6,500	
Accounts Receivable	4,500	
Prepaid Insurance	600	
Office Supplies	200	
Equipment	50,000	
Accumulated Depreciation–Equipment		$ 30,000
Accounts Payable		4,500
Unearned Fees		15,000
Capital Stock		10,000
Retained Earnings		4,400
Dividends	25,000	
Fee Revenue		97,000
Depreciation Expense–Equipment	10,000	
Insurance Expense	1,800	
Miscellaneous Expense	4,000	
Office Supplies Expense	300	
Rent Expense	16,500	
Utilities Expense	1,500	
Wages and Salaries Expense	40,000	
	$160,900	$160,900

(c) *Prepare financial statements.*

Wildwater Expeditions, Inc.
Income Statement
For the Year Ended December 31, 19X3

Fee revenue		$97,000
Expenses:		
Depreciation—equipment	$10,000	
Insurance	1,800	
Miscellaneous	4,000	
Rent	16,500	
Office supplies	300	
Utilities	1,500	
Wages and salaries	40,000	
Total expenses		74,100
Net income		$22,900

Wildwater Expeditions, Inc.
Retained Earnings Statement
For the Year Ended December 31, 19X3

Beginning balance, 1-1-X3	$ 4,400
Add: Net income	22,900
Less: Dividends	(25,000)
Ending balance, 12-31-X3	$ 2,300

Wildwater Expeditions, Inc. **Balance Sheet** **December 31, 19X3**		
Assets		
Cash		$ 6,500
Accounts receivable		4,500
Prepaid insurance		600
Office supplies		200
Equipment	$50,000	
Accumulated depreciation—equipment	(30,000)	20,000
Total assets		$31,800
Liabilities and Stockholders' Equity		
Liabilities:		
Accounts payable	$ 4,500	
Unearned fees	15,000	
Total liabilities		$19,500
Stockholders' Equity:		
Capital stock	$10,000	
Retained earnings	2,300	
Total stockholders' equity		12,300
Total liabilities and stockholders' equity		$31,800

(d) *Prepare and post the closing entries.*

Dec. 31	Fee Revenue	97,000	
	Income Summary		97,000
	To record the closing of the revenue accounts.		
31	Income Summary	74,100	
	Depreciation Expense—Equipment		10,000
	Insurance Expense		1,800
	Miscellaneous Expense		4,000
	Rent Expense		16,500
	Office Supplies Expense		300
	Utilities Expense		1,500
	Wages and Salaries Expense		40,000
	To record the closing of the expense accounts.		
31	Income Summary	22,900	
	Retained Earnings		22,900
	To record the closing of Income Summary.		
31	Retained Earnings	25,000	
	Dividends		25,000
	To record the closing of Dividends.		

Cash				Accounts Receivable		
TB	6,500			TB	4,500	
Bal.	6,500			Bal.	4,500	

Prepaid Insurance				Office Supplies		
TB	2,400	(1)	1,800	TB	500	(5)	300
Bal.	600			Bal.	200	

Equipment		
TB	50,000	

Accumulated Depreciation— Equipment		
		TB	20,000
		(2)	10,000
		Bal.	30,000

Accounts Payable		
	TB	3,000
	(4)	1,500
	Bal.	4,500

Unearned Fees			
(3)	65,000	TB	80,000
		Bal.	15,000

Capital Stock		
	TB	10,000
	Bal.	10,000

Retained Earnings			
		TB	4,400
(C)	25,000	(C)	22,900
		Bal.	2,300

Dividends			
TB	25,000	(C)	25,000
Bal.	0		

Income Summary			
		(C)	97,000
(C)	74,100		
(C)	22,900		
Bal.	0		

Fee Revenue			
		TB	32,000
		(3)	65,000
(C)	97,000		
		Bal.	0

Depreciation Expense–Equipment			
(2)	10,000		
		(C)	10,000
Bal.	0		

Insurance Expense			
(1)	1,800		
		(C)	1,800
Bal.	0		

Miscellaneous Expense			
TB	4,000		
		(C)	4,000
Bal.	0		

Rent Expense			
TB	15,000		
(4)	1,500	(C)	16,500
Bal.	0		

Office Supplies Expense			
(5)	300		
		(C)	300
Bal.	0		

Utilities Expense			
(1)	1,500		
		(C)	1,500
Bal.	0		

Wages and Salaries Expense			
TB	40,000		
		(C)	40,000
Bal.	0		

(e) *Prepare a post-closing trial balance.*

	Debits	Credits
Wildwater Expeditions, Inc.		
Post-Closing Trial Balance		
December 31, 19X3		
Cash	$ 6,500	
Accounts Receivable	4,500	
Office Supplies	200	
Prepaid Insurance	600	
Equipment	50,000	
Accumulated Depreciation—Equipment		$30,000
Accounts Payable		4,500
Unearned Fees		15,000
Capital Stock		10,000
Retained Earnings		2,300
Totals	$61,800	$61,800

(f) *Calculate profit margin.*

Profit Margin = Net Income ÷ Revenues
Profit Margin = $22,900 ÷ $97,000
Profit Margin = 23.61%

Comments: The profit margin indicates that nearly 24 cents of each dollar of revenue is profit. Conversely, we can conclude that 76 cents ($1 – 24 cents) of each dollar of revenue go to cover the expenses of the business. This seems to indicate good profit potential for Wildwater. Better information about the business's operating performance could be obtained by: (1) comparing the margin with past years to identify any trends that may appear and (2) obtaining industry profit margin data from a source such as Robert Morris Associates to learn how Wildwater compares with other businesses providing guided outdoor activities.

KEY TERMS

accounting period, *100*
accrued expenses, *107*
accrued revenue, *109*
Accumulated Depreciation, *105*
adjusted trial balance, *113*
adjusting entries, *102*
carrying amount, *105*
carrying value, *105*
closing temporary accounts
    (closing the accounts), *117*

depreciable cost, *106*
depreciation expense, *105*
estimated residual value, *106*
fiscal year, *100*
going-concern assumption, *102*
Income Summary, *117*
interim financial reports, *100*
net book value, *105*
post-closing trial balance, *121*
profit margin, *123*

temporary accounts, *117*
unadjusted trial balance, *103*
unearned revenue, *108*
useful life of an asset, *105*
valuation account (contra-asset
    account), *105*

SELF-QUIZ

LO 1 1. According to the _____ principle, we should recognize expenses in the same period as the related revenues.

LO 3 2. Key terms related to accounting periods and their definitions are presented below. Match the terms with the definitions.

__a. Accounting period
__b. Fiscal year
__c. Calendar year
__d. Interim financial reports
(1) The specific 12-month accounting period a business adopts

(2) The most popular accounting period

(3) Financial statements provided for periods shorter than a year

(4) The period of time for which we determine net income

LO 1 3. The _____ assumption states that, in the absence of evidence to the contrary, we assume that the enterprise will continue to operate as a viable business.

LO 2 4. Adjusting entries

a. Indicate the account balances are in error and corrections must be made

b. Are often made because some revenues earned have not been recorded and some expenses incurred have not been recorded

c. Are needed only if the trial balance is out of balance

d. Are normally made at the beginning of the accounting period

LO 2 5. Key terms and their definitions are listed below. Match the definitions with the key terms.

___ a. Depreciation expense

___ b. Accumulated depreciation

___ c. Prepaid expense

___ d. Adjusting entries

___ e. Accrued expenses

___ f. Unearned revenues

___ g. Accrued revenues

___ h. Adjusted trial balance

___ i. Unadjusted trial balance

(1) Entries made at the end of the accounting period to record unrecorded expenses and revenues

(2) An expense that has been paid but not yet incurred

(3) Expenses recognized for the expiration of portions of the total lifetime usefulness of long-term assets

(4) Expenses that are incurred but unpaid

(5) Trial balance taken at the end of the accounting period prior to recording adjusting entries

(6) Revenue that the business has earned but not yet received

(7) Trial balance used to prepare the financial statements

(8) Account credited when a cash payment is received for goods or services before the goods or services are delivered

(9) Account representing the cumulative depreciation of the asset since it was acquired

LO 2 6. Five types of adjusting entries are described below. Match the adjusting entry with the description.

___ a. Expiration of prepaid expenses

___ b. Recognition of depreciation expense

___ c. Accrual of unpaid expenses

___ d. Recognition of revenue previously unearned

___ e. Accrual of revenues earned

(1) Insurance Expense	XX	
Prepaid Insurance		XX
(2) Accounts Receivable	XX	
Revenue		XX
(3) Utilities Expense	XX	
Accounts Payable		XX
(4) Unearned Revenue	XX	
Revenue		XX
(5) Depr. Exp.—Equip.	XX	
Accum. Depr.—Equip.		XX

LO 2 7. The accounting year begins with a $375 balance in Office Supplies. During the year, we purchase supplies costing $600, debiting the office supplies account. At the end of the year, an inventory is taken, and office supplies costing $100 are on hand. Prepare the adjusting entry at the end of the year to record the office supplies used.

LO 2 8. On December 1, 19X3, we rent an empty warehouse to another company for the 6-month period beginning December 1 and ending May 31. We receive the entire $200 per month rent in advance and record the transaction by debiting Cash and crediting Unearned Rent Revenue for $1,200. Prepare the necessary adjusting entry on December 31, 19X3, the end of our accounting year.

LO 2 9. After accountants prepare adjusting entries, they journalize them in the _____ _____ and post the entries to the _____ _____.

LO 3 10. Financial statements are prepared from an adjusted trial balance. Each account in the adjusted trial balance will appear on the income statement or on the balance sheet.

a. Identify the types of accounts that appear on the income statement.

b. Identify the types of accounts that appear on the balance sheet.

LO 4 11. Name two types of temporary accounts.

LO 4 12. What are the balances in the temporary accounts after the closing process is complete?

a. All of these accounts will have a debit balance

b. All of these accounts will have a credit balance

c. Some of these accounts will have debit balances and others will have credit balances

d. All of these accounts will have a zero balance at the beginning and end of each accounting period.

LO 5
LO 6
13. Arrange the various steps in the accounting process in order by numbering them from 1 to 7.
- __ Prepare financial statements.
- __ Post to the general ledger.
- __ Analyze transactions.
- __ Close temporary accounts.
- __ Journalize transactions.
- __ Adjust accounts.
- __ Prepare post-closing trial balance.

LO 7 14. _____ is calculated by dividing net income by revenues.

LO 8 15. (Appendix 3-A) On December 1, 19X3, we rent an empty warehouse to another company for the 6-month period beginning December 1 and ending May 31. We receive the entire $200 per month rent in advance and record the transaction by debiting Cash and crediting Rent Revenue for $1,200. Prepare the necessary adjusting entry on December 31, 19X3, the end of our accounting year.

LO 8 16. (Appendix 3-A) During our first year of operations, we purchase $600 of supplies, debiting Office Supplies Expense. At the end of the year, an inventory count determines that $100 of office supplies are on hand. Prepare the adjusting entry at the end of the year to record the office supplies used.

LO 9 17. (Appendix 3-B) True or False? All columns on an accountant's worksheet should sum to the same total.

LO 9 18. Which of the following is not a purpose of preparing a worksheet?
a. Assist in the adjustment process
b. Help calculate net income
c. Determine if journal entries are posted to the correct account
d. Help prepare financial statements

SOLUTIONS TO SELF-QUIZ

1. matching   2. a. 4; b. 2; c. 2; d. 3   3. going concern   4. b   5. a. 3; b. 9; c. 2; d. 1; e. 4; f. 8; g. 6; h. 7; i. 5

6. a. 1; b. 5; c. 3; d. 4; e. 2

7. Office Supplies Expense	875	
Office Supplies		875
8. Unearned Rent Revenue	200	
Rent Revenue		200

9. general journal, general ledger   10. a. revenues and expenses b. assets, liabilities, and stockholders' equity

11. Revenues, expenses, and dividends   12. d   13. 5 3 1 6 2 4 7   14. Profit margin

15. Rent Revenue	1,000	
Unearned Rent Revenue		1,000
16. Office Supplies	100	
Office Supplies Expense		100

17. False

18. c

▌QUESTIONS

Q3-1 A company fails to make an adjusting entry to accrue revenue as of the end of the accounting period. Explain the effect this omission will have on the income statement, the retained earnings statement, and the balance sheet.

Q3-2 Why might a company choose to have its accounting year different from the calendar year?

Q3-3 Comment on the following statement made by a business owner: "The accountants complain about all the work involved in adjusting entries at the end of the monthly accounting period, and I'm tired of hearing it....I say if they keep the books up-to-date during the month like they are supposed to, they wouldn't have all this adjustment stuff to do at the end of the month."

Q3-4 Describe an accounting entry that recognizes an expense without decreasing an asset.

Q3-5 Describe an accounting entry that recognizes revenue without increasing assets.

Q3-6 Describe an accounting entry that involves the receipt of cash from a customer for services performed but does not involve the recognition of revenue.

Q3-7 Why is it necessary to close the temporary accounts?

Q3-8 What are the necessary steps to close temporary accounts?

Q3-9 What is the purpose of an income summary account?

Q3-10 What are the steps in the accounting cycle?

Q3-11 What is the purpose of a post-closing trial balance?

Q3-12 (Appendix 3-A) Company A records the purchase of supplies by debiting the asset account Supplies. Company B records the same transaction by debiting Supplies Expense. Which company is correct? Explain.

Q3-13 (Appendix 3-B) Explain to a new business associate why it is necessary to prepare a worksheet.

Q3-14 (Appendix 3-B) How does a worksheet assist the accountant in preparing financial statements?

EXERCISES

LO 2

E3-1 **Adjusting Entries** The balance of Cleaning Supplies at the end of the accounting period is $815. An inventory count indicates cleaning supplies costing $276 are on hand at the end of the accounting period.

REQUIRED:

Prepare the necessary adjusting entry.

LO 2

E3-2 **Adjusting Entries** Northern Airlines has a balance in Unearned Revenue of $385,000 at the end of the accounting period. Cancelled ticket information indicates that $175,000 of this $385,000 has been earned.

REQUIRED:

Prepare the necessary adjusting entry.

LO 2

E3-3 **Adjusting Entries** The only employee of White Corporation, Helen Gibson, earns $100 per day and works a 5-day week, Monday through Friday. Helen is paid every Friday for the work of that week. The last payday of the accounting period ending December 31, 19X3, is on Friday, December 27. Helen works Monday, December 30, and Tuesday, December 31.

REQUIRED:

a. Prepare the adjusting entry necessary on December 31.
b. Prepare the journal entry on Friday, January 3, 19X4, to record the payment to Helen.

LO 2

E3-4 **Adjusting Entries** On September 1, 19X4, Black Corporation signs a contract with James Farmer requiring Black to manage Farmer's rental cabins for the period from September 1, 19X4, through May 31, 19X5. Black is required to maintain the property in good condition and to provide weekly security inspections. The $450 fee for this service ($50 per month) is collected in advance. Black credits Unearned Fees.

REQUIRED:

Prepare the adjusting entry necessary on December 31, 19X4, Black's year-end.

LO 2

E3-5 **Adjusting Entries** On October 1, 19X1, Green River Supply Corporation purchases a 12-month insurance policy, which provides fire and other protection for the period

October 1, 19X1, through September 30, 19X2. The cost of the policy, $1,800, is paid in advance. Green records the transaction by debiting Prepaid Insurance.

REQUIRED:

Prepare the necessary adjusting entry on December 31, 19X1, the end of Green's accounting period.

LO 4 | **E3-6** | **Closing Entries** Prepare closing entries from the following list of account balances.

Accounts Receivable	$43,500	Utilities Expense	$13,900
Accumulated Depreciation–Equip.	21,000	Income Taxes Payable	7,600
Wages and Salaries Expense	13,200	Rent Expense	3,600
Repairs Revenue	68,500	Income Tax Expense	8,100
Dividends	12,200	Depreciation Expense–Equip.	12,900
Retained Earnings	49,900	Notes Payable	46,600

LO 4,5 | **E3-7** | **Prepare a Post-Closing Trial Balance** Prepare the closing entries and a post-closing trial balance for Reither's Travel Service, Inc. from the adjusted trial balance given below.

Reither's Travel Service, Inc.
Adjusted Trial Balance
December 31, 19X4

	Debits	Credits
Cash	$14,500	
Accounts Receivable	1,650	
Supplies	2,550	
Prepaid Insurance	3,600	
Prepaid Rent	9,000	
Equipment	18,000	
Accumulated Depreciation—Equipment		$ 1,800
Accounts Payable		5,550
Notes Payable		12,000
Unearned Revenue		6,150
Capital Stock		10,000
Retained Earnings		12,800
Dividends	1,800	
Fee Revenue		7,700
Supplies Expense	700	
Utilities Expense	900	
Wages and Salaries Expense	3,300	
Totals	$56,000	$56,000

LO 6 | **E3-8** | **The Accounting Cycle** Using a separate sheet of paper, list the following steps in the accounting cycle in the appropriate order.

Close temporary accounts.
Post to general ledger.
Adjust accounts.
Journalize transactions.
Prepare financial statements.
Analyze transactions.

LO 3, 7   **E3-9   Financial Statements**   The adjusted trial balance for Brown Bag Consulting Corporation is shown below. Brown Bag prepares financial statements on December 31; there were no capital stock transactions during the year.

		Debits	Credits
Brown Bag Consulting Corporation			
Adjusted Trial Balance			
December 31, 19X6			
Cash		$ 1,500	
Accounts Receivable		8,000	
Prepaid Insurance		600	
Office Supplies		400	
Equipment		75,000	
Accumulated Depreciation—Equipment			$ 15,000
Accounts Payable			3,000
Notes Payable			25,000
Unearned Fees			2,000
Wages and Salaries Payable			1,000
Capital Stock			10,000
Retained Earnings			22,400
Dividends		24,000	
Fee Revenue			55,000
Depreciation Expense—Equipment		5,000	
Insurance Expense		1,200	
Miscellaneous Expense		1,200	
Office Supplies Expense		500	
Wages and Salaries Expense		16,000	
Totals		$133,400	$133,400

REQUIRED:

a. Prepare an income statement.
b. Prepare a retained earnings statement.
c. Prepare a balance sheet.
d. Calculate the profit margin.

LO 8   **E3-10   Adjusting Entries (Appendix 3-A)**   Prepare the adjusting entry for Green River in E3-5, assuming it recorded the purchase of the policy by debiting Insurance Expense.

LO 9   **E3-11   Worksheet Preparation (Appendix 3-B)**   Using a separate sheet of paper, determine whether the following items from the adjusted trial balance in a worksheet should be extended to: (a) the Dr. Income Statement column, (b) the Cr. Income Statement column, (c) the Dr. Balance Sheet column, or (d) the Cr. Balance Sheet column of the worksheet.

Notes Payable	Utilities Expense
Dividends	Accounts Payable
Depreciation Expense	Prepaid Rent
Unearned Repair Revenue	Rent Expense
Accumulated Depreciation—Equipment	
Accounts Receivable	
Repair Revenue	
Wages and Salaries Payable	
Retained Earnings	

PROBLEM SET A

LO 1,2,3,7   **P3-1A   Recording and Posting Basic Transactions Including Revenues and Expenses, Adjusting Entries, Preparing Financial Statements, Distinguishing Between Cash and Accrual Basis Income**   Greg Lighthead incorporated his business on March 1, 19X3. Greg will provide sailboard lessons for a fee. The following events occurred during March:

Mar. 1 Greg purchases capital stock for $500 cash in his new corporation, Lighthead Aqua Dimensions, Inc.

2 Greg purchases 4 sailboards at $900 each on account. The boards are estimated to have a useful life of 36 months. Greg will depreciate the boards.

2 Greg signs a contract with Island Breeze Resorts to provide instruction to registered Breeze guests for March, April, and May. Greg receives $1,500 per month for the service and collects $4,500 for the 3 months as payment in advance.

3 Greg purchases liability insurance for the 3-month period of March, April, and May. The cost of the policy is $600 and is paid in cash.

15 Greg provides instruction to Joe Green (not a Breeze guest) and bills Joe $75. Payment is due April 15.

25 Greg receives a $1,000 dividend from the business since the corporation had an outstanding month.

27 Greg places an ad in the *Beach Bulletin* to be run in April and May. The cost is $100 per month, and the amount for the 2 months is paid in full.

Use the following accounts:

	Acct. No.
Cash	100
Accounts Receivable	110
Prepaid Insurance	150
Prepaid Advertising	154
Equipment	230
Accumulated Depreciation–Equipment	231
Accounts Payable	302
Unearned Fees	340
Capital Stock	519
Retained Earnings	550
Dividends	598
Fee Revenue	604
Depreciation Expense-Equipment	712
Insurance Expense	728

REQUIRED:

a. Prepare journal entries to record the transactions, using accrual basis accounting.

b. Post the transactions to the general ledger. Use T-accounts.

c. Prepare the necessary adjusting entries required at the end of March. Greg has a monthly accounting period.

d. Post the adjusting entries to the T-accounts in the general ledger.

e. Prepare an adjusted trial balance.

f. Prepare an income statement for March.

g. Prepare a retained earnings statement for March.

h. Prepare a balance sheet as of March 31.

i. Calculate Lighthead's profit margin.

LO 2   **P3-2A   Adjusting Entries**   Following is a transaction requiring an adjusting entry:

On July 1, 19X7, the Tellico Development Corporation rented the 29th and 30th floors of the Cumberland Building for the 12-month period July 1, 19X7, through June 30, 19X8. The fee of $192,000 ($16,000 per month) is paid in advance.

REQUIRED:

a. Prepare the necessary adjusting entry on the books of Tellico, assuming: (1) it recorded the transaction with a debit to Prepaid Rent, and (2) Tellico's accounting period ends on September 30, 19X7.

b. Prepare the necessary adjusting entry on the books of Cumberland, assuming: it recorded the transaction with a credit to Unearned Revenue, and Cumberland's accounting period ends December 31, 19X7.

LO 1,2,3,7   **P3-3A**   **Recording and Posting Basic Transactions Including Revenues and Expenses, Adjusting Entries, Preparing Financial Statements, Distinguishing Between Cash and Accrual Basis Income**   In 19X3, Ralph Carson resigned from the FBI to establish a business offering security and intelligence gathering services to the corporate community. The following events occurred during the first month of operations:

May 1   Ralph forms the corporation, North American Security and Intelligence (NASI) Inc., by exchanging $35,000 of his personal cash for capital stock in the corporation. The corporation issues Ralph the capital stock.

1   Ralph purchases electronic surveillance and monitoring equipment for $270,000. A cash down payment of $25,000 is made and a $245,000 note payable due in 3 years is given to the vendor. Interest of 12% is payable at the end of each year. The equipment has an expected useful life of 3 years, after which time Ralph expects it to be obsolete. Ralph will depreciate the equipment over its 3-year life.

3   Ralph leases a Mini-Storage warehouse to store the equipment. The warehouse is leased for 6 months at a cost of $50 per month. The first month's rent (prorated to $46 for May) and the last month's rent are paid in advance. Record the payment by debiting Prepaid Rent.

4   Ralph arranges to lease a van on a monthly basis, at a cost of $400 per month. Rent for May 4 through May 31 ($348) is paid.

5   Ralph leases an office from TurnKey Business Services, which includes telephone service and other office support services at a cost of $750 per month. Ralph pays the first 3 months in advance, including a full month's rent for May.

14   Ralph signs a contract with Global Defense Systems to compile intelligence information on individuals who are assigned to Global's classified Lone Wolf project. For this service, Ralph is to receive $1,000 per day. The contract starts May 15 and terminates on December 15. Global has the option to renew the contract for up to an additional 7 months. Contractual arrangements call for Global to pay each month's fees on the 15th day of the following month. For example, the fee for May (17 days at $1,000 per day) is payable on June 15.

15   Ralph hires 3 employees, all with extensive security and intelligence backgrounds, to work with him in the Global contract.

Use the following accounts:

	Acct. No.
Cash	100
Accounts Receivable	110
Prepaid Rent	152
Equipment	230
Accumulated Depreciation—Equipment	231
Interest Payable	318
Wages and Salaries Payable	346
Notes Payable—Noncurrent	408
Capital Stock	519
Retained Earnings	550
Fee Revenue	604
Depreciation Expense—Equipment	710

Interest Expense	730
Rent Expense	762
Wages and Salaries Expense	784

REQUIRED:

a. Prepare journal entries to record the transactions, using accrual basis accounting.
b. Post the transactions to the general ledger. Use T-accounts.
c. Prepare the necessary adjusting entries required at the end of the month. Ralph has a monthly accounting period. Salaries earned but unpaid for the 3 employees for May total $4,000.
d. Post the adjusting entries to the T-accounts in the general ledger.
e. Prepare an adjusted trial balance.
f. Prepare an income statement for May.
g. Prepare a retained earnings statement for May.
h. Prepare a balance sheet as of May 31.
i. Calculate NASI's profit margin.

LO 2,3,7

P3-4A **Preparing Adjusting Entries, Preparing Financial Statements Using an Adjusted Trial Balance** Presented below is a trial balance for Lynn's Window Cleaning Service, Inc. for June 30, 19X8. Lynn closes the books each month.

Lynn's Window Cleaning Service, Inc.
Unadjusted Trial Balance
June 30, 19X8

	Debits	Credits
Cash	$ 14,000	
Accounts Receivable	40,000	
Cleaning Supplies	6,000	
Prepaid Insurance	3,000	
Prepaid Rent	2,000	
Equipment	90,000	
Accumulated Depreciation–Equipment		$ 18,000
Office Equipment	24,000	
Accumulated Depreciation–Office Equipment		6,000
Unearned Revenue		5,000
Accounts Payable		41,000
Capital Stock		10,000
Retained Earnings		84,000
Dividends	3,000	
Revenue		60,000
Advertising Expense	400	
Professional Fees Expense	1,000	
Telephone Expense	350	
Utilities Expense	250	
Wages and Salaries Expense	40,000	
Totals	$224,000	$224,000

Information for adjusting entries as of June 30, 19X8 follows:

(1) Windows cleaned in June but not billed, $4,000.
(2) The $5,000 balance in Unearned Revenue represents an advance payment by Capital Enterprises received on June 1, 19X8, for the cleaning of 500 windows facing Broadway on the north side of Capital's office building. Lynn's supervisor tells her "about 300" of these windows have been cleaned.

(3) Lynn charges the asset account, Cleaning Supplies, for purchases of the various solvents used in cleaning. An inventory was taken by Lynn's supervisor who estimated that there were $2,000 of cleaning supplies on hand at June 30.

(4) On June 1, a $3,000 premium was paid on a comprehensive insurance policy covering the period June 1, 19X8, through November 30, 19X8.

(5) On January 1, 19X8, 9 months' rent, at $500 per month, was paid in advance. The balance in Prepaid Rent represents the prepaid rent remaining at the beginning of the June accounting period.

(6) The equipment is depreciated over its estimated 5-year life.

(7) Office equipment is depreciated over its estimated 10-year life.

(8) Lynn's accounting firm charges $1,000 per month for monthly accounting services, payable at the beginning of the month. In addition to the monthly fee, paid on June 5 for the month of June, the firm advises Lynn that it has accumulated 50 billable hours of work during June on a Tax Court Case involving Lynn's 19X6 business tax returns. The firm's rate is $75 per hour.

(9) Wages owed to employees at June 30, $1,000.

The business uses the following accounts:

	Acct. No.
Cash	100
Accounts Receivable	110
Cleaning Supplies	132
Prepaid Insurance	150
Prepaid Rent	152
Equipment	230
Accumulated Depreciation–Equipment	231
Office Equipment	242
Accumulated Depreciation—Office Equipment	243
Accounts Payable	302
Unearned Revenue	342
Wages and Salaries Payable	346
Capital Stock	519
Retained Earnings	550
Dividends	598
Revenue	600
Advertising Expense	700
Cleaning Supplies Expense	703
Depreciation Expense–Equipment	712
Depreciation Expense–Office Equipment	716
Insurance Expense	728
Professional Fees Expense	750
Rent Expense	762
Telephone Expense	775
Utilities Expense	780
Wages and Salaries Expense	784

REQUIRED:

a. Create a general ledger by opening T-accounts and entering the June 30 unadjusted balances in the accounts.

b. Prepare adjusting entries. To save time, instead of entering the adjustments in the general journal, which is the proper procedure, enter them directly in the T-accounts. Code each adjustment with the number corresponding to the adjustment information. Add T-accounts as necessary.

c. Prepare an adjusted trial balance as of June 30, 19X8.

d. Prepare an income statement for the month of June.

e. Prepare a retained earnings statement for the month of June.

f. Prepare a balance sheet as of June 30, 19X8.
g. Calculate the business's profit margin for June and evaluate the operating performance for June. Discuss what information (that is not given in this problem) you might need to perform the evaluation.

LO 3,4,5   **P3-5A**   **Prepare Financial Statements Using an Adjusted Trial Balance**   An adjusted trial balance for the Atlanta Lawn Service, Inc. is presented below. Atlanta's fiscal year ends December 31.

Atlanta Lawn Service, Inc. Adjusted Trial Balance December 31, 19X4		
	Debits	*Credits*
Cash	$ 35,000	
Accounts Receivable	175,000	
Prepaid Insurance	5,000	
Maintenance Supplies	20,000	
Land	30,000	
Buildings	250,000	
Accumulated Depreciation—Buildings		$ 100,000
Equipment	80,000	
Accumulated Depreciation—Equipment		50,000
Delivery Equipment	100,000	
Accumulated Depreciation—Delivery Equipment		60,000
Accounts Payable		30,000
Interest Payable		2,000
Notes Payable		200,000
Unearned Revenue		25,000
Wages and Salaries Payable		4,000
Capital Stock		10,000
Retained Earnings		79,000
Dividends	50,000	
Revenue		900,000
Professional Fees Expense	24,000	
Advertising Expense	30,000	
Depreciation Expense—Buildings	10,000	
Depreciation Expense—Equipment	8,000	
Depreciation Expense—Delivery Equipment	20,000	
Insurance Expense	3,000	
Miscellaneous Expense	10,000	
Supplies Expense	200,000	
Telephone Expense	6,000	
Utilities Expense	4,000	
Wages and Salaries Expense	400,000	
Totals	$1,460,000	$1,460,000

REQUIRED:

a. Prepare an income statement for the year ended December 31, 19X4.
b. Prepare a retained earnings statement for the year ended December 31, 19X4.
c. Prepare a balance sheet as of December 31, 19X4.
d. Explain why the income statement and retained earnings statement are dated for a designated period of time (the year) ending on December 31, while the balance sheet is dated for a point in time (December 31).

e. You were asked to prepare the statements in this order: income statement, retained earnings statement, and balance sheet. Is this order necessary, or could you prepare the balance sheet or retained earnings statement first? Explain.

f. Prepare the closing entries from the adjusted trial balance. What accounts remain open?

g. Prepare a post-closing trial balance for December 31, 19X4.

LO 3   **P3-6A   Closing Entries**   A listing of account balances is given below:

Accounts Receivable	$27,900	Wages and Salaries Expense	$29,900
Accumulated Deprec.—Bldgs.	11,000	Sales Taxes Payable	6,700
Insurance Expense	10,200	Rent Expense	5,600
Revenue	98,600	Sales Tax Expense	18,700
Dividends	9,200	Deprec. Expense—Bldgs.	12,900
Retained Earnings	78,100	Wages and Salaries Payable	6,600
Miscellaneous Revenue	7,900	Utilities Expense	5,300
Unearned Revenue	44,440	Supplies Expense	13,900

REQUIRED:

Prepare closing entries from the list of account balances.

LO 7   **P3-7A   Adjusting Entries (Appendix 3-A)**   Four account balances from the December 31, 19X6, general ledger of Executive Miniature Golf, Inc. are presented below. These accounts have not been adjusted.

	Debits	*Credits*
Maintenance Supplies	– 0 –	
Maintenance Supplies Expense	$17,500	
Unearned Fees		– 0 –
Fee Revenue		$258,000

Dae Sung Lee, the putting pro and manager of Executive, knows you are taking a college accounting course and asks you to help him make adjusting entries for the supplies and revenue accounts. His bookkeeper is out sick, and these accounts are the only ones that have not been adjusted. You make some inquiries and learn that: (1) the supplies inventory on December 31 is "about $5,000" and that (2) $18,000 of the green fees tickets sold have not been presented for play. Dae Sung states that these tickets are typically purchased as gifts and most of them will be used in the spring.

REQUIRED:

a. Prepare the necessary adjusting entry for the supplies.

b. Suppose that Executive charged (debited) Maintenance Supplies when purchasing supplies, instead of its current procedure of charging Maintenance Supplies Expense. Prepare the appropriate adjusting entry on December 31.

c. Prepare the necessary adjusting entry for revenue.

d. Suppose that Executive credits Unearned Fees when collecting cash for green fees tickets. Prepare the appropriate adjusting entry on December 31.

e. Which account would you recommend be debited for the purchase of supplies? Explain. Which account would you recommend be credited for the collection of green fees tickets? Explain.

LO 9   **P3-8A   Preparing a Worksheet**   The trial balance for Dara's Services International, Inc. at December 31, 19X5, is presented on the next page:

Additional Information:

(1) A count of supplies revealed that $3,900 remained on hand as of December 31.

(2) Dara purchased a 2-year insurance policy for $1,200 on January 1, 19X5.

Dara's Services International, Inc. Trial Balance December 31, 19X5		
	Debits	Credits
Cash	$ 29,100	
Accounts Receivable	3,300	
Office Supplies	5,100	
Prepaid Insurance	1,200	
Prepaid Rent	18,000	
Equipment	36,000	
Accumulated Depreciation—Equipment		$ 3,600
Accounts Payable		11,100
Unearned Revenue		12,300
Notes Payable—Noncurrent		24,000
Capital Stock		10,000
Retained Earnings		29,600
Dividends	3,600	
Fee Revenue		14,400
Wages and Salaries Expense	6,600	
Utilities Expense	2,100	
Totals	$105,000	$105,000

(3) Paid 2 year's rent of $18,000 in advance on January 1, 19X5.

(4) The equipment was purchased on January 1, 19X4. The expected life of the equipment was 10 years at the time of purchase.

(5) Dara's Services International, Inc. was paid $12,300 on December 5 for services to be performed in December and January. On December 31, $9,600 of these services have been performed.

REQUIRED:

a. Prepare a worksheet similar to Illustration 3-15.

b. Prepare an income statement for the year ended December 31, 19X5.

c. Prepare a balance sheet as of December 31, 19X5.

d. Journalize adjusting entries for 19X5.

e. Journalize closing entries for 19X5.

f. Prepare a post-closing trial balance.

g. Calculate the profit margin as of December 31, 19X5.

LO 9

P3-9A   Preparing a Worksheet   The trial balance for Carol's Consulting, Inc. at January 31, 19X3, and additional information follow:

Additional Information:

(1) A count of remaining supplies revealed that $7,580 remained on hand as of January 31.

(2) Prepaid rent of $4,800 expired during the month.

(3) The January 31 balance of Prepaid Insurance should be $21,000.

(4) Depreciation for one month on the office furniture is $875.

(5) One-third of the balance of the unearned fees account was not earned during the month.

(6) Salary expense of $1,800 should be accrued at the end of January.

REQUIRED:

a. Prepare a worksheet similar to the one in Illustration 3-15.

b. Prepare an income statement for the month ended January 31, 19X3.

Carol's Consulting, Inc. Trial Balance January 31, 19X3		
	Debits	Credits
Cash	$ 67,720	
Accounts Receivable	55,900	
Office Supplies	9,010	
Prepaid Rent	12,000	
Prepaid Insurance	28,000	
Office Equipment	84,000	
Accumulated Depreciation—Office Equipment		$ 31,500
Accounts Payable		14,600
Unearned Fees		12,000
Notes Payable—Noncurrent		100,000
Capital Stock		10,000
Retained Earnings		35,330
Fee Revenue		130,000
Miscellaneous Expense	11,400	
Rent Expense	4,800	
Utilities Expense	6,600	
Wages and Salaries Expense	54,000	
Totals	$333,430	$333,430

c. Prepare a balance sheet as of January 31, 19X3.
d. Journalize adjusting entries for January.
e. Journalize closing entries for January.
f. Prepare a post-closing trial balance.

PROBLEM SET B

LO 1,2,3,7   **P3-1B**   **Recording and Posting Basic Transactions Including Revenues and Expenses, Adjusting Entries, Preparing Financial Statements, Distinguishing Between Cash and Accrual Basis Income**   Janet Lopez incorporates her business on September 1, 19X7. Janet's business will provide automobile driver training. The following events occurred during September:

Sept. 1   Janet purchased capital stock in Safeway Driver Training, Inc. for $15,000 cash.

    1   Janet leases 2 automobiles specially equipped for driver instruction. The cars are leased on a monthly basis, and the rent for each car is $450 per month. Janet pays the first 3 months' rent in advance. Record the transaction with a debit to Prepaid Rent.

    1   Janet purchases comprehensive liability insurance for the period September 1, 19X7, through August 31, 19X8. The annual premium, $3,000, is paid on September 1.

    2   Janet obtains a probationary license and certification to provide driver training from the state for the period September 1, 19X7, through August 31, 19X8. The annual fee is $600 and is paid in advance on September 2.

    3   Janet signs a contract with a local private high school to provide driving instruction for the school's students. There are 50 students involved, and the instruction will be started in September and completed by December. The contract calls for each student to receive 4 hours of hands-on driver training and 2 hours of classroom training. The fee for providing the instruction is $15,000, paid in advance on September 3. (50 students, 6 hrs. each, $50 per hr.)

Sept. 4 Janet hires 2 driving instructors. Each instructor will be paid a flat rate of $12 per instructional hour.

30 Instructors are paid for 100 instructional hours provided during September. (Note: This information is also used to prepare the entry to adjust Unearned Fees in Requirement *c*.)

30 Janet receives a $2,000 cash dividend from the business.

Use the following accounts:

	Acct. No.
Cash	100
Prepaid Insurance	150
Prepaid License	151
Prepaid Rent	152
Unearned Fees	340
Capital Stock	519
Retained Earnings	550
Dividends	598
Fee Revenue	604
Insurance Expense	728
License Expense	733
Rent Expense	762
Wages and Salaries Expense	784

REQUIRED:

a. Prepare journal entries to record the transactions, using accrual basis accounting.
b. Post the transactions to the general ledger. Use T-accounts.
c. Prepare the necessary adjusting entries required at the end of September.
d. Post the adjusting entries to the T-accounts in the general ledger.
e. Prepare an adjusted trial balance.
f. Prepare an income statement for September.
g. Prepare a retained earnings statement for September.
h. Prepare a balance sheet as of September 30.
i. Calculate Safeway's profit margin.

LO 2   **P3-2B   Adjusting Entries**   Below is a transaction requiring an adjusting entry:

On November 1, 19X2, Ocoee Rafting Adventures (ORA), Inc., entered into a contract with Ducktown Protection Services. ORA paid Ducktown $24,000 to provide weekend parking and traffic management on the Ocoee River. The period of the contract is November 1, 19X2, through October 31, 19X3.

REQUIRED:

a. Prepare the necessary adjusting entry on the books of ORA, assuming: (1) it recorded the transaction with a debit to Prepaid Professional Fees and (2) ORA's accounting period ends on December 31, 19X2.
b. Prepare the necessary adjusting entry on the books of Ducktown Protection Services, assuming: (1) it recorded the transaction with a credit to Unearned Fees and (2) Ducktown's accounting period ends on March 31, 19X3.

LO 1,2,3,7   **P3-3B   Recording and Posting Basic Transactions Including Revenues and Expenses, Adjusting Entries, Preparing Financial Statements, Distinguishing Between Cash and Accrual Basis of Income**   David Harris incorporated his carpet installation and cleaning business. The following events occur during April 19X3, the first month of operations:

Apr. 1 David purchased for cash $6,000 of capital stock of Reliable Carpet Services, Inc., a newly formed corporation.

1 David purchases 2 carpet shampoo machines at a cost of $1,800 each. The machines have an estimated useful life of 3 years. A cash down payment of $100 is made, and the balance is due in 30 days.

1 David leases a van at a rate of $400 per month and pays the first 3 months in advance.

2 David purchases carpet installation tools. The tools cost $2,700 and have an estimated useful life of 3 years. A cash down payment of $800 is paid, and the balance is due in 90 days.

3 David purchases cleaning solvents and supplies on account. The cost is $500, and payment is due in 30 days.

15 During the first 15 days of April, David installed carpet in 2 houses for Executive Home Builders. The $2,500 fee is billed to Executive.

25 David cleaned the carpet of Lynn Bowman and collected the fee in cash, $100.

29 David received $1,500 from Executive Home Builders as a partial payment of the amount owed for the April 1-15 work.

30 David received cash dividends of $1,000 since the business had a good month.

30 David paid the $3,500 balance due on the April 1 purchase of the shampoo machines.

Use the following accounts:

	Acct. No.
Cash	100
Accounts Receivable	110
Cleaning Supplies	132
Prepaid Rent	152
Equipment	230
Accumulated Depreciation–Equipment	231
Accounts Payable	302
Capital Stock	519
Retained Earnings	550
Dividends	598
Revenue	600
Cleaning Supplies Expense	703
Depreciation Expense–Equipment	712
Rent Expense	762

REQUIRED:

a. Prepare journal entries to record the transactions, using accrual basis accounting.

b. Post the transactions to the general ledger. Use T-accounts.

c. Prepare the necessary adjusting entries required at the end of the month. Supplies on hand on April 30 total $100.

d. Post the adjusting entries to the T-accounts in the general ledger. Supplies on hand April 30 total $100.

e. Prepare an adjusted trial balance.

f. Prepare an income statement for the month of April.

g. Prepare a retained earnings statement for April.

h. Prepare a balance sheet as of April 30, 19X3.

i. Calculate Reliable's profit margin.

LO 2,3   **P3-4B**   **Preparing Adjusting Entries, Preparing Financial Statements Using an Adjusted Trial Balance**   Presented on the next page is a trial balance for Longview Bicycle Repair, Inc. for March 31, 19X5. Longview closes the books each month.

Information for adjusting entries for March 31, 19X5, follows:

(1) Repair work performed in March but not billed, $1,000.

(2) The $2,000 balance in Unearned Revenue represents an advance payment by Smoky Mountain Bike Rentals. The payment was made March 1 and requires Longview to

Longview Bicycle Repair, Inc. Unadjusted Trial Balance March 31, 19X5		
	Debits	Credits
Cash	$ 1,500	
Accounts Receivable	4,000	
Maintenance Supplies	9,000	
Prepaid Insurance	600	
Prepaid Rent	900	
Equipment	18,000	
Accumulated Depreciation–Equipment		$ 3,000
Unearned Revenue		2,000
Accounts Payable		1,000
Capital Stock		10,000
Retained Earnings		15,000
Dividends	900	
Repairs Revenue		6,000
Miscellaneous Expense	500	
Professional Fees Expense	200	
Telephone Expense	100	
Utilities Expense	300	
Wages and Salaries Expense	1,000	
Totals	$37,000	$37,000

perform routine periodic maintenance on Smoky's rental fleet of mountain bikes for the 10-month period March 1 through December 31.

(3) Maintenance supplies inventory on March 31 is $7,000.

(4) On March 1, the premium was paid on a 6-month comprehensive insurance policy covering the period March 1 through August 31.

(5) On March 1, 3 months' rent at $300 per month was paid in advance.

(6) Equipment has an estimated life of 6 years.

(7) Wages owed to employees at March 31, $1,500.

REQUIRED:

a. Create a general ledger by opening T-accounts and entering the March 31 unadjusted balances in the accounts. Add any accounts needed to complete the adjusting entries.

b. Prepare adjusting entries. To save time, instead of entering the adjustments in the general journal, which is the proper procedure, enter them directly in the T-accounts. Code each adjustment with the number corresponding to the adjustment information. Add T-accounts as necessary.

c. Prepare an adjusted trial balance as of March 31, 19X5.

d. Prepare an income statement for the month of March.

e. Prepare a retained earnings statement for the month of March.

f. Prepare a balance sheet as of March 31, 19X5.

g. Calculate Longview's profit margin for March and evaluate Longview's operating performance. Discuss what information (that is not given in this problem) you might need to perform the evaluation.

LO 3,4,5   **P3-5B   Prepare Financial Statements Using an Adjusted Trial Balance**   An adjusted trial balance for Bluegrass Charter Flights, Inc. is presented below. Bluegrass' fiscal year ends December 31.

Bluegrass Charter Flights, Inc.
Adjusted Trial Balance
December 31, 19X9

	Debits	Credits
Cash	$ 12,000	
Accounts Receivable	18,000	
Office Supplies	1,000	
Prepaid Insurance	10,000	
Equipment	500,000	
Accumulated Depreciation–Equipment		$ 200,000
Office Equipment	25,000	
Accumulated Depreciation–Office Equipment		10,000
Accounts Payable		20,000
Interest Payable		30,000
Notes Payable		100,000
Unearned Fees		20,000
Wages and Salaries Payable		5,000
Capital Stock		10,000
Retained Earnings		137,000
Dividends	50,000	
Fee Revenue		500,000
Depreciation Expense–Equipment	50,000	
Depreciation Expense–Office Equipment	5,000	
Fuel Expense	100,000	
Insurance Expense	30,000	
Maintenance Expense	50,000	
Miscellaneous Expense	3,000	
Professional Fees Expense	15,000	
Rent Expense	10,000	
Telephone Expense	2,000	
Utilities Expense	1,000	
Wages and Salaries Expense	150,000	
	$1,032,000	$1,032,000

REQUIRED:

a. Prepare an income statement for the year ended December 31, 19X9.

b. Prepare a retained earnings statement for the year ended December 31, 19X9.

c. Prepare a balance sheet as of December 31, 19X9.

d. Explain why the income statement and retained earnings statement are dated for a designated period of time (the year) ending December 31, while the balance sheet is for a point in time (December 31).

e. You were asked to prepare the statements in this order: income statement, retained earnings statement, and balance sheet. Is this order necessary, or could you prepare the balance sheet or retained earnings statement first? Explain.

f. Prepare closing entries from the adjusted trial balance. What accounts remain open?

g. Prepare a post-closing trial balance for December 31, 19X9.

LO 4   **P3-6B**   **Closing Entries**   A listing of account balances is given below:

Equipment	$ 45,700
Accumulated Deprec.—Equip.	16,000
Wages and Salaries Payable	1,100
Unearned Fees	88,600

Dividends	19,800
Retained Earnings	66,200
Miscellaneous Revenue	9,700
Fee Revenue	114,440
Wages and Salaries Expense	32,400
Rent Payable	7,600
Insurance Expense	5,500
Insurance Premium Payable	16,700
Deprec. Expense—Equip.	10,900
Prepaid Rent	16,600
Utilities Expense	9,700
Supplies Expense	18,800

REQUIRED:

Prepare closing entries from the list of account balances.

LO 8   **P3-7B   Adjusting Entries (Appendix 3-A)**   Four account balances from the December 31, 19X2, general ledger of Glendale Salvage and Demolition, Inc., are presented below. These accounts have not been adjusted.

	Debits	*Credits*
Prepaid Insurance	– 0 –	
Insurance Expense	$24,000	
Unearned Fees		– 0 –
Fee Revenue		$600,000

Mike Steel, the manager, asks you to help him adjust the insurance and fees accounts. You learn that the balance in Insurance Expense is from the payment of the premium for a 1-year liability policy covering the period October 1, 19X2, through September 30, 19X3. Included in the balance of Fee Revenue is an entry for recording the advance payment of $100,000 to demolish a warehouse the state condemned because of asbestos standards. Mike expects the demolition to take place in March 19X3. All other demolition fees have been earned.

REQUIRED:

a. Prepare the necessary adjusting entry for the insurance.
b. Suppose that Glendale charged (debited) Prepaid Insurance when recording the premium payment, instead of its current practice of debiting Insurance Expense. Prepare the appropriate adjusting entry on December 31.
c. Prepare the necessary adjusting entry for the fee accounts.
d. Suppose that Glendale credits Unearned Fees when collecting demolition fees. Prepare the appropriate adjusting entry for December 31.

LO 9   **P3-8B   Preparing a Worksheet**   The trial balance for Travel Time, Inc. at December 31, 19X6, is presented on the next page.

Additional Information:
(1) Used $1,600 of office supplies during 19X6.
(2) Travel Time purchased an 18-month insurance policy on January 1, 19X6, for $3,600.
(3) Paid 1 year's rent in advance on January 1, 19X6.
(4) The equipment was purchased on January 1, 19X5. The expected useful life was 10 years at the time of purchase.
(5) Collected $2,100 of travel deposits in 19X6 for trips to be taken in 19X7. The deposits were credited to the revenue account.

Travel Time, Inc. Trial Balance December 31, 19X6		
	Debits	Credits
Cash	$ 9,100	
Accounts Receivable	13,800	
Office Supplies	4,800	
Prepaid Insurance	3,600	
Prepaid Rent	24,000	
Equipment	36,500	
Accumulated Depreciation—Equipment		$ 3,650
Accounts Payable		11,300
Notes Payable—Noncurrent		30,600
Capital Stock		10,000
Retained Earnings		12,150
Dividends	2,800	
Revenue		36,800
Utilities Expense	1,600	
Wages and Salaries Expense	8,300	
Totals	$104,500	$104,500

REQUIRED:

a. Prepare a worksheet similar to the one in the Illustration 3-15.
b. Prepare an income statement for the year ended December 31, 19X6.
c. Prepare a balance sheet as of December 31, 19X6.
d. Journalize adjusting entries for 19X6.
e. Journalize closing entries for 19X6.
f. Prepare a post-closing trial balance.
g. Calculate the profit margin as of December 31, 19X6.

LO 9

P3-9B **Preparing a Worksheet** The trial balance for Koch Services, Inc. at January 31, 19X7, is presented on the next page.

Additional Information:

(1) A count of office supplies revealed that $12,300 remained on hand as of January 31.
(2) One-third of the prepaid rent expired during the month.
(3) The amount of $15,100 of prepaid insurance remained as of January 31.
(4) Depreciation for the month on the office equipment is $825.
(5) One-half of the balance of the Unearned Fees account was earned during the month.
(6) Salary expense of $4,100 should be accrued at the end of January.

REQUIRED:

a. Prepare a worksheet similar to the one in Illustration 3-15.
b. Prepare an income statement for the month ended January 31, 19X7.
c. Prepare a balance sheet as of January 31, 19X7.
d. Journalize and post adjusting entries for January.
e. Journalize and post closing entries for January.
f. Prepare a post-closing trial balance.

Koch Services, Inc. Trial Balance January 31, 19X7		
	Debits	*Credits*
Cash	$ 56,350	
Accounts Receivable	41,600	
Office Supplies	17,900	
Prepaid Rent	6,600	
Prepaid Insurance	18,600	
Office Equipment	99,000	
Accum. Depr.–Office Equipment		$ 9,900
Accounts Payable		17,600
Unearned Fees		21,960
Notes Payable–Noncurrent		100,000
Wages and Salaries Payable		3,000
Capital Stock		10,000
Retained Earnings		41,990
Fee Revenue		108,300
Miscellaneous Expense	10,700	
Rent Expense	11,600	
Utilities Expense	4,900	
Wages and Salaries Expense	45,500	
Totals	$312,750	$312,750

CRITICAL THINKING AND COMMUNICATING

C3-1

Using Generally Accepted Accounting Principles, which requires accrual accounting, Feldon Corporation reported a quarterly loss in excess of $1 billion for the first quarter of 19X5.

REQUIRED:

a. Does this indicate that Feldon's cash disbursements exceeded cash receipts by $1 billion during the first quarter? Discuss.

b. Assuming Feldon had no contributions from the stockholders during the first quarter and there were no dividends during this period, what impact will this loss have on Feldon's stockholders' equity? Discuss.

c. Does this loss indicate that Feldon was unable to pay its bills during the first quarter? Would a creditor be willing to loan Feldon money, after the reporting of the loss? Discuss.

d. How will this loss impact Feldon's balance sheet? Discuss.

e. Is it possible that Feldon could have shown a net income under cash basis accounting for the first quarter? Discuss.

C3-2

You have been employed as the chief accountant of the Dellwood Property Management Corporation for about 1 year. Sandra Dellwood owns and manages the corporation. You have a good professional relationship with Sandra, a liberal arts major in college who has not had a course in accounting; and she has come to trust your judgment in financial matters related to the company's operations.

A month ago, Sandra signed a $30,000 contract with the Bridgetown Apartments to manage a 250-unit complex. The contract is for 6 months, starting on December 1 and concluding on May 31, calling for a $5,000 per month management fee for the 6-month period. Dellwood's responsibility is to collect monthly rents, arrange for vacant apartments to be cleaned, and rent vacant apartments. The $30,000 was paid to Dellwood in advance on December 1. You recorded the receipt by debiting Cash and crediting Unearned Fees. You are now in the process of preparing financial statements for the year ended December 31 and have submitted your proposed adjusting entries to Sandra for her review. Included in your adjusting entries is an entry debiting Unearned Fees and crediting Fee Revenue for $5,000.

Sandra returns your adjustments with a note requesting you to recognize the entire $30,000 as earned. You meet with her to discuss the request, and she says: "We have the money; we won't have to refund it; so, we may as well recognize it as income. It will improve our income statement and balance sheet, and I'm applying for a loan at the bank. The loan officer, William O'Day, is an old friend and has already approved the loan. However, he suggested that we go ahead and classify the contract as income because we have the cash, and he is confident that we won't have to give it back. The improved financial statements will ensure that the senior vice-president on the bank's loan board won't question the loan."

REQUIRED:

a. Explain the effect that Sandra's reclassification suggestion would have on the income statement, the retained earnings statement, and the balance sheet.
b. How would you, as the chief accountant, respond to Sandra's suggestion?

C3-3   Select two corporations whose operations and products are familiar and obtain their financial statement information (generally available in a library, from a stock brokerage company, or from the corporation itself).

REQUIRED:

a. Compare the two corporation's income statements, retained earnings statements, and balance sheets for account titles and statement formats. How are they alike? How do they differ?
b. Compute each corporation's profit margin. Is it possible to compare these corporations' profit margins and come to confident conclusions? What additional information would be helpful?
c. Both corporations made adjusting entries in their preparation of the financial statement. List the types of adjustments each corporation probably made and why. Are there any special adjustments either corporation made due to its unique line of business?
d. Communicate your findings in a brief written memo and share these memos in class through small group discussions.

C3-4 The financial statements of J.C. Penney Company, Inc. are in Appendix B. Locate Penney's income statements.

REQUIRED:

a. Calculate Penney's profit margins for 1993, 1992, and 1991.
b. Comment on the direction and magnitude of the changes in the profit margins for the 3-year period.

CHAPTER 4

Sales Revenue and Cost of Goods Sold

Robert Good plans to retire at the end of the current business year on December 31, 19X2. He has owned and operated Good's Campus Books, Inc., for 30 years but has arranged to sell it to his manager, Sheila Pell. Sheila has agreed to pay a price equal to 12 times the business's average net income for the last 5 years. Robert believes this is a fair arrangement, but he is worried because the income for the year just ended was disappointing. He wants to know what went wrong and how to turn things around for his last year. His retirement income depends on receiving a favorable price for his business. How can Robert diagnose the problem and focus his attention on the most important ways to improve his business's profitability?

In this chapter, we introduce the components of income of a merchandising business, the concept of gross profit, and a specially formatted income statement designed to reflect the way merchandising businesses earn income. After we cover the components of income and the preparation of financial statements of merchandising businesses, you will see how Robert can use financial statement information in planning to maximize the bookstore's income in his last year before retirement.

1. Describe a multistep income statement and explain why a merchandising business uses it.
2. Record gross sales, sales returns and allowances, and sales discounts and calculate net sales for a merchandising business.
3. Record gross purchases, purchases returns and allowances, purchases discounts, and transportation costs for purchased goods and calculate cost of goods purchased.
4. Describe the periodic method of inventory valuation, contrast it with the perpetual method, and calculate cost of goods sold under the periodic inventory method.
5. Describe the operating expenses of a merchandising business and distinguish between selling expenses and general and administrative expenses.
6. Prepare the adjusting entries for a merchandising business using the periodic inventory method.
7. Prepare the financial statements of a merchandising business, using the adjusted trial balance.
8. Prepare closing entries for a merchandising business.
9. Calculate the cost of goods sold and gross profit ratios and use them to assess profitability.
10. Distinguish between the gross and net methods of recording purchases (Appendix 4-A).

MERCHANDISING OPERATIONS AND INCOME STATEMENTS

Service businesses earn their income by providing services to their customers for fees or commissions. The income statement of any business should reflect the nature of its operations—how it earns income. Service businesses have very straightforward income statements containing only three principal parts: revenues, expenses, and net income. In contrast, merchandising businesses earn their income by buying products from suppliers and then selling those products to their customers.

LO 1

Describe a multistep income statement and explain why a merchandising business uses it.

Merchandising Operations

Some merchandising businesses engage in retail trade, selling products directly to consumers. Grocery stores, drugstores, bookstores, record stores, and consumer electronics stores are examples. Another type of merchandising business sells products only on a wholesale basis to other businesses. For example, industrial electronics dealers buy and sell the basic components used to manufacture radios, televisions, stereos, and other appliances. Still another type of merchandising business sells both to other businesses and to consumers. Lumber yards and auto parts dealers are good examples in this category.

Merchandising Income Statements

Since merchandising businesses earn revenues primarily by selling products to customers, they report their expenses in two main categories: the cost of the goods sold and operating expenses. The condensed, multistep income statement of Good's Campus Books, Inc., in Illustration 4-1 reflects this format.

ILLUSTRATION 4-1 Income Statement of Good's Campus Books, Inc.

Good's Campus Books, Inc. Income Statement For the Year Ended December 31, 19X1	
Net sales	$697,910
Less: Cost of goods sold	447,532
Gross profit	$250,378
Less: Operating expenses	142,728
Income before income taxes	$107,650
Less: Income tax expense	23,200
Net income	$ 84,450

In the first step of the **multistep income statement**, we display the net sales (revenue) and the cost of the goods sold and calculate gross profit. Net sales consists of the total amounts a business receives or expects to be collected for the period's sales of merchandise to customers. **Cost of goods sold** represents the total purchase costs of the goods the business provides to customers for the period. It includes the purchase costs and any costs incidental to the purchase of the goods from suppliers—e.g., the cost of shipping from the supplier's location. The components and calculation of both net sales and cost of goods sold are covered in a later section of this chapter. **Gross profit** is the difference between net sales and the cost of goods sold. Good's Campus Books, Inc., earned a gross profit for 19X1 of $250,378, the difference between net sales (revenue) of $697,910 and cost of goods sold of $447,532. *Gross profit may be interpreted as the portion of net sales that is available to cover operating expenses and income taxes and to produce a profit or net income.*

In the second step of the multistep income statement, we subtract operating expenses from gross profit to derive income before taxes. **Operating expenses** consist of all the expenses of running the business for a period, *other than the cost of goods sold and income taxes.* Operating expenses include salaries, wages, depreciation, rent, and utilities expenses.

In the third step of the multistep income statement, we subtract income tax expense from income before income taxes. Good's Campus Books, Inc., earned net income of $84,450, because it generated a gross profit of $250,378 in 19X1 and incurred operating expenses of $142,728 and income tax expense of $23,200.[1] Illustration 4-2 graphically shows the logical flow of the multistep income statement.

Illustrations 4-1 and 4-2 give you a simple, straightforward picture of the merchandising business's income components. Actually, several important types of transactions make up both net sales and cost of goods sold. In addition, you will find that calculating cost of goods sold is a challenge when the business uses the periodic inventory method (defined later in the chapter). In the follow-

---

[1] A single-step presentation of the same income statement would appear as follows:

Net sales	$697,910
Less: Expenses	613,460
Net income	$ 84,450

ILLUSTRATION 4-2 Multistep Income Statement

ing sections, we acquaint you with the major types of merchandising transactions *in the order they appear in the income statement*—first, net sales; then, cost of goods sold. By learning to account for these transactions and learning to calculate net sales and cost of goods sold, you will better understand merchandising operations and be prepared to analyze the accounting information of merchandising businesses.

Record gross sales, sales returns and allowances, and sales discounts and calculate net sales for a merchandising business.

NET SALES

The term *net* in *net sales* implies that offsetting components make up the overall figure. This is the case. Several transaction components make up the net sales figure, as shown in Illustration 4-3.

ILLUSTRATION 4-3 Calculation of Net Sales

Good's Campus Books, Inc. Income Statement (Partial)		
Gross sales		$736,400
Less: Sales returns and allowances	$27,444	
Sales discounts	11,046	38,490
Net sales		$697,910

Notice that the bottom figure in Illustration 4-3, net sales, is the same number as the net sales figure of Illustration 4-1. Illustration 4-3 shows the detail of how we derive a net sales figure. **Gross sales** equals the sum of the prices of all goods a business sells in a period. **Net sales** equals gross sales less sales returns and allowances and sales discounts. Net sales represents the revenue Good's Campus Books, Inc. actually earned.

The merchandising business does not earn the full sales price for every sales transaction. Sometimes the merchandise sold does not satisfy the customer or is found defective, resulting in sales returns. In a **sales return** transaction, the customer returns goods previously purchased, and the seller gives a refund of the price paid. When a business gives a refund to a customer, it does not earn the revenue originally recorded.

In other cases, the goods sold are *basically* acceptable, but the customer discovers minor flaws in them. The customer often agrees to keep the goods if the business concedes to a reduction in price. A reduction in price given because merchandise is partially flawed is called a **sales allowance**. Sales allowances reduce the amount of the original price actually earned.

Additionally, in the case of credit sales, a merchant frequently offers reductions in payments on purchases to its customers to induce them to pay early. Reductions in payments to induce early payments are called **sales discounts**.

A merchandising business records sales, sales returns and allowances, and sales discounts in separate accounts as transactions occur. Net sales is not recorded directly, but is calculated in the income statement from the other components (as we demonstrate in Illustration 4-3).

Gross Sales

Gross sales is the total amount of revenue a merchandising business would earn if it always collects the full sales prices on all sales transactions—that is, if it gives no discounts, accepts no sales returns, and grants no allowances. A business uses the sales account to record gross sales. Two types of sales transactions combine to make up gross sales: cash sales and credit sales.

In a cash sale, the merchant's employees enter the prices of the merchandise sold or scan the prices marked in bar codes on the merchandise with an optical scanner connected to the cash register. The store manager, other senior employee, or a computer totals the daily sales from all the store's cash registers and records the daily total. Good's Campus Books, Inc. made a total of $2,310 in cash sales for January 27, 19X1, and recorded the sales with the following general journal entry:

Jan. 27	Cash	2,310	
	Sales		2,310
	To record daily cash sales.		

In a credit sale, an employee or a computer (or, in some cases, a sophisticated cash register) lists the customer's purchases on a sales invoice. The prices and quantities of individual products are multiplied, and the product subtotals are added; the terms of payment are noted; and the customer receives a copy of the invoice (or it is mailed, if the goods are shipped to the customer). On January 27, 19X1, Good's Campus Books, Inc. made a sale of used books to College Book Brokers. The details of the sale are shown on the invoice in Illustration 4-4. The entry to record the sale is:

Jan. 27	Accounts Receivable	1,500	
	Sales		1,500
	To record credit sale to College Book Brokers.		

Sales Returns and Allowances

Many businesses accept returned merchandise within a short time after the sale, *whether or not the merchandise is defective*. For example, Nordstrom's, a department store chain based in Seattle, Washington, built a remarkably loyal customer base around its policy that all returns are accepted for full refunds with

ILLUSTRATION 4-4 A Sales Invoice

Good's Campus Books, Inc.
4500 Broad Street
College Place, TX 01122-3456

SALES INVOICE   568234

Date: 1/27/x1   **Invoice Number: 568234**

Sold to   **Shipped to**

College Book Brokers   Buyer
7629 Foundation Dr.
Solstice, CA 93989-4524

Shipping Adv. 61204	**Sales Order** 44332211	**Your P.O.** 24677

Qty.	Description	Unit Price	Amount
200	Introductory Economics (Western College Press)	7.50	1,500.00

Terms: 2/10, n/30
Freight: F.O.B. shipping point

Page total: $ 1,500.00

Prepared By: *RGM*   **Verified by:** *JDG*

no questions asked. While not all merchandising businesses have such generous policies, most accept the return of merchandise that is defective and grant allowances to induce customers to keep merchandise that has only minor defects.

Sales returns and allowances are gross sales dollars that ultimately are not earned. Therefore, when sales returns and allowances occur, they could be debited directly to Sales. That is, the balance of sales for the period could be reduced directly. Would this be good business practice? No, because most merchandising managers need to keep track of sales returns and allowances separately for management reasons.

Every merchandising business can expect a certain percentage of merchandise sold to be returned. Likewise, it can expect to grant allowances up to a certain percentage of gross sales. However, unexpectedly high sales returns and allowances signal that something is wrong. For example, the merchandise it has purchased may be of poor quality, or employees may be mishandling it and causing damage. The manager will want this "signal" so that the manager can take steps to investigate the cause and to correct the situation. Debiting sales returns and allowances directly to Sales buries the returns in the balance of that account, and the manager would have no convenient way to keep track of them. *Thus, a merchandising business records its sales returns and allowances in a separate contra-account to Sales, entitled Sales Returns and Allowances.*

To record sales returns and allowances, the business credits the account that was originally debited to record the sale, either Cash or Accounts Receivable, and debits Sales Returns and Allowances. So, for example, if Good's Campus Books, Inc., gave $50 of cash allowances and allowed $350 in returns of previous credit sales on February 5, 19X1, it would record returns and allowances for the day as follows:

Feb. 5	Sales Returns and Allowances	400	
	Accounts Receivable		350
	Cash		50
	To record the day's sales returns and allowances on cash and credit sales.		

Sales Discounts

Merchants commonly offer sales discounts of 1/2% to 2% to credit-sales customers to encourage them to pay their accounts earlier than the due dates. The specific amount of discount varies, depending on the level of interest rates and the amount of competition. If interest rates are low, businesses tend to offer small discounts; if interest rates are high, they tend to offer high discounts. However, if a particular business offers large sales discounts to attract credit customers, its competitors may have to do the same, regardless of the general level of interest rates.

Typically, merchants offer sales discounts for payment within 10 days. For example, a wholesale business commonly requires payment in full on all invoices within 30 days and offers a 1% discount for payment within 10 days. Such terms are usually abbreviated on invoices. For example, we abbreviate the above terms as 1/10, n/30. The *1* is the discount percent; *10* the discount period in days; *n* means *net*, referring to the full invoice total; and *30*, the period when the full amount is due (in days) if the discount is not taken. You would quote these terms to a customer as "one ten, net thirty."

Because *customers decide after the sale* whether or not to take sales discounts, we initially record credit sales at the full amounts. When customers take advantage of discounts and pay the lesser amounts, we debit the difference to an account entitled Sales Discounts. Notice the terms (2/10, n/30) of Good's Campus Books, Inc.'s sale of used books to College Book Brokers in Illustration 4-4 (lower left area of the invoice). Now assume that College Book Brokers pays for the used books on February 5—within the discount period of 10 days. College Book Brokers pays $1,470, and Good's records the transaction as follows:

Feb. 5	Cash	1,470	
	Sales Discounts	30	
	Accounts Receivable		1,500
	To record cash received for credit sale and discount taken.		

Sales Discounts is a contra-revenue account. It represents revenue the merchant sacrifices to secure cash from customers at an earlier date to have more cash available for business use. Assuming a business has both sales returns and allowances and sales discounts, the revenue section of its income statement would resemble Illustration 4-3 on page 164.

LO 3

Record gross purchases, purchases returns and allowances, purchases discounts, and transportation costs for purchased goods and calculate cost of goods purchased.

PURCHASE TRANSACTIONS

The cost of goods sold figure in a merchandising business's income statement is actually the net amount of several components. Purchase transactions account for several of these components. The aggregate of the costs suppliers bill to a business is the most significant component. However, this total is subject to discounts and returns and allowances; and a business also incurs additional costs such as those for transportation to put goods in place for sale.

Gross Purchases

Typically, we record purchases at the full or gross amounts the sellers charge. For example, on March 15, 19X1, Good's Campus Books, Inc., purchased textbooks costing $2,000 on terms of 2/10, n/30, from Foster Publishing Company. The purchase entry is:

Mar. 15	Purchases	2,000	
	Accounts Payable		2,000
	To record the purchase of textbooks on credit.		

Purchases Returns and Allowances

Just as a merchant's customers may be dissatisfied with goods they buy, the merchant may also find purchased goods unacceptable in quality or condition. A merchant records **purchases returns** when the goods are sent back to the supplier because they are unacceptable. The supplier records them as sales returns. A merchant records **purchases allowances** when the goods are deficient in only minor ways and the supplier concedes an acceptable reduction in the amount owed for the goods.

Suppose on March 20, Good's Campus Books, Inc., returned one-fourth of the textbooks it purchased from Foster Publishing on March 15. Good's entry to record the return is:

Mar. 20	Accounts Payable	500	
	Purchases Returns and Allowances		500
	To record return of textbooks purchased.		

Purchases Returns and Allowances is a *contra-account* whose balance is subtracted from gross purchases to calculate net purchases. (See Illustration 4-5.)

Purchases Discounts

Vendors (suppliers) frequently offer **purchases discounts** for early payment on credit purchases. Tradition dictates that we account for these discounts in a way that mirrors the treatment of sales discounts. An alternative treatment, which some accountants consider theoretically superior, is discussed in Appendix 4-A. According to tradition, we record credit purchases initially at the full prices suppliers charged for the goods purchased. Then, if the business takes a purchase discount, we debit Accounts Payable for the *full amount owed*, credit Cash for the *amount actually paid*, and credit a *contra-account*, Purchases Discounts, for the *amount of the discount taken*. Assume, for example, that on March 24 Good's Campus Books, Inc., paid for the remaining $1,500 in textbooks purchased from Foster Publishing on March 15. We record the payment, which is within the 10-day discount period, as follows:

Mar. 24	Accounts Payable	1,500	
	Cash		1,470
	Purchases Discounts		30
	To record payment for purchase and 2% discount taken.		

Calculating Net Purchases

When a business returns defective goods, receives allowances for goods with minor flaws, or receives discounts from suppliers for paying its accounts early, the correct cost of the purchased goods is net purchases. **Net purchases** equals purchases less purchases returns and allowances and purchases discounts. The net purchases calculation of Good's Campus Books, Inc., for 19X1 is shown in Illustration 4-5.

ILLUSTRATION 4-5 Calculation of Net Purchases

Good's Campus Books, Inc. Income Statement (Partial)	
Purchases	$460,000
Less: Purchases returns and allowances	(5,676)
Purchases discounts	(8,924)
Net purchases	$445,400

Transportation-In

According to GAAP, an asset's cost is its net purchase price plus any costs incidental to placing the asset in the appropriate location for its intended use. Transportation costs, those incurred in moving goods from the seller's to the purchaser's location, are the most common incidental costs. Practice varies widely as to whether the purchaser or the seller pays for transportation costs. As a consequence, purchasers and suppliers make sure that shipping charges are mentioned explicitly in the terms of the purchase transaction.

Businesses traditionally use certain abbreviations, such as *F.O.B. shipping point* and *F.O.B. destination*, to describe the seller's terms for handling shipping charges. The letters *F.O.B.* stand for "free on board," meaning the goods are the property of the buyer at the location referred to. Thus, F.O.B. shipping point means the buyer owns the goods at the point of shipment. The buyer bears the risk that the goods will be lost or damaged in transit, and the buyer pays for any transportation. On the other hand, F.O.B. destination means the seller owns the goods at the point of shipment, and ownership transfers to the buyer when they are delivered. The seller pays the freight and insurance and assumes responsibility for loss or damage to the goods.

We accumulate transportation charges for purchases in a separate account called Transportation-In. If the carrier (railroad, trucking company, airline, etc.) charges separately for freight, we make separate entries for the purchase and the transportation charges. If Good's Campus Books, Inc., purchased $3,000 of T-shirts on April 1, 19X1, with terms of F.O.B. shipping point and $100 freight to be charged directly by the trucking company, the entries are:

Apr. 1	Purchases	3,000	
	Accounts Payable		3,000
	To record credit purchase of goods shipped		
	F.O.B. shipping point.		
5	Transportation-In	100	
	Accounts Payable		100
	To record shipping charges for goods		
	purchased on April 1.		

Frequently, sellers prepay the freight charges on goods purchased F.O.B. shipping point as a service to their customers. When this happens, the seller usually shows the shipping charges as well as the cost of the goods on the seller's invoice. Then, the buyer records the purchase and transportation-in in one entry.

Apr. 1	Purchases	3,000	
	Transportation-In	100	
	Accounts Payable		3,100
	To record purchases and shipping charges		
	prepaid by supplier.		

When suppliers prepay transportation charges and add the charges to their invoices, any cash discounts offered do not apply to the transportation charges.

Cost of Goods Purchased

Since transportation charges are considered part of the total cost of purchased goods, the **cost of goods purchased** equals net purchases plus transportation-in as demonstrated in Illustration 4-6.

ILLUSTRATION 4-6 Calculation of Cost of Goods Purchased

Good's Campus Books, Inc. Income Statement (Partial)	
Purchases	$460,000
Less: Purchases returns and allowances	(5,676)
Purchases discounts	(8,924)
Net purchases	$445,400
Add: Transportation-in	10,123
Cost of goods purchased	$455,523

LO 4

Describe the periodic method of inventory valuation, contrast it with the perpetual method, and calculate cost of goods sold under the periodic inventory method.

ACCOUNTING FOR MERCHANDISE INVENTORIES

The calculation of the cost of goods purchased is only a step in calculating cost of goods sold. When a business purchases goods for resale to its customers, it adds the goods to its merchandise inventory upon delivery. **Merchandise inventory** is a merchandising business's stock of goods available for sale as of a particular point in time. When goods are sold during a period, they flow out of the business's merchandise inventory into the customers' possession. Therefore, for any period, the relationship in Illustration 4-7 holds. That is, the beginning merchandise inventory plus the goods purchased represent the goods available for sale. The goods available for sale less the goods sold equals the goods remaining in the ending merchandise inventory.

ILLUSTRATION 4-7 Inventory and Cost Relationships for a Period

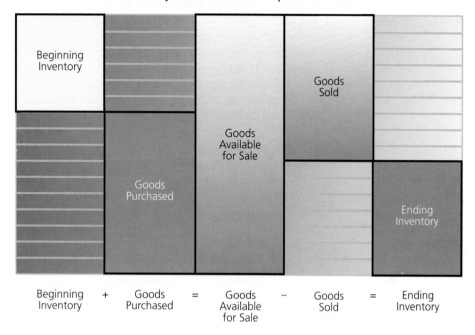

| Beginning Inventory | + | Goods Purchased | = | Goods Available for Sale | – | Goods Sold | = | Ending Inventory |

Consistent with the physical relationship above is a basic cost relationship:

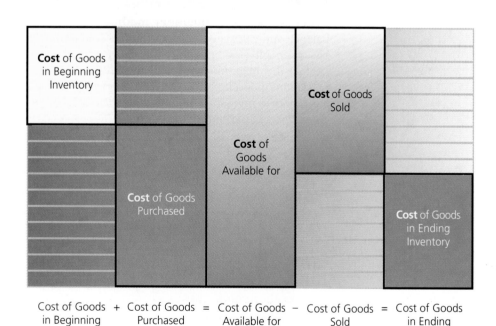

| Cost of Goods in Beginning Inventory | + | Cost of Goods Purchased | = | Cost of Goods Available for Sale | – | Cost of Goods Sold | = | Cost of Goods in Ending Inventory |

The fundamental equation shown at the bottom of Illustration 4-7 governs accounting for inventories and cost of goods sold. However, we have two distinctly different ways to apply this relationship in practice, which lead to two different ways to calculate cost of goods sold. One is the perpetual method of inventory accounting; the other, the periodic method.

The Perpetual Inventory Method

Under the **perpetual inventory method**, we record the costs of purchases and the cost of goods sold on a daily or even a continuous basis. As a business purchases goods, we debit their costs to Merchandise Inventory; as the business sells goods, we credit their costs to Merchandise Inventory and *debit their costs directly to Cost of Goods Sold.* Thus, the inventory balance and the cost of goods sold balance are kept up-to-date *perpetually.*

However, to implement the perpetual inventory method, as a business purchases and sells products, it must keep track of all individual products. Also, the business must keep a separate inventory record for each product it handles to record the physical quantities purchased and sold and their per-unit costs. When a business purchases goods, we add the physical units to the individual inventory record and note the cost per unit. When a business sells goods, we subtract the physical units from the number available and multiply the quantity sold by their unit costs to determine the amount to debit to Cost of Goods Sold. The perpetual inventory method, therefore, can be very intricate and costly to implement. However, availability of relatively inexpensive and powerful computers has made it more feasible to apply the perpetual method to almost any merchandising situation.

The perpetual inventory method contrasts sharply with the periodic inventory method described below. The periodic method is the basis for the discussion in the rest of this chapter. The perpetual method is described in more detail in a later chapter.

The Periodic Inventory Method

Under the **periodic inventory method**, we update the Merchandise Inventory balance and calculate the cost of goods sold *at the end of an accounting period,* based on physical inventory counts. Under the periodic method, we do not change the beginning balance in Merchandise Inventory until the end of an accounting period. We accumulate purchases for the period in Purchases, not in Merchandise Inventory. *We calculate the cost of goods sold as a by-product of the calculation of the ending inventory:*

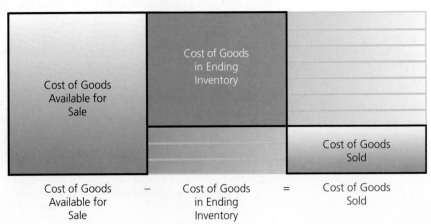

| Cost of Goods Available for Sale | − | Cost of Goods in Ending Inventory | = | Cost of Goods Sold |

Determining the Cost of Ending Inventory. At the end of each period, the business conducts a physical inventory to derive the ending inventory balance independent of purchases and sales of the period. A **physical inventory** is a process of physically counting all goods of each kind in the merchandise inventory as of a particular date. As they count the physical goods on hand, employees also inspect them, set aside spoiled, obsolete, and damaged goods, and count them in separate categories. Employees record the descriptions and tabulate the physical counts of goods on hand. Accounting clerks determine the cost of each inventory item from records of purchases and enter them in the tabulation. They also multiply the costs and quantities and add the individual results to arrive at a total cost of ending inventory, as shown in Illustration 4-8.

ILLUSTRATION 4-8 Periodic Inventory Tabulation

Inventory item number	Quantity counted	x	Unit cost	=	Item amount
1001	25		$ 49.95		$ 1,248.75
1002	56		45.23		2,532.88
1003	3,700		5.01		18,537.00
1004	158		25.00		3,950.00
1005	10		250.00		2,500.00
Total					$28,768.63

Conducting Physical Inventories with Computers. Computers make the process of conducting physical inventories and tabulating the results easier, faster, and more accurate. As they count goods of particular descriptions, employees enter the counts directly in hand-held computers linked to the computer that maintains the inventory records. From its stored records of purchases, the latter computer determines the unit cost of each item. Finally, the computer completes all the arithmetic operations of the inventory tabulation with great speed and accuracy.

COST OF GOODS SOLD

Illustration 4-9 summarizes the calculation of cost of goods sold under the periodic inventory method. The general ledger account balances supply beginning inventory and purchases amounts for the period. Together, they sum to the cost of goods available for sale. The goods available during the period must either

ILLUSTRATION 4-9 Calculation of Cost of Goods Sold

Good's Campus Books, Inc. Income Statement (Partial)	
Inventory, January 1, 19X1	$127,686
Add: Cost of goods purchased	455,523
Cost of goods available for sale	$583,209
Less: Inventory, December 31, 19X1	135,677
Cost of goods sold	$447,532

have been sold during the period or must still be in inventory at the end of the period. Therefore, when the independently derived ending inventory figure is subtracted from the cost of goods available for sale, the result is the correct cost of goods sold for the period.

The detailed calculation of cost of goods sold, including the calculation of net purchases and the cost of goods purchased, can now be examined in Illustration 4-10.

ILLUSTRATION 4-10 Detailed Calculation of Cost of Goods Sold

Good's Campus Books, Inc. Income Statement (Partial)		
Inventory, January 1, 19X1		$127,686
Add: Cost of goods purchased:		
Purchases	$460,000	
Less: Purchases returns and allowances	(5,676)	
Purchases discounts	(8,924)	
Net purchases	$445,400	
Add: Transportation-in	10,123	
Cost of goods purchased		455,523
Cost of goods available for sale		$583,209
Less: Inventory, December 31, 19X1		135,677
Cost of goods sold		$447,532

OPERATING EXPENSES

LO 5
Describe the operating expenses of a merchandising business and distinguish between selling expenses and general and administrative expenses.

Merchandising businesses incur the same types of operating expenses as service businesses. They consist of the costs of wages, salaries, supplies, rent, utilities, depreciation, etc. However, managers of merchandising businesses find it useful to see expenses divided into two categories: selling expenses and general and administrative expenses. **Selling expenses** are directly related to storing, handling, displaying, selling, and shipping or delivering products to customers. For example, the wages and salaries of sales, warehouse, and delivery personnel are selling expenses. On the other hand, expenses that do not relate directly to the selling function such as the wages and salaries of the general managers, accountants, bookkeepers, and office clerks are considered **general and administrative expenses**.

Technically, certain common expenses such as depreciation and utilities expenses—say of a building that houses both a store and administrative offices—can be allocated between the selling category and the administrative and general category. However, managers, in consultation with accountants, may decide to forego the extra detail in the accounts and income statement, unless they actually can manage the expenses separately for the two business functions. The 19X1 operating expenses of Good's Campus Books, Inc., are presented in the partial income statement in Illustration 4-11. Notice that the only costs actually divided between the two functions in this case are wages and salaries expenses. Advertising expense only applies to the selling function. Robert Good apparently has chosen to regard all other expenses exclusively as general and administrative expenses.

ILLUSTRATION 4-11 Operating Expenses

Good's Campus Books, Inc. Income Statement (Partial)		
Selling expenses:		
Advertising expense	$13,555	
Wages and salaries expense	57,500	
		$ 71,055
General and administrative expenses:		
Depreciation expense	$ 8,500	
Insurance expense	2,666	
Supplies expense	8,162	
Utilities expense	12,345	
Wages and salaries expense	40,000	
		71,673
Total operating expenses		$142,728

LO 6

Prepare the adjusting entries for a merchandising business using the periodic inventory method.

ADJUSTING ENTRIES OF A MERCHANDISING BUSINESS

A merchandising business's adjusting and closing entries are similar to those for a service business, except for the entries for merchandise inventory and cost of goods sold. Under the periodic inventory method, no adjustments are made during the accounting period to Merchandise Inventory as a result of transactions that occurred during the accounting period. Also, cost of goods sold is not recorded during the period. At the end of an accounting period, we must adjust Merchandise Inventory to the correct ending amount as determined by a physical inventory, and we must record cost of goods sold. As shown in Illustration 4-10, the beginning inventory balance is $127,686, and the ending inventory balance is $135,677. Merchandise Inventory must be increased by $7,991 ($135,677 − $127,686). The following adjusting entry increases Merchandise Inventory to its correct balance:

Dec. 31	Merchandise Inventory	7,991	
	Cost of Goods Sold		7,991
	To adjust inventory to the ending balance.		

The calculation of cost of goods sold in Illustration 4-10 includes both the beginning and the ending inventory amounts. An increase in inventory during the period (as is the case in Illustration 4-10) has the effect of a net reduction in cost of goods sold, while a decrease in inventory in effect increases cost of goods sold. The adjusting entry for Good's Campus Books, Inc., credits Cost of Goods Sold because inventory increased during the period by $7,991.

The remainder of the calculation of cost of goods sold in Illustration 4-10 is the cost of goods purchased. We refer to this entry as an adjusting entry even though it involves closing the accounts related to purchases. We finish the recording of cost of goods sold by closing the accounts that make up the cost of goods purchased to Cost of Goods Sold. The following entry completes the recording of cost of goods sold:

Dec. 31	Cost of Goods Sold	455,523	
	Purchases Returns and Allowances	5,676	
	Purchases Discounts	8,924	
	Purchases		460,000
	Transportation-In		10,123
	To close cost of goods purchased accounts to Cost of Goods Sold.		

After these two entries, the balances in Merchandise Inventory and Cost of Goods Sold are as follows:

Merchandise Inventory		
Bal.	127,686	
Dec. 31	7,991	
Bal.	135,677	

Cost of Goods Sold			
Dec. 31	455,523	Dec. 31	7,991
Bal.	447,532		

The balances shown in the two accounts are identical to the amounts shown in the calculation of cost of goods sold in Illustration 4-10.

After preparing the adjusting entries, we next prepare an adjusted trial balance—the next step in the accounting cycle. Illustration 4-12 presents the adjusted trial balance for Good's Campus Books, Inc. The information in the trial balance is consistent with the information presented earlier in the chapter.

ILLUSTRATION 4-12 Adjusted Trial Balance

Good's Campus Books, Inc.
Adjusted Trial Balance
December 31, 19X1

	Debits	Credits
Cash	$ 20,000	
Accounts Receivable	85,126	
Merchandise Inventory	135,677	
Supplies	2,664	
Prepaid Insurance	3,000	
Land	50,600	
Equipment	85,000	
Accumulated Depreciation—Equipment		$ 33,500
Accounts Payable		26,795
Wages and Salaries Payable		2,500
Capital Stock		80,000
Retained Earnings		154,822
Sales		736,400
Sales Returns and Allowances	27,444	
Sales Discounts	11,046	
Cost of Goods Sold	447,532	
Advertising Expense	13,555	
Depreciation Expense—Equipment	8,500	
Income Tax Expense	23,200	
Insurance Expense	2,666	
Supplies Expense	8,162	
Utilities Expense	12,345	
Wages and Salaries Expense—Office	40,000	
Wages and Salaries Expense—Sales	57,500	
Totals	$1,034,017	$1,034,017

LO 7
Prepare the financial statements of a merchandising business, using the adjusted trial balance.

FINANCIAL STATEMENTS OF A MERCHANDISING BUSINESS

Illustrations 4-13 through 4-15 show the financial statements that we prepare for Good's Campus Books, Inc., from the adjusted trial balance in Illustration 4-12. They are the income statement, the retained earnings statement, and the balance sheet. Discussion of the statement of cash flows is deferred to a later chapter.

Classified Income Statement

You prepare an income statement, such as the one in Illustration 4-13, from the income statement accounts in the adjusted trial balance in Illustration 4-12. All of the data for preparing the income statement come from the trial balance and

ILLUSTRATION 4-13 Complete Income Statement of Good's Campus Books, Inc.

Good's Campus Books, Inc. Income Statement For the Year Ended December 31, 19X1			
Revenue:			
Gross sales			$736,400
Less: Sales returns and allowances		$ 27,444	
Sales discounts		11,046	38,490
Net sales			$697,910
Cost of goods sold:			
Inventory, January 1, 19X1		$127,686	
Add: Cost of goods purchased:			
Purchases	$460,000		
Less: Purchases returns and allowances	(5,676)		
Purchases discounts	(8,924)		
Net purchases	$445,400		
Add: Transportation-in	10,123		
Cost of goods purchased		455,523	
Cost of goods available for sale		$583,209	
Less: Inventory, December 31, 19X1		135,677	
Cost of goods sold			447,532
Gross profit			$250,378
Selling expenses:			
Advertising expense	$ 13,555		
Wages and salaries expense	57,500		
		$71,055	
General and administrative expenses:			
Depreciation expense–equipment	$ 8,500		
Insurance expense	2,666		
Supplies expense	8,162		
Utilities expense	12,345		
Wages and salaries expense	40,000		
		71,673	
Total operating expenses			142,728
Income before income taxes			$107,650
Income tax expense			23,200
Net income			$ 84,450

the adjusting entries for cost of goods sold, but this income statement organizes the data into several major categories. The major categories correspond to the individual figures in the very simple income statement in Illustration 4-1.

First, Illustration 4-13 begins with a revenue section that corresponds to the calculation presented in Illustration 4-3. Next, the statement displays all of the items making up the cost of goods sold, as shown in Illustration 4-10. We subtract cost of goods sold from net sales revenue to calculate gross profit and deduct operating expenses from gross profit to derive income before income taxes. Finally, we deduct income tax expense from income before income taxes to derive net income. Obviously, Illustration 4-13 is a more detailed presentation of the results of Good's Campus Books, Inc's. 19X1 operations than is Illustration 4-1. Illustration 4-13 contains the type of detail that an owner or manager like Robert Good would want. To communicate summary information to outsiders, Robert would most likely use a condensed income statement, such as Illustration 4-1.

Retained Earnings Statement

The retained earnings statement is generally the simplest of the four major financial statements. This is very evident in Illustration 4-14, which presents the retained earnings statement for Good's Campus Books, Inc. The retained earnings statement begins with the beginning balance in Retained Earnings. To this we add the net income of the period and subtract dividends (not applicable in this case).

ILLUSTRATION 4-14 Retained Earnings Statement

Good's Campus Books, Inc. Retained Earnings Statement For the Year Ended December 31, 19X1	
Retained earnings, January 1, 19X1	$154,822
Net income for the year ended December 31, 19X1	84,450
Retained earnings, December 31, 19X1	$239,272

Classified Balance Sheet

The classified balance sheet of Good's Campus Books, Inc., is shown in Illustration 4-15. It lists the business's asset, liability, and stockholders' equity accounts. Many businesses prepare classified balance sheets. A **classified balance sheet** presents the assets, liabilities, and stockholders' equity accounts arranged in certain customary groupings. While GAAP require no specific format for classifying balance sheet elements, the customary classification format presents assets according to the following groupings:

1. Current assets
2. Long-term investments
3. Property, plant and equipment
4. Intangible assets

Liabilities generally are classified into only two groupings:

1. Current liabilities
2. Noncurrent (or long-term) liabilities

ILLUSTRATION 4-15 Good's Campus Books, Inc.'s Balance Sheet

Good's Campus Books, Inc. Balance Sheet December 31, 19X1		
Assets		
Current assets:		
Cash	$ 20,000	
Accounts receivable	85,126	
Merchandise inventory	135,677	
Supplies	2,664	
Prepaid insurance	3,000	
Total current assets		$246,467
Property, plant, and equipment:		
Land	$ 50,600	
Equipment	$85,000	
Less: Accumulated depreciation	33,500	51,500
Total property, plant, and equipment		102,100
Total assets		$348,567
Liabilities and Stockholders' Equity		
Current liabilities:		
Accounts payable	$ 26,795	
Wages and salaries payable	2,500	
Total current liabilities		$ 29,295
Stockholders' equity:		
Capital stock	$ 80,000	
Retained earnings	239,272	
Total stockholders' equity		319,272
Total liabilities and stockholders' equity		$348,567

Stockholders' equity presents two groupings

1. Contributed (or paid-in) capital
2. Retained earnings

Because Good's Campus Books, Inc., is not complex, its balance sheet only contains two groupings of assets—current assets and property, plant, and equipment—and it only has current liabilities.

Two significant asset and liability classifications are current assets and current liabilities. In relation to assets, the term *current* deals with the length of time before the assets are realized—meaning converted into cash or used. In relation to the term liabilities, *current* refers to how soon the liabilities are due. Current assets and liabilities are assets that a business will realize and liabilities that are due within one year or one operating cycle, whichever is longer. The **operating cycle** of a business is the average period of time it takes from committing resources to providing goods or services to collecting cash from customers. A service business's operating cycle is the period from the time it renders the service until it collects cash from the customer. For a merchandising business, which buys merchandise from wholesalers and resells it to retail customers, the operating cycle is the average period of time between the acquisition of merchandise and receipt of cash from the merchandise's sale. For a manufacturing business, which manufactures a product and sells it to customers, the operating cycle is the average period of time between the acquisition of raw materials and the receipt of cash from the sale of the product.

Since most businesses have shorter operating cycles than one year, they use one year to classify assets and liabilities as current and noncurrent. Some businesses, however, have operating cycles that are longer than one year. For example, construction businesses that enter into long-term contracts to build bridges, highways, buildings, etc., take several years to complete the projects. These businesses generally use a period longer than one year for classification of assets and liabilities as current and noncurrent.

A reader uses a classified balance sheet to assess the business's ability to pay its liabilities when they come due and the extent of the business's investment in various types of assets. A business that has current assets in excess of current liabilities should be able to pay its current liabilities because it will realize the current assets within the same time period that the current liabilities come due. On the other hand, a business with current liabilities greater than its current assets may have to borrow money to pay the liabilities. The noncurrent asset classifications show the amounts and types of assets that a business uses in its long-term operations. The noncurrent liability and stockholders' equity classifications show the sources—borrowing, investments by the owners, and retained earnings—of the business's long-term financing.

Asset Classifications.   Some businesses have classified balance sheets that contain all of the asset classifications listed previously. Other businesses, however, only have some of the classifications in their classified balance sheets, depending on the nature of their operations.

Current assets.   **Current assets** consist of cash and assets that the business reasonably expects to sell, consume, or convert into cash within one year or within one operating cycle, whichever is longer. Current assets generally include cash, short-term investments, notes and accounts receivable, merchandise inventories, prepaid expenses, and unused supplies. Accounts receivable are expected to be converted into cash within a short period, typically 30 to 90 days. Short-term investments (often called trading or *marketable securities*) are temporary investments of cash that the business does not currently need. Investments are classified as short-term if management expects to sell them within a year or an operating cycle. Inventories are goods that the business expects to sell to customers either for cash or for notes or accounts receivable ultimately converted into cash. The business will use or consume prepaid expenses and unused supplies in the short run, within a year.

IBM's 1992 balance sheet reported the following current assets (rounded to the nearest $1 million):

Cash and cash equivalents	$ 4,446,000,000
Marketable securities	1,203,000,000
Receivables	21,604,000,000
Inventories	8,385,000,000
Prepaid expenses and other current assets	4,054,000,000
Total	$39,692,000,000

A classified balance sheet presents current assets in the order of the asset's liquidity. In this context, the term **liquidity** refers to the expected length of time needed to convert an asset into cash. Cash, obviously, is the most liquid asset and is generally listed first in the current asset section. Following cash and in order according to their liquidity are: short-term investments, accounts receivable, notes receivable, and merchandise inventories, respectively. Prepaid expenses and unused supplies are generally not realized in cash and, by convention, are commonly listed last in the current asset section.

Long-term investments. **Long-term investments** include such things as stocks, bonds, and promissory notes that the business does not expect to sell or collect within one year or the operating cycle, whichever is longer. A **promissory note** is a formal, written promise to pay a certain amount of money on a fixed date in the future.

Property, plant, and equipment. **Property, plant, and equipment** include the business's long-lived assets that it uses to sell and/or manufacture a product or to provide a service. Assets commonly classified as property, plant, and equipment are the land and buildings in which the business is housed and the equipment the business uses. For a business such as Good's Campus Books, Inc., this classification might include land and buildings, office equipment, and equipment it uses to provide merchandise to its customers.

The important concepts for classifying assets as property, plant, and equipment are that the assets have relatively long useful lives and that they are used in selling or manufacturing a product or in providing a service. Assets such as land and buildings that the business does not currently use but holds for future expansion or sale should be classified as long-term investments. Property, plant, and equipment assets are sometimes called *plant assets*, *operating assets*, *fixed assets*, *tangible assets*, or *long-lived assets*.

Intangible assets. **Intangible assets** include those that have no physical substance. Examples of intangible assets are patents, copyrights, franchises, and trademarks. The value of these assets results from the rights or privileges granted to the owners of the assets.

Liability Classifications. Liabilities are classified as either current or noncurrent. Most businesses have both of these classifications on their balance sheets.

Current liabilities. **Current liabilities** are those obligations that are due within one year or one operating cycle, whichever is longer. Businesses pay current liabilities with current assets or by incurring new current liabilities. Examples of current liabilities, some of which are shown in Good's Campus Books, Inc.'s balance sheet, are notes payable and accounts payable, wages and salaries payable, interest payable, taxes payable and unearned revenue. Current liabilities are discussed in greater detail in subsequent chapters.

IBM's current liabilities for 1992 are as follows (rounded to the nearest $1 million):

Taxes	$ 979,000,000
Short-term debt	16,467,000,000
Accounts payable	3,147,000,000
Compensation and benefits	3,476,000,000
Deferred income	3,316,000,000
Other accrued expenses and liabilities	9,352,000,000
Total	$36,737,000,000

Noncurrent liabilities. **Noncurrent liabilities** are those obligations that are due in more than one year or one operating cycle, whichever is longer, from the balance sheet date. Examples of noncurrent liabilities are notes and bonds payable and mortgages payable. When the due date for noncurrent liabilities approaches to within one year or one operating cycle, the business reclassifies the liabilities as current. At that point, they meet the definition of a current liability. Noncurrent liabilities, also called *long-term liabilities*, are discussed further in a subsequent chapter.

Stockholders' Equity Classifications. The stockholders' equity section of a corporation's balance sheet shows the amounts of capital stock and retained earnings at the balance sheet date.

Contributed (paid-in) capital. The **contributed capital** of a corporation's balance sheet shows the amount that the stockholders (owners) have invested in the business. Contributed capital is also referred to as **paid-in capital**. So far, you have seen this amount represented by Capital Stock. In a subsequent chapter, we discuss more complex stockholder situations that involve more accounts than just Capital Stock.

Retained earnings. A corporation's **retained earnings** is the cumulative amount of earnings since the corporation's inception less the cumulative amount of dividends. The retained earnings statement presents detailed information about the changes in the amount of retained earnings that occurred during the accounting period, ending at the balance sheet date. Different forms of business organizations (proprietorships and partnerships) have different owners' equity sections in their balance sheets. The owners' equity accounts of these forms of business organizations are discussed in a subsequent chapter.

LO 8

Prepare closing entries for a merchandising business.

CLOSING ENTRIES OF A MERCHANDISING BUSINESS

A merchandising business's closing entries are similar to those for a service business. The only differences are the Cost of Goods Sold balance that was determined as part of the adjusting entries that we discussed earlier and the existence of contra-revenue accounts such as Sales Returns and Allowances and Sales Discounts. First, all of the debit balance income statement accounts (including Cost of Goods Sold) are credited, and their total of $651,950 is debited to Income Summary. Next, all of the credit balance income statement accounts—in this case, there is only Sales—are debited, and the total of $736,400 is credited to Income Summary. When Income Summary is summarized as in Illustration 4-17, we find it has a balance equal to the net income amount of $84,450. This income amount is closed to Retained Earnings in the final entry of Illustration 4-16.

LO 9

Calculate the cost of goods sold and gross profit ratios and use them to assess profitability.

USING THE MULTISTEP INCOME STATEMENT

The multistep income statement of merchandising businesses is no accident. All expenses are basically alike in that they must be covered by revenues before a business generates a profit. Nevertheless, for a merchandising business, the relationship between revenue and cost of goods sold and the resulting gross profit

ILLUSTRATION 4-16 Closing Entries

Dec. 31	Income Summary	651,950	
	Sales Returns and Allowances		27,444
	Sales Discounts		11,046
	Cost of Goods Sold		447,532
	Advertising Expense		13,555
	Depreciation Expense—Equipment		8,500
	Income Tax Expense		23,200
	Insurance Expense		2,666
	Supplies Expense		8,162
	Utilities Expense		12,345
	Wages and Salaries Expense—Office		40,000
	Wages and Salaries Expense—Sales		57,500
	To close the expenses and contra-revenues to Income Summary.		
31	Sales	736,400	
	Income Summary		736,400
	To close revenue to Income Summary.		
31	Income Summary	84,450	
	Retained Earnings		84,450
	To close Income Summary to Retained Earnings.		

ILLUSTRATION 4-17 Income Summary Account

Income Summary				
Dec. 31	651,950	Dec. 31	736,400
Dec. 31	84,450	Bal.	84,450
		Bal.	0

Retained Earnings		
	Bal.	154,822
	Dec. 31	84,450
	Bal.	239,272

is especially important. If a business cannot sell merchandise for more than its cost, then its gross profit will be negative; and with additional expenses to deduct, "it's all downhill from there." Therefore, owners and managers of merchandising businesses give a great deal of attention to trying to manage gross profit.

Gross Profit and Cost of Goods Sold Ratios

Let us now return to the case of Robert Good, who is worried about a drop in the profitability of Good's Campus Books, Inc. in 19X1. Consider the store's income statement for 19X1 compared to its income statement for 19X0 in Illustration 4-18. The side-by-side statements tell us a few things without any additional diagnostic tools. Most importantly, we observe that net sales grew from 19X0 to 19X1, but net income fell—so Mr. Good has reason to be concerned.

In diagnosing what caused this adverse pattern, Robert will want to review the comparative gross profit ratios. The **gross profit ratio** is the ratio of gross profit to the net sales of a given year:

$$\text{Gross Profit Ratio} = \frac{\text{Gross Profit}}{\text{Net Sales}}$$

ILLUSTRATION 4-18 Comparative Income Statements

Good's Campus Books, Inc. Comparative Income Statement For the Years Ended December 31, 19X0 and 19X1		
	19X0	**19X1**
Net sales	$606,878	$697,910
Less: Cost of goods sold	370,196	447,532
Gross profit	$236,682	$250,378
Less: Operating expenses	121,585	142,728
Income before income taxes	$115,097	$107,650
Less: Income tax expense	22,700	23,200
Net income	$ 92,397	$ 84,450

Since cost of goods sold is subtracted from net sales to calculate gross profit, the **cost of goods sold ratio** is the complement of the gross profit ratio:

$$\text{Cost of Goods Sold Ratio} = \frac{\text{Cost of Goods Sold}}{\text{Net Sales}}$$

The two ratios for Good's Campus Books, Inc., for 19X0 and 19X1 reveal a considerable amount about Mr. Good's profitability problem:

	19X0	**19X1**
Cost of goods sold ratio:	$\dfrac{\$370,196}{\$606,878} = .610$	$\dfrac{\$447,532}{\$697,910} = .641$
Gross profit ratio:	$\dfrac{\$236,682}{\$606,878} = .390$	$\dfrac{\$250,378}{\$697,910} = .359$
	1.000	1.000

Using the Cost of Goods Sold and Gross Profit Ratios

The gross profit and cost of goods sold ratios of Good's Campus Books, Inc., tell us that in 19X1, .031 (.641 − .610) more of every net sales dollar went for the cost of goods sold and, therefore, .031 less flowed through to gross profit. That is, of every net sales dollar earned, only .359 became gross profit—to cover operating expenses and generate net income—in 19X1, as opposed to .390 per net sales dollar earned in 19X0. To see the significance of this difference in the cost of goods sold/gross profit split, we multiply the decline in gross profit ratio in 19X1 (.390 − .359) by 19X1 net sales:

$$.031 \times \$697,910 = \$21,635$$

Now we know that, if the gross profit (and cost of goods sold) ratio had been the same in 19X1 as it was in 19X0, Good's Campus Books, Inc., would have had over $20,000 of additional income before taxes than it actually earned in 19X1. This is certainly a significant amount. It shows how small changes in a merchandising business's cost of goods sold/gross profit ratio can have a significant impact on its profitability. It also tells Mr. Good that it would be very worthwhile to investigate the components of cost of goods sold to find out why it was a higher percentage of net sales in 19X1 than it was in 19X0.

INSIGHTS INTO ETHICS

It is now January 10, 19X3. Amy Parks, the accounting clerk at Good's Campus Books, Inc., overheard Frank Diaz, manager of used books, say that the December 31, 19X2, physical inventory included several hundred introductory psychology books that Good's had bought back from students at $15 each. At the end of fall term, Frank assumed the used textbooks would be sold to other students for $30 each at the beginning of spring term. Unfortunately, in December the Psychology Department unexpectedly changed books for spring term; and now the used books must be sold to a broker for only $5 each. Amy realizes immediately that the ending inventory tabulation for 19X1 was overstated, cost of goods sold was thereby understated, and net income was overstated. Amy has always admired Robert Good but has not been particularly fond of Sheila Pell who will soon replace him as the owner. She knows that the price Sheila will pay Robert for the business depends on net income, and she also noticed during 19X2 that Sheila authorized early maintenance and other expenditures to inflate expenses during 19X2. To revise the inventory tabulation and the financial statements will be a lot of work. What should Amy do?

To see just how important managing cost of goods sold and gross profit are in the real world, consider the following ratios of Crown Books Corporation, which operates retail specialty bookstores.

	1990	1991	1992
Cost of goods sold ratio	.783	.781	.785
Gross profit ratio	.217	.219	.215

Notice that the fluctuations from year to year are less than .005 of sales, indicating relatively tight control of costs of goods sold in relationship to sales.

SUMMARY

Describe a multistep income statement and why a merchandising business uses it. The multistep income statements of merchandising businesses consist of three stages. First, we subtract cost of goods sold from net sales to arrive at gross profit. Second, we subtract operating expenses from gross profit to derive net income before income taxes. Third, we subtract income tax expense from income before income taxes to derive net income. Since merchandising businesses earn revenues primarily by selling products to customers, managers and other users of their financial statements find it useful to see expenses split into two main categories: the cost of the goods sold and operating expenses.

	Net Sales
Less:	**Cost of Goods Sold**
Equals:	**Gross Profit**
Less:	**Operating Expenses**
Equals:	**Income Before Income Taxes**
Less:	**Income Tax Expense**
Equals:	**Net Income**

Record gross sales, sales returns and allowances, and sales discounts and calculate net sales for a merchandising business. The prices customers pay or agree to pay for merchandise at the time of sale are the gross sales of the business recorded in Sales. We record sales returns and allowances and sales discounts in *contra-revenue* accounts and subtract their balances from gross sales to derive net sales in the income statement.

	Gross Sales
Less:	**Sales Returns and Allowances**
Less:	**Sales Discounts**
Equals:	**Net Sales**

Record gross purchases, purchases returns and allowances, purchases discounts, and transportation costs for purchased goods and calculate cost of goods purchased. Under the gross method, we record purchases at the full prices suppliers charge. We record purchases returns and allowances and purchases (cash) discounts in contra-accounts and subtract them from gross purchases to calculate net purchases. Further, we record transportation costs of purchases in Transportation-In and add its balance to net purchases to derive the cost of goods purchased.

	Gross Purchases
Less:	**Purchases Returns and Allowances**
Less:	**Purchases Discounts**
Equals:	**Net Purchases**
Add:	**Transportation-In**
Equals:	**Cost of Goods Purchased**

Describe the periodic method of inventory valuation, contrast it with the perpetual method, and calculate cost of goods sold under the periodic inventory method. Under the periodic inventory method, we update the Merchandise Inventory balance and calculate the cost of goods sold *only at the ends of accounting periods*, based on physical inventory counts. We do not change the beginning balance in Merchandise Inventory until the end of an accounting period. We accumulate the components of the cost of goods purchased in separate accounts, not in Merchandise Inventory. At the end of the period, we calculate cost of goods available for sale by adding the cost of goods purchased to the beginning inventory balance. The ending inventory balance from the physical inventory is subtracted to derive cost of goods sold.

	Beginning Inventory
Add:	**Cost of Goods Purchased**
Equals:	**Cost of Goods Available for Sale**
Less:	**Ending Inventory**
Equals:	**Cost of Goods Sold**

Describe the operating expenses of a merchandising business and distinguish between selling expenses and general and administrative expenses. Selling expenses are directly related to storing, handling, displaying, selling, and shipping or delivering products to customers. For example, the wages and salaries of sales, warehouse, and delivery personnel are selling expenses. On the other hand, the wages and salaries of general managers, accountants, bookkeepers, and office clerks are considered general and administrative expenses.

Prepare the adjusting entries for a merchandising business using the perioic inventory method. A merchandising business's adjusting entries are fundamentally the same as those of a service business, and they serve the same function. However, some modifications are required to handle merchandise inventories and cost of goods sold under the periodic inventory method. The cost of goods sold is not accumulated during the period under the periodic inventory method. An adjusting entry is made to adjust Merchandise Inventory to the correct ending balance. A second adjusting entry is made to close purchases-related accounts. Both of these entries are also adjustments to Cost of Goods Sold. After appropriate adjustments are made, the balance in Cost of Goods Sold is the correct amount for the period.

Prepare the financial statements of a merchandising business, using the adjusted trial balance. All the account balances needed for preparation of the income statement, retained earnings statement, and balance sheet are displayed in the adjusted trial balance and need only be formatted into suitable statements.

Prepare closing entries for a merchandising business. A merchandising business's closing entries are the same as those for a service business, with the addition of Cost of Goods Sold and contra-revenue accounts.

Calculate the cost of goods sold and gross profit ratios and use them to assess profitability. We calculate the cost of goods sold and gross profit ratios by dividing their respective amounts by net sales. Because the cost of goods sold is a significant expense to most merchandising businesses, small fluctuations in the cost of goods sold and gross profit ratios usually imply significant effects on net income. The ratios are very useful in assessing the profitability of merchandising businesses.

LO 10

Distinguish between the gross and net methods of recording purchases.

APPENDIX 4-A: RECORDING PURCHASES NET OF DISCOUNTS

Some accountants and managers criticize the traditional method of handling cash discounts on purchases—that is, deducting purchases discounts from gross purchases to derive net purchases. First, purchases discounts are related to the business's cash management, not to its purchasing function. Generally speaking, if the business has adequate cash on hand, it should take all cash discounts on purchases. (In a later chapter, we justify this rule of thumb.) If a business does not take the discounts, the discounts lost are costs of financing purchases using supplier credit, not costs of the goods purchased. From the cash-management perspective, a manager should want the discounts lost categorized as a separate controllable expense, rather than as a component of the net purchases calculation. Thus, many managers and accountants prefer an alternative to the traditional way of accounting for cash discounts on purchases.

Under the alternative method, when a supplier offers a business a cash discount on purchases, we record the purchases at the discounted purchase price. For example, we record the purchase of $4,000 worth of goods under terms of 1/10, n/30 as:

(Date)	Purchases	3,960	
	Accounts Payable		3,960
	To record purchases net of available cash discounts.		

Only the costs necessary to acquire the goods are regarded as part of the purchase cost. When discounts are not taken, in effect, the merchant borrows money from the supplier. In the case above, the period of the loan is 20 days, the difference between the 10-day discount period and the 30 days allowed for full payment. If the merchant does not take the discount offered in the case above, we debit the amount of the discount lost to an expense account entitled Purchases Discounts Lost.

(Date)	Accounts Payable	3,960	
	Purchases Discounts Lost	40	
	Cash		4,000
	To record payments on accounts payable after the discount period.		

Otherwise, if the merchant pays the invoice within 10 days, the payment on the purchase is the discounted amount and we record it as:

(Date)	Accounts Payable	3,960	
	Cash		3,960
	To record payments on accounts payable within the discount periods.		

Under this method, cash discounts on purchases do not enter into calculating net purchases. *Purchases are already recorded net of discounts.* We continue to subtract purchases returns and allowances from purchases to calculate net purchases. Since Purchases Discounts Lost is akin to (and sometimes is combined with) interest expense, we typically report it on the income statement in an other income and expense category or after operating expenses.

REVIEW PROBLEM

The adjusted trial balance for the Small-Fry Toy Corporation is presented on the next page. In addition to the adjusted trial balance, the following information for 19X1 was used to prepare adjusting entries.

Merchandise Inventory, January 1	$ 9,800
Merchandise Inventory, December 31	16,100
Purchases	62,600
Purchases Returns and Allowances	2,300
Purchases Discounts	2,700
Transportation-In	3,100

REQUIRED:

a. Prepare a multistep income statement for 19X1.
b. Prepare a retained earnings statement for 19X1.
c. Prepare a classified balance sheet as of December 31, 19X1.
d. Prepare closing entries.

Small Fry Toy Corporation
Adjusted Trial Balance
December 31, 19X1

	Debits	Credits
Cash	$ 19,500	
Accounts Receivable	8,100	
Merchandise Inventory	16,100	
Supplies	2,700	
Prepaid Insurance	1,400	
Land	8,000	
Building	42,000	
Accumulated Depreciation—Building		$ 11,200
Accounts Payable		5,700
Income Taxes Payable		13,000
Wages and Salaries Payable		4,700
Notes Payable—Noncurrent		8,500
Capital Stock		15,000
Retained Earnings		22,400
Dividends	7,200	
Sales		157,600
Sales Returns and Allowances	3,900	
Sales Discounts	1,800	
Cost of Goods Sold	54,400	
Depreciation Expense—Office	1,600	
Depreciation Expense—Sales	1,200	
Income Tax Expense	13,000	
Insurance Expense	2,700	
Supplies Expense—Office	2,100	
Supplies Expense—Sales	1,500	
Utilities Expense—Office	700	
Utilities Expense—Sales	900	
Wages and Salaries Expense—Office	22,200	
Wages and Salaries Expense—Sales	27,100	
Totals	$238,100	$238,100

SOLUTION:

Planning and Organizing Your Work

1. Prepare a multistep income statement, using revenue and expense accounts from the adjusted trial balance and cost of goods sold information from the additional information presented.
2. Prepare a retained earnings statement, using the retained earnings account in the adjusted trial balance as the beginning balance, net income from the income statement in *b.* above, and the dividends account from the adjusted trial balance.
3. Prepare a classified balance sheet, using asset, liability, and capital stock accounts from the adjusted trial balance and ending retained earnings from the retained earnings statement from *c.* above.
4. Close revenue and expense accounts to Income Summary.
5. Close income summary to Retained Earnings.
6. Close Dividends to Retained Earnings.

(a) *Prepare a multistep income statement for 19X1.*

Small-Fry Toy Corporation
Income Statement
For the Year Ended December 31, 19X1

Revenue:			
Gross sales			$157,600
Less: Sales returns and allowances		$ 3,900	
Sales discounts		1,800	5,700
Net sales			$151,900
Cost of goods sold:			
Merchandise inventory, January 1, 19X1		$ 9,800	
Add Cost of goods purchased:			
Purchases	$62,600		
Less: Purchases returns and allowances	(2,300)		
Purchases discounts	(2,700)		
Net purchases	$57,600		
Add: Transportation-in	3,100		
Cost of goods purchased		60,700	
Cost of goods available for sale		$70,500	
Less: Merchandise inventory,			
December 31, 19X1		16,100	
Cost of goods sold			54,400
Gross profit			$ 97,500
Selling expenses:			
Depreciation expense–sales	$ 1,200		
Supplies expense	1,500		
Utilities expense	900		
Wages and salaries expense	27,100	$30,700	
General and administrative expenses:			
Depreciation expense–office equip.	$ 1,600		
Insurance expense	2,700		
Supplies expense	2,100		
Utilities expense	700		
Wages and salaries expense	22,200	29,300	
Total operating expenses			60,000
Income before income taxes			$ 37,500
Income tax expense			13,000
Net income			$ 24,500

(b) *Prepare a retained earnings statement for 19X1.*

Small-Fry Toy Corporation
Retained Earnings Statement
For the Year Ended December 31, 19X1

Retained earnings, January 1, 19X1	$22,400
Net income for the year ended December 31, 19X1	24,500
	$46,900
Less: Dividends	7,200
Retained earnings, December 31, 19X1	$39,700

(c) *Prepare a balance sheet.*

Small-Fry Toy Corporation
Balance Sheet
December 31, 19X1

Assets

Current assets:			
Cash		$19,500	
Accounts receivable		8,100	
Merchandise inventory		16,100	
Supplies		2,700	
Prepaid insurance		1,400	
Total current assets			$47,800
Property, plant, and equipment:			
Land		$ 8,000	
Building	$42,000		
Less: Accumulated depreciation	11,200	30,800	
Total property, plant, and equipment			38,800
Total assets			$86,600

Liabilities and Stockholders' Equity

Current liabilities:		
Accounts payable	$ 5,700	
Income taxes payable	13,000	
Wages and salaries payable	4,700	
Total current liabilities		$23,400
Long-term liabilities:		
Notes payable–noncurrent		8,500
Stockholders' equity:		
Capital stock	$15,000	
Retained earnings	39,700	
Total stockholders' equity		54,700
Total liabilities and stockholders' equity		$86,600

(d) *Prepare closing entries.*

Dec. 31	Sales	157,600	
	Income Summary		157,600
	To close revenue account.		
31	Income Summary	133,100	
	Sales Returns and Allowances		3,900
	Sales Discounts		1,800
	Cost of Goods Sold		54,400
	Depreciation Expense–Office Equipment		1,600
	Depreciation Expense–Sales		1,200
	Income Tax Expense		13,000
	Insurance Expense		2,700
	Supplies Expense–Office		2,100
	Supplies Expense–Sales		1,500
	Utilities Expense–Office		700
	Utilities Expense–Sales		900
	Wages and Salaries Expense–Office		22,200
	Wages and Salaries Expense–Sales		27,100
	To close contra-revenue and expense accounts.		

Dec. 31	Income Summary	24,500	
	Retained Earnings		24,500
	To close Income Summary to Retained Earnings		
31	Retained Earnings	7,200	
	Dividends		7,200
	To close Dividends.		

KEY TERMS

classified balance sheet, *178*
contributed (paid-in) capital, *182*
cost of goods purchased, *170*
cost of goods sold, *163*
cost of goods sold ratio, *184*
current assets, *180*
current liabilities, *181*
general and administrative expenses, *174*
gross profit, *163*
gross profit ratio, *183*
gross purchases, *168*
gross sales, *164*
intangible assets, *181*

liquidity, *180*
long-term investments, *181*
merchandise inventory, *170*
multistep income statement, *163*
net purchases, *169*
net sales, *164*
noncurrent liabilities, *182*
operating cycle, *179*
operating expenses, *163*
periodic inventory method, *172*
perpetual inventory method, *172*
physical inventory, *173*

promissory note, *181*
property, plant, and equipment, *181*
purchases discounts, *168*
purchases returns and allowances, *168*
retained earnings, *182*
sales allowances, *165*
sales discounts, *165*
sales returns, *164*
selling expenses, *174*

SELF-QUIZ

LO 1 1. Which of the following is *not* a principal part of a merchandising firm's income statement?
a. Operating expenses
b. Net profit
c. Gross profit
d. Cost of goods sold

LO 2 2. Net sales equals gross sales minus _____ _____ _____ _____ and _____ _____.

LO 2 3. Sales discounts is classified as a _____ account.

LO 2 4. Which of the following is the correct meaning of the term *2/10, n/30*?
a. Payment is due between February 10 and November 30.
b. A discount of between 2% and 10% will be given if payment is received within 30 days.
c. A 2% discount will be given if payment is received between 10 to 30 days.
d. A 2% discount will be given if payment is received within 10 days, or the full amount is due within 30 days of purchase.

LO 3 5. Net purchases equals purchases less _____ _____ _____ _____ and _____ _____.

LO 3 6. Which of the following is *not* correct about the term *F.O.B shipping point*?

a. F.O.B. stands for "free on board."
b. The buyer is responsible for the cost of the shipping.
c. The buyer owns the goods when they are shipped.
d. The seller is responsible for purchasing insurance for the shipment.

LO 3 7. True or False? If a good is shipped F.O.B. shipping point, the purchaser is responsible for paying the freight.

LO 3 8. Net purchases plus transportation-in is equal to _____ _____ _____ _____.

LO 4 9. Which of the following is not correct about the perpetual inventory method?
a. Purchased goods are debited directly to Merchandise Inventory.
b. Cost of Goods Sold is debited and Merchandise Inventory is credited with each sale.
c. The perpetual inventory system is usually easy and inexpensive to implement.
d. This method is only associated with businesses containing few individual inventory items.

LO 4 10. Which of the following is a correct computation of cost of goods sold?
a. Beginning Inventory + Net Purchases + Transportation-In – Ending Inventory
b. Ending Inventory + Net Purchases + Transportation-In – Beginning Inventory
c. Goods Available for Sale – Beginning Inventory
d. Beginning Inventory + Net Purchases – Transportation-In – Ending Inventory

LO 4 11. True or False? It is generally not necessary to count inventory to determine cost of goods sold under the periodic inventory system.

LO 4 12. Which of the following is *not* correct about the periodic inventory method?
a. Purchased goods are debited directly to Merchandise Inventory.
b. Cost of goods sold is not calculated until the end of the period.
c. The Merchandise Inventory balance is updated only at the end of the accounting period based on physical inventory counts.
d. The periodic method is often easier and less expensive to implement than the perpetual inventory method.

LO 4 13. What are the two purposes of adjusting Merchandise Inventory under the periodic inventory system?

LO 6 14. True or False? Cost of goods sold is an account on a merchandising business's income statement.

LO 6 15. Indicate whether the following accounts are debited or credited when they are closed.
a. Sales Discounts
b. Sales
c. Purchases Discounts
d. Transportation-In

LO 7 16. What is the label of the amount that represents net sales minus cost of goods sold on a classified income statement?

LO 7 17. What is the only different account on a merchandising company's classified balance sheet compared with that of a service company?

LO 9 18. What is the gross profit ratio if net sales are $50,000 and cost of goods sold is $30,000?

LO 9 19. True or False? The gross profit ratio subtracted from one is equal to the cost of goods sold ratio.

LO 9 20. What does it mean if the gross profit ratio decreases and net sales do not decline?

SOLUTIONS TO SELF-QUIZ
1. b   2. sales returns and allowances, sales discounts   3. contra-revenue   4. d   5. purchases returns and allowances, purchases discounts   6. d   7. True   8. cost of goods purchased   9. c   10. a   11. False   12. a
13. (1) To change inventory on the balance sheet from the beginning balance to the ending balance according to the inventory count   (2) To provide the beginning and ending inventory amounts in the income statement to calculate cost of goods sold
14. True   15. a credited b. debited   c. debited   d. credited   16. Gross profit   17. Merchandise inventory
18. ($50,000 – $30,000) ÷ $50,000 = 40%   19. True   20. Cost of goods sold is higher than before.

QUESTIONS

Q4-1 What are the major differences between how a service business and a merchandising business earns profits?

Q4-2 What are the differences between a service business's and a merchandising business's income statements?

Q4-3 What is the difference between a sales allowance and a sales discount?

Q4-4 How do you compute net sales?

Q4-5 Why do businesses accept returned merchandise even if it is not defective?

Q4-6 Why is Sales Discounts classified as a contra-revenue account?

Q4-7 What is the definition of F.O.B.? Why is it important for an accountant to know the F.O.B. terms of a purchase?

Q4-8 What are the advantages and disadvantages of using the perpetual inventory method compared with using the periodic inventory method?

Q4-9 Why is it necessary to count inventory under the periodic inventory system?

Q4-10 What type of operating expenses does your local drug store incur?

Q4-11 What are the effects of using computers in conducting physical inventories?

Q4-12 What is the purpose of computing a cost of goods sold ratio?

EXERCISES

LO 1   **E4-1** **Determining Gross Profit** Determine gross profit if sales are $500,000 and cost of goods sold is 60% of sales.

LO 2   **E4-2** **Recording Basic Sales Transactions** Prepare journal entries for the following list of events:

Jan. 2 Sold merchandise in exchange for $1,300 cash.
     5 Sold merchandise on credit for $2,100.
   12 One-half of the goods sold on January 5 were defective and were returned.
   21 Sold merchandise for $2,200, of which one-half was paid in cash and the remainder was sold on credit.

LO 2   **E4-3** **Recording Sales Transactions** Prepare journal entries for the Home Builders Supply Corporation for the following list of events:

Mar. 2 Sold building supplies to Charles Smith for $13,500 on account, terms 2/10, n/30.
     7 Sold plumbing fixtures to Fantasy Builders on account for $30,000. No discount was given.
   13 Sold lumber to Abbey Street Stores on account for $8,000, terms 2/10, n/30.
   15 Charles Smith returned $2,000 of building supplies from the March 2 sale.
   21 Payment was received from Abbey Street Stores.
   28 Payment was received from Charles Smith.
   31 Payment was received from Fantasy Builders.

LO 2   **E4-4** **Calculate Sales Discounts** Treetop Corporation, a company that sells precut wooden treehouse kits, had net sales of $184,000, gross sales of $207,000, and sales returns and allowances of $19,175 for 19X4.

REQUIRED:

Calculate the amount of sales discounts given by Treetop for 19X4.

LO 3   **E4-5** **Recording Basic Purchases Transactions** Prepare journal entries for the following list of events. The company uses the periodic inventory method and records purchases at the gross amount.

May 3 Purchased $1,900 of merchandise in exchange for cash.
     5 Purchased $4,300 of merchandise on credit.
   16 One-half of the goods purchased on May 5 were defective and were returned.
   24 Purchased $3,700 of merchandise, of which one-half was paid in cash and the remainder was purchased on credit.

LO 3   **E4-6** **Purchases Discount Transactions** Prepare journal entries for Middaugh's Hobby Shop, Inc., for the following list of events. The company uses the periodic inventory method and records purchases at the gross amount.

July 1 Purchased $5,000 of toy model kits with terms of 1/10, n/30, F.O.B. shipping point.
     9 Ordered $3,500 of remote-controlled racing cars on terms of 2/10, n/30, F.O.B. destination.
   11 Received the remote-controlled cars ordered on July 9. The attached invoice listed the freight charge at $95.
   12 Received a freight bill for $135 due on August 1 for the July 1 purchase.
   13 Returned $600 of the toy model kits purchased on July 1 because they were defective.

July 18 Paid the balance owed for the remote-controlled racing cars received on July 11.
    28 Paid the balance owed for the toy model kits.

LO 10

E4-7   **Recording Purchases Net of Discounts (Appendix)**   Prepare journal entries for the events described in E4-6, assuming Middaugh's Hobby Shop, Inc., uses the net of discount method for recording purchases.

LO 4

E4-8   **Basic Inventory Relationships**   Determine the missing amounts for the following information:

	January	*February*	*March*
Beginning merchandise inventory	$1,400	?	$1,800
Goods purchased	?	?	$2,000
Goods available for sale	$3,100	$5,600	?
Cost of goods sold	$1,100	?	?
Ending merchandise inventory	?	?	$1,100

LO 5

E4-9   **Calculate Operating Expense**   Determine the total selling expenses and the total general and administrative expenses from the total operating expenses listed below. The sales department and the administrative offices are located in the same building. Each function occupies one-half of the total space. Allocate as many of the total operating expenses as you can to the separate categories of selling expenses and general and administrative expenses.

Sales commissions	$13,150
Insurance expense	12,980
Wages and salaries expense—administrative	89,500
Wages and salaries expense—sales	76,890
Advertising expense	31,160
Depreciation expense—building	19,800
Utilities expense	2,985

LO 6

E4-10   **Adjusting and Closing Entries for Cost of Goods Sold**   Prepare the adjusting entries for cost of goods sold from the following list of accounts. (Ignore the absence of other revenue, contra-revenue, and expense accounts that ordinarily would be closed as well.)

Merchandise Inventory, 1/1/X7	$33,500
Merchandise Inventory, 12/31/X7	21,000
Transportation-In	3,200
Purchases	42,000
Purchases Returns and Allowances	4,600
Purchases Discounts	1,100

LO 4,6

E4-11   **Calculating Net Sales, Gross Profit, and Net Income**   Presented on the next page is the adjusted trial balance for Discount Furniture Corporation.

REQUIRED:

Calculate net sales, gross profit, and net income for Discount Furniture Corporation for 19X1 from the information in the adjusted trial balance.

Discount Furniture Corporation Adjusted Trial Balance December 31, 19X1		
	Debits	Credits
Cash	$ 29,400	
Accounts Receivable	12,200	
Merchandise Inventory	44,200	
Supplies	2,200	
Prepaid Insurance	4,400	
Prepaid Rent	11,000	
Equipment	24,000	
Accumulated Depreciation—Equipment		$ 3,600
Accounts Payable		7,400
Income Taxes Payable		8,200
Notes Payable		16,000
Capital Stock		50,000
Retained Earnings		27,700
Dividends	2,400	
Sales		147,000
Sales Returns and Allowances	3,500	
Sales Discounts	8,400	
Cost of Goods Sold	100,400	
Depreciation Expense—Equipment	1,200	
Income Tax Expense	8,200	
Insurance Expense	400	
Rent Expense	1,000	
Supplies Expense	1,200	
Utilities Expense	1,400	
Wages and Salaries Expense	4,400	
Totals	$259,900	$259,900

E4-12 **Preparing an Income Statement from an Adjusted Trial Balance** Using the adjusted trial balance in E4-11, prepare a multistep income statement for Discount Furniture Corporation. Assume that each of the operating expenses are 60% selling and 40% general and administrative.

E4-13 **Preparing a Retained Earnings Statement and a Classified Balance Sheet** Using the adjusted trial balance in E4-11, prepare a retained earnings statement and a classified balance sheet for Discount Furniture Corporation.

E4-14 **Calculate Cost of Goods Sold and Gross Profit Ratios** During 19X1, Kumar's Computer Store had net income of $158,000, operating expenses of $59,600, and cost of goods sold of $679,200.

REQUIRED:

Determine the gross profit and the cost of goods sold ratios for 19X1.

PROBLEM SET A

LO 2,3

P4-1A **Sale and Purchase Transactions** Merino's Sweater Store, Inc., uses the periodic inventory method and the gross method of recording purchases. A list of events for Merino's during the month of October is given below:

Oct. 1 Purchased $3,500 of cashmere sweaters from Liz's Sweater Supply on account with terms of 2/10, n/30. The sweaters were picked up by a Merino's employee.
3 Sold sweaters for $830 cash.
5 Sold sweaters for $760 on credit with terms of 1/10, n/30.
6 Returned $300 of the cashmere sweaters to Liz's Sweater Supply because they were defective.
7 Purchased $1,300 of sweaters, F.O.B. shipping point, from Wool-Enz Company on account with terms of 2/10, n/30. Freight, prepaid by the seller, was $50.
9 Sold sweaters for $660 cash.
12 Sweaters that sold for $200 on October 5 were returned due to defects.
14 Paid for the sweaters purchased on October 7, including the freight prepaid by the seller of $50.
17 Collected cash for the sweaters sold on October 5.
19 Sold sweaters on credit for $4,300 with terms of 1/10, n/30. The customer picked up the sweaters at the store.
26 Paid the balance due on the October 1 purchase.
28 Collected cash for the sweaters sold on October 19.
30 Sold sweaters for $900. One-half was paid in cash and the remainder was on account. The customer took possession of the sweaters at the time of sale.

REQUIRED:

a. Record journal entries for each of the events.
b. Calculate net sales.
c. Calculate cost of goods purchased.

LO 3,4

P4-2A **Accounting for Purchases** Wilner's Hardware Corporation uses the periodic inventory method and the gross method of recording purchases. A list of events for Wilner's during the month of June is given below:

June 1 Purchased $600 of hammers from Armand Company on account with terms of 2/10, n/30, F.O.B. destination. Freight charges of $30 were paid by Armand Company. The hammers were received on June 2.
5 Purchased $4,200 of power drills from Tools International on account with terms of 1/10, n/30, F.O.B. shipping point. Freight charges of $120 were paid by Tools International.
10 Paid the balance due to Tools International for the June 5 purchase.
12 Purchased $2,600 of lawn trimmers from Grass Eater Company on account with terms of 1/10, n/30, F.O.B. shipping point. Freight charges of $190 were paid by Wilner at the time of delivery on June 15.
18 Returned $200 of hammers to Armand Company.
28 Paid the balance due to Armand Company for the June 2 purchase.
30 Paid the balance due to the Grass Eater Company for the June 12 purchase.

REQUIRED:

a. Record journal entries for each of the events.
b. Calculate cost of goods purchased.
c. Calculate cost of goods sold, assuming the beginning and ending balances of Merchandise Inventory are $32,600 and $29,700, respectively.

LO 3,4,6 **P4-3A** **Cost of Goods Sold Relationships** Selected information for Bayer Company for the years ended 19X5 and 19X6 is presented below:

	19X5	19X6
Purchases returns and allowances	2,100	?
Cost of goods sold	10,500	?
Cost of goods purchased	?	?
Net purchases	?	21,500
Transportation-in	1,100	1,500
Ending merchandise inventory	?	4,200
Goods available for sale	20,000	?
Purchases discounts	700	400
Beginning merchandise inventory	3,500	?
Gross purchases	?	24,100

REQUIRED:

a. Fill in the missing information for 19X5 and 19X6.
b. Prepare all appropriate adjusting entries for the accounts shown for 19X6.

LO 1,2,3,4,8 **P4-4A** **Merchandising Income Statement Relationships** Selected information for Ralph's Plumbing Supply, Inc., for the years ended 19X2 and 19X3 is presented below:

	19X2	19X3
Purchases returns and allowances	?	6,000
Net income	37,200	41,100
Gross sales	223,500	?
Cost of goods purchased	?	?
Beginning merchandise inventory	?	?
Sales expense	?	18,100
Cost of goods available for sale	176,100	?
Purchases discounts	2,400	9,200
Gross profit	81,700	?
Sales discounts	?	4,700
Ending merchandise inventory	?	41,900
Net sales	?	221,000
Transportation-in	8,700	4,300
Cost of goods sold	120,100	?
General and administrative expense	27,100	27,300
Purchases	152,600	?
Sales returns and allowances	11,600	9,100
Net purchases	144,500	?

REQUIRED:

a. Fill in the missing information for 19X2 and 19X3.
b. Prepare a classified income statement for Ralph's Plumbing Supply for 19X3.
c. Calculate the gross profit ratios for 19X2 and 19X3.
d. Calculate the cost of goods sold ratios for 19X2 and 19X3.

LO 7,8 **P4-5A** **Preparing Financial Statements and Closing Entries for a Merchandising Business** Presented on the next page is the adjusted trial balance for A. Leathers Corporation.

Additional Information:

Purchases	$218,650
Transportation-in	11,100
Merchandise inventory, January 1, 19X8	64,180
Purchases returns and allowances	8,240
Purchases discounts	4,160

A. Leathers Corporation
Adjusted Trial Balance
December 31, 19X8

	Debits	Credits
Cash	$ 23,800	
Accounts Receivable	14,350	
Merchandise Inventory	99,640	
Supplies	4,400	
Prepaid Insurance	3,600	
Equipment	204,000	
Accumulated Depreciation—Equipment		$ 49,800
Accounts Payable		11,450
Income Taxes Payable		13,200
Notes Payable—Noncurrent		118,000
Capital Stock		60,000
Retained Earnings		68,670
Dividends	8,400	
Sales		313,560
Sales Returns and Allowances	6,200	
Sales Discounts	4,180	
Cost of Goods Sold	181,890	
Depreciation Expense—Equipment (Sales)	9,000	
Depreciation Expense—Equipment (G&A)	1,200	
Income Tax Expense	13,200	
Insurance Expense	4,800	
Supplies Expense	12,200	
Utilities Expense	9,620	
Wages and Salaries Expense (Sales)	9,800	
Wages and Salaries Expense (G&A)	24,400	
Totals	$634,680	$634,680

REQUIRED:

a. Prepare a multistep income statement for A. Leathers Corporation for 19X8. Classify all operating expenses that are not identified as sales-related as general and administrative.
b. Prepare a retained earnings statement for 19X8.
c. Prepare a classified balance sheet for the year ended December 31, 19X8.
d. Prepare the closing entries for 19X8.

LO 6,7,8,9   **P5-6A**   **Preparing Adjusting Entries, Financial Statements, and Closing Entries for a Merchandising Business**   The unadjusted trial balance as of December 31, 19X6 for the Higgins Corporation is shown on the next page.

Additional Information:

(1) A count of remaining supplies revealed that $400 remained on December 31, 19X6.
(2) A 2-year insurance policy was purchased for $2,800 on January 1, 19X6.
(3) Total depreciation of the building for the year was $10,500.
(4) Total depreciation of the equipment for the year was $6,000.
(5) All depreciation expense, supplies expense, and insurance expense are classified as general and administrative expenses.
(6) The December 31, 19X6 amount of merchandise inventory is $43,700.
(7) All advertising expense is categorized as selling.
(8) Wages and salaries owed to employees, but unpaid at December 31, 19X6 were $5,000 for sales personnel and $4,400 for other employees.
(9) The Higgins Corporation pays income taxes at the rate of 28%.

Higgins Corporation Unadjusted Trial Balance December 31, 19X6		
	Debits	Credits
Cash	$39,000	
Accounts Receivable	16,200	
Merchandise Inventory, January 1, 19X6	19,600	
Office Supplies	5,800	
Prepaid Insurance	2,400	
Land	16,000	
Building	84,000	
Accumulated Depreciation—Building		$ 21,000
Equipment	60,000	
Accumulated Depreciation—Equipment		6,000
Accounts Payable		11,400
Notes Payable		8,500
Wages and Salaries Payable		9,400
Capital Stock		50,000
Retained Earnings		69,100
Dividends	14,400	
Sales		315,200
Sales Returns and Allowances	7,800	
Sales Discounts	3,600	
Purchases	125,200	
Transportation-In	6,200	
Purchases Returns and Allowances		5,600
Purchases Discounts		5,400
Advertising Expense	2,800	
Wage and Salaries Expense–Office	44,400	
Wage and Salaries Expense–Sales	54,200	
Totals	$501,600	$501,600

REQUIRED:

a. Prepare adjusting entries for 19X6.

b. Prepare an adjusted trial balance as of December 31, 19X6.

c. Prepare a multistep income statement for Higgins Corporation for 19X6. Classify all operating expenses that are not identified as sales-related as general and administrative.

d. Prepare a retained earnings statement for 19X6.

e. Prepare a classified balance sheet for the year ended December 31, 19X6.

f. Prepare the closing entries for 19X6.

g. Calculate the cost of goods sold and gross profit ratios for Higgins for 19X6.

PROBLEM SET B

LO 2,5   **P4-1B**   **Sale and Purchase Transactions**   Jean's Lighting Store, Inc., uses the periodic inventory method and the gross method of recording purchases. A list of events for Jean's during the month of September is given below:

Sept. 2 Purchased $4,500 of lighting fixtures from Eastern Electric on account with terms of 2/10, n/30. The fixtures were picked up by one of Jean's employees.

3 Sold light fixtures for $2,130 cash.

Sept. 5 Sold chandeliers for $3,260 on credit with terms of 1/10, n/30. The chandeliers were delivered to the customer at the store.

7 Returned $900 of the lighting fixtures to Eastern Electric because they were defective.

8 Purchased $4,300 of bathroom lighting fixtures F.O.B. shipping point from A-One Wholesale Electronics on account with terms of 2/10, n/30. Freight of $250 was paid by A-One.

10 Sold lighting fixtures for $4,660 cash. The fixtures were delivered to the customer at the store.

12 Chandeliers that were sold for $1,700 on September 5 were returned due to defects.

14 Paid for the bathroom lighting fixtures purchased on September 8, including the prepaid freight of $250.

17 Collected cash for the chandeliers sold on September 5.

19 Sold lighting fixtures for $8,300 on credit with terms of 1/10, n/30. The customer took possession of the fixtures at the store.

26 Paid the balance due on the September 2 purchase.

28 Collected cash for the fixtures sold on September 19.

30 Sold bathroom lighting fixtures for $1,800. One-half was paid in cash and the remainder was on account. The customer picked up the fixtures.

REQUIRED:

a. Record journal entries for each of the events.
b. Calculate net sales.
c. Calculate net cost of goods purchased.

LO 3,4

P4-2B **Accounting for Purchases** The Appliance Den, Inc. uses the periodic inventory method. A list of events for The Appliance Den during the month of March is given below:

Mar. 2 Received $900 of blenders purchased from Shaker Company on account with terms of 2/10, n/30, F.O.B. destination. Freight charges of $30 were paid by Shaker Company.

5 Purchased $6,300 of vacuum cleaners from Kauffman Distributors on account with terms of 1/10, n/30, F.O.B. shipping point. Freight charges of $120 were paid by Kauffman Distributors.

10 Paid the balance due to Kauffman Distributors for the March 5 purchase.

12 Purchased $3,900 of toaster ovens from Westend Company on account with terms of 1/10, n/30, F.O.B. shipping point. Freight charges of $190 were paid in cash on delivery by The Appliance Den on March 15.

18 Returned $300 of blenders to Shaker Company.

28 Paid the balance due to Shaker Company for the March 2 purchase.

30 Paid the balance due to Westend Company for the March 12 purchase.

REQUIRED:

a. Record journal entries for each of the events.
b. Calculate cost of goods purchased.
c. Calculate cost of goods sold, assuming the beginning and ending balances of Merchandise Inventory are $48,900 and $44,550, respectively.

LO 3,4

P4-3B **Cost of Goods Sold Relationships** Selected information for Butler Corp. for the years ended 19X1 and 19X2 is presented below and on the next page.

	19X1	*19X2*
Purchases returns and allowances	5,250	5,500
Cost of goods sold	26,250	?

	19X1	19X2
Net cost of goods purchased	?	?
Net purchases	?	53,750
Transportation-in	2,750	3,750
Ending merchandise inventory	?	10,500
Goods available for sale	50,000	?
Purchase discounts	1,750	?
Beginning merchandise inventory	8,750	?
Gross purchases	?	60,250

REQUIRED:

a. Fill in the missing information for 19X1 and 19X2.

b. Prepare all appropriate adjusting entries for the accounts shown for 19X2.

LO 1,2,3 4,8   **P5-4B**   **Merchandising Income Statement Relationships**   Selected information for Ace Auto Parts, Inc., for the years ended 19X8 and 19X9 is presented below:

	19X8	19X9
Purchases returns and allowances	?	3,000
Net income	18,600	20,550
Gross sales	111,750	?
Cost of goods purchased	?	?
Beginning merchandise inventory	?	?
Sales expense	?	9,050
Cost of goods available for sale	88,050	?
Purchases discounts	1,200	4,600
Gross profit	40,850	?
Sales discounts	?	2,350
Ending merchandise inventory	?	20,950
Net sales	?	110,500
Transportation-in	4,350	2,150
Cost of goods sold	60,050	?
General and administrative expense	13,550	13,650
Purchases	76,300	?
Sales returns and allowances	5,800	4,550
Net purchases	72,250	?

REQUIRED:

a. Fill in the missing information for 19X8 and 19X9.

b. Prepare a classified income statement for Ace Auto Parts, Inc., for 19X9.

c. Calculate the gross profit ratios for 19X8 and 19X9.

d. Calculate the cost of goods sold ratios for 19X8 and 19X9.

LO 7,8   **P4-5B**   **Preparing Financial Statements and Closing Entries for a Merchandising Business** Presented on the next page is the adjusted trial balance for N. Suhm Corporation.

Additional Information:

Purchases	$327,975
Transportation-in	16,650
Merchandise inventory, January 1, 19X4	96,270
Purchases returns and allowances	12,360
Purchases discounts	6,240

N. Suhm Corporation		
Adjusted Trial Balance		
December 31, 19X4		
	Debits	Credits
Cash	$ 35,700	
Accounts Receivable	21,525	
Merchandise Inventory	149,460	
Supplies	6,600	
Prepaid Insurance	5,400	
Equipment	306,000	
Accumulated Depreciation—Equipment		$ 74,700
Accounts Payable		17,175
Notes Payable—Noncurrent		177,000
Income Taxes Payable		37,000
Capital Stock		100,000
Retained Earnings		81,335
Dividends	12,600	
Sales		470,340
Sales Returns and Allowances	12,360	
Sales Discounts	6,240	
Cost of Goods Sold	272,835	
Depreciation Expense—Equipment (Sales)	9,100	
Depreciation Expense—Equipment (G&A)	6,200	
Income Tax Expense	37,000	
Insurance Expense	7,200	
Supplies Expense	18,300	
Utilities Expense	14,430	
Wages and Salaries Expense (Sales)	16,300	
Wages and Salaries Expense (G&A)	20,300	
Totals	$957,550	$957,550

REQUIRED:

a. Prepare a multistep income statement for N. Suhm Corporation for 19X4. Classify all operating expenses that are not identified as sales-related as general and administrative.
b. Prepare a retained earnings statement for 19X4.
c. Prepare a classified balance sheet for the year ended December 31, 19X4.
d. Prepare the closing entries for 19X4.

LO 6,7,8,9   **P4-6B** **Preparing Adjusting Entries, Financial Statements, and Closing Entries for a Merchandising Business**   The unadjusted trial balance on December 31, 19X5 for The Silverman Corporation is shown on the next page:

Additional Information:
(1) A count of remaining supplies revealed that $600 remained on December 31, 19X5.
(2) A 2-year insurance policy was purchased for $3,600 on January 1, 19X5.
(3) Depreciation on the equipment for the year was $15,500.
(4) Depreciation for the year on the building was $9,000.
(5) Wages and salaries owed but unpaid at December 31, 19X5 were $6,600 for office personnel and $7,500 for sales employees.
(6) The December 31, 19X5 amount of merchandise inventory is $65,550.
(7) Silverman chooses to view all depreciation expense, supplies expense, and insurance expense as general and administrative expense.
(8) All advertising expense is selling.
(9) Silverman pays income tax at the rate of 28%.

The Silverman Corporation Unadjusted Trial Balance December 31, 19X6		
	Debits	Credits
Cash	$58,500	
Accounts Receivable	24,300	
Merchandise Inventory	29,400	
Office Supplies	8,200	
Prepaid Insurance	3,600	
Land	24,000	
Equipment	126,000	
Accumulated Depreciation—Equipment		$ 31,500
Building	90,000	
Accumulated Depreciation—Building		9,000
Accounts Payable		17,100
Notes Payable		12,750
Wages and Salaries Payable		14,100
Capital Stock		70,000
Retained Earnings		108,650
Dividends	21,600	
Sales		472,800
Sales Discounts	11,700	
Sales Returns and Allowances	5,400	
Purchases	187,800	
Transportation-In	9,800	
Purchases Returns and Allowances		8,400
Purchases Discounts		8,100
Advertising Expense	4,200	
Wage and Salaries Expense–Office	66,600	
Wage and Salaries Expense–Sales	81,300	
Totals	$752,400	$752,400

REQUIRED:

a. Prepare adjusting entries for 19X5.
b. Prepare an adjusted trial balance as of December 31, 19X5.
c. Prepare a multistep income statement for The Silverman Corporation for 19X5. Classify all operating expenses that are not identified as sales-related as general and administrative.
d. Prepare a retained earnings statement for 19X5.
e. Prepare a classified balance sheet for the year ended December 31, 19X5.
f. Prepare the closing entries for 19X5.
g. Calculate the cost of goods sold and gross profit ratios for Silverman for 19X5.

CRITICAL THINKING AND COMMUNICATING

C4-1 Fred Wang owns and operates a regional chain of pet supply stores. Many of Mr. Wang's suppliers offer purchase discounts with the terms of 2/10, n/30. Mr. Wang suspects some of his store managers, hired in the last year, are not paying the suppliers in time to receive the discounts. Mr. Wang's stores record purchases at gross prices and deduct discounts received to derive net purchases. Mr. Wang prefers not to change his accounting method to the "net" method (see Appendix 4-A). Mr. Wang discusses the problem with his accountant, Mrs. Greenleaf, and asks her how to analyze it.

REQUIRED:

a. Explain why Mr. Wang is concerned about his managers not receiving purchases discounts.
b. Describe the analysis that Mrs. Greenleaf should recommend to Mr. Wang and explain how it will help him determine the extent of the problem.
c. Explain to Mr. Wang what the impact of not taking purchases discounts would have on the gross profit ratio.

C4-2 Yvette Bescos owns and operates Yvette's Boutique, Inc. She has been replacing the lines of clothing she carries with well-known designer labels. Yvette believes her net income has been increasing as a result of carrying these labels, but she is concerned about the decline in sales last year. A comparative income statement for her store is given below:

Yvette's Boutique, Inc. Comparative Income Statement For the Years Ended December 31, 19X7 and 19X8		
	19X7	*19X8*
Net sales	$198,000	$195,000
Less: Cost of goods sold	110,000	93,000
Gross profit	$ 88,000	$102,000
Less: Expenses	38,000	39,000
Net income	$ 50,000	$ 63,000

REQUIRED:

a. Calculate the gross profit ratios for 19X7 and 19X8.
b. Explain why Yvette's strategy may cause sales to decline.
c. Advise Yvette whether or not to continue her current strategy.

C4-3 The financial statements of J.C. Penney Company, Inc. a major retail merchandising company, are reprinted in Appendix B at the end of the text. Examine J. C. Penney's income statement carefully. Note two things. The company does not calculate gross profit in the income statement and it includes "occupancy, buying, and warehousing costs" with cost of goods sold.

REQUIRED:

1. Ignore the additional costs included with cost of goods sold and calculate J.C. Penney's gross profit, gross profit percentage, and cost of goods sold percentage for 1991, 1992, and 1993. Use retail sales rather than total revenue in your calculations.
2. Comment on the degree of fluctuation in J.C. Penney's gross profit percentage over the three years.
3. Calculate the effect an increase in cost of goods sold equal to 1% of retail sales would have had on J.C. Penney's net income for 1993.
4. Considering that J.C. Penney operates stores in many different locations, comment on why you think that management lumps "occupancy, buying, and warehousing costs" with cost of goods sold in the income statement.

CHAPTER 5

Cash and Cash Equivalents

Frank Brown, owner of Ready Auto Parts, Inc., believed he really was in touch with the successful business he founded a few years ago—that is, until today. Having just finished a meeting with some officers of his bank, Frank now feels confused. Wanting to establish a line of credit—a pre-arranged loan—that he could draw on as needed to help him finance further business growth, Frank had arranged the meeting. The bankers had ana-lyzed his financial statements and had asked many specific questions Frank could easily answer. Then, when they had asked specifically about how his business controlled its cash and about its liquidity position, Frank felt less prepared. He knows he has done a good job of organizing his business, and he has implemented most of the internal control sug-gestions made by the CPAs who help his account-ing personnel prepare the financial statements each year. However, Frank is no longer familiar with many of the details, and he has never learned about the financial ratios that best measure a busi-ness's liquidity. Before his meeting with the bankers ended, Frank asked for a second meeting in a week to prepare answers to their questions.

This chapter covers the methods businesses commonly use to control cash. A well-designed sys-tem controls cash receipts, cash disbursements, and any cash the business holds. Cash control systems must be "tight" because cash is the asset that employees most easily convert to personal use and it is the business's life-blood—the means by which it pays its bills and survives. The liquidity of a busi-ness is its ability to pay its bills in the short run. At the end of the chapter, we introduce you to the current ratio and the colorfully named acid-test ratio, the toughest of the widely used tests of a business's liquidity position.

1. Describe broad control objectives and control procedures for cash received from credit sales.
2. Describe control procedures for cash received in cash sales transactions.
3. Describe control procedures for cash disbursements, including the voucher system and voucher documents.
4. Describe the operation of a petty cash fund and record petty cash expenditures in the accounting records.
5. Identify the reconciling items that make the business's cash balance differ from the balance on its bank statement.
6. Follow the steps required to prepare a bank reconciliation and record any needed adjustments in the accounting records.
7. Describe two major categories of electronic funds transfers businesses use.
8. Define and explain the accounting for cash equivalents.
9. Define and interpret the current and acid-test ratios.

LO 1

Describe broad control objectives and control procedures for cash received from credit sales.

CONTROL OBJECTIVES AND SYSTEMS FOR CASH

A business cannot earn a profit by being sloppy or inefficient, especially when it must compete with other businesses. It must be effective in achieving its sales, production, and other goals; and it must be efficient in utilizing its assets and personnel to achieve those goals at the least cost. In other words, a business must be disciplined and operate under management's control. A management control system has the following broad objectives:

1. Goals are achieved (effectiveness).
2. Only necessary costs are incurred in achieving goals (efficiency).
3. Activities are conducted only in accordance with management's policies, and all transactions are preauthorized.
4. The assets of the business are safeguarded.
5. The financial reports used by management and prepared for outside users are reliable.

Like all other business functions, the accounting function requires discipline or control. If a business does not control the accounting process carefully, it cannot achieve the objective of ensuring reliable financial reports. Accounting also contributes significantly to the overall control of the business. For example, a business cannot judge the efficiency of its sales department without reliable accounting information about the expenses incurred to support the sales effort.

Different areas of an overall control system will emphasize control objectives to different degrees. Because employees and others can readily convert cash to personal use, cash control systems predominantly focus on *safeguarding cash*. However, a business cannot safeguard its cash unless employees conform *strictly to company policies* and *maintain reliable records*. So, good cash control systems must meet three of the five management control objectives listed above.

Illustration 5-1 gives you an overview of the major components of a cash control system. An overall **cash control system** includes both strong cash receipts and strong cash disbursements controls. Using a bank checking account

ILLUSTRATION 5-1 Overview of a Cash Control System

physically protects cash reserves and disbursements. A checking account is so crucial to cash control that we do not consider cases where this essential control is absent. When a business uses a checking account, the only significant amounts of cash employees actually handle are cash receipts, which should be deposited promptly in the bank. All significant payments should be made by check, and minor expenditures should be made with a petty cash fund. The monthly bank statement is the bank's independent record of the cash transactions and the cash balance. A business should use the bank statement monthly to verify its recorded cash balance by preparing a schedule known as a bank reconciliation.

CONTROL OF CASH RECEIPTS

Processing cash receipts consists of:

1. Receiving and recording cash at the point of receipt
2. Preparing deposit slips and depositing cash in the bank
3. Recording cash receipts in the general journal.

Whenever possible (cost-effective), no employee should be allowed to perform more than one of these basic functions. By separating these responsibilities, no individual employee can commit theft of cash and avoid detection by covering up the theft in the accounting records. Employees who work independently of each other should perform verifications and reconciliations as we describe below.

Control of Cash Receipts from Credit Sales

Ready Auto Parts, Inc.'s system for processing cash receipts on credit sales is shown in Illustration 5-2.

ILLUSTRATION 5-2 Processing Cash Receipts from Credit Sales

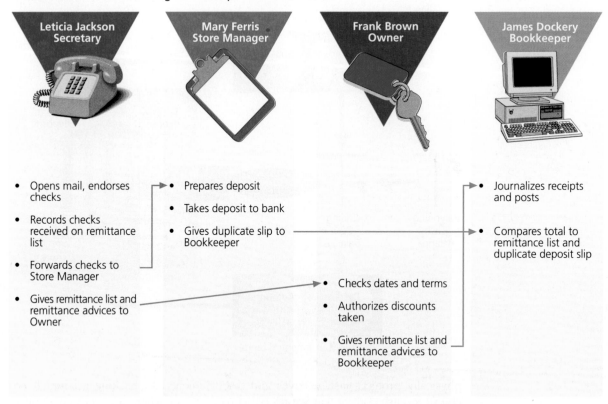

**Leticia Jackson
Secretary**

- Opens mail, endorses checks

- Records checks received on remittance list

- Forwards checks to Store Manager

- Gives remittance list and remittance advices to Owner

**Mary Ferris
Store Manager**

- Prepares deposit

- Takes deposit to bank

- Gives duplicate slip to Bookkeeper

**Frank Brown
Owner**

- Checks dates and terms

- Authorizes discounts taken

- Gives remittance list and remittance advices to Bookkeeper

**James Dockery
Bookkeeper**

- Journalizes receipts and posts

- Compares total to remittance list and duplicate deposit slip

Receiving Cash. Generally, businesses receive cash receipts from credit sales through the mail. Businesses should discourage their customers from remitting currency or coins when paying their accounts. At Ready Auto Parts, Frank Brown's secretary, Leticia Jackson, opens the mail, separates the checks from the rest of the mail, and restrictively endorses each check immediately. A restrictive endorsement, as shown in Illustration 5-3, says that the check may only be deposited to the account of the payee business. After restrictively endorsing the checks, Leticia enters them on a remittance list, like the one shown in Illustration 5-3, that includes the names of the companies or individuals making the payments and the amounts of the checks. After entering and double-checking all the checks, Leticia signs the remittance list, thus taking personal responsibility for its accuracy.

Depositing Cash. Leticia immediately gives the checks to the Store Manager, Mary Ferris, who makes the bank deposits. Mary fills out deposit slips such as the one shown in Illustration 5-4. Notice that the deposit slip includes currency and coins from cash sales (discussed below) as well as checks from credit sales customers. Either Mary or Frank personally delivers the daily deposit to the bank, and Mary then gives a copy of the deposit slip to James Dockery, the bookkeeper.

Authorizing Discounts. Leticia gives the remittance advices to Frank to review and to approve the discounts customers take. Customers should return the

ILLUSTRATION 5-3 Restrictive Endorsement

Back of Check

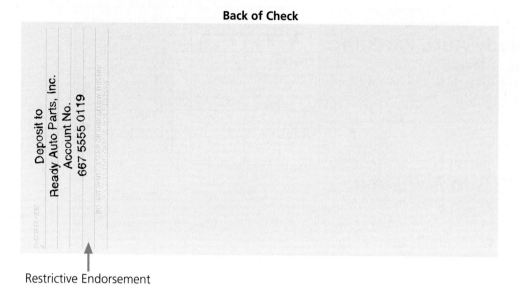

Restrictive Endorsement

Ready Auto Parts, Inc.'s remittance advices (second copies of the original invoices sent to them) when they make payments on their accounts. When customers forget to return remittance advices with their checks, Leticia makes photocopies of the original invoices. The important point is that a document other than the check is ultimately used to record each cash receipt. This procedure separates the incompatible duties of handling the checks for deposit purposes and recording cash receipts.

Before the recording takes place, Frank compares the date of receipt of payment with the due dates for discounts, according to the terms of the original sales transaction. He approves discounts taken by initialing the discount on the remittance advice. When Frank denies a discount, he indicates so on the remittance advice, and James subsequently records only the amount of the payment. The improper discount is not recognized and remains receivable from the customer.

Recording Cash Receipts. Frank gives the remittance advices to James to enter the data using the computer program that posts cash receipts to the accounts receivable account. James uses the program to print a list of the day's entries and to reconcile the list total with the deposit slips and the remittance listing forwarded to him by Mary and Frank, respectively. He corrects any entry errors he has made and reports other discrepancies to Frank immediately.

How Controls Protect Cash Received. Even in a small business like Ready Auto Parts, Inc., control over cash receipts is built not just on the trustworthiness of key employees, but also on basic controls. In Illustration 5-2 and the discussion above, Mary handles checks received only after they are restrictively endorsed, and she does not record cash receipts transactions. James, on the other hand, enters the cash receipts into the computer, but he does not handle any cash. Neither of these employees can take cash from the business and cover up the theft without the cooperation of another employee. The **separation of incompatible duties** works on a common-sense principle of account-

ILLUSTRATION 5-4 Business Deposit Slip

DEPOSIT SLIP	CASH	CURRENCY	1,550	00	00-001
Ready Auto Parts,Inc.		COIN	45	50	555
105 S. Main	CHECKS				
Twin City, MO 11223-4578	Attach list				
Date: _June 10, 19X1_			3,110	00	
North *National* Bank	TOTAL DEPOSIT		4,705	50	
232 North Elm Street, Twin City, MO 11223					

":055500010 ":40566755550119" '4564

Ready Auto Parts, Inc.
Remittance List

Date: 06/10/X1	Page 1	
Maker	**Amount**	
Windler Garage	530	00
Ace Repair	1,060	00
Don's Auto Repair	125	00
Vern's Body Shop	545	00
Bob's Top Shop	850	00
Total	3,110	00

ing control: The likelihood that two or more employees will be dishonest is less than the likelihood that one employee will be dishonest. The separation of incompatible duties denies the single dishonest employee an easy opportunity to harm the business.

So, you might ask: "What about Leticia, who opens the mail and handles *both* the checks and the remittance advices?" Frank has employed her for many years and is absolutely sure of her honesty and integrity. However, even if his judgment is wrong, according to the schematic in Illustration 5-2, there are implicit controls over her role in handling cash. As long as Leticia has no access to accounting records, if she takes checks and converts them to her own use (and destroys the remittance advices), the customers' accounts will not be credited with their payments. Eventually, Frank will try to collect what appear to be past-due accounts, and an investigation will follow. Thus, the virtual certainty of ultimate detection acts as a deterrent, albeit not a perfect one, to the person in Leticia's position in the control system.

LO 2

Describe control procedures for cash received in cash sales transactions.

Controlling Cash Sales

While cash receipts on credit sales generally involve only receipt of checks, cash sales involve the receipt of checks, currency, and coins, as well as giving change to customers. Since receipts on cash sales give rise to greater risks of employee errors and dishonesty, the procedures for controlling cash received from cash sales differ slightly from those involving credit sales. Effective control for cash sales involves the use of cash registers and separation of duties of receiving cash, depositing cash, and recording and reconciling cash received to the cash register record of cash sales. A schematic for processing cash sales is shown in Illustration 5-5.

ILLUSTRATION 5-5 Cash Sales Processing

Cashiers

- Enters sales data in cash register and puts cash received in cash drawer
- Counts cash at end of shift and submits count and cash to Manager

Mary Ferris Store Manager

- Counts cash
- Prepares deposit slip and takes deposit to bank
- Gives copy of deposit slip to Bookkeeper

James Dockery Bookkeeper

- Notes register total on computer
- Compares register total to deposit slip and cash count
- Notifies Owner of major differences
- Enters daily sales and Cash Over or Short

Customer receipt
Tape record of sales

Receipt of Cash Using Cash Registers. Cashiers at Ready Auto Parts, Inc., enter each cash sale into electronic cash registers at the time of sale. As cashiers enter the amounts, customers can see them on a display. As a cash register receives the information entered, it prints this information and the total of each sale on two tapes. One tape provides sales receipts to customers. Because customers generally will pay only for the amount on the receipts, the register cashier is not able to collect more cash than is recorded and keep the difference. The other tape is locked in (inaccessible to the cashier) and keeps a paper record of the sales made with the register. The cash register totals the sales keyed in for a particular shift or for the day and prints the total to the locked-in tape. The cash register is also connected to Ready Auto Parts, Inc.'s computer network, and it transmits its totals to a computer as well. At the end of the shift or end of the day, each cashier is required to count the cash in his or her cash drawer and turn it over to the Store Manager, Mary Ferris.

Depositing Cash. Mary Ferris recounts the cash to check on the accuracy of the cashiers' counts and includes the coins, currency, and checks collected in the daily deposit. As shown in Illustration 5-5, she gives a copy of the deposit slip to the Bookkeeper, James Dockery.

Reconciling Cash Sales to Deposits. James has access to the cash register totals through his computer. He compares the register totals to the cash count on the deposit slip and calls any significant discrepancies to Frank's attention immediately.

Recording Cash Sales. After reconciling and following up on discrepancies, James enters the (corrected) cash count from the deposit slip into the computer, which then records it in Cash and Cash Sales. Minor discrepancies between cash deposited and the cash sales per the cash register tapes are recorded as "cash over or short."

Recording Cash Over or Short. Regardless of how honest and careful the cashiers are, they will make small errors in handling cash from cash sales. Thus, at the end of the workday, the amount of cash sales indicated by the cash register total will differ from the amount of cash on hand for deposit. The discrepancy is recorded in an account called Cash Over or Short. Assume that at the end of business on June 10, 19X1, the cash register total of Ready Auto Parts, Inc., indicates cash sales of $1,597.75, but the cash listed on the deposit slip is only $1,595.50, meaning that there is a cash shortage for the day of $2.25. James would enter the cash shortage as well as the deposit total, and the computer would record these two numbers along with the cash register total in the following general journal entry:

June 10	Cash	1,595.50	
	Cash Over or Short	2.25	
	Cash Sales		1,597.75
	To record day's cash sales.		

On the other hand, if cash sales had been $1,593.25, the amounts recorded would be:

June 10	Cash	1,595.50	
	Cash Over or Short		2.25
	Cash Sales		1,593.25
	To record day's cash sales.		

Over time, the cash shortages and the cash overages should be about equal. Of course, any individually large daily shortages or overages should be investigated—as should any large *cumulative* debit or credit balances in Cash Over or Short. At the end of an accounting period, the balance of Cash Over or Short is closed to Income Summary. In the income statement, a debit balance in Cash Over or Short is shown as part of selling expense or miscellaneous expense. A credit balance is shown as a part of miscellaneous revenue.

Separation of Incompatible Duties.   While Ready Auto Parts, Inc.'s accounting system is not foolproof, the separation of incompatible duties for cash sales should be reasonably effective. James, who has access to the cash register totals, does not have access to the cash. On the other hand, the cashiers and Mary, who physically handle the cash, do not have access to the cash register totals.

If employees with access misappropriate cash, their actions would be detected almost immediately. James would notice a significant discrepancy between the amount of the cash register total and the cash count per the deposit slip—more than would be explained by ordinary cash over or short. He would immediately take his findings to Frank, the owner. The internal cash register tapes serve as a backup in case of an electronic problem with a cash register or the computer network. They are saved for a few months, and Frank occasionally compares a day's tape total to the daily entry for cash sales. This is a reasonable overall check on all the personnel involved in handling and recording cash sales.

CONTROLLING CASH DISBURSEMENTS

LO 3
Describe control procedures for cash disbursements, including the voucher system and voucher documents.

Controlling cash disbursements requires some fairly sophisticated accounting controls. They focus not only on the direct expenditure of funds, but also on the acquisition of goods and services. It makes little difference to a business whether an employee steals cash directly from a cash register or indirectly. For example, an employee might submit fake purchase documents, and the business would issue a check to the employee or to the employee's business without receiving any goods or services in exchange.

Voucher System

To integrate controls over acquisitions and expenditures, many businesses use the voucher system. The **voucher system** takes its name from the word *vouch*, which means to support (with evidence or testimony). The **voucher** is the document on which relevant data about an obligation to pay are summarized for approval, recording, and payment. Illustration 5-6 is the voucher for the June 2, 19X1, receipt by Ready Auto Parts, Inc., of a shipment of mufflers purchased from Quiet Mufflers, Inc. Some small businesses use the voucher system without having a separate voucher document. They merely use a stamp that makes an impression on the supplier's invoice. The impression is a condensed voucher form that employees fill out right on the face of the invoice. This is a simple, cost-saving alternative to the full voucher documentation.

Processing Purchases

Vouchers represent purchase transactions and cash disbursements for both goods and services. They are supported by purchase requisitions, purchase

ILLUSTRATION 5-6 Voucher

(Front of Voucher)

Ready Auto Parts, Inc.
Voucher

Payee:	Quiet Mufflers, Inc.		Voucher No:	**10001**

Address: 666 S. Second Avenue
Rockport, ME 11223

		Date:	06/02/X1
Terms:	2/10, n/30	Date Due:	06/12/X1
		Check No.	221

Date	Invoice Number	Description	Amount
06/02/X1	INV606076	250 Universal Mufflers	5,000

Attach Supporting Document

Supporting Documents Attached ___*CLM*___

Amount and Terms Correct ___*CLM*___   Approved ___*MF*___

(Back of Voucher)

Debit to Account	Amount
754 Purchases	5,000
776 Transportation-In	
Other Accounts: Number Name	
Credit to 212 Vouchers Payable	5,000
Distribution Reviewed and Approved	*MF*

Date Due: 06/12/X1

Amount: 5,000

Discount: 100

Check Amount: 4,900

Payment Approved: *FB*

Check Number: 221

orders, receiving reports, and supplier invoices. The individual responsible for maintaining stocks on hand submits a **purchase requisition**, a request to purchase needed goods. For example, John Thomas, inventory manager, requisitioned the mufflers Ready purchased. John reviews the existing stocks of goods in the store and reorders them when necessary. A **purchase order**, a formal offer to buy goods, is sent to the supplier after a person with authority approves the transaction. A clerk prepares purchase orders at Ready Auto Parts, Inc., and Mary Ferris, store manager, approves them. A **receiving report**, a document completed by the employees who physically receive goods on the business's behalf, contains evidence of the quantities and condition of goods actually received from suppliers. John Thomas signs receiving reports when goods are received. The **supplier's invoice**, the supplier's billing document, contains the descriptions, quantities shipped and prices of goods, the total amount owed, and the terms of credit.

Preparing Vouchers.   Illustration 5-7 presents a schematic of a system for preparing vouchers and controlling cash disbursements, once purchased goods are received. At Ready Auto Parts, Inc., office assistants working for Mary Ferris prepare vouchers from the basic information on the supplier's invoice. They compare the invoice to the requisition, purchase order, and the receiving report so the business recognizes liabilities and pays suppliers only for goods and services actually ordered and received. Only originals or carbon copies of supporting documents are accepted (no photocopies) to reduce the chance of duplicate payments. The assistants also enter on the back of the voucher the "account distribution" of the transaction—the appropriate accounts and amounts to be debited in recording the purchase. (See Illustration 5-6.)

ILLUSTRATION 5-7 Voucher Processing Schematic

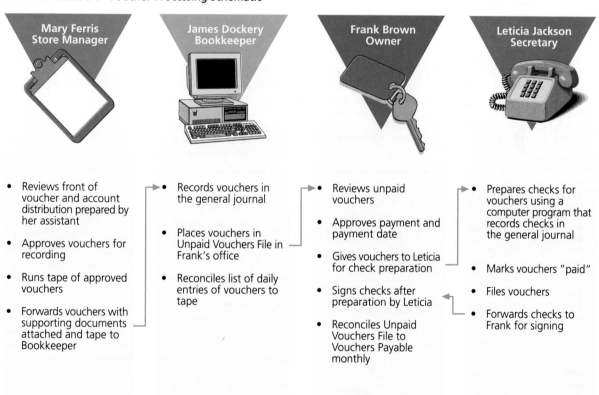

Mary Ferris Store Manager
- Reviews front of voucher and account distribution prepared by her assistant
- Approves vouchers for recording
- Runs tape of approved vouchers
- Forwards vouchers with supporting documents attached and tape to Bookkeeper

James Dockery Bookkeeper
- Records vouchers in the general journal
- Places vouchers in Unpaid Vouchers File in Frank's office
- Reconciles list of daily entries of vouchers to tape

Frank Brown Owner
- Reviews unpaid vouchers
- Approves payment and payment date
- Gives vouchers to Leticia for check preparation
- Signs checks after preparation by Leticia
- Reconciles Unpaid Vouchers File to Vouchers Payable monthly

Leticia Jackson Secretary
- Prepares checks for vouchers using a computer program that records checks in the general journal
- Marks vouchers "paid"
- Files vouchers
- Forwards checks to Frank for signing

Approving Vouchers for Recording.   Mary Ferris examines the underlying documentation attached to each voucher and checks the voucher and the account distribution on the back for accuracy. If satisfied, she initials both sides of the voucher, indicating that it is approved for recording. She also runs a tape of the totals of all vouchers approved for recording each day and passes the tape along to James Dockery with the vouchers.

Recording Vouchers.   James Dockery journalizes and posts the information on the vouchers. By performing this task, he records obligations for all kinds of goods and services. Every acquisition of goods or required payment for services is recorded at the first opportunity, whether it is due the day it is recorded or at some time in the future. Every item results in an entry in the Vouchers Payable account. Purchases of goods and services require debits to the appropriate asset or expense accounts. James Dockery places recorded vouchers in order of the date payment is due in the Unpaid Vouchers file in Mr. Brown's office.

The Unpaid Vouchers file serves two purposes. First, its due-date order ensures timely payment of obligations and taking as many discounts as possible. Second, it also represents the details supporting the balance in the general ledger Vouchers Payable at any time. When the computer completes all posting at the end of a month, Frank compares the sum of the unpaid vouchers to the balance of the general ledger Vouchers Payable and investigates discrepancies.

Approving Vouchers for Payment.   Reviewing vouchers on the day they are due, Frank focuses primarily on the validity of the attached documents. He indicates his approval by writing his initials in the appropriate place on the back of the vouchers and then passes them along to Leticia for check preparation. After Leticia prepares the checks, she presents them to Frank for signature.

Paying Vouchers.   Leticia Jackson prepares checks like the one in Illustration 5-8 for all approved vouchers. Notice that an extension document, called a remittance advice, is attached to the bottom of the check. The **remittance advice** notifies the payee of the purpose of the payment so that Ready Auto Parts, Inc.'s account with the payee will be credited properly. Recall that all expenditures are first recorded as liabilities and the related asset or expense

ILLUSTRATION 5-8 Business Check with Attached Remittance Advice

Ready Auto Parts, Inc.
105 S. Main
Twin City, MO 11223-4578

221

00-001

555

June 12   19 _X1_

PAY TO THE
ORDER OF _Quiet Mufflers, Inc._ $ 4,900.00

Four thousand nine hundred and 00/100 —————————————————— DOLLARS

North
National Bank
232 North Elm Street, Twin City, MO 11223

MEMO _____   _Frank Brown_

":055500010 ":40566755550119" '0221

REMITTANCE ADVICE				**Ready Auto Parts, Inc.**
Date	P.O. No.		Description	Amount
06/12/X1	PO67561		250 Universal Mufflers (Terms: 2/10, n/30) Your Invoice No. INV606076	$5,000.00
			Less applicable discount	100.00
			Net	$4,900.00

accounts are debited. Thus, actual expenditures involve only debits to Vouchers Payable and credits to Cash and Purchases Discounts (where applicable).

After checks are prepared and recorded, Leticia marks the voucher and all the attached documents "Paid" to prohibit their use another time to support duplicate payments. She presents the checks (with the vouchers) to Frank for signature and then mails them to the payees. Finally, she files the paid vouchers by payee.

PETTY CASH FUND

LO 4

Describe the operation of a petty cash fund and record petty cash expenditures in the accounting proceeds.

Although businesses should make most of their cash payments by check, some expenditures are too small to justify the expense and time of preparing a voucher, securing the necessary approvals, and writing a check. Thus, many businesses use a **petty cash fund** from which to make small cash payments.

Setting Up the Petty Cash Fund

Frank Brown decided to establish a petty cash fund on July 1, 19X1. He estimated that $75 should be sufficient for one month's operation of the fund. He gave Leticia Jackson an approved voucher debiting Petty Cash and asked her to prepare a check for his signature payable to "Cash" in the amount of $75. He also asked her to cash the check and to set up and run the petty cash fund. She keeps the petty cash fund in a small metal cash box locked in her desk. The following general journal entry records establishing the petty cash fund:

July 1	Petty Cash	75.00	
	Cash		75.00
	To establish a petty cash fund to be managed by Leticia Jackson.		

The effect of the entry is to transfer $75 from Cash to Petty Cash. Once the petty cash fund is established and recorded, Petty Cash is not debited or credited until the amount of the fund is changed. The amount of the fund is changed when experience indicates that the original amount of the fund is either too small or too large.

Expenditures from Petty Cash

When she makes a payment out of the petty cash fund, Leticia requires the person receiving the cash to sign a **petty cash receipt**. On the petty cash receipt, Leticia records the date, the amount of the expenditure, what the expenditure is for, and the account to which the expenditure should ultimately be posted. As shown in Illustration 5-9, the petty cash receipt also has a space for Leticia's signature as the person with the authority to approve petty cash expenditures.

Leticia places the petty cash receipts in the cash box with the remaining cash. Therefore, *the sum of the petty cash receipts and the remaining cash should always equal the amount of the petty cash fund.* This feature provides an element of control over the use of the petty cash fund. When Leticia performs a count, the amount of cash in the fund should equal the amount at which the fund is established less the amount of the petty cash receipts.

ILLUSTRATION 5-9 Petty Cash Receipt

Petty Cash Receipt

Date: _7/20/X1_   Receipt No.: _5_

Amount: _$3.14_

For: _Typewriter ribbon_   _Judy Gold_
                                  Received by

Charge to: _Office Supplies_   _Leticia Jackson_
                                      Approved by

Replenishment of Petty Cash

At the end of July, Leticia lists the petty cash receipts:

Receipt No.	Purpose	Amount	Debit Account
1	Postage stamps	$22.00	Office Supplies
2	Freight on purchase	7.50	Transportation-In
3	Flowers for office party	15.75	Miscellaneous Expense
4	Coffee service	12.60	Miscellaneous Expense
5	Typewriter ribbon	3.14	Office Supplies
6	Freight on purchase	9.89	Transportation-In
	Total	$70.88	

Only $4.12 remains in the petty cash fund, a balance which probably is insufficient to make another payment. To replenish the fund, Leticia gives the petty cash receipts to Mary Ferris, who prepares a voucher. Frank approves the voucher after reviewing the petty cash expenditures and has Leticia prepare another check payable to "Cash" for $70.88. She cashes the check and puts the $70.88 in the petty cash box, restoring the fund to its original amount of $75. James Dockery would enter the voucher in the general journal as follows:

July 31	Office Supplies	25.14	
	Transportation-In	17.39	
	Miscellaneous Expense	28.35	
	Cash		70.88
	To record the replenishment of the petty cash fund.		

The entry debits the asset and expense accounts that are affected by the cash payments and reduces Cash. Occasionally, the petty cash receipts and remaining balance do not sum to the proper amount—the amount of the petty cash fund. Small discrepancies are debited or credited to Cash Over or Short when the fund is replenished.

Because the entry to replenish petty cash is necessary to record the effects of petty cash payments, it is preferable to replenish the petty cash fund at the end of every accounting period, whether or not the fund is exhausted. Technically, failure to do so results in overstating the amount of Cash and understating the assets and expenses resulting from the petty cash payments in the financial statements. However, the amounts usually are too small to make a material difference, and it may be cost-effective to replenish the fund only as needed. In the balance sheet, petty cash generally is combined with the other cash accounts and the total is shown as the Cash balance.

THE BANK STATEMENT

Once each month, banks mail statements to their depositors. A **bank statement** lists the activity in the depositor's bank account for a month. The bank statement reports the items listed below.

1. The account balance at the beginning of the month
2. Deposits for the month
3. Checks the bank paid during the month
4. Monthly bank service charges and fees for certain transactions
5. The account balance at the end of the month

The information reported in the bank statement is based on the bank's records. Since the customer's account is a liability of the bank, increases such as deposits are called credits and decreases such as paid checks are called debits (or charges). A bank statement is shown in Illustration 5-10.

The bank includes several documents when it mails the statement to the depositor. The depositor's paid checks and copies of any debit or credit memo-

INSIGHTS INTO ACCOUNTING

SEPARATION OF INCOMPATIBLE DUTIES

Below are the first two paragraphs from an actual memo dated February 18, 1994, to all administrators from the Vice President of Business Affairs of a major state university.

Embezzlement. As a result of a major cash loss which recently led to criminal charges against a University employee, a special committee of accountants and auditors has been formed to review and improve University fiscal controls (internal controls). Without delay, however, I want to ask all individuals who have responsibility for University accounts to be aware of several specific fiscal practices which should be followed.

[Payments for] Goods and Services. There should be a clear separation of assigned duties between individuals who are involved in ordering, receiving, and processing payments for goods and services. That is, the same person should not be authorized to (1) place orders for goods/services, (2) certify that goods/services have been received, and (3) approve payment vouchers. It is best to have a different person perform each of these functions, but, as a minimum, the person who certifies that goods and services have been received should not also be authorized to sign and process payment vouchers. Obviously, if a person is in a position to process a payment for goods/services which have not actually been received, internal controls are not adequate to avoid embezzlement.

ILLUSTRATION 5-10 Bank Statement

						Closing Date:		June 30, 19X1
						Statement Date:		July 6, 19X1
						Account No.:		66755550119

North National Bank
232 North Elm Street, Twin City, MO 11223

STATEMENT OF ACCOUNT
Ready Auto Parts, Inc.
105 S. Main
Twin City, MO 11223

	No.	Total
Previous Balance:		9,865.71
Credits:	15	36,145.20
Debits:	14	28,667.00
New Balance:		17,343.91

Checks				Deposits	Date	Balance
					05/31/X1	9,865.71
213	2,525.00	214	637.00	3,531.25	06/02/X1	10,234.96
216	50.00			1,567.83	06/03/X1	11,752.79
NSF	500.00	215	325.00	2,547.12	06/05/X1	13,474.91
218	7,650.00	219	125.00	1,715.15	06/08/X1	7,415.06
				4,705.50	06/10/X1	12,120.56
				2,424.56	06/11/X1	14,545.12
220	1,000.00	221	4,900.00	1,935.80	06/15/X1	10,580.92
				3,598.99	06/17/X1	14,179.91
222	250.00			2,654.33	06/18/X1	16,584.24
				3,636.96	06/23/X1	20,221.20
217	900.00			2,161.89	06/25/X1	21,483.09
				4,286.37	06/26/X1	25,769.46
224	6,370.00	225	3,430.00	1,316.45	06/29/X1	17,285.91
DM	5.00			CM 63.00	06/30/X1	17,343.91

Please refer any discrepancies within ten days for correction.

DM   Debit Memo
CM   Credit Memo
NSF Not Sufficient Funds

randa applied to the depositor's account are sent with the statement. The checks returned with the statement are the depositor's checks that the bank paid during the month. The paid checks returned with the statement are commonly called **canceled checks** because at the time of payment the bank either stamps or perforates the checks to indicate that they have been paid. The debit and credit memoranda are the bank's notifications that the depositor's account has been decreased or increased for certain transactions the bank has handled. A **debit memorandum** reports a decrease in the account for such things as previous bank credit errors or service charges and fees. A **credit memoran-**

dum reports an increase in the depositor's account for such things as previous bank debit errors and notes receivable the bank has collected for the depositor.

When a business deposits all cash receipts in the bank and makes cash disbursements with checks, it may use the bank statement to verify the balance in Cash and recorded cash receipts and cash disbursements. However, only rarely will the ending balance shown on the bank statement agree with the balance of Cash. There are two principal reasons why the two amounts may not be equal:

1. The bank often records checks, deposits, and other increases and decreases in cash on dates different than the ones the business records.
2. Either the bank or the business may have made errors.

Therefore, verifying Cash involves **reconciling** it to the bank balance. At Ready Auto Parts, Inc., Frank Brown reconciles the bank account to Cash each month. The bank reconciliation process permits Frank to discover errors or omissions that got by his cash controls. Large discrepancies will alert him to possible employee theft or fraud.

THE BANK RECONCILIATION

A **bank reconciliation** is a schedule that adjusts the company's cash balance and the balance on the bank statement until they each equal the correct amount of cash as of a given date. The bank reconciliation for Ready Auto Parts, Inc. is shown in Illustration 5-11.

The reconciliation starts with the balance in Cash on June 30, 19X1, $19,958.58. This figure is corrected for unrecorded items and for any errors Ready committed in accounting for its cash. After the adjustments, the correct

ILLUSTRATION 5-11 Bank Reconciliation

Ready Auto Parts, Inc. Bank Reconciliation June 30, 19X1		
Balance per books, June 30, 19X1		$19,958.58
Add: Bank credit for previous excess charges	$ 63.00	
Error in recording Check No. 219	27.00	90.00
		$20,048.58
Less: NSF check of Sterling Auto Body	$ 500.00	
Service charge for NSF check	5.00	505.00
Correct cash balance		$19,543.58
Balance per bank, June 30, 19X1		$17,343.91
Add: Deposit-in-transit at June 30, 19X1	$2,214.67	
Bank error in recording Check No. 218	300.00	2,514.67
		$19,858.58
Less: Outstanding checks:		
No. 223	$ 90.00	
No. 226	25.00	
No. 227	200.00	315.00
Correct cash balance		$19,543.58

balance is $19,543.58. In the lower half of the bank reconciliation, the same procedure is followed, starting with the balance from the bank statement in Illustration 5-10 of $17,343.91 and ending with the correct figure of $19,543.58.

LO 5

Identify the reconciling items that make the business's cash balance differ from the balance on its bank statement.

Finding the Reconciling Items for a Bank Reconciliation

To prepare a bank reconciliation, you must first find the reconciling items and their amounts. If a business's cash balance does not agree with the balance on its bank statement, the difference implies that cash receipts disagree with the credits recorded on the bank statement and/or cash disbursements (checks issued) disagree with the charges on the bank statement. You will find the reconciling items and their amounts by organizing your search into two phases.

Compare Bank Debits to Checks Issued.   When he receives the monthly bank statement, Frank Brown makes a detailed comparison between the debits in the bank statement and the checks issued during the month or on the outstanding check list of the previous month. He traces each check appearing on a bank statement to the check register to be sure the bank has charged the correct amount. When Frank performs this procedure, he places a check mark (✔) in the "Check Cleared" column of that check's entry in the check register. The comparison of bank charges to checks issued will turn up three types of possible discrepancies:

1. Outstanding checks. **Outstanding checks** are those the business has issued and recorded but which have not been presented to the bank for payment. These checks have not appeared as charges on a bank statement and are easily identified as the checks that have not been ✔-marked in the Checks Cleared column of the check register. *Example.* Ready Auto Parts, Inc., had issued the following checks during June 19X1, that the bank had not paid as of June 30:

Check No. 223, issued 06/22	$ 90.00
Check No. 226, issued 06/30	25.00
Check No. 227, issued 06/30	200.00

2. Bank charges. **Bank charges** may be made for check printing charges, other service charges, fees, and for previously deposited checks that have been refused for lack of funds by the banks that they are drawn on. The latter are called **NSF** (nonsufficient funds) **checks**. The former are represented by debit memorandums (DMs) the bank returns with the statement. DMs should be reviewed carefully to make certain that the charges are proper and that the amounts are reasonable. *Example.* Ready deposited a check for $500 from one of its customers on June 2. When the bank tried to collect from that customer's bank, it was refused due to nonsufficient funds. The bank charged (debited) this item back to Ready's account on June 5 and charged a $5 fee at the end of the month for handling it.

3. Errors. Either the company or the bank may have made errors in recording checks, fees, or charges. *Example.* Ready erroneously recorded Check No. 219 at $152, instead of the correct amount, $125. The bank recorded the check correctly on June 8. The bank erroneously recorded Check No. 218 at $7,650 on June 8. Ready correctly recorded it at $7,350.

Compare Bank Credits to Deposits.   Frank also compares deposits per the company's books and deposits-in-transit from last month's reconciliation to deposits per the bank statement. This examination will also turn up three types of possible discrepancies.

1. Deposits-in-transit. **Deposits-in-transit** are amounts the company deposits in the bank but which the bank does not record until the next period. They usually occur on the last day of business of a period. The company closes for the day, prepares its deposit, and takes it to the bank. The bank has an after-hours deposit box that receives deposits after closing time. The bank records the deposit as of the next day, the first day of a new period. *Example.* Ready dropped a deposit of $2,214.67 in the bank's night deposit box on June 30. The bank did not record the deposit until July 1.

2. Bank credits. Bank credits are credits the bank makes to the customer's account, of which the customer was unaware. Banks often collect notes receivable and deposit them directly for their customers. Another such credit is a correction of a past debit error by the bank. The bank sends credit memorandums (CMs) with the bank statements describing such items. *Example.* On June 30 the bank credited Ready's account with a refund of $63.00 of previous excessive service charges that Ready had previously recorded as bank charges.

3. Errors. Either the bank or the company may have made errors in recording deposits or other credits. *Example.* In the case at hand, neither Ready nor the bank made errors of this type.

Preparing a Bank Reconciliation

As noted earlier, a bank reconciliation is composed of two parts. The first part is prepared by reconciling the business's cash balance to the correct amount; the second part is prepared by reconciling the bank balance to the correct amount. Thus, at the end of the reconciliation process, the correct balance per the company's books should equal the correct balance per the bank. If not, an error has been made and the process should be reviewed.

Part 1. *Start with the cash balance per the company's books.* That is, the debit balance of the general ledger Cash account as of the date of the reconciliation, after the cash receipts and cash disbursements totals for the period have been posted to Cash. This is illustrated in the top half of Illustration 5-11. *Example.* Ready's Cash balance in its general ledger account on June 30 was $19,958.58.

Add:

1. Credits from the bank statement that have not yet been recorded as debits to Cash. *Example.* The bank credited Ready with $63 for past excessive charges.

2. Errors discovered *in the company's records* that tended to understate the cash balance—for example, understated deposits or overstated checks. *Example.* Ready overstated Check No. 219 by $27 (thus, understating its cash balance).

Subtract:

1. Debits from the bank statement that have not yet been recorded as credits to Cash. *Example.* The bank charged Ready for an NSF check of $500 and a handling fee of $5.

2. Errors discovered *in the company's records* that tended to overstate the cash balance—for example, overstated deposits or understated checks. *Example.* None in this case.

Calculate the correct cash balance. *Example.* The correct cash balance for Ready as of June 30 is $19,543.58. See the last figure in the top half of Illustration 5-11.

Part 2. *Start with the cash balance per the bank statement.* This stage is illustrated in the bottom half of Illustration 5-11. *Example.* The bank balance from the statement in Illustration 5-10 is $17,343.91.

Add:

1. Deposits-in-transit. *Example.* There was a deposit-in-transit of $2,214.67 that the bank recorded after June 30.
2. Errors discovered *in the bank statement* that tended to understate the bank balance—for example, understated deposits or overstated checks. *Example.* The bank recorded Check No. 218 at $300 in excess of the correct amount.

Subtract:

1. Outstanding checks. *Example.* There were three outstanding checks (223, 226, and 227) totaling $315 at June 30.
2. Errors discovered *in the bank statement* that tended to overstate the cash balance—for example overstated deposits or understated checks. *Example.* None in this case.

Calculate the correct cash balance. *Example.* The correct cash balance for Ready as of June 30 is $19,543.58.

Adjusting Cash for Errors and Omissions

After completing the bank reconciliation, the company should adjust Cash to the correct balance. For Ready Auto Parts, Inc., the bank reconciliation shows a correct cash balance of $19,543.58. However, Cash shows a balance of $19,958.58. To establish the correct balance in Cash, Ready needs to make adjustments for unrecorded items and errors in its *accounting records*. These are the amounts added to and deducted from the "Balance per books" in upper half of the bank reconciliation. Adjustments are *not* made to the accounting records for items added to and deducted from the "Balance per bank," because the bank will ultimately record these items. For example, the bank has already recorded the June 30 deposit on July 1; and it will record the outstanding checks when they are presented for payment. The adjustments for Ready are as follows:

June 30	Accounts Receivable – Sterling Auto Body	505.00	
	Cash		505.00
	To record NSF check returned by bank and related service charge ($5).		
30	Cash	27.00	
	Vouchers Payable		27.00
	To correct error in recording Check No. 219.		
30	Cash	63.00	
	Miscellaneous Expense		63.00
	To record refund of previously recorded excess service charges by the bank.		

Describe two major categories of electronic funds transfers businesses use.

COMPUTER-ASSISTED CASH RECEIPTS AND DISBURSEMENTS

Electronic funds transfers, an innovation in cash receipts and disbursements systems, are cash payments made by computer rather than by coins, currency, or checks. Not only do electronic funds transfers dramatically increase the speed at which payments and receipts occur, but they also cost much less to process than does processing checks. In this section, we discuss two types of electronic funds transfer systems that certain businesses use.

Types of Electronic Funds Transfer Systems

Businesses use two types of electronic funds transfer systems: point-of-sale systems and automated clearing houses.

Point-of-Sale Systems. **Point-of-sale systems** are computer-based cash receipts systems that allow customers to transfer funds immediately from their bank accounts to the merchant's bank account at the time of a sale. On-line terminals that have immediate access to a bank's computer are located at check-out counters or at other locations where sales occur. Inserting a plastic bank account card into the terminal that reads the information encoded on the card, the customer keys in a personal identification number (PIN). Using a cash register or a bar-code reader connected to the terminal, the salesperson enters other information about the transaction.

If the customer and the merchant have accounts at the same bank, the bank's computer transfers the appropriate amount of funds from the customer's account to the merchant's account. If the customer's and merchant's banks are different, a switching and processing center connects the computers of the two banks. The computer at the customer's bank verifies the validity of the card, the encoded information, and whether the customer has sufficient funds in his/her account to cover the amount of the purchase. The customer's account is then reduced by the amount of the purchase, and the merchant's account is increased by the same amount. Both parties to the transaction receive a printed statement (receipt) at the time of the transaction.

Automated Clearing Houses. An **automated clearing house** is a system for the transfer of funds between banks. A traditional bank clearing house processes checks and clears the transfer of funds between banks according to the writer of each check and the payee. In an automated clearing house, the payments must enter the system in the form of electronic data, usually computer-generated magnetic tapes or disks.

For example, consider how a business could pay its suppliers through an automated clearing house. At the end of the month, the company prepares a computer tape or disk that contains information about the names of the payees, bank and customer account identification numbers for each payee, and the amount of each payment. The business then delivers the computer tape to its bank or directly to the automated clearing house. The transfers of funds between banks and adjustment of the various bank accounts take place the same as with paper checks. Because they eliminate the need for the business to write checks and for the payees to receive, endorse, deposit, and send checks, automated clearing houses are efficient.

Control Considerations

Point-of-sale systems essentially are cash receipts systems. In fact, point-of-sale systems enhance control over cash receipts from sales because employees do not physically handle cash or checks. The primary control procedure for these transactions is reconciliation. At the end of each day, a designated employee will retrieve the cash register total on the business's computer and reconcile it to actual cash receipts and the amount credited to the business's bank account directly.

Automated clearing houses, used as described above, essentially are cash disbursement systems. The control procedures for these systems are the same as those for cash disbursements systems that use checks—as discussed in this chapter. The difference is that a computer entry is made on the expenditure tape or disk file for each authorized expenditure, instead of printing a check.

LO 8

Define and explain the accounting for cash equivalents.

CASH EQUIVALENTS

Businesses occasionally accumulate cash balances in excess of amounts needed for current or near future operations. Such accumulations of large cash balances are due to differences in timing between cash inflows and cash requirements for operations. In such cases, the excess cash balance is temporary and is called **idle cash** because it is not being used to support the business's current revenue-generating activities.

As part of sound financial management, businesses often invest the excess cash to earn revenue. Because businesses will need the cash that is invested for operations in a short period of time, however, they consider only certain types of investments as prudent. The types of investments made for this purpose are those that can readily be converted to cash when it is needed for operations. **Cash equivalents**, a term often applied to such temporary investments of excess cash, include certificates of deposit (CDs), U. S. Treasury bills, and commercial paper. Banks issue **certificates of deposit**, which are essentially promissory notes of varying time periods. The government issues U.S. Treasury bills, promissory notes that have maturities of 13 weeks, 26 weeks, and 52 weeks. Corporations issue **commercial paper**, a term used to describe short-term promissory notes. These types of investments are suitable for excess cash because they have relatively short maturities and can be converted to cash on short notice.

Accounting for Cash Equivalents Illustrated

Western Corporation estimates it has $100,000 of cash that it will not need for at least 6 months. To earn additional revenue for the corporation, Western decides on May 1, 19X1, to invest the $100,000 in a 6-month CD from First National Bank. The CD pays interest at the annual rate of 4%. The investment in the CD is recorded in the amount of the investment, which is its cost. The entry to record the investment is as follows:

May 1	Investment in Certificate of Deposit	100,000	
	Cash		100,000
	To record temporary investment in CD.		

In 6 months, on November 1, when the CD matures, Western will receive its initial investment plus interest at the rate of 4%. Unless otherwise indicated, stated interest rates are for a 1-year period. Therefore, the corporation will not receive the full 4% interest because the investment is for only 6 months. The amount of interest received at maturity is: $100,000 x 4% x 6/12 = $2,000. The fraction *6/12* in the calculation of interest is necessary because the investment is for one-half of a year, or 6 months of the 12 months. The general journal entry at the maturity date of the CD is as follows:

Nov. 1	Cash	102,000	
	Investment in Certificate of Deposit		100,000
	Interest Revenue		2,000
	To record proceeds at maturity of CD.		

The end of an accounting period often occurs between the date of an investment and its maturity date. When this occurs, the corporation must make an adjusting entry to accrue the interest earned between the date of the investment and the end of its accounting period. In the previous illustration, assume Western invests in the CD on October 1. On December 31, Western needs to make an adjusting entry to recognize the $1,000 ($100,000 x 4% x 3/12) of interest earned for the 3 months from October 1 to December 31. The adjusting entry to record the accrued interest revenue is as follows:

Dec. 31	Interest Receivable	1,000	
	Interest Revenue		1,000
	To record interest earned on investment in CD.		

Western recognizes the interest revenue for 3 months at the end of its accounting period because, under accrual concepts, revenue is recognized in the period that it is earned. Interest is earned as time passes; therefore, at the end of its accounting period, Western has earned 3 months' interest.

Three months after the end of its accounting period, or March 31, 19X2, the CD matures, and Western receives $102,000 in cash. In this case, the general journal entry at the maturity date of the CD is as follows:

Mar. 31	Cash	102,000	
	Investment in Certificate of Deposit		100,000
	Interest Receivable		1,000
	Interest Revenue		1,000
	To record proceeds at maturity of CD.		

This entry records Western's receipt of the initial investment of $100,000, receipt of the $1,000 interest receivable that is recorded in the adjusting entry at December 31, 19X1—the end of its previous accounting period—and receipt of interest revenue of $1,000 that Western earned for the 3 months from the end of its previous accounting period to the maturity date of the CD.

Cash Equivalents in the Financial Statements

In a classified balance sheet, businesses list current assets in the order of their liquidity. Cash, the most liquid asset, is listed first. Companies usually present cash and temporary investments of cash as a single item and label the amount "Cash and cash equivalents" or "Cash and equivalents." For example, in the 1992 balance sheet of The Walt Disney Company, the first asset presented is cash and cash equivalents of $764,800,000.

Any interest receivable recorded as part of an adjusting entry is usually combined with the temporary investment; and the combined amount consisting of cash, temporary investments, and interest receivable is shown on the balance sheet as a single item. Interest revenue from temporary investments is shown as "Other revenue" in the income statement.

USING INFORMATION ABOUT CONTROLS AND LIQUID ASSETS

Remember Frank Brown's problem from the beginning of the chapter? While satisfied with Frank's expansion plans and the profitability of his present business, the bankers wanted a description of the controls Frank had established for his cash system, and they also wanted to discuss Ready Auto Parts, Inc.'s liquidity position. At their second meeting with Frank, the bankers explained that many small profitable businesses have failed because employees embezzle cash at crucial times and render the businesses unable to pay their bills. However, the bankers are satisfied—even impressed—that a small business such as Ready Auto Parts, Inc., would have the kind of controls Frank had just summarized for them. So, the discussion advanced to the current and acid-test ratios, the final criteria the bankers wished to apply before approving Frank's loan.

Calculating the Current Ratio

Financial statement readers use classified balance sheets to assess the business's liquidity. Of particular interest to creditors—and to potential creditors—is the relationship between current assets and current liabilities. This relationship may be observed with a classified balance sheet since current assets and current liabilities are two of the classifications. A commonly used financial ratio to assess the relative liquidity and debt-paying ability is the current ratio. The **current ratio** compares current assets to current liabilities as of the balance sheet date as follows:

$$\text{Current Ratio} = \frac{\text{Current Assets}}{\text{Current Liabilities}}$$

The current asset and current liabilities sections of Ready Auto Parts, Inc's balance sheet that Frank Brown supplied to the bankers are as follows:

Current Assets		Current Liabilities	
Cash	$ 9,544	Vouchers payable	$25,600
Cash equivalents	10,000	Wages and salaries payable	3,450
Accounts receivable	40,000		
Merchandise inventory	49,000		
Prepaid insurance	360		
Total	$108,904	Total	$29,050

The current ratio of Ready Auto Parts is calculated as follows:

$$\text{Current Ratio} = \frac{\$108,904}{\$29,050} = 3.75$$

Interpreting the Current Ratio

This relationship gives an indication of the business's ability to pay current liabilities with current assets. Because of this relationship, the larger the ratio, the more ability the business has to pay its liabilities as they come due. The bankers told Frank that a current ratio of at least 3.0 would be required for them to grant the loan. Since Ready Auto Parts, Inc., has a current ratio of 3.75, this requirement is satisfied.

Calculating the Acid-Test Ratio

The **acid-test ratio** (or **quick ratio**) compares liquid current assets to current liabilities:

$$\text{Acid-Test Ratio} = \frac{\text{Liquid Current Assets}}{\text{Current Liabilities}}$$

Liquid current assets typically consist of cash, cash equivalents (CDs at banks and readily marketable securities), and net accounts receivable. The acid-test ratio is a more stringent test of a business's **liquidity** than the current ratio because it focuses only on the current assets that can be most readily converted into cash to satisfy current liabilities. In the acid-test ratio, inventories and prepaid expenses are excluded from the numerator because the ability to convert them into cash in the very short run is often doubtful.

Interpreting the Acid-Test Ratio

The acid-test ratio compares the business's liquid assets (cash plus the assets that it can most readily convert to cash) to the amount of liabilities that it will have to pay in the short run. Hence, the ratio is a measure of the business's ability to pay short-term obligations. From this perspective, the larger the ratio, the better. After reviewing all the other information Frank supplied, the bankers decided that they could accept an acid-test ratio of 1.25 or greater. Using the current asset and current liability information presented above, Ready Auto parts, Inc., has an acid-test ratio that is more than adequate, and the bankers approved the loan:

$$\text{Acid-Test Ratio} = \frac{\$59,544}{\$29,050} = 2.05$$

Limitations of the Current and Acid-Test Ratios

While the current and acid-test ratios provide measures of a business's ability to pay its short-run obligations, users of financial statement information should interpret them with care. Most importantly, the numerator of both ratios contains accounts receivable that may or may not be collectible. Those amounts not collected will not be available to pay obligations. Also, the numerator of the current ratio contains merchandise inventories and prepaid expenses. If the business cannot sell inventory items in a short period at the amount shown in the balance sheet, the amount will not be available to pay the business's obligations. Prepaid expenses cannot usually be used to pay business obligations. If the business's financial statements are not audited, users of the financial statements may want to assure themselves that sound valuation principles have been applied to accounts receivable and merchandise inventories and that the amounts shown in the balance sheet can reasonably be expected to be collected or realized from sale. Subsequent chapters cover the problems of collectibility of receivables and proper valuation of receivables and merchandise inventories.

SUMMARY

Describe broad control objectives and control procedures for cash received from credit sales. To be effective in achieving its goals and to efficiently use assets and personnel, a business must operate under management control. To control cash received from credit sales, one employee should open the mail, separate all checks, restrictively endorse the checks, and prepare a remittance list of the checks. This employee should then give the checks to a second employee for deposit. Then, an employee with authority to approve discounts taken by customers should receive the remittance lists and remittance advices. The remittance advices, remittance list, and a copy of the deposit slip should be given to a fourth employee who records the remittances and reconciles the total recorded to the remittance list and the deposit slip.

Describe control procedures for cash received in cash sales transactions. Businesses should use cash registers with locked-in tapes, preferably connected directly to the computer(s) used in their accounting systems, to record cash sales. Cashiers should count their cash drawers at the end of a shift and turn their cash over to the employee who prepares the bank deposit. The employee who prepares the bank deposit should give a copy of the deposit slip to the employee who records cash receipts. The person who records cash receipts should record sales for the day equal to the amount of the cash register totals, the increase in cash in the amount of the total on the deposit slip, and the difference as cash over or short. Large daily or cumulative amounts of cash over or short should be investigated.

Describe control procedures for cash disbursements, including the voucher system and voucher documents. Businesses can achieve control of cash disbursements through use of a voucher system. Original or carbon copies (no photocopies) of requisitions, purchase orders, receiving reports, and supplier invoices should be attached to vouchers. Before being approved for recording, the vouchers should be checked carefully for agreement with the descriptions, quantities, prices, and total charges for goods and services on these underlying support documents. A separate employee should be responsible for recording the vouchers. An employee with authority should monitor vouchers in the Unpaid Voucher File to ensure timely payment and to review and approve the underlying documents before checks are prepared.

Describe the operation of a petty cash fund and record petty cash expenditures in the accounting records. Many businesses use a petty cash fund to make cash payments that are too small to be made efficiently by individual checks. The procedures employed for the operation of a petty cash fund are designed to deter employee misconduct in handling the petty cash fund and to provide documentation for recording petty cash transactions in the accounting records. Because the petty cash fund is periodically reimbursed by check, the controls of the voucher system and bank reconciliation are maintained over petty cash as well as cash in the bank.

Identify the reconciling items that make the business's cash balance differ from the balance on its bank statement.   Any differences between a business's cash balance and its bank statement balance will be due to differences between its recorded receipts and the credits on its bank statement and/or differences between its recorded expenditures and the charges on its bank statement. To find the items to be used in the bank reconciliation, you should systematically compare receipts to bank credits and expenditures to bank charges. You may find credits such as bank collections of notes receivable not recorded among the receipts, charges such as those for check printing that are not recorded as expenditures, and errors in the business's cash balance. You may also find deposits-in-transit not recorded, outstanding checks that have not cleared, and errors on the bank statement.

Follow the steps required to prepare a bank reconciliation and record any needed adjustments in the accounting records.   When a business uses a bank account for all cash receipts and cash disbursements, a bank reconciliation becomes an important procedure for ensuring the accuracy of the accounting records. In a bank reconciliation, the cash balance in the business's records and the bank statement balance are each reconciled to the correct cash balance. In the process, errors the business made and previously unrecorded cash receipts and disbursements are discovered, leading to adjusting entries to Cash. These adjustments never include bank errors or deposits or checks the bank has not yet recorded.

Describe two major categories of electronic funds transfers businesses use.   Cash transactions can be facilitated significantly by electronic funds transfers. Point-of-sale transfers involve on-line terminals at sales check-out counters. Information about the customer and the sale are entered, and computers transfer funds directly from the customer's bank account to the seller's bank account. No currency or checks change hands. However, it is still important to reconcile total funds transferred to cash register totals. Similarly, businesses that wish to pay their bills electronically can send machine-readable files of expenditure information to automated clearing houses. There, computers read the files, and the funds to pay each bill are transferred from the payer's bank account to the payee's bank account. Once again, no cash or checks change hands. However, expenditures should still be properly documented and authorized before they are entered on the file sent to the clearing house.

Define and explain accounting for cash equivalents.   Cash equivalents are temporary investments of cash not currently needed for operations (idle cash). Prudent investments of idle cash are those that can readily be converted to cash when needed for operations. Examples of cash equivalents are U.S. Treasury bills, certificates of deposit (CDs), and commercial paper. Accounting for cash equivalents involves recording the investments, recognizing interest revenue as earned, and recording the proceeds at maturity or liquidation of the investments. In the financial statements, the amount of Cash Equivalents is combined with Cash and shown as a single amount in the balance sheet.

Define and interpret the current and acid-test ratios.   We calculate the current ratio by dividing current assets by current liabilities:

$$\text{Current Ratio} = \frac{\text{Current Assets}}{\text{Current Liabilities}}$$

The current ratio gives an indication of the business's debt-paying ability as of its balance sheet date. Care should be taken in interpreting the current ratio because its numerator includes accounts receivable that may be of questionable collectibility and merchandise inventory that may not be realized at the recorded amount.

The acid-test ratio compares liquid current assets to current liabilities:

$$\text{Acid-Test Ratio } = \frac{\textbf{Liquid Current Assets}}{\textbf{Current Liabilities}}$$

Liquid current assets typically consist of cash, cash equivalents (certificates of deposit at banks and readily marketable securities), and accounts receivable. The ratio is generally thought to be a stringent measure of the business's ability to pay short-run obligations. However, it should be interpreted with care because its numerator may contain receivables of questionable collectibility.

REVIEW PROBLEM 1: PETTY CASH

The Action Sales Corporation is establishing a petty cash fund to facilitate the cash payment of small amounts for which immediate cash is necessary. The petty cash fund is established on September 1, 19X3, in the amount of $150.00. The following payments were made during the month of September.

Petty Cash Voucher	Amount	Purpose
No. 1	$15.00	Transportation-In
No. 2	26.00	Printer Ribbons
No. 3	10.50	Transportation-In
No. 4	7.50	Transportation-In
No. 5	22.60	Flowers
No. 6	18.74	Stationery

The cash count of the petty cash box at the end of the month was $48.56.

REQUIRED:

a. Prepare the journal entry to establish the petty cash fund on September 1, 19X3.
b. Prepare the journal entry to reimburse the petty cash fund at the end of the business day on September 30, 19X3.

SOLUTION:

Planning and Organizing Your Work

1. To establish a petty cash fund, consider the accounts that should be debited and credited and write the necessary journal entry.
2. Sum the amounts of the petty cash receipts and the petty cash fund balance to determine if there is cash over or short.
3. Sum the receipts that apply to individual accounts. Any petty cash expenditure that cannot be identified with a specific account may be considered a miscellaneous expense.
4. Write the journal entry to replenish the petty cash fund, debiting the various asset, expense, and other accounts and crediting Cash.

(a) *Prepare the journal entry to establish fund.*

Sept. 1	Petty Cash	150.00	
	Cash		150.00
	To establish a petty cash fund.		

(b) *Prepare the journal entry to reimburse fund.*

Sept. 30	Miscellaneous Expense	22.60	
	Transportation-In	33.00	
	Office Supplies	44.74	
	Cash Over or Short	1.10	
	Cash		101.44
	To reimburse petty cash fund and record expenses paid and cash shortage.		

REVIEW PROBLEM 2: BANK RECONCILIATION

DuMont Deli, Inc., began business April 1, 19X4, and opened a checking account at the Central Plaza Bank on April 2 with a deposit of $10,000. During the month, deposits of sales receipts were made totaling $15,000 and checks were written totaling $18,500. Thus, the Deli's Cash balance on April 30 was $6,500. The bank statement was received on May 4, indicating a closing date of April 30 and an ending balance of $8,860. The manager compares the canceled checks with the cash disbursements and finds three checks still outstanding: Number 14 to Wheaton Deli Supply for $2,986.00; Number 16 to Bost Bakeries for $48.50; and Number 17 to Central Power Corporation for $199.00.

She also discovered that Check No. 7 had been correctly written for $209.00 in payment of a voucher payable but had been recorded in the books at $290.00. A comparison of the checkbook with the bank statement and the deposit slips identified a check deposited on April 8 in the amount of $210.00 omitted from the Deli's books and a deposit on April 30 of $1,089 that the bank had not yet recorded. The check for $210.00 was from a customer in payment of an account receivable balance. There were two debit memoranda included with the bank statement, indicating an NSF check in the amount of $35.00 from R. A. Brown and a charge for printing checks of $55.00. A credit memo indicated the interest earned for the month was $14.50.

REQUIRED:

a. Prepare a bank reconciliation for DuMont Deli, Inc., as of April 30, 19X4.
b. Prepare general journal entries required to adjust Cash to the correct cash balance.

SOLUTION:

Planning and Organizing Your Work
1. Compare the charges and credits on the bank statement with the check register.
2. Identify each item in the bank reconciliation as one of the following:

   Adjustments to balance per books:
   An unrecorded bank charge to be subtracted from the balance per books.
   An unrecorded bank credit to be added to the balance per books.
   An error overstating Cash to be subtracted from the balance per books.
   An error understating Cash to be added to the balance per books.

   Adjustments to balance per bank:
   An outstanding check to be subtracted from the balance per bank.
   A deposit in transit to be added to the balance per bank.
   An error overstating the bank balance to be subtracted from the balance per bank.
   An error understating the bank balance to be added to the balance per bank.

3. Prepare the bank reconciliation by beginning with the balance per books and adjusting it to the correct balance. Then, begin again with the balance per bank and adjust it to the correct balance. When the two "correct" balances are equal, the reconciliation is complete.

4. Write journal entries to record the adjustments to the balance per books.

(a) *Prepare a bank reconciliation.*

DuMont Deli, Inc. Bank Reconciliation April 30, 19X4		
Balance per books, April 30, 19X4		$6,500.00
Add: Error in recording Check No. 7		
($209.00 recorded as $290.00)	$ 81.00	
Interest earned	14.50	
Deposit not recorded for April 8	210.00	305.50
		$6,805.50
Less: Bank charge, Check Printing	$55.00	
NSF check	35.00	90.00
Correct cash balance		$6,715.50
Balance per bank, April 30, 19X4		$8,860.00
Add: Deposit-in-transit at April 30, 19X4		1,089.00
		$9,949.00
Less: Outstanding checks:		
No. 14	$2,986.00	
No. 16	48.50	
No. 17	199.00	3,233.50
Correct cash balance		$6,715.50

(b) *Prepare journal entries.*

Apr. 30	Cash	290.00	
	Vouchers Payable		290.00
	To reverse effects of Check No. 7 recorded at incorrect amount.		
30	Vouchers Payable	209.00	
	Cash		209.00
	To record Check No. 7 at the correct amount.		
30	Cash	14.50	
	Interest Revenue		14.50
	To record interest revenue credited by the bank.		
30	Cash	210.00	
	Accounts Receivable		210.00
	To record a check deposited on April 8 but not recorded in cash receipts.		
30	Miscellaneous Expense	55.00	
	Cash		55.00
	To record bank charge for check printing.		
30	Accounts Receivable	35.00	
	Cash		35.00
	To record a check returned by the bank due to NSF.		

REVIEW PROBLEM 3: CURRENT AND ACID-TEST RATIOS

The balance sheet of Arapaho Products Corp. included the following current assets and current liabilities:

Current assets:		Current liabilities:	
Cash	$ 3,250	Notes payable	$ 2,500
Cash equivalents	11,200	Vouchers payable	12,500
Accounts receivable (net)	14,200	Sales tax payable	1,800
Merchandise inventory	25,600	Total current liabilities	$16,800
Prepaid insurance	1,800		
Prepaid rent	6,000		
Total current assets	$62,050		

REQUIRED:

Calculate the current and acid-test ratios and discuss what they mean to creditors.

SOLUTION:

Planning and Organizing Your Work

1. Determine which current assets meet the test of being "liquid" current assets and sum them for the numerator of each ratio.
2. Calculate each ratio.
3. Express what the specific value of each ratio means.

Current ratio:

$$\frac{\$62,050}{\$16,800} = 3.7$$

What it means:

Arapaho Products Corp. has $3.70 of current assets for each dollar of current liabilities. The company should be able to pay its current liabilities when due, assuming that receivables and inventory are properly valued. Prepaid expenses usually cannot be used to pay current liabilities.

Acid-test ratio:

$$\frac{\$3,250 + \$11,200 + \$14,200}{\$16,800} = \frac{\$28,650}{\$16,800} = 1.7$$

What it means:

Arapaho Products Corp. has $1.70 in liquid current assets for each dollar in current liabilities. This suggests that the company is able to pay its short-term debts on time if the accounts receivables and current investments are properly valued.

KEY TERMS

acid-test ratio, *231*
automated clearing house, *227*
bank charges, *224*
bank reconciliation, *223*
bank statement, *221*
canceled checks, *222*
cash control system, *208*
cash equivalents, *228*
certificates of deposit (CDs), *228*
commercial paper, *228*
credit memorandum (CM), *222*

current ratio, *230*
debit memorandum (DM), *222*
deposits-in-transit, *225*
electronic funds transfers, *227*
idle cash, *228*
liquidity, *231*
NSF checks, *224*
outstanding checks, *224*
petty cash fund, *219*
petty cash receipt, *219*
point-of-sale systems, *227*
purchase order, *216*

purchase requisition, *216*
quick ratio, *231*
receiving report, *216*
reconciling, *223*
remittance advice, *218*
separation of incompatible
  duties, *211*
supplier's invoice, *217*
voucher, *215*
voucher system, *215*

SELF-QUIZ

LO 1   1. Indicate which of the following broad control objectives of accounting systems are required in a good cash control system. (*Yes, No*)
    ___a. Effectiveness in achieving goals
    ___b. Efficiency in incurring costs
    ___c. Activities in accordance with management's policy
    ___d. Assets safeguarded
    ___e. Reliable financial reports

LO 1   2. Checks received from customers should be immediately _____ _____ to protect them from risk of misappropriation.

LO 2   3. Differences between the actual cash count and the cash receipts recorded on the cash register are called ____ ____ ____ _____.

LO 2   4. Which of the following is *not* a normal element of control over cash received from cash sales transactions?
    a. Recording cash sales with a cash register
    b. Preparation of a daily cash report and cash count by the cashier
    c. Cash recount and preparation of duplicate deposit slips by someone other than the cashier
    d. Deposit of daily cash receipts by the cashier
    e. Reconciliation of cash sales to deposits

LO 3   5. Which of the following items is *not* used to ensure that a payment should be authorized?
    a. Vendor's invoice   c. Shipping report
    b. Receiving report   d. Purchase order

LO 3   6. The Unpaid Voucher File serves both as a due date file to assure payments in time to take discounts and as _____ _____ the balance in the general ledger Vouchers Payable account.

LO 3   7. A control against duplicate payments based on a particular voucher and its supporting documentation would be to _____.

LO 4   8. The petty cash fund is typically reimbursed:
    a. At the end of each accounting period
    b. When the fund is nearly exhausted
    c. On the last day of the fiscal year
    d. All of the above
    e. None of the above

LO 4   9. The contents of a petty cash box should be:
    a. Petty cash receipts
    b. Currency and coins
    c. Petty cash receipts, currency, and coins, which should total to the amount of the petty cash fund
    d. None of the above are correct.

LO 5   10. Interpret these common notations from a bank statement.
    a. DM _____ _____.
    b. CM _____ _____.
    c. NSF _____ _____.

LO 5   11. Canceled checks are checks that
    a. The company has voided before mailing due to errors made in writing the checks
    b. Have cleared the bank and that the bank has canceled because they have been paid
    c. The company has written but which the bank has returned due to a lack of sufficient funds
    d. None of the above

LO 5   12. Debit memoranda are received
    a. From the bank to indicate that a debit has been made on the bank's records to reflect a reduction in our account because of errors or fees the bank charged
    b. From the bank to indicate that it has credited our cash account at the bank and that we should debit Cash in the company books
    c. From the bank to indicate that it has increased our account at the bank
    d. None of the above

LO 5   13. Credit memoranda are received
    a. From the bank to indicate that it has debited our cash account at the bank and that we should credit Cash in the company books
    b. From the bank to indicate that a credit has been made on the bank's records to reflect an increase in our account because of errors or transactions the bank made on our behalf.
    c. From the bank to indicate that it has decreased our account at the bank.
    d. None of the above

LO 5   14. Indicate which one of the following items would be added to the "Balance per books" on a bank reconciliation.
    a. Nonsufficient funds check the bank returned
    b. Interest earned on the account
    c. Outstanding checks at the end of the month
    d. Deposits-in-transit

LO 6   15. An adjusting entry is required as the result of the preparation of a bank reconciliation for:
    a. Deposits-in-transit
    b. Outstanding checks
    c. A bank error
    d. A bank service charge
    e. None of the above

LO 6   16. Journal entries required as the result of the preparation of a bank reconciliation are taken from the reconciling items that adjust the _____ _____ _____ to the corrected cash balance.

LO 7   17. By numbering them 1 and 2, indicate which of the following are the two major categories of electronic funds transfers businesses use.

___a. Bank clearing houses
___b. Point-of-sale systems
___c. Wire fund transfer systems
___d. Federal reserve clearing houses
___e. Automated clearing houses

LO 7 18. Of the two major categories of electronic funds transfer, the _____ transfers customerrs' funds to the business's account and the _____ transfers funds of the business to its creditors.

LO 8 19. Which of the following is not a cash equivalent?
a. Notes receivable
b. Certificates of deposit
c. U.S. Treasury bills
d. Commercial paper

LO 9 20. The current ratio is a measure of
a. Solvency
b. Liquidity
c. Excess cash reserves
d. Quick assets to current liabilities

LO 9 21. The effectiveness of the acid-test ratio is dependent upon the
a. Strength of the bank holding the cash reserves
b. Valuation and marketability of the inventories
c. Amount of prepaid expenses included in current assets
d. Quality and valuation of the account receivable

SOLUTIONS TO SELF-QUIZ

1. a. No b. No c. Yes d. Yes e. Yes   2. restrictively endorsed   3. Cash Over or Short   4. d   5. c
6. details supporting   7. mark the voucher and supporting documentation "paid"   8. d   9. c   10. a. Debit memoranda   b. Credit memoranda   c. Nonsufficient funds   11. b   12. a   13. b   14. b   15. d   16. Balance per books   17. b is 1; e is 2.   18. Point-of-sale system, automated clearing house   19. a   20. b   21. d

QUESTIONS

Q5-1   Briefly explain why the control of cash is critical to the successful operation of a business.

Q5-2   Discuss what is meant by the "separation of incompatible duties" when applied to cash.

Q5-3   Explain how the separation of incompatible duties contributes to the overall control of cash.

Q5-4   Which of the following provides the appropriate steps for processing cash receipts from credit sales received through the mail?
a. Open the mail, separate the envelopes with checks and turn them over to the office manager who removes the checks, prepares a deposit slip, and deposits them in the bank.
b. Open the mail, separate the checks, prepare a remittance list, and turn over the checks and the remittance list to the bookkeeper for recording purposes. The bookkeeper then turns the checks over to the office manager who prepares a deposit slip and makes the deposit.
c. Open the mail and separate the checks from the rest of the mail. With each check being restrictively endorsed, record the amounts and names of the payers on a remittance list, total the remittance list, sign and send a copy of the list to the bookkeeper. The checks are turned over to another employee not associated with bookkeeping to prepare a deposit slip and deposit in the bank.
d. None of the above are adequate to control cash receipts through the mail.

Q5-5   What can be done to ensure that only the discounts actually earned by customers are granted?

Q5-6   The entries for cash received from credit customers, are made from
a. The individual checks since they show both the amount paid and the payer's name and address
b. The remittance list since the checks are deposited shortly after being received
c. The remittance advices or from photocopies of the remittance advices when customers fail to return them with their checks
d. Copies of the customer's purchase orders

Q5-7 Cash received in the course of business should be recorded in the accounting records by
a. The cashier
b. The individual who prepares the bank deposit slips and makes the bank deposits
c. Either a or b above as the cited controls are adequate
d. Neither a nor b since they both handle cash

Q5-8 Indicate which of the following is a part of a voucher system used to control cash disbursements.
a. A properly authorized voucher to support each check written
b. A properly authorized voucher supported by the purchase requisition, purchase order, receiving report, and supplier's invoice
c. Payments of vouchers payable recorded in the general journal
d. An unpaid voucher file
e. All of the above are part of a voucher system

Q5-9 Explain why Cash Over or Short would be debited if the cash received is less than that indicated by the cash register totals and why it would be credited if the cash received is greater than that of the cash register totals.

Q5-10 The petty cash fund is reimbursed at the end of the accounting period so that
a. The amount in the fund will be sufficient to carry the firm through the first month of the new year
b. The financial statements will not be materially misstated by omitting some of the expenses
c. The expenses of the current year paid from the petty cash fund will be included in the current year's income statement and Petty Cash will not be overstated in the balance sheet
d. None of the above

Q5-11 Petty Cash is
a. Debited to record its creation
b. Credited for expenditures made from the account
c. Debited when it is reimbursed
d. Credited when it is reimbursed

Q5-12 A properly completed petty cash receipt includes all of the following except
a. Date of the payment and the amount paid
b. Purpose of expenditure and the account to be charged
c. The signature of the bookkeeper to validate it
d. The signature of the person receiving the payment
e. The signature of the petty cashier

Q5-13 Indicate which one of the following items is added to the "Balance per books" in preparing a bank reconciliation.
a. A bank deposit representing an amount collected from a customer that was omitted from recorded cash receipts
b. An NSF check of a customer returned by the bank
c. A deposit-in-transit
d. The total of the outstanding checks at month-end

Q5-14 Indicate which one of the following items is added to the "Balance per bank" in preparing a bank reconciliation.
a. A bank deposit representing an amount collected from a customer that was omitted from recorded cash receipts
b. An NSF check of a customer returned by the bank
c. A deposit-in-transit
d. The total of outstanding checks at month-end

Q5-15 Indicate which one of the following items is deducted from the "Balance per books" in preparing a bank reconciliation.
  a. A bank deposit representing an amount collected from a customer that was omitted from recorded cash receipts
  b. An NSF check of a customer returned by the bank
  c. A deposit-in-transit
  d. The total of outstanding checks at month-end

Q5-16 Indicate which one of the following items is deducted from the "Balance per bank" in preparing a bank reconciliation.
  a. A bank deposit representing an amount collected from a customer that was omitted from recorded cash receipts
  b. An NSF check of a customer returned by the bank
  c. A deposit-in-transit
  d. The total of outstanding checks at month-end

Q5-17 The correct cash balance on the bank reconciliation represents
  a. A check figure used to find errors in the books or on the bank records
  b. A total, like the total of the trial balance, which proves equality of debits and credits but does not appear elsewhere
  c. The account balance that will appear on the next month's bank statement
  d. The balance of Cash on the books after the adjustments required by the reconciliation have been journalized and posted

Q5-18 Point-of-sale systems and automated clearing houses are two types of electronic funds transfer systems some businesses use. Which two of the following statements regarding these systems are incorrect?
  a. A point-of-sale system transfers funds from one business to another in settlement of accounts with the use of checks.
  b. An automated clearing house transfers funds from one business to another in settlement of accounts without the use of checks by using electronic input.
  c. A point-of-sale system transfers funds immediately from a customer's account to the business's account when the transaction is input using the customer's plastic bank account card at the check-out counter.
  d. An automated clearing house transfers funds immediately from a customer's account to the business's account when the transaction is input using the customer's plastic bank account card at the check-out counter.

Q5-19 "Cash and cash equivalents" is commonly listed on a classified balance sheet. Which of the following statements is correct regarding these assets?
  a. Reflects only current assets banks hold for the company.
  b. Reports company holdings of cash, certificates of deposit, U.S. Treasury bills, commercial paper, and all associated interest accounts.
  c. Is the most liquid of all current assets; thus, is listed first on the balance sheet.
  d. Is listed on the balance sheet at its current market value.

Q5-20 Indicate which of the following statements about the acid-test ratio is incorrect.
  a. The numerator of the equation includes cash, liquid investments, and accounts receivable (net).
  b. The acid-test ratio is a measure of a firm's "liquidity," or its ability to pay its current debt.
  c. The acid-test ratio is very reliable because the items included are not subject to any valuation problems.
  d. The denominator of the equation includes all of the current liabilities.

EXERCISES

LO 1   **E5-1**   **Identifying Control Procedures for Cash Received from Credit Sales**   Indicate which of the following are major components of a cash control system. (*Yes, No*)

___a.   Use of a bank checking account
___b.   Recording receipts from remittance advices
___c.   Prompt deposit of cash receipts (daily)
___d.   Making all disbursements in cash
___e.   Use of a petty cash fund
___f.   Timely recording of cash receipts
___g.   Separation of incompatible duties
___h.   Use of a remittance list
___i.   Authorization required for discounts taken
___j.   Timely preparation of bank reconciliations

LO 2

E5-2 **Identifying Control Procedures for Cash Received from Cash Sales**   Employee duties related to cash received from cash sales include the following:

(1) Recording the cash in the accounting records
(2) Recording the cash received in a cash register
(3) Physical receipt of the payment from the customer
(4) Making the bank deposits
(5) Preparing the bank deposit slips

Complete the following by inserting the numbers of the above statements in the proper blanks.
a. ___ is not compatible with any of the other four.
b. ___ is compatible with 2.
c. ___ is compatible with 5.
d. ___ and 3 are not compatible with 4 and _____.

LO 2

E5-3 **Cash Receipts from Cash Sales**   Which of the following carries the greatest risk of employee error and dishonesty? Explain why the item you select involves a significant risk. Assume that cash registers with locked-in tapes are used for cash sales.
a. An employee who does not open the mail completing deposit slips and depositing cash received from credit customers
b. An employee reconciling all the company's bank statements
c. An employee receiving cash from customers in cash sales
d. An employee completing a daily cash report

LO 3,4,5

E5-4 **Cash Control Systems**   Indicate whether the following statements regarding cash control systems are True (*T*) or False (*F*).
___a.   Small cash shortages do not necessarily indicate dishonesty on the cashier's part.
___b.   An unpaid voucher file is used in conjunction with cash payments.
___c.   Vouchers Payable is not a substitute for Accounts Payable when a voucher system is used.
___d.   Petty Cash is debited when the amount of the fund is to be increased.
___e.   Items added to the "Balance per books" in a bank reconciliation require an adjusting entry at the end of the month.

LO 4

E5-5 **Reimbursement of Petty Cash**   The petty cash box of Horvath-Cochran Corp. has a cash count totalling $34.68 and petty cash receipts as follows:

Voucher	Amount	Expense Category
No. 154	$24.12	Transportation-In
No. 155	29.00	Office Supplies Expense
No. 156	5.00	Miscellaneous Expense
No. 157	24.50	Maintenance Expense
No. 158	45.20	Parts Expense
No. 159	38.42	Maintenance Expense
No. 160	39.20	Office Supplies Expense
No. 161	7.11	Miscellaneous Expense

The debit balance of Petty Cash in the general ledger is $250.00.

REQUIRED:

Prepare the journal entry to reimburse the fund on August 31, 19X3.

LO 5   **E5-6**   **Identifying Reconciling Items**   Indicate which of the following statements related to bank reconciliations is *not* correct. State why the item that you select is incorrect.
   a. Credits shown on the bank statement that have not yet been recorded as debits to the company's Cash should be added to the "Balance per books."
   b. Debits from the bank statement that have not yet been recorded as credits to the company's Cash should be deducted from the "Balance per books."
   c. Debits to Cash that have not yet been recorded on the bank statement should be deducted from the "Balance per bank."
   d. Credits to Cash that have not yet been recorded as debits on the bank statement should be deducted from the "Balance per bank."

LO 5   **E5-7**   **Identifying the Additions and Deductions to be Made in a Bank Reconciliation**   Indicate whether the items listed below are:

   (1) Added to the "Balance per books."
   (2) Deducted from the "Balance per books."
   (3) Added to the "Balance per bank."
   (4) Deducted from the "Balance per bank."

   ___a.   Outstanding checks
   ___b.   Funds collected by the bank for us and added to the bank account
   ___c.   NSF checks of customers returned to us
   ___d.   Deposits-in-transit
   ___e.   Bank charge for printing checks
   ___f.   Interest earned on the checking account for the month
   ___g.   Bank error in omitting one of our deposits
   ___h.   Error in recording checks that overstated the credit to cash

LO 6   **E5-8**   **Recording Adjustments from Bank Reconciliations**   Following are possible treatments of a reconciling item in a bank reconciliation:

   (1) Added to the "Balance per books."
   (2) Deducted from the "Balance per bank."
   (3) Added to the "Balance per books."
   (4) Deducted from the "Balance per bank."

REQUIRED:

a. Journal entries are required for which of the above items:

   (a) 1 and 2 only
   (b) 3 and 4 only
   (c) 1 and 3 only
   (d) 2 and 4 only
   (e) All of the above

b. Explain why the items selected require journal entries.

LO 5   **E5-9**   **Reconciling Items**   An entry credited Cash in the journal for Check No. 3110, a corporate dividend. The check was correctly written for $61,500 and recorded in the journal for $16,500.

REQUIRED:

a. Explain how the item would be treated in a bank reconciliation.
b. Prepare the adjusting entry for the item, if necessary.

LO 5,6   **E5-10**   **Bank Reconciliation**   Use the following information to prepare a bank reconciliation at month-end:

(1) The balance per Cash in the general ledger is $4,350.00 at month-end.
(2) The list of outstanding checks totals $1,780.00.
(3) Bank service charges for the month total $85.00.
(4) Deposits-in-transit total $840.00.
(5) The bank collected $2,500 on a noninterest-bearing note receivable as our agent.
(6) The bank returned an NSF check of Bulloch Concrete Co., our customer, in the amount of $750.00.
(7) The balance per bank statement at month-end is $6,955.00.

LO 5,6   **E5-11**   **Bank Reconciliation and Adjusting Entries**   Use the following information to prepare a bank reconciliation at month-end and prepare any necessary journal entries.

(1) The closing balance per bank statement is $6,000.00.
(2) The list of outstanding checks totals $2,400.00.
(3) Bank service charges for the month total $150.00.
(4) Deposits-in-transit total $1,000.00.
(5) The bank collected $4,000 on a noninterest-bearing note for us.
(6) The bank returned an NSF check of Cullowhee Corp., our customer, in the amount of $500.00.
(7) The balance per Cash in the general ledger is $1,250.00 at month-end.

LO 8   **E5-12**   **Cash Equivalents**   Due to an influx of cash, the Valley Metal Company, Inc., has excess cash after paying current bills and estimating cash needs for the next three months. It made the following investments:

May 30   Valley Metal invests in a 1-month, $10,000 CD from Spring Savings Bank. The certificate pays interest at an annual rate of 6%.
June 29   The Spring Savings Bank CD matures and pays Valley Metal its initial investment plus one month's interest.

REQUIRED:

Prepare the journal entries for the transactions above.

LO 9   **E5-13**   **Current and Acid-Test Ratios**   Clubhouse Grill, Inc., is concerned about its current position with its creditors. Following are Clubhouse's current asset and liability accounts as of June 30, 19X7:

Cash	$20,000	Prepaid Insurance	$ 2,000
Cash Equivalents	10,000	Prepaid Rent	2,000
Petty Cash	300	Notes Payable	40,000
Accounts Receivable (net)	50,700	Accounts Payable	62,000
Merchandise Inventory	80,000	Sales Tax Payable	500
Trading Securities	40,000		

REQUIRED:

Calculate Clubhouse's current and acid-test ratios and comment on what the ratios mean.

PROBLEM SET A

LO 1,2   **P5-1A**   **Controlling Cash Receipts from Credit Sales**   Ramond Barr Inc., has two office employees, Walter and Hazel, and an accountant, Alfred. The major stockholder, Ramond, works full-time in the business. All sales are made on credit with payment due within 10 days of the invoice date. All mail is delivered to the company office during working hours.

a. Describe the critical elements in controlling checks received through the mail.

b. Develop a set of accounting controls for Ramond Barr, Inc., to handle the receipt of payments from customers through the mail that will provide for adequate separation of incompatible duties. Identify the employee performing each function in your system.

LO 3,4   **P5-2A**   **Cash Disbursements, Petty Cash, and the Voucher System**   The Vendall Corporation makes all disbursements by check, excluding small amounts paid out of the petty cash fund. It uses a voucher system to record the disbursements. The system requires an approved voucher accompanied by supporting documentation for each check written. Vendall uses a periodic inventory system and a vouchers payable account.

     The following selected transactions relating to payables and disbursements are presented for Vendall for August:

Aug. 1 Purchased merchandise on account, $490.00, terms 2/10, n/30, Voucher No. 156.

     4 Purchased office supplies on account, $130.00, terms 1/10, n/30, Voucher No. 157.

     8 Purchased a 1-year insurance policy for comprehensive protection and paid the premium in advance, $300.00, Voucher No. 158. Wrote Check No. 145 in payment of Voucher No 158.

   11 Paid Voucher No. 156, taking the discount, with Check No. 146.

   12 Established a petty cash fund for $100.00, Voucher No. 159. Wrote Check No. 147 in payment of Voucher No. 159.

   20 Received a statement from the city for property taxes due, $867.55, Voucher No. 160.

   25 Paid Voucher No. 157 with Check No. 148.

   31 Reimbursed the petty cash fund. The fund contained petty cash vouchers totaling $94 for miscellaneous expenses and $6 cash, Voucher No. 161. Wrote Check No. 149 in payment of Voucher No. 161

REQUIRED:

Prepare the journal entries for the August transactions.

LO 4   **P5-3A**   **Petty Cash Funds, Operation, Reimbursement, and Journal Entries**   Zebra Petting Zoo, Inc., frequently has to write small checks for supplies acquired. Management has decided that a petty cash fund would be appropriate to handle purchases of leftover vegetables from grocery outlets, which are fed to the animals, and for other small disbursements that arise for which immediate cash payment is necessary or desirable.

     Petty cash activities for October 19X6 are presented below:

Oct. 4 The fund is established with $250.00.

     9 $25.00 is disbursed to Ingles Produce Market for a pickup truck load of wilted lettuce (Voucher No. 001).

   15 $32.00 is disbursed for 800 pounds of soft cantaloupe, Fruit Delivery Service (Voucher No. 002).

   21 Postage due was disbursed to a postal worker in the amount $2.10 for a package delivered (Voucher No. 003).

   26 $37.50 is disbursed for 40, fifty-pound bags of dog food in torn bags (Voucher No. 004).

   30 Voucher No. 005 was completed for $2.90 to reimburse Jane Wilsong for postage to mail a package.

   31 The petty cash fund contained $150.25 and Vouchers 001–005 above. The fund was replenished.

REQUIRED:

a. Discuss the types of controls that Zebra might establish for the petty cash system.

b. Prepare general journal entries to record the activities related to the petty cash fund for October.

c. Assume the October 31 replenishment of the fund included a reduction in the size of the fund to $200. Prepare the October 31 journal entry.

d. If Zebra failed to replenish the fund on October 31, identify the errors that would be present in the October 31 balance sheet and income statement for the month.

LO 6

P5-4A **Bank Reconciliations, Determining the Cash Balance per Books, Journal Entries**
The following information relates to Topico Fruit Corporation's June 30, 19X8, bank reconciliation.

(1) The balance per the bank statement at June 30, 19X8, is $3,600.00.
(2) The outstanding checks at June 30, 19X8, total $1,150.00.
(3) Bank service charges total $38.00 for the month of June.
(4) Interest earned on the checking account for the month of June is $4.50.
(5) A deposit of $250.00 was in transit as of the cutoff date, June 30, 19X8. There are no other items affecting the bank reconciliation except the "Balance per books."

REQUIRED:

a. Prepare the part of a bank reconciliation that reconciles the "Balance per bank" to the correct cash balance.
b. Compute the apparent balance in Cash on the books of Topico as of June 30, 19X8.
c. Complete the part of the bank reconciliation that reconciles the "Balance per books" to the correct cash balance.
d. Prepare the journal entries required by the reconciliation.

LO 6

P5-5A **Preparation of a Bank Reconciliation, Journal Entries**   Comet Construction Corp., in preparing the July 31, 19X7, bank reconciliation, identified four checks outstanding at the end of the month: No. 714 for $231.20, No. 716 for $450.50, No. 720 for $711.13, and No. 721 for $196.96. A check for $200.00 from Welbilt Corp. was returned as NSF, and a debit memorandum was included in the amount of $25.50 as a collection fee the bank charged for collecting a 60-day, noninterest-bearing note receivable of $5,000.00. The bank statement reported interest earned on the checking account of $18.00. The comparison of the deposits on the bank statement with the daily receipts deposited per the bank deposit slips found a deposit-in-transit as of July 31 in the amount of $2,310.00 and a deposit on July 17 of $330 the bank recorded in error as $300. The balance per books on July 31 was $742.51, and the balance per bank on July 31 was $4,784.80.

REQUIRED:

a. Prepare a bank reconciliation as of July 31, 19X7, for Comet Construction Corp.
b. Explain how Comet probably identified the outstanding checks.
c. What action should Comet take when it discovers the error in the July 17 deposit?
d. Prepare the journal entries required by the reconciliation.

LO 5

P5-6A **Preparation of a Bank Reconciliation and Related Journal Entries**   Aardvark Pest Control Corporation received its bank statement on August 8 for the month ending July 31, 19X7. The bank statement, a listing of checks written in June and July, and the deposit slips for July are provided on the following pages. Additional information is as follows:

(1) The NSF check had been received from Family Restaurant in payment of May services.
(2) The debit memorandum was for bank service charges.
(3) The balance in Cash on June 30 was $3,410.00.
(4) All checks cleared the bank for the correct amounts.

3rd National Bank of Inverness
P.O. Box 151852
Inverness, FL 31321

STATEMENT OF ACCOUNT: Aardvark Pest Control Corp. CLOSING DATE: Jul. 31, 19X7
5541 S. Thrush Pt. STATEMENT DATE: Aug. 6, 19X7
Inverness, FL 31323 ACCOUNT NO.: 421-11552-01

PREVIOUS BALANCE	CREDITS		DEBITS		NEW BALANCE
	NUMBER	TOTAL	NUMBER	TOTAL	
$3,710.00	7	$12,850.00	12	$5,870.00	$10,690.00

DATE	CHECKS				DEPOSITS	BALANCE
07/01/X7						$ 3,710.00
07/02/X7	830	$125.00				3,585.00
07/03/X7	828	199.00	829	$ 101.00		3,285.00
07/07/X7	831	350.00			$2,400.00	5,335.00
07/11/X7	832	80.00			1,200.00	6,455.00
07/17/X7	833	25.00	834	2,150.00	1,500.00	5,780.00
07/20/X7					2,200.00	7,980.00
07/25/X7	835	870.00			2,650.00	9,760.00
07/30/X7	836	420.00	837	1,210.00	1,900.00	10,030.00
07/31/X7	NSF	300.00	DM	40.00	1,000.00	10,690.00

Partial Listing of Checks Written in June

DATE	CHECK NO.	CHECK CLEARED	AMOUNT
19X7			
Jun. 26	826	✔	418.00
28	827	✔	315.75
30	828		199.00
30	829		101.00
Totals			6,950.75

===== Indicates columns omitted

----- Indicates lines omitted

List of Checks Written in July

DATE	CHECK NO.	CHECK CLEARED	AMOUNT
19X7			
Jul. 1	830		125.00
5	831		350.00
9	832		80.00
15	833		52.00
15	834		2,150.00
22	835		870.00
26	836		420.00
29	837		1,210.00
30	838		660.00
31	839		148.00
Totals			6,065.00

REQUIRED:

a. Determine the outstanding checks as of July 31.
b. Determine the deposits-in-transit as of July 31.
c. Identify the error on Aardvark's books.
d. Compute the cash balance per books on July 31.
e. Prepare a bank reconciliation as of July 31.
f. Prepare the journal entries required by the reconciliation.

Deposit Slips

Date	Deposit Amount
19X7	
Jul. 5	$ 2,400.00
11	1,200.00
16	1,500.00
19	2,200.00
24	2,650.00
29	1,900.00
30	1,000.00
31	350.00
Totals	$13,200.00

LO 9

P5-7A **Calculating and Interpreting the Current and Acid-Test Ratios**   Below are the current assets and current liabilities excerpted from Wal-Mart's 1993 annual report.

(Amounts in thousands)	January 31, 1993	1992
Current assets:		
Cash and cash equivalents	$ 12,363	$ 30,649
Receivables	524,555	418,867
Recoverable costs from sale/leaseback	312,016	681,387
Inventories	9,268,309	7,384,299
Prepaid expenses	80,347	60,221
Total current assets	$10,197,590	$8,575,423
Current liabilities:		
Commercial paper	$ 1,588,825	$ 453,964
Accounts payable	3,873,331	3,453,529
Accrued liabilities	1,042,108	829,381
Accrued federal and state income taxes	190,620	226,828
Long-term debt due within one year	13,849	5,156
Obligations under capital leases due within one year	45,553	34,917
Total current liabilities	$ 6,754,286	$5,003,775

REQUIRED:

a. Calculate Wal-Mart's current ratio for January 31, 1992 and 1993.
b. Explain whether you think the change is significant or not.
c. Calculate Wal-Mart's acid-test ratio for January 31, 1992 and 1993.
d. Explain whether you think the change is significant or not.

PROBLEM SET B

LO 3

P5-1B **Control Procedures for Cash Disbursements, Voucher Systems**   The following *elements* are all used in a cash disbursements control system that includes a voucher system:

1. Purchase requisition
2. Purchase order
3. Receiving report
4. Supplier's invoice
5. Vouchers
6. Checkbook
7. Unpaid Vouchers file
8. Paid Vouchers file
9. Bank reconciliation
10. "PAID" stamp

The following *activities* are used in controlling the payments under a voucher system:

A. Prepare vouchers and accounting distribution
B. Record vouchers
C. File unpaid vouchers
D. File paid vouchers
E. Prepare checks
F. Record checks
G. Sign checks
H. Approve vouchers for recording
I. Approve vouchers for payment
J. Attach documentation
K. Prepare bank reconciliation
L. Recording reconciliation adjustments
M. Review Unpaid Vouchers file
N. Forward vouchers to bookkeeper
O. Run tape of approved vouchers
P. Record check numbers on vouchers
Q. Stamp documents and vouchers paid
R. Post to general ledger

REQUIRED:

Divide the *activities* among four employees—manager, receptionist/clerk, accountant, and office manager—in a manner that will provide a separation of incompatible duties and enhance internal control over disbursements. Relate each of the *elements* to the activities assigned.

LO 3,4   **P5-2B   Cash Disbursements, Petty Cash, and the Voucher System**   The Kendall Corporation makes all disbursements by check, excluding small amounts paid out of the petty cash fund. It uses a voucher system to record the disbursements. The system requires an approved voucher accompanied by supporting documentation for each check written. All payments are made by check. Kendall uses a periodic inventory system and a vouchers payable account.

The following selected transactions related to payables and disbursements are presented for Kendall for August:

Aug. 1 Purchased merchandise on account, $600.00, terms 1/10,n/30, Voucher No. 201.
   4 Purchased office equipment on account, $900.00, Voucher No. 202.
   8 Signed a 1-year rental agreement to rent a warehouse and paid the rent in advance, $3,600.00, Voucher No. 203. Wrote Check No. 120 in payment of Voucher No. 203.
   11 Issued Check No. 121 in payment of Voucher No. 201, taking the discount.
   12 Established a petty cash fund for $200.00, Voucher No. 204. Issued Check No. 122 in payment of Voucher No. 204.
   20 Received a statement from the city for property taxes due, $945.50, Voucher No. 205.
   25 Paid Voucher No. 202 with Check No. 123.
   31 Reimbursed the petty cash fund. The fund contained petty cash receipts totaling $164 for miscellaneous expenses and $36 cash, Voucher No. 206. Issued Check No. 124 in payment of Voucher No. 206.

REQUIRED:

Prepare the journal entries for August for these transactions.

LO 4   **P5-3B   Petty Cash Funds, Operation, Reimbursement, and Journal Entries**   Wilkes Mailing Service, Inc., receives and forwards mail for individuals whose work requires them to relocate frequently. Wilkes takes advantage of special rates for packages with various parcel services and the post office. The result is a large number of small payments each month, which Wilkes classifies as Office Expense. Writing checks for these payments is awkward and time-consuming, and Wilkes has decided to try a petty cash fund to handle these payments and simplify the process.

The following petty cash transactions occurred during April 19X8:

Apr. 1 The petty cash fund is established for $250.00

Receipts completed:

	No.	Amount	Payee
Apr. 2	001	$ 2.90	USPS
3	002	3.85	UPS
5	003	2.90	USPS
6	004	4.52	RPS
7	005	7.40	RRE
7	006	5.90	UPS
8	007	18.92	FX
9	008	7.52	EAF
10	009	5.20	RPS
12	010	2.90	USPS
13	011	24.17	FX
13	012	13.82	UPS
15	013	5.45	USPS
15	014	31.12	EAF
16	015	14.85	RPS
17	016	4.54	UPS
19	017	2.90	USPS
20	018	17.82	FX
22	019	5.80	RPS
23	020	6.80	FX
26	021	5.80	USPS
27	022	6.15	RRE
27	023	6.60	RRE
28	024	5.80	USPS
29	025	2.90	USPS
30	026	7.40	EAF

30 Wilkes reimbursed the fund on April 30, the end of the fiscal year. The cash in the petty cash box was $12.64.

REQUIRED:

a. Write a brief explanation as to how the petty cash fund would work.
b. Prepare the journal entries required to record all of the activities related to the petty cash fund during April 19X8.
c. After replenishing on April 30, Wilkes decided the fund may not be large enough for every month's activity. Prepare the journal entry to increase the fund to $300.00.
d. If Wilkes failed to replenish the fund on April 30, identify the errors in the April 30 balance sheet and the April income statement.

LO 6   **P5-4B   Bank Reconciliations, Determining the Cash Balance per Books, Journal Entries**
The following information relates to the Truck Cap Corporation's August 31, 19X3, bank reconciliation.

(1) The balance per the bank statement at August 31, 19X3, is $5,120.00.
(2) Outstanding checks at August 31, 19X3, total $785.00.
(3) Bank service charges total $22.00 for the month of August.
(4) Interest earned on the checking account for the month of August is $128.60.
(5) A deposit of $400.00 was in-transit at August 31, 19X3. There are no other items affecting the bank reconciliation except the "Balance per books."

REQUIRED:

a. Prepare the part of a bank reconciliation that reconciles the "Balance per bank" to the correct cash balance.

b. Compute the apparent balance in Cash on the books of Truck Cap Corporation at August 31, 19X3.

c. Complete the part of the bank reconciliation that reconciles the "Balance per books" to the correct cash balance.

d. Prepare the journal entries required by the reconciliation.

LO 6   **P5-5B**   **Preparation of a Bank Reconciliation**   Alabama Record Corp., in preparing the December 31, 19X5, bank reconciliation, identified four checks outstanding at the end of the month: No. 326 for $721.00, No. 328 for $150.00, No. 330 for $425.50, and No. 331 for $290.40. A check for $150.00 from Marvin Co. was returned as NSF, and a debit memorandum was included in the amount of $65.00 as a fee the bank charged for check printing. The bank statement reported interest earned on the checking account of $32.10. The comparison of the deposits on the bank statement with the daily receipts deposited per the bank deposit slips found a deposit-in-transit as of December 31, in the amount of $2,200.00, and a deposit on December 17 of $340 was recorded in error by the bank as $430. The balance per books at December 31, 19X5, was $8,972.71. The bank's balance at December 31, 19X5, was $8,266.71.

REQUIRED:

a. Prepare a bank reconciliation as of December 31, 19X5, for Alabama Record Corp.

b. Explain how Alabama probably identified the outstanding checks.

c. What action should Alabama take when it discovers the error in the December 17 deposit.

d. Prepare the journal entries required by the reconciliation.

LO 5   **P5-6B**   **Preparation of a Bank Reconciliation and Related Journal Entries**   Alexia Movorik Corp. received its bank statement on April 7 for the month ending March 31, 19X2. The bank statement, a listing of the checks written in February and March, and the deposit slips for March are provided on the following pages. Additional information is as follows:

(1) The debit memorandum was $45.00 for check printing.

(2) Cash was $2,015.00 on February 28, 19X2, after adjustments.

(3) There was a $500.00 deposit in transit as of February 28, 19X2.

(4) The NSF check had been received from B. B. Ballik, a customer, for payment on account.

(5) All checks cleared the bank at the correct amounts.

REQUIRED:

a. Determine the outstanding checks as of March 31.

b. Determine the deposits-in-transit as of March 31.

c. Identify the error on Movorik's books.

d. Compute the cash balance per books on March 31.

e. Prepare a bank reconciliation as of March 31.

f. Prepare the journal entries required by the reconciliation.

Bank of Gerald
2 South Spring Street
Gerald, MO 63121

STATEMENT OF ACCOUNT: Alexia Movorik Corp.
41 N. Oak Street
Lone Spring, MO 63142

CLOSING DATE: Mar. 31, 19X2
STATEMENT DATE: Apr. 5, 19X2
ACCOUNT NO.: 16-0115

PREVIOUS BALANCE	CREDITS		DEBITS		NEW BALANCE
	NUMBER	TOTAL	NUMBER	TOTAL	
$2,340.50	8	$5,270.00	11	$4,274.50	$3,336.00

DATE	CHECKS				DEPOSITS	BALANCE
03/01/X2						$ 2,340.50
03/01/X2	216	$ 315.50			$ 500.00	2,525.00
03/07/X2	218	145.00	217	$275.00	800.00	2,905.00
03/10/X2	219	190.00			1,300.00	4,015.00
03/22/X2	222	670.00			350.00	3,695.00
03/24/X2	220	25.00			750.00	4,420.00
03/25/X2	221	1,140.00			410.00	3,690.00
03/26/X2	215	84.00			850.00	4,456.00
03/30/X2	224	1,320.00			310.00	3,446.00
03/31/X2	NSF	65.00	DM	45.00		3,336.00

Partial Listing of
Checks Written in February

DATE	CHECK NO.	CHECK CLEARED	AMOUNT
19X7			
Feb. 26	211	✔	246.00
27	212	✔	110.00
27	213	✔	125.00
28	214		426.00
28	215		84.00
28	216		315.50
Totals			6,306.50

List of Checks
Written in March

DATE	CHECK NO.	CHECK CLEARED	AMOUNT
19X2			
Mar. 1	217		275.00
5	218		415.00
9	219		190.00
15	220		25.00
15	221		1,140.00
22	222		670.00
26	223		310.00
29	224		1,320.00
30	225		460.00
31	226		1,435.00
Totals			6,240.00

===== Indicates columns omitted

----- Indicates lines omitted

Deposit Slips	
Date	**Deposit Amount**
19X2	
Mar. 6	$ 800.00
9	1,300.00
21	350.00
23	750.00
24	410.00
25	850.00
29	310.00
30	160.00
31	1,250.00
Totals	$6,180.00

LO 8

P5-7B **Calculating and Interpreting the Current and Acid-Test Ratios** Below are the current assets and current liabilities excerpted from Kmart's 1993 annual report.

(Amounts in millions)	End of January 1993	End of January 1992
Current assets:		
Cash (including temporary investments of $260 and $309, respectively)	$ 611	$ 565
Merchandise inventories	8,752	7,546
Accounts receivable and other current assets	1,146	879
Total current assets	$10,509	$8,900
Current liabilities:		
Long-term debt due within one year	$ 117	$ 39
Notes payable	590	0
Accounts payable—trade	2,959	2,722
Accrued payrolls and other liabilities	1,215	1,014
Taxes other than income taxes	368	322
Income taxes	246	211
Total current liabilities	$ 5,495	$4,308

REQUIRED:

a. Calculate Kmart's current ratio for January 29, 1992, and January 27, 1993. (Some companies such as Kmart choose an accounting period of 52 weeks instead of a calendar year. Hence, the exact day of their fiscal year-ends generally fluctuate one or two days each year.)

b. Explain whether you think the change is significant or not.

c. Calculate Kmart's acid-test ratio for January 29, 1992, and January 27, 1993.

d. Explain whether you think the change is significant or not.

CRITICAL THINKING AND COMMUNICATING

C5-1 Jim Gordon has worked for the Robbins Corporation for many years and is a trusted employee. Unknown to his employer and friends, Jim is experiencing severe financial and personal problems.

One of the duties that Jim performs is the monthly reconciliation of the bank statement and Cash. Jim does not perform any other duties related to cash. Robbins Corporation manages estates and trusts and has receipts and disbursements of several million dollars each month.

Jim Gordon's friend, Roger Simmons, is a systems analyst at the local bank where Robbins maintains its general checking account. Roger has convinced Jim that he has a tip on an investment that can make them both a lot of money. The investment would require $25,000 and would have to be held about 6 months before it could be sold at an expected significant gain.

Roger suggests to Jim that he can transfer $25,000 from Robbins' account to a Swiss account that the two men would have access to. The only problem, states Roger, is that "You will have to figure out a way to conceal the cash shortage until we can sell the investment and put the money back in Robbins' account."

REQUIRED:

a. How might Jim conceal the shortage?
b. What control procedures would identify the concealment?
c. Do you think a scenario such as this happens often in business? Discuss.
d. If the scheme works and the $25,000 is restored to the account, is there anything wrong with what Jim and Roger have done?

C5-2

You have worked for the Watson Sales Corporation since you started college. You spend 2 hours each afternoon and a full day on Saturdays helping with a variety of office tasks, including calling delinquent customers to urge payment, taking bank deposits to the bank, picking up the mail at the post office, filing paid and unpaid invoices, and other office work. You are well-liked by everyone in the office, and your boss has always allowed you an afternoon off to prepare for tests in your classes. It has been a really good experience for you, especially since you are a business major.

One Saturday, while filing invoices, you notice one of the full-time salespersons going through the company's accounting records and occasionally copying down information. You had never seen anyone other than the owner work on the accounting records. You pretend to concentrate on your filing. About a month later, you see the same person again going through the financial records and making notes. You become concerned. It seems to you that the owner has always been careful to lock the accounting records in the safe when he finishes with them.

You like your employer and all of the staff and don't want to "get involved" but wonder if you have some obligation to relate what you have seen to your employer. You also worry that if the salesperson is supposed to be in the records and you report him it will become some sort of office joke at your expense.

REQUIRED:

a. Discuss what kinds of information the salesperson could be getting from the financial records that could be of financial benefit or could provide an advantageous edge to a competitor of the company.
b. Discuss what controls would have prevented this problem from occurring.
c. Discuss your ethical obligation to your employer and to the company with respect to what you have seen.
d. Discuss how you might deal with the problem and meet your obligation.

C5-3

Refer to Appendix B, the financial statements of J.C. Penney Company, Inc., and examine the balance sheet's current asset and current liabilities sections and their accompanying footnotes.

REQUIRED:

a. Are the account titles similar to the text's chart of accounts? How do they differ?
b. How does J.C. Penney define cash equivalents? (See notes to financial statements.) What term does J.C. Penney use for cash equivalents? What additional information would be relevant?

c. Calculate the current and acid-test ratios for all the years presented in the balance sheet. Discuss the significance of your ratio results for the company's creditors.

d. Some financial analysts omit prepaids from the current and acid-test ratios, claiming their inclusion could be misleading. Why?

e. Calculate J.C. Penney's current and acid-test ratios, excluding the prepaids for all years presented in the balance sheet. Compare your results with the ratios you computed in c. What is your conclusion about prepaids and the current and acid-test ratios?

C5-4 Observe a video rental store or other all-cash business's checkout counter for 15 minutes. Based on what you have learned in this chapter, critique its cash controls. What are the store's strengths and weaknesses? What suggestions would you make to management? Prepare a brief memo detailing your observations, analysis, and recommendations.

C5-5 Observe a home shopping channel on television. Describe its cash control procedures for sales. Are all sales on credit? What safeguards do you observe? How do electronic funds transfers affect cash control? How does the network handle returns of merchandise? Prepare a brief memo answering these questions and detailing your personal conclusions regarding this form of shopping from a cash control perspective.

CHAPTER 6

Accounts Receivable and Notes Receivable

Jane Trevor decided several years ago that her business, Trevor's Wholesale Warehouse, Inc., should extend credit to its customers. Since that time, cash sales have stayed about the same each year, but credit sales have grown dramatically. However, the profitability of her business is now down, and Jane wonders if she has carried credit sales growth too far. She would like to have some diagnostic tools to help her determine whether her credit sales are actually hurting, instead of helping, the business.

In this chapter, we introduce you to the costs and benefits of credit sales. One of the costs of credit sales is uncollectible accounts, which present some interesting challenges in accounting for accounts receivable. We show you how to handle these challenges, and you will see how you can use some simple diagnostic tools to keep track of the effect on a business of credit sales and accounts receivable. In addition to learning about credit sales and more about accounts receivable, you will learn about bank card sales such as VISA and MasterCard sales. We will also introduce you to notes receivable and why businesses accept notes receivable, as well as accounts receivable, from customers.

LEARNING OBJECTIVES

1. Explain why businesses grant credit to their customers, why they should expect to experience uncollectible accounts, and how they can control uncollectible accounts expense.
2. Account for estimated uncollectible accounts, uncollectible accounts expense, and subsequent write-offs of uncollectible accounts according to the allowance method.
3. Account for third-party credit card sales and explain how they can reduce problems of collecting on credit sales.
4. Describe a promissory note receivable and distinguish between negotiable and nonnegotiable notes.
5. Calculate explicit and implicit interest on notes receivable.
6. Account for receipt of notes receivable, accrual of interest on notes receivable, and receipt of payment on notes receivable.
7. Account for the discounting of notes receivable.
8. Calculate the number of days-sales-in-receivables and uncollectible-accounts-expense-as-a-percent-of-credit sales and use these tools to diagnose problems.

LO 1

Explain why businesses grant credit to their customers, why they should expect to experience uncollectible accounts, and how they can control uncollectible accounts expense.

CREDIT SALES AND UNCOLLECTIBLE ACCOUNTS

Businesses extend credit to their customers to increase sales. However, inevitably some customers do not pay. The decision to grant credit to customers should satisfy the following criterion: Will granting credit add to profitability? Granting credit involves adding to the firm's assets (accounts receivable), and the business must earn competitive profits on this additional investment. The benefit of granting credit to customers is measured as follows:

Additional Earnings = Additional Sales Revenue –
Cost of Additional Goods Sold –
Additional Expenses Incurred

The expense of uncollectible accounts receivable is one of the additional expenses that results from granting credit.

Uncollectible accounts expense is the estimated portion of a period's credit sales that a business ultimately will not collect from customers. Uncollectible accounts expense can make credit sales unprofitable or, at least, not sufficiently profitable to justify the necessary investment in accounts receivable.

Controlling Uncollectible Accounts Expense

The best protection for any individual business against excessive uncollectible accounts expense is a sound credit policy. A business should establish criteria for screening credit customers and impose control over authorizing credit sales transactions.

Screening Credit Customers. The first rule of a sound credit policy is obvious: "Do not sell goods on credit to those who cannot or will not pay." Though obvious, this rule is not easy to apply. At the time of sale, it is impossible to recognize every customer who ultimately will not pay. As a result, the business must establish criteria to distinguish between customers who are likely to pay and those who are unlikely to pay. Thus, the business must set up procedures to screen potential credit customers in advance of any sales transactions. Personnel other than salespeople should conduct credit screening. This way, conflicts of interest can be avoided, especially if sales personnel are paid commissions on the sales they complete.

Credit Applications. The first-time credit sale customer usually has to apply for credit. A credit application may involve no more than a telephone interview, or it may require detailed financial information provided on elaborate forms. Illustration 6-1 is an application for a Sears charge account. The business granting credit uses such an application to collect certain facts about the applicant's financial condition and history to serve as a basis for credit evaluation. Notice that the Sears application asks the customer for personal information and history under the caption TELL US ABOUT YOURSELF, information about income

ILLUSTRATION 6-1 Sears Credit Application

(ability to pay) under ABOUT YOUR EMPLOYER, and information about credit cards and banking relationships under the caption ABOUT YOUR CREDIT REFERENCES.

If the applicant is a business, the company granting credit often requests financial statements (and income tax returns) to evaluate and to judge the applicant's ability to pay. In addition, the company may consult various credit bureaus or credit rating services such as Dun & Bradstreet, Inc. to obtain a summary of the applicant's credit history. Illustration 6-2 displays an excerpt from a Dun & Bradstreet report showing the most recent payment history of a particular business as reported by its suppliers to Dun & Bradstreet. Notice that this particular business is slow in paying some of its recent bills and is past due with certain amounts—which might make other businesses reluctant to grant it credit.

If the overall credit evaluation of an individual or a business indicates that the applicant is creditworthy, then the company sets up an account in the accounts receivable subsidiary ledger and sets an initial credit limit.

ILLUSTRATION 6-2 Excerpt from a Dun & Bradstreet Report[1]

PAYMENTS REPORTED SALE	PAYING RECORD	HIGH CREDIT	NOW OWES	PAST DUE	SELLING TERMS	LAST WITHIN
(Amounts may be rounded to nearest figure in prescribed ranges)						
02/X5	Ppt-Slow 30	250	50	50		1 Mo
01/X5	Ppt	500				1 Mo
	Lease agreement					
	Ppt-Slow 30	2500	750	100	N15	1 Mo
10/X4	Ppt	5000			N30	
	Ppt	2500		-0-	N30	

* Payment experiences reflect how bills are met in relation to the terms granted. In some instances payment beyond terms can be the result of disputes over merchandise, skipped invoices etc.

Authorizing Credit Sales

Personnel should check the customer's credit status before a credit sale is made.

Retail Credit Sales. In a retail setting, a business often issues its customers plastic credit cards with the customers' account numbers embossed on them. Salesclerks either check the numbers manually against lists of unauthorized accounts, key the numbers into cash registers that are linked to computers, or pass them through devices linked to computers that read the numbers off magnetic strips on the back of the cards. In any case, the sale is rejected if the customer's account is either over the limit or past due or if the customer is otherwise considered unworthy of credit at the time.

Wholesale Credit Sales. In a wholesale or industrial setting, the customer typically sends the seller a written purchase order (which may be preceded by a

---

[1]The report shown is reproduced from an actual computer-printed report from Dun & Bradstreet. However, dates have been changed and the company's name has been omitted. Individual company's credit records change over time; and it would be unfair to print a company's slow-payment record as of a past point in time, when the company may have since improved its record.

INSIGHTS INTO ETHICS

Linda Bonaventure is concerned about her own and a co-worker's welfare. Her co-worker, Larry Farnsworth, and she are salespersons for Sleep Tight Waterbeds. Sleep Tight pays its salespersons basic salaries, 15% commissions on all sales they make, and annual bonuses for high sales performers. Larry has confided in her that he is under financial stress. He and his wife recently bought a home that has needed unexpected emergency repairs. He has had to pay for the repairs, but he hopes to be repaid eventually by his homeowner's insurance company.

Linda has noticed that Larry recently has been very aggressive in his sales tactics and, in at least one case, approved a couple for credit on a very expensive bedroom set after Linda had to turn them down for credit just one week earlier. Management has emphasized time and again that salespersons must be careful to approve credit only for customers with ability to pay.

However, Linda is reluctant to say anything to Larry or to management about the credit approval. Linda and Larry and his wife are good friends and she and Larry are "friendly rivals" on the sales floor. Each year they end up number 1 and 2 in sales for the company. The number 1 salesperson always receives a significantly larger bonus than the others. Until just recently, Linda was ahead of Larry in year-to-date sales. She worries that if she talks to management about the bad credit approval Larry will lose his job because of temporary financial pressure beyond his control and her co-workers will think she told on him to win the top annual bonus. If she talks to Larry, she is apt to lose a good friend because he resents her making judgments about his behavior. However, she is also concerned that given Larry's increased sales volume, if he approves too many uncreditworthy customers, he may do serious damage to the business and jeopardize all of their jobs.

What should Linda do about Larry's behavior?

Can she offer management any advice about how to avoid this type of problem?

telephone order). The sales department transforms the information on the customer's order into an internal sales order, which the credit department reviews. The credit department authorizes the sale only if the customer's current balance is not past due and if the customer's current balance and the proposed sale do not exceed the customer's credit limit. The shipping department should never ship goods to a customer unless credit approval is indicated on the sales order.

LO 2

Account for estimated uncollectible **accounts,** uncollectible accounts expense, and subsequent write-offs of uncollectible accounts according to the allowance method.

ACCOUNTING FOR UNCOLLECTIBLE ACCOUNTS EXPENSE—THE ALLOWANCE METHOD

A sound credit policy does not mean that customers will always pay their accounts. It means only that the amounts of noncollections—called *uncollectible accounts*—will be kept within acceptable limits. According to the matching principle, a business should recognize the amount of uncollectible accounts as an expense in the same period it recognizes related gross revenues. However, accounts receivable are frequently not determined to be uncollectible until some later period. Under the **allowance method** of accounting for receivables, a business anticipates and estimates uncollectible accounts to be recognized as uncollectible accounts expense in the period of sale. The business then records the estimated amount of uncollectible accounts expense in an entry that is independent of any actual write-offs of specific accounts deemed to be uncollectible.

A business can use two approaches for estimating uncollectible accounts expense: the income statement (percentage of sales) approach and the balance sheet (percentage of accounts receivable) approach. We first illustrate the accrual of uncollectible accounts expense under the income statement approach.

Income Statement (Percentage of Sales) Approach

Under the **income statement approach**, a business accrues estimated uncollectible accounts expense based on its past experience with average collections per dollar of credit sales—with appropriate consideration given to changes in economic conditions or credit policy. For example, Trevor's Wholesale Warehouse, Inc. (TWW) made its decision to offer credit to its customers five years ago. Its experience with uncollectible accounts for the five years preceding the current year (19X5) is summarized in Illustration 6-3.

ILLUSTRATION 6-3 Uncollectible Accounts as Percentages of Credit Sales

Year	Credit sales	Uncollectible accounts	Percent of sales uncollectible
19X0	$ 204,000	$ 4,039	1.98%
19X1	214,200	4,984	2.33%
19X2	235,620	4,948	2.10%
19X3	240,332	5,440	2.26%
19X4	252,349	5,252	2.08%
Total	$1,146,501	$24,663	2.15%

Although it has experienced year-to-year fluctuations, TWW has had an average of 2.15% uncollectible credit sales over the last five years. Assume that TWW has maintained a stable credit policy for the past five years, that general economic conditions have been stable, and that conditions in the industry have been relatively unchanged. Under these assumed conditions, TWW may reasonably project its overall average experienced rate of 2.15% uncollectible sales to its credit sales in 19X5. Therefore, as it recognizes credit sales revenues in 19X5, TWW can appropriately accrue uncollectible accounts expense at 2.15% of the new credit sales.

Now, assuming credit sales for January, February, and March totaled $69,767, TWW's entry to accrue the uncollectible accounts expense for the first quarter would be:

Mar. 31	Uncollectible Accounts Expense	1,500	
	Allowance for Uncollectible Accounts		1,500
	To accrue estimated uncollectible accounts expense for the quarter ended March 31. ($69,767 x .0215 = $1,500)		

If the company changes its credit policy or if changes take place in the economy or industry that suggest changes in collectibility of accounts, TWW should adjust its historical percentage for the new conditions before accruing its uncollectible accounts expense.

Allowance for Uncollectible Accounts. As you would expect, the debit entry increases uncollectible accounts expense by $1,500. However, we do not credit Accounts Receivable directly, as you might have expected. Instead, we credit a new account, Allowance for Uncollectible Accounts. The **Allowance for Uncollectible Accounts** is a valuation, or contra-account, representing the cumulative amount of past sales that a business estimates to be uncollectible but has not written off. The Allowance for Uncollectible Accounts typically has a credit balance that offsets the debit balance of Accounts Receivable.

Allowance for Uncollectible Accounts in the Financial Statements. In its balance sheet, a business can combine the balance of Allowance for Uncollectible Accounts with the balance in Accounts Receivable in different ways to disclose net receivables. Two acceptable methods are shown in Illustration 6-4. The $49,570 figure for accounts receivable equals the balance in the general ledger Accounts Receivable account and the amount individual customers actually owe for past sales. The valuation account (Allowance for Uncollectible Accounts) balance of $3,570 is the amount that TWW does not expect to collect.

ILLUSTRATION 6-4 Allowance for Uncollectible Accounts in the Balance Sheet

Direct Disclosure			Indirect (Net) Disclosure		
TWW, Inc. **Balance Sheet (Partial)** **March 31, 19X5**			**TWW, Inc.** **Balance Sheet (Partial)** **March 31, 19X5**		
Current assets:			Current assets:		
Cash		$20,000	Cash		$20,000
Accounts receivable	$49,570		Accounts receivable,		
Less: Allowance for			net of allowance of		
uncollectible			$3,570		
accounts	3,570	46,000			46,000

Either of the two methods shown in Illustration 6-4 is acceptable, but most large public companies use the **indirect (net) method**. They also frequently use the terms "bad debts" or "doubtful accounts" in place of "uncollectible accounts."

As seen in the following excerpt from its March 31, 1993, annual report, Communications Group, Inc. uses the net method for balance sheet disclosure and uses the term "doubtful accounts" in place of "uncollectible accounts."

		March 31	
		1993	1992
Receivables:			
Trade, less allowance for doubtful accounts of $175,000 and $200,000 at March 31, 1993 and 1992		$584,960	$925,650

As an alternative to showing the allowance in the balance sheet, some large companies such as L.A.Gear, Inc. merely report accounts receivable and indicate that they are reported "net." Other companies such as General Electric report accounts receivable "net" in the balance sheet, but they refer the reader to a note following the financial statements that offsets the allowance against gross receivables and derives the net figure disclosed in the balance sheet.

Uncollectible Accounts Expense. In practice, businesses disclose their uncollectible accounts expenses according to two different methods in income statements, depending on the point of view taken regarding the nature of uncollectible accounts. The revenue-reduction or contra-revenue view calls for inclusion of uncollectible accounts expense in the calculation of net revenue. Suppose TWW had sales returns and allowances of $1,575 but had no sales discounts in the quarter ended March 31, 19X5. The net revenue section of its income statement for the the quarter ending on March 31 would appear as in Illustration 6-5.

ILLUSTRATION 6-5 Uncollectible Accounts Expense in the Income Statement

TWW, Inc. Income Statement (Partial) Quarter Ended March 31, 19X5	
Revenue from sales	$69,767
Less: Sales returns and allowances	(1,575)
Uncollectible accounts expense	(1,500)
Net revenue from sales	$66,692

Many large companies such as Reebok International, Inc. only report "net sales" in their income statements, giving no details about the deductions used to derive net sales from total sales revenues.

The selling-expense view implies that uncollectible accounts expense will be included in selling expenses and may not be distinguished from other selling expenses. However, some companies such as Communications Group, Inc. show uncollectible accounts expense (bad debt expense) as a separate expense of the business on a specific line in the income statement as you can see from the following excerpt from its March 1993 annual report.

	1993	1992
Net sales	$4,833,570	$4,252,240
Costs and expenses:		
Cost of sales (exclusive of depreciation and amortization	1,770,060	1,727,710
Selling, general and administrative expenses	1,814,380	2,092,430
Bad debt expense	89,630	260,240
Depreciation and amortization	486,100	425,750

Writing Off Uncollectible Accounts

Suppose TWW sold $300 worth of merchandise to Freida Smith on credit on January 15, 19X5. Assuming that Freida's individual account receivable was paid-up prior to this sale, her individual account would have the following balance on January 15:

Accounts Receivable—Freida Smith	
Jan. 15 300	

Now, suppose Freida did not pay her account and TWW concluded it was uncollectible on October 31, 19X5. Under the allowance method, TWW would make the following general journal entry on October 31:

Oct. 31	Allowance for Uncollectible Accounts	300	
	Accounts Receivable		300
	To write off an uncollectible account.		

TWW posts this entry to Accounts Receivable and Allowance for Uncollectible Accounts general ledger accounts and to Freida Smith's individual account. After the entry is posted, Freida Smith's individual account (shown below) has a zero balance. That is, her $300 balance would have been *written off* TWW's accounts. However, the write-off leaves uncollectible accounts expense unaffected. TWW previously recognized the uncollectible accounts expense with the adjusting entry (accrual) of $1,500 of *estimated* expense it recognized on March 31 to match sales revenues of January, February, and March, 19X5. At the time of the accrual, TWW credited Allowance for Uncollectible Accounts but did not know which specific sales of January, February, or March ultimately would not be collected. Now, Freida Smith's individual account has been specifically identified as uncollectible. Hence, TWW reduces both Accounts Receivable and the allowance account, and it also credits the reduction to Freida's individual account.

Accounts Receivable—Freida Smith			
Jan. 15	300		
		Oct. 31	300

Illustration 6-6 summarizes the allowance method for handling estimated uncollectible accounts expense and actual write-offs of uncollectible accounts. Notice that the accrual of uncollectible accounts expense does not affect Accounts Receivable. Also, notice that the subsequent write-off of a specific customer's account does not affect Uncollectible Accounts Expense.

ILLUSTRATION 6-6 Allowance Method for Uncollectible Accounts

		General Ledger		
	Sales	Accounts Receivable	Allowance for Uncollectible Accounts	Uncollectible Accounts Expense
Jan. 15 Sale	300	300		
Mar. 31 Accrual			1,500	1,500
Oct. 31 Write-off		300 300		

Subsequent Collection of Accounts Previously Written Off. Although it may be unusual, some former customers pay their accounts after the accounts have been written off. Upon subsequent collection, we debit Accounts Receivable and credit Allowance for Uncollectible Accounts for the amount of the payment. The amount of the payment is posted to the general ledger accounts and to the individual customer's account. Thus, we restore the customer's balance to Accounts Receivable and to Allowance for Uncollectible Accounts. After the restoration entry, we record the cash receipt in the usual way:

Dec. 15	Accounts Receivable	300	
	Allowance for Uncollectible Accounts		300
	To restore balance previously written off.		

Dec. 15	Cash	300	
	Accounts Receivable—Freida Smith		300
	To record collection of account previously written off.		

Balance Sheet Approach for Estimating Uncollectible Accounts Expense

An alternative to the income statement (percentage of sales) approach for estimating uncollectible accounts expense is the **balance sheet** (percentage of accounts receivable) **approach**. According to GAAP, both the income statement relationship (match uncollectible amounts with the related sales) and the balance sheet relationship (net receivables should be valued at the amount expected to be collected) must be maintained. A business can use the latter as well as the former relationship as a basis for accruing uncollectible accounts expense.

Aged Schedule of Accounts Receivable.   To apply the balance sheet approach, a business uses an *aged schedule of accounts receivable* to evaluate the makeup of the accounts receivable balance at the end of a period.

Illustration 6-7 shows the last page of TWW's aged schedule of accounts receivable as of March 31, 19X5. At the bottom of the page is a summary of the entire schedule. The schedule identifies the customers by account numbers in the first column and lists all of the individual customers' accounts receivable balances in the last column. The columns in between show the breakdown of each customer's balance according to when the amounts making up the balance are (were) due. For example, the amounts in the second column are "within discount." They represent credit sales to customers within the 10 days prior to March 31. In the next column are sales made 11 to 30 days prior to March 31. These amounts are not yet past due. Then, there are five columns representing sales to customers more than 30 days prior to March 31. These amounts are cat-

ILLUSTRATION 6-7 Aged Schedule of Accounts Receivable

TWW, Inc.
Aged Schedule of Accounts Receivable
March 31, 19X5

CUSTOMER NUMBER	AMOUNT WITHIN DISCOUNT	AMOUNT WITHIN 30 DAYS	AMOUNT 1–30 DAYS PAST DUE	AMOUNT 31–60 DAYS PAST DUE	AMOUNT 61–90 DAYS PAST DUE	AMOUNT 91–120 DAYS PAST DUE	OVER 120 DAYS PAST DUE	CUSTOMER TOTAL
1101						650		650
1102						390	567	957
1103		401						401
1104		445						445
1105		368						368
1106	456							456
1107		679						679
1108			230	120				350
1109				150	400			550
1110	540							540
Page Total	996	1,893	230	270	400	1,040	567	5,396
Total	9,900	17,037	2,070	2,430	3,600	9,360	5,103	49,500
Allowance %	0.80%	1.20%	2.50%	5.50%	9.10%	15.50%	25.90%	
Allowance	79	204	52	134	328	1,451	1,322	3,570

egorized in the columns according to how many days they are past due. For example, Customer 1108's balance of $350 is composed of $230 that is 1 to 30 days past due and $120 that is 31 to 60 days past due.

Estimating the Appropriate Balance for the Allowance for Uncollectible Accounts.

The credit manager should review the amounts in each age category to determine if it is appropriate to apply past experience with collections from each of the age categories. For example, suppose TWW has a history of ultimately collecting 97.5% of accounts once they become past due by 1-30 days. In a "normal" period, TWW should establish a 2.5% allowance for uncollectible accounts in this category of total accounts receivable as shown at the bottom of Illustration 6-7. However, the credit manager may conclude that conditions have changed or that the customers whose accounts are in the particular age category are more or less likely to pay than past experience dictates. In either case, the credit manager should adjust the percentage for that category.

In the above manner, the credit manager or other responsible employee sets appropriate uncollectible percentages for all the age layers. Notice that the percentages increase with the age of the accounts because generally the longer a customer takes to pay, the higher the probability of nonpayment. The appropriate percentages are then multiplied by the total balance in each age category as shown at the bottom of Illustration 6-7, and the allowance amounts are summed across to determine the total allowance estimate. The total allowance estimate of $3,570 in Illustration 6-7 is the estimated amount that will not be collected from the total accounts receivable balance of $49,500 as of March 31, 19X5.

The credit manager compares this total allowance to the *unadjusted balance* in Allowance for Uncollectible Accounts to determine the appropriate expense accrual. Assuming that the *unadjusted* balance in the account is $2,050 at March 31, 19X5, the manager determines the accrual as:

Estimated allowance for uncollectible accounts, March 31, 19X5:	$3,570
Less: Balance in Allowance for Uncollectible Accounts, March 31, 19X5	2,050
Estimated uncollectible accounts expense, January-March, 19X5	$1,520

The journal entry to record the accrual adjustment is:

Mar. 31	Uncollectible Accounts Expense	1,520	
	Allowance for Uncollectible Accounts		1,520
	To adjust the allowance account and to estimate and accrue uncollectible accounts expense for the quarter ended March 31 ($3,570 - $2,050 = $1,520).		

Income Statement and Balance Sheet Approaches Compared

Illustration 6-8 compares the sequence of entries affecting Allowance for Uncollectible Accounts under the balance sheet and income statement approaches. Notice that the only event that differs is the accrual adjustment. Theoretically, the amounts of the accruals and the balances in the account should be the same under both approaches. However, both approaches involve estimations, and different approaches frequently produce different estimates (as we illustrated in the TWW examples above).

The income statement approach is simpler and less costly to apply, and some businesses use it especially for monthly or quarterly accruals. The balance sheet approach, as we have illustrated it, is more detailed and complicated and involves greater cost to implement; but it generally produces more accurate estimates. In addition, because it focuses attention on accounts that are past due and in need of extra collection effort, the review of an aged schedule of accounts receivable is an important part of the management of the collection process. With the widespread proliferation of computers—even in small businesses—preparing an aged schedule of accounts receivable is not the time-consuming task it used to be. Thus, more and more businesses are using the balance sheet approach of estimating the allowance for and accrual of uncollectible accounts expense.

ILLUSTRATION 6-8 Comparing the Income Statement and Balance Sheet Approaches

Income Statement Approach	Balance Sheet Approach
1. Beginning balance, Allowance for Uncollectible Accounts	1. Beginning balance, Allowance for Uncollectible Accounts
2. Deduct write-offs as accounts are deemed uncollectible.	2. Deduct write-offs as accounts are deemed uncollectible.
3. **Estimate and accrue uncollectible accounts expense as a percent of credit sales for the period.**	3. **Estimate appropriate balance in the allowance account from aged schedule of individual accounts and accrue uncollectible accounts expense to achieve the target balance.**
4. Ending balance, Allowance for Uncollectible Accounts	4. Ending balance, Allowance for Uncollectible Accounts

Accounting for Uncollectible Accounts—Direct Write-Off Method

Some businesses use the direct write-off method of accounting for uncollectible accounts receivable—even though it is not acceptable under GAAP. Under the **direct write-off method**, customers' accounts are credited and Uncollectible Accounts Expense is debited when amounts owed are deemed uncollectible. Recall the example of Freida Smith who purchased $300 worth of merchandise on credit from TWW on January 15, 19X5. Under the direct write-off method, TWW would not have accrued any uncollectible accounts expense on March 31 to match against January, February, and March sales as it did under the allowance method. Instead, when TWW deemed Freida's account uncollectible on October 31, it would make the following entry:

Oct. 31	Uncollectible Accounts Expense	300	
	Accounts Receivable—Freida Smith		300
	To write off uncollectible account and		
	to recognize uncollectible accounts expense.		

TWW would post the entry to the general ledger accounts, resulting in a reduction in Accounts Receivable and a recognition of Uncollectible Accounts Expense. When posted to Freida Smith's account, the entry has the same effect as a write-off under the allowance method:

Accounts Receivable—Freida Smith	
Jan. 15　　300	
	Oct. 31　　300

Direct Write-Off Versus Allowance Method— A Matter of Materiality

Many businesses prefer the direct-write-off method because of its simplicity. In addition, the Internal Revenue Code allows taxpayers to use the direct write-off method for recognizing uncollectible accounts expense, but it does not permit the allowance method. Thus, businesses that cannot afford to keep separate records for financial accounting and tax purposes (including many small businesses) use the direct write-off method. However, direct write-off method violates accrual accounting concepts (GAAP). From a GAAP perspective, a business should recognize and match uncollectible accounts expense against the related revenues in the period it recognizes revenues. The direct write-off method recognizes the expense when accounts are written off. This may or may not be the same accounting period in which the sales were made. When it is not the same period, uncollectible accounts expense will be misstated from an accrual perspective. In addition, according to GAAP, a business should not value the accounts receivable above the amounts actually expected to be collected. Under the direct write-off method, however, no allowance for uncollectible accounts is created to offset gross accounts receivable. Thus, the direct write-off method is not acceptable under GAAP.

However, the principle of materiality makes it possible for some businesses to use the direct write-off method and *still not violate GAAP*. **Materiality** is the amount of error or incorrectness in a set of financial statements that could change a decision of a knowledgeable user of the financial statements. By this definition, immaterial amounts of error or incorrectness in financial statements do not matter to users of the statements. Thus, a business may use a simpler, less expensive non-GAAP method of accounting, provided the differences in its financial statements compared to using the GAAP method are *immaterial*.

LO 3

Account for third-party credit card sales and explain how they can reduce problems of collecting on credit sales.

THIRD-PARTY CREDIT CARDS

A business can avoid collection problems and uncollectible accounts expense by accepting third-party credit cards. These credit cards are of two basic types: bank cards and all other credit cards.

Bank Cards

Bank cards such as MasterCard and VISA permit a customer to purchase goods on credit, while the merchant receives immediate cash payment. These cards are called bank cards because the merchant and the customer each have a bank or other financial service business involved in the transaction.

The customer deals with an "issuing bank." The issuing bank takes applications for bank cards from consumers, reviews their credit records, and either issues or denies them bank cards. Once the cards are issued, the issuing banks guarantee payment on all *properly authorized* transactions charged to the card.

The merchant deals with a "service bank." The service bank typically solicits business from merchants by encouraging them to accept bank cards. The service bank evaluates the merchant's actual or likely volume of bank card sales and other cost factors and quotes the merchant a discount rate. Upon depositing the credit card sales slips, the merchant receives an immediate credit to (increase in) his or her bank account for the amount of the sales minus the discount.

Bank cards create a hybrid situation. By accepting bank cards, the merchant gives customers the benefit of credit sales and enjoys a higher sales volume as a result. Compared to regular credit sales, the merchant receives three benefits from the bank card sales arrangement:

1. The merchant receives cash immediately.
2. The merchant avoids any uncollectible account losses from customers.
3. The merchant avoids the costs of credit reviews, collection efforts, and maintenance of customer accounts.

However, the typical discount of $3^1/2$ to 5% offsets these benefits. The amount of the discount depends on a number of factors, including volume of sales and whether authorization is secured by voice (which requires a live operator at the bank to respond) or electronically. The discount is the lowest if the merchant invests in devices that can read the customers' card numbers off the magnetic strips on the backs of the cards and electronically check the status of the cards with a bank card computer system.

Bank card sales revenues and bank card discounts are recorded as of the date of sale. On March 1, 19X5, TWW had bank card sales of $500, and its discount rate is 4%. TWW's entry to record the bank card sales is:

Mar. 1	Cash	480	
	Sales Discounts	20	
	Sales		500
	To record daily bank card sales.		

Other Third-Party Credit Cards

Other third-party credit cards such as American Express cards work in one of two ways. Similar to bank cards, they offer instantaneous payment by working through a bank. Or, if the seller is willing to wait for payment—say six weeks—third-party credit cards offer a lower discount (called a service fee). The seller has the choice of having a higher discount taken out of sales revenues and avoiding uncollectible accounts *and* avoiding waiting for payment or avoiding only the uncollectible accounts problem and enjoying a lower discount. In either case, sales should be stimulated by the seller's willingness to accept the buyer's credit card.

If the seller chooses the full service, the entries for other third-party credit cards are the same as for bank cards. However, if the seller chooses the second alternative, the entries are similar to ordinary credit sales. For example, suppose TWW had $500 of American Express card sales on March 10. The arrangement between TWW and American Express is for TWW to bill American Express for sales and enclose the credit card slips. American Express pays the amounts billed, less a service fee of 2%, in 30 days. TWW's entries to record the sales and subsequent remittance are:

Mar. 10	Accounts Receivable—American Express	490	
	Sales Discounts	10	
	Sales		500
	To record daily American Express card sales.		
Apr. 11	Cash	490	
	Accounts Receivable—American Express		490
	To record collection on American Express card sales.		

LO 4

Describe a promissory note receivable and distinguish between negotiable and nonnegotiable notes.

NOTES RECEIVABLE

Accounts receivable are not the only types of receivables a business may accept from customers or others in exchange for assets. It may also accept promissory notes receivable. A **promissory note** is a written promise by one party (the **maker** of the note) to pay a specified amount of money, usually with interest, to another party (the **payee**) on a specified date at a specified place. Illustration 6-9 is an example of a promissory note.

ILLUSTRATION 6-9 Promissory Note

Corresponding to the labels in Illustration 6-9, the components of the promissory note are:

(a) The **face amount** of the note in numbers; for example, *$1,000*.

(b) The date the note becomes effective—from which interest and the due date are calculated.

(c) The name of the maker of the note—the person or entity who (which) is promising the payment.

(d) The payee of the note to whom (to which) the amount is owed.

(e) The face amount in words; for example, *One thousand and 00/100*.

(f) The location at which it is agreed the payment will be made when due.

(g) The annual **interest rate** that applies to the face amount of the note.

(h) The **period**, **term**, or **duration** of the note in days (or months or years); for example, *one hundred twenty* or *120* days.

(i) Any supplemental information or conditions; for example, the word *unsecured* indicates that there is no particular property of the maker that provides a "collateral" way of settling the note if the maker fails to pay cash.

(j) The number of the note if it is in a series of notes the maker writes.

(k) The signature of the maker or its authorized representative.

A business may accept promissory notes in exchange for almost any consideration (asset or service). For example, a business sometimes accepts notes as payment for sales or services rendered. It sometimes accepts notes in exchange for accounts receivable that have or will become past due. In such cases, the customer cannot pay on time but plans to pay in the future. The seller wants a written promise to pay by a particular date and requires an interest rate that adequately compensates the seller for waiting for payment. In other cases, a business accepts promissory notes in exchange for cash loans—as in many bank lending arrangements.

Negotiable Promissory Notes Receivable

A **negotiable promissory note** is an instrument of debt that the original payee can sell readily to collect cash earlier than the due date of the note. A negotiable promissory note actually can confer equal or greater rights to the buyer (called a **holder in due course**) than to the original payee. However, not all notes are negotiable, and not all buyers are holders in due course. To gain the full benefits of negotiability, the note and the buyer (holder) must satisfy certain conditions specified in the U.S. Uniform Commercial Code (UCC). The UCC is the model statutory law governing commercial transactions and relationships. Most states have adopted the UCC in its entirety. All 50 states and the District of Columbia have adopted Article 3 governing negotiable instruments. It is beyond the scope of this text to go into greater detail about the conditions the UCC sets forth. We assume that all of the notes illustrated in this chapter are negotiable.

A holder in due course of a negotiable note is entitled to collect the note, regardless of any offsetting claims or defenses that the maker might have against the original payee. For example, suppose that Ace Cleaning Supply, Inc., the maker of the note in Illustration 6-9, buys cleaning products from Superior Cleanser Corporation for $1,000 and gives the negotiable note in exchange. If the goods turn out to be defective, Ace can claim an offset against the note (or that it should not be paid at all), *if Superior tries to collect*. However, suppose Superior sells the note to First National Bank in exchange for cash and First National becomes a holder in due course. Ace will have to pay First National in full when the note becomes due and will have no defense due to the defects in the goods. However, do not conclude that negotiable notes are a means for sellers to evade responsibility for defects in goods sold. To the contrary, in the above example, Superior has a responsibility for the defects, whether or not the note is sold—but a holder in due course of a negotiable note does not.

Non-Negotiable Promissory Notes

A **non-negotiable promissory note** is a note that does not satisfy the legal conditions for negotiability. A holder of a non-negotiable promissory note does not have an unconditional right to collect the note. Therefore, the payee of a non-negotiable note will not be able to sell it as readily as a negotiable note and will be less likely to accept such a note from the maker.

ACCOUNTING FOR NOTES RECEIVABLE

You must master a few mechanics to account for notes receivable. Notes have fixed terms to maturity and provide the payee with interest. To allocate interest revenue properly between accounting periods, you will have to determine the due dates and numbers of days in the duration of notes accurately, and you will need to calculate both explicit and implicit interest.

Determining the Due Dates of Notes

Several ways are used to express the duration or due date of a note. Some notes begin the promise to pay section with the words "On demand, I (we) promise to pay...." Such notes are demand notes. **Demand notes** are promissory notes that are due at any time the payee or holder in due course presents them for payment. Other notes are of fixed durations. That is, their due dates are fixed by either a stated period such as 90 days from the date made or by a specified due date. The note in Illustration 6-9 is due 120 days from January 15, 19X1. Therefore, it is due on May 15, 19X1:

January 16–31	16 days
February	28 days
March	31 days
April	30 days
May 1–15	15 days
Total	120 days

LO 5

Calculate explicit and implicit interest on notes receivable.

Interest on Notes

To understand how to account for promissory notes, you must understand interest calculations. **Interest** is the expense a borrower incurs for the use of money owed in fixed-amount agreements such as promissory notes; and it is the revenue the creditor earns for lending the money. An **interest-bearing note** explicitly mentions an interest rate to be applied to the face amount of the note. If an interest rate is not mentioned, the note is said to be **noninterest-bearing**. For example, suppose a purchaser of goods worth $950 gives the seller a note that makes no mention of interest but has a face value of $1,000. The note carries $50 of interest cost to the maker even though no interest rate is mentioned.

We customarily state interest rates in annual terms. For example, if a note such as the one in Illustration 6-9 quotes an interest rate of 12%, it means that the borrower must repay the amount borrowed plus interest of 12% of the amount borrowed for use of the money for one full year. However, the term of a note (the period from the date it is made until its due date) may be for more or less than one year. Thus, you must be able to calculate interest amounts for both fractions and multiples of years. In this chapter, discussion is restricted to periods of less than one year, which usually are expressed in days. For example, notes due in 30, 60, 90, and 120 days are common. Interest for multiple periods and multiple years is covered in a subsequent chapter.

Calculating Explicit Interest. The general formula for calculating explicit interest for a fraction of a year is:

$$\text{Interest} = \text{Principal} \times \text{Rate} \times \text{Time}$$

or

$$I = PRT$$

Principal is the face amount of the note; rate, the stated annual interest rate; and time, the fraction of a year for which interest is being calculated. To illustrate, suppose that a 90-day note was made for a face value of $2,000 (the amount mentioned on the face of the note), with explicit interest at 11%. The interest for 90 days on the note is:

$$\$54.25 = \$2,000 \times 11\% \times \frac{90 \text{ days}}{365 \text{ days}}$$

The calculation means that the amount to be paid when the note is due is $2,054.25, the face amount of $2,000, plus $54.25 interest for 90 days. The amount to be paid when the note is due is called the **maturity value** of the note.

You may use the above formula to calculate interest for any subperiod in the term of a note as well as to calculate the full interest over the term (as illustrated). For example, the interest for the first 30 days of the note of the previous example is:

$$\$18.08 = \$2,000 \times 11\% \times \frac{30 \text{ days}}{365 \text{ days}}$$

Calculating Implicit Interest.   Notes that carry implicit interest do not state interest rates on them. They only mention the promised amount and when it is due. Thus, the face amount of such a note is also its maturity value. However, such notes typically are accepted in exchange for amounts of goods or services worth less than the face amounts. For example, as an alternative to the previous example, a $2,000 noninterest-bearing, 90-day note might be accepted in exchange for goods worth $1,945.75. In this way, the seller of the goods would earn the same $54.25 for waiting 90 days as the payee in the previous example who accepts a note bearing 11% explicit interest.

Use the following formula to calculate implicit interest for fractions of the duration of a note carrying implicit interest:

$$\text{Interest} = \text{Total Interest} \times \frac{\text{Days}}{\text{Term}}$$

Total interest is the difference between the face value of the note and the value exchanged for it (in this example $54.25); days, the number of days for which you wish to calculate interest; and term, the full term of the note in days. To find the amount of interest applicable to 60 days of the note in the preceding example, perform the following calculation:

$$\$36.17 = \$54.25 \times \frac{60 \text{ days}}{90 \text{ days}}$$

LO 6

Account for receipt of notes receivable, accrual of interest on notes receivable, and receipt of payment on notes receivable.

Recording Receipt of Notes Receivable

As mentioned above, a business may accept a note receivable in almost any type of exchange transaction with another entity. A common example is a sales transaction. When Ace Cleaning Supply, Inc., purchased $1,000 worth of cleaning products from Superior Cleanser on January 15, 19X1, with the note in

Illustration 6-9, Superior would have recorded the exchange with an entry such as this:

Jan. 15	Notes Receivable—Ace Cleaning Supply, Inc.	1,000	
	Sales		1,000
	To record sale and note receivable.		

When a business accepts a note in transactions other than the sale of goods, it is usually in exchange for assets other than merchandise or to convert a previous account receivable into a note receivable. Assume Ace Cleaning Supply, Inc. gave the note to Superior Cleanser to pay an account receivable before it became past due. Superior's entry to record the note would have been:

Jan. 15	Notes Receivable—Ace Cleaning Supply, Inc.	1,000	
	Accounts Receivable—Ace Cleaning Supply, Inc.		1,000
	To record acceptance of a note receivable in payment of an account receivable.		

Interest Revenue From Notes Receivable

The interest the maker of a note promises is revenue to the payee (or holder). If the note runs full-term during a single accounting period, the payee can simply postpone recording the revenue until the note is collected.

Recording Interest Upon Receipt of Payment. Ace's $1,000 note made in favor of Superior is due on May 15, 19X1, with 12% interest. The total interest revenue from the note will be $39.45:

$$\$39.45 = \$1,000 \times 12\% \times \frac{120 \text{ days}}{365 \text{ days}}$$

Assuming Superior does not end an accounting period between January 15 and May 15, it can record the revenue from the note upon receipt of the payment.

May 15	Cash	1,039.45	
	Notes Receivable—Ace Cleaning Supply, Inc.		1,000.00
	Interest Revenue		39.45
	To record receipt of payment of a note receivable.		

Accruing Interest on Notes Before Receipt of Payment. However, if the payee ends an accounting period during the term of a note, it *accrues* interest revenue as of the end of the period in proportion to the amount of the term of the note that has passed during the period that is ending. Suppose that, in the previous example, Superior wants to prepare financial statements as of March 31, 19X1. The term of the note is split between quarters, 75 days in the fiscal quarter ended March 31, 19X1 (from January 16 through March 31) and 45 days in the fiscal quarter ended June 30, 19X1 (from April 1 to May 15). Superior should recognize the following amounts of interest earned in the two quarters:

$$\text{Quarter ended March 31:} \quad \$24.66 = \$1,000 \times 12\% \times \frac{75 \text{ days}}{365 \text{ days}}$$

$$\text{Quarter ended June 30:} \quad \$14.79 = \$1,000 \times 12\% \times \frac{45 \text{ days}}{365 \text{ days}}$$

Total interest earned: $39.45

To recognize the splitting of revenue between fiscal periods (in this case, quarters), requires an accrual as of March 31, 19X1, of 75 days' revenue recognized with an adjusting entry:

Mar. 31	Interest Receivable—Note	24.66	
	Interest Revenue		24.66
	To accrue interest on note receivable.		

After the above entry, the balance in Notes Receivable (with respect to this note) will be $1,000 and the balance in Interest Receivable—Note will be $24.66. Superior would recognize the remaining interest revenue in the quarter ended June 30 ($14.79) upon receipt of the payment of the note on May 15, with the entry:

May 15	Cash	1,039.45	
	Notes Receivable		1,000.00
	Interest Receivable—Note		24.66
	Interest Revenue		14.79
	To record receipt of payment and interest on		
	note receivable.		

Recording Dishonored Notes Receivable

When the maker of a note declines to pay on the date it is due, the maker is said to have *dishonored* the note. If the maker dishonors a note, then the payee must make certain entries. While the note's terms cover its original time period and indicate that it is due now, they do not apply to the period subsequent to the due date. However, the maker of the note still owes the payee the full debt. To recognize this may require two entries. First, any accrued interest not previously recognized is recorded with an adjusting entry. Referring to the previous example, suppose Ace Cleaning Supply, Inc. dishonors the $1,000 note on May 15. Further, suppose Superior Cleanser had recorded the accrued interest revenue on the note of $24.66 through March 31. As of May 15, the carrying value of the note (including interest receivable) is $1,024.66. When Ace dishonored the note on May 15, Superior should recognize the remaining interest due on the note of $14.79 with an entry like this:

May 15	Interest Receivable—Note	14.79	
	Interest Revenue		14.79
	To accrue interest on note receivable dishonored.		

At this point, the Notes Receivable balance is $1,000 and the Interest Receivable—Note balance is $39.45—for a total of $1,039.45, the full amount due from Ace. The next entry converts the full amount of the note receivable into an account receivable:

May 15	Accounts Receivable—Ace Cleaning Supply, Inc.	1,039.45	
	Notes Receivable—Ace Cleaning Supply, Inc.		1,000.00
	Interest Receivable—Note		39.45
	To record account receivable for note plus		
	accrued interest dishonored by Ace Cleaning		
	Supply, Inc.		

After May 15, Superior will treat Ace's obligation like any other account receivable except that Ace probably is entitled to accrue interest. Of course, since the note was not paid on time, the collectibility of the account receivable and any interest may be in doubt. Thus, the collectibility of this new account receivable should enter into Superior's evaluation of the adequacy of its Allowance for Uncollectible Accounts balance as described earlier in the chapter.

Allowance Method for Notes Receivable

The GAAP considerations that apply to uncollectible accounts receivable apply equally to notes receivable. Thus, if any risk that notes receivable will not be collected exists, then the business should accrue uncollectible notes expense and set up an allowance for uncollectible notes. A business may ignore this requirement only if it would lead to immaterial effects on its financial statements—as would be the case if a business only accepted an occasional note receivable in the normal course of its business.

LO 7

Account for the discounting of notes receivable.

Discounting Notes Receivable

The payee of a negotiable note has a choice of holding it until it is due or discounting it (selling it) to a third party. The third party may be anyone other than the maker or the payee. Frequently, the third party is a bank. When a payee sells a note to a third party, the third party does the waiting until the note is due. Hence, the third party requires some compensation or interest in return for waiting for the receipt of cash. This is usually handled by setting a selling price that is less than the note's maturity value. This difference is called a **discount**, and the process of selling or assigning a note is called **discounting a note**.

To illustrate, consider a $2,000, 10% note Credit Corporation holds. Credit Corporation received the note on September 15, 19X1, from DBT Corporation in exchange for services provided. The term of the note is 90 days, so it is due on December 14, 19X1. The note's maturity value (face value plus interest) is:

Face value	$2,000.00
Interest	$49.32 = \$2,000 \times 10\% \times \dfrac{90 \text{ days}}{365 \text{ days}}$
Maturity value	$2,049.32

Now, suppose Credit Corporation discounts the note with Federal Bank on September 30. The Bank requires an interest rate of 14% on the note's maturity value. The Bank's interest requirement (discount) is calculated using an interest rate of 14% for 75 days (instead of 90 days because Credit Corporation has held the note for 15 days) and a principal amount equal to maturity value:

$$\$58.95 = \$2,049.32 \times 14\% \times \frac{75 \text{ days}}{365 \text{ days}}$$

The Bank is willing to buy the note for $2,049.32 - $58.95 = $1,990.37. If the Bank then holds the note to maturity, it will receive $2,049.32 and earn $58.95 in interest.

The first thing Credit Corporation must do in recording the discounting transaction is to make sure the note is properly valued in its accounts. If Credit Corporation does not automatically accrue interest monthly, it must now accrue the interest through September 30:

$$\$8.22 = \$2,000 \times 10\% \times \frac{15 \text{ days}}{365 \text{ days}}$$

Sept. 30	Interest Receivable—Note	8.22	
	Interest Revenue		8.22
	To accrue interest on note receivable from DBT		
	Corporation through September 30.		

After the interest is accrued with the above entry, the carrying value of the note is $2,008.22, a combination of the balance in Notes Receivable ($2,000) and Interest Receivable – Note ($8.22). Now, when Credit Corporation discounts the note to the Bank, Credit's cost of receiving cash for the note 75 days before maturity is easily calculated. It is the difference between the carrying value of the note ($2,008.22) and the amount received from the Bank ($1,990.37) or $17.85. Credit Corporation should classify this cost as interest expense, since it is a cost of having cash for a period of time. Credit Corporation would record the discounting of the note to the Bank as follows:

Sept. 30	Cash	1,990.37	
	Interest Expense	17.85	
	Notes Receivable		2,000.00
	Interest Receivable—Note		8.22
	To record discounting of note receivable		
	from DBT Corporation with Federal Bank.		

Discounted Notes Receivable Dishonored

When the original payee of a negotiable note discounts it to a third party (holder), the payee endorses the note. To endorse a note, the payee signs the back of the note, just as one endorses a check. By endorsing the note with an appropriate *qualification*, the endorser of a note can avoid any liability for payment, should the maker dishonor the note. With qualified endorsement, the payee specifically states that he/she does not assume obligation to pay a discounted note if the maker dishonors it. To make qualified endorsement, the endorser writes "Without recourse" above his/her signature. If the holder accepts the endorsed note, the holder accepts the restriction.

Unless the endorsement is qualified, the original payee is obligated to pay the maturity value (plus a small penalty called a *protest fee*) to the holder in the event that the maker dishonors the note. While the note is outstanding, the original payee of a discounted note (with an unqualified endorsement) is said to have a contingent liability. A **contingent liability** is an obligation that depends on the outcome of future events – in this case, the liability of the original payee depends on whether the maker dishonors the note. If the maker fails to pay the note at the maturity date, the holder is obligated to make a reasonable effort to collect. Failing in this effort, the holder sends a *notice of protest*, usually witnessed by a notary public, to any *unqualified* endorser(s) of the note.

Upon receipt of the notice of protest, the unqualified endorser of the note must pay the holder in full, including any protest fee. The note again becomes the endorser's property and is transferred back by the purchaser in exchange for the endorser's payment in full. At this point, the note is treated just like a dishonored note that the endorser held to maturity—by recording it as an account receivable. Assume, for example, that on December 14, DBT Corporation dishonored the $2,000 note originally made in favor of Credit Corporation, which Credit Corporation discounted to Federal Bank. After making a reasonable effort to collect the note from DBT Corporation, the bank sends a notice of protest to Credit Corporation on December 20. The notice demands payment of the note's maturity value, $2,049.32, plus a protest fee equal to 1% of the maturity value, or a total of $2,049.32 + 20.49 = $2,069.81. The entry to record Credit Corporation's payment of the note and fee is:

Dec. 20	Accounts Receivable—DBT Corporation	2,069.81	
	Cash		2,069.81
	To record payment of discounted note		
	dishonored by DBT Corporation.		

Upon paying the bank, Credit Corporation now has the right, once again, to collect from DBT Corporation. Moreover, it has the right to collect interest on the account balance of $2,069.80 for the period until the full amount is paid. Credit should expend all reasonable efforts within legal limits to collect the account, subject to the cost-effectiveness standard. However, a dishonored note is evidence of the maker's unwillingness or inability to pay and, therefore, the collectibility of such an account is generally doubtful. Therefore, Credit may have to write off the account eventually. In the meantime, Credit should not accrue further interest. Although the interest is *earned*, it may not be *collectible*.

LO 8

Calculate the number of days-sales-in-receivables and uncollectible-accounts-expense-as-a-percent-of-credit sales and use these tools to diagnose problems.

USING INFORMATION ABOUT RECEIVABLES

Now, let us return to the problem Jane Trevor faced. She has used credit sales to stimulate sales growth for several years. But, after reviewing her results for 19X5, she is dissatisfied with profits and has asked her accountant to produce the comparative information in Illustration 6-10. Jane has already noted that net income declined from 19X4 to 19X5, while gross sales increased. Although she suspects problems with credit sales, she is not sure. She needs some analytical tools to aid her inquiry.

ILLUSTRATION 6-10 Comparative Financial Data

Trevor's Wholesale Warehouse, Inc. Comparative Financial Data For the Years Ended December 31, 19X4 and 19X5		
	19X4	*19X5*
Income statement data:		
Cash sales	$102,550	$104,675
Credit sales	252,349	275,565
Gross sales	$354,899	$380,240
Less: Sales returns and allowances	(6,536)	(7,558)
Uncollectible accounts expense	(5,359)	(10,595)
Net sales	$343,004	$362,087
Less: Cost of goods sold	212,939	228,144
Gross profit	$130,065	$133,943
Less: Operating expenses	88,725	95,060
Net income	$ 41,340	$ 38,883
Selected balance sheet data:		
Gross accounts receivable (December 31)	$ 45,560	$ 65,240
Less: Allowance for uncollectible accounts	3,450	6,524
Net receivables	$ 42,110	$ 58,716

Days-Sales-in-Receivables

One common financial ratio Jane can use to analyze her accounts receivable is **days-sales-in-receivables**, defined as follows:

$$\text{Days-Sales-in-Receivables} = \frac{\text{Receivables Balance}}{\text{Credit Sales}} \times \text{Days in Period}$$

The receivables balance is the amount of gross receivables as of any balance sheet date (or the average for a period);[2] credit sales, for the period ended on the balance sheet date (a month, a quarter, or a year); and days in the period, the number of days in the period used to measure credit sales. Jane's ratios, using the data in Illustration 6-10 (the period is a year), are:

19X4	19X5
$\frac{\$45,560}{\$252,349} \times 365 \text{ days} = 66 \text{ days}$	$\frac{\$65,240}{\$275,565} \times 365 \text{ days} = 86 \text{ days}$

These comparative ratios tell Jane that on average the receivables her customers owed are 86 days old as of December 31, 19X5; the average receivable was 66 days old as of December 31, 19X4. What can Jane infer from this change?

1. The investment in accounts receivable has grown more than in proportion to credit sales; credit sales grew 9.2%, while receivables grew 43.2%.[3]
2. Her credit sales customers are paying slower at the end of 19X5 than they were at the end of 19X4. This may be due either to a change in customers' abilities to pay or to poor application of credit and collection policies in her business. If employees authorize credit for less credit worthy customers, the new customers will take longer to pay and a higher percentage will fail to pay. If employees do not pursue collections vigorously, customers will take longer to pay.
3. There is a higher risk of customers not paying at all. That is, as a general rule, when customers take longer to pay, more of them fail to pay.
4. Because accounts receivable grew much faster than credit sales, collections have slowed, and the risk of uncollectibility is higher, the allowance for uncollectible accounts should have expanded considerably— and it did, by 89.1%. Such an expansion generally means that uncollectible accounts expense also grew substantially, reducing the profitability of credit sales.

Uncollectible-Accounts-Expense-as-a-Percent-of-Credit Sales

Uncollectible-accounts-expense-as-a-percent-of-credit sales can add further to Jane's diagnosis of her profitability problem. Assume the credit manager of Trevor's Wholesale Warehouse, Inc. wrote off all accounts that should have been written off in 19X5, accurately estimated the required ending allowance for uncollectible accounts, and caused the appropriate adjusting entry to be

---

[2]The average gross receivables for a period is often approximated by adding the beginning and ending balances and dividing by 2.

[3]Growth rates are calculated as follows:

$$\text{Growth Rate} = 100\% \times \left(\frac{\text{New Amount}}{\text{Previous Amount}} - 1 \right)$$

made for the final year-end accrual of uncollectible accounts expense. Under these circumstances, the uncollectible accounts expense is an accurate estimate of the portion of credit sales for the year that will not be collected. Jane can use the uncollectible-accounts-expense-as-a-percent-of-credit sales as an indicator of the profitability effects of credit sales. The percent is calculated as follows:

$$\text{Percent} = 100 \times \frac{\text{Uncollectible Accounts Expense}}{\text{Credit Sales}}$$

The percents for 19X4 and 19X5 are as follows:

19X4	19X5
$100 \times \left(\dfrac{\$5{,}349}{\$252{,}349}\right) = 2.12\%$	$100 \times \left(\dfrac{\$10{,}595}{\$275{,}565}\right) = 3.84\%$

These comparative ratios show a significant change in uncollectible accounts expense. If uncollectible accounts expense had remained the same percent of credit sales in 19X5 as in 19X4 (2.12%), TWW would have saved $4,740 [(3.84% - 2.12%) x $275,565 = $4,740]. The net income of $38,883 would have been higher by $4,740, or by more than 11%.

In summary, the days-sales-in-receivables and uncollectible-accounts-expense-as-a-percent-of-credit sales ratios tell Jane that her customers are paying slower, more are failing or will fail to pay, her investment in receivables has escalated out of proportion to credit sales, and the profitability of credit sales has clearly declined. She definitely will want to investigate her employees' application of TWW's credit and collections policies.

SUMMARY

Explain why businesses grant credit to their customers, why they should expect to experience uncollectible accounts, and how they can control uncollectible accounts expense. Businesses grant credit to customers to increase sales and net income. However, some customers ultimately do not pay their accounts. The best ways to control uncollectible accounts expense are a sound credit policy and a system of authorizing sales only to creditworthy customers.

Account for estimated uncollectible accounts, uncollectible accounts expense, and subsequent write-offs of uncollectible accounts according to the allowance method. A business should recognize uncollectible accounts expense in the same period it records the related credit sales. However, the business does not always know the exact credit sales that will not be collected in the same period as the sales were made. Therefore, as it recognizes uncollectible accounts expense (debited), it increases the contra-receivables account Allowance for Uncollectible Accounts, (credited). When individual accounts are deemed uncollectible, the business writes off accounts in both Accounts Receivable (credit) and Allowance for Uncollectible Accounts (debit). The business may accrue uncollectible accounts expense according to the income statement (percent of credit sales) method or the balance sheet (percent of receivables) method.

Account for third-party credit card sales and explain how they can reduce problems of collecting on credit sales. Third-party credit cards have the advantage of providing credit to customers and immediate cash to merchants. However, credit card companies charge a discount on credit card sales—that is, the cash received is less than the amount of the sale. Merchants may willingly sacrifice the discount to have cash immediately and to avoid uncollectible accounts.

Describe a promissory note receivable and distinguish between negotiable and nonnegotiable notes.   A note receivable is an explicit, written promise by the maker to pay a specific sum on a specific date (or on demand) at a specific location. A negotiable note is one that meets certain criteria so that a holder in due course to whom the payee has sold the note may collect it, regardless of any dispute the maker may have with the original payee. The advantage of a negotiable note is that it can be sold readily. All other notes are nonnegotiable and cannot be sold as readily as negotiable notes.

Calculate explicit and implicit interest on notes receivable.   Whether stated explicitly or not, most notes receivable pay interest to the payee or holder. The following formula is used to calculate interest on short-term notes carrying explicit interest:

$$\text{Interest} = \text{Principal x Rate x Time}$$

Principal is the face amount of the note; rate, the stated annual interest rate; and *time, the fraction of a year* for which interest is being calculated.

   If a short-term note carries no explicit interest rate, interest revenue for a period is calculated according to this formula:

$$\text{Interest} = \text{Total Interest} \times \frac{\text{Days}}{\text{Term}}$$

Total interest is the difference between the note's face value and the value exchanged for it; days, the number of days for which you wish to calculate interest; and term, the full term of the note in days.

Account for receipt of notes receivable, accrual of interest on notes receivable, and receipt of payment on notes receivable.   When a note is issued—usually in exchange for cash or merchandise—we record the note at the value given in exchange for it. Interest revenue on notes receivable is recorded in each accounting period in proportion to the amount of the term of the note that has expired. When payment is received, any remaining interest is recognized as the difference between the carrying value of the note (original value plus accrued interest) and the cash received.

Account for the discounting of notes receivable.   When a payee sells the note to a holder, we say it is discounted. The holder pays less (by the amount of a discount) than maturity value to the original payee or other seller of the note. The seller then recognizes the difference between the discounted maturity value and the seller's carrying value of the note as interest expense.

Calculate the number of days-sales-in-receivables and uncollectible-accounts-expense-as-a-percent-of-credit sales and use these tools to diagnose problems.   Days-sales-in-receivables is calculated according to the following formula:

$$\text{Days-Sales-in-Receivables} = \frac{\text{Receivables Balance}}{\text{Credit Sales}} \times \text{Days in Period}$$

The receivables balance is the amount of gross receivables as of any balance sheet date (or the average for a period); credit sales, the sales for the period ended on the balance sheet date (a month, a quarter, or a year); and days in the period, the number of days in the period used to measure credit sales.

Uncollectible-accounts-expense-as-a-percent-of-credit sales is calculated as follows:

$$\text{Percent} = 100 \times \frac{\text{Uncollectible Accounts Expense}}{\text{Credit Sales}}$$

Managers can use these two ratios to diagnose problems with credit granting, sales authorization, collection efforts, and profitability of credit sales.

REVIEW PROBLEM 1: ACCOUNTS RECEIVABLE

The Smith Corporation uses the allowance method of accounting for uncollectible accounts receivable. Accounts receivable information for Smith Corporation for the year ended 19X1 is presented below:

Cash sales	$ 23,600
Credit sales	170,000
Accounts to be written off, 12-31-X1	2,700
Allowance for uncollectible accounts, 1-1-X1	3,100
Accounts receivable, 12-31-X1, before write-offs	48,720

Smith Corporation
Aged Schedule of Accounts Receivable
December 31, 19X1

CUSTOMER NUMBER	AMOUNT WITHIN DISCOUNT	AMOUNT WITHIN 30 DAYS	AMOUNT 1–30 DAYS PAST DUE	AMOUNT 31–60 DAYS PAST DUE	AMOUNT 61–90 DAYS PAST DUE	AMOUNT 91–120 DAYS PAST DUE	AMOUNT 120 DAYS PAST DUE	CUSTOMER TOTAL
101	3,720		2,190					5,910
102	3,360							3,360
103		4,890	4,810		860	1,020		11,580
104				2,540	920			3,460
105				1,760				1,760
106	2,220							2,220
107					2,220	3,120		5,340
108							960	960
109				1,310				1,310
110		8,930		1,190				10,120
Total	9,300	13,820	7,000	6,800	4,000	4,140	960	46,020
Allowance %	1.5%	3.0%	4.0%	5.0%	7.0%	12.0%	18.0%	
Allowance								

REQUIRED:

a. Prepare all necessary journal entries, assuming that 2.0% of all credit sales will be uncollectible (income statement method).

b. Prepare the balance sheet (direct disclosure method) and income statement (contra-revenue) presentation of accounts receivable, assuming that 2.0% of all credit sales will be uncollectible.

c. Complete the aged schedule of accounts receivable.

d. Calculate uncollectible accounts expense for 19X1 from the information determined in c above (balance sheet method).

SOLUTION:

Planning and Organizing Your Work

1. Calculate uncollectible accounts expense by multiplying the estimated uncollectible percentage times credit sales.
2. Record the uncollectible accounts expense calculated in Step 1.
3. Record the write-off of uncollectible accounts.
4. Determine the balances in Accounts Receivable and Allowance for Uncollectible Accounts.
5. Prepare the income statement and balance sheet presentations.
6. Complete the aged schedule of accounts receivable by multiplying the total in each category times the allowance percentage.
7. Determine the ending balance in the Allowance for Uncollectible Accounts by summing the amounts calculated in Step 6.
8. Determine the uncollectible accounts expense for 19X1 by calculating the amount of increase necessary to bring the Allowance for Uncollectible Accounts to the correct balance calculated in Step 7. (Note: Ignore any previous accrual of uncollectible accounts expense under the income statement method.)

(a) *Prepare all journal entries.*

Dec. 31	Allowance for Uncollectible Accounts	2,700	
	Accounts Receivable		2,700
	To write off uncollectible accounts.		
31	Uncollectible Accounts Expense	3,400	
	Allowance for Uncollectible Accounts		3,400
	To accrue estimated uncollectible accounts expense for the year ended December 31. ($170,000 x 2%)		

(b) *Prepare the balance sheet and income statement presentation.*

The T-accounts for Accounts Receivable and Allowance for Uncollectible Accounts are presented below:

Accounts Receivable			Allowance for Uncollectible Accounts		
End. Bal. 48,720				Beg. Bal. 3,100	
	Write-offs 2,700		Write-offs 2,700		
				Accrual 3,400	
Adj. Bal. 46,020				End. Bal. 3,800	

Therefore, the partial balance sheet would appear as follows:

Smith Corporation
Balance Sheet (Partial)
December 31, 19X1

Current assets:		
Accounts receivable	$46,020	
Less: Allowance for uncollectible accounts	3,800	$42,220

Smith Corporation
Income Statement (Partial)
For the Year Ended December 31, 19X1

Revenue from sales	$193,600
Less: Uncollectible accounts expense	3,400

(c) *Complete the Aged Schedule of Accounts Receivable.*

Smith Corporation
Aged Schedule of Accounts Receivable
December 31, 19X1

CUSTOMER NUMBER	AMOUNT WITHIN DISCOUNT	AMOUNT WITHIN 30 DAYS	AMOUNT 1–30 DAYS PAST DUE	AMOUNT 31–60 DAYS PAST DUE	AMOUNT 61–90 DAYS PAST DUE	AMOUNT 91–120 DAYS PAST DUE	OVER 120 DAYS PAST DUE	CUSTOMER TOTAL
101	3,720		2,190					5,910
102	3,360							3,360
103		4,890	4,810		860	1,020		11,580
104				2,540	920			3,460
105				1,760				1,760
106	2,220							2,220
107					2,220	3,120		5,340
108							960	960
109				1,310				1,310
110		8,930		1,190				10,120
Total	9,300	13,820	7,000	6,800	4,000	4,140	960	46,020
Allowance %	1.5%	3.0%	4.0%	5.0%	7.0%	12.0%	18.0%	
Allowance	140	415	280	340	280	497	173	2,125

(d) *Calculate uncollectible accounts expense for 19X1.*
The calculation of uncollectible accounts expense is shown below:

Estimated allowance for uncollectible accounts, December 31, 19X1 $2,125
Less: Balance in Allowance for Uncollectible Accounts after
       write-offs on December 31, 19X1 ($3,100 - $2,700)   400
Estimated uncollectible accounts expense for 19X1 $1,725

REVIEW PROBLEM 2: NOTES RECEIVABLE

Olympic Corporation received a $15,000, 90-day, 10% note from Mountain, Inc. on December 31, 19X1, in exchange for services performed.

REQUIRED:

a. Prepare the journal entry for Olympic Corp. to record the issuance of the note.
b. Prepare the journal entry for Olympic Corp. to record the recognition of interest and collection of the note.
c. Calculate the proceeds for Olympic if it discounted the note with First National Bank at 12%, 60 days after the note was received.
d. Prepare the journal entries for Olympic if it discounted the note at 12%, 60 days after the note was received.
e. Prepare the journal entry assuming Mountain does not honor the discounted note. Assume a protest fee of $150.

SOLUTION:

Planning and Organizing Your Work

1. Analyze the transaction in which the note is received and record the journal entry.
2. Calculate interest for 90 days on the note. Prepare a journal entry to accrue interest revenue for 90 days and the collection of cash.
3. Calculate the interest First National Bank must receive at maturity of the note (the discount).

4. Deduct the discount from the maturity value of the note—face value plus interest for 90 days—to determine the discounted value (proceeds of discounting).
5. Calculate the carrying value of the note after 60 days—face value plus accrued interest.
6. Compare the discounted value (proceeds) to carrying value to determine the interest expense associated with the discounting.
7. Write the journal entry to accrue interest on the note for 60 days.
8. Write a journal entry to record discounting the note. Debit (credit) Interest Expense with the difference between carrying value and the proceeds of discounting.
9. Prepare a journal entry for the cash payment to First National Bank for the dishonored note at maturity value plus the $150 protest fee.

(a) *Record the issuance of the note.*

19X1			
Dec. 31	Notes Receivable—Mountain, Inc.	15,000.00	
	Revenue		15,000.00
	To record the receipt of the note in exchange for services performed.		

(b) *Record the recognition of interest and collection of the note.*

19X2			
Mar. 31	Cash	15,369.86	
	Notes Receivable—Mountain, Inc.		15,000.00
	Interest Revenue		369.86
	To recognize collection of the note plus interest. ($15,000 x 10% x 90/365 = $369.86)		

(c) *Calculate the proceeds if the note is discounted.*

1. Calculate maturity value: ($15,000 x 10% x 90/365) + $15,000 = $15,369.86
2. Calculate discount: ($15,369.86 x 12% x 30/365)   =   151.59
3. Calculate proceeds: $15,369.86 - $151.59   = $15,218.27

(d) *Record the discounting of the note.*

19X2			
Mar. 1	Interest Receivable—Note	246.58	
	Interest Revenue		246.58
	To accrue interest of $246.58 on note receivable from Mountain. ($15,000 x 10% x 60/365 before discounting).		
1	Cash	15,218.27	
	Interest Expense	28.31	
	Notes Receivable—Mountain, Inc.		15,000.00
	Interest Receivable—Note		246.58
	To record discounting of note receivable from Mountain.		

The cash received is calculated above. The carrying value of the note receivable equals the original amount ($15,000) plus the interest that would have been recognized after 60 days. The interest expense is the difference between the carrying value and the cash received [($15,000 + $246.58) − $15,218.27 = $28.31].

(e) *Prepare the journal entry assuming Mountain does not honor the note.*

19X2			
Mar. 31	Accounts Receivable—Mountain, Inc.	15,519.86	
	Cash		15,519.86
	To record payment of discounted note dishonored by Mountain. ($15,369.86 + $150 protest fee)		

KEY TERMS

allowance for uncollectible
  accounts, *263*
allowance method, *261*
balance sheet approach, *266*
bank card, *269*
contingent liability, *278*
days-sales-in-receivables, *280*
demand notes, *273*
direct write-off method, *268*
discount, *277*
discounting a note, *277*
face amount, *271*

holder in due course, *272*
income statement approach,
  262
indirect (net) method, *263*
interest, *273*
interest-bearing, *273*
interest rate, *271*
maker, *271*
materiality, *269*
maturity value, *274*
negotiable promissory note,
  272

noninterest-bearing, *273*
non-negotiable promissory
  note, *272*
payee, *271*
period (term, duration), *271*
promissory note, *271*
uncollectible accounts expense,
  258
uncollectible-accounts-
  expense-as-a-percent-of-
  credit sales, *280*

SELF-QUIZ

LO 1 1. How do you calculate the additional profits
      from granting credit?
      a. Additional Cost of Goods Sold - Additional
         Sales Revenues
      b. Additional Sales Revenue - Additional Cost
         of Goods Sold
      c. Additional Sales Revenue - Additional Cost
         of Goods Sold - Additional Expenses,
         including Uncollectible Accounts Expense
      d. Additional Sales Revenue - Additional
         Uncollectible Accounts Expense

LO 1 2. True or False? Sales personnel on commission
      should conduct credit screenings since they
      know the most about customers.

LO 1 3. According to the _____ principle, a business
      should recognize the estimated amount of
      uncollectible accounts from a period's sales
      revenues as an expense in the same period it
      recognizes the revenues.

LO 2 4. Which of the following is *not* true about the
      allowance method?
      a. The accrual of uncollectible accounts expense
         is independent of any actual write-offs.
      b. This method uses a contra-asset account
         called Allowance for Uncollectible
         Accounts.
      c. It is consistent with the matching concept.
      d. Uncollectible Accounts Expense is debited
         when amounts owed are deemed uncol-
         lectible.

LO 2 5. True or False? Under the income statement
      approach, businesses accrue estimated uncol-
      lectible accounts expense based on the aver-
      age collections per dollar of credit sales.

LO 2 6. Which of the following statements is *not* true
      under the allowance method?
      a. Recognition of uncollectible accounts
         expense reduces Accounts Receivable.

      b. The write-off of a customer's account
         receivable does not affect Uncollectible
         Accounts Expense.
      c. Uncollectible accounts expense can be pre-
         sented in the income statement as a reduc-
         tion of revenue.
      d. Uncollectible accounts expense can be pre-
         sented in the income statement in the cate-
         gory "Other income and expense."

LO 2 7. To apply the _____ _____ approach, an
      aged trial balance is used to evaluate the
      makeup of the Accounts Receivable balance
      at the end of a period.

LO 2 8. Which of the following is *not* true about the
      direct write-off method?
      a. It is the simplest method of handling uncol-
         lectible accounts.
      b. Uncollectible Accounts Expense is debited
         when amounts owed are deemed uncollectible.
      c. It is consistent with the matching concept.
      d. Subsequent collections of written-off
         accounts are accounted for by a credit to
         Uncollectible Accounts Expense.

LO 3 9. With respect to bank cards, the customer
      deals with an _____ bank and the merchant
      deals with a _____ bank.

LO 4 10. A promissory note is a written promise by the
      _____ of the note to pay a specified amount
      of money to the _____ on a specified date at
      a specified place.

LO 4 11. Which of the following is *not* a component of
      a promissory note?
      a. The signature of the payee
      b. The interest rate
      c. The period, term, or duration
      d. The name of the maker

LO 4 12. True or False? Demand notes are promissory
      notes that are due on a specified date.

LO 5 13. What is the formula for calculating explicit interest?

LO 6 14. It is necessary to accrue _____ _____ on a note receivable if the payee ends an accounting period during the term of the note.

LO 6 15. True or False? When the payee of a note declines to pay on the date it is due, the payee is said to have dishonored the note.

LO 7 16. The process of selling a negotiable note receivable to a third party is called _____ a note.

LO 7 17. Which of the following is *not* true about discounting a note receivable?
   a. The original payee will receive cash before the note is due.
   b. The selling price of the note is usually equal to its maturity value.

   c. The original payee has a contingent liability for the note's maturity value if it is endorsed without qualification.
   d. When a note is dishonored, the holder of the note may collect a protest fee.

LO 8 18. How much is Trevino Corporation's days-sales-in-receivables if Trevino's ending receivable balance and credit sales for the year are $40,000 and $240,000, respectively?

LO 8 19. True or False? The lower the days-sales-in-receivables, the higher the risk that credit customers will not pay.

LO 8 20. True or False? To be useful in analyzing a company's credit policy, a reasonably accurate estimate of uncollectible accounts expense for uncollectible-accounts-expense-as-a-percent-of-credit sales is necessary.

SOLUTIONS TO SELF-QUIZ
1. c   2. False   3. Matching   4. d   5. True   6. a   7. Balance sheet   8. c   9. issuing, service
10. maker, payee   11. a   12. False   13. Interest = Principal x Rate x Time   14. interest revenue   15. False
16. discounting   17. b   18. ($40,000/$240,000) x 365 = 61days   19. False   20. True

QUESTIONS

Q6-1   Why do businesses grant credit to their customers even though they sometimes cannot collect all of the amounts due?

Q6-2   How can uncollectible accounts expense be controlled?

Q6-3   What are the differences between the income statement approach and the balance sheet approach to estimating uncollectible accounts expense?

Q6-4   What are the advantages and disadvantages of using an aged schedule of accounts receivable?

Q6-5   What are the two different formats for disclosing the allowance for uncollectible accounts on the balance sheet?

Q6-6   What are the differences between the direct write-off method and the allowance method of accounting for receivables?

Q6-7   Why do businesses accept third-party credit cards?

Q6-8   What are the differences between bank cards and other third-party credit cards?

Q6-9   What are the two types of promissory notes and how do they differ?

Q6-10   What is a holder in due course?

Q6-11   What is the difference between explicit interest and implicit interest?

Q6-12   Under what circumstances should the allowance method be applied to notes receivable?

Q6-13   What is the difference between a discount on a note and discounting a note?

Q6-14   What are the advantages and disadvantages of a very low number of days-sales-in-receivables?

EXERCISES

LO 2

E6-1   Allowance Method for Uncollectible Accounts   Using the allowance method, record journal entries for the Caster Corporation for the following transactions:

19X0

Mar. 31 Caster estimated that $7,300 of March credit sales will be uncollectible.

Apr. 3 Sold $2,900 of goods on credit to R. Ricketts.

Nov. 28 R. Ricketts' account was deemed to be uncollectible.

19X1

Feb. 3 R. Ricketts paid the $2,900 owed to Caster.

LO 2

E6-2 Income Statement Method Gadgets Unlimited, Inc. decided to grant credit 4 years ago, and it uses the percentage of sales method. Since it has a relatively stable credit experience, Gadgets bases the calculation of uncollectible accounts expense on the average uncollectible percentage over the past 4 years. During 19X1, the company had $420,000 of credit sales.

Years Past	Credit Sales	Uncollectible Accounts
4 years	$325,000	$ 7,800
3 years	380,000	8,360
2 years	360,000	8,280
1 year	435,000	10,614

REQUIRED:

Calculate the 19X1 uncollectible accounts expense given the above information.

LO 2

E6-3 Financial Statement Presentation Using the Allowance Method Given the following information, show the income statement (contra-revenue) and balance sheet (direct disclosure) presentation for the Krish Corporation:

Item	Amount
Allowance for uncollectible accounts (1/1/X2)	$ 5,100
Write-offs for 19X2	23,500
Estimated uncollectible accounts expense for 19X2	29,200
Accounts receivable (12/31/X2)	188,300
Sales revenue	356,000
Sales returns and allowances	21,600

LO 2

E6-4 Balance Sheet Method Bright Lights, Inc. uses an aged schedule of accounts receivable to estimate uncollectible accounts expense. The balance of Allowance for Uncollectible Accounts is $2,900 (credit) after write-offs have been recorded but before uncollectible accounts expense has been estimated. The following summary information is from an aged schedule of accounts receivable:

Age	Accounts Receivable Balance	Percent Uncollectible
Current	$138,000	2%
31–60 days	152,000	4
61–90 days	110,000	6
Over 90 days	85,000	10

REQUIRED:

Write the necessary journal entry to record Uncollectible Accounts Expense for Bright Lights, Inc.

LO 3

E6-5 Accepting Bank Cards To have the benefit of accepting credit sales without having to initiate its own credit system, Premier Jewelry, Inc., accepts only bank cards and cash. The service bank charges a discount rate of 4% on all bank card sales. During January, Premier Jewelry, Inc.'s customers bought $47,600 of jewelry, of which $13,600 was for cash and the remainder was charged to bank cards.

REQUIRED:

Record the necessary journal entries for January sales.

LO 5   **E6-6   Calculating Explicit Interest**   Boone Corporation received a $1,000, 120-day, 13%
            note from J. Lewis.

            REQUIRED:

            Determine the explicit interest and the maturity value of the note.

LO 5   **E6-7   Calculating Implicit Interest**   New Ohio Corporation received an $8,000, noninterest-
            bearing, 90-day note in exchange for goods worth $7,783.

            REQUIRED:

            Calculate the amount of interest that New Ohio Corporation would accrue at the end of
            the fiscal year, 60 days after the note is dated.

LO 6   **E6-8   Accounting for Notes Receivable**   Plaza Laundry, Inc. purchased $5,000 of cleaning
            chemicals on credit from Rodger's Chemical Supply Corporation on August 12, 19X3. On
            December 1, Rodger's Chemical Supply agreed to accept a 90-day, 10% note receivable
            from Plaza Laundry to pay for the account receivable from the purchase on August 12.

            REQUIRED:

            Record the necessary journal entries for the receipt of the note, the accrual of interest on
            December 31, and the collection of the note for Rodger's Chemical Supply Corporation.

LO 6   **E6-9   Recording Dishonored Notes Receivable**   Assuming Plaza Laundry, Inc. dishonors
            the note on the due date, record the journal entry for the note receivable for Rodger's
            Chemical Supply Corporation described in E6-8 above.

LO 7   **E6-10   Calculating the Proceeds for a Discounted Note Receivable**   The Sun Corporation
            discounted at a rate of 15%, a $10,000 face value, 90-day, 12% note receivable 60 days
            after the note was issued.

            REQUIRED:

            Calculate the proceeds to Sun Corporation.

LO 7   **E6-11   Discounting of Notes Receivable**   Record journal entries for the Pei Corporation for
            the following transactions:

            Apr.   1   Sold $8,000 of merchandise to Discount Stores in exchange for a 60-day, 10%
                         note receivable.
                   16   Discounted the note receivable at Last National Bank at 14%.
            May   31   Discount Stores paid the amount due to Last National Bank.

LO 7   **E6-12   Discounted Notes Receivable Dishonored**   Junipers, Inc. discounted a $5,000 note
            from Trillo Corporation to the Second National Bank. The note has a maturity value of
            $5,460. Second National Bank charges a protest fee of 2% of the maturity value for all
            dishonored notes.

            REQUIRED:

            Assuming Trillo dishonors the note, record the journal entry for Junipers.

LO 8 | **E6-13** | **Calculating Days-Sales-in-Receivables and Uncollectible-Accounts-Expense-as-a-Percent-of-Credit Sales** Calculate the days-sales-in-receivables and the uncollectible-accounts-expense-as-a-percent-of-credit sales for Wetscapes, Inc. given the following information for the year 19X1:

Credit sales	$271,890
Accounts receivable	61,289
Uncollectible accounts expense	3,245

PROBLEM SET A

LO 2 | **P6-1A** | **Income Statement Method** The Kumar Corporation uses the allowance method of accounting for accounts receivable. Kumar estimates uncollectible accounts expense to be 3.5% of net credit sales. During 19X5, Kumar had sales on account of $846,300. Sales returns and allowances on credit sales were $11,200, and sales discounts amounted to $4,800. In addition, Kumar deemed $24,200 of accounts receivable to be uncollectible during the year, and it collected $1,300 of accounts receivable written off in prior years. The balance in Allowance for Uncollectible Accounts as of January 1, 19X5, was $21,600. The December 31, 19X5, balance in Accounts Receivable was $207,200.

REQUIRED:

a. Calculate the estimated uncollectible accounts expense for 19X5.
b. Record the journal entries for the 19X5 events given above.
c. Show how Kumar would disclose the estimated uncollectible accounts expense on the 19X5 income statement (contra-revenue method).
d. Show how Kumar would disclose the allowance for uncollectible accounts on the December 31, 19X5, balance sheet using both disclosure formats.

LO 2 | **P6-2A** | **Using an Aged Schedule of Accounts Receivable** Jones Corporation uses the allowance method of accounting for uncollectible accounts receivable. Accounts receivable information for Jones Corporation for the year ended 19X7 is presented below:

Cash sales	$ 354,000
Credit sales	1,275,000
Accounts written off	40,500
Allowance for uncollectible accounts, 1-1-X7	46,500
Accounts receivable, 1-1-X7	453,000

Estimated percent uncollectible:

Age of Receivable	Percent Uncollectible
0 – 30 Days	1.5%
31 – 60 Days	3.0
61 – 90 Days	5.0
91 – 120 Days	6.0
Over 120 Days	10.0

Accounts receivable for Jones Corporation by customer (after write-offs) as of December 31, 19X7 is presented below:

Customer Number	Amount	Time Outstanding
101	$ 37,500	20 days
101	19,100	47 days
213	38,000	130 days
284	13,300	15 days
312	27,000	112 days
330	18,600	40 days
401	46,900	32 days
402	11,100	5 days

Customer Number	Amount	Time Outstanding
569	102,200	12 days
612	24,000	88 days
671	72,300	53 days
691	69,900	27 days

REQUIRED:

a. Prepare an aged schedule of accounts receivable similar to the one in Illustration 6-7. Jones Corporation does not offer sales discounts, but sells on terms of net 30 days.
b. Prepare the journal entry for the accounts written off.
c. Determine uncollectible accounts expense and prepare the journal entry to record it.
d. Show how The Jones Corporation would disclose the estimated uncollectible accounts expense (contra-revenue) and the allowance for uncollectible accounts on the 19X7 financial statements. Use the direct disclosure method for the balance sheet.

LO 2

P6-3A **Determining Missing Information for Accounts Receivable** Tom's Electronics Distributors, Inc. estimates that 2% of all credit sales are uncollectible. Selected information for Tom's Electronics Distributors, Inc. for the years ended 19X8 and 19X9 is presented below:

	19X8	19X9
Accounts receivable, 1/1	$130,000	$140,000
Accounts receivable, 12/31	?	?
Allowance for uncollectible accounts, 1/1	8,400	?
Allowance for uncollectible accounts, 12/31	?	13,600
Credit sales	540,000	?
Collections	?	620,000
Write-offs	6,200	?
Uncollectible accounts expense	?	14,100

REQUIRED:

a. Fill in the missing information for 19X8 and 19X9.
b. Using the direct disclosure method, show how Tom's will disclose accounts receivable and allowance for uncollectible accounts on the 19X8 and 19X9 balance sheet.

LO 6

P6-4A **Accounting for Notes Receivable** The Rojo Corporation had the following transactions during 19X3:

Apr. 1 The Grunstadt Corporation purchased goods at a price of $20,000 from Rojo. Because Grunstadt is a marginal credit risk, Rojo insisted that Grunstadt pay by issuing a 14%, $20,000, 120-day note in exchange for the goods purchased.
July 1 Rojo Corporation loaned $25,000 to one of its best customers, Bill Schwartz, in exchange for a note. The note is due in 1 year and has an interest rate of 12%.
30 Grunstadt Corporation dishonored the note issued on April 1.
Sept. 1 Blanco Corporation, which purchased goods for $10,000 on credit, was unable to pay the amount owed. Rojo accepted a 15%, $10,000, 90-day note in exchange.
Nov. 1 Rojo Corporation loaned $5,000 to a trusted employee in exchange for a note. The note is due in 120 days and has an interest rate of 10%.
30 Blanco paid Rojo Corporation in full.

REQUIRED:

a. Prepare journal entries for the above transactions.
b. Prepare appropriate adjusting entries at December 31, 19X3.

LO 7

P6-5A **Notes Receivable Discounted** The Travis Corp. had the following transactions during 19X6:

Mar. 31 The McGee Corp. purchased goods for $20,000 from Travis. Because the purchase was large and would take several months for McGee to sell, Travis allowed McGee to pay by issuing a 14%, $20,000, 120-day note in exchange for the goods purchased.

Apr. 30 Travis Corp. discounted the note from McGee to the Everglades National Bank at a discount rate of 16%. Travis endorsed the note with no qualifications.

July 29 McGee dishonored the note. Travis made the necessary payment to Everglades National Bank, including a protest fee of $40.

Oct. 1 Abernathy Company, which previously purchased goods for $10,000 on credit, was unable to pay the amount owed. Travis accepted a 15%, $10,000, 90-day note in exchange.

Nov. 30 Travis Corp. discounted the note from Abernathy to the Gator National Bank at a discount rate of 17%. Travis endorsed the note with no qualifications.

Dec. 30 Abernathy paid the Gator National Bank in full.

REQUIRED:

Prepare journal entries for the above transactions.

LO 8

P6-6A **Calculate the Number-of-Days-Sales-in-Receivables and Uncollectible-Accounts-Expense-as-a-Percent-of-Credit Sales and Use these Tools to Diagnose Problems**
The Truly Good Shoe Barn, Inc. has experienced a 40% increase in gross sales in 19X1 compared to 19X0—mostly due to increased credit sales. However, net income increased by only 25%. The president is worried that credit sales may be reducing the company's profitability. The president asks the chief accountant to prepare a schedule of the relevant financial data.

		The Truly Good Shoe Barn, Inc. **Comparative Financial Data** **For the Years Ended December 31, 19X0 and 19X1**	
		19X0	*19X1*
Income statement data:			
Cash sales		$ 90,000	$100,000
Credit sales		160,000	250,000
Gross sales		$250,000	$350,000
Less: Sales returns and allowances		(5,000)	(7,000)
Uncollectible accounts expense		(5,000)	(17,500)
Net sales		$240,000	$325,500
Less: Cost of goods sold		155,000	217,000
Gross profit		$ 85,000	$108,500
Less: Operating expenses		65,000	83,500
Net income		$ 20,000	$ 25,000
Selected balance sheet data:			
Gross accounts receivable (December 31)		$ 32,000	$ 60,000
Less: Allowance for uncollectible accounts		3,200	10,000
Net receivables		$ 28,800	$ 50,000

REQUIRED:

Analyze the data using the number-of-days-sales-in-receivables and uncollectible-accounts-expense-as-a-percent-of-credit sales. Comment on whether the president's concerns about credit sales are well founded.

PROBLEM SET B

P6-1B **Income Statement Method** The Reinbold Corporation uses the allowance method of accounting for accounts receivable. Reinbold estimates uncollectible accounts expense to be 4% of net credit sales. Reinbold deemed $35,100 of accounts receivable to be uncollectible during the year, and it collected $3,200 of accounts receivable written off in prior years. The Allowance for Uncollectible Accounts had a January 1, 19X9, balance of $33,100. The December 31, 19X9, balance in Accounts Receivable was $231,800. Sales information for Reinbold during 19X9 is presented below:

Sales on account	$958,200
Sales returns and allowances on credit sales	16,200
Sales discounts	5,500

REQUIRED:

a. Calculate the estimated uncollectible accounts expense for 19X9.
b. Record the journal entries for the 19X9 events given above.
c. Show how Reinbold would list the estimated uncollectible accounts expense (contra-revenue) on the 19X9 income statement.
d. Show how Reinbold would disclose the allowance for uncollectible accounts on the December 31, 19X9, balance sheet using both disclosure formats.

P6-2B **Using an Aged Schedule of Accounts Receivable** The Schwartz Corp. uses the allowance method of accounting for uncollectible accounts receivable. Accounts receivable information for Schwartz Corp. for the year ended 19X2 is presented below:

Cash sales	$ 427,000
Credit sales	1,476,000
Accounts written off	52,300
Allowance for uncollectible accounts, 1-1-X2	49,100
Accounts receivable, 1-1-X2	432,600
Estimated percent uncollectible:	

Age of Receivable	Percent Uncollectible
0 – 30 Days	2.0%
31 – 60 Days	3.5
61 – 90 Days	4.5
91 – 120 Days	7.0
Over 120 Days	9.0

Accounts receivable information for Schwartz by customer (after write-offs) as of December 31, 19X2 is presented below:

Customer Number	Amount	Time Outstanding
1010	$ 87,500	23 days
1017	27,900	47 days
1213	41,100	130 days
1284	23,300	5 days
3112	42,200	102 days
3430	14,700	33 days
4501	46,200	42 days
4829	60,300	72 days
4902	111,100	19 days
5669	49,400	8 days
6120	6,300	113 days
6671	15,200	58 days
6991	69,900	27 days
7824	33,300	88 days

REQUIRED:

a. Prepare an aged schedule of accounts receivable similar to the one in Illustration 6-7. Schwartz does not offer sales discounts, and sells only on terms of net 30 days.
b. Prepare the journal entry for the accounts written off.
c. Determine uncollectible accounts expense and prepare the journal entry to record it.
d. Show how Schwartz would disclose the estimated uncollectible accounts expense (contra-revenue) and the allowance for uncollectible accounts on the 19X2 financial statements. Use the direct disclosure method for the balance sheet.

LO 2

P6-3B Determining Missing Information for Accounts Receivable Semiconductors Unlimited, Inc. estimates that 3% of all credit sales are uncollectible. Selected information for Semiconductors Unlimited for the years ended 19X6 and 19X7 is presented below:

	19X6	*19X7*
Accounts receivable, 1/1	$210,000	?
Accounts receivable, 12/31	195,000	?
Allowance for uncollectible accounts, 1/1	10,300	?
Allowance for uncollectible accounts, 12/31	?	$ 25,450
Credit sales	?	?
Collections	817,200	890,900
Write-offs	?	19,100
Uncollectible accounts expense	24,600	?

REQUIRED:

a. Fill in the missing information for 19X6 and 19X7.
b. Using the direct disclosure method, show how Semiconductors will disclose accounts receivable and allowance for uncollectible accounts on the 19X6 and 19X7 balance sheets.

LO 6

P6-4B Accounting for Notes Receivable The Trail Corporation had the following transactions during 19X8:

Apr. 1 The Vert Corp. purchased goods at a price of $30,000 from Trail. Because Vert is a marginal credit risk, Trail insisted that Vert pay by issuing a 13%, $30,000, 120-day note in exchange for the goods purchased.

July 1 Trail Corporation loaned $20,000 to one of its best customers, Bill Black, in exchange for a note. The note is due in 1 year and has an interest rate of 14%.

30 Vert Corp. dishonored the note issued on April 1.

Sept. 1 Blanche Company, which purchased goods for $15,000 on credit, was unable to pay the amount owed. Trail accepted a 16%, $15,000, 90-day note in exchange.

Nov. 1 Trail Corporation loaned $10,000 to a trusted employee in exchange for a note. The note is due in 120 days and has an interest rate of 12%.

30 Blanche paid Trail Corporation in full.

REQUIRED:

a. Prepare journal entries for the above transactions.
b. Prepare appropriate adjusting entries at December 31, 19X8.

LO 7

P6-5B Notes Receivable Discounted The Bond Corporation had the following transactions during 19X4:

Mar. 31 The Lane Company purchased goods for $15,000 from Bond. Because this is a large purchase for Lane and it will take Lane several months to sell the goods, Bond allowed Lane to pay by issuing a 13%, $15,000, 120-day note in exchange for the goods purchased.

Apr. 30 Bond Corporation discounted the note from Lane to the Washington National Bank at a discount rate of 15%. Bond endorsed the note with no qualifications.

July 29 Lane dishonored the note. Bond made the necessary payment to Washington National Bank, including a protest fee of $25.

Oct. 1 Cain Company, which previously purchased goods for $25,000 on credit, was unable to pay the amount owed. Bond accepted a 15%, $25,000, 90-day note in exchange.

Nov. 30 Bond Corporation discounted the note from Cain to the Second National Bank at a discount rate of 16%. Bond endorsed the note with no qualifications.

Dec. 30 Cain paid the Second National Bank in full.

REQUIRED:

Prepare journal entries for the above transactions.

LO 8   **P6-6B**   **Calculate the Number-of-Days-Sales-in-Receivables and Uncollectible-accounts-Expense-as-a-Percent-of-Credit Sales and Use these Tools to Diagnose Problems**
The Good Ole Boot Warehouse, Inc. has experienced stagnant gross sales (no growth) for several years. The president believes he can increase credit sales by as much as 50% and total sales by at least 35% by relaxing his credit policy. He asks the controller to prepare a schedule of the relevant financial data for 19X0 (the year just ended) and projections for 19X1.

The Good Ole Boot Warehouse, Inc. Comparative Financial Data For the Years Ended December 31, 19X0 and 19X1		
	Actual 19X0	Projected 19X1
Income statement data:		
Cash sales	$ 80,000	$ 90,000
Credit sales	140,000	210,000
Gross sales	$220,000	$300,000
Less: Sales returns and allowances	(7,000)	(10,000)
Uncollectible accounts expense	(3,000)	(15,000)
Net sales	$210,000	$275,000
Less: Cost of goods sold	130,000	175,000
Gross profit	$ 80,000	$100,000
Less: Operating expenses	45,000	60,000
Net income	$ 35,000	$ 40,000
Selected balance sheet data:		
Gross accounts receivable (December 31)	$ 28,000	$ 60,000
Less: Allowance for uncollectible accounts	2,800	10,000
Net receivables	$ 25,200	$ 50,000

REQUIRED:

Analyze the data using the number-of-days-sales-in-receivables and uncollectible-accounts-expense-as-a-percent-of-credit sales. Comment on whether the company should pursue its plans to relax the credit policy, assuming the controller's projections are accurate.

CRITICAL THINKING AND COMMUNICATING

 C6-1 Odd Job Trading Corporation purchases excess inventory from manufacturers at reduced rates and sells them for highly discounted prices in stores throughout the greater Dallas-Ft. Worth metropolitan area. Because of its low prices, Odd Job Trading Corporation has always operated on a cash only basis. Mr. Dawson, the president of the company, recently attended a meeting of retailers where the speaker discussed the advantages of granting credit. Mr. Dawson always avoided granting credit because he knew that some of his customers would not pay their bills. However, until the meeting, Mr. Dawson did not realize the impact that granting credit would have on his business.

To determine whether or not to grant credit, Mr. Dawson hired Ms. Bosh, a credit consultant. Mr. Dawson asked Ms. Bosh for her recommendations. Mr. Dawson was particularly interested in two issues. First, should he have his own credit operation, accept bank cards, or both? Second, if he initiates his own credit operation, how should he implement it?

REQUIRED:

Summarize the information Ms. Bosh would need to collect to answer Mr. Dawson's questions and how she should analyze the information.

 C6-2 Guillermo Lopez works in the accounts receivable department for Bicycles Unlimited, Inc., a large chain of retailers in the Los Angeles area. One of Guillermo's duties is reviewing credit applications. While reviewing these applications, Guillermo ran across a friend's credit application for an $800 bicycle. On this application, his friend lied by stating he was employed; Guillermo knew that his friend had quit his job several weeks ago. Guillermo's friend met all other conditions for obtaining credit. Bicycles Unlimited, Inc. typically does not verify employment on credit applications under $1,000. Guillermo's friend knows that he reviews credit applications and will be very upset if his credit application is denied. Guillermo also knows that his friend has already interviewed for several jobs, and his chances of having a new job in the near future are good. Guillermo believes it is a virtual certainty that his friend will repay the debt.

REQUIRED:

Should Guillermo allow his friend to obtain credit from Bicycles Unlimited, Inc.? Justify your answer and explain how you think Guillermo should handle the situation.

 C6-3 Refer to the financial statements of J.C. Penney in Appendix B at the end of the text. J.C. Penney is a major retailer with department stores in all 50 states and Puerto Rico. In 1993, Penney's experienced record retail sales of $19 billion, an increase of 5.4% from the previous year. It also experienced a decrease in its cash flow from operations from $1,574 million in 1992 to $286 million in 1993. This change was due primarily to increased credit card usage by customers in the fourth quarter of 1993 compared to the same period of the previous year.

Total customer accounts receivable at the end of 1993 were $4.4 billion, an 8.8% increase over 1992, but in line with 1991's amount. J.C. Penney's policy is to write off accounts when the scheduled minimum payment has not been received for 6 months, if any portion of the balance is more than 12 months past due, or if it is otherwise determined that the customer is unable to pay.

REQUIRED:

a. To what do you attribute the increased credit card usage in late 1993? Consider the state of the economy in 1992 and 1993.

b. Using the information in the annual report, how much did J.C. Penney write off as uncollectible during 1993? (Hint: Look at the change in the allowance accounts and the bad debt expense that was recorded for the year.

c. What recommendations would you make to J.C. Penney to improve its credit policy? Weigh both the potential for increased sales revenue and the possibility of increased write-offs.

CHAPTER 7

Inventories

"Why don't you ever have my size in stock?" asked Marie. Once again, Marie was frustrated at Bob's Discount Shoe Mart, Inc. for not having her size of an attractive style of shoe. Marie wanted to wear the shoes to the spring graduation ceremony at Gulfside College. Although she knew she could probably buy the shoes at European Shoe Boutique, which always carried a complete selection of all sizes in a wide variety of styles, Marie also knew the mall stores charge nearly twice as much for similar shoes. Marie, being a college student, had a limited budget; and she preferred to buy the shoes at Bob's to save money. Marie wondered why a business such as Bob's Discount Shoe Mart, Inc. sold a large volume of shoes but was often out of a particular size or style of shoe. On the other hand, a business such as European Shoe Boutique sold a much smaller volume of shoes but always had a complete selection of sizes and styles. In her accounting class, Marie was beginning to study accounting for merchandise inventories. She wondered if accounting information about inventories could help her understand the different ways the two shoe stores operated.

This chapter discusses accounting for merchandise inventories. You were introduced to this topic in a previous chapter, but many of the issues were deferred to this chapter. Since inventory items are purchased and sold continuously, activities concerning merchandise inventory are a major portion of a merchandising business's operations. Typically, inventory is a merchandising business's largest current asset, and cost of goods sold is usually the largest expense in its income statement. In its 1992 financial statements, General Mills, Inc. reported inventories of $487 million, compared to total current assets of $1.03 billion. Cost of goods sold for General Mills was $4.1 billion, compared to sales of $7.8 billion. For Kmart, the impact of inventories is even more dramatic. For 1991, Kmart reported inventories of $7.5 billion, compared to total assets of $16 billion. Cost of goods sold was $25.9 billion, compared to sales of $34.6 billion.

1. Describe the process for determining inventory quantities at the end of an accounting period.
2. Calculate cost of goods available for sale and allocate it to units in ending inventory and to the units sold during the period.
3. Describe the importance of inventory errors.
4. Apply the alternative methods of assigning costs to ending inventory.
5. Discuss the factors management should consider in selecting an inventory method.
6. Discuss when inventories should be valued at less than cost and calculate the relevant values.
7. Describe perpetual inventory systems and prepare the necessary entries.
8. Apply the two methods of estimating inventories.
9. Calculate and interpret the inventory turnover ratio.

LO 1

Describe the process for determining inventory quantities at the end of an accounting period.

ACCOUNTING FOR MERCHANDISE INVENTORIES AT THE END OF A PERIOD

At the end of an accounting period, a business adjusts Merchandise Inventory to reflect the ending inventory and to calculate the cost of goods sold. These procedures are shown in Illustration 7-1. The first procedure is to determine the number of units of merchandise that are on hand at the end of the period. The second procedure is to assign costs to the ending inventory. The final procedure is to determine cost of goods sold. As you saw in an earlier chapter, the number of units sold is the number of units available for sale less the number of units in ending inventory.

ILLUSTRATION 7-1 End-of-Period Procedures for Merchandise Inventories

Determine units in ending inventory	Assign costs to ending inventory	Determine cost of goods sold

Determining Inventory Quantities

Determining the number of units of merchandise that make up the ending inventory involves taking a physical inventory and analyzing goods in transit at the end of the accounting period.

Taking a Physical Inventory.   Employees commonly take the physical inventory. As an alternative, some businesses take physical inventories for other businesses for a fee. The end result of a physical inventory is the determination of the total cost of the ending inventory. Computers have made the process of conducting physical inventories and tabulating the results easier, faster, and more accurate. Physical inventory procedures were discussed in an earlier chapter where you were introduced to merchandising businesses.

Analyzing Goods In Transit. **Goods in transit** are items of merchandise in the possession of a carrier, such as a trucking, railroad, shipping, or airline company. Since the goods are in the process of being transported, those taking inventory cannot possibly include them in the physical inventory. Therefore, in determining the quantity of the merchandise inventory, a business should analyze the goods in transit at the end of the accounting period for possible inclusion in the ending inventory. The ending inventory should include goods in transit that the business owns at the end of the period.

Remember: Businesses determine the ownership of the merchandise in transit by the terms of the transaction. Goods may be shipped F.O.B. shipping point or F.O.B. destination. For a business, goods in transit may include both items of merchandise it has sold to customers and items of merchandise it has purchased from suppliers.

At the end of 19X1, Donald's TV Store, Inc. had the following goods in transit:

Merchandise Purchases		Merchandise Sales	
Item	Terms	Item	Terms
5 – 19″ televisions	F.O.B. shipping point	2 – 25″ televisions	F.O.B. shipping point
10 – TV stands	F.O.B. destination		

Among the purchases in transit, the 19″ televisions should be included in the ending inventory because Donald's became the owner of them when they were shipped. However, since the company does not become the owner of the TV stands until the carrier delivers them, Donald's should not include them in ending inventory. Ownership of the sold televisions transferred to the customers when Donald's delivered them to the carrier. Therefore, Donald's should not include the sold televisions in the ending inventory. If the televisions had been sold with F.O.B. destination terms, then Donald's would have included them in the ending inventory because the company would have continued to have ownership at the end of the period.

Assigning Inventory Costs

LO 2

Calculate cost of goods available for sale and allocate it to units in ending inventory and to the units sold during the period.

The **cost of goods available for sale** consists of the cost of the beginning inventory plus the cost of purchases during the year. The cost of merchandise inventory purchases should include all costs incurred to get the merchandise to a marketable condition, including acquisition and transportation costs. These costs include:

**Purchase Price – Purchases Discounts and Cash Discounts +
Transportation-In and Insurance-In-Transit**

Conceptually, a business should include such incidental costs as purchasing, handling, and storing in the cost of merchandise inventory. In practice, however, these costs are often difficult to trace directly to individual items of inventory. Typically, a business simply charges these costs to operating expenses for the period. (See a previous chapter for a discussion of the accounting procedures for recording the cost of merchandise inventory purchases.)

At the end of the year, a business allocates the cost of goods available for sale to the units in the ending inventory and to the units sold during the period. The allocation procedures are:

Allocation 1: Assign costs to the units in ending inventory.

Allocation 2: Calculate the cost of goods sold by subtracting the cost of the ending inventory from the cost of goods available for sale.

To illustrate the allocation of the cost of goods available for sale, assume Brown's Garden Supplies, Inc. determines that its cost of goods available for sale is $75,000. This amount consists of beginning inventory of $25,000 and the cost of purchases of $50,000. The physical inventory indicates that 4,000 units are on hand at the end of the year. The per-unit cost of the ending inventory is $5. The allocation of the cost of goods available for sale is shown in Illustration 7-2.

ILLUSTRATION 7-2 Allocation of Cost of Goods Available for Sale

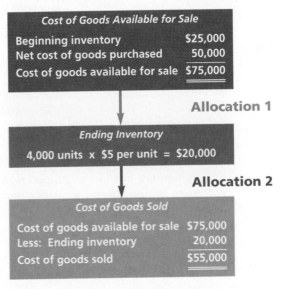

As shown above, the $75,000 cost of goods available for sale is allocated $20,000 to the ending inventory and $55,000 to the cost of goods sold.

THE IMPORTANCE OF INVENTORY ERRORS

LO 3

Describe the importance of inventory errors.

Errors may occur in the process of determining the cost of ending inventory. Such errors include those made in counting the number of items in the inventory or those made in assigning costs to inventory items. When an error occurs in determining the cost of the ending inventory, cost of goods sold, net income, stockholders' equity, and current assets are all misstated in the financial statements. Therefore, for accurate financial reporting, it is important that businesses determine correctly the inventory quantities and assign the correct costs to the units in inventory.

To illustrate the effects of errors in the ending inventory for the current year, consider the three examples shown in Illustration 7-3. In the first example, the ending inventory is stated correctly at $20,000. In the second example, the ending inventory is overstated by $5,000; and in the third example, the ending inventory is understated by $5,000. The errors in ending inventory and the errors in other income statement items that result are highlighted in Illustration 7-3.

ILLUSTRATION 7-3 Effects of Inventory Errors

	Correct Inventory	Ending Inventory Overstated	Ending Inventory Understated
Beginning inventory	$20,000	$20,000	$20,000
Add: Purchases	45,000	45,000	45,000
Cost of goods available for sale	$65,000	$65,000	$65,000
Less: Ending inventory	20,000	25,000	15,000
Cost of goods sold	$45,000	$40,000	$50,000
Sales	$80,000	$80,000	$80,000
Cost of goods sold (above)	45,000	40,000	50,000
Gross profit	$35,000	$40,000	$30,000

When the ending inventory is overstated, cost of goods sold is understated and gross profit is overstated. Conversely, when ending inventory is understated, cost of goods sold is overstated and gross profit is understated.

Because the ending inventory of one year is the beginning inventory of the next year, an inventory error affects not only the current year's income statement, but it also affects the subsequent year's financial statements. To illustrate this point, consider the example in Illustration 7-4. In 19X1, the ending inventory is overstated by $5,000; and this results in the 19X2 beginning inventory also being overstated by $5,000. The ending inventory for 19X2 is stated correctly, as is the 19X3 beginning inventory.

ILLUSTRATION 7-4 Inventory Errors in Subsequent Periods

	19X1	19X2	19X3
Sales	$80,000	$80,000	$80,000
Cost of goods sold:			
Beginning inventory	$20,000	$25,000	$20,000
Net purchases	45,000	45,000	45,000
Cost of goods available	$65,000	$70,000	$65,000
Ending inventory	25,000	20,000	20,000
Cost of goods sold	$40,000	$50,000	$45,000
Gross profit	$40,000	$30,000	$35,000

The 19X1 overstatement of ending inventory causes the 19X1 cost of goods sold to be understated by $5,000 and gross profit to be overstated by $5,000. Cost of goods sold should be $45,000 ($65,000 − $20,000), and gross profit should be $35,000 ($80,000 − $45,000). The effects on 19X2 are just the opposite. The overstatement of beginning inventory causes the cost of goods sold to be overstated by $5,000 and gross profit to be understated by $5,000. Cost of goods sold should be $45,000 ($20,000 + $45,000 − $20,000), and gross profit should be $35,000 ($80,000 − $45,000). For the two-year period, 19X1 and 19X2, the effects of the error in 19X1 cancel out. This is because the effects of the error in 19X2 are equal in amount, but in the opposite direction, of the effects of the error in 19X1. The correct gross profit for the two-year period is $70,000.

Even though the effects of inventory errors cancel out over a two-year period, such errors should be avoided. Although the total gross profit for the two-year period is correct, the individual financial statements for each year are incorrect. Because financial statement users make decisions based on the financial statements of each period, the accountant has an obligation to make sure that each period's financial statements are correct.

The effects of inventory errors on the elements of financial statements may be summarized as shown in Illustration 7-5.

ILLUSTRATION 7-5 Summary of Effects of Inventory Errors

	Cost of Goods Sold	Gross Profit	Net Income	Ending Stockholders' Equity	Ending Current Assets
If ending inventory:					
Overstated	U	O	O	O	O
Understated	O	U	U	U	U
If beginning inventory:					
Overstated	O	U	U	U	no error
Understated	U	O	O	O	no error
U=understated					
O=overstated					

LO 4

Apply the alternative methods of assigning costs to ending inventory.

METHODS USED TO ASSIGN COSTS TO INVENTORIES

The allocation of the cost of goods available for sale to the ending inventory and to cost of goods sold is made more difficult when the business incurs different costs for purchases of an item at different times during a year. For example, the cost of an item that is purchased for inventory may increase during the year. On the other hand, costs may also decrease or fluctuate. In any event, when the cost of inventory items changes during a year, the accountant must decide which costs to assign to the units in the ending inventory. Accountants follow two general approaches to assigning costs to inventory: actual physical flow and assumed cost flow. Under these approaches, the accountant can use these methods:

Approaches	Methods
Actual physical flow	Specific identification
Assumed cost flow	Weighted-average cost First-in, first-out (FIFO) Last-in, first-out (LIFO)

Actual Physical Flow Approach

One method a merchant uses to assign costs to the ending inventory is specific identification. The **specific identification method** keeps track of the actual physical flow of units during the period. That is, using serial numbers or tags and other coding devices, the merchant specifically identifies the actual units remaining in the ending inventory and the actual units sold during the period. The merchant keeps a record of each inventory item's actual cost. When an item is sold, the merchant adds its invoice cost to cost of goods sold and measures the ending inventory at the invoice cost of the unsold inventory items.

For example, assume that during 19X1, Anna's Antiques, Inc. purchased three antique desks for $2,500, $2,650, and $2,700, respectively. At the end of the year, the desk that cost $2,650 remains unsold. Using the specific identification method, the cost of goods sold is $5,200 ($2,500 + $2,700); and the ending inventory is the cost of the unsold desk, or $2,650. Illustration 7-6 demonstrates the specific identification method for these transactions of Anna's Antiques, Inc.

ILLUSTRATION 7-6 Specific Identification Method

While the specific identification method is simple and logical, its use in practice is generally restricted to unique items of high value such as fine jewelry, automobiles, and antique furniture. A criticism of the specific identification method is that when the inventory is composed of identical items, management can choose to sell either lower-cost or higher-cost items, thereby manipulating the income the business reports. For example, if management desires to report higher net income, it can choose to sell the lower-cost units. Conversely, management can report lower net income by selling the higher-cost units. Also, when the inventory consists of a high volume of identical items such as 8.2 oz. tubes of Crest toothpaste or 32 oz. jars of Crisco vegetable oil, the specific identification method is inefficient and other methods are used.

Assumed Cost Flow Approach

To avoid the limitations of the specific identification method, under GAAP businesses may assign costs to the ending inventory by *assuming* some pattern of cost flows related to units of merchandise. Three assumed cost flow methods are:

1. Weighted-average cost
2. First-in, first-out (FIFO)
3. Last-in, first-out (LIFO)

Illustration 7-7 shows what percentages of businesses use the various inventory cost methods.

When a business uses an assumed cost flow method, the assumed cost flow is not required to conform with the actual physical flow of goods. Management must decide what is the appropriate cost flow method for the business. However, once management adopts a particular method, the *consistency principle* requires that the business use the method consistently from year to year.

ILLUSTRATION 7-7 Relative Use of Inventory Methods

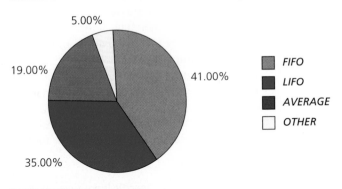

Source: *Accounting Trends and Techniques*, AICPA, 1992.

The consistent use of an inventory costing method allows financial statement users to assess the business's financial position and results of operations consistently across time. Changes in accounting methods disrupt the relationship between financial statements and actual activities of the business.

The three assumed cost flow methods will be illustrated with the following example of Exotic Electronics Corp. and its experience with Model 89X Transformers during 19X1. Illustration 7-8 provides information about the beginning inventory, purchases, sales, and ending inventory of Model 89X during the year.

Exotic Electronics Corp. uses the periodic inventory method. Recall that under the periodic inventory method, we update the Merchandise Inventory balance and Cost of Goods Sold only at the ends of accounting periods, based on physical inventory counts. The information in Illustration 7-8 about the beginning inventory comes from the prior year's ending inventory. The information about the purchases is found in the purchases invoices. The sales invoices provide the information about sales. The ending inventory is the result of the physical inventory taken at the end of 19X1.

ILLUSTRATION 7-8 Model 89X Transformers Inventory Data

Exotic Electronics Corp. Model 89X Transformers				
19X1		Units	Unit Cost	Total Cost
Jan. 1	Beginning inventory	10	$60	$ 600
Mar. 28	Purchase	20	66	1,320
Aug. 22	Purchase	20	70	1,400
Oct. 14	Purchase	25	76	1,900
Cost of goods available for sale		75		$5,220

Ending inventory = 30 units
Sales   = 45 units
Units available = 75 units

Weighted-Average Cost Method.   Under the **weighted-average cost method**, the costs assigned to the ending inventory and to cost of goods sold are based on the average cost per unit, which consists of the combined cost of the beginning inventory and the purchases made during the year. Exotic Electronics Corp. calculates the average cost per unit by the following formula, using the data from Illustration 7-8:

$$\text{Average Cost Per Unit} = \frac{\text{Cost of Goods Available for Sale}}{\text{Number of Units Available for Sale}}$$

$$\$69.60 = \frac{\$5,220}{75}$$

The weighted-average cost method is based on the assumption that all the units available for sale during the year are identical and, therefore, each unit should have the same cost.

Illustration 7-9 shows the application of the weighted-average cost method. First, the average cost per unit is calculated. Then, the resulting weighted-average cost is assigned to the units in ending inventory. Finally, the accountant calculates the cost of goods sold by subtracting the cost of ending inventory from the cost of goods available for sale. To verify the cost of goods sold figure, the number of units sold is multiplied by the average cost per unit (45 x $69.60 = $3,132).

ILLUSTRATION 7-9 Weighted-Average Cost Method

First-In, First-Out Method.   The **first-in, first-out (FIFO)** method *assumes* that the cost of the ending inventory consists of the costs of the most recent purchases, as shown in Illustration 7-10. Illustration 7-10 is based on the same purchases and sales data as those of Illustration 7-8. For Exotic Electronics Corp., the FIFO method *assumes* that the ending inventory of 30 units consists of the 25 units purchased on October 14, plus 5 of the 20 units purchased on August 22. The FIFO method *assumes* that the cost of goods sold consists of the cost of units in beginning inventory and the costs of the earliest purchases during the year. Under FIFO, the 45 units Exotic Electronics Corp. sold are *assumed* to consist of the 10 units that are in the beginning inventory, the 20 units purchased on March 28, and 15 of the units purchased on August 22. Illustration 7-11 shows the allocation of the cost of goods available for sale to the ending inventory and cost of goods sold for the Model 89X Transformers under the FIFO method.

ILLUSTRATION 7-10 FIFO Time Line

The cost of goods sold of $2,970 that is calculated in Illustration 7-11 may be verified by assigning the appropriate costs to the 45 units assumed to be sold, as follows:

Beginning inventory	10 units x $60 =	$ 600
Mar. 28 purchase	20 units x 66 =	1,320
Aug. 22 purchase	15 units x 70 =	1,050
Cost of goods sold	45 units	$2,970

The FIFO assumption that the first units purchased are the first units sold is consistent with the actual physical flow of goods of many businesses. When merchants purchase goods and place them on shelves in their stores, they typically place the newly purchased units behind the units already on the shelves. This minimizes the chances of merchants accumulating old units of merchandise that may spoil or become obsolete. However, to use the FIFO method, the business's actual physical flow of goods is irrelevant. Accountants view FIFO as a cost assumption, not a description of actual flows.

Last-In, First-Out Method. The last-in, first-out (LIFO) method *assumes* that the cost of the ending inventory consists of the costs of the units in beginning inventory and the costs of the earliest purchases made during the period. On the other hand, LIFO *assumes* that the cost of goods sold consists of the costs of the most recent purchases. In other words, the LIFO method *assumes* that the last goods purchased are the first goods sold, hence, the name "last-in, first-out." Illustration 7-12 shows a time line for the LIFO method when applied to the Model 89X Transformers.

ILLUSTRATION 7-11 FIFO Method

Cost of Goods Available for Sale				
Date		Units	Unit Cost	Total Cost
Jan. 1	Beginning inventory	10	$60	$ 600
Mar. 28	Purchase	20	66	1,320
Aug. 22	Purchase	20	70	1,400
Oct. 14	Purchase	25	76	1,900
Cost of goods available for sale		75		$5,220

Ending Inventory			
Date	Units	Unit Cost	Total
Oct. 14	25	$76	$1,900
Aug. 22	5	70	350
Total	30		$2,250

Cost of Goods Sold	
Cost of goods available for sale	$5,220
Less: Ending inventory	2,250
Cost of goods sold	$2,970

ILLUSTRATION 7-12 LIFO Time Line

LIFO *assumes* the ending inventory of 30 units consists of the 10 units in the beginning inventory plus the 20 units purchased on March 28. The 45 units sold are *assumed* to consist of the 25 units purchased on October 14, plus the 20 units purchased on August 22. Illustration 7-13 shows the allocation of the cost of goods available for sale to the ending inventory and to cost of goods sold.

ILLUSTRATION 7-13 LIFO Method

Cost of Goods Available for Sale				
Date		Units	Unit Cost	Total Cost
Jan. 1	Beginning inventory	10	$60	$ 600
Mar. 28	Purchase	20	66	1,320
Aug. 22	Purchase	20	70	1,400
Oct. 14	Purchase	25	76	1,900
Cost of goods available for sale		75		$5,220

Ending Inventory			
Date	Units	Unit Cost	Total Cost
Jan. 1	10	$60	$ 600
Mar. 28	20	66	1,320
Total	30		$1,920

Cost of Goods Sold	
Cost of goods available for sale	$5,220
Less: Ending inventory	1,920
Cost of goods sold	$3,300

The cost of goods sold of $3,300 in Illustration 7-13 may be verified by assigning the appropriate cost to the 45 units assumed to be sold, as follows:

Oct. 14 purchase	25 units x $76 =	$1,900
Aug. 22 purchase	20 units x 70 =	1,400
Cost of goods sold	45 units	$3,300

Under the LIFO method, the assumed flow of costs is not consistent with the actual physical flow of goods for most merchandising businesses.

INTERNATIONAL PERSPECTIVES

Other countries have accounting principles for merchandise inventories that differ from GAAP in the United States. These different principles have developed for various reasons, such as different degrees of self-regulation by the accounting profession, business customs, legal traditions, and rates of inflation. In most countries, the LIFO method is not an acceptable method. LIFO is acceptable, however, in Germany, Italy, the Netherlands, and South Africa, provided that the market value of the inventory is disclosed in the notes to the financial statements.

Comparison of Alternative Inventory Methods

During periods when the costs of merchandise change, the three alternative cost flow assumptions result in different amounts for cost of goods sold and for ending inventory. The previous example for Model 89X Transformers for 19X1 illustrates what happens in a period of increasing costs. Illustration 7-14 presents a comparison of the effects of applying the three inventory methods, assuming net revenues in each case of $4,000.

ILLUSTRATION 7-14 Comparison of Alternative Inventory Methods

	Weighted-Average Cost	FIFO	LIFO
Net revenue	$4,000	$4,000	$4,000
Cost of goods sold:			
Beginning inventory	$ 600	$ 600	$ 600
Purchases	4,620	4,620	4,620
Cost of goods available for sale	$5,220	$5,220	$5,220
Less: Ending inventory	2,088	2,250	1,920
Cost of goods sold	$3,132	$2,970	$3,300
Gross profit	$ 868	$1,030	$ 700

Income Statement Effects

During periods of increasing purchase costs, LIFO results in the highest cost of goods sold and the lowest gross profit, while the FIFO method produces the lowest cost of goods sold and the highest gross profit. The weighted-average cost method smooths out the effects of changing prices and produces measurements of cost of goods sold and gross profit that are between the LIFO and FIFO amounts.

Balance Sheet Effects

The effects of the methods on the cost of inventory reported in the balance sheet are just the opposite of their effects on cost of goods sold. The following presents a comparison of the balance sheet effects of the alternative methods:

	Weighted-Average Cost	FIFO	LIFO
Ending inventory	$2,088	$2,250	$1,920

During periods of increasing costs, the LIFO method produces the lowest amount for ending inventory since it assumes that the inventory consists of the oldest, and lowest, costs. On the other hand, the FIFO method produces the highest amount for ending inventory since it assumes that the inventory consists of the most recent, and highest, costs. The weighted-average cost method produces an amount for ending inventory that is between the amounts produced by the LIFO and FIFO methods.

LO 5

Discuss the factors management should consider in selecting an inventory method.

Factors In Selection of Inventory Methods

Because inventory is such a significant financial statement component for many businesses, management's selection of an inventory method is important. Management should give careful thought to the selection because once a business adopts a method, the *consistency principle* requires that the business use the method in subsequent periods. The following discussion presents some of the factors that management may consider in selecting an inventory method.

Those who support the LIFO method argue that it is the superior method for measuring net income. Since the LIFO method measures cost of goods sold at the most recent costs, they argue that it results in a better matching of current costs (the most relevant costs) and revenues. A going-concern must maintain some minimum level of inventory; and when it sells an item, the business must replace it. Therefore, the appropriate cost to match against revenues is the cost of replacing the item sold. Also, during periods of increasing costs, the LIFO method produces the lowest measurement of net income, which minimizes the amount of income taxes paid. (See Appendix A to this text for an explanation of income taxes.)

During periods of steadily increasing costs of inventory purchases, the LIFO method assigns the higher, recent costs to the cost of goods sold, which produces the lowest net income. On the other hand, the LIFO method assigns the lowest costs to the ending inventory. Critics argue that under the LIFO method, the ending inventory a business reports in its balance sheet does not reflect the value (cost) of its inventory. During periods of steadily decreasing costs of inventory purchases, the effects of LIFO are just the opposite—reporting low cost of goods sold, high net income, high income taxes, and high ending inventory cost.

Supporters of the FIFO method argue that it produces the most realistic measurement of the ending inventory reported in the balance sheet. Under the FIFO method, ending inventory is measured at the most recent costs, which generally approximates the current cost of the inventory. Also, supporters of the FIFO method argue that first-in, first-out more closely approximates the physical flow of goods for most merchandising businesses.

Both the FIFO and LIFO methods have strong points and weak points. Both are acceptable under GAAP. The weighted-average cost method is simply a compromise and is acceptable because it is easy to apply. Management's decision about which inventory costing method to use depends on its expectation about future costs of inventory items and the relative amount of net income and taxable income it desires to report. For example, if management expects inventory costs to increase in the future and wants to report the highest relative amount of income, then it should choose the FIFO method to produce the desired results. On the other hand, if management wishes to minimize the amount of income taxes paid currently, it should choose the LIFO method.

The comparisons of the alternative inventory methods discussed above are valid for periods of increasing costs. During periods of decreasing costs, the comparisons of the methods are just the opposite in their relationships. Because of the effects the selection of an inventory method can have on the income statement and the balance sheet, GAAP require a business to disclose in the financial statements the inventory method that it uses. Financial statement users need to know the inventory costing methods underlying the statements to compare accurately the income and financial position of one business to another. For example, Air Products and Chemicals, Inc. had the following accounting policy disclosure in the notes to the financial statements:

Inventories—To determine the cost of chemical inventories and some gas and equipment inventories in the United States, the company uses the last-in, first-out (LIFO) method. This method assumes the most recent cost is closer to the cost of replacing an item that has been sold. During periods of rising prices, LIFO maximizes the cost of goods sold and minimizes the profit reported on the company's income statement.

LO 6

Discuss when inventories should be valued at less than cost and calculate the relevant values.

INVENTORIES AND THE PRINCIPLE OF CONSERVATISM

The value of merchandise a business holds for resale to customers may decrease below its assigned cost. The decrease in value may be the result of damage or obsolescence that occurs while the inventory is held. For example, the value of personal computers held in inventory may decrease below cost because of technological advances that make the computers obsolete. Items of inventory may be damaged while being handled or while serving as floor samples for customers' inspection. In addition to damage and obsolescence, the value of goods in inventory also may decrease because of a decline in consumer demand for the particular good. In this case, the merchant may have to decrease the selling price below cost to sell the goods. A business should not report inventories in the balance sheet at more than **estimated net realizable value**, which is the estimated selling price less the estimated costs of disposing of the merchandise.

INSIGHTS INTO ETHICS

Amy Brown is the Assistant Controller of Telmax Company. The employees just completed the physical inventory for the current year and she is comparing the inventory costs with the costs of the previous year. She realizes that for most of the inventory items the costs have actually declined since last year. This realization disturbs Amy because just last year she proposed to management that the business change from the FIFO inventory method to the LIFO method. Her proposal claimed that the LIFO method would save income taxes for the business even though it would result in lower net income. Her proposal had been vigorously opposed by Roy Stein, a new employee in the accounting department, who was very vocal about his ambitions to rise to the management ranks of the business. After a meeting with top management, attended by both Amy and Roy in which Roy had argued strongly against Amy's proposal, management accepted the proposal and switched to the LIFO method.

Amy is considering whether to report the information about the declining inventory costs to management. With the benefit of hindsight, she will be admitting that her proposal was wrong and she will have to listen to Roy say, "I told you so." Management probably will discuss switching back to the FIFO method in order to reduce income taxes. Amy knows that switching inventory methods requires Internal Revenue Service approval. Receiving approval for changing inventory methods for two consecutive years is rare at best. On the other hand, since the business's total inventory has increased, it is unlikely that anyone else will discover that the LIFO method is actually penalizing the business. If she just keeps quiet, she may avoid embarrassment and possible damage to her career.

What should Amy do?

When the value of inventory decreases below its cost, the business has incurred a loss. The loss is attributed to the decrease in the inventory's revenue-producing ability and the inability to recover its cost. Under GAAP, the business should report the loss in net income in the period that the decrease in value occurs. This means that a business should not wait until the period it sells the merchandise to report the loss in net income. The measurement of the loss, however, is different for decreases in value that are the result of damage or obsolescence and price decreases.

Damage or Obsolescence

The loss from damaged or obsolete goods is measured as the difference between the cost of the goods and their estimated net realizable value. For example, assume that Carol's Dress Shop, Inc. has five dresses on display in the shop's window. The dresses originally cost $125 each and have a normal selling price of $250 each. The dresses are slightly faded from being in the window, and Carol's estimates that it can sell them for only $100 each. Additionally, Carol's pays its salesclerks a 10% commission on all sales. The estimated net realizable value of each dress is $90, as shown below:

Estimated selling price	$100
Less estimated costs of disposal:	
Sales commission	10
Estimated net realizable value	$ 90

For the five dresses, Carol's has incurred a loss of $175 [5 x ($125 − $90)] that should be reported in net income of the current period. The following entry recognizes the loss:

(Date)	Loss from Damaged Inventory	175	
	Merchandise Inventory		175
	To record estimated loss on damaged inventory.		

In the period that the dresses are sold, Carol's recognizes no income or loss on the sale unless the actual selling price is different from the estimated selling price.

Price Decreases

In the previous discussion, we have illustrated several methods of determining the cost of merchandise inventories. Under GAAP, inventories should be presented in the balance sheet at the lower of cost or market. *Cost*, in lower of cost or market, means the cost of the ending inventory as determined by one of the alternative methods—FIFO, LIFO, or weighted-average cost. When the market value of inventory falls below this cost because of price decreases, the business has incurred a loss that should be recognized immediately by reducing the inventory to market value. For example, in the first quarter of 1986, the price of crude oil decreased dramatically from approximately $35 per barrel to approximately $10 per barrel. This decrease in the price of crude oil caused many oil companies to write down their inventories of crude oil and to recognize a loss.

The loss recognized for some of the companies exceeded $100 million.[1] The term *market value*, as used in this context, means the cost of replacing the inventory item, or *replacement cost*. Reporting inventories at market value when the market value has fallen below cost is called the **lower-of-cost-or-market rule**. Raychem Corporation disclosed the following accounting policy in the notes to the financial statements:

Inventories

Inventories are stated at the lower of cost (principally the first-in, first-out method) or market. Market is determined on the basis of replacement cost or net realizable value. Appropriate consideration has been given to obsolescence and other factors in evaluating net realizable value.

Applying the Lower-Of-Cost-Or-Market Rule

The lower-of-cost-or-market rule is applied by comparing the cost of the inventory as determined by one of the methods previously discussed to the market value of the inventory. In the example that follows, Hi-Fi Electronics, Inc. is a retail business that sells radios and televisions. Illustration 7-15 shows the application of the lower-of-cost-or-market rule to the inventories of radios and televisions for Hi-Fi Electronics, Inc.

ILLUSTRATION 7-15 Determination of Lower of Cost or Market

	Model	Units	Cost per Unit	Market per Unit	Total Cost	Total Market	Lower of Cost or Market
Radios							
	1	20	$ 27	$ 28	$ 540	$ 560	
	2	10	50	44	500	440	
	3	5	64	66	320	330	
Televisions							
	101	3	220	212	660	636	
	102	2	279	285	558	570	
	103	4	456	420	1,824	1,680	
					$4,402	$4,216	
Inventory at lower of cost or market							$4,216

For Hi-Fi Electronics, the market value of the inventory is lower than the cost by $186 ($4,402 − $4,216). Hi-Fi Electronics would make the following journal entry to write down the cost of the inventory to lower of cost or market and to recognize the decline in value:

(Date)	Loss from Decline in Market Value of Merchandise Inventory	186	
	Merchandise Inventory		186
	To record inventory at the lower of cost or market.		

Hi-Fi Electronics would make the entry above *after* recording cost of goods sold in the closing process as previously illustrated. However, if the market

---

[1]"Oil Firms Scramble to Restate Earnings In Wake of SEC Ruling on Write-Down," *The Wall Street Journal* (May 12, 1986), p. 8.

value of $4,216, instead of the cost of $4,402, were used in the closing process, cost of goods sold would include the $186 loss; and it would be double-counted in net income after the entry to reduce merchandise inventory to market. For the subsequent period, Hi-Fi Electronics would use the $4,216 (lower of cost or market) as the beginning inventory.

PERPETUAL INVENTORY PROCEDURES

To this point, the discussions of inventory procedures have dealt with periodic inventory systems. With periodic inventory systems, businesses determine the current inventory only at the end of an accounting period by taking a physical inventory. Some businesses desire to know the amount of inventory on hand at any time during the period. With this information, they can respond more effectively to customer inquiries about merchandise availability and better avoid being out of stock. This information permits managers to have more control over the merchandise inventory and to determine cost of goods sold for periods shorter than a year, without the need of frequent physical inventories. Businesses use a perpetual inventory system to increase control and up-to-date information about inventory.

Recording Perpetual Inventory Transactions

Accounting under perpetual inventory procedures differs from that under periodic inventory procedures in that Merchandise Inventory is continually updated by recording purchases and sales as they occur. Recall that for the periodic method, Merchandise Inventory remains at the beginning amount until the end of the period when the business takes a physical inventory and updates the account balance. Accounts such as Purchases, Purchases Returns and Allowances, Purchases Discounts, and Freight-in that you saw for the periodic method are not used in the perpetual method. For the perpetual method Cost of Goods Sold is posted as sales occur for the cost of merchandise sold to customers.

To illustrate the differences between the two methods, consider the following information for stereo headsets of Don's Stereo Shop, Inc., which uses the FIFO method:

March	1	Beginning inventory is 20 units that cost $50 each.
	10	Sold 10 units at a price of $90 each.
	13	Purchased 20 units at a cost of $60 each.
	20	Sold 8 units at a price of $90 each.

Illustration 7-16 compares the recording in general journal form for both the perpetual and periodic methods.

As shown in Illustration 7-16, the difference between the perpetual and periodic methods is the continual updating of Merchandise Inventory and Cost of Goods Sold. At the end of a period, the entries that you saw for the periodic method to adjust Merchandise Inventory and to establish Cost of Goods Sold are not needed for the perpetual method. The balances of Merchandise Inventory and Cost of Goods Sold are updated when each purchase and sale transaction occurs.

Merchandise Inventory Card

In a perpetual inventory system, purchases of merchandise are *not* recorded in a separate Purchases account. Instead, businesses keep an inventory card simi-

ILLUSTRATION 7-16 Entries for Perpetual and Periodic Methods

	Perpetual Method				Periodic Method		
To record sale of 10 units at $90 each:							
Mar. 10	Cash	900			Cash	900	
	Sales		900		Sales		900
To record cost of 10 units sold at $50 each:							
10	Cost of Goods Sold	500			No Entry		
	Merchandise Inventory		500				
To record purchase of 20 units at $60 each:							
13	Merchandise Inventory	1,200			Purchases	1,200	
	Accounts Payable		1,200		Accounts Payable		1,200
To record sale of 8 units at $90 each:							
20	Cash	720			Cash	720	
	Sales		720		Sales		720
To record cost of 8 units sold at $50 each:							
20	Cost of Goods Sold	400			No Entry		
	Merchandise Inventory		400				

lar to the one in Illustration 7-17 for each type of merchandise in inventory. The **merchandise inventory card** records in both quantities and costs the beginning inventory for the item, purchases of the item and sales of the item. For each item, employees keep a continuous record on the inventory card of the quantity of the item on hand. At any time, the total of all the dollar balances of the inventory cards should agree with Merchandise Inventory in the general ledger. Consider what is recorded in Illustration 7-17. First, there is a balance of 20 units on hand at March 1. These units cost $50 each, or a total of $1,000. On March 10, the business sold 10 units. The inventory card indicates that the 10 units sold have a cost of $50 each, or a total of $500. After the sale, the inventory card indicates that the remaining inventory is 10 units at $50 each, or a total of $500.

The next transaction recorded on the inventory card is a purchase of merchandise on March 13. On that date, Don's purchased 20 units at a cost of $60 each. The inventory card reflects that after the purchase the inventory consists

ILLUSTRATION 7-17 Perpetual Inventory Card

ITEM: Stereo Headsets

DATE	PURCHASED				SOLD				BALANCE		
	VOUCHER #	UNITS	COST	TOTAL	INVOICE#	UNITS	COST	TOTAL	UNITS	COST	TOTAL
Mar. 1									20	50	1,000
10					S-2602	10	50	500	10	50	500
13	V-989	20	60	1,200					10	50	500
									20	60	1,200
20					S-2615	8	50	400	2	50	100
									20	60	1,200

of 10 units at a cost of $50 each, and 20 units at a cost of $60 each. The total cost of inventory after the purchase transaction is $500 + $1,200 = $1,700.

In Illustration 7-17, Don's is using the first-in, first-out inventory method and the cost of the eight units sold on March 20 is $50 per unit, which are the older costs. After the March 20 sale, the remaining inventory consists of 2 units at a per unit cost of $50 and 20 units at a per unit cost of $60, or a total cost of $1,300. Businesses with perpetual inventory systems also may use last-in, first-out and weighted-average cost methods.

The inventory card in Illustration 7-17 is for a business that does not have a computerized accounting system. Businesses that have computerized accounting systems have similar inventory records in their accounting systems, typically stored on magnetic tape or magnetic disks. Modern computers have greatly enhanced the ability of businesses to use perpetual inventory procedures. Consider the number of items of merchandise and the number of sale and purchase transactions of a supermarket or a retailer such as J.C. Penney Company. Without computers, perpetual inventory procedures would require considerable effort. Not only do computers enhance the accounting for merchandise inventory, they also enhance the management of merchandise inventory. With continually updated inventory information, management can be more effective in avoiding being out of stock of merchandise desired by customers. The timely information indicates when inventory on hand of an item is low and merchandise should be ordered. Some computerized inventory systems automatically reorder merchandise when the number of units on hand reaches a predetermined level.

The inventory card, as shown in Illustration 7-17, has columns to record the sales invoices and vouchers used to post increases and decreases in the inventory item. Periodically, the balances of all the inventory cards should be summed and reconciled to the balance of the Merchandise Inventory account in the general ledger. If the two figures do not agree, employees should undertake an investigation to determine the cause of the discrepancy and to make any necessary corrections. Such a reconciling and correcting process contributes to the completeness and accuracy of the recording of the changes in perpetual inventory.

Perpetual Inventories and the Need for Physical Inventories

Since businesses keep a continuous record of merchandise inventory with perpetual inventory systems, it may appear that physical inventories are not needed. The merchandise inventory records, however, only show what inventory *should* be on hand. A physical inventory is needed to determine what inventory actually is on hand. The perpetual inventory records may not show the actual inventory because of shrinkage, breakage, theft, and other causes. Also, employees may have made errors in recording inventory transactions. After the actual inventory on hand is determined by physical inventory, employees should adjust the merchandise inventory card to reflect the correct inventory on hand. After all inventory cards are corrected, the business adjusts Merchandise Inventory in the general ledger to reflect the sum of the corrected inventory cards. For example, assume that the physical inventory determines a shortage of merchandise that cost $85. The entry in general journal form to record the loss is:

Dec. 31	Loss from Inventory Shortage	85	
	Merchandise Inventory		85
	To record loss from inventory shortage.		

Point-of-Sale Systems

Point-of-sale systems for the electronic transfer of funds from customers' bank accounts to the business's bank account are described in an earlier chapter. Some businesses also have point-of-sale systems for updating their inventory records. For example, consider a business that uses an electronic product code reader. Each item of merchandise has a unique code that the electronic reader recognizes. Such a product code is shown below.

The product code reader is connected to the cash register and to the business's computer. When a customer makes a purchase, the product code reader (scanner) identifies the merchandise being purchased. The computer contains information about the prices of merchandise and enters the proper amounts in the cash register. Simultaneously, the computer adjusts the perpetual inventory records of each item of merchandise sold. Some businesses have programmed their computers to order merchandise automatically from suppliers whenever inventory levels drop to a designated amount. Point-of-sale systems enhance the management of inventory levels by instantaneously adjusting the inventory records.

LO 8
Apply the two methods of estimating inventories.

ESTIMATING INVENTORIES

Businesses frequently must estimate the amounts of inventories to prepare interim financial reports and to file an insurance claim should the inventory be lost due to a disaster. Two methods businesses use to estimate inventories are the gross profit method and the retail method. To manage more effectively, retail merchandise businesses often need financial statements prepared more frequently than annually. Managers frequently desire financial statements at least monthly. Also, creditors may desire financial statements on a more frequent basis than annually, perhaps every three months or even monthly. Financial statements prepared for accounting periods shorter than one year are called *interim financial statements*.

Although interim financial statements are as valuable to retail businesses as to any other business, retail businesses often find that both perpetual inventory procedures and frequent periodic physical inventories are too costly. This is because of the varieties and quantities of retail inventories. Many retail businesses use periodic inventory systems and do not keep continuous track of the merchandise on hand and sold in their accounting records. At the end of the annual accounting period, they determine inventory by taking a physical inventory. To avoid the time and expense of a physical inventory when preparing interim financial statements, businesses may estimate the amount of inventory on hand by using the gross profit method or retail method.

Gross Profit Method

The **gross profit method** of estimating inventories relies on the formula for calculation of cost of goods sold:

> **Beginning inventory**
> **Add: Purchases**
> _____
> **Cost of goods available for sale**
> **Less: Ending inventory**
> _____
> **Cost of goods sold**

The gross profit method also assumes that the business's cost of goods sold/sales ratio is relatively stable over time. The steps in applying the gross profit method are as follows:

1. Calculate the cost of goods available for sale by summing the beginning inventory and purchases, both at cost.
2. Calculate *estimated* cost of goods sold by multiplying net sales by the cost of goods sold/sales ratio.
3. Calculate *estimated* ending inventory by subtracting the estimated cost of goods sold from the cost of goods available for sale.

Gross Profit Method Illustrated

Assume the accounting records at the end of a period show the following amounts:

Sales	$112,000
Sales returns and allowances	4,000
Inventory (beginning)	21,000
Purchases	70,000
Transportation-in	5,000

In recent years, the gross profit margin has been relatively stable at 25% of net sales; and nothing has occurred in the current period to indicate any change in that margin. A gross profit margin of 25% means that the cost of goods sold/sales ratio is 75% as shown by the following relationship:

Net sales (as a percent of net sales)	100%
Gross profit (as a percent of net sales)	25%
Cost of goods sold (as a percent of net sales)	75%

The cost of goods sold/sales ratio of 75% is used to estimate the ending inventory:

1. Beginning inventory		$21,000
Purchases	$ 70,000	
Add: Transportation-in	5,000	75,000
Cost of goods available for sale		$96,000
2. Sales	$112,000	
Less: Sales returns and allowances	4,000	
Net sales	$108,000	
Estimated cost of goods sold (75% x $108,000)		81,000
3. Estimated ending inventory		$15,000

Businesses use the gross profit method of estimating inventories in several ways. In estimating inventories when preparing interim financial statements or when estimating inventories destroyed by fires or storms, businesses use the gross profit method to determine the amount of inventory. Also, accountants often use the gross profit method to check the reasonableness of inventory amounts determined by physical inventories.

Retail Method

To use the **retail method** of estimating inventories, the records of the business should have information about the beginning inventory at cost and at retail. The term *at cost* means the cost of the beginning inventory as determined by one of the acceptable inventory methods previously discussed. The term *at retail* means the selling price of the merchandise. In addition to this information about the beginning inventory, the accounting records should show the purchases during the period at both cost and retail and the *net* sales at retail for the period. The net sales at retail consist of the amount of sales entered in Sales during the period less sales returns, allowances, and discounts for the period. The following section describes the steps involved in applying the retail method.

Steps in Applying the Retail Method

1. Calculate the amount of goods available for sale at both cost and retail. Goods available for sale at cost consist of (1) beginning inventory at cost, plus (2) net purchases at cost, plus (3) transportation-in related to the purchases, minus (4) purchase discounts, returns, and allowances. Goods available for sale at retail is the sum of beginning inventory at retail plus net purchases at retail.
2. Determine the cost/retail ratio by dividing the goods available for sale at cost by the goods available for sale at retail.
3. Calculate ending inventory at retail by subtracting net sales, which are at retail, from the goods available for sale at retail.
4. Determine ending inventory at cost by multiplying the ending inventory at retail by the cost/retail ratio determined in Step 2.

These steps in applying the retail method are shown in Illustration 7-18.

ILLUSTRATION 7-18 Applying the Retail Method

Step	Cost	Retail
1. Beginning inventory	$ 60,000	$ 96,000
Purchases	115,000	204,000
Transportation-in	5,000	
Goods available for sale	$180,000	$300,000
2. Cost/retail ratio: $180,000 ÷ $300,000 = 60%		
3. Net sales		250,000
Ending inventory, at retail		$ 50,000
4. Ending inventory, at cost		
($50,000 x 60%)	$ 30,000	

The example shown in Illustration 7-18 may be interpreted as follows:

1. The business had merchandise for sale during the period worth $300,000 at retail prices.
2. The average cost of each $1.00 of merchandise for sale is $.60.
3. Of the merchandise for sale at total retail prices of $300,000, merchandise with total retail prices of $250,000 was sold during the period, leaving $50,000 of merchandise at retail on hand at the end of the period.
4. Since each $1.00 of merchandise at retail has, on average, a cost of $.60, the merchandise on hand at the end of the period must have cost approximately $30,000 (i.e., $50,000 x 60%).

Although the retail method is acceptable for estimating inventory for interim financial statements, the business needs to take a physical inventory at least one time each year for purposes of preparing the annual financial statements. As with the perpetual inventory method, the retail method indicates the cost of inventory that *should* be on hand, not what is actually on hand.

LO 9
Calculate and interpret the inventory turnover ratio.

INVENTORY TURNOVER

Inventory turnover indicates the rate at which inventory passes through a business. The measure compares the volume of inventory sold to the average amount of inventory on hand during the period. To analyze a business's performance, a commonly used measure—that includes the amount of merchandise inventory reported in the financial statements—is the inventory turnover ratio. This ratio is calculated as follows:

$$\text{Inventory Turnover Ratio} = \frac{\text{Cost of Goods Sold}}{\text{Average Inventory}}$$

where

$$\text{Average Inventory} = \frac{\text{Beginning Inventory} + \text{Ending Inventory}}{2}$$

If a business has cost of goods sold of $100,000 and average inventory of $25,000, the inventory would have *turned over* four times ($100,000 ÷ $25,000 = 4) in the period.

Interpreting Inventory Turnover Ratio

The inventory turnover ratio varies for different types of businesses. On the average, family clothing, sporting goods, and department stores have inventory turnover ratios of about four times per year. This implies that they turn over their inventories about once every season. Restaurants, on the other hand, deal mainly in fresh food and have inventory turnover ratios of about 60 times per year, or about once every six days.

The inventory turnover ratio allows financial statement readers to assess how efficiently management utilized its inventory. A business's merchandise inventory requires an investment of capital. To maintain the investment in inventory, a business incurs costs. These costs include: storage of the merchandise, insurance, property taxes, ordering, and handling. By maintaining a relatively low level (high turnover) of inventory, a business can minimize storage, insurance, and property tax costs. Conversely, a relatively high level (low turnover) of inventory tends to minimize ordering and handling costs. There is, however, an implicit cost to low levels of inventory. This implicit cost is lost sales and perhaps poor customer relations from not being able to meet customer demand. Management must often try to balance these inventory costs.

Analyzing Marie's Shoes Experience

In the scenario that opened this chapter, Marie's frustration with the shoe stores resulted from two different approaches to inventory management. European Shoe Boutique's approach is to maintain relatively high levels of inventory to avoid lost sales and to establish a clientele. These customers should provide repeat business because they know the store always has in stock what they want. This approach usually results in the business charging higher prices to cover the costs of maintaining high levels of inventory with low inventory turnover and low sales volume.

Conversely, Bob's Discount Shoe Mart, Inc.'s approach to inventory management involves a minimum level of inventory and high sales volume. The low level of inventory allows such businesses to charge lower prices because of the lower inventory maintenance costs. These businesses experience high inventory turnover. Under this approach, management expects the low prices to attract customers, ever though the business often might not have in stock what the customer wants. If Marie were to examine the financial statements of the two stores and calculate their inventory turnover ratios, she would probably see these two approaches to inventory management reflected in their turnover ratios. Bob's Discount Shoe Mart Inc.'s turnover ratio is probably much higher than that for European Shoe Boutique.

SUMMARY

Describe the process for determining inventory quantities at the end of an accounting period. Businesses determine the number of units of merchandise that make up ending inventory by taking a physical inventory and by analyzing goods in transit at the end of an accounting period. Taking a physical inventory involves following strictly controlled procedures to count each item in the inventory. Businesses analyze goods in transit to ensure that the goods the business owns are included in ending inventory.

Calculate cost of goods available for sale and allocate it to units in ending inventory and to units sold during the period. Cost of goods available for sale consists of the cost of the beginning inventory plus the cost of inventory purchases during the year. Businesses allocate cost of goods available for sale to the units in the ending inventory and to the units sold during the year. The allocation procedures are: (1) assign costs to the units in the ending inventory, and (2) calculate the cost of goods sold by subtracting the cost of the ending inventory from the cost of the goods available for sale.

Describe the importance of inventory errors. By incorrectly determining inventory quantities or by incorrectly assigning costs to the units in inventory, errors may occur in the process of determining the cost of the ending inventory. When an error occurs in determining the cost of the ending inventory, cost of goods sold, net income, stockholders' equity, and current assets are all misstated in the financial statements.

Apply the alternative methods of assigning costs to ending inventory. The fact that prices of inventory items change over time complicates the assignment of costs to goods that are sold and to goods in the ending inventory. Businesses use four methods to assign costs to these two elements: (1) specific identification, (2) weighted-average cost, (3) first-in, first-out (FIFO), and (4) last-in, first-out (LIFO). The inventory methods, except for specific identification, assume some flow of the costs of the units rather than keeping track of the physical flow of units.

Discuss the factors management should consider in selecting an inventory method. Management's decision about which inventory costing method to use depends on its expectations about future costs of inventory items and the relative amounts of net income and taxable income it desires to report. During periods of rising prices, the FIFO method will result in the highest net income and LIFO will result in the lowest taxable income.

Discuss when inventories should be valued at less than cost and calculate the relevant values. Usually, inventories are shown on the balance sheet at cost. While items of inventory are held for resale their values may decline below assigned costs. The decline in value may be the result of damage or obsolescence or changes in consumer demand. When the value of inventory declines below cost, the business has incurred a loss that should be reported in net income in the period that the decline in value below cost occurs.

Describe perpetual inventory systems and prepare the necessary entries. Some businesses desire to know the amount of inventory on hand at any time during the period. This allows greater control over inventory and the determination of cost of goods sold for a period shorter than a year. These businesses use the perpetual inventory system, which keeps a continuous record of merchandise inventory and permits summarizing cost of goods sold at any point in time.

Apply the two methods of estimating inventories. For businesses that use the periodic inventory system, the preparation of interim financial statements using normal end-of-period inventory procedures is often too costly. These businesses prepare interim statements by estimating the cost of inventory at the end of an interim period. Two common methods businesses use to estimate the cost of inventories are the gross profit method and the retail method.

Calculate and interpret the inventory turnover ratio. The inventory turnover ratio is the ratio of cost of goods sold to the average inventory for the period. The ratio shows the rate at which inventory passes through a business and how efficiently the business utilizes its inventory.

REVIEW PROBLEM

The data shown on the next page are given for the inventory transactions of Boutique Clothiers Corporation for the month of March.

REQUIRED:

a. Calculate cost of goods available for sale.
b. Calculate cost of goods sold for March and ending inventory for the month, assuming that Boutique Clothiers Company uses a periodic inventory system using the following methods: (1) FIFO, (2) LIFO, and (3) weighted-average cost.

c. Calculate cost of goods sold for March and ending inventory for the month assuming the Boutique Clothiers Corporation uses a perpetual system using the following methods: (1) FIFO, and (2) LIFO.

Date	Purchases Units	Cost	Sales (Units)	Inventory (Units)
Beg. inventory	300	$5.00		300
Mar. 2	600	$5.25		900
6			400	500
10	250	$5.40		750
13			500	250
20	100	$5.45		350
22	700	$5.50		1,050
28			250	800
31	100	$5.60		900

SOLUTION:

Planning and Organizing Your Work

1. Find the cost of beginning inventory and the cost of each purchase by multiplying the quantity times the unit price.
2. Determine cost of goods available for sale by adding the cost of the beginning inventory plus purchases calculated in Step 1.
3. Determine the cost of the ending inventory (900 units) for each method as shown in "Methods Used to Assign Costs to Inventories" in this chapter.
4. Determine the cost of goods sold for each method by subtracting the ending inventory, calculated in Step 3, from the cost of goods available for sale, calculated in Step 2.
5. Set up answer format as a perpetual inventory card as shown in the Perpetual Inventory Procedures section of this chapter.
6. For the FIFO inventory method, complete the inventory card in chronological order. Start with beginning inventory by entering the data given for units and cost in the Balance columns. Complete the total balance column by multiplying the units times the cost to compute the total balance.
7. For each date, enter the data given and compute total purchased or total sold as appropriate. Recap the effect of the day's activity in the balance columns applying the assumptions of the FIFO inventory method.
8. Determine the cost of goods sold after all the month's given data has been entered and extended (Step 6). Compute cost of goods sold by summing the total sold column of the perpetual inventory card. This total is the sum of all the costs of units sold using the FIFO method. Unit selling prices do not appear on the perpetual inventory card, only unit costs.
9. Determine the cost of ending inventory by referring to the balance column for the last date on the perpetual inventory card.
10. Repeat steps 6–9 for the LIFO method.

(a) *Calculate cost of goods available for sale.*

Date		Units	Unit Cost	Total Cost
Mar. 1	Beg. inventory	300	$5.00	$ 1,500
2	Purchase	600	5.25	3,150
10	Purchase	250	5.40	1,350
20	Purchase	100	5.45	545
22	Purchase	700	5.50	3,850
31	Purchase	100	5.60	560
Cost of goods available for sale		2,050		$10,955

(b) *Calculate cost of goods sold and ending inventory (periodic).*

FIFO

Goods available for sale		$10,955
Ending inventory:		
100 x $5.60	$ 560	
700 x $5.50	3,850	
100 x $5.45	545	
Less: Total ending inventory		4,955
Cost of goods sold		$ 6,000

LIFO

Goods available for sale		$10,955
Ending inventory:		
300 x $5.00 (Beg. inv.)	$1,500	
600 x $5.25	3,150	
Less: Total ending inventory		4,650
Cost of goods sold		$ 6,305

Weighted-Average Cost

Goods available for sale	$10,955
Less: Ending inventory	
(900 x $5.344*)	4,810
Cost of goods sold	$ 6,145

*$10,955 ÷ 2,050 units

(c) *Calculate cost of goods sold and ending inventory (perpetual).*

FIFO

DATE	PURCHASED			SOLD			BALANCE		
	UNITS	COST	TOTAL	UNITS	COST	TOTAL	UNITS	COST	TOTAL
Beg.							300	$5.00	$1,500
Mar. 28	600	$5.25	$3,150				300	$5.00	
							600	$5.25	$4,650
6				300	$5.00		500	$5.25	$2,625
				100	5.25	$2,025			
10	250	$5.40	$1,350				500	$5.25	
							250	$5.40	$3,975
13				500	$5.25	$2,625	250	$5.40	$1,350
20	100	$5.45	$ 545				250	$5.40	
							100	$5.45	$1,895
22	700	$5.50	$3,850				250	$5.40	
							100	$5.45	
							700	$5.50	$5,745
28				250	$5.40	$1,350	100	$5.45	
							700	$5.50	$4,395
31	100	$5.60	$ 560				100	$5.45	
							700	$5.50	
							100	$5.60	$4,955

Cost of goods sold: $2,025 + $2,625 + $1,350 = $6,000 (Sum of the Sold Total column)
Ending inventory: $4,955 (ending balance on inventory card)
Self-check: Cost of goods sold + ending inventory = cost of goods available for sale
$6,000   + $4,955   = $10,955

LIFO

DATE	PURCHASED			SOLD			BALANCE		
	UNITS	COST	TOTAL	UNITS	COST	TOTAL	UNITS	COST	TOTAL
Beg.							300	$5.00	$1,500
Mar. 2	600	$5.25	$3,150				300	$5.00	
							600	$5.25	$4,650
6				400	$5.25	$2,100	300	$5.00	
							200	$5.25	$2,550
10	250	$5.40	$1,350				300	$5.25	
							200	$5.25	
							250	$5.40	$3,900
13				250	$5.40		250	$5.00	$1,250
				200	$5.25				
				50	$5.00	$2,650			
20	100	$5.45	$ 545				250	$5.00	
							100	$5.45	$1,795
22	700	$5.50	$3,850				250	$5.00	
							100	$5.45	
							700	$5.50	$5,645
28				250	$5.50	$1,375	250	$5.00	
							100	$5.45	
							450	$5.50	$4,270
31	100	$5.60	$ 560				250	$5.00	
							100	$5.45	
							450	$5.50	
							100	$5.60	$4,830

Cost of goods sold: $2,100 + $2,650 + $1,375 = $6,125 (Sum of the Sold Total column)
Ending inventory: $4,830 (ending balance on inventory card)
Self-check: Cost of goods sold + ending inventory = cost of goods available for sale
$6,125   + $4,830   = $10,955

KEY TERMS

cost of goods available for sale, *303*
estimated net realizable value, *315*
first-in, first-out (FIFO), *309*
goods in transit, *303*
gross profit method, *322*

inventory turnover, *324*
inventory turnover ratio, *324*
last-in, first-out (LIFO), *310*
lower-of-cost-or-market rule, *317*
merchandise inventory card, *319*

retail method, *323*
specific identification method, *306*
weighted-average cost method, *308*

SELF-QUIZ

LO 1 1. Which of the following should *not* be included in ending inventory?
   a. Goods sold F.O.B. shipping point that are in transit.
   b. Goods sold F.O.B. destination point that are in transit.
   c. Goods purchased F.O.B. shipping point that are in transit.
   d. Goods purchased F.O.B. destination that have arrived on the loading dock.

LO 2 2. Which of the following is *not* a component of the cost of goods available for sale?
   a. Purchases discounts
   b. In-transit insurance costs
   c. Beginning inventory
   d. Transportation-out

LO 2 3. True or False? Cost of goods available for sale is equal to ending inventory plus cost of goods sold.

LO 3 4. Which of the following is *correct* if ending inventory is overstated in 19X1?
   a. Beginning inventory is understated in 19X2.
   b. Stockholders' equity is correctly stated at the end of 19X2.
   c. Gross profit is understated for 19X1.
   d. Cost of goods sold is overstated for 19X1.

LO 4 5. Which of the following is *not* an assumed cost flow method?
   a. Specific identification   c. FIFO
   b. Weighted-average cost   d. LIFO

LO 5 6. Supporters of the FIFO method argue that it produces the most realistic measurement of the _____ _____.

LO 5 7. Which of the following statements about inventory methods is *incorrect* if purchase prices are rising?

a. The LIFO method produces the lowest amount of ending inventory.
b. The FIFO method produces the lowest cost of goods sold.
c. The weighted-average cost method produces the highest gross profit.
d. The LIFO method produces the lowest gross profit.

LO 5 8. True or False? During periods of decreasing costs, the LIFO method minimizes the amount of income taxes paid.

LO 6 9. Reporting inventories at market value when the market value has fallen below cost is called the _____ - _____ - _____ - _____ - _____ rule.

LO 7 10. True or False? Businesses that use a perpetual inventory system record purchases of merchandise in Purchases.

LO 8 11. Which of the following is *not* a correct step in applying the retail method?
   a. Dividing purchases at cost by purchases at retail to determine the cost/retail ratio
   b. Subtracting net sales from goods available for sale at retail to determine ending inventory at retail
   c. Calculating goods available for sale at both cost and retail
   d. Multiplying ending inventory at retail by the cost/retail to determine ending inventory at cost

LO 8 12. Two methods used to estimate inventories are the _____ _____ method and the _____ method.

LO 9 13. True or False? The inventory turnover ratio is calculated by dividing cost of goods sold by average inventory.

SOLUTIONS TO SELF-QUIZ

1. a   2. d   3. True   4. b   5. a   6. ending inventory   7. c   8. False   9. lower-of-cost-or-market
10. False   11. a   12. gross profit, retail   13. True

QUESTIONS

Q7-1   What is the process for determining inventory quantities at the end of an accounting period?

Q7-2   What two allocations of cost of goods available for sale do businesses make at the end of the year?

Q7-3   Why is it important for the accountant to make sure each year's inventory is correctly stated even though most inventory errors automatically correct themselves within two years?

Q7-4 What are three inventory methods that assume a cost flow?

Q7-5 Which inventory flow method would result in net income being stated at the most current value and why?

Q7-6 Which inventory flow method would result in ending inventory on the balance sheet being stated at the most current value and why?

Q7-7 What factors should management consider when selecting an inventory method?

Q7-8 What are the two main reasons why the value of merchandise held for resale to customers may decrease below its assigned cost?

Q7-9 Why do businesses use perpetual inventory procedures?

Q7-10 Why do businesses need physical inventories if they use a perpetual inventory system?

Q7-11 What is the gross profit inventory method and when should it be used?

Q7-12 What is the retail inventory method and when should it be used?

Q7-13 What does the inventory turnover ratio measure?

EXERCISES

LO 2

E7-1 **Assign Inventory Costs** The cost of goods available for sale for Kringle's Christmas Store, Inc. is $189,000. The cost of the ending inventory is $23,000.

REQUIRED:

Determine cost of goods sold.

LO 2,3

E7-2 **Determining Ending Inventory** Determined by a physical count at the end of 19X5, the ending inventory for Catherine's Jewelry Store, Inc. is $139,200. The accounting records revealed that inventory on January 1, 19X5 equaled $105,600. The general ledger shows that Purchases and Transportation-In equal $992,500 and $9,100, respectively. In addition, Catherine's sold jewelry with a cost of $41,600 that was shipped F.O.B. shipping point, and it is still in transit. This shipment was not included in the physical count of ending inventory. Also not included in ending inventory was a $69,300 order in transit that Catherine's purchased from Diamond Wholesalers, F.O.B. destination.

REQUIRED:

Determine for 19X5 the cost of goods available for sale, ending inventory, and cost of goods sold for Catherine's Jewelry Store, Inc.

LO 3

E7-3 **Inventory Errors** A $14,500 overstatement of inventory occurred during a physical count and valuation of inventory at the end of 19X3. In addition, purchases during 19X4 were understated by $9,200.

REQUIRED:

Determine the effects of these errors on cost of goods sold, gross profit, net income, and ending stockholders' equity for 19X3 and 19X4.

LO 4,7

E7-4 **Calculating Ending Inventory and Cost of Goods Sold** The following information is given for the inventory transactions of Altman's Stereo Store, Inc. for the month of May:

	Purchases		Total
Date	*Units*	*Cost*	*Cost*
Beg. inventory	60	$3.50	$210.00
May 4	42	3.60	151.20

Date	Purchases Units	Cost	Total Cost
May 11	84	3.65	306.60
16	55	3.75	206.25
21	40	3.70	148.00
30	50	3.80	190.00

Altman's sold 235 units during May.

REQUIRED:

1. Assuming a periodic inventory system, determine ending inventory and cost of goods sold for Altman's if it uses the following: (1) FIFO, (2) LIFO, and (3) weighted-average cost.
2. Assuming a perpetual inventory system, determine ending inventory and cost of goods sold for Altman's if it uses the following: (1) FIFO, and (2) LIFO.

LO 6

E7-5 Damaged Inventory   Heavy rains caused some flooding at Harold's Haberdashery Corp. Unfortunately, 10 snakeskin Western hatbands that cost $160 each were damaged. Harold's estimates that it can sell each hatband for $120. In addition, Harold's pays a 5% commission on each hatband sold.

REQUIRED:

Determine the net realizable value of the inventory and record the journal entry to record the effects of the damage.

LO 6

E7-6 Lower of Cost or Market   Appliance Warehouse, Inc. is a discount store that sells major appliances. The inventory for Appliance Warehouse is given below:

Model	Units	Cost per Unit	Market Price per Unit
17	20	$ 98.50	$ 89.00
23	14	136.00	142.50
41	55	228.00	213.00
56	40	435.50	472.50
72	70	539.90	501.30
81	10	601.00	610.00

REQUIRED:

Determine the amount of the ending inventory by applying the lower-of-cost-or-market rule and record the journal entry (if any) to adjust the inventory.

LO 7

E7-7 Perpetual Inventory   The Scott Appliance Company began operations on June 1, 19X0. Following are some June transactions:

June 1 Purchased 50 television sets at a cost of $275 per set.
    8 Sold 5 television sets on credit at a price of $325 per set.
   15 Sold 9 television sets for cash at a price of $335 per set.

REQUIRED:

Journalize the transactions for the Scott Appliance Company if it uses a perpetual inventory system.

LO 8

E7-8 Retail Inventory Method   Jasmine's Sporting Goods uses the retail inventory method to estimate ending inventory. During the period, Jasmine's had sales of $130,000.

REQUIRED:

Estimate ending inventory at cost given the following information:

	Cost	Retail
Beginning inventory	$40,000	$ 68,000
Net purchases	98,000	142,000
Transportation-in	2,000	

LO 8   **E7-9   Gross Profit Method**   The accounting records of Stuart's Musicland, Inc. show the following amounts:

Sales	$250,000
Sales returns and allowances	4,000
Inventory (beginning)	45,000
Purchases	205,000
Purchases returns	4,500
Purchases discounts	5,500
Transportation-in	5,000

Stuart's percentage of gross profit to sales is 30%.

REQUIRED:

Using the gross profit method, determine the estimated ending inventory for Stuart's Musicland, Inc.

LO 9   **E7-10   Calculate the Inventory Turnover Ratio**   For 19X1, Singh's Carpet Warehouse, Inc. has cost of goods sold of $400,000 and average inventory of $80,000.

REQUIRED:

Calculate the 19X1 inventory turnover ratio for Singh's Carpet Warehouse, Inc.

PROBLEM SET A

LO 1,2,3   **P7-1A   Inventory Errors**   Maude's Tile Corporation's books were in a shambles; so, it hired Regina Bruce to put the books back in order. During her investigation, Regina found the following facts for the years 19X7 and 19X8:

(1) In-transit purchases of $5,000 shipped F.O.B. shipping point were not included in 19X7 ending inventory, and were recorded in 19X7 purchases.

(2) In-transit sales of merchandise that cost $8,000 shipped F.O.B. destination point were not included in 19X8 ending inventory.

(3) $3,500 of goods were included in the 19X8 ending inventory but were never recorded as a purchase.

(4) In-transit purchases of $6,000 shipped F.O.B. destination point were included in 19X8 ending inventory, but were not recorded as purchases until 19X9.

REQUIRED:

a. Identify which, if any, of the above errors will not be self-correcting in the subsequent year.

b. Determine the effect of each error on 19X7 and 19X8 ending inventory, cost of goods sold, gross profit, and stockholders' equity.

c. Determine the combined effects of all errors on 19X7 and 19X8 ending inventory, cost of goods sold, gross profit, and stockholders' equity.

LO 4

P7-2A **Calculating Inventory** The following inventory transactions of Ann's Dress Shop, Inc. took place in 19X4 and 19X5:

Date	*Purchases* Units	Cost	*Total* Cost
Beg. inventory	90	$62.00	$5,580.00
Mar. 7, X4	30	67.50	2,025.00
May 8, X4	40	71.25	2,850.00
Aug. 8, X4	20	69.50	1,390.00
Nov. 6, X4	50	67.75	3,387.50
Mar. 1, X5	25	71.50	1,787.50
Jun. 6, X5	30	70.00	2,100.00
Oct. 2, X5	60	72.50	4,350.00

Ann sold 180 dresses in 19X4 and 100 dresses in 19X5 as follows:

Date	Units	Sales Price
Apr. 1, X4	90	$100.00
Dec. 7, X4	90	100.00
July 4, X5	100	100.00

REQUIRED:

a. Calculate cost of goods sold and ending inventory for 19X4 and 19X5 if Ann's uses the FIFO inventory method and the periodic system.
b. Calculate cost of goods sold and ending inventory for 19X4 and 19X5 if Ann's uses the LIFO inventory method and the periodic system.
c. Calculate cost of goods sold and ending inventory for 19X4 and 19X5 if Ann's uses the weighted-average cost inventory method and the periodic system.
d. Calculate cost of goods sold and ending inventory for 19X4 and 19X5 if Ann's uses the FIFO inventory method and the perpetual inventory system.
e. Calculate cost of goods sold and ending inventory for 19X4 and 19X5 if Ann's uses the LIFO inventory method and the perpetual inventory system.

LO 6

P7-3A **Lower of Cost or Market** Dinettes Galore, Inc. is a discount store that sells tables and chairs. The inventory for Dinettes Galore is given below:

	Model	Units	Cost per Unit	Market Price per Unit
Tables	15	20	$ 97.50	$ 86.00
	21	14	106.00	111.50
	46	35	207.00	203.00
Chairs	113	60	37.50	41.50
	129	80	40.25	38.00
	144	48	68.00	66.50
	162	32	88.50	97.00

REQUIRED:

Determine the amount of the ending inventory by applying the lower-of-cost-or-market rule and record the journal entry (if any) to adjust the inventory.

LO 8

P7-4A **Retail Inventory** Gunther's Pet Supply Store, Inc. uses the retail inventory method to estimate ending inventory. Information relating to the estimation of inventory is as follows:

	Cost	Retail
Beginning inventory	$ 25,000	$ 48,000
Purchases	108,000	202,000
Transportation-in	5,000	
Purchases discounts	3,500	
Purchases returns and allowances	9,500	
Sales		190,400
Sales discounts		2,200
Sales returns and allowances		3,200

REQUIRED:

a. Calculate net purchases.
b. Calculate net sales.
c. Estimate ending inventory using the retail method.

LO 8

P7-5A **Gross Profit Method** The accounting records of Reid's Rare Books Corp. show the following amounts:

Sales	$153,600
Sales returns and allowances	1,100
Inventory (beginning)	65,500
Purchases	115,000
Purchases returns	2,700
Purchases discounts	1,300
Transportation-in	2,400

Reid's Rare Books Corp. has average annual sales of $140,000 and an average gross profit of $49,000.

REQUIRED:

a. Calculate the gross profit percentage.
b. Estimate the ending inventory.
c. Estimate the amount of the loss Reid's would incur if a fire destroyed everything except for $22,000 of rare books in ending inventory.

LO 9

P7-6A **Inventory Turnover** The accounting records of Classic Stores Corp. provides the following information for 19X1:

Beginning inventory	$120,000
Purchases	790,000
Transportation-in	45,000
Purchases discounts	15,000
Purchases returns and allowances	10,000
Ending inventory	130,000

REQUIRED:

a. Calculate the inventory turnover ratio for 19X1.
b. If asked by management, how would you interpret the ratio that you calculated?

PROBLEM SET B

LO 1,2,3

P7-1B **Inventory Errors** Bubba's Plumbing Supply Corporation's books were disorganized; so, it hired Shirley Williams to put the books back in order. During her investigation, Shirley found the following facts for the years 19X8 and 19X9:

(1) In-transit sales of merchandise that cost $6,000 shipped F.O.B. destination point were not included in 19X8 ending inventory.

(2) In-transit purchases of $2,700 shipped F.O.B. shipping point were not included in 19X8 ending inventory, but were included in 19X8 purchases.

(3) $2,100 of goods were included in the 19X9 ending inventory but were never recorded as a purchase.

(4) In-transit purchases of $4,500 shipped F.O.B. destination point were included in 19X9 ending inventory, and were included in purchases in the following year.

REQUIRED:

a. Identify which, if any, of the above errors will not be self-correcting in the subsequent year.

b. Determine the effect of each error on 19X8 and 19X9 ending inventory, cost of goods sold, gross profit, and stockholders' equity.

c. Determine the combined effects of all errors on 19X8 and 19X9 ending inventory, cost of goods sold, gross profit, and stockholders' equity.

LO 4,7

P7-2B   Calculating Inventory   The following information is for the inventory transactions of Executive Suits, Inc. for 19X2 and 19X3:

		Purchases	*Total*
Date	*Units*	*Cost*	*Cost*
Beg. inventory	40	$ 97.50	$3,900.00
Feb. 2, X2	25	102.00	2,550.00
Apr. 13, X2	30	103.25	3,097.50
Sept. 2, X2	15	106.50	1,597.50
Oct. 30, X2	50	105.40	5,270.00
Feb. 15, X3	20	107.00	2,140.00
Jul. 7, X3	35	103.50	3,622.50
Sept. 28, X3	70	108.00	7,560.00

Executive Suits had sales of 90 suits in 19X2 and 85 suits in 19X3 as follows:

Date	*Units*	*Sales Price*
Mar. 15, X2	45	$150.00
Nov. 25, X2	45	150.00
Jan. 15, X3	45	150.00
Sept. 30, X3	40	150.00

REQUIRED:

a. Calculate cost of goods sold and ending inventory for 19X2 and 19X3 if Executive Suits uses the FIFO inventory method and the periodic system.

b. Calculate cost of goods sold and ending inventory for 19X2 and 19X3 if Executive Suits uses the LIFO inventory method and the periodic system.

c. Calculate cost of goods sold and ending inventory for 19X2 and 19X3 if Executive Suits uses the weighted-average cost inventory method and the periodic system.

d. Calculate cost of goods sold and ending inventory for 19X2 and 19X3 if Executive Suits uses the FIFO inventory method and the perpetual inventory system.

e. Calculate cost of goods sold and ending inventory for 19X2 and 19X3 if Executive Suits uses the LIFO inventory method and the perpetual inventory system.

LO 6

P7-3B   Lower of Cost or Market   Modern Electronics Corp. is a discount store that sells stereos and televisions. The inventory for Modern Electronics Corp. is given below:

	Model	*Units*	*Cost per Unit*	*Market Price per Unit*
Stereos	18	46	$ 89.50	$ 98.00
	25	42	163.00	148.00
	48	60	197.90	187.50

	Model	Units	Cost per Unit	Market Price per Unit
Televisions	131	20	147.50	151.50
	149	32	159.25	138.00
	157	22	219.50	206.50
	173	36	288.50	298.00

REQUIRED:

Determine the carrying value of the ending inventory by applying the lower-of-cost-or-market rule and record the journal entry (if any) to adjust the inventory.

LO 8

P7-4B   **Retail Inventory**   Discount Lawn Furniture, Inc. uses the retail inventory method to estimate ending inventory. Information relating to the estimation of inventory is given below:

	Cost	Retail
Beginning inventory	$ 37,500	$ 72,000
Purchases	162,000	303,000
Transportation-in	7,500	
Purchases discounts	5,250	
Purchases returns	14,250	
Sales		235,600
Sales discounts		1,200
Sales returns		4,400

REQUIRED:

a. Calculate net purchases.
b. Calculate net sales.
c. Estimate ending inventory using the retail method.

LO 8

P7-5B   **Gross Profit Method**   The accounting records of Napa River Wines Corporation show the following amounts:

Sales	$102,400	Purchases returns	$1,800
Sales returns and allowances	700	Purchases discounts	950
Inventory (beginning)	43,600	Transportation-in	1,650
Purchases	79,000		

Napa River Wines Corporation has average annual sales of $104,000 and an average gross profit of $41,600.

REQUIRED:

a. Calculate the gross profit percentage.
b. Estimate the ending inventory.
c. Estimate the amount of the loss Napa River Wines Corporation would incur if a fire destroyed everything except for $13,000 of wine in ending inventory.

LO 9

P7-6B   **Inventory Turnover**   Construction Supply Corp. is attempting to borrow funds from North National Bank. The bank has asked for information about the company's inventory, specifically the inventory turnover ratio. The accounting records of Construction Supply Corp. provide the following information for 19X2:

Beginning inventory	$350,000
Purchases	815,000
Transportation-in	20,000
Purchases discounts	10,000
Purchases returns and allowances	5,000
Ending inventory	410,000

REQUIRED:

a. Calculate the inventory turnover ratio for 19X2.
b. Assuming that the inventory turnover ratio has been averaging about 4:1 in previous years, how would you interpret the ratio that you calculated for 19X2?

CRITICAL THINKING AND COMMUNICATING

C7-1 Special Chips is a newly formed company that specializes in semiconductors. George Castro, the major stockholder and president, is trying to determine which inventory method to select. Since the inventory items are not unique, George has determined that he should not select the specific identification method. George decided he needed help in making the decision; so, he hired Teresa Iglesias to advise him on this matter. George particularly wanted to know what inventory methods are available as well as the effects of the different methods on the company's financial statements.

REQUIRED:

a. Identify the different inventory methods and explain how they work.
b. Assume you are Teresa Iglesias and answer George's questions.

C7-2 The Falcon Corporation has always used the weighted-average cost inventory method. Justine Falcon, the president of the company, asked her bookkeeper to restate inventory under the FIFO and the LIFO methods for the last three years. The bookkeeper presented the following schedule of cost of goods sold under the two methods:

Date	FIFO	Weighted-Average Cost	LIFO
Dec. 31, X1	$13,300	$14,600	$16,200
Dec. 31, X2	13,500	15,200	16,400
Dec. 31, X3	14,210	16,740	18,320

Justine wondered why FIFO always had the lowest cost and LIFO always had the highest cost and the existing method always was in-between.

REQUIRED:

Explain in a written memo why the different methods result in this pattern of cost of goods sold.

C7-3   Refer to the financial statements of J.C. Penney Company reprinted in Appendix B at the end of this text. J.C. Penney is a major retail merchandising company; therefore, merchandise inventory is critical to the company's performance.

REQUIRED:

a. Comment on J.C. Penney's method of accounting for merchandise inventories. Hint: Examine the *Summary of Accounting Policies* located immediately after the statement of cash flows.
b. Calculate the inventory turnover ratios for J.C. Penney for 1993 and 1992 (ignore the additional costs included with cost of goods sold).
c. Comment on the direction of fluctuation in the turnover ratios.
d. Determine the cause of the fluctuation in the turnover ratio. Hint: Calculate the percentage changes in the numerator and the denominator of the turnover ratio.

Operating Assets

The last time Chris Rader had his hair trimmed, the hair stylist asked his advice about an investment. The stylist, Jeff Foreman, is considering purchasing his own business. Jeff currently works in Red's Barber Shop, Inc., and the owner has offered to sell the business to Jeff. Also, Jeff is acquainted with the owner of Nouveau Hair Styling Salon, Inc., who has offered to sell his business to Jeff. The two businesses have similar locations and have the same number of styling chairs, as well as other equipment used in the hair styling business. While the two businesses are similar in the services they provide, Red's is an old, established business and Nouveau is a relatively new business. Chris told Jeff that he needs to assess the relative profitability of the two businesses before making an investment decision.

This chapter presents a discussion of the accounting for the noncurrent, or long-term, productive assets a business uses in its operations. This chapter discusses the accounting for the acquisition, expiration of the service potential through use, and disposal of plant assets. We also discuss other noncurrent, productive assets classified as intangible assets and natural resources. Finally, you will learn one way to evaluate how well the business's assets are performing. Chris can use this approach to evaluate assets and to help Jeff make his decision.

1. Identify the categories of plant assets.
2. Determine which costs are included in the recorded cost of plant assets.
3. Explain the concept of depreciation.
4. Identify the factors used in calculating depreciation.
5. Calculate depreciation expense using several alternative depreciation methods.
6. Compare the alternative depreciation methods and explain the factors that affect management's choice of depreciation methods.
7. Calculate and interpret the return on total assets.
8. Calculate depreciation for partial periods, account for revisions of depreciation rates, and calculate depreciation for income taxes.
9. Analyze and record expenditures related to plant assets during their useful lives.
10. Explain how to record the disposal of plant assets by abandonment and by sale.
11. Identify the accounting issues related to the acquisition and amortization of intangible assets.
12. Apply GAAP to the acquisition and depletion of natural resources.
13. Record exchanges of plant assets for both dissimilar and similar assets (Appendix 8-A).

LO 1

Identify the categories of plant assets.

CATEGORIES OF PLANT ASSETS

Most businesses own tangible productive assets called **plant and equipment**; **property, plant, and equipment**; or **plant assets**. The primary characteristics of plant assets are:

1. They are useful for a period of time exceeding a year.
2. They are acquired to be used in the business's operations and not to be resold to customers.

These assets also are commonly called **fixed assets** or **capital assets**. Although the term *fixed assets* implies that assets are permanent, they do in fact wear out or become obsolete and need to be replaced.

What a business classifies as plant assets depends on the business's nature and its operations. For example, a retail store's plant assets include land and building, merchandise display equipment, office equipment, and delivery equipment; whereas, a manufacturing business's plant assets include land and buildings, manufacturing equipment, delivery trucks, and office equipment. The plant asset classification would also include stand-by equipment that the business uses only during peak time or in case of an emergency. Once the business ceases to use plant assets in its operations, it should cease classifying them as plant and equipment. Unless the business plans to sell these assets within one year or less, it classifies them as long-term investments. If the business plans to resell the plant assets to customers, then it should classify them as inventory. Plant assets are often classified into the following four categories:

1. Land. Businesses often own land as a building site.
2. Land improvements. Examples of land improvements include driveways, sidewalks, parking lots, fences, and lighting.
3. Buildings. The types of buildings that a business owns varies according to the type of business—retail store, factory building, storage building, etc.

4. Equipment. The types of equipment a business owns depends on the nature of its operations. Examples include cash registers, computers, conveyor belts, drill presses, delivery trucks, and office equipment such as desks, chairs, and file cabinets. Illustration 8-1 shows the asset classifications found in the 1992 annual survey of the financial statements of 600 large businesses.

ILLUSTRATION 8-1 Asset Captions in Financial Statements for 1992

Land Captions	
Land	367
Land and improvements	128
Land and buildings	37
Land and other identified assets	17
No caption with term land	21
Buildings Captions	
Buildings	253
Buildings and improvements	210
Buildings and land or equipment	74
Buildings and other identified assets	5
No caption with term buildings	25
Other Asset Captions	
Machinery and/or equipment	454
Machinery and/or equipment with other assets	90
Construction in progress	254
Leasehold improvements	103
Automobiles, marine equipment, etc.	61
Leased assets	71
Furniture, fixtures, etc.	48
Assets leased to others	14

Source: *Accounting Trends and Techniques* (Jersey City, New Jersey: AICPA, 1993).

For many businesses, plant assets are a major portion of the assets reported in their balance sheets. Therefore, not only is the accounting for plant assets important, but management must also safeguard and maintain plant assets. Also, expanding investment in plant assets and replacing existing plant assets as needed are critical management responsibilities.

LO 2

Determine which costs are included in the recorded cost of plant assets.

DETERMINING COSTS OF PLANT ASSETS

Although a business may occasionally self-construct an asset such as a building or a specialized machine, businesses generally acquire plant assets by purchasing them. Regardless of how businesses acquire plant assets, accountants should record them according to the cost principle, which applies to the acquisition of *used* assets as well as to *new* assets. The total recorded cost of a plant asset includes all necessary costs a business incurs to acquire the asset, to put the asset in the proper condition for use, to prepare the site for the asset, and to move the asset to the location of its intended use. Necessary acquisition costs include such expenditures as the purchase price, transportation costs, and insurance while the asset is in transit. The purchase price used in recording the acquisition cost should be the cash outlay, which is the purchase price less any discounts the supplier offered. A business may not always use cash to purchase assets; rather, it may exchange other assets for the purchased asset. In these cases, we determine the purchase price by the fair value of the asset given or the asset received, whichever is more clearly evident. (We discuss the accounting for exchanges of noncash assets in Appendix 8-A to this chapter.)

Land

Land purchases commonly involve costs in addition to the purchase price. Such costs include real estate sales commissions, legal fees, title transfer and registration fees, and survey costs. Accountants should record these costs as part of the cost of the land. If a business acquires land for the site of a new building, all costs the business incurs in preparing the land for construction should also be debited to Land. When a building site already has an existing building, we include the cost of removing the old building, less the amount received as salvage for the materials from the old building, in the cost of the land. Also, we include the cost of clearing, draining, and grading land in the cost of the land. The rationale for including these costs is that they are necessary costs of preparing the land for its intended use—the site of a new building.

For example, assume that on January 4, 19X1, Paul's Print Shop, Inc. incurs the following costs in purchasing land as the site of a new building:

Purchase price		$250,000
Real estate commissions		5,000
Legal and title fees		1,000
Removal of old building	$20,000	
Less: Salvage	7,500	12,500
Clearing and grading		8,000
		$276,500

The purchase of the land and the costs of site preparation are recorded in Land with the following summary entry:

Jan. 4	Land	276,500	
	Cash		276,500
	To record the purchase of land and the cost of site preparation.		

We record land and building costs in separate accounts because land does not deteriorate or become obsolete and, therefore, is not subject to depreciation. (We discuss depreciation later in this chapter.) A building deteriorates and becomes obsolete and, therefore, is subject to depreciation. Thus, we record the cost of a building in a separate account.

Land Improvements

Certain improvements to land—driveways, sidewalks, parking lots, fences, and lighting—have a limited life and are subject to depreciation. We record the cost of these land improvements in Land Improvements rather than in Land so that we may calculate depreciation without confusion. To illustrate the recording of land improvements, assume Paul's Print Shop, Inc. constructs a new parking lot at a cost of $10,000 beside its office building. On April 27, 19X1, Paul's pays the construction company for the parking lot with a $2,000 cash down payment and an $8,000 interest-bearing note payable. Paul's entry to record the cost of the new parking lot is as follows:

Apr. 27	Land Improvements	10,000	
	Cash		2,000
	Notes Payable		8,000
	To record the cost of a new parking lot.		

Buildings

A business may acquire a building either by purchasing an existing structure or by constructing a new building. When a business purchases a building, the cost of the building includes the purchase price and other costs to prepare the building for occupancy such as renovation and repair costs. Repair costs a business incurs to maintain the building after it is put into use, however, are expenses because they are not necessary costs to acquire the building and get it ready for use.

When a business constructs its own building, the cost of the building should include all construction costs. Construction costs include architectural fees, building permits, legal fees, excavation, materials, labor, a portion of administration costs, and insurance during the period of construction—and the interest incurred on loans used to finance the construction of the building. After the building is put into use, such costs as insurance, interest, and repairs and maintenance are expenses, not additional costs of the building itself.

Assume Paul's Print Shop incurs the following costs in constructing a building that it will use in its operations:

Architectural fees	$ 60,000
Building permits and legal fees	5,000
Excavation	75,000
Materials	400,000
Labor	350,000
Administration costs	100,000
Insurance during construction	8,000
Interest on construction loans	96,000
Total cost	$1,094,000

The total cost of the building is $1,094,000, which we debit to Buildings with the following *summary* entry:

(Date)	Buildings	1,094,000	
	Cash, Accounts Payable, etc.		1,094,000
	To record the cost of self-constructed building.		

Equipment

The cost of equipment includes the net purchase price (purchase price less any discounts), freight, insurance during transit, installation, and testing. Assume that on October 31, 19X1, Paul's Print Shop purchases a new binding machine. The price of the machine is $10,000, and the terms are 2/10, n/30; freight cost incurred for shipping the machine is $125; insurance during transit is $25; and installation and testing of the machine is $275. We calculate the cost of the machine and debit it to Equipment as follows:

Purchase price	$10,000	
Less: 2% cash discount	200	
Net purchase price		$ 9,800
Freight		125
Insurance during transit		25
Installation and testing		275
Total cost		$10,225

Oct. 31	Equipment	10,225	
	Accounts Payable		10,225
	To record purchase of binding machine.		

If the equipment is damaged accidentally while in transit or when it is being installed, the cost of repairing the equipment is an expense, not a cost of the equipment, because the repairs are not necessary costs of acquiring the asset.

Group Purchases

Businesses commonly purchase plant assets as a group rather than individually. For example, in one transaction a business purchases a building and the land on which it is located. When a business purchases these assets as a group, we record the various assets separately. As previously discussed, the land is not subject to depreciation. However, the other assets purchased, such as building and equipment, are subject to different rates of depreciation. In recording group purchases, we allocate the purchase price to the individual assets in the group on the basis of their relative fair values. We determine the fair values of the assets by referring to any available price lists or by appraisal. The relative fair value assigned to an asset included in the group of assets purchased is the fair value of that asset as a percent of the total fair value of the group of assets:

Fair Value of Asset

Total Fair Value of Group of Assets

On November 24, 19X1, Paul's Print Shop purchases an existing printing operation that is located in a nearby city. The assets purchased in the transaction include land, building, and equipment. Paul's purchases the printing operation for $90,000 cash. An appraisal of the assets indicates the following fair values: land $25,000, building $60,000, and equipment $15,000—for a total of $100,000. Paul's is able to purchase the group of assets at less than their individual fair values because the former owner was anxious to sell. Based on this information, we assign the $90,000 group purchase price to the individual assets as follows:

	Proportion of Total Fair Value		Allocated Cost
Land	$ 25,000/$100,000	x $90,000	$22,500
Building	60,000/100,000	x 90,000	54,000
Equipment	15,000/100,000	x 90,000	13,500
Total	$ 100,000/$100,000	x $90,000	$90,000

The journal entry below shows how to record the group purchase:

Nov. 24	Land	22,500	
	Buildings	54,000	
	Equipment	13,500	
	Cash		90,000
	To record the group purchase of property, plant, and equipment.		

LO 3
Explain the concept of depreciation.

DEPRECIATION ACCOUNTING

A business purchases plant assets because they can provide useful services to its operations. In fact, an asset can be thought of as a bundle of benefits to be provided to a business as it uses the asset. For example, a delivery truck provides transportation services, and a computer provides computational and word processing services. Plant assets, however, generally have limited useful lives. In other words, except for land, these assets can only provide a limited amount of services. Over the entire useful life of the asset, the *cost of the services* it provides is the cost of the asset less the value received when the asset is sold or traded in on a new asset. **Depreciation** is the process of allocating the cost of the assets to the periods benefited from the services they provide.

In accordance with the matching principle, recording depreciation expense matches the cost of the services provided by plant assets with the related revenues in determining net income. The accounting profession describes depreciation as follows:

> The cost of a productive facility is one of the costs of the services it renders during its useful economic life. Generally accepted accounting principles require that this cost be spread over the expected useful life of the facility in such a way as to allocate it as equitably as possible to the periods during which services are obtained from the use of the facility. This procedure is known as depreciation accounting, a system of accounting which aims to distribute the cost or other basic value of tangible capital assets, less salvage (if any), over the estimated useful life of the unit ... in a systematic and rational manner. It is a process of allocation, not valuation.[1]

The profession's description includes an important distinction about depreciation in accounting—depreciation is a cost allocation process, not a valuation process. In particular, depreciation does *not* attempt to measure the asset's market value. The **current value** is the amount that the asset could be sold for at its current age and in its current condition. We do *not* determine the amount of depreciation expense by measuring the change in the asset's market value that occurs in the accounting period. Businesses acquire plant assets to be used in providing goods and services, not for resale to customers. Therefore, the accounting profession has decided that information about fluctuations in market values of these assets is not as important as information about the original cost sacrificed to use the asset.

---

[1] *Financial Accounting Standards: Original Pronouncements as of July 1, 1992*, ARB No. 43, (Norwalk, Conn.: FASB, 1993), Chap. 9, Sec. C, par. 5.

Recording Depreciation

We record depreciation at the end of each accounting period by a debit to Depreciation Expense and a credit to Accumulated Depreciation. For example, assume that on January 2, 19X1, Paul's Print Shop, Inc. purchases a new computerized printing machine at a cost of $40,000; and depreciation for 19X1 is determined to be $5,000. Paul's entries to record the purchase and the depreciation are as follows:

Jan. 1	Equipment	40,000	
	Cash		40,000
	To record purchase of printing machine.		
Dec. 31	Depreciation Expense—Equipment	5,000	
	Accumulated Depreciation—Equipment		5,000
	To record depreciation for the year.		

Businesses commonly have separate depreciation expense and accumulated depreciation accounts for groups of assets that serve similar functions or common uses. For example, several groupings of assets by function would include buildings, machinery, and equipment, which are usually depreciated at different rates. Groupings of assets by use could include store equipment, factory equipment, and office equipment. These groupings by use allow depreciation expense to be allocated among various organizational components such as manufacturing, sales, and administration.

Depreciation in the Financial Statements

In its December 31, 19X1, balance sheet, Paul's Print Shop, Inc. displays the printing equipment as follows:

| Equipment | $40,000 | |
| Less: Accumulated depreciation | 5,000 | $35,000 |

We call the $35,000 net amount the **carrying amount** or **net book value** of the asset, and it represents the undepreciated cost of the asset as of the balance sheet date. **Accumulated Depreciation** is a contra-asset account. Some accountants refer to Accumulated Depreciation as a **valuation account**. This usage does not mean that Accumulated Depreciation adjusts the asset to its market value. Rather, we adjust the asset to its undepreciated cost, which is the carrying amount or net book value. In this text, we use the term carrying amount instead of net book value.

LO 4
Identify the factors used in calculating depreciation.

FACTORS USED IN CALCULATING DEPRECIATION

In addition to the asset's recorded cost, accountants must know its estimated residual value and estimated useful life.

Estimated Residual Value

The **estimated residual value** is either the estimated net proceeds if the asset is sold or the trade-in value if the asset is traded in on a replacement asset. A business estimates, in the period it acquires the asset, the amounts to be received at the date of disposal. We base the estimate of the residual value generally on the company's experience and on other sources of information such as prices of used assets. If a business incurs costs in disposing of the asset, the residual value is the estimated proceeds less the estimated costs of disposing of the asset. We commonly refer to the estimated residual value as the **estimated salvage value**.

Accountants call the cost of the asset minus the estimated residual value the **depreciable cost**. The depreciable cost of an asset is the total amount subject to depreciation and is the total amount allocated to depreciation expense over the asset's useful life.

Estimated Useful Life

An asset's **estimated useful life** is the estimated period of time that the business can *use* the asset in the business. As a business uses depreciable assets in its operations, they wear out. Eventually, the assets deteriorate to the point that the business can no longer use them; and the business has to replace the assets. For example, as a business uses a delivery truck, it begins to wear out. Eventually, the truck will be completely worn out; and the business will have to replace the old truck with a new truck.

Plant assets may have limited lives due to obsolescence or inadequacy as well as to physical wear. As society makes technological advances, new assets become available and are superior to those the business currently uses. These new assets may provide the same services as the old assets, but at a lower cost, or they may provide higher quality services. Some new assets may even provide higher quality services at a lower cost. For example, the rapid technological advances made in computers quickly rendered existing computers obsolete because the newer computers can process data faster and at a lower cost than the older models. Because of obsolescence, an asset's useful life may be less than its potential physical life. For example, a computer may have a potential physical life of ten years, but because of obsolescence, a business may replace its computers every five years. Consequently, the business should allocate the cost of its computers over five years.

Assets may become inadequate for the needs of a business as it grows or as the nature of its operations changes. For example, a rapidly growing business may become too large for its physical facilities and be forced to relocate its operations to larger facilities.

Useful life may be measured in time, in total units of service (such as machine hours), or in output (number of stampings or castings produced). In the next section on depreciation methods, we illustrate some of the alternative measures of useful life.

LO 5

Calculate depreciation expense using several alternative depreciation methods.

DEPRECIATION METHODS

Within GAAP, many alternative methods for allocating assets' depreciable costs to accounting periods are available. The following discussion illustrates four of the most commonly used methods: straight-line, units-of-production, sum-of-the-years'-digits, and double-declining-balance. Illustration 8-2 shows the use of the various depreciation methods in 1992 by 600 large businesses.

ILLUSTRATION 8-2 Number of Companies Using Various Depreciation Methods*

Straight-line	564
Declining-balance	26
Sum-of-the-years'-digits	12
Accelerated method—not specified	62
Units-of-production	47
Other	5

*The total exceeds 600 because some companies use different depreciation methods for different categories of assets.

Source: *Accounting Trends and Techniques* (Jersey City, New Jersey: AICPA, 1993).

Straight-Line Method

Virtually all types of businesses use the straight-line method, the most popular depreciation method in practice. The **straight-line method** of depreciation allocates an equal amount of depreciation expense to each period in the asset's estimated useful life. Accountants calculate the depreciation expense for each period by dividing the depreciable cost of the asset (cost less estimated residual value) by the number of periods in the asset's estimated useful life:

$$\text{Depreciation Expense Per Year} = \frac{\text{Depreciable Cost}}{\text{Estimated Useful Life (in years)}}$$

An equivalent method for computing straight-line depreciation is:

$$\text{Depreciable Expense Per Year} = \text{Depreciable Cost} \times \text{Straight-Line Rate}$$

The **straight-line rate** is defined as follows:

$$\text{Straight-Line Rate} = \frac{100\%}{\text{Estimated Useful Life}}$$

For example, assume Paul's Print Shop, Inc. purchases a new packaging machine at a cost of $12,000. The machine has an estimated useful life of 4 years, and the residual value is $2,000. The straight-line rate for a useful life of 4 years is 25% (100% ÷ 4). Depreciable cost is $10,000 ($12,000 - $2,000). Depreciation expense per year for the machine using the straight-line method is calculated as follows:

$$\text{Depreciation Expense Per Year} = \frac{\$10,000}{4} = \$2,500$$

Or, equivalently,

$$\text{Depreciation Expense Per Year} = \$10,000 \times 25\% = \$2,500$$

A **depreciation schedule** that shows the allocation of depreciation expense over the machine's useful life is shown in Illustration 8-3. From the depreciation schedule, you can observe four characteristics of the straight-line depreciation method. First, as previously discussed, depreciation expense is an equal amount each period. Second, Accumulated Depreciation increases by an equal amount each time period. Third, the asset's carrying amount decreases by an equal amount each time period. Fourth, the carrying amount at the end of

ILLUSTRATION 8-3 Depreciation Schedule for Straight-Line Method

Period	Depreciable Cost	Depreciation Rate	Depreciation Expense	Accumulated Depreciation	Carrying Amount
At purchase	$10,000	——	——	——	$12,000
End of Year 1	10,000	25%	$2,500	$ 2,500	9,500
End of Year 2	10,000	25%	2,500	5,000	7,000
End of Year 3	10,000	25%	2,500	7,500	4,500
End of Year 4	10,000	25%	2,500	10,000	2,000

the machine's expected useful life is equal to the residual value expected at the time it was acquired.

Units-Of-Production Method

The **units-of-production method** allocates depreciation to time periods based on the asset's output. While the straight-line method allocates an equal amount of depreciation to each time period, the units-of-production method allocates an equal amount of depreciation to each unit the asset produces. We calculate the amount of depreciation allocated to each unit of production by dividing the asset's depreciable cost by the estimated lifetime units of production. The equation for calculating depreciation for each unit of output is:

$$\text{Depreciation Expense Per Unit of Production} = \frac{\text{Depreciable Cost}}{\text{Estimated Total Units of Production}}$$

We calculate the depreciation expense for an accounting period by multiplying the units of production during the accounting period by the depreciation expense per unit of production, as follows:

$$\text{Depreciation Expense} = \frac{\text{Units of Production}}{\text{During the Period}} \times \frac{\text{Depreciation Expense}}{\text{Per Unit of Production}}$$

If Paul's Print Shop decides to use the units-of-production method to depreciate the new packaging machine, management must estimate how many packages the machine can wrap during its useful life. Management bases the estimate of total production on the manufacturer's specifications and any previous experience the business has had with similar machines. Based on the information available, management estimates that the machine can wrap 40,000 packages during its useful life. Using the units-of-production method, the calculation of depreciation expense per unit of output is as follows:

$$\text{Depreciation Expense Per Unit of Production} = \frac{\$10,000}{40,000 \text{ units}} = \$.25 \text{ per unit}$$

If the machine's actual production is 8,000 packages during Year 1, depreciation expense for Year 1 is:

$$\text{Depreciation Expense for Year 1} = 8,000 \text{ units} \times \$.25 \text{ per unit} = \$2,000$$

Assuming Paul's produces 10,000 units in Year 2, 14,000 units in Year 3, and 8,000 units in Year 4, the depreciation schedule for the machine using the units-of-production method is shown in Illustration 8-4. From the depreciation schedule, observe that depreciation expense varies directly in relation to the

ILLUSTRATION 8-4 Depreciation Schedule for Units-of-Production Method

Period	Units of Production	Depreciation per Unit	Depreciation Expense	Accumulated Depreciation	Carrying Amount
At purchase	—	—	—	—	$12,000
End of Year 1	$ 8,000	$0.25	$2,000	$ 2,000	10,000
End of Year 2	10,000	0.25	2,500	4,500	7,500
End of Year 3	14,000	0.25	3,500	8,000	4,000
End of Year 4	8,000	0.25	2,000	10,000	2,000

asset's pattern of production. Likewise, accumulated depreciation *increases* directly in relation to the pattern of production. Finally, the carrying amount *decreases* directly in relation to the pattern of production and, in the end, equals the original estimate of residual value.

Accelerated Depreciation Methods

A group of depreciation methods, called **accelerated depreciation methods**, results in depreciation expense that is higher in the earlier years but is lower during the later years of the asset's useful life. Accelerated depreciation methods are based on the assumption that more of an asset's benefits are consumed during the earlier years than they are in the later years of its useful life. As assets age, they require more maintenance and are out of service more frequently. The following section discusses two commonly used accelerated depreciation methods: the sum-of-the-years'-digits method and the double-declining-balance method.

Sum-of-the-Years'-Digits. The **sum-of-the-years'-digits (SYD) method** allocates depreciation by multiplying the asset's depreciable cost by a fraction for each year. The fraction is sometimes called the *SYD fraction*. The numerator of the fraction for each year is the number of periods in the asset's estimated remaining useful life as of the *beginning* of the period. The denominator of the fraction is the sum of the digits in the asset's estimated useful life. The calculation, expressed in the form of an equation, is as follows:

$$\text{Depreciation Expense} = \text{Depreciable Cost} \times \frac{\textbf{Periods Remaining in Useful Life}}{\textbf{Sum of the Years' Digits}}$$

In the example of the new packaging machine Paul's Print Shop purchased, the estimated useful life is 4 years and the sum of the years' digits is:[2]

$$1 + 2 + 3 + 4 = 10$$

Depreciation for the first year is calculated as follows:

$$\$10,000 \times 4/10 = \$4,000$$

---

[2]For assets that have relatively long estimated useful lives, directly summing the years may be burdensome. The sum of the years may be calculated using the following formula:

$$\text{Sum} = N(N+1) \div 2$$

In the formula, N is equal to the asset's estimated useful life. For example, the sum of the years for a building that has an estimated useful life of 40 years is:

$$40(40 + 1) \div 2 = 820$$

The numerator in the fraction is 4 because the asset's estimated useful life remaining at the beginning of Year 1 is 4 years. Depreciation expense for Year 2 is:

$$\$10,000 \times 3/10 = \$3,000$$

At the beginning of Year 2, the asset's remaining estimated useful life 3 years; therefore, the fraction used is 3/10.

A depreciation schedule for the machine using the sum-of-the-years'-digits method is shown in Illustration 8-5. The depreciation schedule illustrates that the sum-of-the-years'-digits method is an accelerated depreciation method. Depreciation expense is largest in the first year and decreases in each subsequent year. Also, the amounts of the increases in accumulated depreciation and the amounts of the decreases in the asset's carrying amount both decrease in each subsequent period.

ILLUSTRATION 8-5 Depreciation Schedule for the Sum-of-the-Years'-Digits Method

Period	Depreciable Cost	SYD Fraction	Depreciation Expense	Accumulated Depreciation	Carrying Amount
At purchase	$10,000	———	———	———	$12,000
End of Year 1	10,000	4/10	$4,000	$ 4,000	8,000
End of Year 2	10,000	3/10	3,000	7,000	5,000
End of Year 3	10,000	2/10	2,000	9,000	3,000
End of Year 4	10,000	1/10	1,000	10,000	2,000

Double-Declining-Balance. Accountants calculate depreciation expense using the declining-balance method by *multiplying the asset's carrying amount by some percentage of the straight-line depreciation rate.* Common percentages of the straight-line rate used are: 125%, 150%, 175%, and 200%. The choice of which percentage to use depends on how rapidly management desires to depreciate the asset. When it chooses 200% of the straight-line rate, management uses the method called **double-declining-balance**. The term *declining-balance* originates from the fact that the asset's carrying amount, or "balance," declines each period as we record additional depreciation expense. We apply the depreciation rate to this declining balance to calculate each successive period's depreciation expense.

Continuing with the example of the new packaging machine Paul's Print Shop purchased, assume Paul's uses the double-declining-balance method to calculate depreciation. The first step is to determine the straight-line depreciation rate. We determine the straight-line rate by dividing 100% by the asset's estimated useful life (in years). The machine in the example has an estimated useful life of 4 years; therefore, the straight-line rate is 100% ÷ 4 = 25%. To calculate depreciation for the first year, multiply the asset's carrying amount by 200% times the straight-line rate, or 2 x 25% = 50%. For the first year, the carrying amount is the cost of the asset since accumulated depreciation is zero. Notice that, of the depreciation methods presented, *only the double-declining-balance method starts with the asset's cost* rather than with the depreciable cost. Depreciation expense for Year 1 is:

$$\$12,000 \times 50\% = \$6,000$$

We determine depreciation for the second year by multiplying the asset's *carrying amount* at the beginning of the period by 50%. The carrying amount of the machine at the beginning of Year 2 is $6,000:

Machine (at cost)	$12,000
Less: Accumulated depreciation	6,000
Carrying amount (on balance sheet)	$ 6,000

We base depreciation for Year 2 on the carrying amount at the end of Year 1.

$$\$6,000 \times 50\% = \$3,000$$

Illustration 8-6 presents a depreciation schedule for the machine using the double-declining-balance method.

ILLUSTRATION 8-6 Depreciation Schedule for the Double-Declining-Balance Method

Period	Depreciable Cost	Depreciation Rate	Depreciation Expense	Accumulated Depreciation	Carrying Amount
At purchase	——	——	——	——	$12,000
End of Year 1	$12,000	50%	$6,000	$ 6,000	6,000
End of Year 2	6,000	50%	3,000	9,000	3,000
End of Year 3	3,000	50%	1,000*	10,000	2,000
End of Year 4	2,000	50%	0**	10,000	2,000

*Adjusted to $1,000 so that carrying amount is not less than residual value.
**No depreciation is recorded so that carrying amount is not less than residual value.

Notice in the depreciation schedule that the depreciation expense for Year 3 is only $1,000, even though 50% x $3,000 = $1,500. Depreciation in Year 3 is limited to $1,000 because the machine has an estimated residual value of $2,000. *In recording depreciation, as a rule, we do not reduce an asset's carrying amount below its estimated residual value.* Therefore, the amount of depreciation that we record in Year 3 is $1,000; and we record no depreciation in Year 4.

The depreciation schedule illustrates that the double-declining-balance method is an accelerated depreciation method. Similar to the sum-of-the-years'-digits method, depreciation expense is largest in the first year and decreases in each subsequent year. Also, the amounts of the increases in accumulated depreciation and the amounts of the decreases in the asset's carrying amount decrease in each subsequent period.

LO 6

Compare the alternative depreciation methods and explain the factors that affect management's choice of depreciation methods.

COMPARISON OF DEPRECIATION METHODS

Presented in Illustration 8-7 is a comparison of the amounts of depreciation expense for the packaging machine Paul's Print Shop purchased for each year under the four depreciation methods. The schedule shows that the amount of depreciation varies significantly among the depreciation methods. Each of the methods, however, is acceptable under GAAP.

Choosing a Depreciation Method

When management chooses a depreciation method to use for an asset, it commonly considers several factors. One important factor is whether the asset's use-

ILLUSTRATION 8-7 Depreciation Expense Under Different Methods

Year	Straight-Line	Units-of-Production	Sum-of-the Years'-Digits	Double-Declining-Balance
1	$ 2,500	$ 2,000	$ 4,000	$ 6,000
2	2,500	2,500	3,000	3,000
3	2,500	3,500	2,000	1,000
4	2,500	2,000	1,000	—
	$10,000	$10,000	$10,000	$10,000

fulness expires as a result of the amount of usage or of the passage of time. The units-of-production method results in the allocation of depreciation to periods based on the pattern of usage, and this method is particularly appropriate when the usage of the asset varies significantly from period to period.

The straight-line and accelerated depreciation methods assume that the asset's usefulness expires with the passage of time. The straight-line method assumes that an equal amount of the asset's benefits are used up each period. The accelerated methods, however, assume that more benefits expire in the earlier periods of the asset's useful life than they do in the later periods. For example, a machine may be more efficient when it is relatively new than when it becomes older. Therefore, accelerated depreciation results in a better matching of revenues and expenses since the machine produces more service per unit of time when it is new than after it becomes older and less efficient.

Advocates of accelerated depreciation methods also argue that these methods result in more accurate total expense for using the asset. As assets become older, they often require more maintenance and repairs. Since accelerated depreciation expense decreases in these later years, the sum of depreciation, maintenance, and repairs is relatively constant for each period of the asset's useful life.

Management is responsible for selecting the depreciation methods for assets. Managers may rely upon the advice of accountants in making this selection; but in any event, the ultimate responsibility rests with management. In addition to the causes of the expiration of the asset's usefulness, management may also consider the relative amounts of depreciation per year when choosing a method. As shown in Illustration 8-7, the selection among the alternative depreciation methods can significantly affect net income through different patterns of depreciation expense.

Disclosing Depreciation Methods in Financial Statements

In selecting depreciation methods, management should depreciate similar assets using the same method. When management adopts a method for a category of assets, it should use the method consistently to enhance the comparability of the financial statements from period to period. Also, because of the significance of depreciation, the financial statements should disclose the methods of depreciation used for the plant assets presented in the balance sheet.

LO 7
Calculate and interpret the return on total assets.

RETURN ON TOTAL ASSETS

At the beginning of this chapter, we introduced you to the investment decision that Jeff Foreman, the hair stylist, is considering. The owners of both Red's

Barber Shop, Inc. and Nouveau Hair Styling Salon, Inc. have offered Jeff the opportunity to purchase their businesses. Jeff wants to invest in the business that is the more profitable. He has asked Chris Rader to help him assess their profitability.

Jeff asked each current owner to provide him with the most recent financial statements. Jeff has shown these statements to Chris and has asked him what the statements show about the relative profitability of the two businesses. Illustration 8-8 shows the two sets of financial statements.

ILLUSTRATION 8-8 Financial Statements for Red's and Nouveau

Red's Barber Shop, Inc. Income Statement For the Year Ended December 31, 19X3		
Revenue		$86,000
Operating expenses:		
Wages and salaries	$58,000	
Taxes and fees	1,090	
Utilities	1,600	
Interest	240	
Depreciation	1,500	
Repairs	2,900	65,330
Net Income		$20,670

Nouveau Hair Styling Salon, Inc. Income Statement For the Year Ended December 31, 19X3		
Revenue		$89,000
Operating expenses:		
Wages and salaries	$64,000	
Taxes and fees	1,200	
Utilities	1,400	
Interest	4,000	
Repairs	3,000	73,600
Net income		$15,400

Red's Barber Shop, Inc. Balance Sheet December 31, 19X3		
Assets		
Cash		$ 500
Supplies		350
Equipment	$ 2,600	
Less: Accum. deprec.	2,100	500
Land		10,000
Buildings	$30,000	
Less: Accum. deprec.	15,000	15,000
Total assets		$26,350
Liabilities and Stockholders' Equity		
Accounts payable		$ 175
Notes payable		6,000
Capital stock		20,175
Total liabilities and stockholders' equity		$26,350

Nouveau Hair Styling Salon, Inc. Balance Sheet December 31, 19X3		
Assets		
Cash		$ 600
Supplies		375
Equipment	$3,700	
Less: Accum. deprec.	700	3,000
Land		12,000
Buildings	$70,000	
Less: Accum. deprec.	2,300	67,700
Total assets		$83,675
Liabilities and Stockholders' Equity		
Accounts payable		$ 200
Notes payable		75,000
Capital stock		5,000
Retained earnings		3,475
Total liabilities and stockholders' equity		$83,675

Calculating Return on Total Assets

We calculate the return on total assets using the following formula:

$$\textbf{Return on Total Assets} = \frac{\textbf{Net Income + Interest Expense}}{\textbf{Total Assets}}$$

The numerator of the ratio is income before interest expense. We add interest expense to net income because interest is a payment to creditors for the business's use of money to acquire assets. We want to calculate the return on assets without regard to how the business financed the acquisition of its assets.

The calculations of the return on total assets for Red's and Nouveau are as follows:

$$\text{Red's:} \quad \frac{\$20,670 + \$240}{\$26,350} = 79\%$$

$$\text{Nouveau:} \quad \frac{\$15,400 + \$4,000}{\$83,675} = 23\%$$

Interpreting Return on Total Assets

In previous chapters, we discussed ratios used to assess the business's profitability such as return on equity. The return on total assets is another ratio that can be used to assess profitability. This ratio reflects the business's ability to utilize its assets to generate net income. By just looking at the two ratios, it appears that Red's is much more profitable than Nouveau. When using ratio analysis, however, you must be careful to assess whether the ratios may be misleading.

When we study the balance sheets of the two businesses, it becomes apparent that Red's has assets that are much older than Nouveau's assets. We see this by comparing the accumulated depreciation amounts to the assets' costs. For example, Red's building is 50% ($15,000 ÷ $30,000) depreciated as compared to Nouveau's building, which is 3% ($2,300 ÷ $70,000) depreciated. There are two implications for the ratios of return on total assets of this circumstance:

1. The carrying amounts of assets included in the measurement of total assets will be much smaller for older assets than for newer assets because accumulated depreciation is greater relative to the cost of the older assets.
2. Because of inflation, the cost of newer assets will be higher than the cost of assets acquired in earlier years.

Both of these implications result in the denominator being larger (and the ratio being smaller) for the business with newer assets. Also, the business with newer assets will record more depreciation expense than the business with older assets. This leads to lower net income and a smaller return on total assets for the business with the newer assets.

How should the ratios for Red's and Nouveau affect Jeff's decision? Obviously, Red's appears to be more profitable. However, Jeff should keep in mind that he may have to replace the older assets of Red's in the near future and the apparent profitability of Red's may be only a temporary situation. Chris probably should advise Jeff to investigate the replacement cost of Red's assets and assess what the affect of new assets would be on the relative profitability of the two businesses.

LO 8

Calculate depreciation for partial periods, account for revisions of depreciation rates, and calculate depreciation for income taxes.

SPECIAL PROBLEMS IN DEPRECIATION ACCOUNTING

When certain events occur, the accountant must modify the normal depreciation accounting procedures. These special problems are:

1. Calculating depreciation when assets are purchased at times other than the beginning of the fiscal year
2. Revising depreciation rates because of new information
3. Calculating depreciation for income taxes

Depreciation for Partial Years

A business commonly purchases assets during a fiscal year so it can allocate only a partial year's depreciation to the first and last fiscal year within the asset's estimated useful life.

Partial Years for Straight-Line Method. For example, assume that on April 1, 19X1, Paul's Print Shop purchases a machine for $5,600. The machine has an estimated useful life of 5 years and an estimated residual value of $600. Paul's uses the straight-line depreciation method for the machine, and the calendar year is its annual accounting period. Annual depreciation is $1,000, calculated as follows:

$$\frac{\$5,600 - \$600}{5 \text{ years}} = \$1,000$$

For 19X1, however, Paul's uses the machine for only 9 months (April through December); therefore, only 9/12 of the annual depreciation should be allocated to 19X1. The depreciation for 19X1 is 9/12 x $1,000 = $750.

For 19X6, the last year of the machine's useful life, we allocate $250 (3/12 x $1,000) of depreciation to that year. The $250 of depreciation for 19X6 reduces the machine's carrying amount to its estimated residual value.

When a business purchases assets during the month, accountants commonly calculate depreciation for the nearest whole month. For assets purchased in the first half of a month, we allocate a whole month's depreciation for that month. For assets purchased in the second half of a month, we allocate no depreciation for that month.

Partial Years for Sum-of-the-Years'-Digits Method. When a business uses the sum-of-the-years'-digits method, a unique problem arises with purchases made during the year. The problem is due to the use of a different fraction for allocating depreciation for each year of the asset's useful life. Furthermore, each year of useful life overlaps two annual accounting periods. Accountants handle the problem by allocating each year's depreciation expense between the two accounting periods. Assume Paul's Print Shop purchases an asset on May 4, 19X1. The asset cost $4,000 and has an estimated residual value of $400 and an estimated useful life of 4 years. Illustration 8-9 shows the allocation of depreciation for the asset's 4-year estimated useful life to the annual accounting periods.

The asset was purchased on May 4, 19X1; therefore, we allocate the first year's depreciation 8/12 to 19X1 and 4/12 to 19X2. Depreciation expense related to the asset for 19X2 is the four months of the first year's depreciation and the eight months of the second year's depreciation.

ILLUSTRATION 8-9 Allocation of Depreciation Among Annual Accounting Periods

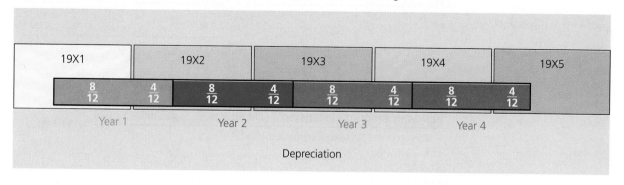

Using the sum-of-the-years'-digits method, the depreciation for each year is calculated as follows:

Useful Life	Sum-of-the-Years'-Digits Depreciation	Allocation of Depreciation						
		8/12	4/12	19X1	19X2	19X3	19X4	19X5
1	$3,600 × 4/10 = $1,440	$960	$480	$960	$ 480			
2	3,600 × 3/10 = 1,080	720	360		720	$360		
3	3,600 × 2/10 = 720	480	240			480	$240	
4	3,600 × 1/10 = 360	240	120				240	$120
				$960	$1,200	$840	$480	$120

Revision of Depreciation Rates

Management's estimates in the period the business acquires the asset determine two factors involved in the calculation of depreciation—the useful life and residual value. Since these estimates involve forecasts of the future, it is not uncommon for the actual useful life or the actual residual value to be different from the earlier estimates of those amounts.

Revised Useful Life. Under GAAP, if management receives new information indicating that the asset's estimated useful life or estimated residual value is different than the original estimates of those amounts, then management should revise the depreciation rates for the remaining estimated useful life. We apply the revised depreciation rate only to the current and future periods remaining in the asset's useful life. Under GAAP, the depreciation recorded in prior periods is *not* adjusted for the revised rate. The accounting profession adopted this rule to avoid the erosion of confidence in financial reporting that might occur if prior years' financial statements are revised as a result of future events.

Assuming the straight-line method, we determine the new annual depreciation expense by dividing the remaining depreciable cost at the time of the revision by the asset's revised remaining estimated useful life. For example, assume Paul's Print Shop purchases a machine on January 2, 19X1, for $14,000. Management estimates that the asset's useful life is 4 years and the estimated residual value is $2,000. Following the straight-line depreciation method, the annual depreciation is: ($14,000 - $2,000) ÷ 4 = $3,000. Based on the machine's condition at the beginning of 19X3, management revises the estimate of its useful life from 4 years to 6 years. At the end of 19X2, the accounts for the machine appear as follows:

Equipment		Accumulated Depreciation–Equipment	
Jan. 2, X1 14,000		Dec. 31, X1 3,000	
		Dec. 31, X2 3,000	
		Bal. 6,000	

We calculate the revised *annual* depreciation as follows:

$$\frac{\textbf{Carrying Amount - Estimated Residual Value}}{\textbf{Revised Remaining Estimated Useful Life}} = \frac{\textbf{\$8,000 - \$2,000}}{\textbf{4}} = \textbf{\$1,500}$$

By depreciating the machine at the rate of $1,500 per year for the remaining 4 years of estimated useful life, we reduce the asset's carrying amount to the estimated residual value of $2,000 at the end of the sixth year, as follows:

Equipment		Accumulated Depreciation–Equipment	
Jan. 2, X1 14,000		Dec. 31, X1 3,000	
		Dec. 31, X2 3,000	
		Dec. 31, X3 1,500	
		Dec. 31, X4 1,500	
		Dec. 31, X5 1,500	
		Dec. 31, X6, 1,500	
		Bal. 12,000	

Revised Residual Value. If management revises the estimate of the asset's residual value, then we depreciate the revised remaining depreciable cost over the remaining estimated useful life to reduce the carrying amount to the revised estimated residual value. For example, Paul's acquires an asset on January 2, 19X1, for $1,400. The asset has an estimated useful life of 6 years and an estimated residual value of $200. Using the straight-line method, annual depreciation is $200 per year ($1,400 - $200) ÷ 6.

After two years have passed, management revises its estimate of the residual value from $200 to zero. The revised annual depreciation is calculated as follows:

Carrying amount of asset $1,400 - (2 x $200) =	$1,000
Revised estimated residual value	0
Remaining depreciable cost	$1,000
Remaining useful life	÷ 4
Revised annual depreciation	$ 250

The revised annual depreciation will reduce the asset's carrying amount to its revised estimated residual value of zero at the end of its useful life.

Depreciation and Income Taxes

For determining taxable income, a business is allowed a deduction for depreciation. The rules for depreciation for income tax purposes are called the **Accelerated Cost Recovery System (ACRS)**. The current ACRS rules were adopted as part of the Tax Reform Act of 1986 and apply to assets purchased since December 31, 1986. In practice, accountants call the current rules

Modified ACRS or **MACRS**. The tax rules classify depreciable property as either real property (buildings) or personal property (equipment). MACRS requires that real property be depreciated using the straight-line method. Residential rental property must be depreciated over 27 1/2 years, and all other real property must be depreciated over 31 1/2 years—regardless of management's estimate of the asset's useful lives.

The tax rules classify personal property into several classes of depreciation periods that range from 3 years to 20 years. MACRS assigns assets to classes based on the type of asset, and the class lives are generally shorter than the asset's useful lives. Personal property may be depreciated using the straight-line method; however, accelerated depreciation is also available under MACRS. If a business elects accelerated depreciation, MACRS specifies the percentage of the asset's cost that the business can take as a depreciation deduction for each year of the asset's class life. The percentages assume that the assets were purchased in the middle of the tax year, regardless of when the assets were actually purchased. The depreciation percentages for 3, 5 and 7-year assets are as follows:

		CLASSES	
Year	3-Year	5-Year	7-Year
1	33.33%	20.00%	14.29%
2	44.45	32.00	24.49
3	14.81	19.20	17.49
4	7.41	11.52	12.49
5	—	11.52	8.93
6	—	5.76	8.92
7	—	—	8.93
8	—	—	4.46
	100.00%	100.00%	100.00%

Notice that the percentages extend for one more year than the class lives due to the mid-year acquisition assumed for MACRS. That is, a 3-year asset assumed to be acquired in the middle of Year 1 would be depreciated for 3 years, to the middle of Year 4. Also, MACRS ignores estimated residual value.

To illustrate the use of the percentages, assume Baker Corporation purchases a machine in the 5-year class on February 1, 19X1, at a cost of $10,000. Annual depreciation deductions for the 6 years are:

19X1	$10,000 x 20.00% =	$ 2,000
19X2	10,000 x 32.00% =	3,200
19X3	10,000 x 19.20% =	1,920
19X4	10,000 x 11.52% =	1,152
19X5	10,000 x 11.52% =	1,152
19X6	10,000 x 5.76% =	576
Total		$10,000

The advantage of accelerated depreciation for income tax purposes is that it results in higher depreciation expense and lower taxable income and taxes early in the asset's life. Deductions are larger in the early years of an asset's life under MACRS than they are for straight-line depreciation. However, the total deductions over the asset's life are always the same because for accelerated depreciation, the deductions are smaller in the later years than they are for straight-line depreciation. While the total deductions are the same for the two methods, the deferral of payments gives the business the "interest free" use of cash due to smaller tax payment for some period of time.

LO 9

Analyze and record expenditures related to plant assets during their useful lives.

EXPENDITURES DURING USEFUL LIFE OF PLANT ASSETS

In the periods after a business acquires plant assets, additional expenditures related to the upkeep, reconditioning, and improvement of them are not uncommon. Examples of such expenditures include the cost of replacing tires and engine tuneups on vehicles and the cost of painting and replacing damaged building components. An accounting issue arises concerning the proper classification of such expenditures. The possible classifications of the expenditures are either as assets, called capital expenditures, or as expenses, called revenue expenditures.

Capital expenditures are those expenditures subsequent to acquisition that extend the asset's useful life beyond its original useful life or those expenditures that enhance the asset's efficiency or effectiveness. Accountants record capital expenditures as assets because they increase the future benefits the asset provides. **Revenue expenditures**, on the other hand, merely maintain the asset's usefulness and keep it functioning at its original capacity. Since revenue expenditures do not create additional future benefits, we record them as expenses of the current period and match them with current revenue.

Repairs

Because they are ordinary and routine expenditures made to maintain the asset in good working order, **repairs** are revenue expenditures. For example, a delivery truck periodically needs tuneups, oil changes, and lubrication, as well as replacement of minor parts. A building needs painting, roofing repairs, plumbing repairs, and electrical repairs. These routine expenditures are necessary to maintain the asset's usefulness, and we record them as debits to an expense account called Maintenance Expense. For example, Paul's Print Shop pays $125 for an engine tuneup on one of its delivery trucks. Paul's entry to record the repair expense is:

(Date)	Maintenance Expense	125	
	Cash		125
	To record cost of engine tuneup.		

Replacements

Occasionally, a business makes a nonroutine, major expenditure that extends the asset's useful life beyond its original estimated useful life. These expenditures, which we call **replacements**, are capital expenditures. We record them as a reduction in the related accumulated depreciation account on the basis that the expenditures *recover* a portion of past depreciation by extending the asset's useful life. For example, Baker purchases a delivery truck for $22,000; it has an estimated useful life of 5 years and an estimated residual value of $2,000. Assuming straight-line depreciation, after 4 years, the truck's remaining depreciable cost is $4,000, as follows:

Cost	$22,000
Less: Accumulated depreciation of 4 years	16,000
Carrying amount	$ 6,000
Less: Estimated residual value	2,000
Remaining depreciable cost	$ 4,000

At the end of the fourth year, Baker performs a major engine overhaul costing $2,000. The overhaul extends the estimated useful life by 2 years to a total of 7 years. Baker records the cost of the overhaul as follows:

(Date)	Accumulated Depreciation-Delivery Equipment	2,000	
	Cash		2,000
	To record cost of engine overhaul.		

The remaining depreciable cost, which the above entry increases to $6,000, should be depreciated over the revised remaining useful life of 3 years. We calculate the revised annual depreciation as follows:

Remaining depreciable cost before replacement	$4,000
Add: Replacement	2,000
Revised remaining depreciable cost	$6,000
Remaining useful life	÷ 3
Revised annual depreciation expense	$2,000

Three years of depreciation at $2,000 per year exactly reduce the truck's carrying amount to its estimated residual value of $2,000.

Improvements

An **improvement,** a subsequent expenditure that makes an asset more efficient or effective, does not necessarily extend the asset's useful life. For example, a business converts a machine from manual operation to computer-controlled operation; and the change results in fewer flaws in the output. This type of expenditure enhances the machine's usefulness, and we consider it a capital expenditure.

Accountants debit the cost of an improvement either to the asset account or to Accumulated Depreciation, depending on whether the cost increases the asset's useful life. To illustrate, assume that on January 2, 19X4, Paul's Print Shop decides to replace the electric motor in a machine with a more powerful motor that will enhance the rate of output but not extend the machine's useful life. The cost of the new motor is $2,000. Paul's purchased the machine 3 years ago, and it has an estimated useful life of 6 years. When the improvement does not increase the asset's useful life, we debit the cost to the asset account as follows:

Jan. 2	Equipment	2,000	
	Cash		2,000
	To record cost of new motor.		

By increasing Equipment, this entry increases the machine's carrying amount and depreciable cost by $2,000. We allocate the machine's revised depreciable cost over its remaining useful life—which is 3 years. We account for the cost of improvements that increase the asset's useful life the same as we account for

INSIGHTS INTO ACCOUNTING

INCOME TAX TREATMENT OF ASBESTOS REMOVAL COSTS

For income tax purposes, the Internal Revenue Service (IRS) has developed rules for what expenditures may be deducted currently and, thereby, reduce current income taxes payable. Expenditures that cannot be deducted currently must be capitalized and deducted over the remaining life of the asset in the form of depreciation. To be deductible currently, the expenditure must be a repair. To be a repair, the expenditure must not extend the life of the asset, adapt it to a different use, materially increase its value, or create a separate asset.

For several years the federal government has been involved in requiring businesses (and others) to remove asbestos insulation because of its apparent link to cancer. A particular business had manufacturing equipment with asbestos as thermal insulation. Federal government regulations would have required the business to monitor continuously the air for asbestos particles, and totally encapsulate the equipment each time routine maintenance or repairs were required. These procedures would have been costly and resulted in loss of manufacturing time.

The business decided it would be less costly in the long run to replace the asbestos insulation on its manufacturing equipment with another thermal lining than to comply with the government regulations concerning the safety measures it would otherwise have to take. The business considered the cost of replacement to be a repair and treated it as a current deduction on its tax return.

The current deduction was disallowed by the IRS. The IRS took the position that the cost was a capital expenditure because the removal of the asbestos added to the value of the equipment because the equipment would be more readily salable with the non-asbestos insulation than with the asbestos in place. It apparently did not matter to the IRS that the business did not intend to sell the equipment, but to continue to use it in manufacturing.

Source: Grant Thornton, *National Tax Alert*, No. 92-40 (September 8, 1992).

replacements—debiting the cost to Accumulated Depreciation. We allocate the revised remaining depreciable cost over the revised remaining useful life.

DISPOSAL OF PLANT ASSETS

LO 10

Explain how to record the disposal of plant assets by abandonment and by sale.

When plant assets wear out or become technologically obsolete, a business commonly disposes of them. A business accomplishes disposal by ceasing to use the asset, by selling the asset, or by trading in the asset on the purchase of a new one. The following sections discuss how a business can use and account for the first two methods of disposal of plant assets. Trade-ins of assets are discussed in Appendix 8-A.

Ceasing to Use

When an asset reaches the end of its estimated useful life, its carrying amount will equal its estimated residual value. At this point, since an asset should not be depreciated below its estimated residual value, a business should cease depreciation of the asset. If the business continues to use the asset, it should not remove the asset account and the related accumulated depreciation account from its accounting records. Thus, the accounting records continue to reflect all assets the business presently uses. However, if for any reason the business ceases to use the asset, it should remove the asset cost and the related accumulated depreciation from its records by a journal entry.

Assume that on January 2, 19X6, Paul's Print Shop ceases to use a machine because it is worn out. Paul's will discard the machine because the cost of transporting the machine is more than its scrap value. An examination of the accounting records reveals the account balances for the machine as shown in the T-accounts below:

Equipment		Accumulated Depreciation—Equipment	
Jan. 2, X1 5,000		Dec. 31, X1 1,000	
		Dec. 31, X2 1,000	
		Dec. 31, X3 1,000	
		Dec. 31, X4 1,000	
		Dec. 31, X5 1,000	
		Bal. 5,000	

The account balances indicate that the machine's carrying amount is zero. We depreciate the machine to zero, in this case, because its estimated residual value is zero. At the time it discards the machine, Paul's should remove the asset cost and the related accumulated depreciation from the accounting records with the entry shown below:

Jan. 2	Accumulated Depreciation—Equipment	5,000	
	Equipment		5,000
	To record discarding of fully depreciated machine.		

After the above entry, both Equipment and Accumulated Depreciation—Equipment have zero balances, as follows:

Equipment		Accumulated Depreciation—Equipment	
Jan. 2, X1 5,000	Jan. 2, X6 5,000		Dec. 31, X1 1,000
Bal. 0			Dec. 31, X2 1,000
			Dec. 31, X3 1,000
			Dec. 31, X4 1,000
			Dec. 31, X5 1,000
		Jan. 2, X6 5,000	
			Bal. 0

Selling the Asset

When a business disposes of an asset by selling it, we record the difference between the asset's carrying amount and the proceeds from the sales transaction as a gain or loss. For example, assume that on January 2, 19X5, Paul's Print Shop sells a machine for $500. The accounting records contain the account balances for the machine as shown in the following T-accounts:

Equipment		Accumulated Depreciation—Equipment	
Jan. 2, X1 3,000		Dec. 31, X1 600	
		Dec. 31, X2 600	
		Dec. 31, X3 600	
		Dec. 31, X4 600	
		Bal. 2,400	

The carrying amount of the machine is $600, as follows:

Equipment (cost)	$3,000
Less: Accumulated depreciation	2,400
Carrying amount	$ 600

The proceeds from selling the machine, $500, are less than the machine's carrying amount. Therefore, Paul's incurs a loss from the sales transaction. The following entry records the sale:

Jan. 2	Cash (or receivable)	500	
	Accumulated Depreciation—Equipment	2,400	
	Loss from Sale of Equipment	100	
	Equipment		3,000
	To record sale of machine.		

The above entry records the receipt of cash (or a promise to pay from the buyer), reduces to zero the balances in Equipment and Accumulated Depreciation—Equipment, and recognizes the loss from the sale of the machine.

If, on the other hand, the proceeds from the sale of the machine are $850, then Paul's would recognize a gain of $250 on the sales transaction as follows:

Proceeds from sale	$850
Carrying amount of machine	600
Gain from sale	$250

The entry to record this transaction is shown below:

Jan. 2	Cash (or receivable)	850	
	Accumulated Depreciation—Equipment	2,400	
	Equipment		3,000
	Gain from Sale of Equipment		250
	To record sale of machine.		

The above entry records the receipt of cash (or a promise to pay from the buyer), reduces to zero the balances in Equipment and Accumulated Depreciation—Equipment, and recognizes the $250 gain from the sale of the machine. Gains and losses from the sale of plant assets are components of net income in the income statement.

Depreciation to the Date of Disposal

When a business disposes of plant assets, regardless of the method of disposal, we record the asset's depreciation expense for the period between the end of the preceding accounting period and the date of disposal. For example, assume Paul's Print Shop purchases a machine on January 2, 19X1, for $9,000. The machine has an estimated useful life of 4 years and an estimated residual value of $1,000, and Paul's uses the straight-line method of depreciation. We calculate annual depreciation expense as follows:

$$(\$9,000 - \$1,000) \div 4 = \$2,000$$

If Paul's sells the machine on June 30, 19X4, for cash of $2,200, we record depreciation for the 6-month period from January 1, 19X4, to June 30, 19X4, *before* we record the sale transaction. Depreciation expense for the 6-month period is 6/12 x $2,000 = $1,000. After recording the depreciation for 19X4, Accumulated Depreciation has a balance of $7,000 [(3 x $2,000) + $1,000]. The sale of the machine results in a $200 gain, calculated as follows:

Proceeds from sale	$2,200
Carrying amount of machine ($9,000 – $7,000)	2,000
Gain from sale	$ 200

The entries to record the depreciation and the sales transaction are shown below:

Jun. 30	Depreciation Expense—Equipment	1,000	
	Accumulated Depreciation—Equipment		1,000
	To record depreciation on machine that was sold.		
30	Cash	2,200	
	Accumulated Depreciation—Equipment	7,000	
	Equipment		9,000
	Gain from Sale of Equipment		200
	To record sale of machine.		

Failure to record depreciation to the date of sale causes the financial statements to be incorrect in that depreciation expense would be understated and a gain (loss) from disposal would be understated (overstated).

INTANGIBLE ASSETS

LO 11
Identify the accounting issues related to the acquisition and amortization of intangible assets.

Accountants generally describe **intangible assets** as noncurrent, or long-term, assets without physical existence. Examples of intangible assets are patents, copyrights, trademarks and trade names, franchises, and goodwill. Some current assets such as accounts and notes receivable also do not have physical existence; however in accounting, the term *intangible assets* refers only to noncurrent, nonphysical assets.

Because they grant a legal right or represent favorable economic circumstances, intangible assets have value to a business. An example of a legal right granted is the sole right to sell a product or to use a process. A favorable economic circumstance would be a unique business location. In accordance with the matching principle, we allocate the cost of intangible assets such as the cost of plant assets to the periods the assets benefit. **Amortization** is the process of allocating the cost to periods benefited and is the same process as depreciation of plant assets. GAAP require that the period of time over which a business amortizes intangible assets cannot exceed 40 years. Also, a business generally uses the straight-line method to calculate amortization expense. As shown in Illustration 8-10, we present intangible assets in the balance sheet in a separate section following plant assets. We present intangible assets at cost net of accumulated amortization.

Patents

The federal government grants patents through the U.S. Patent Office. A **patent** gives the holder the exclusive right to use the product or process for a period

ILLUSTRATION 8-10 Partial Balance Sheet

Plant Assets:			
Land		$50,000	
Building	$125,000		
Less: Accumulated depreciation	30,000	95,000	
Equipment	$ 69,000		
Less: Accumulated depreciation	13,000	56,000	$201,000
Intangible Assets:			
Patents (at cost less amortization)		$24,000	
Goodwill (at cost less amortization)		18,000	42,000
			$243,000

of 17 years. The government grants patents to encourage inventions of new products or processes. Consistent with the cost principle, we record patents at their acquisition costs. We amortize the cost of the patent over its legal life or useful life, whichever is shorter. Although the legal life of a patent is 17 years, its useful life is often shorter because of new inventions and other factors.

To illustrate the accounting for patents, assume Product Research, Inc. purchased a patent for $9,000 on April 2, 19X1. Management estimates that the patent will be useful for only 6 years even though its legal life is 17 years. Product Research should record the patent at cost as shown in the following journal entry:

Apr. 2	Patents	9,000	
	Cash		9,000
	To record acquisition of patent.		

At the end of 19X1, the following entry records amortization for 9 months (April through December). Amortization for the 9 months is $1,125 ($9,000 x 1/6 x 9/12).

Dec. 31	Patent Amortization Expense	1,125	
	Patents		1,125
	To record patent amortization.		

By tradition, accountants record amortization directly to the asset account, as illustrated in the entry above, rather than to an accumulated amortization account.

Research and Development

Under GAAP, accountants do not record the costs of research and development activities as assets. Rather, we record these costs as expenses.[3] **Research and development** activities involve the search for and the application of knowledge to new products or processes. Although research and development does not result in recorded intangible assets, we discuss the costs of these activities in this section because they sometimes result in patents and copyrights.

Research and development costs are significant for many businesses. Large businesses such as DuPont and IBM spend billions of dollars annually on

---

[3]*Accounting for Research and Development Costs*, Statement No. 2 para. 12. (Stamford, Conn: FASB, 1974).

research and development. IBM's 1992 Annual Report contains the following note to the financial statements:

Research, Development and Engineering

Research, development and engineering expenses amounted to $6,522 million in 1992, $6,644 million in 1991, and $6,554 million in 1990.

Included in these amounts were expenditures of $5,083 million in 1992, $5,001 million in 1991, and $4,914 million in 1990 for a broad program of research and development activities covering basic scientific research in a variety of fields and the application of scientific advances to the development of new and improved products and their uses. In addition, expenditures for product-related engineering amounted to $1,439 million, $1,643 million, and $1,640 million for the same three years.

We do not record intangible assets for research and development costs because it is often virtually impossible to identify the costs of individual projects and the amounts (if any) and timing of the future benefits of these costs are highly uncertain. For these reasons, the FASB decided that all businesses should record the costs of research and development as expenses and disclose the amounts of the costs in their financial statements.

For example, assume Hi-Tech Labs, Inc. incurred costs of $1,800,000 for research and development activities during 19X1. The *summary* entry to record these costs is:

(Date)	Research and Development Expense	1,800,000	
	Cash		1,800,000
	To record the costs of research and development for the year.		

In the notes to its 19X1 financial statements, Hi-Tech Labs should disclose that during the year it incurred costs of $1,800,000 related to research and development activities.

Copyrights

Similar to patents, the federal government grants **copyrights**. The government grants copyrights to authors, painters, musicians, sculptors, software engineers, and others. Copyrights give them and their heirs the exclusive right to their creative works for the lifetime of the creator plus 50 years. For example, composers of popular music obtain copyrights on the songs they compose to prohibit their work from being copied without their permission. When a business purchases a copyright, we record the cost as an intangible asset; and we amortize that cost over the useful life of the copyright, not to exceed 40 years.

Trademarks and Trade Names

Trademarks and **trade names** are words, symbols, or other devices that identify or distinguish a product or a business. Examples of trade names are Coke, Kleenex, and Chevrolet. The U.S. Patent Office grants the right of exclusive use of a registered trademark or trade name to the creator or original user for a period of 20 years. Additional 20-year registrations are granted so long as the business continuously uses the trademark or trade name.

If a business purchases a trademark or trade name, we record it at the acquisition cost. If a business develops a trademark or trade name internally,

INSIGHTS INTO ACCOUNTING

WHAT'S IN A NAME? BILLIONS

Marlboro is the best-known brand on the face of the earth. But how much is it worth? About $31 billion, twice its annual revenue, says *Financial World*. The magazine takes on one of the toughest tasks in business: putting dollar values on brand names.

Conventional accounting doesn't have an accepted way to value the trade names businesses back with millions in marketing money. *Financial World* used its own complex formula to pin down brands' value.

The most valuable brands after Marlboro: Coca-Cola, worth $24.4 billion; Budweiser, $10.2 billion; Pepsi-Cola, $9.6 billion; and Nescafe instant coffee, $8.5 billion. Only eight brands—including megasellers Coke and Barbie and luxury names Hennessy, Hermes and Louis Vuitton—would sell for more than twice their annual revenue. "What it says is that the folks running these companies are very, very smart," says the Senior Editor of *Financial World*. "They have maximized whatever cachet the brand has."

Source: Martha T. Moore, "What's in a Name? Billions," *USA Today* (August 12, 1992), p. 1B.

the recorded cost includes attorneys' fees, registration fees, costs of successful legal defense, and other costs related to developing and retaining the trademark or trade name. We amortize the cost of trademarks and trade names over the estimated period benefited, not to exceed 40 years.

Franchises

A **franchise** is a legal agreement in which one party (franchisor) grants the exclusive right to another party (franchisee) to market a product or provide a service within a designated geographical area. Examples of franchise businesses include Shell service stations, McDonald's restaurants, and General Motors dealers. In many franchise agreements, the franchisee must pay the franchisor an initial fee plus yearly fees that are based on some factor such as net sales revenue. The initial fee is the cost of the franchise that we record as the franchisee's intangible asset. We amortize the cost of the franchise over the term of the franchise, or over 40 years if the term of the agreement exceeds 40 years. We record the yearly fee the franchisee pays to the franchisor as an expense of the franchisee when incurred in accordance with the matching principle.

McDonald's 1992 Annual Report contains the following note to its financial statements:

Franchise Agreements

Franchise arrangements, with franchisees who operate in various geographical locations, generally provide for initial fees and continuing payments to the Company based upon a percent of sales, with minimum rent payments. Among other things, franchisees are provided the use of restaurant facilities, generally for a period of 20 years. They are required to pay related occupancy costs which include property taxes, insurance, maintenance and a refundable, noninterest-bearing security deposit. On a limited basis, the Company receives notes from franchisees. Generally the notes are secured by interests in restaurant equipment and franchises.

(In millions of dollars)	1992	1991	1990
Minimum rents:			
Owned sites	$ 538.7	$ 494.5	$ 439.8
Leased sites	353.3	303.7	250.0
	$ 892.0	$ 798.2	$ 689.8
Percentage fees	$1,120.6	$ 970.4	$ 914.0
Initial fees	18.2	17.9	16.0
Revenues from franchised restaurants	$2,030.8	$1,786.5	$1,619.8

Goodwill

In accounting terminology, **goodwill** refers to the business's ability to generate earnings at a higher rate than is normal for the industry in which the business operates. We attribute goodwill to such factors as superior management, unique location, superior work force, and monopolistic access to a scarce resource. Under GAAP, however, accountants record goodwill only when a business purchases another entire business or a major portion of the operating assets of another business. The amount of goodwill recorded in such cases is the measure of the excess of the purchase price over the fair value of the identifiable assets purchased.

Jeff's Purchase of Red's Barber Shop

In the scenario at the beginning of this chapter, assume Jeff purchased Red's Barber Shop, Inc. for $50,000. Jeff must now record the assets and liabilities of Red's Barber Shop that he acquired when he purchased Red's. We show below the carrying amounts of the assets and liabilities from Red's balance sheet in Illustration 8-8 immediately before Jeff's purchase (except for cash, which the owner of Red's will keep). Also, the second column shows the fair values of the assets and liabilities at the time of the purchase. Jeff obtained the fair values from distributors' price lists and from an appraisal of the property's value.

Item	Carrying Amount	Fair Value
Sales supplies	$ 350	$ 350
Equipment (net)	500	1,825
Land	10,000	20,000
Buildings (net)	15,000	25,000
Accounts payable	(175)	(175)
Notes payable	(6,000)	(7,000)
Total net assets	$19,675	$40,000

Recall that Jeff paid $50,000 for Red's Barber Shop. In recording the purchase, Jeff records the assets and liabilities of Red's at their fair values, which net to $40,000. Jeff would allocate to goodwill the $10,000 excess purchase price over the fair values of the purchased net assets. Jeff should record the purchase of Red's with the following entries:

(Date)	Cash	50,000	
	Capital Stock		50,000
	Cash purchase of stock to begin new business.		

(Date)			
	Sales Supplies	350	
	Equipment	1,825	
	Land	20,000	
	Buildings	25,000	
	Goodwill	10,000	
	Accounts Payable		175
	Notes Payable		7,000
	Cash		50,000
	To record purchase of Red's Barber Shop, Inc.		

Under GAAP, the "advantages" represented by goodwill are always assumed to have a finite life span. We amortize recorded goodwill, therefore, over the estimated period of benefit, not exceeding 40 years.

LO 12

Apply GAAP to the acquisition and depletion of natural resources.

NATURAL RESOURCES

Natural resources consist of such things as oil and gas, mineral deposits, and standing timber. As businesses pump oil and gas, mine mineral deposits, and cut timber, the assets are depleted. For this reason, natural resources are commonly called "wasting" assets. When natural resources are pumped, mined, or cut, they become inventory to be sold. Under the cost principle, accountants record natural resources at cost. Generally, we allocate the cost to periods in accordance with the matching principle using the units-of-production method. Accountants call the process of allocating the cost of natural resources **depletion**, and it is similar to depreciation and amortization.

Assume that on January 2, 19X1, Southern Mines Corporation purchases a mineral deposit for $5,200,000. Southern's entry to record the purchase of the mineral deposit is:

Jan. 2	Mineral Deposits	5,200,000	
	Cash		5,200,000
	To record the purchase of a mineral deposit.		

Based on tests performed by geologists, the estimated deposit consists of 2,000,000 tons of ore. Furthermore, the estimated land value for the property after mining operations are completed is $200,000. As shown below, we calculate the depletion per ton by dividing the depletable cost (cost of the deposit less the estimated residual value) by the estimated tons of ore that can be mined from the deposit:

For Southern Mines, the depletion per ton is $2.50, calculated as follows:

$$(\$5,200,000 - \$200,000) \div 2,000,000 \text{ tons} = \$2.50 \text{ per ton}$$

We calculate the amount of depletion to be recorded for a period as shown below:

If, during the first year, Southern mines 300,000 tons of ore, we debit $750,000 (300,000 tons x $2.50/ton) to inventory as shown by the following *summary* entry:

Dec. 31	Mineral Inventory	750,000	
	Accumulated Depletion		750,000
	To record the cost of ore mined for the year.		

In the entry above to record the depletion, the credit is to the contra-asset account Accumulated Depletion. In the financial statements, Southern would show Mineral Deposits along with Accumulated Depletion as follows:

| Mineral deposits | $5,200,000 | |
| Less: Accumulated depletion | 750,000 | $4,450,000 |

Some businesses follow the practice of crediting the asset account directly for depletion, similar to recording amortization of intangible assets.

If Southern sells 200,000 tons of the ore, then we debit $500,000 (200,000 tons x $2.50/ton) to Depletion Expense as follows:

(Date)	Depletion Expense	500,000	
	Mineral Inventory		500,000
	To record depletion expense on ore sold during the year.		

The amount shown as Depletion Expense in the entry above is the cost of ore sold during the period.

SUMMARY

Identify the categories of plant assets. In financial statements, plant assets are often classified into four categories: land, land improvements, buildings, and equipment.

Determine which costs are included in the recorded cost of plant assets. We record plant assets according to the cost principle. The total recorded cost of plant assets includes all necessary costs incurred to acquire the asset. The necessary costs include the purchase price, transportation costs, and insurance while in transit.

Explain the concept of depreciation. Depreciation is the process of allocating the cost of assets to the periods benefited from the services they provide. The cost of an asset to be allocated over its useful live is the cost of the asset less the value received when the asset is sold or traded for another asset.

Identify the factors used in calculating depreciation. The factors are:

1. *Cost.* The amount the business records as the cost of the asset at the time of acquisition.
2. *Estimated residual value.* Either the estimated net proceeds if the asset is sold or the trade-in value if the business trades in the asset on a replacement asset.
3. *Estimated useful life.* The estimated period of time that the business can use the asset.

Calculate depreciation expense using several alternative depreciation methods. The alternative depreciation methods include:

1. *Straight-line method.* Allocates a constant amount of depreciation to each period of the asset's estimated useful life.
2. *Units-of-production method.* Allocates depreciation to time periods based on the asset's output.
3. *Accelerated methods.* Allocates a higher amount of depreciation to the earlier periods of estimated useful life and a lower amount to the later periods. Two commonly used accelerated methods are the sum-of-the-years'-digits method and the double-declining-balance method.

Compare the alternative depreciation methods and explain the factors that affect management's choice of depreciation methods. An important factor for management to consider is whether the asset's usefulness expires as a result of the amount of usage or of the passage of time. The units-of-production method allocates depreciation based on the amount of usage of the asset. Both the straight-line method and the accelerated methods allocate depreciation based on the passage of time. The straight-line method allocates the same amount of depreciation to each period, and the accelerated methods allocate a higher amount to the early years. Another factor management needs to consider is the relative effect on net income of the alternative depreciation methods.

Calculate and interpret the return on total assets. The return on total assets is the ratio of net income plus interest expense to total assets. The ratio can be used to assess the business's ability to utilize its assets to generate net income.

Calculate depreciation for partial periods, account for revisions of depreciation rates, and calculate depreciation for income taxes. Calculating depreciation for partial periods involves allocating a proportionate amount of depreciation to the first and last time periods in the asset's estimated useful life. For the sum-of-the-years'-digits method, special care must be taken because for each year two different fractions enter into the calculation of depreciation. If management revises its estimates of the asset's useful life or residual value, management should revise the depreciation rates for the remaining estimated useful life. We apply the revised rate only to the current and future periods remaining in the asset's useful life. Businesses calculate depreciation for income taxes according to the Modified Accelerated Cost Recovery System. This system classifies depreciable property as either personal property or as real property. MACRS classifies personal property into several classes of depreciation periods that range from 3 years to 20 years. MACRS depreciates real property using the straight-line method.

Analyze and record expenditures related to plant assets during their useful lives. We classify expenditures during the asset's useful life as capital expenditures or as revenue expenditures. Capital expenditures extend the asset's useful life beyond its original life or enhance the asset's efficiency or effectiveness. Capital expenditures include replacements and improvements. Accountants record capital expenditures as assets. Revenue expenditures such as repairs maintain the asset's usefulness. Accountants record revenue expenditures as expenses.

Explain how to record the disposal of plant assets by abandonment and by sale. When a business abandons a plant asset, we remove its cost and accumulated depreciation accounts from the accounting records. Also, the business recognizes a loss for any remaining carrying amount of the asset. When a business sells a plant asset, we recognize a gain or loss for the difference between the proceeds of the sale and the asset's carrying amount.

Identify the accounting issues related to the acquisition and amortization of intangible assets. Intangible assets are noncurrent productive assets without physical existence. We record intangible assets at the amount of cost incurred in acquiring the asset in accordance with the cost principle. Under the matching principle, we allocate the costs of intangible assets that are used up to the periods the assets benefit. The cost allocation process for intangible assets is similar to straight-line depreciation.

Apply GAAP to the acquisition and depletion of natural resources. In accordance with the cost principle, we record natural resources at the amount of costs incurred in acquiring the assets. Accountants call the cost allocation process for natural resources depletion, and it is similar to units-of-production depreciation.

LO 13

Record exchanges of plant assets for both dissimilar and similar assets.

APPENDIX 8-A: EXCHANGING ASSETS

Businesses frequently dispose of one asset and acquire another asset by exchanging the assets with another business or individual. The assets exchanged may be **similar**—meaning that the assets exchanged serve the same function—or **dissimilar**—meaning that the assets exchanged serve different functions. An exchange of a computer for another computer involves similar assets. An exchange of a computer for a drill press involves dissimilar assets. Frequently, an exchange also involves a cash payment by one of the parties to make equal the fair values of the assets exchanged. The accounting for the exchange of assets involves three steps on the date of the exchange:

1. Determine the value (cost) of the asset(s) acquired.
2. Determine any gain or loss from assets given, if applicable.
3. Record in a single entry the acquisition of a new asset, the disposal of the old asset, and any applicable gain or loss.

Whether there is a gain or loss from the disposal of the old asset—and the calculation of the cost of the new asset—depends on whether the exchange involves dissimilar or similar assets.[4]

Exchange of Dissimilar Assets

In an exchange involving dissimilar assets, the new asset's recorded cost is equal to the old asset's fair value plus the amount of any cash paid to the other party to the exchange. Also, we always recognize a gain or loss from an exchange involving dissimilar assets. The gain or loss is equal to the difference between the old asset's carrying amount and its fair value on the date of the exchange.

Assume that on January 4, 19X1, Paul's Print Shop exchanges a computer and $14,700 cash for a delivery truck. On the date of the exchange, the computer has a carrying amount of $3,000 (original cost of $4,500 and accumulated depreciation of $1,500). By appraisal, Paul's determines that the computer's fair value is $3,500.

Step 1: Based on this information, the acquisition cost of the truck is $18,200:

Fair value of computer	$ 3,500
Cash paid	14,700
Cost of truck	$18,200

Step 2: Paul's calculates a gain of $500 on the disposal of the computer, according to the following calculation:

Fair value of computer	$3,500
Carrying amount of computer	3,000
Gain from disposal	$ 500

Step 3: Paul's entry to record the exchange is shown below:

Jan. 4	Delivery Equipment	18,200	
	Accumulated Depreciation—Office Equipment	1,500	
	Office Equipment		4,500
	Cash		14,700
	Gain from Disposal		500
	To record exchange of computer for delivery truck.		

---

[4]*Accounting for Nonmonetary Exchanges*, APB Opinion No. 29 (New York, NY: AICPA, 1973), para. 18–26.

If, on the other hand, the computer's fair value is only $2,000, we apply the three steps as follows:

Step 1: The cost of the truck is $16,700, determined as follows:

Fair value of computer	$ 2,000
Cash paid	14,700
Cost of truck	$16,700

Step 2: In this case, Paul's would calculate a loss from the disposal of the computer of $1,000:

Fair value of computer	$2,000
Carrying amount of computer	3,000
Loss from disposal	$1,000

Step 3: Paul's entry to reflect these circumstances is:

Jan. 4	Delivery Equipment	16,700	
	Accumulated Depreciation—Office Equipment	1,500	
	Loss from Disposal	1,000	
	Office Equipment		4,500
	Cash		14,700
	To record exchange of computer for delivery truck.		

Exchange of Similar Assets

When a productive asset wears out, a business commonly trades in the old asset on the purchase of a new one. For example, when a delivery truck wears out, the business purchases a new delivery truck by trading in the old truck and paying cash to the truck dealer. The proper accounting for the exchange of similar assets depends on whether the transaction results in a loss or gain.

Loss Recognized When Incurred. When a business exchanges one of its assets for a similar asset, the business incurs a loss if the asset's carrying amount exceeds the trade-in allowance received for the old asset. GAAP require that businesses recognize losses in the period they occur, regardless of whether similar or dissimilar assets are exchanged. For example, on July 1, Paul's Print Shop trades in a computer it owns toward the purchase of a new computer. The cost of the old computer is $10,000, and accumulated depreciation (including depreciation to the date of the exchange) is $8,800. The price of the new computer is $15,000, and Paul's receives a trade-in allowance of $1,000 for the old computer. So, Paul's must pay $14,000 in cash.

Step 1: Based on this information, the acquisition cost of the new computer is $15,000:

Fair value of computer	$ 1,000
Cash paid	14,000
Cost of new computer	$15,000

Step 2: Paul's calculates a loss of $200 from the disposal of the old computer:

Step 3: Paul's entry to record the exchange is as follows:

July 1	Office Equipment (new)	15,000	
	Accumulated Depreciation—Office Equipment	8,800	
	Loss from Disposal	200	
	Office Equipment (old)		10,000
	Cash		14,000
	To record trade-in of old computer on a new computer.		

The above entry accomplishes several things: it reduces old Office Equipment and the related Accumulated Depreciation—Office Equipment to zero; it records the new computer at its purchase price; it records the loss from the disposal; and it records the cash paid for the difference between the price of the new computer and the trade-in allowance received on the old computer.

Gain Not Recognized Immediately. A gain on the exchange of similar productive assets occurs when the trade-in allowance received for the old asset exceeds its carrying amount at the date of exchange. In determining that a business has realized a gain, however, we must be careful that the indicated trade-in allowance is the old asset's fair value, not an inflated trade-in allowance resulting from a list price of the new asset that exceeds its normal selling price.

In the previous example of an exchange of computers, assume that instead of a trade-in allowance of $1,000, Paul's receives a trade-in allowance of $1,600, which represents the old computer's fair value. Therefore, the cash payment required is $13,400. With this new assumption, the exchange transaction results in a $400 gain because the trade-in allowance of $1,600 exceeds the old computer's $1,200 carrying amount by $400. In the case of a gain, GAAP provide that we do not recognize the gain at the time of the exchange. Instead, we record the new computer at the carrying amount of the old computer plus the cash payment. This amount is commonly called the **cost basis** of the new asset.

Step 1: We calculate the new computer's recorded amount as the old computer's carrying amount plus the cash payment:

Carrying amount of old computer ($10,000 − $8,800)	$ 1,200
Cash payment	13,400
Cost basis of new computer	$14,600

Step 2: We calculate the amount of the gain:

Fair value of old computer	$1,600
Carrying amount of old computer	1,200
Gain (unrecognized)	$ 400

In this case, the gain is not recognized at the time of the exchange because accountants consider the exchange of similar assets not to be the end of the old asset's earning process. In effect, the new asset's recorded cost is reduced from its fair value by the unrecognized gain. The new computer's recorded cost, calculated as $14,600, is the new computer's $15,000 fair value less the $400 unrecognized gain. By reducing the new computer's total recorded cost by the amount of the unrecognized gain, we recognize the gain in net income over the computer's estimated useful life through lower amounts of annual depreciation expense.

Step 3: Paul's entry to record the exchange transaction is:

July 1	Office Equipment (new)	14,600	
	Accumulated Depreciation—Office Equipment	8,800	
	Office Equipment (old)		10,000
	Cash ($15,000 – $1,600)		13,400
	To record trade-in of old computer on a new computer.		

Income Tax Treatment of Exchanges of Assets

For purposes of computing income taxes, special rules exist for exchanges of assets. The tax rules classify asset exchanges as either "like-kind exchanges" or "non-like-kind exchanges." These classifications are close to the similar and dissimilar classifications used for financial statements.

Like-kind exchanges do not result in the recognition of taxable gains or losses. The tax basis of the asset received is the tax basis of the asset given up in the exchange. **Non-like-kind exchanges** result in the recognition of taxable gains and losses. The amount of the gain or loss is the difference between the tax basis of the asset given up and the fair value of the asset received. The tax basis of the asset received is its fair value at the time of the exchange.

REVIEW PROBLEM A: PLANT ASSET PURCHASE AND DEPRECIATION

Allison Crib Corporation purchased a new lathe on January 2, 19X1, for cash of $145,000. In addition, Allison has to pay transportation costs of $3,500 and installation costs of $1,500. The estimated life is 5 years, and the lathe has an estimated residual value of $30,000.

REQUIRED:

a. Determine the cost of the lathe.
b. Record the journal entry for the purchase of the lathe on January 2, 19X1.
c. Determine depreciation expense for each year using: (1) straight-line, (2) sum-of-the-years'-digits, and (3) double-declining-balance methods.
d. Determine depreciation expense for each year for tax purposes using MACRS, assuming that the lathe is classified as 5-year property.

SOLUTION:

Planning and Organizing Your Work

1. Determine the sum of all relevant costs in acquiring and installing the lathe.
2. Record the journal entry for the acquisition of the lathe, using the sum determined in Step 1.
3. Calculate the depreciation expense for each method, using the formulas given in the chapter under Depreciation Methods.
4. Calculate the depreciation expense for tax purposes using the percentages given for 5-year property in the table provided on page 361.

(a) *Determine the cost of the lathe.*

Purchase price	$145,000
Transportation	3,500
Installation	1,500
Total	$150,000

(b) *Record the purchase.*

Jan. 2	Equipment	150,000	
	Cash		150,000
	To record the acquisition of a lathe.		

(c) *Determine the depreciation expense.*

Straight-Line Method

($150,000 - $30,000) ÷ 5 = $24,000 per year

Sum-of-the-Years'-Digits Method

Year	Calculation	Depreciation Expense
1	5/15 x $120,000	$40,000
2	4/15 x 120,000	32,000
3	3/15 x 120,000	24,000
4	2/15 x 120,000	16,000
5	1/15 x 120,000	8,000

Double-Declining-Balance Method

Year	Calculation	Depreciation Expense	Carrying Amount
			$150,000
1	40% x $150,000	$60,000	90,000
2	40% x 90,000	36,000	54,000
3	40% x 54,000	21,600	32,400
4	$32,400 - $30,000*	2,400	30,000
5		0	30,000

*An asset cannot be depreciated below its estimated residual value.

(d) *Determine the depreciation expense for tax purposes.*

MACRS Method

Year	Calculation	Depreciation Expense
1	20.00% x $150,000	$ 30,000
2	32.00% x 150,000	48,000
3	19.20% x 150,000	28,800
4	11.52% x 150,000	17,280
5	11.52% x 150,000	17,280
6	5.76% x 150,000	8,640
Total		$150,000

REVIEW PROBLEM B: DISPOSAL OF PLANT ASSETS

Gigantic Cleaners, Inc. purchased a computer on January 2, 19X1, for $125,000. The computer had an estimated useful life of 5 years and an estimated residual value of $25,000.

REQUIRED:

a. Record the journal entry for the sale of the computer if Gigantic sells it for $20,000 on December 31, 19X5.
b. Record the journal entry for the sale of the computer if Gigantic sells it for $40,000 on December 31, 19X5.
c. Record the journal entry for the sale of the computer if Gigantic sells it for $35,000 on December 31, 19X4.

SOLUTION:

Planning and Organizing Your Work

1. Calculate the accumulated depreciation and the carrying amount for the asset that is sold.
2. Determine the gain or loss from the sale of the asset by subtracting the sold asset's carrying amount from the proceeds from the sale.
3. Record the disposition of the asset by removing the asset and the related accumulated depreciation and by recording the cash proceeds and the gain or loss calculated in Step 2 above.

(a) *Record the entry for the sale on December 31, 19X5, for $20,000.*

Accumulated depreciation: ($20,000 x 5 years)	=	$100,000
Carrying amount ($125,000 – $100,000)	=	25,000
Loss ($25,000 – $20,000)	=	5,000

19X5			
Dec. 31	Cash	20,000	
	Accumulated Depreciation—Equipment	100,000	
	Loss from Sale of Equipment	5,000	
	Equipment		125,000
	To record sale of computer.		

(b) *Record the entry for the sale on December 31, 19X5, for $40,000.*

Accumulated depreciation: ($20,000 x 5 years)	=	$100,000
Carrying amount ($125,000 – $100,000)	=	25,000
Gain ($40,000 – $25,000)	=	15,000

19X5			
Dec. 31	Cash	40,000	
	Accumulated Depreciation—Equipment	100,000	
	Equipment		125,000
	Gain from Sale of Equipment		15,000
	To record sale of computer.		

(c) *Record the entry for the sale on December 31, 19X4, for $35,000.*

Accumulated depreciation: ($20,000 x 4 years)	=	$80,000
Carrying amount ($125,000 – $80,000)	=	45,000
Loss ($45,000 – $35,000)	=	10,000

19X4			
Dec. 31	Cash	35,000	
	Accumulated Depreciation—Equipment	80,000	
	Loss from Sale of Equipment	10,000	
	Equipment		125,000
	To record sale of computer.		

REVIEW PROBLEM C: ACQUISITION AND DEPLETION OF NATURAL RESOURCES

Star Corporation purchased a silver mine for $950,000 on January 2, 19X1. A geological survey company has estimated that 250,000 ounces of recoverable silver are in the mine. The estimated land value of the property after mining is $400,000.

REQUIRED:

a. Record the purchase of the silver mine.
b. Calculate the depletion per ounce.
c. Record depletion for the year ended December 31, 19X1, if 60,000 ounces of silver are mined and 50,000 ounces are sold.

SOLUTION:

Planning and Organizing Your Work
1. Record the purchase of the silver mine at cost.
2. Calculate depletion per ounce by dividing the cost less estimated residual value by the estimated recoverable amount of silver.
3. Record the depletion for the silver that is mined and add the amount to inventory.
4. Record the sale of silver.

(a) *Record the purchase of the mine.*

19X1			
Jan. 2	Mineral Deposits	950,000	
	Cash		950,000
	To record the purchase of the silver mine.		

(b) *Calculate depletion per ounce.*

$$(\$950,000 - \$400,000) \div 250,000 \text{ ounces} = \$2.20 \text{ per ounce.}$$

(c) *Record the mining and sale of silver.*

19X1			
Dec. 31	Mineral Inventory (60,000 x $2.20)	132,000	
	Accumulated Depletion		132,000
	To record the cost of the silver ore mined for the year.		
	Depletion Expense (50,000 x $2.20)	110,000	
	Mineral Inventory		110,000
	To record depletion expense on silver ore sold.		

KEY TERMS

SELF-QUIZ

LO 1 1. Which of the following is *not* a plant asset category?
a. Land improvements
b. Buildings
c. Inventory
d. Equipment

LO 2 2. Which of the following would *not* be included in the cost of land purchased as a site for a new building?
a. Real estate commissions
b. Removal of old building
c. Architectural fees
d. Clearing and grading

LO 2 3. True or False? The cost of constructing a driveway should be included in the cost of a building.

LO 4 4. Which of the following is typically *not* used when calculating depreciation?
a. Estimated useful life
b. Estimated benefit from using the asset
c. Estimated residual value
d. Depreciable cost

LO 5 5. The _____ depreciation method does *not* directly use the depreciable cost in the computation of depreciation expense.

LO 6 6. Which method would have the highest depreciation expense in the first year of an asset's life of 4 years (ignore residual value)?
a. Sum-of-the-years'-digits method
b. Pay-as-you-go method
c. Double-declining-balance method
d. Straight-line method

LO 7 7. State the formula to calculate return on total assets.

LO 7 8. True or False? Return on total assets tends to be higher when a company has older assets rather than newer assets.

LO 8 9. True or False? Management should restate prior years' depreciation of an asset if they receive new information indicating that the asset's estimated useful life is different than the original estimate.

LO 8 10. The _____ _____ _____ _____ _____ is used to depreciate assets for tax purposes.

LO 9 11. Repairs are _____ expenditures, and replacements are _____ expenditures.

LO 9 12. True or False? While an improvement makes an asset more efficient or effective, it does not necessarily extend the asset's useful life.

LO 10 13. True or False? Disposal of an asset may be accomplished by ceasing to use it.

LO 10 14. When a business disposes of plant assets, we record the asset's depreciation expense for the period between the end of the preceding accounting period and the _____ _____ _____.

LO 11 15. When a business purchases a copyright, we record the cost as an intangible asset and we amortize that cost over the useful life of the copyright, not to exceed _____ years.

LO 11 16. True or False? Goodwill is recorded anytime a business is able to generate earnings at a higher rate than is normal for the industry in which the business operates.

LO 12 17. Natural resources are commonly called _____ assets.

LO 12 18. Depletion, or the cost allocation process for natural resources, is similar to the _____-_-_____ depreciation method.

LO 13 19. Accounting for the exchange of assets involves three steps on the date of the exchange. Name these steps.

LO 13 20. What is the new asset's recorded cost in an exchange involving dissimilar assets?
a. The new asset's fair value plus the amount of any cash paid.
b. The old asset's fair value plus the gain recorded on the exchange.
c. The new asset's fair value less the amount of cash paid.
d. The old asset's fair value plus the amount of any cash paid.

LO 13 21. When does a gain occur on an exchange of similar productive assets?
a. When the cash paid out is greater than the recorded loss.
b. When the trade-in allowance received for the old asset exceeds its carrying amount.
c. When the old asset's carrying amount exceeds the new asset's fair value and cash is paid.
d. When the old asset's fair value exceeds the new asset's fair value and cash is paid.

SOLUTIONS TO SELF-QUIZ

1. c   2. c   3. False   4. b   5. double-declining-balance   6. c   7. (Net Income + Interest Expense) ÷ Total Assets   8. True   9. False   10. Modified Accelerated Cost Recovery System   11. revenue, capital   12. True   13. True   14. date of disposal   15. 40   16. False   17. wasting   18. units-of-production   19. Step 1: Determine the value (cost) of the asset(s) acquired.   Step 2: Determine any gain or loss on assets given, if applicable.   Step 3: Record in a single entry the acquisition of a new asset, the disposal of the old asset, and any applicable gain or loss.   20. d   21. b

QUESTIONS

Q8-1   What are four commonly used categories of plant assets?

Q8-2   What comprises the total recorded cost of a plant asset?

Q8-3   How should the cost of a group purchase be allocated to each item in the group?

Q8-4   Why do we depreciate an asset?

Q8-5   What factors are needed to calculate depreciation?

Q8-6   What are the basic differences between straight-line and accelerated depreciation methods?

Q8-7   What factors should be considered when choosing a depreciation method?

Q8-8   What action should management take if it receives new information indicating that the asset's estimated useful life or estimated residual value is different than the original estimates of these amounts?

Q8-9   What is the advantage of using accelerated depreciation for income tax purposes?

Q8-10 What are the differences between a capital expenditure and a revenue expenditure?

Q8-11 What are the differences between repairs, replacements, and improvements?

Q8-12 What is the interpretation of the return on total assets ratio?

Q8-13 What is the effect on the financial statements if a company fails to record depreciation to the date of sale?

Q8-14 Why would a company abandon an asset with a carrying amount greater than zero?

Q8-15 What are the differences among depreciation, amortization, and depletion?

Q8-16 Why do intangible assets have value to a business?

Q8-17 What is the difference between a patent and a copyright?

Q8-18 How do we account for research and development costs?

Q8-19 Why do companies record depletion for the cost of their natural resources?

Q8-20 (Appendix 8-A) When can a gain be recognized from an exchange of similar assets?

Q8-21 (Appendix 8-A) What is the tax treatment of like-kind exchanges of assets?

EXERCISES

LO 1,2

E8-1   **Costs Included In Plant Assets**   Mo Yost's Commercial Art Service, Inc. made the following expenditures:
a. Purchased a tract of land with an unusable building for $287,500, which does not include a real estate commission of $12,500.
b. Paid an architect $39,000 to design a studio.
c. Delinquent taxes on the land of $3,900 were paid.
d. Demolished the building at a cost of $19,000 and paid an additional $3,500 to clear and grade the land.
e. Constructed a studio building at a cost of $457,200 excluding the cost of building permits and legal fees of $6,000.
f. Interest expense during construction was $18,400.

REQUIRED:

Determine the capitalized cost of the land and studio building for Mo Yost's Commercial Art Service, Inc.

LO 1,2

E8-2   **Costs Included in Plant Assets**   Pep Twins, Inc. bought a new hydraulic lift for its auto repair shop. The lift had a list price of $40,000, but the dealer gave Pep

Twins a 10% reduction. Pep Twins paid a shipping firm $1,000 to pick up and deliver the lift. Insurance during transit was $500. In addition, Pep Twins had to pay $600 to reinforce the floor on which the lift would be placed. Normal installation fees on the lift were $750, but the installers broke a part and charged an additional $250. Pep Twins paid the installers the full amount requested.

REQUIRED:

Determine the cost of the equipment.

LO 2

E8-3 **Group Purchases** Billy Bob's Hardware, Inc. bought land, building, and a parking lot for $210,000 to open a store in a new location. The following information relates to acquired assets:

Asset	Appraised Value	Former Carrying Amount
Land	$140,000	$100,000
Building	100,000	60,000
Parking lot	40,000	40,000

REQUIRED:

Determine the amount of cost to be allocated to the land, building, and parking lot.

LO 5

E8-4 **Calculating Depreciation** Denisha Higgins purchased a video camera for $22,000 for her video production company. The camera has an estimated residual value of $2,000 at the end of its useful life. It is estimated that the camera has an expected useful life of 4 years, or it can be used on 250 jobs.

REQUIRED:

Determine the annual depreciation expense for:
a. Straight-line depreciation method
b. Units-of-production method if 50 jobs are shot in the first year; 100 jobs in Year 2; 75 jobs in Year 3, and 25 jobs in Year 4.

LO 5

E8-5 **Calculating Depreciation** Frank's Canvas Factory, Inc. purchased equipment for $165,000 with an estimated residual value of $15,000 on January 2, 19X1. The estimated useful life of the equipment is 5 years.

REQUIRED:

a. Determine the depreciation expense for each year if Frank's Canvas Factory, Inc. uses the sum-of-the-years'-digits method.
b. Show how the equipment would appear on the December 31, 19X3, balance sheet.

LO 5

E8-6 **Calculating Depreciation Expense** The Automated Laundry Corp. bought a triple-capacity washing machine for $8,000. The machine has an estimated life of 4 years, and it is to be depreciated using the double-declining-balance depreciation method.

REQUIRED:

Determine depreciation expense for each year if the estimated residual value is:
a. $0
b. $3,000

LO 7

E8-7 **Calculating Return on Total Assets** Feliciano Corporation's net income for the year ended December 31, 19X5, is $38,500. Interest expense was $140 for 19X5. Total assets on December 31, 19X5, is $322,000.

REQUIRED:

Calculate Feliciano Corporation's return on total assets for 19X5.

LO 8

E8-8 **Calculating Depreciation Expense for Partial Periods** Wolf's Pet Supplies, Inc. purchased $13,000 of store equipment on October 1, 19X3. The equipment has an estimated residual value of $1,000 and an estimated useful life of 6 years.

REQUIRED:

Determine depreciation expense for 19X3 and the carrying amount of the equipment at Wolf's accounting year-end of December 31, 19X4, using the straight-line method.

LO 8

E8-9 **Calculating Depreciation Expense for Partial Periods** Hahn's Meat Packing Corporation purchased a new conveyor belt on August 1, 19X5, at a cost of $20,000. The belt has a 3-year useful life and will be depreciated using the sum-of-the-years'-digits method. The estimated residual value is $2,000, and Hahn's accounting year-end is December 31.

REQUIRED:

Determine depreciation expense for the machine for 19X5, 19X6, 19X7, and 19X8.

LO 8

E8-10 **Revision of Depreciation Rates** Honey's Pancake House, Inc. acquired a restaurant on January 2, 19X2, for $220,000. The restaurant had an estimated residual value of $20,000 and an estimated useful life of 20 years when it was acquired. On January 2, 19X7, it was determined that the restaurant would only have an estimated useful life of 10 more years with $0 estimated residual value.

REQUIRED:

Determine the depreciation expense for 19X7 if Honey's uses the straight-line method.

LO 9

E8-11 **Capital versus Revenue Expenditures** Determine if each of the following items are capital (*C*) expenditures or revenue (*R*) expenditures:
___a. A major overhaul was performed on a service vehicle that had broken down.
___b. Purchased new tires for a delivery van.
___c. A new wing was added to a store.
___d. The roof of a building is replaced with a new one. The roof extended the life of the building.
___e. Repaired a leaky roof.
___f. A machine was modified so that it will use 10 percent less energy after the modification.
___g. A crumbling wall was plastered and painted.

LO 8

E8-12 **Replacements** Ellis Print Shop, Inc. has a printing press that it purchased on January 1, 19X6, at a cost of $20,000. The company uses the straight-line depreciation method. The estimated residual value was $4,000, and the estimated useful life was 4 years. On January 1, 19X8, Ellis replaced the press's motor at a cost of $6,000. This will extend the life of the press by 3 years. The residual value is now estimated to be $3,000.

REQUIRED:

Record the journal entry on January 1, 19X8, for the replacement and the journal entry on December 31, 19X8, to record 19X8's depreciation expense.

LO 10

E8-13 **Disposal of Plant Assets** Barne's Manufacturing, Inc. purchased equipment for $79,000 on January 2, 19X1, with an estimated life of 7 years and an estimated salvage value of $2,000. This asset is depreciated using the straight-line method.

REQUIRED:

Determine the gain or (loss) on disposal of the asset and record the journal entry on January 2, 19X5, if Barne's receives:
a. $0
b. $46,000

LO 10

E8-14 Disposal of Plant Assets Ewing Supply Corporation purchased equipment for $320,000 on January 2, 19X2, with an estimated life of 5 years and an estimated salvage value of $20,000. The asset is depreciated using the sum-of-the-years'-digits method.

REQUIRED:

Determine the cash received if Ewing's disposed of the asset on December 31, 19X4, at a gain of $23,000.

LO 10

E8-15 Disposal of Plant Assets Pam's Pancake House, Inc. purchased a griddle on July 1, 19X0, at a cost of $20,000. The asset was depreciated using the straight-line method. The griddle had an estimated useful life of 5 years and an estimated residual value of $0. Pam's sold the griddle on October 1, 19X3. Pam's Pancake House has a June 30 fiscal year-end.

REQUIRED:

Record the necessary journal entries for the sale on October 1, 19X3, if the griddle is sold for:
a. $6,000
b. $15,000

LO 11

E8-16 Amortization of Intangible Assets Determine the annual amortization for the following intangible assets:
a. A patent was purchased from another company for $80,000. The patent has an expected economic life of 10 years.
b. A copyright was acquired for $25,000. The copyright has an expected economic life of 45 years.
c. An artist developed a trademark. The artist was paid $12,000, and an additional $3,000 in legal fees were incurred to process the application for the trademark. The trademark has an expected economic life of 75 years.
d. A company with net assets having a fair value of $780,000 was purchased for $900,000. The goodwill is expected to have an economic life of 20 years.

LO 11

E8-17 Amortization of Intangible Assets Bill Smythe bought a Burger Bun Franchise on January 2, 19X1. The franchise fee is $20,000 and gives Smythe the exclusive right to sell Burger Buns for 20 years.

REQUIRED:

a. Record the journal entry on January 2, 19X1, for the purchase of the franchise right.
b. Record the journal entry on December 31, 19X1, for the first year's amortization of the franchise right, using straight-line amortization.

LO 11

E8-18 Research and Development During 19X1, Delta Computers, Inc. spent $400,000 in cash to research and develop a line of software. On August 14, 19X1, the software was copyrighted and is expected to be profitable for 5 years.

REQUIRED:

Record the necessary journal entries in 19X1 relating to the new line of software.

LO 12   **E8-19** **Depletion of Natural Resources** Geo Exploration Corp. purchased an offshore tract for $360,000 on January 2, 19X5. Based on test wells, geologists estimate that 240,000 barrels of oil can be recovered. The tract has no residual value.

REQUIRED:

If 50,000 barrels are pumped from the well and 40,000 barrels are sold during 19X5, determine the amount debited to inventory and the amount of depletion expense for the year ended 19X5.

LO 13   **E8-20** **Disposal of Plant Assets by Exchange (Appendix 8-A)** John's Delivery Service, Inc. exchanged an old delivery truck for a new one. On the date of exchange, the old truck had a carrying amount of $7,000. The original cost was $16,000, and accumulated depreciation was $9,000. The new truck has a list price of $20,000. A trade-in allowance of $5,500 was allowed on the old truck. Therefore, John's paid an additional $14,500 in cash to purchase the new truck.

REQUIRED:

Record the journal entry for the exchange.

LO 13   **E8-21** **Disposal of Plant Assets by Exchange (Appendix 8-A)** Marlin's Auto Sales, Inc. exchanged a used service truck and paid cash of $6,000 for an air conditioning system. On the date of exchange, the accumulated depreciation on the truck was $14,000, and the original cost was $23,500 The fair value of the used truck is $11,000 and the fair value of the air conditioning system is estimated to be $17,000.

REQUIRED:

Determine the gain or (loss) on the disposal of the truck and record the journal entry.

LO 13   **E8-22** **Disposal of Plant Assets by Exchange (Appendix 8-A)** Abalone's Lunch Meats, Inc. exchanged a used refrigeration unit and paid cash of $35,000 for a new unit. On the date of exchange, the accumulated depreciation on the refrigeration unit was $53,000; and the original cost was $82,000. The trade-in allowance for the old refrigeration unit was $39,000.

REQUIRED:

Record the journal entry for the exchange of assets.

PROBLEM SET A

LO 2,5   **P8-1A** **Purchase and Depreciation of Equipment** Metalwork International Corp. paid $190,000 on January 2, 19X4, for a computerized machine to fabricate metal machine parts. In addition, Metalwork incurred transportation costs of $3,000, installation fees of $11,000, testing costs of $2,500, and removal cost of the old equipment being replaced of $3,500. The machine has an estimated useful life of 5 years and no estimated residual value.

REQUIRED:

a. Record the journal entry for the asset's acquisition.
b. Calculate annual depreciation expense using the straight-line method.
c. Calculate the annual depreciation expense for all 5 years using the sum-of-the-years'-digits method.

 d. Calculate the annual depreciation expense for all 5 years using the double-declining-balance method.

 e. Show how the fabrication machine would appear on the December 31, 19X6, balance sheet if the double-declining-balance method is used.

LO 5

P8-2A **Depreciation Methods** On January 1, 19X2, Smithers Incorporated bought a high-speed production machine for $330,000. The machine has an estimated useful life of 5 years and an estimated residual value of $30,000. The machine should be able to produce 1,500,000 good units of output over its productive life. Estimated production is given below:

Year	Output
19X2	300,000
19X3	500,000
19X4	400,000
19X5	200,000
19X6	100,000

REQUIRED:

 a. Prepare a depreciation schedule if Smithers uses the straight-line method.

 b. Prepare a depreciation schedule if Smithers uses the units-of-production method and actual production equals estimated production.

 c. Prepare a depreciation schedule if Smithers uses the sum-of-the-years'-digits method.

 d. Prepare a depreciation schedule if Smithers uses the double-declining-balance method.

LO 9

P8-3A **Calculate and Interpret Return on Total Assets** Hamburger Heaven, Inc. has the following income statement for 19X1:

Hamburger Heaven, Inc. Income Statement For the Year Ended December 31, 19X1		
Revenues		$78,000
Cost of goods sold		41,000
Gross profit		$37,000
Expenses:		
Advertising	$ 2,700	
Depreciation	6,500	
Insurance	900	
Interest	2,400	
Wages and salaries	14,000	26,500
Net income		$10,500

Hamburger Heaven's balance sheet for December 31, 19X1, shows assets of $112,500, liabilities of $30,000, and stockholders' equity of $82,500.

REQUIRED:

 a. Calculate the return on total assets for Hamburger Heaven, Inc.

 b. While talking to owners of other restaurants in the area, you learn that most of them are experiencing returns on total assets of 18–20 percent. What could be the causes of the differences between Hamburger Heaven's return on total assets as compared to those of the other competitors? What steps would you advise Hamburger Heaven to take to improve its return on total assets?

LO 8

P8-4A **Partial Period Depreciation** On April 1, 19X7, Microware Enterprises, Inc. purchased a high-speed floppy disk copier for $9,000. The copier has an estimated useful life of 4 years and an estimated residual value of $1,000. Microware's fiscal year ends December 31.

REQUIRED:

a. Determine depreciation expense for 19X7 and 19X8 if Microware uses the straight-line depreciation method.
b. Determine depreciation expense for 19X7 and 19X8 if Microware uses the sum-of-the-years'-digits depreciation method.
c. Determine depreciation expense for 19X7 and 19X8 if Microware uses the double-declining-balance depreciation method.

LO 2,5,8

P8-5A **Group Purchase, Depreciation Methods, and Revision of Estimates** On January 2, 19X1, Joanne Bern Corp. opened a machining operation by buying an existing factory. The purchase price of the factory was $4,000,000 and included the land, the factory building, and equipment. Relevant information concerning all three assets is given below:

	Appraised Value	Estimated Useful Life	Estimated Residual Value
Land	$2,500,000		
Building	2,000,000	4 years	$200,000
Equipment	500,000	5 years	25,000

REQUIRED:

a. Record the journal entry for the group purchase on January 2, 19X1.
b. Record the journal entry for depreciation expense for 19X1, assuming the straight-line method is used.
c. Record the journal entry for depreciation expense for 19X1, assuming the double-declining-balance method is used.
d. Assume Bern uses straight-line depreciation for all assets. On January 2, 19X3, it becomes apparent that the equipment will last another 5 years and have no residual value. Record the journal entry for 19X3's depreciation of the equipment.

LO 9

P8-6A **Capital versus Revenue Expenditures** Atley Atwater Corp. purchased a delivery van on January 1, 19X4, at a total cost of $20,000. The van will be depreciated using straight-line depreciation over its estimated 4-year life. Residual value is estimated to be $2,000. On February 7, 19X5, Atley takes the truck to Phil's Repair Shop for a tuneup, oil change, belt replacement, and brake job. The total bill is $400. On January 4, 19X6, the van is taken back to Phil's for replacement of the engine at a cost of $1,500.

REQUIRED:

a. Record the journal entry for the asset's acquisition.
b. Record the journal entry for the work done on February 7, 19X5.
c. Record the journal entry on December 31, 19X5 for depreciation expense.
d. Record the journal entry on January 4, 19X6, for the replacement of the engine, assuming it will extend the life of the asset by 1 year but not change the estimated residual value. Also, record the journal entry for depreciation expense on December 31, 19X6.
e. Record the journal entry on January 4, 19X6, assuming that the engine replacement significantly improves the fuel economy of the truck but does not extend its useful life. Also record the journal entry for depreciation expense on December 31, 19X6.

LO 10

P8-7A **Disposal of Assets** Kennel Kare, Inc. purchased a grooming station on September 1, 19X6, for $7,150. The grooming station has an estimated useful life of 5 years and an estimated residual value of $550. Kennel Kare uses the straight-line depreciation method. On June 30, 19X8, Kennel Kare sold the grooming station.

REQUIRED:

a. Determine the gain or (loss) on disposal if Kennel Kare received $4,700 for the grooming station.

b. Record the journal entry for the disposal of the grooming station.

c. Determine the gain or (loss) on disposal if Kennel Kare received $750 for the grooming station.

LO 10

P8-8A **Disposal of Assets** Martin Manufacturing, Inc. purchased a stamping machine on January 3, 19X7. The machine had a cost of $20,000, an estimated useful life of 5 years, and an estimated residual value of $5,000. Martin uses straight-line depreciation and has a December 31 year-end. The machine was disposed of on April 30, 19X9. Two independent situations are given below for the disposal of the asset.

REQUIRED:

a. Record the necessary journal entries in 19X9 if Martin sold the asset for $16,000.

b. Record the necessary journal entries in 19X9 if Martin sold the asset for $5,000.

LO 11

P8-9A **Calculation and Amortization of Goodwill** On January 2, 19X2, Lonestar Corporation purchased the assets of Texas International for $1,300,000. The fair value of the assets purchased are as follows:

Asset	Fair Value
Merchandise inventory	$190,000
Equipment	480,000
Land	290,000
Office equipment	35,000
Supplies	4,000

REQUIRED:

a. Calculate the amount of goodwill.

b. Record the entry for the purchase of the assets from Texas International.

c. Record the entry for the amortization of goodwill for 19X2.

LO 12

P8-10A **Depletion of Natural Resources** On January 3, 19X4, Ironore Mining Corporation bought a mine in the Appalachian Mountains. Experts employed by the company estimated that the mine has deposits of 20,000,000 tons of coal. The mine cost $3,900,000, and an additional $200,000 was spent on legal fees to obtain necessary operating permits. The land is estimated to be worth $100,000 after all the ore has been mined. During 19X4, 4,000,000 tons were mined and 3,500,000 tons were sold for $.60 per ton cash. During 19X5, 5,000,000 tons were mined and sold for $.60 per ton cash. The mine ceased operations on June 4, 19X6, after an additional 1,000,000 tons had been mined since January 1, 19X6. All remaining coal was sold for $.50 per ton cash. Ironore sold the mine to a real estate developer for $200,000 on June 10, 19X6.

REQUIRED:

a. Record the journal entry for the purchase of the mine.

b. Record the journal entries in 19X4 for the mining and sale of coal.

c. Record the journal entries in 19X5 for the mining and sale of coal.

d. Record the journal entries in 19X6 for the mining and sale of coal.

e. Record the journal entry for the sale of the mine on June 10, 19X6.

LO 13

P8-11A **Exchange of Assets (Appendix 8-A)** Chico Corporation purchased a computerized checkout system to replace a group of cash registers by trading in the cash registers and paying $50,000. On the date of exchange, the accumulated depreciation for the cash registers was $28,000; and the original cost was $50,000. The fair value of the computerized checkout system is estimated to be $80,000.

REQUIRED:

a. Prepare the journal entry necessary to record this exchange if the assets are considered to be similar in nature.
b. Prepare the journal entry necessary to record this exchange if the asset exchanged for the checkout system is a building originally costing $50,000 and with accumulated depreciation of $28,000.

PROBLEM SET B

LO 2,5   **P8-1B   Purchase and Depreciation of Equipment**   Hardwood Furniture, Inc. paid $105,000 for a computerized sawing station to fabricate parts for furniture on January 2, 19X1. In addition, Hardwood incurred transportation costs of $2,100, installation fees of $8,700, testing costs of $4,200, and removal cost of the old equipment being replaced of $10,000. The machine has an expected life of 4 years and an estimated residual value of $5,000.

REQUIRED:

a. Record the journal entry for the asset's acquisition.
b. Calculate annual depreciation expense using the straight-line method.
c. Calculate the annual depreciation expense for all 4 years using the sum-of-the-years'-digits method.
d. Calculate the annual depreciation expense for all 4 years using the double-declining-balance method.
e. Show how the sawing station would appear on the December 31, 19X3, balance sheet if the double-declining-balance method is used.

LO 5   **P8-2B   Depreciation Methods**   On January 1, 19X4, Cousins, Inc. bought a high-speed production machine for $425,000. The machine has an estimated useful life of 5 years and an estimated residual value of $25,000. The machine should be able to produce 1,600,000 good units of output over its productive life. Estimated production is given below:

Year	Output
19X4	200,000
19X5	500,000
19X6	300,000
19X7	200,000
19X8	400,000

REQUIRED:

a. Prepare a depreciation schedule if Cousins uses the straight-line method.
b. Prepare a depreciation schedule if Cousins uses the units-of-production method and actual production equals estimated production.
c. Prepare a depreciation schedule if Cousins uses the sum-of-the-years'-digits method.
d. Prepare a depreciation schedule if Cousins uses the double-declining-balance method.

LO 7   **P8-3B   Calculate and Interpret Return on Total Assets**   Assume you are a management consultant. One of your clients, Tigert's Tapes and CDs, Inc., is unhappy with its performance. You are presented with the following income statement:

Tigert's Tapes and CDs, Inc.		
Income Statement		
For the Year Ended December 31, 19X1		
Revenues		$320,000
Cost of goods sold		180,000
Gross profit		$140,000
Expenses:		
Advertising	$12,000	
Depreciation	26,000	
Insurance	3,000	
Interest	18,000	
Wages and salaries	60,000	119,000
Net income		$ 21,000

Tigert's balance sheet shows total assets of $840,000. The property, plant, and equipment section of the balance sheet is as follows:

Land		$ 80,000
Building	$560,000	
Less: Accumulated depreciation	30,000	530,000
Equipment	$ 96,000	
Less: Accumulated depreciation	6,000	90,000

REQUIRED:

a. Calculate the return on total assets for Tigert's Tapes and CDs.
b. Should your client be unhappy with its performance? Why?
c. Suggest some actions your client might take in order to improve its performance.

LO 8   **P8-4B   Partial Period Depreciation**   On April 1, 19X8, We Rentit All, Inc. purchased a mini-computer system for $30,000 to account for its rentals. The computer has an estimated useful life of 4 years and an estimated residual value of $5,000. We Rentit All's fiscal year-end is December 31.

REQUIRED:

a. Determine depreciation expense for 19X8 and 19X9 if We Rentit All uses the straight-line depreciation method.
b. Determine depreciation expense for 19X8 and 19X9 if We Rentit All uses the sum-of-the-years'-digits depreciation method.
c. Determine depreciation expense for 19X8 and 19X9 if We Rentit All uses the double-declining-balance depreciation method.

LO 2,5,8   **P8-5B   Group Purchase, Depreciation Methods, and Revision of Estimates**   On January 2, 19X6, Hank Stern Corp. purchased an existing radio station. The purchase price of the station was $12,000,000 and included the land, the building, and equipment. Relevant information concerning all three assets is given below:

	Appraised Value	Estimated Useful Life	Estimated Residual Value
Land	$ 4,000,000		
Building	10,000,000	10 years	$1,000,000
Equipment	2,000,000	5 years	100,000

REQUIRED:

a. Record the journal entry for the group purchase on January 2, 19X6.
b. Record the journal entry for depreciation expense for 19X6, assuming the straight-line method is used.
c. Record the journal entry for depreciation expense for 19X6, assuming the double-declining-balance method is used.
d. Assume Stern uses straight-line depreciation for all of his assets. On January 2, 19X8, it becomes apparent that the equipment will last another 5 years and have no residual value. Record the journal entry for 19X8's depreciation of the equipment.

LO 9   **P8-6B   Capital Versus Revenue Expenditures**   Mary Jones Corp. purchased a used bus to give guided tours on January 1, 19X4, at a total cost of $20,000. The bus will be depreciated using straight-line depreciation over its estimated 5-year life. Residual value is estimated to be $2,000. On February 7, 19X4, Mary takes the bus to Tony's Repair Shop to fix leaking windows and the air conditioner. The total bill is $500. On January 3, 19X5, the bus is taken back to Tony's for replacement of the engine at a cost of $2,200.

REQUIRED:

a. Record the journal entry for the asset's acquisition.
b. Record the journal entry for the work done on February 7, 19X4.
c. Record the journal entry on December 31, 19X4, for depreciation expense.
d. Record the journal entry on January 3, 19X5, for the replacement of the engine assuming it will extend the life of the asset by 1 year but not change the estimated residual value. Also, record the journal entry for depreciation expense on December 31, 19X5.
e. Record the journal entry on January 3, 19X5, assuming that the engine replacement significantly improves the fuel economy of the bus but does not extend its useful life. Also record the journal entry for depreciation expense on December 31, 19X5.

LO 10   **P8-7B   Disposal of Assets**   Auto Wash, Inc. purchased an automated car wash on October 1, 19X7, for $21,850. The car wash has an expected life of 4 years and an estimated residual value of $1,850. Auto Wash uses the straight-line depreciation method. On April 1, 19X9, Auto Wash sold the automated car wash.

REQUIRED:

a. Determine the gain or (loss) on disposal if Auto Wash received $12,700 for the automated car wash.
b. Record the journal entry for the disposal of the automated car wash.
c. Determine the gain or (loss) on disposal if Auto Wash received $8,750 for the automated car wash.

LO 10   **P8-8B   Disposal of Assets**   Marlin Boats, Inc. purchased a mold injection machine on January 3, 19X2. The machine had a cost of $125,000, an estimated useful life of 8 years, and an estimated residual value of $5,000. Marlin uses straight-line depreciation and has a December 31 year-end. The machine was disposed of on April 30, 19X4. Three independent situations are given below for the disposal of the asset.

REQUIRED:

a. Record the necessary journal entries in 19X4 if Marlin sold the asset for $90,000.
b. Record the necessary journal entries in 19X4 if Marlin sold the asset for $92,000.
c. Record the necessary journal entries in 19X4 if Marlin sold the asset for $88,000.

LO 11

P8-9B   Calculation and Amortization of Goodwill   On January 2, 19X1, Dakota Corporation purchased the assets of North Company for $890,000. The fair value of the assets purchased are as follows:

Asset	Fair Value
Merchandise inventory	$160,000
Equipment	195,000
Land	160,000
Delivery equipment	65,000
Supplies	15,000

REQUIRED:

a. Calculate the amount of goodwill.
b. Record the entry for the purchase of the assets from North Company.
c. Record the entry for the amortization of goodwill for 19X1.

LO 12

P8-10B   Depletion of Natural Resources   On January 3, 19X2, Geld Mining Corporation bought a mine in the Sierra Mountains. Experts employed by the company estimated that the mine has deposits of 10,000 ounces of gold. The mine cost $1,910,000, and an additional $5,000 was spent on legal fees to obtain necessary operating permits. The land is estimated to be worth $15,000 after all the gold has been mined. During 19X2, 2,000 ounces were mined and 1,750 ounces were sold for $240 per ounce cash. During 19X3, 2,500 ounces were mined and sold for $260 per ounce cash. The mine ceased operations on June 4, 19X4, after 5,000 ounces had been mined since January 1, 19X4. All remaining gold was sold for $280 per ounce cash. Geld sold the mine to a real estate developer for $290,000 on June 10, 19X4.

REQUIRED:

a. Record the journal entry for the purchase of the mine.
b. Record the journal entries in 19X2 for the mining and sale of gold.
c. Record the journal entries in 19X3 for the mining and sale of gold.
d. Record the journal entries in 19X4 for the mining and sale of gold.
e. Record the journal entry for the sale of the mine on June 10, 19X4.

LO 13

P8-11B   Exchange of Assets (Appendix 8-A)   Harpo Corporation purchased a crane to replace a block and tackle system by trading in the block and tackle system and paying $140,000. On the date of exchange, the accumulated depreciation for the block and tackle system was $39,000; and the original cost was $60,000. The fair value of the crane is estimated to be $175,000.

REQUIRED:

a. Prepare the journal entry necessary to record this exchange if the assets are considered to be dissimilar in nature.
b. Prepare the journal entry necessary to record this exchange if the assets are considered similar in nature.

CRITICAL THINKING AND COMMUNICATING

C8-1   Ed Lohmann owns a chain of toy stores. Ed, having just acquired a new store, asked his auditor how the store should be depreciated. The accountant told Ed that there are several alternatives that could create significant differences on the balance sheet and income statement. Ed was confused about the many alternatives available and asked Hillary Karlinsky, the company accountant, to explain why different methods are acceptable and what factors should be considered when selecting a method.

REQUIRED:

Assuming the role of Hillary Karlinsky, write a memo explaining why different methods are acceptable and what factors Ed should consider.

C8-2 Helene Caudill owns a chain of discount office supply stores. Over the past 2 years, Helene has added 5 additional stores for a total of 9 stores. Helene purchased all the new stores and depreciates them using the sum-of-the-years'-digits method. The stores have an estimated useful life of 10 years. Selected financial information for her chain of stores for the last 2 years is given on the next page.

	19X4	*19X5*
Sales	$1,400,000	$2,325,000
Net income	280,000	320,000
Return on total assets	28%	21%

Helene is concerned about the decline in the return on total assets ratio and is considering slowing down or eliminating the expansion of her business.

REQUIRED:

Explain why the return on assets is declining and advise Helene if she should slow or eliminate the expansion.

C8-3 Todd Kesterson is a new accounting clerk for Compusoft, Inc., a computer software company. His supervisors asked Todd to prepare a memo detailing the accounting treatment for two independent situations described below. His supervisors are not sure why the accountants do not treat these two similar situations the same.

Situation 1. Compusoft purchased the copyright on a new spreadsheet package for $1,000,000 from Number Crunching Incorporated. Number Crunching Incorporated is in the business of developing software packages, which it then sells to companies such as Compusoft to market. This package should have a useful life of 5 years before it becomes obsolete.

Situation 2. Compusoft's own research and development group has developed a new word processing package at a cost of $1,000,000. The company views the new software as superior to anything currently on the market. The average useful life of word processing packages is 5 years. After 5 years, newer improved packages usually replace existing ones.

REQUIRED:

a. Explain the appropriate accounting treatment for each of the two situations.
b. Draft the memo as if you were Todd.

C8-4 Gwyn Lopez was assigned to inspect physically the plant assets of Twyla Corporation. During the inspection, Gwyn noticed a group of machines that were not in use. These machines were rusted and in very poor condition. Gwyn checked the numbers attached to the machines and determined that the machines were only partially depreciated. Gwyn scheduled a meeting with the controller of the plant and discussed the possibility of writing off the machines since they appeared to be obsolete. The controller told Gwyn that the company was already having a bad year and, therefore, writing off the machines would aggravate the situation and would cause him to receive a poor performance evaluation. The controller suggested that they should wait for a more profitable year to write off the equipment.

REQUIRED:

If you were Gwyn's friend, what would you advise her to do?

C8-5 Refer to the financial statements of J.C. Penney reprinted in Appendix B at the end of this text. In considering the requirements of this case, remember that Penney's is a retail merchandising company.

REQUIRED:

a. Locate Penney's depreciation accounting policy in the *Summary of Accounting Policies* immediately after the statement of cash flows. Determine the estimated useful lives for the various categories of assets. Evaluate the depreciation method used by Penney's.

b. Calculate the return on total assets for 1993, 1992, and 1991. For net income in the ratio as discussed in the chapter, use the amount in Penney's income statements named "Income before extraordinary charge and cumulative effect of accounting changes."

c. Comment on the direction of fluctuation in the return on total assets ratios.

d. By analyzing the changes in the numerators and denominators of the ratios, determine the possible causes for the fluctuations in the ratios.

CHAPTER 9

Current Liabilities and Long-Term Notes and Loans Payable

Katherine Schmidt has just put her life savings and the proceeds of a loan from her parents into buying a women's apparel shop called Fashion Ready-Wear, Inc. As the name implies, the shop specializes in women's ready-to-wear clothes that are copies of high-fashion originals. Katherine, who did her college degree in "Textiles and Related Arts" at Western University, has been with a major department store for ten years and had progressed to buyer of women's fashions before leaving to run her own business. So, she feels very capable of competing in the retail market for women's off-the-rack apparel, including buying the best fashions and managing the inventory. However, she feels less capable to run the other important aspects of her newly acquired business. In the words of experienced businesspeople, "She's never met a payroll." And, payroll is one of Katherine's concerns. The previous owners of the business warned her that the Internal Revenue Service had shut them down for a week during the Christmas peak selling season last year for nonpayment of payroll taxes. They also warned Katherine about the difficulty of managing cash flows and credit during the peak selling seasons.

Katherine knows that shutting the doors of a retail business, even for a few days, during one of the peak selling seasons can mean an unprofitable year and possible financial distress or failure (bankruptcy). So, now having purchased the business in September, she wants to be prepared to finance her first peak Christmas season; and she wants to know if the business is in good shape for utilizing the necessary sources of credit.

In this chapter, you will learn about the current liabilities that are used to finance a business and how their various features may make them more or less desirable as sources of funds. You will also learn some of the simple tools for evaluating the current liability position of a business. Finally, you will learn how to account for bank loans and notes payable.

1. Describe the various types of current liabilities businesses incur and the factors that affect which ones they utilize.
2. Calculate the interest rate implicit in losing discounts on accounts payable.
3. Account for short-term notes payable.
4. Account for short-term bank loans.
5. Calculate and interpret the number of days-purchases-in-payables and the percent utilization of a line of credit.
6. Account for long-term notes with constant principal payments.
7. Find the present value of an amount to be received in some future period, calculate the present value of a long-term note, and account for the note from issue to maturity.
8. Find the amount of the constant payments required to pay off an installment note and account for installment notes from issue to maturity.

LO 1

Describe the various types of current liabilities that businesses incur and the factors that affect which ones they utilize.

CURRENT LIABILITIES

Liabilities are a business's obligations to provide assets or services to other businesses or individuals in the future. Liabilities arise out of present and past activities or transactions. For example, when a business employs a person to work a particular day, the business has an obligation to pay that person. Similarly, when a business purchases merchandise from another business on credit, it is obligated to pay for the merchandise at a later date. These obligations are liabilities because they require the business to provide assets to other entities for things that have already happened.

Estimated and Contingent Liabilities

Many liabilities are quite definite; a debtor owes a specific amount of money due at a specific time. However, two types of liabilities are not so definite—estimated liabilities and contingent liabilities.

Estimated liabilities are those whose exact amounts will not be known until future events take place. They require estimation whenever a business prepares a balance sheet. For example, Computer Sales Corporation sells personal computers and warrantees them for one-year periods, following expiration of the manufacturers' typical 90-day warrantees. At any balance sheet date, Computer Sales has an obligation for repairs to or replacement of the computers it has sold within the last 15 months. However, Computer Sales does not know the exact amount of the obligation and must estimate an amount based on its past experience, modified for current conditions.

Contingent liabilities are potential obligations only. They depend on the outcomes of future events to determine *whether* the business must pay and, in some cases, how much the business must pay. For example, in the event that the maker of a promissory note does not pay, the endorser of the note must pay the holder (buyer). Until the maker actually defaults, the endorser's obligation is a liability *contingent* on the maker's future actions. Contingent liabilities also arise from disputed claims. Assume a customer sues Computer Sales for damages arising from the failure of computer equipment to perform adequately. Computer Sales maintains that the equipment performs properly and that it is the software the customer uses that is causing the problem. Whether an obligation exists in such a case depends on the outcome of a trial, arbitration, or settlement negotiations. Computer Sales would not even recognize such a potential obligation on its balance sheet as a liability unless it is *probable* that it will lose the suit *and* the amount awarded the plaintiff is *reasonably estimable*. Computer Sales would disclose other contingent liabilities in notes at the end of its financial statements, rather than recognizing them as specific amounts in its balance sheet.[1]

This chapter and a later chapter cover a variety of business liabilities. However, further discussion of contingent liabilities is beyond the text's scope.

Current and Long-Term Liabilities

A liability's **term to maturity** refers to the period of time until the liability must be paid. In accounting, we classify liabilities according to their terms to maturity. **Current liabilities** are those that must be satisfied within a short period by paying cash, providing other current assets, or incurring other current liabilities. According to GAAP, current liabilities generally include all liabilities due within one year or within one operating cycle, *whichever is longer.* In an earlier chapter, we defined a business's **operating cycle** as the average period of time it takes from committing of resources to provide goods or services to collecting cash from customers. In certain industries such as distilling, shipbuilding, high-rise construction, and research contracting, the operating cycle exceeds one year. In most other businesses, including virtually all merchandising businesses, the operating cycles are shorter than one year. When this is the case, we use one year to define what is "current." Liabilities that are not due within one year (or within one operating cycle, if longer) generally are referred to as **noncurrent liabilities**, **long-term liabilities**, or **long-term debts**.

TYPICAL CURRENT LIABILITIES

Before we begin discussion of some types of loans and notes payable, we list and describe the typical liabilities businesses incur. Not all of these liabilities are new to you. We briefly introduced such liabilities as accounts payable and wages and salaries payable in earlier chapters. Here, we include them in an expanded list, because it is possible to trade off the use of one type of liability for another in managing a business—as you will see very soon. In addition, several of the liabilities mentioned below will receive further coverage in this chapter.

Current Liabilities

Businesses incur a variety of current liabilities, including the portion of noncurrent liabilities to be paid in the short term.

Accounts Payable. Accounts payable consist of the amounts a business owes to outside suppliers of goods and services as of a point in time.

---

[1]"Accounting for Contingencies," *Statement of Financial Accounting Standards No. 5* (Stamford, Conn.: FASB, 1975), paras. 8–11 and 38.

Short-Term Notes Payable.   Notes payable represent written promises to pay specified amounts on specified dates at specified places to particular payees (or bearers of the notes). Short-term notes payable are due within one year (or within one operating cycle, if longer). A note payable of a debtor (maker of the note) is a note receivable to a payee. A previous chapter covers basic features common to both notes receivable and notes payable.

Short-Term Bank Loans.   Short-term bank loans are designed to help a business with short-term needs to finance assets such as accounts receivable and inventory.

Wages and Salaries Payable.   Wages and salaries payable consist of the amounts a business owes to employees for hours or periods already worked.

Payroll Taxes Payable.   Payroll taxes payable are the unpaid amounts of employee and employer payroll taxes and premiums a business owes to federal and state governments. Employee taxes include federal, state, and local income taxes withheld from employees' pay, as well as the employees' portions of social security and Medicare taxes deducted from their pay. Employer taxes consist of the employer's share of social security taxes, state and federal unemployment tax (or premiums), and workers' compensation insurance premiums.

Income Taxes Payable.   Proprietorships and partnerships are not taxed on their incomes *per se*. Instead, the owners of proprietorships and partnerships are taxed on the incomes they derive from those types of businesses. Corporations, on the other hand, are generally required to pay estimated (accrued, but unpaid) income taxes to the respective governments at least quarterly. Until a business makes these payments, the balances due are liabilities.

Current Portion of Long-Term Liabilities.   Liabilities whose terms are more than one year are often paid in installments or portions that are due at shorter intervals of one or more months. At each balance sheet date, a business evaluates such liabilities, determines the portions that are due within the coming 12 months, and reclassifies them from noncurrent to current liabilities.

Liability Trade-Offs

Some liabilities such as accounts payable, wages and salaries payable, and taxes payable arise more or less spontaneously in the course of business. Businesses use other liabilities such as bank loans and notes payable more deliberately to satisfy specific financing objectives—for example, to minimize total interest costs. The factors that affect whether a firm should borrow from one source of credit versus another are interest costs and other terms, loan arrangement costs, collateral requirements, and creditor restrictions on the business. Katherine Schmidt needs to understand these factors and how she can use different types of liabilities to finance Fashion Ready-Wear, Inc. through the peak season.

LO 2
Calculate the interest rate implicit in losing discounts on accounts payable.

FINANCING OF PURCHASES THROUGH ACCOUNTS PAYABLE

A business such as Fashion Ready-Wear, Inc. that purchases goods and services on account, in effect, borrows from the supplier of those goods or services.

Fashion Ready-Wear's suppliers offer terms of 2/10, n/30. Based on these terms, Fashion Ready-Wear may effectively borrow funds to finance each purchase for ten days at no interest cost. However, if it takes longer to pay than ten days, the business incurs a cost of borrowing from the supplier—the loss of the 2% discount on every purchase. This can have a profound effect on Fashion Ready-Wear's profitability.

Advantage of Accounts Payable as a Financing Source

Borrowing by not taking discounts on accounts payable has one great advantage—virtually no arrangement costs or arrangement requirements. A purchaser who has established credit with a supplier does not have to notify the supplier if it does not intend to take discounts on its purchases. Therefore, the purchaser can borrow spontaneously—without any arrangement costs.

Katherine Schmidt will want to purchase $150,000 in new inventory from Southwest Distributors Corporation for the Christmas buying season. If she purchases the goods on November 15 under the usual terms, 2/10, n/30, she automatically has two payment plans.

First, in general journal format, Fashion Ready-Wear records the season's purchases as follows:

19X1			
Nov. 15	Purchases	150,000	
	Accounts Payable		150,000
	To record purchases.		

If Katherine pays for the purchases in ten days, her entry to record the cash disbursement is:

Nov. 25	Accounts Payable	150,000	
	Cash		147,000
	Purchases Discounts		3,000
	To record payment for purchases—		
	2% discount taken.		

She would not pay sooner, because the first ten days of credit are free (she keeps her money and does not lose the discount). On the other hand, she may merely wait and pay $150,000 on December 15:

Dec. 15	Accounts Payable	150,000	
	Cash		150,000
	To record payment for purchase after discount		
	period expired.		

In this latter case, she will have simply borrowed the supplier's money for an additional 20 days at a cost of $3,000—the loss of the discount. During the extra 20 days, Katherine can collect and accumulate receipts from sales to pay for the purchases and other costs of running the business. So, not taking discounts on accounts payable is a form of financing the business—a form of borrowing.

Equivalent Annual Interest Rate on Accounts Payable

The $3,000 discount lost in the above example seems like a minor amount compared to the purchases. However, borrowing from suppliers for longer than the discount period can be very costly, indeed. In the case above, the discount was 2% for payment in 10 days. For keeping the money for an additional 20 days,

Fashion Ready-Wear, Inc. pays 2% interest. To find the *effective (equivalent) annual interest rate* for discounts lost, use the following formula:

$$\text{Effective Annual Rate} = \text{Discount Rate} \times \frac{\textbf{365 days}}{\textbf{Additional Days to Payment}}$$

$$36.5\% = 2\% \times \frac{365 \text{ days}}{20 \text{ days}}$$

So, we see that not taking discounts in this case is effectively equivalent to paying 36.5% interest per year. Under most conditions, such a rate is exhorbitant and will have an adverse impact on profits.

Thus, despite the ease with which Katherine will be able to use her suppliers' money, the effective interest rate is high, as illustrated above. In addition, the terms of payment are fixed. Katherine must be able to sell the apparel purchased on November 15 and collect sufficient cash from her customers by December 15 to pay for the purchases and all the other costs of running the business during that period. This may be impossible if many of the sales are on credit and not collectible until later, say, after January 1.

Like other retailers, Katherine may wish to look to other forms of borrowing to get her business through its peak season. For example, she might offer negotiable notes payable to her suppliers at better terms (for her) than those for normal terms of accounts payable. Because the notes would be negotiable and the suppliers can discount (sell) them, they may be willing to accept better terms. Alternatively, she may arrange for a bank loan. The following sections describe the characteristics of and the accounting for these alternatives.

SHORT-TERM NOTES PAYABLE

LO 3

Account for short-term notes payable

The important components of short-term promissory notes are covered in the earlier chapter on Accounts Receivable and Notes Receivable. But, some minor differences exist in how notes payable are handled relative to notes receivable. For example, the maker of a note does not change accounting for a note when a note is discounted (sold by the original payee to a subsequent holder). To the maker of the note, the liability is the same, regardless of who ultimately will be paid.

Here, we cover short-term notes that are written for single payments of both principal and interest at fixed dates 1 to 12 months from the date they are made. You will recall from the earlier chapter that the interest rate of a single-payment note is sometimes explicitly stated, for example, 10%. In such cases, the "face" amount of the note is the amount borrowed. In other cases, when no interest is stated, the face amount is more than the amount borrowed (the maker receives an amount discounted from face value). In such cases, the interest is implicit and is measured by the amount of the discount. In either case, the accounting requirements are to record the notes at the time they are made, recognize interest and properly value the notes at financial statement dates, and record payment of the notes at time of maturity.

Interest-Bearing Notes Payable

Suppose that on November 25, 19X1, Southwest Distributors agrees to accept Fashion Ready-Wear's note payable for $147,000 to pay its account payable for the November 15 purchase of inventory. The note matures in 75 days. Its purpose is to permit Fashion Ready-Wear, Inc. to postpone payment for the large quantity of merchandise purchased in anticipation of the Christmas selling season until after it sells the inventory and collects cash from its customers. Also, the interest rate of 12% is much preferred to losing discounts by paying ordinary accounts payable late. Katherine's entry to record the note is:

Nov. 25	Accounts Payable	150,000	
	Notes Payable—Southwest Distributors Corp.		147,000
	Purchases Discounts		3,000
	To record issue of 12% note payable to Southwest Distributors Corp. in payment of accounts payable less 2% discount taken.		

Fashion Ready-Wear has a fiscal year-end of January 31. Therefore, Katherine would calculate the appropriate interest accrual for the 67 days from November 25 to January 31 as follows (Remember: PRT or Principal x Rate x Time)

$$\$3,238.03 = \$147,000 \times 12\% \times \frac{67 \text{ days}}{365 \text{ days}}$$

Katherine's entry is:

19X2			
Jan. 31	Interest Expense	3,238.03	
	Interest Payable		3,238.03
	To record interest through year-end on 12% note payable to Southwest Distributors Corp.		

The note is due on February 8, 19X2. At that time, another 8 days' interest has accrued:

$$\$386.63 = \$147,000 \times 12\% \times \frac{8 \text{ days}}{365 \text{ days}}$$

Katherine's entry to record payment of the note and to record further interest for February is:

Feb. 28	Interest Expense	386.63	
	Interest Payable	3,238.03	
	Notes Payable—Southwest Distributors Corp.	147,000.00	
	Cash		150,624.66
	To record interest on and payment of 12% note payable to Southwest Distributors.		

The total cost of the note to Fashion Ready-Wear is $3,624.66, which is more than the $3,000 discount that was lost in the earlier example. However, under the note payable option, Katherine pays $3,624.66 to borrow $147,000 for 75 days; whereas, under the account payable option, she pays $3,000 to borrow $147,000 for only 20 days. Just as important, Fashion Ready-Wear probably needs the extra 55 days to generate the cash collections on its peak-season sales to pay for the loan. Thus, assuming its suppliers are willing to accept Katherine's notes, using the notes to finance purchases for the peak season is superior to losing discounts on purchases for postponed payments. The suppliers will accept the notes as payments for accounts payable, provided they are negotiable and can be discounted on favorable terms.

Noninterest-Bearing Notes Payable

All of the above advantages also apply to a note payable that carries no explicit interest rate. For example, suppose Fashion Ready-Wear, Inc. gives Southwest Distributors a $150,750, 75-day note to pay its account payable of $147,000 on November 25. The key interest calculations are as follows:

$$\text{Total interest cost (discount)} = \$150{,}750 - \$147{,}000 = \$3{,}750$$
$$\text{Daily interest cost} = \$3{,}750 \div 75 \text{ days} = \$50$$
$$\text{Interest expense November–January} = \$50 \times 67 \text{ days} = \$3{,}350$$
$$\text{Interest expense for February} = \$50 \times 8 \text{ days} = \$400$$

Katherine's entry to record issue of this alternative note that carries *implicit* interest is:

Nov. 25	Accounts Payable	150,000	
	Discounts on Notes Payable	3,750	
	Notes Payable—Southwest Distributors Corp.		150,750
	Purchases Discounts		3,000
	To record issue of note payable to Southwest Distributors Corp. in settlement of account.		

Notice that the discounted note is recorded at $150,750. However, the net account payable that it paid is only $147,000 ($150,000 less the purchase discount of $3,000). Thus, to complete its initial valuation, the $3,750 of implicit interest that ultimately will be paid is recognized as a discount on the note payable. The discount is recognized with a debit to a contra-liability account called Discounts on Notes Payable. If Katherine prepared a balance sheet as of November 25, she would use the contra-account to value the note properly on the balance sheet as follows:

Current liabilities:		
Notes payable—Southwest Distributors Corp.	$150,750	
Less: Discounts on notes payable	3,750	$147,000

No payments of interest are made on the discounted note. But, as of January 31, the end of Fashion Ready-Wear's fiscal year, Katherine records $3,350 of the total $3,750 discount as interest expense of the year ending on that date.

19X2			
Jan. 31	Interest Expense	3,350	
	Discounts on Notes Payable		3,350
	To record interest through year-end on note payable to Southwest Distributors Corp.		

The note would then appear as follows on the January 31, 19X2, balance sheet:

Current liabilities:		
Notes payable—Southwest Distributors Corp.	$150,750	
Less: Discounts on notes payable	400	$150,350

At the time the note is paid on February 8, Katherine recognizes the rest of the discount as interest.

Feb. 8	Interest Expense	400	
	Notes Payable—Southwest Distributors Corp.	150,750	
	Discounts on Notes Payable		400
	Cash		150,750
	To record interest on and payment of note payable to Southwest Distributors Corp.		

LO 4
Account for short-term bank loans.

SHORT-TERM BANK LOANS

In the preceding example, the problem of the fixed term to payment and high effective interest rate on accounts payable is solved by issuing a note to the supplier. However, suppose Katherine purchased the inventory that needed to be financed for the peak season from several suppliers. These circumstances require Katherine to negotiate the acceptance of a note by each of the suppliers. Under these circumstances, Katherine will probably prefer to arrange a bank loan so that she can take discounts on all of the accounts payable. The bank loan requires effort to arrange, may require a loan origination fee, and probably will impose some restrictions on Fashion Ready-Wear, Inc. However, these disadvantages are offset by substantial savings in interest costs and the security of prearranged financing.

Short-Term Borrowing Needs

When a business approaches a bank for a loan, the bank typically requires the applicant to supply copies of current and past financial statements, along with information about its business history and plans. The bank will do a credit analysis of the business, including an investigation of its past record of paying its creditors. The bank will evaluate the applicant's plans, including its probable ability to repay a loan. The bank will also look at the specific purpose that the business has for the loan and will counsel the business about the more suitable type of loan for its needs. For example, if the business plans to grow and requires permanent additions to buildings and equipment, then a long-term loan may be more suitable. On the other hand, the business may have a short-term, seasonal need to expand its inventory and accounts receivable during its busy selling season, as in the case of Fashion Ready-Wear, Inc.

Revolving Lines of Credit.   A short-term, revolving line of credit is suitable for the latter type of need. A **short-term, revolving line of credit** is a bank's commitment to advance funds on demand to a borrower up to a limit and for a period it sets. If a bank approves a line of credit for a borrower, it usually sets an absolute limit on the loan and a flexible limit. A flexible limit is generally tied to something that reflects the customer's need to borrow the money. For example, a flexible limit might be set as an amount equal to "50% of the cost of inventory on hand *plus* 80% of accounts receivable that are less than 90 days old." The customer can then borrow up to the amount of the flexible limit but not more than the absolute limit. The absolute limit is the maximum amount the bank expects the customer will need or the maximum amount the customer can be expected to repay—whichever is less. The flexible limit escalates with the needs of the customer, thereby providing the customer with additional financing on an "as needed" basis.

When Katherine bought Fashion Ready-Wear, Inc. she understood that the previous owners had negotiated a line of credit with a bank. The bank had agreed to lend Fashion Ready-Wear amounts up to 50% of its inventory total and 50% of its accounts receivable—but not to exceed $200,000. On November 25, Fashion Ready-Wear has inventory of $200,000 and accounts receivable of $140,000. This means that it can borrow up to $170,000 [(.5 x $200,000) + (.5 x $140,000)] on its line of credit by simply calling its bank loan officer and requesting that the money be transferred to its account. However, after the busy season is over and inventory and accounts receivable resettle to off-season levels of $70,000 and $50,000, respectively, the maximum loan amount will be $60,000 [(.5 x $70,000) + (.5 x $50,000)]. If Fashion Ready-Wear borrows more than this during the busy time, it will have to repay at least part of the loan as its accounts receivable and inventory levels drop.

Other Short-Term Lending Terms. Other customary terms are used for short-term bank loans such as the one described above. First, banks making such loans generally require that the customer pledge its inventory and accounts receivable as collateral for the loan, which means that the bank may take the assets in settlement if the customer does not repay the loan on time. Second, the loan is usually a "demand" loan, which means that the bank can *require that it be repaid in full at any time*. The bank usually requires that the customer pays the loan balance in full once each year (in the off-season). Third, the interest rate is often flexible; that is, it is tied to a "base" rate that fluctuates with the rate at which the Federal Reserve Bank makes loans to other banks, called the *rediscount rate*. Bank base rates vary with conditions in the economy and the Federal Reserve System's policy of either expanding or contracting the money supply. A business borrowing on a revolving line of credit is likely to be quoted "base plus one" or "base plus two."[2] If the base rate is 8%, the customer will pay an annual effective rate of 9% or 10%, respectively. Fourth, interest on the loan balance is payable each month or quarter. Fifth, the bank makes a commitment to provide funds to the borrower up to the applicable limit. If the borrower does not use the full credit available, the bank often charges a small rate on the unused portion of the commitment, say, 1% or 2%. Sixth, the bank may require that the borrower maintain a minimum balance in the borrower's accounts with the bank; or the bank may adjust the interest rate downward if the borrower maintains such a balance. Seventh, the bank may require the borrower to sign a special note (non-negotiable) agreeing to all the other required terms and conditions. If the borrower is required to pledge assets as collateral or to maintain a minimum balance, the borrower must disclose these facts in notes at the end of the financial statements.

Accounting for Short-Term Bank Loans

The bank agreed to charge Fashion Ready-Wear, Inc. 10% per year with interest payable for each month on the tenth day of the following month. On November 25, Fashion Ready-Wear borrows $147,000 to pay its total accounts payable on

---

[2]The often quoted base rate that large banks charge their most creditworthy customers is called the *prime rate*.

its seasonal purchases in time to take the discounts. Katherine's entries to record the two transactions are:

19X1			
Nov. 25	Cash	147,000	
	Notes Payable—Bank		147,000
	To record borrowing against revolving line of credit.		
25	Accounts Payable	150,000	
	Cash		147,000
	Purchases Discounts		3,000
	To record payment for purchases less 2% discount taken.		

On December 10, 19X1, interest is due for the month of November. We calculate interest in this case in the same way that we do for short-term notes receivable as described earlier:

$$\$201.37 = \$147{,}000 \times 10\% \times \frac{5 \text{ days}}{365 \text{ days}}$$

Katherine would accrue this amount as of November 30, 19X1:

Nov. 30	Interest Expense	201.37	
	Interest Payable		201.37
	To record accrued interest on short-term bank borrowing.		

When payment is made, Katherine records it as follows:

Dec. 10	Interest Payable	201.37	
	Cash		201.37
	To record payment of accrued interest on short-term bank borrowing.		

Since interest costs are paid monthly, the entry to record repayment of the loan would include only interest not previously paid. For example, if Fashion Ready-Wear repays its loan on February 10, Katherine would remit the principal amount plus interest for January (which would have been accrued on January 31) plus interest for the 10 days in February:

$$\$1{,}248.49 = \$147{,}000 \times 10\% \times \frac{31 \text{ days}}{365 \text{ days}}$$

$$\$402.74 = \$147{,}000 \times 10\% \times \frac{10 \text{ days}}{365 \text{ days}}$$

19X2			
Feb. 10	Interest Payable	1,248.49	
	Interest Expense	402.74	
	Notes Payable—Bank	147,000.00	
	Cash		148,651.23
	To record repayment of short-term bank loan with accrued interest.		

The total interest cost of the loan would be:

November	$ 201.37
December	1,248.49
January	1,248.49
February	402.74
Total	$3,101.09

Thus, the bank loan alternative provides advantages over losing discounts on accounts payable similar to the advantages of issuing negotiable notes payable to individual suppliers—a longer, more flexible term and lower effective interest cost. The bank loan also provides the additional advantage of prearranged financing with only one entity—the bank.

ANALYZING AND INTERPRETING INFORMATION ABOUT CURRENT LIABILITIES

LO 5
Calculate and interpret the number of days-purchases-in-payables and the percent utilization of a line of credit.

Let us now return to the basic problem that Katherine Schmidt faces. As she looks forward to the peak selling season, she needs:

1. Sufficient financing to purchase a large quantity of inventory and
2. Postponement of repayment over a sufficient period to recover cash from the sales of the seasonal inventory to repay the financing.

She believes the bank line of credit is her best source of financing because the terms fit her needs and the line of credit is already arranged. However, this special financing will allow her to meet her out-of-pocket expenses such as wages and salaries, payroll taxes, and employee benefits only if the business is in good financial condition going into the peak season. To determine Fashion Ready-Wear, Inc.'s short-term financial condition going into the peak season, Katherine wants some diagnostic tools to indicate whether the business is up-to-date in paying its bills and has borrowing power in its line of credit. Illustration 9-1 shows the financial statements of Fashion Ready-Wear for October 19X1.

Days-Purchases-in-Payables

Two indicators of short-term financial condition are **days-purchases-in-payables** and **percent utilization of a line of credit**. The former can be used to infer how promptly a business has been paying its accounts payable; the latter can be used to determine whether credit is available to the business when it needs it.

To calculate days-purchases-in-payables, you must first calculate purchases. This is often the case when businesses do not publish financial statements with the full detail of cost of goods sold included. To calculate purchases (cost of goods purchased), recall the following calculation of cost of goods sold from an earlier chapter:

Beginning inventory (BI)
Add: Purchases (P)
Cost of goods available for sale
Less: Ending inventory (EI)
Cost of goods sold (COGS)

ILLUSTRATION 9-1 Fashion Ready-Wear, Inc.'s Financial Statements

Fashion Ready-Wear, Inc.
Income Statement
For the Month Ended October 31, 19X1

Net sales	$150,000
Cost of goods sold	75,000
Gross profit	$ 75,000
Expenses	65,000
Net income	$ 10,000

Fashion Ready-Wear, Inc.
Balance Sheet
September 30 and October 31, 19X1

	Sept. 30		Oct. 31	
Assets				
Cash		$ 10,000		$ 40,000
Accounts receivable		90,000		80,000
Inventory		75,000		70,000
Store equipment	$200,000		$200,000	
Less: Accumulated depreciation	122,000	78,000	125,000	75,000
Total assets		$253,000		$265,000
Liabilities and Owner's Equity				
Accounts payable		$ 30,000		$ 20,000
Notes payable—bank		20,000		10,000
Wages and salaries payable		6,000		5,000
Income taxes payable		3,000		2,000
Owner's capital		194,000		228,000
Total liabilities and owner's equity		$253,000		$265,000

In symbol form, the relationship is:

$$P + BI - EI = COGS$$

We solve this equation for cost of purchases (P), thusly:

$$P = COGS - BI + EI, \text{ or}$$

$$P = COGS + (EI - BI), \text{ or}$$

$$P = COGS + \text{(Change in Inventory)}$$

In other words, since goods purchased are either sold during the period or remain in ending inventory at the end of the period, purchases equals cost of goods sold plus any increase in inventory. When purchases are less than cost of goods sold, the business draws down its inventory to make sales. Then, purchases equals cost of goods sold less the decrease in inventory. Thus, Ready-Wear's purchases for October must have been:

$$\text{Purchases} = \$75,000 + (\$70,000 - \$75,000)$$
$$\text{Purchases} = \$75,000 + (-\$5,000) = \$70,000$$

Now, using the calculated purchases figure, we determine the days-purchases-in-payables using the following equation:

$$\textbf{Days-Purchases-in-Payables} = \frac{\textbf{Accounts Payable Balance}}{\textbf{Purchases}} \textbf{ x Days in Period}$$

$$\text{Days-Purchases-in-Payables} = \frac{\$20,000}{\$70,000} \text{ x 31 days} = 8.86 \text{ days}$$

The value of 8.86 days tells us that the Accounts Payable balance of $20,000 is equal to approximately 9 days purchases, or that the accounts are, on average, about 9 days old. Since Fashion Ready-Wear, Inc. buys on terms of 2/10, n/30, accounts that are, on average, 9 days old are within the 10-day discount period. We interpret this information as favorable, since it implies that Fashion Ready-Wear has had the ability to pay its accounts on a timely basis and not lose purchases discounts.

As you can see, the days-purchases-in-payables is a useful diagnostic tool, especially when the terms of purchases are known. However, a word of caution is in order. Note that the number of days-purchases-in-payables and the age of the payables are average figures. Both are based on the average day's purchases for the period. They can be quite accurate when applied to one month's data. However, purchases may fluctuate significantly over a period as long as a year, especially in a seasonal business. Therefore, great caution should be used in making inferences from annual calculations.

Percent Utilization of a Line of Credit

The percent utilization of a line of credit is a straightforward indicator. We calculate it as follows:

$$\textbf{Percent Utilization} = \frac{\textbf{Loan Balance}}{\textbf{Maximum Available Loan}} \textbf{ x 100\%}$$

For a revolving line of credit such as Fashion Ready-Wear has arranged, the maximum available loan is the flexible loan limit or the absolute limit, whichever is less. Fashion Ready-Wear's bank has agreed to loan it amounts up to 50% of its inventory total and 50% of its accounts receivable—but not to exceed $200,000. We calculate the flexible limit on October 31 as follows:

$$(.5 \text{ x } \$70,000) + (.5 \text{ x } \$80,000) = \$75,000$$

Since the flexible limit is less than the absolute limit of $200,000, it is used in calculating the percent utilization:

$$\textbf{Percent Utilization} = \frac{\$10,000}{\$75,000} \textbf{ x 100\% = 13.3\%}$$

The value of 13.3% tells us that the revolving line of credit is not being heavily utilized as of October 31 and that a significant borrowing capacity is ready for utilization as the peak selling season approaches.

Together, the approximately 9 days-purchases-in-payables, the relatively low utilization of the line of credit, and the cash balance of $40,000 (up from

$10,000 at the end of September) imply that Fashion Ready-Wear is in relatively good condition to enter the peak selling season. To achieve a more precise conclusion would require an analysis of expected cash inflows (including borrowings) and outflows (including interest and repayments).

LONG-TERM NOTES AND LOANS PAYABLE

A business often arranges long-term loans when it requires additional financing for long-run expansions of its assets and when the necessary capital is not available from either the owners or internally from past earnings. Long-term borrowings may be in the form of long-term notes payable or bonds payable (described in a later chapter). A business may borrow money from a bank, giving a long-term note in exchange, and then spend the cash on needed assets. Or, the supplier of the assets may accept a long-term note in exchange for the assets.

LO 6

Account for long-term notes with constant principal payments.

Long-Term Notes With Constant Principal Payments

On January 1, 19X1, Centex Retail Store, Inc. gave a $5,000, 5-year, 12% note payable to Quality Equipment, Inc. in exchange for store equipment that is worth $5,000. The terms of the note call for semiannual interest payments and $500 semiannual payments of principal on June 30 and December 31 of 19X1 through 19X5. Illustration 9-2 shows the first-year history of the note.

ILLUSTRATION 9-2 First-Year History of a Long-Term Note Payable

	19X1
January 1, balance	$5,000
Accrued interest, Jan.–June	300
Payment on June 30	(800)
July 1, balance	$4,500
Accrued interest, July–Dec.	270
Payment on December 31	(770)
December 31, balance	$4,000

In the same way that we illustrated for short-term notes earlier in this chapter, Centex accrues interest every 6 months on this note. However, Centex prefers to measure time in months, not days. For the first six months, it accrues $300:

$$I = PRT = \$5,000 \times 12\% \times \frac{6 \text{ months}}{12 \text{ months}} = \$300$$

The two payments in Illustration 9-2 each consists of the $500 payment of principal plus the interest accrued since the previous payment—a total of $800 on June 30 and $770 on December 31. Because Centex pays $500 of the principal every 6 months, the principal amount of the note declines. As a result, the amount of interest accrued and paid at each date declines. Thus, Centex accrues $270 for the July-December period of 19X1, because the July 1 balance is $4,500 after the first principal payment. Because the principal payment remains constant, the total payment declines as the 6-month interest declines. Centex's entries for the first year of the note are representative of all the subsequent years:

19X1			
Jan. 1	Equipment	5,000	
	Notes Payable—Noncurrent		5,000
	To record purchase of equipment and issue of 5-year note to Quality Equipment.		
June 30	Interest Expense	300	
	Notes Payable—Noncurrent	500	
	Cash		800
	To record interest and semiannual payment on 5-year note payable to Quality Equipment.		
Dec. 31	Interest Expense	270	
	Notes Payable—Noncurrent	500	
	Cash		770
	To record interest and semiannual payment on 5-year note payable to Quality Equipment.		

Illustration 9-3 shows the complete history of the 5-year note. Notice that the above interest and payment pattern repeats every January-June and every July-December from 19X1 to 19X5. Interest is accrued on the beginning balance and is paid along with $500 of the principal amount of the note. Notice that the December 31 balance (last line) declines from $4,500 on December 31, 19X1, to $0 on December 31, 19X5, the maturity date of the note.

ILLUSTRATION 9-3 Five-Year History of Note Payable

	19X1	19X2	19X3	19X4	19X5
January 1, balance	$5,000	$4,000	$3,000	$2,000	$1,000
Accrued interest, Jan.-June	300	240	180	120	60
Payment on June 30	(800)	(740)	(680)	(620)	(560)
July 1, balance	$4,500	$3,500	$2,500	$1,500	$ 500
Accrued interest, July-Dec.	270	210	150	90	30
Payment on December 31	(770)	(710)	(650)	(590)	(530)
December 31, balance	$4,000	$3,000	$2,000	$1,000	$ 0

LO 7

Find the present value of an amount to be received in some future period, calculate the present value of a long-term note, and account for the note from issue to maturity.

Notes That Require Initial Valuation

Accounting for the note in the above example is straightforward because the principal payments are constant and the interest payments are simply added on. Conveniently, the note's face amount equaled the equipment's cash value at the time it was purchased. Thus, no question is raised about the proper valuation of the equipment or the liability. However, these conditions are not always met. Sometimes, the cash value of an asset purchased with a note does not equal the note's face amount. At other times, the cash value of the asset acquired cannot be established, except implicitly from the terms of the note. To handle such situations, we use the concept of the "present value" of future cash payments.

Concept of Present Value.   The **present value** of an amount to be received in the future is the amount that a rational person would accept now in exchange for the right to receive the future amount. Intuitively, **future values** always exceed the equivalent present values:

Present Value < Future Value

Why do rational individuals attach smaller present values to future sums? Because they can invest the money they currently hold and earn additional funds during the time they would have to wait to receive the future funds. For example, if they can invest funds to earn 12% interest for one year, then $1 invested currently would be worth $1.12 one year from now. Thus, $1 is the present value of $1.12 to be received after one year. If the $1 is invested for two years, it will be worth $1.25 in two years; and $1 is the present value of $1.25 to be received in two years:

Beginning principal, Year 1	$1.0000	← Present Value
Add interest at 12% per year	0.1200	
Beginning principal, Year 2	$1.1200	
Add interest at 12% per year	0.1344	
Ending principal, Year 2	$1.2544	
Ending principal rounded to nearest cent	$1.25	← Future Value

Notice that the interest earned in Year 1, in turn, earns interest in Year 2. We call interest earned on principal *and* previous interest amounts **compound interest**. Compound interest calculations reduce to a simple mathematical formula:

$$FV = PV(1 + i)^n$$

FV stands for the future value of a current or present value (*PV*) invested. The term, *n*, is the number of periods for which the amount is invested; and the term, *i*, is the interest rate. Using the example above in which $n = 2$, $i = 12\%$, and $PV = \$1$:

$$FV = \$1(1 + .12)^2 = \$1.2544$$

Turning this relationship around gives us a formula for the present value of an amount to be received in the future.

$$PV = \frac{FV}{(1 + i)^n}$$

$$PV = \frac{\$1}{(1 + .12)^2} = \$.7972$$

This says that the present (cash) equivalent value of $1 to be received at the end of 2 years is $.7972. To prove that the present value formula is correct, we repeat our previous detailed interest calculations, beginning with a first-year principal amount of $.7972:

Beginning principal, Year 1	$0.7972	← Present Value
Add interest at 12% per year	0.0957	
Beginning principal, Year 2	$0.8929	
Add interest at 12% per year	0.1071	
Ending principal, Year 2	$1.0000	← Future Value

Earlier we said that $1 invested for two years at 12% will equal $1.2544. Therefore, we can say that $1 is the present value of $1.2544. We can get the same result by multiplying the $1.2544 times the present value of $1 to be received after two years:

$$PV = \$1.2544 \times .7972 = \$1.000$$

Thus, we can find the present value of any future amount by simply multiplying the future amount by the present value of $1 to be received after the same number of periods.

Present Value Tables.   Since the present-value-future-value relationship reduces to a mathematical formula, anyone who solves it for a particular interest rate and number of periods achieves the same result. However, the calculations can be tedious without a calculator or computer assistance. To save unnecessary effort, tables of present values are available. Table 1 in Appendix C to this text displays the present value of one dollar to be received after 1 to 25 periods at interest rates from 1% to 18%. To use the table, find the intersection of the column of the desired interest rate and the row of the relevant waiting period (n). For example, the present value of $1 to be received after 14 years at 11% interest is $.2320.

Valuing Notes Payable Using Present Values.   Quality Equipment, Inc. offers merchants such as Centex Retail Store a special payment plan. The entire price charged for equipment is due in a lump sum at the end of two years. On July 1, 19X1, the first day of its fiscal year, Centex purchases equipment under the plan for an agreed-upon payment of $9,000 to be made on June 30, 19X3. Centex makes a noninterest-bearing note payable to Quality Equipment for $9,000. Quality custom-configured the equipment for Centex, so there is no market value of comparable equipment to refer to in establishing its value. In this case, the present value of the payment is a reasonable approximation of the equipment's value, assuming Centex is competent and rational in accepting the payment arrangement. Indeed, Centex probably should calculate the present value of the payment to determine whether the equipment is "worth" its equivalent cash price.

If the prevailing interest rate to Centex for borrowed funds is 9% per year, $.8417 is the present value of $1 to be received (paid) after two years (see the intersection of the $n=2$ row and the 9% column of Table 1, Appendix C). Therefore, $7,575.30 is the present value of $9,000 ($9,000 x .8417 = $7,575.30). $7,575.30 is the value of the liability at the date of purchase and the value to Centex of the equipment purchased in exchange for the liability. Centex would record the transaction thus:

19X1			
July 1	Equipment	7,575.30	
	Discount on Notes Payable	1,424.70	
	Notes Payable—Noncurrent		9,000.00
	To record purchase of equipment and issue of		
	note payable to Quality Equipment.		

Notice that we record the note payable at face value, but we also record the difference between its face value and its present value in Discount on Notes Payable. Thus, the note's carrying value (face value less discount) is equal to its present value, the value of the liability and of the equipment.

Interest on Notes Valued Using Present Values. By just knowing the implicit interest rate and the number of periods used to derive the note's present value, the note's entire history can be scheduled in advance as in Illustration 9-4. Only one terminal payment is required and, therefore, interest is compounded annually.

ILLUSTRATION 9-4 History of a Two-Year Discounted Note Payable

Balance, July 1, 19X1	$7,575.30
Fiscal 19X2 interest @ 9%*	681.78
Balance, June 30, 19X2	$8,257.08
Fiscal 19X3 interest @ 9%#	742.92
Balance, June 30, 19X3	$9,000.00

*Recall that Centex's fiscal year begins July 1.
#Compound interest calculations often lead to rounding differences. It is customary to "adjust" the final interest accrual to correct any difference and force the final value of the liability to the exact amount to be paid at maturity. In this case, the final interest accrual was reduced by $.22 to eliminate a rounding difference ($8,257.08 x .09 = $743.14).

Centex would record interest expense and the single payment as follows:

19X2			
June 30	Interest Expense	681.78	
	Discount on Notes Payable		681.78
	To record interest on 2-year note payable to Quality Equipment, Inc.		
19X3			
June 30	Interest Expense	742.92	
	Discount on Notes Payable		742.92
	To record interest on 2-year note payable to Quality Equipment, Inc.		
June 30	Notes Payable—Noncurrent	9,000.00	
	Cash		9,000.00
	To record payment of 2-year note payable to Quality Equipment, Inc.		

Notice that Centex does not credit the amount of interest expense to an interest payable account. Instead, it deducts the accrued interest from (credits it to) Discount on Notes Payable. This process is called *amortizing the discount.* Interest is then calculated on the note's larger carrying value (face value less the unamortized remainder of the discount) in the second year. The second year's amortization of the discount reduces it to zero; and, thus, the note's carrying value equals its face value at the time it is paid:

	Note Payable	Discount	Carrying Value
Balance, July 1, 19X1	$9,000.00	$1,424.70	$7,575.30
Fiscal 19X2 interest (amortization) @ 9%		(681.78)	
Balance, June 30, 19X2	9,000.00	742.92	8,257.08
Fiscal 19X3 interest (amortization) @ 9%		(742.92)	
Balance, June 30, 19X3	9,000.00	0.00	9,000.00

We do not use the same straight-line methodology for amortizing the discount and recognizing interest that we use on short-term notes. Under the straight-line method, we would have divided the total discount of $1,424.70 ($9,000 − $7,575.30) by the number of days of the loan to get a daily interest accrual. Then, we would have multiplied the daily accrual times the number of days in each accrual period. That methodology would have allocated an equal amount of interest to both years in the life of the note:

	Note Payable	Discount	Carrying Value
Balance, July 1, 19X1	$9,000.00	$1,424.70	$7,575.30
Fiscal 19X2 interest @ 9%		(712.35)	
Balance, June 30, 19X2	9,000.00	712.35	8,287.65
Fiscal 19X3 interest @ 9%		(712.35)	
Balance, June 30, 19X3	9,000.00	0.00	9,000.00

However, the straight-line methodology ignores the compound interest *implicit* in the present value that permitted us to value the note initially. The difference between a "straight-line" allocation of the total interest cost to 19X2 and 19X3 and the allocation based on the interest rate times the note's increasing carrying value is not very great. Nevertheless, the interest rate method is considered to be more "correct." The difference is generally immaterial over periods shorter than a year, and the straight-line methodology illustrated earlier is widely used for short-term notes.

Long-Term Installment Loans

LO 8

Find the amount of the constant payments required to pay off an installment note, and account for installment notes from issue to maturity.

Installment loans present some additional challenges, both in financing a business and in accounting for the liabilities. Many loans require multiple payments of interest and principal. Technically, they all could be called installment loans. However, it is customary to use the term **installment loan** only to describe a loan that is repaid with a *series of equally spaced payments of a constant amount*. One of the challenges is to determine the constant amount of the installment payments required to repay a loan at a particular interest rate over a particular number of installments. For example, what annual payment is required in each of 5 years to repay a $10,000 loan at 11% interest? To determine the answer, you first have to understand the concept of an annuity value.

Concept of an Annuity Value. An **annuity** is any series of equal payments to be paid or received at the ends of a series of fixed periods. Annuities are described by the amount of the payments and the number and length of the periods. For example, a $1,000, 5-year annuity is a series of $1,000 amounts to be paid or received at the end of each year for 5 years illustrated by this time line:

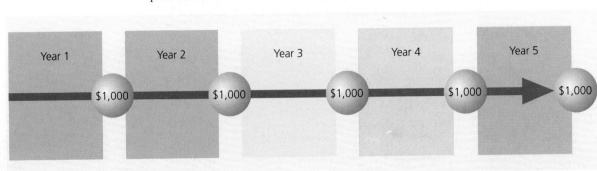

The first payment in the annuity series is paid or received at the end of the first year; the second payment, at the end of the second year, etc. A stream in which the amounts are paid or received at the beginnings of the periods is called an **annuity due**. However, most liabilities requiring constant payments fit the pattern of an annuity rather than an annuity due.

An **annuity value** is the *sum* of the present values of each of the individual $1 amounts paid or received at the end of each of a specified number of periods in a $1 annuity. *To calculate the annuity value of $1 to be received at the end of, say, each of 5 years at 11% interest, we add the present values of each of the individual payments:*

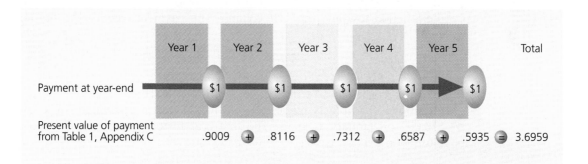

This calculation tells us that an individual who could earn 11% interest on money invested would be willing to pay $3.6959 for the right to receive $1 at the end of each year for 5 years. Note that the above total of the 5 present values, rounded to three decimal places (3.696), can be found at the intersection of the 11% column and the 5-period row of Table 2 in Appendix C. Table 2 contains the annuity values corresponding to $1 annuities for all the periods and at all the interest rates included in Table 1.

Present Value of an Annuity. Since the annuity value from the table is the present value of an annuity of $1 payments, it can be multiplied by the amount of the payments of annuities of any sizes to get their present values:

$$PV = AV \times PMT$$

PV here represents the total present value of the entire annuity; *AV*, the annuity value factor from Table 2; and *PMT*, the amount of each payment in the annuity. The total present value at, say, 13% of the $1,000, 5-year annuity illustrated in the time line above is:

Amount of each payment	$1,000.00
Annuity value from Table 2	
for 5 periods at 13%	x 3.517
Present value of the payments	$3,517.00

Receiving the rights to the $1,000 annuity is the economic equivalent of having $3,517.00 invested at 13% interest today. Thus, we can interpret the $3,517.00 present value as the amount a rational individual would be willing to pay for $1,000 to be received at the end of each of 5 years, assuming the individual could earn 13% on money he or she invests.

Installments Required to Repay a Note Payable.   Now, by simply turning the above present value formula around (that is, solving for *PMT*), we have a relationship that will tell us the size of a series of payments required to repay a loan.

$$PMT = \frac{PV}{AV}$$

The required payment size is the present value (the amount borrowed or the value of the goods purchased with a note) *divided by* the appropriate annuity value factor. Now, we return to the problem posed earlier: How much must each of 5 equal annual payments be to repay a $10,000 loan at 11% interest? The appropriate annuity value of 3.696 is found in Table 2 at the intersection of the 5-period row and the 11% column. The payment (rounded to the nearest cent) is:

$$PMT = \frac{\$10,000}{3.696} = \$2,705.63$$

Accounting for Long-Term Installment Notes Payable.   Suppose the note in the above example is made payable to a bank in exchange for a loan of $10,000 on January 1, 19X1. The first-year history of the note is shown in Illustration 9-5.

ILLUSTRATION 9-5 First-Year History of Installment Note

	19X1
January 1, balance	$10,000.00
Accrued interest, Jan.–Dec.	1,100.00
Payment on December 31	(2,705.63)
December 31, balance	$ 8,394.37
Implicit principal payment	$ 1,605.63

Notice that interest is accrued at the interest rate on which the installment calculation was based, 11%, times the January 1 balance. Since the payment is fixed at $2,705.63, we derive the **implicit principal payment** by subtracting the interest component from the total payment ($1,605.63 = $2,705.63 – $1,100.00). The implicit principal payment is the amount by which the first installment payment reduces the principal amount owed on the note. Here are the entries to record the issue of the note and to recognize interest expense and the first year's payment:

19X1 Jan. 1	Cash Notes Payable—Noncurrent To record issue of 5-year installment note payable to Bank.	10,000.00	10,000.00
Dec. 31	Notes Payable—Noncurrent Interest Expense Cash To record interest and payment on 5-year installment note payable to Bank.	1,605.63 1,100.00	2,705.63

The entry for interest and the annual payment for the first year is representative of the subsequent years' entries. However, because the principal amount of the loan declines with each payment, the subsequent year's interest expense declines; and the amount of each year's payment that reduces the principal amount increases. These patterns are reflected in the 5-year history of the note in Illustration 9-6.

ILLUSTRATION 9-6 History of an Installment Note Payable*

	19X1	19X2	19X3	19X4	19X5
January 1, balance	$10,000.00	$8,394.37	$6,612.12	$4,633.82	$2,437.91
Accrued Interest, Jan.–Dec.	1,100.00	923.38	727.33	509.72	267.72
Payment on December 31	(2,705.63)	(2,705.63)	(2,705.63)	(2,705.63)	(2,705.63)
December 31, balance	$ 8,394.37	$6,612.12	$4,633.82	$2,437.91	$ 0.00
Implicit principal payment	$ 1,605.63	$1,782.25	$1,978.30	$2,195.91	$2,437.91

*In multiple-period present value and annuity calculations, there is always some rounding difference. Rounding differences will prevent the calculations used in accounting for long-term debts to come out exactly even. Accountants commonly adjust the last interest accrual to make the numbers work out evenly. We follow this practice throughout this chapter, and you will need to do the same in solving some of the exercises and problems at the end of the chapter.

For example, interest for 19X2 is $923.38 ($8,394.37 x 11%), rather than the $1,100.00 of 19X1. Thus, $1,782.25 of 19X2's installment is a reduction of principal—in contrast to $1,605.63 in 19X1. The principal payments implicit in each year's installment in Illustration 9-6 reduce the liability's carrying value to zero after the fifth payment—as they should.

Balance Sheet Disclosure of Long-Term Obligations

Because long-term installment obligations generally have one or more remaining installments due within one year, a portion of the long-term obligation is a current liability. For example, in the case of the long-term installment note of Illustration 9-6, the carrying value of $8,394.37 as of December 31, 19X1, can be broken down into the following present values:

Installment due December 31, 19X2 ($2,705.63 x .9009*)	$2,437.50
Installments due after December 31, 19X2 ($8,394.37 – $2,437.50)	5,956.87
Total	$8,394.37

*Present value of $1 for one year at 11% interest.

The issuer of the installment note in this case would disclose the note in its December 31, 19X1, balance sheet as follows:

Current liabilities	
Current portion of noncurrent notes payable	$2,437.50
Noncurrent liabilities	
Notes payable—noncurrent	$5,956.87

Year-End Accrued Interest on Long-Term Installment Notes

If the installment note of Illustration 9-6 had been issued on July 1, 19X1, but the issuer's fiscal year ended on December 31 (as assumed above), accounting for the note would change slightly. The issuer would accrue one-half year's interest at December 31 each year and the other half at the time of the annual payment. The entries for the first year in the life of the note would be:

19X1			
July 1	Cash	10,000.00	
	Notes Payable—Noncurrent		10,000.00
	To record issue of 5-year installment note payable to Bank.		
Dec. 31	Interest Expense	550.00	
	Interest Payable—Installment Note		550.00
	To accrue interest expense on 5-year installment note payable to Bank.		
19X2			
June 30	Notes Payable—Noncurrent	1,605.63	
	Interest Expense	550.00	
	Interest Payable—Installment Note	550.00	
	Cash		2,705.63
	To record interest and payment on 5-year installment note payable to Bank.		

SUMMARY

Describe the various types of current liabilities that businesses incur and the factors that affect which ones they utilize.   Liabilities are a business's obligations to provide assets or services to other businesses or individuals in the future. They arise out of present and past activities or transactions. Many liabilities are quite definite—however, two types of liabilities are not so definite, estimated liabilities and contingent liabilities. Current liabilities are those that must be satisfied within one year or within one operating cycle, whichever is longer. Typical current liabilities include accounts payable, short-term notes payable, short-term bank loans, wages and salaries payable, payroll taxes payable, income taxes payable, and the current portion of long-term debt. The factors that affect whether a firm should borrow from one source of credit versus another are interest costs and other terms, loan arrangement costs, collateral requirements, and creditor restrictions on the business.

Calculate the interest rate implicit in losing discounts on accounts payable.   To find the effective (equivalent) annual interest rate for discounts lost, use the following formula:

$$\text{Effective Annual Rate} = \text{Discount Rate} \times \frac{365 \text{ days}}{\text{Additional Days to Payment}}$$

Account for short-term notes payable.   Accounting for short-term notes payable consists of three stages. First, record the liability at time of issue, including a discount for noninterest-bearing notes. Second, accrue interest or amortize the discount on financial statement dates that come before the note is paid. Finally, recognize payment of the note along with any accrued interest.

Account for short-term bank loans. Accounting for short-term bank loans is comparable to accounting for short-term notes payable. However, bank loans often require monthly or quarterly payment of interest.

Calculate and interpret the number of days-purchases-in-payables and the percent utilization of a line of credit. Days-purchases-in-payables is calculated according to this formula:

$$\text{Days-Purchases-in-Payables} = \frac{\text{Accounts Payable Balance}}{\text{Purchases}} \times \text{Days in Period}$$

Where the cost of purchases (P) is calculated as follows, if it is not given directly in the income statement:

$$P = COGS + (\text{Change in Inventory})$$

The percent utilization of a line of credit is a straightforward indicator. We calculate it as follows:

$$\text{Percent Utilization} = \frac{\text{Loan Balance}}{\text{Maximum Available Loan}} \times 100\%$$

Account for long-term notes with constant principal payments. When a company issues a long-term note with constant principal payments, accounting for the note is straightforward. Interest payable and interest expense are accrued on financial statement dates, and further interest and payments are recorded on payment dates. Payments include a constant amount of principal and a declining interest component due to the effect of the principal payments.

Find the present value of an amount to be received in some future period, calculate the present value of a long-term note, and account for the note from issue to maturity. When a single-payment note is issued for an asset whose value cannot be determined independently, then the note's current cash equivalent value must be derived using present value calculations (or tables). If the note's term to maturity spans more than one year, interest should be accrued or amortized on a compound-interest basis rather than on a straight-line basis. Compound interest calculations lead to a pattern of increasing interest accruals. Interest is accrued in one period on the original principal plus all previously accrued interest. As the discount on a note is amortized, the carrying value increases, increasing the base for calculating subsequent interest and amortizations.

Find the amount of the constant payments required to pay off an installment note, and account for installment notes from issue to maturity. Installment notes present all the problems of multiple-year notes plus some. Specifically, it is necessary to determine the exact constant payment amount that will pay off the installment note in the specified period at the specified interest rate. It is also necessary to calculate the portion of each installment payment that is interest and the implicit amount of payment of the note's principal. With each payment, the principal portion reduces the note's principal. As a consequence, over the term to maturity of an installment note, the interest portion of each payment declines and the principal portion increases.

REVIEW PROBLEM A: SHORT-TERM NOTES PAYABLE

On May 1, 19X5, Mountain View Nursing Home, Inc. borrowed $100,000 cash from the Colonial Bank and signed a $100,000, 90-day, 12% interest-bearing note dated May 1. On the same day, Mountain View Nursing Home purchased 50 special-care beds from Medical Technology, Inc. for $200,000, paid $100,000 cash, and signed a 90-day, nonin-terest-bearing note dated May 1, with a face value of $102,958.90. Mountain View has a June 30 year-end.

REQUIRED:

a. Prepare journals entries to record the issue of the notes.
b. Prepare the necessary adjusting entries on June 30.
c. Show the presentation of the notes in the June 30 balance sheet.
d. Prepare the journal entries to record the payment of the notes.

SOLUTION:

Planning and Organizing Your Work

1. Determine what value you should assign to the notes in your entries to record them. Record interest-bearing notes in one account, Notes Payable, at their face values, which usually equal the values received in exchange for them. Record noninterest-bearing notes in two accounts. Record their face values, which equal their maturity values and include implicit interest, in Notes Payable. Record the difference between their face values and the values received in exchange for them in Discounts on Notes Payable. Thus, in both cases, the initial carrying values of the notes equal the values received in exchange for them.
2. Write the journal entries to record the issuing of the notes.
3. Calculate interest accruals using the following formula for interest-bearing notes:

$$\text{Interest} = \text{Principal x Rate x Time}$$

or

$$I = PRT$$

where principal is the face amount of the note, rate the annual interest rate; and time the fraction of a year for which interest is being calculated.
Calculate interest accruals using the following formula for noninterest-bearing notes:

$$\text{Interest} = \text{Total Interest x } \frac{\text{Days}}{\text{Term}}$$

where total interest is the discount at issue or the difference between the face value of the note and the value exchanged for it, days the number of days for which you wish to calculate interest, and term the full term of the note in days.
4. Write the adjusting journal entries to accrue interest on the notes at June 30. Interest on interest-bearing notes is recorded in Interest Expense and Interest Payable; interest expense on noninterest-bearing notes reduces Discounts on Notes Payable.
5. Show the financial statement presentation of the notes. Show the notes' face values as notes payable in the current liabilities section of the balance sheet. In the case of an interest-bearing note, show the interest payable as a separate current liability. In the case of a noninterest-bearing note, offset the unamortized balance of the discount against the face value to show the carrying value of the note, which equals the original discounted value plus accrued interest to date.
6. Calculate the additional interest accruals through the maturity dates of the notes. Write journal entries to recognize the further (previously unaccrued) interest expense and the cash payment to pay off the notes in full.

(a) *Record the issue of notes.*
The issue of the May 1 note to Colonial Bank:

19X5			
May 1	Cash	100,000.00	
	Notes Payable		100,000.00
	To record issue of 90-day, 12%, $100,000 face value note to Colonial Bank.		

The interest on the Colonial note is not recorded on May 1 because no interest is owed at that date. Interest expense is incurred over the term of the note.

The issue of the May 1 note to Medical Technology, Inc.:

May 1	Equipment	200,000.00	
	Discounts on Notes Payable	2,958.90	
	Cash		100,000.00
	Notes Payable		102,958.90
	To record issue of 90-day, $102,958.90 face value note to Medical Technology, Inc.		

The net amount of the note to Medical Technology is calculated as follows:

Cost of equipment	$200,000.00
Less: Cash paid	100,000.00
Net amount of note	$100,000.00

The difference between the face value of the note and the net amount of the note represents interest to be paid over the term of the note:

Face value of note	$102,958.90
Net amount of note	100,000.00
Interest to be paid over term of note	$ 2,958.90

Since the interest is not a liability at the time the note is issued (interest is incurred over the 90-day term of the note), the $2,958.90 is recorded in a contra-liability account, Discounts on Notes Payable, thus reducing the liability to the amount owed ($100,000) at the date the note is issued.

(b) *Prepare the adjusting entries on June 30.*
To adjust for the Colonial note:

19X5			
June 30	Interest Expense	1,972.60	
	Interest Payable		1,972.60
	To record accrual of interest expense.		
	[$100,000 x .12 x (60/365)] = $1,972.60		

To adjust for the Medical Technology note:

June 30	Interest Expense	1,972.60	
	Discounts on Notes Payable		1,972.60
	To record recognition of interest expense.		
	[$2,958.90 x (60/90)] = $1,972.60		

(c) *Show presentation of notes in balance sheet.*

Current Liabilities

Notes payable—Colonial Bank		$100,000.00
Interest payable		1,972.60
Notes payable—Medical Technology, Inc.	$102,958.90	
Less: Discounts on notes payable	986.30	101,972.60

The June 30 balance in Discounts on Notes Payable: $2,958.90 − $1,972.60 = $986.30.

(d) *Prepare journal entries for the payment of the notes.*

The payment of the Colonial note:

19X5			
July 30	Interest Expense (1)	986.30	
	Interest Payable (2)	1,972.60	
	Notes Payable (3)	100,000.00	
	Cash		102,958.90
	To record payment of Colonial note.		

(1) 100,000 × .12 × (30/365) = 986.30
(2) 100,000 × .12 × (60/365) = 1,972.60
(3) 100,000 + [100,000 × .12 × (90/365)] = 102,958.90

Due date of note: Count 90 days; do not include date of note (May 1); do include date of payment:

May	30 days (May 2 through May 31)
June	30 days (June 1 through June 30)
July	30 days (July 1 through July 30)
	90 days = July 30

The payment of the Medical Technology note:

July 30	Interest Expense (1)	986.30	
	Notes Payable	102,958.90	
	Discounts on Notes Payable (1)		986.30
	Cash		102,958.90
	To record payment of Medical Technology, Inc. note.		

(1) Amortize remaining amount of discount: $2,958.90 × (30/90)

REVIEW PROBLEM B:　LONG-TERM INSTALLMENT LOANS

J. M. Teerlink Corporation has arranged to borrow $50,000 from a bank on October 1, 19X4 in exchange for an installment note payable to the bank. The note, repayable in 10 semiannual installments over 5 years, carries an interest rate of 8%, compounded semiannually. Teerlink's fiscal year-end is December 31.

REQUIRED:

a. Calculate the amount of each of Teerlink's 10 semiannual note payments.
b. Prepare the journal entry to accrue interest expense as of December 31, 19X4.
c. Prepare the journal entry to recognize interest expense and payment when the first semiannual note payment is due.

SOLUTION:

Planning and Organizing Your Work

1. Find the amount of the installment payments by first finding the annuity factor for 10 periods at the appropriate interest rate. In this case, the stated interest rate is an *annual* rate of 8%, but the payments are due and interest is compounded *semiannualy*. Thus, you should divide the annual rate by 2 to get the appropriate semiannual rate of 4%. The annuity factor will be at the intersection of the row for 10 periods (n) and the column for 4% compound interest in Table 2, Appendix C. Then find the amount of an installment by dividing the amount of the loan by the annuity factor.

2. Find the interest expense for 6 months of the loan (one semiannual period) by multiplying the interest rate of 4% by the balance of the loan at the beginning to the period, in this case $50,000. For accrual purposes, the amount of the semiannual interest

expense may be allocated proportionately to sub-periods within payment periods. Since the period from October 1, to December 31, is 3 months, accrue one-half of the 6-month interest amount at December 31, crediting Interest Payable.

3. Use one entry to accrue an additional 3-month's interest and recognize the first payment on March 31, 19X5. Credit Cash for the amount of the payment. Debit Interest Expense for the additional interest, Interest Payable for the previously accrued interest, and Note Payable—Noncurrent for the difference between the sum of the two interest amounts and the payment amount.

(a) *Calculate the amount of each of the payments.*

The annuity factor in Table 2, Appendix C, for 10 periods at a rate of 4% is 8.111. The amount of a payment is:

$$PMT = \frac{\$50,000}{8.111} = \$6,164.47$$

(b) *Prepare the journal entry to accrue interest expense as of December 31, 19X4.*

Interest expense=$50,000 x 4% ÷ 2=$1,000

19X4			
Dec. 31	Interest Expense	1,000.00	
	Interest Payable		1,000.00
	To accrue interest expense as of year end on installment note payable.		

(c) *Prepare the journal entry to recognize interest expense and payment when the first semiannual note payment is due.*

19X5			
Mar. 31	Interest Payable	1,000.00	
	Interest Expense	1,000.00	
	Notes Payable—Noncurrent	4,164.47	
	Cash		6,164.47
	To accrue interest expense and record payment on installment note payable.		

KEY TERMS

annuity, *418*
annuity due, *419*
annuity value, *419*
compound interest, *415*
contingent liabilities, *400*
current liabilities, *401*
days-purchases-in-payables, *410*
effective annual interest rate, *404*

estimated liabilities, *400*
future value, *414*
implicit principal payment, *420*
installment loan, *418*
liabilities, *400*
long-term debts, *401*
long-term liabilities, *400*
noncurrent liabilities, *400*

operating cycle, *401*
percent utilization of a line of credit, *410*
present value, *414*
short-term, revolving lines of credit, *407*
term to maturity, *401*

SELF-QUIZ

LO 1   1. An example of a contingent liability is
    a. The obligation of a retailer of mountain bikes for a one-year product warranty
    b. Social security taxes withheld from employees
    c. A noninterest-bearing note payable
    d. A lawsuit brought against us seeking $100,000 for breach of contract

LO 1   2. An example of an estimated liability is
    a. The obligation of the endorser of a note receivable sold to the bank
    b. A lawsuit against us by the Internal Revenue Service seeking additional income taxes
    c. Payments we will have to make related to the warranty on products sold

d. The amount of merchandise we expect to purchase on account during the next fiscal year

LO 1 3. Current liabilities are
   a. Liabilities due within 30 days
   b. Liabilities that we expect to pay
   c. Liabilities due within one year or within one operating cycle, whichever is shorter
   d. Liabilities due within one year or within one operating cycle, whichever is longer

LO 2 4. Berry Corporation purchases merchandise 2/5, n/30. The effective annual interest rate of not taking the purchase discount is
   a. 2%
   b. 29%
   c. 40%
   d. 24%

LO 2 5. 2/10, n/30 purchase discounts
   a. Provide for the effective borrowing of funds for 30 days at no interest cost
   b. Provide for the effective borrowing of funds for 20 days at no interest cost
   c. Provide for the effective borrowing of funds for 10 days with no interest cost
   d. Allow a 10% discount if paid within 2 days

LO 3 6. Interest-bearing notes payable
   a. Include the interest in the face (maturity) value of the note
   b. Require the payment of the face value of the note plus interest
   c. Are a more expensive way of borrowing than noninterest-bearing notes
   d. Require the payment of only the face value of the note

LO 3 7. Noninterest-bearing notes payable
   a. Allow funds to be borrowed without an interest charge
   b. Require the payment of the face value of the note plus an interest charge
   c. Require payment of only the face value of the note
   d. Are a less expensive way of borrowing than interest-bearing notes

LO 4 8. Short-term, revolving lines of credit
   a. Are good ways to finance permanent additions to buildings and equipment
   b. Are good ways to finance short-term, seasonal needs to expand inventory and accounts receivable

   c. Are commitments by banks to advance funds on demand up to the limits and periods in the agreement
   d. Both b and c

LO 4 9. Customary terms for short-term bank loans include
   a. The pledging of inventory and accounts receivable as collateral
   b. The right of the bank to require that it be paid in full at any time
   c. A flexible interest rate that fluctuates with the rate at which the Federal Reserve Bank makes loans to other banks
   d. All of the above

LO 5 10. Warner Corporation had cost of goods sold of $100,000, beginning inventory of $15,000, and ending inventory of $20,000. Its purchases during the period were
   a. $95,000
   b. $120,000
   c. $105,000
   d. $100,000

LO 5 11. Matrix Corporation has a monthly (assume 30 days) accounting period. Purchases for the month were $200,000 and the balance in Accounts Payable at the end of the accounting period was $50,000. The days-purchases-in-payable were:
   a. 120
   b. 7.5
   c. 4
   d. .25

LO 6 12. True or False? Cash payments of notes with constant principal payments decrease over the term of the note since interest is added to the required principal payment.

LO 7 13. If the cash value of an asset acquired cannot be established, except implicitly from a note's terms, we use the concept of the _____ _____ of future cash payments.

LO 7 14. True or False? Future values always exceed equivalent present values.

LO 8 15. If a long-term obligation has one or more installments due within one year, a portion of the long-term installment is a(n) _____ _____.

SOLUTIONS TO SELF-QUIZ

1. d   2. c   3. d   4. b   5. c   6. b   7. c   8. d   9. d   10. c   11. b   12. True   13. present value
14. True   15. current liability

QUESTIONS

Q9-1 Do the liabilities included on a balance sheet dated December 31, 19X4, include the cost of purchases on account that the company will make in January 19X5? Explain.

Q9-2 What two conditions must exist to recognize a contingent liability in the balance sheet?

Q9-3 What is the operating cycle of a business?

Q9-4 How can the operating cycle of a business affect the classification of a liability as current or noncurrent?

Q9-5 List four typical current liabilities.

Q9-6 A company purchases merchandise, terms 2/10, n/30. Calculate the effective annual interest rate of failing to take the purchases discount.

Q9-7 A company borrows $100,000 cash and signs a 60-day noninterest-bearing note. Will the maturity value of the note equal $100,000? Explain.

Q9-8 On November 1, 19X7, a company purchases merchandise for $10,000 and signs a 90-day, 9%, interest-bearing note for $10,000. A company spokesperson says that the company will not incur any interest expense for the year ended December 31, 19X7, because the interest will not be paid until 19X8. Do you agree?

Q9-9 On November 1, 19X7, a company purchases merchandise for $10,000 and signs a 90-day, noninterest-bearing note for $10,221.92. Show how the note payable would be presented in a November 1, 19X7, balance sheet.

Q9-10 If a bank approves a line of credit for a borrower, it usually sets an absolute limit and a flexible limit on the loan. Briefly describe how a bank might determine each limit.

Q9-11 What is the mathematical formula for calculating compound interest?

Q9-12 What is the process of amortizing the discount on a note payable?

Q9-13 What is an installment loan?

Q9-14 What is an annuity?

EXERCISES

LO 2

E9-1 Implicit Interest Rate on Lost Discounts The Brown Sage Corporation purchases merchandise from three suppliers. The terms offered by each supplier are:

Supplier A: 1/10, n/30
Supplier B: 2/15, n/30
Supplier C: 3/10, n/45

REQUIRED:

For each supplier, calculate the effective annual interest rate of failing to take purchases discounts.

LO 3

E9-2 Short-Term Notes Payable, Interest-Bearing Pepper Corporation records purchases at gross and its accounting period ends on December 31.

19X2

Oct. 15 Purchased $10,000 of merchandise from Turner Corporation terms 2/10, n/30.
     25 Gave Turner a 90-day, 8%, interest-bearing note for $9,800.
Dec. 31 Accrued interest owed Turner.

19X3
Jan. 23 Paid the Turner note.

REQUIRED:

Record journal entries on the books of Pepper Corporation for the above events.

LO 3

E9-3 **Short-Term Notes Payable, Noninterest-Bearing** Pepper Corporation records purchases at gross and its accounting period ends on December 31.

19X2
Oct. 15 Purchased $10,000 of merchandise from Turner Corporation, terms 2/10, n/30.
     25 Gave Turner a 90-day, noninterest-bearing note for $9,993.32.
Dec. 31 Recognized interest expense.

19X3
Jan. 23 Paid the Turner note.

REQUIRED:

Record journal entries on the books of Pepper Corporation for the above events.

LO 3

E9-4 **Presentation of Interest-Bearing and Noninterest-Bearing Notes on the Balance Sheet** On December 1, 19X6, the Greenwich Corporation borrowed $50,000 cash from the Fidelity Trust Corporation and signed a note.

REQUIRED:

a. Show the presentation of the liability to Fidelity on the December 31, 19X6, balance sheet of Greenwich, assuming the note was a 60-day, 7%, $50,000 interest-bearing note.
b. Show the presentation of the liability to Fidelity on the December 31, 19X6, balance sheet of Greenwich, assuming the note was a 60-day, noninterest-bearing note for $50,575.34.

LO 4

E9-5 **Short-Term Bank Loans** The Industrial Bank agreed to loan Bargain Mart, Inc. up to 40% of its inventory and 40% of its accounts receivable during the next 3 years, with the amount of the loan not to exceed $1,000,000. On June 15, 19X1, Bargain Mart exercised the line of credit and had the bank transfer $200,000 to its account. Interest on the loan, at the rate of 9%, is payable monthly on the 10th day of the following month.

REQUIRED:

a. Prepare a journal entry to record the loan on June 15, 19X1.
b. Prepare the journal entry to accrue interest on June 30, 19X1.
c. Prepare the July 10, 19X1, journal entry to record the payment of interest for June.
d. Assuming Bargain Mart has a July 31 year-end, prepare the adjusting entry necessary on July 31, 19X1.

LO 5

E9-6 **Number of Days-Purchases-in-Payables** The following information is available for the Dryden Corporation for the accounting year ended December 31, 19X6.

Purchases $25,000,000
Accounts payable, 12/31/X6   900,000

Dryden makes all purchases on account, terms 2/10, n/30.

REQUIRED:

a. Calculate the days-purchases-in-payables.
b. Comment on what the calculation in *a* tells us about Dryden.

LO 6

E9-7 **Long-Term Notes with Constant Principal Payments** On January 1, 19X2, SuperPet Stores, Inc. gave a $16,000, 4-year, 10% note to Rapid Construction Corporation in exchange for remodeling one of the company's stores. The remodeling is worth $16,000. The terms of the note call for semiannual interest payments and $2,000 semiannual payments of principal on June 30 and December 31 over the 4-year term of the note.

REQUIRED:

Prepare the journal entries for June 30 and December 31, 19X2.

LO 7

E9-8   **Valuing Notes Payable Using Present Values**   Fontasia Corporation exchanged a note payable for equipment from Computers Unlimited, Inc. on January 1, 19X3. There is no market value for comparable equipment to refer to in establishing value. Fontasia agreed to pay $20,000 on December 31, 19X4. The prevailing interest rate to Fontasia for borrowed funds is 8%.

REQUIRED:

Determine the value of the note and prepare the journal entry to record the purchase of equipment.

LO 8

E9-9   **Determining Installment Loan Payments**   Boomer Corporation issued a 9% installment note payable to the bank in exchange for $30,000. Boomer is to repay the note in equal payments at the end of each year for 5 years.

REQUIRED:

Calculate the amount of each payment and the amount of implicit principal paid on the first installment.

PROBLEM SET A

LO 2,3

P9-1A   **Short-Term Notes Payable, Interest-Bearing; Implicit Interest Rate in Losing Discounts**   Selected transactions for the American Information Corporation are given below. American's annual accounting period ends on August 31.

19X1

May   1   Purchased merchandise from the Green Corp. for $100,000, terms 1/10, n/30.
      11 Gave the Green Corp. a $99,000, 10%, 180-day note in payment of the open account.
      12 Borrowed $250,000 from the Western Trust Corp. and gave Western a one-year, 9%, note for $250,000.

REQUIRED:

a. If American had elected to pay Green on May 31, calculate its implicit interest rate.
b. Prepare journal entries to record the transactions on May 1, 11, and 12.
c. Prepare necessary adjusting entries on August 31.
d. Show the presentation of the liabilities in the August 31, 19X1, balance sheet.
e. Prepare journal entries to record payment of the Green note on November 7, 19X1, and the Western note on May 12, 19X2.

LO 3

P9-2A   **Short-Term Notes Payable, Noninterest-Bearing**   Selected transactions for the American Information Corporation are given below. American's annual accounting period ends on August 31.

19X1

May   1   Purchased merchandise from the Green Corporation for $100,000, terms 1/10, n/30.

May 11 Gave the Green Corporation a $103,882.19, 180-day, noninterest-bearing note in payment of the open account. The note has a net value of $99,000.

  12 Borrowed $250,000 from the Western Trust Corp. and gave Western a one-year, noninterest-bearing note for $272,500.

REQUIRED:

a. Prepare journal entries to record the transactions on May 1, 11, and 12.
b. Prepare necessary adjusting entries on August 31.
c. Show the presentation of the liabilities in the August 31, 19X1, balance sheet.
d. Prepare journal entries to record payment of the Green note on November 7, 19X1, and the Western note on May 12, 19X2.

LO 4   **P9-3A   Short-Term Bank Loans**   The Cascades Country Club, Inc. arranged a line of credit with the Atlantic National Bank that provides for a loan of up to 40% of its pro-line golf club inventory and 50% of its most recent month's green fees (receivable). This line of credit extends over a one-year period. Interest on any loans made is payable monthly on the 15th day of the following month. The interest rate is 7.75%. The maximum loan available is $1,600,000.

On March 13, 19X2, Cascades had Atlantic transfer $300,000 to its account under the terms of the agreement. On May 5, 19X2, Cascades had Atlantic transfer another $200,000 to its account.

Cascades' accounting year ends on June 30.

REQUIRED:

a. List some other terms, in addition to the ones mentioned, that are customary for short-term loans like the one above.
b. Prepare all journal entries necessary in Cascades' records for the transactions related to the line of credit for the period March 13, 19X2, through June 30, 19X2. Include year-end adjusting entries.
c. Calculate the percent utilization of Cascades' line of credit. Explain its significance.

LO 5   **P9-4A   Days-Purchases-in-Payables**   The Jackson Home Center, Inc. has the following information available for the accounting year ended December 31, 19X8.

Jackson Home Center, Inc. Income Statement For the Year Ended December 31, 19X8	
Sales	$6,000,000
Cost of goods sold	4,000,000
Gross profit	$2,000,000
Operating expenses	1,500,000
Net income	$ 500,000

On December 31, 19X7, and December 31, 19X8, Jackson's balance sheets report merchandise inventories of $400,000 and $450,000, respectively, and Accounts Payable balances of $100,000 and $110,000, respectively. All accounts payable are owed to merchandise vendors, and Jackson purchases nearly all of its merchandise under 2/10, n/30 terms.

REQUIRED:

a. Calculate the purchases for 19X8.
b. Calculate the days-purchases-in-payables on December 31, 19X8.
c. Discuss what you can infer from Jackson's days-purchases-in-payables.

LO 7, 8   **P9-5A**   **Long-Term Notes Payable**   Jet Technologies, Inc. issued an 8% installment note payable to United Bank on January 1, 19X1, in exchange for $200,000. Jet Technologies is to repay the note in equal payments at the end of each year for four years. Jet Technologies also exchanged a note payable for equipment from Turbine Corporation on July 1, 19X1. There is no market value for comparable equipment to refer to in establishing value. The terms of the note called for Jet Technologies to pay $150,000 on June 30, 19X4, to repay the note. The prevailing interest rate to Jet Technologies for borrowed funds is 8%.

REQUIRED:

a. Determine the annual payment for the installment note issued to United Bank.
b. Determine the present value of the note issued to Turbine Corporation.
c. Record all necessary journal entries for 19X1 and 19X2.
d. Show the balance sheet disclosure of both notes as of December 31, 19X1.

PROBLEM SET B

LO 2,3   **P9-1B**   **Short-Term Notes Payable, Interest-Bearing; Implicit Interest Rate in Losing Discounts**   Selected transactions for the Data Management Corporation are given below. Data's annual accounting period ends on September 30.

19X4
Jun.   1   Purchased merchandise from the Hacker Corp. for $30,000, terms 2/10, n/30.
       11   Gave the Hacker Corp. a $29,400, 8%, 180-day note in payment of the open account.
       25   Borrowed $50,000 from the Future Bank and gave Future a one-year, 9.5%, note for $50,000.

REQUIRED:

a. If Data Management had elected to pay Hacker on July 1, calculate its implicit interest rate.
b. Prepare journal entries to record the transactions on June 1, 11, and 25.
c. Prepare necessary adjusting entries on September 30.
d. Show the presentation of the liabilities in the September 30, 19X4, balance sheet.
e. Prepare journal entries to record payment of the Hacker note on December 8, 19X4, and the Future note on June 25, 19X5.

LO 2,3   **P9-2B**   **Short-Term Notes Payable, Noninterest-Bearing**   Selected transactions for the Data Management Corporation are given below. Data's annual accounting period ends on September 30.

19X4
Jun.   1   Purchased merchandise from the Hacker Corp. for $30,000, terms 2/10, n/30.
       11   Gave the Hacker Corp. a $30,559.89, 180-day, noninterest-bearing note in payment of the open account. The note has a net value of $29,400.
       25   Borrowed $50,000 from the Future Bank and gave Future a one-year, noninterest-bearing note for $54,750.

REQUIRED:

a. Prepare journal entries to record the transactions on June 1, 11, and 25.
b. Prepare necessary adjusting entries on September 30.
c. Show the presentation of the liabilities in the September 30, 19X4, balance sheet.
d. Prepare journal entries to record payment of the Hacker note on December 8, 19X4, and the Future note on June 25, 19X5.

LO 4

P9-3B **Short-Term Bank Loans** The Highland Tennis Club, Inc. arranged a line of credit with the Valley National Bank that provides for a loan of up to 50% of its tennis merchandise inventory and 60% of its most recent month's court fees (receivable). This line of credit extends over a one-year period. Interest on any loans made is payable monthly on the 10th day following the end of the month. The interest rate is 11%. The maximum loan available is $400,000.

On May 7, 19X1, Highland had Valley transfer $150,000 to its account under the terms of the agreement. On June 5, 19X1, Highland had Valley transfer another $200,000 to its account.

Highland's accounting year ends on August 31.

REQUIRED:

a. Prepare all journal entries necessary on Highland's books to record transactions related to the line of credit for the period May 7, 19X1, through August 31, 19X1. Include year-end adjusting entries.
b. Calculate the percent utilization of Highland's line of credit. Explain its significance.

LO 5

P9-4B **Days-Purchases-in-Payables** The Big Sky Building Supply Corporation has the following information available for the accounting year ended July 31, 19X6.

Big Sky Building Supply Corporation Income Statement For the Year Ended July 31, 19X6	
Sales	$9,000,000
Cost of goods sold	6,000,000
Gross profit	$3,000,000
Operating expenses	2,000,000
Net income	$1,000,000

On July 31, 19X5, and July 31, 19X6, Big Sky's balance sheets report merchandise inventories of $600,000 and $550,000, respectively, and Accounts Payable balances of $150,000 and $140,000, respectively. All accounts payable are owed to merchandise vendors, and Big Sky purchases nearly all of its merchandise under 2/10, n/30 terms.

REQUIRED:

a. Calculate the purchases for 19X6.
b. Calculate the days-purchases-in-payables on July 31, 19X6.
c. Discuss what you can infer from Big Sky's days-purchases-in-payables.

LO 7, 8

P9-5B **Long-Term Notes Payable** Kennel Corporation issued a 10% installment note payable to Partners Loan Corporation on January 1, 19X4, in exchange for $100,000. Kennel is to repay the note in equal payments at the end of each year for 4 years. Kennel Corporation also exchanged a note payable for equipment from K-9 Corporation on July 1, 19X4. There is no market value for comparable equipment to refer to in establishing value. The terms of the note called for Kennel Corporation to pay $300,000 on June 30, 19X8, to repay the note. The prevailing interest rate to Kennel Corporation for borrowed funds is 10%.

REQUIRED:

a. Determine the annual payment for the installment note issued to Partners Loan Corporation.
b. Determine the present value of the note issued to K-9 Corporation.

   c. Record all necessary journal entries for 19X4 and 19X5.

   d. Show the balance sheet disclosure of both notes as of December 31, 19X4.

CRITICAL THINKING AND COMMUNICATING

C9-1 A foreign government recently sued Western Corporation and sought damages over the alleged improper installation of a component that was part of a nuclear power plant. Western contested the charge.

REQUIRED:

   a. Is this a contingent liability or an estimated liability? Discuss.

   b. Should a liability related to this litigation be reported on Western's balance sheet? Discuss.

C9-2 Interview a commercial loan officer at a local bank about his or her job. Inquire about the types and duration of loans most commonly granted. What kind of collateral is best? What factors affect the negotiated interest rate? How does the bank evaluate a prospective business loan? Obtain a loan application and a truth in lending statement.

REQUIRED:

In class, share and compare your findings with other students. Write a brief summary of your opinion and conclusions regarding short-term and long-term bank financing.

C9-3 Refer to the J.C. Penney Company, Inc. financial statements in Appendix B at the end of the text. Find in the "Notes to Financial Statements" the details of short-term debt, long-term debt, and changes in long-term debt.

REQUIRED:

   a. Briefly state what short-term debt and long-term debt contain. How do these terms compare with what you have read in this chapter? Define at least one of these new terms.

   b. Referring to the section on changes in long-term debt, why did long-term debt have a net decrease pf $242 million in 1993?

   c. Read "Management's Discussion and Analysis of Financial Condition and Results of Operations" about financial position. Does it agree with your conclusions about the cause of the decrease in long-term debt.

   d. Calculate days-purchases-in-payables for 1993 and 1992. Is the company, in your opinion, better off in 1993?

CHAPTER 10

Bonds and Other Long-Term Liabilities

The Chief Operating Officer has just informed Miklos Kronis, the chief financial officer (CFO) of Midwestern Alliance Corporation, that the company must replace some of its equipment immediately or stop essential operations. The equipment, which has an estimated useful life of 10 years is available from a supplier at a cash price of $100,000. The question is: How should the company finance its purchase?

The company has only enough cash to meet its regular bills, so it must raise new equity capital or borrow the necessary funds. Miklos faces two limiting factors, however. First, Mr. Conrad, who is the Chairman, Chief Executive Officer (CEO), and majority shareholder of the corporation, neither wishes to invest more equity in Midwestern nor to have new (or existing) owners dilute his majority share. Second, the bank that provides Midwestern with its revolving line of credit has placed restrictions, called debt covenants, on the corporation's ability to borrow from other sources. Specifically, Midwestern will default on its line of credit if its debt-equity ratio exceeds 1.0 (or 1-to-1).

Ordinarily, Miklos would feel free to choose among the various long-term financing (borrowing) plans available—for example, a long-term installment note payable, issuing bonds payable, leasing the equipment under a capital lease, or leasing under an operating lease. He would normally choose the financing plan that costs the least (had the lowest present value). Unfortunately, in this case, Miklos now has to worry more about the financing plan's impact on the corporation's debt-equity ratio.

In this chapter, you will learn about using present value methodology to establish the values of bonds and capital leases. You will learn to account for bonds and leases. You also will learn how to calculate the debt-equity ratio, how to interpret it, and how to apply it in the case of a debt restriction. Finally, you will be exposed to the controversial topic of off-balance-sheet financing.

1. Describe the important features of bonds businesses issue as a form of borrowing; explain why some bonds are issued at face value, some at discounts, and some at premiums and record issues of bonds.
2. Calculate total interest cost of bond issues and record interest expense, including amortization of discounts and premiums, using the straight-line and interest-methods.
3. Accrue interest expense and amortize discounts and premiums between interest payment dates, account for bond issue costs, and account for bonds issued between interest payment dates.
4. Account for investments in bonds.
5. Explain the difference between capital leases and operating leases.
6. Account for the assets and liabilities recognized under capital leases.
7. Calculate and interpret the debt-equity ratio as an indicator of potential financial distress, and recognize its limitations when off-balance-sheet financing is used.

LO 1

Describe the important features of bonds businesses issue as a form of borrowing; explain why some bonds are issued at face value, some at discounts, and some at premiums and record issues of bonds.

BONDS

One of the many ways businesses can borrow is by selling or issuing bonds. **Bonds** are debt securities—meaning they are debts represented by transferable certificates. The borrower or debtor is called the **issuer of bonds**; the lenders or creditors are called **bondholders**. Bonds differ from negotiable notes (which are also transferable) in several respects:

1. The terms of bonds are usually longer than those for notes.
2. The total amount of debt or borrowing represented by an "issue" of bonds is broken down into separate debt securities of relatively small denominations (amounts).
3. Costs are associated with issuing bonds, and costs may be associated with retiring them.
4. All individual bonds are covered by one legal contract of indebtedness called a bond indenture.

The **bond indenture** for a bond issue contains all the debt's terms and conditions. Bond indentures include such things as: number of bonds that may be issued under the agreement, denomination of the bonds, interest rate paid on the bonds, term of the bonds, and any restrictions the debt imposes on the issuer of the bonds. Common restrictions limit the issuer's amount of total debt and the amount of dividends that may be paid to stockholders.

Bonds are most often issued in denominations of $1,000 each. So, if an issuer wishes to raise $3,000,000 by issuing bonds, it would issue 3,000 bonds at $1,000 each. The **denominations of bonds** are also referred to as their par values, face values, principal amounts, and maturity values. The interest rate stated in the indenture is usually called the **stated**, **nominal**, or **coupon rate**. It specifies the annual rate of interest to be paid on the bonds' face value. Frequently, interest on bonds is paid semiannually. So, for example, an issuer of $1,000 bonds that have a stated rate of 11% to be paid semiannually, pays two payments of $55 each year per bond.

The **full term** of a bond is the total number of years between the date it can be first issued and the date it matures. At any date subsequent to the first date a bond can be issued, the time remaining before it matures is referred as the **term to maturity**, or the remaining term of the bond.

Together, the face value, term (full or remaining), interest rate, and frequency of payment of a bond determine the stream of payments the issuer makes to the bondholder. Suppose, for example, that Ace Corporation issues a $1,000, 5-year, 9% bond, paying interest semiannually on June 30 and December 31 of each year. These terms imply that someone who buys such a bond on or after January 1, but before June 30 of the first year of its full term, will receive the following stream of payments from Ace:

Year 1	June 30	Interest	$ 45
	Dec. 31	Interest	45
Year 2	June 30	Interest	45
	Dec. 31	Interest	45
Year 3	June 30	Interest	45
	Dec. 31	Interest	45
Year 4	June 30	Interest	45
	Dec. 31	Interest	45
Year 5	June 30	Interest	45
	Dec. 31	Interest	45
	Dec. 31	Principal	1,000
Total			$1,450

Registered bonds are issued in the buyer's name. The issuer enters the buyer's name on the bond certificate and in a bond register. The issuer makes interest and principal payments only to the *registered* owners of the bonds and enters the payments in the bond register. The owners of registered bonds cannot transfer them directly to purchasers. They must turn the bond certificates in to the issuer, who then reissues certificates registered in the new owner's name. **Bearer** or **coupon bonds** are not registered. Instead, the bond certificates have detachable coupons that are redeemed for interest payments with the issuer or the issuer's agent (usually a bank). The bearer (owner) of the bonds surrenders them when they mature in exchange for payment of the principal amount.

Bonds differ from long-term notes payable in another way. Individual bonds are generally *not* structured on an installment basis. However, a special kind of bonds, called serial bonds, have the same effect. Borrowers issue **serial bonds** under indentures specifying that certain subsets of the total issue of bonds will be due at different maturity dates. Serial bond indentures identify by serial numbers which bonds in the issue are due at which maturity dates. For the issuer, the series of due dates for subsets of a serial bond issue has an effect similar to an installment loan arrangement. Bonds issued under indentures that specify that all the bonds are due at the same date are called **term bonds**. We cover only term bonds in this text.

Values of Bonds at Issue

Most bonds are sold for cash. However, they rarely are sold precisely for their face values. If they are sold for less than face value, we say they are sold at a **discount**. If they are sold for more than face value, we say they are sold at a **premium**. Discounts and premiums result from differences between the nominal (stated) rate of interest on the bond and the market rate (also called the prevailing rate) that investors can receive on other investments of about equal risk and duration.

To see this, consider 100 bonds Beta Corporation issued on April 1, 19X1. Each bond has a face value of $1,000, nominal interest rate of 10%, annual interest payments on March 31, and a 5-year term. Now, consider how much a buyer would be willing to pay Beta for the bond if the interest rate for comparable investments at the time of issue is 8%, 10%, or 12%. To determine these amounts, we find the present value of the bond's interest and principal payments at each of these interest rates as shown in Illustration 10-1.

ILLUSTRATION 10-1 Present Value of a Bond

March 31	Bond Payments	8 % (Premium Case)		10 % (Par Value)		12 % (Discount Case)	
		Present Value Factor	Present Value	Present Value Factor	Present Value	Present Value Factor	Present Value
19X2	$ 100.00	0.9259	$ 92.59	0.9091	$ 90.91	0.8929	$ 89.29
19X3	100.00	0.8573	85.73	0.8264	82.64	0.7972	79.72
19X4	100.00	0.7938	79.38	0.7513	75.13	0.7118	71.18
19X5	100.00	0.7350	73.50	0.6830	68.30	0.6355	63.55
19X6	100.00	0.6806	68.06	0.6209	62.09	0.5674	56.74
19X6	1,000.00	0.6806	680.60	0.6209	620.93	0.5674	567.40
Total present values			$1,079.86		$1,000.00		$927.88

The dates and payments implied by the terms of the bonds are shown in the first and second columns of Illustration 10-1. We find the present value factors in Table 1 of Appendix C at the intersections of the appropriate interest rate columns and the rows representing the numbers of years to payment. We multiply these factors times the payment amounts to derive the present values of the individual payments. Then, we sum the present values of the payments to get the present values of the bonds for each interest rate.

Now consider the middle case (the face-value case) in Illustration 10-1. Recall that interest payments are determined by the nominal rate of 10% and the note's face value. If the prevailing rate for similar investments is the same as the nominal rate, then this investment pays the same rate on the face value as does any other comparable investment. The investor, therefore, would be willing to pay Beta face value of $1,000 for it.

However, if the prevailing rate is higher than 10%, then an investor would not be willing to pay Beta face value for the bond, but something less than face value. Illustration 10-1 shows that if the prevailing rate is 12%, the investor would be willing to pay $927.88. If the investor buys the bond for $927.88, it is equivalent to investing this amount in any other comparable investment that pays 12%. In other words, the bondholder will actually earn 12% on the bond if it is purchased at $927.88. The 12% is known as the effective interest rate of the bond purchased at this price. The **effective interest rate** is the interest rate at which the present value of all the payments due on a bond (or other long-term obligation) equals the proceeds from issuing the bond.

If the prevailing rate is lower than the nominal rate, investors will pay Beta more than face value for the bond. According to Illustration 10-1, if the prevailing rate is 8%, investors will pay $1,079.86 for the bond. At this price, the bond has an effective interest rate of 8%.

Recording Bond Issues

To illustrate the recording of bond issues, we assume that Beta issued 100 of the bonds described in Illustration 10-1 on April 1, 19X1, at each of the prices illustrated. When Beta issues the bonds, it receives assets and incurs a liability. If the bonds are issued at face value, for cash, Beta's entry to record the issue is very straightforward:

19X1			
Apr. 1	Cash	100,000	
	Bonds Payable		100,000
	To record issue of 100, $1,000 bonds at face.		

In Beta's balance sheet, bonds issued at face value are presented as follows:

Noncurrent liabilities	
10% bonds payable, due March 31, 19X6, issued at face value	$100,000

When bonds are issued at a lower price than face value, the difference is recorded in a separate contra-liability account, Discount on Bonds Payable. If Beta sold the 100 bonds at $927.88, the entry is:

19X1			
Apr. 1	Cash	92,788	
	Discount on Bonds Payable	7,212	
	Bonds Payable		100,000
	To record issue of 100, $1,000 bonds at $927.88.		

In Beta's balance sheet, bonds issued at a discount are presented as follows:

Noncurrent liabilities		
10% bonds payable, due March 31, 19X6		
Face value	$100,000	
Less: Unamortized discount	7,212	$92,788

When bonds are issued at a price higher than face value, the difference is recorded in a separate valuation account, Premium on Bonds Payable. If Beta sold the 100 bonds at $1,079.86, the entry is:

19X1			
Apr. 1	Cash	107,986	
	Bonds Payable		100,000
	Premium on Bonds Payable		7,986
	To record issue of 100, $1,000 bonds at $1,079.86.		

In Beta's balance sheet, bonds issued at a premium are presented as follows:

Noncurrent liabilities		
10% bonds payable, due March 31, 19X6		
Face value	$100,000	
Add: Unamortized premium	7,986	$107,986

LO 2

Calculate total interest cost of bond issues and record interest expense, including amortization of discounts and premiums, using the straight-line and interest methods.

Total Bond Interest Cost

When bonds are issued at face value, total interest cost over the term of the bonds equals the sum of the interest payments. Total interest cost also equals the difference between the total payments (principal and interest) and the proceeds from issuing the bonds. The interest cost for any period is the interest that applies to that period at the stated interest rate. For example, if Beta Corporation's 5-year, 10% bonds illustrated above are issued at face value, the total interest cost over the term of the bonds is $50,000, the sum of five, $10,000 annual interest payments. Total interest cost also equals the sum of the interest and principal payments, $150,000, less the proceeds of issue, $100,000.

However, when a bond is sold at a premium or discount, the premium or discount becomes part of the calculation of the bond's interest cost. The total interest costs of the premium and discount cases for Beta's bonds described in Illustration 10-1 are shown in Illustration 10-2.

ILLUSTRATION 10-2 Total Interest Cost Calculations

		Discount Case	Premium Case
Payments to be made:			
March 31,19X2	Interest	$ 10,000	$ 10,000
March 31,19X3	Interest	10,000	10,000
March 31,19X4	Interest	10,000	10,000
March 31,19X5	Interest	10,000	10,000
March 31,19X6	Interest	10,000	10,000
March 31,19X6	Principal	100,000	100,000
Total payments		$150,000	$150,000
Less: Proceeds of sale		92,788	107,986
Total interest cost—full term		$ 57,212	$ 42,014

When we add the discount of $7,212 to the interest payments of $50,000, we get a total interest cost of $57,212 over the term of the bonds. When we subtract the premium of $7,986 from the $50,000 in interest payments, we get a net interest cost of $42,014 over the term of the bonds. These amounts for total interest cost agree with the figures in Illustration 10-2, found by subtracting total proceeds from total payments.

Interest Expense: Straight-Line Amortization of Discounts and Premiums

If bonds are issued at face value, recognizing interest expense is relatively straightforward. If Beta Corporation issues its 100, 10% bonds at face value on April 1, 19X1, it will pay $10,000 in interest payments on each subsequent March 31 for 5 years. Beta would make an entry like the following one on each interest payment date, starting with March 31, 19X2:

19X2			
Mar. 31	Interest Expense	10,000	
	Cash		10,000
	To record interest expense and annual interest payment on 10% bonds payable.		

If Beta issues the bonds at a discount or premium, it will recognize a greater or lesser amount of interest cost over the term of the bonds by the amount of the discount or premium. Thus, the amount of the discount or premium must be allocated (amortized) to the periods in the full term of the bonds. The simplest method of amortization is the straight-line method, which allocates an equal portion of the discount or premium to each period in the term of the bonds. In the case where the total discount at issue was $7,212, Beta would allocate $1,442 to each year ($7,210 ÷ 5). This allocation increases interest expense Beta recognizes and reduces the balance in Discount on Bonds Payable:

19X2			
Mar. 31	Interest Expense	11,442	
	Discount on Bonds Payable		1,442
	Cash		10,000
	To record interest expense, amortization of		
	discount, and annual interest payment on 10%		
	bonds payable.		

After the first year's amortization of the discount, Beta would present the bonds issued at a discount in its balance sheet as follows:

Noncurrent liabilities
  10% bonds payable, due March 31, 19X6
    Face value $100,000
    Less: Unamortized discount   5,770 $94,230

In the case where the total premium at issue was $7,986, Beta would allocate $1,597 per year ($7,986 ÷ 5). This allocation reduces Beta's interest expense and the balance in Premium on Bonds Payable thus:

19X2			
Mar. 31	Interest Expense	8,403	
	Premium on Bonds Payable	1,597	
	Cash		10,000
	To record interest expense, amortization of premium,		
	and annual interest payment on 10% bonds payable.		

After the first year's amortization of the premium, Beta would present the bonds issued at a premium in its balance sheet as follows:

Noncurrent liabilities
  10% bonds payable, due March 31, 19X6
    Face value $100,000
    Add: Unamortized premium   6,389 $106,389

In the case of both premiums and discounts, the straight-line method of amortization accomplishes two things. First, the sum of the interest expense amounts recognized in the periods in the term of the bonds equals the total interest cost over the term of the bonds. In Illustration 10-2, the total interest costs of bonds issued at a discount or at a premium is $57,212 or $42,014, respectively. The Interest Expense columns in Illustration 10-3 agree with these

INSIGHTS INTO ACCOUNTING

Below is an advertisement, called a "tombstone," that appeared in *The Wall Street Journal* on May 23, 1994. It announces the issue of $100 million in senior subordinated debentures. Debentures are unsecured bonds. Holders of subordinated debentures have the usual rights of creditors to payments of their claims before owners receive any proceeds of liquidation of the assets of a corporation, but their claims come after the claims of other creditors. Notice that the advertisement contains a disclaimer that it is neither an offer to sell nor a solicitation of an offer to buy the debentures. Security regulations prevent sellers of new issues of securities from offering them for sale without providing the prospective buyers with a disclosure document, called a prospectus, that has been registered with the Securities and Exchange Commission. Notice that the offer price is quoted as 99.266% (of face or par value), which means that the debentures will be issued at a discount and the effective interest rate will be slightly higher than the stated interest rate of 11%. The four companies listed at the bottom of the advertisement are investment banking firms that are underwriting this issue of debentures. They will receive a percentage of the proceeds as a commission and they guarantee some minimum level of proceeds to the issuer.

This announcement is neither an offer to sell nor a solicitation of an offer to buy these securities.
The offer is made only by the Prospectus.

New Issue / May 23, 1994

$100,000,000

Santa Fe Energy Resources, Inc.

11% Senior Subordinated Debentures Due 2004

Price 99.266% and accrued interest, if any, from May 25, 1994

Copies of the Prospectus may be obtained in any State in which this
announcement is circulated only from such of the undersigned
as may legally offer these securities in such State.

Salomon Brothers Inc

Dillon, Read & Co. Inc.

Lazard Frères & Co.

Chemical Securities Inc.

ILLUSTRATION 10-3 Straight-Line Amortization of Bond Discount and Premium

	Discount Case			
Date	Interest Payment	Amortization	Interest Expense	Discount Balance
April 1, 19X1				$7,212
March 31, 19X2	$10,000	$1,442	$11,442	5,770
March 31, 19X3	10,000	1,442	11,442	4,328
March 31, 19X4	10,000	1,442	11,442	2,886
March 31, 19X5	10,000	1,442	11,442	1,444
March 31, 19X6	10,000	1,444	11,444	0
Totals	$50,000	$7,212	$57,212	

	Premium Case			
Date	Interest Payment	Amortization	Interest Expense	Premium Balance
April 1, 19X1				$7,986
March 31, 19X2	$10,000	$1,597	$ 8,403	6,389
March 31, 19X3	10,000	1,597	8,403	4,792
March 31, 19X4	10,000	1,597	8,403	3,195
March 31, 19X5	10,000	1,597	8,403	1,598
March 31, 19X6	10,000	1,598	8,402	0
Totals	$50,000	$7,986	$42,014	

figures, based on adding the discount amortizations or subtracting the premium amortizations to interest paid, respectively.

Second, the discount or premium account balance is reduced to zero just at the time the principal amount is due. This is illustrated in the right-hand columns of the discount and premium panels of Illustration 10-3. As a consequence, whether bonds are issued at a premium, at a discount, or at face value, Beta's entry to record their retirement at full term is the same:

19X6 Mar. 31	Bonds Payable	100,000	
	Cash		100,000
	To record payment at maturity of 10% bonds payable.		

Interest Method of Amortization

The straight-line method not only is the simplest method of amortization, but for this reason, also is the most frequently used. However, it is not the most theoretically correct or preferred method. The preferred method is called the effective interest method or just the "interest method." Under the **interest method of amortization**, all payments to bondholders are considered installments on a loan, whether they are interest or principal payments. *Interest expense is determined by applying the effective interest rate to the bonds' carrying value.* The difference between the interest payments and interest expense is the amount of amortization to be applied to bond discount or premium.

To illustrate, consider again Beta Corporation's 100, 5-year bonds with face values of $1,000 and interest of 10%, payable annually. Look at the numbers at the top of the Carrying Value columns of Panels A and B of Illustration 10-4.

ILLUSTRATION 10-4 Interest Method of Amortization

	Panel A: 10% Bonds Sold at a Discount to Yield 12%				
Date	Interest Expense	Interest Payment	Amortization of Discount	Unamoritized Discount	Carrying Value
April 1, 19X1				$7,212	$ 92,788
March 31, 19X2	$11,135	$10,000	$1,135	6,077	93,923
March 31, 19X3	11,271	10,000	1,271	4,806	95,194
March 31, 19X4	11,423	10,000	1,423	3,383	96,617
March 31, 19X5	11,594	10,000	1,594	1,789	98,211
March 31, 19X6	11,789	10,000	1,789	0	100,000
Total expense	$57,212				

	Panel B: 10% Bonds Sold at a Premium to Yield 8%				
Date	Interest Expense	Interest Payment	Amortization of Premium	Unamoritized Premium	Carrying Value
April 1, 19X1				$7,986	$107,986
March 31, 19X2	$ 8,639	$10,000	$1,361	6,625	106,625
March 31, 19X3	8,530	10,000	1,470	5,155	105,155
March 31, 19X4	8,412	10,000	1,588	3,567	103,567
March 31, 19X5	8,285	10,000	1,715	1,852	101,852
March 31, 19X6	8,148	10,000	1,852	0	100,000
Total expense	$42,014				

The numbers are the proceeds of issue or carrying values of the 10% bonds, assuming they were issued on April 1, 19X1, at a discount to yield 12% interest (carrying value of $92,788) or at a premium to yield 8% interest (carrying value of $107,986).

Panel A of Illustration 10-4 applies the interest method to the discount case. Under this method, Beta Corporation determines its interest expense for the year ended March 31, 19X2, by multiplying the effective interest rate of 12% times the carrying value of the bond liability as of April 1, 19X1. Thus, the first year interest expense is $11,135 ($92,788 x 12%). Since the interest payment is $10,000, more interest expense is recorded than is owed and paid. Beta recognizes the difference of $1,135 as the amount of the amortization of the discount for the first year. By reducing the discount by this amount, the carrying value of the debt is increased. In effect, the reduction of the discount adds *interest recorded but not paid* to the balance owed (carrying value) of the liability.

Beta then applies the 12% interest rate to the higher carrying value at March 31, 19X3, resulting in a higher interest expense ($11,271) in the second year. This pattern continues until the discount is fully amortized at the maturity date of the bonds. Total interest expense for the full term of the bonds ($57,212) is equal to the total payments less the proceeds of issue. Moreover, as the carrying value of the liability increases, interest expense increases commensurate with it.

Panel B illustrates the premium case. Beta determines its interest expense for the year ended March 31, 19X2, by multiplying 8% times the carrying value of the bond liability as of April 1, 19X1 ($8,639 = $107,986 x 8%). Since the interest payment is $10,000, Beta will accrue $1,361 less interest than is paid. The difference is the amount of the amortization of the premium for the first year. By reducing the premium by this amount, Beta decreases the debt's carrying value, reflecting the fact that a larger amount was paid than the interest expense recorded for the year.

Beta Corporation then applies the 8% interest rate to the lower carrying value at March 31, 19X3, resulting in a lower interest expense ($8,530) in the second year. This pattern continues until the premium is fully amortized at the maturity date of the bonds. Total interest expense for the full term of the bonds ($42,014) is equal to the total payments less the proceeds of issue. Moreover, as the carrying value of the liability decreases, interest expense decreases commensurate with it.

When the Straight-Line Method Is Acceptable

Although the interest method of expense recognition and discount amortization is preferred, it is sometimes acceptable to use the straight-line method. The straight-line method is acceptable unless the difference between the methods is material. A **material difference** in the amounts appearing in financial statements is one that could alter the decision of a qualified and informed individual who takes the care to analyze the financial statements. What is material in a particular case is a matter of judgment for those who prepare the business's financial statements. The differences between the two methods for the previous example are shown in Illustration 10-5. In this particular case, the maximum difference between the interest expense recognized in any given year under the two methods is $345—in the fifth year for the discount case. Since the total annual interest payment is $10,000, it appears unlikely that this difference would be judged material. Therefore, the straight-line method would probably be acceptable in this example.

ILLUSTRATION 10-5 Differences Between Straight-Line and Interest Methods of Amortization

Panel A: 10% Bonds Sold at a Discount to Yield 12%			
Year Ended	Interest Method*	Straight-Line*	Difference
March 31, 19X2	$1,135	$1,442	$307
March 31, 19X3	1,271	1,442	171
March 31, 19X4	1,423	1,442	19
March 31, 19X5	1,594	1,442	−152
March 31, 19X6	1,789	1,444	−345
Totals	$7,212	$7,212	$ 0

Panel B: 10% Bonds Sold at a Premium to Yield 8%			
Year Ended	Interest Method*	Straight-Line*	Difference
March 31, 19X2	$1,361	$1,597	$236
March 31, 19X3	1,470	1,597	127
March 31, 19X4	1,588	1,597	9
March 31, 19X5	1,715	1,597	−118
March 31, 19X6	1,852	1,598	−254
Totals	$7,986	$7,986	$ 0

*Minor differences due to rounding.

LO 3

Accrue interest expense and amortize discounts and premiums between interest payment dates, account for bond issue costs, and account for bonds issued between interest payment dates.

Accruing Interest Between Interest Payment Dates

To this point, we have considered only recognizing interest expense and amortizing discounts and premiums at the times interest payments are made. However, if financial statements are prepared at other dates in the bond issuer's fiscal year, we must accrue interest expense with an adjusting entry. Suppose, for example, that Beta Corporation, the issuer of the bonds described in Illustration 10-3, ends its fiscal year on December 31 instead of March 31. Beta will accrue interest for the first time on December 31, 19X1, for the 9-month period, April through December. Assuming straight-line amortization of the discount as in Illustration 10-3, interest expense for the 9-month period of $8,581.50 consists of two parts. First, Beta takes three-fourths of one year's interest payment, $7,500, and adds to it three-fourths of one year's amortization of discount, $1,081.50 ($1,442 x 3/4). Beta's adjusting entry is:

19X1			
Dec. 31	Interest Expense	8,581.50	
	Discount on Bonds Payable		1,081.50
	Interest Payable		7,500.00
	To accrue interest and amortize discount on 10% bonds payable.		

After the 9 month's amortization of the discount, Beta would disclose its bonds issued at a discount in its balance sheet as follows:

Noncurrent liabilities		
10% bonds payable, due March 31, 19X6		
Face value	$100,000.00	
Less: Unamortized discount	6,130.50	$93,869.50

For the period January through March, 19X2, Beta would recognize interest expense in two parts: one-fourth of the annual payment, $2,500, plus $360.50 ($1,442 x 1/4), for a total of $2,860.50. Beta's entry to recognize interest expense and the interest payment on March 31, 19X2, is:

19X2			
Mar. 31	Interest Expense	2,860.50	
	Interest Payable	7,500.00	
	Discount on Bonds Payable		360.50
	Cash		10,000.00
	To accrue interest, amortize discount, and record interest payment on 10% bonds payable.		

For the premium case, Beta would accrue interest on December 31 equal to three-fourths of the first year's interest payment less amortization of premium: $7,500 less $1,197.75 ($1,597 x 3/4), or $6,302.25. Beta's year-end accrual entry is:

19X1			
Dec. 31	Interest Expense	6,302.25	
	Premium on Bonds Payable	1,197.75	
	Interest Payable		7,500.00
	To accrue interest and amortize premium on 10% bonds payable.		

After the first year's amortization of the premium, Beta would show the bonds issued at a premium in its balance sheet as follows:

Noncurrent liabilities		
10% bonds payable, due March 31, 19X6		
Face value	$100,000.00	
Add: Unamortized premium	6,788.25	$106,788.25

For the period January through March, 19X2, Beta will recognize interest expense equal to the other one-fourth of its annual payment, $2,500, less $399.25, the remaining one-fourth of the first year's amortization of premium ($1,597 x 1/4), or $2,100.75. Beta's entry to recognize interest expense and the interest payment on March 31, 19X2, is:

19X2			
Mar. 31	Interest Expense	2,100.75	
	Interest Payable	7,500.00	
	Premium on Bonds Payable	399.25	
	Cash		10,000.00
	To accrue interest, amortize premium, and record interest payment on 10% bonds payable.		

Bond Issue Costs

Issuers usually incur some costs to issue bonds. These costs include costs of printing the bonds, registering them with the state or the Securities and Exchange Commission, advertising, etc. Issue costs represent part of the total cost of borrowing money from bondholders. Like interest costs, bond issue costs are recognized as expenses over the full term of the bonds. First, we record issue costs when they are incurred in a deferred expense account called Bond Issue Costs. A deferred expense account is a debit-balance account, customarily shown as an asset in the balance sheet. It is somewhat akin to prepaid expenses such as prepaid insurance. If, in the continuing example, Beta Corporation incurred issue costs of $6,600, it would record the costs initially with this entry:

19X1			
Apr. 1	Bond Issue Costs	6,600	
	Cash (or Accounts Payable)		6,600
	To record issue costs on 10% bonds payable.		

Next, we recognize issue costs as expenses according to a simple rule of thumb: *Recognize issue costs as expense in the same periods and in proportion to interest expense.* Under the straight-line method of amortization, interest costs are recognized at a constant rate per year. Under this method, the bond issue costs would also be amortized on a straight-line basis. For the period from April through December, Beta should amortize three-fourths of one year's portion of its issue costs, or $990 (($6,600 ÷ 5) x 3/4). Beta's accrual entry is:

19X1			
Dec. 31	Bond Issue Expense	990	
	Bond Issue Costs		990
	To amortize issue costs on 10% bonds payable.		

Issuing Bonds Between Interest Payments

Because bonds are often issued in large numbers to many different buyers, it is inconvenient to make interest payments to different bondholders in unique amounts, covering different periods. This is especially true for coupon bonds, since the coupons are preprinted and are redeemable for uniform amounts of interest. Therefore, issuers customarily make the same interest payment on each payment date to each bondholder, regardless of whether the bondholder held the bonds for the full interval of payment. However, when bonds are issued between interest payments, the bondholder does not earn all the interest that will be paid at the first subsequent payment date. Thus, the issuer charges the bondholder at the time of bond purchase for any interest that has accrued from the last interest payment date.

Suppose Beta Corporation, whose bond indenture requires that it pay a full year's interest of $10,000 to its bondholders on March 31, 19X2, issues its bonds on July 1, 19X1, instead of April 1, 19X1. The bondholders should not receive $2,500 of the annual interest payment on March 31, 19X2—the amount that would have accrued for the period April through June, 19X1. To handle this difference between the annual interest payment and the amount to which the bondholders actually are entitled, Beta simply charges the bondholders in advance for interest through June 30, 19X1, at the time they buy the bonds (July 1). If the bondholders otherwise would have paid face value for the bonds, then they should actually pay face value plus accrued interest of $2,500. That is, the bondholders would pay $102,500 for the bonds, and Beta would record the transaction thus:

19X1			
July 1	Cash	102,500	
	Interest Expense		2,500
	Bonds Payable		100,000
	To record issue of 100, $1,000 bonds at face value plus accrued interest of $2,500.		

Notice that Beta credits the interest the bondholders paid to Interest Expense. At this point, the balance in Beta's Interest Expense, which is ordinarily a debit-balance account, is a credit of $2,500.

Beta's actual interest expense for the year ended December 31, 19X1, should be $5,000—interest on $100,000 at 10% for one-half year (July 1 to December 31). However, since the bondholders paid for $2,500 additional interest, Beta accrues a full three-fourths of one year's interest expense at December 31:

19X1			
Dec. 31	Interest Expense	7,500	
	Interest Payable		7,500
	To accrue interest expense on 10% bonds payable.		

The credit balance in Interest Expense of $2,500 from the previous entry is offset by this debit of $7,500. Between these two entries, Beta records $5,000 interest expense—the correct interest expense for 19X1. At the same time, Beta's Interest Payable balance is $7,500 from the entry above. This is composed of the $5,000 interest the bondholders earned plus the $2,500 of accrued interest they paid at the time of purchase. On March 31, 19X2, Beta accrues further interest expense and pays the bondholders their first interest payment, which is recorded as follows:

19X2			
Mar. 31	Interest Expense	2,500	
	Interest Payable	7,500	
	Cash		10,000
	To accrue interest expense and record the annual interest payment on 10% bonds payable.		

LO 4
Account for investments in bonds.

INVESTMENTS IN BONDS

The bonds of corporations and of certain government entities, including the federal government, are attractive investments because they provide fixed principal and interest payments to the investor. With the exception of so-called junk bonds, bonds as a class generally are less risky as investments than common stocks of corporations.

In general, businesses buy bonds for one of two reasons: as long-term investments or as short-term investments. Only by holding bonds to maturity can an investor realize the fixed schedule of interest or principal payments. If bonds are sold before maturity, the prices they bring—that is, their fair or market values—may be less or more than their carrying values, depending on whether current interest rates are higher or lower than the bonds' interest rates. Thus, when bonds are bought and then sold before maturity, gains and losses usually arise.

Readily marketable bonds, such as those traded on the major securities exchanges, may be purchased as short-term or long-term investments. A controversy arises when such bonds are purchased and held while their market prices increase or decrease relative to their carrying values. Many accountants, financial analysts, and investors believe that, since ready market prices are available for such bonds, gains and losses should be recognized in each accounting period that the securities are held, as well as when they are finally sold or redeemed. Many companies that invest in bonds dispute this position, arguing that bonds can always be held to maturity and, therefore, the investor need not realize any gains or losses in market values over the terms of the bonds.

The FASB, in a recent pronouncement, basically recognized some merit in both arguments and struck a compromise between the two positions. The FASB's position requires investments in bonds to be classified into three categories that are accounted for by different methods:

1. Investments in bonds held to maturity
2. Investments in bonds available for sale
3. Short-term investments (trading securities)[1]

The accounting methods for bonds held to maturity and trading bonds represent two extremes. We will cover the two extremes first. Then, we will examine the way we account for bonds available for sale.

Investments in Bonds Held to Maturity

For bonds to be classified as **bonds held to maturity,** the business must have a "positive intent and ability to hold those [bonds] to maturity."[2] That is, there must not be any foreseeable intent or need to sell the bonds to secure cash. Accounting for bonds that are held to maturity generally mirrors the issuing corporation's accounting.

Suppose Omega Corporation purchased all 100 of Beta Corporation's $1,000 face value, 10%, 5-year bonds on July 1, 19X1. Omega paid Beta $95,250 plus accrued interest of $2,500 for the bonds and recorded the transaction thus:

19X1 July 1			
	Investment in Beta Bonds	95,250	
	Interest Revenue	2,500	
	Cash		97,750
	To record purchase of Beta Corporation bonds at a discount plus accrued interest.		

---

[1] "Accounting for Certain Investments in Debt and Equity Securities," *Statement of Financial Accounting Standards No. 115* (Norwalk, CT: FASB, May 1993), par. 6.

[2] *Ibid.*, par. 7.

Unlike the issuer of bonds, the purchaser does not use a discount account but records the bonds in the investment account at net cost or carrying value (including brokerage fees or other costs, if any). The bonds would be shown in the investments section of Omega's balance sheet at carrying value:

Investments:	
Beta Corporation 10% bonds purchased at a discount	$92,250

The accrued interest Omega purchased at July 1 is not part of its cost of the long-term investment. Omega debits its Interest Revenue for $2,500, giving that normally credit-balance account a temporary debit balance.

Assuming Omega's fiscal year ends on December 31, 19X1, it would accrue additional interest revenue and amortize a portion of the discount on the bonds. The discount on the bonds is $4,750 ($100,000 − 95,250). Assuming the straight-line method of amortization is used, Omega should amortize $1,000 per year ($4,750 ÷ 4.75 years). Omega will accrue interest revenue through December at three-fourths of the annual interest payment (from April 1 to December 31), $7,500, plus one-half of the annual discount amortization, $500:

19X1			
Dec. 31	Interest Receivable	7,500	
	Investment in Beta Bonds	500	
	Interest Revenue		8,000
	To accrue interest revenue and amortize discount		
	through year-end on Beta Corporation bonds.		

This entry brings the Interest Revenue balance to $5,500:

Interest accrued through December 31	$7,500	
Less: Accrued interest paid at July 1	2,500	$5,000
Amortization of discount (July 1–December 31)		500
Interest revenue (July 1–December 31)		$5,500

On March 31, 19X2, when it receives the first interest payment from Beta, Omega makes the following entry to record the receipt and another one-fourth year's interest accrual ($2,500) and amortization ($250):

19X2			
Mar. 31	Cash	10,000	
	Investment in Beta Bonds	250	
	Interest Receivable		7,500
	Interest Revenue		2,750
	To accrue interest revenue, amortize discount, and		
	record interest received on Beta Corporation bonds.		

Assuming Omega holds the Beta Corporation bonds to maturity, the discount will be fully amortized and the bonds' carrying value will be the face value of $100,000 at the receipt of the final payment from Beta. When the bonds held to maturity are within one year of maturity, Omega should reclassify them as current assets in the balance sheet.

Investments in Bonds as Trading Securities

Trading securities are those purchased and held for resale in the short-term. The objective of short-term investments in trading securities is not so much to earn interest (dividends) on these securities as to realize gains due to market price increases. Short-term investments are always classified as current assets in the balance sheet. Bonds purchased as short-term investments are initially recorded at their purchase costs, including brokerage fees and commissions. Interest revenue is recognized on the face amount of the bonds at the stated interest rate. The major difference in accounting for short-term investments in bonds is that at the end of each accounting period, their carrying values are compared to their current market values, and the unrealized gains and losses in value are recognized as if they are realized gains and losses.

Suppose Geneva Corporation buys the following bonds on July 1, 19X1, for purposes of holding them for a short period and reselling them for gains:

100, $1,000, 8% bonds of Paris, Inc., due December 31, 19X5, for $100,000
100, $1,000, 9% bonds of Rome Corp., due December 31, 19X3, for $97,107

Both of these companies' bonds pay interest semiannually on June 30 and December 31. Geneva could record the investments in one entry as follows:

19X1			
July 1	Investment in Paris, Inc. Bonds	100,000	
	Investment in Rome Corp. Bonds	97,107	
	Cash		197,107
	To record purchase of Paris, Inc. and Rome Corp.		
	bonds as short-term investments.		

On December 31, 19X1, Geneva recognizes interest revenue with the following entries:

19X1			
Dec. 31	Cash	4,000	
	Interest Revenue		4,000
	To record interest received from Paris, Inc.		
	Cash	4,500	
	Interest Revenue		4,500
	To record interest received from Rome Corp.		

Now, assume interest rates have fallen slightly since July 1. Based on present value reasoning, if interest rates fall, the market values of bonds with fixed payment schedules should increase. Because increases and decreases in interest rates tend to affect all bonds in the same way, bond prices tend to rise and fall together—more so than stock prices. A comparison of the carrying values and current market values of the Paris, Inc. and Rome Corp. bonds as of December 31 shows the following:

	Carrying Value	Current Market Value	Increase (Decrease)
Paris, Inc. 10% bonds	$100,000	$101,632	$1,632
Rome Corp. 9% bonds	97,107	98,721	1,614
	$197,107	$200,353	$3,246

Geneva would record the unrealized holding gains with the following journal entry:

19X1			
Dec. 31	Investment in Paris, Inc. Bonds	1,632	
	Investment in Rome Corp. Bonds	1,614	
	Unrealized Gain (Loss) from Investments		3,246
	To record unrealized gains on trading securities.		

Unrealized Gain (Loss) from Investments is closed to Income Summary and, therefore, is included in the current period's income on the income statement. In addition, the bonds' carrying values are now their market values as of December 31, 19X1.

Now, assume that on February 1, 19X2, Geneva sells the Paris bonds for $103,000. It records the sale as follows:

19X2			
Feb. 1	Cash	103,000	
	Investment in Paris, Inc. Bonds		101,632
	Gain from Sale of Investments		1,368
	To record unrealized gains on trading securities.		

Notice that only the incremental amount above the December 31 market value of the bonds is recognized as an additional gain from the sale of the bonds.

Investments in Bonds Available for Sale

If bonds are not held to maturity or held for short-term trading, the FASB considers them to be **bonds available for sale**. That is, they could be liquidated at any time, but they may not be, depending on circumstances. Bonds available for sale should be classified as current if they will mature within a year (or longer operating cycle) or if management intends to sell them within that period. We account for investments in securities available for sale in a manner similar to short-term investments. However, we amortize discounts and premiums, and we do not include unrealized gains and losses in current income. Referring to Geneva's transactions in the Paris, Inc. and Rome Corp. bonds, assume Geneva did not purchase the bonds as short-term investments and is not holding them to maturity. Interest revenue from the Rome bonds would consist of $4,500 interest received plus $579 amortization of discount on a straight-line basis. The increase in the carrying value of the bonds from amortization of the discount decreases the unrealized gain. Geneva's December 31 entry to record the increase in their market values is:

19X1			
Dec. 31	Investment in Paris, Inc. Bonds	1,632	
	Investment in Rome Corp. Bonds	1,035	
	Unrealized Gain (Loss) from Available for Sale		
	Securities		2,667
	To record unrealized gains on bond investments.		

Unlike the case of short-term investments, Unrealized Gain (Loss) from Available for Sale Securities is not a temporary account that is closed to Income Summary. Instead, it is a valuation account in stockholders' equity. Thus, the unrealized gains and losses on securities available for sale are not included in current income.

When the Paris, Inc. bonds are sold on February 1, Geneva makes the following entry:

19X2 Feb. 1	Cash	103,000	
	Unrealized Gain (Loss) from Available for Sale Securities	1,632	
	Investment in Paris, Inc. Bonds		101,632
	Gain from Sale of Investments		3,000
	To record realized gain on securities.		

Notice that we clear the previous gain in market value recorded in Unrealized Gain (Loss) with this entry (debit of $1,632). We also recognize the entire cumulative gain between cost and selling price at the time of sale, when the gain becomes a realized gain. This treatment contrasts to the inclusion in current income of previous unrealized holding gains in the case of short-term investments in bonds.

LO 5

Explain the difference between capital leases and operating leases.

LEASE OBLIGATIONS

Businesses often lease (rent) assets rather than purchasing them. Virtually any asset a business might use can be leased as well as purchased. Major airlines often lease the aircraft that are their primary means of providing services to their customers. Some businesses even lease the potted plants they use to decorate their premises.

By leasing assets, businesses may avoid some or all of the risks of ownership such as obsolescence and costs of maintenance. They also avoid the necessity of raising the funds required to purchase the assets.

Types of Leases

Leases may be short-term (less than one year) or long-term. They may also be operating leases or capital leases. **Operating leases** are short-term or long-term leases that involve strictly renting assets for use in the lessee's (renter's) business. No special rights or privileges are acquired, and the lessor (owner) bears all of the risks of ownership. **Capital leases** are long-term leases that involve the lessee's acquisition of at least some significant ownership rights and obligations, in addition to the use of the assets over the term of the lease.

Operating Leases.   An operating lease agreement does not represent many formidable challenges to accountants. The major problem is to allocate rent payments as expenses to the periods covered by the lease arrangement. Suppose, for example, that Gamma Corporation rents a computer for 2 years under a lease calling for advance rent of $1,800 plus rent payments of $150 per month. The computer's owner (lessor), Alpha Computers, agrees under the lease to maintain the computer and to pay for all parts and labor required to keep it in satisfactory working condition.

The total rent expense for the 2-year lease is $5,400 ($1,800 + $3,600), or an average of $225 per month. A key question in allocating a portion of the total rent expense to each month is the pattern of benefits expected from the rented asset(s). In this case, assume the computer is expected to benefit Gamma's business equally in each of the 24 months the lease covers. This implies that an equal amount of rent should be recognized as expense in each month.

First, Gamma recognizes the initial payment of $1,800 as prepaid rent, thus:

(Date)	Prepaid Rent	1,800	
	Cash		1,800
	To record prepayment of rent under operating lease agreement.		

Then, each month Gamma pays the monthly rent and amortizes the prepaid rent to recognize $225 of total rent expense. Gamma's entries for each month is of this form:

(Date)	Rent Expense	225	
	Cash		150
	Prepaid Rent		75
	To record rent expense and amortize prepaid rent.		

At the end of the 2 years, the operating lease will have expired, the Prepaid Rent balance will be zero, Gamma will return the computer to the owner and will have no further rights or obligations under the operating lease.

Capital Leases. Although many leases simply involve the lessees' renting of assets, accountants have long recognized that some leases are *in substance* purchases of assets.[3] Such leases, called capital leases, are effectively the same as the "rent-to-own" arrangements appliance and furniture stores offer to consumers. Instead of involving only the temporary use of assets for rental fees, the lessee (renter) also acquires some property rights over the course of the lease. Whether a particular lease is a rental agreement or a special kind of purchase is a matter of judgment. Thus, different accountants and managers might come to different conclusions about any given lease. As a result, the Financial Accounting Standards Board has set forth criteria, any one (or more) of which identify a lease as a capital lease. The criteria may be *paraphrased* as follows:[4]

1. The lease transfers the ownership of the property to the lessee by the end of the lease term.
2. The lease contains an option to purchase the assets at less than their expected fair value at the end of the term of the lease.
3. The lease term is equal to 75% or more of the estimated remaining economic life of the leased property.
4. At the beginning of the lease term, the present value of the minimum lease payments equals or exceeds 90% of the fair value of the leased property to the lessor at the start of the lease term.[5]

LO 6

Account for the assets and liabilities recognized under capital leases.

Accounting for Capital Leases

Now, suppose Gamma Corporation leases a computer on January 1, 19X1, for 5 years at an annual rental of $2,000. At the end of the lease term, the computer becomes Gamma's property. This lease arrangement conforms to Criterion 1

---

[3]"Accounting for Leases," *Statement of Financial Accounting Standards No. 13* (Stamford, CT: FASB, 1976), pars. 61 and 63.

[4]*Ibid.*, par. 7.

[5]Note: Criteria 3 and 4 apply only if more than 25% of the asset's estimated total economic life remains at the start of the lease term.

and must be accounted for as a capital lease. Accounting for capital leases roughly approximates the accounting that would be accorded an asset that is financed entirely with borrowed funds. Assume Gamma Corporation can borrow funds over 5 years at an interest rate of, say, 12%. From Table 2 in Appendix C, we see that the present value of each $1 paid annually for 5 years at 12% is 3.605. Thus, the lease is equivalent to borrowing $7,210 ($2,000 x 3.605) and spending the proceeds of the loan on the computer.

The capital lease treatment requires that the computer be recognized as an asset and the lease obligation be recognized as a liability. Gamma's journal entry to recognize initially both the asset and liability in this case is:

19X1			
Jan. 1	Equipment Under Capital Lease	7,210	
	Long-Term Lease Payable		7,210
	To record acquisition of a computer under a long-term capital lease agreement.		

Assets Leased Under Capital Leases. Once Gamma makes the above entry, the computer is depreciated just as it would be if it had been purchased for cash. That is, depreciation is recognized according to the method Gamma uses for any similar asset. Assuming a useful life of 6 years, expected residual value of $1,000, and straight-line depreciation, Gamma recognizes depreciation expense of $1,035 (($7,210 − $1,000) ÷ 6) each year. At the end of the first year, the asset would appear in Gamma's balance sheet thus:

Property, plant, and equipment:		
Equipment leased under capital lease	$7,210	
Less: Accumulated depreciation	1,035	$6,175

Capital Lease Liabilities. The lease obligation is treated just like other long-term installment obligations such as the long-term notes illustrated in a previous chapter. Illustration 10-6 summarizes the history of the lease liability.

ILLUSTRATION 10-6 History of a Capital Lease Liability

Year	Balance Jan. 1	+ Annual Interest Expense	− Annual Payment	= Balance Dec. 31
19X1	$7,210.00	$865.20	$2,000.00	$6,075.20
19X2	6,075.20	729.02	2,000.00	4,804.22
19X3	4,804.22	576.51	2,000.00	3,380.73
19X4	3,380.73	405.69	2,000.00	1,786.42
19X5	1,786.42	213.58	2,000.00	0.00

At the beginning of 19X1, the lease liability equals $7,210, the present value of the payments of the five, $2,000 lease installments. The liability would be disclosed in two parts in the January 1 balance sheet as follows:

Current liabilities:	
Current portion of long-term lease	$1,786.00
Noncurrent liabilities:	
Long-term lease	$5,424.00

The current portion of the liability is the present value of the $2,000 payment due on December 31, 19X1 ($2,000 x .8929 = $1,786). The noncurrent portion is the present value of the remaining four payments ($7,210 − $1,786 = $5,424).

The interest in any year of the lease is equal to the beginning carrying value times the interest rate used to determine the liability's original present value (12%). During 19X1, Gamma accrues a total of $865.20 in interest expense ($7,210 x 12%). Gamma's entries to accrue the interest and pay the annual installment are:

19X1			
Dec. 31	Interest Expense—Long-Term Lease	865.20	
	Long-Term Lease Payable		865.20
	To accrue interest on long-term capital lease.		
31	Long-Term Lease Payable	2,000.00	
	Cash		2,000.00
	To record annual payment on long-term capital lease.		

According to the first line of Illustration 10-6, the net effect of these two entries is to reduce the principal amount of Gamma's liability by $1,134.80, the difference between the accrued interest and the lease payment. The reduction in principal leaves a new balance as of December 31, 19X1, of $6,075.20. To calculate approximately the same balance, we can multiply the payment amount times the annuity factor from Table 2 in Appendix C for 4 years at 12%: $2,000 x 3.037 = $6,074. This new balance would appear in the December 31, 19X1, balance sheet as follows:

Current liabilities	
Current portion of long-term lease	$1,786.00
Noncurrent liabilities	
Long-term lease	$4,289.20

DEBT-EQUITY RATIO AND OFF-BALANCE-SHEET FINANCING

LO 7
Calculate and interpret the debt-equity ratio as an indicator of potential financial distress, and recognize its limitations when off-balance-sheet financing is used.

Let us return to Miklos Kronis' problem of financing $100,000 of new equipment for Midwestern Alliance Corporation. Miklos has asked the supplier about the possibility of acquiring the equipment under either an operating or capital lease; he has talked to the company's commercial bank about a long-term installment loan, which will require $2,000 in various loan-origination costs; and he has consulted an investment banker about issuing bonds. He now focuses on financing the equipment over a 5-year period. Five years balances off the equipment's expected useful life (10 years) against the risk of early obsolescence. Miklos definitely dislikes still having to pay for assets after they are no longer useful.

Miklos rules out issuing bonds, because the registration process will take too long and the issuing costs will be high. Midwestern Alliance can borrow long-term funds at 9% annual interest. The cash payments for the other three options and their present values (at the 9% interest rate) are shown in Illustration 10-7. Payments in Illustration 10-7 on the line labeled End of Year 0

ILLUSTRATION 10-7 Comparative Cash Payments and Present Values

End of Year	Present Value of $1	Installment Note		Capital Lease		Operating Lease	
		Cash Payments	Present Value	Cash Payments	Present Value	Cash Payments	Present Value
0	1.0000	$ 2,000	$ 2,000	$ 24,000	$ 24,000	$ 21,000	$21,000
1	.9174	25,500	23,394	24,000	22,018	21,000	19,266
2	.8417	25,500	21,463	24,000	20,200	21,000	17,675
3	.7722	25,500	19,691	24,000	18,532	21,000	16,216
4	.7084	25,500	18,065	24,000	17,002	21,000	14,877
5	.6499	25,500	16,573		0		0
Totals		$129,500	$101,186	$120,000	$101,752	$105,000	$89,034

should be interpreted as payments at the beginning of Year 1. Notice that, in effect, the lease alternatives require that the major annual payments start immediately; whereas only the loan origination costs will be required immediately under the installment note alternative.

According to the calculations in Illustration 10-7, the operating lease has the lowest present value—meaning the lowest equivalent cost of the equipment in present cash-equivalent terms. However, Miklos expects the equipment to be worth at least $25,000 at the end of 5 years ($16,248 in present value terms) and to have perhaps as many as 5 additional years of useful life. Under the operating lease, the company will have to return the equipment to the supplier at the end of the 5-year lease. Thus, in pure economic terms, Miklos prefers either the installment note or the capital lease. Although either the note or capital lease will cost about $12,000 more than the operating lease in present value terms, at the end of 5 years, the company will own the equipment. Since the residual value of the equipment is over $16,000 in present value terms, the loan and capital lease are the better forms of financing. Miklos further prefers the loan, because it requires only $2,000 in "up-front" costs, whereas the capital and operating leases require a full year's payment of $24,000 and $21,000, respectively, upon delivery of the equipment.

However, before making a final decision on a financing plan, Miklos must consider the effects of the plans on Midwestern's debt-equity ratio. Therefore, as soon as he was faced with the equipment acquisition issue, he asked the Accounting Department to prepare the balance sheet in Illustration 10-8.

Debt-Equity Ratio

The **debt-equity ratio**, defined below, is one of the most popular financial indicators.

$$\text{Debt-Equity Ratio} = \frac{\text{Total Liabilities}}{\text{Total Stockholders' Equity}}$$

The debt-equity ratio most directly measures the relationship between the business's debt financing and equity financing. The more a business relies on debt, the higher its ratio will be. Also, the more a business relies on debt, the more fixed payment obligations it has and the higher the probability that it might not be able to pay all of its bills. Therefore, the debt-equity ratio is considered an indicator of potential financial distress or insolvency. Creditors often use the

ILLUSTRATION 10-8   Midwestern Alliance Balance Sheet

Midwestern Alliance Corporation Balance Sheet		
Assets		
Current assets:		
Cash		$ 40,000
Accounts receivable		60,000
Inventory		50,000
Prepaid expenses		5,000
Total current assets		$155,000
Property, plant, and equipment	$900,000	
Less: Accumulated depreciation	400,000	500,000
Total assets		$655,000
Liabilities and Stockholders' Equity		
Current liabilities:		
Accounts payable		$ 30,000
Notes payable		80,000
Wages and salaries payable		10,000
Taxes payable		5,000
Total current liabilities		$125,000
Noncurrent liabilities		175,000
Total liabilities		$300,000
Stockholders' equity:		
Capital stock		$ 20,000
Paid-in capital in excess of par		200,000
Retained earnings		135,000
Total stockholders' equity		$355,000
Total liabilities and stockholders' equity		$655,000

debt-equity ratio to restrict a borrower's tendency to overuse debt and to risk insolvency—as the bank has done to Midwestern Alliance Corporation.

Recall that under its revolving line of credit agreement with the bank, Midwestern may not let its debt-equity ratio exceed 1.0. Based on its balance sheet in Illustration 10-8, before the equipment acquisition, Midwestern's debt equity ratio is .845:

$$\text{Debt-Equity Ratio} = \frac{\$300,000}{\$355,000} = .845$$

However, if Midwestern acquires the equipment with the long-term install-ment loan or the capital lease, at least $77,752 of new debt will be recorded (the present value of the 4 remaining payments under the capital lease in Illustration 10-7). That would change Midwestern's debt-equity ratio to 1.064.

$$\text{Debt-Equity Ratio} = \frac{\$377,752}{\$355,000} = 1.064$$

Thus, the installment loan and the capital lease arrangement are infeasible under Midwestern's line of credit agreement with its bank. Midwestern can acquire the equipment only through the operating lease arrangement under which no new debt will show up on its balance sheet.

Off-Balance-Sheet Financing

By acquiring the equipment under an operating lease, Midwestern is accepting an economically less favorable arrangement just to avoid having debt financing show up on its balance sheet (and be included in calculating its debt-equity ratio). This is an example of off-balance-sheet financing. **Off-balance-sheet financing** is any scheme or system through which a business effectively acquires or retains property rights in assets without showing the assets or a source of funds on its balance sheet. In the extreme form of off-balance-sheet financing, companies work with suppliers or other creditors specifically to structure leases and other arrangements so they need not be recognized as debt obligations. The purpose is to present to the world a balance sheet with less debt. If analysts of their financial statements are not careful, they will underestimate those companies' risks of financial distress. For example, is Midwestern Alliance Corporation less likely to have financial difficulty under the operating lease than under the installment loan or capital lease? Probably not. In fact, Midwestern must make annual rent payments that are only marginally less than those for the capital lease and installment loan payments. If it is unable to make a rent payment, Midwestern will lose the equipment, which is essential to its ongoing operations. Thus, because of off-balance-sheet financing, the debt-equity ratio is limited in its ability to measure a company's exposure to financial distress due to debt obligations.

SUMMARY

Describe the important features of bonds businesses issue as a form of borrowing; explain why some bonds are issued at face value, some at discounts, and some at premiums and record issues of bonds. Bonds are a major source of debt financing, especially for large corporations. Bonds are debt obligations represented by securities that holders can exchange. Bearer bonds can be exchanged without notifying the issuer; whereas registered bonds can be exchanged only by returning them to the issuer and having them reissued to the new owner. Serial bonds are paid off in a series of retirements over a period of years and have the characteristics of installment loans to the issuer. The bond indenture is the agreement between the issuer and all holders of a particular issue of bonds. The indenture sets forth the full term of the bonds and the stated, nominal, or coupon rate of interest. When the market rate is less than the coupon rate of interest, buyers are willing to pay more than face value for the bonds; and they sell at a premium such that they yield the market rate on the higher carrying value. When the market rate is greater than the coupon rate of interest, buyers are unwilling to pay face value for the bonds; and they sell at a discount such that they yield the market rate on the lower carrying value. Bonds are recorded in the bond liability account at face value, and the premium or discount is recorded in a separate valuation account or contra-liability account, respectively.

Calculate total interest cost of bond issues and record interest expense, including amortization of discounts and premiums using the straight-line and interest methods. When bonds are issued at a discount or premium, the bonds are valued at face value plus any premium or minus any discount. Total interest expense equals the interest payments plus any discount or minus any premium. The discount or premium is amortized—most commonly according to the straight-line method. To recognize interest expense in each period, the total discount or premium is divided by the number of periods to maturity of the bonds to determine the amount of amortization. Then the amount of amortization is added to or subtracted from the interest payment for a period to determine the interest expense for the period. Under the interest method, the effective interest rate is found by determining the rate that equates the present value of the bonds' interest and principal payments to the proceeds from issue. This rate is applied to the beginning-of-period carrying value of the bonds to determine interest expense for the period. The difference between interest expense and the interest payment is the amount of discount or premium amortized. If the difference between methods is immaterial, a business may use the simpler straight-line method to amortize discounts and premiums.

Accrue interest expense and amortize discounts and premiums between interest payment dates, account for bond issue costs, and account for bonds issued between interest payment dates.   When financial statements fall between payment dates, proportional amounts of the payments and amortizations are accrued on the financial statement dates. Bond issue costs are recognized at issue as prepaid expenses and are amortized over the remaining term of the bonds in proportion to interest expense. When bonds are issued between interest payment dates, the issuer charges the buyers the interest that has accrued since the last payment, records this amount as a credit to interest expense, and then pays and debits interest expense for the full payment next due.

Account for investments in bonds.   Accounting for investments in bonds differs, depending on the bonds' classification as: held to maturity, short-term, or available for sale. Buyers account for investments in bonds held to maturity in a way that virtually mirrors the issuers' recognition of interest payments and amortizations of premiums and discounts. The only exception is that buyers recognize the bonds' carrying value in a single account—no discount or premium accounts are used. Holders of short-term investments in bonds purchase them for short-term resale and short-term gains. They account for interest earned at face value of the bonds times the stated interest rate. However, in addition, they add (deduct) increases (decreases) in the market values of the bonds to their carrying values and recognize these unrealized gains (losses) as current income. In contrast, bonds available for sale (not bought for short-term trading or for holding to maturity) are accounted for in a third way. They are treated similarly to short-term investments. However, the unrealized gains and losses are not closed to Income Summary or included in current income. Instead, the unrealized gains and losses are accumulated in a stockholders' equity account. When the securities are sold, their previous unrealized gains (losses) are reversed from this account and included in an overall realized gain or loss that is included in current income.

Explain the difference between capital leases and operating leases.   Leases have become increasingly popular as a means of acquiring needed assets. Assets are provided strictly for the lessee's temporary use under an operating lease in exchange for rent payments, possibly including advance payments. The only problem in accounting for such leases, known as operating leases, is to recognize rent paid as expense according to the benefits derived from the leased assets. This generally requires that advanced rent payments be set up in a prepaid rent account and amortized over the life of the lease. On the other hand, capital leases involve acquisition of at least some property rights in the leased assets.

Account for the assets and liabilities recognized under capital leases. When assets are acquired under capital leases, the assets and the capital lease liabilities are valued at the present value of the lease payments. The asset is then amortized (depreciated) in the same way other similar assets in the business would be amortized (depreciated). And the lease is treated like other long-term, installment liabilities.

Calculate and interpret the debt-equity ratio as an indicator of potential financial distress, and recognize its limitations when off-balance-sheet financing is used. The debt-equity ratio is one of the most popular financial indicators.

$$\text{Debt-Equity Ratio} = \frac{\text{Total Liabilities}}{\text{Total Stockholders' Equity}}$$

The more a business relies on debt, the higher its ratio will be. Also, the more a business relies on debt, the more fixed payment obligations it has and the higher the probability that it might not be able to pay all of its bills. Therefore, the debt-equity ratio is considered an indicator of potential financial distress or insolvency. However, when companies work with suppliers or other creditors specifically to structure leases and other arrangements so they need not be recognized as debt obligations, the debt-equity ratio is limited in its ability to measure a company's exposure to financial distress. Analysts should, therefore, be aware of off-balance-sheet financing and take it into account separately.

REVIEW PROBLEM A: BONDS PAYABLE AND INVESTMENTS IN BONDS

On January 2, 19X1, Day Corporation issued 1,000, $1,000 face value, 8% bonds that pay interest annually on December 31 of each year for 5 years. Crandall Corporation purchased the entire bond issue with an effective interest rate of 10%.

REQUIRED:

a. Calculate the price of the bonds when issued.
b. Record Day Corporation's issuance of the bonds.
c. Record Day Corporation's interest expense and amortization of discount for 19X1 and 19X2, using the straight-line method.
d. Record the interest expense and amortization of discount for 19X1 and 19X2, using the interest method.
e. Record Crandall Corporation's investment in the bonds.
f. Record the interest revenue and amortization of discount for 19X1 if Crandall classified the bonds as held to maturity.
g. Assuming Crandall classifies the bonds as short-term investments, record the interest revenue, and unrealized holding gain for 19X1. The bonds have a market value of $945,000 on December 31, 19X1.
h. Assuming Crandall classifies the bonds as available for sale, record the interest revenue, amortization of discount, and unrealized holding gain for 19X1. The bonds have a market value of $945,000 on December 31, 19X1.

SOLUTION:

Planning and Organizing Your Work

1. Determine the bonds' annual cash flows and multiply the cash flows times 10% present value factors for the appropriate time periods. Sum the discounted cash flows.

2. Record the bonds' issuance by debiting Cash for the amount determined in Step 1, crediting Bonds Payable at face value, and debiting the difference to the discount account.
3. Calculate the annual amortization of the discount by dividing the total discount by the term of the bond issue. Record the amortization of the discount and the payment of interest. The amortization of the discount plus the cash paid for interest equals the debit to Interest Expense. The amounts are the same for both years since the straight-line method is used..
4. Multiply the bonds' carrying value at the beginning of 19X1 and 19X2 by the effective interest rate of 10% to determine the interest expense for each year. Record the payment of interest for each year. The difference between interest expense and the interest payment is credited to the bond discount account for each year.
5. Record the investment in bonds. Debit Investments in Bonds and credit Cash for the amount computed in Step 1.
6. Compute interest revenue by the same procedure as in Step 4. Record interest revenue and the collection of interest. The difference between interest revenue and interest collected is added to the debit balance in Investments in Bonds.
7. Follow the procedures in Step 6 for bond investments classified as short-term; but ignore amortization. Adjust (debit) the investment account by the increase in market value after you record interest and amortization. Credit Unrealized Gain (Loss) from Investments.
8. Follow the procedures in Step 6 for bond investments classified as available for sale. Adjust (debit) the investment account by the increase in market value after you record interest and amortization. Credit Unrealized Gain (Loss) from Available-for-Sale Securities (a component of stockholders' equity).

(a) *Calculate the price of the bonds.*

December 31	Payment*	10% Present Value Factor	Present Value
19X1	$ 80,000	0.9091	$ 72,728
19X2	80,000	0.8264	66,112
19X3	80,000	0.7513	60,104
19X5	80,000	0.6830	54,640
19X6	80,000	0.6209	49,672
19X6	1,000,000	0.6209	620,900
Total present value			$924,156

*1,000 bonds x $1,000 x 8%

(b) *Record the issuance of the bond on January 2, 19X1.*

Discount on bonds = $100,000 − $924,156 = $75,844

19X1			
Jan. 2	Cash	924,156	
	Discount on Bonds Payable	75,844	
	Bonds Payable		1,000,000
	To record issue of 1,000, $1,000 8% bonds		
	for $924,156.		

(c) *Record the interest expense and amortization of discount for 19X1 and 19X2, using the straight-line method (same entry for both years).*

Interest payment = $1,000,000 x 8% = $80,000
Amortization of discount = $75,844 ÷ 5 = $15,169

19X1–19X2 Dec. 31	Interest Expense	95,169	
	Cash		80,000
	Discount on Bonds Payable		15,169
	To record interest expense, amortization of discount, and annual interest payment on 8% bonds payable.		

(d) *Record the interest expense and amortization of discount for 19X1 and 19X2, using the interest method.*

Interest expense 19X1 = $924, 156 × 10% = $92,416
Amortization of discount = $92,416 − $80,000 = $12,416
Interest expense 19X2 = ($924,156 + $12,416) × 10% = $93,657
Amortization of discount = $93,657 − $80,000 = $13,657

19X1 Dec. 31	Interest Expense	92,416	
	Cash		80,000
	Discount on Bonds Payable		12,416
	To record interest expense, amortization of discount, and annual interest payment on 8% bonds payable.		

19X2 Dec. 31	Interest Expense	93,657	
	Cash		80,000
	Discount on Bonds Payable		13,657
	To record interest expense, amortization of discount, and annual interest payment on 8% bonds payable.		

(e) *Record Crandall Corporation's investment.*

19X1 Dec. 31	Investments in Bonds	924,156	
	Cash		924,156
	To record purchase of Day Corporation bonds at a discount.		

(f) *Record the interest revenue and amortization of discount for 19X1 if Crandall classified the bond as held to maturity.*

19X1 Dec. 31	Cash	80,000	
	Investments in Bonds	12,416	
	Interest Revenue		92,416
	To record interest revenue, amortize discount, and record collection of interest.		

(g) *Record the interest revenue and unrealized holding gain for 19X1.*

Unrealized gain = $945,000 − $924,156 = $20,844

19X1 Dec. 31	Cash	80,000	
	Interest Revenue		80,000
	To record interest received from Day Corporation.		
	Investments in Bonds	20,844	
	Unrealized Gain (Loss) from Investments		20,844
	To record unrealized gain on short-term investments.		

(h) *Record the interest revenue, amortization of discount, and unrealized holding gain for 19X1.*

19X1			
Dec. 31	Cash	80,000	
	Investments in Bonds	12,416	
	Interest Revenue		92,416
	To record interest received from Day Corporation and amortization of discount.		
	Investments in Bonds	8,428	
	Unrealized Gain (Loss) from Available-for-Sale		
	Securities		8,428
	To record unrealized gain on bond investment.		

REVIEW PROBLEM B: ACCOUNTING FOR LEASES

On January 1, 19X2, Hostettler Corporation acquired new equipment under a 5-year lease calling for annual payments of $10,000 starting immediately. Although the equipment will revert back to the owner at the end of the lease term, its expected useful life is 5 years, and it is expected to have no market value at the end of the lease term. Hostettler, whose fiscal year-end is December 31, can borrow funds to acquire such equipment at 11%. Hostettler uses straight-line depreciation for similar equipment it has purchased.

REQUIRED:

a. Prepare the journal entry to recognize the first lease payment, including any assets and liabilities, if appropriate.
b. Prepare a journal entry or entries to recognize any necessary accruals or adjustments of of December 31, 19X2.
c. Prepare a journal entry to recognize the lease payment of January 1, 19X3.
d. Demonstrate the relationship between the balance of any lease obligation that you have recognized and the remaining lease payments at January 1, 19X3.

SOLUTION:

Planning and Organizing Your Work

1. First, determine if the lease is an operating lease or a capital lease by comparing its terms to the 4 criteria for capital leases listed in the chapter. In this case, the lease term is more than 75% of the remaining economic life of the equipment. Therefore, the lease is a capital lease.
2. Next, determine the value of the lease liability and the cost of the equipment. In this case, the lease is an annuity due. The value of the liability on January 1, 19X2 is equal to the present value of the remaining annuity of $10,000 each year for 4 years at 11%. The cost of the equipment is the value of the lease plus the first payment of $10,000 on January 1, 19X2. Debit Equipment Under Capital Lease with the value of the equipment, credit Long-Term Lease Payable with the value of the lease, and credit Cash with the first payment.
3. Find the depreciation expense for the year by applying the straight-line method to the cost of the equipment less any salvage value (none). Prepare the adjusting entry, debiting Depreciation Expense and crediting Accumulated Depreciation—Equipment Under Capital Lease.
4. Find the interest expense for the year by multiplying the beginning of the year carrying value of the lease liability by the effective interest rate. Prepare the adjusting entry, debiting Interest Expense and crediting Long-Term Lease Payable.
5. Recognize the payment by debiting Long-Term Lease Payable and crediting Cash for the amount of the payment.

6. Calculate the present value of the remaining annuity of 3 payments and compare to the balance in Long-Term Lease Payable. Ignore small rounding differences.

(a) *Prepare the journal entry to recognize the first lease payment.*

Annuity value of $1 paid at the end of each of 4 years at 11% (from Table 2, Appendix C): 3.102. Value of the lease liability: $10,000 x 3.102 = $31,020. Cost of the equipment: $31,020 + $10,000 = $41,020.

19X2			
Jan. 1	Equipment Under Capital Lease	41,020	
	Long-Term Lease Payable		31,020
	Cash		10,000
	To record acquisition of equipment under a long-term capital lease agreement.		

(b) *Prepare a journal entry or entries to recognize any necessary accruals or adjustments as of December 31, 19X2.*

Depreciation expense: $41,020 ÷ 5
Interest expense: $31,020 x 11%

19X2			
Dec. 31	Depreciation Expense	8,204	
	Accumulated Depreciation—Equipment Under Capital Lease		8,204
	To record depreciation of equipment under a long-term capital lease agreement.		
31	Interest Expense	3,412	
	Long-Term Lease Payable		3,412
	To record interest expense on a long-term capital lease.		

(c) *Prepare a journal entry to recognize the payment on January 1, 19X3.*

19X3			
Jan. 1	Long-Term Lease Payable	10,000	
	Cash		10,000
	To record payment on a long-term capital lease		

(d) *Demonstrate the relationship between the balance of the lease obligation and the remaining lease payments at January 1, 19X3.*

Present value of remaining lease payments:

Lease payment	$10,000
Times annuity of $1 each year for 3 years at 11%	x 2.444
Present value of remaining payments	$24,440

Balance in Long-Term Lease Payable:

Lease balance, January 1, 19X2	$31,020
Interest for 19X2	3,412
Payment on January 1, 19X3	(10,000)
Lease balance, January 1, 19X3	$24,432

KEY TERMS

bearer or coupon bonds, *439*	discount, *439*	operating leases, *455*
bondholders, *438*	effective interest rate, *440*	premium, *439*
bond indenture, *438*	full term, *438*	registered bonds, *439*
bonds, *438*	interest method of	serial bonds, *439*
bonds available for sale, *454*	amortization, *445*	stated, nominal, or coupon
bonds held to maturity, *451*	issuer of bonds, *438*	rate, *438*
capital leases, *455*	material difference, *447*	term bonds, *439*
debt-equity ratio, *459*	off-balance-sheet financing,	term to maturity, *439*
denominations of bonds, *438*	*461*	trading securities, *453*

SELF-QUIZ

LO 1 1. Which of the following is *not* a difference between bonds and negotiable notes?
a. The terms of the bonds are usually longer than those of notes.
b. The total amount of bond debt is broken down into relatively small denominations.
c. More costs are associated with issuing notes than with issuing bonds.
d. All individual bonds are covered by a bond indenture.

LO 1 2. Which of the following statements is *false*?
a. If a bond sells for more than face value, it is sold at a premium.
b. If the nominal interest rate exceeds the market interest rate for a comparable investment, a bond will sell at a discount.
c. If the nominal interest rate equals the interest rate for a comparable investment, a bond will sell at face value.
d. If a bond sells for less than face value, it is sold at a discount.

LO 2 3. Which of following represents total interest cost of a bond?
a. The sum of the interest payments for any bond
b. The sum of the interest payments for bonds issued at face value
c. The sum of the interest payments plus the premium for bonds issued at greater than face
d. The sum of the interest payments plus the discount for a bond issued at greater than face

LO 3 4. Which of the following statements is *not* correct about bond issue costs?
a. These include costs of registering and printing the bonds.
b. These costs should be included in a deferred expense account.
c. The deferred expense account should be classified as a contra-liability on the balance sheet.
d. The costs should be recognized as expenses over the full term of the bonds.

LO 4 5. The three classifications of investments in bonds are: _____ ___ _____, _____ ___ _____, and _____ _____.

LO 5 6. Which of the following is *not* a criterion for identifying a capital lease?
a. The lease transfers the ownership of the property to the lessee by the end of the lease term.
b. The lease contains an option to purchase the assets at less than their expected fair value at the end of the lease term.
c. The lease term is equal to 75% or more of the leased property's estimated remaining economic life.
d. The lessor agrees to perform all maintenance on the leased property and to pay all taxes and insurance relating to the property.

LO 7 7. State the formula for the debt-equity ratio.

SOLUTIONS TO SELF-QUIZ
1. c   2. b   3. b   4. c   5. held to maturity, available for sale, short-term investments   6. d
7. Total Liabilities ÷ Total Stockholders' Equity

QUESTIONS

Q10-1   What are the differences between a registered bond and a coupon bond?

Q10-2   What are the differences between a serial bond and a term bond?

Q10-3   What are the procedures for issuing a bond?

Q10-4   What is the difference between the interest method and the straight-line method of premium or discount amortization?

Q10-5   When is it acceptable to use the straight-line method of interest amortization?

Q10-6   What is the rule of thumb for recognizing bond issue cost expense?

Q10-7   Why are bonds attractive investments?

Q10-8   What are the requirements for bonds to be classified as held to maturity?

Q10-9   What are the differences between an operating lease and a capital lease?

Q10-10 What does the debt-equity ratio measure?

EXERCISES

LO 1

E10-1   Value of Bonds at Issue   Vernon Corporation sold an issue of 100, $1,000, 5-year, 8% bonds. The bonds pay interest annually.

REQUIRED:

Calculate the selling price of the bond issue if a comparable investment would yield:
a. 8%
b. 10%
c. 6%

LO 1

E10-2   Recording Bond Issues   Knight Corporation sold a $500,000, 5-year, 9% bond issue. The bonds pay interest annually.

REQUIRED:

Record the issuance of the bonds, assuming they were sold for:
a. $500,000
b. $485,000
c. $529,000

LO 2

E10-3   Straight-Line Method of Amortization of Discounts   Western Corporation sold a $100,000, 5-year, 7% bond issue for $94,000 on January 2, 19X5. The bonds pay interest annually on December 31 of each year, and the discount is amortized using the straight-line method.

REQUIRED:

Record the journal entry for the accrual of interest expense, amortization of discount, and payment of interest on December 31, 19X5 and 19X6.

LO 2

E10-4   Straight-Line Method of Amortization of Premiums   Eastern Corporation sold a $1,000,000, 10-year, 9% bond issue for $1,150,000 on January 2, 19X7. The bonds pay interest annually on December 31 of each year, and the premium is amortized using the straight-line method.

REQUIRED:

Record the journal entry for the accrual of interest expense, amortization of premium, and payment of interest on December 31, 19X7 and 19X8.

LO 2   **E10-5**   **Interest Method of Amortization of Discounts**   McBurger Corporation sold a $500,000, 10-year, 9% bond issue for $469,275 on January 2, 19X8. The bonds pay interest annually on December 31 of each year, and the discount is amortized using the interest method. The effective rate of interest is 10%.

REQUIRED:

Record the journal entry for the accrual of interest expense, amortization of discount, and payment of interest on December 31, 19X8 and 19X9.

LO 2   **E10-6**   **Interest Method of Amortization of Premiums**   Elise, Inc. sold a $200,000, 5-year, 12% bond issue for $223,340 on January 2, 19X1. The bonds pay interest annually on December 31 of each year, and the premium is amortized using the interest method. The effective rate of interest is 9%.

REQUIRED:

Record the journal entry for the accrual of interest expense, amortization of premium, and payment of interest on December 31, 19X1 and 19X2.

LO 3   **E10-7**   **Accruing Interest Between Interest Payment Dates**   F.I.A. Corporation sold a $1,000,000, 10-year, 9% bond issue for $1,200,000 on April 1, 19X2. The bonds pay interest annually on March 31 of each year, and the premium is amortized using the straight-line method. F.I.A. Corporation's fiscal year ends on December 31.

REQUIRED:

Record the journal entry for the recognition of interest expense on December 31, 19X2, and the payment of interest on March 31, 19X3.

LO 4   **E10-8**   **Bond Issue Costs**   Alpha Corporation paid $24,000 in bond issue costs when issuing a 12-year, 10% bond on April 1, 19X3. Alpha Corporation uses the straight-line method of amortization. Alpha's fiscal year ends on December 31.

REQUIRED:

Record the issue costs for the bond on April 1, 19X3, and the amortization of the issue costs on December 31, 19X3.

LO 4   **E10-9**   **Investments in Bonds Held to Maturity**   Canseco, Inc. purchased 1,000 of the $500 face value, 12%, 10-year bonds of Palmero Corporation on January 1, 19X4. The bonds pay interest annually beginning on December 31, 19X4. Canseco paid $524,000 for the bonds. Canseco classifies the bonds as bonds held to maturity. Canseco uses the straight-line amortization method to amortize premiums or discounts on bond investments.

REQUIRED:

Record the purchase of the bonds on January 1, 19X4, and the recognition of interest revenue on December 31, 19X4.

LO 4   **E10-10**   **Short-Term Investments in Bonds**   Jordan, Inc. purchased 2,000 of the $100 face value, 10%, 5-year bonds of Harper Corporation on January 1, 19X5. The bonds pay interest annually beginning on December 31, 19X5. Jordan paid $192,000 for the bonds.

Harper Corporation bonds had a market value of $92 per bond on December 31, 19X5. Jordan classifies the bonds as short-term investments.

REQUIRED:

Record the purchase of the bonds on January 1, 19X5, the recognition of interest revenue on December 31, 19X5, and the recognition of the unrealized gain or loss for 19X5.

LO 5   **E10-11**   **Operating Leases**   Price Corporation rents a private branch exchange telephone system for 3 years under a lease calling for advance rent of $3,600 plus monthly rent payments of $150 per month.

REQUIRED:

Record the initial payment of $3,600 and the payment of the first month's rent. Assume Price will receive equal benefits from the system each month.

LO 6   **E10-12**   **Capital Leases**   DeMaris Corporation leased a delivery truck for 5 years on January 1, 19X6. The estimated life of the truck is 5 years; and, therefore, the lease is considered a capital lease. The annual payments are $6,000 for 5 years beginning December 31, 19X6, which, at DeMaris' borrowing rate of 9%, makes them equivalent to borrowing $23,340—the truck's fair value.

REQUIRED:

Record the initial entry for the lease and the first payment on December 31, 19X6.

LO 7   **E10-13**   **Calculating the Debt-Equity Ratio**   Audionics, Inc. has total assets and total liabilities of $1,850,000 and $392,000, respectively.

REQUIRED:

Calculate the debt-equity ratio for Audionics.

PROBLEM SET A

LO 1, 2   **P10-1A**   **Bond Transactions, Straight-Line Method**   The Maurro Corporation uses the straight-line method for amortizing bond discounts and premiums. The following transactions took place during 19X2 and 19X3:

19X2

Jan.   2 Issued 1,000, $1,000 face value, 8% bonds that pay interest annually on December 31 of each year for 5 years. The bonds sold for $1,100,000.
  3 Bond issue costs of $5,000 are paid.

July   1 Issued 500, $1,000 face value, 7% bonds dated January 1, 19X2, that pay interest annually on January 2 of each year for 10 years. The bonds sold for $481,000 (excluding accrued interest).

Dec. 31 Paid the interest due on the 8% bonds issued on January 2, 19X2.

19X3

Jan.   2 Paid the interest due on the 7% bonds issued on July 1, 19X2.

Dec. 31 Paid the interest due on the 8% bonds issued on January 2, 19X2.

REQUIRED:

a. Record all necessary journal entries for 19X2.
b. Record all necessary journal entries for 19X3.
c. Show the balance sheet presentation for bonds payable and bond issue costs as of December 31, 19X3.

LO 1, 3   **P10-2A**   **Bond Transactions, Interest Method**   On January 2, 19X4, Laddie, Inc. issued 500, $1,000 face value, 9% bonds that pay interest annually on December 31 of each year for 5 years. At the time of issue, comparable bonds pay interest at the rate of 8%. Laddie, Inc. uses the interest method of amortization.

REQUIRED:

a. Determine the bonds' selling price.
b. Record the issue of the bonds on January 2, 19X4.
c. Record the payment of interest on December 31, 19X4.
d. Record the payment of interest on December 31, 19X5.

LO 1, 2, 3   **P10-3A**   **Prepare a Bond Amortization Table**   On July 1, 19X2, Eagle Corporation issued $100,000 of 12% bonds that pay interest annually on June 30 of each year for 5 years. Eagle Corporation uses the interest method of amortization.

REQUIRED:

a. Prepare a table similar to that in Illustration 10-4 (page 446) if comparable bonds pay interest at the rate of 8%.
b. Prepare a table similar to that in Illustration 10-4 (page 446) if comparable bonds pay interest at the rate of 15%.
c. Record all necessary entries for 19X2 and 19X3 if the bonds are issued at a rate of 8%.
d. Record all necessary entries for 19X2 and 19X3 if the bonds are issued at a rate of 15%.

LO 4   **P10-4A**   **Investment in Bonds**   Transcontinental, Inc. purchased 3 bond issues on January 1, 19X8. All bonds pay interest annually on December 31 of each year. Transcontinental uses the straight-line method of amortization. Information for these issues is given below:

Bond	Interest Rate	Face Value	Purchase Price	Dec. 31, X8 Price	Dec. 31, X9 Price	Term
Deer Corp.	8%	$100,000	$ 95,786	$ 97,152	$ 97,022	5-year
Clear Corp.	9%	50,000	51,162	50,894	50,912	10-year
Pappas Corp.	10%	180,000	194,200	199,400	200,120	10-year

Transcontinental classifies the investment in Deer Corp. and Clear Corp. bonds as available for sale and that in Pappas Corp. as bonds held to maturity. No additional purchases or sale of bond investments occurred after the purchase of the 3 bonds.

REQUIRED:

a. Record Transcontinental's purchase of the bonds.
b. Record the journal entries for recognition of interest and amortization of premium or discount for all 3 bond issues on December 31, 19X8.
c. Record the journal entries for unrealized gains or losses for 19X8 and 19X9.

LO 5, 6   **P10-5A**   **Operating and Capital Leases**   Lee Corporation leased equipment for 5 years from Lor Company on January 2, 19X3. Lee Corporation agreed to pay Lor Company $25,000 on December 31 of each year. The equipment will revert to Lor Company at the end of the lease. The equipment has an estimated useful life of 5 years. Lee uses the straight-line depreciation method for similar equipment. Assume Lee can borrow money from a bank at an interest rate of 10%.

REQUIRED:

a. Determine if this lease is an operating lease or a capital lease and explain your answer.
b. Assuming the lease is a capital lease, determine the initial value of the leased asset and liability.

c. Assuming the lease is a capital lease, record the inception of the lease on January 2, 19X3.

d. Assuming the lease is a capital lease, record the depreciation of the equipment, the lease payment, and the accrual of interest on December 31, 19X3, and December 31, 19X4.

e. Assuming the lease is an operating lease, record the lease payment on December 31, 19X3.

PROBLEM SET B

LO 1, 2   **P10-1B**   **Bond Transactions, Straight-Line Method**   The Richards Corporation uses the straight-line method for amortizing bond discounts and premiums. The following transactions took place during 19X5 and 19X6:

19X5

Jan.   2   Issued 500, $1,000 face value, 11% bonds that pay interest annually on December 31 of each year for 5 years. The bonds sold for $470,000.

         3   Bond issue costs of $2,500 are paid.

July   1   Issued 1,000, $1,000 face value, 8% bonds dated January 1, 19X5, that pay interest annually on January 2 of each year for 10 years. The bonds sold for $1,190,000 (excluding accrued interest).

Dec. 31   Paid the interest due on the 11% bonds issued on January 2, 19X5.

19X6

Jan.   2   Paid the interest due on the 8% bonds issued on July 1, 19X5.

Dec. 31   Paid the interest due on the 11% bonds issued on January 2, 19X5.

REQUIRED:

a. Record all necessary journal entries for 19X5.

b. Record all necessary journal entries for 19X6.

c. Show the balance sheet presentation of bonds payable and bond issue costs as of December 31, 19X6.

LO 1, 3   **P10-2B**   **Bond Transactions, Interest Method**   On January 2, 19X3, Prince Corporation issued 1,000, $1,000 face value, 8% bonds that pay interest annually on December 31 of each year for 5 years. At the time of issue, comparable bonds pay interest at the rate of 10%. Prince Company uses the interest method of amortization.

REQUIRED:

a. Determine the bonds' selling price.

b. Record the issue of the bonds on January 2, 19X3.

c. Record the payment of interest on December 31, 19X3.

d. Record the payment of interest on December 31, 19X4.

LO 1, 2, 3   **P10-3B**   **Bond Amortization Table**   On October 1, 19X1, Buckeye Corporation issued $500,000 of 8% bonds that pay interest annually on September 30 of each year for 5 years. Buckeye Corp. uses the interest method of amortization.

REQUIRED:

a. Prepare a table similar to that of Illustration 10-4 (page 446) if comparable bonds pay interest at the rate of 6%.

b. Prepare a table similar to that of Illustration 10-4 (page 446) if comparable bonds pay interest at the rate of 10%.

c. Record all necessary entries for 19X1 and 19X2 if the bonds are issued at a rate of 6%.

d. Record all necessary entries for 19X1 and 19X2 if the bonds are issued at a rate of 10%.

LO 4

P10-4B **Investment in Bonds** PanEurope, Inc. purchased 3 bond issues on January 1, 19X3. All bonds pay interest annually on December 31 of each year. PanEurope uses the straight-line method of amortization. Information for these issues is given below:

Bond	Interest Rate	Face Value	Purchase Price	Dec. 31, X3 Price	Dec. 31, X4 Price	Term
Steelman Corp.	8%	$200,000	$191,572	$194,304	$194,044	5-year
Hurwitz Corp.	9%	100,000	102,324	101,788	101,824	10-year
Menendez Corp.	10%	360,000	388,400	398,800	400,240	10-year

PanEurope classifies the investment in Steelman Corp. and Hurwitz Corp. as bonds as available for sale and that in Menendez Corp. as bonds held to maturity. No additional purchases or sale of bond investments occurred after the purchase of the 3 bonds.

REQUIRED:

a. Record PanEurope's purchase of the bonds.

b. Record the journal entries for recognition of interest and amortization of premium or discount for all 3 bond issues on December 31, 19X3.

c. Record the journal entries for unrealized gains or losses for 19X3 and 19X4.

LO 5, 6

P10-5B **Operating and Capital Leases** See Corporation leased equipment for 5 years from Sor, Inc. on January 2, 19X2. See Corporation agreed to pay Sor, Inc. $15,000 on December 31 of each year. The equipment will revert to Sor, Inc. at the end of the lease. The equipment has an estimated useful life of 5 years. See uses the straight-line depreciation method for similar equipment. Assume See can borrow money from a bank at an interest rate of 10%.

REQUIRED:

a. Determine if this lease is an operating lease or a capital lease and explain your answer.

b. Assuming the lease is a capital lease, determine the value of the leased asset and liability.

c. Assuming the lease is a capital lease, record the inception of the lease on January 2, 19X2.

d. Assuming the lease is a capital lease, record the depreciation of the equipment, the lease payment, and the accrual of interest on December 31, 19X2, and December 31, 19X3.

e. Assuming the lease is an operating lease, record the lease payment on December 31, 19X2.

CRITICAL THINKING AND COMMUNICATING

C10-1 Leather Works Corporation is a conservative company that has always relied on contributed capital to finance expansion. There is no long-term debt on the balance sheet. Mary Shearling, the president of Leather Works Corporation, told the treasurer Herman Schwartz to investigate using long-term debt to finance an attractive business opportunity for Leather Works.

REQUIRED:

Write a memo for Herman Schwartz explaining the different types of long-term debt financing alternatives.

C10-2 Aerobics World is a national chain of fitness clubs. The following information is abstracted from Aerobics World's 19X7 and 19X8 balance sheet.

	19X7	19X8
Total liabilities	$4,500,000	$5,900,000
Total stockholders' equity	9,000,000	9,100,000

Aerobics World is considering a large expansion of its operation. It plans to lease several new fitness clubs in a series of strip shopping centers being opened in the coming year by a real estate investment company. The leases offered by the investment company do not meet any of the criteria for capital leases, so they can be treated as operating leases. However, Aerobics World does not have sufficient cash to buy the neccessary $500,000 of fitness equipment and other furnishings for the new clubs. Management does not want to incur the costs of issuing additional stock to raise capital from owners. Unfortunately, one of the existing long-term creditors of the company insisted on a debt covenant requiring Aerobics World's debt-equity ratio to remain below 65%. This rules out borrowing the $500,000. The equipment manufacturer offered to lease the equipment to Aerobics World, but the lease, when appropriately discounted, covered 90% of the fair value of the equipment. Thus, the lease would have to be capitalized and treated like debt, which would also violate the covenant.

At an officers meeting, Aerobics World's chief financial officer proposed a scheme. Aerobics World would ask the equipment manufacturer to customize the equipment by affixing to it Aerobics World's own nameplate with the company's logo. Then, they would ask the equipment manufacturer to raise the cash price of the equipment substantially, but adjust the required lease payments only slightly to cover the costs of customizing. Thus, the present value of the lease payments would be less than 90% of the new "fair value" of the equipment and the lease could be treated as an operating lease. The other officers at first objected to the plan, but when a phone call to the equipment manufacturer won easy cooperation, they approved the scheme and went ahead with it.

REQUIRED:

Comment on the CFO's scheme for financing the equipment for the fitness clubs. Do you see any way that the definitional criteria for capital leases could be changed to prevent such schemes? Do you see any way the long-term creditor could have written a debt covenant that might have prevented the scheme?

C10-3 Refer to the financial statements of J.C. Penney Company, Inc. in Appendix B at the end of the text. Find the balance sheet.

REQUIRED:

1. Calculate J.C. Penney's total debt and its debt-equity ratio for 1991, 1992, and 1993. Hint: Subtract total stockholders' equity from total liabilities and stockholders' equity to calculate total liabilities.
2. What are the implications of the changes in J.C. Penney's debt-equity ratios over the 3 years?

CHAPTER 11

Stockholders' Equity

Josh Adams went home from college for the holidays to visit his parents and to see old friends from high school. During dinner one evening, between discussions of football games played the past weekend, Josh's father told the family about the terrific investments he had recently made. In particular, Josh's father seemed pleased that all stocks in which he had invested had shown increases in earnings per share. Josh's father even had an article from a financial magazine that summarized earnings per share and the change in earnings per share for several hundred companies. Josh's father had invested in the stocks of some of these companies.

As Josh considered his father's enthusiasm and excitement, he started to wonder about this number called earnings per share. Josh had seen financial statements before in his accounting course at school. He knew that net income was a measure of business performance. However, his father was excited about earnings per share, not net income, and the magazine article evaluated companies based solely on earnings per share. Josh wondered about the validity of ignoring all the other information that financial statements present and simply looking at earnings per share.

Of the three forms of business organizations—sole proprietorship, partnership, and corporation—the corporation is by far the primary form of business in the United States in terms of the numbers of transactions, the dollar amounts of transactions, total assets, and the numbers of employees. This dominance exists even though the number of businesses organized as proprietorships and partnerships exceeds the number of corporations. Some characteristics of corporations, such as ease of raising capital and ease of transferring ownership, encourage the development of large businesses. In fact, virtually all large businesses in the United States are organized as corporations. For example, General Electric had total assets of $193 billion at the end of 1992, and General Motors Corporation had total revenues of $133 billion for 1992. The Fortune 500 Companies as a group had total assets at the end of 1992 of over $2.5 trillion.[1]

[1]*Fortune* (April 19, 1993), p. 202.

This chapter presents a discussion of the characteristics of the corporate form of business and the fundamental transactions involving owners—issuing stock and paying dividends. In addition, we discuss transactions that affect retained earnings and transactions in the company's own equity securities. These transactions include cash, stock dividends, and treasury stock transactions.

LEARNING OBJECTIVES

1. Describe the organization and management of a corporation, and state the advantages and disadvantages of the corporate form of business organization.
2. Explain how a corporation is formed and account for organization costs.
3. Describe the characteristics of the components of stockholders' equity.
4. Account for the issuance of common and preferred stock in exchange for cash and noncash assets and account for stock subscriptions.
5. Account for the declaration and payment of cash dividends.
6. Calculate the stated, cumulative, and participating dividends on preferred stock.
7. Describe the recording of stock dividends and stock splits.
8. Account for the purchase and reissuance of treasury stock.
9. Describe how businesses report the retirement of stock in their financial statements.
10. Discuss the accounting for appropriations of retained earnings.
11. Calculate and interpret earnings per share.

THE CORPORATION

LO 1

Describe the organization and management of a corporation, and state the advantages and disadvantages of the corporate form of business organization.

A **corporation** is a legal entity separate from its owners, created when a state government grants a **charter**. Thus, a corporation comes into existence in accordance with the applicable statutes and continues to exist as a legal entity only as permitted by those statutes. The separate legal status of corporations distinguishes them from sole proprietorships and partnerships and results in some differences in accounting that we discuss in this chapter. The state laws grant to a corporation most of the privileges persons possess. Exceptions include those privileges that only a person can exercise such as the rights to vote and to hold public office. Aside from these exceptions, corporations assume most of the duties and responsibilities of persons such as paying taxes and conducting their affairs in accordance with applicable laws.

One way to classify corporations is by the purpose for which they were created—profit and not-for-profit. Many corporations are organized to carry on a business to earn a **profit**. Examples include IBM and General Motors. Other organizations, however, are **not-for-profit**, yet are organized as corporations. These not-for-profit organizations are charitable, educational, and medical organizations. Examples include the United Way and the American Accounting Association.

Another way to classify corporations is by the nature of their ownership. Virtually all large corporations are **publicly-owned corporations**. These corporations, such as American Express and McDonald's, have thousands of owners (stockholders); and their stocks are traded on the national stock exchanges. Other corporations have only a few owners. Corporations with relatively few owners are called **privately-owned corporations**. A family business is often organized as a privately-owned corporation, and the members of the family are the owners of the corporation.

Organization of a Corporation

The stockholders, as owners of the corporation, collectively have the authority to appoint the manager of the business. The stockholders delegate their authority to an elected board of directors, which establishes the corporation's broad operating policies. Appointed by the board of directors, the corporate officers manage the day-to-day operations of the corporation. In managing the operations, the officers are responsible for implementing the policies the directors establish. We show the organizational structure of a corporation in Illustration 11-1.

ILLUSTRATION 11-1 Organization Chart of a Corporation

Stockholders. The **stockholders** are the owners of the corporation. Technically, stockholders participate in management of a corporation only indirectly by electing the board of directors. However, individual stockholders may serve as directors if elected by the stockholders or as officers if appointed by the board of directors. Direct stockholder involvement in management is more typical in small, privately-owned corporations, but is less typical in large corporations. Stockholders also indirectly participate in management by voting on certain issues, including selection of an independent auditor, changes in the number of shares authorized, and proposed mergers and acquisitions at the annual stockholders' meeting.

State laws generally require corporations to hold annual meetings of the stockholders. At these meetings, stockholders elect directors and vote on other matters. Not all stockholders can attend the meeting, however. For large corporations, stockholders are located across the nation; and for some corporations, ownership is international. Stockholders who are unable to attend the stockholders' meeting may delegate their votes to an agent. By signing a legal document called a **proxy**, a stockholder allows the agent to cast the number of votes to which he or she is entitled. Typically, the agent is a current officer of the corporation.

Stockholders have the rights granted by the charter and specified by the various state laws and regulations. Generally, the rights of the common stockholders are as follows:

1. The right to vote in meetings of stockholders.
2. The right to dispose of their shares of stock as they please.
3. The right to share *pro rata* (meaning in proportion to their ownership shares) with the other common stockholders in any dividends the board of directors declare.
4. The right to have the *first* opportunity to purchase additional shares of stock the corporation issues.
5. The right to share *pro rata* with other common stockholders in any assets remaining after the settlement of the creditors' and preferred stockholders' claims upon liquidation of the corporation.

Dividends (Number 3, above) are distributions, usually cash, a corporation makes to its stockholders. Dividends distributed to stockholders are similar to withdrawals of partners and proprietors. The **preemptive right** (Number 4, above) of common stockholders allows them to purchase additional shares. It also allows stockholders the opportunity to maintain their proportion of ownership when the corporation issues additional shares. For example, assume that Paul Johnson owns 100 shares of the Southeast Design, Inc.'s 1,000 outstanding shares, or 10% of the shares. If the corporation undertakes to issue an additional 500 shares, the preemptive right gives Paul the first opportunity to purchase 50 of the additional shares. The purchase of the additional shares means that Paul owns 150 of the 1,500 shares now outstanding, which maintains Paul's 10% ownership of the corporation.

Board of Directors.   Laws and regulations delegate to the board of directors the authority to establish the corporation's business policies. The directors are also responsible for protecting the stockholders and creditors, and they appoint the officers of the corporation to whom they delegate the authority to implement the policies they establish. In addition, the directors are also responsible for declaring dividends, approving contracts, approving major borrowing arrangements, and setting executive compensation.

Laws or regulations do not prescribe the exact composition of the board of directors. For most publicly-owned corporations, the board consists of several officers of the corporation, along with a number of outside directors who are not employees of the corporation. Outside director membership on the board is desirable because it allows the board to monitor independently the performance of management.

Management. The board of directors appoints the corporation's managers and gives them the responsibility of implementing the business policies the board adopts and for carrying on the business's operations. The officers of a corporation generally include the president, vice president(s), controller, treasurer, and secretary. The president, or chief operating officer of the corporation, reports directly to the board. Many corporations have several vice presidents, each responsible for a specific function such as production, marketing, finance, and human resources (personnel). The controller is the chief accounting officer responsible for preparing financial statements, tax returns, other required regulatory reports, internal financial and operating reports, and budgets. The treasurer is responsible for managing the corporation's funds. In addition to maintaining the minutes of meetings of stockholders and the board of directors, the secretary is also responsible for the stockholder records.

Advantages of a Corporation

The corporate form of business offers several advantages over sole proprietorships and partnerships.

Separate Legal Entity. A corporation is a legal entity and separate from its owners. Under U.S. law, a corporation has the rights and responsibilities of a person. Through its agents, a corporation conducts its affairs and can enter into contracts; purchase, own, and sell property; and hire and dismiss employees. It can also sue and be sued in the courts, independent of its owners.

Limited Stockholder Liability. Since a corporation is a separate legal entity, it is responsible for its actions and debts. Laws limit creditors' claims against a corporation to the total amount of the corporation's assets. The stockholders are not liable for the claims of creditors of the corporation. That is, if the corporation's assets do not fully satisfy creditor claims, stockholders are *not* required to make up the difference. Laws limit the risk stockholders assume to losing their investments in the corporation. For investors in the corporation's stock, the limited liability aspect of the corporate form of business has great appeal. In contrast, proprietors and partners may be liable for debts of proprietorships and partnerships; and creditors may make claims against their personal assets to satisfy the debts of their businesses.

Lack of Mutual Agency. In the corporate form of business, mutual agency does not exist. The stockholders, acting as owners, cannot bind the corporation to contracts. For example, a stockholder cannot purchase land in the name of the corporation. For partnerships, however, mutual agency does exist; and a partnership can be bound by the actions of any partner. Because of the lack of mutual agency, stockholders do not have to be as concerned as partners do about the other owners with whom they associate in a business enterprise.

Ease of Transferring Ownership. Shares of stock represent the stockholders' ownership of the corporation. Stockholders can transfer shares of stock to others whenever they please. The transfer of ownership neither affects the corporation's operations nor requires the approval of other stockholders.

Ease of Raising Capital. Because of the previously discussed characteristics of a corporation, it is possible to raise large amounts of capital. In particular, limited stockholder liability, lack of mutual agency, and the ease of transferring ownership make it possible to have a large number of owners who each invest relatively small amounts of money. The only limit on a corporation's capital-raising potential is its ability to employ the invested capital profitably.

Continuity of Existence. The time specified in the charter and the state laws where it is incorporated define the life of a corporation. When the time specified in the charter expires, renewing the charter extends the life of the corporation. In contrast to a partnership, the death or withdrawal of an owner does not affect the life of the corporation.

Professional Management. Many corporations are owned by large numbers of stockholders. They have neither the skill nor the time to manage the corporation. To solve this problem, corporations hire professional managers to run the corporation's day-to-day operations. This situation creates a separation between the owners and management. While professional management is an advantage of corporations, the separation of owners and managers sometimes creates some disadvantages. For example, if there is a lack of communication between management and the owners, the owners may not be able to observe the managers' actions. Thus, managers may make decisions that are not in the best interests of the owners.

Disadvantages of a Corporation

When compared to proprietorships and partnerships, corporations also have the disadvantages of increased government regulation and certain aspects of income taxation.

Government Regulation. Corporations are subject to the control and regulation of the state where incorporated. Generally, state laws and regulations require corporations to submit numerous reports to state agencies. In addition, publicly-owned corporations that operate across state lines and have a relatively large number of stockholders are regulated under federal statutes administered by the Securities and Exchange Commission (SEC). Among other things, federal laws require that quarterly and annual financial statements, as well as other reports, be filed on a timely basis with the SEC. Fulfilling the requirements of the various laws and regulations imposes significant costs on corporations.

Taxation of Income. The owners of a special class of corporations, known as "S corporations," are taxed as if they are partners of a partnership. The S corporations themselves are not taxed. The incomes of all other corporations, known as "C corporations," are subject to both federal and state income taxes. (Refer to Appendix A of this text to learn about income taxation of corporations; and, henceforth, when we mention corporations, we refer to C corporations.) Together, state and federal income taxes can amount to more than 40% of a corporation's pre-tax earnings. Furthermore, when a corporation distributes after-tax earnings to the owners as dividends, the dividends are taxable income of the stockholders. This is called **double taxation of corporations**. First, the corporation's income is taxed and when paid to the stockholders as dividends the income is taxed again. In contrast to C corporations, the incomes of proprietorships, partnerships and S corporations are taxable only once as their owners' personal incomes.

Explain how a corporation is formed and account for organization costs.

FORMING A CORPORATION

In most states, corporations are formed by obtaining a charter from the state. To obtain a charter, at least three incorporators must submit an application to the appropriate state agency.

Articles of Incorporation and Bylaws

The application that incorporators submit contains a document called the **articles of incorporation**, which is a contract between the corporation and the state. The articles of incorporation contains information about the name and address of the corporation, the purpose of the corporation, the different classes and authorized shares of stock, the voting and dividend rights of each class of stock, and the life of the corporation.

Once the state agency approves the application and after the incorporators pay all fees, the state grants the charter; and the corporation comes into existence. The corporation is then able to sell stock to the incorporators and to others who become the owners (stockholders) of the corporation. The stockholders then hold a meeting to elect the board of directors. The directors adopt **bylaws** to govern the corporation's conduct and appoint officers of the corporation to manage the business's operations.

Organization Costs

Organization costs, those incurred in forming a corporation, include fees paid to the state to obtain a charter, legal fees incurred in preparing the application for a charter, promoters' fees, printing fees for stock certificates, and any other costs incurred. We record organization costs as intangible assets because they, at least conceptually, benefit the corporations throughout their lives.

When the business incurs organization costs, we debit the amount to an asset account called Organization Costs. We amortize the intangible asset over its useful life; but according to GAAP, the amortization period should not exceed 40 years. In practice, businesses usually amortize organization costs over 5 years. This practice developed because federal income tax laws and regulations permit amortization over 5 years. Since the amortization of organization costs is immaterial for many corporations, the 5-year amortization period is the easiest way to account for the organization costs. To illustrate accounting for organization costs, assume Home Furnishings, Inc. incurs $8,500 of organization costs on January 2, 19X1. The entry to record the intangible asset is as follows:

19X1			
Jan. 2	Organization Costs	8,500	
	Cash		8,500
	To record costs incurred in forming the corporation.		

If Home Furnishings elects to amortize the organization costs over 5 years, it would make the entry shown below on December 31, 19X1, to record the first year's amortization:

19X1			
Dec. 31	Organization Costs Amortization Expense	1,700	
	Organization Costs		1,700
	To record one year's amortization of organization cost: ($8,500 ÷ 5 = $1,700).		

Notice that we make the credit directly to Organization Costs account rather than to Accumulated Amortization. This treatment is consistent with the amortization of other intangible assets discussed in previous chapters.

STOCKHOLDERS' EQUITY

With the exception of the stockholders' equity section of the balance sheet, the financial statements of corporations are consistent with those of other forms of business enterprises. Also, the GAAP for assets, liabilities, revenues, and expenses are the same for corporations as they are for proprietorships and partnerships. We show the stockholders' equity section of a corporation's balance sheet in Illustration 11-2. It recognizes that, in general, there are two classes of corporate stock—common stock and preferred stock.

An important reporting objective of the stockholders' equity section is to distinguish the *sources of stockholders' equity*. The two principal sources, as presented in Illustration 11-2, are *contributed capital* and *retained earnings*. **Contributed capital** represents the stockholders' claim to the corporation's net assets due to the purchase of the corporation's capital stock. Contributed capital consists of the sum of the capital stock accounts (preferred and common) and the additional paid-in capital accounts for both preferred and common stock. The stockholders' equity section presents detailed information about contributed capital such as: classes of stock that the corporation has issued, par or stated values of the stock issued, total shares authorized of each class, and total shares issued of each class. The *par value* of stock represents the corporation's legal capital. We discuss par value and legal capital below in the section titled "Capital Stock."

ILLUSTRATION 11-2 Partial Balance Sheet

Stockholders' Equity	
Contributed capital:	
Preferred 8% stock, $100 par value, 50,000 shares authorized and issued	$ 5,000,000
Additional paid-in capital, preferred	800,000
Common stock, $1 par value, 100,000 shares authorized, 80,000 shares issued	80,000
Additional paid-in capital, common	9,600,000
Total contributed capital	$15,480,000
Retained earnings	8,230,000
Total stockholders' equity	$23,710,000

A corporation's **retained earnings** consist of the cumulative net income from the business, less the cumulative dividends paid out to stockholders from the beginning of the corporation's life. Another way of describing retained earnings is that it represents the corporation's net income that is retained in the business. The following sections present a discussion of the components of contributed capital.

Capital Stock

When an investor purchases shares of stock, the stockholder receives from the corporation a stock certificate such as the one shown in Illustration 11-3. The **stock certificate** is evidence of ownership of shares in a corporation and indicates the name of the stockholder and the class and number of shares owned. When a stockholder decides to transfer ownership, usually by selling shares, he or she must endorse the stock certificate on the reverse side of the certificate and send it to the corporation secretary. The secretary will then cancel the old certificate and issue a new certificate to the new stockholder.

ILLUSTRATION 11-3 Stock Certificate

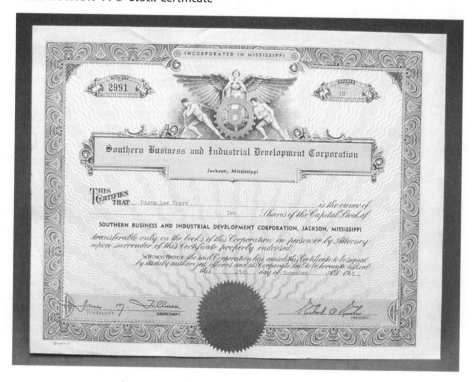

Corporations that have more than a few stockholders normally record information about stock ownership in a **stockholders' ledger**, a subsidiary ledger to the company's capital stock accounts. Each stockholder has a separate account in the ledger. The stockholders' ledger may be a book in a manual system or a file on an electronic data storage device in a computerized system. We show a stockholders' ledger account in Illustration 11-4. Each stockholder's account has information about the number of shares owned, the stock certificate numbers, and the dates of purchase and sale of shares by the stockholder.

Large corporations have millions of shares of stock outstanding, and investors transfer thousands of shares daily. Large corporations usually engage **registrars** and **transfer agents** to handle these tasks. The corporation gives its registrar and transfer agent (usually large banks or trust companies) the responsibilities of transferring the corporation's stock. In addition, the registrar is responsible for maintaining stockholder records and supplying the corporation with a list of stockholders for stockholders' meetings and for dividend payments.

ILLUSTRATION 11-4 Stockholders' Ledger

Angela Freeland
4518 Pecos Avenue
Austin, TX 78730-4518

	CERTIFICATES ISSUED			CERTIFICATES CANCELLED		SHARES OWNED
DATE	CERTIFICATE NO.	NO. OF SHARES	DATE	CERTIFICATE NO.	NO. OF SHARES	
19X2						
Aug. 28	1012	500				500
Dec. 12	1532	100				600
			19X7			
			Oct. 16	1532	100	500

When a stockholder decides to transfer ownership of the shares, he or she endorses the stock certificate and sends the certificate to the transfer agent through a stockbroker. The transfer agent then cancels the old certificate, prepares a new certificate, and forwards it to the registrar. The registrar then updates the corporation's stockholder records and records the change in ownership of the shares. The registrar then sends the new certificate to the new stockholder.

Authorized and Issued Shares. A corporation's **authorized shares** are the number of shares of stock the corporation can issue. The articles of incorporation include the number of shares of preferred and common stock that the state authorizes the corporation to issue. To increase the authorized shares, a corporation must amend its charter by making application to the state to change the number of authorized shares. Commonly, corporations apply for more authorized shares than they initially intend to issue. Then, in the future, if they decide to raise additional capital by selling more shares of stock, they have authorized shares available immediately without having to amend their charters. The partial balance sheet in Illustration 11-2 shows the number of authorized shares for each class of stock. Also, the balance sheet shows the number of shares of stock that the corporation has issued for each class of stock.

Par and No-Par Value Stock. The shares of stock a corporation issues may be either par value stock or no-par value stock. If the stock has a par value, the corporation's charter specifies the amount of the par value, which is printed on the stock certificate. The corporation's organizers designate the par value of stock, which may be $100, $10, $1, $.10, $.01, or any other amount. Under the state incorporation laws, the **par value** of the stock issued determines the corporation's legal capital. The amount of **legal capital** is the minimum amount of contributed capital for the number of shares issued. In concept, the amount of legal capital is for the protection of creditors in that a corporation cannot pay dividends that would reduce stockholders' equity below legal capital. In practice, creditors are concerned more with the corporation's assets and earning power when evaluating its ability to pay interest and principal.

Usually, the par value of stock is set arbitrarily low and bears no relationship to the stock's market value. In determining the par value to specify, the organizers usually select an amount that is less than the stock's expected market value. In some states, if stock is sold at an amount below par value, the pur-

HISTORICAL PERSPECTIVES

STOCKS AS OBJET'S D'ART

In addition to representing ownership of a company, many stock certificates were exalted to the status of near-works of art. Numerous entrepreneurs did not hesitate to engage skilled painters, etchers, and both steel, and copper-plate engravers to provide the artistic embellishment of their stock certificates.

In the past, the collection of these documents was the hobby of only a few individual bankers and financiers. But its popularity is spreading. To an increasing extent, share certificates are being taken out of safe-deposit boxes and, once elegantly framed, hung as decorations on walls.

Source: Kristina Piwecki and George Alexander, "Stocks and Shares as Objets d'Art," *swiss Business*, No. 4 (July 1990): 61.

chasers may subsequently be assessed for the deficiency if corporation assets are not sufficient to satisfy creditor claims upon liquidation. Also, some state laws forbid the issuance of stock at an amount below par value.

Some corporations elect not to assign a par value to stock, and this results in stock, called **no-par value** stock. An advantage of no-par value stock is that the corporation can sell it at any price without creating a deficiency in legal capital. Also, the absence of a par value on the stock certificate avoids the possibility of investors mistakenly believing that the par value is the stock's market value. Some states allow a corporation to assign a **stated value** to no-par value stock, and the stated value is the corporation's legal capital. In other states, the entire amount received from selling no-par value stock is considered legal capital.

Common Stock

A corporation may issue two classes of stock: common stock and preferred stock. Common stockholders have all of the rights discussed previously in this chapter, including the right to vote at stockholders' meetings. **Common stock** represents the claims of the common stockholders to the corporation's net assets. However, when a corporation liquidates (goes out of business), it must satisfy all creditors' claims to corporate assets and the preferred stockholders before it can distribute any assets to common stockholders. Moreover, the corporation may not issue dividends to common stockholders unless a positive balance remains in Retained Earnings after the corporation meets the dividend preferences of preferred stockholders (described in a subsequent section). If a corporation is authorized to issue only one class of stock, it must be common stock.

Preferred Stock

Preferred stock has several characteristics that differ from those of common stock. **Preferred stock** is generally nonvoting stock, but it does entitle the stockholders to certain preferences relative to those of common stockholders. Preferred stock usually affords preferred stockholders preferences as to dividends and preferences as to assets upon liquidation. A corporation may issue several classes of preferred stock with each class having unique features such as different dividend rates.

LO 4

Account for the issuance of common and preferred stock in exchange for cash and noncash assets and account for stock subscriptions.

ACCOUNTING FOR ISSUANCE OF COMMON STOCK

When a corporation sells common stock, it receives either cash or noncash assets. When the investor pays fully for the shares, the corporation issues stock certificates for the shares of stock purchased. The shares of stock the corporation sells may be either par value stock or no-par value stock.

Sale of Par Value Common Stock for Cash

When a corporation sells par value stock for cash, we credit the total par value of the stock to Common Stock. For example, assume that on April 1, 19X1, Scientific Products Corp. sells 100 shares of $10 par value common stock for cash of $10 per share. We show Scientific's entry to record the sale and issuance of the stock as follows:

19X1			
Apr. 1	Cash	1,000	
	Common Stock		1,000
	To record the sale and issuance of common stock.		

When the corporation sells par value stock at an amount greater than par value, we credit the excess to **Paid-In Capital in Excess of Par**. Assume that, in the previous example, the corporation sells the 100 shares of stock for $25 cash per share instead of $10 per share. Scientific's entry to record the sale and issuance or the stock is as follows:

19X1			
Apr. 1	Cash	2,500	
	Common Stock		1,000
	Paid-In Capital in Excess of Par–Common		1,500
	To record the sale and issuance of common stock.		

The balance of Common Stock is Scientific Products Corp.'s legal capital. The corporation's contributed capital, however, is the sum of the balances of Common Stock and Paid-In Capital in Excess of Par–Common.

Sale of No-Par Value Common Stock for Cash

The accounting for the issuance of no-par value stock depends on whether the directors assigned a stated value to the stock. Assume the directors of Home Furnishings, Inc. assign a stated value of $5 per share to its no-par value stock. We record the sale and issuance of 100 shares for $50 cash per share on August 10 as follows:

Aug. 10	Cash	5,000	
	Common Stock		500
	Paid-In Capital in Excess of Stated Value–Common		4,500
	To record the sale and issuance of common stock.		

Notice that the stated value assigned to the no-par value stock functions similarly to a par value. The stated value determines the amount credited to Common Stock, and the balance in that account is the corporation's legal capital. We credit proceeds from the sale of the stock that are in excess of the stated value to Paid-In Capital in Excess of Stated Value–Common. The sum of the balances of Common Stock and Paid-In Capital in Excess of Stated Value–Common is the corporation's total contributed capital.

If the directors do *not* assign a stated value to no-par value stock, we consider legal capital to be the entire amount of the proceeds from the sale of the stock. If the directors of Home Furnishings, Inc. do not assign a stated value to its no-par value stock, we record the sale and issuance of 100 shares for $50 per share as follows:

Aug. 10	Cash	5,000	
	Common Stock		5,000
	To record the sale and issuance of no-par value stock.		

Sale of Common Stock for Noncash Assets

In the previous examples, the corporation sells stock for cash. However, the corporation also may sell stock in exchange for noncash assets. For example, assume that on September 28, Appliance Sales, Inc. exchanges 10,000 shares of $10 par value stock for a parcel of land that the previous owner had offered to sell for $275,000. We record the purchase of the land and the sale of stock at the stock's fair value, or the land's fair value, whichever is more clearly evident. If the stock is traded actively, we can determine the stock's fair value by referring to the currently quoted price. In some cases, however, stock is not traded actively; and the fair value of the noncash asset is more clearly evident. In any event, the board of directors should approve the value assigned to the exchange of stock for noncash assets. Assume that the stock of Appliance Sales, Inc. is traded actively and the current market price per share is $25. We show Appliance's entry to record the transaction below:

Sept. 28	Land	250,000	
	Common Stock		100,000
	Paid-In Capital in Excess of Par–Common		150,000
	To record the issuance of 10,000 shares of $10 par value common stock in exchange for land.		

Stock Subscriptions

Corporations commonly sell stock for cash and immediately issue the shares of stock. However, corporations sometimes sell shares of stock on a subscription basis. When the corporation sells shares of stock through a **stock subscription**, the purchaser signs an agreement to pay a specified price for the shares at some future date(s). The purchaser may pay for the shares in a single payment or in installments.

In a stock subscription transaction, the purchaser enters into a contractual agreement to purchase the shares of stock. The promise to pay for the shares of stock creates a receivable for the corporation, and we debit it to an account called Subscriptions Receivable. Since the corporation may sell either common or preferred stock on a subscription basis, the account should specify to which it applies. Since the shares are not fully paid for at the time the corporation enters into the stock subscription agreement, the corporation does not issue the shares to the purchaser. At the time the corporation collects the stock subscription and the shares are fully paid for, the corporation issues the shares to the investor. At the time the corporation enters into the stock subscription, we credit the par value or stated value of the subscribed shares to a temporary stockholders' equity account called Stock Subscribed, designated as either common or preferred. When the shares are fully paid for and issued, we transfer the amount credited to Stock Subscribed to either Common Stock or to Preferred Stock.

Accounting for Stock Subscriptions. To illustrate the accounting for stock subscriptions, assume that Ace Glass Corporation receives subscriptions for 20,000 shares of common stock on April 1, 19X1. The common stock has a par value of $5 per share, and the subscription price is $12 per share. We show Ace's entry to record the stock subscription below:

19X1			
Apr. 1	Subscriptions Receivable–Common	240,000	
	Stock Subscribed–Common		100,000
	Paid-In Capital in Excess of Par–Common		140,000
	Received stock subscriptions for 20,000, $5 par-value shares of common stock at $12 per share.		

Notice that in the entry above, we credit only the par value of the subscribed shares to Stock Subscribed–Common. However, we credit the amount that the purchaser agrees to pay in excess of the par value to Paid-In Capital in Excess of Par–Common.

Assume that on June 1, 19X1, Ace Glass Corporation receives the first installment of $60,000 for the subscribed shares. Ace's entry to record the receipt of the payment is as follows:

19X1			
Jun. 1	Cash	60,000	
	Subscriptions Receivable–Common		60,000
	To record receipt of cash for stock subscriptions.		

In most states, the corporation cannot issue the stock until all of the subscribed shares are paid fully. Therefore, even though the investor has paid for the equivalent of 5,000 shares ($60,000 ÷ $240,000 x 20,000 shares), the corporation does not issue any shares.

Stock Subscriptions in the Balance Sheet. In the corporation's balance sheet, we display subscriptions receivable as an asset—usually a current asset since, in most cases, the corporation collects the receivable within one year of the date of the balance sheet. If Ace Glass Corporation receives no additional payments during June, a balance sheet dated June 30, 19X1, would show subscriptions receivable of $180,000 ($240,000 − $60,000) in the current assets section. We display the account, Stock Subscribed–Common, in the stockholders' equity section of the balance sheet as part of contributed capital. We show the partial balance sheet sections for the example in Illustration 11-5.

ILLUSTRATION 11-5 Partial Balance Sheet

Assets	
Current assets	
Subscriptions receivable, common stock	$ 180,000
Stockholders' Equity	
Contributed capital:	
Common stock, $5 par value, 500,000 shares authorized,	
200,000 shares issued and outstanding	$1,000,000
Common stock subscribed but not issued, 20,000 shares	100,000
	$1,100,000
Paid-in capital in excess of par, common	640,000
Total contributed capital	$1,740,000

If Ace collects the remaining subscriptions in July, all of the subscribed shares would be paid for fully; and the corporation would issue the stock certificates. The following entries summarize Ace's collection of the remaining subscription price and the issuance of the shares:

19X1			
Jul. 31	Cash	180,000	
	Subscriptions Receivable–Common		180,000
	To record receipt of cash for stock subscriptions.		
31	Stock Subscribed–Common	100,000	
	Common Stock		100,000
	To record the issuance of 20,000 shares of $5 par value common stock.		

We transfer only the par value of the shares issued from Stock Subscribed—Common to the permanent Common Stock. At the time of initially recording the stock subscription, we credit the agreed-upon price *in excess of par value* to Paid-In Capital in Excess of Par–Common. Therefore, it is unnecessary to record additional paid-in capital when the corporation issues the subscribed shares.

ACCOUNTING FOR ISSUANCE OF PREFERRED STOCK

The accounting for the sale and issuance of preferred stock is the same as for common stock, except account titles specify they are for preferred stock. For example, if Ace Glass Corporation sells 1,000 shares of $100 par value preferred stock for $125 cash per share, its entry to record the sale and issuance is:

(Date)	Cash	125,000	
	Preferred Stock		100,000
	Paid-In Capital in Excess of Par–Preferred		25,000
	To record the sale of 1,000 shares of $100 par value preferred stock.		

Similar to Common Stock, we credit Preferred Stock for the par value of the shares. State laws include the par value of preferred stock in the corporation's total legal capital. We credit the proceeds in excess of the par value to Paid-In Capital in Excess of Par–Preferred. Both Preferred Stock and Paid-In Capital in Excess of Par–Preferred are part of the corporation's contributed capital.

Corporations may also sell preferred stock on a subscription basis. The accounting for preferred stock subscriptions is the same as for common stock subscriptions, except the account titles are designated as preferred stock.

ACCOUNTING FOR DIVIDENDS

LO 5

Account for the declaration and payment of cash dividends.

Only the corporation's board of directors have the authority to declare dividends. Generally, state corporation laws require that a company have positive retained earnings, which means a credit balance in Retained Earnings, before the directors can declare dividends. To illustrate the accounting for cash dividends, assume that the board of directors of Vacation Travel, Inc. meets on December 1, 19X1, and declares a cash dividend of $2 per share to the common stockholders of record on December 15, 19X1. The dividend is payable on December 28,

19X1, and 10,000 shares of common stock are outstanding. Therefore, the total amount of the dividends declared is $20,000 ($2 x 10,000 shares).

Notice that the description of the dividend declaration indicates three dates—declaration, record, and payment. The **declaration date** is the date that the board of directors meets and declares the dividend. Similar to withdrawals by partners and proprietors, dividends are not expenses of the business, but distributions of earnings. When directors declare a dividend, the company is obligated legally to make the dividend payment. It is common for corporations to declare dividends more than one time a year, for example, quarterly. At the time the directors declare dividends, the company commonly follows the practice of debiting a temporary retained earnings account entitled Dividends. On the declaration date, Vacation Travel, Inc. records the dividend and the related liability as shown in the following entry:

19X1			
Dec. 1	Dividends	20,000	
	Dividends Payable		20,000
	To record the declaration of dividends.		

During the year, we accumulate the amounts of the several dividend declarations in Dividends. At the end of the fiscal year, we close Dividends directly to Retained Earnings. We do *not* close Dividends to Income Summary because it is *not* an expense. Assume Vacation Travel, Inc. declares the same amount of dividends each quarter of the fiscal year. The following entry shows Vacation's closing entry for Dividends:

19X1			
Dec. 31	Retained Earnings	80,000	
	Dividends		80,000
	To close Dividends to Retained Earnings.		

The second date indicated in the description of the dividend declaration is the record date. The **record date** is the date the board of directors designates for determining who owns what number of shares of stock and, therefore, who is entitled to receive the dividend. The company's stock registrar compiles the list of owners of shares of stock and the number of shares as of the record date and sends it to the company to use in paying the dividend. If a stockholder sells shares of stock between the declaration date and the record date, the new owner is entitled to receive the dividends. The new owner is the stockholder as of the designated record date. Conversely, if a stockholder sells shares after the record date, but before the corporation pays the dividend, the former owner is entitled to receive the dividends, because he or she is the owner as of the record date. When investors sell stock after the record date, the stock sells "ex dividend," meaning without the right to the dividend that the directors declared.

The third date indicated in the description of the dividend declaration is the **payment date**. The payment date is the date that the corporation actually pays the dividends. We record the dividend payment as a decrease in Dividends Payable and as a decrease in Cash, as shown in the following entry for Vacation Travel, Inc.:

19X1			
Dec. 28	Dividends Payable	20,000	
	Cash		20,000
	To record the payment of cash dividends.		

Occasionally, a company will declare dividends that are payable in noncash assets such as items of inventory or shares of another company's stock that the dividend-paying company owns. The accounting for noncash dividends is the same as for cash dividends except that at the time of payment, we decrease the noncash asset account rather than Cash. The amount at which the company records a noncash dividend is a complex issue that more advanced accounting texts discuss.

ANALYSIS OF DIVIDEND POLICY

To illustrate the analysis of dividend policy, consider the case of Jennifer Johnson. Jennifer has money to invest and is studying her stockbroker's research reports on two companies that are possible investment opportunities. These two companies are Midwestern Industries, Inc. and Scientific Products, Inc. Securities of both companies trade on a national stock exchange. Jennifer has two investment goals: current cash returns and long-term growth potential. With these goals in mind, she is comparing the two companies' current cash dividend policies. The research reports contained the following information about the companies:

	Midwestern Industries, Inc.	Scientific Products, Inc.
Current price of stock	$25 per share	$12 per share
Current dividend	$2 per share	$.30 per share
Earnings growth rate	10% per year	14% per year

Jennifer wants to know how to use this information to compare the two investment opportunities to determine which one better meets her investment goals. Investment analysts use two ratios to compare companies' dividend policies: dividend payout ratio and dividend yield ratio. In the following sections, we discuss how analysts compute and interpret these two ratios.

Computing Dividend Payout and Dividend Yield

Dividend payout is the ratio of dividends per share to earnings per share:

$$\text{Dividend Payout} = \frac{\text{Dividends Per Share}}{\text{Earnings Per Share}}$$

The income statements for the current year shows that earnings per share (discussed later in this chapter) for Midwestern Industries and Scientific Products are $4 per share and $2 per share, respectively. Using the EPS information and the dividend information for the two companies given above, we compute dividend payout as follows:

Midwestern Industries: $\quad \text{Dividend Payout} = \dfrac{\$2.00}{\$4.00} = 50\%$

Scientific Products: $\quad \text{Dividend Payout} = \dfrac{\$.30}{\$2.00} = 15\%$

Dividend yield is the ratio of dividends per share to market price per share:

$$\text{Dividend Yield} = \frac{\text{Dividends Per Share}}{\text{Market Price Per Share}}$$

Using the information given above, we compute dividend yield for the two companies as follows:

Midwestern Industries: Dividend Yield $= \dfrac{\$2.00}{\$25} = $ 8%

Scientific Products: Dividend Yield $= \dfrac{\$.30}{\$12} = $ 2.5%

Now that we have computed the ratios for the investment opportunities, we next discuss the interpretation of the two ratios.

Interpretation of Dividend Payout and Dividend Yield

Investors receive income from investments in common stocks in two forms: current cash dividends and appreciation in the price of the stock (commonly called capital gains because of their treatment for income tax purposes). The dividend payout ratio shows what percentage of current earnings the company pays to its owners in the form of dividends. When companies pay dividends that are less than earnings, they have more net assets available to invest in projects that generate future income and future increases in the stock's value. Most companies have established dividend payout policies, and they are reluctant to deviate from those policies. In particular, stock market participants view downward deviations as a signal from management that future earnings will be depressed from historic levels. On the other hand, companies generally do not raise dividend payout levels unless they lack opportunities to efficiently invest the net assets generated by operations. Therefore, investors may not view news of an increase in the dividend payout for a company as positive information. Thus, management is careful to explain any change in dividend policy to avoid confusion.

The dividend payout ratio varies among companies, and there is no correct dividend payout. Companies that we consider to be growth firms have lower cash dividend payouts than do mature, slow-growing companies because growth companies usually have more attractive investment opportunities available to them. The cash dividend payouts for Midwestern Industries and Scientific Products are 50% and 15%, respectively. This information seems to indicate that Scientific Products is a growth firm that retains earnings for investment rather than paying out earnings as dividends.

The dividend yield shows the relationship between current dividends and the stock's market price. Dividend yield is analogous to the interest yield on a savings account at the bank—i.e., it represents the current earnings on the investment. As with dividend payout, there is no correct dividend yield. Growth companies tend to have lower dividends because they retain earnings to invest and this causes the stock's market price to rise. The dividend yields for Midwestern Industries and Scientific Products are 8% and 2.5%, respectively. These ratios reinforce the conclusion that Scientific Products is more of a growth firm than is Midwestern Industries. The retention of earnings to invest in profitable projects results in a low dividend payout and a low dividend yield.

Recall that Jennifer Johnson has two investment goals: current cash income and long-term growth potential. With the inverse relationship between current dividend yield and long-term growth, it may not be possible to invest in a single stock that satisfies both of Jennifer's goals. A possible investment strategy would be to invest some in each of the two companies since one (Midwestern Industries) has a relatively high dividend yield and the other (Scientific Products) appears to have long-term growth potential.

LO 6

Calculate the stated, cumulative, and participating dividends on preferred stock.

PREFERRED STOCK DIVIDENDS

The most common special feature of preferred stock is a preference as to dividends. Stock certificates specify the amount of dividends to which a class of preferred stock is entitled. They also express the amount of preferred dividends in two ways: as a stated dollar amount per share or as a percentage of par value per share. For example, $9 preferred stock, $100 par value, means that the *annual* dividend is $9 per share. If a certificate describes the stock as 10% preferred stock, $50 par value, the annual dividend is $5 per share (10% x $50 = $5 per share).

The preferred stock dividend preference does *not* give preferred stockholders an absolute right to dividends. The declaration of dividends by the board of directors entitles the preferred stockholders to dividends. In deciding to declare dividends, the board of directors takes into consideration such things as the company's current cash position, future cash requirements, and potential investment opportunities.

Cumulative and Noncumulative

With respect to dividend preference, preferred stock may be either noncumulative or cumulative. If preferred stock is **noncumulative**, in any single year that characteristic entitles preferred stockholders to the stated amount of dividends before the common stockholders can receive any dividends. If the board of directors decides not to declare dividends for a year, the preferred stockholders' right to receive a dividend for that year lapses. The dividend preference only means that preferred stockholders must receive their dividends before the common stockholders are entitled to any dividends *when dividends are declared*.

If preferred stock is **cumulative**, the right to receive the annual amount of the stated dividend does not expire when the board of directors fails to declare dividends in a given year. Rather, the right to receive the preferred dividends carries over to future years; and the undeclared dividends are called **dividends in arrears**. For example, assume Home Furnishings, Inc. has preferred stock outstanding as follows: 8% cumulative preferred stock, $100 par value, 10,000 shares outstanding. During 19X1, the board of directors does not declare dividends because the company has insufficient cash to pay dividends. At the end of 19X1, dividends in arrears on the preferred stock are $80,000 ($100 x 8% x 10,000 shares).

The general rule is that in any year, the cumulative characteristic entitles preferred stockholders to receive all of the dividends in arrears and the current year's dividends before the common stockholders receive any dividends. However, dividends in arrears are not a liability of the corporation. The corporation is not obligated to pay dividends until the board of directors declares them. Therefore, at the end of 19X1, Home Furnishings, Inc.'s balance sheet does *not* list a liability for the preferred dividends in arrears. However, to inform the users of the financial statements adequately, the corporation should disclose the fact that dividends are in arrears and the amount in either the notes to the financial statements or the body of the statements. The following footnote discloses the preferred dividends in arrears for the previous example:

> As of January 1, 19X2, the company is in arrears by $80,000, or $8 per share, on dividends to preferred stockholders. The company must pay all dividends in arrears, as well as current dividends, to preferred stockholders before dividends may be paid to common stockholders.

In 19X2, Home Furnishings, Inc.'s cash position has improved; and on December 15, 19X2, the board of directors declares dividends of $250,000. The corporation will distribute dividends to the preferred and common stockholders as follows:

Total dividends declared		$250,000
Preferred dividends in arrears from 19X1	$80,000	
19X2 preferred dividends	80,000	
Total preferred dividends		160,000
Remainder to the common stockholders		$ 90,000

Participating and Nonparticipating

When the stock certificate limits the dividends on preferred stock to the stated amount, as in the above example, the preferred stock is called **nonparticipating**. Most preferred stock is nonparticipating. However, a corporation may issue **participating preferred stock** that allows preferred stockholders to receive dividends in excess of the stated amount in certain circumstances. If preferred stock is fully participating, the corporation first allocates preferred stockholders their stated dividend amount. Next, the corporation allocates common stockholders dividends up to the percentage of par value represented by the stated preferred dividend. Finally, the preferred and common stockholders share any additional dividends on an equal percent of par values.

For example, during 19X1, assume Atlantic Distributing Corp. has the following stock outstanding:

6% preferred stock, $100 par value, fully participating, 10,000 shares outstanding;
Common stock, $10 par value, 50,000 shares outstanding

At the end of 19X1, the board of directors declares dividends of $150,000. We allocate the dividends first to preferred stockholders according to the stated dividend amount:

$$6\% \times \$100 \times 10,000 \text{ shares} = \$60,000$$

Next, we allocate the common stockholders' dividends up to 6% of the par value of the common stock:

$$6\% \times \$10 \times 50,000 \text{ shares} = \$30,000$$

After these two initial allocations, we calculate the dividends remaining to be shared by the preferred and common stockholders as follows:

Dividends declared		$150,000
Allocated to preferred	$60,000	
Allocated to common	30,000	90,000
To be shared by preferred and common		$ 60,000

We allocate the $60,000 of dividends to preferred and common stockholders in proportion to the par values of their stock as follows:

Par value of preferred: 10,000 shares x $100 = $1,000,000
Par value of common: 50,000 shares x $10 =   500,000
             Total $1,500,000

$$\text{Portion allocated to preferred} = \frac{\$1,000,000}{\$1,500,000} \times \$60,000 = \$40,000$$

$$\text{Portion allocated to common} = \frac{\$500,000}{\$1,500,000} \times \$60,000 = \$20,000$$

The total dividends allocated to preferred stockholders is $100,000 ($60,000 + $40,000); to common stockholders, $50,000 ($30,000 + $20,000). As a percent of total par value, the preferred stockholders receive 10% ($100,000 ÷ $1,000,000), and the common stockholders receive the same percent of total par value, or 10% ($50,000 ÷ $500,000).

PREFERRED STOCK ASSETS UPON LIQUIDATION

Preferred stockholders generally have a preference as to the corporation's assets upon liquidation. When a corporation goes out of business and is liquidated, creditors' claims are settled first. Preferred stockholders have the next priority to any remaining assets. The amount of assets that the preferred stockholders are entitled to upon liquidation is the par value of the preferred stock or a larger stipulated liquidation value. The claim to assets of the cumulative preferred stockholders includes any dividends in arrears. No assets are distributed to the common stockholders until the preferred stockholders' claims are settled. After the creditors' and preferred stockholders' claims are settled fully, the common stockholders are then entitled to any remaining assets.

LO 7
Describe the recording of stock dividends and stock splits.

STOCK DIVIDENDS

If the board of directors decides not to pay cash dividends to conserve the company's assets for some purpose such as expansion or investment, the directors may decide to distribute a stock dividend. In this way, the directors are giving the stockholders something that represents their interest in the company's reinvested earnings. When a company issues common stock to its own common stockholders without receiving any assets in return, it gives a **stock dividend**.

While cash dividends reduce both the company's assets and stockholders' equity, stock dividends have no effect on assets or on the amount of total stockholders' equity because the company does not distribute assets to the stockholders. The accounting profession has decided to account for a stock dividend by transferring the market value of the shares issued from retained earnings to contributed capital. We call the procedure of transferring an amount from retained earnings to contributed capital **capitalizing retained earnings**.

Stockholders find stock dividends desirable because, although they own more shares, the market price per share is not often affected significantly.[2] This is especially true whenever the company maintains the cash dividend per share after the stock dividend. Therefore, many stockholders believe that a stock dividend represents a distribution of the company's retained earnings in the amount of the market price of the shares issued.[3] Actually, the common stockholders have the same equity in the company's net assets after the stock dividends as they did before the dividend. For example, Modern Office Supplies, Inc. has stockholders' equity as shown in Illustration 11-6; and Cindy Stepp owns 10,000 shares of the common stock.

ILLUSTRATION 11-6 Partial Balance Sheet

Contributed capital:	
Common stock, $1 par value, 200,000 shares authorized, 100,000 shares issued and outstanding	$ 100,000
Paid-in capital in excess of par value	900,000
Total contributed capital	$1,000,000
Retained earnings	260,000
Total stockholders' equity	$1,260,000

The shares of stock Stepp owns represent a 10% ownership interest in the company (10,000 shares ÷ 100,000 shares outstanding = 10%). We calculate the book value per share of the stock as follows:

$$BV = \frac{\textbf{Total Stockholders' Equity}}{\textbf{Number of Shares Outstanding}}$$

$$BV = \frac{\$1,260,000}{100,000 \text{ shares}}$$

$$BV = \$12.60 \text{ per share}$$

The total book value of the shares Stepp holds is:

$$10,000 \text{ shares} \times \$12.60 \text{ per share} = \$126,000$$

Now, assume Modern Office Supplies, Inc. declares a 5% stock dividend on June 15. A 5% stock dividend means that stockholders receive an additional 5 shares of stock for each 100 shares they own. Stepp owns 10,000 shares and receives an additional 500 shares (5% x 10,000 shares = 500 shares). However, her ownership interest in Modern Office Supplies, Inc. remains at 10%, calculated as follows:

$$\frac{\textbf{Number of Shares Owned after Stock Dividend}}{\textbf{Number of Shares Outstanding}}$$

[2]"Restatement and Revision of Accounting Research Bulletins," *Accounting Research Bulletin No. 43* (New York, NY: AICPA, 1953), Chap. 7, Sec. B, par. 10.

[3]*Ibid.*

$$\frac{10{,}500 \text{ shares}}{105{,}000 \text{ shares outstanding}} = 10\%$$

After the stock dividend, we calculate the book value per share as follows:

$$BV = \frac{\textbf{Total Stockholders' Equity}}{\textbf{Number of Shares Outstanding}}$$

$$BV = \frac{\$1{,}260{,}000}{105{,}000 \text{ shares}}$$

$$BV = \$12.00 \text{ per share}$$

The book value of the 10,500 shares owned after the stock dividend is equal to $126,000 (10,500 shares x $12 per share = $126,000). Therefore, a stock dividend affects neither the ownership interests nor the book values of the total shares stockholders own.

If the market price per share of the stock at the time the company declares the stock dividend is $16, we record the stock dividend declaration by capitalizing $80,000 of retained earnings (100,000 shares x 5% x $16 = $80,000). In the entry to record the stock dividend that is shown below, we credit the *par value* of the stock to be issued to Stock Dividend Distributable; and we credit the market price in excess of par value to Paid-In Capital—Stock Dividend.

June 15	Retained Earnings	80,000	
	Stock Dividend Distributable		5,000
	Paid-In Capital—Stock Dividend		75,000
	To record 5% stock dividend when market price per share is $16.		

On June 30, when the company issues the shares of stock, it makes the following entry:

June 30	Stock Dividend Distributable	5,000	
	Common Stock		5,000
	To record distribution of stock dividend.		

If the company prepares financial statements between the declaration date and the distribution date of the stock dividend, we classify Stock Dividend Distributable as part of contributed capital in stockholders' equity. The account is not a liability because it is the result of an equity transaction; and it is satisfied by the company's issuance of the common stock, *not* by transferring assets or by incurring other liabilities. The stockholders' equity section of a balance sheet prepared between the declaration date and the distribution date is shown in Illustration 11-7.

ILLUSTRATION 11-7 Partial Balance Sheet

Contributed capital:	
Common stock, $1 par value, 200,000 shares authorized, 100,000 shares issued and outstanding	$ 100,000
Stock dividend distributable	5,000
Paid-in capital in excess of par value	975,000
Total contributed capital	$1,080,000
Retained earnings	180,000
Total stockholders' equity	$1,260,000

After the stock dividend, total stockholders' equity remains at the amount of $1,260,000. However, the recorded amount of the stock dividend increases contributed capital and decreases retained earnings.

Large Stock Dividends

The board of directors may sometimes decide to distribute a large stock dividend to decrease the market price per share of its common stock. A **large stock dividend** is defined as greater than 20–25% of the outstanding shares. Over time, the market price per share of a successful corporation that reinvests some or all of its earnings increases. The price may become so high that many investors become hesitant to purchase shares. Thus, to encourage wider ownership of the company's stock, the directors may declare a large stock dividend to decrease the market price of the shares.

Because a large stock dividend significantly reduces the market price of the shares, stockholders do *not* perceive the dividend as a distribution of retained earnings as they do for small stock dividends. Therefore, the amount of retained earnings capitalized for large stock dividends is not equal to the market value of the shares issued. Instead, the amount of retained earnings capitalized is the amount required to satisfy state corporation laws concerning minimum legal capital. Usually, this amount is par value or stated value for no-par stock in some states.

Computer Supplies, Inc. has 10,000 shares of $100 par value common stock outstanding when it declares a 50% stock dividend. When the company declares the stock dividend, the market price per share of the stock is $150. However, we capitalize only the par value of $500,000 (50% x 10,000 x $100 = $500,000) of the stock to be issued. Computer Supplies records the declaration of the stock dividend as follows:

(Date)	Retained Earnings	500,000	
	Stock Dividend Distributable		500,000
	To record the declaration of a 50% stock dividend.		

Notice that the par value, not the market price per share, affects the retained earnings capitalized as shown in the above entry for a large stock dividend.

Stock Splits

The board of directors may also reduce the market price per share of the stock by declaring a stock split. In a **stock split**, the company calls in the outstanding shares and replaces them with a multiple of the number of shares previously outstanding. Common multiples are 2, 3, or 4 shares of new stock for each old share. Actually, the company may exchange any number of new shares for each old share. Companies describe stock splits by their exchange ratios. For example, a 2-for-1 stock split means that stockholders receive 2 shares of new stock for each share owned prior to the stock split.

Food Distributors, Inc. has 100,000 shares of $10 par value stock and declares a 2-for-1 stock split. The stock split declaration requires the company to amend the charter to reduce the par value of the stock from $10 to $5 per share and to double the number of shares authorized. The company calls in the old shares and replaces each $10 par value share with 2 of the new $5 par value shares. The company then cancels the old shares.

A stock split does not affect the corporation's net assets or stockholders' equity, and there is *no effect* on retained earnings. Therefore, we do not need a formal entry to record a stock split. However, the company should include information about the stock split in its stockholder records. Also, the company should modify the description of the stock in its balance sheet. The description of the common stock in the stockholders' equity section before and after the stock split is shown below. Notice that the stock split does not change the balance of Common Stock.

Before the stock split:	
Common stock, $10 par value, 100,000 shares authorized, 100,000 shares issued and outstanding	$1,000,000
After the stock split:	
Common stock, $5 par value, 200,000 shares authorized, 200,000 shares issued and outstanding	$1,000,000

LO 8

Account for the purchase of treasury stock.

TREASURY STOCK TRANSACTIONS

Corporations sometimes reacquire shares of their previously issued stock. We call the reacquired shares of stock **treasury stock**. The company may reacquire shares by purchase from the stockholders or by the stockholders donating the shares to the company. The distinction between treasury stock and unissued shares (authorized shares that have not been issued) is that the company has issued treasury stock but the shares are no longer outstanding, whereas the company has never issued unissued shares. Treasury stock is similar to unissued shares in that shares of treasury stock may be resold. Also, like unissued shares, shares of treasury stock do not carry the usual stockholder rights such as the rights to vote and receive dividends, as well as the preemptive right.

Corporations repurchase outstanding shares of stock for various reasons, including:

1. At some time in the future to distribute to executives as part of stock compensation plans
2. To use at a later date in acquiring other businesses
3. To increase the market price of the shares that remain outstanding. By keeping dividends constant and buying back shares, dividends per share increase, which may favorably affect the market price of a share.

In all but the last case, companies can accomplish the same purpose with authorized but previously unissued stock. However, sufficient unissued shares may not always be available.

Purchasing Treasury Stock

The purchase of treasury stock is similar to cash dividends in that each reduces both the corporations' assets and stockholders' equity. Also, the purchase of treasury stock results in a distribution of corporate assets to certain stockholders, similar to the payment of cash dividends. For this reason, the corporation laws of most states limit both treasury stock purchases and dividends to the amount of the corporation's retained earnings. The cost of the treasury stock reduces the amount of retained earnings available for dividends.

When a company purchases treasury stock, we generally record the stock at the cost of the reacquired shares. For example, on May 19, Atlantic Beverage Corp. purchases 5,000 of the outstanding shares of its $10 par value common stock for $36 per share. We debit the total cost of the reacquired shares to Treasury Stock. The par or stated value of the stock or the amount at which the shares were previously issued does not affect the entry. Atlantic's entry to record the purchase is as follows:

May 19	Treasury Stock	180,000	
	Cash		180,000
	To record the purchase of 5,000 shares of treasury stock for $36 per share.		

Treasury Stock in the Financial Statements

As shown in Illustration 11-8, we classify Treasury Stock in the financial statements as a reduction in total stockholders' equity, *not* as an asset. Sometimes Treasury Stock is called a contra-stockholders' equity account. Notice that in the stockholders' equity section of the balance sheet in Illustration 11-8, we modify the description of common stock to indicate the number of previously outstanding shares that the company reacquired. While we modify the number of shares outstanding (from 40,000 to 35,000), the number of shares issued remains unchanged at 40,000 shares.

ILLUSTRATION 11-8 Partial Balance Sheet

Stockholders' Equity	
Contributed capital:	
Common stock, $10 par value, 50,000 shares authorized,	
40,000 shares issued, 35,000 shares outstanding	$ 400,000
Paid-in capital in excess of par value—common	1,200,000
Total contributed capital	$1,600,000
Retained earnings	600,000
Total	$2,200,000
Less: Treasury stock, 5,000 shares at cost	180,000
Total stockholders' equity	$2,020,000

Reissuing Treasury Stock

A company may reissue shares of treasury stock just as it may issue previously unissued stock. When a company reissues treasury stock, it increases the number of shares outstanding; and we should modify the description of the stock in the stockholders' equity section of the balance sheet. The reissuance of treasury stock increases both the corporation's assets and stockholders' equity. The company may reissue treasury stock for an amount equal to its cost, greater than its cost, or less than its cost.

Reissuing Treasury Stock at Cost. Assume that on August 20, Atlantic Beverage Corp. reissues for cash 2,000 of the shares of treasury stock at the original cost of $36 per share. Atlantic's entry to record the reissuance of the treasury stock is as follows:

Aug. 20	Cash	72,000	
	Treasury Stock		72,000
	To record the sale of 2,000 shares of treasury stock		
	for $36 per share.		

As a result of the reissuance, we should modify the stockholders' equity section of the balance sheet as shown in Illustration 11-9. By comparing Illustration 11-8 and Illustration 11-9, you will notice that while the number of shares issued remains at 40,000, the number of shares outstanding increases by the number of shares of treasury stock reissued. Also, stockholders' equity increases by $72,000, which is the amount of proceeds the corporation received from reissuing the treasury stock.

ILLUSTRATION 11-9 Partial Balance Sheet

Stockholders' Equity	
Contributed capital:	
Common stock, $10 par value, 50,000 shares authorized,	
40,000 shares issued, 37,000 shares outstanding	$ 400,000
Paid-in capital in excess of par value—common	1,200,000
Total contributed capital	$1,600,000
Retained earnings	600,000
Total	$2,200,000
Less: Treasury stock, 3,000 shares at cost	108,000
Total stockholders' equity	$2,092,000

Reissuing Treasury Stock at More Than Cost.   Assume Atlantic Beverage Corp. reissues the 2,000 shares of treasury stock for $60 per share, instead of $36 per share. Although the reissuance price is in excess of the cost of the treasury stock, we do *not* recognize a gain. Under GAAP, a corporation may not recognize a gain or a loss in transactions involving its own equity securities.[4] Rather, we view the difference between the proceeds from reissuing the treasury stock and the original cost of the treasury stock as an increase or as a decrease in contributed capital or, in some cases, as a decrease in retained earnings. As a result of reissuing the 2,000 treasury shares at $60 per share, Atlantic Beverage would make the following entry:

Aug. 20	Cash	120,000	
	Treasury Stock		72,000
	Paid-In Capital—Treasury Stock Transactions		48,000
	To record the sale of 2,000 shares of treasury stock		
	for $60 per share; original cost of $36 per share.		

In the stockholders' equity section of the balance sheet, we classify Paid-In Capital—Treasury Stock Transactions as a component of total contributed capital, the same as Paid-In Capital in Excess of Par from the original issuance of the stock.

Reissuing Treasury Stock at Less Than Cost.   When the corporation reissues treasury stock at a price that is less than the original cost, it does not recognize

---

[4]"Reporting the Results of Operations," *Accounting Principles Board Opinion No. 9* (New York, NY: AICPA, 1966), par. 28.

a loss. We report the difference between the cost and the reissue price of the treasury stock as a reduction in Paid-In Capital—Treasury Stock Transactions. If the balance of the account is less than the amount needed to absorb the deficiency in the reissuance price, then we debit any excess to Retained Earnings. Assume that on October 12, Atlantic Beverage Corp. reissues the remaining 3,000 shares of treasury stock at a price of $24 per share. It records the reissuance of the treasury stock with the following entry:

Oct. 12	Cash	72,000	
	Paid-In Capital—Treasury Stock Transactions	36,000	
	Treasury Stock		108,000
	To record the sale of 3,000 shares of treasury stock at $24 per share. Cost of the shares is $36 per share.		

In this case, the $48,000 balance in Paid-In Capital—Treasury Stock Transactions (from the sale of treasury stock in the previous example) is sufficient to absorb the $36,000 deficiency in the reissuance price.

On the other hand, if the company reissues the 3,000 shares of treasury stock at a price of $16 per share, the $48,000 balance is not sufficient to absorb the $60,000 deficiency in the reissuance price. In this case, the following entry records Atlantic's reissuance of the treasury stock:

Oct. 12	Cash	48,000	
	Paid-In Capital—Treasury Stock Transactions	48,000	
	Retained Earnings	12,000	
	Treasury Stock		108,000
	To record the sale of 3,000 shares of treasury stock at $16 per share. Cost of the shares is $36 per share.		

RETIREMENT OF STOCK

LO 9
Describe how businesses report the retirement of stock in their financial statements.

A corporation may reacquire some of its previously outstanding shares with no intention of reissuing the shares. The company may retire or cancel the reacquired shares, but only with the approval of the stockholders. When the company retires stock, we should remove from the accounts all amounts related to the original issuance of the shares. For example, assume that on January 22, Adams Corporation reacquires 500 shares of its outstanding common stock at a price of $20 per share. The common stock has a par value of $5 per share, and the company originally issued it at a price of $20 per share. Adams records the reacquisition and retirement of the shares with the following entry:

Jan. 22	Common Stock	2,500	
	Paid-In Capital in Excess of Par—Common	7,500	
	Cash		10,000
	To record the reacquisition and retirement of 500 shares of common stock at $20 per share.		

If the company reacquires the shares at a price that is less than the original issue price, we credit the difference to contributed capital in an account called Paid-In Capital—Retirement of Stock. For example, assume that Adams Corporation reacquires 500 shares of stock at a price of $16 per share. The following entry records Adams's reacquisition and retirement of the shares:

Jan. 22	Common Stock	2,500	
	Paid-In Capital in Excess of Par—Common	7,500	
	Cash		8,000
	Paid-In Capital—Retirement of Stock		2,000
	To record the reacquisition and retirement of 500 shares of common stock at $16 per share.		

Conversely, if the company reacquires the shares at a price that is more than the original issue price, we debit the difference first to Paid-In Capital—Retirement of Stock. If this account does not have a balance at least equal to the difference, we debit the excess to Retained Earnings. For example, assume that Adams Corporation reacquires 500 shares of stock at a price of $28 per share. Adams Corporation previously had not retired any shares of stock. Adams records the reacquisition and retirement of the shares with the following entry:

Jan. 22	Common Stock	2,500	
	Paid-In Capital in Excess of Par—Common	7,500	
	Retained Earnings	4,000	
	Cash		14,000
	To record the reacquisition and retirement of 500 shares of common stock at $28 per share.		

APPROPRIATIONS OF RETAINED EARNINGS

LO 10

Discuss the accounting for appropriations of retained earnings.

When a corporation has a contingency that may require a significant amount of assets at some future date, the board of directors may decide to restrict the payment of dividends to accumulate assets to meet the contingency. Examples of such contingencies include a possible loss from a lawsuit or future investments such as a plant expansion. In restricting the payment of dividends, the board of directors may segment retained earnings into appropriated and unappropriated amounts. We call the restriction on the amount of retained earnings available for dividends an **appropriation of retained earnings**. The amount of unappropriated retained earnings is available for dividend declaration. The existence of unappropriated retained earnings does not necessarily mean that sufficient cash is available to pay dividends. After the contingency is satisfied, the board of directors will generally remove the restriction on dividend payments. In the accounting records, we reclassify the appropriated retained earnings as unappropriated retained earnings.

Assume Western Supply Corporation plans a future plant expansion that is anticipated to cost $800,000. To restrict dividend payments, the board appropriates retained earnings in the amount of $800,000. In the accounting records, Western records the appropriation as follows:

(Date)	Retained Earnings	800,000	
	Retained Earnings Appropriated		800,000
	To record resolution of board of directors appropriating retained earnings.		

The company presents the appropriation of retained earnings in the stockholders' equity section of the balance sheet as shown in Illustration 11-10.

Recently, the appropriation of retained earnings on the balance sheet has become a rare practice. Rather, management discusses restrictions on dividend

ILLUSTRATION 11-10 Partial Balance Sheet

Stockholders' Equity		
Contributed capital:		
Common stock, $10 par value, 500,000 shares authorized and issued		$5,000,000
Paid-in capital in excess of par value—common		1,500,000
Total contributed capital		$6,500,000
Retained earnings:		
Appropriated for future plant expansion	$ 800,000	
Unappropriated	1,950,000	2,750,000
Total stockholders' equity		$9,250,000

payments in the notes to the financial statements. By discussing the restrictions in the notes, the chances for misunderstanding the nature of appropriated retained earnings are reduced. Some users of financial statements may believe that appropriated retained earnings results in the accumulation of a fund of cash that the company can use. The amount of the dividend restriction, however, does not necessarily result in such a fund because the company may invest the cash not paid as dividends in assets such as inventories and plant assets or use the cash to pay off liabilities such as notes payable.

LO 11

Calculate and interpret earnings per share.

EARNINGS PER SHARE

At the beginning of this chapter, we introduced you to Josh Adam's uncertainty about using one number, earnings per share, to evaluate a company's performance. We will explain how to calculate earnings per share, how to interpret the number, and then discuss some limitations of using the ratio.

Calculating Earnings Per Share

Earnings per share (EPS) is the ratio of net income available to the common stockholders to the number of shares of common stock outstanding. We will use the stockholders' equity section of Southeast Products, Inc., presented in Illustration 11-11, to illustrate the calculation of earnings per share.

ILLUSTRATION 11-11 Partial Balance Sheet

Stockholders' Equity	
Contributed capital:	
Preferred 8% stock, $100 par value, 50,000 shares authorized and issued	$ 5,000,000
Additional paid-in capital, preferred	800,000
Common stock, $1 par value, 100,000 shares authorized, 80,000 shares issued	80,000
Additional paid-in capital, common	9,600,000
Total contributed capital	$15,480,000
Retained earnings	8,230,000
Total stockholders' equity	$23,710,000

In addition to the information about stockholders' equity, assume Southeast Products' net income for 19X1 is $752,000. First, we must determine the amount of net income available to the common stockholders by subtracting preferred stock dividends from net income. The preferred dividends are $400,000 (8% x $100 x 50,000). The amount of net income available to the common stockholders is $352,000 ($752,000 – $400,000). Next, we divide net income available to common stockholders by the number of shares of common stock outstanding to calculate earnings per share as:

$$\text{EPS} = \frac{\$352,000}{80,000 \text{ shares}} = \$4.40 \text{ per share}$$

Interpreting Earnings Per Share

In the numerator of earnings per share, dividends of the preferred stockholders have been deducted from net income, and the result is the amount of net income available to common stockholders. Dividing by the number of shares of common stock outstanding produces earnings per common share. The usual interpretation of EPS is that the greater the amount of the ratio, the better the company's performance. EPS gives common stockholders a means of assessing the company's performance relative to the number of shares they own. When EPS increases, it means that the company has generated more resources with which to pay dividends (assuming cash is available), and/or invest in projects that will generate future earnings.

Limitations of Earnings Per Share

Relying solely on EPS to evaluate a company's performance may lead to misleading results. Investors should be concerned with what contributes to EPS; that is, with the components of net income (revenues, expenses, gains, and losses). Investors should evaluate whether the current magnitude of EPS is a long-term condition or merely temporary. For example, current EPS may be high because the company liquidated a portfolio of investments for a large gain. The large gain will not be a recurring item; and, therefore, future EPS would be expected to decline. On the other hand, current EPS may be depressed because the company decided to sell an unprofitable operation even though it would realize a large current period loss from the sale. Future EPS may increase as a result of this action, since the loss from the sale is not a recurring item, and the losses that the operation generated will not reduce future earnings. While the financial press focuses on EPS, the other information presented in the company's financial statements provides useful insight into its interpretation.

SUMMARY

Describe the organization and management of a corporation, and state the advantages and disadvantages of the corporate form of business organization. A corporation is a legal entity that is separate from its owners. The separate legal status of a corporation results in accounting for owners' equity, different from that of proprietorships and partnerships. A corporation has most of the rights and duties of a person. Corporations may be classified as profit and not-for-profit corporations and as publicly-owned and privately-owned corporations.

The stockholders own a corporation, but their authority is exercised by an elected board of directors. The board of directors establishes the corporation's broad business policies and appoints the management to carry on the business's day-to-day operations.

The corporate form offers several advantages to business organizations, especially limited stockholder liability, lack of mutual agency, ease of transferring ownership, and ease of raising capital. The disadvantages of corporations include the double taxation of income and the extent of government regulation.

Explain how a corporation is formed and account for organization costs. A corporation is created when the state government grants a charter to the incorporators. We record the costs of forming the corporation as an intangible asset, called Organization Costs, that we amortize over its useful life, not to exceed 40 years.

Describe the characteristics and components of stockholders' equity. The stockholders' equity of a corporation includes the major components of contributed capital and retained earnings. Contributed capital is the total proceeds received from selling preferred stock and common stock. The corporation's minimum legal capital is the par or stated value of common stock. Retained earnings is the cumulative earnings that the business has reinvested in itself.

Account for the issuance of common and preferred stocks in exchange for cash and noncash assets and account for stock subscriptions. A corporation sells common and preferred stock and receives either cash or noncash assets in exchange. The contributed capital that we record from the issuance of stock is the amount of cash received or the fair value of noncash assets received. The corporation may sell stock on a subscription basis, in which the investor agrees to pay for the stock at some future date(s). In this case, the stock in not issued until the investor pays the full purchase price.

Account for the declaration and payment of cash dividends. The board of directors of a corporation has the authority to declare dividends. On the declaration date of a dividend, a liability is recorded for the amount of the dividend and the temporary retained earnings account Dividends is debited by the same amount. As part of the closing process, Dividends is closed to Retained Earnings. Ownership of stock on the record date determines the stockholders who are entitled to receive the dividend. On the payment date, the liability for the dividend is settled by the payment of the dividend.

Calculate the stated, cumulative, and participating dividends on preferred stock. The stock certificate states the amount of dividends that the preferred stockholders are entitled to receive. The preferred stock may be either cumulative or noncumulative. Cumulative preferred stockholders are entitled to receive the stated dividends each year. If the directors do not declare dividends for a year, those cumulative preferred dividends accumulate and must be satisfied before common stockholders receive any dividends. Participating preferred stockholders are entitled to participate with the common stockholders in dividends in excess of the stated amount.

Describe the recording of stock dividends and stock splits. Small stock dividends result in the capitalization of retained earnings equal to the stock's market price. For large stock dividends, retained earnings are capitalized in the amount necessary for minimum legal capital, which usually is par or stated value of the stock issued as a dividend. Stock splits do not result in any formal entry in the accounts of the corporation.

Account for the purchase and reissuance of treasury stock. Previously issued shares of stock that the corporation reacquires are called treasury stock. Treasury stock is recorded at cost and is presented as a reduction of stockholders' equity in the balance sheet. When treasury stock is reissued, an increase or decrease in contributed capital may result.

Describe how businesses report the retirement of stock in their financial statements. When the stockholders approve the retirement of stock, all amounts related to the original issuance of the stock are removed from the accounts.

Discuss the accounting for appropriations of retained earnings. Companies use appropriations of retained earnings to inform stockholders and others that a portion of retained earnings will not be paid out as dividends. We record appropriations of retained earnings by transferring the appropriated amount from Retained Earnings to Retained Earnings–Appropriated.

Calculate and interpret earnings per share. Earnings per share is the ratio of earnings available to the common shareholders (net income less preferred dividends) to the number of shares of common stock outstanding. EPS provides common stockholders a means of assessing the company's performance relative to the number of shares they own.

REVIEW PROBLEM A: ISSUING STOCK AND PAYING DIVIDENDS

Great Graphics became a corporation on January 2, 19X1. It was authorized to issue 1,000,000 shares of common stock and 10,000 shares of preferred stock. Great Graphics had net income of $445,000 during 19X1 and the following transactions occurred:

19X1

Jan.	2	Issued 45,000 shares of $5 par value common stock for $30 per share.
	5	Issued 10,000 shares of cumulative, 8%, $100 par value preferred stock for $110 per share.
June	30	Exchanged 5,000 shares of common stock for a parcel of land with a market value of $165,000.
Sept.	1	Declared an 8% preferred stock dividend payable on September 30.
	1	Declared a $1.00 per share common stock dividend payable on September 30.
	30	Paid the preferred stock dividend declared on September 1.
	30	Paid the common stock dividend declared on September 1.
Oct.	19	Received a stock subscription for 20,000 shares of common stock at a price of $28 per share.
Dec.	1	Received cash payment in full for subscribed stock and issued the stock.

REQUIRED:

a. Prepare the journal entries for the transactions above.
b. Prepare the stockholders' equity section of the December 31, 19X1, balance sheet.

SOLUTION:

Planning and Organizing Your Work

1. Analyze each transaction and prepare the journal entry.
2. Prepare the stockholders' equity section of the balance sheet using the information from Step 1. Remember that Dividends is closed to Retained Earnings at the end of the period.

(a) *Prepare journal entries.*

19X1			
Jan. 2	Cash ($30 x 45,000)	1,350,000	
	Common Stock ($5 x 45,000)		225,000
	Paid-In Capital in Excess of Par–Common		
	($30 – $5) x 45,000		1,125,000
	To record the issuance of common stock for $30 per share on January 2.		
5	Cash ($110 x 10,000)	1,100,000	
	Preferred Stock ($100 x 10,000)		1,000,000
	Paid-In Capital in Excess of Par–Preferred		
	($110 – $100) x 10,000		100,000
	To record the issuance of preferred stock for $110 per share.		
Jun. 30	Land	165,000	
	Common Stock ($5 x 5,000)		25,000
	Paid-In Capital in Excess of Par–Common		
	($165,000 – $25,000)		140,000
	To record the exchange of stock for a parcel of land.		
Sept. 1	Dividends (8% x $1,000,000)	80,000	
	Dividends Payable		80,000
	To record the declaration of an 8% preferred stock cash dividend.		
1	Dividends (45,000 + 5,000) x $1	50,000	
	Dividends Payable		50,000
	To record the declaration of a $1 per share common stock cash dividend.		
30	Dividends Payable	80,000	
	Cash		80,000
	To record the payment of the preferred dividend.		
30	Dividends Payable	50,000	
	Cash		50,000
	To record the payment of the common dividend.		
Oct. 19	Subscriptions Receivable–Common ($28 x 20,000)	560,000	
	Stock Subscribed–Common ($5 x 20,000)		100,000
	Paid-In Capital in Excess of Par–Common		
	($28 – $5) x 20,000		460,000
	To record common stock subscribed.		
Dec. 1	Cash	560,000	
	Subscriptions Receivable–Common		560,000
	To record cash received for subscribed stock		
1	Stock Subscribed–Common	100,000	
	Common Stock		100,000
	To record issuance of common stock.		

(b) *Prepare the stockholders' equity section.*

Stockholders' Equity

Contributed capital:		
Preferred 8% stock, $100 par value, 10,000 shares authorized		
and issued		$1,000,000
Paid-in capital in excess of par, preferred		100,000
Common stock, $5 par value, 1,000,000 shares authorized,		
70,000 shares issued		350,000
Paid-in capital in excess of par, common		1,725,000
Total contributed capital		$3,175,000
Retained earnings*		315,000
Total stockholders' equity		$3,490,000

*$445,000 – $50,000 – $80,000

REVIEW PROBLEM B: STOCK DIVIDENDS, STOCK SPLITS, AND TREASURY STOCK

The stockholders' equity section for Carol Ann Corporation is given below:

Carol Ann Corporation
Partial Balance Sheet
December 31, 19X0

Stockholders' Equity

Contributed capital:	
Common stock, $5 par value, 1,000,000 shares authorized,	
200,000 shares issued	$1,000,000
Paid-in capital in excess of par value	2,000,000
Total contributed capital	$3,000,000
Retained earnings	1,700,000
Total	$4,700,000
Less: Treasury stock, 10,000 shares at a cost of $12 per share	120,000
Total stockholders' equity	$4,580,000

REQUIRED:

Prepare journal entries for each of the following **independent events** of 19X1.
a. Declared a 10% stock dividend when the market price of stock is $18 per share.
b. Declared a 40% stock dividend when the market price of stock is $16 per share.
c. Declared a 2-for-1 stock split.
d. Distributed the stock dividend in (a) above.
e. Purchased 1,000 shares of treasury stock for $20 per share.
f. Sold 2,000 shares of treasury stock at $10 per share.
g. Sold 3,000 shares of treasury stock at $15 per share.
h. Retired 5,000 shares of common stock at $14 per share.
i. Appropriated $300,000 of retained earnings for potential loss from litigation.

SOLUTION:

Planning and Organizing Your Work
1. Analyze each transaction.
2. Determine if the stock dividend is large or small.

3. If the stock dividend is small, use the stock's market value to determine the amount of retained earnings to capitalize.
4. If the stock dividend is large, use the stock's par or stated value to determine the amount of retained earnings to capitalize.
5. Record purchases of treasury stock at cost.
6. Record the difference between the reissuance price of treasury stock and its original cost as either an increase or a decrease in paid-in capital (or retained earnings if necessary).
7. Remove all amounts related to the original issuance of stock for retirement of stock.

(a) *Declared a 10 % stock dividend.*
Retained earnings: $18 x 200,000 shares x 10%

19X1	Retained Earnings	360,000	
	Stock Dividend Distributable*		100,000
	Paid-in Capital — Stock Dividend**		260,000
	To record the declaration of a 10% stock dividend.		
	*$5 x 200,000 shares x 10%		
	**($18 – $5) x (200,000 x 10%)		

(b) *Declared a 40 % stock dividend.*
Retained Earnings: $5 x 200,000 shares x 40%

19X1	Retained Earnings	400,000	
	Stock Dividend Distributable		400,000
	To record the declaration of a 40% stock dividend.		

(c) *Declared a 2-for-1 stock split.*

No entry required. Show Common Stock at $2.50 par ($5 ÷ 2) and 400,000 (200,000 x 2) shares issued.

(d) *Distributed stock dividend.*

19X1	Stock Dividend Distributable	100,000	
	Common Stock		100,000
	To record the distribution of the stock dividend.		

(e) *Purchased treasury stock for $20 per share.*

19X1	Treasury Stock	20,000	
	Cash		20,000
	To record the purchase of 1,000 shares of treasury stock for $20 per share.		

(f) *Sold treasury stock for $10 per share.*
Cash: $10 x 2,000 shares
Treasury Stock: $12 x 2,000 shares
Retained Earnings: $24,000 – $20,000

19X1	Cash	20,000	
	Retained Earnings	4,000	
	Treasury Stock		24,000
	To record the sale of 2,000 shares of treasury stock below cost.		

(g) *Sold treasury stock for $15 per share.*
Cash: $15 x 3,000 shares
Treasury Stock: $12 x 3,000 shares
Paid-In Capital—Treasury Stock Transactions: $45,000 – $36,000

19X1	Cash	45,000	
	Paid-In Capital—Treasury Stock Transactions		9,000
	Treasury Stock		36,000
	To record the sale of 3,000 shares of treasury stock above cost.		

(h) *Retired common stock for $14 per share.*
Common Stock: $5 x 5,000 shares

19X1	Common Stock	25,000	
	Paid-In Capital in Excess of Par——Common*	50,000	
	Paid-In Capital—Retirement of Stock**		5,000
	Cash		70,000
	To record the retirement of 5,000 shares of common stock.		
	*($2,000,000/200,000 shares) x 5,000		
	**($15-$14) x 5,000		

(i) *Appropriated retained earnings.*

19X1	Retained Earnings	300,000	
	Retained Earnings Appropriated		300,000
	To record resolution of board of directors appropriating retained earnings.		

KEY TERMS

appropriation of retained earnings, *505*
articles of incorporation, *483*
authorized shares, *486*
bylaws, *483*
capitalizing retained earnings, *498*
charter, *478*
common stock, *487*
contributed capital, *484*
corporation, *478*
cumulative preferred stock, *495*
dividend declaration date, *492*
dividend payment date, *492*
dividend payout, *493*
dividend record date, *492*
dividend yield, *493*
dividends, *480*
dividends in arrears, *495*

double taxation of corporations, *482*
earnings per share (EPS), *506*
large stock dividend, *500*
legal capital, *486*
noncumulative preferred stock, *495*
nonparticipating preferred stock, *496*
no-par value, *487*
not-for-profit, *478*
organization costs, *483*
Paid-In Capital in Excess of Par, *488*
participating preferred stock, *496*
par value, *486*
preemptive right, *480*
preferred stock, *487*

privately-owned corporations, *478*
profit, *478*
proxy, *480*
publicly-owned corporations, *478*
registrars, *485*
retained earnings, *484*
stated value, *487*
stock certificate, *485*
stock dividend, *497*
stock split, *500*
stockholders, *479*
stockholders' ledger, *485*
stock subscription, *489*
transfer agents, *485*
treasury stock, *501*

SELF-QUIZ

LO 1 1. Corporations with thousands of owners are called _____ corporations, and corporations with relatively few owners are called _____ corporations.

LO 1 2. True or False? The preemptive right of common stockholders is the right to receive dividends.

LO 1 3. Which of the following is *not* typically a common stockholder's right?

a. To vote in meetings of stockholders

b. To have the first opportunity to purchase additional shares of stock

c. To run the daily operations of the company

d. To dispose of their shares of stock as they please

LO 2 4. Which of the following is *not* an advantage of a corporation?

a. Reduction of taxes

b. Limited stockholders' liability

c. Continuity of existence

d. Ease of raising capital

LO 2 5. Organization costs must be amortized over a period that should not exceed _____ years.

LO 3 6. Which of the following is *not* typically found in the stockholders' equity section of a corporation's balance sheet?

a. Net income

b. Common stock

c. Retained earnings

d. Paid-in Capital in Excess of Par

LO 3 7. True or False? Par value of stock is typically equal to the stock's market value.

LO 3 8. Both Preferred Stock and Paid-In Capital in Excess of Par–Preferred are part of the corporation's _____ capital.

LO 4 9. True or False? Common stock may be issued in exchange for noncash assets such as land.

LO 5 10. Which of the following events relating to dividends requires no journal entries?

a. Declaration of dividends

b. Date of record

c. Date of payment

d. Simultaneous declaration and payment

LO 6 11. If the preferred stock is _____, the right to receive the annual amount of the stated dividend does not expire when the board of directors fails to declare dividends in a given year.

LO 7 12. Which of the following is a *correct* statement about stock dividends?

a. They decrease assets when declared.

b. They decrease assets when distributed.

c. They do not require declaration by the board of directors.

d. They cause the capitalization of retained earnings.

LO 7 13. True or False? A stock split reduces retained earnings.

LO 8 14. Which of the following is *not* a true statement about treasury stock?

a. Treasury stock is shown at the end of the stockholders' equity section of the balance sheet.

b. Treasury stock is always recorded at the stock's original par value.

c. Treasury stock reduces stockholders' equity.

d. Treasury stock reduces shares outstanding when it is acquired.

LO 9 15. If a company retires shares at a price less than their original issue price, we credit the difference to an account called _____ _____– _____ _____ _____.

LO 10 16. Which of the following is *not* a correct statement about the appropriation of retained earnings?

a. Most corporations frequently practice it.

b. It is used to restrict the payment of dividends in order to meet a future contingency.

c. The decision to appropriate retained earnings is made by the board of directors.

d. It is shown separately from unappropriated retained earnings on the balance sheet.

LO 11 17. _____ ___ _____ is the ratio of net income available to the common shareholders to the number of shares of common stock outstanding.

SOLUTIONS TO SELF-QUIZ

1. publicly-owned, privately-owned   2. False   3. c   4. a   5. 40   6. a   7. False   8. contributed   9. True
10. b   11. cumulative   12. d   13. False   14. b   15. Paid-In Capital—Retirement of Stock   16. a
17. Earnings per share

QUESTIONS

Q11-1 What are the differences among a corporation, a partnership, and a sole proprietorship?

Q11-2 Describe the role of the board of directors of a corporation.

Q11-3 Describe the duties of the president, controller, and treasurer of a corporation?

Q11-4 What are the advantages and disadvantages of a corporation?

Q11-5 How is a corporation formed?

Q11-6   What are the advantages of no-par value stock compared to par value stock?

Q11-7   What are the differences between common stock and preferred stock?

Q11-8   How does a corporation sell shares of stock through a stock subscription?

Q11-9   Why do corporations pay dividends?

Q11-10   What is the difference between participating and nonparticipating preferred stock?

Q11-11   Explain the differences between cumulative and noncumulative preferred stock.

Q11-12   Why do corporations declare stock dividends?

Q11-13   What is the difference between the accounting treatment of a small stock dividend and a large stock dividend?

Q11-14   Why are small stock dividends accounted for differently than large stock dividends?

Q11-15   What is the difference between a stock dividend and a stock split?

Q11-16   What is the interpretation of the dividend yield ratio?

Q11-17   Why do firms acquire treasury stock?

Q11-18   What is the difference between acquiring treasury stock and retiring common stock?

Q11-19   Why do companies appropriate retained earnings?

Q11-20   What are the implications of relying solely on current EPS to evaluate a company's performance?

EXERCISES

LO 2

E11-1   **Organization Costs**   Yates Corporation incurred the following costs during formation:

Charter fees paid to the state	$1,900
Legal fees to prepare charter	4,300
Promoters' fees	3,700
Printing of stock certificates	1,100

REQUIRED:

Record the journal entry for the payment of organization costs and first-year amortization of organization costs if Yates Corporation amortizes these costs over 5 years. Assume a full year's amortization is appropriate for the first year.

LO 3

E11-2   **Stockholders' Equity Section**   Prepare the stockholders' equity section in good form for the Castle Corporation given the following information:

a. Paid-in Capital in Excess of Par–Common and Preferred Stock are $268,000 and $400,000, respectively.

b. There is $189,000 of retained earnings.

c. There are 100,000 shares of $2 par value common stock authorized and 20,000 shares issued.

d. There are 50,000 shares of 8%, $100 par value preferred stock authorized and issued.

LO 4

E11-3   **Common Stock**   Prepare journal entries for the following independent common stock transactions:

a. Sold 5,000 shares of $10 par value common stock for $48 per share.

b. Sold 10,000 shares of no-par value common stock with a stated value of $5 per share for $40 per share.

c. Sold 2,000 shares of no-par value common stock (no stated value) for $42 per share.

d. Exchanged 6,000 shares of $5 par value common stock for a parcel of land that the previous owner offered to sell for $125,000.

LO 4   **E11-4**   **Stock Subscriptions**   Stone Concrete Corporation receives subscriptions for 50,000 shares of common stock on July 1, 19X2. The common stock has a par value of $2 per share, and the subscription price is $15 per share. On October 1, 19X2, Stone Corporation received payment of one-third of the total subscription price, and it received the balance on November 1, 19X2.

REQUIRED:

Prepare all journal entries for the stock subscription and subsequent receipts of cash.

LO 5   **E11-5**   **Issuance of Preferred Stock**   Bilko Corporation sells 5,000 shares of $100 par value preferred stock for $110 per share.

REQUIRED:

Record the journal entry for the issuance of the preferred stock.

LO 5   **E11-6**   **Cash Dividends**   On December 1, 19X1, the board of directors of Technology Incorporated declared a cash dividend of $2.50 per share to the common stockholders of record on December 20, 19X1. The dividend is payable on December 30, 19X1, and 20,000 shares of common stock are outstanding.

REQUIRED:

Prepare journal entries for the declaration and payment of dividends.

LO 6   **E11-7**   **Stated and Cumulative Dividends**   Edwards Furniture, Incorporated has 50,000 shares of 8%, $100 par value, cumulative preferred stock. During 19X3, the board of directors did not declare dividends. In 19X4 and 19X5, Edwards' board of directors decided to pay all dividends required.

REQUIRED:

Determine the total amount of dividends paid to preferred stockholders in 19X4 and in 19X5.

LO 6   **E11-8**   **Participating Dividends**   Texoma International Corporation has the following stock outstanding:

8% preferred stock, $100 par value, fully participating, 10,000 shares outstanding; Common stock, $30 par value, 100,000 shares outstanding.

At the end of 19X6, the board of directors declared dividends of $400,000.

REQUIRED:

Determine the amount of dividends to be paid to preferred and common stockholders.

LO 7   **E11-9**   **Small Stock Dividend**   Uncle Jimmy's Corporation has 20,000 shares of $2 par common stock outstanding on June 30, 19X2, when the market price is $24 per share. The board of directors declares a 10% stock dividend to be distributed on July 15, 19X2.

REQUIRED:

Record the necessary journal entries for the declaration and distribution of the stock dividend.

LO 7   **E11-10**   **Large Stock Dividend**   Assume that Uncle Jimmy's board of directors declares a 50% stock dividend, instead of a 10% stock dividend, as given in E11-9.

REQUIRED:

Record the necessary journal entries for the declaration and distribution of the stock dividend.

LO 7   **E11-11**   **Stock Splits**   Imelda's Shoes, Inc. has 1,000,000 shares authorized and 200,000 shares issued and outstanding of $15 par value common stock and declares a stock split.

REQUIRED:

Show how Common Stock would appear on the balance sheet:
a. Before the stock split
b. After a 2-for-1 stock split
c. After a 3-for-1 stock split.

LO 7   **E11-12**   **Dividend Ratios**   Audionics Corporation reported $2,350,000 net income and paid $1,200,000 in dividends for 19X3. The market price per common share of stock and number of shares of common stock outstanding on December 31, 19X3, is $31.00 per share and 1,000,000 shares, respectively.

REQUIRED:

Calculate the dividend payout and dividend yield ratios for 19X3.

LO 8   **E11-13**   **Purchase of Treasury Stock**   Moon Distillers, Inc. purchased 3,000 shares of its $5 par value common stock for $59 per share on October 31, 19X4.

REQUIRED:

Prepare the journal entry to record the purchase of treasury stock.

LO 8   **E11-14**   **Sale of Treasury Stock**   The stockholders' equity section for Squire Corporation is given below:

Squire Corporation **Partial Balance Sheet** **December 31, 19X5**	
Stockholders' Equity	
Contributed capital:	
Common stock, $10 par value, 1,000,000 shares authorized,	
150,000 shares issued	$1,500,000
Paid-in capital in excess of par—common	4,400,000
Paid-in capital—treasury stock	100,000
Total contributed capital	$6,000,000
Retained earnings	2,800,000
Total	$8,800,000
Less: Treasury stock, 10,000 shares at a cost of $38 per share	380,000
Total stockholders' equity	$8,420,000

REQUIRED:

Record the necessary journal entry to record the sale of 4,000 shares of treasury stock in 19X6 at:
a. $35 per share
b. $50 per share

LO 9

E11-15 **Retirement of Stock** On March 13, 19X7, Cass Corporation retired 7,500 shares of its outstanding common stock at a price of $40 per share. The common stock has a par value of $10 per share and originally was issued at a price of $32 per share.

REQUIRED:

Record the journal entries for the retirement of the shares.

LO 11

E11-16 **Earnings Per Share** Domingo Company has 100,000 shares of $1 par value common stock and 50,000 shares of 6%, $100 par value cumulative preferred stock outstanding on December 31, 19X9. Net income during 19X9 for Domingo company is $790,000.

REQUIRED:

Determine earnings per share for Domingo's common stockholders for 19X9.

PROBLEM SET A

LO 3,4,5,6

P11-1A **Stock Transactions** Trans-International Corporation was formed on January 2, 19X2. The following stock transactions occurred during 19X2:

19X2
Jan.   2 Sold 50,000 shares of $5 par common stock for $35 per share (1,000,000 shares authorized).
       3 Sold 10,000 shares of $100 par, 6%, nonparticipating preferred stock for $122 per share (50,000 shares authorized).
June   1 Received subscriptions for 5,000 shares of the $5 par common stock at $37 per share.
July 31 Received cash for the full amount of the stock subscriptions of June 1.
Dec.   1 Declared the annual cash dividend to preferred stockholders of record on December 20.
       1 Declared a cash dividend of $2.00 per share to the common stockholders of record on December 20.
      30 Paid the preferred stock dividend declared on December 1.
      30 Paid the common stock dividend declared on December 1.

REQUIRED:

a. Prepare journal entries for the transactions listed above.
b. Prepare the stockholders' equity section of the balance sheet as of December 31, 19X2, if the ending balance in Retained Earnings is $49,000 (after Dividends and Income Summary are closed).

LO 3,4

P11-2A **Determine Missing Values** The stockholders' equity section for the Sunnie Corporation is presented below:

Contributed capital:	
Preferred 8% stock, $50 par value, 50,000 shares authorized	
and _____ issued	$500,000
Paid-in capital in excess of par, preferred	150,000
Common stock, $5 stated value, 1,000,000 shares authorized,	
100,000 shares issued	?
Common stock subscribed but not issued, 20,000 shares	100,000
Paid-in capital in excess of stated value, common	600,000
Total contributed capital	$?
Retained earnings	945,000
Total stockholders' equity	$?

REQUIRED:

a. Calculate the number of shares of preferred stock issued.
b. Calculate the issue price per share of preferred stock.
c. Calculate the issue price per share of common stock, assuming the price of the subscribed stock is the same as the common stock issued.
d. Calculate total stockholders' equity.

LO 5,6   **P11-3A   Preferred and Common Dividends**   The Musket Corporation paid $60,000 of dividends in 19X2, $450,000 in 19X3, and $600,000 in 19X4. During this time, there were 50,000 shares of 8%, $20 par preferred stock outstanding and 200,000 shares of $5 par common stock outstanding.

REQUIRED:

a. Calculate the dividends paid to common and preferred stockholders for each of the 3 years if the preferred stock is noncumulative and nonparticipating.
b. Calculate the dividends paid to common and preferred stockholders for each of the 3 years if the preferred stock is cumulative and nonparticipating (no dividends were paid in 19X0 and 19X1).
c. Calculate the dividends paid to common and preferred stockholders for each of the 3 years if the preferred stock is cumulative and fully participating (no dividends were paid in 19X0 and 19X1).

LO 7,8,9,10   **P11-4A   Stockholders' Equity Transactions**   The stockholders' equity section for Candee Corporation is given below:

| **Candee Corporation** |
| **Partial Balance Sheet** |
| **December 31, 19X0** |

Stockholders' Equity	
Contributed capital:	
Common stock, $1 par value, 1,000,000 shares authorized,	
100,000 shares issued	$ 100,000
Paid-in capital in excess of par—common	1,400,000
Paid-in capital—treasury stock transactions	50,000
Total contributed capital	$1,550,000
Retained earnings	700,000
Total stockholders' equity	$2,250,000

The following events occurred during 19X1:

Jan. 15 Declared a 10% stock dividend when the market price was $20 per share.
         31 Distributed the stock dividend declared on January 15.
May 15 Purchased 3,000 shares of treasury stock at $18 per share.
July 10 Appropriated $150,000 of retained earnings to finance future plant expansion.
Aug. 15 Sold 1,000 shares of treasury stock at $16 per share.
Nov. 19 Retired 5,000 shares of common stock at $17 per share.
Dec.   2 Sold 750 shares of treasury stock at $20 per share.

REQUIRED:

a. Record the necessary journal entries for 19X1.
b. Prepare the stockholders' equity section on December 31, 19X1, assuming net income of $90,000 for the year.
c. Record the journal entry for January 15, assuming a 40% stock dividend, instead of a 10% stock dividend.

LO 11   **P11-5A**   **Book Value Per Share and Earnings per Share**   The stockholders' equity section for the Traymond Corporation is presented below:

Contributed capital:

Preferred 8% stock, $100 par value, 10,000 shares authorized and issued	$1,000,000
Paid-in capital in excess of par, preferred	200,000
Common stock, $5 par value, 1,000,000 shares authorized, 100,000 shares issued	500,000
Paid-in capital in excess of par, common	300,000
Total contributed capital	$2,000,000
Retained earnings	600,000
Total stockholders' equity	$2,600,000

REQUIRED:

a. Determine the earnings per share for common and preferred stock if the preferred stock is noncumulative, nonparticipating, has a redemption price of $110, and net income is $250,000.

PROBLEM SET B

LO 3,4,5,6   **P11-1B**   **Stock Transactions**   The Montoya Corporation was formed on January 2, 19X6. The following stock transactions occurred during 19X6:

19X6

Jan.   2   Sold 40,000 shares of $1 par common stock for $20 per share (100,000 shares authorized).

      3   Sold 8,000 shares of $100 par, 8%, nonparticipating preferred stock for $115 per share (10,000 shares authorized).

June   3   Received subscriptions for 10,000 shares of common stock at $19 per share.

July   29   Received cash for the full amount of the stock subscriptions of June 3.

Dec.   2   Declared the annual cash dividend to preferred stockholders of record on December 21.

      2   Declared a cash dividend of $1.50 per share to the common stockholders of record on December 21.

    28   Paid the preferred stock dividend declared on December 2.

    29   Paid the common stock dividend declared on December 2.

REQUIRED:

a. Prepare journal entries for the transactions listed above.

b. Prepare the stockholders' equity section of the balance sheet as of December 31, 19X6, if the ending balance in Retained Earnings is $38,000 (after Dividends and Income Summary are closed).

LO 3,4   **P11-2B**   **Determine Missing Values**   The stockholders' equity section for the Wallack Corporation is presented on the next page:

REQUIRED:

a. Calculate the number of shares of preferred stock issued.

b. Calculate the issue price per share of preferred stock.

c. Calculate the issue price per share of common stock, assuming the price of the subscribed stock is the same as the common stock issued.

d. Calculate total stockholders' equity.

Contributed capital:

Preferred 8% stock, $50 par value, 50,000 shares authorized and _____ issued	$400,000
Paid-in capital in excess of par, preferred	50,000
Common stock, $4 stated value, 1,000,000 shares authorized, 75,000 shares issued	?
Common stock subscribed but not issued, 20,000 shares	80,000
Paid-in capital in excess of stated value, common	570,000
Total contributed capital	$?
Retained earnings	425,000
Total stockholders' equity	$?

LO 5,6

P11-3B **Preferred and Common Dividends** The Fife Corporation paid $90,000 of dividends in 19X7, $600,000 in 19X8, and $500,000 in 19X9. During this time, there were 75,000 shares of 8%, $20 par preferred stock outstanding and 300,000 shares of $5 par common stock outstanding.

REQUIRED:

a. Calculate the dividends paid to common and preferred stockholders for each of the 3 years if the preferred stock is noncumulative and nonparticipating.
b. Calculate the dividends paid to common and preferred stockholders for each of the 3 years if the preferred stock is cumulative but not participating (no dividends were paid in 19X5 and 19X6).
c. Calculate the dividends paid to common and preferred stockholders for each of the 3 years if the preferred stock is cumulative and fully participating (no dividends were paid in 19X5 and 19X6).

LO 7,8,9,10

P11-4B **Stockholders' Equity Transactions** The stockholders' equity section for Leslie Corporation is given below:

Leslie Corporation
Partial Balance Sheet
December 31, 19X4

Stockholders' Equity

Contributed capital:	
Common stock, $2 par value, 1,000,000 shares authorized, 200,000 shares issued	$ 400,000
Paid-in capital in excess of par—common	800,000
Paid-in capital—treasury stock transactions	70,000
Total contributed capital	$1,270,000
Retained earnings	420,000
Total stockholders' equity	$1,690,000

The following events occurred during 19X5:

Jan.   2   Declared a 15% stock dividend when the market value was $10 per share.
Feb.   5   Distributed the stock dividend declared on January 2.
June 15 Purchased 4,000 shares of treasury stock at $9.50 per share.
July   10 Appropriated $90,000 of retained earnings to finance future plant expansion.
Aug. 25 Sold 1,500 shares of treasury stock at $8 per share.
Nov.   9   Retired 6,000 shares of common stock at $7 per share.
Dec. 22 Sold 1,000 shares of treasury stock at $12 per share.

REQUIRED:

a. Record the necessary journal entries for 19X5.
b. Prepare the stockholders' equity section on December 31, 19X5, assuming net income of $80,000 for the year.
c. Record the journal entry for January 2, assuming a 50% stock dividend, instead of a 15% stock dividend.

LO 9,10 **P11-5B** **Earnings Per Share**   The stockholders' equity section for the Crane Corporation is presented below:

Contributed capital:

Preferred 8% stock, $100 par value, 5,000 shares authorized and issued	$ 500,000
Paid-in capital in excess of par, preferred	150,000
Common stock, $4 par value, 500,000 shares authorized, 100,000 shares issued	400,000
Paid-in capital in excess of par, common	240,000
Total contributed capital	$1,290,000
Retained earnings	710,000
Total stockholders' equity	$2,000,000

REQUIRED:

a. Determine the earnings per share for common and preferred stock if the preferred stock is noncumulative, nonparticipating, has a redemption price of $120, and net income is $175,000.

CRITICAL THINKING AND COMMUNICATING

C11-1

Mr. Spear, the sole owner of a small furniture manufacturer, was contemplating forming a corporation. Mr. Spear's company has experienced consistent sales growth in the past 5 years. As a result of the increase in sales, Mr. Spear was contemplating expansion of his factory, which would require a large capital investment. Mr. Spear's management style consists of running every aspect of the business himself.

Because of the complexity of the decision to incorporate, Mr. Spear hired Mr. Rodgers, a member of a major accounting firm, as a consultant to help determine whether or not to incorporate. If Mr. Spear does incorporate, he contemplates issuing stock to the public.

REQUIRED:

a. Explain to Mr. Spear the procedures necessary to incorporate.
b. Explain to Mr. Spear the advantages and disadvantages of forming a corporation.
c. What advice would you give Mr. Spear about incorporating his business? Defend your answer.

C11-2

Martha Borg is considering an investment in Cyclonics Corporation. Martha prefers to invest in companies that have strong potential for rapid growth. She has been extremely impressed by the large increases in earnings per share for Cyclonics over the last 3 years. Selected financial data for Cyclonics follow:

	19X3	*19X4*	*19X5*
EPS	$1.07	$1.46	$2.33
Sales	$780,000	$792,000	$793,000
Shares outstanding	1,000,000	750,000	425,000

REQUIRED:

Examine the information above. Explain how Martha should interpret this information and how she might use it in making her investment decision.

C11-3 The common stock of We-Haul, Incorporated is traded on a national stock exchange. Barbara Coe, the CEO of We-Haul, is evaluating the company's dividend policy. For the past several years, the company's dividend payout ratio has been constant at 20%. Barbara is considering two options that she thinks might increase the market price of the stock:

1. Increasing the dividend payout ratio to 50%.
2. Supplementing the current dividend by also distributing a stock dividend.

REQUIRED:

a. Discuss Barbara's two dividend policy options. What are the possible investor reactions to the two alternative dividend actions?
b. What other actions might Barbara consider to increase the market price of We-Haul's stock?

C11-4 The financial statements of J.C. Penney Company, Inc. are reprinted in Appendix B at the end of the text. On the income statement is the earnings per share information. Notice that the company reports numerous EPS numbers for each year. Discussion of the various EPS figures are the subject of more advanced accounting texts. For purposes of this case, use the EPS number called "Primary, Income before extraordinary charge and cumulative effect of accounting changes."

REQUIRED:

a. Calculate the dividend payout ratio for 1991–1993. You can find both the numerators and denominators for this ratio in the *Supplemental Information*, located after the financial statements, entitled Five Year Financial Summary.
b. Calculate the dividend yield for 1991–1993. You can find the market price of the stock in the *Supplemental Information* entitled Quarterly Data. For calculating this ratio, use the fourth quarter average market price (i.e., average of the high and low for the fourth quarter).
c. Analyze J.C. Penney's dividend policy using the ratios you calculated in Requirements a and b. Would you classify J.C. Penney as a growth company? Why?

C11-5 Refer to the J.C. Penney Company, Inc. Annual Report in Appendix B to answer the following questions.

REQUIRED:

a. The "Consolidated Statements of Income" discloses two different sets of earnings per common share numbers. What are they called? Do the *Notes to Consolidated Financial Statements* assist you in understanding how they were computer? Explain in your own words what significance these earnings per share numbers have.
b. Did J.C. Penney Company declare cash or stock dividends in 1991, 1992, or 1993? If so, in what year and how much?
c. What year(s) did J.C. Penney Company's stock split?
d. Is the preferred stock cumulative or participating? Does it have any other features?
e. What is the par value of J.C. Penney's preferred and common stock? How many shares of each are authorized and issued? In 1994, is the board of directors hoping to authorize more stock? If so, how many additional shares? Who must approve the increase?
f. What does LESOP stand for? What is it? What percentage ownership does the LESOP have of J.C. Penney's stock?

g. Was any preferred or common stock issued or retired in 1991? 1992, or 1993? If so, when and how much?

h. Do the financial statements or notes disclose any market price data for common or preferred J.C. Penney stock?

i. After answering the above questions, do you find that the disclosures regarding J.C. Penney's stockholders' equity are adequate and user-friendly? Write a brief paper explaining your position.

CHAPTER 12

Unincorporated Businesses

When Ray Johnson graduated from college five years ago, he began a business that sells compact discs and cassette tapes, as well as some related items. At first, business was slow. Recently, since he began advertising frequently on the local cable television system, Ray's business has grown rapidly. In fact, Ray's business is so good that he is considering expanding. A national developer of shopping malls is building a new mall across town from Ray's current location. Ray believes there is enough business to support another store, and he is considering renting space in the new mall.

However, Ray is concerned about finding financing for his new store. In the last year, the local banks have been hesitant to loan money to small businesses, and Ray is looking for alternative sources of financing. Ray's Uncle Hank recently took early retirement from a major business and has approached Ray about investing in the business. Hank has suggested that they form a partnership, but Ray has some concerns about the partnership form of business. Since Hank wants to be a passive investor, not involved in the day-to-day operations, Ray is uncertain about how he and Hank would divide the profits. Also, Ray has read in the newspapers about the increasing number of small businesses declaring bankruptcy, and he wants to know how a partnership would affect his personal finances if the business fails.

Previous chapters in this text emphasize the corporation form of business to present and illustrate various accounting concepts, principles, and procedures that apply to business enterprises. Sole proprietorship and partnership forms of business are alternatives to corporations. Proprietorships and partnerships offer certain advantages compared to those of the corporate form of business, but they also have some disadvantages. This chapter discusses accounting procedures that sole proprietorship and partnership forms of business use. While GAAP for assets, liabilities, owners' equity, revenues, and expenses apply to unincorporated businesses, this chapter presents some unique applications of those principles to sole proprietorships and partnerships.

1. Account for the transactions of a sole proprietorship.
2. Describe the advantages and disadvantages of the partnership form of business.
3. Record in the accounting records the formation of a partnership.
4. Calculate and record the allocation of partnership net income and losses to the partners according to the partnership agreement.
5. Prepare partnership financial statements.
6. Explain and record the various forms of partnership dissolution.
7. Record the transactions related to the liquidation of partnerships.

LO 1

Account for the transactions of a sole proprietorship.

ACCOUNTING FOR SOLE PROPRIETORSHIPS

Although usually small in size, most businesses in the United States are sole proprietorships. A **sole proprietorship** is a business owned by one person. Most sole proprietorships are operated as a business separate from the personal affairs of the owner. The accounting records and financial statements should reflect the transactions, assets, and liabilities of the business separately from those of the owner. Legally, however, a sole proprietorship is *not* a separate entity from the owner. All of the business's net income is allocated to the owner who is legally obligated for the business's liabilities. A sole proprietorship exists as long as the owner wants it to exist or until the owner dies.

A person establishes a sole proprietorship by investing assets in a business. In the business records, the owner should record the invested assets at their current fair values. The fair value of the invested net assets is also recorded in the owner's capital account. The owner's capital account represents the owner's equity interest in the business's net assets. For example, on January 2, 19X1, Casay Calloway invested in a building, subject to a mortgage, and $10,000 cash to begin her business, Casay's Casual Clothes. The fair value of the building is $100,000, and the mortgage value is $80,000. Casay's makes the following entry to record the investment:

19X1			
Jan. 2	Cash	10,000	
	Buildings	100,000	
	Mortgage Payable		80,000
	Casay Calloway, Capital		30,000
	To record investment of assets to begin business.		

Normally, the owner of a business depends on the business for living expenses and, therefore, withdraws cash periodically from the business. Since the owner and the business are not legally separate entities, no formal declaration is required as is the case for dividends of a corporation. When the owner withdraws cash, the business records the amount of the withdrawal in a temporary owner's equity account, called owner's Withdrawals. Withdrawals reduce net assets, but they are not expenses of the business. Assume that on January 31, 19X2, Casay withdraws $1,000 from her business. Casay records the withdrawal as follows:

19X2			
Jan. 31	Casay Calloway, Withdrawals	1,000	
	Cash		1,000
	To record owner's withdrawal.		

At the end of an accounting period, revenue and expense accounts are closed to Income Summary. For a sole proprietorship, Income Summary is closed to the owner's **Capital account** rather than to Retained Earnings as for corporations. Assume Casay's net income for 19X1 is $15,000. Casay would make the following entry to close Income Summary:

Dec. 31	Income Summary	15,000	
	Casay Calloway, Capital		15,000
	To close Income Summary to owner's capital.		

Additionally, owner's Withdrawals is closed to owner's Capital at the end of an accounting period. Assume that for 19X1, Casay withdrew a total of $12,000. The following entry is made to close Withdrawals:

19X1			
Dec.31	Casay Calloway, Capital	12,000	
	Casay Calloway, Withdrawals		12,000
	To close owner's withdrawals to owner's capital.		

After posting the closing entries, the balance in owner's Capital equals the amount of net assets.

THE NATURE OF PARTNERSHIPS

LO 2

Describe the advantages and disadvantages of the partnership form of business.

State laws regulate partnerships, and most states have adopted the Uniform Partnership Act to regulate partnerships within their jurisdictions. Section 16 of the Uniform Partnership Act defines a **partnership** as "an association of two or more persons to carry on as co-owners a business for profit." The provisions of the Act apply to the formation, operation, and dissolution of partnerships. The following sections discuss certain unique characteristics of partnerships.

Voluntary Association

According to its definition, a partnership is not a legal entity, but an association of two or more individuals. In forming a partnership, individuals are free to choose with whom they wish to carry on a business and cannot be forced against their will into joining a partnership. The reasons for the voluntary association feature of partnerships are:

1. Each partner is responsible for the acts of his or her partners, so long as the acts are within the scope of the partnership.
2. Each partner is personally responsible for partnership liabilities.

For example, a partner can enter into a contract on behalf of the partnership. If the contract causes financial distress for the partnership, the law may require individual partners to satisfy partnership liabilities. Given the responsibilities partners assume, it is reasonable to give individuals such freedom to choose with whom to be associated in a business.

Partnership Agreement

A **partnership agreement**, the agreement between two or more persons, governs their association as partners and constitutes a contract that creates the partnership without additional legal formalities. A partnership may be formed by the oral agreement of two or more individuals. However, *written* partnership agreements are usually considered to be a better business practice because written agreements are less likely to be misunderstood. The partnership agreement is an important document to the business's smooth operation and to relations between the partners. A well-written agreement anticipates all important aspects of the partnership and, at a minimum, should include the following:

1. The nature of the business
2. Each partner's rights and duties
3. Each partner's initial investment
4. Subsequent additional investments and withdrawals
5. How partnership income and losses are to be shared
6. Procedures for dissolution of the partnership

Limited Life

Any event or act that terminates the partnership agreement also terminates the partnership. The admission of a new partner, the withdrawal or death of a partner, voluntary dissolution by the partners, and bankruptcy terminate partnerships. Also, some partnership agreements specify that the partnership is for a limited time, such as the time required for the completion of a project; and when the specified event occurs, the partnership terminates. For example, individuals may form a partnership for the purpose of developing new computer software. When the partnership completes development of the software, the partnership terminates.

Unlimited Liability

Under partnership law, each partner is personally liable for all partnership liabilities. If a partnership encounters financial difficulties and cannot pay all of its liabilities, the partnership's creditors must first satisfy their claims out of the partnership's assets. When the partnership's assets are insufficient, creditors may then satisfy their claims out of the partners' personal assets. If one or more partners are insolvent, then the creditors may call upon the remaining partners' assets to satisfy their claims. Also, the law could require any partner to satisfy all of the partnership's liabilities. Hence, each partner has unlimited liability for the partnership's obligations. This feature of partnerships is particularly important when considered in conjunction with the mutual agency feature discussed in the following section.

An exception to the unlimited liability of partnerships exists for limited partnerships. In a **limited partnership**, the liability of the limited partners is only for the amount of their investment in the partnership. However, limited partnerships must have at least one general partner who has unlimited liability.

Mutual Agency

Normally, each partner is an agent of the partnership. This characteristic, referred to as **mutual agency**, means that any partner can enter into a binding agreement on behalf of the partnership, provided the agreement relates to the scope of the partnership's business. For example, a partner in an office equipment business can enter into contracts to purchase and sell office equipment, lease store space, and hire salespersons. A partner could not, however, bind the partnership to the purchase of a sailing yacht because that sort of transaction is not within the scope of an office equipment business.

Co-Ownership of Partnership Property

When the partners admit an individual to a partnership, the new partner's investment may be cash or other property. Property that partners invest in a partnership becomes the partnership's property and is owned jointly by all of the partners. Thus, if the property invested in the partnership increases in value, all the partners share in the increase.

Participation in Partnership Income

Each partner has a right to share in partnership income. Likewise, each partner also shares in partnership losses. As previously indicated, the partnership agreement should specify how partners share income and losses. If the partnership agreement is silent about the sharing of income and losses, the Uniform Partnership Act requires that income and losses be shared equally. Also, if the partnership agreement specifies how income is shared but is silent about losses, the Act requires that losses be shared in the same way as income. Accounting for the distribution of partnership income and losses is discussed in a subsequent section of this chapter.

Summary of Advantages and Disadvantages

There are both advantages and disadvantages to the partnership form of business. The primary disadvantages are limited life, unlimited liability, and mutual agency. Also, the transfer of an ownership interest in a partnership is not as easy as it is for corporations (described in a previous chapter). Some of the advantages of partnerships include the ability to pool the resources and talents of two or more persons, the ease of formation and dissolution, and the freedom of action afforded the partners. Also, because they are not legal entities, partnerships are not subject to income taxes. However, the individual partners are subject to income taxes on their shares of partnership income. Appendix A of this text discusses certain income tax aspects of the various forms of business organizations.

LO 3
Record in the accounting records the formation of a partnership.

FORMATION OF A PARTNERSHIP

The partnership agreement should specify the assets each partner is to invest at the time they form the partnership. The assets they invest may consist of either cash or noncash assets such as inventory and property, plant, and equipment. When partners invest noncash assets in the partnership, they must agree on the assets' valuation. The general rule is that partners should value noncash assets at their fair values at the dates of investment.

Investment of Noncash Assets

To give the investing partner proper credit for his or her investment in the partnership, we record the investment of noncash assets at fair value. The fair values of noncash assets fluctuate; and, therefore, the fair value of an asset at the date the partners form the partnership may be different than its previously recorded cost. The partners determine the fair value of noncash assets by checking current price lists or by having an appraisal performed. In any event, partners have to agree to the fair values assigned to noncash assets invested; and they should specify these amounts in the partnership agreement. We record additional investments by partners in the same way we do initial investments.

Accounting for Partnership Equity

In earlier chapters of this text, GAAP are discussed in the context of a corporation form of business. Those accounting principles also apply to the proprietorship and partnership forms of business. Thus, the recording of assets, liabilities, revenues, and expenses is consistent for both proprietorships and partnerships. However, differences arise between the two forms of business concerning owners' equity. For a proprietorship, there is only a single owner. Therefore, there is only one capital account and one withdrawals account. On the other hand, since a partnership has two or more owners, separate capital and withdrawals accounts are established for each partner. Illustration 12-1 demonstrates the differences in owners' equity for a proprietorship owned by Jones and a partnership consisting of Roberts and Stewart.

ILLUSTRATION 12-1 Owners' Equity T-Accounts

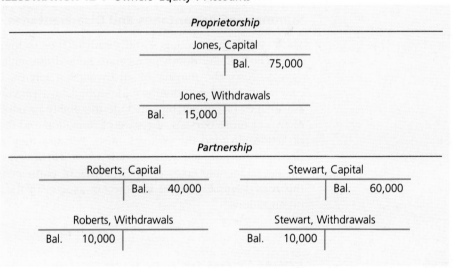

The balance in a partner's capital account on any date consists of the cumulative effect of the partner's initial investment in the partnership, plus any subsequent investments, plus the partner's share of partnership income, less the partner's share of losses, less withdrawals by the partner. In the balance sheet of a partnership, we display separately the balance of each partner's capital account in the partners' equity section, as shown in the partial balance sheet in Illustration 12-2.

We record the investment of assets in the partnership by debiting the appropriate asset account(s) and crediting the investing partner's capital account. For example, assume Lane and Morgan agree to form a partnership. The partnership agreement specifies that Lane is to invest cash of $25,000 and Morgan is to invest

ILLUSTRATION 12-2 Partial Balance Sheet

Liabilities and Partners' Equity		
Current liabilities	$15,000	
Noncurrent liabilities	50,000	
Total liabilities		$ 65,000
Partners' equity:		
Roberts, Capital	$30,000	
Stewart, Capital	50,000	
Total partners' equity		80,000
Total liabilities and partners' equity		$145,000

inventory. Current price lists for the merchandise indicate that the inventory's value is $30,000, and Lane and Morgan agree that $30,000 is the fair value. The following is the general journal entry to record the formation of the partnership:

(Date)	Cash	25,000	
	Merchandise Inventory	30,000	
	Lane, Capital		25,000
	Morgan, Capital		30,000
	To record initial investment of cash and inventory by partners.		

Partnerships may also assume liabilities in conjunction with an investment. For example, assume Lane makes an additional investment of a building that has a fair value of $100,000 at the date of investment and is subject to a $80,000 mortgage. We record Lane's additional investment in the partnership by the following general journal entry:

(Date)	Buildings	100,000	
	Mortgage Payable		80,000
	Lane, Capital		20,000
	To record additional investment by Lane.		

LO 4

Calculate and record the allocation of partnership net income and losses to the partners according to the partnership agreement.

ACCOUNTING FOR PARTNERSHIP INCOME AND LOSSES

According to the terms specified in the partnership agreement, partners share partnership net income and net losses. The income allocated to partners consists of compensation for services partners perform and a monetary return on the capital they invest in the partnership. Ideally, the basis for allocating partnership income to the partners should reflect these two elements of partnership income. The following sections discuss the several bases for allocating partnership income: specified ratio, ratio of invested capital, and allowances for salaries and interest with the remainder at a specified ratio.

Specified Ratio

When partners use a specified ratio to allocate partnership income, the ratio should reflect the relative contributions of the partners. If partners provide the same quantity and quality of services and invest equal amounts of capital, then an equal sharing of partnership income is appropriate. On the other hand, an unequal sharing of income is appropriate when partners provide different amounts of service to the partnership and when there are differences in the amounts of invested capital. Other factors that may result in an unequal sharing of income include superior managerial or technical skills, valuable business contacts, and an established customer base.

Assume the partnership agreement of Ames, Baker, and Cook specifies that income and losses are to be shared 40% by Ames, 30% by Baker, and 30% by Cook. This ratio reflects that Ames is assuming management responsibility for the partnership. At the end of 19X1, we close all partnership revenue and expense accounts to Income Summary. The balance of Income Summary is $40,000, which is the income of the partnership for the year. We allocate the partnership income to the partners as follows:

Ames:	$40,000 x	40% =	$16,000
Baker:	40,000 x	30% =	12,000
Cook:	40,000 x	30% =	12,000
	Total	100%	$40,000

The general journal entry to allocate income to the partners is as follows:

19X1			
Dec. 31	Income Summary	40,000	
	Ames, Capital		16,000
	Baker, Capital		12,000
	Cook, Capital		12,000
	To close Income Summary and to allocate partnership income.		

Ratio of Invested Capital

For many businesses, the amount of invested capital is an important factor in their success. For these businesses, the allocation of partnership income based on the ratio of the partners' invested capital results in a fair allocation. For example, assume the partnership agreement of Banes and Corbett specifies that they will share partnership income in the ratio of their capital accounts. Throughout 19X1, the balances of Banes's and Corbett's capital accounts are $50,000 and $75,000, respectively. Partnership net income for 19X1 is $30,000. We calculate each partner's share of partnership income by multiplying net income of $30,000 by the ratio of that partner's capital account balance to the total of the capital account balances of $125,000 ($50,000 + $75,000). The calculations for Banes and Corbett are shown below:

Banes:	$30,000 x ($50,000 / $125,000) =	$12,000
Corbett:	$30,000 x ($75,000 / $125,000) =	18,000
	Total partnership income	$30,000

The entry to record the allocation of partnership income is as follows:

19X1			
Dec. 31	Income Summary	30,000	
	Banes, Capital		12,000
	Corbett, Capital		18,000
	To close Income Summary and to allocate partnership income.		

For purposes of calculating the ratio, invested capital may be the beginning balance of the partners' capital accounts, the ending balance, or, if partners expect their capital accounts to fluctuate, the weighted-average balance. The partnership agreement should specify how partners determine invested capital. Assume the partnership agreement of Davis and Edwards specifies that partners are to share partnership net income in the ratio of the weighted-average balances of the partners' capital accounts. Income for 19X1 is $60,000, and the partners have the following activities in their capital accounts during 19X1:

	Davis	Edwards
Beginning balance	$100,000	$60,000
Additional investment, April 1	40,000	
Additional investment, July 1		40,000
Withdrawals, October 1		(40,000)
Ending balance	$140,000	$60,000

We calculate the weighted-average capital account balances below. The fractions in the Portion of Year column are the number of months of the year that the specified capital account balance existed.

Davis

Dates	Balance		Portion of Year	Product
1/1 to 3/31	$100,000	x	3/12	$ 25,000
4/1 to 12/31	140,000	x	9/12	105,000
			Weighted-average balance	$130,000

Edwards

Dates	Balance		Portion of Year	Product
1/1 to 6/30	$ 60,000	x	6/12	$30,000
7/1 to 9/30	100,000	x	3/12	25,000
10/1 to 12/31	60,000	x	3/12	15,000
			Weighted-average balance	$70,000

We calculate each partner's share of partnership net income by multiplying income of $60,000 by the ratio of that partner's weighted-average capital balance to the total of the weighted-average capital balances of $200,000 ($130,000 + $70,000). We show the calculations for Davis and Edwards below:

Davis:	$60,000 x ($130,000 / $200,000) = $39,000
Edwards:	$60,000 x ($70,000 / $200,000) = 21,000
	Total partnership net income $60,000

The general journal entry to record the allocation of partnership net income is as follows:

19X1			
Dec. 31	Income Summary	60,000	
	Davis, Capital		39,000
	Edwards, Capital		21,000
	To close Income Summary and to allocate		
	partnership income.		

Allowances for Salaries and Interest

When partners provide unequal services to the partnership, the partnership agreement may specify that partners use salary allowances in allocating net income to recognize the differences in the amount of services. Similarly, when partners' capital contributions are unequal, they may use allowances for interest on invested capital to recognize the differences. If both services and contributed capital are unequal, then the partners may use allowances for both salaries and interest to allocate partnership net income. When partners use salary and interest allowances, they allocate any residual income or loss according to the ratio specified in the partnership agreement. If the agreement does not specify a ratio, then partners share residual income and losses equally as required by the Uniform Partnership Act.

While salary and interest allowances are common provisions of partnership agreements, it is important to note that these distributions are not expenses of the partnership. Although called salaries and interest, they are merely means of allocating net income to the partners. The allowances are not partnership expenses because a partnership is not a legal entity but an association of persons; and the partners cannot pay themselves salaries and interest. Corporations, on the other hand, are legal entities; and salaries and interest paid to employees, who are also owners, are expenses of the corporation. When comparing the financial statements of partnerships and corporations, you should keep this difference in mind and adjust the analysis accordingly.

The following sections illustrate the allocation of partnership income using allowances for salaries and interest.

Allowance for Salaries and Specified Ratio. Assume the partnership agreement of Johnson and Key provides that Johnson is to receive a salary of $30,000 and Key is to receive a salary of $20,000. They are to share equally any residual income or loss. The partners agreed to the difference in the salary allowances because of Johnson's established contacts with customers. Partnership income for 19X1 is $85,000, and we show the allocation to Johnson and Key in Illustration 12-3.

ILLUSTRATION 12-3 Allocation of Partnership Income

	Johnson	Key	Total
Income to be allocated			$85,000
Salaries	$30,000	$20,000	(50,000)
			$35,000
Residual shared equally	17,500	17,500	(35,000)
Total income allocated to each partner	$47,500	$37,500	$ 0

Allowances for Interest and Specified Ratio. Assume the partnership agreement of Lowell and Morris provides that partners are to receive annually an allowance for interest of 12% of the weighted-average capital balances. They are to allocate the remainder, after the allowances for interest, 60% to Lowell and 40% to Morris. The balance of Lowell's capital account remained at $100,000 throughout 19X1. The balance of Morris's capital account is $80,000 on January 1, 19X1; and the only transaction affecting his capital account during 19X1 is an additional investment of $40,000 on October 1, 19X1. The weighted-average balance of Morris's capital account is $90,000, calculated as follows:

		Morris		
Dates	Balance		Portion of Year	Product
1/1 to 9/30	$ 80,000	x	9/12	$60,000
10/1 to 12/31	120,000	x	3/12	30,000
	Weighted-average balance			$90,000

Partnership net income is $32,800 for 19X1, and we show the allocation to the partners in Illustration 12-4.

ILLUSTRATION 12-4 Allocation of Partnership Income

	Lowell	Morris	Total
Income to allocate			$32,800
Interest:			
Lowell			
$100,000 x 12%	$12,000		(12,000)
Morris			
$90,000 x 12%		$10,800	(10,800)
			$10,000
Residual shared 60/40	6,000	4,000	(10,000)
Total income allocated to each partner	$18,000	$14,800	0

Allowances for Salaries and Interest and Specified Ratio. The partnership agreement of Newman and Owen provides for salaries of $24,000 for Newman and $20,000 for Owen. In addition, the partners are to receive interest at the rate of 12% on their weighed-average capital balances. For 19X1, the weighted-average capital balances for Newman and Owen are $100,000 and $120,000, respectively. Finally, the partners are to allocate the remainder, after the salaries and interest, 70% to Newman and 30% to Owen. We show the allocation of the partnership net income of $60,000 for 19X1 to the partners in Illustration 12-5.

ILLUSTRATION 12-5 Allocation of Partnership Income

	Newman	Owen	Total
Income to allocate			$60,000
Salaries	$24,000	$20,000	(44,000)
			$16,000
Interest:			
Newman			
$100,000 x 12%	12,000		(12,000)
Owen			
$120,000 x 12%		14,400	(14,400)
			$(10,400)
Residual shared 70/30	(7,280)	(3,120)	10,400
Total income allocated to each partner	$28,720	$31,280	$ 0

The allocation of income for Newman and Owen shown in Illustration 12-5 demonstrates an important point about allocating partnership income and losses. Notice that the partnership income of $60,000 is not sufficient to cover both the salaries and interest. Nevertheless, *the partners should follow the provisions of the partnership agreement and allocate the salaries and interest as planned, with the resulting negative remainder allocated to the partners as specified in the agreement.* Also, if a partnership incurs a net loss for the year, the partners should continue to allocate salaries and interest to the partners as specified in the agreement and the resulting larger negative remainder allocated according to the agreement.

LO 5

Prepare partnership financial statements.

PARTNERSHIP FINANCIAL STATEMENTS

The financial statements of partnerships are similar to those of corporations. The differences arise in the owners' equity section of the balance sheet because of the differences in the ownership structure of the two forms of business. The partners' equity section of the partnership balance sheet reflects the multiple owners' capital accounts. Partnership income statements are the same as corporate income statements except partnerships do not incur income taxes. We illustrated previously the partners' equity section of a partnership balance sheet in Illustration 12-2.

Instead of a retained earnings statement, a partnership prepares a **statement of partners' capital**. We show a statement of partners' capital in Illustration 12-6. The purpose of the statement is to show the changes in each partner's capital account that occurred during the period. The statement starts with each partner's capital balance at the beginning of the period. Next, it shows increases in the capital account balances. Increases consist of additional investments by the partners and the allocation of net income. After the increases, the statement shows the decreases in the capital accounts. Decreases consist of withdrawals by the partners and allocations of net losses. Finally, the statement presents the capital account balances at the end of the period.

ILLUSTRATION 12-6 Statement of Partners' Capital

	Newman	Owen	Total
Newman and Owen			
Statement of Partners' Capital			
For the Year Ended December 31, 19X1			
Capital, January 1	$ 80,000	$100,000	$180,000
Add: Additional investments	40,000	40,000	80,000
Net income	28,720	31,280	60,000
	$148,720	$171,280	$320,000
Less: Withdrawals	20,000	24,000	44,000
Capital, December 31	$128,720	$147,280	$276,000

LO 6

Explain and record the various forms of partnership dissolution.

PARTNERSHIP DISSOLUTION

When a change in the association of partners occurs, the partnership is *legally* dissolved. Dissolution of a partnership occurs when the partners admit a new partner to the partnership, when a partner withdraws from the partnership, or upon the death of a partner. The admission of new partners and the withdrawal of existing partners can occur through a variety of transactions, all of which dissolve the existing partnership. Upon the dissolution of a partnership, partners must either wind up the affairs of the partnership or form a new partnership.

Admission of a New Partner

The admission of a new partner may occur in two ways:

1. One or more of the original partners may sell all or part of their partnership interests to the new partner.
2. The new partner may invest assets in the partnership.

In either case, the original partners must approve the admission of the new partner. Also, since a new association is formed, the partners should prepare a new partnership agreement that describes the features of the new association.

Sale of an Interest in the Partnership.   Assume the capital balances of Charles Stevens and Jay Tilton are $80,000 and $100,000, respectively. Stevens agrees to sell his $80,000 interest in the partnership to Karen Burns for $95,000. If Tilton agrees to the transaction, the following general journal entry records the transfer of Stevens's interest to Burns:

(Date)	Stevens, Capital	80,000	
	Burns, Capital		80,000
	To record the transfer of Stevens's equity to Burns.		

We show the effects of this transaction on the net assets and the partners' capital accounts in the T-accounts in Illustration 12-7.

ILLUSTRATION 12-7 Partnership T-Accounts

This transaction is external to the partnership and does not affect partnership net assets, which remain at $180,000. Therefore, the entry merely transfers Stevens's recorded equity in the partnership of $80,000 to Burns's capital account. The price negotiated by Stevens and Burns does not affect the entry because the exchange is between the two individuals and does not involve partnership assets. As a result, even though Burns paid Stevens $95,000 for the interest in the partnership, the entry only transfers the $80,000 recorded interest. The $15,000 Stevens received in excess of his capital account balance is, in effect, profit for Stevens from the sale of his partnership interest.

In the transaction above, Burns purchased all of Stevens's interest in the partnership; and, assuming Tilton agrees, they form a new partnership consisting of Tilton and Burns. Instead of completely buying out one partner, the partners may admit a new partner by selling a portion of each of the original partners' interests. Assume that instead of Burns purchasing all of Stevens's interest, Burns purchases one-half of each of the partners' interests, paying Stevens $47,500 and Tilton $65,000. Again, this transaction is external to the partnership; and the prices paid for the two interests do not affect the partnership assets. We show the entry to record this transaction as follows:

(Date)	Stevens, Capital	40,000	
	Tilton, Capital	50,000	
	Burns, Capital		90,000
	To record the transfer of one-half of the equity of		
	Stevens and Tilton to Burns.		

We show the effects of this transaction on the net assets and partners' capital accounts in Illustration 12-8.

ILLUSTRATION 12-8 Partnership T-Accounts

Since the transaction does not affect partnership assets, the transfer is for one-half of Stevens's recorded equity (1/2 x $80,000) and for one-half of Tilton's recorded equity (1/2 x $100,000). As a result of this transaction, the partners form a new partnership consisting of Stevens, Tilton, and Burns.

Investment of Assets in a Partnership. As previously stated, the partners may admit a new partner to the partnership by having the new partner invest assets. In this case, the investment affects partnership assets. Therefore, the amount the new partner invests and the partners' shares of total equity agreed to affects the entry to record the transaction. Assume that Stevens and Tilton agree to admit Burns to the partnership. Under the agreement, Burns is to receive a one-fourth interest in exchange for investing $60,000 cash in the partnership. After Burns's investment, the net assets are $240,000 ($180,000 + $60,000) and partnership equity is as follows:

Stevens, Capital	$ 80,000
Tilton, Capital	100,000
Burns, Capital	60,000
Total	$240,000

In this case, the $60,000 Burns invested for a one-fourth interest is equal to one-fourth of the net assets after the investment and one-fourth of the new partnership equity (1/4 x $240,000 = $60,000). We show the entry to record Burns's investment below:

(Date)	Cash	60,000	
	Burns, Capital		60,000
	To record investment by Burns for a one-fourth interest in the partnership.		

We show the effects of this transaction on the net assets and the partners' capital accounts in Illustration 12-9.

ILLUSTRATION 12-9 Partnership T-Accounts

Although Burns receives a 25% interest for her investment, the income and loss sharing ratio may be different from the capital ratios. The new partnership agreement should specify the income and loss sharing ratio to which the partners agree.

Bonus to the Original Partners.   Because of the cost principle, the carrying amount of assets over time does not necessarily represent their fair value. For example, plant assets may have increased in value since the business purchased them; however, we do not record the increase in value. As a result, the recorded amount of partnership equity may be an amount that is less than the fair value of the partnership's net assets. In this case, when partners admit a new partner by having the new partner invest assets in the partnership, the amount invested may be more than the new partner's share of the partnership net assets and equity.

Assume Stevens and Tilton agree to admit Burns to the partnership. The agreement specifies that Burns is to receive a one-fourth interest in exchange for investing $80,000 cash in the partnership. After Burns's investment, the total partnership net assets and equity will be $260,000 as follows:

Stevens, Capital	$ 80,000
Tilton, Capital	100,000
Burns, investment	80,000
Total	$260,000

In this transaction, Burns is giving a bonus of $15,000 to Stevens and Tilton, calculated as follows:

Investment	$80,000
One-fourth interest (1/4 x $260,000)	65,000
Bonus to the old partners	$15,000

When the new partner gives a bonus, we allocate the bonus to the old partners based on their original income and loss sharing ratio. Because it represents income from the increases in the assets' fair values that have not been recorded, we use the income and loss sharing ratio to allocate the bonus to the old partners. If Stevens and Tilton share income and losses equally, we allocate the $15,000 bonus $7,500 to each. The following entry records the admission of the new partner and the allocation of the bonus to the old partners:

(Date)	Cash	80,000	
	Stevens, Capital		7,500
	Tilton, Capital		7,500
	Burns, Capital		65,000
	To record investment by Burns for a one-fourth interest in the partnership.		

Bonus to the New Partner. As an inducement to join the partnership, the old partners may be willing to give a larger interest in the partnership than the amount of investment the new partner makes. The old partners are willing to give a bonus to a new partner because the individual may have some desirable talent, possess an established customer base, or the partnership may need additional capital to expand operations.

Assume Stevens and Tilton agree to admit Burns to the partnership. Burns is to receive a one-fourth interest in exchange for a cash investment of $40,000. After Burns's investment, the total partnership net assets and equity will be $220,000 as follows:

Stevens, Capital	$ 80,000
Tilton, Capital	100,000
Burns, investment	40,000
Total	$220,000

In this case, Burns receives a bonus of $15,000, calculated as follows:

One-fourth interest (1/4 x $220,000)	$55,000
Investment	40,000
Bonus to Burns	$15,000

We always allocate to the old partners in their original income and loss sharing ratio the bonus given to a new partner. Assume Stevens and Tilton share income and losses in the ratio of 1/3 − 2/3, respectively. We show the entry to record Burns's admission to the partnership below:

(Date)	Cash	40,000	
	Stevens, Capital	5,000	
	Tilton, Capital	10,000	
	Burns, Capital		55,000
	To record investment by Burns for a one-fourth interest in the partnership.		

Withdrawal from a Partnership

Because a partnership is a voluntary association of two or more individuals, a partner can withdraw at any time he or she chooses. A well-written partnership agreement should anticipate that partners may withdraw and should specify the procedures to be followed. In general, a partner can withdraw by two ways:

1. Selling his or her interest in the partnership (previously covered).
2. Withdrawing assets from the partnership.

As shown in the right side of Illustration 12-10, partners have several ways of withdrawing assets.

ILLUSTRATION 12-10 Forms of Partnership Withdrawals

The following sections illustrate the accounting for each way of withdrawing from a partnership. For each of the examples, assume that partners Rhonda Addison, Jill Bailey, and Roy Carey have the capital balances listed below:

Addison, Capital	$ 80,000
Bailey, Capital	100,000
Carey, Capital	60,000
Total	$240,000

Withdrawal of Assets Equal to Recorded Equity. As previously mentioned, the partnership agreement should specify the procedures required when a partner withdraws. When a partner withdraws by taking partnership assets, a common procedure is to restate partnership assets and equity to their current fair values. Also, an audit may be performed to ensure that the partnership records are in order. An advantage of restating the assets to their current fair values is that the withdrawing partner's capital account reflects the current fair value of his or her equity. In such cases, the agreement usually provides that the withdrawing partner take assets equal to his or her restated capital account.

Assume that Carey decides to withdraw from Addison, Bailey, and Carey. The agreement specifies that at the time of withdrawal, a partner is to receive assets equal to the balance in his capital account after it is restated to reflect the current fair values of partnership assets. The partners agree that the present carrying amounts of the assets are equal to their current fair values. If Carey takes a promissory note, instead of cash, equal to the balance in his capital account of $60,000, the following entry is needed to record the withdrawal:

(Date)	Carey, Capital	60,000	
	Notes Payable (to Carey)		60,000
	To record the withdrawal of Carey from the partnership.		

The withdrawal of Carey reduces the partnership's net assets by $60,000. We show the effects of the transaction on the net assets and partners' capital accounts in the T-accounts in Illustration 12-11.

ILLUSTRATION 12-11 Partnership T-Accounts

Withdrawal of Assets Worth More Than Recorded Equity. A partner may sometimes decide to withdraw, and the remaining partners may decide not to restate the partnership assets to their current fair values. If the recorded amounts of assets are less than their current fair values, then the withdrawing partner's recorded equity is less than its current fair value. To be fair, the withdrawing partner should receive assets worth more than his or her recorded equity and equal to his or her share of the net assets' fair value. Another reason why a withdrawing partner may receive assets worth more than his or her recorded equity is that the other partners are willing to give the partner a bonus to induce the withdrawal. When a partner withdraws and takes assets worth more than his or her recorded equity, the partners deduct the excess amount from the remaining partners' capital accounts according to their income and loss sharing ratio.

Assume in the partnership of Addison, Bailey, and Carey, the income and loss sharing ratio is 25/50/25, respectively. Carey decides to withdraw from the partnership, and the partners agree not to restate the assets to their current fair values. The partners also agree that the current fair value of partnership assets is $40,000 higher than their recorded amounts. If the partners restate assets, they would credit Carey's capital account for his share of the increase, or $10,000

(25% x $40,000). This means that the current fair value of Carey's equity is $70,000 ($60,000 + $10,000). The partners agree to giving Carey $70,000 cash when the withdrawal occurs. We allocate the additional amount given to a withdrawing partner to the remaining partners according to their relative income and loss sharing ratio. For Addison and Bailey, we calculate their relative ratio as follows:

$$\text{Addison:} \quad 25\% \div (25\% + 50\%) = 1/3$$
$$\text{Bailey:} \quad 50\% \div (25\% + 50\%) = 2/3$$

Therefore, we allocate Addison $3,333.33 (1/3 x $10,000) and Bailey $6,666.67 (2/3 x $10,000). The entry to record Carey's withdrawal is as follows:

(Date)	Carey, Capital	60,000.00	
	Addison, Capital	3,333.33	
	Bailey, Capital	6,666.67	
	Cash		70,000.00
	To record the withdrawal of Carey from the partnership.		

Withdrawal of Assets Worth Less Than Recorded Equity. A partner sometimes withdraws and takes assets that are worth less than his or her recorded equity. This situation may arise for two reasons. First, the carrying amount of partnership assets may be more than their current fair values, and the partners decide not to restate the assets. Second, the withdrawing partner may be so anxious to withdraw that he or she is willing to accept less than recorded equity. Assume that Carey is anxious to withdraw from the partnership of Addison, Bailey, and Carey and agrees to accept $54,000 cash even though his recorded equity is $60,000. We allocate the amount of the equity in excess of the assets Carey takes, $6,000, to the remaining partners in their relative income and loss sharing ratio. If the income and loss sharing ratio for the partnership is 25/50/25, then we allocate Addison $2,000 ($6,000 x 1/3) and Bailey $4,000 ($6,000 x 2/3). The entry to record Carey's withdrawal is as follows:

(Date)	Carey, Capital	60,000	
	Addison, Capital		2,000
	Bailey, Capital		4,000
	Cash		54,000
	To record the withdraw of Carey from the partnership.		

Death of a Partner

When a partner dies, a partnership terminates because the association is broken. The partnership agreement should specify the procedures partners will follow upon the death of a partner. Normal procedures include:

1. Determining the fair values of partnership assets
2. Closing the books to determine partnership income or loss since the end of the previous accounting period
3. Allocating partnership income or loss to the partners so that the partner capital accounts are stated at the appropriate balances as of the date of death
4. Having an audit performed to ensure that the partnership records are in order

The final disposition of the deceased partner's equity must be agreed to by his or her estate and by the remaining partners. The estate of the deceased partner may sell his or her interest to one or more of the remaining partners or to an outsider; or the estate may withdraw assets from the partnership. The entries for these transactions resulting from the decisions of the deceased partner's estate are the same as those discussed previously for withdrawals by living partners.

LO 7

Record the transactions related to the liquidation of partnerships.

PARTNERSHIP LIQUIDATION

Liquidating a partnership involves ending its operations, settling its debts, and either requiring additional contributions from partners to settle the debts or distributing assets to them. The procedures normally followed for liquidation include: closing the books and allocating partnership income or loss to the partners, selling partnership assets to convert them to cash, allocating gains and losses from selling the assets to partners in their income and loss sharing ratio, paying partnership creditors, and distributing cash to partners equal to the balances in their capital accounts. Although many situations can arise leading to partnership liquidation, we discuss only three:

1. Partners sell partnership assets for a gain.
2. Partners sell partnership assets for a loss, and there is sufficient partner equity.
3. Partners sell partnership assets for a loss, and one partner has insufficient equity.

Assets Sold for a Gain

Because of declining demand for their services, Rita Davis, Jackson Ewing, and Donald Fox decide to end operations. The income and loss sharing ratio for the partners is 25/50/25, respectively. After closing the accounts and allocating partnership net income, the partnership has the balance sheet shown in Illustration 12-12.

ILLUSTRATION 12-12 Partnership Balance Sheet

Davis, Ewing, and Fox Balance Sheet October 1, 19X1			
Assets		**Liabilities and Partners' Equity**	
Cash	$ 10,000	Accounts payable	$ 10,000
Accounts receivable	50,000	Davis, capital	80,000
Merchandise inventory	120,000	Ewing, capital	100,000
Equipment (net)	70,000	Fox, capital	60,000
		Total liabilities and	
Total assets	$250,000	partners' equity	$250,000

The next step in the liquidation is for the partners to convert all noncash assets to cash by selling them. When they sell the assets, partners normally incur a gain or loss. In the entry to record the sale of assets, we credit or debit the gain or loss to an account called Gain (Loss) from Realization. In the process of converting the assets to cash, assume: (1) The partners collect only $49,500 of the accounts receivable. (2) The partners sell the merchandise inventory for $125,000. (3) The partners sell the equipment for $77,500. We show the entries to record these transactions as follows:

(1) (Date)	Cash	49,500	
	Gain (Loss) from Realization	500	
	Accounts Receivable		50,000
	To record collection of accounts receivable.		
(2) (Date)	Cash	125,000	
	Merchandise Inventory		120,000
	Gain (Loss) from Realization		5,000
	To record sale of merchandise inventory.		
(3) (Date)	Cash	77,500	
	Equipment		70,000
	Gain (Loss) from Realization		7,500
	To record sale of equipment.		

Notice that we credit gains to Gain (Loss) from Realization, and we debit losses to the account. After the partners sell all of the assets, Gain (Loss) from Realization has either a debit balance, if there is a net loss incurred in selling the partnership assets, or a credit balance, if there is a net gain from selling the assets. The three transactions of the Davis, Ewing, and Fox partnership result in a net gain of $12,000. The T-account shown below presents the three entries in Gain (Loss) from Realization.

	Gain (Loss) from Realization	
(1)	500	(2)	5,000
		(3)	7,500
		Bal.	12,000

We then allocate the net gain to the partners according to their income and loss sharing ratio. The entry to allocate the gain is as follows:

(Date)	Gain (Loss) from Realization	12,000	
	Davis, Capital		3,000
	Ewing, Capital		6,000
	Fox, Capital		3,000
	To close Gain (Loss) from Realization.		

We show the effects of the above entry on the partners' capital accounts in Illustration 12-13.

The next step in the liquidation process is for the partners to pay the creditors. Before the partners distribute any cash to themselves, they must first pay any creditors. By paying creditors before distributing cash to themselves, they avoid the risk of insufficient cash to pay the creditors. We show the entry to record the payment of creditors below:

(Date)	Accounts Payable	10,000	
	Cash		10,000
	To record the payment of creditors.		

ILLUSTRATION 12-13 Partnership T-Accounts, Gain from Realization

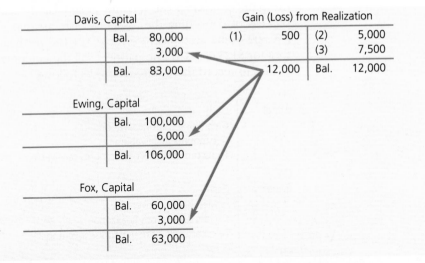

After the partners sell the assets and pay the creditors, the only balance sheet accounts with balances are Cash and the partners' capital accounts, as shown in Illustration 12-14.

ILLUSTRATION 12-14 Partnership Balance Sheet, Gain from Realization

Davis, Ewing, and Fox Balance Sheet December 1, 19X1			
Assets		**Partners' Equity**	
Cash	$252,000	Davis, capital	$ 83,000
		Ewing, capital	106,000
		Fox, capital	63,000
Total assets	$252,000	Partners' equity	$252,000

The final step in the liquidation process is for the partners to distribute the cash to themselves in the amount of their capital account balances. Notice that the capital account balances are not in the income and loss sharing ratio. Partners distribute the cash to themselves according to their capital balances. The entry to record the distribution of the cash to the partners is as follows:

(Date)	Davis, Capital	83,000	
	Ewing, Capital	106,000	
	Fox, Capital	63,000	
	Cash		252,000
	To record final distribution of cash to partners according to balances in their capital accounts.		

After this entry, all partnership accounts are closed, all partnership assets have been distributed, and the operations of the partnership have ceased.

Assets Sold for a Loss—Sufficient Partner Equity

In the previous example of a partnership liquidation, the partners sold their partnership assets for a net gain. However, the sale of assets sometimes results in a net loss. Assume that, instead of selling the assets for $252,000, the partnership of Davis, Ewing, and Fox only realizes $200,000 from the sale of the partnership assets. The carrying amount of the assets sold is $240,000, and the partners incur a loss of $40,000. The sale of the assets may be summarized in a single entry as follows:

(Date)	Cash	200,000	
	Gain (Loss) from Realization	40,000	
	Accounts Receivable		50,000
	Merchandise Inventory		120,000
	Equipment		70,000
	To record collection of accounts receivable and sale of merchandise inventory and equipment.		

After converting the assets to cash, the partners allocate the net loss incurred to the capital accounts according to their income and loss sharing ratio of 25/50/25. We show the entry to allocate the loss and to close Gain (Loss) from Realization below:

(Date)	Davis, Capital	10,000	
	Ewing, Capital	20,000	
	Fox, Capital	10,000	
	Gain (Loss) from Realization		40,000
	To close Gain (Loss) from Realization.		

We show the effects of the entry on the partners' capital balances in the T-accounts in Illustration 12-15.

ILLUSTRATION 12-15 Partnership T-Accounts, Loss from Realization

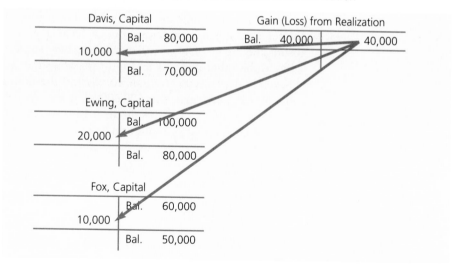

Before partners distribute any cash to themselves, they must pay the creditors. We show the entry to record the payment of the creditors below:

(Date)	Accounts Payable	10,000	
	Cash		10,000
	To record payment of creditors.		

The balance sheet shown in Illustration 12-16 presents the balances of the partnership accounts after creditors are paid.

ILLUSTRATION 12-16 Partnership Balance Sheet, Loss from Realization

Davis, Ewing, and Fox Balance Sheet December 1, 19X1			
Assets		*Partners' Equity*	
Cash	$200,000	Davis, capital	$ 70,000
		Ewing, capital	80,000
		Fox, capital	50,000
Total assets	$200,000	Partners' equity	$200,000

The balance sheet shows that even though converting the assets to cash results in a loss, all of the partners have sufficient equity to absorb their share of the loss. Therefore, the liquidation of the partnership may proceed by distributing the remaining cash to the partners according to the balances in their capital accounts. The entry to record the distribution of cash is as follows:

(Date)	Davis, Capital	70,000	
	Ewing, Capital	80,000	
	Fox, Capital	50,000	
	Cash		200,000
	To record final distribution of cash to partners according to their capital account balances.		

Assets Sold for a Loss—One Partner Has Insufficient Equity

In the previous example, all partners have sufficient equity to absorb the loss incurred in converting the partnership assets to cash. Sometimes, however, a partner may not have a large enough balance in his or her capital account to absorb the share of loss. In such cases, the partner with insufficient equity is liable to the other partners and must make up the deficit. Assume that, because of severely depressed economic conditions, the noncash assets of Davis, Ewing, and Fox can only generate $20,000 of cash. Since the assets have a carrying amount of $240,000, this results in a loss of $220,000. We show the entry to summarize the conversion of partnership assets to cash below:

(Date)	Cash	20,000	
	Gain (Loss) from Realization	220,000	
	Accounts Receivable		50,000
	Merchandise Inventory		120,000
	Equipment		70,000
	To record collection of accounts receivable and sale of merchandise inventory and equipment.		

The next entry allocates the loss to the partners in their income and loss sharing ratio:

(Date)	Davis, Capital	55,000	
	Ewing, Capital	110,000	
	Fox, Capital	55,000	
	Gain (Loss) from Realization		220,000
	To close Gain (Loss) from Realization.		

We show the effects of this entry on the partners' capital accounts in Illustration 12-17.

ILLUSTRATION 12-17 Partnership T-Accounts, Partner with Insufficient Equity

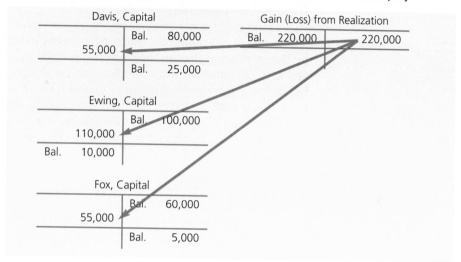

After the partners pay the accounts payable of $10,000, the account balances of the partnership are as shown in Illustration 12-18.

ILLUSTRATION 12-18 Partnership Balance Sheet, Partner with Insufficient Equity

Davis, Ewing, and Fox Balance Sheet December 1, 19X1			
Assets		*Partners' Equity*	
Cash	$20,000	Davis, capital	$ 25,000
		Ewing, capital	(10,000)
		Fox, capital	5,000
Total assets	$20,000	Partners' equity	$ 20,000

As the balance sheet shows, Ewing's capital account balance is insufficient to absorb his share of the loss. Ewing is responsible for investing additional assets in the amount of his capital account's deficit. Assuming Ewing has personal assets of $10,000, the entry to record the additional investment is as follows:

(Date)	Cash	10,000	
	Ewing, Capital		10,000
	To record additional investment by Ewing.		

After Ewing's additional investment, the partnership has cash of $30,000, which the partners distribute to Davis and Fox according to the balances in their capital accounts.

(Date)	Davis, Capital	25,000	
	Fox, Capital	5,000	
	Cash		30,000
	To record final distribution of cash to partners according to their capital account balances.		

After this entry, all partnership account balances are zero; and the partners have liquidated the partnership.

A partner who has insufficient equity to absorb his or her share of a loss realized from converting the partnership assets to cash is sometimes personally insolvent. Assume that, in the previous example, Ewing is personally insolvent and cannot contribute funds to eliminate his deficit. In such cases, we allocate the deficit in the insolvent partner's capital account to the other partners according to their relative income and loss sharing ratio. Davis and Fox share income and losses 25/25, respectively. Therefore, we allocate each one half of the $10,000 deficit in Ewing's capital account. The entry to allocate Ewing's deficit is as follows:

(Date)	Davis, Capital	5,000	
	Fox, Capital	5,000	
	Ewing, Capital		10,000
	To allocate Ewing's deficit to the remaining partners in their relative income and loss sharing ratio.		

Allocating Ewing's deficit to the other partners does not relieve Ewing of his liability for the deficit. In this case, Davis and Fox join Ewing's personal creditors with respect to rights to Ewing's personal assets.

After we allocate Ewing's deficit to Davis and Fox, the capital account balances of both Ewing and Fox are zero. The capital account balance of Davis is $20,000, which is equal to the amount of cash of the partnership. The final step is to record the distribution of the cash to Davis with the following entry:

(Date)	Davis, Capital	20,000	
	Cash		20,000
	To record final distribution of cash according to partners' capital account balances.		

Ray Johnson's Partnership Decision

At the beginning of this chapter, Ray Johnson considered forming a partnership with his Uncle Hank. The discussion in this chapter addresses the concerns that Ray had about the partnership. Keep in mind that one advantage of the partnership form of business over proprietorships is that it allows a business to grow by joining individuals who can provide more resources than just one individual. Hank's willingness to invest capital in the business is why Ray considers forming a partnership with Hank.

One of Ray's questions involved the division of profits. Since Hank wants to be a passive investor, not involved in daily management, Ray should structure the partnership agreement to provide a management salary for himself. On the other hand, the agreement should provide interest to Hank for the capital that he would invest. The division of any residual income (or losses) is a matter that Ray and Hank will have to negotiate. It is important that the partnership agreement accurately reflect what Ray and Hank agree to and that the agreement contemplates all contingencies. It is probably well worth the cost for Ray to engage an attorney experienced in partnership law to prepare the agreement.

Another concern Ray had was how the partnership would affect him personally if the business fails. One of the disadvantages of the partnership form of business is the partners' personal liability for the partnership's debts. Also, since individual partners can enter into business transactions on behalf of the partnership, Ray's decision may depend on how well he knows and trusts Hank. For instance, Ray's personal finances could be affected dramatically if Hank were to commit the partnership to debts and then the business fails. Ray might be called upon to pay some of the partnership debts with his personal assets.

Ultimately, Ray will have to weigh the advantages and disadvantages of partnerships relative to other forms of businesses. A corporation is another form of business that offers both advantages and disadvantages relative to proprietorships and partnerships. (We discuss corporations in previous chapters of this text.)

SUMMARY

Account for the transactions of a sole proprietorship.   A sole proprietorship is a business owned by one person. Accounting for a sole proprietorship differs from a corporation only in accounting for owner's equity. The owner's investment is recorded in his or her capital account. Income Summary is closed to owner's Capital. Withdrawals of assets by the owner are recorded in owner's Withdrawals, which is closed to owner's Capital.

Describe the advantages and disadvantages of the partnership form of business. A partnership is an association of two or more persons to carry on a business for profit as co-owners. The advantages of the partnership form of business include the ability to pool the resources and talents of more than one person, the ease of formation and dissolution, and the freedom of action afforded the partners. Disadvantages include limited life, unlimited liability, mutual agency, and restrictions on transferring an ownership interest.

Record in the accounting records the formation of a partnership.   Individuals form partnerships by contributing cash and/or noncash assets to the partnership. We record the assets that the partners invest at their fair values at the time of the investment. At the same time, we record each partner's capital at the fair value of the assets that each invested in the partnership.

Calculate and record the allocation of partnership net income and losses to the partners according to the partnership agreement.   A partner's capital account is increased by investments and his or her share of partnership income and is decreased by withdrawals and his or her share of partnership losses. Partnership net income and losses may be allocated to partners according to a specified ratio, the ratio of invested capital, or allowances for salaries and interest with the remainder at a specified ratio.

Prepare partnership financial statements.   Accounting for partnerships differs from corporations only for partners' equity. A separate capital account is maintained for each partner. Other than displaying each partner's capital account in the partners' equity section of the balance sheet and the preparation of a statement of partners' capital, financial statements for partnerships are the same as for corporations.

Explain and record the various forms of partnership dissolution.   Partners legally dissolve partnerships when a change in the association of the partners occurs. Partnership dissolution results from the admission of a new partner, the withdrawal of a partner, or the death of a partner. When dissolution occurs, partners must either wind up the affairs of the association and liquidate the partnership or form a new partnership.

Record the transactions related to the liquidation of partnerships. Partnership liquidations involve closing the books and allocating partnership income or loss to the partners, selling partnership assets, allocating gains and losses from selling assets to the partners, paying partnership creditors, and distributing cash to the partners.

REVIEW PROBLEM

Harold Gabris and Sarah Golaan form a partnership on January 1, 19X4, to provide household maintenance services in their local area. Gabris contributes $5,000 in cash and a carpet cleaner with a cost of $2,300 and a fair value of $1,500. Golaan contributes $4,000 in cash, a commercial vacuum cleaner worth $1,200, and a truck with a fair value of $2,500. During the first year of operations, they generated $95,000 in revenue and incurred $34,500 in expenses. Gabris and Golaan each withdrew $12,000 during the year. By the end of the year, business volume had grown high enough to need another partner to work in the business.

On January 2, 19X5, Stevesen is admitted to the partnership upon contributing $25,000 to the partnership assets. The partners agree to share profits 35%, 35%, 30% to Gabris, Golaan, and Stevesen, respectively. The revenues for the year total $165,000, and the expenses incurred total $66,000. During the year each of the partners withdrew $15,000.

REQUIRED:

a. Record the journal entries affecting capital accounts for 19X4 and prepare a statement of partners' capital. They operate on a calendar year basis.
b. Record the journal entries affecting capital accounts for 19X5 and prepare a statement of partners' capital.

SOLUTION:

Planning and Organizing Your Work

1. Analyze the formation of the partnership and prepare the journal entries. Remember that noncash assets contributed to a partnership are recorded at their fair values.
2. For 19X4, close the $60,500 balance in Income Summary to the partners' capital accounts according to their income and loss distribution agreement. Close the partners' withdrawals accounts to their capital accounts.
3. Prepare the 19X4 statement of partners' capital using the information from your journal entries.
4. Repeat the procedures (including the admission of the new partner) for 19X5 using the information provided.

(a) *Record journal entries for 19X4 and prepare a statement.*
The equipment is recorded at fair value.

19X4			
Jan. 1	Equipment	1,500	
	Cash	5,000	
	Gabris, Capital		6,500
	To record investment in partnership.		

The equipment and the truck are both recorded at fair value.

Jan. 1	Equipment	1,200	
	Truck	2,500	
	Cash	4,000	
	Golaan, Capital		7,700
	To record investment in partnership.		

(Date)	Gabris, Withdrawals	12,000	
	Golaan, Withdrawals	12,000	
	Cash		24,000
	To record partners' withdrawals during year.		

Dec. 31	Income Summary	60,500	
	Gabris, Capital		30,250
	Golaan, Capital		30,250
	To close Income Summary to Capital.		

The profits are shared equally under the Uniform Partnership Act because the partners made no mention of a ratio for sharing profits and losses.

Dec. 31	Gabris, Capital	12,000	
	Golaan, Capital	12,000	
	Gabris, Withdrawals		12,000
	Golaan, Withdrawals		12,000
	To close withdrawals to Capital.		

Gabris and Golaan
Statement of Partners' Capital
December 31, 19X4

	Gabris	Golaan	Total
Beginning capital, 1/1/X4	$ 0	$ 0	$ 0
Investments by partners	6,500	7,700	14,200
Income for 19X4	30,250	30,250	60,500
Subtotal	$36,750	$37,950	$74,700
Partners' withdrawals	12,000	12,000	24,000
Ending capital, 12/31/X4	$24,750	$25,950	$50,700

(b) *Record journal entries for 19X5 and prepare a statement.*

19X5			
Jan. 2	Cash	25,000	
	Stevesen, Capital		25,000
	To record Stevesen's admission to partnership.		

(Date)	Gabris, Withdrawals	15,000	
	Golaan, Withdrawals	15,000	
	Stevesen, Withdrawals	15,000	
	Cash		45,000
	To record partners' withdrawals during year.		

Dec. 31	Income Summary	99,000	
	Gabris, Capital		34,650
	Golaan, Capital		34,650
	Stevesen, Capital		29,700
	To close Income Summary to Capital.		
	Gabris ($99,000 x .35 = $34,650)		
	Golaan ($99,000 x .35 = $34,650)		
	Stevesen ($99,000 x .30 = $29,700)		

Dec. 31	Gabris, Capital	15,000	
	Golaan, Capital	15,000	
	Stevesen, Capital	15,000	
	Gabris, Withdrawals		15,000
	Golaan, Withdrawals		15,000
	Stevesen, Withdrawals		15,000
	To close withdrawals to Capital.		

Gabris, Golaan, and Steveson
Statement of Partners' Capital
December 31, 19X5

	Gabris	Golaan	Stevesen	Total
Beginning capital, 1/1/X5	$24,750	$25,950	$ 0	$ 50,700
Investment by Stevesen			25,000	25,000
Subtotal	$24,750	$25,950	$25,000	$ 75,700
Income for 19X5	34,650	34,650	29,700	99,000
Subtotal	$59,400	$60,600	$54,700	$174,700
Partners' withdrawals	15,000	15,000	15,000	45,000
Ending capital, 12/31/X5	$44,400	$45,600	$39,700	$129,700

KEY TERMS

capital account, *529*
co-ownership of partnership
  property, *531*
limited life, *530*

limited partnership, *530*
mutual agency, *530*
partnership, *529*
partnership agreement, *529*

sole proprietorship, *528*
statement of partners' capital,
  538
unlimited liability, *530*

SELF-QUIZ

LO 1 1. True or False. Owners of sole proprietorships are not responsible for their business's liabilities.

LO 1 2. To what account is Income Summary closed in a sole proprietorship?

LO 1 3. What does the balance in an owner's capital account equal after the year-end closing entries are made?

LO 2 4. Indicate which of the following items are part of the definition of the term *partnership*:

    ___ a. Amalgamation
    ___ b. Conglomeration
    ___ c. Association
    ___ d. Two or more persons
    ___ e. Three or more persons
    ___ f. Four or more persons
    ___ g. Business for profit
    ___ h. Legal entity
    ___ i. Limited liability

    ___ j. Mandatory
    ___ k. Voluntary
    ___ l. Regulatory
    ___ m. Shareholder
    ___ n. Co-owner
    ___ o. Co-resident
    ___ p. Co-director

LO 2 5. Indicate which of the following are among the minimum key elements of a partnership agreement:

    ___ a. Business nature
    ___ b. Projected cash flows
    ___ c. State of incorporation
    ___ d. Income sharing agreement
    ___ e. Chart of accounts
    ___ f. Trial balance
    ___ g. Original investments
    ___ h. Subsequent investments and withdrawals

___ i. Partner's previous business experience

___ j. Dissolution procedures

LO 2   6. Indicate which of the following are considered to be disadvantages of the partnership form of business organization:

___ a. Ease of formation

___ b. Unlimited liability

___ c. Freedom of action

___ d. Limited life

___ e. Pooling resources

___ f. Mutual agency

LO 2   7. A partnership agreement may be

a. Oral

b. Written

c. a and b

d. None of the above

LO 3   8. Assets invested in a partnership are recorded at

a. The lower of depreciated cost or fair value

b. The lower of cost or fair value

c. Fair value

d. Depreciated cost

LO 3   9. Partnership capital balances include the cumulative effect of

a. Initial investments

b. Subsequent investments

c. Shares of income

d. Shares of losses

e. Withdrawals

f. All of the above

g. None of the above

LO 3   10. Partner's investments may include which of the following?

a. Cash assets

b. Noncash assets

c. Noncash assets subject to debt claims

d. Only a and b above

e. a, b, and c above

LO 4   11. In calculating the allocation of partnership income to partners, where no mention is made of income sharing in the partnership agreement, which of the following ratios would be used?

a. Ratio of beginning capital balances

b. Ratio of weighted-average capital balances

c. Ratio of ending capital balances

d. None of the above

LO 4   12. Indicate which of the following distributions would be made last in allocating partnership income to the partners, where interest on capital balances and salary allowances to partners are involved

a. Specified ratio

b. Salary allowance

c. Interest on capital balances

d. None of the above would be last.

LO 4   13. For the most equitable distribution of partnership income based on invested capital, the partnership agreement should specify which of the following is considered invested capital?

a. Beginning capital

b. Ending capital

c. Weighted-average capital

d. None of the above

LO 5   14. A statement of partners' capital should include all of the following *except*

a. Partners' beginning capital balances

b. Partners' investments during the period

c. Partners' share of income for the period

d. Partners' withdrawals during the period

e. Partners' ending capital balances

f. Partners' payments of loans

LO 6   15. Partnerships are dissolved when

a. A new partner is admitted

b. Partner withdraws

c. Partner dies

d. Partners agree to dissolve

e. All of the above

f. None of the above

LO 6   16. When partners agree to sell a portion of their respective interests to a new partner, the journal entry to record the transaction on the partnership books includes

a. Debiting Cash for the investment

b. Debiting the capital account of the new partner

c. Debiting the capital accounts of the old partners

d. None of the above

LO 6   17. When partners agree to admit a new partner to the partnership in exchange for an investment of cash or other assets in the partnership, the new partner's capital account can reflect an amount

a. Equal to the investment

b. Greater than the investment

c. Less than the investment

d. Any of the above

e. None of the above

LO 6   18. When a partner elects to withdraw, the amount of cash or other assets paid in settlement of the partner's capital interest may be

a. Worth more than the withdrawing partner's recorded equity

b. Worth less than the withdrawing partner's recorded equity

c. Worth an amount equal to the withdrawing partner's recorded equity

d. Any of the above

e. None of the above

LO 6   19. When a partner dies, the partners should

a. Retire all partnership debt

b. Close the books of the partnership

c. Determine the fair value of the partnership assets

d. b and c
e. None of the above

20. Partnership dissolution (without liquidation) results in
   a. Closing the business and selling the assets
   b. Creating a new partnership and replacing the old one
   c. Terminating the old partnership agreement
   d. b and c
   e. None of the above

LO 7 21. The liquidation of a partnership results in
   a. Closing the business and selling the assets
   b. Creating a new partnership and replacing the old one
   c. Terminating the old partnership agreement
   d. b and c only
   e. None of the above

LO 7 22. Which of the following is *not* associated with the liquidation of a partnership?
   a. Converting partnership assets to cash
   b. Paying creditors
   c. Admitting a new partner
   d. Closing the books and allocating income or losses to the partners' capital accounts

LO 7 23. In converting partnership assets to cash, any differences between the proceeds of sale and the carrying amount of the assets sold should be recorded as a
   a. Debit to the partners' equity accounts
   b. Debit to the partners' withdrawals accounts
   c. Debit or credit to Gain (Loss) from Realization
   d. Debit or credit to Income Summary
   e. None of the above

SOLUTIONS TO SELF-QUIZ

1. False	2. Owner's Capital	3. Net assets of the business	4. c, d, g, k, n	5. a, d, g, h, k	6. b, d, and f	7. c
8. c	9. f	10. e	11. d	12. a	13. c	14. f	15. e	16. c	17. d	18. d	19. d	20. d	21. a
22. c	23. c					

QUESTIONS

Q12-1 Define sole proprietorship.

Q12-2 What determines the life of a sole proprietorship?

Q12-3 What makes up an owner's capital account in a sole proprietorship?

Q12-4 Define partnership.

Q12-5 List six important elements that should be included in a partnership agreement.

Q12-6 Match the following terms with the definitions below:
   a. Limited life
   b. Unlimited liability
   c. Mutual agency
   d. Co-ownership of partnership property

   ___ (1) Each partner is an agent of the partnership and has the ability to bind the partnership to business agreements within the scope of the business.
   ___ (2) The business will be terminated when a partner withdraws, a new partner is admitted, the partners voluntarily terminate the agreement, bankruptcy terminates the agreement, or the agreed life of the entity expires.
   ___ (3) Each partner risks not only the assets invested in the business but also personal assets.
   ___ (4) Specific assets a partner invests in a partnership business are not necessarily available to that partner upon withdrawal from the partnership.

Q12-7 If the partnership agreement sets a ratio for distribution of profits but ignores the topic of losses, any losses incurred will be shared
   a. Equally
   b. In the ratio of capital balances
   c. In the same ratio as profits
   d. None of the above

Q12-8 Which of the following is *not* an advantage of the partnership form of business organization?
   a. Ability to pool the resources of several owners
   b. Ease of formation and dissolution
   c. Unlimited liability of the partners
   d. Freedom of action afforded partners

Q12-9 How are partnership income and losses distributed if the partnership agreement is silent about the sharing of income and losses?

Q12-10 Explain how the assets invested in a partnership should be recorded.

Q12-11 Discuss why it might be appropriate to provide for interest on partners' capital balances and to distribute the remainder in a predetermined ratio.

Q12-12 Discuss why it might be appropriate to provide for salary allowances to partners and to distribute the remainder in a predetermined ratio.

Q12-13 Discuss why it might be appropriate to provide for interest on partners' capital balances, salary allowances, and for distributing the remainder of partnership income in a predetermined ratio.

Q12-14 List events that could alter the partnership agreement and terminate the partnership.

Q12-15 Does altering the partnership agreement and, hence, terminating the partnership necessarily mean that the assets will be disposed of and that the business will cease to exist as a going-concern? Explain.

Q12-16 When partners agree to sell a portion of their respective interests to an incoming partner, what happens to the cash the incoming partner pays?

Q12-17 Discuss what happens to the equity created when an incoming partner receives a capital interest that is less that the amount invested.

Q12-18 Discuss what happens when a new partner receives a capital interest that exceeds the amount invested in the partnership.

Q12-19 What could be the justification for paying a retiring partner more than the balance reflected in that partner's capital account?

Q12-20 Discuss the accounting procedures that would be followed when a partner dies.

Q12-21 Explain the difference between partnership dissolution and partnership liquidation.

Q12-22 Discuss what happens if in a partnership liquidation the cash realized from the sale of the partnership assets is insufficient to cover the claims of the partnership creditors.

Q12-23 In a partnership liquidation, after the allocation of losses from conversion of the partnership assets, one of the partners has a capital balance that is insufficient to absorb the partner's share of the loss. Discuss how the resulting debit balance in the deficient partner's capital account is disposed of.

EXERCISES

LO 3

E12-1 **Allocation of Income in a Sole Proprietorship** Mike Hartmann is a student who started a word processing business to help support himself while in school. Mike purchased a computer and a printer for $4,000 to start his business. During Hartmann's first year, he had revenues of $14,000 and expenses of $2,000 in connection with his business.

REQUIRED:

a. Prepare the necessary journal entries at the end of the first year to close Hartmann's revenue, expense, and income summary accounts. Assume that all of Hartmann's expenses were for supplies he used.

b. If Hartmann has total assets of $26,000 at the end of his first year of business, what are his liabilities at that time?

LO 1

E12-2   Journal Entries for a Sole Proprietorship   Richard Ray owns and runs his own pool maintenance business. He started the business by investing $4,000 of his own cash on March 1, 19X4. On November 1, 19X4, Richard withdrew $1,000 for personal use to take a vacation. During 19X4, Richard had revenues of $16,000 and expenses of $5,500 relating to this business.

REQUIRED:

a. Prepare the necessary journal entries for each of the following:
   1. Richard's investment to start his business.
   2. Richard's withdrawal of cash from his business.
   3. To close Income Summary.
   4. To close Withdrawals.
b. What is the net worth of Richard's business on January 19X5?

LO 3

E12-3   Formation of a Partnership   Abell, Babec, and Cadore agree to form a partnership to practice accounting. They agree to each contribute $10,000 to the partnership and to share profits and losses equally.

REQUIRED:

Prepare the journal entry or entries to record the partners' investments.

LO 3

E12-4   Formation of a Partnership   Martha Walters and Ivan Recuso form a partnership to provide computer repair services. Walters has been repairing computers part-time in her garage for the last several months. She brings to the partnership testing equipment that had cost her $8,000 last year and $3,000 in cash. Recuso is investing cash in an amount to make his investment equal to hers. They agree that the testing equipment has a fair value of $6,500.

REQUIRED:

Prepare the journal entries to record each partner's investment in the partnership.

LO 4

E12-5   Partnership Income Distribution   Clark and Clendenny had 19X8 beginning capital balances of $35,000 and $45,000, respectively. Income for 19X8 is $60,000.

REQUIRED:

Prepare the journal entries to distribute the income to Clark and Clendenny for the two following cases:
a. There is no written agreement as to the distribution of profits and losses.
b. Income is distributed in the ratio of beginning capital balances.

LO 4

E12-6   Partnership Income Distribution   Thibodeaux and Swafford share income and losses by allocating 6% interest on weighted-average capital balances for the year and dividing the remainder in the ratio of 3 to 2. The weighted-average capital balances were $80,000 and $40,000 for the year, respectively.

REQUIRED:

Prepare the journal entry to distribute income of $60,000 for the period. Show calculations.

LO 4

E12-7   Partnership Income Distribution   Hilliard and Hariman share income and losses by using a salary allowance of $5,000 and $10,000, respectively, with the remainder distributed 35/65.

REQUIRED:

Prepare the journal entry to distribute income of $14,000 for the period. Show calculations.

LO 4 · E12-8 **Partnership Loss Distribution** Califano and Christoffersen operate a retail store as partners. The partnership agreement calls for income and losses to be distributed with 8% interest on beginning capital balances, salaries of $10,000 and $12,000, respectively, and any remainder in the ratio of 40/60. The loss for the year was $6,000. Beginning capital balances were $20,000 and $30,000, respectively.

REQUIRED:

Prepare the journal entry to record the distribution of the loss to the partners. Show calculations.

LO 4,5 · E12-9 **Partnership Income Distribution and Statement of Partners' Capital** McCoy and Wade began 19X8 with January 1 capital balances of $35,000 and $45,000, respectively. McCoy's withdrawals for the year totaled $25,000, and Wade's withdrawals totaled $20,000. Net income for the year ended December 31, was $60,000. The partnership agreement is silent regarding the distribution of profits and losses.

REQUIRED:

Prepare a statement of partners' capital at year-end.

LO 6 · E12-10 **Admission of a New Partner, Sale of Existing Interest** Rice and Rhoades share profits and losses equally. On January 1, 19X9, when their capital balances are $40,000 and $60,000, respectively, they admit Reid to the partnership by each selling one-half of their interest to Reid. Reid pays a total of $60,000 for the interests acquired.

REQUIRED:

Prepare the journal entry to reflect Reid's admission to the partnership.

LO 6 · E12-11 **Admission of a New Partner, Investment of Assets** Secore and Seay admit Brown to a one-fourth interest in the partnership with an investment of $50,000 in cash. At the time of Brown's admission, the former partners had capital balances of $50,000 and $60,000, respectively. Secore and Seay's income and loss ratio was 50/50.

REQUIRED:

Prepare the journal entry to record the admission of Brown to the partnership. Show calculations.

LO 6 · E12-12 **Withdrawal of Assets Greater Than Recorded Equity** Adam Mitchell, Colleen Grace, and Richard Mellon have worked together for many years. Mellon elects to retire and in accordance with the partnership agreement, Mellon is to receive cash equal to 125% of his capital account balance at the date of withdrawal. Capital balances at this time are $145,000, $155,000, and $100,000, respectively. The partners have always shared income and losses equally.

REQUIRED:

Prepare the journal entry to record Mellon's withdrawal from the partnership, assuming there is ample cash for settlement. Show calculations.

LO 6 **E12-13** **Withdrawal of Assets Less Than Recorded Equity** Johansson, Brank, Wilson, and Isenhower share income and losses in the ratio 40%, 20%, 20%, 20%. Marcus Isenhower is withdrawing from the partnership and is to receive an amount of cash equal to 90% of his capital balance. The capital balances at the date of withdrawal are $100,000, $50,000, $60,000, and $40,000, respectively.

REQUIRED:

Prepare the journal entry to record Isenhower's withdrawal from the partnership, assuming there is ample cash for settlement. Show calculations.

LO 7 **E12-14** **Partnership Liquidation** Barnes and Corbin have decided to terminate the operation of their partnership. Their assets consist of $5,000 in cash and inventory with a carrying amount of $95,000. Their only liability is an account payable of $10,000. Their capital balances are $40,000 and $50,000, respectively, and they share profits and losses equally.

REQUIRED:

a. Prepare the journal entries to record the sale of the inventory for $85,000, the distribution of the loss to the partners, and the final disposition of the cash.
b. Post the journal entries to T-accounts to illustrate the liquidation.

PROBLEM SET A

LO 1 **P12-1A** **Owner's Capital in a Sole Proprietorship** On March 1, 19X2, Harrison Hord invested $5,000 cash and an office building containing a computer and some furniture to start his own consulting business. The computer and office furniture were appraised at $2,000 and $6,000, respectively. Harrison had bought the building in 19X0 for $120,000 by putting $12,000 down and financing the $108,000 balance. The balance on the mortgage is now $106,000. A recent appraisal placed the value of the land the building sits on at $45,000 and the value of the building at $90,000.

During 19X2, Hord earned $214,000 in revenues from his consulting business and incurred $68,000 in expenses.

REQUIRED:

a. Prepare the journal entry necessary to record Harrison Hord's initial investment in his business.
b. Prepare the journal entry to close Hord's Income Summary at the end of 19X2.

LO 2,3,5 **P12-2A** **Partnership Formation** On April 1, 19X8, Pepin and Pentz agree to form a partnership to sell and install residential water-softening equipment. The partners agree that Pepin will invest tools and equipment, which cost $8,000, and have a current fair value of $6,000 together with cash of $14,000; and Pentz will invest a truck, which cost $15,500 and has a fair value of $9,500 together with sufficient cash to equal Pepin's investment.

REQUIRED:

a. Prepare the journal entry to record the partners investments.
b. Prepare a balance sheet for the Pepin and Pentz partnership at April 1, 19X8.

LO 4 **P12-3A** **Accounting for Partnership Income and Losses** Freis, Fritag, and Friedlander own and operate a go-cart track. The business has been operating for 3 years; and the partners have beginning capital balances of $10,000, $15,000, and $25,000, respectively. The partners work part-time in the business and have different amounts of time available to work at the track. They have been sharing profits and losses equally and have decided that a different distribution of profits and losses may be more equitable.

The following plan has been adopted: salaries of $6,000, $4,000, and $3,000, respectively; interest of 8% on the beginning capital balances; and the remainder shared equally.

REQUIRED:

a. Calculate the distribution of income or loss to partners assuming income of $38,000.
b. Prepare the journal entry to close Income Summary to partners' capital accounts under Requirement a.
c. Calculate the distribution of income or loss to partners, assuming a loss of $10,000.
d. Prepare the journal entry to close Income Summary to partners' capital accounts under Requirement c.

LO 4,5   **P12-4A**   **Accounting for Partnership Income and Losses; Partnership Financial Statements**
Cross-Bayou Nursery buys bedding plants and resells them to landscapers. The partners, B. Kinnear and G. King, have beginning capital balances of $35,000 each and share profits and losses by allowing interest of 5% on beginning capital balances, salaries of $15,000 and $20,000, respectively, and the remainder shared equally. During the fiscal year ended July 31, 19X9, Cross-Bayou reported revenues of $235,000 and expenses of $190,000.

REQUIRED:

a. Prepare the journal entries to close the revenue and expense accounts and to distribute the income to the partners' capital accounts. Show the calculation of the distribution of income.
b. Prepare a statement of partner's capital for the year ended July 31, 19X9. There were no withdrawals during the period.

LO 4,5,6   **P12-5A**   **Partnership Dissolution, Admission of a Partner with Sale of Existing Interests**
On January 1, 19X1, Tiger and Tisdale, with capital balances of $45,000 and $55,000, respectively, have tired of working full-time in the Limousine Service and agree to admit Stiles to a one-fourth interest in the partnership by each selling Stiles one-fourth of their existing interests. Stiles pays a total of $40,000 for the interest, the cash being given to Tiger and Tisdale in proportion to their capital balances. They agree to share profits 40%, 40%, 20%. During 19X1, the business generates revenues of $400,000, while incurring expenses of $220,000. The partners withdrew $30,000 each during the year.

REQUIRED:

a. Prepare the journal entry to record Stiles's admission to the partnership.
b. Prepare the journal entries to close the accounts on December 31, 19X1.
c. Prepare a statement of partners' capital as of December 31, 19X1.

LO 4,5,6   **P12-6A**   **Partnership Dissolution, Withdrawal of a Partner with Bonus to Withdrawing Partner**   Crew, Mull, and Dray share profits 40%, 30%, 30% and have capital balances of $60,000, $80,000, and $80,000, respectively, on January 1, 19X2. During the year, revenues total $220,000, and expenses incurred total $110,000. Crew, Mull, and Dray each withdrew $25,000 during the year.

Roberta Crew has elected to retire. The other partners have agreed that she should receive an amount $5,000 higher than the reported capital balance at year-end because the fair value of the assets is greater than the carrying amount.

REQUIRED:

a. Prepare the journal entries to close the accounts of the partnership as of December 31, 19X2, and to distribute income to the partners.

b. Prepare the journal entry to record Crew's withdrawal from the partnership on December 31, 19X2.

c. Prepare a statement of partners' capital for the year ended December 31, 19X2.

LO 4,7   **P12-7A**   **Partnership Liquidation, Gain or Loss from Realization, Remaining Cash to Partners**   The Helms Family Store has been operated as a partnership for many years by Hal, Fred, and Doris. They have shared income equally over the years. Their current balance sheet is shown below:

Helms Family Store Balance Sheet December 31, 19X8			
Cash	$ 80,000	Accounts payable	$ 30,000
Supplies	25,000	H. Helms, capital	15,000
Inventory	125,000	F. Helms, capital	90,000
Equipment	140,000	D. Helms, capital	135,000
Accumulated depreciation	(100,000)		
	$270,000		$270,000

In the course of the liquidation, the supplies are sold for $29,000; inventory, for $100,000; and equipment, for $10,000, all at an auction on December 31, 19X8.

REQUIRED:

a. Prepare the entries to record the sale of the supplies, inventory, and equipment.

b. Prepare the entries to record the payment of the accounts payable and to distribute the gain or loss to the partners' capital accounts.

c. Assume any partner with a deficit balance in capital after the distribution of losses pays the amount of the deficit into the partnership. Prepare the journal entry to record this payment.

d. Prepare the entry to distribute the cash to the partners and to close the books.

e. Explain why the cash in Requirement d was not distributed equally to all the partners in view of their agreement to share profits equally.

PROBLEM SET B

LO 1   **P12-1B**   **Accounting for a Sole Proprietorship**   Jeanne Ward started a word processing business in her home by investing $400 in cash and contributing her personal computer with a fair value of $1,600. During her first year of business, Jeanne billed revenues of $8,200 and incurred expenses of $1,600. She also withdrew $800 from her business for personal use. During her second year, Jeanne made no further investments or withdrawals from her business. Because of referrals, her revenues climbed to $14,600 and her expenses were $3,400.

REQUIRED:

a. Prepare the appropriate journal entry to record Jeanne's initial investment to start her business.

b. Prepare the appropriate journal entry to record Jeanne's withdrawal of cash from her business.

c. Prepare the appropriate journal entry to close Jeanne's Income Summary at the end of her first year of operations.

d. What is the balance in Jeanne's capital account at the beginning of her third year in business?

LO 2,3,5   **P12-2B**   **Partnership Formation**   Salzano and Salzillo agree to form a partnership on August 5, 19X5, for the purpose of manufacturing and selling custom silver jewelry. Both are master crafters and have their own tools, which they will invest in the business. Salzano and Salzillo agree that their tools have fair values of $4,500 and $6,000 respectively. They further agree to invest sufficient cash such that each partner will have a beginning capital balance of $25,000.

REQUIRED:

a. Prepare the journal entry to record the partners' investments.

b. Prepare a balance sheet for the Salzano and Salzillo partnership at August 5, 19X5, immediately after formation.

LO 4   **P12-3B**   **Accounting for Partnership Income and Losses**   Bucca, Casho, and DeVita operate a car wash as partners. The partners have beginning capital balances of $15,000, $15,000, and $20,000, respectively. Each partner works part-time in the business. They are seeking a more equitable distribution of profits and losses.

     The following plan has been adopted: salaries of $3,000, $4,000, and $5,000, respectively; interest of 6% on the beginning capital balances; and the remainder shared equally.

REQUIRED:

a. Calculate the distribution of income or loss to partners, assuming income of $24,000.

b. Prepare the journal entry to close Income Summary to partners' capital accounts under Requirement a.

c. Calculate the distribution of income or loss to partners, assuming a loss of $6,000.

d. Prepare the journal entry to close Income Summary to partners' capital accounts under Requirement c.

LO 4,5   **P12-4B**   **Accounting for Partnership Income and Losses; Partnership Financial Statements** Aldret and Arvey operate a carpet and rug cleaning service. The partners have beginning capital balances of $25,000 and $35,000, respectively. They share profits and losses by allowing interest of 8% on capital beginning balances, salaries of $8,000 and $12,000 respectively, with the remainder shared equally. During the fiscal year ended March 31, 19X6, Carpet Cleaners Company reported revenues of $190,000 and expenses of $95,000.

REQUIRED:

a. Prepare the journal entries to close the revenue and expense accounts and to distribute the income to the partners' capital accounts. Show the calculation of the distribution of income.

b. Prepare a statement of partners' capital for the year ended March 31, 19X6. There were no withdrawals during the period.

LO 4,5,6   **P12-5B**   **Partnership Dissolution, Admission of a Partner with Investment of Assets and Bonus to Original Partners**   Panagos and Trainor have successfully operated a bowling alley for 3 years. They have capital accounts of $125,000 and $175,000, respectively, and share profits and losses equally. The need to add 12 lanes caused them to seek a new partner with ample funds. Sara Owle has indicated a willingness to invest $200,000 for a 35% interest in capital and a 1/3 share in the profits. The agreement was completed, and Sara invested the cash on January 4, 19X7, the beginning of the fiscal year. During 19X7, the business generates revenues of $485,000, while incurring expenses of $275,000. The partners withdrew $50,000 each during the year.

REQUIRED:

a. Prepare the journal entry to record Owle's admission to the partnership.

b. Prepare the journal entries to close the accounts on December 31, 19X7.

c. Prepare a statement of partners' capital as of December 31, 19X7.

LO 4,5,6   **P12-6B**   **Partnership Dissolution, Withdrawal of a Partner with Bonus from Withdrawing Partner**   Borke, Radcliff, and Smart have capital balances of $45,000, $65,000, and $40,000, respectively, after closing the accounts on December 31, 19X8. During 19X9, revenues earned were $190,000, and expenses incurred were $120,000. Each of the partners withdrew $12,000 during the year. Smart has decided to retire as of December 31, 19X9, and the partners agree that Smart will receive $40,000 in settlement of the partnership interest because the assets are overvalued. The partners share profits and losses 30%, 50%, 20%, respectively.

REQUIRED:

a. Prepare the journal entries to close the accounts of the partnership as of December 31, 19X9, and to distribute the income to the partners.
b. Prepare the journal entry to record Smart's withdrawal from the partnership on December 31, 19X9.
c. Prepare a statement of partners' capital for the year ended December 31, 19X9.

LO 4,7   **P12-7B**   **Partnership Liquidation, Gain or Loss from Realization, Settlement with Capital-Deficient Partner**   Li, Ho, and Chin have decided to liquidate their partnership and retire. They share profits and losses in the ratio 40%, 40%, 20%, respectively. The balance sheet as of December 31, 19X6, after closing, is shown below:

Li, Ho, and Chin Balance Sheet December 31, 19X6			
Cash	$ 7,000	Accounts payable	$20,000
Supplies	1,500	Li, capital	5,000
Inventory	22,500	Ho, capital	15,000
Equipment	69,000	Chin, capital	10,000
Accumulated depreciation	(50,000)		
	$50,000		$50,000

In the course of the liquidation, supplies are sold for $1600; inventory, for $15,000; and equipment, for $10,000. Assume that any partner with a deficit balance after the distribution of losses from the liquidation of assets is unable to pay the amount owed.

REQUIRED:

a. Prepare the entries to record the sale of the supplies, inventory, and equipment.
b. Prepare the entry to distribute the gain or loss to the partners' capital accounts.
c. Prepare the entry to pay the liabilities.
d. Prepare the entry to adjust the partners' capital balances to absorb the deficit balance of the deficient partner.
e. Prepare the entry to distribute the cash to the partners.

CRITICAL THINKING AND COMMUNICATING

C12-1   Rocker, Mellon, and Barche have operated a partnership for 15 years. They started on a handshake and have done business that way ever since. On August 14, this year, Barche died suddenly. Since there is no written agreement as to the means of settlement with Barche's estate or family, Rocker and Mellon have come to you, their accountant, to ask what needs to be done. You explain that you are not an attorney and advise them that they should retain one. They agree to retain an attorney and ask you what accounting procedures will be required and what questions they should ask the attorney since they wish to continue to operate the business.

REQUIRED:

Provide a written response in the form of a letter to Rocker and Mellon.

C12-2 Jody Ham and Gerald Ham, brothers, have decided to enter into a partnership. The two brothers are master mechanics who specialize in tuning racing motorcycles.

Jody, now 25 years old, has been tuning motorcycles since he was 5. He is known in racing circles as something of a genius. His services are highly sought-after on the racing circuit. Gerald, a skilled mechanic in his own right, does not have the reputation of brother Jody; but as an ex-racer, he is a valuable part of the team because he can test ride the bikes that Jody is tuning and give his brother accurate feedback about the bikes. Also, Gerald has the capital to finance the partnership. Together, Jody and Gerald plan to offer their services to factory racing teams.

They already have offers of contracts for the upcoming year, which could total as much as $400,000. The operation will require a $100,000 investment in equipment. Gerald will provide the capital by investing $150,000 cash in the partnership. Jody will not make an investment.

REQUIRED:

The brothers come to you and ask for help with an equitable profit-sharing agreement. Propose a plan and show a projected distribution of profits, assuming a net income of $150,000.

CHAPTER 13

Investments in Stocks, Business Combinations, and Consolidated Financial Statements

While walking along University Avenue on his way to lunch, Mark Litton noticed a large, white 18-wheeler pass him. The three logos painted on the side of the truck caught Mark's attention. They were for three popular restaurant chains: KFC (Kentucky Fried Chicken), Pizza Hut, and Taco Bell. Mark assumed the truck delivered supplies to the three restaurants. In assuming the three restaurants were separate companies, Mark wondered how they were related.

An undergraduate business student at a large Midwestern university, Mark went to the university library to do some research on the relationship, if any, among the three restaurants. Mark read some stock investment reference sources, and he was amazed to learn that another well known company—PepsiCo, Inc.—owned the three restaurant chains. This discovery aroused Mark's curiosity. How did the restaurants become part of PepsiCo? How did PepsiCo include in its financial statements information about the chains?

This chapter discusses accounting for investments in another company's equity securities. One corporation may purchase stock in another corporation for the purpose of influencing or controlling the other company or simply for the purpose of investing to earn income. You will see that the level of ownership determines how we account for the investment. We also discuss the preparation of consolidated financial statements when the level of ownership allows one company to control another company.

1. Discuss the effects of the level of ownership on the method a company uses to account for investments in stocks.
2. Account for investments in stock, using the market method.
3. Account for investments in stock, using the cost method.
4. Account for investments in stock, using the equity method.
5. Prepare consolidated balance sheets at the date of acquisition.
6. Use a consolidation worksheet to prepare consolidated financial statements at the date of acquisition and for subsequent periods (Appendix 13-A).

LO 1

Discuss the effects of the level of ownership on the method a company uses to account for investments in stocks.

INVESTMENTS IN STOCK

Some corporations invest in the equity securities of other corporations. Some of these investments are short-term, and we classify them as current assets on the balance sheet. Companies make short-term investments to generate income from cash that the companies currently do not need in their business operations. Such investments are part of their cash management programs.

Corporations intend for some investments in the equity securities of other corporations to be long-term, and we classify them as noncurrent assets in the balance sheet. Companies make these investments for various reasons, including: to earn a favorable rate of return on the investment and to influence or control the other corporation's policies. The reasons for wanting to invest in and control another corporation may be to expand, diversify, or enhance the production, marketing, and financing success of the investing corporation. For example, when General Motors Corporation acquired controlling ownership of Electronic Data Services (EDS), the purpose was to gain control of the computer-systems expertise of EDS. This expertise is valuable to General Motors not only because of the growing demand for computer services by other businesses, but also because GM could use the expertise to modernize its own operations.

Similar to other assets, long-term investments in corporate securities are initially recorded at cost. Cost includes the purchase price plus any other costs such as brokerage fees the company incurs in acquiring the securities. For subsequent periods, companies account for long-term investments in stocks by the market method, the cost method, the equity method, or with consolidated financial statements. The appropriate method for the company to use depends on the level of influence the investor company (company that owns the stock) is able to exert on the investee company (the company whose stock the investor owns) and, in some cases, whether quoted market prices are available. The level of influence may be insignificant, significant, or controlling. Illustration 13-1 presents the guidelines followed in selecting the appropriate accounting method.

ILLUSTRATION 13-1 Accounting Methods for Stock Investments

Ownership Percentage	Presumed Influence	Accounting Method
Less than 20%	Insignificant	Market or cost methods
20% to 50%	Significant	Equity method
More than 50%	Controlling	Consolidated financial statements

In applying the guidelines presented in Illustration 13-1, the accountant should use judgment. The relationship between the ownership percentages and the levels of influence are merely guidelines, and the accountant should assess the level of influence by considering the circumstances. For example, an investor may own 20% of the voting stock of a corporation but has no significant influence because another investor owns the remaining 80% of the voting stock. With such an ownership interest, the 80% investor is able to control the investee company's operations and to ignore the wishes of the 20% investor.

Insignificant Influence

When the level of ownership does not allow the investor to exert significant influence on the investee company's management decisions, the investor should account for the investments in stock using the market method or the cost method. These methods apply to investments in both common and preferred stocks. They also apply to both long-term and short-term investments in stocks.

LO 2

Account for investments in stock using the market method.

Available Market Prices—Market Method.   If the investments are in stocks for which fair values are available, GAAP require the company to use the **market method**—that is, to present the investments in the balance sheet at the fair values of the stocks as of the balance sheet date. GAAP consider the stocks to have available fair values if sales prices or bid and ask prices are available currently on a national securities exchange (such as the New York Stock Exchange) or in the over-the-counter market.[1] The over-the-counter market refers to stocks that the public purchases and sells, but these transactions do not occur on an organized stock exchange. The National Association of Securities Dealers Automated Quotation systems (NASDAQ) or the National Quotation Bureau report price quotations for stocks traded over-the-counter.

   Long-term investments.   Long-term investments in stocks accounted for by the market method are called **available-for-sale securities**. To illustrate the application of the market method to long-term investments, assume the Oaks Company has the following transactions in 19X1, involving investments in long-term equity securities:

Stock Transactions in 19X1
May 5	Purchased 500 shares of Sand Corporation common stock for $12,500 ($25 per share) and 800 shares of Stone Company common stock for $38,400 ($48 per share). These investments represent less than 20% of the outstanding voting stock of each company, and there is no possibility that Oaks Company will have any significant influence on either investee. (For simplicity, assume there are no commissions from the stock purchases.)
June 30	Stone Company paid dividends of $2 per share that it declared on June 15, 19X1.
Dec. 31	Market prices per share: Sand Company $27 per share and Stone Company $40 per share.

Investment in Stock.   On May 5, 19X1, Oaks records the investments at cost as shown in the following entry:

---

[1]"Accounting for Certain Investments in Debt and Equity Securities," *Statement of Financial Accounting Standards No. 115* (Norwalk, Conn.: FASB, 1993), pars. 3–14.

19X1			
May 5	Investment in Sand Corporation Stock	12,500	
	Investment in Stone Company Stock	38,400	
	Cash		50,900
	To record purchase of 500 shares of Sand		
	Corporation common stock for $25 per share		
	and 800 shares of Stone Company common		
	stock for $48 per share.		

Dividends Received. On June 30, 19X1, Oaks records the dividends received. Since the declaration date and the payment date are in the same accounting period, it may record the dividends earned on the payment date.

19X1			
June 30	Cash	1,600	
	Dividends Revenue		1,600
	To record dividends received from Stone Company of		
	$2 per share.		

Year-End Adjustment. At the end of an accounting period, we must calculate the market value of each investment to determine the amount to be presented in the balance sheet. On December 31, 19X1, the market price of Oaks' investments are calculated as follows:

Investment	Number of Shares	Market Prices	Market Value	Carrying Amount	Increase (Decrease)
Sand Corporation	500	$27	$13,500	$12,500	$ 1,000
Stone Company	800	40	32,000	38,400	(6,400)
			$45,500	$50,900	$(5,400)

The calculations indicate that the market prices of the investments have changed since the date of purchase (May 5). The market value of the investment in Sand Corporation's stock increased by $1,000, and the market value of the investment in Stone Company's stock decreased by $6,400. The market method requires that Oaks present investments on the balance sheet at a total amount of $45,500, the total market price. This results in the offsetting of the unrealized gains and losses of the two stocks. Oaks records the following entry to adjust the investments to their total market values:

19X1			
Dec. 31	Unrealized (Gain) Loss from Available-for-Sale		
	Securities	5,400	
	Investment in Sand Corporation Stock	1,000	
	Investment in Stone Company Stock		6,400
	To adjust long-term investments in stocks to current		
	market prices.		

The net effect of the above journal entry on long-term investments is to reduce them to the total market price at the balance sheet date of $45,500. Because the investments are long-term, we do *not* include Unrealized Loss from Available-for-Sales Securities in the calculation of net income. That is, it is *not* closed to Income Summary at the end of the accounting period. Rather, we present it as a contra-stockholders' equity account in the balance sheet, similar to Treasury Stock. We present the investments in the noncurrent asset section of the balance sheet and the unrealized loss in the stockholders'equity section of the balance sheet as follows:

Investments:	
Long-term investments in equity securities (at market)	$ 45,500
Stockholders' Equity:	
Contributed capital:	
Common stock	$130,000
Paid-in capital in excess of par	350,000
Retained earnings	270,000
Total paid-in capital and retained earnings	$750,000
Less: Unrealized loss from available-for-sale securities	5,400
Total stockholders' equity	$744,600

To continue the example, assume Oaks Company has the following transactions in 19X2, involving investments in long-term investments in equity securities:

Stock Transactions in 19X2	
June 18	Sold all the shares of Sand Corporation common stock for $14,000. The sale is entered into due to a change in investment policy by the management of Oaks.
Sept. 30	Received a cash dividend from Stone Company of $1 per share.
Oct. 15	Purchased 400 shares of Shale Company common stock for $12,000. The 400 shares represent 1% of the voting stock of Shale.
Dec. 31	Market prices per share: Stone Company $45 per share and Shale Company $31 per share.

Sale of Stock.   When a company sells a long-term investment in stock, *we record a realized gain or loss for the difference between the proceeds from the sale and the original cost of the shares sold.*

Calculation of realized gain (loss) from sale of Sand Corporation stock:	
Selling price	$14,000
Original cost	12,500
Gain	$ 1,500

The amount of the realized gain or loss recorded is not affected by the previously recorded unrealized gain or loss related to the stock sold. On June 18, 19X2, Oaks records the sale of the shares of Sand Corporation as follows:

19X2			
June 18	Cash	14,000	
	Unrealized (Gain) Loss from Available-for-Sale		
	Securities	1,000	
	Investment in Sand Corporation Stock		13,500
	Gain from Sale of Investments		1,500
	To record the sale of 500 shares of Sand Corporation stock for $28 per share.		

Dividends Received. On September 30, 19X2, Oaks records the dividends received as follows:

19X2			
Sept. 30	Cash	800	
	Dividends Revenue		800
	To record the receipt of cash dividends from Stone Company of $1 per share.		

Investment in Stock. Oaks records the purchase of the Shale Company stock at cost by the entry shown below:

19X2			
Oct. 15	Investment in Shale Company Stock	12,000	
	Cash		12,000
	To record the purchase of 400 shares of Shale Company common stock for $30 per share.		

Year-End Adjustment. On December 31, 19X2, we calculate the total market price and the total cost of Oaks' investments on hand as follows:

Investment	Number of Shares	Market Prices	Market Value	Carrying Amount	Increase (Decrease)
Stone Company	800	$45	$36,000	$32,000	$4,000
Shale Company	400	31	12,400	12,000	400
			$48,400	$44,000	$4,400

The calculations indicate that the market price of both investments has increased. This means that Oaks should record the net gain of $4,400 in Unrealized (Gain) Loss from Available-for-Sale Securities. Oaks makes the following entry to record the change in market prices of the investments:

19X2			
Dec. 31	Investment in Stone Company Stock	4,000	
	Investment in Shale Company Stock	400	
	Unrealized (Gain) Loss from Available-for-Sale		
	Securities		4,400
	To adjust long-term investments to current market prices.		

After the above entry, Unrealized (Gain) Loss from Available-for-Sale Securities that the company presents as a contra-stockholders' equity account in the balance sheet has a debit (loss) balance of $2,000. We can reconcile this amount by comparing the original cost of $50,400 ($38,400 + $12,000) of the two investments to the total current market value of $48,400. This comparison shows that there has been a net $2,000 unrealized loss on the two investments.

Short-term investments. The application of the market method to short-term investments in stock is similar to that for long-term investments, which we discussed in the preceding section. However, there is one major exception. For short-term investments, we include the unrealized change in market value for each period in net income rather than accumulate it in the stockholders' equity valuation account. Also, when the investments are sold, we include in net income the change in market value from the beginning of the period to the date of sale. In other words, we make no distinction between realized and unrealized changes in the market value of short-term investments in stocks. We include changes in value in net income in the period they occur, whether or not the investments are sold.

LO 3

Account for investments in stock using the cost method.

Market Prices Not Available—Cost Method. We use the cost method for investments in stocks where the investor is unable to exert significant influence on the investee company's decisions *and* where market prices for the stocks are not available. The application of the cost method is the same for both long-term and short-term investments. Under the **cost method**, the investment is initially recorded at cost; and the investment is carried at cost until the securities are sold. Any dividends received from the investment are recorded as dividend revenue. Because the investor has no significant influence on the investee's operating and financing decisions, the investor should recognize revenue when the investee declares dividends.

Investment in Stock. On July 2, Dynamic Research, Inc. purchases 100 of the 2,500 outstanding shares of JJM Corporation's common stock. The market price of the stock is $49 per share, and the broker's commission is $215. Dynamic's purchase of the shares is recorded with the following entry:

July 2	Investment in JJM Corporation Stock	5,115	
	Cash		5,115
	To record the purchase of 100 shares of common stock at $49 per share plus commission of $215.		

Notice that, in the above entry, the entire cost of the shares is debited to Investment in JJM Corporation Stock. The par or stated value of the stock is not relevant to the *investor* company's recording of the purchase.

When the investee company declares cash dividends, the investor company recognizes dividends earned. Since the dividend declaration by the investee's board of directors creates the right for stockholders to receive the dividends, under the realization concept, the investor should recognize dividends as revenue when declared rather than when received.

Dividends Declared. On December 10, 19X1, the directors of the JJM Corporation declare cash dividends of $4 per share, payable on January 5, 19X2, to owners of record on December 20, 19X1. If Dynamic does not intend to sell the stock before December 20, it should record the dividends on December 10 with the entry shown below:

19X1			
Dec. 10	Dividends Receivable	400	
	Dividends Revenue		400
	To record dividends of $4 per share on common stock of JJM Corporation.		

On December 31, 19X1, the end of Dynamic's annual accounting period, Dividends Revenue is closed to Income Summary. On January 5, 19X2, when the dividend is received, Dynamic makes the following entry:

19X2			
Jan. 5	Cash	400	
	Dividends Receivable		400
	To record the receipt of dividends from JJM		
	Corporation.		

Stock dividends of JJM Corporation do *not* result in income for Dynamic Research; therefore no entry is required to record the stock dividend. Stock dividends do, however, reduce the cost per share of the stock owned. For example, assume JJM Corporation declares a 10% stock dividend. Before the stock dividend, the cost per share of the stock Dynamic Research, Inc. owned is $51.15 ($5,115 ÷ 100 shares). After the stock dividend, Dynamic owns 110 shares; and the cost per share is $46.50 ($5,115 ÷ 110 shares). Thus, Dynamic would calculate gains and losses on any subsequent sales of the shares by using the $46.50 cost per share amount.

Stock Sold.   When all or part of an investment is sold, the difference between the cost of the shares and the proceeds from the sale is recorded as a gain or loss. For example, assume Dynamic Research sells 50 of the JJM Corporation's shares at $70 per share and pays a broker's commission of $175. The sale results in a gain of $1,000 calculated as follows:

Proceeds from sale:	
50 shares x $70 per share	$3,500
Less: Commission	175
	$3,325
Cost (after stock dividend):	
50 shares x $46.50 per share	2,325
Gain	$1,000

Dynamic records the sale of the shares with the following entry:

(Date)	Cash	3,325	
	Investment in JJM Corporation Stock		2,325
	Gain from Sale of Investments		1,000
	To record sale of 50 shares of stock for $70 per		
	share less $175 commission.		

On the other hand, if Dynamic sells the 50 shares for $40 per share, less a broker's commission of $150, it incurs a loss of $475, calculated as follows:

Proceeds from sale:	
50 shares x $40 per share	$2,000
Less: Commission	150
	$1,850
Cost (after stock dividend):	
50 shares x $46.50 per share	2,325
Loss	$ 475

Dynamic's entry to record the sale is shown below:

(Date)	Cash	1,850	
	Loss from Sale of Investments	475	
	Investment in JJM Corporation Stock		2,325
	To record sale of 50 shares at $40 per share less commission of $150.		

LO 4

Account for investments in stock, using the equity method.

Significant Influence—Equity Method

When the long-term investment in another company's common stock is large enough that the investor is able to exert significant influence on the investee company's operating and financial policies, we account for the investment using the **equity method**. Stock ownership may indicate the ability to exert significant influence on the investee company's policies in several ways, including: representation on the board of directors, participation in policy making, material intercompany transactions, interchange of managerial personnel, or technological dependency.[2]

Under the equity method, we initially record the investment at cost. Because of the influence the investor can exert on the investee's policies, however, the investor recognizes as income the earning of income by the investee. The investor has the ability to influence the investee's declaration of dividends. If the investor were to recognize income based on dividends, the investor would be able to influence the timing of the recognition of income from the investment.

The investee's net assets are increased by its net income and are decreased by its cash dividends. Therefore, the investment account is increased for the investor's share of the investee's net income and is reduced for the investor's share of the investee's cash dividends. As a result, conceptually, under the equity method of accounting for long-term investments in stock, the balance of the investment account represents the investor's equity (proportionate share as a stockholder) in the investee company's net assets.

Investment in Stock. Assume Oaks Company purchases 10,000 shares of Water Company common stock for $250,000 cash on January 2, 19X1. The 10,000 shares represent 25% of Water Company's voting stock. Assuming Oaks can exert significant influence on Water Company's policies, Oaks should account for the investment using the equity method. Oaks' investment is recorded at cost as shown in the following entry:

19X1			
Jan. 2	Investment in Water Company Stock	250,000	
	Cash		250,000
	To record the purchase of 10,000 shares of Water Company common stock for $25 per share.		

Dividends Declared. Assume the Water Company declares cash dividends of $1 per share on August 15, 19X1. Under the equity method, Oaks Company records its share of the dividends with the following entry:

---

[2] "The Equity Method of Accounting for Investments in Stock," *Accounting Principles Board Opinion No. 18* (New York, NY: AICPA, 1971), par. 17.

19X1 Aug. 15	Dividends Receivable	10,000	
	Investment in Water Company Stock		10,000
	To record the receipt of dividends of $1 per share.		

Recognition of Income. For 19X1, Water Company reports net income of $84,000. Under the equity method, Oaks Company records its 25% share of Water Company's earnings as shown in the following entry:

19X1 Dec. 31	Investment in Water Company Stock	21,000	
	Income from Water Company		21,000
	To record share of net income of Water Company (25% x $84,000).		

At the end of the accounting period, Income from Water Company is closed to Income Summary and is included in Oaks Company's net income.

The relationship between the investor's investment account and the investee's net assets is shown in Illustration 13-2. When the 25% interest in Water Company is initially purchased for $250,000, Water Company's net assets are $1,000,000. The balance in the investment account represents the investor's 25% interest in Water Company's net assets. The dividends Water Company declares reduces its net assets by $40,000, and Oaks Company recognizes the decrease in the net assets by reducing the investment account by $10,000 ($40,000 x 25%). On the other hand, Water Company's net income increases its net assets by $84,000. Oaks Company recognizes this increase in the investee's net assets by increasing the investment account by $21,000 ($84,000 x 25%). Notice that the balance in the investment account of $261,000 is equal to 25% of the investee's net assets of $1,044,000.

ILLUSTRATION 13-2 Investee and Investor T-Accounts

Oaks Company			Water Company		
Investment in Water Company Stock			Net Assets		
Purchase	250,000	Dividends 10,000	Bal.	1,000,000	Dividends 40,000
Income	21,000		Net income	84,000	
Bal.	261,000		Bal.	1,044,000	

CONTROL—PARENT AND SUBSIDIARY RELATIONSHIPS

LO 5
Prepare consolidated balance sheets at the date of acquisition.

One corporation sometimes owns a majority (more than 50%) of another corporation's voting stock and is said to **control** the investee company. The investor company, called the **parent company**, is able to control the investee company, called the **subsidiary company**, by electing a majority of the members of the subsidiary's board of directors. In this way, the parent can control (not just influence) the subsidiary's operating, financing, and investing policies. Most large corporations in the United States are actually parent and subsidiary companies. The companies exist as separate entities because of certain economic, tax, and legal advantages. Many large, publicly-owned companies consist of a parent and numerous subsidiaries.

Parent and subsidiary companies are separate legal entities. This means that each company has the rights and duties of a corporation and that each company maintains its own accounting records and prepares its own financial statements. However, under GAAP, parent companies generally also must prepare consolidated financial statements. **Consolidated financial statements** are prepared as though the parent and subsidiary companies are one entity. This view represents the economic substance of the relationship, since the parent company can control the subsidiary companies' resources and operations. Preparing consolidated financial statements is a complex topic that is covered in advanced accounting texts. The next section, however, presents an overview of preparing consolidated balances sheets.

PREPARING CONSOLIDATED BALANCE SHEETS

In the consolidated balance sheet, the assets and liabilities of the parent and subsidiaries are combined so that, for example, cash is reported as the combined amount of the parent's and subsidiaries' cash. However, in preparing a consolidated balance sheet, duplicate balance sheet items are eliminated to avoid double-counting them. Duplicate balance sheet items exist because of transactions between the parent and the subsidiaries. A primary example of duplicate amounts is the investment in subsidiary account in the parent's accounting records and the assets and liabilities recorded in the subsidiary's accounting records. If the parent's investment account and the subsidiary's individual asset and liability accounts are both reported in the consolidated balance sheet, net assets would be double-counted. Also, since the parent company owns the subsidiary's common stock, stockholders' equity would be double-counted. To avoid the duplicate amounts from being reported, the parent's investment account and the subsidiary's stockholders' equity accounts are eliminated in the preparation of the consolidated balance sheet.

For example, Illustration 13-3 shows the balance sheets for Plant Corp. and Simko, Inc. Plant owns 100% of Simko's common stock. The consolidated balance sheet for Plant Corp. and its subsidiary (Simko) is also presented in Illustration 13-3. Notice that Investment in Simko Stock from Plant's individual balance sheet and Simko's stockholders' equity are not included in the consolidated balance sheet.

ILLUSTRATION 13-3 Consolidation of Balance Sheets

	Plant Corp. and Simko, Inc. Balance Sheets July 1, 19X1		
Assets	*Plant Corp.*	*Simko, Inc.*	*Consolidated Balance Sheet*
Current assets	$ 25,000	$ 17,000	$ 42,000
Investment in Simko	90,000		
Plant assets (net)	100,000	103,000	203,000
Total assets	$215,000	$120,000	$245,000
Liabilities and Stockholders' Equity			
Liabilities	$ 80,000	$ 30,000	$110,000
Stockholders' equity	135,000	90,000	135,000
Total liabilities and stockholders' equity	$215,000	$120,000	$245,000

In Appendix 13-A, we discuss the preparation of consolidated financial statements using worksheets. Also, in the appendix we discuss more complex consolidation issues.

PepsiCo's Consolidated Financial Statements

Mark Litton located PepsiCo, Inc.'s 1993 annual report in the university library. In the notes to the consolidated financial statements, Mark read the following description of PepsiCo's consolidation practices:

> **Principles of Consolidation.** The financial statements reflect the consolidated accounts of PepsiCo., Inc. and its controlled affiliates. Intercompany accounts and transactions have been eliminated. Investments in affiliates in which PepsiCo exercises significant influence but not control are accounted for by the equity method, and the equity in net income is included in selling, general, and administrative expenses in the Consolidated Statement of Income.

Mark read that PepsiCo's business consists of three primary segments: beverages, restaurants, and snack foods. The beverage segment had net sales of $8.6 billion in 1993. Brands of beverages include: Pepsi-Cola, 7 Up, and Lipton Original ice tea. The snack food segment had net sales of $7 billion in 1993. Brands of snack foods include: Lay's potato chips, Fritos, and Doritos. The restaurant segment had 1993 net sales of $9.4 billion. PepsiCo acquired Pizza Hut in 1977; Taco Bell in 1978; and KFC in 1986.

PepsiCo's annual report demonstrates how the corporate form of business allows businesses to expand and diversify through acquistions of ownership of existing companies. Businesses have the option of getting into a line of business by starting a new operation or by investing in an existing business. When the business follows the investment in existing business option, the investments may result in a level of ownership sufficient to control the investee company. Even though these acquired companies continue to exist as legally separate corporations, the consolidated financial statements reflect the financial position and results of operation as though they were one company.

SUMMARY

Discuss the effects of the level of ownership on the method a company uses to account for investments in stock. Levels of stock ownership are classified as: insignificant influence, significant influence, and controlling. Insignificant influence is presumed when the level of ownership is less than 20% of the voting stock. If market prices are available, investor companies use the market method to account for the investments. If market prices are not available, they use the cost method. Significant influence is presumed when the level of voting stock ownership is 20% or more. When significant influence is present, the investor company uses the equity method to account for the investment. A controlling level exists with voting stock ownership of more than 50%. When control exists, the investor company (parent) prepares consolidated financial statements.

Account for investments in stock, using the market method. Under the market method, the investor company records the investment in stock at cost at the date it acquires the stock. Dividends earned are recorded at the date the investee company declares them. At the end of each subsequent accounting period, the investor company adjusts the carrying amount of the investments to their market prices on that date. If the investment is considered long-term, the adjustment (unrealized gain or loss) is recorded in a contra-stockholders' equity account. If the investment is considered long term, the adjustment to current market prices is included in that period's income as though it were a realized gain or loss.

Account for investments in stock, using the cost method. Under the cost method, the investor company records the investment at cost. The company makes no adjustments to the carrying amount until it sells the investment. Dividends earned are recorded at the date the investee company declares them.

Account for investments in stock, using the equity method. At the date of investment in the stock, the investor company records the investment at cost. Under the equity method, the investment account is decreased for dividends received from the investee company. The investment account is increased and income is recorded for the investor's share of the investee's net income.

Prepare consolidated balance sheets at the date of acquistion. When a company controls another company through ownership of a majority of the voting stock, a parent and subsidiary company relationship exists and consolidated financial statements are prepared. The preparation of consolidated balance sheets involves eliminating duplicate amounts in the separate balance sheets of the two companies and summing the remaining amounts to prepare the consolidated balance sheet.

APPENDIX 13-A: CONSOLIDATION WORKSHEETS AND COMPLEX CONSOLIDATION ISSUES

CONSOLIDATED BALANCE SHEET AT THE DATE OF ACQUISITION

LO 6
Use a consolidation worksheet to prepare consolidated financial statements at the date of acquisition and for subsequent periods.

The process of preparing a consolidated balance sheet involves using a consolidation worksheet such as the one shown in Illustration 13-4. To illustrate the preparation of a consolidated balance sheet, assume that on January 2, 19X1, Parent Company purchases 100% of the 800 shares of $100 par value common stock of Subsidiary, Inc. Subsidiary's common stock has a carrying value of $126,000, and Parent Company paid that amount for the shares of stock. On the acquisition date, a consolidated balance sheet is prepared using the worksheet in Illustration 13-4.

In the worksheet, the first two columns present the two companies' separate balance sheets that are prepared from their separate ledger accounts after appropriate adjusting entries have been made. The next two columns, one for debits and one for credits, are for recording elimination entries needed to avoid double-counting amounts in the separate balance sheets resulting from intercompany transactions. Even though these are called "entries," they are *not* recorded in the journals or ledgers of either the parent or the subsidiary, both of which keep separate accounting records. The entries appearing in the consolidation worksheet are used solely to prepare the consolidated financial statements. The final column in the worksheet presents the consolidated balance sheet. The procedures for determining the consolidated amounts are also discussed below.

The elimination entry in the worksheet is labeled "(a)." In more complex consolidation examples, several elimination entries are required; and labeling the entries aids in interpreting the worksheet. In this example, the single entry is to eliminate Investment in Subsidiary in Parent's balance sheet and Subsidiary's stockholders' equity accounts. In preparing consolidated balance sheets, this elimination entry is always required. After these amounts are eliminated, combining the two balance sheets results, in effect, in the investment account being replaced by Subsidiary's individual assets and liabilities.

The consolidated balance sheet in the worksheet in Illustration 13-4 is determined by summing the amounts in each row, including the debits and credits in the Eliminations columns. For example, cash of $42,000 in the consolidated balance sheet is determined by summing Parent's cash of $24,000 and Subsidiary's cash of $18,000. Notice that Parent's Investment in Subsidiary does not have a balance in the Consolidated Balance Sheet column because the $126,000 debit in the first column is exactly offset by the $126,000 credit in the third column. Also, Subsidiary's Common Stock and Retained Earnings are eliminated in the same way. The consolidated balance sheet, therefore, shows only Parent's stockholders' equity accounts. This reflects the fact that the only "outside" stockholders of the combined entities are those of Parent.

ILLUSTRATION 13-4 Consolidation Worksheet

Parent Company and Subsidiary
Worksheet for Consolidated Balance Sheet
January 2, 19X1

	PARENT COMPANY	SUBSIDIARY, INC.	ELIMINATIONS		CONSOLIDATED BALANCE SHEET
			DEBITS	CREDITS	
Assets					
Cash	24,000	18,000			42,000
Accounts Receivable	30,000	26,000			56,000
Inventories	80,000	52,000			132,000
Investment in Subsidiary	126,000			(a) 126,000	
Plant Assets (net)	120,000	100,000			220,000
	380,000	196,000			450,000
Liabilities and Stockholders' Equity					
Current Liabilities	26,000	10,000			36,000
Noncurrent Liabilities	129,000	60,000			189,000
Common Stock	150,000	80,000	(a) 80,000		150,000
Retained Earnings	75,000	46,000	(a) 46,000		75,000
	380,000	196,000	126,000	126,000	450,000

Once the consolidation worksheet is completed, it is used to prepare the consolidated balance sheet in the same format as the balance sheet of an individual company.

Less Than 100 Percent Acquisition

Recall that consolidated financial statements are required when the parent owns more than 50% of the investee company's voting stock. To illustrate the preparation of a consolidated balance sheet when less than 100% of the voting stock is purchased, assume that, rather than purchasing 100% of Subsidiary, Inc., Parent Co. purchases 80% of the common stock. The carryng value of 80% of Subsidiary's stock is $100,800 ($126,000 x 80%). Parent pays carrying value for the shares. The worksheet for preparing the consolidated balance sheet at the acquisition date based on the new assumption is presented in Illustration 13-5.

ILLUSTRATION 13-5 Consolidation Worksheet

Parent Company and Subsidiary
Worksheet for Consolidated Balance Sheet
January 2, 19X1

	PARENT COMPANY	SUBSIDIARY, INC.	ELIMINATIONS DEBITS	ELIMINATIONS CREDITS	CONSOLIDATED BALANCE SHEET
Assets					
Cash	49,200	18,000			67,200
Accounts Receivable	30,000	26,000			56,000
Inventories	80,000	52,000			132,000
Investment in Subsidiary	100,800			(a) 100,800	
Plant Assets (net)	120,000	100,000			220,000
	380,000	196,000			475,200
Liabilities and Stockholders' Equity					
Current Liabilities	26,000	10,000			36,000
Noncurrent Liabilities	129,000	60,000			189,000
Common Stock	150,000	80,000	(a) 80,000		150,000
Retained Earnings	75,000	46,000	(a) 46,000		75,000
	380,000	196,000			
Minority Interest				(a) 25,200	25,200
			126,000	126,000	475,200

When a company purchases more than 50%, but less than 100%, of another company's voting stock, it purchases a **majority interest** in the investee's net assets. In these circumstances, the other stockholders are said to have a **minority interest** in the subsidiary company's net assets. In the worksheet in Illustration 13-5, when Investment in Subsidiary Stock of $100,800 debit and Common Stock and Retained Earnings of Subsidiary of $126,000 credit ($80,000 + $46,000) are eliminated, a residual credit of $25,200 remains to balance the elimination entry. The $25,200 credit is the minority interest of the other stockholders (20% x $126,000 = $25,200). The minority interest is presented in the consolidated balance sheet, but in practice the presentation is not uniform. Some companies present minority interest in the noncurrent liabilities section; other companies present minority interest as part of stockholders' equity; and some companies present minority interest as a separate classification between noncurrent liabilities and stockholders' equity. In any case, two sets of outside stockholders are now represented in the consolidated balance sheet, the stockholders of Parent and the stockholders of Subsidiary. Illustration 13-6 shows the liabilities and stockholders' equity section of the consolidated balance sheet with the minority interest presented in stockholders' equity. This approach is used throughout the remainder of this textbook.

ILLUSTRATION 13-6 Partial Consolidated Balance Sheet

Liabilities and Stockholders' Equity

Liabilities:		
Current liabilities	$ 36,000	
Noncurrent liabilities	189,000	
Total liabilities		$225,000
Stockholders' equity:		
Common stock	$150,000	
Minority interest, Simko	25,200	
Retained earnings	75,000	
Total stockholders' equity		250,200
Total liabilities and stockholders' equity		$475,200

Acquisition at More Than Book Value

Companies do not always pay book value for the purchased shares of a subsidiary. Quite often the purchase price is in excess of the shares' book value. An investor has three reasons for paying more than book value for the stock:

1. The fair values of the investee company's assets are more than their recorded carrying values.
2. The fair values of the investee company's liabilities are less than their recorded carrying values.
3. The investor's expectations about the investee's future earnings justify paying more than carrying value.

When the cost of the investment is in excess of its carrying value, the accounting profession requires that any excess cost first be assigned to the investee company's assets and liabilities to recognize their fair values in the consolidated balance sheet. Any remaining excess of cost over carrying value is presented as goodwill in the consolidated balance sheet.

Assume Parent Company purchases 80% of Subsidiary, Inc.'s common stock for $118,000 on January 2, 19X1. Consistent with the previous example, the carrying value of the stock is $100,800 ($126,000 x 80%). Also, assume that the carrying values of Subsidiary's assets and liabilities are equal to their fair values. The worksheet for preparing the consolidated balance sheet is presented in Illustration 13-7. Notice that in the elimination entry, $17,200 of goodwill emerges. This is the difference between the cost of the investment of $118,000 and the carrying value of the interest acquired in Subsidiary's net assets of $100,800 ($126,000 x 80%). **Goodwill** is the excess of cost over the fair value of the net assets. Since the fair values and carrying values of Subsidiary's assets and liabilities are equal, the excess of cost over carrying value is presented as purchased goodwill in the consolidated balance sheet.

Consolidated Balance Sheet Subsequent to Acquisition Date

For accounting periods subsequent to the acquisition date, the basic procedures for preparing a consolidated balance sheet are the same. Assume that for 19X1, Subsidiary has net income of $12,000 and pays dividends of $10,000. Under the equity method of accounting for investments in stocks, Parent makes the following entries to (1) record its 80% share of the dividends and (2) record its 80% share of the net income:

ILLUSTRATION 13-7 Consolidation Worksheet

Parent Company and Subsidiary
Worksheet for Consolidated Balance Sheet
January 2, 19X1

	PARENT COMPANY	SUBSIDIARY, INC.	ELIMINATIONS		CONSOLIDATED BALANCE SHEET
			DEBITS	CREDITS	
Assets					
Cash	32,000	18,000			50,000
Accounts Receivable	30,000	26,000			56,000
Inventories	80,000	52,000			132,000
Investment in Subsidiary	118,000			(a) 118,000	
Plant Assets (net)	120,000	100,000			220,000
	380,000	196,000			
Goodwill			(a) 17,200		17,200
					475,200
Liabilities and Stockholders' Equity					
Current Liabilities	26,000	10,000			36,000
Noncurrent Liabilities	129,000	60,000			189,000
Common Stock	150,000	80,000	(a) 80,000		150,000
Retained Earnings	75,000	46,000	(a) 46,000		75,000
	380,000	196,000			
Minority Interest				(a) 25,200	25,200
			143,000	143,200	475,200

19X1 (Date)	Cash	8,000	
	Investment in Subsidiary		8,000
	To record dividends received from Subsidiary (80% x $10,000).		
Dec. 31	Investment in Subsidiary	9,600	
	Income from Subsidiary		9,600
	To record share of net income of Subsidiary (80% x $12,000).		

To simplify the example, assume Parent has only one other transaction in 19X1, which is a loan to Subsidiary of $5,000. The loan is still owed on December 31, 19X1.

The worksheet to prepare the consolidated balance sheet at December 31, 19X1, is shown in Illustration 13-8. In the Parent Company column, cash increased by $3,000 from the previous Illustration 13-7. This increase is the $8,000 dividend received from Subsidiary minus the $5,000 loan made to Subsidiary. Also, Investment in Subsidiary increased by $1,600, which is the excess of Parent's share of Subsidiary's net income over its share of Subsidiary's dividends. Retained Earnings of Parent increased by its $9,600 share of Subsidiary's net income.

For Subsidiary, cash increased by $7,000 from the previous example, which is the $2,000 excess of net income over dividends ($12,000 – $10,000) plus the

$5,000 loan from Parent. For simplicity, it is assumed that all other asset accounts are unchanged. Current liabilities increased by $5,000 for the loan from Parent. Finally, Retained Earnings increased by $2,000, which is the excess of net income over dividends ($12,000 – $10,000).

In the Eliminations columns, the entry to Investment in Subsidiary and Retained Earnings of Subsidiary reflect the changed amounts as explained above. Minority interest has increased by $400, which is the minority interest's share of the increase in Subsidiary's retained earnings [20% x ($12,000 – $10,000)]. A second elimination entry, labeled (b), is needed to eliminate Receivable from Subsidiary of $5,000 in Parent's balance sheet and $5,000 of Current Liabilities in Subsidiary's balance sheet. These amounts are eliminated because they are not an asset and a liability of the consolidated entity. To report them in the consolidated balance sheet would overstate both assets and liabilities because an entity cannot owe money to itself.

Other Consolidation Issues

In Illustration 13-8, Goodwill is shown in the Consolidated Balance Sheet column at its original amount of $17,200. Under GAAP, goodwill is an intangible asset that should be amortized over its useful life, not exceeding 40 years.[3] For simplicity in the example, goodwill is not amortized.

For periods subsequent to the acquisition date, consolidated income statements also are prepared. In simplistic examples such as in the previous discussion, the consolidated income statement is prepared by summing the revenues and expenses of the separate companies. In practice, however, consolidated income statements are affected by complex intercompany transactions that must be eliminated. These complexities are discussed in advanced accounting texts.

Purchase Versus Pooling-of-Interests Accounting

The discussion of accounting for business combinations in this chapter has followed the purchase method, which treats the business combination as a purchase of assets. Under the **purchase method**, the acquired company's assets and liabilities are reported at their fair values on the date of the business combination. Any excess of the cost of the purchase over the fair value of the net assets acquired is reported as goodwill. A business combination accounted for by the purchase method often involves the exchange of cash or other assets for the net assets acquired.

Another way of accounting for a business combination is the pooling-of-interests method (pooling). Under the **pooling-of-interests method**, the combining company's net assets are reported in the consolidated financial statements at their carrying values immediately preceding the combination. The pooling method is used for combinations that involve the exchange of common stock.

Alternative Methods. While the purchase and pooling methods are alternative ways of accounting for business combinations, they are not alternative methods for the same business combination. *APB Opinion No. 16* specifies 12 criteria that must be met for the combination to be accounted for as a pooling.[4]

---

[3]"Intangible Assets," *Accounting Principles Board Opinion No. 17* (New York, NY: AICPA, 1970), pars. 27–28.

[4]"Business Combinations," *Accounting Principles Board Opinion No. 16*, (New York, NY: AICPA, 1970), pars. 45–48.

ILLUSTRATION 13-8 Consolidation Worksheet

Parent Company and Subsidiary
Worksheet for Consolidated Balance Sheet
January 2, 19X1

	PARENT COMPANY	SUBSIDIARY, INC.	ELIMINATIONS DEBITS	ELIMINATIONS CREDITS	CONSOLIDATED BALANCE SHEET
Assets					
Cash	35,000	25,000			60,000
Accounts Receivable	30,000	26,000			56,000
Receivable from Subsidiary	5,000			(b) 5,000	
Inventories	80,000	52,000			132,000
Investment in Subsidiary	119,600			(a) 119,600	
Plant Assets (net)	120,000	100,000			220,000
	389,600	203,000			
Goodwill			(a) 17,200		17,200
					485,200
Liabilities and Stockholders' Equity					
Current Liabilities	26,000	15,000	(b) 5,000		36,000
Noncurrent Liabilities	129,000	60,000			189,000
Common Stock	150,000	80,000	(a) 80,000		150,000
Retained Earnings	84,600	48,000	(a) 48,000		84,600
	389,600	203,000			
Minority Interest				(a) 25,600	25,600
			150,200	150,200	485,200

If all 12 criteria are met, the combination *must* be accounted for as a pooling. Otherwise, the purchase method must be followed. Two of the criteria are:

1. The combination must be completed in a single transaction.
2. One company must exchange shares of its common stock for at least 90% of the other company's voting stock.

Comparison of the Balance Sheet Effects. Because of inflation, the combining company's net assets reported under the purchase method will be greater than if the pooling method is used. Also, no goodwill is recognized under the pooling method because the net assets are reported at their carrying values.

Comparison of Income Statement Effects. Under the purchase method, the acquired company's earnings are included in the combined company's net income only from the date of the combination. Under the pooling method, the combining company's earnings are included in the combined company's net income for the entire year in which the combination occurs, regardless of the date of the combination. Also, operating expenses will usually be greater under the purchase method because the net assets are reported at fair value rather than at carrying value. This affects expenses such as cost of goods sold and depreciation. Amortization expense will usually be greater under the purchase method because no goodwill is recognized under the pooling method.

Illustration 13-9 shows that both the purchase and pooling methods are used in practice, but the use of the purchase method is much greater.

ILLUSTRATION 13-9 Number of Purchases and Poolings

	1991	1990	1989	1992
Poolings	16	10	18	17
Purchases	160	190	219	182

Source: *1993 Accounting Trends and Techniques*, p. 53.

REVIEW PROBLEM A: ACCOUNTING FOR INVESTMENTS IN STOCK

Greer Corporation purchased 5,000 shares of Hogg Corporation's common stock for $30 per share on January 2, 19X1. During 19X1, Hogg Corporation declared and subsequently paid a dividend of $2 per common share. Hogg Corporation earned $5 per share during 19X1. The market price of Hogg Corporation stock on December 31, 19X1 is $33 per share. Greer considers the investment to be long-term.

REQUIRED:

a. Record Greer Corporation's purchase of Hogg Corporation stock.
b. Record the necessary entries if Greer Corporation uses the market method of accounting for the investment in Hogg Corporation stock.
c. Record the necessary entries if Greer Corporation uses the equity method of accounting for investment in Hogg Corporation stock.
d. Record Greer's sale of 2,000 shares of Hogg Corporation stock on June 30, 19X2, for $32.50 per share. Assume that Greer Corporation uses the cost method of accounting for the investment in Hogg. Hogg pays a broker's fee of $900.

SOLUTION:

Planning and Organizing Your Work

1. Record the purchase of Hogg Corporation stock at cost.
2. Calculate the dividends Greer received to determine dividends earned under the market method. Record the entries for the recognition and collection of dividends.
3. Record the entry to adjust Hogg stock to market value and record the unrealized gain or loss under the market method.
4. Record the entry to reduce Greer's Investment in Hogg Corporation Stock account for Greer's dividends from Hogg for the equity method.
5. Record the entry to recognize Greer's share of Hogg's income under the equity method.
6. Record cash received minus the broker's commission from the sale and recognize the appropriate gain or loss on the sale.

(a) *Record the purchase.*

19X1 Jan. 2	Investment in Hogg Corporation Stock*	150,000	
	Cash		150,000
	To record the purchase of 5,000 shares of stock for $30 per share.		
	*($30 x 5,000 shares)		

(b) *Prepare market method entries.*

(Date)	Dividends Receivable	10,000	
	Dividends Revenue		10,000
	To record dividend revenue of $2 per share.		
(Date)	Cash	10,000	
	Dividends Receivable		10,000
	To record the receipt of dividends declared.		
Dec. 31	Investment in Hogg Corporation Stock*	15,000	
	Unrealized Gain (Loss) from Available-for-Sale		
	Securites		15,000
	To adjust long-term investments in stocks to current		
	market prices.		
	*($33 − $30) x 5,000 shares		

(c) *Prepare equity method entries.*

(Date)	Dividends Receivable	10,000	
	Investment in Hogg Corporation Stock		10,000
	To record the declaration of dividends by the		
	investee of $2 per share.		
(Date)	Cash	10,000	
	Dividends Receivable		10,000
	To record the receipt of dividends declared.		
Dec. 31	Investment in Hogg Corporation Stock*	25,000	
	Income from Hogg Corporation		25,000
	To record share of income earned by the investee		
	of $5 per share.		
	* ($5 x 5,000 shares)		

(d) *Record the sale of long-term investments.*
Cash: ($32.50 x 2,000 shares) − $900
Gain: $64,100 − $60,000

19X2			
June 30	Cash [($32.50 x 2,000 shares) − $900]	64,100	
	Investment in Hogg Corporation Stock *		60,000
	Gain from Sale of Investments ($64,100 − $60,000)		4,100
	To record sale of 2,000 shares of stock for $32.50		
	per share less $900 commission.		
	*$30.00 x 2,000 shares		

REVIEW PROBLEM B: PREPARING A CONSOLIDATED BALANCE SHEET

Patrice Corporation acquired 100% of the common stock of Sliver Corporation on January 4, 19X4, for $10,000 cash. Immediately before the businesses combined, each company's balance sheet looked like this:

	Patrice	*Sliver*
Cash and other current assets	$40,000	$15,000
Accounts payable	$15,000	$ 5,000
Stockholders' equity	25,000	10,000
Total liabilities and stockholders' equity	$40,000	$15,000

REQUIRED:

a. Prepare the journal entry to record the purchase by Patrice of Sliver's stock.

b. Prepare the consolidated balance sheet immediately after purchase.

SOLUTION:

Planning and Organizing Your Work

1. Record the purchase of Sliver Corporation stock at cost.
2. Modify Patrice Corporation's balance sheet to reflect the purchase.
3. Set up Patrice's and Sliver's balance sheets in a format similar to that of Illustration 13-3 and prepare a consolidated balance sheet.

(a) *Record the purchase.*

19X4			
Jan. 4	Investment in Sliver Corporation Stock	10,000	
	Cash		10,000
	To record the purchase of 100% of Sliver's stock.		

(b) *Prepare consolidated balance sheet.*

Patrice Corporation and Sliver Corporation			
Balance Sheets			
January 4, 19X4			
Assets	*Patrice Corp.*	*Sliver Corp.*	*Consolidated Balance Sheet*
Current assets	$30,000	$15,000	$45,000
Investment in Sliver	10,000		
Total assets	$40,000	$15,000	$45,000
Liabilities and Stockholders' Equity			
Accounts payable	$15,000	$ 5,000	$20,000
Stockholders' equity	25,000	10,000	25,000
Total liabilities and stockholders' equity	$40,000	$15,000	$45,000

KEY TERMS

available-for-sale securities, *571*
consolidated financial
  statements, *579*
control (of a corporation), *578*
cost method, *575*

equity method, *577*
goodwill, *584*
majority interest, *583*
market method, *571*
minority interest, *583*

parent company, *578*
pooling-of-interests method,
  586
purchase method, *586*
subsidiary company, *578*

SELF-QUIZ

LO 1 1. Which of the following is *not* a method of accounting for long-term investments in stocks?

a. Cost

b. Equity

c. Market

d. Net realizable value

LO 2 2. For short-term investments, we include the unrealized change in market value for each period in _____ _____.

LO 2,3 3. When the level of ownership does not allow the investor to exert significant influence on the investee company's management decisions, the investor should account for the investments in stock using the _____ method or the _____ method.

LO 2 4. The account, Unrealized Loss (Gain) from Long-Term Investments, is disclosed in the financial statements as a(n)

a. Footnote

b. Contra-account in the stockholders' equity section of the balance sheet

c. Contra-account to Long-Term Investments

d. Account on the income statement

LO 2 5. Courtney Corporation's sole long-term investment is 1,000 shares in Brent Corporation common stock. Courtney does not have significant influence or control over Brent. The stock was purchased in 19X1 at a price of $20 per share. At December 31, 19X1, the market price was not available. What should be the carrying value of the investment on Courtney's 19X1 balance sheet?

a. $20,000

b. $0

c. Disclose investment only in a footnote to the balance sheet.

d. Ignore; The investment is immaterial.

LO 4 6. The declaration of dividends on an investment affects the investments account when a company uses which of the following methods?

a. Market

b. Cost

c. Equity

d. Consolidated financial statements

LO 5 7. Which of following is *not* a reason why investors are willing to pay more than book value for another company's stock?

a. The fair value of the assets of an investee company exceeds their recorded values.

b. The fair value of the liabilities of an investee company are less than their recorded values.

c. The par value of a company's stock is less than the issue price.

d. Expected future earnings of the investee are optimistic.

LO 6 8. True or False? A company may select either the purchase or pooling-of-interests method for its business combinations.

LO 6 9. Under the purchase method of business combinations, assets and liabilities of the acquired company are reported in the consolidated balance sheet at their _____ _____ value; while under the pooling-of-interests method, the _____ value is used.

LO 6 10. True or False? Only the earnings of the subsidiary from date of acquisition are consolidated with the parent company under the purchase method of business combinations.

SOLUTIONS TO SELF-QUIZ

1. d   2. net income   3. market, cost   4. b   5. a   6. c   7. c   8. False   9. fair market, carrying   10. True

---

QUESTIONS

Q13-1 Why does a company have short-term investments?

Q13-2 What reasons would a company have for owning long-term investments?

Q13-3 What is included in the cost of investments?

Q13-4 What two factors determine whether long-term investments are accounted for by the market, cost, equity, or consolidated financial statements methods?

Q13-5 True or False? The ownership percentage is the only factor used to determine the level of influence one company has over another.

Q13-6 What is the main difference in applying the market method to short-term investments versus long-term investments?

Q13-7 When would an investor use the cost method instead of the market method for investments?

Q13-8 Under the equity method for long-term investments, what does the investment account represent?

Q13-9 What accounting method does a parent company use for long-term investments during the year? At year-end?

Q13-10 Why do companies prepare consolidated financial statements?

Q13-11   When consolidated financial statements are prepared, what account is eliminated?

Q13-12   True or False? Consolidating entries are adjusting entries of the parent company.

Q13-13   True or False? When a company acquires control or influence over another, the investee company makes a journal entry reflecting the acquisition value.

Q13-14   (Appendix) Define majority interest.

Q13-15   (Appendix) Who has a minority interest in a corporation?

Q13-16   (Appendix) What two accounts may be found on a consolidated balance sheet that will not be on the parent's balance sheet?

Q13-17   Identify the account on the parent's balance sheet that disappears during the consolidating process.

Q13-18   (Appendix) Why would an investor acquire a company for more than its carrying value?

Q13-19   (Appendix) Explain the purchase method for business combinations.

Q13-20   (Appendix) How does the pooling-of-interests method of business combinations impact the consolidated financial statements?

EXERCISES

LO 1

E13-1   **Investments in Stock, Market Method**   Oklahoma Instruments, Inc. purchased 10% of the 10,000 shares of common stock of BMOC Corporation on January 3, 19X8, for $30 per share. Oklahoma Instruments intends to retain the investment in BMOC for more than one year. BMOC reported earnings of $3.50 per share and declared dividends of $1.25 per share for 19X8 on December 31. The dividends will be paid on January 15, 19X9. The market price of BMOC on December 31, 19X8, is $31.50 per share.

REQUIRED:

Record the purchase of BMOC, the recognition of income, the adjustment to current market price, and the receipt of dividends by Oklahoma Instruments.

LO 2

E13-2   **Year-End Adjustments, Market Method**   Kinsman Corporation invested in Franconia Corporation's common stock for $10,000 and Easton Corporation's common stock for $20,000 in 19X0. Kinsman did not exert significant influence or ownership over either of these long-term investments. In preparing year-end adjustments, the accountant has compiled the following information:

Year-End	Franconia's Market Value	Easton's Market Value
19X0	$11,000	$18,000
19X1	12,000	16,000
19X2	13,000	20,000

REQUIRED:

Record the year-end adjusting entries required due to the market fluctuations in the value of these long-term investments.

LO 2

E13-3   **Short-Term Investments, Market Method**   Hamilton Corporation purchased 1,000 shares of Jaime Corporation's common stock for $40 per share. Hamilton is planning to hold the stock as a short-term investment. During the year, Hamilton received a $1.00 per share dividend; and at year-end, the Jaime stock was selling for $42 per share. Subsequently, Hamilton sold the Jaime stock for $44 per share.

REQUIRED:

Record for Hamilton the purchase of the Jaime common stock, the receipt of dividends, the year-end adjustment, and its subsequent sale.

LO 3

E13-4 **Sale of Investments, Cost Method** Outdoors Unlimited purchased 2,000 shares of Trailblazers Incorporated on February 24, 19X0, for $80.25 per share. Trailblazer intended to retain the stock for more than one year at the time of purchase. Outdoors Unlimited sold 2,000 shares of Trailblazers Incorporated on March 13, 19X3, for $81.00 per share and paid a broker's fee of $600.

REQUIRED:

Record the sale of Trailblazers Incorporated stock, using the cost method.

LO 4

E13-5 **Investments in Stock, Equity Method** Quick Express, Inc., purchased 40% of the 80,000 shares of common stock of Fax-It Corporation on January 3, 19X1, for $25 per share. Fax-It reported earnings of $2.50 per share and declared dividends of $1 per share for 19X1. The dividends will be paid on February 15, 19X2.

REQUIRED:

Record the purchase of the Fax-It stock, the recognition of income, and the recognition of dividends by Quick Express, Inc. using the equity method.

LO 2,4

E13-6 **Long-Term Investments, Market and Equity Methods** In January, the Viking Corporation purchased, as long-term investments, 5% of Homewood Corporation's common stock for $50,000 and 30% of Flossmoor Corporation's common stock for $125,000. During the year, Homewood had net income of $100,000 and declared dividends of $10,000. Flossmoor had net income of $300,000 and paid dividends of $75,000. The market value of both stocks at year-end was the same as the January purchase price.

REQUIRED:

Prepare the journal entries for Viking Corporation to record this information.

LO 5

E13-7 **Consolidated Balance Sheet** Erin Corporation acquired 100% of Jonathan Corporation's common stock on June 4, 19X4, for $10,000 cash. Immediately before the businesses combined, each company's balance sheet looked like this:

	Erin	Jonathan
Cash and other assets	$60,000	$30,000
Accounts payable, etc.	$40,000	$20,000
Stockholders' equity	20,000	10,000
Total liabilities and stockholders' equity	$60,000	$30,000

REQUIRED:

a. Prepare Erin's journal entry to record the purchase of Jonathan's stock.
b. Prepare the journal entry, if any, to record Erin's purchase of Jonathan's stock on Jonathan's books.
c. Prepare the consolidated balance sheet immediately after the purchase.

LO 6

E13-8 **Consolidated Balance Sheet Worksheet (Appendix 13-A)** Primo Corporation purchased 100% of the Segundo Corp. common stock on January 2, 19X2, for $196,000.

REQUIRED:

On a separate sheet of paper, complete the partially completed worksheet below to prepare a consolidated balance sheet for Primo and Segundo.

Primo Corporation and Subsidiary
Worksheet for Consolidated Balance Sheet
January 2, 19X1

| | PRIMO CORPORATION | SEGUNDO CORP. | ELIMINATIONS | | CONSOLIDATED BALANCE SHEET |
			DEBITS	CREDITS	
Assets					
Cash	41,500	14,700			
Accounts Receivable	32,300	21,900			
Inventories	91,700	57,300			
Investment in Segundo	196,000				
Plant Assets (net)	379,600	167,200			
	741,100	261,100			
Liabilities and Stockholders' Equity					
Current Liabilities	117,800	51,700			
Noncurrent Liabilities	183,200	13,400			
Common Stock	300,000	50,000			
Retained Earnings	140,100	146,000			
	741,100	261,100			

PROBLEM SET A

LO 2,4

P13-1A **Investments in Stock** Rose Corporation had never made any long-term investments in marketable equity securities. During 19X2, it decided to invest in Blackjack Company, Greta Company, and Harcor Company. All investments are classified as long-term. The following information relates to the stock of these companies and other 19X2 results.

	Blackjack	Greta	Harcor
Acquisition price	$45,000	$33,000	$90,000
Number of shares	1,000	1,500	4,500
Ownership percentage	10%	15%	30%
Earnings per share	$ 9.00	$ 6.00	$ 4.00
Dividends per share	$ 3.00	$ 2.50	$ 2.50
Market price per share on December 31, 19X2	$ 41.00	$ 22.50	$ 19.00

REQUIRED:

a. Prepare the journal entries for the purchases of the investments.
b. Prepare the journal entries to record the recognition of income and the receipt of dividends for the investments.
c. Prepare the journal entries to record the adjustment to the investment account if the market method is used for investments where the ownership percentage is less than 20%.
d. Show how these investments would appear on Rose Corporation's balance sheet and how they would affect the income statement.

LO 5

P13-2A **Consolidated Balance Sheet** Palatka Corporation acquired 100% of Saint Johns Corporation's common stock on September 4, 19X4, for $20,000 cash. Immediately before the businesses combined, each company's balance sheet looked like this:

	Palatka	*Saint Johns*
Cash and other assets	$80,000	$45,000
Accounts payable, etc.	$15,000	$25,000
Stockholders' equity	65,000	20,000
Total liabilities and stockholders' equity	$80,000	$45,000

REQUIRED:

a. Prepare the journal entry to record Palatka's purchase of Saint Johns' stock.

b. Prepare the consolidated balance sheet immediately after the purchase.

LO 6

P13-3A **Consolidated Balance Sheet (Appendix 13-A)** Pop Corporation purchased 75% of Son Company's common stock on January 2, 19X3, for $216,000. Assume the carrying values of Son Company's assets and liabilities are equal to their fair values. Pop has a $5,000 account receivable from Son.

Pop Corporation and Subsidiary
Worksheet for Consolidated Balance Sheet
January 2, 19X3

	POP CORPORATION	SON COMPANY	ELIMINATIONS DEBITS	ELIMINATIONS CREDITS	CONSOLIDATED BALANCE SHEET
Assets					
Cash	84,000	38,000			
Accounts Receivable	60,000	48,000			
Inventories	130,000	98,000			
Investment in Son	216,000				
Plant Assets (net)	270,000	208,000			
	760,000	392,000			
Goodwill					
Liabilities and Stockholders' Equity					
Current Liabilities	27,000	15,000			
Noncurrent Liabilities	263,000	125,000			
Common Stock	284,000	150,000			
Retained Earnings	186,000	102,000			
	760,000	392,000			
Minority Interest					

REQUIRED:

a. Calculate goodwill.

b. Calculate the minority interest.

c. On a separate piece of paper, complete the partially completed worksheet to prepare a consolidated balance sheet for Pop and Son.

PROBLEM SET B

LO 2,4

P13-1B Investments in Stock Broccoli Corporation had never made any long-term investments in marketable equity securities. During 19X6, it decided to invest in Bush Company, Ranger Company, and Bean Company. All investments are classified as long-term. The following information relates to the stock of these companies and other 19X6 results.

	Bush	*Ranger*	*Bean*
Acquisition price	$60,000	$42,000	$81,000
Number of shares	2,000	1,500	4,500
Ownership percentage	10%	16%	40%
Earnings per share	$ 5.50	$ 5.00	$ 3.50
Dividends per share	$ 1.50	$ 1.20	$ 0.75
Market price per share on December 31, 19X6	$31.00	$24.50	$19.00

REQUIRED:

a. Prepare the journal entries for the purchases of the investments.
b. Prepare the journal entries to record the recognition of income and the receipt of dividends for the investments.
c. Prepare the journal entries to record the adjustment to the investment account if the market method is used for investments where the ownership percentage is less than 20%.
d. Show how these investments would appear on Broccoli Corporation's balance sheet and how they would affect the income statement.

LO 5

P13-2B Consolidated Balance Sheet Perry Corporation acquired 100% of Santa Fe Corporation's common stock on March 4, 19X4, for $50,000 cash. Immediately before the businesses combined, each company's balance sheet looked like this:

	Perry	*Santa Fe*
Cash and other assets	$80,000	$50,000
Accounts payable, etc.	$15,000	
Stockholders' equity	65,000	$50,000
Total liabilities and stockholders' equity	$80,000	$50,000

REQUIRED:

a. Prepare the journal entry to record Perry's purchase of Santa Fe's stock.
b. Prepare the consolidated balance sheet immediately after the purchase.

LO 5

P13-3B Consolidated Balance Sheet (Appendix 13-A) Plum Corp. purchased 85% of Seay, Inc.'s common stock on January 2, 19X7, for $324,000. Assume the book values of Seay Inc.'s assets and liabilities are equal to their fair values. Plum has $8,000 of accounts receivable from Seay.

REQUIRED:

a. Calculate goodwill.
b. Calculate the minority interest.
c. On a separate sheet of paper, complete the partially completed worksheet to prepare a consolidated balance sheet for Plum and Seay.

Plum Corp. and Subsidiary
Worksheet for Consolidated Balance Sheet
January 2, 19X7

	PLUM CORP.	SEAY, INC.	ELIMINATIONS		CONSOLIDATED BALANCE SHEET
			DEBITS	CREDITS	
Assets					
Cash	126,000	57,000			
Accounts Receivable	90,000	72,000			
Inventories	195,000	147,000			
Investment in Seay	324,000				
Plant Assets (net)	405,000	312,000			
	1,140,000	588,000			
Goodwill					
Liabilities and Stockholders' Equity					
Current Liabilities	41,000	22,000			
Noncurrent Liabilities	394,000	188,000			
Common Stock	426,000	225,000			
Retained Earnings	279,000	153,000			
	1,140,000	588,000			
Minority Interest					

CRITICAL THINKING AND COMMUNICATING

C13-1 You are the auditor of Modern Electronics Company. You recently informed the chief financial officer (CFO) that a new accounting standard will require that the company's portfolio of long-term investments in stocks will have to be accounted for by the market method (instead of the cost method) beginning with the next set of financial statements. The CFO was very upset at this development and replied: "These are long-term investments, why should the company's performance be judged on changes in the market price of the stocks when the company has no intention of selling the stocks?"

REQUIRED:

Write a letter to the CFO explaining the accounting for long-term investments in stocks and how the financial statements are affected. Be sure and respond to his concern about judging the company's performance when there is no intention to sell the stocks.

C13-2 The financial statements of J.C. Penney Company are reprinted in Appendix B at the end of this text. For this, case you will need to locate the summary of accounting policies, recent accounting standards, and notes to the financial statements.

REQUIRED:

a. Refer to the summary of accounting policies and comment on the accounting policies used for investments in equity securities (not debt).
b. Find the recent accounting standard disclosure concerning debt and equity securities. The Securities and Exchange Commission requires this disclosure even though J.C. Penney has not yet adopted FASB *Statement No. 115*. Why does the Securities and

Exchange Commission require such a disclosure? How might the information be useful to the readers of the financial statements?

c. One of the notes to the financial statements concerns investments. The footnote has two main categories of investments. One, fixed income securities and asset-backed certificates, is carried at amortized cost. The other, equity securities, is carried at market. Using only the disclosures about equity securities:

1. Fill in the T-account for equity securities for 1992 and 1993.

Investments in Equity Securities

1991 Ending balance (at cost)	$18	Assume no sales during 1992.
Net purchases (at cost)	?	
1992 Ending balance (at cost)	?	Assume no sales during 1993.
Net purchases (at cost)	?	
1993 Ending balance (at cost)		

2. Reconstruct the adjusting journal entries for 1992 and 1993 to revalue J.C. Penney's investments in equity securities to market.

CHAPTER 14

Statement of Cash Flows

Peter Chang owns 1,000 shares of Davis Corporation's common stock, which he purchased recently for $6,000. During the current year of 19X2, he knows that Davis Corporation declared cash dividends of $.25 per share. When Peter analyzed the company's balance sheet and income statement for 19X2 (shown in Illustration 14-1 on pages 603–604), he discovered that net income for the year was $14,400, or $1.20 per share. Puzzled about why dividends were less than 25% of earnings, Peter further studied the statements and noticed that cash declined from $8,000 at the beginning of the year to $1,000 at the end of the year. Peter wants to know what happened to the cash since net income was $14,400 and the cash dividends declared certainly did not use up all the cash. While doing his study, Peter noticed another financial statement called the statement of cash flows. Unfamiliar with this statement, he wonders if it might answer the mystery of the disappearing cash.

When a company prepares a *complete set of financial statements*, it includes a statement of cash flows with the income statement, balance sheet, and retained earnings statement.[1] A **statement of cash flows** is a financial statement that displays a business's cash receipts and cash disbursements for a period according to categories of business activities—operating activities, financing activities, and investing activities. The statement shows the reader the business's cash sources and how the business used the cash during the period. Readers use this information in answering such questions as: Why did the company pay little or no cash dividends when it had significant net income? or, How did the company finance the purchase of new plant assets? This chapter presents a discussion of the statement of cash flows, including its usefulness, and describes techniques for preparing the statement.

---

[1]"Statement of Cash Flows," *Statement of Financial Accounting Standards No. 95* (Stamford, Conn.: FASB, 1987), par. 3.

1. Explain the purpose of a statement of cash flows.
2. Describe the operating, investing, and financing classifications of cash flow activities.
3. Explain how to prepare a statement of cash flows.
4. Analyze accrual basis accounting information to determine the effects on cash flows.
5. Describe the indirect method of reporting cash flows from operating activities.
6. Prepare a statement of cash flows using a worksheet (Appendix 14-A).

LO 1

Explain the purpose of a statement of cash flows.

PURPOSE OF A STATEMENT OF CASH FLOWS

The accounting profession has identified information about a business's cash flows as an objective of financial reporting as indicated by the following paragraph:

> Financial reporting should provide information to help present and potential investors and creditors and other users in assessing the amounts, timing, and uncertainty of prospective cash receipts from dividends or interest and the proceeds from the sale, redemption, or maturity of securities or loans. The prospects for those cash receipts are affected by an enterprise's ability to generate enough cash to meet its obligations when due and its other cash operating needs, to reinvest in operations, and to pay cash dividends.[2]

Accountants designed the statement of cash flows to meet this objective by assisting investors, creditors, and other readers of the financial statements in assessing such factors as follow:

- The business's ability to generate positive cash flows in future periods
- The business's ability to meet its obligations and to pay dividends
- Reasons for differences between the amount of net income and the related cash flows from operations
- Both the cash and noncash aspects of the business's investing and financing activities for the period.[3]

Complete Set of Financial Statements

Illustration 14-1 presents a complete set of financial statements for the Davis Corporation. The financial statements presented include a comparative balance sheet for 19X1 and 19X2, an income statement for 19X2, a retained earnings statement for 19X2, and a statement of cash flows for 19X2.

The statement of cash flows shown in Illustration 14-1 classifies cash receipts and cash disbursements according to operating, investing, and financing activities. The general format of a statement of cash flows is depicted visually in Illustration 14-2.

---

[2]"Objectives of Financial Reporting by Business Enterprises." *Statement of Financial Accounting Concepts No. 1* (Stamford, Conn.: FASB, 1978), par. 37.

[3]*Ibid.*, par. 5.

ILLUSTRATION 14-1 Davis Corporation Financial Statements

Davis Corporation
Comparative Balance Sheet
December 31, 19X1 and 19X2

	19X1	19X2	
Assets			
Current assets:			
Cash	$ 8,000	$ 1,000	← Difference is net decrease in cash of $7,000
Accounts receivable	12,000	14,000	
Rent receivable	0	400	
Merchandise inventory	14,000	13,000	
Prepaid insurance	2,000	1,800	
Total current assets	$36,000	$30,200	
Plant assets:			
Office equipment	$ 2,300	$ 2,700	
Accumulated depreciation—office equipment	(1,000)	(1,250)	
Buildings	40,000	45,000	
Accumulated depreciation—buildings	(6,000)	(8,000)	
Land	35,000	30,000	
Total plant assets	$ 70,300	$68,450	
Total assets	$106,300	$98,650	
Liabilities and Stockholder's Equity			
Current liabilities:			
Notes payable	$ 5,000	$10,000	
Accounts payable	8,000	2,300	
Wages and salaries payable	500	750	
Dividends payable	1,500	1,800	
Income taxes payable	1,850	1,950	
Total current liabilities	$16,850	$16,800	
Noncurrent liabilities:			
Notes payable—noncurrent	40,000	15,000	
Total liabilities	$56,850	$31,800	
Stockholders' equity:			
Common stock, $1 par value	$ 10,000	$12,000	
Paid-in capital in excess of par-common	25,000	30,000	
Paid-in capital—stock dividend	0	4,000	
Retained earnings	14,450	20,850	
Total stockholders' equity	$ 49,450	$66,850	
Total liabilities and stockholders' equity	$106,300	$98,650	

ILLUSTRATION 14-1 (Continued) Davis Corporation Financial Statements

Davis Corporation
Income Statement
For the Year Ended December 31, 19X2

Revenues:		
Sales	$84,800	
Rent	2,600	
Total revenues		$87,400
Cost of goods sold		44,000
Gross profit		$43,400
Expenses:		
Wages and salaries expense	$21,000	
Depreciation expense—office equipment	550	
Depreciation expense—buildings	2,000	
Interest expense	800	
Income tax expense	7,250	
Other operating expenses	400	
Total expenses		(32,000)
Gain from sale of property		3,000
Net income		$14,400

Davis Corporation
Statement of Cash Flows
For the Year Ended December 31, 19X2

Cash flows from operating activities:		
Collections from customers	$82,800	
Rent received	2,200	
Payments to suppliers	(48,700)	
Payments to employees	(20,750)	
Interest paid	(800)	
Income taxes paid	(7,150)	
Payments for other operating expenses	(200)	
Net cash flows from operating activities		$7,400
Cash flows from investing activities:		
Purchase of office equipment	$ (700)	
Building addition	(5,000)	
Sale of land	8,000	
Net cash flows from investing activities		2,300
Cash flows from financing activities:		
Payment of 10% note	$(25,000)	
Common stock issued	6,000	
Cash dividends paid	(2,700)	
Net proceeds from short-term notes	5,000	
Net cash used by financing activities		(16,700)
Net decrease in cash		$ (7,000)

ILLUSTRATION 14-1 (Continued) Davis Corporation Financial Statements

Davis Corporation Retained Earnings Statement For the Year Ended December 31, 19X2		
Balance, January 1		$14,450
Add: Net income for 19X2		14,400
Total		$28,850
Less: Cash dividends declared	$3,000	
Stock dividends declared	5,000	8,000
Balance, December 31		$20,850

ILLUSTRATION 14-2 Format of Statement of Cash Flows

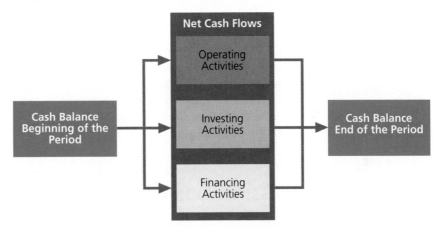

For each of the three activity classifications, we sum the cash receipts and cash disbursements and present a net cash inflow or outflow. Then, we sum the net cash flows for the three classifications and present the total as the change in cash for the period. The change in cash in the statement of cash flows ($7,000) equals the difference between the cash balances in the comparative balance sheet ($8,000 − $1,000).

A statement of cash flows plays a complementary role with a balance sheet and income statement in providing a *complete* picture of the business's assets and financial structure (liabilities and stockholders' equity) and how those assets, liabilities, and equities changed during a period. A balance sheet provides information about the assets, liabilities, and stockholders' equity of a business at a *moment in time*. However, the balance sheet provides an incomplete picture because it provides no information about how changes in those elements occur from period to period. Both an income statement and a statement of cash flows provide information about how changes in the business's net assets occurred during a period. The information an income statement provides is about changes in net assets resulting from revenue and expense transactions of the business. On the other hand, a statement of cash flows provides more detailed information about how particular assets, liabilities, and stockholders' equity elements changed as a result of cash receipts and cash disbursements from the business's operating, investing, and financing activities.

The statement of cash flows is useful for identifying the business's cash sources and how the business used that cash. Also, the statement of cash flows can be used in conjunction with other financial statements to explain changes in the business's financial position. While balance sheets and income statements provide information about these activities, they present only partial information. For example, a financial statement reader (such as Peter Chang who was introduced at the beginning of this chapter) might ask the following question concerning the Davis Corporation: "How is it possible that with net income of $14,400, cash on the comparative balance sheet *decreased* by $7,000 ($8,000 − $1,000) for the year even though the company declared only $3,000 of dividends?"

Interpreting the Statement of Cash Flows

An examination of the statement of cash flows reveals the following response to Peter Chang's question about the disappearing cash: Even though net income is $14,400, operating activities actually generated net cash flows of only $7,400. Also, investing activities generated net cash flows of $2,300, resulting from the sale of land less the purchase of new assets. Finally, financing activities used net cash of $16,700, resulting from the net effects of issuing common stock, paying off debt of $25,000, paying the $3,000 cash dividends, and increasing short-term borrowings. The net effect of these transactions is a $7,000 decrease in cash for the year. Overall, rather than paying greater dividends, Davis Corporation paid off a large portion of its long-term debt. Certainly, such a detailed analysis of Davis Corporation would be difficult without the statement of cash flows.

LO 2

Describe the operating, investing, and financing classifications of cash flow activities.

CLASSIFICATION OF CASH FLOWS

As you see in Illustration 14-1, the statement of cash flows classifies the business's cash receipts and cash payments according to the categories of operating, investing, and financing activities.

Operating Activities

A business's normal operations result in both cash receipts and cash disbursements. Cash receipts result from selling merchandise and providing services. The cost of goods sold and other operating expenses result in cash disbursements. The revenues and expenses reported in the income statement, however, do not coincide with the cash receipts and cash disbursements. Under GAAP, we prepare the income statement on an accrual basis, which means we record the revenues when earned and expenses when incurred. The receipts and payments of cash for these revenues and expenses may occur in either an earlier or later period than the period we report the revenues and expenses.

All transactions and events that are not classified as either investing or financing activities are classified as operating activities. Cash flows from operating activities generally are the *cash effects* of the transactions—selling or producing goods or providing services—included to determine net income. Illustration 14-3 presents a listing of the types of transactions that are classified as operating activities for the statement of cash flows.

In some cases, the classification of certain transactions depends on the business's nature. For example, it is generally assumed that property, plant, and

ILLUSTRATION 14-3 Cash Flows From Operating Activities

Cash Inflows	Cash Outflows

*Cash sales to customers
*Collections of both short-term and
    long-term receivables from credit sales
    to customers
*Cash receipts of interest and dividends
 Refunds from suppliers
 Cash collected from settlements of
    lawsuits
	*Payments to suppliers for goods and
	    services
	*Payments of both short-term and
	    long-term payables resulting from the
	    purchase of goods and services
	*Payments of taxes, fines, and other fees
	*Payments of interest
	 Payments to settle lawsuits
	 Refunds to customers
	 Contributions to charities

*Illustrated in the statement of cash flows in Illustration 14-1.

equipment acquisitions and sales are part of the business's investing activities because the business uses such assets for a long time to produce revenue. Some businesses, such as a dealer in used construction equipment, earn net income by purchasing property, plant, and equipment and then, in a short period of time, reselling those assets at a profit. In the latter case, we classify the purchase and sale of property, plant, and equipment as an operating activity, rather than as an investing activity, because, in effect, those transactions are merely inventory transactions.

Direct Method of Calculating Cash Flows From Operating Activities.   The statement of cash flows in Illustration 14-1 presents cash flows from operating activities using the direct method. The **direct method** of presenting cash flows from operating activities shows major classes of cash receipts and cash payments and their sum. The sum is net cash flows from operating activities.

Indirect Method of Calculating Cash Flows From Operating Activities.   An alternative approach to reporting cash flows from operating activities is the indirect or reconciliation method. The **indirect method** begins with net income and shows the adjustments necessary to determine cash flows from operating activities. This chapter emphasizes the direct method because we believe it reports cash flows from operating activities more clearly. We illustrate the indirect method later in the chapter.

Investing Activities

Businesses enter into various kinds of investing activities that result in cash receipts and cash disbursements. These transactions involve purchasing and selling assets that are classified in the balance sheet as short-term and long-term investments, plant assets, and intangible assets. Also, lending and collecting loans are considered investing activities. Illustration 14-4 lists the kinds of transactions that are considered investing activities in the statement of cash flows.

In Illustration 14-4, the collection of loans listed as a cash inflow needs further explanation. Normally, we classify the collection of loan principal as a cash flow from an investing activity. If the loan is a receivable from the sale of goods or services, then the cash inflow is considered an operating activity as shown in Illustration 14-3. Also, all collections of interest and dividends are considered operating activities.

ILLUSTRATION 14-4 Cash Flows From Investing Activities

Cash Inflows	Cash Outflows
Collections of loans	Payments in the form of loans to others
*Cash received from the sale of plant assets (including land)	Payments to purchase stocks and bonds of other companies
Cash received from the sale of intangible assets	*Payments to purchase plant assets (including land)
	Payments to purchase intangible assets

*Illustrated in the statement of cash flows in Illustration 14-1.

Financing Activities

Various cash receipts and cash disbursements occur as a result of the business's financing activities. Financing activities include:

1. Obtaining assets from owners, repaying assets to owners, and providing owners with returns in the form of withdrawals or dividends
2. Obtaining loans from creditors and repaying the principal amount of the loans

Illustration 14-5 presents a listing of the kinds of transactions that are considered financing activities in the statement of cash flows.

ILLUSTRATION 14-5 Cash Flows From Financing Activities

Cash Inflows	Cash Outflows
*Proceeds from issuing common and preferred stock	*Payments of common and preferred dividends
Proceeds from issuing bonds	Payments to purchase treasury stock
*Proceeds from other short-term and long-term borrowings	*Repayments of principal amounts to creditors

*Illustrated in the statement of cash flows in Illustration 14-1.

Transactions involving repayments to creditors need further explanation. As you saw in the discussion of operating activities, repayments of borrowings from suppliers for the purchase of goods and services are considered operating activities. Repayments of other types of short-term and long-term borrowings are considered financing activities in the statement of cash flows. Examples of short-term borrowings classified as financing activities would include repaying amounts borrowed under lines of credit agreements with banks. Long-term borrowings classified as financing activities would include long-term notes payable and bonds payable.

LO 3
Explain how to prepare a statement of cash flows.

PREPARING THE STATEMENT OF CASH FLOWS

To prepare a statement of cash flows, accountants analyze the accounts to identify the cash receipts and cash disbursements associated with the three classifications of operating, investing, and financing activities. The framework for the analysis of accounts relies on the characteristics of the double-entry accounting system and the balance sheet equation. In particular, any change in Cash is associated with a change in another account. We know from the accounting equation (Assets = Liabilities + Stockholders' Equity) that if the amount of cash increases, either the other assets must decrease by an equal amount or liabilities and stockholders' equity must increase by an equal amount. Similarly, if the amount of cash decreases, either other assets must increase by an equal amount or liabilities and stockholders' equity must decrease by an equal amount.

The Accounting Equation

These relationships may be depicted by manipulating the accounting equation as follows:

$$\textbf{Assets = Liabilities + Stockholders' Equity}$$

$$\textbf{Cash + Other Assets = Liabilities + Stockholders' Equity}$$

$$\textit{C + OA = L + SE}$$

Subtracting other assets (*OA*) from both sides of the equation results in the following expression of the accounting equation:

$$\textit{C = L + SE - OA}$$

As we account for a business's transactions and other activities, change (Δ) in one side of the equation must be accompanied by an equal change in the other side of the equation or the balance will not be retained:

$$\Delta\textit{C} = \Delta\textit{L} + \Delta\textit{SE} - \Delta\textit{OA}$$

This final equation shows that a change in cash must be accompanied by an equal change in liabilities or stockholders' equity in the *same* direction, or an equal change in other assets in the *opposite* direction. For example, assume a business has the following balance sheet totals:

$$\textit{C} \quad = \quad \textit{L} \quad + \quad \textit{SE} \quad - \quad \textit{OA}$$
$$\$10,000 = \$12,000 + \$38,000 - \$40,000$$

The purchase of an asset for $3,000 cash results in a decrease in cash of $3,000 and an increase in other assets of $3,000 as follows:

$$\textit{C} \quad = \quad \textit{L} \quad + \quad \textit{SE} \quad - \quad \textit{OA}$$
$$\$10,000 = \$12,000 + \$38,000 - \$40,000$$
$$\underline{(3,000) = \hspace{4.5cm} - \quad \underline{3,000}}$$
$$\$\,7,000 = \$12,000 + \$38,000 - \$43,000$$

Notice that the equation remains in balance after including the effects of the transaction.

If the business borrows $6,000 from the bank, the effect is an increase in cash of $6,000 and an increase in liabilities of $6,000:

$$\textit{C} \quad = \quad \textit{L} \quad + \quad \textit{SE} \quad - \quad \textit{OA}$$
$$\$\,7,000 = \$12,000 + \$38,000 - \$43,000$$
$$\underline{6,000 = \quad \underline{6,000}}$$
$$\$13,000 = \$18,000 + \$38,000 - \$43,000$$

Again, the equation remains in balance after including the effects of the transaction.

Remember that Cash is a debit-balance account; therefore, increases in cash are accompanied by credits to a noncash account(s). For example, the issuance of common stock for cash results in a debit (increase) in Cash and a credit to Common Stock. On the other hand, decreases in cash are accompanied by debits to a noncash account(s). For example, the purchase of a plant asset for cash results in a credit to Cash and a debit to a plant asset account.

Accountants use these relationships in analyzing the accounts to prepare a statement of cash flows. The account analysis consists of *analyzing the changes in the noncash balance sheet accounts to explain the changes in cash for the period*. The account analysis is complicated by the fact that not all changes in noncash accounts result in a cash inflow or outflow. For example, the purchase of a building by incurring a mortgage payable does not have an immediate effect on cash. Also, depreciation expense does not involve an entry to Cash. To prepare the statement of cash flows, the accountant must sort through the changes in the noncash balance sheet accounts and *identify those transactions and events that change the noncash accounts and involve cash receipts and disbursements*.

Sources of Information

To perform the account analysis described in the previous section, the accountant should have the following sources of information:

- *Comparative balance sheet.* The accountant needs a balance sheet for the end of the current period and a balance sheet for the end of the previous period to determine the *net* change in Cash and the noncash balance sheet accounts for the period.
- *Income statement.* The accountant uses an income statement for the current period to determine the cash flows from operating activities. The income statement provides information about the revenue and expenses for the period, including noncash expenses such as depreciation.
- *Summary transaction data.* The accountant can obtain summary information about the components of changes in account balances by analyzing the general ledger accounts. The summary information about transactions is needed because the comparative balance sheet only shows the *net* changes in the various account balances. For example, a $1,000 increase in Equipment may be the result of a purchase of equipment costing $1,000, or the result of a $2,000 purchase and the disposal of equipment that originally cost $1,000. Acquisitions and dispositions of plant assets are shown as separate investment activities on a statement of cash flows.

LO 4

Analyze accrual basis accounting information to determine the effects on cash flows.

PREPARING A STATEMENT OF CASH FLOWS— AN ILLUSTRATION

In Illustration 14-1, the statement of cash flows for Davis Corporation is presented. Following is a discussion of how we developed that statement from the company's accrual basis records.

In addition to the company's financial statements, shown in Illustration 14-1, we derived the following information from analyzing Davis Corporation's accounts:

1. Prepaid Insurance is related to "Other operating expenses" shown on the income statement.
2. New office equipment was purchased at a cost of $700.
3. Worn-out and fully depreciated office equipment was discarded. The equipment cost $300 when purchased.
4. A new storage room was added to the building at a cost of $5,000.
5. Depreciation expense, office equipment, is $550.
6. Depreciation expense, building, is $2,000.
7. Land that cost $5,000 was sold for $8,000.
8. $25,000 of the 10% note payable was paid.
9. A 10% stock dividend was declared when the market price of the stock was $5 per share.
10. After the stock dividend, common stock was issued for $6 per share.
11. Cash dividends of $3,000 were declared.

Cash Flows From Operating Activities

The analysis of cash flows from operating activities consists of identifying *relevant* income statement amounts. We then adjust the income statement amounts for any changes in related balance sheet accounts. The result of the adjustment is the amount of cash flow from the identified activity.

Collections From Customers. If a business has only cash sales, the amount of sales revenue it reports in the income statement is the amount of cash it collected from customers. However, when a business has credit sales, we adjust the amount of sales revenue for the change in accounts receivable. A decrease in accounts receivable for the period means that cash collections from customers for the period exceed sales revenue on the accrual basis. Conversely, an increase in accounts receivable means that cash collections from customers was less than sales revenue in the income statement.

Illustration 14-1 shows sales revenue in the income statement of $84,800 for 19X2 and accounts receivable in the comparative balance sheet increased from $12,000 at the beginning of the year to $14,000 at the end of the year. With this information, a summary of sales revenue transactions is:

		Accounts Receivable		
Beg. Bal.	12,000			
Sales	84,800		**Collections**	**82,800**
End. Bal.	14,000			

The T-account summary shows that for accounts receivable to increase, cash collections from customers must be less than sales revenue recorded on the accrual basis. In other words, if we know that sales revenue, which increase accounts receivable, are $84,800, but that the Accounts Receivable balance increased by $2,000, then we know that collections must have been $82,800. In general, the following relationships exist:

$$\text{Cash Collections from Customers} = \text{Sales Revenue} \begin{cases} - \text{ Increase in Accounts Receivable} \\ or \\ + \text{ Decrease in Accounts Receivable} \end{cases}$$

We show the $82,800 cash collections from customers in the statement of cash flows in Illustration 14-1 as a cash *inflow* from operating activities.

Rent Received. The analysis of rent received is similar to cash collected from customers. The analysis begins with rent revenue from the income statement. We then adjust the amount of rent revenue for any change in rent receivable in the comparative balance sheet. In general, we use the following relationships to calculate rent received:

$$\text{Rent Received} = \text{Rent Revenue} \begin{cases} - \text{ Increase in Rent Receivable} \\ or \\ + \text{ Decrease in Rent Receivable} \end{cases}$$

Illustration 14-1 shows that rent revenue in the income statement is $2,600 for 19X2 and that rent receivable in the comparative balance sheet increased by $400 during 19X2. The rent revenue transactions may be summarized as follows:

Rent Receivable			
Beg. Bal.	0		
Rent Revenue	2,600	**Receipts**	**2,200**
End. Bal.	400		

Rent revenue increases rent receivable, and receipts of rent payments decrease rent receivable. Since rent receivable increased by $400 for Davis Corporation during 19X2, rent revenue must exceed receipts of rent payments by $400. Therefore, to calculate rent received, we reduce rent revenue by the $400 increase in rent receivable. We show the rent received in the statement of cash flows in Illustration 14-1 as a cash *inflow* from operating activities.

Payments to Suppliers. The analysis of cash payments to suppliers begins with cost of goods sold from the income statement. Cost of goods sold is different from cash payments for purchases of merchandise inventory in two respects:

1. Cost of goods sold is different from purchases by the amount of the change in merchandise inventory for the period.
2. Purchases are different from cash payments to suppliers of merchandise by the change in accounts payable for the period.

The calculation of cash payments to suppliers involves the following two adjustments:

$$\text{Purchases} = \text{Cost of Goods Sold} \begin{cases} + \text{ Increase in Merchandise Inventory} \\ or \\ - \text{ Decrease in Merchandise Inventory} \end{cases}$$

$$\text{Cash Payments to Suppliers} = \text{Purchases} \begin{cases} + \text{ Decrease in Accounts Payable} \\ or \\ - \text{ Increase in Accounts Payable} \end{cases}$$

For Davis Corporation, cost of goods sold in the income statement is $44,000 for 19X2; and merchandise inventory in the comparative balance sheet decreased from $14,000 to $13,000 during 19X2. The merchandise inventory transactions may be summarized as follows:

Merchandise Inventory

Beg. Bal.	14,000		
Purchases	**43,000**	Cost of goods sold	44,000
End. Bal.	13,000		

With the amount of purchases calculated as $43,000, the purchases transactions may be summarized thus:

Accounts Payable

		Beg. Bal.	8,000
Payments	**48,700**	Purchases	43,000
		End. Bal.	2,300

We show the cash payments to suppliers of $48,700 in the statement of cash flows in Illustration 14-1 as a cash *outflow* from operating activities.

Payments to Employees. The income statement amount with which to begin the analysis of cash payments to employees is wages and salaries expense. The balance sheet account related to wages and salaries expense is Wages and Salaries Payable. The calculation of payments to employees is:

$$\text{Cash Payments to Employees} = \text{Wages and Salaries Expense} \begin{cases} + \text{ Decrease in Wages and Salaries Payable} \\ or \\ - \text{ Increase in Wages and Salaries Payable} \end{cases}$$

In Illustration 14-1, Davis Corporation reports wages and salaries expense in the income statement of $21,000 for 19X2. Wages and salaries payable in the comparative balance sheet increased $250 during 19X2. We summarize the wages and salaries transactions as follows:

Wages and Salaries Payable

		Beg. Bal.	500
Payments	**20,750**	Expense	21,000
		End. Bal.	750

We show the cash payments to employees of $20,750 in the statement of cash flows in Illustration 14-1 as a cash *outflow* from operating activities.

Interest Paid. The analysis of interest paid begins with interest expense in the income statement. We then adjust the amount of interest expense for any change in interest payable as follows:

$$\text{Interest Paid} = \text{Interest Expense} \begin{cases} + \text{ Decrease in Interest Payable} \\ or \\ - \text{ Increase in Interest Payable} \end{cases}$$

In Illustration 14-1, Davis Corporation reports interest expense in the income statement of $800. Since no interest payable is shown in either the balance sheet at the beginning of the year or the balance sheet at the end of the year, interest paid must be equal to interest expense. We summarize the interest transactions thus:

Interest Payable

		Beg. Bal.	0
Payments	**800**	Expense	800
		End. Bal.	0

We show the cash payments of $800 for interest in the statement of cash flows in Illustration 14-1 as a cash *outflow* from operating activities.

Income Taxes Paid. The analysis of income taxes paid is similar to the analyses of cash payments for wages and salaries and interest payments. We adjust the amount of income tax expense for any change in income taxes payable as follows:

$$\text{Income Taxes Paid} = \text{Income Tax Expense} \begin{cases} + \text{ Decrease in Income Taxes Payable} \\ or \\ - \text{ Increase in Income Taxes Payable} \end{cases}$$

For Davis Corporation, we summarize the income taxes transactions as follows:

Income Taxes Payable

		Beg. Bal.	1,850
Payments	**7,150**	Expense	7,250
		End. Bal.	1,950

We show income taxes paid of $7,150 in the statement of cash flows in Illustration 14-1 as a cash *outflow* from operating activities.

Payments for Other Operating Expenses. The analysis of operating expenses begins with operating expenses shown in the income statement in Illustration 14-1. Included in other operating expenses are: rent, insurance, utilities, property taxes, etc. To calculate cash payments, the amount of operating expenses requires two adjustments for changes in related balance sheet accounts: prepaid expenses and expenses payable. These adjustments are:

$$\text{Cash Payments for Operating Expenses} = \text{Operating Expenses} \begin{cases} + \text{ Increases in Prepaid Expenses} \\ or \\ - \text{ Decreases in Prepaid Expenses} \\ and \\ + \text{ Decreases in Expenses Payable} \\ or \\ - \text{ Increases in Expenses Payable} \end{cases}$$

For Davis Corporation, the "Other operating expenses" shown in the income statement in Illustration 14-1 has a related prepaid expenses account. However, there is no related payable account. Therefore, we summarize the other operating expenses transactions as follows:

Prepaid Insurance

Beg. Bal.	2,000		
Payments	**200**	Expense	400
End. Bal.	1,800		

We show the cash payments of $200 for other operating expenses in the statement of cash flows in Illustration 14-1 as a cash *outflow* from operating activities.

Gain From Sale of Property (Land).   The income statement in Illustration 14-1 shows a gain from the sale of property (land) of $3,000. The gain from the sale of land is not analyzed in determining cash flows from operating activities because we classify cash received from the sale of plant assets as an investing activity (as shown in Illustration 14-4). We analyze the gain from the sale of land below in the discussion of investing activities.

Cash Flows From Investing Activities

The statement of cash flows in Illustration 14-1 shows that in 19X2, Davis Corporation had three cash flows resulting from investing activities.

Purchase of Office Equipment.   During 19X2, Davis Corporation purchased new office equipment at a cost of $700. In the statement of cash flows, this amount is shown as a cash *outflow* from investing activities. The listing of information obtained from analyzing the accounts, however, shows that office equipment was affected by three transactions described in Items 2, 3 and 5 on page 611. Transaction 2 is the purchase of new office equipment described above, and Transaction 3 is the discarding of worn-out and fully depreciated office equipment. At the time Davis discarded the equipment, it made the following entry:

(Date)	Accumulated Depreciation—Office Equipment	300	
	Office Equipment		300
	To record the disposal of fully depreciated office equipment.		

As you can see in this entry, no cash flows occurred as a result of this transaction. Therefore, this transaction is not included in the statement of cash flows because it does not result in either a cash inflow or a cash outflow.

Transaction 5 is for depreciation of the office equipment for 19X2. Recording depreciation expense also does not include cash flows, as shown in Davis's following entry to record depreciation expense:

19X2			
Dec. 31	Depreciation Expense—Office Equipment	550	
	Accumulated Depreciation—Office Equipment		550
	To record depreciation expense.		

The transactions affecting office equipment may be summarized as follows:

Office Equipment				Accumulated Depreciation—Office Equip.			
Beg. Bal.	2,300					Beg. Bal.	1,000
Purchase	**700**	Disposal	300	Disposal	300	Expense	550
End. Bal.	2,700					End. Bal.	1,250

Notice that the beginning and ending balances of the two accounts can be reconciled to the amounts in the comparative balance sheet. This reconciliation provides assurance that no transactions involving office equipment are omitted from the analysis.

Building Addition.   During 19X2, Davis Corporation added a new storage room at a cost of $5,000 to its building. We show this transaction as a cash *outflow* in the statement of cash flows. Transaction 6 on page 611 for depreciation expense is also related to the building. As you have seen, recording depreciation expense does not involve cash flows. The transactions related to the building may be summarized thus:

Building			Accumulated Depreciation—Building		
Beg. Bal.	40,000			Beg. Bal.	6,000
Addition	**5,000**			Expense	2,000
End. Bal.	45,000			End. Bal.	8,000

Sale of Land. During 19X2, Davis Corporation sold land. In the statement of cash flows, we report the transaction as a cash *inflow* from investing activities in the amount of $8,000. The comparative balance sheet shows a decrease in land of $5,000. The difference is the gain from the sale of $3,000 that is shown in the income statement. The entry Davis made when it sold the land shows that the cash inflow is $8,000.

(Date)	Cash	8,000	
	Land		5,000
	Gain from Sale of Property		3,000
	To record the sale of property.		

The transaction involving land is shown in the accounts as follows:

Land			
Beg. Bal.	35,000	Sale	5,000
End. Bal.	30,000		

Cash Flows From Financing Activities

For 19X2, Davis Corporation reports four cash flow transactions from financing activities.

Payment of 10% Note. Davis Corporation paid off $25,000 of the 10% note payable during 19X2. In the statement of cash flows, we show the transaction as a cash *outflow* from financing activities. In the accounts, the transaction is shown thus:

Notes Payable—Noncurrent			
		Beg. Bal.	40,000
Payment	**25,000**		
		End. Bal.	15,000

Common Stock Issued. In 19X2, Davis Corporation had two transactions involving common stock. The first transaction is the 10% stock dividend Davis declared when the market price of the stock was $5 per share. The stock dividend is not a "large" stock dividend. Therefore, the stock dividend is recorded by capitalizing the market price of the stock issued as the dividend. As shown by the following entry, the stock dividend does not involve cash flow:

(Date)	Retained Earnings	5,000	
	Common Stock		1,000
	Paid-In Capital—Stock Dividend		4,000
	To record 10% stock dividend (10% x 10,000 x $5).		

The other transaction involving common stock is the issuance of 1,000 shares for $6 per share. In the statement of cash flows, we show this transaction as a cash inflow of $6,000 from financing activities. The effect on cash flows of this transaction can be seen by examining Davis's entry to record the issuance of the stock:

(Date)	Cash	6,000	
	Common Stock		1,000
	Paid-In Capital In Excess of Par–Common		5,000
	To record the issuance of $1 par value stock		
	for $6 per share.		

The common stock transactions for 19X2 may be summarized as follows:

Common Stock		
Beg. Bal.	10,000
Dividend	1,000
Issuance	**1,000**
End. Bal.	12,000

Paid-In Capital In Excess of Par—Common		
Beg. Bal.	25,000
Issuance	**5,000**
End. Bal.	30,000

Paid-In Capital—Stock Dividend		
Beg. Bal.	0
Dividend	4,000
End. Bal.	4,000

Cash Dividends Paid. The analysis of cash dividends paid begins with the amount of cash dividends declared. To calculate the amount of cash dividends paid, we adjust the amount declared for the change in dividends payable, as follows:

$$\text{Cash Dividends Paid} = \text{Cash Dividends Declared} \begin{cases} + \text{ Decrease in Dividends Payable} \\ or \\ - \text{ Increase in Dividends Payable} \end{cases}$$

The amount of cash dividends declared is $3,000 (from additional information Item 11 on page 611 or from the retained earnings statement in Illustration 14-1). The comparative balance sheet shows that dividends payable increased by $300 during 19X2. In the statement of cash flows, we show cash dividends paid of $2,700 as a cash *outflow* from financing activities. We summarize the cash dividends transactions as follows:

Dividends Payable			
Payments **2,700**	Beg. Bal.	1,500
	Declared	3,000
	End. Bal.	1,800

Net Proceeds From Short-Term Notes. Many businesses maintain lines of credit with banks as well as other sources of short-term credit such as commercial paper. Borrowings from these sources occur during the year as the business needs funds, and repayments occur within a relatively short period of time. During 19X2, Davis Corporation had net proceeds of $5,000 from these sources. That is, the borrowings exceeded repayments by $5,000. For this type of debt, the borrowings and repayments may be shown as a net cash inflow or a net cash outflow. Since Davis Corporation had net proceeds, in the statement of cash flows, we show $5,000 as a cash *inflow* from financing activities.

Additional Considerations in Preparing the Statement

The preparation of a statement of cash flows sometimes involves certain additional considerations that are discussed below.

Cash and Cash Equivalents.   As discussed in an earlier chapter, businesses sometimes have cash on hand that is not temporarily needed in their daily operations. Rather than let the cash be idle, businesses invest it in short-term, highly liquid securities (e.g., U.S. Treasury bills) to earn income. These temporary investments of excess cash are called **cash equivalents**. In a statement of cash flows, cash should be combined with or include cash equivalents.[4] Cash plus cash equivalents is used because in evaluating a business's cash flows, it matters little to a reader whether the cash is on hand, on deposit in a bank, or invested temporarily in *highly liquid assets*. In preparing a statement of cash flows, cash and short-term investments that management designates as cash equivalents are combined and treated as a single item.

In the notes to its October 31, 1992, annual report, General Cinema Corporation describes cash and cash equivalents as follows:

Cash and equivalents

Cash equivalents consist of liquid investments which are readily convertible into cash. Cash and equivalents are stated at cost plus accrued interest, which approximates market. At October 31 cash and equivalents consisted of the following:

(In thousands)	1992	1991
Cash	$ 19,162	$ 18,189
Bank obligations	45,160	800,813
Corporate obligations	254,115	474,696
Other cash equivalents	112,291	325,270
Total cash and equivalents	$430,728	$1,618,968

Noncash Investing and Financing Activities.   A statement of cash flows reports only the business's cash receipts and cash disbursements. For this reason, there may be some significant transactions that did not involve either receiving or paying cash. Some common examples of noncash investing and financing transactions include the following:

1. *Acquiring assets by assuming liabilities.* A business may purchase land and buildings by assuming a mortgage payable.
2. *Acquiring assets by issuing stock.* A company may purchase assets such as plant assets and intangible assets by issuing preferred or common stock directly to the seller.
3. *Exchanges of nonmonetary assets.* Companies commonly trade one asset to another company or individual for a more desirable asset.
4. *Issuance of stock to repay loans.* A company may repay a loan by issuing preferred or common stock to the creditor.

To present a complete picture of the business's investing and financing activities, significant noncash investing and financing transactions are presented

---

[4]*Ibid.*, par. 7.

in a separate schedule following the statement of cash flows or in the notes to the financial statements.[5] An example of a separate schedule of noncash investing and financing activities is shown in Illustration 14-6.

ILLUSTRATION 14-6 Schedule of Noncash Investing and Financing Activities

Preferred stock issued to settle noncurrent debt	$ 125,000
Purchase of land and building by assumption of mortgage payable	890,000
Exchange of land in Texas for land in Washington	100,000
	$1,115,000

Other noncash transactions such as stock dividends, stock splits, and appropriations of retained earnings are neither investing nor financing activities and are not reported in the schedule of noncash investing and financing activities. Information about these noncash transactions is generally reported in the retained earnings statement or in schedules and notes explaining changes in stockholders' equity.

LO 5

Describe the indirect method of reporting cash flows from operating activities.

ALTERNATIVE PRESENTATION OF CASH FLOWS FROM OPERATING ACTIVITIES

The indirect method of reporting cash flows from operating activities begins with net income and adjusts for items that are included in net income but did not affect cash flows from operating activities. There are three types of adjustments to net income.

Noncash Expenses

Certain expenses that are included in net income do not result in a cash outflow. The primary noncash expenses are depreciation and amortization. The offsetting entry for these expenses is to an accumulated depreciation account and to an intangible asset account, respectively. The cash flows associated with these transactions occur at the time of purchase and disposal of the related assets and are classified then as investing activities.

Adjustments to Convert Revenues and Expenses to the Cash Basis

Revenues and expenses are recognized on the accrual basis at times that may be different than the time of the related cash flows. The adjustments to net income for these items involve analyzing changes in receivables, inventories, prepaid expenses, and payables that are related to revenues and expenses.

Nonoperating Items

Gains and losses from investing and financing transactions are included in net income, but the transactions are not considered operating activities. These gains and losses are from disposals of plant assets and settlements of long-term liabili-

---

[5]*Ibid.*, par. 32.

ties. *These transactions are considered investing and financing activities.* Therefore, the gains and losses associated with these transactions should be removed from net income in calculating cash flows from operating activities.

The Indirect Method—An Illustration

Illustration 14-7 presents Davis Company's statement of cash flows following the indirect method of reporting cash flows from operating activities. Notice that only the operating activities section is different from the statement of cash flows in Illustration 14-1, which follows the direct method.

ILLUSTRATION 14-7 Statement of Cash Flows (Indirect Method)

Davis Corporation Statement of Cash Flows For the Year Ended December 31, 19X2			
Cash flows from operating activities:			
Net income		$ 14,400	
Noncash expense:			
Depreciation		2,550	
Adjustments to convert revenues and expenses to cash basis			
Increase in accounts receivable	$(2,000)		
Increase in rent receivable	(400)		
Decrease in merchandise inventory	1,000		
Decrease in prepaid insurance	200		
Decrease in accounts payable	(5,700)		
Increase in wages and salaries payable	250		
Increase in income taxes payable	100	(6,550)	
Adjustment for nonoperating item:			
Gain on sale of land		(3,000)	
Net cash flows from operating activities			$ 7,400
Cash flows from investing activities:			
Purchase of office equipment		$ (700)	
Building addition		(5,000)	
Sale of land		8,000	
Net cash flows from investing activities			2,300
Cash flows from financing activities:			
Payment of 10% note		$(25,000)	
Common stock issued		6,000	
Cash dividend paid		(2,700)	
Net proceeds from short-term notes		5,000	
Net cash used by financing activities			(16,700)
Net decrease in cash			$(7,000)

Although the FASB expressed a clear preference for the direct method of reporting cash flows from operating activities, most businesses use the indirect method. The reasons they usually offer for using the indirect method involve past practice and cost. Historically, they have used the indirect method. Also, changing their accounting systems to collect information to prepare the statement using the direct method would be too costly. Presented in Illustration 14-8 are the results of a survey of 600 large corporations about their reporting of cash flows.

ILLUSTRATION 14-8 Method of Reporting Cash Flows From Operating Activities

	1991	1990	1989
Indirect method	585	585	583
Direct method	15	15	17
Total	600	600	600

Source: *Accounting Trends and Techniques*, 1992, p. 392.

SUMMARY

Explain the purpose of a statement of cash flows. The primary purpose of a statement of cash flows is to provide information about the business's cash receipts and cash disbursements during a period. A secondary objective of the statement is to provide information about the business's investing and financing activities during a period. Classifying cash flows in the statement into categories of operating, investing, and financing activities serve these two purposes.

Describe the operating, investing, and financing classifications of cash flow activities. Cash receipts and cash disbursements from operating activities are the cash effects of revenue and expense transactions. Investing activities include transactions that involve acquiring and disposing of productive assets, investing in securities, and investing in intangible assets. Financing activities include transactions with stockholders (owners) and creditors.

Explain how to prepare a statement of cash flows. To prepare a statement of cash flows, accountants analyze the accounts to identify the cash receipts and cash disbursements associated with operating, investing, and financing activities. The information accountants use includes comparative balance sheets, income statements, and additional information from the business's accounts.

Analyze accrual basis accounting information to determine the effects on cash flows. In preparing the statement of cash flows, we adjust income statement amounts for the differences between the timing of related cash flows and the timing of revenue and expense recognition under accrual accounting.

Describe the indirect method of reporting cash flows from operating activities. The indirect method begins with net income and adjusts for items that are included in net income but did not affect cash flows from operating activities. These adjustments are for noncash expenses, adjustments to convert revenues and expenses to the cash basis, and nonoperating items.

APPENDIX 14-A: USING A WORKSHEET TO PREPARE THE STATEMENT OF CASH FLOWS

In earlier chapters, we discussed how accountants use a worksheet to prepare the income statement and balance sheet. For complex situations involving numerous adjustments, accountants also use a worksheet to facilitate the preparation of the statement of cash flows. In this Appendix, we give a comprehensive example to illustrate the use of a worksheet for preparing a statement of cash flows. The worksheet we demonstrate is for the indirect method for cash flows from operating activities. We chose this approach because of its widespread use in the business world. A similar worksheet method is available for the direct method.

LO 6

Prepare a statement of cash flows using a worksheet.

PREPARING THE WORKSHEET

The worksheet for preparing Davis Corporation's statement of cash flows is presented in Illustration 14-9. The worksheet consists of five columns. The first column is for listing the names of the accounts. The remaining four columns are for listing the dollar amounts of and changes in the account balances. We use the following steps in preparing the worksheet:

1. Enter the beginning balances of the balance sheet accounts in the first dollar column, and enter the ending balances in the fourth dollar column.
2. List the accounts with debit balances first, followed by the accounts with credit balances. This convention means that accumulated depreciation accounts are listed with the credit balances (such as liabilities) rather than as contra-asset accounts as presented in the balance sheet. Listing the accounts in this order facilitates the analysis of the changes in account balances. Recall that any credit change to an account balance is a possible increase in cash and any debit is a possible decrease in cash.
3. After entering the account balances, sum the debits and credits in each column to make sure that they are equal in each of the two columns. If the debits and credits are not equal, you have made an error in entering the data in the worksheet. Before proceeding, locate and correct the error(s).
4. Enter relevant components of the changes in accounts in the Account Analysis columns. These entries (1) represent changes in the account balances and (2) allow the determination of cash flows from operating, investing, and financing activities, which are listed at the bottom of the worksheet. For some changes in account balances, more than one entry is necessary to explain the change. For example, in Illustration 14-9, two entries are needed to explain the $400 increase in office equipment: (1) a $700 debit (Entry f) and (2) a $300 credit (Entry g). Notice that the two entries net to a $400 debit, which explains the $400 increase in office equipment from a balance of $2,300 at December 31, 19X1, to $2,700 at December 31, 19X2. *Remember: The data for the entries come from the income statement, statement of retained earnings, and analysis of the general ledger accounts.*

   The entries on the worksheet summarize the effects of the various transactions that changed the account balances during the period. For example, Entry (g) is a debit to Accumulated Depreciation—Office Equipment and a credit to Office Equipment. For every entry representing a component of the change in one account balance, there is an offsetting entry(ies) to other accounts of equal amount. Some of these offsetting entries involve an increase or a decrease in cash. However, we do not enter the changes in cash on the Cash line at the top of the worksheet. Instead, we enter them at the bottom of the worksheet in the proper activity category of the statement of cash flows. The statement substitutes for entries in the change columns of the Cash line. For example, the payment on the 10% note payable (Entry q) is a debit to Note Payable and a credit (decrease in cash) in the "Financing activities" category at the bottom of the worksheet.

Other entries explain changes in noncash accounts, but the related transaction(s) have no effect on cash. For example, the disposal of fully depreciated office equipment (Entry g) noted above results in a credit to Office Equipment and a debit to Accumulated Depreciation—Office Equipment. Since cash is not affected by the transaction, we make no entry to the statement of cash flows section of the worksheet.

The bottom portion of the worksheet allows the preparer to enter the change in cash as a cash inflow or outflow from operating, investing, or financing activities. The worksheet preparer must be knowledgeable about the classification of cash flows to complete the worksheet. The terms Increases and Decreases in the Account Analysis columns in the bottom portion of the worksheet represent cash inflows (increases) and cash outflows (decreases), respectfully. After fully explaining the changes in all noncash accounts with appropriate entries, the cash flows statement at the bottom of the worksheet is also complete and it (Entry u) explains the change in Cash at the top of the worksheet.

5. After analyzing all account balance changes, sum the Debits and Credits columns to make sure that the debits equal the credits.

Analyzing the Changes in Accounts

Presented below is an analysis of the selected transactions of Davis Corporation that we use in preparing the entries in the worksheet.

Net Income. The worksheet presented prepares the cash flows from operating activities according to the indirect method. We begin the analysis of the accounts by analyzing net income. After the analysis of net income, we analyze the accounts in the order presented in the balance sheets in Illustration 14-1.

In the statement of cash flows, we classify net income as a source of cash inflow from operating activities. Note that the worksheet entries are used solely for preparing the statement of cash flows; they are *not* posted to the accounts. The worksheet entry is:

| (a) | Operating Activities, Net Income | 14,400 | |
| | Retained Earnings | | 14,400 |

Accounts Receivable. The increase in accounts receivable means that the cash Davis collected from customers is $2,000 less than the revenue reported in the income statement. The change in accounts receivable is one adjustment required to convert net income to cash flows from operating activities. Therefore, to calculate cash flows from operating activities, we deduct the $2,000 increase in accounts receivable from net income. *Rule of thumb:* A debit change to any noncash account is offset by a credit (decrease) to cash. A credit change to any noncash account is offset by a debit (increase) to cash. The worksheet entry in the Account Analysis columns is:

| (b) | Accounts Receivable | 2,000 | |
| | Operating Activities, Increase in Accounts Receivable | | 2,000 |

ILLUSTRATION 14-9 Cash Flow Worksheet

Davis Corporation
Worksheet for Statement of Cash Flows
For the Year Ended December 31, 19X2

	ACCOUNT BALANCES 12/31/X1	ACCOUNT ANALYSIS DEBITS		ACCOUNT ANALYSIS CREDITS		ACCOUNT BALANCES 12/31/X2
Debits						
Cash	8,000			(u)	7,000	1,000
Accounts Receivable	12,000	(b)	2,000			14,000
Interest Receivable		(c)	400			400
Merchandise Inventory	14,000			(d)	1,000	13,000
Prepaid Insurance	2,000			(e)	200	1,800
Office Equipment	2,300	(f)	700	(g)	300	2,700
Buildings	40,000	(h)	5,000			45,000
Land	35,000			(i)	5,000	30,000
Total debits	113,300					107,900
Credits						
Accumulated Depr.–Off. Equip.	1,000	(g)	300	(j)	550	1,250
Accumulated Depr.–Buildings	6,000			(k)	2,000	8,000
Accounts Payable	8,000	(m)	5,700			2,300
Notes Payable	5,000			(l)	5,000	10,000
Wages and Salaries Payable	500			(n)	250	750
Dividends Payable	1,500			(o)	300	1,800
Income Taxes Payable	1,850			(p)	100	1,950
Notes Payable—Noncurrent	40,000	(q)	25,000			15,000
Common Stock	10,000			(r)	1,000	
				(s)	1,000	12,000
Paid-In Capital–Stock Dividend	0			(r)	4,000	4,000
Paid-In Capital in Excess of Par– Common	25,000			(s)	5,000	30,000
Retained Earnings	14,450	(r)	5,000			
		(t)	3,000	(a)	14,400	20,850
Total credits	113,300					107,900

		Increases		Decreases		
Cash flows from:						
Operating activities:						
Net income		(a)	14,400			
Increase in accounts receivable				(b)	2,000	
Increase in interest receivable				(c)	400	
Decrease in merchandise inventory		(d)	1,000			
Decrease in prepaid insurance		(e)	200			
Gain from sale of land				(i)	3,000	
Depreciation expense–office equip.		(j)	550			
Depreciation expense–building		(k)	2,000			
Decrease in accounts payable				(m)	5,700	
Increase in wages and salaries pay.		(n)	250			
Increase in income taxes payable		(p)	100			
Investing activities						
Purchased office equipment				(f)	700	
Building addition				(h)	5,000	
Sale of land		(i)	8,000			
Financing activities						
Increase in short-term notes pay.		(l)	5,000			
Increase in dividends payable		(o)	300			
Payment of notes payable				(q)	25,000	
Issued common stock		(s)	6,000			
Cash dividend declared				(t)	3,000	
Decrease in cash		(u)	7,000			
Totals			91,900		91,900	

Rent Receivable. The increase in rent receivable means that Davis's cash collections of rent are *less* than the rent revenue reported in the income statement. Therefore, to calculate cash flows from operating activities, we deduct the $400 increase in rent receivable from net income. The worksheet entry is:

| (c) | Rent Receivable | 400 | |
| | Operating Activities, Increase in Rent Receivable | | 400 |

Merchandise Inventory. The decrease in merchandise inventory means that Davis's purchases are *less* than the cost of goods sold reported in the income statement. Therefore, to calculate cash flows from operating activities, we add the decrease in merchandise inventory to net income. The worksheet entry is:

| (d) | Operating Activities, Decrease in Merchandise Inventory | 1,000 | |
| | Merchandise Inventory | | 1,000 |

Prepaid Insurance. The $200 decrease in prepaid insurance means that expenses Davis used in calculating net income are *more* than the cash payments for those expenses. Therefore, we add the $200 decrease in prepaid insurance to net income in calculating cash flows from operating activities. The worksheet entry is:

| (e) | Operating Activities, Decrease in Prepaid Insurance | 200 | |
| | Prepaid Insurance | | 200 |

Office Equipment. The $400 increase in office equipment is the result of two transactions. A $700 increase is the result of Davis's purchase of new office equipment, and it is a cash outflow from investing activities. The worksheet entry is:

| (f) | Office Equipment | 700 | |
| | Investing Activities, Purchase of Office Equipment | | 700 |

Also, Davis discarded worn-out and fully depreciated office equipment that originally cost $300. This transaction does not affect cash flows. However, we make an entry in the worksheet so that all changes in account balances are analyzed. The worksheet entry is:

| (g) | Accumulated Depreciation—Office Equipment | 300 | |
| | Office Equipment | | 300 |

Buildings. Davis's building addition of $5,000 is a cash outflow from investing activities. The worksheet entry is:

| (h) | Building | 5,000 | |
| | Investing Activities, Building Addition | | 5,000 |

Land. The sale of land resulted in a gain of $3,000 as reported in the income statement. In the statement of cash flows, we classify the sale of a plant asset as an investing activity. Therefore, we deduct the gain from the sale of land from net income in determining cash flows from operating activities. We classify the entire amount of proceeds from the sale of $8,000 as a cash inflow from investing activities. The worksheet entry is:

(i)	Investing Activities, Sale of Land	8,000	
	Land		5,000
	Operating Activities, Gain from Sale of Land		3,000

Accumulated Depreciation—Office Equipment. The recording of depreciation expense decreases net income, but there is no effect on cash flows. Therefore, to calculate cash flows from operating activities, we add the amount of depreciation expense to net income. The worksheet entry is:

| (j) | Operating Activities, Depreciation Expense—Office Equipment | 550 | |
| | Accumulated Depreciation—Office Equipment | | 550 |

Accumulated Depreciation—Buildings. The analysis of the accumulated depreciation for the building is the same as for the office equipment. The worksheet entry is:

| (k) | Operating Activities, Depreciation Expense—Building | 2,000 | |
| | Accumulated Depreciation—Building | | 2,000 |

Notes Payable. The increase in short-term notes payable is a cash inflow from financing activities. The worksheet entry is:

| (l) | Financing Activities, Increase in Notes Payable | 5,000 | |
| | Notes Payable | | 5,000 |

Accounts Payable. The $5,700 decrease in accounts payable means that the purchases amount Davis used in the determination of net income is *less* than the cash payments to suppliers. Therefore, to calculate cash flows from operating activities, we deduct the decrease in accounts payable from net income. The worksheet entry is:

| (m) | Accounts Payable | 5,700 | |
| | Operating Activities, Decrease in Accounts Payable | | 5,700 |

Wages and Salaries Payable. The $250 increase in wages and salaries payable means that the wages and salaries expense Davis deducted in the determination of net income is *more* than the cash payments made to employees. Therefore, to calculate cash flows from operating activities, we add the increase in wages and salaries payable to net income. The worksheet entry is:

| (n) | Operating Activities, Increase in Wages and Salaries Payable | 250 | |
| | Wages and Salaries Payable | | 250 |

Dividends Payable. The $300 increase in dividends payable means that cash payments for dividends are less than the dividends Davis declared. In the statement of cash flows, we classify the payment of cash dividends as a financing activity. Therefore, we deduct the increase in dividends payable from dividends declared in the calculation of cash flows from financing activities. The worksheet entry is:

| (o) | Financing Activities, Increase in Dividends Payable | 300 | |
| | Dividends Payable | | 300 |

Income Taxes Payable. The $100 increase in income taxes payable means that income taxes expense Davis deducted in the determination of net income is more than cash payments made to the government(s) for income taxes. Therefore, to calculate cash flows from operating activities, we add the increase in income taxes payable to net income. The worksheet entry is:

| (p) | Operating Activities, Increase in Income Taxes Payable | 100 | |
| | Income Taxes Payable | | 100 |

Notes Payable—Noncurrent. In the statement of cash flows, we classify the $25,000 decrease in the note payable as a cash outflow from financing activities. The worksheet entry is:

| (q) | Notes Payable—Noncurrent | 25,000 | |
| | Financing Activities, Payment of Note Payable | | 25,000 |

Common Stock and Additional Paid-In Capital. During 19X2, Davis had two transactions that affect common stock and additional paid-in capital. The first transaction is the stock dividend. The stock dividend does not involve cash flows, but we enter the effects on the accounts in the worksheet so that we include all changes in the accounts. The worksheet entry is:

(r)	Retained Earnings	5,000	
	Common Stock		1,000
	Paid-In Capital—Stock Dividend		4,000

The second transaction that affects common stock and additional paid-in capital is Davis's issuance of stock. The issuance of common stock results in a cash inflow from financing activities. The worksheet entry is:

(s)	Financing Activities, Issued Common Stock	6,000	
	Common Stock		1,000
	Paid-In Capital in Excess of Par—Common		5,000

Retained Earnings. Retained earnings is affected by several transactions. We analyze the stock dividend above, and we analyze the net income effect at the beginning of this section. Davis's retained earnings is also reduced by the declaration of cash dividends. In the statement of cash flows, we classify cash dividends as a cash outflow from financing activities. The worksheet entry is:

| (t) | Retained Earnings | 3,000 | |
| | Financing Activities, Cash Dividend Declared | | 3,000 |

Cash. After the changes in all noncash accounts are analyzed, the final step to complete the worksheet is to enter the change in cash. The offsetting entry to the $7,000 credit to Cash is the last amount entered in the Debits column. This procedure results in the Debits and Credits columns being equal, assuming that no mistakes have occurred in preparing the worksheet. The worksheet entry is:

| (u) | Decrease in Cash | 7,000 | |
| | Cash | | 7,000 |

Preparing the Statement

After the worksheet is complete, all the information needed to prepare the statement of cash flows is contained in the bottom portion of the worksheet. The statement prepared according to the indirect method is presented in Illustration 14-7 on page 620.

REVIEW PROBLEM

Prepare a statement of cash flows using the direct method for the Neeley Corp. from the financial statements and additional information that follow:

Neeley Corp. Comparative Balance Sheet December 31, 19X1 and 19X2		
	19X1	*19X2*
Assets		
Current assets:		
Cash	$ 18,000	$ 26,000
Accounts receivable	36,000	33,800
Interest receivable	3,500	6,000
Merchandise inventory	72,000	65,000
Prepaid insurance	2,700	2,500
Total current assets	$132,200	$133,300
Plant assets:		
Equipment	$ 53,000	$ 68,000
Accumulated depreciation—equipment	(2,500)	(2,800)
Buildings	80,000	123,500
Accumulated depreciation—buildings	(4,000)	(7,000)
Land	22,000	72,000
Total plant assets	$148,500	$253,700
Total assets	$280,700	$387,000
Liabilities and Stockholder's Equity		
Current liabilities:		
Accounts payable	$ 12,200	$ 3,100
Wages and salaries payable	14,300	6,900
Interest payable	1,300	1,000
Dividends payable	1,500	2,000
Income taxes payable	200	0
Total current liabilities	$ 29,500	$ 13,000
Noncurrent liabilities:		
Notes payable—noncurrent	0	20,000
Bonds payable	0	50,000
Total liabilities	$ 29,500	$ 83,000
Stockholders' equity:		
Common stock, $10 par	$150,000	$190,000
Paid-in capital in excess of par—common	50,000	60,000
Retained earnings	51,200	54,000
Total stockholders' equity	$251,200	$304,000
Total liabilities and stockholders' equity	$280,700	$387,000

Neeley Corp.
Income Statement
For the Year Ended December 31, 19X2

Revenues:		
Sales	$90,000	
Interest	4,200	
Total revenue		$94,200
Cost of goods sold		68,000
Gross profit		$26,200
Expenses:		
Wages and salaries expense	$10,100	
Depreciation expense—equipment	1,500	
Depreciation expense—buildings	3,000	
Interest expense	1,700	
Income taxes expense	1,000	
Insurance expense	2,800	
Total expenses		(20,100)
Loss from sale of equipment		(800)
Net income		$ 5,300

Neeley Corp.
Retained Earnings Statement
For the Year Ended December 31, 19X2

Balance, January 1	$51,200
Add: Net income for 19X2	5,300
Total	$56,500
Less: Cash dividends declared	2,500
Balance, December 31	$54,000

Additional Information:

(a) Equipment was purchased for $20,000 cash.

(b) Equipment with a cost of $5,000 and a book value of $3,800 was sold for $3,000.

(c) An addition to the building was added at a cost of $43,500. The addition was paid for in cash.

(d) Borrowed $70,000 cash by issuing a $20,000 10% note payable and $50,000 of bonds.

(e) Acquired land with a fair value of $50,000 by exchanging 4,000 shares of common stock for the land.

SOLUTION:

Planning and Organizing Your Work

1. Analyze the change in each balance sheet account to determine the cash inflows and cash outflows. You may find it helpful to analyze the account changes by using T-accounts as demonstrated in the chapter.

2. Make note of changes in balance sheet accounts resulting from noncash investing and financing activities.

3. Classify each cash flow as resulting from operating, investing, or financing activities.

4. Prepare the statement of cash flows in the proper format.

5. Prepare the supplementary schedule for noncash investing and financing activities.

Neeley Corp.
Statement of Cash Flows
For the Year Ended December 31, 19X2

Cash flows from operating activities		
Collections from customers (1)	$92,200	
Interest received (2)	1,700	
Payments to suppliers (3)	(70,100)	
Payments to employees (4)	(17,500)	
Interest paid (5)	(2,000)	
Income taxes paid (6)	(1,200)	
Payments for insurance (7)	(2,600)	
Net cash flows from operating activities		$ 500
Cash flows from investing activities		
Purchase of equipment (8)	$(20,000)	
Sale of equipment (given)	3,000	
Building addition (9)	(43,500)	(60,500)
Net cash used from investing activities		
Cash flows from financing activities		
Issue of 10% note payable (10)	$20,000	
Issue of bond payable (11)	50,000	
Cash dividend paid (12)	(2,000)	
Net cash flows from financing activities		68,000
Net increase in cash		$ 8,000
Schedule of noncash investing and financing activities		
Purchase of land in exchange for common stock (13)		$50,000

(1)	Accounts Receivable			(2)	Interest Receivable		
Beg. Bal.	36,000			Beg. Bal.	3,500		
Sales	90,000	**Receipt**	**92,200**	Interest Rev.	4,200	**Receipt**	**1,700**
End. Bal.	33,800			End. Bal.	6,000		

(3)	Merchandise Inventory			(3)	Accounts Payable		
Beg. Bal.	72,000					Beg. Bal.	12,200
Purchases	**61,000**	Cost of		**Payments**	**70,100**	Purchases	61,000
		Goods Sold	68,000			End. Bal.	3,100
End. Bal.	65,000						

(4)	Wages and Salaries Payable			(5)	Interest Payable		
		Beg. Bal.	14,300			Beg. Bal.	1,300
Payments	**17,500**	Wages and		**Payments**	**2,000**	Interest Exp.	1,700
		Salary Exp.	10,100			End. Bal.	1,000
		End. Bal.	6,900				

(6)	Income Taxes Payable			(7)	Prepaid Insurance		
		Beg. Bal.	200	Beg. Bal.	2,700		
Payments	**1,200**	Income Taxes		**Payments**	**2,600**	Ins. Exp.	2,800
		Expense	1,000	End. Bal.	2,500		
		End. Bal.	0				

(8)	Equipment		
Beg. Bal.	53,000		
Purchases	**20,000**	Sold	5,000
End. Bal.	68,000		

(9)	Buildings		
Beg. Bal.	80,000		
Purchases	**43,500**		
End. Bal.	123,500		

(10)	Notes Payable—Noncurrent		
		Beg. Bal.	0
		Receipt	**20,000**
		End. Bal.	20,000

(11)	Bonds Payable		
		Beg. Bal.	0
		Receipt	**50,000**
		End. Bal.	50,000

(12)	Dividends Payable		
		Beg. Bal.	1,500
Payments	**2,000**	Declared	2,500
		End. Bal.	2,000

(13)	Land		
Beg. Bal.	22,000		
Acquired	50,000		
End. Bal.	72,000		

(13)	Common Stock		
		Beg. Bal.	150,000
		Issued for	
		Land	40,000
		End. Bal.	190,000

(13)	Paid-In Capital in Excess of Par—Common		
		Beg. Bal.	50,000
		Issued for	
		Land	10,000
		End. Bal.	60,000

KEY TERMS

cash equivalents, *618*
direct method, *607*

indirect method, *607*
statement of cash flows, *601*

SELF-QUIZ

LO 1   1. True or False? The statement of cash flows is not one of the statements included in a complete set of financial statements.

LO 1   2. True or False? The statement of cash flows should help the user assess a business's ability to meet its obligations and to pay dividends.

LO 2   3. Which of the following is *not* a cash flow from an operating activity?
   a. Cash receipts of dividends
   b. Payments of interests
   c. Payments of dividends
   d. Refunds to customers

LO 2   4. Which of the following is *not* a cash flow from an investing activity?
   a. Payment of principal on bonds payable

   b. Cash received from the sale of investments in stocks
   c. Payments in the form of loans to others
   d. Collections of loans

LO 2   5. Which of the following is *not* a cash flow from a financing activity?
   a. Payment of dividends to stockholders
   b. Payment to purchase treasury stock
   c. Proceeds from sale of property, plant, and equipment
   d. Proceeds from issuing bonds

LO 3   6. To perform account analysis in preparing a statement of cash flows, the accountant needs a _____ _____ _____, the_____ _____, and summary transaction data.

LO 4   7. True or False? Short-term notes payable can be included in cash equivalents.

LO 5   8. Which of the following is *not* a noncash investing and financing activity?
  a. Purchase of land and building by assuming a mortgage payable
  b. Declaring a stock dividend
  c. Issuing stock to repay loans
  d. Trading one asset for a similar asset of another company

LO 5   9. Which of the following would *not* be an adjustment to net income using the indirect method?
  a. Increase in notes payable to bank
  b. Decrease in accounts receivable
  c. Depreciation expense
  d. Loss from sale of land

SOLUTIONS TO SELF-QUIZ

1. False   2. True   3. c   4. a   5. c   6. comparative balance sheet, income statement   7. False   8. b   9. a

QUESTIONS

Q14-1   What are the purposes of a statement of cash flows?

Q14-2   What is the difference between the direct method and the indirect method of calculating cash flows from operating activities?

Q14-3   What are some examples of cash flows from operating activities?

Q14-4   What are some examples of investing activities?

Q14-5   What are some examples of financing activities?

Q14-6   How does the accountant use account analysis to help prepare the statement of cash flows?

Q14-7   What balance sheet account(s) and income statement items are analyzed to determine cash payments to employees?

Q14-8   How do we report noncash investing and financing activities?

Q14-9   (Appendix) What are the four steps in preparing a statement of cash flows using a worksheet?

EXERCISES

LO 2   **E14-1**   **Operating, Investing, and Financing Activities**   The following events occurred during 19X1. Determine if each event should be classified as an operating activity (*O*), investing activity (*I*), financing activity (*F*), or not on the statement of cash flows (*NS*).
  ___ a. Purchased property, plant, and equipment
  ___ b. Collected cash from customers
  ___ c. Sold land held for investment
  ___ d. Paid dividends
  ___ e. Issued common stock
  ___ f. Paid suppliers of merchandise
  ___ g. Collected interest
  ___ h. Distributed stock dividends
  ___ i. Paid wages and salaries due employees
  ___ j. Retired bonds payable

LO 2   **E14-2**   **Cash Flow Impact**   Determine if each of the items presented in E14-1 would be a cash inflow (*I*), a cash outflow (*O*), or have no effect (*NE*) on cash flow.

LO 3,4

E14-3   **Operating Cash Flows**   Determine the impact on cash flows from operating activities for each of the following items:

(1) Wages and Salaries Payable has a beginning balance of $3,200 and an ending balance of $1,100. Wages and salaries expense is $15,900.

(2) Prepaid Rent has a beginning balance of $2,800 and an ending balance of $1,600. Rent expense is $11,500.

(3) Accounts Receivable has a beginning balance of $5,900 and an ending balance of $6,300. Credit sales total $39,000.

(4) Income Taxes Payable has a beginning balance of $2,100 and an ending balance of $2,900. Income Taxes Expense is $6,900.

(5) Interest Receivable has a beginning balance of $1,900 and an ending balance of $1,600. Interest revenue is $3,700.

LO 3,4

E14-4   **Investing Cash Flows**   Determine the impact on cash flows from investing activities for each of the following items:

(1) Land held for investment has a beginning balance of $178,000 and an ending balance of $199,000. No land was sold.

(2) Notes receivable has a beginning balance of $28,000 and an ending balance of $44,000. No notes receivable were collected.

(3) Buildings has a beginning balance of $1,297,000 and an ending balance of $1,639,000. No buildings were sold.

(4) Equipment with a cost of $530,000 and accumulated depreciation of $210,000 is sold. The loss on sale of equipment is $45,000.

LO 3,4

E14-5   **Financing Cash Flows**   Determine the impact on cash flows from financing activities for each of the following items:

(1) Dividends Payable has a beginning balance of $9,200 and an ending balance of $3,800. Dividends declared is $18,500.

(2) Bonds Payable has a beginning balance of $470,000 and an ending balance of $770,000. No bonds were retired.

(3) Mortgage Payable has a beginning balance of $629,000 and an ending balance of $625,100. No additional mortgage loans were obtained.

(4) Notes Payable—Noncurrent has a beginning balance of $83,000 and an ending balance of $62,000. Additional cash of $30,000 was borrowed by issuing a long-term note payable.

(5) Common Stock has a beginning balance of $1,200,000 and an ending balance of $1,350,000. Paid-In Capital in Excess of Par-Common has a beginning balance of $4,700,000 and an ending balance of $5,150,000. No common stock was retired.

LO 3,4

E14-6   **Investment Account Analysis**   The account balances relating to equipment during 19X1 for the Taylor Company are as follows:

	Beginning Balance	*Ending Balance*
Equipment	$75,000	$145,000
Accumulated Depreciation	25,000	34,000

Equipment with an original cost of $16,000 and a book value of $12,000 was sold for $15,000.

REQUIRED:

Calculate the cash inflow from the sale of equipment and the cash outflow to purchase new equipment.

LO 4

E14-7   **Schedule of Noncash Investing, Financing Activities**   Prepare a schedule of noncash investing and financing activities for the Stone Company if the following transactions occurred during 19X1:

(1) Issued $500,000 (fair value) of preferred stock in exchange for land and building.
(2) Acquired $175,000 of equipment with a capital lease.
(3) Traded $240,000 of land in California for land with an equivalent fair market value in Florida.
(4) Purchased a $300,000 parking garage by assuming a mortgage payable.

LO 5

E14-8   Operating Cash Flows, Indirect Method   For each of the following items, determine if they would be added (+), subtracted (–), or neither (N) when adjusting net income to derive cash flows from operating activities.

___ a. Increase in accounts payable
___ b. Gain from sale of equipment
___ c. Depreciation expense
___ d. Uncollectible accounts expense
___ e. Amortization of goodwill
___ f. Decrease in wages and salaries payable
___ g. Loss from sale of land
___ h. Decrease in interest receivable
___ i. Decrease in accounts receivable
___ j. Interest revenue

LO 3,4

E14-9   Operating Section of a Statement of Cash Flows   A partial comparative balance sheet and income statement for the Truax, Inc. are presented below and on the next page.

REQUIRED:

Prepare the cash flow from operating activities section of Truax, Inc.'s statement of cash flows for the year ended December 31, 19X3. Use the direct method.

Truax, Inc. Comparative Balance Sheet (Partial) December 31, 19X2 and 19X3		
	19X2	*19X3*
Current assets:		
Cash	$ 4,100	$ 3,800
Accounts receivable	13,300	14,900
Merchandise inventory	16,600	14,600
Prepaid rent	1,000	1,200
Total current assets	$35,000	$34,500
Current liabilities:		
Accounts payable	$ 2,100	$ 1,800
Wages and salaries payable	2,000	2,650
Interest payable	4,500	3,900
Income taxes payable	1,400	0
Total current liabilities	$10,000	$ 8,350

Truax, Inc.
Income Statement
For the Year Ended December 31, 19X3

Sales		$66,400
Cost of goods sold		40,800
Gross profit		$25,600
Expenses:		
Wages and salaries expense	$12,900	
Depreciation expense—equipment	1,500	
Income taxes expense	1,000	
Interest expense	1,400	
Rent expense	2,300	
Total expenses		19,100
Net income		$ 6,500

LO 3,4

E14-10   Investment Section of a Statement of Cash Flows   A partial comparative balance sheet and additional information are as follows:

Truax, Inc.
Comparative Balance Sheet (Partial)
December 31, 19X2 and 19X3

	19X2	19X3
Assets		
Long-term investments	$13,500	$ 8,900
Plant assets:		
Equipment	23,000	28,000
Accumulated depreciation–equipment	(2,500)	(4,000)
Land	14,000	17,500
Total noncurrent assets	$48,000	$50,400

Additional Information:
(1) Long-term investments were sold at cost. No long-term investments were purchased.
(2) Equipment was purchased for $5,000 cash. No equipment was sold.
(3) Land was purchased for $3,500 cash. No land was sold.

REQUIRED:

Prepare the cash flow from investing activities section of Truax, Inc.'s statement of cash flows for the year ended December 31, 19X3.

LO 3,4

E14-11   Financing Section of a Statement of Cash Flows   A partial comparative balance sheet for Truax, Inc. is shown on the next page.

Additional Information:
(1) Long-term notes payable of $5,000 were paid.
(2) Common stock was issued for $3,000.
(3) Net income was $6,500. All dividends declared were paid.

REQUIRED:

Prepare the cash flow from financing activities section of Truax, Inc.'s statement of cash flows for the year ended December 31, 19X3.

Truax, Inc.
Comparative Balance Sheet (Partial)
December 31, 19X2 and 19X3

	19X2	19X3
Noncurrent liabilities:		
Note payable—noncurrent	$20,000	$15,000
Stockholders' equity:		
Common stock, $10 par	$20,000	$22,000
Additional paid-in capital	10,000	11,000
Retained earnings	23,000	28,550
Total stockholders' equity	$53,000	$61,550

PROBLEM SET A

LO 2,3

P14-1A   Determining the Change in Cash   The Cash balance on January 1, 19X4, for the Pickens Corporation was $285,900. The following items occurred during 19X4:

(1)	Cash collected from customers	$493,800
(2)	Proceeds from issuing common stock	221,000
(3)	Purchase of equipment	79,100
(4)	Sale of building	99,300
(5)	Interest paid	29,900
(6)	Payments on long-term borrowings	129,400
(7)	Payments to suppliers	198,500
(8)	Dividends paid	87,700
(9)	Income taxes paid	41,200
(10)	Long-term borrowings	192,000
(11)	Interest collected	39,400
(12)	Wages and salaries paid	119,800

REQUIRED:

a. Determine the cash balance on December 31, 19X4.
b. Classify each item as either an operating (*O*), investing (*I*), or financing (*F*) activity.
c. Prepare a statement of cash flows for 19X4 using the direct method.

LO 3,4

P14-2A   Cash Flow Information From Financial Statements   Financial statements for Clarinda's Prime Rib Corp. are as shown on the next page.

REQUIRED:

Determine the following for 19X6:
a. Cash collected from customers
b. Interest collected
c. Wages and salaries paid
d. Payments to suppliers of merchandise
e. Interest paid
f. Income taxes paid
g. Dividends paid (Only cash dividends are declared.)
h. Proceeds from issue of common stock
i. Proceeds from issue of notes payable
j. Purchase of building and land (No building or land was sold.)

Clarinda's Prime Rib Corp.
Comparative Balance Sheet
December 31, 19X5 and 19X6

	19X5	19X6
Assets		
Current assets:		
Cash	$ 50,000	$ 75,000
Accounts receivable	145,000	210,000
Interest receivable	12,500	25,000
Merchandise inventory	105,000	165,000
Total current assets	$312,500	$475,000
Plant assets:		
Equipment	$ 20,000	$ 20,000
Accumulated depreciation—equipment	(6,500)	(13,500)
Buildings and land	130,000	282,500
Accumulated depreciation—building	(6,000)	(14,000)
Total plant assets	$137,500	$275,000
Total assets	$450,000	$750,000
Liabilities and Stockholders' Equity		
Current liabilities:		
Accounts payable	$110,000	$132,500
Wages and salaries payable	28,500	30,000
Interest payable	4,000	5,000
Dividends payable	0	17,500
Total current liabilities	$142,500	$185,000
Notes payable—noncurrent	0	125,000
Total liabilities	$142,500	$310,000
Stockholders' equity:		
Common stock, $10 par	$112,500	$150,000
Paid-in capital in excess of par—common	112,500	150,000
Retained earnings	82,500	140,000
Total stockholders' equity	$307,500	$440,000
Total liabilities and stockholders' equity	$450,000	$750,000

Clarinda's Prime Rib Corp.
Income Statement
For the Year Ended December 31, 19X6

Revenues:		
Sales	$1,550,000	
Interest	50,000	
Total revenue		$1,600,000
Cost of goods sold		1,250,000
Gross profit		$ 350,000
Expenses:		
Wages and salaries expense	$ 175,000	
Depreciation expense—equipment and buildings	15,000	
Interest expense	40,000	
Income taxes expense	20,000	
Total expenses		250,000
Net income		$ 100,000

LO 5

P14-3A **Cash Flows From Operating Activities, Indirect Method** An abbreviated income statement for Thomas Company for 19X7 is presented below:

Sales	$1,100,000
Cost of goods sold	(614,000)
Gross profit	$ 486,000
Operating expenses	(160,000)
Depreciation expense	(36,000)
Net income before taxes	$ 290,000
Income taxes expense	(130,000)
Net income	$ 160,000

Beginning and ending balances in Thomas Company's current asset and current liability accounts for 19X7 were as follows:

	Beg. Balance	*End. Balance*
Cash	$176,000	$190,000
Accounts Receivable	565,000	590,000
Merchandise Inventory	378,000	367,000
Dividends Payable	36,000	29,000
Prepaid Rent	89,000	86,000
Accounts Payable	277,000	272,800
Wages and Salaries Payable	57,700	59,900
Income Taxes Payable	62,000	42,000

REQUIRED:

a. Determine which of the current assets and current liabilities should be subtracted or added to net income in determining cash flows from operating activities.
b. Prepare the cash flows from operating activities section of the statement of cash flows for 19X7, using the indirect method.

LO 3,4,5

P14-4A **Statement of Cash Flows** Financial statements and additional information for the Atlas Company are as follows:

Atlas Company Comparative Balance Sheet December 31, 19X8 and 19X9		
	19X8	*19X9*
Assets		
Current assets:		
Cash	$ 4,500	$ 6,500
Accounts receivable	9,000	8,450
Interest receivable	875	1,500
Merchandise inventory	18,000	16,250
Prepaid insurance	675	625
Total current assets	$33,050	$33,325
Plant assets:		
Equipment	$13,250	$17,000
Accumulated depreciation—equipment	(625)	(700)
Buildings	20,000	30,875
Accumulated depreciation—buildings	(1,000)	(1,750)
Land	5,500	18,000
Total plant assets	$37,125	$63,425
Total assets	$70,175	$96,750

Liabilities and Stockholders' Equity

Current liabilities:		
Accounts payable	$ 3,050	$ 775
Wages and salaries payable	3,575	1,725
Interest payable	325	250
Dividends payable	375	500
Income taxes payable	50	0
Total current liabilities	$ 7,375	$ 3,250
Noncurrent liabilities:		
Notes payable—noncurrent	0	17,500
Total liabilities	$ 7,375	$20,750
Stockholders' equity:		
Common stock, $1 par	$12,500	$22,500
Paid-in capital in excess of par—common	37,500	40,000
Retained earnings	12,800	13,500
Total stockholders' equity	$62,800	$76,000
Total liabilities and stockholders' equity	$70,175	$96,750

Atlas Company
Income Statement
For the Year Ended December 31, 19X9

Revenues:		
Sales	$32,500	
Interest	1,050	
Total revenue		$33,550
Cost of goods sold		17,000
Gross profit		$16,550
Expenses:		
Wages and salaries expense	$ 2,525	
Depreciation expense—equipment	2,575	
Depreciation expense—building	750	
Interest expense	425	
Income taxes expense	250	
Insurance expense	700	
Total expenses		(7,225)
Gain from sale of equipment		1,000
Net income		$10,325

Atlas Company
Retained Earnings Statement
For the Year Ended December 31, 19X9

Balance, January 1	$12,800
Add: Net income for 19X9	10,325
Total	$23,125
Less: Cash dividends declared	9,625
Balance, December 31	$13,500

Additional Information:

(1) Equipment was purchased for $7,750 cash.

(2) Equipment with a cost of $4,000 and a carrying value of $1,500 was sold for $2,500.

(3) A small building was purchased at a cost of $10,875. The building was purchased for cash.

(4) Borrowed $17,500 cash by issuing a 10% note payable.

(5) Acquired land with a fair value of $12,500 by exchanging 10,000 shares of common stock for the land.

REQUIRED:

a. Prepare a statement of cash flows using the direct method.

b. Prepare a statement of cash flows using the indirect method.

LO 6   **P14-5A   Statement of Cash Flows Worksheet (Appendix 14-A)**   Prepare a statement of cash flows for the Atlas Company. Use the five-column worksheet format presented in Illustration 14-9 (page 624). The Atlas Company data are presented in P14-4A.

PROBLEM SET B

LO 2,3   **P14-1B   Change in Cash**   The Cash balance on January 1, 19X1, for the Staggs Corporation was $331,500. The following items occurred during 19X1:

(1)	Cash collected from customers	$673,800
(2)	Proceeds from issuing bonds	176,000
(3)	Purchase of building	97,100
(4)	Sale of equipment	149,300
(5)	Interest paid	29,900
(6)	Payments on note payable	219,400
(7)	Payments to suppliers	98,900
(8)	Dividends paid	57,700
(9)	Taxes paid	93,200
(10)	Proceeds from issuing common stock	122,000
(11)	Interest collected	63,400
(12)	Wages and salaries paid	215,100

REQUIRED:

a. Determine the cash balance on December 31, 19X1.

b. Classify each item as either an operating (*O*), investing (*I*), or financing (*F*) activity.

c. Prepare a statement of cash flows for 19X1 using the direct method.

LO 3,4   **P14-2B   Cash Flow Information From Financial Statements**   Financial statements for Fazzio's Pizza Company are as shown on the next page.

REQUIRED:

Determine the following for 19X3:

a. Cash collected from customers

b. Interest collected

c. Wages and salaries paid

d. Payments to suppliers of merchandise

e. Interest paid

f. Income taxes paid

g. Dividends paid (Only cash dividends were declared.)

h. Proceeds from issue of common stock

i. Proceeds from issue of notes payable

j. Purchase of building and land (No building or land was sold.)

Fazzio's Pizza Company
Comparative Balance Sheet
December 31, 19X2 and 19X3

	19X2	19X3
Assets		
Current assets:		
Cash	$ 85,000	$ 127,500
Accounts receivable	246,500	357,000
Interest receivable	21,250	42,500
Merchandise inventory	178,500	280,500
Total current assets	$531,250	$ 807,500
Plant assets:		
Equipment	$ 34,000	$ 34,000
Accumulated depreciation—equipment	(11,050)	(22,950)
Buildings and Land	221,000	480,250
Accumulated depreciation—building	(10,200)	(23,800)
Total plant assets	$233,750	$ 467,500
Total assets	$765,000	$1,275,000
Liabilities and Stockholders' Equity		
Current liabilities:		
Accounts payable	$187,000	$ 225,250
Wages and salaries payable	48,450	51,000
Interest payable	6,800	8,500
Dividends payable	0	29,750
Total current liabilities	$242,250	$ 314,500
Notes payable—noncurrent	0	212,500
Total liabilities	$242,250	$ 527,000
Stockholders' equity:		
Common stock, $10 par	$191,250	$ 255,000
Paid-in capital in excess of par—common	191,250	255,000
Retained earnings	140,250	238,000
Total stockholders' equity	$522,750	$ 748,000
Total liabilities and stockholders' equity	$765,000	$1,275,000

Fazzio's Pizza Company
Income Statement
For the Year Ended December 31, 19X3

Revenues:		
Sales	$2,635,000	
Interest	85,000	
Total revenue		$2,720,000
Cost of goods sold		2,125,000
Gross profit		$ 595,000
Expenses:		
Wages and salaries expense	$ 297,500	
Depreciation expense—equipment and buildings	25,500	
Interest expense	68,000	
Income taxes expense	34,000	
Total expenses		425,000
Net income		$ 170,000

LO 5

P14-3B **Cash Flows From Operating Activities, Indirect Method** An abbreviated income statement for Carrera Corporation for 19X4 is presented below:

Sales	$1,650,000
Cost of goods sold	(921,000)
Gross profit	$ 729,000
Operating expenses	(240,000)
Depreciation expense	(54,000)
Net income before taxes	$ 435,000
Income taxes expense	(195,000)
Net income	$ 240,000

Beginning and ending balances of Carrera Corporation's current asset and current liability accounts for 19X4 were as follows:

	Beg. Balance	End. Balance
Cash	$264,000	$285,000
Accounts receivable	847,500	885,000
Merchandise inventory	567,000	550,500
Dividends payable	67,000	59,000
Prepaid rent	133,500	129,000
Accounts payable	415,500	409,200
Wages and salaries payable	86,550	89,850
Income taxes payable	93,000	63,000

REQUIRED:

a. Determine which of the current assets and current liabilities should be subtracted or added to net income in determining cash flows from operating activities.
b. Prepare the cash flows from operating activities section of the statement of cash flows for 19X4, using the indirect method.

LO 3,4,5

P14-4B **Statement of Cash Flows** Financial statements and additional information for the Hercules Company are as follows:

Hercules Company Comparative Balance Sheet December 31, 19X5 and 19X6		
	19X5	*19X6*
Assets		
Current assets:		
Cash	$ 27,000	$ 39,000
Accounts receivable	54,000	50,700
Interest receivable	5,250	9,000
Merchandise inventory	108,000	97,500
Prepaid insurance	4,050	3,750
Total current assets	$198,300	$ 199,950
Plant assets:		
Equipment	$ 79,500	$102,000
Accumulated depreciation—equipment	(3,750)	(4,200)
Buildings	120,000	185,250
Accumulated depreciation—buildings	(6,000)	(10,500)
Land	33,000	108,000
Total plant assets	$222,750	$380,550
Total assets	$421,050	$580,500

Liabilities and Stockholders' Equity

Current liabilities:		
Accounts payable	$ 18,300	$ 4,650
Wages and salaries payable	21,450	10,350
Interest payable	1,950	1,500
Dividends payable	2,250	3,000
Income taxes payable	300	0
Total current liabilities	$ 44,250	$ 19,500
Noncurrent liabilities:		
Notes payable—noncurrent	0	105,000
Total liabilities	$ 44,250	$124,500
Stockholders' equity:		
Common stock, $5 par	$ 75,000	$135,000
Paid-in capital in excess of par—common	225,000	240,000
Retained earnings	76,800	81,000
Total stockholders' equity	$376,800	$456,000
Total liabilities and stockholders' equity	$421,050	$580,500

Hercules Company
Income Statement
For the Year Ended December 31, 19X6

Revenues:		
Sales	$165,000	
Interest	6,300	
Total revenue		$171,300
Cost of goods sold		102,000
Gross profit		$ 69,300
Expenses:		
Wages and salaries expense	$ 15,150	
Depreciation expense—equipment	15,450	
Depreciation expense—building	4,500	
Interest expense	2,550	
Income taxes expense	1,500	
Insurance expense	4,200	
Total expenses		(43,350)
Gain from sale of equipment		6,000
Net income		$ 31,950

Hercules Company
Retained Earnings Statement
For the Year Ended December 31, 19X6

Balance, January 1	$ 76,800
Add: Net income for 19X6	31,950
Total	$108,750
Less: Cash dividends declared	27,750
Balance, December 31	$ 81,000

Additional Information:

(1) Equipment was purchased for $46,500 cash.

(2) Equipment with a cost of $24,000 and a carrying value of $9,000 was sold for $15,000.

(3) A small building was purchased at a cost of $65,250. The building was purchased for cash.

(4) Borrowed $105,000 cash by issuing a 9% note payable.

(5) Acquired land with a fair value of $75,000 by exchanging 12,000 shares of common stock for the land.

REQUIRED:

a. Prepare a statement of cash flows using the direct method.

b. Prepare a statement of cash flows using the indirect method.

LO 6   **P14-5B**   **Statement of Cash Flows, Worksheet (Appendix 14-A)**   Prepare a statement of cash flows for the Hercules Company using the five-column worksheet format presented in Illustration 14-9 (page 624). The Hercules Company data is presented in P14-4B.

■CRITICAL THINKING AND COMMUNICATING

C14-1   Sandberg Company is a large national chain of drug stores. It had the following reported net income for the past 5 years (000 omitted):

19X1	19X2	19X3	19X4	19X5
$100	$1,100	$2,200	$2,400	$6,800

During this period, most financial analysts thought Sandberg was a well-run company and represented a good investment. David Kirsten, a well-respected accounting professor, disagreed with the optimistic analysis of Sandberg Company. Professor Kirsten calculated the cash flow generated from operating activities (000 omitted) for 19X1 through 19X5 as follows:

19X1	19X2	19X3	19X4	19X5
$(1,900)	$(600)	$100	$1,100	$2,600

REQUIRED:

a. Explain how net income amounts could differ from the cash flows from operating activities by such a substantial amount.

b. Why was Professor Kirsten's analysis so pessimistic?

c. What mitigating factors could possibly make Sandberg Company a good investment?

C14-2   Bethany Benson, the president of Ampflo Corporation, is confused about why depreciation expense is added to net income and why gain from sale of land is subtracted from net income on Ampflo's indirect-method statement of cash flows.

REQUIRED:

Write a memo to Bethany Benson explaining why these two adjustments are made to net income.

C14-3   The financial statements of J.C. Penney Company reprinted in Appendix B at the end of this text present statements of cash flows for 1991, 1992, and 1993.

REQUIRED:

a. What method of preparing the operating activities section of the statements does J.C. Penney use?

b. Comment on the direction and magnitude of fluctuations in each of the operating, investing, and financing activities sections of the statements.

c. In the operating activities section, identify what you think were the major causes of the fluctuations that occurred.

d. What is your assessment of the overall cash flow performance of J.C. Penney for the three-year period?

CHAPTER 15

Financial Statement Analysis

Just over one year ago, Brian Boerne took over as Chief Executive Officer of Flatland Distributing Corporation, a distributor of auto parts. He promised the Board of Directors that he could turn around Flatland's downward trend in earnings. The Board entered into an agreement with Boerne to award him a bonus in 19X3, based on the increase in Flatland's earnings in 19X2 over 19X1. However, as a condition of the bonus agreement, the Board stipulated that Flatland's overall performance for 19X2 must receive a favorable evaluation from an independent analyst. The agreement states that the overall analysis will include relative profitability (rate of return on equity), earnings quality and persistence, cash flows, efficiency of asset utilization, reliance on and servicing of short-term and long-term debt, and financial condition and risk of financial distress. Boerne and the Chairperson of the Board jointly chose Deidre Washington as the independent analyst.

In this chapter, you will learn how to analyze a complete set of financial statements. You will learn about the concept of general purpose financial statements and about the other sources of information available to financial statement analysts. You will see the relationships among income statement components, accounting methods, and the important concepts of earnings quality and persistence. You will also learn about the tools of financial analysis and how to structure a written analysis.

1. Define financial statement analysis and describe the relationship between a business's net income and its future cash flows.
2. Define the various components of net income recognized under GAAP and relate them to the concepts of income persistence and quality.
3. Describe the tools of financial statement analysis, including the key questions underlying financial statement analysis.
4. Perform an analysis of a complete set of financial statements.
5. Organize and write an analysis of a set of financial statements.
6. Describe what an independent auditors' report adds to financial statements.
7. Describe the effects of general inflation and specific price changes on businesses, their owners, and financial statement users (Appendix 15-A).

FINANCIAL STATEMENT ANALYSIS

LO 1

Define financial statement analysis and describe the relationship between a business's net income and its future cash flows.

Financial statement analysis is the art of systematically utilizing (1) financial statement data, (2) ratios and other statistics calculated from financial statement data, and (3) information related to the financial statements to answer questions about a business and to make predictions about its future.

Future Cash Flow Orientation

As the FASB notes in the objectives of financial reporting quoted in an earlier chapter, users of financial statements generally want to make predictions about the business's future cash flows. Since financial statement data generally describe past events and conditions, they do not relate directly to the prediction of future cash flows. Nevertheless, the processes that a business has used in the recent past will tend to be the same ones that the firm will use in the future, perhaps with some modification, to continue to generate cash flows. Therefore, analysts use analysis of financial statement information as a basis for formulating predictions about the future.

How Accounting Net Income Relates to Future Cash Flows

Among the most analyzed aspects of any business are its net income and profitability (a measure of relative performance based on income). However, current net income does not measure current cash flows. So, how can the analysis of earnings satisfy the objective of predicting future cash flows? Earnings convey information about future cash flows by matching expenses (which are generally measured in terms of cash paid or promised to be paid for goods and services) with revenues earned (which are generally measured in terms of cash received or to be received). When we match expenses with revenues earned to determine accounting net income, we ignore the exact timing of the related cash flows. Thus, for any given period, income and cash flows are not the same. However, by systematically matching the flows according to the earning process, earnings convey the long-run (average) cash-generating ability of the current earning process.

In general, we can make the following assertions about cash flows and net income:

1. Over the life of a business, accounting net income equals cash flows from all sources, except borrowings and repayments of debt and transactions with owners. In other words, lifetime income approximately equals cash flows from operations and investment activities—the cash flows the business generates for itself (not from owners and creditors).
2. Therefore, over the life of the business, average income (per period) approximately equals average cash flows from operations and investment activities. In other words, average income is an approximation of average cash flows per period.
3. If a business continues in operation indefinitely, providing the same volume of goods and services at the same prices and using the same inputs at the same prices, current income is an approximation of the average net cash flows per period the business will generate *in the future.*

This latter concept may seem naive, since the future is never the same as the present or past. Yet, financial statement analysts can directly build on this concept to forecast the future. First, the analyst will want to evaluate net income to determine how well it approximates steady-state future cash flows. We call this the income persistence problem. Next, the analyst may wish to judge the net income for any bias—especially optimistic bias management introduces by choosing particular accounting principles and methods. We call this the income quality problem. Finally, the analyst must predict how a particular firm's future will be different from its past and adjust net income to achieve a better prediction of the actual (non-steady-state) future. Thus, successful analysts are the ones who have the best insight into the future.

PERSISTENCE AND QUALITY OF INCOME

In this course, we cannot cover all there is to know about forecasting a company's future. We can, however, teach you the concepts an analyst needs to form *the platform for a forecast* of future earnings and cash flows. **Income persistence** is the tendency for a component of income to continue in future periods under steady-state (no change) assumptions. **Income quality** is the degree to which management does not exercise or does not have the opportunity to manipulate the firm's income to paint an optimistic picture of ongoing income.

Income Persistence

Income statements are formatted to segregate income components or segments with regard to their persistence. Illustration 15-1 conceptually represents an income statement that contains at least one of every kind of income component recognized under GAAP. The components of overall net income in Illustration 15-1 that are preceded by a bullet (•) are intentionally separated from revenues and expenses under GAAP. These income components are believed to have different relationships to future cash flows than do revenues and expenses.

Revenues and Expenses.   From earlier chapters, you are aware that revenues and expenses are the increases and decreases in the business's assets and liabilities that relate to its *continuing* processes of supplying products or services to customers. As we mentioned earlier, revenues and expenses are representative of the business's ability to generate cash flows in the future under steady-state assumptions—that is, by continuing to do in the future what it has done in the current period.

ILLUSTRATION 15-1 Components of Net Income Under GAAP*

Revenues
Expenses
•Gains (losses) other than from providing products or services to customers
Income (loss) from continuing operations before taxes
Provision for income taxes (income tax expense)
Income (loss) from continuing operations
•Income (loss) from discontinued operations—net of taxes:
Income (loss) from operating discontinued segment(s)
Gain (loss) on disposition of discontinued segment(s)
Income before extraordinary items
•Extraordinary items (gains or losses) — net of taxes
Income before cumulative effects on prior years of changes in accounting principles
•Cumulative effects of changes in accounting principles—net of taxes
Net income

*Adapted from "Recognition and Measurement in Financial Statements of Business Enterprises," *Statement of Financial Accounting Concepts No. 5* (Stamford, Conn.: FASB, 1984), par. 34.

Gains and Losses. Gains and losses are associated with the business's cash flows, and they are *normal* parts of doing business. For example, whenever a business retires or sells assets such as property, plant, or equipment, it generally recognizes a gain or loss. Similarly, whenever a business pays off debt before it is due, it generally incurs a gain or loss. However, gains and losses arise from events and transactions that are incidental to providing products and services to customers. Moreover, gains and losses usually occur less frequently and at less regular intervals than do revenues and expenses, especially in smaller businesses. Therefore, gains and losses, if material, are segregated from revenues and expenses in the income statement. With material gains and losses displayed in income statements separately, analysts can factor them into their predictions of future cash flows in a different way than routine revenues and expenses.

Income (Loss) From Continuing Operations. Income from continuing operations before taxes equals revenues minus expenses plus gains minus losses. The income tax provision (expense) is subtracted to calculate income from continuing operations (after taxes).

Income (Loss) From Discontinued Operations. Discontinued operations (including the gain or loss on discontinuing them) contribute to the net income of the current period. Therefore, income (loss) from discontinued operations belongs somewhere in the income statement. However, if operations are not continuing, they have no implications for future cash flows. Therefore, analysts interested in predicting the business's future cash flows would not want revenues, expenses, and gains or losses from discontinued operations mingled with those from continuing operations.

Extraordinary Items. **Extraordinary items** are similar to gains and losses from a bookkeeping perspective, but here the similarity ends. The transactions or circumstances giving rise to extraordinary items are *not normal* parts of doing business and are not expected to repeat themselves in the foreseeable future.[1] For example, suppose that a business had property, plant, and equipment located in a foreign country. If a material amount of loss resulted from the sale of some or all of these assets, the result would be a loss on the income statement. The loss would be included in the income from the business's continuing operations because it is *normal* for any business occasionally to sell some of its assets. However, suppose a material amount of loss occurred because the government of the foreign country confiscated assets of the business that one of its executives used to commit an illegal act in that country. The loss would be considered extraordinary, because the rare illegal act of an executive is not a normal part of the firm's operations and should not recur in the foreseeable future.

Because extraordinary items are not a normal part of the business and are not expected to recur, they do not have implications for the business's future cash flows. Therefore, they are segregated from other income statement components.

Cumulative Effects of Changes in Accounting Principles. The cumulative effects of changes in accounting principles are the effects on beginning retained earnings of using one method of accounting instead of another—for example, straight-line versus accelerated depreciation. When a firm changes from one accounting method to another there are two effects:

1. A current effect on net income of the change in accounting methods
2. An effect on the beginning balance in retained earnings, which should be adjusted as if the new method had always been in use

This second (cumulative) effect of the change does not relate to future income or future cash flows; it is a measurement adjustment. However, in its *Opinion No. 20*, the Accounting Principles Board requires that cumulative effects of changes in accounting principles generally be shown in a separate category on the current income statement.[2] This reporting standard presumably discourages management from making inappropriate accounting changes or attempting to make changes to increase income artificially. Analysts always can pick out the effects of the changes and segregate them from ongoing income components.

Quality of Income

Quality of income is much spoken about among financial analysts, but it is difficult to describe concisely how to analyze it. One thing is clear, however. If management tries to manipulate the amount of net income, analysts cannot rely on the net income figure to the same extent that they could if management remained neutral. How can management manipulate income? In a surprising variety of ways. First, management can select among GAAP those principles that produce the desired effect on income but do not fit the circumstances as well as

---

[1]*Accounting Principles Board Opinion No. 30* (New York: AICPA, 1973), par. 20.

[2]*Ibid.*, par. 18. There are some categories of accounting changes for which an adjustment to prior years' financial statements are *required*. But they represent only a *few* exceptions to the rule, stated in par. 18 of *APB Opinion 20*.

other principles. For example, a growing business facing rising prices selects FIFO instead of LIFO, straight-line instead of accelerated depreciation, and point-of-sale recognition of revenue instead of the installment sales method for risky installment sales. Each of these choices, if not the most appropriate in the circumstances, will bias net income upward. Second, management makes numerous estimates and judgments in applying GAAP. For example, management ultimately is responsible for estimating the useful lives and residual values of assets, future warrantee costs, and future losses on uncollectible accounts. Management can systematically over- and underestimate these accounting variables in the directions that have desired effects on income. Finally, management can engage in outright fraud or deception. The most common intentional deception in financial reporting is overstating revenues. Methods range from recording the subsequent year's sales early—as revenue of the current year—to shipping goods before year-end to customers that did not order them (and recording the sales returns in the subsequent year when the goods are returned).

The difficulty in analyzing quality of income is that, if management is manipulating income, they do not openly disclose their actions. In the financial reports of companies, notes to the financial statements disclose the accounting methods and many of the estimates used—but often only in broad terms. However, professional analysts follow companies for years, observe the judgments that their managers make, and compare them to peer firms and their managers. Over time, companies gain reputations for high or low quality earnings and analysts make adjustments accordingly.

TOOLS OF FINANCIAL STATEMENT ANALYSIS

LO 3

Describe the tools of financial statement analysis, including the key questions underlying financial statement analysis.

The tools of financial statement analysis consist of common-size and percent-change financial statements and various financial ratios, many of which you are familiar with from earlier chapters. Common-size financial statements support a technique known as vertical analysis; while percent-change financial statements support horizontal analysis.

Common-Size Financial Statements

Common-size financial statements are those whose numerical amounts are re-expressed as percents of an important summary figure. In common-size balance sheets, all individual asset and liability balances are re-expressed as percents of total assets (total liabilities plus owners' equity). Illustration 15-2 is the common-size version of the Flatland Distributing Corporation's balance sheets for 19X1 and 19X2. In common-size income statements, all dollar amounts are re-expressed as percents of gross or net sales (whichever is the beginning figure in the particular income statement). Illustration 15-3 is the common-size version of Flatland's 19X1 and 19X2 income statements.

The common-size percents of financial statement component amounts are calculated according to the following formula:

$$\text{Common-Size Percent} = \frac{\text{Component Amount}}{\text{Base Amount}} \times 100\%$$

ILLUSTRATION 15-2 Comparative Balance Sheet With Common-Size Percents

Flatland Distributing Corporation **Comparative Balance Sheet** **December 31, 19X1 and 19X2**				
	19X1		19X2	
	Amount	*Percent*	*Amount*	*Percent*
Assets				
Cash	$ 155,000	3.6%	$ 85,250	1.6%
Accounts receivable (net of allowance of $35,000 and $50,000, respectively)	465,000	10.8%	720,750	13.4%
Inventory	850,000	19.8%	1,283,500	23.8%
Prepaid expenses	95,000	2.2%	109,250	2.0%
Total current assets	$1,565,000	36.5%	$2,198,750	40.8%
Land	1,125,000	26.2%	1,125,000	20.9%
Buildings	1,250,000	29.1%	1,500,000	27.8%
Accumulated depreciation	(300,000)	(7.0%)	(350,000)	(6.5%)
Equipment	750,000	17.5%	1,050,000	19.5%
Accumulated depreciation	(100,000)	(2.3%)	(130,000)	(2.4%)
Total assets	$4,290,000	100.0%	$5,393,750	100.0%
Liabilities and Stockholders' Equity				
Accounts payable	$ 250,000	5.8%	$ 382,628	7.1%
Notes payable	600,000	14.0%	900,000	16.7%
Wages and salaries payable	30,000	0.7%	40,000	0.7%
Taxes payable	52,000	1.2%	75,000	1.4%
Total current liabilities	$ 932,000	21.7%	$1,397,628	25.9%
Notes payable—noncurrent	750,000	17.5%	1,200,000	22.2%
Total liabilities	$1,682,000	39.2%	$2,597,628	48.2%
Common stock	$ 100,000	2.3%	$ 100,000	1.9%
Paid-in capital in excess of par	900,000	21.0%	900,000	16.7%
Retained earnings	1,608,000	37.5%	1,796,122	33.3%
Total stockholders' equity	$2,608,000	60.8%	$2,796,122	51.8%
Total liabilities and stockholders' equity	$4,290,000	100.0%	$5,393,750	100.0%

Thus, the base amounts in each statement are expressed as 100%. In Illustration 15-2, the percent next to 19X1 total current assets of $1,565,000 is calculated as follows:

$$36.5\% = \frac{\$1,565,000}{\$4,290,000} \times 100\%$$

Similarly, in Illustration 15-3, the percent next to selling expense of $687,470 for 19X2 is calculated as follows:

$$11.5\% = \frac{\$687,470}{\$5,978,000} \times 100\%$$

Vertical Analysis. One application of common-size statements is vertical analysis. **Vertical analysis** of financial statements is the analysis of the percentage composition of the components of a particular statement for a particular year. Looking at Illustration 15-3, for instance, we note that in 19X2 Flatland's

ILLUSTRATION 15-3 Comparative Income Statement With Common-Size Percents

Flatland Distributing Corporation
Comparative Income Statement
For the Years Ended December 31, 19X1 and 19X2

	19X1 Amount	19X1 Percent	19X2 Amount	19X2 Percent
Net sales	$4,900,000	100.0%	$5,978,000	100.0%
Cost of goods sold	3,332,000	68.0%	4,065,040	68.0%
Gross profit	$1,568,000	32.0%	$1,912,960	32.0%
Selling expense	$ 539,000	11.0%	$ 687,470	11.5%
Depreciation expense	60,000	1.2%	80,000	1.3%
Interest expense	126,150	2.6%	189,902	3.2%
Other administrative expenses	514,500	10.5%	538,020	9.0%
Total expenses	$1,239,650	25.3%	$1,495,392	25.0%
Income before taxes	$ 328,350	6.7%	$ 417,568	7.0%
Income tax expense	95,222	1.9%	129,446	2.2%
Net income	$ 233,128	4.8%	$ 288,122	4.8%

cost of goods sold and gross profit were 68% and 32% of net sales, respectively, and that net income was 4.8% of net sales. Vertical analysis can be coupled with comparing the percentages of various components of a statement in two successive years, which can reveal important changes. For example, we note from Illustration 15-2 that Flatland's total liabilities went from about 39% of total liabilities and stockholders' equity in 19X1 to about 48% in 19X2. From this change, it is clear that Flatland is relying more heavily on debt financing.

Common-Size Analysis. Common-size analysis involves the analysis of the common-size percents of two or more entities. Analysts frequently want to compare one entity with another, but they would prefer not to let the different sizes of the entities interfere with their analyses. The common-size percents adjust all numbers in the entities' financial statements to the same scale, 100%. This focuses the analysts' attention on relevant relationships. For example, Illustration 15-4 compares Flatland's 19X2 common-size income statement with its industry averages. You can see immediately that Flatland has a higher cost-of-goods-sold percent, making its gross profit percent lower. Although its other expenses are a

ILLUSTRATION 15-4 Common-Size Analysis

	Flatland	Industry
Net sales	100.0%	100.0%
Cost of goods sold	68.0%	65.0%
Gross profit	32.0%	35.0%
Selling expense	11.5%	11.5%
Depreciation expense	1.3%	1.3%
Interest expense	3.2%	3.5%
Other administrative expenses	9.0%	9.5%
Total expenses	25.0%	25.8%
Income before taxes	7.0%	11.0%
Income tax expense	2.2%	3.4%
Net income	4.8%	7.6%

smaller percent of net sales, they do not fully compensate for the higher cost-of-goods-sold percent. Thus, Flatland's percent of net income to net sales is lower than that of its industry in general. This quick analysis suggests that Flatland may have an opportunity to improve its profitability by improving its control of the costs of its purchases.

Percent-Change Financial Statements

Percent-change financial statements are simply conventional financial statements with changes and percents of changes added. Illustrations 15-5 and 15-6 contain the Flatland percent-change balance sheets and income statements, respectively. To calculate the amounts of changes, subtract the earlier year amount from the later year amount. Calculate the percents of changes as follows:

$$\text{Percent Change} = \frac{\text{Later Year Amount} - \text{Earlier Year Amount}}{\text{Earlier Year Amount}} \times 100\% = \frac{\text{Amount of Change}}{\text{Earlier Year Amount}} \times 100\%$$

For example, the percent change in net accounts receivable in Illustration 15-5 and the percent change in interest expense in Illustration 15-6, respectively, are calculated as follows:

$$55.0\% = \frac{\$720{,}750 - \$465{,}000}{\$465{,}000} \times 100\% = \frac{\$255{,}750}{\$465{,}000} \times 100\%$$

$$50.5\% = \frac{\$189{,}902 - \$126{,}150}{\$126{,}150} \times 100\% = \frac{\$63{,}752}{\$126{,}150} \times 100\%$$

Looking at the rates of change across periods in components of financial statements is termed **horizontal analysis**. The change percents represent rates of growth or decline in financial statement components and can provide many insights about the business's activities. For instance, we know from looking at Illustration 15-6 that Flatland's net sales, cost of goods sold, and gross profit all grew by about the same percent, 22%, in 19X2. While its other expenses grew at a slower rate, 20.6%, income tax expense grew by 35.9%. Thus, Flatland's net income grew by 23.6% on the net sales growth of 22%. Ordinarily, we would expect net income to grow by a larger percent than net sales, because some expenses do not increase, or increase very little, in the short run as sales are expanded.

Financial Ratios

Financial ratios are numerical statistics that represent important relationships between financial statement amounts. The debt-equity ratio, for example, reveals the relationship between debt and equity financing. It also measures the amount of financial risk (risk of insolvency or bankruptcy) the business is bearing. Although ratios may reveal some of the same insights that common-size and percent-change financial statements reveal, they are much more flexible. A financial ratio can be calculated to represent almost any relevant relationship between financial statement amounts. Ratios are not confined to information contained in any one financial statement. For example, rate-of-return ratios, such as rate of return on total assets, use numbers from the income statement in their numerators and numbers from the balance sheet in their denominators.

ILLUSTRATION 15-5 Comparative Balance Sheet With Percent Changes

Flatland Distributing Corporation Comparative Balance Sheet December 31, 19X1 and 19X2				
	19X1	*19X2*	*Change*	*Percent*
Assets				
Cash	$ 155,000	$ 85,250	$ (69,750)	(45.0%)
Accounts receivable (net of allowance of $35,000 and $50,000, respectively)	465,000	720,750	255,750	55.0%
Inventory	850,000	1,283,500	433,500	51.0%
Prepaid expenses	95,000	109,250	14,250	15.0%
Total current assets	$1,565,000	$2,198,750	$ 633,750	40.5%
Land	1,125,000	1,125,000	0	0.0%
Buildings	1,250,000	1,500,000	250,000	20.0%
Accumulated depreciation	(300,000)	(350,000)	(50,000)	16.7%
Equipment	750,000	1,050,000	300,000	40.0%
Accumulated depreciation	(100,000)	(130,000)	(30,000)	30.0%
Total assets	$4,290,000	$5,393,750	$1,103,750	25.7%
Liabilities and Stockholders' Equity				
Accounts payable	$ 250,000	$ 382,628	$ 132,628	53.1%
Notes payable	600,000	900,000	300,000	50.0%
Wages and salaries payable	30,000	40,000	10,000	33.3%
Taxes payable	52,000	75,000	23,000	44.2%
Total current liabilities	$ 932,000	$1,397,628	$ 465,628	50.0%
Notes payable—noncurrent	750,000	1,200,000	450,000	60.0%
Total liabilities	$1,682,000	$2,597,628	$ 915,628	54.4%
Common stock	$ 100,000	$ 100,000	$0	0.0%
Paid-in capital in excess of par	900,000	900,000	0	0.0%
Retained earnings	1,608,000	1,796,122	188,122	11.7%
Total stockholders' equity	$2,608,000	$2,796,122	$ 188,122	7.2%
Total liabilities and stockholders' equity	$4,290,000	$5,393,750	$1,103,750	25.7%

Although a ratio depicting any financial statement relationship may be calculated, certain ratios have the status of being time-honored. Many analysts employ them because they help answer important questions about the business's financial condition or performance. In earlier chapters, we have introduced you to many of these frequently used ratios and have showed you how to interpret and use them in decisions. In this chapter, we incorporate them into our analysis of Flatland's financial statements.

Key Questions Underlying Financial Statement Analysis

Because financial statement analysis is an art, rather than a science, there is no single best way to structure an analysis of a particular set of statements. However, we believe the analysis must answer the following key questions about the business and, therefore, the questions form a working framework to guide you:

ILLUSTRATION 15-6 Comparative Income Statement With Percent Changes

Flatland Distributing Corporation
Comparative Income Statement
For the Years Ended December 31, 19X1 and 19X2

	19X1	19X2	Change	Percent
Net sales	$4,900,000	$5,978,000	$1,078,000	22.0%
Cost of goods sold	3,332,000	4,065,040	733,040	22.0%
Gross profit	$1,568,000	$1,912,960	$ 344,960	22.0%
Selling expense	$ 539,000	$ 687,470	$ 148,470	27.5%
Depreciation expense	60,000	80,000	20,000	33.3%
Interest expense	126,150	189,902	63,752	50.5%
Other administrative expenses	514,500	538,020	23,520	4.6%
Total expenses	$1,239,650	$1,495,392	$ 255,742	20.6%
Income before taxes	$ 328,350	$ 417,568	$ 89,218	27.2%
Income tax expense	95,222	129,446	34,224	35.9%
Net income	$ 233,128	$ 288,122	$ 54,994	23.6%

- How profitable is the business?
- What is the composition of the business's current cash flows?
- Does the business utilize its assets efficiently?
- Is the business able to service (pay) its debts satisfactorily?
- How risky is the business?

In the next section, we present the analysis of the Flatland statements according to this framework. In each subsection of the analysis (corresponding to one of the key questions), we raise additional, more detailed questions to guide you.

Standards for Analyzing Financial Statements

To answer the key questions of financial statement analysis, some standards of comparison are useful. Many of the questions cannot be answered in absolute terms. For example, what level of profitability is satisfactory? In a market-based economy, the standard is a competitive standard. That is, *a business is earning satisfactory profits when it is earning as much as any firm could with the same amount invested in assets at the same risk.* If a firm cannot earn such profits, the owners will want to withdraw their investments and invest them elsewhere.

Some of the standards of comparison that are used in financial statement analysis are:

1. Prior years' financial statements
2. Industry comparisons
3. The plans of the business

We confine our analysis in the next section to the first standard primarily because basing the analysis on multiple standards would become too complex for this text. Comparing the current year to the immediate past year (and other prior years) indicates the direction that the business has taken and may reveal important trends that could persist into the future and influence future cash flows. To facilitate this type of analysis, most companies prepare comparative financial statements for at least two years. Because the standard of comparison for this type of analysis is so readily available, it is the type of analysis most frequently performed.

In contrast, outside analysts often experience problems obtaining information on industry statistics and the plans of a business. It is sometimes impossible to define the industry of a business. For example, at one time, Quaker Oats Company and its Subsidiaries operated in two major industries, groceries and toys (the latter through its Fisher-Price subsidiary). It would have been incorrect to compare the performance of Quaker to either the toy industry or to the grocery industry alone. Yet, there were few or no other companies operating in only those two industries.

Securing information about a business's plans may be equally frustrating. Managers rarely like to reveal their plans to outsiders, except in the sketchiest terms, because competitors may use the knowledge of the firm's plans to their advantage. Thus, outside analysts often find it difficult to secure useful information about plans at the level of detail they would like to have to compare to actual financial statements.

LO 4

Perform an analysis of a complete set of financial statements.

APPLICATION OF FINANCIAL STATEMENT ANALYSIS

In this section, we first list a set of detailed subquestions for each major question or category to guide the analysis. Then, we provide sets of observations derived from (1) the common-size financial statements (Illustrations 15-2 and 15-3); (2) the percent-change financial statements (Illustrations 15-5 and 15-6); and (3) the ratio values defined, calculated, and interpreted under the applicable questions.

Business Profitability

To judge a business's overall profitability from its comparative financial statements, you will want to address the following detailed questions:

- Is the business increasing or decreasing in profitability?
- What accounts for its increasing or decreasing profitability?
- Does it earn a satisfactory return on assets?
- Does it earn a satisfactory return on owners' investment?
- Are there questions about the quality of earnings?
- Are there questions about earnings persistence?

Common-Size and Percent-Change Evidence. Illustration 15-6 (percent-change income statement) shows us that net sales increased by an impressive 22% in 19X2 (over 19X1). Cost of goods sold and, therefore, gross profit also increased by 22%. Net income increased by only slightly more than net sales (23.6%). With gross profit increasing by the same percent as net sales, the expenses other than cost of goods sold must explain how net income increased by a slightly higher percent. In Illustration 15-6, we note that selling expense, depreciation expense, and interest expense all increased by greater percents than did net sales and gross profit. However, other administrative expenses hardly increased at all; and, thus, income before and after taxes grew by larger percents than net sales.

Because cost of goods sold and gross profit increased in proportion to sales, they remained at 68% and 32% of net sales, respectively (Illustration 15-3). Net income also remained a constant 4.8% of net sales.[3]

Profitability Ratios. Illustration 15-7 defines and interprets the major **profitability ratios** and calculates them for Flatland's 19X1 and 19X2 financial statements. As we would expect from the common-size financial statements, the gross margin ratio (which is also the percent of gross profit to net sales) and the profit margin ratio (which is the percent of net income to net sales) did not change between 19X1 and 19X2. However, the return on assets improved from 11.4% to 12.5%, and return on equity improved from 9.2% to 10.7%. Thus, we conclude that while the profitability of each sales dollar did not change, Flatland did improve its rates of return by modest amounts.

Earnings Persistence and Quality. Flatland made no changes in accounting methods that would affect the quality of earnings. Moreover, it uses no accounting principles or estimates that suggest it is trying to bias the measurement of income upward. However, we will return later to the issues of quality and persistence of earnings.

Cash Flows

Profitability is the business's lifeblood. If a business can be profitable in the long run, it should survive and even grow. However, in the short run, the flow of cash through the business determines whether or not it is in a healthy financial position; that is, whether it is able to invest in all needed assets, pay its bills on time, and have reserve funds available to absorb unexpected demands for expenditures. In analyzing cash flows, we want to know:

- Are cash flows from operations positive or negative?
- Are cash flows from operations increasing or decreasing?
- Were cash flows from operations able to supply the necessary funds for investments in noncurrent assets?
- Did financing activities supply or use material amounts of cash?
- Did investing activities supply or use material amounts of cash?

Statement of Cash Flows Information. No customary ratios are designed specifically to answer the above questions. However, the statement of cash flows is tailor-made for this analysis. Flatland's statement of cash flows appears in Illustration 15-8.

Analysis of Cash Flows. Flatland's operations consumed net cash of $169,750 in 19X2 in contrast to net cash generated by operations of $52,628 in 19X1. Inventories increased by much more than accounts payable, requiring significantly higher payments for inventory purchases than for the cost of goods sold. Accounts receivable increased significantly, indicating that collections lagged significantly behind sales. These are the big contributing factors in the negative cash flows from operations in 19X2. Because of the negative cash flow from operations, Flatland apparently had to increase its short-term notes payable to banks.

---

[3]Actually, since net income grew by more than net sales, you would expect net income to be a larger percent of net sales in 19X2 than in 19X1. This is indeed the case. The percentages to two decimal accuracy are 4.82% and 4.75%, respectively. However, when rounded to one decimal place as in Illustration 15-3, the slight difference disappears.

ILLUSTRATION 15-7 Profitability Ratios

Ratio	Definition	19X1	19X2
Profit Margin *Interpretation:* Indicates net profitability of each dollar of sales.	$\dfrac{\text{Net Income}}{\text{Net Sales}}$	$\dfrac{\$233,128}{\$4,900,000} = .048$	$\dfrac{\$288,122}{\$5,978,000} = .048$
Gross Margin *Interpretation:* Indicates the amount of each sales dollar available to cover expenses and to provide a profit	$\dfrac{\text{Gross Profit}}{\text{Net Sales}}$	$\dfrac{\$1,568,000}{\$4,900,000} = .32$	$\dfrac{\$1,912,960}{\$5,978,000} = .32$
Return on Assets *Interpretation:* Rate of return earned on all resources used. When compared to other firms, indicates the business's competitiveness in employing assets; also indicates the business's ability to generate competitive returns to suppliers of capital.	$\dfrac{\text{Before Tax Income + Interest Expense}}{\text{Average Total Assets}}$	$\dfrac{\$328,350 + \$126.150}{(\$3,679,872^a + \$4,290,000)/2} = .114$ [a]The 19X1 beginning total assets amount of $3,679,872 was reconstructed from the ending balance and the changes in assets recognized in the statement of cash flows for 19X1.	$\dfrac{\$417,568 + \$189,902}{(\$4,290,000 + \$5,393,750)/2} = .125$
Return on Owners' Equity *Interpretation:* This is the rate of return earned on resources owners provide. When compared to other firms of comparable risk to owners, it indicates the business's ability to earn competitive returns to owners. If the same ratio is calculated "before tax" and compared to return on assets, it indicates leverage effects from using debt to finance assets.	$\dfrac{\text{Net Income}}{\text{Average Owners' Equity}}$	$\dfrac{\$233,128}{(\$2,474,872^b + \$2,608,000)/2} = .092$ [b]The 19X1 beginning owners' equity amount of $2,474,872 was derived from the ending balance plus 19X1 dividends less 19X1 income.	$\dfrac{\$288,122}{(\$2,608,000 + 2,796,122)/2} = .107$

ILLUSTRATION 15-8 Comparative Statement of Cash Flows

Flatland Distributing Company Comparative Statement of Cash Flows For the Years Ended December 31, 19X1 and 19X2		
	19X1	*19X2*
Cash flows from operating activities:		
Net income	$ 233,128	$ 288,122
Depreciation expense	60,000	80,000
Increase in accounts payable	30,000	132,628
Increase in wages payable	2,000	10,000
Increase in taxes payable	5,000	23,000
Increase in accounts receivable	(125,000)	(255,750)
Increase in inventory	(150,000)	(433,500)
Increase in prepaid expenses	(2,500)	(14,250)
Net cash flows from operating activities	$ 52,628	$(169,750)
Cash flows from investing activities:		
Building improvements	$(125,000)	$(250,000)
Equipment purchases	(150,000)	(300,000)
Net cash used by investing activities	$(275,000)	$(550,000)
Cash flows from financing activities:		
Net proceeds of notes payable to banks	$ 100,000	$ 300,000
Proceeds of notes—noncurrent	350,000	550,000
Repayments of noncurrent notes	(150,000)	(100,000)
Dividends paid	(80,000)	(100,000)
Net cash used by financing activities	$ 220,000	$ 650,000
Net decrease in cash	$ (2,372)	$ (69,750)

Flatland invested in substantial amounts of noncurrent assets financed by additional long-term borrowings. It also paid $100,000 in dividends and repaid $100,000 in previous long-term borrowings.

On balance, net new borrowings (financing) were less than the investment in noncurrent assets and the negative cash flow from operations. Thus, cash declined by $69,750 in 19X2.

Utilization of Assets

Efficient utilization of assets is important to the long-run success of a company. If a business can earn the same income by investing in fewer assets and using them more efficiently, then its rates of return on assets and equity will be higher and more competitive. An analysis of asset utilization should answer these detailed questions:

- Are asset turnovers increasing or decreasing?
- Are receivables being collected more or less promptly?
- Are inventories becoming older on average and possibly obsolete?

Common-Size and Percent-Change Information. From the percent-change balance sheets (Illustration 15-5), we note that the following assets increased by more than the increase in net sales (22%): accounts receivable (55%), inventory (51%), equipment (40%), and total assets (25.7%). On the other hand, cash, land, and buildings did not increase in proportion to net sales. However, with at least some assets and total assets increasing by substantially higher percents than net sales, we expect to see some decline in efficiency of utilization of assets.

Also, as we would expect, accounts receivable, inventory, and equipment all increased as percents of total assets from 19X1 to 19X2.

Asset Utilization Ratios.   Illustration 15-9 defines and interprets the major **asset utilization ratios** and calculates them for Flatland's 19X1 and 19X2 financial statements. Notice that total asset turnover increased slightly, meaning that, compared to 19X1, Flatland was able to generate marginally more net sales per dollar of investment in assets in 19X2. On the other hand, the turnovers of both receivables and inventory declined. The slower turnovers mean that Flatland increased its investment in accounts receivable and inventory per dollar of net sales generated. The increase in relative investment, in turn, means that these assets are not being used as efficiently. The age of receivables and days' supply of inventory express the inefficiency in another way. Assuming Flatland sells to its customers on terms requiring full payment in 30 days, the aging of receivables from 37 days at the end of 19X1 to 47 days at the end of 19X2 is particularly troubling. Flatland seems to have gone from having a moderate amount of accounts receivable past due to having a substantial amount past due.

Quality and Persistence Issues.   The slowdown of inventory turnover and increase in age of accounts receivable raise questions of quality and persistence of earnings. The slowdown in inventory, which is due to the large increase in ending inventory, may be due to inventory obsolescence. That is, Flatland may be stockpiling types of previously purchased merchandise that are not selling, while at the same time purchasing and stocking adequate supplies of the types that are selling. The effect causes inventory to grow more than in proportion to sales—just what we observe for 19X2. If Flatland has obsolete inventory, it should be written off or written down, resulting in a loss. To understand how sensitive Flatland's 19X2 results could be to this issue, consider that it would only require a write-off or write-down of 7% of December 31, 19X2, inventory to wipe out the entire $89,000 increase in income before taxes in 19X2.

The growth in accounts receivable relative to net sales and the corresponding increase in average age also raise valuation and income questions. The increase in age of receivables is an indicator of deterioration in collectibility of the accounts. Yet, the following analysis shows that the balance of the allowance for uncollectible accounts is actually a smaller percent of gross receivables (net receivables plus the allowance) at the end of 19X2 than it was at the end of 19X1.

	19X1	19X2
Allowance for Uncollectible Accounts	$\dfrac{\$35,000}{\$465,000 + \$35,000} = 7\%$	$\dfrac{\$50,000}{\$720,750 + \$50,000} = 6.5\%$
Gross Accounts Receivable		

Given the circumstances, it is safe to say that the allowance for uncollectible accounts should be larger than reported at December 31, 19X2. This would require an adjustment that would also increase uncollectible accounts expense for the year and decrease income before and after taxes.

ILLUSTRATION 15-9 Asset Utilization Ratios

Ratio	Definition	19X1	19X2
Asset Turnover *Interpretation:* Indicates efficiency with which total resources are utilized. Higher turnovers imply greater efficiency.	$$\frac{\text{Net Sales}}{\text{Average Total Assets}}$$	$$\frac{\$4,900,000}{(\$3,679,872^a + \$4,290,000)/2} = 1.23$$ [a]The 19X1 beginning total assets amount of \$3,679,872 was reconstructed from the ending balance and the changes in assets recognized in the statement of cash flows for 19X1.	$$\frac{\$5,978,000}{(\$4,290,000 + \$5,393,750)/2} = 1.24$$
Receivables Turnover *Interpretation:* Indicates efficiency of collection of trade accounts receivable.	$$\frac{\text{Net Credit Sales}^b}{\text{Average Net Trade Receivables}}$$ [b]All of Flatland's sales are made on credit.	$$\frac{\$4,900,000}{(\$340,000^c + \$465,000)/2} = 12.2$$ [c]The 1991 beginning net receivables amount was derived from the ending balance less the increase shown in the statement of cash flows.	$$\frac{\$5,978,000}{(\$465,000 + \$720,750)/2} = 10.1$$
Age of Accounts Receivables *Interpretation:* Average number of days to collect trade receivables. Indicates efficiency of collection of trade accounts. Also, indicates degree to which customers are past due in payment, if terms of credit are known.	$$\frac{\text{Gross Trade Receivables}}{\text{Net Credit Sales}} \times 365 \text{ days}$$	$$\frac{\$500,000^d}{\$4,900,000} \times 365 = 37.2$$ [d]Gross receivables was derived by adding the allowance for bad debts amount back to the net receivables amount in the balance sheet.	$$\frac{\$770,750^d}{\$5,978,000} \times 365 = 47.1$$ [d]Gross receivables was derived by adding the allowance for bad debts amount to the net receivables amount in the balance sheet.
Inventory Turnover *Interpretation:* Number of times an amount equal to average inventory on hand was sold. Indicates frequency of conversion of inventory into sales or efficiency of utilization of inventory.	$$\frac{\text{Cost of Goods Sold}}{\text{Average Inventory}}$$	$$\frac{\$3,332,000}{(\$700,000^e + \$850,000)/2} = 4.3$$ [e]The 19X1 beginning inventory amount was derived from the ending balance less the increase shown in the statement of cash flows.	$$\frac{\$4,065,040}{(\$850,000 + \$1,283,500)/2} = 3.8$$
Days' Supply in Inventory *Interpretation:* Average number of days' supply in inventory. Indicates availability and efficiency of utilization of inventory; also possible overstocking, obsolescence, etc.	$$\frac{\text{Inventory}}{\text{Cost of Goods Sold}} \times 365 \text{ days}$$	$$\frac{\$850,000}{\$3,332,000} \times 365 = 93.1$$	$$\frac{\$1,283,500}{\$4,065,040} \times 365 = 115.2$$

After examining the above issues, we conclude that the earnings Flatland reported are probably overstated due to understatement of the allowance for uncollectible accounts and may also be overstated due to unrecognized inventory obsolescence (or other inventory valuation errors). Thus, we cannot rate highly the quality of the reported net income. Moreover, to the extent that net income contains overstatement errors, we cannot expect the overstated amounts to persist.

Servicing Debt

An important part of an analysis of a business is its debt-servicing record and its general financial condition. To have a healthy financial condition, the business should not only have paid all of its bills that have already become due, but it should also be in a position to continue to do so. A firm's continuing ability to pay its bills is a function of the degree to which it relies on debt financing, its liquidity, its profitability, and its reserve funds, if any. An analysis of debt servicing ability should answer these questions:

- What is the business's liquidity position?
- What is the business's solvency position?
- Is it relying on debt financing more or less?
- Does it have reserve funds to act as a cushion against cash inadequacy?

Common-Size and Percent-Change Information. From the percent-change balance sheet in Illustration 15-5, we note that current liabilities and noncurrent liabilities increased by 50% and 60%, respectively, while total liabilities and stockholders' equity increased by only 25.7%. Thus, we expect to see in Illustration 15-2 that both current liabilities and noncurrent liabilities have increased as percents of total liabilities and stockholders' equity.

Liquidity Ratios. Illustration 15-10 defines, interprets, and calculates the major **liquidity ratios** for Flatland for 19X1 and 19X2. All of the ratios have deteriorated except the working capital ratio, which remained relatively unchanged between December 31, 19X1, and December 31, 19X2. We note further that, if a substantial portion of Flatland's inventory should be written down or written off, or should its allowance for uncollectible accounts be increased significantly, all of its liquidity ratios, except the age of accounts payable, would worsen.

Solvency Ratios. Illustration 15-11 defines and interprets the major **solvency ratios** and calculates them for Flatland's 19X1 and 19X2 financial statements. All of Flatland's solvency ratios have deteriorated between 19X1 and 19X2 because of its greater reliance on debt financing (and negative 19X2 cash flow from operations).

Reserve Funds. **Reserve funds**, like cash flows, are not measured by ratios. Reserve funds represent the margin of protection a business has against sudden financial distress. Reserve funds consist of three components. First, a business may have assets in excess of what is required to produce its products or services for customers. This type of reserve funds is usually held in the form of cash reserves, certificates of deposit, or marketable securities. However, in some cases, other assets such as land not required for new facilities can be liquidated in time of need to meet short-run cash requirements. The second source of reserve funds consists of prearranged amounts of new debt or equity funds. For example, many businesses arrange lines of credit with banks that exceed what they expect to need, the excess being reserve funds in case plans do not work

ILLUSTRATION 15-10 Liquidity Ratios

Ratio	Definition	19X1	19X2
Working Capital Ratio *Interpretation:* Interpreted as an indicator of short-term liquidity or ability to pay short-term obligations with current assets.	$\dfrac{\text{Current Assets}}{\text{Current Liabilities}}$	$\dfrac{\$1,565,000}{\$932,000} = 1.68$	$\dfrac{\$2,198,750}{\$1,397,628} = 1.57$
Quick (Acid Test) Ratio *Interpretation:* Liquid current assets usually include cash, marketable securities, receivables, and other highly liquid assets. Therefore, this is a more severe test of immediate ability to pay short-term obligations than is the current ratio.	$\dfrac{\text{Liquid Current Assets}}{\text{Current Liabilities}}$	$\dfrac{\$620,000}{\$932,000} = .665$	$\dfrac{\$806,000}{\$1,397,628} = .577$
Working Capital to Total Assets *Interpretation:* Indicator of relative amount of current assets financed by long-term debt and owners' equity. May be interpreted as an indicator of short-term liquidity or ability to pay short-term obligations.	$\dfrac{\text{Working Capital}}{\text{Total Assets}}$	$\dfrac{\$633,000}{\$4,290,000} = .148$	$\dfrac{\$801,122}{\$5,393,750} = .149$
Age of Accounts Payable *Interpretation:* Indicates the apparent age of accounts payable in terms of an average day's purchases and, therefore, the timeliness of payment of payables.	$\dfrac{\text{Accounts Payable}}{\text{Purchases}} \times 365 \text{ days}$	$\dfrac{\$250,000}{\$3,482,000^*} \times 365 = 26.2$ *Purchases is derived by adding the increase in inventory (statement of cash flows) to the cost of goods sold.	$\dfrac{\$382,628}{\$4,498,540^*} \times 365 = 31.0$ *Purchases is derived by adding the increase in inventory (statement of cash flows) to the cost of goods sold.

ILLUSTRATION 15-11 Solvency Ratios

Ratio	Definition	19X1	19X2
Times Interest Earned *Interpretation:* Indicates the business's ability to generate sufficient funds to pay its minimum debt service requirements. The larger the ratio, the more comfortably the business is able to meet its obligations.	$$\frac{\text{Pre-Tax Income + Interest Expense}}{\text{Interest Expense}}$$	$$\frac{\$328{,}350 + \$126{,}150}{\$126{,}150} = 3.60$$	$$\frac{\$417{,}568 + \$189{,}902}{\$189{,}902} = 3.199$$
Cash Flows to Total Debt *Interpretation:* Indicates the business's ability to generate sufficient cash to pay its debt service requirements. The larger the ratio, the more comfortably the business is able to meet its obligations.	$$\frac{\text{Cash Flows From Operations}}{\text{Year-End Total Debt}}$$	$$\frac{\$52{,}628}{\$1{,}682{,}000} = .031$$	$$\frac{\$(169{,}750)}{\$2{,}597{,}628} = \text{---}^{*}$$ *Cannot be calculated due to negative numerator.
Total Debt to Total Assets *Interpretation:* Proportion of assets provided by creditors. Indicates magnitude of debt service burden and potential for insolvency.	$$\frac{\text{Year-End Total Liabilities}}{\text{Year-End Total Assets}}$$	$$\frac{\$1{,}682{,}000}{\$4{,}290{,}000} = .392$$	$$\frac{\$2{,}597{,}628}{\$5{,}393{,}750} = .482$$
Total Debt to Owners' Equity *Interpretation:* Amounts of resources provided by creditors relative to owners. Indicates magnitude of debt service burden and potential for insolvency.	$$\frac{\text{Year-End Total Liabilities}}{\text{Year-End Owners' Equity}}$$	$$\frac{\$1{,}682{,}000}{\$2{,}608{,}000} = .645$$	$$\frac{\$2{,}597{,}628}{\$2{,}796{,}122} = .929$$

out as expected. The third source of reserve funds consists of completely new debt and equity funds that can be tapped when financial distress appears imminent. This last source of funds suffers a potentially serious drawback. When reserve funds are needed quickly—that is, when financial distress is imminent—the business may not look particularly attractive to new lenders or owners. Still, economically, if a business is able to earn competitive returns on assets invested in the long run, then it should be able to secure adequate funds to survive, even if temporarily it is in peril of financial failure.

In the case of Flatland, we have little hard evidence about reserve funds, except that its position has deteriorated. Its cash balance declined 45% in 19X2, and it has no marketable securities. It has land that may not be in use or needed for planned expansion, but there is no concrete evidence that it could be sold readily or without impairing current or planned operations. Total debt has increased by more than 50% in 19X2, and total debt to total equity is approximately 1:1 as a result. Thus, the only probable source of reserve funds would be new financing by existing or new owners. This is the most difficult form of reserve funds to raise in the short run. In summary, Flatland's reserve funds situation may not be critical, but it has clearly deteriorated in 19X2.

Risk Analysis

Investors and creditors are interested in the amount, timing, and risk associated with a business's future cash flows. Risk is the potential that future cash flows will be less than expected. Two components make up the overall risk of a business, business risk and financial risk.

Business Risk.   **Business risk** stems from the nature of the business and the markets in which it operates. Businesses operating in markets in which demand for products or services fluctuate widely face greater business risk than do those operating in more stable markets. Consider three industries that provide people with three essentials: the food products industry (food), the automobile industry (transportation), and the residential housing industry (shelter). The food products industry is generally considered to have more stable demand and less business risk than the automobile industry or the housing industry. Because the typical expenditure for a house or a car is greater than that for food, consumers often postpone expenditures for new houses and cars when they are pessimistic about the economic future. Food, on the other hand, is a daily necessity for everyone. Industries with less business risk tend to experience more stable net incomes and cash flows from operations

Financial Risk.   **Financial risk** is the added risk that a business incurs when it uses debt financing. Debt financing does two things to the riskiness of a business. It increases the volatility of earnings and cash flows from operations through the leverage effect (explained below); and it introduces the risk of bankruptcy. Bankruptcy occurs when a business is forced to quit operating, liquidate its assets, and pay off its debts because it was not able to pay the principal and interest on its debts as a going concern.

Leverage Effects.   **Leverage** is the effect of using debt financing to complement owners' capital to provide the necessary funds to operate a business. Leverage has two effects—a beneficial effect and a risk effect. The beneficial aspect of leverage is the effect on the rate of return on owners' equity of borrowing to finance assets. The best way to describe this effect is by example. Suppose a business is considering investing $100,000 in required assets for a new operation that is expected to earn $10,000 per period, or a *rate of return on assets* of 10% ($10,000 ÷ $100,000). However, suppose the business borrows $50,000 of the required new investment and asks the owners to contribute the other $50,000. Suppose further that the interest rate required on the borrowed funds is 8%, or $4,000 per period. The rate of return to the creditor on the borrowed funds is obviously 8% ($4,000 ÷ $50,000). The rate of return to the owners on their investment of $50,000 (the rate of return on equity) is calculated as follows:

Total return on new operation	$10,000
Less: Required interest on debt	4,000
Net return on equity investment	$ 6,000

Rate of return on equity: $6,000 ÷ $50,000 = 0.12 = 12%

Notice that because the creditors in this case require an interest rate less than the expected rate of return on assets, the owners can expect a rate of return on equity greater than the expected rate of return on assets. This illustrates the beneficial leverage effect of liabilities on rate of return on owners' equity.

However, this same effect can be negative if the operation does not prove to be as profitable as expected. For example, if the operation earns only $5,000 (5%) on the total $100,000 investment, the creditors are still entitled to their $4,000. This leaves only $1,000 for the owners, which is a rate of return of only 2%. Moreover, if the operation earns less than 4% on assets (less than $4,000) overall, the creditors must still be paid $4,000; and the business must derive the funds from some other source. A simple comparison of several rates of return on assets and the related return on equity for the above example shows how the return to the owners becomes more volatile with leverage.

Return on Assets	Return on Equity
0%	–8%
2	–4
4	0
6	4
8	8
10	12
11	14
12	16

As you can see, a range of 0% to 12% in return on assets, which would also be the return on equity if the investment were funded entirely by owners' capital, corresponds to a range of returns on equity from –8% to 16% with 50% debt financing.

In summary, the financing of business operations with liabilities provides an opportunity for the rate of return on owners' investments to be enhanced. However, it also means that the rate of return on equity will be very low or negative if results of operations are less than expected and, in general, the rate of return on equity will be more volatile than otherwise. Therefore, one important decision for management is how extensively to utilize liabilities in the financing of the business.

Analyzing Risk.   Numerous techniques are available for analyzing the risk associated with the business's future operating cash flows and net income. They range from straightforward observation and logical analysis to sophisticated statistical techniques. The latter are beyond the scope of this text.

Applying simple observation and analysis to Flatland's situation indicates that its risk has increased during 19X2. Flatland's industry, wholesale auto parts, is relatively low risk from a demand perspective. That is, cars always need repairs; and when times are tough, people hang on to their cars longer and repair them rather than buying new cars. However, the auto parts business is very competitive. As a small distributor of auto parts, Flatland's chief source of business risk is that its customers, small independent auto parts retailers, will be driven out of business or taken over by the large chain auto parts stores. There is no evidence in the financial statements and no other information that would suggest that Flatland's business risk condition changed during 19X2.

Flatland's increased reliance on debt has, however, increased its financial risk. The proportion of its assets financed by debt (total debt to total assets ratio) went from 39% at December 31, 19X1, to 48% at December 31, 19X2. Thus, it will have higher fixed interest charges in the future, and its earnings will tend to be more volatile. Moreover, there is some greater probability of insolvency and bankruptcy.

LO 5

Organize and write an analysis of a set of financial statements.

WRITING AN ANALYSIS OF FINANCIAL STATEMENTS

Above all else, you should remember to be brief when writing an analysis of a set of financial statements. Financial statements contain many individual numbers and may be accompanied by many explanatory notes. You write an analysis to capture only the essentials from this potentially vast array of data. Thus, successful analysts must be able to recognize those things that are important and to ignore those that are unimportant. What is important is a matter of judgment, which is why financial statement analysis was defined earlier as an art. The beginner should look for significant changes in financial statement components and ratios from year-to-year. More sophisticated analysts with experience and knowledge of the business being analyzed will pick out more subtle cues. For example, experienced analysts will focus sometimes on components of financial statements and ratios that do not change significantly—because the analysts have reasons to expect that the ratios or components *should have changed* significantly. Illustration 15-12 is the brief analysis provided to the Board of Directors of Flatland as part of the performance review of Brian Boerne, the new chief executive officer.

LO 6

Describe what an independent auditors' report adds to financial statements.

AUDITORS' REPORTS

One aspect of an analysis of financial statements is the question of reliability. Even the best analysis cannot overcome significant errors in the financial statements or intentional misstatements or omissions. Audits of financial statements are conducted to enhance their trustworthiness and, thereby, their credibility. Management prepares and presents financial statements for use by outsiders. Management knows the most about the business and, therefore, is in the best

ILLUSTRATION 15-12 Financial Analysis

February 1, 19X3

To the Board of Directors, Flatland Distributing Corporation:

I have analyzed the comparative financial statements of Flatland Distributing Company for the years ended 19X1 and 19X2. The statements given to me for analysis are unaudited. Except as otherwise noted, I have assumed that the financial statements are accurate and have based my analysis solely on the information in the statements. My findings and recommendations are outlined below.

Profitability. Flatland's sales increased by 22% in 19X2. Cost of goods sold increased by the same percent as sales, and all other expenses increased by a greater percent, except other administrative expenses. Other administrative expenses increased by only 5%, permitting income before and after income taxes to increase by 27% and 24%, respectively. Gross margin remained constant and profit margin increased, but by less than a tenth of a percent of net sales. Thus, profitability per sales dollar remained unchanged. Rate of return on average assets and rate of return on average equity increased modestly from 11.4% to 12.5% and from 9.2% to 10.7%, respectively. However, as will be discussed below, the debt-equity ratio increased from 65% to 93% in 19X2. Had the proportion of equity remained constant, the rate of return on average equity would have been 9.8% in 19X2, cutting growth in return to one-half of the growth reported.[4]

Cash Flows. Because collections lagged and purchases apparently were accelerated relative to sales, receivables and inventory increased substantially and caused cash flows from operations to be a negative $170,000. Net increases in current and noncurrent borrowings totaling $750,000 were not sufficient to cover the negative operating cash flows, pay dividends of $100,000, and provide for new investments in buildings and equipment totaling $550,000. Thus, cash decreased by approximately $70,000.

Asset Utilization. Overall asset turnover improved marginally during 19X2. However, inventory turnover decreased, and the average age of receivables at year-end increased from 37 to 47 days. The decrease in inventory turnover and increase in age of receivables raise questions about the efficiency of investments in these assets. Moreover, inventory and receivables are commonly susceptible to realization problems. (See accounting issues below.)

Liquidity and Solvency. Flatland is relying more heavily on current debt at the end of 19X2, principally in the form of accounts payable and notes payable to banks, which together increased by more than 50%. Thus, in spite of the large increases in accounts receivable and inventory, both the working capital and quick ratios deteriorated, indicating a decline in liquidity. If receivables are omitted from the quick assets due to the slowdown in collections, the quick ratio would have dropped from .17 to .06. The average age of accounts payable went from 21 to 31 days. While this does not indicate any serious late payment problems, Flatland apparently is losing many more discounts on purchases at the end of 19X2 than at the end of the previous year.

---

[4]If the debt-equity ratio had remained at 64.5%, and assets grew to $5,393,750, equity would have been $3,278,875 at the end of 19X2 ($5,393,750 ÷ 1.645). The return on equity would have been .098 [$288,122 ÷ (($2,608,000 + $3,278,875) ÷ 2)].

Flatland also increased its long-term notes by a net amount of $450,000. Its debt increased by 54%, while total assets increased by 26%. Thus, Flatland is a much more heavily leveraged company at the end of 19X2 than it was at the end of the previous year. While the leverage effect was sufficient to cause a small improvement in the return on equity as noted above, Flatland is more financially risky as well. That is, all indicators point to a deterioration in solvency or, in other words, a higher probability of financial distress.

Summary. Flatland's net income increased by about 24% on an increase in sales of 22%, and the rates of return on assets and equity increased modestly. However, the investments in receivables and inventory ballooned by over 50%, causing cash flows from operations to be negative. As a result, financing through short-term and long-term debt increased by 50% or more; and both liquidity and solvency have deteriorated. The cash balance declined by 45%. In light of the increase in debt, the significant decline in available cash suggests that Flatland's sources of reserve funds are minimal, except for possible additional equity funds. Thus, in summary, the increase in income and the accompanying modest increase in return on equity were achieved at a cost of substantially increased financial risk for Flatland's stockholders. In other words, Flatland's performance in 19X2 was "mixed."

Accounting Issues. Analysis of the turnover of inventory and age of receivables suggests two common accounting valuation problems. First, the receivables are significantly older at the end of 19X2 than they were at the end of the previous year. Such deterioration in the age of receivables generally is associated with a deterioration in collectibility. Yet, the allowance for uncollectible accounts actually is a smaller percent of gross receivables at December 31, 19X2 than it was at December 31, 19X1. Thus, I conclude that the allowance and uncollectible account expense could be understated. Second, inventory increased by 51%, while sales grew by only 22%. Although no specific conclusions can be drawn from such a disparity in growth rates, commonly such a disparity implies obsolete inventory that may need to be written off. Either an increase in uncollectible account expense or a write-off of inventory, or both, would mean that net income is less than reported.

Recommendations. While income has increased and Mr. Boerne will be interested in claiming a bonus and stock options as his agreement with the Board provides. Flatland's overall performance, taking into account cash flow and financial risk, is actually mixed. If the Board sees these other aspects of performance to be of importance to the stockholders, perhaps a more detailed contract with Mr. Boerne should be written to include other indicators besides net income and profitability ratios. In addition, having an incentive contract with Mr. Boerne raises a conflict of interest issue. Mr. Boerne's performance is judged from financial statements based on his own decisions, estimates, and other judgments. The Board, therefore, should consider engaging an outside certified public accountant to audit the financial statements, thus reducing the effects of any management bias and the risk of errors.

Sincerely,

Deidre Washington
Financial Consultant

position to make choices about accounting systems, accounting principles, and the appropriate format for the enterprise's financial statements. However, many decisions outsiders make affect management's welfare. Financial statements may influence elections of boards of directors who, in turn, hire and fire managers. Boards often base management bonuses on accounting net income.

As a consequence, management may have incentives to bias information presented through financial statements. Managers have been known to go so far as to produce fraudulent financial statements. Even if management is not biased, they are often too close to the situation to see the potential for inadvertent errors; and they may not detect fraud perpetrated by employees.

For all of these reasons, an *independent* examination of the relationship between the financial statements and underlying events, transactions, and circumstances makes the financial statements more valuable to outside users. An independent audit involves a significant amount of testing, analyzing, and evaluating the financial statements and the underlying accounting system that produced them. Although audits are not exhaustive investigations for reasons of cost-effectiveness, they are designed to give reasonable assurance that financial statements are not materially in error or misleading.

Standard Auditors' Reports

The standard **independent auditors' report** appears in Illustration 15-13. Notice that the report consists of three paragraphs. The first paragraph identifies the financial statements and management's and the auditors' relative responsibilities for them. Notice that the auditors never accept the primary responsibility for the business's financial statements. Management must always retain that responsibility. The second paragraph, called the scope paragraph, indicates that the examination was conducted according to generally accepted auditing standards, which are broad standards that apply primarily to the quality of the auditor's conduct of an audit examination.

Notice that the auditors warn the users of the financial statements about certain limitations of audit examinations. For example, audits are planned to give *reasonable assurance* (not complete certainty) that the financial statements are not *materially* misstated (as opposed to free from *all* error). Therefore, audits involve examining evidence on a *test* basis (as opposed to exhaustive examination). The third paragraph, called the opinion paragraph, begins with the words, "in our opinion," which again emphasizes the lack of complete assurance or perfect certainty. It goes on to say that in the auditors' opinion the financial statements fairly present what they are supposed to present in all material respects in accordance with GAAP.

The particular wording of the report in Illustration 15-13 is called by several names, including a "clean opinion," an "unqualified opinion" and a "standard opinion." All of these names mean the same thing. The auditors, their examination, and the financial statements satisfied several criteria:

1. The auditors were independent of the firm whose financial statements were audited.
2. The audit was conducted according to generally accepted auditing standards, and no restrictions were placed on the scope of the auditors' examination by management or by circumstances that prevented examination of material elements of the financial statements.
3. There were no material misstatements or omissions in the financial statements relative to the requirements imposed by GAAP that were not corrected by management.
4. There were no changes in an accounting principle or method that had a material effect on the financial statements.
5. There were no major uncertainties that, if resolved one way or the other, would make the financial statements seem misleading after the fact.

ILLUSTRATION 15-13 Standard Auditors' Report

To the Board of Directors and Stockholders of ABC Company:

We have audited the accompanying balance sheets of ABC Company as of December 31, 19X1 and 19X0, and the related statements of income, retained earnings, and cash flows for the years then ended. These financial statements are the responsibility of the company's management. Our responsibility is to express an opinion on these financial statements based on our audits.

We conducted our audits in accordance with generally accepted auditing standards. Those standards require that we plan and perform the audit to obtain reasonable assurance about whether the financial statements are free of material misstatement. An audit includes examining, on a test basis, evidence supporting the amounts and disclosures in the financial statements. An audit also includes assessing the accounting principles used and significant estimates made by management, as well as evaluating the overall financial statement presentation. We believe that our audit provides a reasonable basis for our opinion.

In our opinion, the financial statements referred to above present fairly, in all material respects, the financial position of ABC Company as of December 31, 19X1 and 19X0, and the results of its operations and its cash flows for the years then ended in conformity with generally accepted accounting principles.

Count & Footes, CPAs

February 29, 19X2

6. There was no substantial doubt about the business's ability to continue as a going concern in the short run.
7. There were no other auditors for whose work on the audit the primary auditor will not take responsibility.
8. No other matters that, in the auditors' opinion, should be called to the attention of users of the financial statements.

Any departure from the above conditions requires a departure from the auditors' standard report. There are several different types of such departures. Users of financial statements should always read the auditors' report and note any nonstandard wording. It is helpful to know that most departures from the standard report result in extra paragraphs describing the departures or their causes.

Other Financial Statement Services and Reports by Accountants

Frequently, small businesses find audits too costly to be cost-effective. CPAs can perform two other levels of service for such businesses. Sometimes, CPAs *compile* financial statements from the business's basic records. This level of service is suited to very small businesses that do not have regular staff accountants qualified to prepare financial statements according to GAAP. Although compilation services do not involve any testing or analysis of the underlying data, banks and other users often prefer that CPAs prepare the financial statements of such firms. For more sophisticated businesses that do not require audits but want some assurance that their statements are not significantly in error, CPAs conduct financial statement *reviews*. Financial statement reviews involve studies of the business, inquiries of management, analyses of the financial statements, and other similar procedures. Although financial statement reviews offer some assurance that the financial statements are not significantly in error, they fall far short of the work performed and the assurance achieved in an audit. Therefore, it is important to read the auditors' report on a set of financial statements carefully to determine the level of assurance provided.

SUMMARY

Define financial statement analysis and describe the relationship between a business's net income and its future cash flows.   Financial statement analysis is the art of systematically utilizing (1) financial statement data, (2) ratios and other statistics calculated from financial statement data, and (3) information related to the financial statements to answer questions about a business and to make predictions about its future.

In general, we can make the following assertions about cash flows and net income:

1. Over the life of a business, accounting net income equals cash flows from all sources, except borrowings and repayments of debt and transactions with owners. In other words, lifetime income approximately equals cash flows from operations and investment activities—the cash flows the business generates for itself (not from owners and creditors).
2. Therefore, over the life of the business, average income (per period) approximately equals average cash flows from operations and investment activities. In other words, average income is an approximation of average cash flows per period.
3. If a business continues in operation indefinitely, providing the same volume of goods and services at the same prices and using the same inputs at the same prices, current income is an approximation of the average net cash flows per period the business will generate *in the future*.

Define the various components of net income recognized under GAAP and relate them to the concepts of income persistence and quality.   To help analysts build on earnings to predict future cash flows, the income statement is segregated into segments of income according to their relative persistence. Income from *continuing* operations is segregated from other, more transitory components of income. Within income from continuing operations, material gains and losses are isolated and reported separately. Gains and losses are normal in any business, but they only indirectly relate to the provision of products and services to customers and generally occur less frequently and at less regular intervals than do ordinary expenses and revenues. Income from *discontinued* operations and *extraordinary* gains and losses are totally separated from income from continuing operations because they clearly are not expected to be repeated. Finally, the cumulative effects of changes in accounting principles and methods are reported separately as components of current net income. These effects are not the results of any earning process *per se*. They only arise from the differences in methods of accounting for the same facts.

Describe the tools of financial statement analysis, including the key questions underlying financial statement analysis. The tools of financial statement analysis consist of common-size and percent-change financial statements and various financial ratios. Common-size financial statements support a technique known as vertical analysis, while percent-change financial statements support horizontal analysis.

An analysis of financial statements should answer the following key questions about a business:

- How profitable is the business?
- What is the composition of the business's current cash flows?
- Does the business utilize its assets efficiently?
- Is the business able to service (pay) its debts satisfactorily?
- How risky is the business?

Perform an analysis of a complete set of financial statements. An analysis of a complete set of financial statements requires using various tools of analysis selectively to answer the above key questions.

Organize and write an analysis of a set of financial statements. Financial statements contain many individual numbers and may be accompanied by many explanatory notes. You write an analysis to capture only the essentials from this potentially vast array of data. Thus, successful analysts must be able to recognize those things that are important and to ignore those that are unimportant. What is important is a matter of judgment, which is why financial statement analysis was defined as an art. Above all else, you should remember to be brief when writing an analysis of a set of financial statements.

Describe what an independent auditors' report adds to financial statements. Management prepares and presents financial statements for use by outsiders. Management knows the most about the business and, therefore, is in the best position to make choices about accounting systems, accounting principles, and the appropriate format for the enterprise's financial statements. However, many decisions outsiders make affect management's welfare. As a consequence, management may have incentives to bias information presented through financial statements. *Independent* examinations, called audits, of the relationship between the financial statements and underlying events, transactions, and circumstances enhance the trustworthiness of the financial statements and, thereby, make them more valuable to outside users.

APPENDIX 15-A: THE EFFECTS OF CHANGING PRICES ON BUSINESSES AND FINANCIAL STATEMENTS

One of the important assumptions underlying financial accounting is that the monetary unit, the dollar in the U.S., is stable in size over time. The **stable monetary unit assumption** means that, even though prices change over time, assets, liabilities, revenues, and expenses are still recorded and reported in financial statements according to the cost principle. You will recall that the **cost principle** requires that the values assigned to assets and liabilities be the amounts paid for the assets and the amounts received for the liabilities in the original exchanges in which the assets are acquired and the liabilities are incurred. In many cases, the differences between current and historical prices existing at the times of the original transactions are negligible. However, over many years of price changes, the current prices of such long-lived assets as buildings and equipment depart significantly from original costs. Moreover, if most prices increase over time, each dollar currently buys less, in general, than the dollars a business paid many years earlier for assets that are still in service. Although these differences usually are ignored within the financial accounting process, changing prices affect businesses; and they affect how users should interpret financial statements. To understand these issues, you must first be able to distinguish between general price changes and specific price changes.

GENERAL PRICE CHANGES

LO 7

Describe the effects of general inflation and specific price changes on businesses, their owners, and financial statement users.

General price changes refer to the general trend in prices in the economy as a whole, in a major sector of the economy, or in a region of the country. General price changes popularly are referred to as **inflation** if prices are generally rising or as **deflation** if prices are generally declining. General price changes are measured by pricing specified bundles of goods and services at different times. The aggregate price of the specified bundle is then compared between points in time to determine whether the prices of the goods and services have generally increased or declined. For example, suppose the total price of a broad cross-section of consumer goods (houses, cars, food, fuel, clothing, etc.) had the following aggregate prices at the ends of the years 19X0–19X9.

19X0	$20,454	19X5	$24,682
19X1	20,949	19X6	26,227
19X2	21,696	19X7	28,101
19X3	22,817	19X8	30,219
19X4	23,768	19X9	31,299

To find out the percent change in prices between any base year (say, 19X4) and any subsequent year (say, 19X5), we perform the following calculation:

$$\left(\frac{\text{Total Price in Subsequent Year}}{\text{Total Price in Base Year}} - 1 \right) \times 100\%$$

$$\left(\frac{\$24,682}{\$23,768} - 1 \right) \times 100\% = 3.85\%$$

This calculation tells us that, on average, prices of consumer goods at the end of 19X5 were 3.85% higher than prices of consumer goods at the end of 19X4. One obvious consequence of this increase in average prices is that a given amount of money would buy less in 19X5 than it did in 19X4.

For ease of expression, the prices of the bundles of goods are commonly expressed in index numbers instead of money. For example, 19X4 can be selected as a "base year"; and its price index number is arbitrarily set equivalent to a value of 100. Then, all of the other years' prices can be expressed relative to this base with the formula:

$$\left(\frac{\text{Total Price in Other Year}}{\text{Total Price in Base Year}} \right) \times 100$$

Using this method, the price index numbers of the specified bundle of goods at the ends of years 19X0–19X9 are re-expressed as:

19X0	86.06	19X5	103.85
19X1	88.14	19X6	110.35
19X2	91.28	19X7	118.23
19X3	96.00	19X8	127.14
19X4	100.00	19X9	131.69

SPECIFIC PRICE CHANGES

While prices may generally rise or fall together creating general trends of inflation or deflation, respectively, not all prices follow the trends. **Specific price changes** are changes in the prices of particular goods or services, irrespective of general trends. The prices of some goods and services fall in periods of inflation, while the prices of some goods may rise in times of deflation. Moreover, the prices of various goods do not rise or fall at the same rates. For example, during the 1970s, a period of relatively high general inflation, the price of crude oil rose faster than the general trend; whereas, in the 1980s, a period of relatively low but persistent inflation, the price of crude oil actually dropped substantially. During both decades, the prices of certain electronic products such as color television sets, personal computers, and compact tape and disc players tended to drop. The point is that, while prices may generally be inflating or deflating, the prices of specific products or services may behave quite differently from the average trend.

CONSEQUENCES OF PRICE CHANGES

To see the consequences of price changes for businesses, consider a simple example of a small business, ItemStore, Inc. that buys and sells Items. ItemStore starts at the beginning of 19X1 with an investment of $50,000, $20,000 of which it borrows on a 2-year, 10% note, payable at the end of 19X2. The $50,000 is invested in an inventory of 1,000 items at a cost of $10 each and $40,000 worth of equipment with an expected life of 2 years. During its first two years, ItemStore experiences the following operations and other events:

a. The firm sells 10,000 Items (inventory "turns over" 10 times) each year.
b. The purchase price and selling price of an Item are $10 and $15, respectively.
c. The firm depreciated the equipment on a straight-line basis.
d. The firm accrued interest payable of $2,000 on the note each year.
e. The firm paid income taxes on its income before taxes at 30%.
f. The firm paid cash dividends equal to its net income.
g. At the end of 19X2, the firm liquidated its inventory (did not replace inventory sold as year-end approached), retired its fully depreciated equipment (no gain or loss), and repaid the note with interest.

ItemStore's income statements for 19X1 and 19X2 are as follows:

	19X1	19X2
Net sales revenue	$150,000	$150,000
Cost of goods sold	(100,000)	(100,000)
Depreciation expense	(20,000)	(20,000)
Interest expense	(2,000)	(2,000)
Income before taxes	$ 28,000	$ 28,000
Income tax expense	(8,400)	(8,400)
Net income	$ 19,600	$ 19,600

Illustration 15-14 presents ItemStore's 2-year history in accounting-equation format.[5]

ILLUSTRATION 15-14 Two-Year Accounting History of ItemStore

Transactions and Events	Cash	+ Inventory	+ Equipment	− Accumulated Depreciation	= Note	+ Contributed Capital	+ Retained Earnings
19X1:							
Owners invest	30,000					30,000	
Borrowing	20,000				20,000		
Investment	(50,000)	10,000	40,000				
Sales	150,000						150,000
Purchases	(100,000)	100,000					
Cost of sales		(100,000)					(100,000)
Depreciation				(20,000)			(20,000)
Interest					2,000		(2,000)
Taxes	(8,400)						(8,400)
Dividends	(19,600)						(19,600)
Balances	22,000	10,000	40,000	(20,000)	22,000	30,000	0
19X2:							
Sales	150,000						150,000
Purchases	(90,000)	90,000					
Cost of sales		(100,000)					(100,000)
Depreciation				(20,000)			(20,000)
Interest					2,000		(2,000)
Taxes	(8,400)						(8,400)
Dividends	(19,600)						(19,600)
Repay note	(24,000)				(24,000)		
Retire equipment			(40,000)	40,000			
Balances	30,000	0	0	0	0	30,000	0

Illustration 15-14 shows us some of the business implications of financial accounting. Notice that when a firm follows a policy of paying dividends equal to net income, its Retained Earnings balance remains zero and its contributed capital remains intact. Moreover, if a firm goes through its life cycle following such a policy and then liquidates its assets and pays its liabilities, it will end its life with cash and contributed capital equal to the owners' cumulative invest-

[5]For convenience in presenting a single picture capturing ItemStore's 2-year history, several shortcuts are taken in Illustration 15-14. Increases and decreases in accounts are expressed algebraically instead of as debits and credits. Revenues and expenses are entered directly into Retained Earnings instead of to temporary accounts that would be closed to Retained Earnings. Finally, all sales and purchases are assumed to be for cash.

ments—in this case $30,000. In the case illustrated, the owners would have a choice between:

1. Withdrawing the $30,000 and having ItemStore go out of business
2. Borrowing $20,000 again, combining it with the $30,000 remaining investment of the owners, reinvesting in new inventory and equipment, and continuing the business as before

Some Consequences of General Inflation

When general inflation or deflation take place, owners of businesses and creditors experience purchasing power gains and losses. Constant dollar accounting can be used to measure these effects of changes in general prices.

Purchasing Power Gains and Losses. Assume that prices did not change during the 2 years of ItemStore's existence. The owners will be as well off at the end of 19X2, if their $30,000 is returned to them, as they were when they invested that amount. Moreover, they will have enjoyed total dividends of $19,600 in each of the 2 years. Under this assumption, accounting net income measures the amount of benefits the owners enjoy as a result of investing in ItemStore. However, suppose the general price level rose from 86.06 at the time of the owners' investment at the beginning of 19X1 to 91.28 at the end of 19X2. This means that it would take $91.28 to purchase at the end of 19X2 what could be purchased at the beginning of 19X1 for $86.06. By extension, the $30,000 returned to the owners at the end of 19X2 would only have the purchasing power of $28,284.40 in 19X1:

$$\$30,000 \ \text{x} \ \frac{86.06}{91.28} = \$28,284.40$$

The owners, therefore, have lost some of the purchasing power of their original investments while they enjoyed the dividends they received. Thus, in times of inflation, net income alone does not measure the benefits of ownership. To measure the owners' net benefits, it is necessary to offset the loss in purchasing power of their investments against the income recognized (or, in this case, the dividends paid).

Constant Dollar Accounting. If the owners in the above example wanted to know just how well off they have been made over 2 years as a result of their investments, they would face a problem of nonconstant dollars. That is, their investment of $30,000, the first dividend of $19,600, the second dividend of $19,600 and the return of their investment of $30,000 occurred at times of different-sized dollars (different purchasing power). Adding and subtracting these amounts is like "adding and subtracting apples and oranges"—to quote the classic complaint about the stable monetary unit assumption. Logically, the amounts measured in different-sized dollars must be re-expressed in the same-sized units. To do this, the dollars of one point in time are converted to dollars of another point in time that would have the same purchasing power. The conversions are made according to the following formula:

$$\text{Transaction Amount} \ \text{x} \ \frac{\textbf{Base Price Index}}{\textbf{Price Index at Time of Transaction}}$$

The base price index is the price index for the point in time whose dollars are used as the constant monetary units to express all other amounts. The investment history of the investors in ItemStore is re-expressed in constant, end-of-19X2 dollars as follows:

19X2 Return of investment	$30,000 x (91.28 ÷ 91.28) =	$30,000.00
19X2 Dividends	$19,600 x (91.28 ÷ 91.28) =	19,600.00
19X1 Dividends	$19,600 x (91.28 ÷ 88.14) =	20,298.25
Less: Original investment	$30,000 x (91.28 ÷ 86.06) =	(31,819.66)
Constant-dollar income (in 19X2 dollars)		$38,078.59

The owners of ItemStore received dividends for 19X1 and 19X2 totaling $39,200. However, the above calculation tells us that the net effect of the owners' investment in ItemStore for 2 years was $38,078.59 as expressed in 19X2 dollars. Thus, the owners lost purchasing power equivalent to $1,121.41 in 19X2 dollars ($39,200.00 – $38,078.59).

Debtor Gains From Inflation. One aspect of the above example is the business's use of debt to finance some of its investment in assets. Because the owners did not invest all the necessary funds to run the business, they transferred some of the purchasing power loss on the total required investment to the creditors. ItemStore borrowed $20,000 at the beginning of 19X1. At the end of 19X2, it paid back $20,000 plus $4,000 of accrued interest. However, the amount borrowed is the equivalent of $21,213.11 in end-of-19X2 dollars [$20,000 x (91.28 ÷ 86.06)]. Therefore, the creditors lost $1,213.11 in purchasing power. This is a benefit to the owners because they had the use of the assets purchased with the creditors' money without suffering a purchasing power loss on that portion of ItemStore's total investment in assets.

As a general rule, debtors gain and creditors lose purchasing power in times of inflation. However, since businesspeople, bankers, and investors are generally aware of this effect of general inflation, interest rates are higher when higher inflation is expected and lower when lower inflation (or deflation) is expected. Therefore, only unexpected inflation leads to *real gains* for debtors and *real losses* for creditors.

Some Consequences of Specific Price Changes

While general inflation and deflation affect the owners' purchasing power, specific price changes affect the business. Specific price changes can affect the business's ability to carry on future operations at the same level physically and they disrupt the relationship between current income and future cash flows.

Let us now *suppose there was no general inflation* from the beginning of 19X1 to the end of 19X2. Assume, also, that there were no specific price changes either. If the owners wish to continue the business, ItemStore may simply borrow $20,000 again, combine it with the owners' remaining investment of $30,000, reinvest in inventory and equipment, and carry on the business as usual. However, let us suppose that the specific cost of Items was increased to $12 each just at the end of 19X2 and the cost of the equipment used in the business had increased to $50,000. If the owners decide to withdraw their investment of $30,000 at the end of 19X2 and discontinue the business, these specific price changes are irrelevant. However, if the business is to continue, the specific price changes are significant.

Erosion of Capital.   The required total investment in assets has increased from $50,000 to $62,000—$50,000 for equipment plus $12,000 for inventory (1,000 Items x $12). If the debt-to-equity investment proportions are held constant, the business would borrow 40% of $62,000, or $24,800. This leaves a required equity investment of $37,200, or $7,200 more than the owners' remaining investment. Some would say, therefore, that the dividends paid in 19X1 and 19X2 were excessive, because they jeopardized the business's ability to continue its activities at the same volume. By extension, net income did not measure income because the income could not be spent on dividends to the owners without requiring new investment to continue the same volume of business. This tends to violate our intuition that income is disposable—that is, income may be withdrawn or distributed without diminishing the business's ability to continue.

Prediction of Future Operating Flows.   The specific price changes also mean that analysts may be missing information that is relevant for predicting future cash flows. The 19X1 and 19X2 income statements are based on old prices that definitely do not apply to the future. Unless analysts know that the replacement equipment will cost $50,000 in early 19X3 and that Items will cost $12 each, they might forecast different costs based on the 19X1 and 19X2 income statements. In addition, the firm will have to raise its selling price to maintain its profitability. This may or may not be possible, depending on aggregate demand and competition in its industry. If they do not know about the specific price changes, analysts may not anticipate these issues.

Supplemental Inflation and Current Cost Information

For many years, the limitations of the stable monetary unit assumption in times of changing prices were debated. The SEC and FASB were keenly aware of the implications of inflation and specific price changes for businesses, owners, creditors, and analysts of financial statements. Their awareness was particularly acute during the 1970s when inflation was high and significant specific price changes took place. The FASB issued *Statement of Financial Accounting Standards No. 33* in September 1979, *requiring* large, publicly-held corporations to provide supplemental information with their financial statements.[6] The supplements are too intricate to define and explain here, but they revealed certain aspects of the effects on the business of both general and specific price changes. However, in 1984, the FASB issued *SFAS No. 82*, making the general-inflation information voluntary.[7] Then, in 1986, the FASB issued *SFAS No. 89*, making the specific-price information voluntary.[8]

---

[6]"Financial Reporting and Changing Prices," *Statement of Financial Accounting Standards No. 33* (Stamford, Conn.: FASB, 1979).

[7]"Financial Reporting and Changing Prices: Elimination of Certain Disclosures," *Statement of Financial Accounting Standards No. 82* (Stamford, Conn.: FASB, 1984).

[8]"Financial Reporting and Changing Prices," *Statement of Financial Accounting Standards No. 89* (Stamford, Conn.: FASB, 1986).

REVIEW PROBLEM

The Bluegrass Distribution Corporation specializes in grass seeds. It sells a large variety of seeds to accommodate differing climates and conditions. Most of its business is with state highway departments and large contractors, and all sales are on credit. Bluegrass's financial statements for the years 19X2 and 19X3 are as follows:

Bluegrass Distribution Corporation
Comparative Balance Sheet (Unaudited)
December 31, 19X2 and 19X3

	19X2	19X3
Assets		
Cash	$110,000	$130,000
Accounts receivable	95,000	125,000
Allowance for uncollectible accounts	(3,000)	(2,500)
Inventory	205,000	290,000
Supplies	2,000	2,500
Prepaid expenses	4,000	3,000
Total current assets	$413,000	$548,000
Land	60,000	60,000
Buildings and equipment	250,000	400,000
Accumulated depreciation	(100,000)	(125,000)
Total assets	$623,000	$883,000
Liabilities and Stockholders' Equity		
Accounts payable	$ 52,000	$ 61,000
Notes payable	40,000	50,000
Wages and salaries payable	5,000	5,000
Taxes payable	4,000	5,000
Total current liabilities	$101,000	$121,000
Notes payable—noncurrent	0	100,000
Total liabilities	$101,000	$221,000
Common stock	$100,000	$110,000
Paid-in capital in excess of par	300,000	340,000
Retained earnings	122,000	212,000
Total stockholders' equity	$522,000	$662,000
Total liabilities & stockholders' equity	$623,000	$883,000

Bluegrass Distribution Corporation
Comparative Income Statement (Unaudited)
For the Years Ended December 31, 19X2 and 19X3

	19X2	19X3
Net sales	$1,200,000	$1,400,000
Cost of goods sold:		
Beginning inventory	$ 180,000	$ 205,000
Purchases (net)	720,000	900,000
Cost of goods available	$ 900,000	$1,105,000
Ending inventory	205,000	290,000
Cost of goods sold	$ 695,000	$ 815,000
Gross profit	$ 505,000	$ 585,000

Continued

	19X2	19X3
Selling expenses	$150,000	$175,000
Depreciation expense	15,000	25,000
Administrative expenses	160,000	170,000
Total operating expenses	$325,000	$370,000
Operating income before taxes	$180,000	$215,000
Interest expense	4,000	15,000
Income before taxes	$176,000	$200,000
Income tax expense	52,800	60,000
Net income	$123,200	$140,000

Bluegrass Distribution Corporation
Comparative Statement of Retained Earnings (Unaudited)
For the Years Ended December 31, 19X2 and 19X3

	19X2	19X3
Retained earnings, beginning	$ 48,800	$122,000
Net income	123,200	140,000
Dividends declared	(50,000)	(50,000)
Retained earnings, ending	$122,000	$212,000

Bluegrass Distribution Corporation
Comparative Statement of Cash Flows
For the Years Ended December 31, 19X2 and 19X3

	19X2	19X3
Cash flows from operating activities:		
Net income	$123,200	$ 140,000
Depreciation expense	15,000	25,000
Increase in accounts payable	5,000	9,000
Increase in taxes payable	200	1,000
Decrease in prepaid expenses	100	1,000
Increase in accounts receivable (net)	(6,000)	(30,500)
Increase in inventory	(25,000)	(85,000)
Increase in supplies	0	(500)
Net cash flows from operating activities	$112,500	$ 60,000
Cash flows from investing activities:		
Purchase of building and equipment	(25,000)	(150,000)
Net cash flows from investing activities	$ (25,000)	$(150,000)
Cash flows from financing activities:		
Payment of dividends	(50,000)	(50,000)
Net proceeds from short-term notes	5,000	10,000
Noncurrent note issued	0	100,000
Common stock issued	0	50,000
Net cash flows from financing activities	$ (45,000)	$ 110,000
Net increase in cash	$ 42,500	$ 20,000

Additional Information:
Beginning 19X2 balances:

Total assets	$539,600
Receivables (net)	86,000
Stockholders' equity	448,800

REQUIRED:

a. Calculate the following profitability ratios for 19X2 and 19X3: profit margin, gross margin, return on assets, and return on stockholders' equity. Comment briefly about Bluegrass's profitability.

b. Analyze the statement of cash flows and comment on the health of Bluegrass's cash flows for 19X3.

c. Calculate the following asset utilization ratios for 19X2 and 19X3: asset turnover, receivables turnover, age of accounts receivable, inventory turnover, and days' supply in inventory. Comment briefly about Bluegrass's asset utilization.

d. Calculate the following liquidity ratios for 19X2 and 19X3: working capital ratio, quick ratio, working capital to total assets, and age of accounts payable. Comment briefly about Bluegrass's liquidity.

e. Calculate the following solvency ratios for 19X2 and 19X3: times interest earned, cash flows to total debt, total debt to total assets, and total debt to stockholders' equity. Comment briefly about Bluegrass's solvency.

f. Based on the limited information you have about Bluegrass, evaluate the persistence and quality of Bluegrass's income.

SOLUTION:

Planning and Organizing Your Work

1. For each of the ratio (key question) categories recall the ratio definitions or review them in Illustrations 15-7, 9, 10, or 11. Calculate the ratios for 19X2 and 19X3 and comment on their individual and collective implications.

2. Examine the statement of cash flows. Consider the cash flows for operating, investing, and financing activies. Comment of their individual and collective implications.

3. Examine the contents of the income statement and review your analyses of all of the previous categories. Consider whether there appear to be any transitory components of net income that will not persist at some level in the future and comment on them. Consider whether there appear to be overstatements or understatements of assets and liabilities and related income statement components that suggest that net income is biased relative to steady-state future cash flows. Comment.

(a) *Calculate profitability ratios.*

$$\text{Profit Margin} = \frac{\text{Net Income}}{\text{Net Sales}}$$

19X2   **19X3**

$$\frac{\$123,200}{\$1,200,000} = .103 \qquad \frac{\$140,000}{\$1,400,000} = .100$$

$$\text{Gross Margin} = \frac{\text{Gross Profit}}{\text{Net Sales}}$$

19X2   **19X3**

$$\frac{\$505,000}{\$1,200,000} = .421 \qquad \frac{\$585,000}{\$1,400,000} = .418$$

$$\text{Return on Assets} = \frac{\text{Before-Tax Income} + \text{Interest Expense}}{\text{Average Total Assets}}$$

19X2   **19X3**

$$\frac{\$176,000 + 4,000}{(\$539,600 + \$623,000)/2} = .310 \qquad \frac{\$200,000 + 15,000}{(\$623,000 + \$883,000)/2} = .286$$

$$\text{Return on Stockholders' Equity} = \frac{\text{Net Income}}{\text{Average Stockholders' Equity}}$$

19X2	*19X3*
$\dfrac{\$123,200}{(\$448,800 + \$522,000)/2} = .254$	$\dfrac{\$140,000}{(\$522,000 + \$662,000)/2} = .236$

Comment on profitability: Bluegrass has very strong profitability. The two years are nearly identical with a very slight downward movement in 19X3.

(b) *Analyze the statement of cash flows.*
Cash flow from operating activities for 19X2 is a healthy $60,000, but it is down from $125,000 in 19X2, primarily because of significant increases in the investments in accounts receivable and inventory. Investment in new plant and equipment of $150,000 and dividends of $50,000 were sufficiently greater than cash flows from operating activities to require issue of a noncurrent note for $100,000 and new owner contributions of capital totaling $50,000. The additional debt financing, however, did put the company in a weaker solvency position (see part e).

(c) *Calculate asset utilization ratios.*

$$\text{Asset Turnover} = \frac{\text{Net Sales}}{\text{Average Total Assets}}$$

19X2	*19X3*
$\dfrac{\$1,200,000}{(\$539,600 + \$623,000)/2} = 2.06$	$\dfrac{\$1,400,000}{(\$623,000 + \$883,000)/2} = 1.86$

$$\text{Receivables Turnover} = \frac{\text{Net Credit Sales}}{\text{Average Net Trade Receivables}}$$

19X2	*19X3*
$\dfrac{\$1,200,000}{(\$86,000 + \$92,000)/2} = 13.5$	$\dfrac{\$1,400,000}{(\$92,000 + \$122,500)/2} = 13.1$

$$\text{Age of Accounts Receivable} = \frac{\text{Gross Trade Receivables}}{\text{Credit Sales}} \times 365$$

19X2	*19X3*
$\dfrac{\$95,000}{\$1,200,000} \times 365 = 28.9 \text{ days}$	$\dfrac{\$125,000}{\$1,400,000} \times 365 = 32.6 \text{ days}$

$$\text{Inventory Turnover} = \frac{\text{Cost of Goods Sold}}{\text{Average Inventory}}$$

19X2	*19X3*
$\dfrac{\$695,000}{(\$180,000 + \$205,000)/2} = 3.6$	$\dfrac{\$815,000}{(\$205,000 + \$290,000)/2} = 3.3$

$$\text{Days' Supply in Inventory} = \frac{\text{Inventory}}{\text{Cost of Goods Sold}} \times 365 \text{ days}$$

19X2	*19X3*
$\dfrac{\$205,000}{\$695,000} \times 365 = 107.7 \text{ days}$	$\dfrac{\$290,000}{\$815,000} \times 365 = 129.9 \text{ days}$

Comment on asset utilization: Some downward trend is noted in the utilization of assets. Asset turnover has decreased; the age of receivables has increased; and inventory turnover has decreased. When viewed in the context of Bluegrass's outstanding profitability, the moderate downward trend in asset utilization is not a cause for concern; but the causes of the increased age of receivables and increased days' supply in inventory should be determined.

(d) *Calculate liquidity ratios.*

$$\text{Working Capital Ratio} = \frac{\text{Current Assets}}{\text{Current Liabilities}}$$

19X2	*19X3*
$\dfrac{\$413,000}{\$101,000} = 4.09$	$\dfrac{\$548,000}{\$121,000} = 4.53$

$$\text{Quick (Acid Test) Ratio} = \frac{\text{Liquid Current Assets}}{\text{Current Liabilities}}$$

19X2	*19X3*
$\dfrac{\$110,000 + \$92,000}{\$101,000} = 2.00$	$\dfrac{\$130,000 + \$122,500}{\$121,000} = 2.09$

$$\text{Working Capital to Total Assets} = \frac{\text{Working Capital}}{\text{Total Assets}}$$

19X2	*19X3*
$\dfrac{\$413,000 - \$101,000}{\$623,000} = .50$	$\dfrac{\$548,000 - \$121,000}{\$883,000} = .48$

$$\text{Age of Accounts Payable} = \frac{\text{Accounts Payable}}{\text{Purchases}} \times 365 \text{ days}$$

19X2	*19X3*
$\dfrac{\$52,000}{\$720,000} \times 365 = 26.4 \text{ days}$	$\dfrac{\$61,000}{\$900,000} \times 365 = 24.7 \text{ days}$

Comment on liquidity: The liquidity ratios show a very strong liquidity. Bluegrass's strong position of current assets to current liabilities combined with its profitability make it a good credit risk for short-term creditors.

(e) *Calculate solvency ratios.*

$$\text{Times Interest Earned} = \frac{\text{Pre-Tax Income} + \text{Interest Expense}}{\text{Interest Expense}}$$

19X2	*19X3*
$\dfrac{\$176,000 + \$4,000}{\$4,000} = 45.00$	$\dfrac{\$200,000 + \$15,000}{\$15,000} = 14.33$

$$\text{Cash Flows to Total Debt} = \frac{\text{Cash Flows From Operations}}{\text{Year-End Total Debt}}$$

19X2	*19X3*
$\dfrac{\$112,500}{\$101,000} = 1.11$	$\dfrac{\$60,000}{\$221,000} = .27$

$$\text{Total Debt to Total Assets} = \frac{\text{Year-End Total Liabilities}}{\text{Year-End Total Assets}}$$

19X2   **19X3**

$$\frac{\$101,000}{\$623,000} = .16 \qquad \frac{\$221,000}{\$883,000} = .25$$

$$\text{Total Debt to Stockholders' Equity} = \frac{\text{Year-End Total Liabilities}}{\text{Year-End Stockholders' Equity}}$$

19X2   **19X3**

$$\frac{\$101,000}{\$522,000} = .19 \qquad \frac{\$221,000}{\$662,000} = .33$$

Comment on solvency: Although Bluegrass's solvency ratios have weakened somewhat, the reason is clear. It issued a $100,000 long-term note and increased its short-term borrowing. As a result, the solvency ratios weakened from the very strong 19X2 levels. It remains strong with a sound debt to equity ratio and coverage of interest. The 19X3 ratios, combined with profitability, give Bluegrass strong solvency.

(f) *Evaluate the persistence and quality of income.*
The persistence of Bluegrass's income looks good. It did not have any extraordinary items, discontinued operations, accounting changes, or even any gains or losses on the income statements. It would be important to evaluate the impact of certain economic conditions on Bluegrass's customers' demands for grass seed.

The quality of income is difficult to evaluate from the information given. We would evaluate this by looking at the accounting methods Bluegrass is using to see if there appears to be a bias toward maximizing income. We would want to evaluate receivables in view of their increase in age to be sure the allowance account is adequate and look at the inventory for obsolete seed or spoilage because of the significant increase in inventory. We would be more comfortable with the quality of earnings issue if Bluegrass had its financial statements audited by an independent CPA firm.

KEY TERMS

SELF-QUIZ

LO 1 1. The item that best describes financial statement analysis is
   a. Analysis of a transaction to determine the best way to record it in the financial statements
   b. Art of using financial statement data and information to answer questions about a business and to make predictions about its future
   c. Analysis of documentation supporting business transactions
   d. None of the above

LO 1 2. In general, which of the following statements about cash flows and net income is correct?
   a. Net income will always be less than cash flows.
   b. Net income will always be greater than cash flows.
   c. Over the life of a business, average income per period approximately equals average cash flows from operations and investment activities.
   d. Net income has no relationship to cash flows.

LO 2 3. Income persistence is
   a. Tendency for a component of income to continue in future periods under steady-state assumptions
   b. Very low for extraordinary gains
   c. Higher for revenues than it is for gains
   d. All of the above

LO 2 4. A high quality of income means
   a. High net income
   b. Absence of extraordinary transactions or discontinued operations in the income statement
   c. Degree to which management does not manipulate the firm's income to present an optimistic picture of ongoing income
   d. All of the above

LO 2 5. Which of the following component(s) of the income statement is (are) highest in income persistence?
   a. Revenues and expenses
   b. Extraordinary items
   c. Cumulative effect of an accounting change
   d. Gains and losses

LO 3 6. The tools of financial statement analysis consist of
   a. Common-size and percent-change financial statements and various financial ratios
   b. Trial balance
   c. Journals and ledgers
   d. None of the above

LO 3 7. Common-size financial statements
   a. Express all financial statement numbers as a percent of the company's retained earnings
   b. Support a technique known as vertical analysis
   c. Support a technique known as horizontal analysis
   d. Both a and b

LO 3 8. Vertical analysis
   a. Refers to the evaluation of financial information for different years; for example, 19X1, 19X2, and 19X3
   b. Refers to calculating financial ratios and presenting them in a vertical format
   c. Refers to the analysis of the percentage composition of the components of a particular statement for a particular year
   d. None of the above

LO 3 9. Percent-change financial statements
   a. Are a form of horizontal analysis
   b. Involve only one year's financial statements
   c. Show rates of growth or decline in financial statement components
   d. Both a and c

LO 3 10. Financial ratios
   a. Can be calculated to represent almost any relevant relationship between financial statement amounts
   b. Are more flexible than common-size financial statements
   c. Are numerical statistics that represent important relationships between financial statement amounts
   d. All of the above

LO 3 11. Once ratios and percents are computed in financial statement analysis, they are usually compared with other information. The standard of comparison used in this chapter is
   a. Prior years' ratios and percents
   b. Industry comparisons
   c. Plans of the business
   d. None of the above

LO 4 12. Select the group of profitability ratios
   a. Asset turnover, receivables turnover, inventory turnover
   b. Profit margin, gross margin, return on assets
   c. Working capital ratio, quick ratio, age of accounts payable
   d. Times interest earned, cash flows to total debt, total debt to owners' equity

LO 4 13. Select the group of asset utilization ratios
   a. Days' supply in inventory, inventory turnover, asset turnover
   b. Return on owners' equity, return on assets, profit margin
   c. Total debt to total assets, times interest earned, cash flows to total debt
   d. Quick ratio, working capital ratio, working capital to total assets

LO 5 14. A well-written analysis of a set of financial statements
   a. Comments about each item contained in the statements
   b. Captures only the essentials from the vast array of data included in the statements
   c. Is brief
   d. Both b and c

LO 6 15. An unqualified opinion in the independent auditors' report provides assurances that
   a. Management of the company is effective
   b. Financial statements are free of errors
   c. Financial statements probably are not materially misstated
   d. All transactions of the company have been verified

LO 7 16. (Appendix) Excluding the effect of interest, during a period of inflation, the party that owes money (debtor)
   a. Incurs a purchasing power loss
   b. Incurs a purchasing power gain
   c. Has neither a purchasing power gain nor loss
   d. None of the above

LO 8 17. (Appendix) Excluding the effect of interest, during a period of inflation, the party that is owed money (creditor)
   a. Incurs a purchasing power loss
   b. Incurs a purchasing power gain
   c. Has neither a purchasing power gain nor loss
   d. None of the above

SOLUTIONS TO SELF-QUIZ

1. b   2. c   3. d   4. c   5. a   6. a   7. b   8. c   9. d   10. d   11. a   12. b   13. a   14. d
15. c   16. b   17. a

QUESTIONS

Q15-1   How does the analysis of the income statement, which is prepared under the accrual method, help predict future cash flows?

Q15-2   Define financial statement analysis.

Q15-3   Explain why gains and losses are lower in income persistence than are revenues and expenses.

Q15-4   Explain how a company having an audit by an independent CPA firm can improve income quality.

Q15-5   Give two examples of ways that the management of a company might manipulate income.

Q15-6   Explain how a common-size income statement is prepared.

Q15-7   Give an example of how a common-size income statement can be used to identify important information.

Q15-8   The usual base figure (the important summary figure) in the common size-balance sheet is: _____.

Q15-9   What is vertical analysis?

Q15-10   What is horizontal analysis?

Q15-11   Explain how a percent-change balance sheet is prepared.

Q15-12   Is financial statement analysis an art or a science? Discuss.

Q15-13   As part of analyzing the financial statements of Green Company, you compute a working capital ratio of 1:8 and a quick ratio of 1:1. Describe the possible implications of this information.

Q15-14   Five key questions, which can act as a framework, must be answered in the analysis of financial statements. List them.

Q15-15   Does an analyst who is primarily interested in a business's solvency have any interest in its profitability? Discuss.

Q15-16   What is meant by the term *utilization of assets*?

Q15-17   Distinguish between liquidity and solvency.

Q15-18   What are three components of reserve funds?

Q15-19   Distinguish between business risk and financial risk.

Q15-20   What is leverage? Give an example of the beneficial effect and the risk effect of leverage.

Q15-21   (Appendix) Describe how a purchasing power loss occurs. Is such a loss recognized in income statements prepared under GAAP?

EXERCISES

LO 2,3,4   **E15-1**   **Concepts of Income Persistence and Quality, Tools of Financial Statement Analysis, Performing Analysis**   Match the terms and the definitions.

____ a. Income persistence
____ b. Income quality
____ c. Common-size financial statements
____ d. Vertical analysis
____ e. Percent-change financial statements
____ f. Horizontal analysis
____ g. Financial ratios
____ h. Business risk
____ i. Financial risk
____ j. Beneficial leverage effect
____ k. Risk leverage effect
____ l. Reserve funds

(1) Risk associated with the nature of the business and the markets in which it operates

(2) Tendency for a component of income to continue in future periods under steady-state assumptions

(3) Statements whose numerical amounts are re-expressed as percents of an important summary figure

(4) Rate of return on assets: 15%; interest rate on borrowed funds: 12%

(5) Rate of return on assets: 8%; interest rate on borrowed funds: 12%

(6) Numerical statistics that represent important relationships between financial statement amounts

(7) Looking at rates of change in gross profit from 19X1 to 19X2

(8) Conventional financial statements with changes and percents of changes added

(9) Line of credit with a bank that exceeds what the business is expected to need

(10) Degree to which management does not manipulate the firm's income to paint an optimistic picture of ongoing income

(11) Analysis of the percentage composition of the components of a particular statement for a particular year

(12) Added risk that a business incurs when it uses debt financing

LO 3,4,5   **E15-2**   **Common-Size Income Statement**   Prepare a common-size comparative income statement for the Diaz Corporation for 19X5 and 19X6 and briefly comment on any significant trends that are identified.

Diaz Corporation Comparative Income Statement For the Years Ended December 31, 19X5 and 19X6		
	19X5	*19X6*
Net sales	$287,000	$350,000
Cost of goods sold	206,000	262,500
Gross profit	$ 81,000	$ 87,500
Selling and administrative expenses	60,000	64,000
Income before taxes	$ 21,000	$ 23,500
Income tax expense	6,300	7,050
Net income	$ 14,700	$ 16,450

LO 3,4,5 **E15-3** **Common-Size Balance Sheet** Prepare a common-size comparative balance sheet for the Canner Corporation for 19X3 and 19X4 and briefly comment on any significant trends that are identified.

Canner Corporation Comparative Balance Sheet June 30, 19X3 and 19X4		
	19X3	*19X4*
Assets		
Cash	$ 60,000	$ 35,000
Accounts receivable (net)	100,000	140,000
Inventory	125,000	140,000
Prepaid expenses	10,000	10,000
Total current assets	$295,000	$325,000
Land	50,000	50,000
Buildings and equipment	400,000	400,000
Accumulated depreciation	(200,000)	(240,000)
Total assets	$545,000	$535,000
Liabilities and Stockholders' Equity		
Accounts payable	$210,000	$205,000
Wages and salaries payable	2,000	2,000
Total current liabilities	$212,000	$207,000
Contributed capital	$200,000	$200,000
Retained earnings	133,000	128,000
Total stockholders' equity	$333,000	$328,000
Total liabilities and stockholders' equity	$545,000	$535,000

LO 3,4,5 **E15-4** **Percent-Change Income Statement** A comparative income statement for the Jefferson Supply, Inc. for 19X1 and 19X2 is presented on the next page

REQUIRED:

Prepare a percent-change comparative income statement and briefly comment on any significant changes.

Jefferson Supply, Inc. Comparative Income Statement For the Years Ended December 31, 19X1 and 19X2		
	19X1	*19X2*
Net sales	$600,000	$582,000
Cost of goods sold	420,000	419,000
Gross profit	$180,000	$163,000
Selling and administrative expenses	100,000	100,000
Income before taxes	$ 80,000	$ 63,000
Income tax expense	24,000	18,900
Net income	$ 56,000	$ 44,100

LO 3,4,5

E15-5 **Percent-Change Balance Sheet** Prepare a percent-change comparative balance sheet for the Cross Walk Corp. and briefly comment on any significant changes that are identified.

Cross Walk Corp. Comparative Balance Sheet July 31, 19X8 and 19X9		
	19X8	*19X9*
Assets		
Cash	$ 51,450	$ 28,000
Accounts receivable (net)	75,000	72,000
Inventory	95,550	130,000
Prepaid expenses	4,000	5,000
Total current assets	$226,000	$235,000
Land	20,000	20,000
Buildings and equipment	250,000	260,000
Accumulated depreciation	(100,000)	(120,000)
Total assets	$396,000	$395,000
Liabilities and Stockholders' Equity		
Accounts payable	$110,000	$140,000
Wages and salaries payable	1,000	1,000
Total current liabilities	$111,000	$141,000
Capital stock	$150,000	$150,000
Retained earnings	135,000	104,000
Total stockholders' equity	$285,000	$254,000
Total liabilities and stockholders' equity	$396,000	$395,000

LO 4

E15-6 **Financial Ratios** Use the codes presented below to classify the listed ratios as profitability ratios, asset utilization ratios, liquidity ratios, or solvency ratios.

PR = profitability ratio
AR = asset utilization ratio
LR = liquidity ratio

SR = solvency ratio

Ratios

___ a. Times interest earned
___ b. Asset turnover
___ c. Age of accounts payable
___ d. Profit margin
___ e. Quick (acid test) ratio
___ f. Total debt to total assets
___ g. Working capital ratio
___ h. Return on assets
___ i. Total debt to owners' equity
___ j. Age of accounts receivable
___ k. Gross margin
___ l. Inventory turnover
___ m. Days' supply in inventory
___ n. Working capital to total assets
___ o. Cash flow to total debt
___ p. Receivables turnover
___ q. Return on owners' equity

LO 4,5   **E15-7**   **Calculation of Profitability Ratios**   The income statement and additional financial information for the Orange Grove Company is presented below for the years 19X6 and 19X7.

Orange Grove Company Comparative Income Statement For the Years Ended December 31, 19X6 and 19X7		
	19X6	*19X7*
Net sales	$850,000	$890,000
Cost of goods sold	552,500	596,300
Gross profit	$297,500	$293,700
Selling and administrative expenses*	200,000	200,000
Income before taxes	$ 97,500	$ 93,700
Income tax expense	29,250	28,110
Net income	$ 68,250	$ 65,590

*Includes $10,000 interest expense in 19X6 and $20,000 interest expense in 19X7.

Additional Information:

	19X6	*19X7*
Average total assets	$700,000	$900,000
Average owners' equity	300,000	325,000

REQUIRED:

Use the information to calculate the profit margin, gross margin, return on assets, and return on owners' equity for 19X6 and 19X7. Briefly comment about what the ratios reveal about Orange Grove's profitability.

LO 4,5   **E15-8**   **Asset Utilization Ratios**   The Danzen Corporation has a local customer base in an area where a large military complex has been closed down. Danzen has been experiencing cash flow problems.

REQUIRED:

Use the following selected information to calculate the receivables turnover, age of accounts receivables, inventory turnover, and days' supplies in inventory for 19X3 and 19X4. Comment on what the ratios reveal.

	19X3	19X4
Net credit sales	$4,650,000	$4,200,000
Cost of goods sold	3,255,000	3,024,000
Average inventory	500,000	550,000
Ending inventory	500,000	600,000
Average net receivables	387,500	450,000
Ending gross receivables	425,000	475,000

LO 4   **E15-9**   **Liquidity Ratios**   Selected information from the balance sheet and income statement of Med Help, Inc. is provided below:

Cash	$ 15,700
Accounts receivable (net)	88,000
Marketable securities	11,000
Supplies	36,000
Prepaid expenses	9,000
Land, buildings, and equipment (net)	450,000
Total assets	$609,700
Accounts payable	$125,000
Notes payable–current	40,000
Notes payable–noncurrent	200,000
Purchases of supplies	300,000

REQUIRED:

a. Use the information to calculate the following liquidity ratios: working capital ratio, quick (acid test) ratio, working capital to total assets, and age of accounts payable.
b. Based on the limited information from these ratios, would you, as a seller of medical supplies, extend credit to Med Help? Explain your reasoning.

LO 4,5   **E15-10**   **Solvency Ratios**   Selected information from the balance sheet and income statement of Cable Tech Corp. is presented below:

Total liabilities	$ 6,000,000
Owners' equity	9,000,000
Total assets	15,000,000
Pre-tax income	1,200,000
Interest expense	300,000
Cash flows from operations	1,500,000

REQUIRED:

a. Use the information to calculate the following solvency ratios: times interest earned, cash flows from operations to total debt, total debt to total assets, and debt-equity.
b. Briefly comment about what these ratios reveal about Cable's solvency.

LO 7   **E15-11**   **Effects of General Inflation (Appendix)**   Judy Morris paid $15,000 for a 5-acre tract of land in 19X2 when the general price index was 125. She sold the land in 19X7 for $16,500 when the general price index was 150.

REQUIRED:

Calculate the gain from the sale of the land, assuming a stable dollar, and calculate the gain or loss in constant 19X7 dollars.

PROBLEM SET A

LO 1   **P15-1A**   **Relationship of Net Income to Cash Flows and Future Cash Flows**   The graph presented below shows the net income and the net cash flows for Northeast Digital Company over a 10-year period. Digital is a growth company; and over this period, it has not paid dividends or made other distributions to shareholders. It has not engaged in any significant financing activities.

REQUIRED:

a. Speculate as to the cause of the cash flows being less than net income in years X1 and X5 and higher than net income in the other years.
b. Assuming any items between the $100 million increments on the Y axis represent $50 million increments, add the net income over the 10-year period and divide by 10 to compute average income.
c. Add the cash flows over the 10-year period and divide by 10 to compute average cash flows.
d. Compare the averages in c and d and discuss the income persistence exhibited by Northeast's income figures.

Financial Statements to be Used with Problems 2A through 6A

The American Apple Corp. (AAC) buys and exports apples, pears, oranges, and grapefruits to Japan, South Korea, and Thialand. All sales are in U.S. dollars. AAC's financial statements for the years 19X8 and 19X9 are presented on the following pages.

Additional Information (in Thousands):

Beginning 19X8 balances:

Total assets	$56,555
Receivables (net)	24,500
Owners' equity	11,250

American Apple Corp.
Comparative Balance Sheet
September 30, 19X8 and 19X9

| | (Thousands) | |
	19X8	19X9
Assets		
Cash	$ 6,500	$ 5,480
Investment in securities	2,000	2,000
Accounts receivable	26,000	32,000
Allowance for uncollectible accounts	(1,000)	(1,000)
Inventory	15,000	18,000
Supplies	100	125
Prepaid expenses	200	175
Total current assets	$48,800	$56,780
Land	1,500	1,800
Buildings and equipment	10,000	15,000
Accumulated depreciation	(2,000)	(2,500)
Total assets	$58,300	$71,080
Liabilities and Stockholders' Equity		
Accounts payable	$10,500	$14,000
Notes payable	7,000	9,000
Wages and salaries payable	50	60
Taxes payable	500	600
Total current liabilities	$18,050	$23,660
Bonds payable	24,000	24,000
Notes payable—noncurrent	4,000	8,000
Total liabilities	$46,050	$55,660
Common stock	$ 5,000	$ 5,000
Paid-in capital in excess of par	3,000	3,000
Retained earnings	4,250	7,420
Total stockholders' equity	$12,250	$15,420
Total liabilities & stockholders' equity	$58,300	$71,080

American Apple Corp.
Comparative Income Statement
For the Years Ended September 30, 19X8 and 19X9

| | (Thousands) | |
	19X8	19X9
Net sales	$90,000	$ 98,000
Cost of goods sold:		
Beginning inventory	$14,000	$ 15,000
Purchases (net)	80,000	86,000
Cost of goods available	$94,000	$101,000
Ending inventory	15,000	18,000
Cost of goods sold	$79,000	$83,000
Gross profit	$11,000	$15,000

Continued

Selling expenses	$3,300	$3,000
Depreciation expense	400	500
Administrative expenses	2,000	2,500
Total operating expenses	$5,700	$6,000
Operating income before taxes	$5,300	$9,000
Interest expense	(2,600)	(3,200)
Interest revenue	160	160
Income before taxes	$2,860	$5,960
Income tax expense	860	1,790
Net income	$2,000	$4,170

American Apple Corp.
Comparative Statement of Retained Earnings
For the Years Ended September 30, 19X8 and 19X9

	(Thousands)	
	19X8	*19X9*
Retained earnings, beginning	$3,250	$4,250
Net income	2,000	4,170
Dividends declared	(1,000)	(1,000)
Retained earnings, ending	$4,250	$7,420

American Apple Corp.
Comparative Statement of Cash Flows
For the Years Ended September 30, 19X8 and 19X9

	(Thousands)	
	19X8	*19X9*
Cash flows from operating activities:		
Net income	$ 2,000	$ 4,170
Depreciation expense	400	500
Increase in accounts payable	200	3,500
Increase in taxes payable	50	100
Increase (decrease) in wages payable	(5)	10
Decrease in prepaid expenses	0	25
Increase in accounts receivable (net)	(500)	(6,000)
Increase in inventory	(1,000)	(3,000)
Increase in supplies	0	(25)
Net cash flows from operating activities	$ 1,145	$ (720)
Cash flows from investing activities:		
Purchase of land	$ 0	$ (300)
Purchase of building and equipment	(1,000)	(5,000)
Net cash flows from investment activities	$(1,000)	$(5,300)
Cash flows from financing activities:		
Payment of dividends	$(1,000)	$(1,000)
Net proceeds from current notes	500	2,000
Noncurrent note issued	0	4,000
Net cash flows from financial activities	$ (500)	$ 5,000
Net increase in cash	$ (355)	$(1,020)

LO 3,4,5

P15-2A **Common-Size and Percent-Change Analysis of Income Statements** Refer to American Apple Corp.'s (AAC's) financial statements (pages 696–697).

REQUIRED:

a. Perform a vertical analysis of AAC's income statements by preparing a common-size comparative income statement for 19X8 and 19X9.
b. Comment on information the common-size income statement reveals.
c. Perform a horizontal analysis of AAC's income statements by preparing a percent-change comparative income statement from 19X8 to 19X9.
d. Comment on information the percent-change comparative income statement reveals.

LO 3,4,5

P15-3A **Common-Size and Percent-Change Analysis of Balance Sheets** Refer to American Apple Corp.'s (AAC's) financial statements (pages 696–697).

REQUIRED:

a. Perform a vertical analysis of AAC's balance sheets by preparing a common-size comparative balance sheet for 19X8 and 19X9.
b. Comment on information the common-size comparative balance sheet reveals.
c. Perform a horizontal analysis of AAC's balance sheets by preparing a percent-change comparative balance sheet from 19X8 to 19X9.
d. Comment on information the percent-change comparative balance sheet reveals.

LO 3,4,5

P15-4A **Analysis of Cash Flows Statements** Refer to American Apple Corp.'s (AAC's) financial statements (pages 696–697).

REQUIRED:

a. Evaluate AAC's cash flows from operating activities for 19X8 and 19X9.
b. Evaluate AAC's cash flows from investing activities for 19X8 and 19X9.
c. Evaluate AAC's cash flows from financing activities for 19X8 and 19X9.

LO 3,4,5

P15-5A **Profitability and Asset Utilization Ratios** Refer to American Apple Corp.'s (AAC's) financial statements (pages 696–697).

REQUIRED:

a. Calculate AAC's profit margin, gross margin, return on assets, and return on stockholders' equity for 19X8 and 19X9. Summarize what they indicate about AAC's profitability.
b. Calculate AAC's asset turnover, receivables turnover, age of receivables, inventory turnover, and days' supply in inventory. Summarize what they indicate about AAC's asset utilization.

LO 3,4,5

P15-6A **Liquidity and Solvency Ratios** Refer to American Apple Corp.'s (AAC's) financial statements (pages 696–697).

REQUIRED:

a. Calculate AAC's working capital ratio, quick ratio, working capital to total assets, and age of accounts payable. Summarize what they indicate about AAC's liquidity.
b. Calculate AAC's times interest earned, cash flows to total debt, total debt to total assets, and debt-equity. Summarize what they indicate about AAC's solvency.

PROBLEM SET B

LO 1   **P15-1B**   **Relationship of Net Income to Cash Flows and Future Cash Flows**   The graph below shows the net income and the net cash flows for the Texas Communications Company over a 10-year period.

TCC has not paid dividends or made other distributions to shareholders. It has, however, engaged in some other significant financing activities.

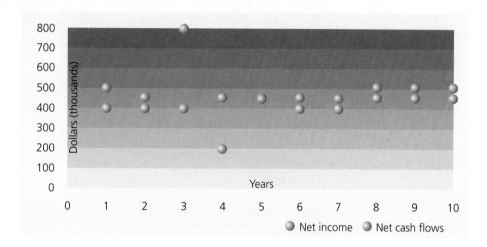

REQUIRED:

a. Speculate as to the cause of the cash flows being slightly above net income for all years except 19X3 and 19X4. Indicate possible events that could account for the 19X3 and 19X4 disparities.

b. Assuming any items between the $100 thousand increments on the Y axis represent $50 thousand increments, add the net income over the 10-year period and divide by 10 to compute average income.

c. Add the cash flows over the 10-year period and divide by 10 to compute average cash flows.

d. Compare the averages in c and d and discuss the income persistence evidenced by TCC's income figures.

Financial Statements to be Used with Problems 2B through 6B

Ohio Laser Supply (OLS), Inc. carries a complete supply of toner imaging cartridges and font cartridges for all popular laser printers. It supplies large companies and government agencies on a just-in-time basis and ships anywhere in the United States overnight. Its sales have expanded significantly; but it is experiencing some problems stocking the rapidly expanding line of laser cartridges. OLS's financial statements for the years 19X0 and 19X1 are presented on the following pages.

Additional Information (in Thousands):

Beginning 19X0 balances:

Total assets	$34,625
Receivables (net)	6,100
Owners' equity	5,610

Ohio Laser Supply, Inc.
Comparative Balance Sheet
October 31, 19X0 and 19X1

	(Thousands) 19X0	19X1
Assets		
Cash	$ 4,000	$ 1,000
Investment in securities	5,000	1,000
Accounts receivable	7,000	10,000
Allowance for uncollectible accounts	(300)	(400)
Inventory	4,000	8,000
Supplies	200	90
Prepaid expenses	100	110
Total current assets	$20,000	$19,800
Land	2,000	2,000
Buildings and equipment	20,000	35,000
Accumulated depreciation	(4,000)	(6,800)
Total assets	$38,000	$50,000
Liabilities and Stockholders' Equity		
Accounts payable	$ 6,500	$11,500
Notes payable	5,000	7,000
Wages and salaries payable	10	15
Taxes payable	290	185
Total current liabilities	$11,800	$18,700
Bonds payable	10,000	10,000
Notes payable—noncurrent	8,000	9,000
Total liabilities	$29,800	$37,700
Common stock	$ 1,000	$ 1,000
Paid-in capital in excess of par	6,000	6,000
Retained earnings	1,200	5,300
Total stockholders' equity	$ 8,200	$12,300
Total liabilities & stockholders' equity	$38,000	$50,000

Ohio Laser Supply, Inc.
Comparative Income Statement
For the Years Ended October 31, 19X0 and 19X1

	(Thousands) 19X0	19X1
Net sales	$80,000	$120,000
Cost of goods sold:		
Beginning inventory	3,500	4,000
Purchases (net)	56,500	95,000
Cost of goods available	$60,000	$ 99,000
Ending inventory	4,000	8,000
Cost of goods sold	$56,000	$ 91,000
Gross profit	$24,000	$ 29,000

Continued

Selling expenses	$ 6,000	$ 7,000
Depreciation expense	1,500	2,800
Administrative expenses	8,000	8,000
Total operating expenses	$15,500	$17,800
Operating income before taxes	$ 8,500	$11,200
Interest expense	(2,300)	(2,600)
Interest revenue	300	60
Income before taxes	$ 6,500	$ 8,660
Income tax expense	1,950	2,600
Net income	$ 4,550	$ 6,060

Ohio Laser Supply, Inc.
Comparative Statement of Retained Earnings
For the Years Ended October 31, 19X0 and 19X1

	(Thousands)	
	19X0	*19X1*
Retained earnings, beginning	$(1,390)	$1,200
Net income	4,550	6,060
Dividends declared	(1,960)	(1,960)
Retained earnings, ending	$ 1,200	$5,300

Ohio Laser Supply, Inc.
Comparative Statement of Cash Flows
For the Years Ended October 31, 19X0 and 19X1

	(Thousands)	
	19X0	*19X1*
Cash flows from operating activities:		
Net income	$ 4,550	$ 6,060
Depreciation expense	1,500	2,800
Increase in accounts payable	500	5,000
Increase (decrease) in taxes payable	290	(105)
Increase (decrease) in wages payable	(5)	5
Decrease (increase) in prepaid expenses	10	(10)
Decrease in supplies	0	110
Increase in accounts receivable (net)	(600)	(2,900)
Increase in inventory	(500)	(4,000)
Net cash flows from operating activities	$ 5,745	$ 6,960
Cash flows from investing activities:		
Sale of marketable securities	$ 0	$ 4,000
Purchase of building and equipment	(1,000)	(15,000)
Net cash flows from investment activities	$(1,000)	$(11,000)
Cash flows from financing activities:		
Payment of dividends	$(1,000)	$ (1,960)
Net proceeds from current notes	500	2,000
Noncurrent note issued	0	1,000
Net cash flows from financial activities	$ (500)	$ 1,040
Net increase in cash	$ (355)	$ (3,000)

LO 3,4,5   **P15-2B   Common-Size and Percent-Change Analysis of Income Statements**   Refer to Ohio Laser Supply's (OLS's) financial statements (pages 700–701).

REQUIRED:

a. Perform a vertical analysis of OLS's income statements by preparing a common-size comparative income statement for 19X0 and 19X1.
b. Comment on information the common-size income statement reveals.
c. Perform a horizontal analysis of OLS's income statements by preparing a percent-change comparative income statement from 19X0 to 19X1.
d. Comment on information the percent-change comparative income statement reveals.

LO 3,4,5   **P15-3B   Common-Size and Percent-Change Analysis of Balance Sheets**   Refer to Ohio Laser Supply's (OLS's) financial statements (pages 700–701).

REQUIRED:

a. Perform a vertical analysis of OLS's balance sheets by preparing a common-size comparative balance sheet for 19X0 and 19X1.
b. Comment on information the common-size comparative balance sheet reveals.
c. Perform a horizontal analysis of OLS's balance sheets by preparing a percent-change comparative balance sheet from 19X0 to 19X1.
d. Comment on information the percent-change comparative balance sheet reveals.

LO 3,4,5   **P15-4B   Analysis of Cash Flows Statements**   Refer to Ohio Laser Supply's (OLS's) financial statements (pages 700–701).

REQUIRED:

a. Evaluate OLS's cash flows from operating activities for 19X0 and 19X1.
b. Evaluate OLS's cash flows from investing activities for 19X0 and 19X1.
c. Evaluate OLS's cash flows from financing activities for 19X0 and 19X1.

LO 3,4,5   **P15-5B   Profitability and Asset Utilization Ratios**   Refer to Ohio Laser Supply's (OLS's) financial statements (pages 700–701).

REQUIRED:

a. Calculate OLS's profit margin, gross margin, return on assets, and return on stockholders' equity for 19X0 and 19X1. Summarize what they indicate about OLS's profitability.
b. Calculate OLS's asset turnover, receivables turnover, age of receivables, inventory turnover, and days' supply in inventory. Summarize what they indicate about OLS's asset utilization.

LO 3,4,5   **P15-6B   Liquidity and Solvency Ratios**   Refer to Ohio Laser Supply's (OLS's) financial statements (pages 700–701).

REQUIRED:

a. Calculate OLS's working capital ratio, quick ratio, working capital to total assets, and age of accounts payable. Summarize what they indicate about OLS's liquidity.
b. Calculate OLS's times interest earned, cash flow to total debt, total debt to total assets, and debt-equity. Summarize what they indicate about OLS's solvency.

CRITICAL THINKING AND COMMUNICATING

C15-1

Kathleen Gordon is the chief accountant of Microtech, Inc.,a newly organized company that makes speakers for personal computers. Kathleen and her assistant are in the process of recommending to management the accounting methods that the new company will use, and she has come to you for advice.

She explains that the new company will be applying for a substantial loan soon, and management is interested in presenting the financial statements "in the best possible light" to improve its chances of getting a loan under favorable terms.

She tells you she is considering recommending the use of straight-line depreciation and the adoption of "reasonably optimistic estimated asset lives and salvage values."

Kathleen explains to you that she places a high value on her integrity as an accountant and asks you if you believe that her proposal is "an ethically proper recommendation."

REQUIRED:

Write Kathleen a letter expressing your views about her proposal.

C15-2
A large and well-known steel company in the United States uses the last-in, first-out (LIFO) method of inventory valuation. It has been using LIFO for many years; and as a result, the value of its steel inventory is measured in very old (World War II era) and, therefore, very low prices. The value of its steel inventory, reported in the balance sheet at the low LIFO prices, is about $1 billion less than the current cost of the inventory, an amount representing more than a third of the company's total assets.

REQUIRED:

a. Discuss how the inventory valuation of the steel company would affect the company's financial ratios.
b. What would you recommend to financial analysts calculating financial ratios for the steel company?

C15-3
Refer to the financial statements of J.C. Penney Company, Inc. in Appendix B at the end of the text. Find the balance sheet and income statement.

REQUIRED:

a. Calculate J.C. Penney's profitability ratios for 1991, 1992, and 1993. 1990 year-end total assets and stockholders' equity were $12,325 million and $4,394 million, respectively. In calculating gross margin, ignore the fact that J.C. Penney includes certain other costs with cost of goods sold.
b. What are the implications of the changes in J.C. Penney's profitability ratios over the 3 years?

CHAPTER 16

Concepts of Financial Statements and International Accounting

Chris Rose recently inherited a substantial sum of money from a close relative. To finish her college education without additional student loans, Chris wants to invest her money to provide a steady stream of cash flows.

Chris has a close friend whose family owns DeAngelis Construction, Inc., and she is considering their offer of part ownership by investment of her inheritance. DeAngelis Construction, Inc., appears to be very successful and prudently managed. It specializes in constructing regional mail distribution centers for the U.S. Postal Service. While interested in this investment, Chris has a reservation about the company's policy of cash withdrawals by owners. DeAngelis limits withdrawals to one-half of the net income of the current period. While Chris believes the policy is generally very prudent, she is concerned about the availability of a steady stream of cash flows to finance her education.

The construction projects that DeAngelis performs for the U.S. Postal Service take approximately three years to complete. Chris knows that DeAngelis only works on one project at a time. While a distribution center is under construction, DeAngelis incurs costs such as building materials, construction equipment, and the wages and salaries of employees. Chris knows that businesses normally only recognize revenue at the completion of the earning process, which she thinks would be at the time the construction project is completed.

Chris has asked to see DeAngelis's financial statements before she makes a final decision. Because of the nature of the company's operations, Chris expects to see a pattern of two years of large net losses, in the first two years of a project, and then a third year of large net income, at the completion of the project. DeAngelis's policy concerning cash withdrawals would mean that Chris would not have any cash flows for the two years of net losses. Clearly, this pattern of cash flows would not be acceptable given Chris' investment goal of steady cash flows for college.

This chapter presents a discussion of the concepts underlying financial statements. A conceptual framework for financial statements is necessary to develop generally accepted accounting principles that maximize the usefulness of the financial statements to those who read and use the information in them. Also, a conceptual framework enhances the consistency among the various Generally Accepted Accounting Principles.

Much of the discussion in this chapter is based on the FASB's Conceptual Framework. Other parts of the discussion are based on assumptions and principles that existed and were practiced before the FASB developed its Conceptual Framework and that continue to be an important part of financial accounting. Many of the concepts presented in this chapter have been discussed in previous chapters of this text. Some of the concepts will be new to you. In any event, an understanding of the conceptual framework that underlies generally accepted accounting principles should enhance your understanding of financial accounting. This chapter concludes with a discussion of how companies account for transactions with parties in other countries and for their own international operations.

LEARNING OBJECTIVES

1. Identify the objectives of financial statements.
2. Explain the qualitative characteristics of useful financial statement information.
3. Define the elements of financial statements.
4. Discuss financial statement recognition and measurement.
5. Describe the assumptions underlying financial statements.
6. Identify the modifying conventions that alter the application of GAAP.
7. Record foreign currency transactions in the accounts.

THE FASB'S CONCEPTUAL FRAMEWORK

The Conceptual Framework began taking form in 1973, at the inception of the FASB, and its final piece was issued in December, 1984. Obviously, the framework's development was a time-consuming effort. Why was a conceptual framework needed? The FASB answers this with the following statement:

> A conceptual framework is a *constitution*, a coherent system of interrelated objectives and fundamentals that can lead to consistent standards and that prescribes the nature, function, and limits of financial accounting and financial statements. The objectives identify the goals and purposes of accounting. The fundamentals are underlying concepts of accounting, concepts that guide the selection of events to be accounted for, the measurement of those events, and the means of summarizing and communicating them to interested parties. Concepts of that type are fundamental in the sense that other concepts flow from them and repeated reference to them will be necessary in establishing, interpreting, and applying accounting and reporting standards.[1]

As shown in Illustration 16-1, the FASB's **Conceptual Framework** consists of: objectives of financial statements, qualitative characteristics of useful information, elements of financial statements, and recognition and measurement in financial statements.

---

[1]*Scope and Implications of the Conceptual Framework Project* (Stamford, Conn.: FASB, 1976), p. 2.

ILLUSTRATION 16-1 FASB's Conceptual Framework

LO 1
Identify the objectives of financial statements.

Objectives of Financial Statements

As you learned in previous chapters, the end product of the accounting process is the financial statements. Financial statements are the business's primary means of reporting information to owners, creditors, and other users about its financial position at the end of the period and about the results of its operations during the period. In developing the **objectives of financial statements**, the FASB considered issues such as the following:

Who are the users of financial statements?
What is the nature of the decisions users make?
What kinds of information are financial statements capable of communicating to these users for making their decisions?

In answering these questions, the FASB specified objectives in *SFAC No. 1*:

1. Financial [statements] should provide information that is useful to present and potential investors and creditors and other users in making rational investment, credit, and similar decisions. The information should be comprehensible to those who have a reasonable understanding of business and economic activities and are willing to study the information with reasonable diligence.
2. Financial [statements] should provide information to help present and potential investors and creditors and other users in assessing the amounts, timing, and uncertainty of future cash receipts from the business and the proceeds from the sale, redemption, or maturity of ownership interests or loans. Since investors' and creditors' cash flows are related to cash flows of the business, financial [statements] should provide information to help investors, creditors, and others assess the amounts, timing, and uncertainty of future cash inflows to the related business.
3. Financial [statements] should provide information about the assets of a business, the claims to those assets (liabilities and stockholders' equity), and other effects of transactions, events, and circumstances that change its assets and claims to those assets.[2]

The first objective states a broad concern that financial statements be useful to individual users in making investment, credit, and other similar decisions. The objectives then move to the more narrow concerns that financial statements provide information that is useful for assessing the amounts, timing, and uncertainty of future cash flows and information about the business's financial position and performance.

---

[2]"Objectives of Financial Reporting by Business Enterprises," *Statement of Financial Accounting Concepts No. 1* (Stamford, Conn.: FASB, 1978), p. 2. In this Statement, the FASB actually uses the more inclusive information set of financial reporting, rather than financial statements.

After the FASB reached its conclusions regarding the objectives of financial statements, its next step was to explore the qualitative characteristics that make financial statements useful for those making the types of decisions discussed.

Qualitative Characteristics of Useful Information

LO 2
Explain the qualitative characteristics of useful financial statement information.

In *SFAC No. 2*, the FASB established three levels of **qualitative characteristics** of useful financial statement information. The FASB intends for accountants to use the qualitative characteristics to answer questions concerning the amount of information to provide in the financial statements, the manner in which to present the information, and which alternative accounting methods to use in recording transactions and events. As presented in Illustration 16-2, the three levels of characteristics are decision usefulness, relevance and reliability, and comparability and consistency.[3]

ILLUSTRATION 16-2 Qualitative Characteristics

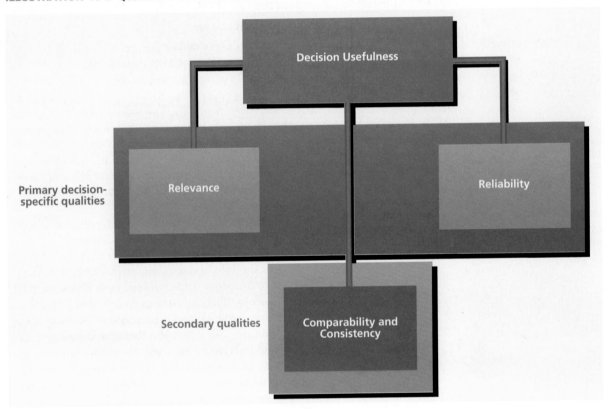

Decision Usefulness. **Decision usefulness** is the primary qualitative characteristic of financial statement information. It requires that the information be useful in making investment, credit, and other decisions. If information is not useful, then it has no value; and any cost incurred in providing the information cannot be justified.

Relevance. The characteristic of **relevance** means that the information is capable of making a difference in a decision. To be relevant, information must

---

[3]"Qualitative Characteristics of Useful Financial Reporting Information," *Statement of Financial Accounting Concepts No. 2* (Stamford, Conn.: FASB, 1980), par. 6–20.

709

have predictive value, feedback value, and timeliness. **Predictive value** is the ability to help users form predictions about the outcomes of events. Information has **feedback value** if it can improve decision makers' capabilities to predict by providing feedback about earlier expectations. The feedback may confirm that the prediction model the decision maker uses is appropriate, or the feedback may suggest changes in the prediction model that would improve subsequent predictions. **Timeliness** of information means that the information is available to the user before it loses its capacity to influence decisions. Delays in providing the information causes a loss in its ability to be useful in decision making and, therefore, a loss of any relevance that otherwise may have existed.

Reliability.   **Reliability** assures that the information is reasonably free from error and bias and faithfully represents what it intends to represent. To be reliable, information must have representational faithfulness, and it must be verifiable and neutral. **Representational faithfulness** is the degree of correspondence or agreement between financial statement numbers and the assets, liabilities, transactions, and events those numbers intend to represent. **Verifiability** is the quality that results in a high degree of agreement among independent measurers. For example, if 10 accounting students were asked to compute depreciation expense for an asset with a cost of $1,000, estimated useful life of 10 years, estimated residual value of zero, and using the straight-line method, hopefully, there would be a high degree of agreement (verifiability) among the 10 students' answers. On the other hand, if the 10 students were asked to estimate the useful life of a particular asset, there would probably be a wide range of answers and, therefore, less verifiability. **Neutrality** means that in choosing an accounting method, there is freedom from bias towards a predetermined result.

Relationship Between Relevance and Reliability.   To be useful, information cannot be completely void of either relevance or reliability. Both qualities must exist to some degree. For example, an estimate of a new business's net income for each of the next 10 years might be highly relevant to the stockholder. On the other hand, an estimate of that information would probably be unreliable; and, therefore, the information would have limited usefulness. While both qualities must exist to some degree, there are trade-offs; information that is highly relevant but has low reliability or information with high reliability but low relevance may still be decision useful.

Comparability and Consistency.   Information about a particular business becomes more useful if it can be compared with similar information about other businesses and with similar information about the same business for some other time period. **Comparability** is the quality of financial statement information that enables users to identify similarities in and differences between two businesses or within a single business between two or more periods. **Consistency** of financial statement information means using the same accounting methods for a business from period to period.

LO 3
Define the elements of financial statements.

Elements of Financial Statements

In previous chapters, you were introduced to many of the **elements of financial statements**. Below are the definitions presented in *SFAC No. 6*.[4] These definitions tend to be more technical than the ones we used to introduce the elements.

---

[4]"Elements of Financial Statements," *Statement of Financial Accounting Concepts No. 6* (*SFAC No. 6* replaced *SFAC No. 3*). (Stamford, Conn.: FASB, 1985), pp. 1–2.

Assets are probable future economic benefits obtained or controlled by a particular entity as a result of past transactions or events.

Liabilities are probable future sacrifices of economic benefits arising from present obligations of a particular entity to transfer assets or provide services to other entities in the future as a result of past transactions or events.

Equity is the residual interest in the assets of an entity that remains after deducting its liabilities. In a business enterprise, the equity is the ownership interest.

Investments by owners are increases in equity of a particular business enterprise resulting from transfers to it from other entities of something valuable to obtain or increase ownership interests (or equity) in it. Assets are most commonly received as investments by owners, but that which is received may also include services or satisfaction or conversion of liabilities of the enterprise.

Distributions to owners are decreases in equity of a particular business enterprise resulting from transferring assets, rendering services, or incurring liabilities by the enterprise to owners. Distributions to owners decrease ownership interest (or equity) in an enterprise.

Comprehensive income is the change in equity of a business enterprise during a period from transactions and other events and circumstances from nonowner sources. It includes all changes in equity during a period except those resulting from investments by owners and distributions to owners.

Revenues are inflows or other enhancements of assets of an entity or settlement of its liabilities (or a combination of both) from delivering or producing goods, rendering services, or other activities that constitute the entity's ongoing major or central operations.

Expenses are outflows or other using up of assets or incurrences of liabilities (or a combination of both) from delivering or producing goods, rendering services, or carrying out other activities that constitute the entity's ongoing major or central operations.

Gains are increases in equity (net assets) from peripheral or incidental transactions of an entity and from all other transactions and other events and circumstances affecting the entity except those that result from revenues or investments by owners.

Losses are decreases in equity (net assets) from peripheral or incidental transactions of an entity and from all other transactions and other events and circumstances affecting the entity except those that result from expenses or distributions to owners.

Because many of the other elements are defined in their terms, assets and liabilities appear to be the primary definitions. For example, "Revenues are inflows or other enhancements of assets of an entity or settlement of its liabilities (or a combination of both)...," and "Losses are decreases in equity (net assets)...."

Recognition and Measurement in Financial Statements

LO 4

Discuss financial statement recognition and measurement.

The FASB presents the recognition and measurement concepts in *SFAC No. 5*.[5] Because the concepts adopted are consistent with accounting principles current-

---

[5]"Recognition and Measurement in Financial Statements of Business Enterprises," *Statement of Financial Accounting Concepts No. 5* (Stamford, Conn.: FASB, 1984).

ly used in practice and, therefore, do not imply changes in financial statements that some accountants and scholars strongly favor, this Statement was the most controversial. **Recognition** in accounting refers to recording the effects of events and transactions formally in the financial statements as assets, liabilities, revenues, expenses, etc.. A recognized item is shown in the financial statements in both words and amounts. **Measurement** in accounting refers to assigning a numerical amount to the information that is recognized. There are two aspects to measurement: choosing the characteristic to be measured and choosing the measurement scale. For example, many transactions are measured using the characteristic of the exchange price observed in the transaction and the measurement scale of the actual dollar amounts exchanged.

The recognition criteria presented in *SFAC No. 5* are divided into fundamental criteria that apply to all recognition decisions and additional guidance in applying the fundamental criteria to the elements of earnings.

Fundamental Recognition Criteria. According to *SFAC No. 5*, a business should recognize information about an item when the following four criteria are met:

1. *Definitions.* The item meets the definition of an element of financial statements.
2. *Measurability.* The item has a relevant attribute measurable with sufficient reliability.
3. *Relevance.* The information about the item is capable of making a difference in user decisions.
4. *Reliability.* The information is representationally faithful, verifiable, and neutral.[6]

Notice that the recognition criteria rely heavily on the definitions of financial statement elements from *SFAC No. 6* and the qualitative characteristics from *SFAC No. 2*.

Additional Guidance for Applying the Fundamental Criteria to the Elements of Earnings. Because of the importance of net income in reporting on the business's performance, the FASB issued additional guidance for the recognition of revenues and gains and for expenses and losses.

Revenues and gains. The additional guidance is intended to provide a higher level of assurance of the existence and amounts of revenues and gains. Recognition of revenues and gains involves consideration of two factors: Revenues must be realized and earned.

1. *Realized.* Revenues and gains are realized when merchandise, services, or other assets are exchanged for cash or claims to cash.
2. *Earned.* Revenues and gains are considered to have been earned when the entity has accomplished what it must do to be entitled to the revenues. Gains are the result of transactions that are not part of the normal operations of the business, such as the sale of an operating asset at a price that is more than the carrying amount of the asset. As a result, the realization and the earning of gains usually occur simultaneously.[7]

The two criteria that revenues must be realized and earned are generally met at the time the business delivers merchandise to or performs services for cus-

---

[6]*Ibid.,* par. 63.
[7]*Ibid.,* par. 83.

tomers. There are, however, some exceptions to the "time of sale" recognition of revenues. These exceptions include the percentage-of-completion method and the installment method for recognition of revenue.

Percentage-of-completion method. Under the **percentage-of-completion method**, businesses that enter into long-term construction projects recognize revenue before they complete the contract. Recall from the beginning of this chapter that Chris Rose has the opportunity to invest in DeAngelis Construction, Inc. She is concerned that a business in long-term construction projects will not provide her with a steady stream of cash flows for her to use to finance her college education. Recall also DeAngelis Construction's policy of limiting withdrawals from the business to one-half of the current year's net income. Chris asked to see DeAngelis's financial statements to assess the cash flow potential. We present DeAngelis Construction's income statement for the last three years (19X1 – 19X3) in Illustration 16-3.

ILLUSTRATION 16-3 Income Statement of DeAngelis Construction, Inc.

DeAngelis Construction, Inc. Income Statement For the Years Ended December 31, 19X3, 19X2, and 19X1			
	19X3	*19X2*	*19X1*
Revenue from long-term contracts	$975,000	$850,000	$825,000
Costs of construction	682,500	595,000	577,500
Gross profit	$292,500	$255,000	$247,500
General and administrative expenses	125,000	115,000	109,000
Net income	$167,500	$140,000	$138,500

In reading the notes to the financial statements, Chris learned that DeAngelis uses the percentage-of-completion method to account for long-term construction projects. Chris does not really understand this method of accounting, so she asked the Chief Accountant of DeAngelis, Josh O'Neal, to explain how this method affects the financial statements.

Josh O'Neal pulled from the file cabinet a contract that DeAngelis Construction had just entered into. DeAngelis Construction received a contract from the U.S. Government to construct a mail distribution center in Atlanta. The contract is for $1,200,000. DeAngelis estimates that it will cost $900,000 to construct the building and that it will take 3 years to complete the project beginning in 19X4. If it follows normal revenue recognition procedures, DeAngelis will show no revenues or net income for 19X4 and 19X5 and revenues of $1,200,000 and gross profit of $300,000 in 19X6. If DeAngelis reports these amounts, the financial statements will imply that DeAngelis generated no revenues in 19X4 and 19X5. Assuming that DeAngelis incurs the $900,000 of estimated costs evenly throughout the 3 years it takes to complete the building, gross profit statements would appear as shown in Illustration 16-4.

This sort of financial reporting would not convey what really happened. (Using the language of *SFAC No. 2*, the information would not be representationally faithful.) Since its contract is with the federal government, DeAngelis will receive the contracted price when it completes the building and meets all

ILLUSTRATION 16-4 *Estimated* Partial Income Statements

DeAngelis Construction, Inc. Partial Income Statements (Estimated) For the Years Ending December 31, 19X6, 19X5, and 19X4			
	19X6	*19X5*	*19X4*
Revenue from long-term contracts	$1,200,000	$0	$0
Costs of construction	900,000	0	0
Gross profit (loss)	$ 300,000	$0	$0

the specifications. Therefore, DeAngelis is earning revenue as it performs the tasks involved in constructing the distribution center.

To overcome the reporting problems of recognizing revenue for long-term construction contracts at their completion, businesses use the percentage-of-completion method when they can make reliable estimates of costs. Using this method, businesses recognize revenue and gross profit each period during the term of the construction as they make progress towards completion. We measure progress towards completion by the ratio of costs incurred in the period to the total estimated cost of the project. The calculation of the amount of revenue recognized in a period is shown in Illustration 16-5.

ILLUSTRATION 16-5 Percentage-of-Completion Method

According to the calculation in Illustration 16-5, DeAngelis would recognize revenue in each period and arrive at gross profit by recognizing as expenses the actual costs incurred during the period. We present the application of the percentage-of-completion method for the new contract in Illustration 16-6.

ILLUSTRATION 16-6 Percentage-of-Completion Calculations

	Costs Incurred During Period	*Total Costs*	*Percent Complete*	*Total Revenue*	*Revenue Recognized*
19X4	$300,000	$900,000	33 1/3%	$1,200,000	$ 400,000
19X5	300,000	900,000	33 1/3%	1,200,000	400,000
19X6	300,000	Balance of contract price			400,000
Totals	$900,000				$1,200,000

The amounts of gross profit that DeAngelis would recognize each period is presented in Illustration 16-7.

Notice that, in this example, we assume actual total costs turned out to be exactly equal to estimated total costs. In an actual project, this is not likely to occur; and businesses that use the percentage-of-completion method periodically revised their accounting estimates. Also, if reliable estimates are not available,

ILLUSTRATION 16-7 Gross Profit—Percentage-of-Completion Method

	19X6	19X5	19X4
Revenue from long-term contracts	$400,000	$400,000	$400,000
Costs of construction	300,000	300,000	300,000
Gross profit (loss)	$100,000	$100,000	$100,000

businesses should not use the percentage-of-completion method because the measure of progress on the project is not sufficiently reliable to be used in recognizing revenue.

In reading the financial statements of DeAngelis Construction, Inc. for 19X3, 19X2, and 19X1 presented in Illustration 16-3, Chris is pleased with the net income reported in the income statements, but what about cash flows? Josh O'Neal explained to Chris that the terms of the contracts require that the government must pay a portion of the contract price to DeAngelis each period. These are called *progress payments*, and they are based on the portion of the project that has been completed. Therefore, DeAngelis does have sufficient cash flow each period, and it can make distributions to owners.

Many businesses engage in projects with long-term production processes, and they use the percentage-of-completion method. The following quote is from the 1991 Annual Report of General Motors Corporation, and it describes GM's revenue recognition policy for part of its operations:

> Certain sales under long-term contracts, primarily in the defense business, are recorded using the percentage-of-completion method of accounting. Under this method, sales are recorded equivalent to costs incurred plus a portion of the profit expected to be realized on the contract, determined based on the ratio of costs incurred to estimated total costs at completion. Profits expected to be realized on contracts are based on the Corporation's estimates of total sales value and cost at completion. These estimates are reviewed and revised periodically throughout the lives of the contracts, and adjustments to profits resulting from such revisions are recorded in the accounting period in which the revisions are made.

Installment method. Another alternative to recognizing revenue, called the *cash basis*, recognizes revenue when cash is collected. Businesses use the cash basis to account for credit sales when there is significant uncertainty about whether the cash will be collected. The installment method is a form of the cash basis of revenue recognition. Under the **installment method**, each receipt of cash from a credit sale is considered to consist of a recovery of part of the cost of the goods sold and part of the gross profit from the sale. The installment method is implemented by first calculating the gross profit percentage of the sale. As shown in Illustration 16-8, each cash collection generates gross profit equal to the amount of cash collected times gross profit percentage. Implicitly, cost of goods sold is the remainder of the amount of cash collected. For example, if a sale has a gross profit percentage of 30%, each cash collection would be considered as 30% gross profit and 70% (100–30%) cost of goods sold.

Assume that Martinez Construction Machinery Corp. had credit sales of $2,000,000 in 19X1, its first year of operations. The cost of the goods sold on credit sales is $1,500,000. The total gross profit is, therefore, $500,000 ($2,000,000 – $1,500,000). The gross profit percentage is 25% ($500,000 ÷ $2,000,000), and the cost of goods sold percentage is 75% (100–25%). Martinez decided to use the installment method to recognize revenue because the con-

ILLUSTRATION 16-8 Installment Method

struction industry is in a recession and Martinez is uncertain about whether all the customers will be able to make cash payments for the machinery they purchased. Cash collections of the credit sales turn out to be as follows:

19X1	$800,000
19X2	600,000
19X3	600,000

The calculation of the gross profit recognized from the credit sales is presented in Illustration 16-9.

ILLUSTRATION 16-9 Calculation of Gross Profit—Installment Method

Year	Cash Collected	Gross Profit Percentage	Gross Profit Recognized
19X1	$ 800,000	25%	$200,000
19X2	600,000	25%	150,000
19X3	600,000	25%	150,000
Totals	$2,000,000		$500,000

As you can see from Illustration 16-9, we consider the installment method to be a cash basis of revenue recognition because the business recognizes gross profit in the period that it collects cash.

Expenses and losses SFAC No. 5 also presents criteria for the recognition of expenses and losses. Accountants call the recognition criterion for expenses the **matching principle** because traditionally accountants try to "match" the timing of expense recognition with related revenue recognition. Therefore, under accrual accounting concepts, we recognize expenses when the business incurs them in its earning process. In other words, we recognize expenses when they contribute to the business's earning of revenues. The matching principle often leads to recognition of expenses at times different from those when costs are incurred. We present this concept in Illustration 16-10.

In many cases when there is no apparent direct relationship between some expenses and revenues, the process of matching expenses with revenues is difficult. For example, is there a direct link between costs incurred in repairing the business's roof and revenues earned? To deal with this problem, accountants recognize expenses based on the types of costs that the business incurs. Some costs provide future benefits by contributing to the earning of revenues in both the current and future periods. We record these costs as assets initially, and they represent unexpired costs. Merchandise inventory, prepaid insurance, and

ILLUSTRATION 16-10 Matching Principle

property, plant, and equipment are examples of costs that generate revenues in current and future periods. Other costs such as advertising, repairs, and salaries benefit the business in earning revenues only in the current period; and we record these costs as expenses in the period the business incurs them. Sometimes costs such as advertising indirectly benefit the business in earning future revenues as well, but the relationship between the costs and future revenues is so indirect or difficult to measure that we simply ignore it and recognize the costs as expenses in the period incurred.

We recognize some unexpired costs as expenses based on a direct relationship between the expiration of the costs and revenues that the business earns. The best example of this direct relationship is merchandise inventory. In the period the business sells merchandise, we recognize revenue; and we record the cost of the merchandise as cost of goods sold and match it with the related revenue in the income statement in the same period.

Other unexpired costs clearly contribute to the earning of revenues in both the current and future periods, but we cannot observe the same direct relationship to specific revenues. We recognize these costs as operating expenses of current and future periods, based on accepted allocation procedures. For example, we allocate the cost of a delivery van to current and future periods in the form of a systematic allocation of depreciation expense.

The following note is from the Annual Report of Santa Anita Operating Company:

> (The) Operating Company has adopted an accounting practice whereby the revenues associated with thoroughbred horse racing at Santa Anita Racetrack are reported as they are earned. Costs and expenses associated with thoroughbred horse racing revenues are charged against income in those periods in which the thoroughbred horse racing revenues are recognized. Other costs and expenses are recognized as they actually occur throughout the year.

When an asset (unexpired cost) is reduced or eliminated or a liability increased because of events and circumstances not related to the earning of revenue, the business recognizes a loss rather than an expense. For example, if a tornado destroys an uninsured building, the business will recognize a loss equal to the building's carrying amount (unexpired cost) on the date the tornado destroyed it.

UNDERLYING ASSUMPTIONS

The accounting profession developed generally accepted accounting principles over time. Underlying these principles are the following assumptions: business entity, going-concern, time periods, and stable-dollar unit.

Business Entity Assumption

We assume that information gathered and recorded in the accounts are for a specific business entity. As a result of this assumption, we can be confident that the financial statements report only the business entity's financial position and results of operations. Accountants have to be careful to distinguish the business's transactions from those of the owner. For example, if Rick Jones pays some of his personal living expenses with the cash of his business, Jones Cleaning Service, the accountant should not record these payments as business expenses. Rather, the accountant would record the payments as owner withdrawals.

Another result of the **business entity assumption** is that when one business owns other businesses, one set of financial statements may be prepared for the group of businesses. These financial statements are called *consolidated financial statements*, and they were discussed in an earlier chapter. The assumption underlying consolidated financial statements is that even though several separate legal business entities exist under the same owners' control, they operate as though they are one economic business entity. Therefore, the consolidated financial statements report the financial position and results of operations of the single economic business entity.

Going-Concern Assumption

When accounting for a business entity, accountants assume that the business will continue to operate indefinitely, unless there is evidence that the business is about to cease operations. The **going-concern assumption**, as discussed in a previous chapter, records as assets, rather than expenses, costs that will generate revenues in both the current and future periods. For example, when a business purchases equipment that it expects to use for five years, it records the cost of the equipment as an asset. Through depreciation, the business allocates the cost of the equipment to expenses of the periods the equipment benefits.

Time Periods Assumption

Accountants assume that the life of a business can be divided into a series of equal time periods—or the **time periods assumption**. These time periods are generally years, quarters, or months. Although most businesses prepare financial statements annually, some may prepare them every three months, or quarterly. Recall from a previous chapter that financial statements for a period shorter than a year are called *interim financial statements*.

While accountants strive to report accurate financial statements for the time periods, this process requires management to make many estimates and to exercise considerable judgment. As you saw in previous chapters, the adjustment process at the end of an accounting period requires management to make estimates of the useful lives of depreciable assets and to exercise judgment about items such as the collectibility of receivables. The adjustment process is required because the business's transactions do not always fit nicely into the time periods the financial statements cover.

Stable-Dollar Assumption

When recording the effects of transactions in the accounts, accountants measure the amounts in dollars. Under the **stable-dollar assumption**, accountants assume the U.S. dollar is a reasonably constant unit of measure. As a result, accountants do not make adjustments in the financial statement amounts for the dollar's changing value.

Although accountants assume the dollar is reasonably constant, we know the value of the dollar does change. Over the past several decades, the value of the U.S. dollar has been declining because the prices of goods and services have been rising. This phenomenon is called *inflation*. Many accountants believe inflation has a significant impact on financial statements, and that we should adjust financial statement amounts for its effects. For example, compare the net incomes of two similar companies. One company purchased its building 10 years earlier than the other did. While both buildings may be identical in all aspects, except the date of purchase, the company that purchased the building at the earlier date will show a higher amount of net income. That is, the older building will cost less because of inflation; therefore, depreciation expense will be less, and the result is higher net income.

LO 6
Identify the modifying conventions that alter the application of GAAP.

MODIFYING CONVENTIONS (CONSTRAINTS)

The application of accounting principles is sometimes altered by several **modifying conventions** that the accounting profession has adopted. These modifying conventions also are called *constraints*. The modifying conventions discussed below include cost/benefits, materiality, and conservatism.

Cost/Benefits

The **cost/benefits convention** requires that information presented in financial statements should provide benefits to the users that exceed the costs of preparing and using the information. The benefits of using information result in better decisions, and the costs of information include those of gathering and presenting the information. Also, users of information incur a cost in processing information through their decisions models.

The cost/benefits convention is difficult to apply in practice. Reasonable estimates for the cost of presenting information are available, but attempts to estimate the costs of using information are elusive at best. Quantitative estimates of the benefits of using information are impossible to obtain. Nevertheless, the convention of cost/benefits is frequently offered in practice as the reason for not providing some kinds of information in the financial statements.

Materiality

The **materiality convention** involves judgments about whether errors and omissions in financial statements are of sufficient size to cause the financial statements to be misleading. If an item is judged to be immaterial, then GAAP does not have to be followed in accounting for the item.

An example of how businesses use the materiality convention is their accounting policies to determine whether they will treat certain costs as expenses in the current period or capitalize and depreciate them over their useful lives. Businesses commonly set some dollar level below which they merely expense purchases of assets in the period of purchases. They capitalize purchases of assets above that amount. This policy results in expensing small purchases such as pencil sharpeners, wastebaskets, and staplers. Large purchases such as computers, copying machines, and telephone systems are capitalized. Under GAAP, these businesses should technically capitalize and depreciate all of the purchases over their useful lives. The materiality convention, however, allows these businesses to expense the small purchases in the current period because the effects on the financial statements between expensing and capitalizing is not large enough to influence decisions—that is, are not *material*.

Conservatism

Conservatism in financial reporting is a means of dealing with uncertainty. When accountants make estimates and judgments about items such as the useful lives of assets, whether revenue should be recognized, and whether gains or losses should be recognized, they are often trying to predict what will happen in an uncertain future time period. For example, assume two estimates exist about the amount of a future payment the business will be required to make. The accountant believes that both estimates are equally likely to occur. The conservatism convention requires that the accountant use the less optimistic estimate in presenting the financial statements.

A popular misconception about conservatism is that accountants deliberately understate net assets and net income. This sort of practice would cause the statements to be unreliable. As discussed earlier in this chapter, reliability is one of the primary qualitative characteristics of useful financial statement information. Therefore, the deliberate misstatement of financial statements amounts is an inappropriate interpretation of the conservatism convention.

In a previous chapter you saw an example of conservatism when we applied the lower-of-cost-or-market method to merchandise inventories. Under this method, we recognize as losses the decreases in the market values of merchandise in the period those decreases occur. We do not recognize increases in market values, however, until the increases are realized in the form of sales to outside parties. The justification given for recognizing losses when the value changes and not recognizing increases in value on the same basis is the convention of conservatism.

INTERNATIONAL OPERATIONS

In recent years, the level of foreign business activity has risen rapidly. This development is the result of governments' relaxation of trade restrictions and companies' search for new markets. Many businesses have operations in other countries, and some operate throughout the world. These companies are called multinational companies. Some companies sell to customers located in foreign countries. Similarly, some companies make purchases from suppliers located in foreign countries. These transactions are called import and export transactions. Other companies have subsidiaries that are located in foreign countries, while some companies have both import and export transactions and foreign subsidiaries. The following sections discuss accounting for both of these types of arrangements.

LO 7

Record foreign currency transactions in the accounts.

Foreign Currency Transactions

When a U.S. company sells to a foreign customer or purchases from a foreign supplier, the transaction may be settled in either U.S. dollars or in a foreign currency. The settlement currency depends on the agreement between the parties to the transaction. From the perspective of a U.S. company, a **foreign currency transaction** is a one that calls for settlement in a currency other than the U.S. dollar.

Foreign currency transactions affect accounting in the recording of the transactions. Foreign currency amounts have to be translated into U.S. dollar equivalents, and translation requires the use of exchange rates. An **exchange rate** is the value of one currency expressed in terms of another currency. Exchange rates change daily as the supplies of and demands for currencies change. Illustration 16-11 presents some examples of exchange rates.

ILLUSTRATION 16-11 Foreign Exchange Rates

Currency	Rates in U.S. dollars
British pound	$1.52
Canadian dollar	.76
French franc	.17
Japanese yen	.01
German mark	.60

Source: *The Wall Street Journal* (August 23, 1993), p. C15.

To see how exchange rates are used for translation, assume a U.S. citizen purchases a product from a French company. The price of the product is 500 francs. To pay for the purchase, the U.S. citizen must buy French francs. If the exchange rate between U.S. dollars and francs is $.17 per franc, it costs $85 ($.17 x 500) to purchase the 500 francs needed to settle the transaction. (Note: Included in this exchange rate is the fee the foreign currency dealer charges for handling the transaction.)

Foreign Currency Purchases Transactions. To illustrate the accounting for a foreign currency purchases transaction, assume that on May 2, Southern Import Co., a U.S. corporation, purchases goods from a Japanese company. The invoice states that the price for the goods is 1,000,000 yen. On the date of the purchase, the exchange rate for yen is $.008 per yen. Southern should record the purchases on the date of the purchase at the U.S. dollar equivalent amount, which is $8,000 (1,000,000 x $.008). The following entry records the purchase:

May 2	Purchases	8,000	
	Accounts Payable		8,000
	To record the purchase of goods from Japanese		
	company for 1,000,000 yen (1,000,000 x $.008).		

On May 12, when the payment of the invoice is due, the exchange rate for yen has changed to $.0082. Therefore, to purchase the 1,000,000 yen to pay the invoice costs $8,200 (1,000,000 x $.0082). Southern's entry to record the payment is:

May 12	Accounts Payable	8,000	
	Exchange Loss	200	
	Cash		8,200
	To record payment of accounts payable		
	(1,000,000 yen x $.0082).		

Because the yen *increased* in value relative to the U.S. dollar between the date of purchase and the payment date, Southern incurred an exchange loss. If the yen had decreased in value during this time period, Southern would have realized an exchange gain. Accounting standards require that the net amount of exchange gains and losses for a period should be included in the determination of net income for the period.[8]

Foreign Currency Sales Transactions. The accounting for a foreign currency sales transaction follows the same concepts as accounting for foreign currency purchases transactions. At the date of sale, the transaction is recorded using the exchange rate on that date. For example, assume that on June 5, Eastern Export Co., a U.S. corporation, sells merchandise to a British company. The sales price is 10,000 British pounds, and the exchange rate is $1.75 per pound. Eastern's entry to record the sale is as follows:

June 5	Accounts Receivable	17,500	
	Sales		17,500
	To record sales revenue (10,000 pounds x $1.75).		

The exchange rate on the date that Eastern receives payment is used to record the receipt of cash. The following entry records the receipt of cash, assuming that the exchange rate has changed to $1.80 per pound on July 15 when Eastern receives payment.

July 15	Cash	18,000	
	Accounts Receivable		17,500
	Exchange Gain		500
	To record receipt of cash (10,000 pounds x $1.80).		

An exchange gain is realized because the value of the British pound *increased* during the time period. If the value of the pound had *decreased*, Eastern would have incurred an exchange loss. Notice that the relationship between the direction of exchange rate changes and exchange gains and losses for sales transactions is opposite that of purchases transactions.

Intervening Financial Statement Date

At the end of an accounting period, accounts receivable and payable from foreign currency transactions may be unsettled. Accounting standards require that

---

[8]"Foreign Currency Translation," *Statement of Financial Accounting Standards No. 52* (Stamford, Conn.: FASB, 1987), par. 15.

the receivables and payables should be adjusted to reflect the exchange rates at the end of the accounting period. The resulting exchange gains and losses should be recognized in net income for the period.[9]

In the previous example, assume that Eastern Export Co.'s fiscal year ends on June 30. The exchange rate on that date is $1.82 per pound. Eastern's entry at the end of the accounting period is as follows:

June 30	Accounts Receivable	700	
	Exchange Gain		700
	To record exchange gain at the end of the period.		
	[($1.82 – $1.75) x 10,000 pounds]		

On July 15, when Eastern receives payment, the exchange rate is $1.80; and the following entry is recorded:

July 15	Cash	18,000	
	Exchange Loss	200	
	Accounts Receivable		18,200
	To record receipt of cash (10,000 pounds x $1.80).		

Notice that the net exchange gain is $500 ($700 – $200), which is the same amount recorded previously when there is no intervening financial statement date. However, a $700 exchange gain is recorded in the year of sale; and a $200 exchange loss is recorded in the year of cash receipt. This method reflects fluctuations in exchange rates in the periods in which they occur.

Translation of Foreign Currency Financial Statements

U.S. foreign subsidiaries commonly keep their accounting records and prepare financial statements in terms of the currency of the country in which they operate. The financial statements of a foreign subsidiary should be consolidated with those of its U.S. parent. This requires that the subsidiary's statements be translated into U.S. dollars because consolidated financial statements prepared in different currencies yield meaningless results.

Accounting standards require that the assets and liabilities of foreign currency financial statements be translated into U.S. dollars using the exchange rates at the date of the financial statements. Stockholders' equity accounts are translated using the exchange rates at the dates the securities were issued, and revenue and expense accounts are translated at the average exchange rate for the period.[10]

SUMMARY

Identify the objectives of financial statements. Financial statements should provide information that is useful in making rational investment, credit, and similar decisions. The information should help users in assessing the amounts, timing, and uncertainty of future cash flows. Also, financial statements should provide information about the business's financial position.

Explain the qualitative characteristics of useful financial statement information. There are three levels of qualitative characteristics of useful financial statement

[9]*Ibid.*

[10]*Ibid.*, par. 12.

information: (1) decision usefulness, (2) relevance and reliability, and (3) comparability and consistency.

Define the elements of financial statements. The FASB defined ten elements of financial statements. These elements are assets, liabilities, equity, investments by owners, distributions to owners, comprehensive income, revenues, expenses, gains, and losses.

Discuss financial statement recognition and measurement. The fundamental recognition criteria include definitions, measurability, relevance, and reliability. Additional recognition criteria for revenues and gains are that they be realized and earned. Additional recognition criteria for expenses are included in the matching principle. Losses are recognized when unexpired costs are reduced or eliminated because of events and circumstances unrelated to the business's normal operations. Measurement in accounting involves choosing the characteristic to be measured and selecting the measurement scale. Generally, the actual exchange price related to a transaction is used for measurement in financial accounting.

Describe the assumptions underlying financial statements. The assumptions underlying financial accounting include business entity, going-concern, time periods, and stable-dollar.

Identify the modifying conventions that alter the application of Generally Accepted Accounting Principles. The conventions that alter the application of GAAP include cost/benefits, materiality, and conservatism.

Record foreign currency transactions in the accounts. Companies that have foreign currency transactions account for them by using the exchange rate at the date of the transaction. Exchange gains and losses that result from fluctuations in exchange rates are recognized in net income in the period the rates change.

REVIEW PROBLEM

1. A conceptual framework is
   a. A set of specific accounting rules
   b. A list of specific accounting procedures that are acceptable for reporting business transactions
   c. A theory developed to explain current accounting standards
   d. A coherent system of interrelated objectives and fundamentals of financial accounting and financial statements
2. The objectives of financial statements
   a. Have not yet been defined by the FASB
   b. Require straight-line depreciation for plant assets
   c. State that the objective of business is to earn a profit
   d. State that information provided in financial statements should be useful in making investment and credit decisions
3. In the FASB's *SFAC No. 2*, qualitative characteristics of financial statement information
   a. Require financial statement information to be relevant, reliable, and have the qualities of comparability and consistency
   b. Require that assets minus liabilities equal equity

    c. Are the basis for the going-concern assumption

    d. None of the above

4. The FASB's *SFAC No. 6*, "Elements of Financial Statements,"

    a. Defines consistency and comparability

    b. Defines the objectives of financial statements

    c. Defines assets, liabilities, equity, revenues, expenses, gains, and losses

    d. Defines the underlying assumptions of accounting

5. The FASB's *SFAC No. 5*, on recognition and measurement,

    a. Discusses the parties who use financial statements

    b. Requires revenue to be recognized when the cash is collected

    c. Establishes four criteria for recognition of items in financial statements

    d. Requires expenses to be recognized in the period they are paid

6. Underlying assumptions to accounting principles

    a. Include the business entity assumption, the going-concern assumption, the time periods assumption, and the stable-dollar assumption

    b. Assume financial statements are used primarily by creditors

    c. Assume revenues are recognized when cash is collected

    d. None of the above

7. Modifying conventions in accounting

    a. Include the going-concern assumption

    b. Establish the goals and objectives of financial statements

    c. Include the costs/benefits, materiality, and conservatism conventions

    d. None of the above

SOLUTION:

1. d (p. 706)
2. d (p. 707)
3. a (p. 708–9)
4. c (p. 709–10)
5. c (p. 710–11)
6. a (p. 717)
7. c (p. 718–19)

KEY TERMS

assets, *710*
business entity assumption, *717*
comparability, *709*
comprehensive income, *710*
Conceptual Framework, *706*
conservatism, *719*
consistency, *709*
cost/benefits convention, *718*
decision usefulness, *708*
distributions to owners, *710*
elements of financial
   statements, *709*
equity, *710*
exchange rate, *720*
expenses, *710*
feedback value, *709*

foreign currency transaction,
   720
gains, *710*
going-concern assumption,
   717
installment method, *714*
investments by owners, *710*
liabilities, *710*
losses, *710*
matching principle, *715*
materiality convention, *719*
measurement, *711*
modifying conventions, *718*
neutrality, *709*
objectives of financial
   statements, *707*

percentage-of-completion
   method, *712*
predictive value, *709*
qualitative characteristics, *708*
recognition, *711*
relevance, *708*
reliability, *709*
representational faithfulness,
   709
revenues, *710*
stable-dollar assumption, *718*
time periods assumption, *717*
timeliness, *709*
verifiability, *709*

SELF-QUIZ

LO 1 1. The FASB's objectives of financial statements
   a. Were the next logical step to explore after identifying the qualitative characteristics that make financial statements useful
   b. State a broad concern that financial statements should be useful to individual users in making investment and credit decisions
   c. Provide definitions of expenses and revenues
   d. Establish criteria for the recognition of revenue

LO 1 2. The FASB's objectives of financial statements do not include the following objective
   a. Financial statements should provide information about assets, liabilities, and stockholders' equity.
   b. Financial statements should be useful to individual users in making investment and credit decisions.
   c. Financial statements should provide information useful in assessing the business's future cash flows.
   d. Financial statements be prepared on the cash basis of accounting.

LO 1 3. A conceptual framework
   a. Provides specific accounting rules outlining the proper treatment of specific transactions
   b. Functions as a "constitution" for financial reporting
   c. Is a coherent system of interrelated objectives and fundamentals
   d. Both b and c

LO-2 4. The *primary* qualitative characteristic of financial statement information is:
   a. Timeliness
   b. Decision usefulness
   c. Neutrality
   d. Conservatism

LO 2 5. Comparability of financial statement information
   a. Is the quality of financial statement information that enables users to identify similarities in and differences between two businesses
   b. Is a characteristic that makes financial statement information useful
   c. Refers to the process of matching revenues and expenses
   d. Both a and b

LO 2 6. Consistency of financial statement information
   a. Is the quality of financial statement information that enables users to identify similarities and differences between two businesses

   b. Means using the same accounting methods for a business from period to period
   c. Refers to the process of matching revenues and expenses
   d. Has the same meaning as comparability

LO 3 7. Examples of elements of financial statements, as defined in the FASB Concepts Statement, are
   a. Relevance and reliability
   b. Revenues and expenses
   c. Gains and losses
   d. Both b and c

LO 3 8. Comprehensive income, as defined in the FASB's elements statement, is
   a. Revenues – Expenses
   b. Assets – Liabilities
   c. Includes all changes in equity during a period, including those resulting from investments from owners and distributions to owners
   d. Includes all changes in equity during a period, except those resulting from investments from owners and distributions to owners

LO 4 9. Recognition in accounting refers to
   a. Assigning a numerical amount to accounting information
   b. Posting information from journals to ledgers
   c. Formally recording the effects of events and transactions in the financial statements
   d. None of the above

LO 4 10. Measurement in accounting refers to
   a. The difference between revenues and expenses
   b. Assigning a numerical amount to information that is recognized
   c. Formally recording the effects of events and transactions in the financial statements
   d. None of the above

LO 4 11. Two factors required for the recognition of revenue are
   a. Cash must be received and the revenue earned.
   b. Revenue must be earned, and it must be from a prior transaction or event.
   c. Revenue must be earned and realized.
   d. Both a and c

LO 4 12. Expenses are recognized
   a. In the period they are paid
   b. In the period they contribute to the earning of revenue
   c. In the period after they are paid
   d. Only if they provide future benefit to the business

LO 5 13. The owner of a business pays her house payment out of the business's cash. The accountant debits Withdrawals and credits Cash to record the transaction. This accounting treatment is based on what underlying assumption?
a. Business entity
b. Going-concern
c. Time period
d. Stable-dollar

LO 5 14. A company spends $100,000 to pay rent in advance, and the amount is not refundable. The accountant debits Prepaid Rent and credits Cash to record the transaction. This accounting treatment is based on what underlying assumption?
a. Business entity
b. Going-concern
c. Stable-dollar
d. None of the above

LO 5 15. A company makes an estimate of the amount of uncollectible accounts at year-end and prepares a journal entry debiting Uncollectible Accounts Expense and crediting Allowance for Uncollectible Accounts. This accounting treatment is based on what underlying assumption?
a. Business entity
b. Going-concern
c. Time periods
d. Stable-dollar

LO 6 16. The cost/benefits convention suggests that
a. Only information that does not involve a cost to prepare should be presented in financial statements.

b. Information about a business's costs and the benefits of these costs should be included in the financial statements.
c. Information should be presented in the financial statements only if the benefits of using the information exceed the costs of preparing and using the information.
d. None of the above

LO 6 17. A business computes the cost of the merchandise inventory at the end of the accounting period and does not include the small amount of transportation costs incurred when the items were purchased as part of the inventory cost. This accounting treatment is based on
a. Materiality
b. Stable-dollar assumption
c. Going-concern assumption
d. Matching principle

LO 6 18. Conservatism in accounting is
a. The deliberate understatement of net assets and net income
b. A reluctance to change current accounting standards
c. A tendency to select the least optimistic estimate from a set of estimates that are equally likely to occur
d. None of the above

LO 7 19. True or False? GAAP require that receivables and payables for unsettled foreign currency transactions be adjusted to reflect the exchange rates at the end of the accounting period.

SOLUTIONS TO SELF-QUIZ

1. b	2. d	3. d	4. b	5. d	6. b	7. d	8. d	9. c	10. b	11. c	12. b	13. a	14. b
15. c	16. c	17. a	18. c	19. True									

QUESTIONS

Q16-1 Why is a conceptual framework for financial accounting and reporting needed?

Q16-2 In developing the objectives of financial statements, what important questions did the FASB consider?

Q16-3 The FASB specified three objectives of financial statements. Which is considered the broadest and most fundamental?

Q16-4 The characteristic of relevance in financial reporting means that the information is capable of making a difference in a decision. To be relevant, information must have _____ _____, _____ _____, and _____.

Q16-5 Reliability assures that the information is reasonably free from error and bias and faithfully represents what it intends to represent. To be reliable, information must have _____ _____; and it must be _____ and _____.

Q16-6   Is it possible for accounting information to be useful and be completely void of either relevance or reliability? Explain.

Q16-7   Distinguish between comparability and consistency, as these terms relate to qualitative characteristics of financial statement information.

Q16-8   Distinguish between revenues and gains.

Q16-9   Distinguish between expenses and losses.

Q16-10   Which two definitions contained in the FASB's "Elements of Financial Statements" can be viewed as the primary definitions? Why?

Q16-11   What four conditions should be met before accounting information is recognized? (1) _____, (2) _____, (3) _____, and (4) _____.

Q16-12   The recognition of revenue requires that the revenue be _____ and _____.

Q16-13   Two accounting methods that are exceptions to the "time of sale" recognition of revenues include: (1) _____ and (2) _____.

Q16-14   When a business incurs a cost, how does it determine if the cost is classified as an asset or an expense?

Q16-15   Many of the adjusting entries made in the business's accounting records are required because of the time periods assumption. Explain.

Q16-16   What is the difference between a foreign currency transaction and foreign currency translation?

EXERCISES

LO 1

E16-1   Objectives of Financial Statements   Identify several different parties who use financial statements.

LO 1

E16-2   Objectives of Financial Statements   One objective of financial statements places a lot of importance on helping decision makers assess a business's cash flows. Does this mean the FASB is expressing a preference for the cash basis of accounting over the accrual basis of accounting? Discuss.

LO 2

E16-3   Qualitative Characteristics   To be reliable, accounting information must have representational faithfulness, and it must be verifiable and neutral. Rate the following accounting items, as to their relative reliability, using the following scale:

ST   = Strong
F   = Fair
WK = Weak

____ a. Cost of equipment
____ b. Amount of prepaid insurance at the end of the accounting period
____ c. Depreciation expense on equipment
____ d. Value of ending inventory determined by a physical count
____ e. Value of the ending inventory determined by an estimate based on the gross profit method
____ f. Liability related to the warranty of products
____ g. Uncollectible Accounts Expense determined under the allowance method of accounting
____ h. Uncollectible Accounts Expense determined under the direct write-off method
____ i. Liability to pay health care benefits to employees after they retire
____ j. Utility expense for the accounting period
____ k. Amount of cash

LO 2 **E16-4** **Qualitative Characteristics** To be relevant, accounting information must be capable of making a difference in a decision. The information must have predictive value, feedback value, and timeliness. Rate the following accounting items, as to their degree of relevance to a potential creditor, using the following scale:

ST = Strong
F   = Fair
WK = Weak

___ a. Net income of a business
___ b. Organization costs of a business
___ c. Amount of purchases discounts lost
___ d. Current assets and current liabilities of a company
___ e. Projection of future cash flows for the next accounting year
___ f. Supplies on hand at the end of the period
___ g. Depreciation expense for the period

LO 3 **E16-5** **Elements of Financial Statements** Listed below are the elements of financial statements as defined by the FASB and their summarized definitions. Match the elements and the definitions.

Elements

___ (1) Assets
___ (2) Liabilities
___ (3) Equity
___ (4) Investments by owners
___ (5) Distributions to owners
___ (6) Comprehensive income
___ (7) Revenues
___ (8) Expenses
___ (9) Gains
___ (10) Losses

Summarized Definitions

a. Increases in net assets from peripheral transactions
b. Increases in equity resulting from transfers to a business of something of value to obtain ownership interests
c. Includes all changes in equity during a period that result from transactions and other events and circumstances, *except* investments by owners and distributions to owners
d. Probable future economic benefits controlled by an entity as a result of past transactions or events
e. Residual interest in the assets of an entity, after deducting its liabilities
f. Outflows of net assets from activities that constitute the entity's ongoing major or central operations
g. Decreases in equity resulting from transferring assets, rendering services, or incurring liabilities to owners
h. Decreases in equity from peripheral transactions
i. Inflows of net assets from activities that constitute the entity's ongoing major or central operations
j. Probable future sacrifices of economic benefits arising from present obligations

LO 3 **E16-6** **Revenues and Gains, Expenses and Losses** Baxter Computer Warehouse, Inc. sells computers and computer components through mail-order operations. Identify the following items as revenues (*R*), gains (*G*), expenses (*E*), or losses (*L*).

___ a. Increases in equity resulting from the sale of computers
___ b. Increase in equity resulting from selling short-term investments at an amount above cost
___ c. Decrease in equity resulting from selling a copy machine Baxter uses in its own operations at an amount below book value

___ d. Decrease in equity resulting from payment of monthly phone bill

___ e. Decrease in equity from payment of a penalty to the federal government for the violation of an environmental code

___ f. Increase in equity resulting from cash awarded in litigation against a competitor

___ g. Decrease in equity resulting from the payment of advertising

___ h. Decrease in equity resulting from the payment of employee salaries

LO 4

E16-7 **Recognition and Measurement, Percentage-of-Completion** In January 19X3, the Biaz Group, Inc. was awarded a contract to install underground cables connecting the major structures of a large regional university. The contract was for $9,000,000. Biaz estimates that it will cost $8,000,000 and take 2 years to complete. Biaz incurs construction costs of $3,000,000 in 19X3 and $5,000,000 in 19X4. The contract is completed in 19X4.

REQUIRED:

Complete the following partial income statements showing Biaz's operating results, assuming; (1) traditional "time of completion" revenue recognition procedures and (2) the percentage-of-completion method.

Normal revenue recognition method:

	19X3	*19X4*
Revenue, long-term contracts	_____	_____
Costs of contracts	_____	_____
Gross profit (loss)	_____	_____

Percentage-of-completion method:

	19X3	*19X4*
Revenue, long-term contracts	_____	_____
Costs of contracts	_____	_____
Gross profit (loss)	_____	_____

LO 4

E16-8 **Recognition and Measurement, Installment Method** In January 19X4, the Bradley Corporation sold the GGH Development Company a track of land for $9,000,000. The land cost Bradley $6,000,000. The GGH Company makes the following payments to Bradley, including interest at 10% on the unpaid balance.

	Principal	*Interest on Unpaid Balance*	*Total Payment*
12-31-X4	$5,000,000	$90,000	$5,090,000
12-31-X5	3,000,000	40,000	3,040,000
12-31-X6	1,000,000	10,000	1,010,000

Bradley Corporation uses the installment method to recognize gross profit because GGH has been experiencing financial trouble, and it is not certain that Bradley will collect the full amount of the contract. Bradley recognizes the interest received on the unpaid balance as interest revenue.

REQUIRED:

a. Complete the following table to show the total revenue Bradley recognized in each of the 3 years under the installment method.

	Principal Collected	*GP%*	*Gross Profit Recognized*	*Interest Revenue Recognized*
12-31-X4	_____	____	_____	_____
12-31-X5	_____	____	_____	_____
12-31-X6	_____	____	_____	_____

b. Complete the following table to show the total revenue Bradley recognized in each of the 3 years, assuming the traditional "time of sale" method was used.

	Principal Collected	GP%	Gross Profit Recognized	Interest Revenue Recognized
12-31-X4	_____	____	_____	_____
12-31-X5	_____	____	_____	_____
12-31-X6	_____	____	_____	_____

LO 5

E16-9 **Underlying Assumptions**   Listed below are four underlying assumptions of accounting principles and a set of items. Identify the assumption most directly related to each item.

Assumptions

Business entity assumption (*BE*)
Going-concern assumption (*G*)
Time periods assumption (*TP*)
Stable-dollar assumption (*SD*)

Items

____ a. Adjusting entries made at the end of the accounting period, accruing and deferring various items

____ b. Preparing a single income statement that includes the operations of both Ford Motor Company and Ford Credit Corporation

____ c. Classifying costs that will benefit future accounting periods as assets

____ d. A tract of land purchased in 1967 for $100,000 and a tract of land purchased in 1994 for $100,000 added together to show the total cost of land reported on the balance sheet

____ e. Classifying a payment out of the business's bank account for the personal living expenses of the owner as withdrawals

____ f. Reporting production equipment on the balance sheet at its carrying amount, although its fair market value is less

____ g. Selling land that cost $100,000 twenty years ago for $125,000, and reporting a gain of $25,000

LO 6

E16-10 **Modifying Conventions**   Listed below are three modifying conventions adopted by the accounting profession and a set of items describing a particular accounting treatment. Identify the modifying convention most closely related to each item.

Modifying Conventions

Cost/benefits (*CB*)
Materiality (*M*)
Conservatism (*C*)

Items

____ a. A company estimates the life of an asset to be from 4 to 6 years and elects to depreciate the asset over 4 years.

____ b. The lower-of-cost-or-market inventory valuation method is used.

____ c. A company has accounts payable to several hundred different suppliers and reports the total as a single amount on the balance sheet.

____ d. All items of supplies and equipment costing under $50 are expensed when purchased.

____ e. Transportation-in is ignored when valuing ending inventory.

____ f. A company uses the LIFO cost flow method for valuing ending inventory in a period of rising prices.

____ g. A company elects to depreciate its assets under the double-declining-balance method of depreciation.

____ h. The effect of purchases discounts are ignored when calculating the cost of the ending inventory.

___ i. Costs that may have future benefit are expensed in the year incurred.

___ j. The ending merchandise inventory is presented as a single number. The costs of distinct categories of items making up the total inventory are not disclosed.

LO 7　　**E16-11　Foreign Currency Transactions**　Worldwide Imports, Inc. purchased goods from Great Brit Export Corporation on December 1, 19X3, for 9,000 British pounds and paid for the purchase on January 10, 19X4. The exchange rate for a British pound was $1.75 on December 1, $1.90 on December 31, and $1.80 on January 10. Both companies use a calendar year as their fiscal year.

REQUIRED:

Record all necessary journal entries for both Worldwide Imports, Inc. and Great Brit Export on December 10 and December 31, 19X3, and January 10, 19X4.

PROBLEM SET A

LO 1　　**P16-1A　Objectives of Financial Statements**　"Objectives of Financial Reporting by Business Enterprises" was the first concepts statement the FASB issued in the development of a conceptual framework of accounting.

REQUIRED:

a. Discuss why establishing objectives is a logical first step in a conceptual framework.
b. What process might the FASB have used to arrive at the objectives?

LO 2　　**P16-2A　Qualitative Characteristics**　The primary qualitative characteristic of financial statement information is that it be useful in making investment, credit, and other decisions. Decision usefulness is based on the primary decision-specific qualities of relevance and reliability and the secondary qualities of comparability and consistency.

REQUIRED:

a. Identify some types of financial information that are not useful in making investment, credit, and other decisions.
b. Discuss what kinds of decisions might be included under the "other" category when classifying decisions as investment, credit, or other.
c. Discuss the relationship between relevance and reliability as to how they affect usefulness. Can information be useful if it is void of either relevance or reliability?
d. Distinguish between comparability and consistency and discuss how they affect usefulness.
e. Discuss how the establishment of qualitative characteristics can lead to better accounting standards.

LO 3　　**P16-3A　Elements of Financial Statements**　Issues related to the elements of financial statements are presented below.

REQUIRED:

a. The Mountain Ski Resort, Inc. regards the cable weather channel as a valuable resource in operating its business. Discuss whether this asset meets the definition of an asset for Mountain's financial accounting purposes.
b. A competitor is suing MicroSolutions Software Company for violation of a copyright. MicroSolutions is contesting the litigation but believes it has a reasonable chance of losing. Discuss whether this potential loss meets the definition of a liability.

c. Discuss why comprehensive income is not increased by investments by owners and decreased by distributions to owners.

d. Explain how distinguishing between expenses and losses and between revenues and gains might help a decision maker better project the business's future cash flows.

LO 4   **P16-4A**   **Expense Recognition**   Accountants match the timing of expense recognition with revenue recognition when it is practical. Two expenses of a merchandising company are presented below:

1. Cost of goods sold
2. Depreciation

REQUIRED:

a. Which expense is the easier to match against revenue? Discuss.
b. Which expense is the more difficult to match against revenue? Discuss.

LO 4   **P16-5A**   **Percentage-of-Completion Method**   In 19X4, the New England Construction Corporation enters into a contract to construct an oil storage facility in Saudi Arabia. The project is scheduled to take 4 years to complete at a cost of $12,000,000. New England is to be paid $15,000,000 for the contract. Information related to the contract during the 4-year period follows:

Year	Cost Incurred Current Period	Estimated Costs to Complete at End of Period
19X4	$3,000,000	$9,000,000
19X5	4,000,000	5,000,000
19X6	4,000,000	1,000,000
19X7	1,000,000	-0-

REQUIRED:

a. Prepare a partial income statement down to gross profit for the contract over the 4-year period, assuming the revenue is recognized in the period the contract is completed.
b. Prepare a partial income statement down to gross profit for the contract over the 4-year period, assuming the percentage-of-completion method is used.
c. Which method provides better information about New England's operating results? Discuss the circumstances under which each method should be used.

LO 1,2,3,4   **P16-6A**   **Conceptual Framework**   Four concepts statements the Financial Accounting Standards Board issued discuss issues fundamental to financial statements of business enterprises. These statements and the issues they represent are assigned the following identifying codes:

OBJ = "Objectives of Financial Reporting by Business Enterprises"
QC   = "Qualitative Characteristics of Useful Financial Statement Information"
ELE   = "Elements of Financial Statements"
R&M = "Recognition and Measurement in Financial Statements of Business Enterprises"

REQUIRED:

An assortment of items, consisting of comments, terms, questions, and statements that relate to the concepts statements are presented below. Using the appropriate identifying code, match each item to the appropriate concepts statement.

Items

___ a. If information is not useful, then it has no value; and any cost incurred in providing the information is not justified.

___ b. Assign a numerical amount to the information that is recognized.

___ c. Financial statements should help investors, creditors, and others to assess future cash flows from the business and from their interest in the business.

___ d. Assets are probable future economic benefits.

___ e. What kinds of information are financial statements capable of communicating to users?

___ f. Information in financial statements should be relevant.

___ g. Expenses are decreases in net assets from producing goods or services.

___ h. Information in financial statements should be reliable.

___ i. Information about a business is more useful if it can be compared with similar information about other businesses.

___ j. Financial statements should provide information about the assets of a business and the claims to the assets.

___ k. Determine when we formally record the effects of events and transactions in the financial statements as assets, liabilities, expenses, revenues, etc.

___ l. Liabilities are probable future sacrifices of economic benefits.

___ m. Equity is the residual interest in the assets of an entity.

___ n. What kinds of decisions do users of financial statements make?

___ o. Revenues are increases in net assets of an entity from providing goods or services.

___ p. Who are the users of financial statements?

___ q. Financial statements should provide information to investors, creditors, and others to help them make good investment and credit decisions.

LO 7

P16-7A **Foreign Currency Transactions** The Everything French Corporation buys and sells French merchandise in the United States on a regular basis and has a December 31 fiscal year-end. The following transactions took place during 19X4:

19X4

Jan. 26 Purchased merchandise from Conehead, Inc., a French company, for 10,000 francs when the exchange rate for the franc was $0.18.

Mar. 17 Paid Conehead, Inc. when the franc had an exchange rate of $0.19.

Apr. 2 Sold 19,000 francs of merchandise to Eiffel Corporation when the franc had an exchange rate of $0.17.

June 15 Sold 34,000 francs of merchandise to Bon Soir Corporation when the franc had an exchange rate of $0.16.

Aug. 17 Collected 19,000 francs from Eiffel Corporation for the April 2 sale when the franc had an exchange rate of $0.17.

Oct. 3 Purchased merchandise from Mirage, Inc. for 22,000 francs when the franc had an exchange rate of $0.17.

Dec. 1 Collected 34,000 francs from the Bon Soir Corporation when the franc had an exchange rate of $0.19.

REQUIRED:

a. Record all necessary journal entries. (The franc has an exchange rate on December 31 of $0.15.)

b. Calculate Everything French's net exchange gain or loss from entering into the foreign currency transactions.

PROBLEM SET B

LO 1

P16-1B **Objectives of Financial Statements** In developing the objectives of financial statements, one of the issues the FASB considered was the kinds of information financial statements are capable of communicating to users.

REQUIRED:

a. Discuss the types of information that financial statements are capable of communicating to users.
b. Discuss the types of information that financial statements are not capable of communicating to users.

LO 2   **P16-2B**   **Qualitative Characteristics, Relevance and Reliability**   Many investors believe that a projection of future operating results, based on the current information available to management, should be included in the financial statements.

REQUIRED:

a. Evaluate the relevance of such information.
b. Evaluate the reliability of such information.

LO 3   **P16-3B**   **Elements of Financial Statements**   Equity is one of the elements of financial statements the FASB defined.

REQUIRED:

a. Equity can essentially be defined in two ways. What are the two definitions?
b. List three elements of financial statements (excluding comprehensive income) that have the effect of increasing equity.
c. List three elements of financial statements that have the effect of decreasing equity.
d. Which of the elements in b and c are included in comprehensive income?

LO 4   **P16-4B**   **Recognition of Revenues**   The MegaSub Sandwich Shop, Inc. has franchised its operations. It sells franchises for $50,000 each, which gives the franchisee the exclusive right to use the MegaSub logo and recipes in a specified territory for 10 years. The $50,000, which is payable at the contract signing date, also entitles the franchisee to free technical assistance from the MegaSub Home Office and to the benefits of a nationwide advertising program conducted by the Home Office.

REQUIRED:

a. What two factors are important to the recognition of revenue?
b. Apply these two criteria to determine if MegaSub should recognize the $50,000 as revenue in the period it signs the contract with the franchisee.

LO 4   **P16-5B**   **Percentage-of-Completion-Method**   In 19X6, the Hubbard Group, Inc. entered into a contract with the Atlanta Center for Disease Control to study the effects of exposure to carbon dioxide among urban residents. Hubbard estimates the project will take 3 years. The contract is for $2,500,000, and the estimated costs of the project are $2,000,000. Information related to the contract over the 3-year period follows:

Year	Cost Incurred Current Period	Estimated Costs to Complete at End of Period
19X6	$ 300,000	$1,700,000
19X7	400,000	1,300,000
19X8	1,300,000	-0-

REQUIRED:

a. Prepare a partial income statement down to gross profit for the contract for the 3-year period, assuming the revenue is recognized in the period the contract is completed.

b. Prepare a partial income statement down to gross profit for the contract for the 3-year period, assuming the percentage-of-completion method is used.

c. Which method provides better information about Hubbard's operating results? Discuss the circumstances under which each method should be used.

LO 5

P16-6B **Going-Concern Assumption**   When accounting for a business entity, accountants assume the business will continue to operate indefinitely, unless there is evidence to the contrary.

REQUIRED:

a. Discuss how the going-concern assumption affects accounting principles.

b. If accountants were to assume that there is evidence to the contrary and that a business is not a going-concern, discuss how this might affect the way financial statements are prepared.

LO 7

P16-7B **Foreign Currency Transactions**   Jewel Corporation buys and sells Japanese merchandise in the United States on a regular basis and has a December 31 fiscal year-end. The following transactions took place during 19X8:

19X8

Jan. 16 Purchased merchandise from Plume, Inc., a Japanese company, for 800,000 yen when the yen had an exchange rate of $0.018.

Mar. 7 Paid Plume, Inc. when the yen had an exchange rate of $0.020.

Apr. 5 Sold 2,900,000 yen of merchandise to Hattari Corporation when the yen had an exchange rate of $0.016.

June 25 Sold 2,400,000 yen of merchandise to Bon Soup Corporation when the yen had an exchange rate of $0.015.

Aug. 7 Collected 2,900,000 yen from Hattari Corporation for the April 5 sale when the yen had an exchange rate of $0.016.

Oct. 13 Purchased merchandise from Viscount, Inc. for 4,200,000 yen when the yen had an exchange rate of $0.019.

Dec. 4 Collected 2,400,000 yen from the Bon Soup Corporation when the yen had an exchange rate of $0.020.

REQUIRED:

a. Record all necessary journal entries. (The yen has an exchange rate on December 31 of $0.017.)

b. Calculate the net exchange gain or loss from entering into the foreign currency transactions.

CRITICAL THINKING AND COMMUNICATING

C16-1   One of the traditional and long-debated issues in financial reporting centers around the primary qualitative characteristic of financial statement information: that it should be useful in making investment, credit, and other decisions.

While everyone agrees with the idea of usefulness, the difficult choices emerge when the primary decision qualities of relevance and reliability are considered. The problem is that the two characteristics often conflict. Some types of information that are highly relevant may be difficult to present with the reliability normally considered necessary for inclusion in financial statements.

REQUIRED:

a. Discuss the relationship between relevance and reliability as these concepts apply to financial statements.

b. Use a brainstorming approach and attempt to identify financially related information that is highly relevant but low in reliability.

C16-2 Jokes can sometimes illustrate and identify important issues that are anything but funny. The following story has probably been told at more than one after-dinner speech:

> The CEO needed a new controller. She interviewed the short list of candidates. Her interview included the following question: "What is two plus two?" Most candidates, of course, responded: "Four." Not the candidate who got the job. He responded: "What do you want it to be?"

REQUIRED:

a. While this story may be amusing, discuss the importance of reliability of financial information.
b. Discuss forces that exist in the business environment which could pressure accountants to produce accounting information that is not neutral.
c. How should the accounting profession respond to such forces?

C16-3 Comparability is the quality of financial statement information about a particular business that enables users to identify similarities in and differences between two businesses.

Although comparability is a characteristic that makes financial statement information useful, Generally Accepted Accounting Principles (GAAP) allow businesses to use different accounting methods. For example, one company might use straight-line depreciation to depreciate property, plant, and equipment; and another company might use double-declining-balance depreciation. Both depreciation methods are in accordance with GAAP. As another example, one company might use the FIFO cost flow assumption for inventory valuation, and another company might use the LIFO cost flow assumption.

REQUIRED:

a. Discuss how the quality of comparability improves the usefulness of financial statement information.
b. Why do you think GAAP allow different accounting methods?
c. Should GAAP require all businesses to use the same accounting methods?

C16-4 In Appendix B at the end of the text, the financial statements of J.C. Penney Company, Inc. are reprinted. Immediately following the consolidated statements of cash flows, you will find the *Summary of Accounting Policies*. Read J.C. Penney's accounting policies for deferred charges and advertising.

REQUIRED:

a. Discuss J.C. Penney's accounting policies for deferred charges and for advertising. Include in your discussion how the policies relate to the matching principle.
b. Discuss how the policies are affected by the time periods and going-concern assumptions and by the materiality and conservatism modifying conventions.

Tax Aspects of Business Decisions

One of the significant factors that any business decision-maker must consider is the impact that the United States federal income tax will have on business decisions. Over the years since the enactment of the first income tax law in 1913, the U.S. tax system has become so complex that no business decision-maker can hope to make effective decisions without considering a wide range of tax factors. Only a tax expert can be expected to really understand the complexities and interrelationships of the various areas of tax law. Not only has the law become exceedingly complicated, but it has also become extremely dynamic, with changes being enacted by Congress every year. Nevertheless, the decision-maker, while not a tax expert, must have a grasp of the fundamental concepts of the tax laws in order to formulate alternatives in making business decisions. The purpose of this appendix is to introduce you to some of the fundamental tax aspects of business decisions. Specific business decisions discussed include:

1. The form of business decision
2. The method of accounting decision
3. Capital expenditure decisions
4. Various other decisions.

Before making a final decision on any business plan, the conscientious decision-maker should consult a professional tax advisor in order to insure that no tax factor has been overlooked.

THE FORM OF BUSINESS DECISION

One of the first decisions faced by a manager is the decision as to which form of business to adopt:

1. Sole proprietorship
2. Partnership
3. Special corporation known as an S corporation
4. Regular corporation known as a C corporation.

What are the tax aspects of this decision? For example, will more taxes be paid if the business is a corporation? Does any tax apply upon formation of a business? What about the tax aspects of withdrawing money from the business? If the business has losses, is there any tax benefit? We discuss each of the forms of business separately in the following paragraphs.

Sole Proprietorship Taxation

A sole proprietorship is *not* a separate, taxable entity. Rather, all the income and deduction items for the business are simply included on the personal tax return of the individual who owns the business. A personal tax return consists of a Form 1040 (along with several supporting forms and schedules) that is filed with the Internal Revenue Service (IRS). Income from all sources is taxable unless some specific statute exempts it. For example, interest income earned on bonds that are issued by municipalities (cities, counties, states, or state agencies) is specifically exempt from federal income taxation. No expense item is deductible unless some specific statute authorizes the deduction. However, there is a far-reaching tax statute that authorizes deductions for all expenses that are related to a profit-seeking business. In addition to business-related expenses, individuals may deduct certain *personal* expenses such as medical expenses (to the extent that the medical expenses exceed a Congressionally-determined threshold or "floor" amount), contributions made to certain charitable organizations, interest paid on home mortgages, property taxes paid to local governments, and certain other personal expenses. Finally, every individual taxpayer is allowed to deduct an amount called the "personal exemption," which is an amount that is arbitrarily determined by Congress. To determine the tax liability for a particular tax year, all the income items minus all the deduction items produce an amount called "taxable income," which is multiplied by the tax rates that apply for that year.

As an example of determining personal tax liability, assume that taxpayer Glen Berg, a professor in the College of Engineering at a large university, had the following items of income and expense for the year 19X1:

University salary	$50,000
Gain from selling antique clock purchased two months ago	500
Dividend income on Microsoft, Inc. stock	275
Interest income on municipal bonds	2,000
Interest payments on his home mortgage	(8,000)
Food and clothing expenses	(5,000)
Contribution to United Way	(300)
Other allowable personal deductions and the personal exemption	(3,500)

Based on the above data, Professor Berg's taxable income would be $38,975, computed as follows:

Gross income:		
Salary	$50,000	
Gain on property sale	500	
Dividend income	275	
Interest income on municipal bonds	0*	$50,775
Deductions:		
Interest payments on his home mortgage	(8,000)	
Food and clothing expenses	0*	
Contribution to United Way	(300)	
Other allowable personal deductions and the personal exemption	(3,500)	(11,800)
Taxable income		$38,975

*Interest income on municipal bonds is exempt, and no statute authorizes deductions for personal living expenses.

Congress changes the tax rates almost every year.[1] For the sake of example, we will assume that the tax rates applicable to single taxpayers are 20% on the

[1]In 1993, the lowest tax rate for a single, individual taxpayer was 15% of the first $22,100 of taxable income. As taxable income increases, the rate becomes 28%, then 31%, then 36%, and finally 39.6%.

first $20,000 of income and 30% on all amounts above that. Professor Berg's tax liability would be $9,693, computed as follows:

		Taxable Income		Tax Amount
20%	x	$20,000	=	$4,000
30%	x	18,975	=	5,693
		$38,975		$9,693

If Professor Berg were to start a sole proprietorship business, the results of that business would be added to his personal tax return. Assume that early in 19X1, Professor Berg decides to start a business called CompuCar and operate it as a sole proprietorship. He contributes $8,000 to a bank account set up for the business. He has invented a voice-activated computer device that monitors automobile mileage and keeps records of which category of travel the driver has dictated to the device. The driver simply gets into the car, says "business" or "personal," and the device keeps track of the mileage in each category. At the end of the year, the driver asks for a printout of the number of miles in each category. During 19X1, Professor Berg successfully manufactured and marketed the device to several car manufacturers and earned $20,000 in sales revenue. He also incurred $3,000 of business-related expenses. From the $17,000 of extra income (net of expenses), Professor Berg withdrew $10,000 and spent it on a vacation trip to Australia. The facts are summarized as follows:

University salary	$50,000
Gain from selling antique clock purchased two months ago	500
Dividend income on Microsoft, Inc. stock	275
Interest income on municipal bonds	2,000
Interest payments on his home mortgage	(8,000)
Food and clothing expenses	(5,000)
Contribution to United Way	(300)
Other allowable personal deductions and the personal exemption	(3,500)
Payment to bank account to start CompuCar business	(8,000)
Sales revenue for CompuCar	20,000
Business expenses for CompuCar	(3,000)
Withdrawal of cash from CompuCar	10,000

The contribution of the $8,000 cash to a bank account to start the business has no tax impact. For tax purposes, Professor Berg simply adds $20,000 to his gross income and increases his deductions by $3,000, so his taxable income becomes $55,975. In addition, the fact that he withdrew $10,000 for his personal use is of no tax consequence. He had $17,000 of additional taxable profit ($20,000 revenue less $3,000 expense), and whether he spent that profit or left it in the business does not affect his tax liability.

Professor Berg has already calculated his tax liability (without the business income) to be $9,693 (as shown in the previous example). The quick way to calculate the new liability is to realize that, at a taxable income level of $38,975, the tax rate on the *next* dollar of income is 30%. In other words, his *marginal tax rate* is 30%. The **marginal tax rate** is the tax rate that would apply if the taxpayer were to receive an additional dollar of taxable income. The extra income of $17,000 (net of expenses) can be multiplied by the marginal tax rate to produce $5,100 of additional taxes. His new tax liability is $14,793 ($9,693 + $5,100). Alternatively, he could calculate his liability in the same manner as shown in the previous example:

		Taxable Income		Tax Amount
20%	x	$20,000	=	$ 4,000
30%	x	35,975	=	10,793
		$55,975		$14,793

As shown by the above examples, the taxpayer who wants to consider the tax factors of operating a business as a sole proprietorship need only be concerned with what the marginal tax rate is for his or her personal tax return. Whether any cash is withdrawn from the business is irrelevant for tax purposes. There is no tax upon *forming* the business, only on the profits generated after the business is operating. But, what if the business incurs losses instead of profits? Assuming that the owner of the business is actively involved in the business and that the business is truly a profit-seeking business, these losses can be used to offset other income on the personal tax return, thus reducing the tax liability.[2]

Assume that Professor Berg's CompuCar business incurred $7,000 in losses during 19X1 (instead of $17,000 of profits). Without the business, his taxable income was $38,975. When the loss from the business is applied to his personal tax return, the taxable income is reduced to $31,975. The tax liability is reduced to $7,593 as shown below:

		Taxable Income		Tax Amount
20%	x	$20,000	=	$4,000
30%	x	11,975	=	3,593
		$31,975		$7,593

An alternative way of calculating the tax effect of the $7,000 loss is simply to realize that the $7,000 loss will offset income that is being taxed at a marginal rate of 30%. Thus, the loss will produce *tax savings* of $2,100 ($7,000 x 30%). Without CompuCar, the tax liability was $9,693 (as shown in our first example). With CompuCar producing a $7,000 loss, the new tax liability is $9,693 minus $2,100 of tax savings, or $7,593.

To summarize, if a taxpayer wants to form a sole proprietorship, such a business, if profitable, will cause additional taxes to be paid at the taxpayer's personal marginal tax rate. Money withdrawn from the business will have no tax effect. If the business incurs losses, the amount of the loss will produce tax savings at the taxpayer's personal marginal tax rate.

---

[2]If the owner does *not* play a significant role in the management of the business, the loss is called a "passive activity loss" and can only be deducted against other "passive" activities that have profits. In this appendix, the owners always play a significant role in the management of the business, so that none of the business ventures are passive activities.

Partnership Taxation

Partnerships are quite similar to sole proprietorships, with the major difference being that there is more than one owner. Like sole proprietorships, partnerships are not separate taxable entities. Rather, each owner of the business simply reports to the IRS his or her share of the income and deduction items from the business.

S Corporation Taxation

The owners of corporations can make a special election to be treated in a manner similar to partnerships for tax purposes. The tax laws that provide these special rules are in Subchapter S of the Internal Revenue Code. Hence, these corporations are called S corporations. Each owner of an S corporation reports his or her share of the income and deduction items on his or her personal tax return.

The net income from the business flows through the S corporation or through the partnership to the individual tax returns of the owners. Thus, the tax liability is the same whether the business is operated as a partnership or as an S corporation. Given this fact, should the taxpayer be indifferent as to which form of business is chosen? No, because there are restrictions placed on S corporations that partnerships do not have. S corporations are limited to 35 shareholders, while partnerships may have any number of partners. Furthermore, only individuals may be S corporation shareholders, while partners may be individuals, other partnerships, or corporations.

In spite of the restrictions placed on S corporations, there is a nontax reason that may convince owners to operate the business as an S corporation rather than as a partnership. All corporations have "limited liability." That is, if the corporate business is sued, the owners' potential losses are limited to the amount of their original investments in the business. On the other hand, partnerships have unlimited liability. If the partnership is sued, the partners could lose their original investment in the business and their personal assets as well.[3]

C Corporation Taxation

Unlike proprietorships, partnerships, and S corporations, the C corporation is a taxable entity separate from its owners.[4] Because of its separate entity status, "double taxation" may apply. **Double taxation** means that the same income is taxed twice, once at the corporate level and once at the shareholder level. When a C corporation earns taxable income, it must pay tax based on its own set of tax rates. If the income earned by the corporation is distributed to the shareholders, this income is treated as dividend income to them, and the shareholders must pay another tax on this same income.

Assume that Professor Glen Berg had items of income and expense for the year 19X1 exactly as shown in the first example in this appendix. He decides to operate CompuCar as a C corporation, and he convinces one of his colleagues,

---

[3]There is a special form of partnership called a limited partnership where the so-called limited partners risk only the amount of their original investment. However, even a limited partnership must have at least one "general" partner who has unlimited liability.

[4]The laws that govern the taxation of regular corporations come from Subchapter C of the Internal Revenue Code, hence the name C corporations.

Professor Debra Seymour, to be a 40% owner in the business. She contributes $3,200 in return for 40% of the stock, and Professor Berg contributes $4,800 in return for 60% of the stock. Neither of the two shareholders will be paid a guaranteed salary, but each will withdraw money from the business if it is profitable. For the year 19X1, CompuCar had $20,000 in revenues and $3,000 in business expenses. Professor Berg withdrew $6,000 and Professor Seymour withdrew $4,000.

For the sake of example, assume that the tax rates for corporations are 15% on the first $25,000 of taxable income and 35% on all amounts above that.[5] CompuCar has taxable income of $17,000. The $10,000 in cash that was distributed to the two shareholders would be classified as a dividend payment. Dividend payments are not deductible by the corporation that pays them. CompuCar's tax liability would be $2,550.

For the C corporation:

		Taxable Income		Tax Amount
15%	x	$17,000	=	$2,550
35%	x	0	=	0
		$17,000		$2,550

Professor Berg received $6,000 in dividend income and the tax could be calculated by adding the $6,000 to the $38,975 of taxable income that Professor Berg had without CompuCar, producing taxable income of $44,975, as shown below:

For Professor Berg:

		Taxable Income		Tax Amount
20%	x	$20,000	=	$ 4,000
30%	x	24,975	=	7,493
		$44,975		$11,493

Alternatively, the $6,000 of dividend income could be multiplied by the marginal tax rate of 30%, to yield an *additional* tax of $1,800. Since his tax liability without CompuCar was $9,693, his tax liability with the dividend from CompuCar is $11,493 ($9,693 + $1,800).

Assuming that Professor Seymour's marginal tax rate is also 30%, she would pay *additional* taxes of $1,200 ($4,000 dividend income x 30%). Thus, double taxation results in $5,550 of taxes being paid. A comparison of the total tax that results when CompuCar is a C corporation versus when CompuCar is a partnership or S corporation follows:

---

[5]The tax rates for corporations change occasionally. In 1993, the actual rates were 15% on the first $50,000 of taxable income, 25% on the next $25,000, 34% on the next $25,000, 39% on the next $235,000, back to 34% on additional amounts of taxable income up to $10,000,000, 35% on the next $5,000,000, 38% on the next $3,333,333, then back to 35% on all additional amounts of taxable income above $18,333,333.

Form of Business	Tax on CompuCar Business	Additional Tax on Prof. Berg	Additional Tax on Prof. Seymour	Total
C corporation	$2,550	$1,800	$1,200	$5,550
S corporation or partnership	N/A	3,060[a]	$2,040[b]	5,100
Difference				$ 450

[a]($17,000 business profit) x (60% ownership interest) x (30% marginal tax rate) = $3,060.
[b]($17,000 business profit) x (40% ownership interest) x (30% marginal tax rate) = $2,040.

Thus, operating the business as a C corporation would cost an additional $450 in taxes compared to operating as a partnership or as an S corporation.

Does the fact that double taxation applies mean that there is never any tax advantage in choosing to operate a business as a C corporation? No, sometimes it may be advantageous tax-wise to operate as a C corporation because there are ways to avoid double taxation or to reduce its effects. The most straightforward way to reduce double taxation is to reduce the taxes on the corporation. This can be done by structuring the payments to the shareholders in such a way that they are deductible by the corporation. Payments that qualify as business expenses are deductible; whereas payments that qualify as dividends are not. Three common examples of deductible business expenses are salary payments, interest payments, and rental payments. Thus, paying the shareholder a salary rather than dividends would avoid double taxation.

Rather than reducing the tax paid by the corporation, another way to reduce the effects of double taxation is to reduce the tax paid by the shareholders. This can be done by reducing, or completely eliminating, the cash distributions paid to the shareholders. That is, the shareholders must agree to leave their money inside the corporation. The corporation would be taxed, but not the shareholders.

The Appropriate Decision on the Form of Business

If you were a decision-maker trying to decide what form of business to adopt, just what would the previous discussion tell you? Basically, there is no clear-cut rule as to which form of business is the most advantageous from a tax planning perspective. The decision-maker must be able to make accurate predictions about the future in order to make the appropriate choice. For example, will the business earn profits from its operations or are losses likely? How many owners will there be? Will the owners need to withdraw cash from the business? What are the relative tax rates on individuals versus corporations? Is Congress likely to change these rates in the future? If you, as the decision-maker, can make accurate predictions, then some guidelines can be given. In considering the following guidelines, assume that there will be more than one owner so the decision is between operating the business as a partnership, an S corporation, or a C corporation. Also assume that there will be no more than 35 owners and none of the owners will be partnerships or corporations, so the S election is always allowable.

1. First, assume that losses will occur during the first years of the business. In this case, the decision-maker should reject the C corporation form because the losses cannot be passed through to the owners' individual tax returns. Either an S corporation or partnership would allow losses to

be passed through, and these losses would offset income from other sources, thus saving taxes. If the owners want to have limited liability, choose the S corporation form.

2. Next, assume that profits will occur during the first years of the business, and the owners will not make cash withdrawals of these profits. In this case the decision turns on the relative tax rates that apply to C corporations and to individuals. If the rates are higher on individuals, then reject the partnership or S corporation form and choose the C corporation. The examples and discussion given in this appendix show that, at low levels of taxable income, the rates are higher on individuals, but as income level increases, the C corporation rates become higher. Congress could change this situation at any time, so the decision-maker needs to keep tabs on potential changes in tax rates.

3. Finally, assume that profits will occur during the first years of the business, and the owners will make at least some cash withdrawals of these profits. Now the choice becomes more complicated because withdrawals from C corporations *might* be treated as taxable dividend income to the recipient shareholders (and as nondeductible dividend payments by the C corporation), but withdrawals from S corporations and partnerships are not taxable to the recipients. On the other hand, the withdrawals might be deductible by the C corporation if they can be characterized as salary, interest, or rental payments to the shareholders. To make a tax-advantageous decision, the decision-maker must predict the amount of the withdrawals, as well as the tax rates that apply to the owners and to C corporations.

The above guidelines represent only a cursory overview of the tax aspects of choosing a form of business. There are many other factors to be considered that are beyond the scope of this appendix.[6]

THE METHOD OF ACCOUNTING DECISION

In accounting for routine transactions, individual taxpayers, S corporations, and partnerships are allowed to choose between the cash method and the accrual method of accounting. C corporations are also allowed to choose between these two methods unless the C corporation is "too large," in which case the C corporation must use the accrual method. The tax law currently defines a C corporation as too large to elect the cash method if it has more than five million dollars in gross receipts. In addition to these two methods, a taxpayer who sells a non-inventory asset (e.g., a machine that was used in production or land that was held for investment purposes) under a deferred-payment contract (i.e., one where at least some part of the sales price is collected in a year after the year of sale) is allowed to use the installment method of accounting for that particular sale, regardless of whether the cash or accrual method is used for the more routine transactions.

---

[6]Some of these factors are (a) the impact of the personal holding company tax, (b) the impact of the accumulated earnings tax, (c) the taxes that apply at the state level, (d) the power of the IRS to treat certain C corporations as if they were partnerships, etc.

The Cash Method

In general, the cash method of accounting requires the recognition of taxable income when cash is received and the recognition of deductions when cash is paid. However, there are some major exceptions to this general rule. One exception is that borrowing money does not cause taxable income, and repaying the principal does not produce a deduction. This rule makes intuitive sense because borrowing increases both an asset and a liability, so the taxpayer's net worth is not increased. Another exception to the general rule is that a payment for an asset that will continue to exist past the end of the year is not deductible when paid. Rather, the amount paid for such an asset (e.g., the amount paid for a building or for prepaid insurance) is deductible over several periods as depreciation or amortization. A third exception is that taxpayers with inventory for sale to customers must use the accrual method for the inventory. That is, no deduction is allowed when inventory is purchased, but only when the inventory is sold. If the inventory is sold on credit, the revenue from the sale must be recognized at the point of sale, not deferred until the cash is collected.

The tax law also provides that the receipt of anything with a fair market value (except accounts receivable arising from the sale of inventory) causes taxable income. For example, if a plumber received some shares of stock with a fair market value of $1,000 in return for his plumbing services, he would have taxable income even though he uses the cash method of accounting. This principle even applies when the taxpayer does not receive an asset. For example, if a taxpayer borrowed $1,000 in cash, there would be no taxable income at the time of borrowing the money. But, if this taxpayer were later to be released from the obligation to repay the debt, the release from the obligation would be treated as $1,000 of taxable income. The taxpayer's total liabilities would decrease as a result of the release from the debt, but total assets would not change. Therefore, the release from the obligation would increase the taxpayer's net worth.

Suppose that on January 1, 19X1, taxpayer Buddy Hamilton opened a sole proprietorship business known as Southern Landscape Enterprises. Southern Landscape Enterprises sold landscaping services and lawn maintenance equipment. Mr. Hamilton's cash receipts and disbursements for the year were as follows:

Receipts:	
Cash sales of inventory and landscaping	$ 50,000
Cash collections for sales of landscaping made on credit (credit sales for the year totaled $85,000)	40,000
Cash borrowed from the bank	100,000
	$190,000
Disbursements:	
Purchases of delivery trucks (only 15% of the cost is deductible as depreciation)	$100,000
Wages paid to employees ($1,500 is owed for work performed at the end of the year)	20,000
Rent for office space, paid in advance for two years on January 1, 19X1	45,000
Inventory purchased ($25,000 of the inventory was sold during the year)	60,000
	$225,000

In addition to the above cash receipts and disbursements, Mr. Hamilton accepted the use of a sail boat for one day in return for landscaping services. The fair market value of the one day's use of the sail boat was $300. The taxable income for Southern Landscape Enterprises determined under the cash basis would be $7,800, determined as follows:

Gross income:		
Cash sales of inventory and landscaping	$50,000	
Collections for sales of landscaping on credit	40,000	
Fair market value of sail boat use	300	$90,300
Deductions:		
Depreciation on delivery trucks	$15,000	
Wages	20,000	
Rent	22,500	
Cost of inventory sold	25,000	82,500
Taxable income		$ 7,800

The Accrual Method

Under the accrual method of accounting for tax purposes, amounts are included in gross income when they are earned, without regard to when cash is collected. Amounts are deducted when expenses are incurred, without regard to when cash is paid. These rules are basically the same rules used by accountants in financial reporting to investors.[7]

Assume that Mr. Hamilton, of the previous example, incurred all the same receipts and disbursements, but Mr. Hamilton uses the accrual method of accounting in calculating his taxable income. His taxable income would be $51,300, determined as follows:

Gross income:		
Cash sales of inventory and landscaping	$50,000	
Sales of landscaping on credit	85,000	
Fair market value of sail boat use	300	$135,300
Deductions:		
Depreciation on delivery trucks	$15,000	
Wages	21,500	
Rent	22,500	
Cost of inventory sold	25,000	84,000
Taxable income		$ 51,300

Obviously, the most significant difference between Mr. Hamilton's taxable income under the cash method and under the accrual method is in accounting for the landscaping sales made on credit. Under the accrual method, all these sales count as taxable income, while under the cash method only the collections on these sales produce taxable income. The examples show clearly why the cash method is frequently the better choice for tax purposes. The cash

---

[7]There are several differences between accrual accounting for tax purposes and generally accepted accounting principles. These differences are beyond the scope of this appendix.

method allows more flexibility in the timing of income recognition. Although Mr. Hamilton sold $85,000 of landscaping services on credit, under the cash method he only recognized $40,000 of taxable income from these sales because he only collected $40,000 in cash. Under the cash method Mr. Hamilton can control how much taxable income he wants to recognize in a particular year by controlling how much effort he puts into collecting on credit sales of his landscaping services. He can control his deductions by accelerating or delaying his cash payments for wages or rent.

The Installment Sales Method

The installment sales method is a special accounting method that allows taxpayers to spread over more than one year the recognition of gain on the sale of non-inventory assets if the sale is under a "deferred-payment contract." A **deferred-payment contract** provides that some or all of the sales price will be collected *after* the end of the year of sale. If the taxpayer uses the cash method or the accrual method to account for a deferred-payment sale of a non-inventory asset at a gain, the entire gain would have to be recognized in the year of sale. It may not be obvious why this is true for the cash method. The following example shows a deferred-payment contract accounted for under the cash method.

In 19X1, taxpayer Michelle Prater, who uses the cash method of accounting for tax purposes, sold land used in her business to Bradford Brown for a price of $10,000, to be collected as follows: (1) $4,000 in 19X1 and (2) $6,000 (plus interest at a market rate) in 19X2. Ms. Prater had a cost in the land of $8,000. Consequently, the realized gain for 19X1 amounted to $2,000 ($10,000 − $8,000). Were it not for the tax statute allowing the installment method, this entire $2,000 gain would have to be recognized when realized in 19X1. To understand the transaction, observe the diagram that follows, where P represents taxpayer Prater, B represents taxpayer Brown, and FMV represents fair market value:

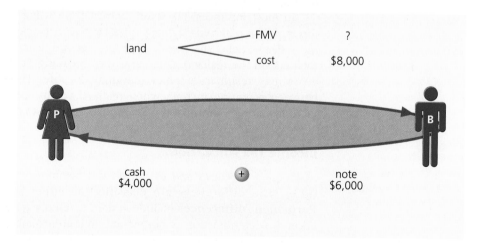

The FMV of the land must be $10,000; otherwise, why would the two parties agree to the exchange? Taxpayer Prater could calculate her realized gain as follows: FMV of property given up ($10,000) less cost of property given up ($8,000) = gain realized ($2,000). Taxpayer Prater would like to argue that she should not have to include the entire $2,000 gain in taxable income because she has not yet collected the entire sales price in cash. However, the cash method requires that anything with a fair market value must be counted in determining receipts. Since the $6,000 note presumably has a $6,000 market value, she is considered to have collected the entire $10,000 sales price in the year of sale and must recognize the $2,000 gain.

Even though the taxpayer in the above example is using the cash method for her normal, routine transactions, she is allowed to use the installment method for this particular transaction. A summary statement of the installment method would be this: if only a portion of the sales price is collected during the year, then only a portion of the total gain is recognized for that year. The following example shows how to apply the installment method.

Assume the same facts as the previous example, except that Ms. Prater elects to use the installment method in accounting for the sale for tax purposes. Although the total realized gain is $2,000, to calculate the amount of realized gain to recognize on the tax return, set up a ratio where the numerator is the amount of cash collected in one year and the denominator is the total amount of cash that will be collected over all years. Then multiply this ratio by the total realized gain. If the ratio is 25%, then 25% of the total cash has been collected, and 25% of the total realized gain should be recognized. In this example, the formula for 19X1 is:

($4,000 cash collected ÷ $10,000 total cash to be collected) x ($2,000 realized gain)

The ratio is 40%, so 40% of $2,000, or $800, should be recognized as gain in 19X1. In 19X2, the formula would be:

($6,000 cash collected ÷ $10,000 total cash to be collected) x ($2,000 realized gain)

Thus, 60% of $2,000, or $1,200, should be recognized as gain in 19X2. In short, as each portion of the cash is collected, a like portion of the gain is recognized. (In addition to the $6,000 cash, taxpayer Brown will pay interest accrued on the note and this amount must be recognized by Prater as ordinary interest income.)

In most instances, taxpayers benefit from using the installment method of reporting for deferred-payment sales for two reasons. First, this method permits the seller to delay the payment of tax. Second, it sometimes results in a lower total tax on the realized gain, since the spreading of the gain over a number of years may result in a lower marginal tax rate. Thus, when given a choice between reporting income when realized versus spreading the recognition of that income over the period cash is collected, most taxpayers prefer the latter.

Income Tax Allocation

Accounting revenues and expenses and taxable income and deductions often differ. The differences are classified as either permanent or temporary. **Permanent differences** include certain revenues and expenses that are included in the determination of net income, but are excluded in the determination of taxable income. An example of a permanent difference is tax-exempt interest earned on investments in bonds issued by state and local governments. The interest earned is included as interest revenue in the determination of accounting net income. However, such interest earned is not subject to federal income taxes and is not included in the determination of taxable income. Permanent differences are included in a corporation's income before deducting taxes. But, they are excluded from the calculation of the corporation's taxable income and, therefore, from the calculation of the income tax expense reported in the income statement.

Temporary differences are certain revenues and expenses that are included in the determination of *accounting* net income either in a later or an earlier period than the period in which they are included in the determination of *taxable* income. The installment sale example above is a case in point. A corporation may use the installment sales method for tax purposes, but recognize the entire realized gains from installment sales in the period of sale for accounting purposes. These choices lead to a difference in accounting for transactions in any given period, but eventually the transactions have the same effect on accounting income and taxable income over the life of the business. Hence, they are called temporary differences. Consider the example of the installment sale and how it would affect the accounting and taxable incomes of the business in the two periods and in total.

Installment Sale			
	Period of Sale	*Period Following Sale*	*Two-Period Total*
Accounting treatment:			
Income from installment sale	$2,000	$ 0	$2,000
Income tax expense @ 40%	800	0	800
After-tax effect	$1,200	$ 0	$1,200
Tax treatment:			
Income from installment sale	$ 800	$1,200	$2,000
Income tax owed @ 40%	320	480	800
After-tax effect	$ 480	$ 720	$1,200

Notice that the effect of the installment sale transaction is the same over two periods for both tax and accounting purposes. However, the income and related tax expense are recorded entirely in the period of sale for accounting purposes, but are spread over two periods for tax purposes. These differences are completely legitimate because the accounting and tax systems serve different purposes. The objectives of financial accounting include presenting information about a) the financial position and b) changes in the financial position, including revenues and expenses resulting from events and transactions of the period. This information is designed to be relevant for making investment, credit, and other economic decisions about businesses. On the other hand, the income tax laws are intended primarily to generate funds for governments and may be modified to achieve social, political and administrative objectives. For example, one reason to allow taxpayers to use the installment sales method is to improve collection of taxes because they are levied in the period in which cash is collected from customers and is available to pay taxes.

Management has an obligation to choose the best methods for both accounting and tax purposes, leading to the kind of disparities illustrated above between income tax expense and the taxes actually owed for the period. How do we handle the disparity within financial accounting? We recognize differences between income tax expense and taxes owed for a period in deferred tax asset and liability accounts. In the case above, the journal entries recording income tax expense for the two years for the installment sale are as follows:

Year of Sale	Income Tax Expense	800	
	Income Taxes Payable		320
	Deferred Income Tax Liability		480
	To record income tax expense, taxes payable and deferred taxes on installment sale.		
Follow-ing year	Income Tax Expense	0	
	Deferred Income Tax Liability	480	
	Income Taxes Payable		480
	To record taxes payable on income previously recognized but not subjected to income tax in the period realized.		

In the above journal entries we ignore income and expenses from all other sources and even make a zero entry to income tax expense just to illustrate a point. Notice that in the year of sale the full tax consequences of realizing $2,000 of income from the installment sale are recognized. However, because the taxpayer corporation uses the installment sale method for tax purposes, only $320 is actually currently owed to the IRS in that year. We say that the other $480 is deferred to the future and will be due in the following year, when the second installment of $6,000 is received. At that time, $480 is owed to the IRS. However, since the full income from the sale was previously recognized for accounting purposes, no further income tax expense is recognized in the following year. Instead, the income taxes previously deferred are now currently due and the second journal entry above moves them from the deferred category to the current liability "income taxes payable."

Occasionally, corporations have the opposite problem from a deferred tax liability. That is, deductions are postponed for tax purposes that are recognized currently as expenses. Or, revenues are recognized currently for tax purposes that will be recognized for accounting purposes in some future period. These conditions lead to higher current taxes and lower future taxes. Most corporations do not adopt such patterns as conscious strategies. They occur because of unavoidable differences between tax law and generally accepted accounting principles.

If a corporation experiences such a pattern, it may result in a deferred tax asset—a kind of long-term prepaid expense. Generally accepted accounting principles permit corporations to recognize such an asset, but only if the benefits of lower future tax bills are virtually guaranteed.[8]

CAPITAL EXPENDITURE DECISIONS

A taxpayer's capital expenditure decision will be affected by the tax laws if that expenditure will produce a tax deduction for the taxpayer at some time. A tax deduction produces tax savings, and the tax savings reduce the cost of the expenditure. Depending on the type of asset purchased, the tax laws might allow (a) an immediate tax deduction for the full cost of the asset (this is called "expensing"), (b) tax deductions that are spread out over several years as

---

[8]"Accounting for Income Taxes," *Statement of Financial Accounting Standards No. 96* (Stamford, Conn.: FASB, 1987), Summary.

depreciation, or (c) no tax deduction at all (if the asset is not depreciable under the law). If the purchase price of several assets is the same, the asset that produces tax deductions the fastest has the lowest net cost. This is true because tax savings that are spread out far into the future are not worth as much in a present value sense as tax savings that come immediately. Thus, other things being equal, the decision-maker should choose to purchase the asset with the lowest net cost, meaning the asset that provides the earliest deductions.

Assume that taxpayer Vickie Mays owns a sole proprietorship, and she is considering the purchase of an asset for the business. The business generally has a rate of return on invested capital of 12% per year, and her marginal tax rate is 30%. She is considering the purchase of either Machine #1, which can be depreciated over 10 years using the straight-line method, or Machine #2, which is eligible for immediate expensing under the tax laws. Both machines cost $10,000. Assuming that she is indifferent about the qualities of the two machines, the analysis in Illustration A-1 indicates that she should purchase Machine #2 because it has the lowest net cost (using present value analysis).

The example in Illustration A-1 demonstrates the basic principle that the faster an asset can be written off (depreciated) for tax purposes, the less expen-

ILLUSTRATION A-1 Analyses of After-Tax Machine Costs

Machine #1

Year	1 Cost	2 Tax Savings	3 Present Value of Tax Savings	4 Net Cost (1 − 3)
1	$10,000	$ 300[1]	$ 300[2]	$9,700
2	0	300	268[3]	(268)
3	0	300	239[3]	(239)
4	0	300	214[3]	(214)
5	0	300	191[3]	(191)
6	0	300	170[3]	(170)
7	0	300	152[3]	(152)
8	0	300	133[3]	(133)
9	0	300	121[3]	(121)
10	0	300	108[3]	(108)
	$10,000	$3,000	$1,896	$8,104

[1]Tax deduction for the year of $10,000 x 30% marginal tax rate.
[2]Since the tax savings come immediately, no discounting is required.
[3]The present value of $300 discounted at 12% for N years, where N = the year − 1. For example, the present value factor from Appendix C for year 2 at 12% is .8929. $300 x .8929 = $267.87, or approximately $268.

Machine #2

Year	1 Cost	2 Tax Savings	3 Present Value of Tax Savings	4 Net Cost (1 − 3)
1	$10,000	$3,000[1]	$3,000[2]	$7,000
2–10	0	0	0	0
	$10,000	$3,000	$3,000	$7,000

[1]($10,000 tax deduction for the year) x (30% marginal tax rate).
[2]Since the tax savings come immediately, no discounting is required.

sive that asset is. How fast an asset can be written off is a function of (a) what type of property it is and (b) what the tax laws allowed in the year the asset was purchased. Every few years, Congress changes the rate at which assets can be written off. In general, there are three broad categories of depreciation rules. We present these broad categories below. However, space does not permit us to go into all the details that apply to each category.

For assets put into service before the beginning of 1981, acceptable methods of depreciation included straight-line, sum-of-the-years'–digits, and various declining balance methods. The period over which these assets could be written off was based on the taxpayer's estimate of the useful life of the asset. Up to $4,000 of certain assets could have been expensed in the year of purchase.

For assets put into service during the years 1981 through 1986, depreciation was based on the Accelerated Cost Recovery System (ACRS). Instead of the taxpayer estimating the useful life of an asset (which led to frequent arguments with the IRS), all assets were divided into categories (e.g., 3-year, 5-year, 10-year, or 15-year assets) depending on what type of property they were. For example, automobiles were assigned to the 3-year class and computers were assigned to the 5-year class, etc. For each class, the IRS published tables that indicated the amount of depreciation that was allowed for each year. The cost of an automobile used for business was written off over three years at the rate of 25% for the first year, 38% for the second year, and 37% for the third year. Up to $5,000 of the costs of certain assets could have been expensed in the year of purchase.

For assets put into service during 1987 and later years, the Modified Accelerated Cost Recovery System (MACRS) applies. Basically, the categories of assets were redefined so that there were more classes, slower depreciation rates were required, and tables were issued for the new classes. Up to $10,000 of the costs of certain assets could be expensed in the year of purchase.[9]

The ACRS and MACRS rules make no attempt to match the cost of purchasing an asset against the revenues produced by that asset over its useful life. However, even though the matching concept is no longer present, the rules have reduced the number of arguments with the IRS. The taxpayer making capital expenditure decisions no longer needs to estimate the useful life of assets but needs access to the tables showing how much depreciation is available for the assets under consideration.

OTHER IMPLICATIONS FOR DECISION-MAKING

In planning for the effect of taxes on income in general, every business decision-maker should have some familiarity with capital gains and losses and the alternative minimum tax. We discuss each of these topics briefly below.

Capital Gains and Losses

For many, many years Congress gave preferential tax treatment to gains on the sale of capital assets. Basically, capital assets are those assets that taxpayers buy to hold as investments (e.g., stocks and bonds, land, etc.) instead of those assets that are part of a business (e.g., inventory, accounts receivable). The preferential treatment was in the form of a significantly lower rate of tax. For exam-

---

[9]Starting in 1993, the $10,000 amount increased to $17,500.

ple, as recently as 1986, an individual taxpayer could be in the 50% marginal tax bracket for ordinary forms of income but the tax on capital gain income was only 20%. So much tax planning effort went into trying to convert ordinary income into capital gain income that some tax commentators called this activity "the second most popular indoor sport in America." Congress had granted the preferential treatment because it felt that it was unfair to tax such gains at the highest rates applicable. For example, if a taxpayer bought stock in 1950 for $1,000 and sold it in 1980 for $20,000, the entire $19,000 gain would be taxed in 1980, even though the appreciation in the market value of the stock took place gradually over a 30-year period. With the graduated tax rates of the U.S. tax system, the bunching of all the income into one year could put the taxpayer into a high marginal tax bracket. A lower rate of tax was a method to compensate the taxpayer for the fact that the income was all bunched into one year. Congress also thought that taxing capital gain income at ordinary income rates impaired the mobility of capital. That is, if a taxpayer who holds stock with $19,000 of appreciation thinks that he or she will have to pay a 50% tax on the sale of this stock, the taxpayer will simply continue to hold the stock instead of selling it and using the money to re-invest in some other asset. A lower rate of tax would encourage taxpayers to sell more often, and the money that was channeled into other investments would stimulate the economy.

However, in 1986 Congress passed a massive tax reform act that changed the relative difference in tax rates on ordinary income versus capital gain. Currently, the tax rate on capital gains for an individual is the same as the rate applied to ordinary income at low levels of taxable income, but the capital gain tax rate cannot exceed 28%. So, some taxpayers may be paying 15% on ordinary income and 15% on capital gains because their total income does not exceed the 15% bracket. Other taxpayers may have more total income that forces them into higher brackets, so they pay 39.6% on ordinary income and 28% on capital gains.

As part of this tax reform act, Congress left in the law the statutory web of rules dealing with capital gains and losses. In particular, Congress left in the law the provision that capital losses could only be deducted against the total of capital gains plus up to $3,000 of ordinary income. If a taxpayer had capital losses of, say, $10,000, but no capital gains, then only $3,000 of the capital losses could be deducted in the year they were incurred (assuming that the taxpayer had at least $3,000 of ordinary income). The remaining $7,000 of capital losses could be carried forward to the next year and matched against all capital gains plus up to $3,000 of ordinary income in that year. Thus, whenever a taxpayer has capital losses in excess of $3,000, an incentive exists for the income to be capital gain rather than ordinary income, as shown in the following example.

Assume that taxpayer Kathleen Kelly has ordinary income of $50,000 in Year 1. During the year she sold 100 shares of stock for $12,000. The stock had a cost of $21,000, so she has a capital loss of $9,000. She also sold another block of stock at a gain of $2,000. Of the $9,000 capital loss, she can deduct $2,000 against her capital gain income and another $3,000 against her ordinary income. The other $4,000 of the net capital loss can be carried forward to Year 2 and matched against any capital gains she has in Year 2. If she has no capital gains in Year 2, she can deduct another $3,000 of the capital loss carryover amount against ordinary income, leaving $1,000 to carry forward to Year 3. If Kathleen could convert $4,000 of her Year 1 ordinary income into capital gain, she would have a total capital gain of $6,000. In that case, she could deduct $6,000 of her capital loss against her capital gain and $3,000 of the capital loss against ordinary income. This would be preferable because the entire $9,000 capital loss would reduce taxes in Year 1 rather than in later years. Because of the time value of money, an immediate reduction in tax liability is worth more than an equal reduction in the liability for a later year.

In the above example, the key to a successful tax planning strategy was the ability of the taxpayer to convert what would have been ordinary income into capital gain income. The following example illustrates one way to accomplish this.

Taxpayer Bill Nelson has a $10,000 capital loss that he incurred this year, in addition to his $100,000 salary (ordinary income). If he has no capital gains, then he will only be able to deduct the capital loss at the rate of $3,000 per year. He also has an antique automobile (held for investment purposes, with a cost of $12,000) that he wants to sell, but it is in need of some repairs. The auto has a market value of $17,000 without any repairs but could be sold for $21,000 if Mr. Nelson incurs $4,000 of repair work. The repair work would be deductible as an investment expense. The results of Mr. Nelson's selling the auto with or without doing the repair work are shown below:

	Seller Does Repairs	Seller Does Not Do Repairs
Selling price of asset	$21,000	$17,000
Less: cost of asset	12,000	12,000
Capital gain	$ 9,000	$ 5,000
Less: repair expense	4,000	0
Net cash flow before taxes	$ 5,000	$ 5,000

Although Mr. Nelson would be just as well off cash-wise under either alternative before considering taxes, the choice of incurring the repair expense (and increasing the selling price by a like amount) leads to increasing his capital gain by $4,000. Thus, of his $10,000 capital loss, he could deduct all of it in the current year ($9,000 of the loss would be deducted against the capital gain and the other $1,000 would be deducted against ordinary income). If he does not incur the repair expense, his capital gain is only $5,000, meaning that, of his $10,000 capital loss, he could deduct $5,000 of it against his capital gain and $3,000 of it against his ordinary income, but $2,000 of the loss would have to be carried over to the next year. Thus, there is an incentive for Mr. Nelson to generate a larger discretionary capital gain.

It may not seem obvious that Mr. Nelson in the above example has *converted* ordinary income into capital gain by incurring the repair expense, but effectively that is the result. By deducting the repairs, Mr. Nelson has reduced his ordinary income. But, because these repair costs will result in a higher selling price for the auto, the reduction in ordinary income is *replaced* by an increase in capital gain.[10] Thus, what would have been ordinary income has been converted to capital gain.

---

[10]One proviso is in order, however. The repair expenses must be allowable as ordinary deductions for this strategy to work. If the IRS were to decide that the $4,000 really represented *improvements,* rather than repairs, then the $4,000 repair expense would be added to the cost of the auto and the capital gain would still be $5,000 [$21,000 – ($12,000 + $4,000)].

Alternative Minimum Tax

Historically, some taxpayers having very sizable economic incomes have been able to arrange their affairs so as to incur little, if any, regular income tax. Examples of how they have been able to do this include (a) arranging for a large part of their income to be in an excluded category (such as interest income from municipal bonds) or (b) claiming large amounts of accelerated depreciation deductions. In an effort to insure that such individuals would still be required to pay a minimum amount of tax, Congress enacted a provision called the "alternative minimum tax." This tax applies only if it exceeds a tax-payer's regular tax. In other words, taxpayers are subject to a dual tax system: the regular tax system and the alternative minimum tax (AMT) system.[11] The AMT system does not apply if it results in a lower tax than the regular tax system. This is often the case because the AMT system has lower rates and a larger exemption amount. However, sometimes the AMT system produces a larger tax than the regular tax system because the AMT system does not allow as many income exclusions or deferrals (such as accelerated depreciation). The following example demonstrates the type of situation to which the alternative minimum tax is intended to apply.

Sally Harris, a single business executive, received a salary of $75,000 in 19X8 (a year when she claimed $3,000 of cash charitable contribution deductions and personal exemptions were $2,000). In addition to this salary, she exercised some of her "incentive stock options (ISOs)." These ISOs allowed her to purchase the stock of her employer for $10,000 even though the stock's actual fair market value was $75,000. The $65,000 excess of the fair market value over the purchase price represents economic income since it is an increase in her wealth. However, this economic income is not reflected in her regular taxable income calculations. Assume that regular tax rates are 20% of the first $20,000 of taxable income and 30% on all amounts above that.

Gross income			$75,000
Less:			
Charitable contributions in cash			(3,000)
Personal exemption			(2,000)
Regular taxable income			$70,000

		Taxable Income		Tax Amount
20%	x	$20,000	=	$ 4,000
30%	x	50,000	=	15,000
		$70,000		$19,000

As illustrated below, however, Sally's liability to the IRS will actually be much higher than this because of the application of the alternative minimum tax.

The computational structure for the alternative minimum tax is as follows:

---

[11]The alternative minimum tax applies to C corporations as well as to individuals. In this appendix, we discuss its impact only on individuals.

Regular Taxable Income
± Tax Preference Adjustments

= Alternative Minimum Taxable Income (AMTI)
− Exemption Amount

= Alternative Minimum Tax Base
x AMT rates

= Alternative Minimum Tax (AMT)

Whereas "taxable income" is the name given to the base for the regular income tax, the base for the alternative minimum tax is alternative minimum taxable income less the exemption amount. The Internal Revenue Code does not have a name for this, but for convenience, we can call it the "AMT base." The starting point in its determination is taxable income (TI) computed in the regular way. Regular TI is then adjusted as shown in the above formula. Like any tax, the alternative minimum tax is computed by multiplying a rate times a base. For this tax, the rate is 26% when the base is less than $175,000 and 28% when the base equals or exceeds $175,000.

Because of the exemption amount, the alternative minimum tax can never apply to low-income taxpayers. Exemption amounts vary from $33,750 for single taxpayers to $45,000 for married couples.[12]

The adjustments to regular taxable income are specified in the Code and are called "tax preference items." In a general sense, you could say that a tax preference occurs anytime that a taxpayer's economic income escapes (regular) taxation because of a Code provision, administrative practice, or judicial doctrine. Congress felt that some tax preferences were being overused. Those that Congress designates as overused are listed in the Code as tax preference items and must be added back to or subtracted from regular taxable income in calculating AMTI.

One of the items that Congress designated as a tax preference item was the bargain element in incentive stock options. For regular TI purposes, a taxpayer who exercises an incentive stock option at a time when the fair market value of the stock exceeds the exercise price need not include this "bargain element" in income. However, since this bargain element does represent economic income, it must be added to regular TI in calculating AMTI.

Another tax preference item is the adjustment for the personal exemption. Under the AMT system, the exemption amount is $33,750 for single taxpayers and $45,000 for married couples. The much smaller personal exemption (around $2,000, with the exact amount depending on the particular year) allowed under the regular tax system must be added back to regular TI and the AMT exemption amount subtracted in order to arrive at the AMT base.

Consider the case of Sally Harris of the previous example. She calculated her 19X8 regular tax liability to be $19,000. However, Sally will have to pay more than this because her alternative minimum tax is $22,470, determined as follows:

---

[12]As AMTI increases in size, the exemption amount is phased out. This phase-out is ignored for purposes of this discussion.

Regular TI	$ 70,000
Adjustments:	
Bargain element in ISOs	65,000
Personal exemption	2,000
AMTI	$137,000
AMT exemption	(33,750)
AMT base	$103,250
AMT rate	26%
AMT	$ 26,845

Perhaps a more intuitive understanding of the AMT can be reached by calculating the AMT base in a "direct" manner (rather than by making adjustments to regular TI) and comparing the result to the calculation of regular TI:

	Regular Tax System	AMT System
Salary	$75,000	$ 75,000
Economic income from stock options	N/A	65,000
Less:		
Charitable contributions in cash	(3,000)	(3,000)
Personal exemption	(2,000)	N/A
AMT exemption	N/A	(33,750)
Tax base	$70,000	$103,250

For planning purposes, taxpayers need to be aware of the impact of both the regular tax and the alternative minimum tax. The following example illustrates the tax aspects of making a choice between alternative investments and demonstrates clearly that being aware of the basic concepts of the alternative minimum tax is necessary in order to make appropriate investment decisions.

Assume that taxpayer Chris Young received a large inheritance in 19X2. Inherited money is not taxable, but he was drawing a salary and expected to have taxable income of $42,000 for tax year 19X2, excluding the income from some investments he was considering purchasing with his inheritance. He was considering two potential investments, each costing the same amount. Investment #1 consisted of some standard municipal bonds that paid $64,000 in interest income per year. Under the regular tax system, interest income on municipal bonds is not taxable. Investment #2 consisted of some municipal bonds that qualified as "private activity bonds" because the city that issued them would turn the proceeds over to private developers to build a stadium for the city. Under the regular tax system, interest income on private activity bonds is not taxable. These bonds paid $68,000 in interest income per year. Mr. Young felt that he should purchase Investment #2 because these bonds paid more and because the interest income on both investments was tax-exempt. However, he was wise enough to consult his tax advisor about his decision.

His tax advisor informed Mr. Young that both investments were indeed tax-exempt, but only from the regular tax. The income from the private activity bonds of Investment #2 would be subject to the alternative minimum tax (while the income from Investment #1 was exempt from both the regular tax and the AMT). Assuming that Mr. Young chose investment #2 and had no other tax preference adjustments, his regular tax and his alternative minimum tax could be determined as follows:

	Regular Tax System	AMT System
Gross income:		
From salary	$42,000	$42,000
From private activity bonds	N/A	68,000
Less:		
Personal exemption	(2,000)	N/A
AMT exemption	N/A	(33,750)
Tax base	$40,000	$76,250
Tax liability	$10,000[1]	$19,825[2]

[1](20% x first $20,000) + (30% x next $20,000) = $10,000
[2]26% x $76,250 = $19,825.

By investing in the private activity bonds of Investment #2, Mr. Young would have an additional $9,825 of tax liability ($19,825 − $10,000) because he would have to pay the AMT instead of the regular tax. The after-tax income from his investment would thus be $58,175 ($68,000 interest income − $9,825 additional tax). On the other hand, Investment #1 would produce no additional tax liability because these bonds were not subject to either the regular tax or the alternative minimum tax. Therefore, the after-tax income from Investment #1 would be $64,000, and Mr. Young would be better off selecting Investment #1.

SUMMARY

This appendix has introduced some of the fundamental tax aspects of some important business decisions. Deciding on the form of business requires (a) knowledge of how sole proprietorships, partnerships, S corporations, C corporations, and their owners are taxed and (b) predictions about how much income will be earned and retained by the business. Deciding on the method of accounting in general requires recognition of (a) the flexibility that results from the cash method and (b) the tax deferral opportunities available with the use of the installment method. Making capital expenditure decisions requires (a) knowledge of the available tax depreciation methods and (b) recognition of the effect these depreciation methods have on the after-tax cost of the assets. Finally, tax planning for the effect of taxes on income in general requires an understanding of (a) the distinction between ordinary income and capital gain and (b) the effect of the alternative minimum tax.

J.C. Penney Company, Inc. 1993 Annual Report

MANAGEMENT'S

DISCUSSION

AND ANALYSIS

OF FINANCIAL

CONDITION AND

RESULTS OF

OPERATIONS

Results of operations (In millions except per share data)

	1993	1992	1991
Retail sales, per cent increase (decrease)	5.4	11.2	(1.0)
Gross margin, per cent of retail sales[1]			
FIFO	31.3	31.5	30.9
LIFO	31.5	31.7	31.5
Selling, general, and administrative expenses, per cent of retail sales[1]	23.7	24.7	25.6
Pre-tax income of other businesses	$ 149	$ 125	$ 91
Effective income tax rate	39.3	38.3	43.5
Net income[2,3]	$ 940	$ 777	$ 80
Per share[2,3]	$ 3.53	$ 2.95	$ .20

[1]Ratios for 1992 and 1991 reflect the reclassifications made to conform with 1993, as described on page 18.
[2]Excluding the effects of an extraordinary charge and the cumulative effect of an accounting change, after tax income was $944 million, or $3.55 per share, in 1993.
[3]Excluding the effects of nonrecurring items and the cumulative effect of an accounting change, after tax income was $528 million, or $2.00 per share, in 1991.

Net income was $940 million in 1993, an increase of 20.9 per cent from $777 million in 1992. Fully diluted earnings per share improved to $3.53 per share from $2.95 per share in 1992. Net income in 1993 was reduced by an extraordinary charge, net of tax, of $55 million, or 21 cents per share, for the premium and unamortized issuing costs related to retired debt. Net income was increased by $51 million, or 19 cents per share, for the cumulative effect of implementing Financial Accounting Standards Board Statement No. 109, *Accounting for Income Taxes.* Excluding the impact of the extraordinary charge and the cumulative effect of the accounting change, net income was $944 million, or $3.55 per share. 1993 net income also included a charge of $14 million, or 5 cents per share, for the impact of the tax rate increase on deferred taxes. Increased sales volume in both stores and catalog, resulting from the Company's strategy of offering fashion, quality, and price to its customers, as well as an aggressive national advertising campaign, were largely responsible for the improvement. Contributing to increased profits were well managed selling, general, and administrative expenses. These expenses, as a per cent of retail sales, declined significantly in 1993.

Net income was $777 million in 1992, an increase of 47.2 per cent from $528 million in 1991, excluding the impact in 1991 of nonrecurring items and the cumulative effect of an accounting change. On a comparable basis, fully diluted earnings per share improved to $2.95 per share from $2.00 per share in 1991. Higher sales volume due to increased unit sales, resulting from the shift in the Company's strategy to more affordable pricing, was largely responsible for the improvement. Selling, general, and administrative expenses, as a per cent of retail sales, declined significantly in 1992.

Net income was $80 million in 1991 and fully diluted earnings per share was 20 cents. Net income in 1991 was reduced by a provision for nonrecurring items and the cumulative effect of an accounting change. Nonrecurring items in 1991 amounted to $395 million before income taxes, and reflected certain changes in strategy. The Company made a strategic business decision in 1991 to hold only regional shopping center investment joint ventures in its real estate investment portfolio and to dispose of all other projects as soon as practicable. As a result of this decision, a provision of $220 million was made to record the costs to dispose of the properties the Company planned to exit. Also, in 1991, a decision was made to downsize or discontinue several non-core retail operations. This decision reflected a change in business strategy to deemphasize experimental businesses and to focus on the Company's core business, resulting in a provision of $115 million. In addition, nonrecurring items included a provision of $60 million for the costs associated with consolidating and streamlining various Company activities. In 1993, the Company completed the disposition of all its non-regional shopping center properties, and continued to close unproductive stores and implement cost cutting measures. The restructuring was substantially complete at the end of 1993. In 1991, the Company adopted Financial Accounting Standards No. 106, Employers' Accounting for Postretirement Benefits Other Than Pensions, that resulted in a one-time charge to earnings of $184 million, net of taxes, or 79 cents per share.

Excluding the effects of the nonrecurring items and the cumulative effect of the accounting change in 1991, income declined 8.5 per cent to $528 million from $577 million in 1990. The decline in 1991 was due to a 1.0 per cent decline in sales volume and an increase in the income tax rate. On a comparable basis, earnings per share declined from $2.16 in 1990 to $2.00 in 1991.

Revenue (In millions)	1993	Per cent increase (decrease)	1992	Per cent increase (decrease)	1991
JCPenney stores	$14,056	4.4	$13,460	12.1	$12,007
Catalog	3,514	11.0	3,166	5.5	3,002
Drug stores	1,413	2.2	1,383	16.0	1,192
Total retail sales*	18,983	5.4	18,009	11.2	16,201
JCPenney Insurance	475	22.5	388	18.3	328
JCPenney National Bank	120	2.0	118	(1.1)	119
Total revenue	$19,578	5.7	$18,515	11.2	$16,648

1993 and 1991 comprised 52 weeks, and 1992 comprised 53 weeks.
*On a comparable 52-week basis, total retail sales increased 6.9 per cent in 1993 and 9.8 per cent in 1992.

Sales of all JCPenney stores in 1993 increased 4.4 per cent while comparable store sales increased 4.0 per cent. The sales gain was primarily the result of the Company's strategy of offering fashion and quality merchandise to its customers at competitive, affordable prices; a new national television advertising campaign; and the increased emphasis on developing its private brands. On a comparable 52 week basis, sales of JCPenney stores increased 5.8 per cent in 1993, and comparable store sales increased 5.3 per cent. JCPenney store sales increased approximately 6 per cent in each of the merchandise divisions (women's, men's, children's and family shoes, and home and leisure). Sales of all JCPenney stores, on a 52 week basis, increased 10.9 per cent in 1992, and comparable store sales increased 9.7 per cent.

Catalog sales increased 11.0 per cent in 1993 to a record $3,514 million. The results were impacted by significant growth in the number of new customers, gains from specialty catalogs, and improved synergy with JCPenney stores' merchandise mix. The Company's decision to accept the Discover Card in April 1993 contributed to 1993's growth in attracting new customers.

Drug store sales increased 2.2 per cent in 1993. On a comparable 52 week basis, drug store sales increased 4.2 per cent in 1993, primarily as a result of higher mail order pharmacy sales.

Gross margin on a FIFO basis, as a per cent of retail sales, declined in 1993 to 31.3 per cent from 31.5 per cent in 1992, due to a more promotional environment during the holiday season. This ratio increased in 1992 as compared with 1991 due to lower markdowns. The decline in this ratio in 1991 as compared with 1990 was due to increased markdowns in the first half of 1991.

In 1991, based on its strategy to lower retail prices, the Company elected to apply an internally developed LIFO index (rather than one prepared by the U.S. Government for all department stores) to measure more accurately increases and decreases in JCPenney retail prices. Because of the continued decline in retail prices, there was deflation in the Company's LIFO index in 1993, 1992, and in 1991. As a result, there was a LIFO credit of $36 million in 1993, as compared with a credit of $32 million in 1992 and a $91 million credit in 1991.

Gross margin on a LIFO basis, as a per cent of retail sales, was 31.5 per cent in 1993, as compared with 31.7 per cent in 1992 and 31.5 per cent in 1991.

SG&A expenses increased in 1993 by 1.4 per cent from 1992's level. As a per cent of sales, SG&A expenses declined in 1993 to 23.7 per cent from 24.7 per cent in 1992, reflecting the Company's continuing efforts to control costs across all operating and support areas.

SG&A expenses increased in 1992 by 7.0 per cent, reflecting higher salaries and personnel related costs resulting from increased sales volume and planned increases in advertising associated with a national television advertising campaign and increased distribution of circulars. SG&A expenses declined in 1991 by 3.1 per cent, reflecting the Company's efforts to reduce costs across all operating and support areas. In 1992, the SG&A expense ratio declined to 24.7 per cent from 25.6 per cent in 1991 and 26.2 per cent in 1990, as a result of higher sales volume and well managed expenses.

Net interest expense and credit costs (In millions)	**1993**	1992	1991
Finance charge revenue	$ **(523)**	$ (509)	$ (567)
Interest expense, net	**241**	258	308
Credit costs			
Bad debt expense	**95**	122	175
Operating expenses (including third party credit costs)	**260**	261	260
Net interest expense and credit costs	$ **73**	$ 132	$ 176

Net interest expense and credit costs declined 44.7 per cent in 1993 to $73 million, primarily as a result of lower bad debt and interest expense. Interest expense declined as a result of the debt restructuring program (described on page 13) initiated by the Company to take advantage of declining interest rates. Net interest expense and credit costs was $132 million in 1992, a decline of 25.0 per cent from $176 million in 1991. The decline in 1992 was also due to lower bad debt and interest expense.

The effective income tax rate for 1993 was 39.3 per cent as compared with 38.3 per cent in 1992 and 43.5 per cent in 1991. The 1993 rate included a one-time, non-cash charge of $14 million for the revaluation of deferred taxes, as required by Statement No. 109, Accounting for Income Taxes. Excluding the adjustment for deferred taxes, the 1993 effective income tax rate was 38.3 per cent, which approximates the expected rate for 1994. The 1993 rate increased from 1992's rate due to the legislated Federal income tax rate increase from 34 per cent to 35 per cent. The 1993 rate was reduced by the tax effect of dividends on allocated leveraged employee stock ownership plan (LESOP) shares, in accordance with Statement No. 109. The 1992 effective income tax rate declined from 1991's rate primarily due to the $21 million charge to income tax expense in 1991 for prior years' tax audit adjustments.

Pre-tax income of other businesses (In millions)	1993	1992	1991
JCPenney Insurance	$ 120	$ 101	$ 78
JCPenney National Bank	29	24	13
Total	$ 149	$ 125	$ 91

JCPenney Insurance, which markets life, accident and health, and credit insurance, continued its growth trend which began in 1989. Pre-tax income was $120 million, an increase of $19 million or 19.3 per cent over 1992. This growth resulted from favorable trends in both premiums earned and lower loss ratios. Premium income for 1993 was $416 million, an increase of $83 million or 25 per cent over 1992. The growth in premium income resulted from an increase of 1.2 million policies, 25 per cent more than in 1992. Increases in renewal premiums of $59 million resulted from the increased sales over the past three years coupled with favorable policy retention. Pre-tax income was $101 million in 1992, an increase of 27.9 per cent over 1991, primarily due to increased premiums. During the past two years, JCPenney Insurance has expanded its market share through relationships with other credit card issuers in both the United States and Canada to solicit their customers. These relationships included 17 companies in the United States and three companies in Canada.

JCPenney National Bank offers Visa and MasterCard credit cards. At the end of the year, about 403 thousand credit cards were active. Pre-tax income improved in both 1993 and 1992, as a result of lower interest rates and a reduction in bad debt expense.

Financial position. The Company generated $286 million in cash from operating activities in 1993 as compared with $1,574 million in 1992 and $911 million in 1991. The change in 1993 was due to an increase in customer accounts receivable, particularly in the fourth quarter when the utilization of the JCPenney credit card increased to 47.5 per cent of sales from 46.6 per cent in 1992's comparable period. Additionally, $425 million of securitized accounts receivable were amortized. The primary contributions to increased cash flow in 1992 were higher net income and declines in customer accounts receivable.

Total customer receivables serviced by the Company were $4.4 billion at the end of 1993, $352 million or 8.8 per cent higher than the level at the end of 1992. The increase in customer receivables was due to the higher sales volume in 1993. In 1993, the Company established the JCPenney Card Bank, National Association, which issues JCPenney credit cards to customers in five states. The customer accounts receivable owned by the Card Bank are fully consolidated for reporting purposes in the total customer receivables serviced by the Company. Customer receivables serviced totaled $4.0 billion at the end of 1992, $411 million or 9.3 per cent below the level at the end of 1991. The decline in 1992 customer receivables serviced reflected a reduction in the utilization of the JCPenney credit card, increased usage of third party credit cards, as well as faster repayments by customers. Customer receivables serviced were $4.4 billion at the end of 1991, or 8.6 per cent below the level at the end of 1990.

Merchandise inventories, on a FIFO basis, increased to $3.8 billion in 1993, up 7.1 per cent from 1992 and are in line with recent sales volumes. FIFO inventories increased 10.2 per cent in 1992 and 4.9 per cent in 1991.

Net property, plant, and equipment, at $3.8 billion, was $63 million above the level of the preceding year. Cash requirements for capital expenditures in 1993 were $480 million, $26 million above 1992. Capital expenditures were $516 million in 1991. The Company presently expects capital expenditures of approximately $500 million in each of the next three years.

Investments, at $1.2 billion, increased $191 million in 1993, primarily due to growth in JCPenney Insurance investments.

Accounts payable and accrued expenses increased 5 per cent to $2.1 billion in 1993 primarily as a result of the increase in trade accounts payable due to the $287 million increase in merchandise inventories. Accounts payable and accrued expenses were $2.0 billion in 1992 and $1.6 billion in 1991.

During 1993, the Company continued a program to restructure its debt and securitized accounts receivable portfolio to take advantage of the lower interest rate environment. The program, which was initiated in 1992, restructured and refinanced $2.6 billion of high cost debt, including both on and off-balance-sheet debt, through various methods including calls, open market purchases, defeasance, and scheduled retirements. Additionally, in February 1994, $350 million of zero coupon notes yielding 13 per cent matured. The restructured debt was financed with operating cash flow and lower cost debt. The weighted average annual interest rate on the restructured and refinanced debt was 10 per cent. In connection with the program, the Company issued $1.25 billion of fixed rate debt in 1993 and 1992 with maturities of five, 10, and 30 years, with a weighted average annual interest rate of 6.1 per cent. As a result, the program will produce annual financing cost savings in excess of $120 million.

Total debt at year end 1993 included $379 million of borrowings by the LESOP, which is guaranteed by the Company. The source of funds to repay the LESOP debt will be dividends from the Series B preferred stock and cash contributions by the Company, totaling approximately $50 million semi-annually through July 1998.

Stockholders' equity was $5.4 billion at the end of 1993, an increase of $660 million from the previous year due primarily to the increase in net income.

On March 9, 1994, the Board of Directors declared an increase in the regular quarterly dividend to 42 cents per share, or an indicated annual rate of $1.68 per share. The regular quarterly dividend on the Company's outstanding stock was payable on May 1, 1994, to stockholders of record on April 8, 1994. The Board also approved on March 9, 1994, the purchase of up to 10 million shares of the Company's common stock to offset dilution caused by the issuance of common shares under the Company's equity compensation and benefit plans. The shares will be purchased from time to time on the open market or through privately negotiated transactions. On March 10, 1993, the Board of Directors declared a two-for-one split of the Company's common stock and increased the quarterly dividend to 36 cents per share from 33 cents per share, or an indicated annual rate of $1.44 compared with $1.32 per share in 1992.

The Company anticipates that the major portion of its cash requirements during the next few years to finance its operations, update its stores, and expand will continue to be generated internally from operations. The Company will continue to review all expenditures to maximize financial returns and maintain financial flexibility.

Impact of inflation and changing prices. The impact of inflation on the Company has lessened in recent years as the rate of inflation has declined. Inflation causes increases in the cost of doing business, including capital expenditures. The effect of rising costs cannot always be passed along to customers by adjusting prices because of competitive conditions. By striving to control costs, the Company attempts to minimize the effects of inflation on its operations.

INDEPENDENT AUDITORS' REPORT

To the Stockholders and Board of Directors of J.C. Penney Company, Inc.:

We have audited the accompanying consolidated balance sheets of J.C. Penney Company, Inc. and Subsidiaries as of January 29, 1994, January 30, 1993, and January 25, 1992, and the related consolidated statements of income, reinvested earnings, and cash flows for the years then ended. These consolidated financial statements are the responsibility of the Company's management. Our responsibility is to express an opinion on these consolidated financial statements based on our audits.

We conducted our audits in accordance with generally accepted auditing standards. Those standards require that we plan and perform the audit to obtain reasonable assurance about whether the financial statements are free of material misstatement. An audit includes examining, on a test basis, evidence supporting the amounts and disclosures in the financial statements. An audit also includes assessing the accounting principles used and significant estimates made by management, as well as evaluating the overall financial statement presentation. We believe that our audits provide a reasonable basis for our opinion.

In our opinion, the consolidated financial statements referred to above present fairly, in all material respects, the financial position of J.C. Penney Company, Inc. and Subsidiaries as of January 29, 1994, January 30, 1993, and January 25, 1992, and the results of their operations and their cash flows for the years then ended in conformity with generally accepted accounting principles.

As discussed on page 25, the Company adopted the provisions of the Financial Accounting Standards Board's Statement of Financial Accounting Standards No. 106, Employers' Accounting for Postretirement Benefits Other Than Pensions, in 1991. Also, as discussed on page 27, the Company adopted the provisions of the Financial Accounting Standards Board's Statement of Financial Accounting Standards No. 109, Accounting for Income Taxes, in 1993.

KPMG Peat Marwick

KPMG Peat Marwick
200 Crescent Court, Dallas, Texas 75201
February 24, 1994

COMPANY STATEMENT ON FINANCIAL INFORMATION

The Company is responsible for the information presented in this Annual Report. The consolidated financial statements have been prepared in accordance with generally accepted accounting principles and are considered to present fairly in all material respects the Company's results of operations, financial position, and cash flows. Certain amounts included in the consolidated financial statements are estimated based on currently available information and judgment of the outcome of future conditions and circumstances. Financial information elsewhere in this Annual Report is consistent with that in the consolidated financial statements.

The Company's system of internal controls is supported by written policies and procedures and supplemented by a staff of internal auditors. This system is designed to provide reasonable assurance, at suitable costs, that assets are safeguarded and that transactions are executed in accordance with appropriate authorization and are recorded and reported properly. The system is continually reviewed, evaluated, and where appropriate, modified to accommodate current conditions. Emphasis is placed on the careful selection, training, and development of professional managers.

An organizational alignment that is premised upon appropriate delegation of authority and division of responsibility is fundamental to this system. Communication programs are aimed at assuring that established policies and procedures are disseminated and understood throughout the Company.

The consolidated financial statements have been audited by independent auditors whose report appears above. This audit was conducted in accordance with generally accepted auditing standards, which includes the consideration of the Company's internal controls to the extent necessary to form an independent opinion on the consolidated financial statements prepared by management.

The Audit Committee of the Board of Directors is composed solely of directors who are not officers or employees of the Company. The Audit Committee's responsibilities include recommending to the Board for stockholder approval the independent auditors for the annual audit of the Company's consolidated financial statements. The Committee also reviews the audit plans, scope, fees, and audit results of the auditors; internal audit reports on the adequacy of internal controls; non-audit services and related fees; the Company's ethics program; status of significant legal matters; the scope of the internal auditors' plans and budget and results of their audits; and the effectiveness of the Company's program for correcting audit findings. Company personnel, including internal auditors, meet periodically with the Audit Committee to discuss auditing and financial reporting matters.

William R. Howell
Chairman of the Board
and Chief Executive Officer

Robert E. Northam
Executive Vice President
and Chief Financial Officer

For the Year	1993	1992	1991
Revenue			
Retail sales	$ 18,983	$ 18,009	$ 16,201
Other revenue	595	506	447
Total revenue	19,578	18,515	16,648
Costs and expenses			
Cost of goods sold, occupancy, buying, and warehousing costs	12,997	12,297	11,099
Selling, general, and administrative expenses	4,508	4,446	4,154
Costs and expenses of other businesses	446	381	356
Net interest expense and credit costs	73	132	176
Nonrecurring items	—	—	395
Total costs and expenses	18,024	17,256	16,180
Income before income taxes, extraordinary charge, and cumulative effect of accounting changes	1,554	1,259	468
Income taxes	610	482	204
Income before extraordinary charge and cumulative effect of accounting changes	944	777	264
Extraordinary charge on debt redemption, net of income taxes of $35	(55)	—	—
Cumulative effect of accounting change for income taxes	51	—	—
Cumulative effect of accounting change for postretirement health care benefits, net of income taxes of $116	—	—	(184)
Net income	$ 940	$ 777	$ 80
Earnings per common share			
Primary			
Income before extraordinary charge and cumulative effect of accounting changes	$ 3.79	$ 3.15	$ .99
Extraordinary charge on debt redemption, net	(.23)	—	—
Cumulative effect of accounting change for income taxes	.21	—	—
Cumulative effect of accounting change for postretirement health care benefits	—	—	(.79)
Net income	$ 3.77	$ 3.15	$ .20
Fully diluted			
Income before extraordinary charge and cumulative effect of accounting changes	$ 3.55	$ 2.95	$ .99
Extraordinary charge on debt redemption, net	(.21)	—	—
Cumulative effect of accounting change for income taxes	.19	—	—
Cumulative effect of accounting change for postretirement health care benefits	—	—	(.79)
Net income	$ 3.53	$ 2.95	$ .20

See Notes to Consolidated Financial Statements on pages 18 through 29.

CONSOLIDATED

STATEMENTS

OF INCOME

(In millions except per share data)
J.C. Penney Company, Inc. and Subsidiaries

CONSOLIDATED

BALANCE

SHEETS

(In millions except share data)
J.C. Penney Company,
Inc. and Subsidiaries

Assets	1993	1992	1991
Current assets			
Cash and short term investments of $156, $405, and $126	$ 173	$ 426	$ 137
Receivables, net	4,679	3,750	4,131
Merchandise inventories	3,545	3,258	2,897
Prepaid expenses	168	157	163
Total current assets	8,565	7,591	7,328
Properties, net	3,818	3,755	3,633
Investments	1,182	991	442
Deferred insurance policy acquisition costs	426	372	313
Other assets	797	758	728
	$ 14,788	$ 13,467	$ 12,444

Liabilities and Stockholders' Equity	1993	1992	1991
Current liabilities			
Accounts payable and accrued expenses	$ 2,139	$ 2,038	$ 1,565
Short term debt	1,284	907	471
Current maturities of long term debt	348	—	237
Deferred taxes	112	64	60
Total current liabilities	3,883	3,009	2,333
Long term debt	2,929	3,171	3,354
Deferred taxes	1,013	1,012	968
Bank deposits	581	538	530
Insurance policy and claims reserves	540	462	353
Other liabilities	477	570	718
Stockholders' equity			
Preferred stock, without par value: Authorized, 25 million shares — issued, 1 million shares of Series B LESOP convertible preferred	648	666	684
Guaranteed LESOP obligation	(379)	(447)	(509)
Common stock, par value 50¢: Authorized, 500 million shares — issued, 236, 235, and 233 million shares	1,003	955	857
Reinvested earnings	4,093	3,531	3,156
Total stockholders' equity	5,365	4,705	4,188
	$ 14,788	$ 13,467	$ 12,444

See Notes to Consolidated Financial Statements on pages 18 through 29.

	1993	1992	1991
Reinvested earnings at beginning of year	$ 3,531	$ 3,156	$ 3,413
Net income	940	777	80
Unrealized change in equity securities	1	(1)	5
Two-for-one stock split	—	(59)	—
Common stock dividends declared	(339)	(309)	(308)
Preferred stock dividends declared, net of taxes	(40)	(33)	(34)
Reinvested earnings at end of year	$ 4,093	$ 3,531	$ 3,156

See Notes to Consolidated Financial Statements on pages 18 through 29.

For the Year	1993	1992	1991
Operating activities			
Net income	$ 940	$ 777	$ 80
Extraordinary charge, net of income taxes	55	—	—
Cumulative effect of accounting change for income taxes	(51)	—	—
Nonrecurring items and cumulative effect of accounting change	—	—	695
Deferred tax effects	—	—	(268)
Depreciation and amortization	316	310	316
Amortization of original issue discount	48	58	53
Deferred taxes	100	48	109
Change in cash from:			
Customer receivables	(352)	411	413
Securitized customer receivables amortized	(425)	(36)	(214)
Inventories, net of trade payables	(196)	(27)	(293)
Other assets and liabilities, net	(149)	33	20
	286	1,574	911
Investing activities			
Capital expenditures	(480)	(454)	(516)
Investment in asset-backed certificates	(12)	(419)	—
Purchases of investment securities	(351)	(325)	(169)
Proceeds from sales of investment securities	215	195	149
	(628)	(1,003)	(536)
Financing activities			
Increase (decrease) in short term debt	377	436	(433)
Issuance of long term debt	1,015	280	500
Payments of long term debt	(875)	(677)	(104)
Premium on debt retirement	(76)	—	—
Common stock issued, net	37	39	7
Preferred stock retired	(18)	(18)	(13)
Dividends paid, preferred and common	(371)	(342)	(342)
	89	(282)	(385)
Net increase (decrease) in cash and short term investments	(253)	289	(10)
Cash and short term investments at beginning of year	426	137	147
Cash and short term investments at end of year	$ 173	$ 426	$ 137
Supplemental cash flow information			
Interest paid	$ 253	$ 265	$ 267
Interest received	$ 51	$ 71	$ 22
Income taxes paid	$ 486	$ 322	$ 259

See Notes to Consolidated Financial Statements on pages 18 through 29.

CONSOLIDATED

STATEMENTS OF

CASH FLOWS

(In millions)

J.C. Penney Company, Inc. and Subsidiaries

17

Reclassifications. Certain amounts for prior years have been reclassified in the Consolidated Statements of Income to conform with the classifications used in 1993. Previously, these amounts were included in "Selling, general, and administrative expenses," "Interest expense, net," "Finance charge revenue," and "Costs and expenses of other businesses." The "Net interest expense and credit costs" caption in the Consolidated Statements of Income includes net interest expense, finance charge revenue, and credit operating costs, including bad debt expense. These reclassifications had no effect on net income. In the Consolidated Balance Sheets, the assets and liabilities of JCPenney Insurance, JCPenney National Bank, and JCP Realty, Inc., which were included in "Other assets" and "Other liabilities," respectively, in prior years, have been fully consolidated. All prior year data throughout this report has been restated to conform with the classifications used in 1993.

Basis of consolidation. The consolidated financial statements present the results of J.C. Penney Company, Inc. and all of its wholly-owned and majority-owned subsidiaries. All significant intercompany transactions and balances have been eliminated in consolidation.

Definition of fiscal year. The Company's fiscal year ends on the last Saturday in January. Fiscal year 1993 ended January 29, 1994, 1992 ended January 30, 1993, and 1991 ended January 25, 1992. They comprised 52 weeks, 53 weeks, and 52 weeks, respectively. The accounts of JCPenney Insurance and JCPenney National Bank are on a calendar year basis.

Retail sales. Retail sales include merchandise and services, net of returns, and exclude sales taxes.

Earnings per common share. Primary earnings per share are computed by dividing net income less dividend requirements on the Series B LESOP convertible preferred stock, net of tax, by the weighted average common stock and common stock equivalents outstanding. Fully diluted earnings per share also assume conversion of the Series B LESOP convertible preferred stock into the Company's common stock. Additionally, it assumes adjustment of net income for the additional cash requirements, net of tax, needed to fund the LESOP debt service resulting from the assumed replacement of the preferred dividends with common stock dividends. The number of shares used in the computation of fully diluted earnings per share was 261 million in 1993, 258 million in 1992, and 234 million in 1991.

Cash and short term investments. Cash invested in instruments with remaining maturities of three months or less from time of investment is reflected as short term investments. The carrying value of these instruments approximates market value due to their short maturities.

Merchandise inventories. Substantially all merchandise inventories are valued at the lower of cost (last-in, first-out) or market, determined by the retail method.

Depreciation. The cost of buildings and equipment is depreciated on a straight line basis over the estimated useful lives of the assets. The principal annual rates of depreciation are 2 per cent for buildings, 5 per cent for warehouse fixtures and equipment, 10 per cent for selling fixtures and equipment, and 20 per cent for data center equipment. Improvements to leased premises are amortized on a straight line basis over the expected term of the lease or their estimated useful lives, whichever is shorter.

Deferred charges. Expenses associated with the opening of new stores are written off in the year of the store opening, except those of stores opened in January, which are written off in the following fiscal year. Deferred policy acquisition costs, principally marketing costs and commissions incurred by JCPenney Insurance to secure new insurance policies, are amortized over the expected premium-paying period of the related policies.

Investments. Fixed income investments (principally bonds), held by JCPenney Insurance, are carried at amortized cost. Marketable equity securities are carried at market value. Investments also include JCP Receivables, Inc. asset-backed certificates held by the Company, which are carried at amortized cost.

Insurance policy and claims reserves. Liabilities established by JCPenney Insurance for future policy benefits are computed using a net level premium method including assumptions as to investment yields, mortality, morbidity, and persistency based on the Company's experience. Liabilities for unpaid claims are charged to expense in the period that the claims are incurred.

Advertising. Costs for newspaper, television, radio, and other media are expensed as incurred, and were $523 million in 1993, $503 million in 1992, and $398 million in 1991. Direct response advertising consists primarily of catalog preparation and printing costs, which are charged to expense over the period during which the benefits of the catalogs are expected, not to exceed six months. Catalog advertising reported in prepaid expense on the balance sheet was $88 million at the end of 1993, as compared with $79 million and $81 million at the end of 1992 and 1991, respectively.

Finance charge revenue and bad debt expense, on customer accounts receivable owned by the Company, are included in the "Net interest expense and credit costs" line of the Consolidated Statements of Income. Finance charge revenue was $523 million in 1993, $509 million in 1992, and $567 million in 1991. Bad debt expense was $95 million in 1993, $122 million in 1992, and $175 million in 1991.

Nonrecurring items amounted to $395 million in 1991, and included recognition of the costs to dispose of certain real estate properties, the write-off of investments in several experimental businesses, and costs associated with consolidating and streamlining various Company activities. There were no nonrecurring items in 1993 or 1992.

Income taxes. The Financial Accounting Standards Board issued Statement No. 109, Accounting for Income Taxes, in February 1992. This statement requires an asset and liability approach to accounting for differences between the tax basis of an asset or liability and its reported amount in the financial statements. Previously, the Company accounted for income taxes under APB Opinion No. 11. The Company adopted Statement No. 109 effective January 31, 1993, and recorded a $51 million cumulative adjustment, reducing deferred taxes on the balance sheet, and increasing net income by the same amount.

Postemployment benefits. The Financial Accounting Standards Board issued Statement No. 112, Employers' Accounting for Postemployment Benefits, in November 1992. This statement, which is required to be adopted in 1994, requires employers to recognize the obligation to provide postemployment benefits on an accrual basis if certain conditions are met. The impact on the Company of adopting this standard is expected to be immaterial.

Debt and equity securities. The Financial Accounting Standards Board issued Statement No. 115, *Accounting for Certain Investments in Debt and Equity Securities,* in May 1993. This statement, which is required to be adopted in 1994 and reflected prospectively, requires that, except for debt securities classified as "held to maturity," investments in debt and equity securities be reported at fair value. Changes in unrealized gains and losses for securities classified as "available for sale" are recorded directly to stockholders' equity, net of applicable income taxes. Had this statement been adopted at year end 1993, assets and deferred taxes on the balance sheet would be increased $119 million and $45 million, respectively, and stockholders' equity would be increased $74 million, with no change in net income.

Advertising. The American Institute of Certified Public Accountants issued Statement of Position No. 93-7, *Reporting on Advertising Costs,* in December 1993. This SOP, which is effective in 1994, requires that all advertising costs be expensed as incurred or the first time the advertising takes place, except for direct response advertising, which can be capitalized and written off over the period during which the benefits are expected. The Company's reporting of advertising costs is in conformance with the provisions of this statement.

Receivables (In millions)	1993	1992	1991
Customer receivables serviced	$ 4,410	$ 4,068	$ 4,489
Customer receivables sold	725	1,150	1,186
Customer receivables owned	3,685	2,918	3,303
Less allowance for doubtful accounts	59	69	79
Customer receivables, net	3,626	2,849	3,224
JCPenney National Bank receivables	587	538	539
Other receivables	466	363	368
Receivables, net	$ 4,679	$ 3,750	$ 4,131

The Company believes that the carrying value of existing customer and bank receivables is the best estimate of fair value because of their short average maturity and bad debt losses can be reasonably estimated and have been reserved.

The Company's policy is to write off accounts when the scheduled minimum payment has not been received for six consecutive months, if any portion of the balance is more than 12 months past due, or if it is otherwise determined that the customer is unable to pay. Collection efforts continue subsequent to write off, and recoveries are applied as a reduction of bad debt losses. Concentrations of credit risk with respect to customer receivables are limited due to the large number of customers comprising the Company's credit card base and their dispersion across the country.

During the period 1988 to 1990, the Company transferred portions of its customer receivables to a trust which, in turn, sold certificates representing undivided interests in the trust in public offerings. Certificates sold during this period totaled $1,400 million. No gain or loss was recognized at the date of sale. The $250 million of certificates sold in 1988 were completely amortized by the end of 1992. Of the $800 million certificates sold in 1990, $425 million were amortized in 1993. As of January 29, 1994, $725 million of the certificates were outstanding and the balance of the receivables in the trust was $1,642 million. The Company owns the remaining undivided interest in the trust not represented by the certificates and will continue to service all receivables for the trust.

19

In 1993 and 1992, the Company purchased $12 million and $419 million, respectively, of its asset-backed certificates in the open market. The fair value of this total investment of $431 million at the end of 1993 was $510 million based upon quoted market value. The fair value of the $419 million investment at the end of 1992 was $465 million.

Cash flows generated from receivables in the trust are dedicated to payment of interest on the certificates (fixed rates ranging from 8.70% to 9.625%), absorption of defaulted accounts in the trust, and payment of servicing fees to the Company. The reserve funds are fully funded ($112 million at January 29, 1994). Reserves are available if cash flows from the receivables become insufficient to make such payments. None of the reserve funds has been utilized as of January 29, 1994. Additionally, the Company has made available to the trust irrevocable letters of credit of $138 million that may be drawn upon should the reserve funds be exhausted. None of the letters of credit was in use as of January 29, 1994.

In connection with the sale of $375 million of certificates in 1990, the Company entered into two offsetting interest rate swap agreements with a commercial bank, each having a notional principal amount of $375 million. Because these interest rate swap agreements are offsetting, their net fair value at the end of 1993 and 1992 was zero. Currently, the Company has no interest rate exposure from these offsetting interest rate swap agreements which terminate when all certificates have been settled in the year 2000. Under one swap the Company receives a fixed rate and pays a floating rate while under the second swap, the Company pays a fixed rate and receives a floating rate. Because of the offsetting nature of these swaps, there is no financial statement impact. The credit risk has been minimized by the selection of a high credit quality commercial bank as counter party. As long as the Company holds both swap positions, there is effectively no credit risk since there is no net exchange of cash flows.

Merchandise inventories (In millions)

	1993	1992	1991
Merchandise inventories, at lower of cost (FIFO) or market	$ 3,791	$ 3,540	$ 3,211
LIFO reserve	(246)	(282)	(314)
Merchandise inventories, at LIFO cost	$ 3,545	$ 3,258	$ 2,897

Substantially all of the Company's inventories are measured using the last-in, first-out (LIFO) method of inventory valuation. Since 1991, the Company has applied internally developed indices that more accurately measure increases and decreases in its own retail prices. From 1974 through 1990, the Company used the Bureau of Labor Statistics price indices applied against inventory selling values to arrive at an inventory valuation. The cumulative effect of this change on reinvested earnings at the beginning of 1991 was not determinable. However, the effect of using the internal indices instead of the Bureau of Labor Statistics price indices at the end of 1991 was to increase net income by approximately $100 million, or 39 cents per share.

Properties (In millions)

	1993	1992	1991
Land	$ 213	$ 212	$ 205
Buildings			
Owned	2,119	2,016	1,838
Capital leases	219	237	244
Fixtures and equipment	2,693	2,703	2,649
Leasehold improvements	575	544	569
	5,819	5,712	5,505
Less accumulated depreciation and amortization	2,001	1,957	1,872
Properties, net	$ 3,818	$ 3,755	$ 3,633

At January 29, 1994, the Company owned 245 retail stores, four catalog distribution centers, one store distribution center, its home office facility, and the insurance company corporate office building.

Capital expenditures (In millions)

	1993	1992	1991
Land	$ 1	$ 8	$ 7
Buildings	119	189	209
Fixtures and equipment	276	270	238
Leasehold improvements	63	27	52
Total capital expenditures	$ 459	$ 494	$ 506

Expenditures for existing stores, primarily modernizations and updates, were $130 million in 1993, as compared with $76 million in 1992 and $134 million in 1991. Expenditures for new stores opened in 1993, 1992, and 1991 were $162 million, $130 million, and $172 million, respectively.

Investments at year end 1993 totalled $1,182 million, and consisted of fixed income securities and asset-backed certificates carried at amortized cost (shown in the table below) and equity securities carried at market value. The market value of investments is based on quoted market prices.

Equity securities were $80 million (cost, $71 million) at year end 1993, $29 million (cost, $22 million) at the end of 1992, and $27 million (cost, $18 million) at the end of 1991. Gross unrealized gains and losses at year end 1993 were $10 million and $1 million, respectively. Net unrealized investment gains on equity securities included in stockholders' equity were $6 million, net of deferred income taxes of $3 million.

The market values of investments carried at amortized cost were as follows:

Investments (In millions)	1993 Amortized Cost	1993 Market Value	1992 Amortized Cost	1992 Market Value	1991 Amortized Cost	1991 Market Value
U.S. Government obligations	$ 139	$ 153	$ 138	$ 142	$ 48	$ 52
Corporate securities	280	302	210	224	193	210
Mortgage-backed securities	158	164	148	159	140	154
Asset-backed certificates	431	510	419	465	—	—
Other	94	92	47	45	34	35
Total	$ 1,102	$ 1,221	$ 962	$1,035	$ 415	$ 451

Gross unrealized gains and losses were $125 million and $6 million, respectively, at year end 1993.

Investments carried at amortized cost had scheduled maturities at year end 1993, as follows:

(In millions)	Amortized Cost	Market Value
Due in one year or less	$ 12	$ 12
Due after one year through five years	147	153
Due after five years through ten years	567	657
Due after ten years	201	218
	$ 927	$1,040
Mortgage-backed securities	158	164
Other	17	17
Total	$1,102	$1,221

Net realized investment gains are included in "Other revenue" on the Consolidated Statements of Income. These gains were $14 million in 1993, $12 million in 1992, and $5 million in 1991.

The Company limits the credit risk by diversifying its investments by industry and geographic region.

Accounts payable and accrued expenses (In millions)	1993	1992	1991
Trade payables	$ 1,034	$ 944	$ 610
Accrued salaries, vacations, profit-sharing, and bonuses	311	308	256
Taxes, including income taxes	234	238	209
Workers' compensation and public liability insurance	126	116	112
Common dividend payable	85	77	77
Other	349	355	301
Total	$ 2,139	$ 2,038	$ 1,565

Short term debt (In millions)	1993	1992	1991
Commercial paper	$ 1,284	$ 887	$ 414
Master notes and other	—	20	57
Short term debt	$ 1,284	$ 907	$ 471
Average short term debt outstanding	$ 1,350	$ 1,154	$ 754
Peak outstanding	$ 2,327	$ 1,675	$ 1,489
Average interest rates	3.2%	3.7%	5.6%

Long term debt (In millions)	1993	1992	1991
Original issue discount			
Zero coupon notes and 6% debentures, due 1992 to 1994 and 2006, $700 at maturity, yields 13.5% to 15.1%, effective rates 12.5% to 13.2%	$ 101	$ 401	$ 359
Debentures and notes			
5.375% to 7.125%, due 1998 to 2023	1,000	—	—
8.25% to 8.875%, due 1992 to 2022	250	366	269
9% to 10%, due 1992 to 2021	1,000	1,750	2,007
Guaranteed LESOP notes, 8.17%, due 1998*	379	447	509
Present value of commitments under capital leases	127	141	160
Other..	72	66	50
Long term debt	$ 2,929	$ 3,171	$ 3,354
Average long term debt outstanding	$ 2,471	$ 2,683	$ 2,827
Average interest rates	9.9%	10.5%	10.2%

For further discussion, see LESOP on page 26.

The fair value for long term debt at the end of 1993 and 1992, excluding capital leases, exceeded the recorded amount by $219 million and $265 million, respectively. The fair value of these instruments was determined based on the interest rate environment and the Company's credit rating.

The Company has in place interest rate swap contracts that were entered into shortly after the issuance of $250 million aggregate principal amount of 8.25 per cent sinking fund debentures in August 1992. These are four year agreements with a notional principal amount totalling $250 million. Under the swap agreements, the Company receives a fixed rate payment and disburses a floating rate payment. The counter parties to these contracts are high credit quality commercial banks. Consequently, credit risk, which is inherent in all swaps, has been minimized to a large extent. The accounting treatment for these contracts, which serve to hedge the 8.25 per cent debentures, is to record the net interest received or paid as an adjustment to interest expense on a current basis. Gains or losses resulting from market movements are not recognized. The fair value of these interest rate swaps at the end of 1993 and 1992 was $13 million and $4 million, respectively.

Changes in long term debt (In millions)	1993	1992	1991
Increases			
5.375% to 9.75% notes, due 1997 to 2023	$ 1,000	$ 250	$ 500
Amortization of original issue discount	48	43	53
Other	16	30	5
	1,064	323	558
Decreases			
Transfers to current maturities of long term debt	348	—	237
8.375% to 12.75% debentures, bonds, and notes, due 1995 to 2021, retired in 1992 and 1993.	872	423	—
Other, including LESOP amortization	86	83	102
	1,306	506	339
Net increase (decrease) in long term debt	$ (242)	$ (183)	$ 219

Maturities of long term debt (In millions)	Long term debt	Capital leases
1994	$ 352	$ 24
1995	2	18
1996	6	19
1997	257	15
1998	587	16
1999 to 2003	821	53
Thereafter	845	19
Total	$ 2,870	164
Less future interest and executory expenses		37
Present value		$ 127

Committed bank credit facilities available to the Company as of January 29, 1994, amounted to $1.25 billion. In 1993, the Company entered into two syndicated revolving credit facility agreements. These facilities include a $450 million, one-year revolver and an $800 million, five-year revolver with a group of 39 domestic and international banks. These facilities, which replaced the $500 million confirmed lines of credit and the $750 million International Revolving Credit Facility, support commercial paper borrowing arrangements. Neither of the borrowing facilities was in use as of January 29, 1994.

Preferred stock. In 1988, a leveraged employee stock ownership plan (LESOP) was adopted (see page 26 for further discussion). The LESOP purchased approximately 1.2 million shares of a new issue of Series B convertible preferred stock from the Company. These shares are convertible into shares of the Company's common stock at a conversion rate equivalent to 20 shares of common stock for each share of preferred stock. The conversion price is $30.00 per common share. The convertible preferred stock may be redeemed at the option of the Company or the LESOP, under certain limited circumstances. The redemption price may be satisfied in cash or common stock or a combination of both at the Company's sole discretion. The dividends are cumulative, are payable semi-annually on January 1 and July 1, and yield 7.9 per cent. The convertible preferred stock issued to the LESOP has been recorded in the stockholders' equity section of the consolidated balance sheet, and the "Guaranteed LESOP obligation," representing borrowings by the LESOP, has been recorded as a reduction of stockholders' equity.

The preferred dividend is payable semi-annually at an annual rate of $2.37 per common equivalent share. Preferred dividends declared were $52 million in 1993, $53 million in 1992, and $54 million in 1991; on an after tax basis, the dividends amounted to $31 million in 1993, $33 million in 1992, and $34 million in 1991.

In 1990, the Board of Directors declared a dividend distribution of one new preferred stock purchase right on each outstanding share of common stock and authorized the redemption of the old preferred stock purchase rights for five cents per share totalling $12 million. The preferred stock purchase rights, in accordance with the rights agreement, entitle the purchase, for each right held, of 1/400 of a share of Series A junior participating preferred stock at a price of $140. The rights are exercisable upon the occurrence of certain events and are redeemable by the Company under certain circumstances, all as described in the rights agreement.

Common stock. On March 9, 1994, the Board of Directors increased the quarterly common dividend to 42 cents per share, or an indicated annual rate of $1.68 per share. The regular quarterly dividend on the Company's outstanding common stock was payable on May 1, 1994, to stockholders of record on April 8, 1994. The Board of Directors also approved on March 9, 1994, the purchase of up to 10 million shares of the Company's common stock to offset dilution caused by the issuance of common shares under the Company's equity compensation and benefit plans. The shares will be purchased from time to time on the open market or through privately negotiated transactions.

The quarterly common dividend was 36 cents per share in 1993, and 33 cents per share in 1992 and 1991, or an indicated annual rate of $1.44 per share in 1993, and $1.32 per share in 1992 and 1991. Common dividends declared were $339 million in 1993, $309 million in 1992, and $308 million in 1991.

On March 10, 1993, the Board of Directors declared a two-for-one stock split in the form of a stock dividend, which was payable May 1, 1993, to stockholders of record on April 12, 1993.

The Company will request stockholder approval at its May 20, 1994 Annual Meeting of Stockholders to increase the authorized number of shares of common stock from 500 million to 1.25 billion shares.

Changes in outstanding common stock	Shares (In thousands)			Amounts (In millions)		
	1993	1992	1991	1993	1992	1991
Balance at beginning of year	234,778	233,302	233,122	$ 955	$ 857	$ 850
Two-for-one stock split	—	—	—	—	59	—
Common stock issued	1,308	1,476	180	48	39	7
Balance at end of year	236,086	234,778	233,302	$1,003	$ 955	$ 857

There were approximately 53,000 stockholders of record at year end 1993. In addition, the Company's savings plans, including the LESOP, had 111,000 participants and held 36.1 million shares of the Company's common stock. The savings plans also held 1.1 million shares of preferred stock, convertible into 21.6 million shares of common stock. On a combined basis, these plans held approximately 22 per cent of the Company's common shares after giving effect to the conversion of the preferred stock at the end of fiscal year 1993.

23

1993 Equity Compensation Plan and 1993 Non-Associate Directors' Equity Plan. In May 1993, stockholders approved the 1993 Equity Compensation Plan (1993 Plan), which replaced the expiring 1989 Equity Compensation Plan. Under the 1993 Plan, 11.6 million shares of common stock were reserved for issuance upon the exercise of options and stock appreciation rights and for the payment of stock awards over the five-year term of the 1993 Plan. No discount options nor tax benefit rights may be issued under the 1993 Plan. Participants in the 1993 Plan are generally to be selected management associates of the Company and its subsidiaries and affiliates as determined by the committee administering the 1993 Plan. It is anticipated that approximately 2,000 associates will be eligible to participate. No awards may be made under the 1993 Plan after May 31, 1998. In May 1993, stockholders also approved the 1993 Non-Associate Directors' Equity Plan (Directors' Plan). Under the Directors' Plan, 90,000 shares of common stock were reserved for issuance upon the exercise of stock options and the payment of stock awards over the five-year term of the Directors' Plan. Each director who is presently not an active employee of the Company will automatically be granted annually an option to purchase 800 shares, in tandem with an award of 200 restricted shares of common stock. An initial grant/award in this same amount will also automatically be granted to each new Non-Associate Director upon his or her first being elected as a director. Such stock options will become exercisable six months from the date of grant, but shares acquired upon such exercise will not be transferable until a director terminates service.

Stock options	1993		1992		1991	
	Shares (In thousands)	Weighted average option price	Shares (In thousands)	Weighted average option price	Shares (In thousands)	Weighted average option price
Balance at beginning of year	8,844	$ 27.42	9,490	$ 26.31	3,820	$ 24.11
Granted	159	41.24	574	35.10	6,048	27.29
Exercised	(752)	24.49	(974)	21.02	(206)	12.85
Expired and cancelled	(16)	26.89	(246)	27.66	(172)	28.20
Balance at end of year	8,235	$ 27.96	8,844	$ 27.42	9,490	$ 26.31

At year end 1993, options covering 2.2 million shares were exercisable and 11.6 million shares were reserved for future grants.

Interest expense (In millions)	1993	1992	1991
Short term debt	$ 43	$ 43	$ 42
Long term debt	246	281	288
Income on short term investments	(14)	(48)	(19)
Interest capitalized	(4)	(14)	(12)
Other, net*	(30)	(4)	9
Interest expense, net	$ 241	$ 258	$ 308

*1993 and 1992 include $34 million and $28 million, respectively, of interest income from the Company's investment in asset-backed certificates.

Rent expense (In millions)	1993	1992	1991
Minimum rent on noncancelable operating leases	$ 236	$ 244	$ 251
Rent based on sales	37	35	33
Minimum rent on cancelable personal property leases	92	107	91
Real estate taxes and common area costs	145	134	120
Total	$ 510	$ 520	$ 495

The Company conducts the major part of its operations from leased premises which include retail stores, distribution centers, warehouses, offices, and other facilities. Almost all leases will expire during the next 20 years; however, most leases will be renewed or replaced by leases on other premises.

Minimum annual rents under noncancelable operating leases and subleases (In millions)

	Gross rents	Net rents*
1994	$ 247	$ 173
1995	232	163
1996	217	152
1997	197	141
1998	184	125
Thereafter	973	718
Total	$ 2,050	$ 1,472
Present value		$ 900
Weighted average interest rate		10%

Rents are shown net of their estimated executory costs, which are principally real estate taxes, maintenance, and insurance.

Retirement plans (In millions)

	1993	1992	1991
Pension			
Service cost	$ 50	$ 46	$ 37
Interest cost	123	122	114
Actual (return) loss on assets	(236)	(90)	(332)
Net amortization and deferral	59	(90)	180
Pension credit	(4)	(12)	(1)
Postretirement health care			
Service cost	3	6	5
Interest cost	24	27	26
Total	27	33	31
LESOP expense	50	49	48
Total retirement plans	$ 73	$ 70	$ 78

Pension plan. JCPenney's principal pension plan, which is noncontributory, covers substantially all United States employees who have completed 1,000 or more hours of service within a period of 12 consecutive months and have attained 21 years of age. In addition, the Company has an unfunded, noncontributory, supplemental retirement program for certain management employees. In general, benefits payable under the principal pension plan are determined by reference to a participant's final average earnings and years of credited service up to 35 years.

In 1993, the Company lowered its discount rate to 7.25 per cent due to the continuation of a lower interest rate environment. The discount rate was also lowered in 1992 to 8 per cent from 9 per cent in 1991. In 1992, the salary progression rate was reduced from 6 per cent to 4 per cent because of lower inflation. The impact of these changes increased the Company's obligation at year end 1993 and 1992. Accordingly, the Company made a cash contribution of $65 million to the plan in 1993 and expects to make a cash contribution to the plan in 1994. The 1993 contribution was the first since 1983.

Postretirement health care benefits. The Company's retiree health care plan (Retiree Plan) covers medical and dental services and eligibility for benefits is based on age and years of service. The Retiree Plan is contributory and the amounts paid by retired employees have increased in recent years and are expected to continue to do so. For certain groups of employees, Company contributions toward the cost of retiree coverage will be based on a fixed dollar amount which will vary with years of service, age, and dependent coverage. The Retiree Plan is funded on a pay-as-you-go basis by the Company and retiree contributions. The Company adopted the Financial Accounting Standards Board Statement No. 106, Employers' Accounting for Postretirement Benefits Other Than Pensions, for its Retiree Plan in 1991.

In 1993 and 1992, the Company modified several postretirement health care assumptions. The discount rate was lowered from 8 per cent to 7.25 per cent in 1993 and from 9 per cent to 8 per cent in 1992. The health care trend rate was lowered from 12 per cent to 10 per cent for 1994 with gradual reductions to 6 per cent by 2003 and beyond. In 1992, the health care trend rate was lowered from 13 per cent to 12 per cent. The health care trend rate change represents a modification from previous assumptions because of favorable experience and a lower inflation environment. The changes in plan assumptions had no significant impact on the Company's obligation at year end 1993. A one per cent increase in the health care trend rate would increase the amount reported for the accumulated obligation by $28 million and would result in $2 million additional expense for 1993.

LESOP. The Company's LESOP, adopted in 1988, is a defined contribution plan which covers substantially all United States employees who have completed at least 1,000 hours of service within a period of 12 consecutive months, and if hired on or after January 1, 1988, have attained 21 years of age.

The LESOP borrowed $700 million at an interest rate of 8.17 per cent through a 10 year loan guaranteed by the Company. The LESOP used the proceeds of the loan to purchase a new issue of convertible preferred stock from the Company. The Company used the proceeds from the issuance of preferred stock to the LESOP to purchase 28 million common shares of the Company in the open market.

The Company has reflected the guaranteed LESOP borrowing as long term debt on the Consolidated Balance Sheet. A like amount of "Guaranteed LESOP obligation" was recorded as a reduction of stockholders' equity. The convertible preferred stock issued to the LESOP for cash was recorded in the stockholders' equity section. As the Company makes contributions to the LESOP, these contributions, plus the dividends paid on the Company's preferred stock held by the LESOP, will be used to repay the loan. As the principal amount of the loan is repaid, the "Guaranteed LESOP obligation" is reduced accordingly.

The amount of compensation cost recorded by the Company represents its cash contribution to the LESOP.

The following table sets forth the status of the Company's retirement plans:

	December 31		
Retirement plans (In millions)	**1993**	1992	1991
Pension			
Present value of accumulated benefits			
Vested	**$ 1,367**	$ 1,227	$ 976
Non-vested	**80**	73	67
	$ 1,447	$ 1,300	$ 1,043
Present value of actuarial benefit obligation	**$(1,781)**	$(1,694)	$(1,373)
Net assets at fair market value	**1,800**	1,585	1,561
Unrecognized transition asset, net of unrecognized losses	**216**	259	(64)
Net prepaid pension cost	**$ 235**	$ 150	$ 124
Postretirement health care benefits			
Accumulated benefit obligation			
Retirees	**$ 246**	$ 205	$ 191
Fully eligible active participants	**51**	82	77
Other active participants	**41**	43	42
	338	330	310
Unrecognized net loss	**(10)**	(7)	—
Net liability	**$ 328**	$ 323	$ 310
Key assumptions			
Rate of return on pension plan assets	**9.5%**	9.5%	9.5%
Discount rate	**7.25%**	8.0%	9.0%
Salary progression rate	**4.0%**	4.0%	6.0%

Total assets and equity (In millions)	Savings plans December 31			Pension December 31		
	1993	1992	1991	1993	1992	1991
JCPenney preferred and common stock	$3,030	$2,200	$1,720	$ —	$ —	$ —
Equity securities	117	103	79	1,424	1,232	1,188
Fixed income investments	1,091	1,061	902	302	275	279
LESOP loan obligation, including accrued interest of $17, $20, and $21	(431)	(498)	(560)	—	—	—
Other assets, net	47	37	32	74	78	94
Net assets	$3,854	$2,903	$2,173	$1,800	$1,585	$1,561

Changes in fair value of net assets (In millions)	Savings plans December 31			Pension December 31		
	1993	1992	1991	1993	1992	1991
Net assets at beginning of year	$2,903	$2,173	$1,823	$1,585	$1,561	$1,284
Company contribution	50	49	48	65	—	—
Participants' contributions	184	169	156	—	—	—
Gains	984	794	400	236	93	332
LESOP interest expense	(35)	(40)	(45)	—	—	—
Benefits paid	(232)	(242)	(209)	(86)	(69)	(55)
Net assets at end of year	$3,854	$2,903	$2,173	$1,800	$1,585	$1,561

Taxes. Taxes other than income taxes, over half of which were payroll taxes, totalled $416 million in 1993, as compared with $386 million in 1992 and $372 million in 1991.

The Financial Accounting Standards Board issued Statement No. 109, Accounting for Income Taxes, in February 1992. This statement requires an asset and liability approach to accounting for differences between the tax basis of an asset or liability and its reported amount in the financial statements (temporary differences). Deferred taxes are determined by applying the provisions of enacted tax laws, and adjustments are required for changes in tax laws and rates. The Company adopted Statement No. 109 effective January 31, 1993. Deferred taxes reflected on the balance sheet were reduced by $51 million, and a cumulative adjustment was recorded to increase net income by the same amount, using current tax rates in effect at the beginning of fiscal 1993.

The Omnibus Budget Reconciliation Act of 1993, which was signed into law on August 10, 1993, included an increase in the statutory Federal income tax rate from 34 per cent to 35 per cent, retroactive to January 1, 1993. This change in the tax rate resulted in higher taxes on operating income in 1993 as well as a one-time, non-cash tax expense totalling $14 million for the revaluation of deferred taxes on the balance sheet as required by Statement No. 109.

Deferred tax assets and liabilities reflected on the Company's consolidated balance sheet at January 29, 1994, were measured using enacted tax rates expected to apply to taxable income in the years in which those temporary differences are expected to be recovered or settled. The major components of deferred tax liabilities (assets) at January 29, 1994, were as follows:

Temporary differences (In millions)	Deferred (Asset)	Deferred Liability	Net (Asset) Liability
Retirement plans	$ (191)	$ 154	$ (37)
Restructuring reserve	(49)	—	(49)
Worker's compensation/public liability	(78)	—	(78)
Leases	(36)	388	352
Accounts receivable	(22)	—	(22)
Inventories	(23)	125	102
Depreciation	—	704	704
Deferred policy acquisition costs	—	147	147
Other	(153)	159	6
Total	$ (552)	$1,677	$1,125

No valuation allowances were considered necessary as of January 31, 1993 or January 29, 1994. The Company believes that the existing deductible temporary differences will be offset by future reversals of differences generating taxable income.

Deferred taxes, under APB Opinion No. 11 in 1992 and 1991, consisted principally of accumulated depreciation and accounting for leases.

27

Income tax expense (In millions)	1993	1992	1991
Current			
Federal	$ 443	$ 372	$ 196
State and local	67	62	62
	510	434	258
Deferred			
Federal	80	29	(29)
State and local	20	19	(25)
	100	48	(54)
Total	$ 610	$ 482	$ 204
Effective tax rate	39.3%	38.3%	43.5%

Reconciliation of tax rates	Amounts (In millions)			Per cent of pre-tax income		
	1993	1992	1991	1993	1992	1991
Federal income tax at statutory rate	$ 544	$ 428	$ 159	35.0	34.0	34.0
State and local income taxes, less federal income tax benefit	58	53	25	3.7	4.2	5.1
Revaluation of deferred taxes	14	—	—	.9	—	—
Tax effect of dividends on allocated LESOP shares	(9)	—	—	(.5)	—	—
Interest, net of tax, on prior years' audit adjustments	—	—	21	—	—	4.6
Tax credits and other	3	1	(1)	.2	.1	(.2)
Total	$ 610	$ 482	$ 204	39.3	38.3	43.5

Segment reporting. The Company operates predominantly in one industry segment consisting of selling merchandise and services to consumers through retail department stores that include catalog departments. Total assets for that industry segment at the end of the last three years were $12,888 million, $11,820 million, and $10,987 million, respectively.

QUARTERLY DATA
(Unaudited)

(In millions except per share data)	First 1993	1992	1991	Second 1993	1992	1991	Third 1993	1992	1991	Fourth 1993	1992	1991
Retail sales	**$ 3,964**	3,793	3,433	**3,963**	3,789	3,456	**4,735**	4,342	3,937	**6,321**	6,085	5,375
Per cent increase (decrease)	**4.5**	10.5	(2.7)	**4.6**	9.6	(3.5)	**9.1**	10.3	(1.4)	**3.9**	13.2	2.2
Total revenue	**$ 4,106**	3,918	3,538	**4,106**	3,912	3,567	**4,888**	4,472	4,050	**6,478**	6,213	5,493
Per cent increase (decrease)	**4.8**	10.7	(2.2)	**5.0**	9.7	(2.8)	**9.3**	10.4	(1.0)	**4.3**	13.1	2.5
LIFO gross margin	**$ 1,280**	1,233	1,107	**1,191**	1,164	1,036	**1,530**	1,395	1,250	**1,985**	1,920	1,709
LIFO gross margin, per cent of retail sales	**32.3**	32.5	32.2	**30.1**	30.7	30.0	**32.3**	32.1	31.8	**31.4**	31.6	31.8
Selling, general, and administrative expenses, per cent of retail sales	**25.9**	26.7	28.4	**25.8**	27.1	27.8	**24.2**	25.0	26.3	**20.8**	21.7	22.0
Income before extraordinary charge and cumulative effect of accounting changes	**$ 172**	136	80	**112**	80	31	**221**	186	116	**439**	375	37
Net income (loss)	**$ 206**	136	(104)	**112**	80	31	**185**	186	116	**437**	375	37
Income per share before extraordinary charge and cumulative effect of accounting changes												
Primary	**$ .68**	.54	.31	**.43**	.31	.10	**.88**	.75	.46	**1.80**	1.55	.12
Fully diluted	**$ .65**	.52	.31	**.42**	.31	.10	**.83**	.70	.46	**1.65**	1.42	.12
Net income (loss) per common share												
Primary	**$ .82**	.54	(.48)	**.43**	.31	.10	**.73**	.75	.46	**1.79**	1.55	.12
Fully diluted	**$ .78**	.52	(.48)	**.42**	.31	.10	**.69**	.70	.46	**1.64**	1.42	.12
Dividends per common share	**$ .36**	.33	.33	**.36**	.33	.33	**.36**	.33	.33	**.36**	.33	.33
Common stock price range												
High	**$ 45**	34	28	**49**	36	29	**52**	38	27	**56**	40	29
Low	**$ 36**	27	24	**41**	32	24	**39**	33	24	**49**	36	24

29

Credit Operations. The following table presents the results of the Company's proprietary credit card operation, measuring on an all-inclusive basis the costs of granting, operating, and financing credit, net of finance charge revenue. Revenue, costs, and expenses contained in the table below relate to all customer accounts receivable generated and serviced by the Company, including those recorded as sold under asset securitization transactions. This presentation is designed to measure on an "economic basis" the total pre-tax cost of providing the JCPenney credit card to customers.

Pre-tax cost of JCPenney credit card (In millions)	1993	1992	1991
Finance charge revenue			
On receivables owned	$ (523)	$ (509)	$ (567)
On receivables sold	(129)	(166)	(197)
Total	(652)	(675)	(764)
Bad debt expense	128	171	240
Operating expenses (including			
in-store costs)	265	270	275
Cost of capital	399	417	496
Total	792	858	1,011
Pre-tax cost of JCPenney credit	$ 140	$ 183	$ 247
Per cent of JCPenney credit sales	1.6%	2.2%	3.1%

The cost of capital shown above represents the cost of financing both Company-owned accounts receivable and securitized accounts receivable. The cost of the sold receivables is the actual interest paid to certificate holders. The owned accounts receivables are financed with both debt and equity capital. The debt component uses the total Company weighted average interest rate, while the equity component uses the Company's minimum return on equity objective of 16 per cent. On a combined basis, for both owned and sold receivables, the debt and equity components of the total capital requirements were 88 per cent debt and 12 per cent equity, which approximates the finance industry standard debt to equity ratio.

	1993		1992		1991	
Credit sales	Amounts (In billions)	Per cent of eligible sales	Amounts (In billions)	Per cent of eligible sales	Amounts (In billions)	Per cent of eligible sales
JCPenney credit card	$ 8.8	46.4	$ 8.4	46.6	$ 7.9	49.3
American Express, Discover, MasterCard, and Visa	2.9	15.4	2.4	13.2	2.0	12.3
Total	$11.7	61.8	$10.8	59.8	$ 9.9	61.6

Key JCPenney credit card information (In millions)	1993	1992	1991
Number of accounts serviced with balances	17.2	17.5	18.3
Total customer receivables serviced	$ 4,410	$ 4,068	$ 4,489
Average customer receivables financed	$ 3,767	$ 3,901	$ 4,288
Average account balances (in dollars)	$ 256	$ 231	$ 244
Average account maturity (months)	4.0	4.1	4.7

Financing costs incurred by the Company to finance its operations, including those costs related to off-balance-sheet liabilities were as follows:

(In millions)	1993	1992	1991
Interest expense, net	$ 241	$ 258	$ 308
Interest portion of LESOP debt payment	35	40	45
Off-balance-sheet financing costs			
Interest imputed on operating leases	97	96	95
Asset-backed certificates interest	87	105	117
Total	$ 460	$ 499	$ 565

Debt to capital ratio shown in the table below includes both debt recorded on the Company's Consolidated Balance Sheet as well as off-balance-sheet debt related to operating leases and the securitization of a portion of the Company's customer accounts receivable.

(In millions)	1993	1992	1991
Short term debt, net of short term investments	$ 1,128	$ 502	$ 345
Long term debt, including current maturities	3,277	3,171	3,591
	4,405	3,673	3,936
Off-balance-sheet debt			
Present value of operating leases	900	950	900
Securitization of accounts receivable, net	294	731	1,186
Total debt	$ 5,599	$ 5,354	$ 6,022
Consolidated equity	$ 5,365	$ 4,705	$ 4,188
Total capital	$10,964	$10,059	$10,210
Per cent of total debt to capital	51.1%	53.2%	59.0%

31

FIVE YEAR

FINANCIAL

SUMMARY

(In millions except per
share data)
J.C. Penney Company,
Inc. and Subsidiaries

	1993[1]	1992	1991[2]	1990	1989[3]
Results for the year					
Total revenue	**$ 19,578**	18,515	16,648	16,736	16,405
Retail sales	**$ 18,983**	18,009	16,201	16,365	16,103
Per cent increase (decrease)	**5.4**	11.2	(1.0)	1.6	8.6
LIFO gross margin, per cent of retail sales	**31.5**	31.7	31.5	31.4	33.4
FIFO gross margin, per cent of retail sales	**31.3**	31.5	30.9	31.7	33.2
Selling, general, and administrative expenses, per cent of retail sales	**23.7**	24.7	25.6	26.2	25.8
Depreciation and amortization	**$ 316**	310	316	299	275
Income taxes	**$ 610**	482	204	255	368
Income before extraordinary charge and cumulative effect of accounting changes	**$ 944**	777	264	577	802
Net income	**$ 940**	777	80	577	802
Earnings per common share					
Primary					
Before extraordinary charge and cumulative effect of accounting changes	**$ 3.79**	3.15	.99	2.30	3.16
Net income	**$ 3.77**	3.15	.20	2.30	3.16
Fully diluted					
Before extraordinary charge and cumulative effect of accounting changes	**$ 3.55**	2.95	.99	2.16	2.93
Net income	**$ 3.53**	2.95	.20	2.16	2.93
Per common share					
Dividends	**$ 1.44**	1.32	1.32	1.32	1.12
Stockholders' equity	**$ 21.53**	19.17	17.33	18.38	17.81
Return on stockholders' equity	**20.1**	18.6	12.0	13.3	20.8
Financial position					
Receivables, net	**$ 4,679**	3,750	4,131	4,303	4,872
Merchandise inventories	**$ 3,545**	3,258	2,897	2,657	2,613
Properties, net	**$ 3,818**	3,755	3,633	3,532	3,268
Capital expenditures	**$ 459**	494	506	601	520
Total assets	**$ 14,788**	13,467	12,444	12,256	12,635
Total debt	**$ 4,561**	4,078	4,062	4,114	4,207
Stockholders' equity	**$ 5,365**	4,705	4,188	4,394	4,353
Number of common shares outstanding at year end	**236**	235	233	234	240
Weighted average common shares					
Primary	**239**	236	234	236	244
Fully diluted	**261**	258	234	260	268
Number of employees at year end (In thousands)	**193**	192	185	196	198

[1]*Excluding the impact of the tax rate increase on deferred taxes, after tax income was $958 million, or $3.60 per share, on a fully diluted basis.*

[2]*Excluding the effect of nonrecurring items and the cumulative effect of an accounting change, after tax income was $528 million, or $2.00 per share, on a fully diluted basis.*

[3]*Excluding the effect of nonrecurring items, after tax income was $822 million, or $3.00 per share, on a fully diluted basis.*

	1993	1992	1991	1990	1989
JCPenney stores					
Number of stores					
Beginning of year	**1,266**	1,283	1,312	1,328	1,355
Openings	**24**	33	38	46	38
Closings	**(44)**	(50)	(67)	(62)	(65)
End of year	**1,246**	1,266	1,283	1,312	1,328
Gross selling space (In million sq. ft.)	**113.9**	114.4	114.5	114.4	112.8
Sales including catalog desks (In millions)	**$ 16,846**	15,698	14,277	14,616	14,469
Comparative store sales per cent increase (decrease)[1]	**6.4**	9.7	(1.5)	0.0	6.8
Sales per gross square foot[1]	**$ 146**	137	125	127	127
Catalog					
Number of catalog units					
JCPenney stores	**1,246**	1,266	1,283	1,312	1,328
Freestanding sales centers and merchants	**543**	640	697	626	501
Drug stores	**101**	128	134	136	126
Other, principally outlet stores	**14**	14	16	16	16
Total	**1,904**	2,048	2,130	2,090	1,971
Number of distribution centers	**6**	6	6	6	6
Distribution space (In million sq. ft.)	**11.4**	11.4	11.4	11.4	11.4
Sales (In millions)	**$ 3,514**	3,166	3,002	3,220	3,205
Drug stores					
Number of stores					
Beginning of year	**548**	530	487	471	434
Openings	**35**	30	46	22	39
Closings	**(77)**	(12)	(3)	(6)	(2)
End of year	**506**	548	530	487	471
Gross selling space (In million sq. ft.)	**4.6**	5.2	5.0	4.8	4.7
Sales (In millions)	**$ 1,413**	1,383	1,192	1,097	987
Sales per gross square foot[1]	**$ 235**	211	201	198	189
JCPenney Insurance (In millions)					
Premium income	**$ 416**	333	286	221	165
Policies and certificates in force	**5.8**	4.6	4.3	4.1	3.5
Amount of life insurance in force	**$ 7,627**	6,552	5,419	5,268	3,797
Total assets	**$ 1,246**	1,033	857	764	739

[1]1992 is presented on a 52 week basis.

FIVE YEAR

OPERATIONS

SUMMARY

J.C. Penney Company,
Inc. and Subsidiaries

33

Through several established programs, the Company continued its commitment to enhance the general environment of the communities in which it does business. Charitable contributions, community service, environmental affairs, and minority/women supplier development are major efforts reflecting this commitment.

Community relations. During 1993, the Company's charitable contributions totalled $23 million nationwide. Of our total contributions, over one-third were given in the area of health and welfare, including the Company's support to nearly 1,000 United Way organizations. The 1993 United Way campaign raised a record $13.8 million in JCPenney associate and unit pledges for local United Ways.

The Company's community relations programs continue to focus on kindergarten through grade twelve education and the support of volunteerism. 15 per cent of contributions were invested in education, including the replication of the JCPenney High Performance Schools Project, a project on school-based management, to two school districts in San Antonio, Texas. $650 thousand was donated to 640 colleges and universities through the Matching Gift Program, and 200 children of JCPenney associates received college scholarships through the JCPenney Super Scholars program.

Major commitments in our focal area of supporting volunteerism include the expansion of our Golden Rule Award Program to 174 markets. These awards publicly honor community volunteers and support their work with contributions. The James Cash Penney Awards for Community Service provide similar recognition to JCPenney associates for outstanding volunteer activities. The two programs contributed approximately $1.7 million to local charitable organizations.

Minority and women-owned businesses. JCPenney's Minority Supplier Development Program has been active since 1972. During 1993, purchases from minority and women-owned businesses were $406 million and $102 million, respectively. In addition to the purchasing of products and services, the Company had relationships with 36 minority-owned banks. The Company recognized, through its Minority Supplier Development Awards Program, eight minority owned-businesses and ten JCPenney associates for their contributions to the Minority Supplier Development Program.

In order to explore ethnic markets more closely, the Fashion Influences catalog was introduced and aimed at a multicultural audience. The catalog's circulation has grown from 400,000 to over 800,000 in just two years. At the same time, a special segment manager was appointed for each of the four merchandise divisions to help find appropriate merchandise for the Fashion Influences catalog as well as those stores that have large ethnic populations within their consumer base.

Environmental affairs. JCPenney is committed to doing business in an environmentally responsible manner. At the center of this commitment stands a determination to make environmental considerations a part of corporate decision making and policy.

Leadership for this effort comes from an Environmental Affairs Committee composed of senior officers. Under their direction, the Company continuously seeks to assure that its operations, to the fullest extent feasible, preserve and improve the environment and protect the health and safety of associates, customers, and communities where JCPenney does business. The Committee has set forth a Statement of Principles on the Environment reflecting the Company's commitment to these goals.

The Company also has an Environmental Issues Task Force consisting of various subcommittees that are studying specific matters such as merchandise packaging, recycling, and trash disposal.

Significant progress has been made towards the Company's environmental goals, especially in recycling. For example, JCPenney is using recycled-content paperboard for all apparel, jewelry, and gift boxes. An environmental packaging recognition award for JCPenney associates has been introduced to encourage the reduction of unnecessary merchandise packaging. In addition, stores are recycling most of the corrugated cardboard boxes in which merchandise shipments are received. The Company also continues to explore sources of high-quality, reasonably priced recycled-content paper for its advertising supplements, catalogs, and other printed matter, and to utilize them where feasible.

An office paper and plastic recycling program is in place in the Company's home office in Plano, Texas, and in a number of other facilities around the country, and a test has been launched in retail stores. State and local officials have recognized one such program, developed by associates at the Manchester, Connecticut, Catalog Distribution Center, as a model for other businesses.

Also, the Company has formal guidelines for evaluating and substantiating environmental themes and claims proposed for merchandise, packaging, labeling, and promotions.

Copies of A Special Report Update on the Company's Environmental Responsibility, including the Company's Statement of Environmental Principles, may be obtained as indicated on page 37 of this Annual Report.

Equal employment opportunity. The Company adheres to a policy of equal employment opportunity. The following employment information summary represents associates of J.C. Penney Company, Inc. and wholly-owned subsidiaries, excluding facilities in Puerto Rico and Canada. The information provided delineates minority and female representation in major job categories.

Employment information	Total employed		Per cent female		Per cent minority	
	1993	1989	**1993**	1989	**1993**	1989
Officials, managers, and professionals	**19,205**	18,959	**47.7**	40.6	**12.0**	10.1
Management trainees	**628**	1,359	**62.7**	62.3	**34.2**	18.1
Sales workers	**99,506**	107,799	**87.7**	87.9	**19.1**	16.4
Office and clerical workers	**33,847**	26,207	**89.2**	90.2	**18.3**	16.0
Technicians, craft workers, operatives, laborers and service workers	**38,911**	42,129	**68.4**	70.9	**24.3**	20.9
Total...	**192,097**	196,453	**80.0**	79.8	**19.3**	16.7

The Company is aware that many of its stockholders are interested in matters of corporate governance. JCPenney shares this interest and is, and for many years has been, committed to assuring that the Company is managed in a way that is fair to all its stockholders, and which allows its stockholders to maximize the value of their investment by participating in the present and future growth of JCPenney.

Independent Board of Directors. In keeping with its long-standing practice, the Company's Board continues to be an independent board under any reasonable definition. All but one director have principal occupations or employment outside of the Company. Nominees for directors are selected by a committee composed entirely of directors who are not Company employees. The wide diversity of expertise, experience, and achievements that the directors possess in business, investments, large organizations, and public affairs allows the Board to most effectively represent the interests of all the Company's stockholders.

Independent committees. The principal standing committees of the Board of Directors are composed entirely of directors who are not employees of the Company. These committees include the Audit Committee, Benefit Plans Review Committee, Committee on Directors, Personnel and Compensation Committee, and the Public Affairs Committee. These committees, as well as the entire Board, consult with and are advised by outside consultants and experts in connection with their deliberations as needed.

Executive compensation. A significant portion of the cash compensation received by the Company's executive officers consists of performance incentive compensation payments derived from compensation plan "values." The amounts of these plan values are directly related to the annual and long-term sales and earnings of the Company and, consequently, vary from year to year based upon Company performance. The total compensation package for the Company's executive officers is set by the Personnel and Compensation Committee, which is composed entirely of directors who are not employees of JCPenney and which receives the advice of independent outside consultants. Please refer to the Company's 1994 Proxy Statement for a report from the Company's Personnel and Compensation Committee describing how compensation determinations are made.

Confidential voting. The Company has previously adopted a confidential voting policy statement. Under this policy, all proxy (voting instruction) cards, ballots, and vote tabulations which identify the particular vote of a stockholder are kept secret from the Company, its directors, officers, and employees. Proxy cards are returned in envelopes directly to the tabulator, who receives and tabulates the proxies. The final tabulation is inspected by inspectors of election who are independent of the Company, its directors, officers, or employees. The identity and vote of a stockholder is not disclosed to the Company, its directors, officers, or employees, or any third party except (i) to allow the independent election inspectors to certify the results of the vote; (ii) as necessary to meet applicable legal requirements and to assert or defend claims for or against the Company; (iii) in the event of a proxy solicitation based on an opposition proxy statement filed, or required to be filed, with the Securities and Exchange Commission; or (iv) in the event a stockholder has made a written comment on such material.

CORPORATE

GOVERNANCE

TABLE C-1 Present Value of $1 To Be Received After *n* Period(s)—Compound Interest Rates

n	1.00%	2.00%	3.00%	4.00%	5.00%	6.00%	7.00%	8.00%	9.00%	10.00%	11.00%	12.00%	13.00%	14.00%	15.00%	16.00%	17.00%	18.00%
1	.9901	.9804	.9709	.9615	.9524	.9434	.9346	.9259	.9174	.9091	.9009	.8929	.8850	.8772	.8696	.8621	.8547	.8475
2	.9803	.9612	.9426	.9246	.9070	.8900	.8734	.8573	.8417	.8264	.8116	.7972	.7831	.7695	.7561	.7432	.7305	.7182
3	.9706	.9423	.9151	.8890	.8638	.8396	.8163	.7938	.7722	.7513	.7312	.7118	.6931	.6750	.6575	.6407	.6244	.6086
4	.9610	.9238	.8885	.8548	.8227	.7921	.7629	.7350	.7084	.6830	.6587	.6355	.6133	.5921	.5718	.5523	.5337	.5158
5	.9515	.9057	.8626	.8219	.7835	.7473	.7130	.6806	.6499	.6209	.5935	.5674	.5428	.5194	.4972	.4761	.4561	.4371
6	.9420	.8880	.8375	.7903	.7462	.7050	.6663	.6302	.5963	.5645	.5346	.5066	.4803	.4556	.4323	.4104	.3898	.3704
7	.9327	.8706	.8131	.7599	.7107	.6651	.6227	.5835	.5470	.5132	.4817	.4523	.4251	.3996	.3759	.3538	.3332	.3139
8	.9235	.8535	.7894	.7307	.6768	.6274	.5820	.5403	.5019	.4665	.4339	.4039	.3762	.3506	.3269	.3050	.2848	.2660
9	.9143	.8368	.7664	.7026	.6446	.5919	.5439	.5002	.4604	.4241	.3909	.3606	.3329	.3075	.2843	.2630	.2434	.2255
10	.9053	.8203	.7441	.6756	.6139	.5584	.5083	.4632	.4224	.3855	.3522	.3220	.2946	.2697	.2472	.2267	.2080	.1911
11	.8963	.8043	.7224	.6496	.5847	.5268	.4751	.4289	.3875	.3505	.3173	.2875	.2607	.2366	.2149	.1954	.1778	.1619
12	.8874	.7885	.7014	.6246	.5568	.4970	.4440	.3971	.3555	.3186	.2858	.2567	.2307	.2076	.1869	.1685	.1520	.1372
13	.8787	.7730	.6810	.6006	.5303	.4688	.4150	.3677	.3262	.2897	.2575	.2292	.2042	.1821	.1625	.1452	.1299	.1163
14	.8700	.7579	.6611	.5775	.5051	.4423	.3878	.3405	.2992	.2633	.2320	.2046	.1807	.1597	.1413	.1252	.1110	.0985
15	.8613	.7430	.6419	.5553	.4810	.4173	.3624	.3152	.2745	.2394	.2090	.1827	.1599	.1401	.1229	.1079	.0949	.0835
16	.8528	.7284	.6232	.5339	.4581	.3936	.3387	.2919	.2519	.2176	.1883	.1631	.1415	.1229	.1069	.0930	.0811	.0708
17	.8444	.7142	.6050	.5134	.4363	.3714	.3166	.2703	.2311	.1978	.1696	.1456	.1252	.1078	.0929	.0802	.0693	.0600
18	.8360	.7002	.5874	.4936	.4155	.3503	.2959	.2502	.2120	.1799	.1528	.1300	.1108	.0946	.0808	.0691	.0592	.0508
19	.8277	.6864	.5703	.4746	.3957	.3305	.2765	.2317	.1945	.1635	.1377	.1161	.0981	.0829	.0703	.0596	.0506	.0431
20	.8195	.6730	.5537	.4564	.3769	.3118	.2584	.2145	.1784	.1486	.1240	.1037	.0868	.0728	.0611	.0514	.0433	.0365
21	.8114	.6598	.5375	.4388	.3589	.2942	.2415	.1987	.1637	.1351	.1117	.0926	.0768	.0638	.0531	.0443	.0370	.0309
22	.8034	.6468	.5219	.4220	.3418	.2775	.2257	.1839	.1502	.1228	.1007	.0826	.0680	.0560	.0462	.0382	.0316	.0262
23	.7954	.6342	.5067	.4057	.3256	.2618	.2109	.1703	.1378	.1117	.0907	.0738	.0601	.0491	.0402	.0329	.0270	.0222
24	.7876	.6217	.4919	.3901	.3101	.2470	.1971	.1577	.1264	.1015	.0817	.0659	.0532	.0431	.0349	.0284	.0231	.0188
25	.7798	.6095	.4776	.3751	.2953	.2330	.1842	.1460	.1160	.0923	.0736	.0588	.0471	.0378	.0304	.0245	.0197	.0160

TABLE C-2 Present Value of an Annuity of $1 for n Period(s)—Compound Interest Rates

n	1.00%	2.00%	3.00%	4.00%	5.00%	6.00%	7.00%	8.00%	9.00%	10.00%	11.00%	12.00%	13.00%	14.00%	15.00%	16.00%	17.00%	18.00%
1	.9901	.9804	.9709	.9615	.9524	.9434	.9346	.9259	.9174	.9091	.9009	.8929	.8850	.8772	.8696	.8621	.8547	.8475
2	1.970	1.942	1.913	1.886	1.859	1.833	1.808	1.783	1.759	1.736	1.713	1.690	1.668	1.647	1.626	1.605	1.585	1.566
3	2.941	2.884	2.829	2.775	2.723	2.673	2.624	2.577	2.531	2.487	2.444	2.402	2.361	2.322	2.283	2.246	2.210	2.174
4	3.902	3.808	3.717	3.630	3.546	3.465	3.387	3.312	3.240	3.170	3.102	3.037	2.974	2.914	2.855	2.798	2.743	2.690
5	4.853	4.713	4.580	4.452	4.329	4.212	4.100	3.993	3.890	3.791	3.696	3.605	3.517	3.433	3.352	3.274	3.199	3.127
6	5.795	5.601	5.417	5.242	5.076	4.917	4.767	4.623	4.486	4.355	4.231	4.111	3.998	3.889	3.784	3.685	3.589	3.498
7	6.728	6.472	6.230	6.002	5.786	5.582	5.389	5.206	5.033	4.868	4.712	4.564	4.423	4.288	4.160	4.039	3.922	3.812
8	7.652	7.325	7.020	6.733	6.463	6.210	5.971	5.747	5.535	5.335	5.146	4.968	4.799	4.639	4.487	4.344	4.207	4.078
9	8.566	8.162	7.786	7.435	7.108	6.802	6.515	6.247	5.995	5.759	5.537	5.328	5.132	4.946	4.772	4.607	4.451	4.303
10	9.471	8.983	8.530	8.111	7.722	7.360	7.024	6.710	6.418	6.145	5.889	5.650	5.426	5.216	5.019	4.833	4.659	4.494
11	10.368	9.787	9.253	8.760	8.306	7.887	7.499	7.139	6.805	6.495	6.207	5.938	5.687	5.453	5.234	5.029	4.836	4.656
12	11.255	10.575	9.954	9.385	8.863	8.384	7.943	7.536	7.161	6.814	6.492	6.194	5.918	5.660	5.421	5.197	4.988	4.793
13	12.134	11.348	10.635	9.986	9.394	8.853	8.358	7.904	7.487	7.103	6.750	6.424	6.122	5.842	5.583	5.342	5.118	4.910
14	13.004	12.106	11.296	10.563	9.899	9.295	8.745	8.244	7.786	7.367	6.982	6.628	6.302	6.002	5.724	5.468	5.229	5.008
15	13.865	12.849	11.938	11.118	10.380	9.712	9.108	8.559	8.061	7.606	7.191	6.811	6.462	6.142	5.847	5.575	5.324	5.092
16	14.718	13.578	12.561	11.652	10.838	10.106	9.447	8.851	8.313	7.824	7.379	6.974	6.604	6.265	5.954	5.668	5.405	5.162
17	15.562	14.292	13.166	12.166	11.274	10.477	9.763	9.122	8.544	8.022	7.549	7.120	6.729	6.373	6.047	5.749	5.475	5.222
18	16.398	14.992	13.754	12.659	11.690	10.828	10.059	9.372	8.756	8.201	7.702	7.250	6.840	6.467	6.128	5.818	5.534	5.273
19	17.226	15.678	14.324	13.134	12.085	11.158	10.336	9.604	8.950	8.365	7.839	7.366	6.938	6.550	6.198	5.877	5.584	5.316
20	18.046	16.351	14.877	13.590	12.462	11.470	10.594	9.818	9.129	8.514	7.963	7.469	7.025	6.623	6.259	5.929	5.628	5.353
21	18.857	17.011	15.415	14.029	12.821	11.764	10.836	10.017	9.292	8.649	8.075	7.562	7.102	6.687	6.312	5.973	5.665	5.384
22	19.660	17.658	15.937	14.451	13.163	12.042	11.061	10.201	9.442	8.772	8.176	7.645	7.170	6.743	6.359	6.011	5.696	5.410
23	20.456	18.292	16.444	14.857	13.489	12.303	11.272	10.371	9.580	8.883	8.266	7.718	7.230	6.792	6.399	6.044	5.723	5.432
24	21.243	18.914	16.936	15.247	13.799	12.550	11.469	10.529	9.707	8.985	8.348	7.784	7.283	6.835	6.434	6.073	5.746	5.451
25	22.023	19.523	17.413	15.622	14.094	12.783	11.654	10.675	9.823	9.077	8.422	7.843	7.330	6.873	6.464	6.097	5.766	5.467

TABLE C-3 Future Value of $1 Due in *n* Periods

	1.00%	1.25%	1.50%	1.75%	2.00%	3.00%	4.00%	5.00%	6.00%	7.00%	8.00%	9.00%	10.00%	12.00%	14.00%	15.00%
1	1.0100	1.0125	1.0150	1.0175	1.0200	1.0300	1.0400	1.0500	1.0600	1.0700	1.0800	1.0900	1.1000	1.1200	1.1400	1.1500
2	1.0201	1.0252	1.0302	1.0353	1.0404	1.0609	1.0816	1.1025	1.1236	1.1449	1.1664	1.1881	1.2100	1.2544	1.2996	1.3225
3	1.0303	1.0380	1.0457	1.0534	1.0612	1.0927	1.1249	1.1576	1.1910	1.2250	1.2597	1.2950	1.3310	1.4049	1.4815	1.5209
4	1.0406	1.0509	1.0614	1.0719	1.0824	1.1255	1.1699	1.2155	1.2625	1.3108	1.3605	1.4116	1.4641	1.5735	1.6890	1.7490
5	1.0510	1.0641	1.0773	1.0906	1.1041	1.1593	1.2167	1.2763	1.3382	1.4026	1.4693	1.5386	1.6105	1.7623	1.9254	2.0114
6	1.0615	1.0774	1.0934	1.1097	1.1262	1.1941	1.2653	1.3401	1.4185	1.5007	1.5869	1.6771	1.7716	1.9738	2.1950	2.3131
7	1.0721	1.0909	1.1098	1.1291	1.1487	1.2299	1.3159	1.4071	1.5036	1.6058	1.7138	1.8280	1.9487	2.2107	2.5023	2.6600
8	1.0829	1.1045	1.1265	1.1489	1.1717	1.2668	1.3686	1.4775	1.5938	1.7182	1.8509	1.9926	2.1436	2.4760	2.8526	3.0590
9	1.0937	1.1183	1.1434	1.1690	1.1951	1.3048	1.4233	1.5513	1.6895	1.8385	1.9990	2.1719	2.3579	2.7731	3.2519	3.5179
10	1.1046	1.1323	1.1605	1.1894	1.2190	1.3439	1.4802	1.6289	1.7908	1.9672	2.1589	2.3674	2.5937	3.1058	3.7072	4.0456
11	1.1157	1.1464	1.1779	1.2103	1.2434	1.3842	1.5395	1.7103	1.8983	2.1049	2.3316	2.5804	2.8531	3.4785	4.2262	4.6524
12	1.1268	1.1608	1.1956	1.2314	1.2682	1.4258	1.6010	1.7959	2.0122	2.2522	2.5182	2.8127	3.1384	3.8960	4.8179	5.3503
13	1.1381	1.1753	1.2136	1.2530	1.2936	1.4685	1.6651	1.8856	2.1329	2.4098	2.7196	3.0658	3.4523	4.3635	5.4924	6.1528
14	1.1495	1.1900	1.2318	1.2749	1.3195	1.5126	1.7317	1.9799	2.2609	2.5785	2.9372	3.3417	3.7975	4.8871	6.2613	7.0757
15	1.1610	1.2048	1.2502	1.2972	1.3459	1.5580	1.8009	2.0789	2.3966	2.7590	3.1722	3.6425	4.1772	5.4736	7.1379	8.1371
16	1.1726	1.2199	1.2690	1.3199	1.3728	1.6047	1.8730	2.1829	2.5404	2.9522	3.4259	3.9703	4.5950	6.1304	8.1372	9.3576
17	1.1843	1.2351	1.2880	1.3430	1.4002	1.6528	1.9479	2.2920	2.6928	3.1588	3.7000	4.3276	5.0545	6.8660	9.2765	10.7613
18	1.1961	1.2506	1.3073	1.3665	1.4282	1.7024	2.0258	2.4066	2.8543	3.3799	3.9960	4.7171	5.5599	7.6900	10.5752	12.3755
19	1.2081	1.2662	1.3270	1.3904	1.4568	1.7535	2.1068	2.5270	3.0256	3.6165	4.3157	5.1417	6.1159	8.6128	12.0557	14.2318
20	1.2202	1.2820	1.3469	1.4148	1.4859	1.8061	2.1911	2.6533	3.2071	3.8697	4.6610	5.6044	6.7275	9.6463	13.7435	16.3665
21	1.2324	1.2981	1.3671	1.4395	1.5157	1.8603	2.2788	2.7860	3.3996	4.1406	5.0338	6.1088	7.4002	10.8038	15.6676	18.8215
22	1.2447	1.3143	1.3876	1.4647	1.5460	1.9161	2.3699	2.9253	3.6035	4.4304	5.4365	6.6586	8.1403	12.1003	17.8610	21.6447
23	1.2572	1.3307	1.4084	1.4904	1.5769	1.9736	2.4647	3.0715	3.8197	4.7405	5.8715	7.2579	8.9543	13.5523	20.3616	24.8915
24	1.2697	1.3474	1.4295	1.5164	1.6084	2.0328	2.5633	3.2251	4.0489	5.0724	6.3412	7.9111	9.8497	15.1786	23.2122	28.6252
25	1.2824	1.3642	1.4509	1.5430	1.6406	2.0938	2.6658	3.3864	4.2919	5.4274	6.8485	8.6231	10.8347	17.0001	26.4619	32.9190
26	1.2953	1.3812	1.4727	1.5700	1.6734	2.1566	2.7725	3.5557	4.5494	5.8074	7.3964	9.3992	11.9182	19.0401	30.1666	37.8568
27	1.3082	1.3985	1.4948	1.5975	1.7069	2.2213	2.8834	3.7335	4.8223	6.2139	7.9881	10.2451	13.1100	21.3249	34.3899	43.5353
28	1.3213	1.4160	1.5172	1.6254	1.7410	2.2879	2.9987	3.9201	5.1117	6.6488	8.6271	11.1671	14.4210	23.8839	39.2045	50.0656
29	1.3345	1.4337	1.5400	1.6539	1.7758	2.3566	3.1187	4.1161	5.4184	7.1143	9.3173	12.1722	15.8631	26.7499	44.6931	57.5755
30	1.3478	1.4516	1.5631	1.6828	1.8114	2.4273	3.2434	4.3219	5.7435	7.6123	10.0627	13.2677	17.4494	29.9599	50.9502	66.2118

TABLE C-4 Future Value of an Ordinary Annuity of $1 Per Period

	1.00%	1.25%	1.50%	1.75%	2.00%	3.00%	4.00%	5.00%	6.00%	7.00%	8.00%	9.00%	10.00%	12.00%	14.00%	15.00%
1	1.0000	1.0000	1.0000	1.0000	1.0000	1.0000	1.0000	1.0000	1.0000	1.0000	1.0000	1.0000	1.0000	1.0000	1.0000	1.0000
2	2.0100	2.0125	2.0150	2.0175	2.0200	2.0300	2.0400	2.0500	2.0600	2.0700	2.0800	2.0900	2.1000	2.1200	2.1400	2.1500
3	3.0301	3.0377	3.0452	3.0528	3.0604	3.0909	3.1216	3.1525	3.1836	3.2149	3.2464	3.2781	3.3100	3.3744	3.4396	3.4725
4	4.0604	4.0756	4.0909	4.1062	4.1216	4.1836	4.2465	4.3101	4.3746	4.4399	4.5061	4.5731	4.6410	4.7793	4.9211	4.9934
5	5.1010	5.1266	5.1523	5.1781	5.2040	5.3091	5.4163	5.5256	5.6371	5.7507	5.8666	5.9847	6.1051	6.3528	6.6101	6.7424
6	6.1520	6.1907	6.2296	6.2687	6.3081	6.4684	6.6330	6.8019	6.9753	7.1533	7.3359	7.5233	7.7156	8.1152	8.5355	8.7537
7	7.2135	7.2680	7.3230	7.3784	7.4343	7.6625	7.8983	8.1420	8.3938	8.6540	8.9228	9.2004	9.4872	10.0890	10.7305	11.0668
8	8.2857	8.3589	8.4328	8.5075	8.5830	8.8923	9.2142	9.5491	9.8975	10.2598	10.6366	11.0285	11.4359	12.2997	13.2328	13.7268
9	9.3685	9.4634	9.5593	9.6564	9.7546	10.1591	10.5828	11.0266	11.4913	11.9780	12.4876	13.0210	13.5795	14.7757	16.0853	16.7858
10	10.4622	10.5817	10.7027	10.8254	10.9497	11.4639	12.0061	12.5779	13.1808	13.8164	14.4866	15.1929	15.9374	17.5487	19.3373	20.3037
11	11.5668	11.7139	11.8633	12.0148	12.1687	12.8078	13.4864	14.2068	14.9716	15.7836	16.6455	17.5603	18.5312	20.6546	23.0445	24.3493
12	12.6825	12.8604	13.0412	13.2251	13.4121	14.1920	15.0258	15.9171	16.8699	17.8885	18.9771	20.1407	21.3843	24.1331	27.2707	29.0017
13	13.8093	14.0211	14.2368	14.4565	14.6803	15.6178	16.6268	17.7130	18.8821	20.1406	21.4953	22.9534	24.5227	28.0291	32.0887	34.3519
14	14.9474	15.1964	15.4504	15.7095	15.9739	17.0863	18.2919	19.5986	21.0151	22.5505	24.2149	26.0192	27.9750	32.3926	37.5811	40.5047
15	16.0969	16.3863	16.6821	16.9844	17.2934	18.5989	20.0236	21.5786	23.2760	25.1290	27.1521	29.3609	31.7725	37.2797	43.8424	47.5804
16	17.2579	17.5912	17.9324	18.2817	18.6393	20.1569	21.8245	23.6575	25.6725	27.8881	30.3243	33.0034	35.9497	42.7533	50.9804	55.7175
17	18.4304	18.8111	19.2014	19.6016	20.0121	21.7616	23.6975	25.8404	28.2129	30.8402	33.7502	36.9737	40.5447	48.8837	59.1176	65.0751
18	19.6147	20.0462	20.4894	20.9446	21.4123	23.4144	25.6454	28.1324	30.9057	33.9990	37.4502	41.3013	45.5992	55.7497	68.3941	75.8364
19	20.8109	21.2968	21.7967	22.3112	22.8406	25.1169	27.6712	30.5390	33.7600	37.3790	41.4463	46.0185	51.1591	63.4397	78.9692	88.2118
20	22.0190	22.5630	23.1237	23.7016	24.2974	26.8704	29.7781	33.0660	36.7856	40.9955	45.7620	51.1601	57.2750	72.0524	91.0249	102.4436
21	23.2392	23.8450	24.4705	25.1164	25.7833	28.6765	31.9692	35.7193	39.9927	44.8652	50.4229	56.7645	64.0025	81.6987	104.7684	118.8101
22	24.4716	25.1431	25.8376	26.5559	27.2990	30.5368	34.2480	38.5052	43.3923	49.0057	55.4568	62.8733	71.4027	92.5026	120.4360	137.6316
23	25.7163	26.4574	27.2251	28.0207	28.8450	32.4529	36.6179	41.4305	46.9958	53.4361	60.8933	69.5319	79.5430	104.6029	138.2970	159.2764
24	26.9735	27.7881	28.6335	29.5110	30.4219	34.4265	39.0826	44.5020	50.8156	58.1767	66.7648	76.7898	88.4973	118.1552	158.6586	184.1678
25	28.2432	29.1354	30.0630	31.0275	32.0303	36.4593	41.6459	47.7271	54.8645	63.2490	73.1059	84.7009	98.3471	133.3339	181.8708	212.7930
26	29.5256	30.4996	31.5140	32.5704	33.6709	38.5530	44.3117	51.1135	59.1564	68.6765	79.9544	93.3240	109.1818	150.3339	208.3327	245.7120
27	30.8209	31.8809	32.9867	34.1404	35.3443	40.7096	47.0842	54.6691	63.7058	74.4838	87.3508	102.7231	121.0999	169.3740	238.4993	283.5688
28	32.1291	33.2794	34.4815	35.7379	37.0512	42.9309	49.9676	58.4026	68.5281	80.6977	95.3388	112.9682	134.2099	190.6989	272.8892	327.1041
29	33.4504	34.6954	35.9987	37.3633	38.7922	45.2189	52.9663	62.3227	73.6398	87.3465	103.9659	124.1354	148.6309	214.5828	312.0937	377.1697
30	34.7849	36.1291	37.5387	39.0172	40.5681	47.5754	56.0849	66.4388	79.0582	94.4608	113.2832	136.3075	164.4940	241.3327	356.7868	434.7451

GLOSSARY

The chapter in which the word first appears or is uniquely defined is indicated in parentheses.

A

Accelerated Cost Recovery System (ACRS) (8): The rules for depreciation for income tax purposes.

Accelerated depreciation methods (8): A group of depreciation methods that result in depreciation expense that is higher in the earlier years but is lower during the later years of a plant asset's estimated useful life.

Account (2): A subclassification of the accounting equation used for storing and summarizing information about transactions that affect a particular element of the business's financial position.

Accountability (I): The process by which individuals and groups demonstrate to others that they have properly or effectively discharged their responsibilities.

Account balance (2): The balance at the end of the period consisting of the beginning balance plus increases during the period minus decreases during the period.

Accounting (I): The process of systematically and selectively capturing financial data, recording these data, summarizing them, and preparing statements that communicate to decision makers relevant information about economic entities, transactions, and events.

Accounting cycle (2): The sequence of procedures accountants follow to complete the financial accounting process, consisting of analyzing transactions, recording transactions to journals, posting journal entries to ledger accounts, recording adjusting entries, preparing the financial statements, and closing all temporary accounts.

Accounting entity concept (1): The concept that the accounting process focuses on specific, separate economic entities.

Accounting equation (1): The equation that governs the relationship among the three accounting elements expressed as assets equal liabilities plus owner's equity.

Accounting period (3): The period of time for which a business determines net income.

Accounting period concept (1): The concept that financial statements or other reports should be prepared at regular intervals such as every month, quarter, or year.

Accounts payable (1): Amounts owed to suppliers for goods and services purchased on credit.

Accounts receivable (1): Payments due from customers for products or services previously provided on a credit basis.

Accrual basis of accounting (2): Revenues are recorded in the period that they are earned, and expenses are recorded in the period that they are incurred.

Accrued expenses (3): Incurred but unpaid expenses.

Accrued revenue (3): Revenue earned by a business but not yet received.

Accumulated depreciation (3, 8): The cumulative depreciation of the assets since they were acquired; a valuation (contra-asset) account.

Acid-test ratio (5): Liquid current assets divided by current liabilities.

Adjusted trial balance (3): A trial balance prepared after posting the adjusting entries.

Adjusting entries (3): Those entries needed to adjust the accounts to their proper balances to conform with GAAP for purposes of preparing appropriate financial statements.

Allowance for uncollectible accounts (6): A valuation account representing the cumulative amount of past sales that a business estimates to be uncollectible but has not written off.

Allowance method (6): A method of accounting for accounts receivable in which the business anticipates and estimates uncollectible accounts to be recognized as uncollectible accounts expense in the period of sale.

Amortization (8): The process of allocating the cost of intangible assets to the periods benefited by the asset.

Annuity (9): Any series of equal payments to be paid or received at the ends of a series of fixed periods.

Annuity due (9): Any series of equal payments to be paid or received at the beginnings of a series of fixed periods.

Annuity value (9): The present value of an annuity of $1 equal to the sum of the present values of each of the individual $1 amounts received at the end of each of a specified number of periods in a $1 annuity.

Appropriation of retained earnings (11): A restriction on the amount of retained earnings available for dividends.

Articles of incorporation (11): A contract between the corporation and the state which incorporators submit to states to obtain a charter.

Assets (1, 16): Probable future economic benefits owned or controlled by a business as a result of past transactions or events.

Asset utilization ratios (15): A group of ratios that assess a business's ability to efficiently use assets to generate long-run profitability.

Authorized shares (11): The number of shares of stock a corporation can issue.

Automated clearing house (5): A electronic system for the transfer of funds between banks.

Available-for-sale securities (13): Long-term investments in stocks and bonds that are not held to maturity or held for short-term trading. Such securities generally are accounted for by the market method.

B

Balance sheet (1): The financial statement that communicates a business's financial position at a specific point in time.

Balance sheet approach (6): A method for estimating uncollectible accounts expense in which a business accrues estimated uncollectible accounts expense based on its past experience with the percentage of accounts receivable that are estimated to be uncollectible.

Bank card (6): Card that permit a customer to purchase goods on credit, while the merchant receives immediate cash payment.

Bank charges (5): Various charges made by the bank reducing the amount in a customer's bank account for such things as check printing, service fees, and NSF items.

Bank reconciliation (5): A schedule that adjusts the company's cash balance and the balance on the bank statement until they each equal the correct amount of cash as of a given date.

Bank statement (5): A statement prepared by the bank showing the activity in the depositor's bank account for a month.

Bearer or coupon bonds (10): Bonds that have detachable coupons that are redeemed for interest payments with the issuer or the issuer's agent. The bearer (owner) of the bonds surrenders them when they mature in exchange for payment of the principal amount.

Bondholders (10): The creditors or lenders who purchase bonds.

Bond indenture (10): A document containing all the debt's terms and conditions.

Bonds (10): Debt securities.

Bonds available for sale (10): Bonds that are neither held to maturity nor held for short-term trading.

Bonds held to maturity (10): In accounting for long-term investments, a classification of bonds in which no gains or losses are recorded until the bonds are sold. To qualify, the business must have a positive intent and ability to hold the bonds to maturity.

Bookkeeping (I): The mechanical and clerical aspects of the accounting process.

Business entity assumption (16): The assumption that information gathered and recorded in accounts is for a specific business entity. The financial statements report the financial position and results of operations of a single economic business entity.

Businesses (I): Private organizations operated to earn profits for their owners.

Business risk (15): The risk associated with the nature of the business and the markets in which it operates.

Bylaws (11): Specific rules adopted by the board of directors to govern the corporation's conduct.

C

Canceled checks (5): Paid checks that have been stamped or perforated by the bank at the time of payment.

Capital account (12): The account used by proprietorships and partnerships to record the residual interest owners have in the business assets after deducting its liabilities.

Capital assets (8): Tangible productive assets owned by a business that are useful for more than one year and are acquired to be used in the business's operations, not to be resold.

Capital expenditures (8): Those expenditures subsequent to the acquisition that extend the plant asset's useful life beyond its original useful life or those expenditures that enhance the asset's efficiency or effectiveness.

Capitalizing retained earnings (11): The process of transferring an amount from retained earnings to contributed capital resulting from such events as a stock dividend.

Capital leases (10): Long-term leases that involve the lessee's acquisition of at least some significant ownership rights and obligations, in addition to the use of the assets over the term of the lease.

Capital stock (1, 2): One component of stockholders' equity. It is the amount of the investments in the business that stockholders make.

Carrying amount (3, 8): An amount representing the undepreciated cost of a plant asset as of the balance sheet date.

Carrying value (3): See *carrying amount*.

Cash basis of accounting (2): Revenues are recorded only in the period that cash payments are received from customers; and expenses are recorded only in the period that cash payments are made.

Cash control systems (5): Systems designed to provide adequate control of both cash receipts and cash disbursements.

Cash equivalents (5, 14): Temporary investments of excess cash in short-term, highly liquid securities.

Certificates of deposit (5): Promissory notes of varying time periods issued by banks.

Charities (I): Private organizations that are operated not for profit but for humanitarian purposes.

Charter (11): A document required by state governments to establish a corporation.

Chart of accounts (2): A list of all account names and account numbers used by a business.

Classified balance sheet (4): A balance sheet that presents the assets and liabilities arranged in certain customary groupings, such as current assets; long-term investments; property, plant, and equipment; and intangible assets.

Closing temporary accounts (3): The process of transferring temporary account balances to owners' capital.

Commercial paper (5): Short-term promissory notes issued by corporations.

Common-size financial statements (15): Financial statements whose numerical amounts are re-expressed as percent of an important summary figure.

Common stock (11): The residual ownership interest of the common stockholders in the corporation's net assets.

Comparability (16): The quality of financial statement information that enables users to identify similarities in and differences between two businesses or within a single business between two or more periods.

Compound interest (9): Interest earned or paid on principal and previous interest amounts.

Comprehensive income (16): The change in equity of a business during a period from transactions and other events and circumstances from nonowner sources.

Conceptual Framework (16): A coherent system of interrelated objectives and fundamentals that can lead to consistent standards and that prescribes the nature, function, and limits of financial accounting and financial statements developed by the FASB.

Conservatism (16): A modifying convention that deals with uncertainty by requiring accountants to use the least optimistic estimate in presenting financial statements.

Consistency (16): The quality of financial statement information that means using the same accounting methods for a business from period to period.

Consolidated financial statements (13): Financial statements prepared as though the parent and subsidiary were one corporation.

Contingent liabilities (6, 9): Potential obligations that depend on the outcome of future events to determine whether the business must pay.

Contributed capital (4, 11): The stockholders' claim to the corporation's net assets due to the purchase of the corporation's capital stock.

Control (6, 13): Steps taken by management to ensure that goals are achieved, only necessary costs are incurred, activities are conducted in accordance with management's policies, assets of the business are safeguarded, and financial reports are reliable. Also, when one corporation owns a majority of another corporation's voting stock.

Co-ownership of partnership property (12): Property invested by partners in a partnership becomes the partnership's property and is owned jointly by all of the partners.

Copyrights (8): Exclusive right granted by the federal government to creative works for the lifetime of the creator plus 50 years.

Corporation (1, 11): A legal entity separate from its owners created when a state government grants a charter.

Cost basis (8): In exchanges of assets, the carrying amount of the old asset plus the cash payment.

Cost/benefits convention (16): A modifying convention that requires that information presented in financial statements should provide benefits to the users that exceed the costs of preparing and using the information.

Cost method (13): A method used to account for investments in stocks where the investor is unable to exert significant influence on the investee company's decisions and where market prices for the stock are not available. Under this method, the investment is initially recorded at cost and is carried at cost until the securities are sold.

Cost of goods available for sale (7): The cost of the beginning inventory plus the cost of purchases during the year, including transportation costs. Also, the sum of the beginning balance in finished goods plus the cost of goods manufactured.

Cost of goods purchased (4): Net purchases plus transportation-in.

Cost of goods sold (4): The total purchase costs of the goods the business provides to customers for the period.

Cost of goods sold ratio (4): Cost of goods sold divided by net sales.

Cost principle (1, 15): Requires that the amounts of assets and liabilities recorded in the accounting records should be the amounts paid (or promised to be paid) for the assets when acquired or the amounts received for the liabilities when incurred.

Credit (2): The right side of a T-account.

Credit balance (2): An account balance which occurs when the sum of credits exceeds the sum of debits.

Credited (2): Recording an amount on the right side of a T-account.

Credit memorandum (5): A document reporting an increase in the bank account.

Cumulative preferred stock (11): A type of preferred stock that allows preferred stockholders an annual stated amount of dividends before the common stockholders can receive any dividends. The right to receive the dividend does not expire if the board of directors fails to declare dividends in a given year. Instead, the right to receive the preferred dividends carries over to future years.

Current assets (4): Cash and assets that the business reasonably expects to sell, consume, or convert into cash within one year or within one operating cycle, whichever is longer.

Current liabilities (4, 9): Those obligations due within one year or within one operating cycle, whichever is longer, and that must be satisfied by paying cash, providing other current assets, or incurring other current liabilities.

Current ratio (5): Current assets divided by current liabilities.

Current value (8): The amount that the asset could be sold for at its current age and in its current condition.

D

Days-purchases-in-payables (9): Accounts payable divided by purchases times the days in the period.

Days-sales-in-receivables (6): Accounts receivable divided by credit sales times days in the period.

Debit (2): The left side of a T-account.

Debit balance (2): An account balance which occurs when the sum of debits exceeds the sum or credits.

Debited (2): Recording an amount on the left side of a T-account.

Debit memorandum (5): A document reporting a decrease in the bank account.

Debt-equity ratio (10): Total liabilities divided by total stockholders' equity.

Decision usefulness (16): The primary qualitative characteristic of financial statement information that requires the information to be useful in making investment, credit, and other decisions.

Declaration date (11): The date that the board of directors declares the dividend and is legally bound to pay the dividend on a stated payment date.

Deflation (15): General decreases in prices.

Demand notes (6): Promissory notes that are due at any time the payee or holder in due course presents them for payment.

Denominations of bonds (10): The amounts that appear on the face of the bonds, also referred to as par values, face values, principal amounts and maturity values.

Depletion (8): The process of allocating the cost of natural resources to the periods benefited by the assets.

Deposits-in-transit (5): Deposits made and recorded by the business but not received by the bank in time to appear on the current bank statement.

Depreciable cost (3, 8): The cost of the plant asset minus the estimated residual value.

Depreciation (8): The process of allocating the cost of the assets to the periods benefited from the services they provide.

Depreciation expense (3): The expense that recognizes the expiration of portions of the total lifetime usefulness of plant assets.

Depreciation schedule (8): A schedule showing the allocation of depreciation expense over the plant asset's useful life.

Direct method (14): A method of presenting cash flows from operating activities showing major classes of cash receipts and cash payments and their sum.

Direct write-off method (6): A method of accounting for uncollectible accounts in which accounts receivable and customers' accounts are credited and Uncollectible Accounts Expense is debited when amounts owed are deemed to be uncollectible. The method is not acceptable under GAAP, but is acceptable under the Internal Revenue Code.

Discount (6, 10): When notes or bonds are sold for less than face or maturity value, the discount is the difference between the selling price and the face or maturity value.

Discounting a note (6): The process of selling or assigning a note.

Dissimilar assets (8): In accounting for exchanges of plant assets, assets that serve different functions.

Distributions to owners (1, 16): Decreases in the equity of a business resulting from transferring assets, rendering services, or incurring liabilities by the business to owners.

Dividend payout (11): Dividends per share divided by earnings per share.

Dividends (1, 2, 11): Distributions by corporations to its stockholders.

Dividends in arrears (11): The undeclared dividends on cumulative preferred stock from previous years.

Dividend yield (11): Dividends per share divided by the market price per share.

Double-declining-balance method (8): A method of depreciation that allocates depreciation expense by multiplying the asset's carrying amount by 200% of the straight-line rate.

Double-entry rule (1): Each change in an element of the accounting equation must be matched by at least one change that has an equal, but opposite, effect.

Double taxation of corporations (11): The fact that corporations pay tax on their pre-tax earnings and stockholders must include dividends (distributions of a corporation's after-tax earnings) in taxable income.

E

Earnings per share (EPS) (11): The ratio of net income available to the common stockholders to the number of shares of common stock outstanding.

Economic entities (I): Any entity that carries on economic activities such as buying or selling products or providing or consuming services.

Effective annual interest rate (9): The interest rate at which the present value of all the payments due on a bond equal the proceeds of issuing the bond.

Effective interest rate (10): The interest rate at which the present value of all the payments due on a bond equal the proceeds of issuing the bond.

Electronic funds transfers (5): A system that manages the transfer of cash electronically, rather than by coins, currency, or checks.

Elements of financial statements (16): Classes of items included in financial statements as defined by the FASB.

Equity (16): The residual interest in the assets of an entity that remains after deducting its liabilities. In a business, the equity is the ownership interest. Also, the notion in cost allocation that suggests that the allocation base should result in allocations that are perceived to be fair.

Equity method (13): A method used to account for long-term investments in another company's stock that is large enough that the investor is able to exert significant influence on the investee company's operating and financial policies. Under this method, the investment is initially recorded at cost, and the investor recognizes in its net income the earning of income by the investee.

Estimated liabilities (9): Liabilities whose exact amounts will not be known until future events occur.

Estimated net realizable value (7): Estimated selling price less the estimated costs of disposing of the merchandise.

Estimated residual value (estimated salvage value) (3, 8): Either the estimated net proceeds if the plant asset is sold or the trade-in value if the plant asset is traded in on a replacement asset.

Estimated useful life (8): The estimated period of time that the business can use the plant asset in the business.

Exchange rate (16): The value of one currency expressed in terms of another currency.

Expenses (1, 16): Decreases in net assets caused by the revenue-producing activities during a specific period. Outflows or other using up of assets or incurrences of liabilities from delivering or producing goods, rendering services, or carrying out other activities that constitute the entity's ongoing major or central operations.

Extraordinary items (15): Items that create gains or losses but are not normal parts of doing business and are not expected to repeat themselves in the foreseeable future.

F

Face amount (6): The amount stated on a bond or promissory note as the principal amount due at maturity.

Feedback value (16): A characteristic of relevance that information should be able to improve decision makers' capabilities to predict by providing feedback about earlier expectations.

Financial accounting (I): An area of accounting that specializes in the processes and principles used to prepare financial statements.

Financial auditing (I): An independent investigative activity through which public accountants lend credibility to the financial statements or other representations of economic entities.

Financial position (1): The relationship among assets, liabilities, and owner's equity.

Financial ratios (15): Numerical statistics that represent important relationships between financial statement amounts.

Financial risk (15): The risk incurred when a business uses debt financing.

Financial statement analysis (15): The art of systematically utilizing (1) financial statement data, (2) ratios and other statistics calculated from financial statement data, and (3) information related to the financial statements to answer questions about a business and to make predictions about its future.

Financial statements (I): Standardized reports prepared by organizations for use by outsiders such as owners and prospective owners of a business, lenders, customers, and creditors.

First-in, first-out (FIFO) (7): A method of assigning cost to the ending inventory assuming that the cost of the units in ending inventory consists of the costs of the most recent units purchased.

Fiscal year (3): The specific twelve-month accounting period a business adopts.

Fixed assets (8): Tangible productive assets owned by a business that are useful for more than one year and are acquired to be used in the business's operations, not to be resold.

Foreign currency transaction (16): A transaction that calls for settlement in a currency other than the U.S. dollar.

Franchise (8): A legal agreement in which one party grants the exclusive right to another party to market a product or provide a service within a designated geographical area.

Full term (10): The total time between the date the bond can first be issued and the date it matures.

Future value (9): The value of an amount or series of amounts invested in the present for a specific time period and interest rate.

G

Gains (16): Increases in equity from peripheral or incidental transactions of an entity and from all other transactions and other events and circumstances affecting the entity except those that result from revenues or investments by owners.

General and administrative expenses (4): Expenses that do not relate directly to the selling function.

General journal (2): A chronological listing of transactions.

General ledger (2): A collection of all the business's accounts.

Generally Accepted Accounting Principles (1): Professional standards to which the financial statements published and distributed by U.S. businesses must conform.

General price changes (15): The general trend in prices in the economy as a whole, in a major sector of the economy, or in a region of the country.

Going-concern assumption (3, 16): In the absence of evidence to the contrary, the assumption that the business will continue to operate indefinitely.

Goods in transit (7): Items of merchandise in the possession of a carrier, such as a trucking, railroad, or airline company.

Goodwill (8, 13): The business's ability to generate earnings at a higher rate than is normal for the industry in which the business operates. Goodwill is only recorded when an entire business or a major portion of a business is purchased. Also, the excess of cost over the fair value of the net assets.

Government accounting (I): A category of accounting consisting of the same activities as private accounting—but performed in cities, counties, and state and federal agencies.

Governments (I): Public organizations formed to supply essential public services to the citizenry and to the state.

Gross profit (4): The difference between net sales and the cost of goods sold.

Gross profit method (7): A method of estimating inventories for interim financial statements using a cost of goods sold to sales ratio.

Gross profit ratio (4): Gross profit divided by net sales.

Gross purchases (4): Purchases recorded at the full (gross) amounts the sellers charge.

Gross sales (4): The sum of the prices of all goods a business sells in a period.

H

Holder in due course (6): The buyer of a negotiable promissory note having equal or greater rights than the original payee.

Horizontal analysis (15): Analysis of the rates of change across periods in the components of a particular financial statement.

I

Idle cash (5): Accumulations of cash balances in excess of amounts needed for current or near future operations.

Implicit principal payment (9): The amount by which an installment payment reduces the principal amount owed on a note, determined by subtracting the interest component from the total payment.

Improvements (8): A subsequent expenditure that makes a plant asset more efficient or effective, but does not necessarily extend the asset's useful life.

Income persistence (15): The tendency for a component of income to continue in future periods under steady-state (no change) assumptions.

Income quality (15): The degree to which management does not exercise or does not have the opportunity to manipulate the firm's income to paint an optimistic picture of ongoing income.

Income statement (1): The financial statement that communicates the revenues, expenses, and net income of a business for a period of time.

Income statement approach (6): A method in which a business accrues and estimates uncollectible accounts expense based on its past experience with average collections per dollar of credit sales.

Income Summary (3): A temporary account to which all revenue and expense accounts are closed.

Independent auditor's report (15): A report prepared by an independent auditor for the purpose of issuing an opinion whether financial statements fairly present what they are supposed to present in all material respects in conformance with GAAP.

Indirect method (14): A method of presenting cash flows from operating activities the begins with net income and shows the adjustments necessary to determine cash flows from operating activities.

Indirect (net) method (6): A method of reporting the effect of uncollectible accounts on the balance sheet in which accounts receivable are reported net of the allowance for uncollectible accounts.

Inflation (15): General increases in prices.

Installment loan (9): A loan that is repaid with a series of equally spaced payments of a constant amount.

Installment method (16): A method of recognizing revenue from an installment sale where each receipt of cash is considered to consist of a recovery of part of the cost of the goods sold and part of the gross profit from the sale used when there is significant uncertainty about whether the cash will be collected.

Intangible assets (4, 8): Noncurrent assets that have no physical substance such as patents, copyrights, franchises, and trademarks.

Interest (6): The expense a borrower incurs and the revenue or income a lender earns for the use of the money owed in fixed-amount agreements such as promissory notes.

Interest-bearing note (6): A debt instrument that expressly states an interest rate to be applied to the face amount of the note.

Interest method of amortization (10): A method of amortization in which interest expense is determined by applying the implicit interest rate to the bond's carrying value and amortization of premium or discount is the difference between interest expense and interest paid.

Interest rate (6): The percentage rate that applies to the face amount of the note.

Interim financial reports (3): Financial statements for a period less than a year.

Internal audit (I): An investigation by accountants of an economic entity designed to determine whether: employees and departments conform to management (or government) policies; functions in the organization are performed at reasonable cost; and a department or division is fully meeting its goals and objectives.

Internal Revenue Code (2): Rules for federal taxation issued by the Internal Revenue Service.

Inventory turnover (7): The rate at which inventory passes through a business.

Inventory turnover ratio (7): Cost of goods sold divided by average inventory.

Investments by owners (1, 16): Increases in equity of a business resulting from transfers to it other entities of cash or other assets from entities that wish to obtain or increase their ownership interests.

Issuer of bonds (10): An entity that borrows by issuing debt securities called bonds.

J

Journal entry (2): The recording of one event or transaction in the general journal.

Journalizing (2): The process of recording a transaction.

L

Large stock dividend (11): A stock dividend that is greater than 20-25% of the outstanding shares.

Last-in, first-out (LIFO) (7): A method of assigning cost to the ending inventory assuming that the cost of the units in ending inventory consists of the costs of the earliest units purchased.

Legal capital (11): The minimum amount of contributed capital for the number of shares issued.

Leverage (15): The effect of using debt financing to complement owner's capital to provide the necessary funds to operate a business.

Liabilities (1, 9, 16): Probable future sacrifices or economic benefits arising from present obligations of a business to transfer assets or provide services to other entities in the future as a result of past transactions or events.

Like-kind exchanges (8): Exchanges of similar plant assets for which no taxable gain or loss may be recognized.

Limited life (12): The characteristic of a partnership that any event or act that terminates the partnership agreement terminates the partnership.

Limited partnership (12): A form of partnership in which the general partner has unlimited liability, but the limited partners are liable only for the amount of their investment in the partnership.

Liquidity (4, 5): The expected length of time needed to convert an asset into cash.

Liquidity ratios (15): A group of ratios that assess a business's ability to meet its current obligations as they come due.

Long-term investments (4): Assets a business does not expect to sell or collect within one year or within the operating cycle, whichever is longer.

Losses (16): Decreases in equity from peripheral or incidental transactions of an entity and from all other transactions and other events and circumstances affecting the entity except those that result from expenses or distributions to owners.

Lower-of-cost-or-market rule (7): Reporting inventories at market value when the market value has fallen below cost.

M

Majority interest (13): When a company owns more than 50% of another company's voting stock.

Maker of a note (6): The party who makes a written promise to pay.

Managerial accounting (I): An area of accounting that specializes in preparing information for use by managers in making decisions about the current and future activities of economic entities.

Market method (13): Presenting investments in the balance sheet at the fair values of the stocks as of the balance sheet date.

Matching principle (2, 16): The accounting principle that states that expenses incurred to produce products and services should be recognized in the same period that revenues from those products and services are recognized.

Material difference (10): Amount of an error or omission in financial statements that could alter the decision of a qualified and informed individual who takes the care to analyze the financial statements.

Materiality (6, 16): The amount of error or incorrectness in a set of financial statements that could change a decision of a knowledgeable user of financial statements. A modifying convention that involves judgments about whether errors and omissions in financial statements are of sufficient size to cause the financial statements to be misleading.

Maturity value of a note or bond (6): The amount to be paid when the note or bond is due.

Measurement (16): To assign a numerical amount to the information that is recognized in the accounts.

Merchandise inventory (4): A merchandising business's stock of goods available for sale as of a particular point in time.

Merchandise inventory card (7): A record in both quantities and costs of the beginning inventory of each item, purchases of the item, and sales of the item.

Minority interest (13): Other stockholders when one investor owns more than 50% of the voting stock in a subsidiary.

Modified Accelerated Cost Recovery System (MACRS) (8): The most current rules for depreciation for income tax purposes.

Modifying conventions (16): Constraints on the application of accounting principles adopted by the accounting profession.

Monetary measurement concept (1): The concept that the focus of accounting is on business events, resources, and obligations that can be expressed in money terms.

Multistep income statement (4): An income statement divided into sections giving details of such items as sales, cost of goods sold, operating expenses, and income taxes.

Mutual agency (12): The characteristic of a partnership that makes each partner an agent of the partnership, and is therefore able to enter into binding agreements on behalf of the partnership.

N

Natural resources (8): Wasting assets such as oil, gas, mineral deposits, and stands of timber.

Negotiable promissory note (6): An debt instrument that the original payee can sell readily to collect cash earlier than the due date of the note.

Net book value (3, 8): An amount representing the undepreciated cost of a plant asset as of the balance sheet date.

Net income (1, 2): The excess of revenues over expenses for a period.

Net loss (2): The excess of expenses over revenues for a period.

Net purchases (4): Purchases less purchases returns and allowances and purchases discounts.

Net sales (4): The total amounts a business receives or expects to be collected for the period's sales of merchandise to customers expressed as gross sales less sales returns and allowances and sales discounts.

Neutrality (16): A characteristic of reliability that means that in choosing an accounting method, there is freedom from bias towards a pre-determined result.

Noncumulative preferred stock (11): A type of preferred stock that allows preferred stockholders a stated amount of dividends before the common stockholders can receive any dividends. However, if no dividend is declared for a year, the preferred stockholders right to receive dividends for that year lapses.

Noncurrent liabilities (long-term liabilities or long-term debts) (4, 9): Those obligations due in more than one year or more than one operating cycle, whichever is longer, from the balance sheet date.

Noninterest-bearing note (6): A debt instrument that does not state an interest rate to be applied to the face amount of the note.

Non-like-kind exchanges (8): Exchanges of dissimilar plant assets for which a taxable gain or loss is recognized.

Non-negotiable promissory note (6): A debt instrument that does not satisfy the legal conditions for negotiability.

Nonparticipating preferred stock (11): A type of preferred stock in which the stock certificate limits the dividends on preferred stock to the stated amount.

No-par value stock (11): Stock issued without a par value.

Not-for-profit (11): An entity organized to conduct business with some other purpose than earning a profit, such as charities, educational institutions, and certain medical organizations.

NSF checks (5): Checks that the banks that they are drawn on refuse to pay for lack of funds in the maker's accounts.

O

Objectives of financial statements (16): Objectives developed by the FASB to provide broad guidelines for financial statements prepared by businesses.

Off-balance-sheet financing (10): Any scheme or system through which a business effectively acquires or retains property rights in assets for future payments without showing the assets or the related liabilities on its balance sheet.

Operating cycle (4, 9): The average period of time between committing resources to providing goods or services and collecting cash from customers.

Operating expenses (4): All the expenses of running the business for a period other than the cost of goods sold.

Operating leases (10): Short-term or long-term leases that involve strictly renting assets for use in the lessee's business. No special rights or privileges are acquired, and the lessor bears all of the risks of ownership.

Organization costs (11): Costs incurred in forming a corporation.

Outstanding checks (5): Checks that a business has issued and recorded but which have not be presented to the bank for payment.

P

Paid-In Capital in Excess of Par (11): The account used to record the difference between the par value of the stock and the selling price when the selling price is greater than the par value.

Parent company (13): The investor company who is able to control the investee.

Participating preferred stock (11): A type of preferred stock in which the stockholder has the right to participate in dividends in excess of the stated amount in certain circumstances.

Partnership (1, 12): An association of two or more persons to carry on a business as co-owners.

Partnership agreement (12): The agreement between two or more persons that governs their association as partners and constitutes a contract that creates that partnership.

Par value (11): The amount printed on the stock certificate and established by the corporation's charter. The par value of the stock issued determines the corporation's legal capital.

Patents (8): The exclusive right granted by the federal government to use the product or process for a period of 17 years.

Payee (6): The party to whom money is owed.

Payment date (11): The date that the corporation actually pays the dividends that have been previously declared by the board of directors.

Percentage-of-completion method (16): A method that recognizes revenue for long-term construction contracts by dividing the total estimated cost by the cost incurred in the current period and multiplying the resulting percentage by the total revenue on the project.

Percent-change financial statements (15): Conventional financial statements with changes and percents of changes added.

Percent utilization of a line of credit (9): Loan balance divided by the maximum available loan.

Period (term, duration) of a note (6): The length of time for which the promissory note is in effect.

Periodic inventory method (4): A method of accounting for inventory in which the balance in Merchandise Inventory is updated at the end of the accounting period as a result of taking a physical inventory.

Perpetual inventory method (4): A method of accounting for inventory in which the costs of purchases and the cost of goods sold are recorded on a daily, or even a continuous, basis.

Petty cash fund (5): A fund used to make small cash payments.

Petty cash receipts (5): Documents providing evidence of disbursements made from the petty cash fund stating the purpose of the payments, the amounts, the dates, and other pertinent information.

Physical inventory (4): A process of physically counting all goods of each kind in the merchandise inventory as of a particular date, assigning costs to them and calculating an inventory balance.

Plant assets (plant and equipment, or property, plant, and equipment) (8): Tangible productive assets owned by a business that are useful for more than one year and are acquired to be used in the business's operations, not to be resold.

Point-of-sale systems (5): Computer-based cash receipts systems that allow customers to transfer funds immediately from their bank accounts to the merchant's bank account at the time of a sale.

Pooling-of-interests method (13): A method of accounting for business combinations in which the acquired company's net assets are reported in the consolidated financial statements at their book values immediately preceding the combination. This method is used for combinations that involve the exchange of common stock.

Post-closing trial balance (3): A trial balance prepared immediately after closing.

Posting (2): The process of recording transactions in the general ledger accounts.

Predictive value (16): A characteristic of relevance that the information should help users form predictions about the outcomes of events.

Preemptive right (11): The right of common stockholders to purchase additional shares before the shares are offered for sale to others.

Preferred stock (11): Generally nonvoting stock, entitling the stockholder to certain preferences relative to those of common stockholders.

Premium (10): When bonds are sold for more than face value, the premium is the difference between the face value and the selling price.

Present value (9): The amount that a rational person would accept now in exchange for the right to receive an amount in the future.

Private accounting (I): A broad category of accounting consisting of all accounting activities required to meet the information needs of private-sector managers and of outside users such as prospective owners and lenders.

Privately-owned corporations (15): Corporations whose shares are held by a relatively few number of owners. The shares are not traded on stock exchanges.

Profitability ratios (15): A group of ratios that assess a business's ability to earn a profit in the future.

Profit margin (3): The amount of net income as a percent of revenues, stated as net income divided by revenues.

Promissory note (4, 6): A written promise by one party to pay a specified amount of money, usually with interest, to another party on a specified date at a specified place.

Property, plant, and equipment (4): The long-lived assets that the business uses to sell and/or manufacture a product or to provide a service.

Proprietorship (1): A business owned by an individual.

Proxy (11): A legal document giving an agent power to cast a stockholder's votes at stockholders' meetings.

Public accounting (I): A category of accounting in which accountants provide professional accounting services to individuals, businesses, government units, and other entities for fees.

Publicly-owned corporations (11): Corporations whose shares are publicly traded on stock exchanges.

Purchase method (13): A method of accounting for business combinations in which the acquired company's assets and liabilities are reported at their fair values on the date of the business combination, with any excess of the cost over the fair value of the net assets reported as goodwill.

Purchase order (5): A formal offer to buy goods sent to the supplier after it has been properly authorized.

Purchase requisition (5): A request to purchase needed goods prepared by the person responsible for maintaining the stock on hand.

Purchases allowances (4): Adjustments to the amount owed for goods resulting from minor deficiencies in the goods.

Purchases discounts (4): Reductions in amounts owed to encourage early payments.

Purchases returns (4): A reduction in the amount owed because flawed or unacceptable goods are returned to the supplier.

Q

Qualitative characteristics (16): Characteristics of decision-useful financial statement information consisting of primary and secondary qualities.

Quick ratio (5): Liquid current assets divided by current liabilities.

R

Rate of return on stockholders' equity (1): Net income divided by average owners' equity.

Realization principle (2): The accounting principle that revenues should be recognized in the period they are earned if they either are collected in cash or they will be collected from customers in the future.

Receiving report (5): A document containing evidence of the quantities and condition of goods actually received from suppliers completed by employees who physically receive goods on the business's behalf.

Recognition (16): The recording of effects of events and transactions formally in the accounts as assets, liabilities, revenues, expenses, etc.

Recognize (2): To record in an account.

Reconciling the bank statement (5): The process of verifying the balance in the cash account against the bank balance of cash by taking into account appropriate adjustments to both balances.

Record date (11): The date the board of directors designates for determining who owns what number of shares of stock and, therefore, who is entitled to receive the dividend.

Registered bonds (10): Bonds issued in the buyer's name and recorded by the issuer in a bond register.

Registrar (11): The person or business who is responsible for transferring the corporation's stock.

Relevance (16): A primary qualitative characteristic of financial statement information that requires the information to be capable of making a difference in a decision.

Reliability (16): A primary qualitative characteristic of financial statement information that assures that the information is reasonably free from error or bias and faithfully represents what it intends to represent.

Remittance advice (5): A document attached to a check that notifies the payee of the purpose of the payment. Also, a duplicate invoice sent by the payee that may be returned with payment and serves the same purpose.

Repairs (8): Ordinary and routine revenue expenditures to maintain the plant asset in good working condition.

Replacements (8): Nonroutine, capital expenditures that extend a plant asset's useful life beyond its original estimated useful life.

Representational faithfulness (16): A characteristic of reliability that requires a high degree of correspondence between financial statement numbers and the assets, liabilities, transactions, and events those numbers intend to represent.

Research and development (8): The search for and the application of knowledge to new products or processes.

Reserve funds (15): Consist of dispensable assets, arranged but unused sources of credit, and untapped sources of new credit and equity capital. Reserve funds represent the margin of protection a business has against sudden financial distress.

Retail method (7): A method of estimating inventories for interim financial statements using a cost to retail ratio for the goods available for sale.

Retained earnings (1, 4, 11): The cumulative net income of a corporation less the cumulative dividends paid to stockholders from the beginning of the corporation's life.

Retained earnings statement (1): A financial statement that reflects the effects on the business of net income and dividends for a period of time.

Return on total assets (8): The sum of net income and interest expense divided by total assets.

Revenue expenditures (8): Those expenditures that merely maintain the plant asset's usefulness and keep it functioning at its original capacity.

Revenues (1, 16): Increases in net assets that result directly from providing products or services to customers during a specific period. Inflows or other enhancements of assets of a business or settlement of its liabilities from delivering or producing goods, rendering services, or other activities that constitute the entity's ongoing major or central operations.

S

Sales allowance (4): A reduction in the price given because merchandise is partially flawed.

Sales discounts (4): Reductions in payments to induce early payments.

Sales return (4): A refund given to the customer when merchandise previously purchased is returned.

Selling expenses (4): Expenses directly related to storing, handling, displaying, selling, and shipping or delivering products to customers.

Separation of incompatible duties (5): A control measure that makes it impossible for a dishonest employee to cover up theft of cash without cooperation of another employee.

Serial bonds (10): Bonds issued under indentures that specify that certain subsets of the total issue of bonds are due at different maturity dates.

Short-term, revolving lines of credit (9): A bank's commitment to advance funds on demand to a borrower up to a limit and for a specific period.

Similar assets (8): In accounting for exchanges of plant assets, assets that serve the same function.

Slide (2): An error that results from adding or dropping one or more zeros from a number.

Sole proprietorship (12): A business owned by one person.

Solvency ratios (15): A group of ratios that assess a business's ability to generate sufficient cash to meets its obligations.

Specific identification method (7): A method of assigning costs to the ending inventory by tracking the actual physical flow of units during the period.

Specific price changes (15): Changes in the prices of particular goods or services, irrespective of general trends.

Stable-dollar assumption (15, 16): The assumption that the U.S. dollar is a reasonably constant unit of measure and that, even though prices change, assets, liabilities, revenues, and expenses are still recorded and reported in the financial statements according to the cost principle.

Stated, nominal, or coupon rate (10): The interest rate stated in the bond indenture.

Stated value (11): A corporation's legal capital if the corporation assigns a value to no-par value stock.

Statement of cash flows (1, 14): A financial statement that displays a business's cash receipts and cash disbursements for a period according to categories of business activities—operating activities, financing activities, and investing activities.

Statement of financial position (1): A financial statement that communicates the financial position of a business by listing the corporation's assets, liabilities, and stockholders' equity. Also known as a *balance sheet*.

Statement of partners' capital (12): The statement of owner's equity for a partnership.

Straight-line method (8): A method of depreciation that allocates an equal amount of depreciation expense to each period in the asset's estimated useful life.

Straight-line rate (8): 100% divided by the estimated useful life.

Stock certificate (11): A document providing evidence of ownership of shares in a corporation.

Stock dividend (11): When a company issues common stock to its own common stockholders without receiving any assets in return.

Stockholders (1, 11): The owners of the corporation.

Stockholders' equity (1): The residual interest owners have in the business's assets after deducting its liabilities.

Stockholders' ledger (11): A subsidiary ledger containing the information about stock ownership.

Stock split (11): A method of reducing the market price per share accomplished by replacing the outstanding shares with a multiple number of the shares previously outstanding.

Stock subscription (11): A sale of shares of stock in which the purchaser agrees to pay a specified price for the shares at some future date(s).

Subsidiary company (13): The investee controlled by the parent corporation.

Sum-of-the-years'-digits method (8): A method of depreciation that allocates depreciation expense by multiplying the asset's depreciable cost by a fraction for each year.

Supplier's invoice (5): The supplier's billing document containing descriptions, quantities shipped, prices of goods, the total amount owed, and the terms of credit.

T

T-account (2): The simplest representation of an account resembling the letter T and consisting of the account title, the left (debit) side and the right (credit) side.

Taxable income (2): The basis on which the amount of income tax is determined.

Tax rate (2): The percentage rate applied to taxable income to determine the amount of income tax.

Temporary accounts (3): Accounts that are closed at the end of the accounting period.

Term bonds (10): Bonds issued under indentures that specify that all the bonds are due at the same date.

Term to maturity (9, 10): The period of time until a liability must be paid. The time remaining before a bond matures.

Timeliness (16): An objective of accounting systems that requires that information be supplied with sufficient lead time to permit management to assimilate and use it in the decision at hand. A characteristic of relevance that requires information to be available to the user before it loses its capacity to influence decisions.

Time periods assumption (16): The assumption that the life of a business can be divided into a series of equal time periods.

Trademarks (trade names) (8): Words, symbols, or other devices that identify or distinguish a product or a business. If registered with the federal government, exclusive right may be granted to use the trademark or trade name for a period of 20 years.

Trading securities (10): Bonds and equity securities that are purchased and held for resale in the near future.

Transaction (I, 1): A voluntary exchange between economic entities, typically involving a sale/purchase of products or services that changes an economic entities' financial position.

Transfer agent (11): The person or business who is responsible for transferring the corporation's stock.

Transposition error (2): The reversal of two digits during the process of recording the number.

Treasury stock (11): Reacquired shares of previously issued stock.

Trial balance (2): A list of debits and credits from the general ledger accounts used to test the equality of debits and credits.

U

Unadjusted trial balance (3): A trial balance prepared before posting the adjusting entries.

Uncollectible accounts expense (6): The estimated portion of a period's credit sales that a business ultimately will not collect from customers.

Uncollectible-accounts-expense-as-a-percent-of-credit sales (6): Uncollectible accounts expense divided by credit sales.

Unearned revenue (3): Payment received in advance of delivering the goods or performing the services.

Units-of-production method (8): A method of depreciation that allocates depreciation expense to the time periods based on the plant asset's output.

Unlimited liability (12): The characteristic of a partnership that holds each partner personally liable for all partnership liabilities.

Useful life of an asset (3): The period of time the business estimates it can use the asset in its operations.

V

Valuation account (contra-asset account) (3, 8): An account that reduces another account to its correct balance for presentation in the financial statements. For example, Accumulated Depreciation is the valuation account for the related plant asset account.

Verifiability (16): A characteristic of reliability that results from a high degree of agreement among independent measurers.

Vertical analysis (15): Analysis of the percentage composition of the components of a particular financial statement for a particular year.

Voucher (5): The document on which relevant data about an obligation to pay are summarized for approval, recording, and payment under a voucher system.

Voucher system (5): An integrated control system in which adequate support documents (vouchers) are prepared for all acquisitions and expenditures.

W

Weighted-average cost method (7): A method of assigning costs to the ending inventory based on the average cost per unit, which consists of the combined cost of the beginning inventory and the purchases made during the year.

Withdrawals (1): Distributions by proprietorships or partnerships.

INDEX